PEARSON ALWAYS LEARNING

Psychology
Core Concepts

A Custom Edition for Housatonic Community College

Taken from:
Psychology: Core Concepts, Seventh Edition
by Philip G. Zimbardo, Robert L. Johnson, and Vivian McCann

*What Every Student Should Know About Reading and
Studying the Social Sciences*
by Sally A. Lipsky and Arden B. Hamer

Cover Art: Courtesy of PhotoDisc/Getty Images.

Taken from:

Psychology: Core Concepts, Seventh Edition
by Philip G. Zimbardo, Robert L. Johnson, and Vivian McCann
Copyright © 2012, 2009, 2006 by Pearson Education, Inc.
Upper Saddle River, New Jersey 07458

What Every Student Should Know About Reading and Studying the Social Sciences
by Sally A. Lipsky and Arden B. Hamer
Copyright © 2010 by Pearson Education, Inc.
Boston, Massachusetts 02116

This special edition published in cooperation with Pearson Learning Solutions.

All trademarks, service marks, registered trademarks, and registered service marks are the property of their respective owners and are used herein for identification purposes only.

Pearson Learning Solutions, 501 Boylston Street, Suite 900, Boston, MA 02116
A Pearson Education Company
www.pearsoned.com

Printed in the United States of America

3 4 5 6 7 8 9 10 VOCR 17 16 15 14 13

000200010271303476

TF

ISBN 10: 1-256-77804-4
ISBN 13: 978-1-256-77804-2

What Every Student Should Know About Reading and Studying the Social Sciences

CONTENTS

PREFACE

Many students begin college with little or no guidance about the requirements and expectations of courses in higher education. The purpose of this book is to provide practical information about how to approach and learn content for a college-level Social Science course. This book is best used from the start of the semester as a complement to the text and other course materials. Included in this book are recommended practices for beginning the term, reading and studying from a textbook, listening and taking notes in class, and preparing for exams. Students are expected to apply and evaluate select strategies as they proceed through the semester.

Text Features

- **The Study Cycle**, described in Chapter 1, provides students with a strategic plan for how to approach out-of-class work. With simple yet important steps, the Study Cycle provides a framework by which students utilize the strategies described in subsequent chapters.
- **Select, Sort, and Solidify**, also introduced in Chapter 1, are the three steps integrated throughout subsequent chapters. Learning is a process; these steps provide students with a basis for acquiring a deeper understanding of content in their Social Science course. Specific strategies for selecting, sorting, and solidifying information are presented for chapter topics—textbook reading, in-class note taking, and preparing for exams.
- **Examples** of how students apply the **Select, Sort, and Solidify** process are presented in each chapter. These examples include textbook pages, in-class notes, and study guides and review sheets for a variety of Social Science courses.
- **Student Comments** are interspersed within chapters. The comments are from college students who completed a course in which they had to implement and assess a variety of learning strategies in Social Science courses. Their remarks and suggestions help to guide and motivate beginning college students.

- **Summary Charts,** located at the ends of selected chapters, provide an overview of strategies presented within the chapter. Students are directed to use the chart as they plan approaches for reading and studying content in their Social Science course.
- **Taking Action** is a five-step process that follows each Summary Chart. Students are directed to reflect on and assess information presented in the chapter by applying strategies to a specific assignment, class session, or test. Students check off strategies on a sheet, cut out the sheet, and then use it as a bookmark to remind them of their plan.
- **The Checklist of Strategies,** presented in the last chapter, is a means for students to periodically assess strategies that they have and/or have not implemented in their Social Science course. As a culminating exercise, students **Prioritize and Apply** five strategies that will help them improve the effectiveness and efficiency of their learning.

INTRODUCTION: TO THE STUDENT

The intent of this handbook is to help you make sense of information that you will encounter in your Social Science course, both in the textbook and in the classroom. By following the strategies presented in this book, you will maximize the effectiveness and the efficiency by which you read, study, and learn content for your Social Science course.

What Are the Social Sciences?

The Social Sciences represent branches of learning that study elements of human experience from differing perspectives. The Social Sciences can include a variety of disciplines: Anthropology, Criminology, Economics, Geography, History, Political Science, Psychology, Religious Studies, and Sociology. Professionals in each of these fields have differing viewpoints and approaches toward studying topics. For example, Social Science professionals might examine the topic of **GENDER** accordingly:

- *Anthropologists*—Differences between males and females in western versus non-western cultures.
- *Criminologists*—Profiles and patterns of males and females within a criminal justice system.
- *Economists*—Current spending trends of males and females.
- *Historians*—Impact of females in the work force during and after WWII.
- *Political Scientists*—Civic engagement and voting patterns of males and females.
- *Psychologists*—Behavioral and emotional differences of males and females.
- *Sociologists*—Roles of males and females within and across ethnic groups in our society.

Among the Social Science disciplines there are many overlapping aspects of study. However, you should be mindful of the specialized point of view for the course that you are enrolled in currently. An awareness of the perspective within a Social Science discipline will help you to better understand the content that you are learning. Therefore, as you read the textbook, listen in class, take notes, and prepare for exams in your Social Science course, be aware of the specialized point of view for that subject area.

1

JUMP START THE SEMESTER

The start of a semester can be a confusing and overwhelming time for college students, especially for first-time students. One way to ease initial apprehensions is to approach your college academics as you would a new full-time job. That is, from the start, work at being conscientious, diligent, and productive—you will impress not only your college instructors, but also yourself!

The First Week

- **Attend class.** During the first week of classes, instructors talk about important information not covered again in the semester, such as setup and requirements for the course and explanations about information on the syllabus. Also, many instructors begin lecturing the first day.
- **Read the syllabus.** The syllabus, or course outline, is an important document for all courses. A syllabus is similar to a contract created by the instructor for students. Instructors usually hand out the syllabus during the first class session, or at least the first week of classes. Review the syllabus closely since it provides information about:
  - *Contacting your instructor.* Take note of your instructor's office hours, location of the office, phone number and email address. Also, how does your instructor want you to contact him? Some instructors prefer email; others prefer that you come to their office.

- ◆ *Attendance policy*. Note your instructor's policies regarding class absences. Is class attendance part of your overall grade in the course? What constitutes an "excused" versus an "unexcused" absence? How many classes can you miss before you are penalized? Also, what should you do if you are sick or have a personal emergency—how do you contact your instructor, and how do you get information about missed class work?
- ◆ *Assignments*. Make note of due dates, explanations, and other expectations of the instructor.
- ◆ *Grading*. How will you be evaluated in the course? Be aware of requirements and point values for assignments, papers, projects, quizzes, exams, and any other means of evaluation.
- ◆ *Late assignment policy*. As with class attendance, instructors can have widely differing procedures for turning in late assignments. First, will your instructor accept a late assignment? Will you be penalized for turning in an assignment past the due date? What constitutes a reasonable excuse?
- **Buy textbooks and supplies.** Go to the campus bookstore; this is the most expedient way to purchase texts, supplemental materials (handbooks, DVDs), and supplies. Go early—you will avoid crowds and have a better chance of purchasing used and, therefore, cheaper texts. (Be sure to purchase a copy with the least amount of text marking and highlighting.) Also, keep your sales receipt and do not write in the text until you are sure you will use it for the course. Most bookstores have return policies, including a limited time period by which to return textbooks.
- **Obtain a planner or calendar.** Keep track of academic requirements (assignments, projects, papers, quizzes, exams, class cancellations, extra labs, study/review sessions), as well as personal and social activities. In upcoming weeks, you easily can forget or feel overwhelmed with mounting activities and obligations. Using a planner or calendar daily will help you manage your time and feel a greater sense of control regarding academic and personal responsibilities.
- **Preview the textbook.** Take note of the following features:
  - ◆ *Abbreviated or brief table of contents*. Provides an overview of topics covered in the text.

- *Expanded table of contents*. Provides more details regarding topics and layout of the textbook.
- *Preface or introduction*. The author explains the approach of the text, the main features within the text, and suggested approaches for reading the text.
- *Glossary*. Defines terminology used in the text.
- *Index*. An alphabetical directory of subjects, people, and/or events in the text.
- *Appendix*. Can include answer keys; extra charts, timelines, or other illustrative materials; a list of sources; and other materials to enhance text content.
- *Supplemental materials*. Is there a Website, CD, podcast, or manual that accompanies the text?

Begin the Study Cycle

For the vast majority of students, academic success in college involves considerable more time and effort than in high school. Generally speaking, for *each hour spent in class*, college students should expect to spend 2 hours doing out-of-class work for that course. Thus, for a course that meets 3 hours per week, be prepared to spend 6 hours doing course work out of class. Like many college students, you might be unaware of what specifically you should be doing during this time for out-of-class course work. The **Study Cycle** (below), along with specific strategies described in subsequent chapters, provides you with a strategic plan for your out-of-class work.

The Study Cycle

review lecture notes ⟹ read text and other course materials

go to class and take notes

go to class and take notes

read text and other course materials

review lecture notes

review lecture notes

read text and other course materials

go to class and take notes

The **Study Cycle** is a series of simple, yet important steps to implement throughout the semester *for each course*. Put these recommended steps into action starting with the first week of the term.

Keep in mind that descriptions of specific strategies for listening, taking notes, reading, and reviewing are provided in subsequent chapters.

1. **Go to class and take notes.** Take supplies—paper and pen, laptop, textbook, planner—and sit near the front. (Chapter 3 provides strategies for in-class note taking.)

⇩

⇩

2. **Review your in-class notes** as soon as possible after class. Make time to organize, add to, and emphasize information within your notes. (See Chapter 3.)

⇩

⇩

3. **Read the assigned material** and create a study guide. (Chapter 2 provides detailed information about how to read, study, and learn from your textbook.)

⇩

⇩

4. **Go to class and take notes.** Be alert, ready to listen and write or type.

⇩

⇩

5. **Review your in-class notes** within 24 hours after class. Organize, add to, emphasize, and summarize information within your notes.

⇩

⇩

6. **Continue to read** assigned pages in your text or other materials. Use information in the readings to clarify questions you might have about lecture material.

⇩

⇩

7. **Go to class and take notes.** Be an active and selective listener—jot down key ideas and ask questions.

⇩

⇩

8. **Review notes.** Look over your *current notes* as well as <u>*all of the notes*</u> you have taken so far in the semester. By reviewing all of your notes, you will be *learning* as you go along, as opposed to cramming right before the exam. (See Chapter 4.)

⇩

⇩

9. **Continue to read and work** in your text. Highlight, summarize, and answer questions.

⇩

⇩ ⇨   ⇨   ⇨   ⇨   ⇨   ⇨   ⇨   ⇨

Repeat this cycle weekly throughout the semester. Notice how easy it is to spend 6 hours per week preparing and studying for each course! Bear in mind that by conscientiously applying these steps, you will be well on your way to excelling in your college coursework.

Three-Step Course of Action

In your Social Science course you likely are required to go beyond simple recall of information. To excel in the course you must obtain a deeper and more complex level of understanding of content. Learning strategies that assist you with acquiring this deeper understanding of Social Science content are described within each chapter of this handbook. The strategies are organized according to three steps: select, sort, and solidify.

1. **SELECT**. Begin with the question: ***What do I need to know for this course?*** To answer this question, you have to make decisions about what is important information for assignments, quizzes, tests, papers, and so on. You will be picking out key ideas as you read the text, listen in class, take notes, and study for exams.

2. **SORT**. In order to maximize your understanding, you need to <u>do</u> something with the key ideas you selected previously. For this step focus on the question: ***How can I summarize, organize, or personalize the information I need to know?*** To answer this question, you will employ strategies that help you clarify new and complex Social Science concepts, as well as make sense of the large amounts of material you will encounter.

3. **SOLIDIFY**. Besides understanding important content, you want to remember this information for an upcoming assignment, class discussion, or exam. For this step, consider the question: ***What can I do to retain information for future use?*** To answer this question, you will combine and reorganize ideas, review and reinforce key concepts, and consolidate material for future application.

The following chapters present specific strategies that guide you through this process of selecting, sorting, and solidifying information for your Social Science course. These strategies will maximize your learning as you proceed through the Study Cycle, that is; as you read your Social Science textbook, take notes and participate in class, and review and prepare for upcoming exams.

Student Comments

- As a freshman, I never paid attention to my course syllabi. As a result, I never knew what was due or what was happening in class. Now I look at the syllabus almost every day. It surprises me that I know so much more about what is going on in class!

  –Jacquí
- The Study Cycle helped me figure out what to do and how to study. In high school I never had to study, so when I started college I had no idea what to do outside of class.

  –Sam

2

READ THE TEXTBOOK

Importance of the Textbook

Your text is a valuable tool that helps you develop a thorough understanding of a Social Science course discipline. Some college instructors refer to the textbook regularly; others rarely mention the text or particular reading assignments. Either way, almost all college instructors assume that you are keeping up with reading the appropriate text chapters. Keep in mind that it is your responsibility to know what chapters and materials you should be reading for each course. Refer to the course syllabus regularly to keep track of assigned chapters, pages, and due dates. If the course syllabus does not contain specific reading assignments, look for the lecture topic on the syllabus. Then use the text index to find the corresponding pages to read.

Here are simple yet worthwhile suggestions for how to use your textbook before, during, and after class.

- **Before class.** Read—or at least skim—your text assignment before each class. Reading an assignment beforehand allows you to:
  - Become familiar with the topic, which prepares you to listen actively in class. Gaining even basic knowledge of a topic before a lecture will strengthen your understanding of in-class material.
  - Recognize names, terms, and other content-specific language that will be used in class.
  - Obtain a general idea of the organization of the material, which will strengthen the overall orderliness and clarity of the notes you take during class.

- **During class.** Have your textbook available during class.
  - ♦ If your instructor uses the text as a main source of information, highlight and write on chapter pages as your instructor talks.
  - ♦ Instructors often refer to illustrations and graphic materials in the text. Have those pages available to view during class.
  - ♦ When class material seems confusing and unclear, jot down the corresponding text pages. After class, reread those pages and add clarifying explanations and examples within your class notes.
  - ♦ If your instructor emphasizes particular text pages in class, make note of the pages. Your instructor considers this information to be important and, therefore, the information likely will be on an upcoming exam.
- **After class.** The textbook is a valuable tool after class when reviewing your lecture notes. As you go back through your class notes, refer to the text chapter in order to:
  - ♦ Fill in missing information and details in your notes.
  - ♦ Clarify confusing portions by adding explanations, examples, and application scenarios.
  - ♦ Deepen your understanding of a complex topic by reading multiple case studies and varied perspectives and analyses of the topic.

Characteristics of Social Science Textbooks

Certain characteristics are common to Social Science textbooks:

- **Content-specific vocabulary.** Knowledge of vocabulary is a foundation of understanding text material. Social Science text chapters tend to be full of terms common to the particular discipline. These terms may or may not be bolded, italicized, or defined. When reading, pay special attention to terms since they often are a significant part of class discussion, assignments, and exams.
- **Numerous names and dates.** Placing too much attention on the many names and dates in a chapter can make reading tedious and overwhelming. Instead, focus on main ideas, selecting only the names and dates that you likely need to know for an assignment or test.
- **Graphics.** Boxed inserts, pictures, charts, and graphs are interspersed within text pages. Graphics summarize large quantities

of information or difficult concepts, thus don't omit them when reading.

- **Examples and case studies.** Also, don't skip examples or case studies. These features help you to apply abstract information to concrete situations, making concepts and theories more relevant and understandable.

- **Text and chapter features.** Be aware of useful text features, including the table of contents, glossary, and index. In addition, utilize chapter features—such as learning objectives, list of terms, summary, and review questions—to familiarize yourself with content and organization before reading and to check your comprehension after reading.

- **Cause and effect connections.** As you read, pay attention to how one event or occurrence triggers another. In particular, focus on **watershed events**; that is, actions, experiences, or incidents that result in *significant changes*. Here are two examples of watershed events in recent history:

  I. Starting in 1989, three opposition groups challenged President Mikhail Gorbachev's leadership in the Soviet Union. → In August 1991, attempted coup of Gorbachev by conservatives in government. → Gorbachev under arrest. → Coup collapsed. → December 1991, Gorbachev relinquished his power. → Commonwealth of Independent States formed. → Official collapse of European communism in Soviet Union and Eastern Europe. *The attempted coup of Gorbachev followed by the relinquishing of his power was a watershed event because it resulted in the collapse of communism in a major world region.*

  II. Early 1970's, a woman raped in Texas. → Two young lawyers challenged Texas law that abortion was criminal act. → Legal case reached Supreme Court. → Justices struck down Texas law as violation of a woman's right to reproductive privacy. *This case, Roe v. Wade, was a watershed event because it resulted in significant changes throughout the country in women's access to abortions.*

These Features Tend to be Unique in History Textbooks

- Sequential presentation of information.
- Long, uninterrupted passages, which can obscure main ideas.

- Densely written passages with each sentence containing important information.
- <u>Many</u> names and dates.
- Minimal text aids, with the exception of timelines that place key events in proper context.

How to Approach History Textbooks

Page 12 contains a passage from a 39-page chapter in an introductory-level History textbook. The passage is part of the first of five sections within the chapter. The chapter covers the years 1933–1945, the period leading up to and during World War II.

Look at the passage. Take note of these elements, which are typical of college-level History textbooks:

- The lack of bold print words, definitions, pictures, and illustrations.
- The compactness of the print and the lack of white spaces.
- The many dates.

Then examine the summary notes that a student jotted in the margins in order to better understand and remember information in this passage. The student followed this sequence before, during, and after reading the History text chapter:

Before

- Read the chapter outline in the detailed table of contents at the beginning of the text and on the first page of the chapter.
- Looked at the timeline at the beginning of the section. This helped to put chapter events into context.
- Turned chapter headings and sub-headings into questions, using open-ended question words: *what, why,* and *how.* Questions included:
  - *What were Hitler's goals?*
  - *How did Hitler plan to achieve his goals?*
  - *How did Germany rearm?*
  - *What was the League of Nations?*
  - *Why did the League of Nations fail?*

During

- Read the first paragraph twice since it was important yet confusing. Rereading the first paragraph set the stage for understanding the remainder of the section.
- In the section "Hitler's Goals," marked the goals and how Hitler intended to achieve them.
- In the section "Germany Rearms," marked signal words ("*The first problem*," "*At last*") and intervening events. This helped him follow the sequence of ideas.
- Looked in the index to find more information about the League of Nations. Added information that helped him better understand this topic.

After

- Answered the questions formed before reading.
- Reviewed his text markings.
- Outlined information in the section in preparation for the lecture and an upcoming quiz.

Select, Sort, Solidify

Successfully reading and learning from a text doesn't just happen. Instead, you will need to plan strategically how you will understand and remember information within the text. These approaches will help you to read and study text material effectively and efficiently.

Strategies to SELECT Text Information

Before Reading

The following strategies help you answer the question: *What text material do I need to know for the upcoming assignment, quiz, or test?*

- *Identify your purpose for reading.* Knowing your purpose tends to increase both interest and concentration when reading. Clarify *why* you are reading the material, which can be one or more of the following reasons:
  - To gain basic background knowledge.
  - To prepare for class discussions.

(Continued)

AGAIN THE ROAD TO WAR (1933–1939)

World War I and the Versailles treaty had only a marginal relationship to the world depression of the 1930s. In Germany, however, where the reparations settlement had contributed to the vast inflation of 1923, economic and social discontent focused on the Versailles settlement as the cause of all ills. Throughout the late 1920s, Adolf Hitler and the Nazi Party denounced Versailles as the source of all of Germany's troubles. The economic woes of the early 1930s seemed to bear them out. Nationalism and attention to the social question, along with party discipline, had been the sources of Nazi success. They continued to influence Hitler's foreign policy after he became chancellor in January 1933. Moreover, the Nazi destruction of the Weimar constitution and of political opposition meant that Hitler himself totally dominated German foreign policy. Consequently, it is important to know what his goals were and how he planned to achieve them. *Germany: nationalism, unrest, strict rules*

HITLER'S GOALS ← *important!!*

From the first expression of his goals in a book written in jail, *Mein Kampf (My Struggle)*, to his last days in the underground bunker in Berlin where he killed himself, Hitler's racial theories and goals were at the center of his thought. He meant to go far beyond Germany's 1914 boundaries, which were the limit of the vision of his predecessors. He meant to bring the entire German people—the *Volk*—understood as a racial group, together into a single nation. *acquire land* *unite people*

The new Germany would include all the Germanic parts of the old Habsburg Empire, including Austria. This virile and growing nation would need more space to live, or *Lebensraum*, that would be taken from the Slavs, who, according to Nazi theory, were a lesser race, fit only for servitude. The removal of the Jews, another inferior race according to Nazi theory, would purify the new Germany. The plans required the conquest of Poland and Ukraine as the primary areas for German settlement and for providing badly needed food. Neither *Mein Kampf* nor later statements of policy were blueprints for action. Rather, Hitler was a brilliant improviser who exploited opportunities as they arose. He never lost sight of his goal, however, which would almost certainly require a *inferior races* *1) Slavs* *2) Jews*

major war. (See "Hitler Describes His Goals in Foreign Policy.")

Germany Rearms When Hitler came to power, Germany was far too weak to permit a direct approach to reach his aims. The first problem he set out to resolve was to shake off the fetters of Versailles and to make Germany a formidable military power. In October 1933, Germany withdrew from an international disarmament conference and also from the League of Nations. Hitler argued that because the other powers had not disarmed as they had promised, it was wrong to keep Germany helpless. These acts alarmed the French, but were merely symbolic. In January 1934, Germany signed a nonaggression pact with Poland that was of greater concern to France, for it undermined France's chief means of containing the Germans. At last, in March 1935, Hitler formally renounced the disarmament provisions of the Versailles treaty with the formation of a German air force, and soon he reinstated conscription, which aimed at an army of half a million men. *no disarmament started draft* *became military power* *left League of Nations*

The League of Nations Fails Growing evidence that the League of Nations could not keep the peace and that collective security was a myth made Hitler's path easier. In September 1931, Japan occupied Manchuria. China appealed to the League of Nations. The league dispatched a commission under a British diplomat, the earl of Lytton (1876–1951). The *Lytton Report* condemned the Japanese for resorting to force, but the powers were unwilling to impose sanctions. Japan withdrew from the League and kept control of Manchuria.

When Hitler announced his decision to rearm Germany, the League formally condemned that action, but it took no steps to prevent it. France and Britain felt unable to object forcefully because they had not carried out their own promises to disarm. Instead, they met with Mussolini in June 1935 to form the so-called Stresa Front, promising to use force to maintain the status quo in Europe. This show of unity was short lived, however. Britain, desperate to maintain superiority at sea, violated the spirit of the Stresa accords and sacrificed French security needs to make a separate naval agreement with Hitler. The pact allowed him to rebuild the German fleet to 35 percent of the British navy. Hitler had taken a major step toward his goal without provoking serious opposition. Italy's expansionist ambitions in Africa, however, soon brought it into conflict with the Western powers. *League didn't prevent German arming* *Britain naval agreement w/Hitler* *Hitler: no major objectors*

Source: Kagan, Donald; Ozment, Steven; Turner, Frank M., *Western Heritage: The Combined Volume*, 9th Edition, © 2007, p. 409. Reprinted by permission of Pearson Education, Inc., Upper Saddle River, NJ.

- ◆ To clarify material presented in class.
- ◆ To deepen your understanding.
- ◆ To learn information that will be on the exam.
- ◆ To use in a class assignment.

- *Review homework or notes from previous class.* This will help you put the new information in context of what your instructor is presenting in class.

- *Reduce distractions.* Minimizing external and internal distractions will maximize your concentration and alertness while reading.
  - ◆ Be rested, well-fed, and alert.
  - ◆ Move away from friends, TV, IM, and other outside sources of distractions.

- *Preview the chapter.* Flip through the pages and take note of:
  - ◆ The main topics.
  - ◆ How information is organized.
  - ◆ Pictures, graphics, bold print, italicized words, and other visual aids. Look at these before you read so that they don't disrupt your concentration while you are reading.
  - ◆ Key terms. Look up terms you don't understand; write definitions in the margins or on index cards.
  - ◆ Introductions, summaries, and chapter questions.
  - ◆ Overall difficulty level of the material.

Student Comments

- A reading plan helps me manage my time so that I finish each reading assignment. My Sociology textbook has long chapters. I first look at the whole chapter and write down the amount of time I need to read. So far I am getting each chapter read on time.

  –Kylie

- A strategy I use is to look at bold headings and important words before reading. This helps me know what I have to focus on as I read.

  –Ana

Strategies to SORT Text Information

During Reading

Employ strategies that help you clarify and understand text material. Answer the question: *How can I summarize, organize, or personalize text information that I need to know?*

- *Break up reading into logical segments.* Concentrate on one section of the chapter at a time.
- *Turn section headings into questions.* Read to discover answers to your questions. Use the words "what," "how," or "why" when formulating questions. For example: *What are key characteristics of Social Science texts? How do I know what text material is important? Why should I preview a chapter?*
- *Mark, write, and highlight in your book.*
  - Highlight or underline important terms or phrases. Be careful to identify just the main points, that is, highlight no more than 20% of a text page.
  - Use margins to paraphrase and summarize key ideas.
  - Add numbers to call attention to the order of ideas.
  - Use color and symbols to emphasize importance.
- *Pay special attention to examples, illustrations, and graphics.* These features will help you understand important concepts.
- *Recite aloud.* After reading a section, look away and restate key information *in your own words*. If you can't do it, read the section again!
- *Make personal connections.* Add your own examples. Link text information with real-life situations.
- *Refer back to your lecture notes* when reading after a class. Focus on how the text and class information fit together. Clarify your class notes by adding information from your text.
- *Take periodic breaks.* Afterward, *review the previous section* before starting to read the next.

Strategies to SOLIDIFY Text Information

After Reading

You want to maximize your ability to remember important text material. Employ strategies that answer the question: *What can I do to retain text information for future use?*

- *Review the chapter.*
  - ◆ Reread your marginal notes.
  - ◆ Answer beginning-of-chapter learning objectives or focus questions. In your own words, answer end-of-chapter comprehension questions.
  - ◆ Define and give examples for important terms and concepts. Know *who* key people are and *why* they are important.
- *Develop a study guide.* Condense and summarize important text information. You can utilize a variety of formats:
  - ◆ Review charts and timelines.
  - ◆ Concept or mind maps.
  - ◆ Questions and answers.
  - ◆ Summary outlines.
  - ◆ Study cards.
- *Recite aloud.* As you review, talk aloud to yourself in order to provide auditory reinforcement of important information.

Student Comments

- I use textbook marking for most of my assignments. Marking text pages helps with my comprehension and retention because it makes me read more in depth. I jot down a note or two about what I just read, and then move on to the next paragraph. It's extremely helpful to me in Psychology, which requires a lot of reading.

  –Jen

Example of Textbook Marking

A student followed this sequence when reading the section, "Classical Conditioning," (see following pages) in the Psychology textbook.

Classical Conditioning

The story of habituation could hardly be more straightforward. We experience a stimulus, respond to it, and then stop responding after repeated exposure. We've learned something significant, but we haven't learned to forge connections between two stimuli. Yet a great deal of learning depends on associating one thing with another. If we never learned to connect one stimulus, like the appearance of an apple, with another stimulus, like its taste, our world would remain what William James (1891) called a "blooming, buzzing confusion"—a world of disconnected sensory experiences.

BRITISH ASSOCIATIONISM

Knowledge = connecting stimuli

Several centuries ago, a school of thinkers called the *British Associationists* believed that we acquire virtually all of our knowledge by connecting one stimulus with another: the sound of our mother's voice with her face, for example. Once we form these associations, we need only recall one element of the pair to retrieve the other. Even thinking about a sensation often triggers it. For example, as you read about your mother's face, you might have pictured her in your mind. The British Associationists, who included David Hartley (1707–1757) and John Stuart Mill (1806–1873), believed that simple associations provided the mental building blocks for more complex ideas. Your understanding of this paragraph, they surely would have suggested, stems from thousands of linkages you've formed between the words in it—like *sound* and *voice*—and other words, which are in turn linked to simple concepts, which are in turn linked to more complex concepts . . . and, well, you get the picture.

PAVLOV'S DISCOVERIES

The Rolling Stones may be the only major rock band to accurately describe the process of classical conditioning. One of their well-known songs refers to a man salivating like one of Pavlov's dogs whenever the object of his affection calls his name. Not bad for a group of non-psychologists!

The history of science teaches us that many discoveries arise from *serendipity*, or accident. Yet it takes a great scientist to capitalize on serendipitous observations that others regard as meaningless flukes. As French microbiologist Louis Pasteur, who discovered the process of pasteurizing milk, observed, "Chance favors the prepared mind." So it was with the discoveries of Russian scientist Ivan Pavlov. His landmark understanding of classical conditioning emerged from a set of unforeseen observations that were unrelated to his main research interests.

Pavlov - initial research in digestion

Pavlov's primary research was digestion in dogs—in fact, his discoveries concerning digestion, not classical conditioning, earned him the Nobel Prize in 1904. Pavlov placed dogs in a harness and inserted a *cannula,* or collection tube, into their salivary glands to study their salivary responses to meat powder. In doing so, he observed something unexpected: He found that dogs began salivating not only to the meat powder itself, but to previously neutral stimuli that had become associated with it, such as research assistants who brought in the powder. Indeed, the dogs even salivated to the sound of these assistants' footsteps as they approached the laboratory. The dogs seemed to be anticipating the meat powder and responding to stimuli that signaled its arrival.

dogs salivate at SIGNAL of food

We call this process of association **classical conditioning** (or **Pavlovian or respondent conditioning**): a form of learning in which animals come to respond to a previously neutral stimulus that had been paired with another stimulus that elicits an automatic response. Yet Pavlov's initial observations were merely anecdotal, so like any good scientist he put his informal observations to a more rigorous test.

classical (Pavlovian or respondent) conditioning
form of learning in which animals come to respond to a previously neutral stimulus that had been paired with another stimulus that elicits an automatic response

conditioned stimulus (CS)
initially neutral stimulus

THE CLASSICAL CONDITIONING PHENOMENON *know this!*

Here's how Pavlov first demonstrated classical conditioning systematically (see **Figure 6.2**).

(1) He started with an initially neutral stimulus, called the **conditioned stimulus (CS)**. In this case, Pavlov used a metronome, a clicking pendulum that keeps time (in other studies, Pavlov used a tuning fork or whistle; contrary to urban legend, Pavlov didn't use a bell). This stimulus doesn't elicit much, if any, response from the dogs. Interestingly, the term

CS

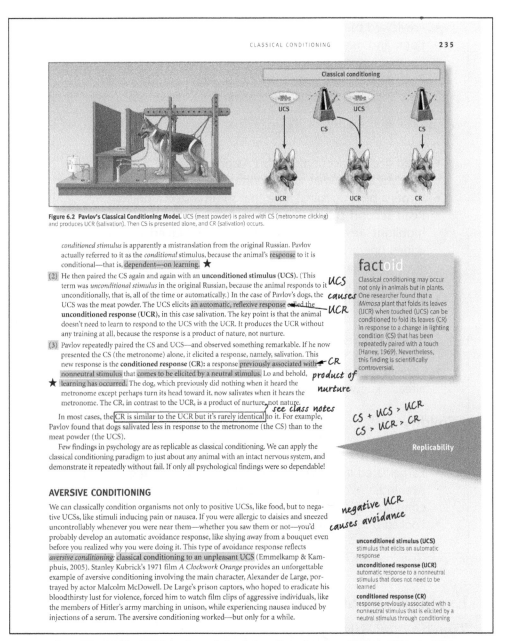

Classical conditioning

UCS   UCS

CS   CS

UCR   UCR   CR

Figure 6.2 Pavlov's Classical Conditioning Model. UCS (meat powder) is paired with CS (metronome clicking) and produces UCR (salivation). Then CS is presented alone, and CR (salivation) occurs.

conditioned stimulus is apparently a mistranslation from the original Russian. Pavlov actually referred to it as the *conditional* stimulus, because the animal's response to it is conditional—that is, dependent—on learning. ★

(2) He then paired the CS again and again with an **unconditioned stimulus (UCS)**. (This term was *unconditional stimulus* in the original Russian, because the animal responds to it unconditionally, that is, all of the time or automatically.) In the case of Pavlov's dogs, the UCS was the meat powder. The UCS elicits an automatic, reflexive response called the **unconditioned response (UCR)**, in this case salivation. The key point is that the animal doesn't need to learn to respond to the UCS with the UCR. It produces the UCR without any training at all, because the response is a product of nature, not nurture.

[margin notes:] UCS causes UCR

(3) Pavlov repeatedly paired the CS and UCS—and observed something remarkable. If he now presented the CS (the metronome) alone, it elicited a response, namely, salivation. This new response is the **conditioned response (CR)**: a response previously associated with a nonneutral stimulus that comes to be elicited by a neutral stimulus. Lo and behold, learning has occurred. The dog, which previously did nothing when it heard the metronome except perhaps turn its head toward it, now salivates when it hears the metronome. The CR, in contrast to the UCR, is a product of nurture, not nature.

[margin notes:] CR — product of nurture   see class notes

In most cases, the CR is similar to the UCR but it's rarely identical to it. For example, Pavlov found that dogs salivated less in response to the metronome (the CS) than to the meat powder (the UCS).

[margin notes:] CS + UCS > UCR   CS > UCR > CR

Few findings in psychology are as replicable as classical conditioning. We can apply the classical conditioning paradigm to just about any animal with an intact nervous system, and demonstrate it repeatedly without fail. If only all psychological findings were so dependable!

Replicability

AVERSIVE CONDITIONING

We can classically condition organisms not only to positive UCSs, like food, but to negative UCSs, like stimuli inducing pain or nausea. If you were allergic to daisies and sneezed uncontrollably whenever you were near them—whether you saw them or not—you'd probably develop an automatic avoidance response, like shying away from a bouquet even before you realized why you were doing it. This type of avoidance response reflects *aversive conditioning*: classical conditioning to an unpleasant UCS (Emmelkamp & Kamphuis, 2005). Stanley Kubrick's 1971 film *A Clockwork Orange* provides an unforgettable example of aversive conditioning involving the main character, Alexander de Large, portrayed by actor Malcolm McDowell. De Large's prison captors, who hoped to eradicate his bloodthirsty lust for violence, forced him to watch film clips of aggressive individuals, like the members of Hitler's army marching in unison, while experiencing nausea induced by injections of a serum. The aversive conditioning worked—but only for a while.

[margin notes:] negative UCR causes avoidance

factoid

Classical conditioning may occur not only in animals but in plants. One researcher found that a *Mimosa* plant that folds its leaves (UCR) when touched (UCS) can be conditioned to fold its leaves (CR) in response to a change in lighting condition (CS) that has been repeatedly paired with a touch (Haney, 1969). Nevertheless, this finding is scientifically controversial.

unconditioned stimulus (UCS)
stimulus that elicits an automatic response

unconditioned response (UCR)
automatic response to a nonneutral stimulus that does not need to be learned

conditioned response (CR)
response previously associated with a nonneutral stimulus that is elicited by a neutral stimulus through conditioning

---

Select

- Previewed the section; looked at headings, bold print, illustrations, and marginal notes.
- Formed a general idea of the type of information presented. Realized the topic was complicated, with confusing terms (i.e. *conditioned* vs. *unconditioned*, *stimulus* vs. *response*).

Sort

- Read first subsection "British Associationism." Stopped and thought about what was important to know.
- Wrote a brief marginal note that summarized a point.
- Read second subsection "Pavlov's Discoveries." Decided to highlight key words that defined bold-faced terms. Also, added brief marginal notations that summarized and emphasized key ideas.
- Repeated process for remaining subsections.
- Used abbreviations and symbols ("→" = connection; "*" = important).
- Circled a phrase she did not understand. Wrote a reminder to check class notes for more explanations.
- Looked for associations between the text and what she already knew. Realized she needed more examples.

Solidify

- Reviewed her text notes the following day.
- Participated in the weekly group review session the following evening. Worked on creating examples of classical conditioning.
- Looked over text and notes before next class session.

Examples of Study Guides

Timeline for History Text Chapter

A student followed this sequence when previewing and reading the History chapter:

Select

- Looked at syllabus—a 50-point multiple choice chapter test was scheduled for the next week.
- Previewed the chapter. Realized the information was presented sequentially, building up to the Holocaust and ending with the creation of Israel.
- Noted particular names and terms (many of which were bold-faced in the text) which likely he needed to know. Used these dates, names, and terms to guide his reading and answer the question: *What do I need to know for this course?*

Sort

- After reading each section, wrote dates in the margin and highlighted key names and terms associated with each date.
- Added information in the margins that he remembered hearing from his grandfather, who served in the army during WWII.

Solidify

- Created a timeline summarizing key points (below). Wrote dates on left side of the paper, jotted down key points, then highlighted important terms and names.
- Used the study guide to review the chapter material: (1) Covered one side of the paper and quizzed himself. (2) Focused on explanations for highlighted words. (3) Cut the events side of the chart into strips and re-organized the events without looking at dates.

Holocaust Timeline

1920	Nazi Party formed.
1929	Heinrich **Himmler** was appointed head of the **SS**, Hitler's elite guard known for brutality.

(Continued)

Holocaust Timeline *(Continued)*

1930s	*Hitler Jugend*—Hitler Youth—was established to spread anti-Semitic and nationalistic propaganda to young boys.
1933	Hitler became Chancellor on January 30.
1933	*Enabling Act* gave Hitler total dictatorial power for four years.
1933–38	Nazis boycotted Jewish businesses; forbade intermarriage between Jews and Germans.
1933	Joseph **Goebbels** appointed minister of propaganda for the Nazi party.
1933	Nazis built first concentration camps in Germany, modeled after Native American reservations in the U.S.
1934	Adolf Hitler became *der Fuhrer*, or leader, of Germany after the death of Hindenburg.
1935	*Nuremberg Racial Laws* deprived German Jews of their citizenship.
1937	*Buchenwald* concentration camp established in Germany. Notorious for medical experiments—amputations, lethal germs, & poisons—performed on human subjects.
1938	*Anschluss*—Germany invaded Austria, though invasion is portrayed as a union.
1938	*Kristallnacht*—Jewish property was attacked in Germany on the "night of broken glass."
1939	World War II officially began with declaration of war on Germany by Britain and France.
1939	*Blitzpogrom*—three million Polish Jews were subjected to rape and murder.
1941	United States entered war as a result of **Pearl Harbor**.
1942	Hitler proposed the **Final Solution** of the "Jewish problem"; the Holocaust truly begins.
1943	**Warsaw Uprising**—Ghetto uprising by Jews.
1945	Advancing Allied Armies discover Nazi extermination camps; 6 million Jews murdered.
1948	Creation of the nation Israel.

Question-and-Answer Study Guide for Psychology Text

A student followed this sequence as she previewed and read the section in the Psychology text:

Select

- Determined that the instructor would lecture on Classical Conditioning in class.
- Previewed the section by looking at headings, bold print, and illustrations.
- Turned each heading into a question, writing on notebook paper (below).

Sort

- Read each subsection, then stopped to answer the question. If could not answer, reread.
- Answered each question in own words; wrote answer below the question, underlining some key words (below).
- Changed or expanded question to fit content, as needed.

Solidify

- After reading, went back and recited the answers without looking at notes.
- Checked each answer before moving on to the next question.

Question: *What is Classical Conditioning?*
Answer: Subjects taught automatic responses to new stimulus after frequent pairing of new + initial stimulus. Has these factors:

- Conditioned Stimulus (CS) – Subject has no response to CS at start of experiment. Response dependent on learning.

(Continued)

- <u>Unconditioned Stimulus (UCS)</u> – What the subject responds to (ex: food).
- <u>Unconditioned Response (UCR)</u> – Automatic, reflexive response (ex: saliva).
- <u>Conditioned Response (CR)</u> – Same response as UCR, but happens w/o food, just to CS.

Question: *Who discovered Classical Conditioning?*
Answer: <u>Ivan Pavlov</u>.
Question: *What is British Associationism?*
Answer: Developed idea that <u>knowledge made by connecting stimuli</u>. Students recall information by remembering one stimulus which leads to another. Thousands of connections needed for complex knowledge.
Question: *How did Pavlov discover Classical Conditioning?*
Answer: Researched digestion initially. Noticed that, before actually tasting powder, dogs would salivate at sound of research assistants bringing meat powder.
Question: *What is Aversive Conditioning?*
Answer: Subject presented with something negative, like pain (UCS) paired with something they want to avoid, like smoking. Then begin to associate negative UCS with what they want to avoid. Used to train subjects to <u>avoid</u> certain activities or stimuli.

Summary Chart

The chart is an overview of text strategies presented in this chapter. Use the chart as you plan approaches for reading and studying content in your Social Science course.

SELECT	SORT	SOLIDIFY
BEFORE:	DURING:	AFTER:

✓ Know your purpose for reading.
✓ Review homework or notes from the previous class.
✓ Reduce distractions.
✓ Preview the chapter.
	✓ Turn section headings into questions. Read to discover answers.
	✓ Mark, write, and highlight in your book.
	✓ Pay attention to examples, illustrations, and graphics.
	✓ Recite aloud.
	✓ Make personal connections.
	✓ Refer back to class notes.
	✓ Review previous section.
		✓ Review the chapter:
		  o Marginal notes.
		  o Chapter questions.
		  o Key terms, concepts, and people.
		✓ Develop a study guide:
		  o Review charts and timelines.
		  o Concept or mind maps.
		  o Questions and answers.
		  o Summary outlines.
		  o Study cards.
		✓ Recite aloud.

Student Comments

- I use textbook markings in my Anthropology class because my instructor teaches mainly from the book. Also, I use concept maps to link what I am reading. Concept maps help me combine my thoughts with the new ideas that I am learning.

–José

- Graphic organizers help me a lot. I'm an artistic and visual learner, so I use many charts, outlines, and diagrams that show relationships between the information I'm reading.

–Terrell

Text Strategies: Taking Action

Take time to stop, reflect, and apply the information presented in this chapter. Follow these five steps, using the sheets on the subsequent pages:

1. Identify a current reading assignment for your Social Science course. Fill in course name, the chapter or pages, and due date.

2. Place a check next to the strategies you will use for this assignment. You should do *all* of the four strategies from the **SELECT** column, *at least three* of the seven strategies from the **SORT** column, and *at least one* of the three strategies from the **SOLIDIFY** column.

3. Cut out the strip. Use it as a bookmark to remind you of your reading plan.

4. Afterward, take a moment to evaluate your success.

5. Repeat these steps for your next reading assignment, using another sheet. Build on previous approaches that worked for you.

Course: Chapter or pages: Due date:

SELECT	**SORT**	**SOLIDIFY**
BEFORE:	DURING:	AFTER:
___Know your purpose for reading.	___Turn section headings into questions. Read to discover answers.	___Review the chapter: o Marginal notes. o Chapter questions. o Key terms, concepts, and people.
___Review home-work or notes from the previous class.	___Mark, write, and highlight in your book.	
___Reduce distractions.	___Pay attention to examples, illustrations, and graphics.	___Develop a study guide: o Review charts and timelines. o Concept or mind maps. o Questions and answers. o Summary outlines. o Study cards.
___Preview the chapter.	___Recite aloud.	
	___Make personal connections.	
	___Refer back to class notes.	
	___Review previous section.	___Recite aloud.

Evaluate Your Success: *For this assignment, which strategies helped you to understand and remember information? Highlight or circle each strategy that assisted you with reading and studying more effectively.*

Course: Chapter or pages: Due date:

SELECT	SORT	SOLIDIFY
BEFORE:	**DURING:**	**AFTER:**
___Know your purpose for reading. ___Review home-work or notes from the previ-ous class. ___Reduce distrac-tions. ___Preview the chapter.	___Turn section headings into questions. Read to discover answers. ___Mark, write, and highlight in your book. ___Pay attention to examples, illus-trations, and graphics. ___Recite aloud. ___Make personal connections. ___Refer back to class notes. ___Review previous section.	___Review the chapter: o Marginal notes. o Chapter questions. o Key terms, concepts, and people. ___Develop a study guide: o Review charts and timelines. o Concept or mind maps. o Questions and answers. o Summary out-lines. o Study cards. ___Recite aloud.

Evaluate Your Success: *For this assignment, which strategies helped you to understand and remember information? Highlight or circle each strategy that assisted you with reading and studying more effectively.*

3

TAKE IN-CLASS NOTES

Importance of Taking Notes in Class

Be prepared to take notes in *each* class session. Whatever the class format—be it conventional lecture, guest speaker, video or movie, or group presentation—be ready to listen attentively and take notes. Subject matter covered in class is a summary of what your instructor has identified as significant within the Social Science discipline and, therefore, the information likely will appear on an upcoming test. The majority of questions on exams in lower-level Social Science courses tend to come from materials covered during class time. Note taking, either on paper or with a computer, is a vital aspect of identifying and understanding important information presented in class.

Format of Class Notes

Most Social Science classes encompass one or more of the following formats for class notes.

- **Traditional lecture notes.** In more conventional classes, the instructor talks during most of class time. Students are expected to write or type a summary of the content presented by the instructor. Topics presented in class often parallel content in a textbook or other reading assignment. During class the instructor sometimes asks questions to spark student input or includes activities to reinforce important concepts.

- **Web-based notes.** Many instructors place lecture notes on a Web-based program. If you are in this situation, *do* preview the notes before each class. Bring the notes to class, either hard copies or on your laptop. Refer to these notes throughout the class session, adding to the information that is discussed, highlighting ideas that are emphasized, and jotting references to text pages and other readings.

- **PowerPoint® notes**. Many instructors use Microsoft PowerPoint presentations in class. Most PowerPoint slides are a bare-bones listing of topics; therefore, it is important that you add explanations, examples, and other details during class. If the PowerPoint slides are available beforehand, print them out and write on the hard copies, adding and highlighting information discussed during the class session.

- **Skeleton notes**. At times an instructor provides a skeleton outline of lecture notes which students can purchase from a copy center or print from the Internet. These notes contain only main topics with plenty of white space for students to add details, examples, and further explanations.

- **Audio notes**. Increasingly instructors make lecture material available to download on an MP3 player or computer, especially in large lecture classes. If you are ill and cannot attend class, use the podcast or audio material to keep abreast of lecture material. Also, listen to the audio content when doing other activities—such as walking, exercising, or laundry—in order to review and reinforce lecture material. However, do not rely on a podcast or audio material to replace regular class attendance. You are more likely to pay closer attention when listening and taking notes in the classroom. Furthermore, you will pick up helpful cues when in the same room as the instructor and other students.

A common characteristic of all five formats of class notes is the need for students to actively listen and decide what information *is* or *is not* important. If you think material is important—write it down. If you are not sure if an idea is important—write it down, also. Since you will be taking time after class to review and edit your notes, it is best to err on the side of including extra ideas, as opposed to too few ideas. Note taking during class is part of active decision making, that is, selecting, sorting, and solidifying Social Science content. No matter what the format, the following strategies will maximize your ability to understand and remember in-class material.

Select, Sort, Solidify

Importantly, *go to every class*. As mentioned previously, you are more likely to create clear, understandable notes when you are sitting in the classroom, as opposed to listening only to a podcast or copying another student's notes. The following strategies will assist you to listen actively and take notes that enhance your understanding and remembering of class content.

Strategies to SELECT In-Class Material

Begin by deciding what information is important. Answer the question: *What in-class material do I need to know for the upcoming assignment, quiz, or test?*

Before Class
Obtain background and familiarity with topics to be discussed in class:

- **Review information on the course syllabus.** Notice which topics will be covered during the class session.
- **Skim homework and notes from the previous class.** This will focus your attention and prepare you to listen.
- **Skim the corresponding text chapter.** Quickly read the introduction and summary, headings and subheadings, bold-faced and italicized words, and graphic features. For a more thorough background and deeper understanding, read the entire chapter.
- **Obtain online notes.** Make online notes available to use during class by either printing out hard copies or bringing your laptop.

During Class
- **Sit in middle-front of the classroom.** You will see and hear more clearly and minimize surrounding distractions, especially in large auditorium-style classrooms.
- **Listen selectively—focus on ideas** (as opposed to words). Concentrate on:
  - *Main ideas* about the topic.
  - *Explanations, details, and examples* that support each main idea.
  - *Relationships or connections* among the ideas. Your notes should reflect how ideas are related or organized. Here are six common ways ideas are presented in the content of a lecture:

- **Definitions.** Content includes either a formal or informal meaning of terms or concepts. In your notes, paraphrase the definitions, adding explanations and examples.
- **Examples.** Content includes illustrations that describe, explain, and/or personalize important terms or concepts. In your notes, leave space to add your own examples after class.
- **Cause and effect.** Content includes how an idea or event triggers another. In your notes, make sure this cause/effect connection is obvious.
- **Order.** Content presented as an order of importance or a time order. In your notes, use numbers (1, 2, 3 . . .) to emphasize the order of ideas or steps in a sequence.
- **Compare and contrast.** Content presents similarities and differences among ideas. After class, summarize the information by creating a chart, with one column listing similarities and the other listing differences.
- **Rationale.** Content provides details that clarify the reasons *why* something happened. In your notes, provide clear, concrete, and substantial explanations.

- **Be attentive of verbal cues.** Every instructor provides verbal cues, or signals, indicating the importance of particular information. For example, an instructor asks questions, repeats or paraphrases information, or talks louder or slower. If your instructor emphasizes an idea, include it in your notes!

- **Be attentive of non-verbal cues.** Likewise, be aware of your instructor's behaviors and mannerisms that indicate ideas are important. For example, an instructor writes on the board, uses hand gestures, paces, or makes eye contact.

- **Use phrases, abbreviations, and symbols.** Often speed is a factor when taking notes in class. Therefore, eliminate unnecessary words—write in phrases and not whole sentences. Also, eliminate unnecessary letters—use abbreviations and symbols.

- **Utilize Web notes.** On your Web notes, highlight ideas that the instructor emphasizes. In addition, add details and examples that help to explain information.

- **Ask questions.** Let the instructor know if you are confused or uncertain about content. Ask questions to clarify information and help you stay alert during class time.

Strategies to SORT In-Class Material

Employ strategies that help you clarify and understand in-class material. Answer the question: *How can I summarize, organize, or personalize in-class information that I need to know?*

After Class

- **Review notes soon after each class.** Within 24 hours after class, take the time to look over your notes and check for understanding.
- **Make additions or changes**, as needed, to clarify information in your notes.
  - ◆ *Organize* ideas.
  - ◆ *Paraphrase* ideas in your own words.
  - ◆ *Add* examples and explanations.
  - ◆ *Fill in* text information.
  - ◆ *Highlight* or *underline* key terms and concepts.
- **Think about upcoming tests.** Identify broad ideas and concepts which are potential essay questions. Look for individual items and details which might be short answer questions. Also, recognize potential case study and application questions.

Strategies to SOLIDIFY In-Class Material

Employ strategies that maximize your ability to remember in-class material. Answer the question: *What can I do to retain in-class information for future use?*

After Class

- **Review weekly.** Set aside a block of time (such as Sunday evening) to go back through your in-class notes. Note the continuation and transition of ideas and how topics relate to each other.
- **Participate in study/review sessions.** Ask and answer questions with other classmates.
- **Make sample test questions** from your notes.
- **Recite aloud.** As you review, talk aloud to yourself to provide auditory reinforcement.

Student Comments

- When I review my notes after each class I notice that I am better prepared for the next class and am able to follow the instructor's lectures much more easily.

  —Taurena

- My instructor posts her lecture notes online. I print out the notes before class and read over them. When I print them out I change them to double spaced, so that in class I can add examples and other information from the instructor.

  —Chris

- In Art History, I was so uninterested and was struggling to stay awake during class. I forced myself to become interested. I started looking at the architecture on campus, went to gallery exhibits, and even talked to other people about what I was learning. Now I find myself genuinely interested in the subject and am able to grasp more in class. Sitting through an hour and a half of lecture has become <u>a lot</u> easier.

  —Amiel

Examples of Notes

Notes from Sociology Class

A student followed this sequence before, during, and after class (see her notes on the following page):

Sort

- Before class, reviewed the syllabus and saw that the instructor would start a new chapter.
- Skimmed the chapter. Noted the title, overview, color-coded headings and sub-headings, abundance of illustrations, reading tips, and sample test questions.
- At start of class, headed the notepaper with date, chapter title, and topic written on the board.
- As instructor spoke, focused on writing main ideas and key terms, with supporting explanations and examples underneath.

(Continued)

- Left spaces between topics. Used phrases, abbreviations, and symbols.
- Asked the instructor a question about "social vs. biological differences." Wrote down the example that the instructor provided.

Select

- That evening, went back through the in-class notes. Highlighted key words; added summary (**Each had . . .**), text reference (**see p. 331**), and emphasis (**def., know . . .**).

Solidify

- Each Monday morning, reviewed consecutive Sociology class notes. Wrote down questions for weekly study group.

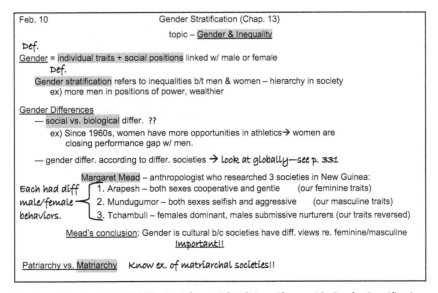

Based on: Macionis, J. J. (2008). *Sociology,* 12th Edition, Chapter 13, Gender Stratification, p. 329–355. Published by Pearson Prentice Hall, Upper Saddle River, NJ.

Web Notes from Political Science Class

A student followed this sequence before, during, and after class:

Sort

- Before class, downloaded that day's notes (see following page), in outline format, onto his laptop computer. Previewed the outline—the right column was empty in order for students to add information from class and textbook.
- Skimmed Chapter 15. Was struck by the length (40 pages) and density of the material. Decided to allow lots of time after class to read and add text information.
- During class, highlighted terms and information that the instructor emphasized. In the right column, typed in additional explanations and examples derived from class discussion.

Select

- Set aside blocks of study time that evening and the following afternoon. As he read a section of the chapter, he reviewed the corresponding material within his class notes.
- Added text information in the right column of the notes.

Solidify

- Referred to notes when completing the 20-question Chapter Review Test.
- Reviewed class and text material out loud with two classmates each Monday evening. Focused on answering the end-of-chapter Discussion Questions since the test will consist of essay questions.

Date: **October 24**	Topic: **Political Parties**	Text Chapter: **15**
I. Major political parties as "umbrella" organizations.		Umbrella means includes a range of issues, coalitions, & interest groups.
II. Religion and Political Parties.		
A. First Amendment: separation of state & church.		Citizens free to practice any religion, but gov't cannot establish a religion -- p. 579
B. Merging of religion & politics.		
1. 1980s: influence of evangelical Christians.		called the Religious Right
2. grassroots networking.		
3. Christian Coalition partnered with Republican Party.		p. 580-1: example in Missouri
4. 1994: Republicans voted into office at all levels.		**influx of CC into politics produced Republican majority w/ conservative agenda
III. Models of Political Parties.		
A. Pragmatic party model: sponsor candidates to control government.		know difference b/t models
B. Responsible party model: sponsor candidates to shape public policy.		
C. Characteristics of Political Parties.		vs. Interest Groups
1. Nominate candidates under own label.		1. don't nominate
2. Have party platform with wide range of policy positions.		2. narrow range of issues
3. Subject to state and local laws.		3. private organizations—no gov't. rules

Based on: Shea, D. M., Green, J. C., & Smith, C. E. (2007). *Living Democracy,* National ed., Chapter 15, Political Parties, p. 579–619. Published by Pearson Prentice Hall, Upper Saddle River, NJ.

Summary Chart

This is an overview of note-taking strategies presented in the chapter. Use the chart as you plan approaches for listening and taking notes in your Social Science course.

SELECT	SORT	SOLIDIFY
BEFORE:	AFTER:	AFTER:

✓ Review syllabus.
✓ Skim homework and previous notes.
✓ Skim related text chapter.
✓ Have online notes ready.
	✓ Review notes soon after class.
	✓ Make additions or changes to clarify information.
	  o Organize ideas.
	  o Add examples and explanations.
		✓ Review weekly.
		✓ Participate in study/review sessions.
		✓ Make sample test questions.
		✓ Recite aloud.

SELECT *(Continued)*	**SORT** *(Continued)*
DURING:	AFTER: *(Continued)*
✓ Sit in middle-front of the classroom. ✓ Listen selectively; focus on ideas. ✓ Be attentive of verbal and non-verbal cues. ✓ Use phrases, abbreviations, and symbols in notes. ✓ Utilize Web notes. ✓ Ask questions.	o Fill in text information. o Highlight or underline key terms and concepts.

Student Comments

- My Political Science instructor is very unorganized—I cannot follow his lectures. I have to rewrite my notes after class and follow the organization in the class textbook.

  –Yoshi

- I used to view each day's notes as separate entities. Then I started looking for patterns and soon was able to associate the topics from one lecture to the next. Now I understand more and am more interested in what my professor is saying!

  –Marta

Note-Taking Strategies: Taking Action

Reflect on and apply information presented in this chapter. Follow these five steps, using sheets on the subsequent pages:

1. Fill in the name of your Social Science course, date of the class session, and topic covered.

2. Place a check next to the strategies you will use for this class.
   - In the **SELECT** column, choose *at least two* of the four strategies to do BEFORE class and *at least two* of the six strategies to do DURING class.

◆ In the **SORT** column, choose *at least one* of the two strategies to do AFTER class.

◆ In the **SOLIDIFY** column, choose *at least two* of the four strategies to do AFTER class.

3. Cut out the sheet. As a reminder, place it in your notebook or post it on your computer.

4. Afterward, take a moment to evaluate your success.

5. Repeat these steps for another class session, building on approaches that have worked.

Course: Date: Topic:

SELECT	SORT	SOLIDIFY
BEFORE:	AFTER:	AFTER:
___Review syllabus.	___Review notes soon after class.	___Review weekly.
___Skim homework and previous notes.	___Make additions or changes to clarify information.	___Participate in study/review sessions.
___Skim related text chapter.	o Organize ideas.	___Make sample test questions.
___Have online notes ready.	o Add examples and explanations.	___Recite aloud.
DURING:	o Fill in text information.	
___Sit in middle-front of the classroom.	o Highlight or underline key terms and concepts.	
___Listen selectively; focus on ideas.		
___Be attentive of verbal and non-verbal cues.		
___Use phrases, abbreviations, and symbols in notes.		
___Utilize Web notes.		
___Ask questions.		

Evaluate Your Success: *Highlight or circle each strategy that assisted you to listen and take notes more effectively.*

Course: Date: Topic:

SELECT	**SORT**	**SOLIDIFY**
BEFORE:	AFTER:	AFTER:
___Review syllabus.	___Review notes soon after class.	___Review weekly.
___Skim homework and previous notes.	___Make additions or changes to clarify information.	___Participate in study/review sessions.
___Skim related text chapter.	o Organize ideas.	___Make sample test questions.
___Have online notes ready.	o Add examples and explanations.	___Recite aloud.
DURING:	o Fill in text information.	
___Sit in middle-front of the classroom.	o Highlight or underline key terms and concepts.	
___Listen selectively; focus on ideas.		
___Be attentive of verbal and non-verbal cues.		
___Use phrases, abbreviations, and symbols in notes.		
___Utilize Web notes.		
___Ask questions.		

Evaluate Your Success: *Highlight or circle each strategy that assisted you to listen and take notes more effectively.*

4

PREPARE FOR EXAMS

Common Types of Exams

Exams in Social Science courses tend to be a combination of objective questions, especially multiple choice items, and essay questions. Rote memorization rarely is adequate to pass exams. Instead, expect that test questions will require higher-level thinking, including application of main ideas and analysis of case studies.

Multiple Choice Questions

Beginning college students frequently are surprised by the difficulty of multiple choice exam questions. Students assume that they will recognize the answer and are confused when the language used in the exam is very different from that in the textbook or lecture notes. At the college level, it is important that you *understand* information and not just memorize what is in your notes or the textbook. Many multiple choice questions on Social Science exams are application questions—that is, you need to utilize information learned in class in a new situation.

Here are some general strategies for tackling multiple choice items:

- *Read carefully.* Look for key words used in the main statement and in the choices of answers.
- *Eliminate.* Narrow down possibilities; cross off answers that you know are wrong.
- *Look for specifics.* Often the more detailed option is the best choice.

- *Look for true options.* Read the main statement with each option, especially when faced with multiple options, such as "a + b" or "none of the above." Then, consider whether that answer is "true" or "false." You are seeking a "true" option(s) as the best answer.
- *Be aware of negatives.* Be careful if a statement contains *not* or *except.*
- *Use clues.* Other questions, especially questions that contain repeated terms or statements, often contain clues about how to answer an item.
- *Guess.* If you are unsure of an answer, take an educated guess in case you run out of time and cannot come back to complete items.

Essay Questions

Exams in the Social Science disciplines often include essay questions. Here are several strategies for answering essay questions:

- *Carefully read the question.* Identify the directive words—those words that indicate the direction or path of your answer. The following chart lists common directive words. The second column explains what type of information you should include in your answer. Directive words provide guidance regarding content and organization of your answer. Note that essay questions often have more than one directive word, such as the example on page 43.
  - ◆ **Directive words:** Use this chart to guide your preparation for essay questions.

Directive Words	What I Should Include in My Answer
Compare	Indicate similarities of ideas; how things are alike (can also include differences).
Contrast	Indicate differences or disparities between or among ideas.
Define	Give a formal definition or meaning, plus further explanation and/or examples.
Critique	Critically analyze and assess an issue; make reference to expert authority or reasons that can support and strengthen your answer.
Describe	Report about, focusing on fundamental characteristics and details (use adjectives/adverbs).

Directive Words	What I Should Include in My Answer
Discuss	Provide points of view or arguments concerning an issue.
Explain	Clarify—provide details; give reasons for—describe why.
Evaluate	Assess or appraise an issue; refer to expert authority or reasons that can support and strengthen your answer.
Identify	Name or label items, often within classifications or categories.
Illustrate	Provide complete examples; add explanations and descriptions.
Justify	Make a case for a statement or point of view by providing reasons and evidence.
List	Place items one after another; note any particular order, such as chronological or level of importance.
Relate	Show how two or more ideas are connected, such as similarities or cause/effect.
Summarize	Go over the main points; review key ideas, omit less important details and examples.
Trace	Order information sequentially; show progression of steps/events.

Source: Lipsky, Sally A. (2008) *College Study: The Essential Ingredients*, 2nd Edition, p. 134. Published by Pearson Prentice Hall, Upper Saddle River, NJ. Reprinted by permission of the publisher.

- *Answer each part of a question in order.* Many questions have multiple parts. Answer each part thoroughly in the order presented. Your instructor will be looking for the same order when reading your answer.
- *Make an outline.* Your answer should include:
  - **Introduction.** Present your thesis. For a short essay, your introduction can be a simple rephrasing of the question.
  - **Body.** Develop each main idea. Include explanations, evidence, examples, and other specifics.
  - **Conclusion.** Summarize your main points.

- *Keep your instructor in mind as you compose your answer.* Remember, your instructor may be assessing hundreds of answers to the same questions. Therefore, your job is to show *clearly* how well you understand the material. Be thorough, yet concise.

- *Use signal or transition words and phrases* to help organize your writing and help your instructor to understand your answer. The chart below provides examples of signal words for each directive word.

Directive Words	Examples of Signal Words and Phrases
Compare	*same as, similarly, likewise, both, as, equal to*
Contrast	*versus, but, on the other hand, nevertheless, in contrast to, instead of*
Define	*to name, labeled by, characterized by*
Critique	*evaluate, critical assessment of, according to*
Describe	*to characterize, labeled with, differentiate, detailed*
Discuss	*a viewpoint, another side of the issue, conversely*
Explain	*to clarify, to detail, shed light on*
Evaluate	*to assess, in appraisal of, in agreement with*
Identify	*a type of, to recognize, distinguished by*
Illustrate	*for instance, such as, to illustrate, a type of, for example*
Justify	*for this reason, because, to verify, to validate*
List	*in addition, also, further, secondarily, next, final, above all, ultimately*
Relate	*linked by, associate with, connected to, as a result, similar to*
Summarize	*in conclusion, to reiterate, in brief, again, to sum up*
Trace	*first, afterward, then, next, followed by, subsequently, currently*

- *Reread your answer, mouthing the words* so that you "hear" your answer. As you reread, ask yourself: Is my answer well-organized and straightforward? Are my main ideas clearly worded at the beginning of each paragraph, followed by adequate supporting details and examples? Are there any grammatical or spelling errors?

Example of Essay Question and Answer

Sociology Exam Question:

One of the greatest social changes during the last half of the 20th century was the rapid influx of women into the labor force. Describe and illustrate how each of the items listed below was affected by this influx of working women. Also, explain the evolution of each item into the 21st century.

1. Married life
2. Child rearing
3. Family income
4. Workplace culture
5. National economic growth

Here's how a student tackled this question:

- Carefully read the question, noting the three directive words: *describe, illustrate,* and *explain.*
- Realized that in order to answer each part of the question, she will *describe* (provide explanations/details) and *illustrate* (provide examples) <u>each</u> of the five listed items. Then, she will *explain* (give reasons for) interrelated development of the five items through the years.
- Constructed a brief outline, which helped to organize her thoughts in preparation for writing her answer, consisting of eight paragraphs:
<u>Paragraph #1.</u> Short introductory paragraph.

(Continued)

Paragraphs #2–6. Each of these five paragraphs included descriptions and illustrations of how an element was influenced by the influx of working women.

Paragraph #7. A longer paragraph included explanations of the interconnected progression of the five elements through the start of 21st century.

Paragraph #8. Concluding paragraph summed up key points.

- Composed the essay, keeping in mind the need to be thorough yet concise.
- Used signal words: *first, then, characterized by, for example, typically, for instance,* and *in conclusion.*
- When finished writing, she silently reread her essay, checking to make sure that she responded to each part of the question and that her ideas made sense. She corrected several spelling and punctuation errors.

Select, Sort, Solidify

Effective test-taking begins with effective planning. First, find out as much as possible about the test—types of questions, point values, material covered, and suggested study approaches. In addition, see if your instructor will provide sample questions. If need be, seek out a student who had the instructor previously and ask about types of test questions, difficulty level, and recommendations for study.

Strategies to SELECT Content for Exams

Begin by answering the question: *What course information do I need to know for this exam?*

- **Begin studying 5–7 days before an exam.** For a major test, you are more likely to avoid cramming and rote memorization if you start the study process a week early.
- **Review materials daily.** Plan study time so that you are reviewing test-related materials daily—in-class notes, textbook and other readings, and outside assignments.
- **Divide up the material.** Progress at a steady pace throughout the week.

Student Comments

- I recommend using short study periods. I always have had problems concentrating and found that it is much better for me to start studying a week before an exam. By reading and studying a little bit each day, I am able to learn the material much better.

  –Kim

- I have a <u>lot of</u> information to learn in my Art History course. I came close to failing the first test. For the next test, I divided up the information and reviewed it in short study periods. This strategy helped me digest the new material, which made a <u>big</u> impact on my test grade.

  –Gavin

Strategies to SORT Content for Exams

Utilize strategies that help you clarify and understand course content. Answer the question, *How can I summarize, organize, or personalize information that I need to know for the exam?*

- **Combine lecture and text information.** Consolidate key ideas, noting overlapping information. Focus on information that you likely will need to know for the test.
- **Create a visual summary of important ideas.** Use idea maps, charts, timelines, graphs, or Venn diagrams to help you organize main ideas and related details.
- **Create application scenarios.** Make information meaningful and relevant to you.

Strategies to SOLIDIFY Content for Exams

Employ strategies that maximize your ability to remember material for the exam. Answer the question: *What can I do to retain information to use on the exam?*

- **Review briefly.** Skim the information studied in previous sessions before moving on to a new section or topic.
- **Recite aloud.** Repeatedly saying key points out loud helps to store the information in your mind—information that you ultimately want to remember for the exam.

Student Comments

- For Economics, I usually have information scattered throughout my notes. After class I have to look at the text chapter and reorganize my notes. When taking the exam I picture my reorganized notes and can usually recall what I need to know.

  –Cheri

- There is a lot of information in my History course that is not necessary when learning concepts that inevitably will be on the exam. I pick and choose only information that I feel is important, which makes my studying much more efficient.

  –Noah

- **Test your knowledge with practice questions.** Use questions in the chapter or in supplemental materials—jot down your answers. Or, create your own questions that are typical of the type that will be on the exam.
- **Study with others.** Share and discuss key ideas, examples, areas of uncertainty, and study aids. Quiz one another; use practice questions from the text or create your own questions.

Study Groups are small groups of students who meet to review information from a shared class. A well-functioning group can help you learn the material for these reasons:

- You understand the material better if you explain it to someone else.
- You hear explanations different from your instructor's presentation of content.
- You have specific questions discussed and answered by other people.

Form a study group that is *productive* for you. Avoid a group that socializes too much or that relies heavily on one or two individuals to do the bulk of the work. In order to form a study group that is effective, utilize these criteria:

- **Ask only serious students**—not just your friends. A group of three or four people usually works the best.
- **Agree on an organizational plan** at the beginning, including specific meeting days, beginning and ending times, and locations.
- **Designate specific assignments** for each member to prepare for the next meeting.
- **Designate a person to keep the group on track** at each meeting; that is, someone to bring the group's attention back to studying whenever members' attention strays.

- **Get adequate sleep.** Sleep greatly affects your concentration and your memory. Students need an average of 7–9 hours of sleep per night. Be mindful of getting enough sleep each night, especially the week before a major test.

Student Comments

- I like to study with my friends who are in the same class, but <u>only</u> if everyone wants to study. Generally, I am the person who takes charge of the group and keeps everyone on track.

–Ellie

Examples of Review Sheets

Review Chart for Psychology Exam

A student used these steps in preparing for his Psychology exam:

Select

- On Sunday evening, developed a plan to prepare for the upcoming test on Friday.
- Divided the material according to "research methods." Wrote down this plan.

(Continued)

Sort

- Combined information from the text chapter and corresponding lecture notes.
- Created a visual summary chart (below).

Solidify

- Tested his knowledge by answering these questions:
  - ◆ For each research method describe a *specific situation* using that method (application).
  - ◆ Explain *why* each item in the last column is classified as a "Disadvantage."
- Went to the weekly peer-led study group on Wednesday evening, where he could review with others.
- Was in bed by midnight each night.
- Before class on Friday morning, reviewed the summary chart briefly, saying the information out loud to himself.

Research Methods				
When to Review	**Method**	**Description**	**Advantage**	**Disadvantage**
Sun.	Observation	systematic study of behavior in natural setting	normal setting	no cause/effect; $$; difficult
Mon.	Case Study	detailed information gathered about specific individuals	detailed information	takes a lot of time
Tues.	Surveys	lots of people answer questions re. behaviors or attitudes	very efficient	random sample; false consensus effect

Tues.	Correlation	relationship between two variables	development of hypotheses	cannot establish cause/effect
Wed.	Experiment	manipulation of variables	can establish cause/effect	bias and error
Thurs.	Review ALL the material!			

Review Chart for History Exam

A student used these steps in preparing for her History exam:

Select

- Since the unit exam was next Friday, she started reviewing lecture notes and corresponding text chapters during the weekend.
- Divided her study time according to the four countries involved.

Sort

- Created a summary chart (next page). Filled in the chart as she reviewed class and text material.

Solidify

- Attended her instructor's review session during Wednesday's class. The instructor gave practice essay questions, which she added to her chart.
- Wrote answers to the essay questions. Shared and discussed answers during Thursday's Supplemental Instruction review session.
- Quickly reviewed the chart again before class on Friday.

Great Depression & Rise of Totalitarianism after World War I

Country	Time Period	Important People	Important Terms & Events	Significance	Essay Practice Questions
Russia	1917–1941	• Czar Nicholas • V.I. Lenin • Stalin • Trotsky	• Russian Revolution • Socialist Party • Bolshevik Revolution • Totalitarianism • Communism	• Czar Nicholas executed. • Lenin and Totalitarian/ Communist party came to power. • Lenin removes Russia from WWI.	• *Trace* development of governments in Russia.
Italy	1920s	• Mussolini	• Black Shirts • March on Rome • The Corporate State • Populist tactics • Fascism	• First dictators in Europe; caused by economic problems.	• *Describe* conditions leading to rise of Mussolini.
Germany	1920–1933	• Hitler • Hindenburg	• War reparations SA • Dawes Plan SS • Nazi party Reichstag • Mein Kampf • Enabling Act • Brown Shirts	• Post-WWI economic crisis & unhappiness allowed Hitler to come to power. • 1933: Hitler elected Chancellor of Germany.	• *Identify* steps Hitler took to power. *Connect* steps to political and economic conditions.

United States	1924–1933	• Hoover • Franklin Roosevelt • Keynes	• Dawes Plan • Stock Market Crash • Great Depression • Unemployment • Declining Capital • Isolationism • New Deal WPA • Public works projects • Fireside chats	• 1929: Stock market crashes, Wall Street crumbles, Great Depression. • Worldwide financial collapse. • Conditions of depression bring reform in U.S.	• *List* causes of Stock Market Crash. • *List* effects of Great Depression.

Summary Chart

This chart is an overview of test preparation strategies presented in this chapter. Use the chart as you prepare for exams in your Social Science courses.

SELECT	SORT	SOLIDIFY
✓ Begin studying 5–7 days before an exam. ✓ Review materials daily. ✓ Divide up the material.	✓ Combine lecture and text information. ✓ Create a visual summary of important ideas. ✓ Create application scenarios.	✓ Review briefly. ✓ Test your knowledge with practice questions. ✓ Study with others. ✓ Get adequate sleep.

Student Comments

- For my Labor Economics class, I needed to know five ways unions better the economy. I read the material out loud to myself over and over again until I was able to hear myself say this information inside my head. When taking the test, I was able to hear the five ways in my head, just like I had rehearsed.

–Jess

- When I was a freshman I never studied in advance of an exam, I would stay up late the night before and cram. This didn't work at all! Now I start to study about a week in advance and make sure that I get a good night's sleep before the exam. As a result, my grades are much higher, and I'm not as stressed.

–JJ

Test Preparation Strategies: Taking Action

Reflect on and apply information presented in this chapter. Follow these five steps, using the sheets on the following page:

1. Fill in the name of your Social Science course and date of the exam.
2. Place a check next to the strategies you will use for this exam.
   - ◆ In the **SELECT** column, choose *at least two* of the three strategies.
   - ◆ In the **SORT** column, choose *at least two* of the three strategies.
   - ◆ In the **SOLIDIFY** column, choose *at least two* of the four strategies.
3. Cut out the sheet. Place it in your notebook or planner, or post it on your computer as a reminder of your plan.
4. Afterward, take a moment to evaluate your success.
5. Repeat these steps for the next test, building on previous approaches that have worked for you.

Course: _____   Exam Date: _____

SELECT	SORT	SOLIDIFY
___Begin studying 5–7 days before an exam. ___Review materials daily. ___Divide up the material.	___Combine lecture and text information. ___Create a visual summary of important ideas. ___Create application scenarios.	___Review briefly. ___Test your knowledge with practice questions. ___Study with others. ___Get adequate sleep.

Evaluate Your Success: *Highlight or circle each strategy that assisted you with understanding and remembering content for your exam.*

Course: Exam Date:

SELECT	SORT	SOLIDIFY
___Begin studying 5–7 days before an exam. ___Review materials daily. ___Divide up the material.	___Combine lecture and text information. ___Create a visual summary of important ideas. ___Create application scenarios.	___Review briefly. ___Test your knowledge with practice questions. ___Study with others. ___Get adequate sleep.

Evaluate Your Success: *Highlight or circle each strategy that assisted you with understanding and remembering content for your exam.*

Course: Exam Date:

SELECT	SORT	SOLIDIFY
___Begin studying 5–7 days before an exam. ___Review materials daily. ___Divide up the material.	___Combine lecture and text information. ___Create a visual summary of important ideas. ___Create application scenarios.	___Review briefly. ___Test your knowledge with practice questions. ___Study with others. ___Get adequate sleep.

Evaluate Your Success: *Highlight or circle each strategy that assisted you with understanding and remembering content for your exam.*

5

MAKE IMPROVEMENTS

Checklist of Strategies

An important part of learning college-level course content is to analyze periodically what you have and have not accomplished. For each strategy listed in the chart, honestly assess yourself at this point in the semester.

For Your Social Science Course Are You:	Yes, Often	Some-times	No, Never
Checking the course syllabus regularly?			
Writing down due dates and assignments?			
Skimming notes, homework, and text readings before class?			
Going to each class?			
Listening selectively and writing down key ideas?			
Asking and answering questions during class?			
Reviewing notes soon after each class?			
Making additions and changes as needed to clarify class notes?			

For Your Social Science Course Are You:	Yes, Often	Some-times	No, Never
Keeping up with reading and reviewing assignments weekly?			
Reducing distractions when you read and study?			
Breaking up your reading into sections?			
Focusing on key ideas and connections among these ideas when reading?			
Turning section headings into questions; reading to discover answers?			
Marking and highlighting important text information?			
Creating study guides that summarize and organize text material?			
Using supplemental materials, such as CDs and Websites?			
Seeking out answers to questions, including visiting your instructor during office hours, a graduate assistant, or tutor?			
Using campus resources, such as academic support or tutorial center, writing center, or advising office?			
Beginning to prepare 5–7 days before an exam?			
Combining and summarizing text and lecture material?			
Practicing how to apply the information and answer test questions?			
Reciting aloud as you study?			
Studying with other students who are doing well in the course?			
Sleeping regularly, usually 7–9 hours per night?			

Prioritize and Apply

What do you need to do to improve how effectively and efficiently you are learning information for your Social Science course? From the previous chart, select and prioritize five strategies to apply for your Social Science course. For each item, write a detailed description of how you will implement that strategy *now*.

Strategy	Description of How You Will Apply
1.	
2.	
3.	
4.	
5.	

Review this list weekly throughout the remainder of the semester. Use this as a guide to improve how you read, study, and learn content for your Social Science course.

Psychology: Core Concepts

BRIEF CONTENTS

CONTENTS

CHAPTER 11   Social Psychology   458

CHAPTER 12   Psychological Disorders   514

TO THE STUDENT . . .

There is one simple formula for academic success, and the following demonstration will show you what it is. Study this array of letters for a few seconds:

I B M U F O F B I C I A

Now, without peeking, write down as many of the letters as you can (in the correct order).

Most people remember about five to seven letters correctly. A few people get them all. How do these exceptional few do it? They find a pattern. (You may have noticed some familiar initials in the array above: IBM, UFO, FBI, CIA.) Finding the pattern greatly eases the task because you can draw on material that is already stored in memory. In this case, all that needs to be remembered are four "chunks" of information instead of 12 unrelated letters.

The same principle applies to material you study for your psychology class. If you try to remember each piece of information as a separate item, you will have a difficult time. But if instead you look for patterns, you will find your task greatly simplified—and much more enjoyable.

USING PSYCHOLOGY TO LEARN PSYCHOLOGY

So, how can you identify the patterns? Your friendly authors have developed several learning features that will make meaningful patterns in the text stand out clearly:

Core Concepts We have organized each major section of every chapter around a single big idea called a Core Concept. For example, one of the four Core Concepts in Chapter 5, *Memory*, says:

> ### Core Concept 5.4
>
> **Human memory is an information-processing system that works constructively to encode, store, and retrieve information.**

The Core Concept, then, becomes the central theme around which about 10 pages of material—including several new terms—are organized. As you read each chapter, keeping the Core Concept in mind will help you encode the new terms and ideas related to that concept, store them in your memory, and later retrieve them when you are being tested. To borrow an old saying, the Core Concepts become the "forest," while the details of the chapter become the "trees."

Key Questions Each Core Concept is introduced by a Key Question that also serves as a main heading in the chapter. Here, for example, is a Key Question from the *Memory* chapter:

5.4 KEY QUESTION
Why Does Memory Sometimes Fail Us?

Key Questions such as this will help you anticipate the most important point, or the Core Concept, in the section. In fact, the Core Concept always provides a brief answer to the Key Question. Think of the Key Question as the high beams on your car, helping you focus on what lies ahead. Our Key Questions should also serve as guides for you in posing questions of your own about what you are reading.

Both the Key Questions and the Core Concepts later reappear as organizing features of the Chapter Summary.

Psychology Matters Psychology has many captivating connections with events in the news and in everyday life, and we have explored one of these connections at the end of each major section in every chapter. To illustrate, here are some examples from the *Memory* chapter:

- Would You Want a "Photographic" Memory?
- "Flashbulb" Memories: Where Were You When . . . ?
- On the Tip of Your Tongue

Such connections—practical, down to earth, and fascinating—will help you link your study of psychology with your real-life experiences. They will also help you critically evaluate many of the psychological ideas you encounter in the media—as when you see news stories that begin with "psychological research shows that . . ." By the end of this course, you will become a much wiser consumer of such information.

Psychology Matters: Using Psychology to Learn Psychology A special Psychology Matters section in every chapter explains how you can apply new knowledge from the chapter to make your studying more effective. For example, in Chapter 2, *Biopsychology, Neuroscience, and Human* Nature, we tell you how to put your understanding of the brain to work for more efficient learning. Similarly, at the end of Chapter 9, *Motivation and Emotion*, we explain how to use the psychological concept of "flow" to boost your academic motivation. Thus, Using Psychology to Learn Psychology not only reinforces points that you have studied but also brings the material home with immediate and practical applications to your life in college.

Do It Yourself! Throughout the book we have scattered active-learning demonstrations like the one in which you were asked to memorize the letters I B M U F O F B I C I A. Besides being fun, these activities have the serious purpose of illustrating important principles discussed in the text. In Chapter 5, for example, one *Do It Yourself!* box helps you find the capacity of your short-term memory; another lets you test your "photographic memory" ability.

Check Your Understanding Whether you're learning psychology, soccer, or the saxophone, you need feedback on your progress, and that's exactly what you will get from the Check Your Understanding quizzes. These quizzes appear at the end of every major section in the chapter, offering you a quick checkup indicating whether you have assimilated the main points from what you have read. Some questions call for simple recall; others call for deeper analysis or application of material. Some are multiple-choice questions; some are short-answer essay questions. These exercises will help you determine how well you have mastered the material.

MyPsychLab Integration Throughout the text, you will find marginal icons that link to important videos, simulations, podcasts, and activities you can find on MyPsychLab. New to this edition, we have developed reading activities (called **Read on MyPsychLab**) that will allow you to explore interesting topics more deeply. There are many more resources on MyPsychLab than those highlighted in the text, but the icons draw attention to some of the most high-interest materials. If you did not receive an access code with your text, you can purchase access at www.mypsychlab.com.

Connection Arrows Links to important topics discussed in other chapters are often cross-referenced with an arrow in the margin, as you can see in the sample here. These links will help you integrate your new knowledge with information you have already learned, or will show you where in a later chapter you can find out more

Watch the **Video** at **MyPsychLab**

Listen to the **Podcast** at **MyPsychLab**

Explore the **Concept** at **MyPsychLab**

Simulate the **Experiment** at **MyPsychLab**

Study and **Review** at **MyPsychLab**

Read the **Document** at **MyPsychLab**

about what you are reading. Connecting these concepts in your mind will help you remember them.

Marginal Glossary The most important terms appear in **boldface**, with their glossary definitions readily accessible in the margin. We list these key terms again in the Chapter Summary. Then, at the end of the book, a comprehensive Glossary gathers together all the key terms and definitions from each chapter in one easy-to-find location.

Chapter Summaries We have written our Chapter Summaries to provide you with an overview of main points in each chapter—to help you preview and review the chapter. The summaries are organized around the Key Questions and Core Concepts introduced within the chapter to facilitate review and mastery of chapter material. But we offer one caution: Reading the Chapter Summary will not substitute for reading the entire chapter! Here's a helpful hint: We recommend that you read the summary before you read the rest of the chapter to get a flavor of what's ahead, then reread the summary after you finish the chapter. Reading the summary before will provide a framework for the material so that it can be more easily encoded and stored in your memory. And, naturally, reviewing the summary after reading the chapter will reinforce what you have just learned so that you can retrieve it when needed on an examination.

THINKING LIKE A PSYCHOLOGIST

Learning all the facts and definitions of psychology won't make you a psychologist. Beyond the facts, *thinking like a psychologist* requires learning some *problem-solving* skills and *critical thinking* techniques that any good psychologist should possess. With this goal in mind, we have added two unique features to this book.

Chapter-Opening Problems Each chapter begins with an important problem that you will learn how to solve with the tools you acquire in your reading. Examples of the chapter-opening problems include testing the claim that sweet treats give children a "sugar high," evaluating claims of recovered memories, and judging the extent to which the people we call "geniuses" are different from the rest of us.

Critical Thinking Applied At the end of each chapter, you will be asked to consider issues disputed among psychologists and issues raised in the media, such as the nature of the unconscious mind and the effects of subliminal persuasion. Each of these issues requires a skeptical attitude and the application of a special set of critical thinking skills that we will introduce in Chapter 1.

DISCOVERING PSYCHOLOGY VIDEOS

At the end of each chapter, you will notice viewing guides for Discovering Psychology, a 26-part video series produced by WGBH and Annenberg Media and narrated by the lead author of this textbook, Phil Zimbardo. The videos provide an overview of historic and current theories of human behavior and feature many of the researchers and studies introduced in this textbook. You can access the Discovering Psychology videos and additional viewing resources through MyPsychLab (www.mypsychlab.com), the online companion to this textbook.

   We have one final suggestion to help you succeed in psychology: This book is filled with examples to illustrate the most important ideas, but you will remember these ideas longer if you generate your own examples as you study. This habit will make the information yours as well as ours. And so we wish you a memorable journey through the field we love.

Phil Zimbardo
Bob Johnson
Vivian McCann

TO THE INSTRUCTOR . . .

Psychology has undergone remarkable changes since 2008, when we finished writing the previous edition of *Psychology: Core Concepts*. Here are just a few examples of the new developments we have included in this seventh edition:

- The brain's "default network," involving parts of the temporal lobe, the prefrontal cortex, and the cingulate cortex, becomes active when people focus their attention internally—when they are remembering personal events, making plans, or imagining the perspectives of others. Unfortunately, daydreamers activating this default network while studying will probably not remember the material they have just studied.

- New research shows that analgesics such as Tylenol, normally used to treat physical pain, can reduce the painful *psychological* sensations resulting from social rejection and ruminating about unhappy relationships.

- Also in the realm of sensation, taste researcher Linda Bartoshuk has discovered a "Rosetta Stone," enabling her to compare objectively the intensities of taste sensations experienced by different individuals.

- Meanwhile, perceptual psychologists have recently used brain scans to confirm the assertion that Americans and Asians perceive scenes differently.

- Brain scans have also enabled researchers to assess patients who have been classified as in *persistent vegetative states*—and predict which ones might improve.

- In healthy individuals, scans have detected changes in the brains of volunteers who have undergone intensive training in meditation. The changes are most obvious in brain areas associated with memory, emotional processing, attention, and stress reduction.

- As cognitive psychologists continue to puzzle over the Flynn effect, IQ scores continue to rise—but new studies show that the rise is slowing in developed countries of the West.

- Cognitive research also shows that one in four auto accidents results from the driver failing to notice hazardous conditions while using a cell phone—a bad decision probably deriving from a mistaken belief in multitasking. (Perhaps future research will determine whether the IQs of these drivers fall above or below the rising average.)

- New research by our own Phil Zimbardo shows that decisions can also be influenced by a personality trait that he calls *time perspective*—referring to a past, present, or future orientation.

- However, the ultimate influence on our decisions lies in natural selection, according to evolutionary psychologists—who have recently proposed a major new and controversial modification of Maslow's famous *hierarchy of needs*.

In all, we have included some 350 new references in this new edition—gleaned from literally thousands we have perused. Which is to say that psychological knowledge continues to grow, with no end in sight. As a result, many introductory textbooks have grown to daunting proportions. Meanwhile, our introductory courses remain the same length—with the material ever more densely packed. We cannot possibly introduce students to all the concepts in psychology, nor can our students possibly remember everything.

The problem is not just one of volume and information overload; it is also a problem of meaningfulness. So, while we have aimed to cover less detail than do the more encyclopedic texts, we have not given you a watered-down "brief edition" book. The result is an emphasis on the most important and meaningful ideas in psychology.

Our inspiration for *Psychology: Core Concepts* came from psychological research: specifically, a classic study of chess players by Dutch psychologist and chess master Adriaan de Groot (1965). His work, as you may recall, involved remembering the locations of pieces on a chessboard. Significantly, when the pieces were placed on the board at random, chess experts did no better than novices. Only when the patterns made sense—because they represented actual game situations—did the experts show an advantage. Clearly, meaningful patterns are easier to remember than random assignments.

In applying de Groot's findings to *Psychology: Core Concepts*, our goal has been to present a scientific overview of the field of psychology within meaningful patterns that will help students better remember what they learn so that they can apply it in their own lives. Thus, we have organized each major section of every chapter around a single, clear idea that we call a Core Concept, which helps students focus on the big picture so they don't become lost in the details.

From the beginning, our intention in writing *Psychology: Core Concepts* has been to offer students and instructors a textbook that combines a sophisticated introduction to the field of psychology with pedagogy that applies the principles of psychology to the learning of psychology, all in a manageable number of pages. Even with all the new material we have included, the book remains essentially the same size—which, of course, meant making some tough decisions about what to include, what to delete, and what to move into our extensive collection of ancillary resources.

Our goal was to blend great science with great teaching and to provide an alternative to the overwhelmingly encyclopedic tomes or skimpy "brief edition" texts that have been traditionally offered. We think you will like the introduction to psychology presented in this book—both the content and the pedagogical features. After all, it's a text that relies consistently on well-grounded principles of psychology to teach psychology.

NEW TO THIS EDITION

This edition of *Psychology: Core Concepts* is certainly no perfunctory revision or slapdash update. And here's why . . .

We have reconceptualized our goal of helping students learn to "think like psychologists." These days, of course, everyone emphasizes *critical thinking*. The new edition of *Psychology: Core Concepts,* however, gives equal weight to that other essential thinking skill: *problem solving*.

To encourage the sort of problem solving psychologists do, every chapter begins with a Problem, a feature we introduced in the last edition. The Problem grows out of the opening vignette and requires, for its solution, material developed in the chapter. In this edition, we have focused on helping readers discover, throughout each chapter, the "clues" that lead to the solution of the problem.

But we have not neglected critical thinking. Throughout the text, we deal with common psychological misconceptions—such as the notion that venting anger gets it "out of your system" or the belief that punishment is the most effective way of changing behavior. And in our Critical Thinking Applied segment at the end of each chapter, we also focus on an important psychological issue in the popular media or an ongoing debate within the field:

- Can "facilitated communication" help us understand people with autism?
- Left vs. right brain: Do most of us use only one side of the brain?
- Can our choices be influenced by subliminal messages?
- Do people have different "learning styles"?
- The recovered memory controversy: How reliable are reports of long-forgotten memories of sexual abuse?
- Gender issues: Are we more *alike* or more *different?*
- The "Mozart Effect": Can music make babies smarter?

- The Unconscious reconsidered: Has modern neuroscience reshaped Freud's concept of the unconscious mind?
- Do lie detectors really detect lies?
- The person-situation controversy: Which is the more important influence on our behavior?
- Is terrorism "a senseless act of violence, perpetrated by crazy fanatics"?
- Insane places revisited: Did Rosenhan get it right?
- Evidence-based practice: Should clinicians be limited by the tested-and-true?
- Is change really hazardous to your health?

But that's not all. We have made extensive updates to the text (in addition to the new research listed above). And we have improved the pedagogical features for which *Psychology: Core Concepts* is known and loved. To give a few examples, we have:

- added **MyPsychLab** icons throughout the margins to highlight important videos, simulations, podcasts, and additional resources for students to explore online. New to this edition, we have created **Read on MyPsychLab** activities that allow students to read and answer questions about many interesting topics more deeply online.
- shifted the focus of psychology's **six main perspectives** to practical applications, giving a concrete example of a real-life problem for each.
- clarified and updated our discussion of the **scientific method** to reflect more accurately how research is done in a real-world context.
- added material on interpreting **correlations**—to help students use the notions of correlation and causation more accurately in their everyday lives.
- simplified and consolidated our discussion of the **split-brain experiments**.
- updated material on **flashbulb memories**, using up-to-date examples.
- created a new section on **cognitive theories of intelligence**.
- added a new Psychology Matters piece entitled "Not Just Fun and Games: The Role of Child's Play in Life Success," telling of the growing role of **self-control** in life success, and how parents and teachers can help nurture this important ability.
- added new material on **Vygotsky's theory**, including *scaffolding* and the *zone of proximal development*, plus new material on neural development in adolescence.
- revised and expanded the sections on **daydreaming** and on both **REM** and **NREM** sleep to reflect important new research.
- changed the order of topics in the Motivation and Emotion chapter, bringing in new material on practical ways of **motivating people**, updating the section on **sexual orientation**, and presenting a revised *hierarchy of needs* based in **evolutionary psychology**.
- added new material on cross-cultural differences in **shyness**, Carol Dweck's research on **mindset**, and individual differences in **time perspective**.
- updated the section on **positive psychology**.
- updated the **Heroic Defiance** section, including new examples from the recent Egyptian protests and new material on events at the Abu Ghraib prison.
- added new examples of recent replications of **Milgram's obedience experiment**.
- added new material on **bullying, the jigsaw classroom,** and **stereotype lift**.
- reconceptualized **depression** in terms of **Mayberg's model**, which emphasizes three factors: biological vulnerability, external stressors, and abnormality of the mood-regulation circuits in the brain. Also presented the new studies on the value of **exercise** in combating depression and the anxiety disorders.
- added new material on **psychopathy**—which is attracting increasing interest but is not a DSM-IV disorder.
- discussed the growing rift within **clinical psychology** (and between APA and APS) over empirically supported treatments and empirically based practice.

- updated the information on **telehealth therapy** strategies.
- connected the discussion of **traumatic stress** to the 2011 earthquake in Japan.
- added a new Do It Yourself! **The Undergraduate Stress Questionnaire: How Stressed Are You?**

We think you will find the seventh edition up-to-date and even more engaging for students than the previous edition. But the changes are not limited to the book itself. Please allow us to toot our horns for the supplements available to adopters.

TEACHING AND LEARNING PACKAGE

The following supplements will also enhance teaching and learning for you and your students:

Instructor's Manual Written and compiled by Sylvia Robb of Hudson County Community College, includes suggestions for preparing for the course, sample syllabi, and current trends and strategies for successful teaching. Each chapter offers integrated teaching outlines, lists the *Key Questions, Core Concepts*, and *Key Terms* for each chapter for quick reference, an extensive bank of lecture launchers, handouts, and activities, crossword puzzles, and suggestions for integrating third-party videos, music, and Web resources. The electronic format features click-and-view hotlinks that allow instructors to quickly review or print any resource from a particular chapter. This resource saves prep work and helps you maximize your classroom time.

Test Bank Written by Jason Spiegelman of Community College of Baltimore County, has provided an extensively updated test bank containing more than 2,000 accuracy-checked questions, including multiple choice, completion (fill-in-the-blank and short answer), and critical essays. Test item questions have been also written to test student comprehension of select multimedia assets found with MyPsychLab for instructors who wish to make MyPsychLab a more central component of their course. In addition to the unique questions listed previously, the Test Bank also includes all of the *Check Your Understanding* questions from the textbook and all of the test questions from the *Discovering Psychology* Telecourse Faculty Guide for instructors who wish to reinforce student use of the textbook and video materials. All questions include the correct answer, page reference, difficulty ranking, question type designation, and correlations to American Psychological Association (APA) Learning Goal/Outcome. A new feature of the Test Bank is the inclusion of rationales for each correct answer and the key distracter in the multiple-choice questions. The rationales help instructors reviewing the content to further evaluate the questions they are choosing for their tests and give instructors the option to use the rationales as an answer key for their students. Feedback from current customers indicates this unique feature is very useful for ensuring quality and quick response to student queries. A two-page Total Assessment Guide chapter overview makes creating tests easier by listing all of the test items in an easy-to-reference grid. The Total Assessment Guide organizes all test items by text section and question type/level of difficulty. All multiple-choice questions are categorized as factual, conceptual, or applied.

The Test Bank comes with **Pearson MyTest,** a powerful assessment-generation program that helps instructors easily create and print quizzes and exams. Questions and tests can be authored online, allowing instructors ultimate flexibility and the ability to efficiently manage assessments anytime, anywhere! Instructors can easily access existing questions and then edit, create, and store them using simple drag-and-drop and Word-like controls. Data on each question provide information relevant to difficulty level and page number. In addition, each question maps to the text's major section and learning objective. For more information, go to www.PearsonMyTest.com.

NEW Interactive PowerPoint Slides These slides, available on the Instructor's Resource DVD (ISBN 0-205-58439-7), bring the *Psychology: Core Concepts* design right into the classroom, drawing students into the lecture and providing wonderful interactive activities, visuals, and videos. A video walk-through is available and provides clear guidelines on using and customizing the slides. The slides are built around the text's learning objectives and offer many links across content areas. Icons integrated throughout the slides indicate interactive exercises, simulations, and activities that can be accessed directly from the slides if instructors want to use these resources in the classroom.

A Set of Standard Lecture PowerPoint Slides Written by Beth M. Schwartz, Randolph College, is also offered and includes detailed outlines of key points for each chapter supported by selected visuals from the textbook. A separate *Art and Figure* version of these presentations contains all art from the textbook for which Pearson has been granted electronic permissions.

Classroom Response System (CRS) Power Point Slides Classroom Response System questions ("Clicker" questions) are intended to form the basis for class discussions as well as lectures. The incorporation of the CRS questions into each chapter's slideshow facilitates the use of "clickers"—small hardware devices similar to remote controls, which process student responses to questions and interpret and display results in real time. CRS questions are a great way to get students involved in what they are learning, especially because many of these questions address specific scientific thinking skills highlighted in the text. These questions are available on the Instructor's Resource DVD (ISBN 0-205-85439-7) and also online at http://pearsonhighered.com/irc.

Instructor's Resource DVD (ISBN 0-205-85439-7) Bringing all of the Seventh Edition's instructor resources together in one place, the Instructor's DVD offers both versions of the PowerPoint presentations, the Classroom Response System (CRS), the electronic files for the Instructor's Manual materials, and the Test Item File to help instructors customize their lecture notes.

The NEW MyPsychLab The NEW MyPsychLab combines original online materials with powerful online assessment to engage students, assess their learning, and help them succeed. MyPsychLab ensures students are always learning and always improving.

- New video: New, exclusive 30-minute video segments for every chapter take the viewer from the research laboratory to inside the brain to out on the street for real-world applications.
- New experiments: A new experiment tool allows students to experience psychology. Students do experiments online to reinforce what they are learning in class and reading about in the book.
- New BioFlix animations: Bring difficult-to-teach biological concepts to life with dramatic "zoom" sequences and 3D movement.
- eText: The Pearson eText lets students access their textbook anytime, anywhere, in any way they want it, including listening to it online.
- New concept mapping: A new concept-mapping tool allows students to create their own graphic study aids or notetaking tools using preloaded content from each chapter. Concept maps can be saved, e-mailed, or printed.
- Assessment: With powerful online assessment tied to every video, application, and chapter of the text, students can get immediate feedback. Instructors can see what their students know and what they don't know with just a few clicks. Instructors can then personalize MyPsychLab course materials to meet the needs of their students.
- New APA assessments: A unique bank of assessment items allows instructors to assess student progress against the American Psychological Association's Learning Goals and Outcomes. These assessments have been keyed to the APA's latest progressive Learning Outcomes (basic, developing, advanced) published in 2008.

Proven Results Instructors and students have been using MyPsychLab for nearly ten years. To date, more than 500,000 students have used MyPsychLab. During that time, three white papers on the efficacy of MyPsychLab were published. Both the white papers and user feedback show compelling results: MyPsychLab helps students succeed and improve their test scores. One of the key ways MyPsychLab improves student outcomes is by providing continuous assessment as part of the learning process. Over the years, both instructor and student feedback have guided numerous improvements, making MyPsychLab even more flexible and effective.

Please contact your local Pearson representative for more information on MyPsychLab. For technical support for any of your Pearson products, you and your students can contact http://247.pearsoned.com.

NEW MyPsychLab Video Series (17 episodes) This new video series offers instructors and students the most current and cutting-edge introductory psychology video content available anywhere. These exclusive videos take the viewer into today's research laboratories, inside the body and brain via breathtaking animations, and onto the street for real-world applications. Guided by the Design, Development and Review team, a diverse group of introductory psychology instructors, this comprehensive series features 17 half-hour episodes organized around the major topics covered in the introductory psychology course syllabus. For maximum flexibility, each half-hour episode features several brief clips that bring psychology to life:

- *The Big Picture* introduces the topic of the episode and provides the hook to draw students fully into the topic.
- *The Basics* uses the power of video to present foundational topics, especially those that students find difficult to understand.
- *Special Topics* delves deeper into high-interest and cutting-edge topics, showing research in action.
- *In the Real World* focuses on applications of psychological research.
- *What's in It for Me?* These clips show students the relevance of psychological research to their own lives.

Available in MyPsychLab and also on DVD to adopters of Pearson psychology textbooks (ISBN 0-205-03581-7).

***Discovering Psychology* Telecourse Videos** Written, designed, and hosted by Phil Zimbardo and produced by WGBH Boston in partnership with Annenberg Media, this series is a perfect complement to *Psychology: Core Concepts*. *Discovering Psychology* is a landmark educational resource that reveals psychology's contribution not only to understanding the puzzles of behavior but also to identifying solutions and treatments to ease the problems of mental disorders. The video series has won numerous prizes and is widely used in the United States and internationally. The complete set of 26 half-hour videos is available for purchase (DVD or VHS format) from Annenberg Media. The videos are also available online in a streaming format that is free (www.learner.org), and, for the convenience of instructors and students using *Psychology: Core Concepts*, links to these online videos have been included in the MyPsychLab program that accompanies the textbook. A student Viewing Guide is found at the end of every chapter within *Psychology: Core Concepts*, with additional Viewing Guide resources also available online within MyPsychLab.

***Discovering Psychology* Telecourse Faculty Guide (ISBN 0-205-69929-4)** The Telecourse Faculty Guide provides guidelines for using *Discovering Psychology* as a resource within your course. Keyed directly to *Psychology: Core Concepts*, the faculty guide includes the complete Telecourse Study Guide plus suggested activities; suggested essays; cited studies; instructional resources, including books, articles, films, and websites; video program test questions with answer key; and a key term glossary. Test questions for *Discovering Psychology* also reappear in the textbook's test bank and MyTest computerized test bank.

Student Study Guide (ISBN 0-205-25299-0) This robust study guide, written by Jane P. Sheldon of University of Michigan-Dearborn, is filled with guided activities and in-depth exercises to promote student learning. Each chapter includes worksheets that give students a head start on in-class note taking; a full list of key terms with page references; a collection of demonstrations, activities, exercises, and three short practice quizzes; and one comprehensive chapter exam with critical-thinking essay questions and concept maps to help you study for your quizzes and exams. The appendix includes answers to all of the practice activities, tests, and concept maps.

ACCESSING ALL RESOURCES

For a list of all student resources available with *Psychology: Core Concepts*, Seventh Edition, go to www.mypearsonstore.com, enter the text ISBN (0-205-18346-8), and check out the "Everything That Goes with It" section under the book cover.

For access to all instructor supplements for *Psychology: Core Concepts*, Seventh Edition go to http://pearsonhighered.com/irc and follow the directions to register (or log in if you already have a Pearson user name and password). Once you have registered and your status as an instructor is verified, you will be e-mailed a log-in name and password. Use your log-in name and password to access the catalog. Click on the "online catalog" link, click on "psychology" followed by "introductory psychology," and then the Zimbardo/Johnson/McCann, *Psychology: Core Concepts,* Seventh Edition text. Under the description of each supplement is a link that allows you to download and save the supplement to your desktop.

You can request hard copies of the supplements through your Pearson sales representative. If you do not know your sales representative, go to http://www.pearsonhighered.com/replocator/ and follow the directions. For technical support for any of your Pearson products, you and your students can contact **http://247.pearsoned.com.**

A NOTE OF THANKS

Nobody ever realizes the magnitude of the task when taking on a textbook-writing project. Acquisitions Editor Amber Chow and Executive Editor Stephen Frail deftly guided (and prodded) us through this process. The vision of the seventh edition confronted reality under the guidance of Deb Hanlon, our tenacious Senior Development Editor, who made us work harder than we had believed possible. Assistant Editor Kerri Hart-Morris managed our spectacular ancillaries package.

The job of making the manuscript into a book fell to Shelly Kupperman, our Production Project Manager at Pearson Education; Andrea Stefanowicz, our Senior Project Manager at PreMediaGlobal; and Kim Husband, our copyeditor. We think they did an outstanding job—as did our tireless photo researcher, Ben Ferrini.

We are sure that none of the above would be offended if we reserve our deepest thanks for our spouses, closest colleagues, and friends who inspired us, gave us the caring support we needed, and served as sounding boards for our ideas. Phil thanks his wonderful wife, Christina Maslach, for her endless inspiration and for modeling what is best in academic psychology. He has recently passed a milestone of 50 years of teaching the introductory psychology course, from seminar size to huge lectures to more than 1,000 students. Phil continues to give lectures and colloquia to college and high school groups throughout the country and overseas. He still gets a rush from lecturing and from turning students on to the joys and fascination of psychology. His new "psych rock star" status comes mostly from generations of students who have grown up watching him perform on the *Discovering Psychology* video series in their high school and college psychology courses.

Bob is grateful to his spouse, best friend, and best editor Michelle, who has for years put up with his rants on topics psychological, his undone household chores, and much gratification delayed—mostly without complaint. She has been a wellspring of understanding and loving support and the most helpful of reviewers. His thanks, too, go to Rebecca, their daughter, who has taught him the practical side of developmental psychology—and now, much to her own astonishment and an undergraduate lapse into sociology, possesses her own graduate degree in psychology. In addition, he is indebted to many friends, most of whom are not psychologists but who are nevertheless always eager to raise and debate interesting issues about the applications of psychology to everyday life. Readers will find topics they have raised throughout the book and especially in the chapter-opening "problems" and in the critical thinking sections at the end of each chapter.

Vivian's thanks go first to her husband, Shawn, and their sons, Storm and Blaze. All three of these amazing men are endless sources of love, support, inspiration, fun, and delight. They also generously allow Vivian to use them as examples of a multitude of concepts in her classes! Vivian also appreciates the many students, friends, and colleagues who have both encouraged and challenged her over the years.

We would especially like to thank Michelle Billies, Nikita Duncan, George Slavich, and Christina Zimbardo for their exceptional help as we revised and prepared this edition for print.

Many psychological experts and expert teachers of introductory psychology also shared their constructive criticism with us on every chapter and feature of the seventh edition of this text:

Thomas Beckner, *Trine University*
Chris Brill, *Old Dominion University*
Allison Buskirk-Cohen, *Delaware Valley College*
Christie Chung, *Mills College*
Elizabeth Curtis, *Long Beach City College*
Linda DeKruif, *Fresno City College*
Meliksah Demir, *Northern Arizona University*
Roger Drake, *Western State College of Colorado*
Denise Dunovant, *Hudson County Community College*
Arthur Frankel, *Salve Regina University*
Marjorie Getz, *Bradley University*
Nancy Gup, *Georgia Perimeter College*
Carrie Hall, *Miami University*
Jeremy Heider, *Stephen F. Austin State University*
Allen Huffcutt, *Bradley University*
Kristopher Kimbler, *Florida Gulf Coast University*
Sue Leung, *Portland Community College*
Brian Littleton, *Kalamazoo Valley Community College*
Annette Littrell, *Tennessee Tech University*
Mark Loftis, *Tennessee Tech University*
Lillian McMaster, *Hudson County Community College*

Karen Marsh, *University of Minnesota–Duluth*
Jim Matiya, *Florida Gulf Coast University*
Nancy Melucci, *Long Beach City College*
Jared Montoya, *The University of Texas at Brownsville*
Suzanne Morrow, *Old Dominion University*
Katy Neidhart, *Cuesta College*
Donna Nelson, *Winthrop University*
Barbara Nova, *Dominican University of California*
Elaine Olaoye, *Brookdale Community College*
Karl Oyster, *Tidewater Community College*
Sylvia Robb, *Hudson County Community College*
Nancy Romero, *Lone Star College*
Beverly Salzman, *Housatonic Community College*
Hildur Schilling, *Fitchburg State College*
Bruce Sherwin, *Housatonic Community College*
Hilary Stebbins, *Virginia Wesleyan College*
Doris Van Auken, *Holy Cross College*
Matthew Zagummy, *Tennessee Tech University*

We also thank the reviewers of the previous editions of *Psychology: Core Concepts* and hope that they will recognize their valued input in all that is good in this text:

Gordon Allen, *Miami University*
Beth Barton, *Coastal Carolina Community College*
Linda Bastone, *Purchase College, SUNY*
Susan Beck, *Wallace State College*

Michael Bloch, *University of San Francisco*
Michele Breault, *Truman State University*
John H. Brennecke, *Mount San Antonio College*
T. L. Brink, *Crafton Hills College*

Jay Brown, *Southwest Missouri State University*
Sally S. Carr, *Lakeland Community College*
Saundra Ciccarelli, *Gulf Coast Community College*
Wanda Clark, *South Plains College*
Susan Cloninger, *The Sage Colleges*
John Conklin, *Camosun College (Canada)*
Michelle L. Pilati Corselli *(Rio Hondo College)*
Sara DeHart-Young, *Mississippi State University*
Janet DiPietro, *John Hopkins University*
Diane Finley, *Prince George's Community College*
Krista Forrest, *University of Nebraska at Kearney*
Lenore Frigo, *Shasta College*
Rick Froman, *John Brown University*
Arthur Gonchar, *University of LaVerne*
Peter Gram, *Pensacola Junior College*
Jonathan Grimes, *Community College of Baltimore County*
Lynn Haller, *Morehead State University*
Mary Elizabeth Hannah, *University of Detroit*
Jack Hartnett, *Virginia Commonwealth University*
Carol Hayes, *Delta State University*
Karen Hayes, *Guilford College*
Michael Hillard, *Albuquerque TVI Community College*
Peter Hornby, *Plattsburgh State University*
Deana Julka, *University of Portland*
Brian Kelley, *Bridgewater College*
Sheila Kennison, *Oklahoma State University*
Laurel Krautwurst, *Blue Ridge Community College*
Judith Levine, *Farmingdale State College*
Dawn Lewis, *Prince George's Community College*
Deborah Long, *East Carolina University*

Margaret Lynch, *San Francisco State University*
Jean Mandernach, *University of Nebraska, Kearney*
Marc Martin, *Palm Beach Community College*
Richard Mascolo, *El Camino College*
Steven Meier, *University of Idaho*
Nancy Mellucci, *Los Angeles Community College District*
Yozan Dirk Mosig, *University of Nebraska*
Melinda Myers-Johnson, *Humboldt State University*
Michael Nikolakis, *Faulkner State College*
Cindy Nordstrom, *Southern Illinois University*
Laura O'Sullivan, *Florida Gulf Coast University*
Ginger Osborne, *Santa Ana College*
Vernon Padgett, *Rio Hondo College*
Jeff Pedroza, *Santa Ana College*
Laura Phelan, *St. John Fisher College*
Faye Plascak-Craig, *Marian College*
Skip Pollock, *Mesa Community College*
Chris Robin, *Madisonville Community College*
Lynne Schmelter-Davis, *Brookdale County College of Monmouth*
Mark Shellhammer, *Fairmont State College*
Christina Sinisi, *Charleston Southern University*
Patricia Stephenson, *Miami Dade College*
Mary Ellen Dello Stritto, *Western Oregon University*
Mario Sussman, *Indiana University of Pennsylvania*
John Teske, *Elizabethtown College*
Stacy Walker, *Kingwood College*
Robert Wellman, *Fitchburg State University*
Alan Whitlock, *University of Idaho*

Finally, we offer our thanks to all of the colleagues whose feedback has improved our book. Thanks also to all instructors of this most-difficult-to-teach course for taking on the pedagogical challenge and conveying to students their passion about the joys and relevance of psychological science and practice.

If you have any recommendations of your own that we should not overlook for the next edition, please write to us! Address your comments to Dr. Robert Johnson, CoreConcepts7@gmail.com.

ABOUT THE AUTHORS

Philip Zimbardo, PhD, Stanford University professor, has been teaching the introductory psychology course for 50 years and has been writing the basic text for this course, as well as the faculty guides and student workbooks, for the past 35 years. In addition, he has helped to develop and update the PBS-TV series, *Discovering Psychology,* which is used in many high school and university courses both nationally and internationally. He has been called "The Face and Voice of Psychology" because of this popular series and his other media presentations. Phil also loves to conduct and publish research on a wide variety of subjects, as well as teach and engage in public and social service activities. He has published more than 400 professional and popular articles and chapters, including 50 books of all kinds. He recently published a trade book on the psychology of evil, *The Lucifer Effect,* that relates his classic Stanford Prison Experiment to the abuses at Iraq's Abu Ghraib Prison. His new book is *The Time Paradox,* but his new passion is helping to create wise and effective everyday heroes as part of his Heroic Imagination Project. Please see these websites for more information: www.zimbardo.com; www.prisonexp.org; www.PsychologyMatters.org; www.theTimeParadox.com; www.LuciferEffect.com; www.HeroicImagination.org.

Robert Johnson, PhD, taught introductory psychology for 28 years at Umpqua Community College. He acquired an interest in cross-cultural psychology during a Fulbright summer in Thailand, followed by many more trips abroad to Japan, Korea, Latin America, Britain, and, most recently, to Indonesia. Currently, he is working on a book on the psychology in Shakespeare. Bob is especially interested in applying psychological principles to the teaching of psychology and in encouraging linkages between psychology and other disciplines. In keeping with those interests, he founded the Pacific Northwest Great Teachers Seminar, of which he was the director for 20 years. Bob was also one of the founders of Psychology Teachers at Community Colleges (PT@CC), serving as its executive committee chair during 2004. That same year, he also received the Two-Year College Teaching Award given by the Society for the Teaching of Psychology. Bob has long been active in APA, APS, the Western Psychological Association, and the Council of Teachers of Undergraduate Psychology.

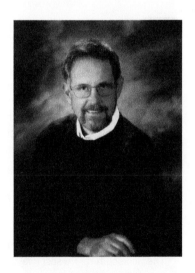

Vivian McCann, a senior faculty member in psychology at Portland Community College in Portland, Oregon, teaches a wide variety of courses, including introductory psychology, human relations, intimate relationships, and social psychology. Born and raised in the California desert just 10 miles from the Mexican border, she learned early on the importance of understanding cultural backgrounds and values in effective communication and in teaching, which laid the foundation for her current interest in teaching and learning psychology from diverse cultural perspectives. She loves to travel and learn about people and cultures and to nurture the same passions in her students. She has led groups of students on four trips abroad, and in her own travels has visited 24 countries so far. Vivian maintains a strong commitment to teaching excellence and has developed and taught numerous workshops in that area. She has served on the APA's Committee for Psychology Teachers at Community Colleges (PT@CC) and is an active member of the Western Psychological Association and APS. She is also the author of *Human Relations: The Art and Science of Building Effective Relationships.*

1 Mind, Behavior, and Psychological Science

"AFTER THE KIDS HAD ALL THAT SUGAR—THE CAKE, ICE CREAM, PUNCH, and candy—they were absolutely bouncing off the walls!" said one of our friends who was describing a birthday party for her 8-year-old daughter.

I must have had a skeptical look on my face, because she stopped her story short and asked, "You don't believe it?" Then she added, "You psychologists just don't believe in common sense, do you?"

I responded that what people think of as "common sense" can be wrong, reminding her that common sense once held that Earth was flat. "Perhaps," I suggested, "it might be wrong again—this time about the so-called 'sugar high' people think they observe.

"It could have been just the excitement of the party," I added.

"*Think* they observe?" my friend practically shouted. "Can you *prove* that sugar doesn't make children hyperactive?"

"No," I said. "Science doesn't work that way. But what I *could* do," I ventured, "is perform an experiment to test the idea that sugar makes children 'hyper.' Then we could see whether your claim passes or fails the test."

My timing wasn't the best for getting her involved in a discussion of scientific experiments, so let me pose the problem to you.

PROBLEM: How would psychology test the claim that sugar makes children hyperactive?

We invite you to think about how we might set up such an experiment. We could, for example, give kids a high-sugar drink and see what happens. But because people often see only what they expect to see, our expectations about sugar and hyperactivity could easily influence our observations. So how could we design an experiment about sugar and hyperactivity that also accounts for our expectations? It is not an easy problem, but we will think it through together, and by the end of this chapter, you will have the tools you need to solve it.

Every chapter in the book will begin with a problem such as this—a problem aimed at getting you actively involved in learning psychology and thinking critically about some important concepts in the chapter. Solving the problem with us, rather than just passively reading the words, will make the concepts more meaningful to you and more easily remembered (see Chapter 5 to find out why).

The important concept illustrated by the "sugar high" problem is one of the most fundamental concepts in all of psychology: using the *scientific method* to explore the mind and behavior. But before we get into the details of the scientific method, let's clarify what we mean by the term *psychology* itself.

1.1 KEY QUESTION
What Is Psychology—and What Is It *NOT?*

"I hope you won't psychoanalyze me," says the student at the office door. It is a frequent refrain and an occupational hazard for professors of psychology. But students need not worry about being psychoanalyzed, for two reasons. First, not all psychologists diagnose and treat mental problems—in fact, those who do are actually in the minority among professors of psychology. Second, only a few psychologists are actually *psychoanalysts.* The term *psychoanalysis* refers to a highly specialized and relatively uncommon form of therapy. You will learn more about the distinction between psychologists and psychoanalysts later in the chapter—but, in the meantime, don't fret that your professor will try to find something wrong with you. In fact, your professor is much more likely to be interested in helping you learn the material than in looking for signs of psychological disorder.

So, you might wonder, if psychology is not all about mental disorders and therapy, what *is* it all about?

psychology   The science of behavior and mental processes.

The term **psychology** comes from *psyche,* the ancient Greek word for "mind," and the suffix *-ology,* meaning "a field of study." Literally, then, *psychology* means "the study of the mind." Most psychologists, however, use the broader definition given in our Core Concept for this section of the chapter:

> ## Core Concept 1.1
>
> **Psychology is a broad field, with many specialties, but fundamentally psychology is the science of behavior and mental processes.**

One important point to note about this definition: Psychology includes not only *mental processes* but also *behaviors.* In other words, psychology's domain covers both *internal* mental processes that we observe only indirectly (such as thinking, feeling, and desiring) as well as *external,* observable behaviors (such as talking, smiling, and running). A second important part of our definition concerns the *scientific* component of psychology. In brief, the science of psychology is based on objective, verifiable evidence—not just the opinions of experts and authorities, as we often find in nonscientific fields. We will give a more complete explanation of the science of psychology in the last part of this chapter. For now, though, let's take a closer look at what psychologists actually do.

Psychology: It's More Than You Think

Psychology covers more territory than most people realize. As we have seen, not all psychologists are therapists. Many work in education, industry, sports, prisons, government, churches and temples, private practice, human relations, advertising, and in the psychology departments of colleges and universities (see Figure 1.1). Others work for engineering firms, consulting firms, and the courts (both the judicial and the NBA variety). In these diverse settings, psychologists perform a wide range of tasks, including teaching, research, testing, and equipment design—as well as psychotherapy. In fact, psychology's specialties are too numerous to cover them all here, but we can give you a taste of the field's diversity by first dividing psychology into three broad groups.

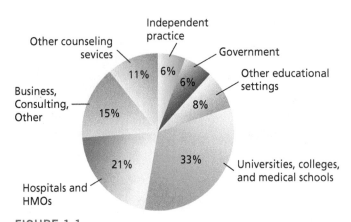

FIGURE 1.1

Work Settings of Psychologists

Source: 2009 Doctorate Employment Survey, APA Center for Workforce Studies. March 2011.

Three Ways of Doing Psychology Broadly speaking, psychologists cluster into three main categories: *experimental psychologists, teachers of psychology,* and *applied psychologists.* Some overlap exists among these groups, however, because many psychologists take on multiple roles in their work.

Experimental psychologists (sometimes called *research psychologists*) constitute the smallest of the three groups. Nevertheless, they perform most of the research that creates new psychological knowledge (Frincke & Pate, 2004).[1] For example, an experimental psychologist would be well equipped to study the effects of sugar on hyperactivity in children. While some experimental psychologists can be found in industry or private research institutes, the majority work at a college or university, where most also teach.

Teachers of psychology are traditionally found at colleges and universities, where their assignments typically involve not only teaching but also research and publication. Increasingly, however, psychologists can be found at community colleges and high schools, where their teaching load is higher because these institutions generally do not require research (American Psychological Association, 2007b; Johnson & Rudmann, 2004).

Applied psychologists use the knowledge developed by experimental psychologists to tackle human problems of all kinds, such as toy or equipment design, criminal analysis, and psychological treatment. They work in a wide variety of places, ranging from schools, clinics, and social service agencies to factories, airports, hospitals, and casinos. All told, about two-thirds of the doctoral-level psychologists in the United States work primarily as applied psychologists (Kohout & Wicherski, 2000; Wicherski et al., 2009).

experimental psychologists Psychologists who do research on basic psychological processes—as contrasted with applied psychologists. Experimental psychologists are also called research psychologists.

teachers of psychology Psychologists whose primary job is teaching, typically in high schools, colleges, and universities.

applied psychologists Psychologists who use the knowledge developed by experimental psychologists to solve human problems.

Applied Psychological Specialties Some of the most popular applied specialties include:

- *Industrial and organizational psychologists* (often called *I/O psychologists*) specialize in personnel selection and in tailoring the work environment to maximize productivity and morale. They may, for example, create programs to motivate employees or to improve managers' leadership skills. I/O psychologists also conduct market research and examine current issues such as attitudes toward pregnancy in the workplace (Shrader, 2001). 📖

- *Sports psychologists* help athletes improve their performance by planning effective practice sessions, enhancing motivation, and learning to control emotions under pressure. Some focus exclusively on professional athletes, and others work with recreational athletes. Sports psychologists may also, for example, study various types of personalities and their relation to high-risk endeavors such as firefighting, parachuting, or scuba diving.

Read about I/O Psychology at **MyPsychLab**

---

[1]Throughout this book, you will find citations in parentheses, calling your attention to a complete bibliographic reference found in the References section, beginning on p. R-1, near the end of this book. These brief in-text citations give the authors' last names and the publication date. With the complete references in hand, your library can help you find the original source.

Applying psychological principles of learning and motivation, sports psychologists work with athletes to improve performance.

CONNECTION CHAPTER 13

Clinical psychologists help people deal with mental disorders and other psychological problems (p. 558).

Explore the Concept Psychologists at Work at **MyPsychLab**

psychiatry   A medical specialty dealing with the diagnosis and treatment of mental disorders.

- *School psychologists* are experts in teaching and learning. They deal with issues impacting learning, family or personal crises influencing school performance, or social conditions such as gangs, teen pregnancy, or substance abuse. They sometimes diagnose learning or behavioral problems and work with teachers, students, and parents to help students succeed in school. Many school psychologists work for school districts, where their work includes administering, scoring, and interpreting psychological tests.

- *Clinical and counseling psychologists* help people improve social and emotional adjustment or work through difficult choices in relationships, careers, or education. Almost half of all doctoral-level psychologists list clinical or counseling psychology as their specialty (Wichersky et al., 2009).

- *Forensic psychologists* provide psychological expertise to the legal and judicial system. One of the most recently recognized specialties in psychology, forensic psychology has gained rapid popularity due in part to such TV shows as *Criminal Minds, Profiler,* and *CSI.* And, while a real day in the life of forensic psychologists may not be as glamorous or fast paced as their television counterparts, the field is burgeoning with opportunities. Forensic psychologists may test inmates in prisons or forensic hospitals to determine readiness for release or fitness to stand trial, evaluate testimony in cases of rape or child abuse, or help with jury selection (Clay, 2009; Huss, 2001).

- *Environmental psychologists* aim to improve human interaction with our environment. They may, for example, study the impact of inner-city garden spaces on children's academic performance or determine how best to encourage environmentally friendly behavior such as recycling. In private practice, environmental psychologists sometimes help clients maintain their commitment to sustainability or conduct workshops teaching people the mental health benefits of interacting with nature (Novotney, 2009).

More information on career possibilities in psychology can be found in *Careers in Psychology for the Twenty-First Century,* published by the American Psychological Association (2003a) and available online at www.apa.org/careers/resources/guides/careers.pdf. ✳

Psychology Is Not Psychiatry

Just as beginning psychology students may think all psychologists are clinical psychologists, they also may not know the distinction between *psychology* and *psychiatry.* So let's clear up that confusion, just in case you encounter a test question on the topic.

Virtually all psychiatrists, but only some psychologists, treat mental disorders—and there the resemblance ends. **Psychiatry** is a medical specialty, not part of psychology at all. Psychiatrists hold MD (Doctor of Medicine) degrees and, in addition, have specialized training in the treatment of mental and behavioral problems, typically with drugs. Therefore, psychiatrists are licensed to prescribe medicines and perform other medical procedures. Consequently, psychiatrists tend to treat patients with more severe mental disorders (such as schizophrenia) and also to view patients from a *medical* perspective, as persons with mental "diseases."

By contrast, psychology is a much broader field that encompasses the whole range of human behavior and mental processes, from brain function to social interaction and from mental well-being to mental disorder. For most psychologists, graduate training emphasizes research methods, along with advanced study in a specialty such as those listed earlier. Moreover, while psychologists usually hold doctoral degrees, their training is not usually *medical* training, and thus they are not generally licensed to prescribe medications (Carlat, 2010; Practice Directorate Staff, 2005). Psychologists, then, work in a wide variety of fields, all of which view people from a *psychological* perspective. This perspective is illustrated by clinical and counseling psychologists, who are likely to view the people they are helping as clients rather than patients.

So, now you know that psychiatry is not psychology. Next, we'll look at something else that often gets confused with psychology: *pseudo-psychology.*

Thinking Critically about Psychology and Pseudo-Psychology

TV series like *Medium* and *Supernatural* continue a long tradition of programs that play on people's fascination with claims of mysterious powers of the mind and supernatural influences on our personalities. Your daily horoscope does the same thing—never mind that astrology has been thoroughly debunked (Schick & Vaughn, 2001). Neither is there any factual basis for graphology (the bogus science of handwriting analysis), fortune telling, or the supposed power of subliminal messages to influence our behavior. All these fall under the heading of **pseudo-psychology:** unsupported psychological beliefs masquerading as scientific truth.

Fortune tellers, astrologers, and other practitioners of pseudo-psychology don't bother to verify their claims with careful research—nor do their clients engage in critical thinking about such practices.

pseudo-psychology Erroneous assertions or practices set forth as being scientific psychology.

Certainly horoscopes and paranormal claims can be fun as pure entertainment, but it is important to know where fact-based reality ends and imagination-based fantasy begins. After all, you wouldn't want to stake an important decision about your health or welfare on false information, would you? Thus, one of the goals of this text is to help you *think critically* when you hear extraordinary claims about behavior and mental processes.

What Is Critical Thinking? Those who talk about critical thinking often find themselves in the position of Supreme Court Justice Potter Stewart, who famously was unable to define *pornography* but concluded, "I know it when I see it." Like Justice Stewart, your fearless authors (Phil, Bob, and Vivian) cannot offer a definition of critical thinking with which everyone will agree. Nevertheless, we are willing to jump into the fray with a list of six **critical thinking skills** we wish to emphasize in this text. Each is based on a specific question we believe should be asked when confronting new ideas.

critical thinking skills This book emphasizes six critical thinking skills, based on the following questions: What is the source? Is the claim reasonable or extreme? What is the evidence? Could bias contaminate the conclusion? Does the reasoning avoid common fallacies? Does the issue require multiple perspectives?

1. **What is the source?** Does the person making the claim have real expertise in the field? Suppose, for example, you hear a newscast on which a politician or pundit declares that juvenile lawbreakers can be "scared straight." The story explains that, in the program, first-time offenders receive near-abusive treatment from felons who try to scare them away from a life of crime with tales of harsh prison life. Such programs have, in fact, been tried in several states (Finckenauer et al., 1999). But does the person making the claim have any real knowledge of the subject? Does the claimant have legitimate credentials, or is he or she merely a self-proclaimed "expert?" One way to find out is to go online and examine the individual's references and standing within the field. Also, find out whether the source has something substantial to gain from the claim. If it's a medical breakthrough, for example, does the claimant stand to make money from a new drug or medical device? In the case of a "scared straight" program, is the source trying to score political points or get votes?

2. **Is the claim reasonable or extreme?** Life is too short to be critical of everything, of course, so the trick is to be selective. How? As the famous astronomer Carl Sagan once said about reports of alien abductions, "Extraordinary claims require extraordinary evidence" (Nova Online, 1996). Critical thinkers, then, are skeptical

of claims touted as "breakthroughs" or "revolutionary." Certainly, there are occasionally breakthroughs or revolutionary new treatments that work—but they are relatively rare. Most new scientific developments are extensions of existing knowledge. So, claims that conflict with well-established knowledge should raise a red flag. For example, beware of ads that promise to help you quit smoking or lose weight with little or no effort. In the case of "scared straight" programs or any other quick fix for a difficult problem, remember that simple solutions to complex problems rarely exist.

3. **What is the evidence?** This is one of the most important guidelines to critical thinking, and you will learn more about what constitutes scientific evidence in the last section of this chapter. For now, though, beware of **anecdotal evidence** or testimonials proclaiming the dramatic effects of a new program. These first-hand accounts tend to be quite convincing, so they often lure us into believing them. Testimonials and anecdotes, though—no matter how compelling—are not *scientific evidence*. They merely represent the experiences of a few carefully selected individuals. It would be risky, and perhaps even dangerous, to assume that what seems true for some people must also be true for everyone.

What does the evidence say about "scared straight" programs? Not only do they not work, but they can also actually inoculate juveniles against fears about prison. Surprising as it may seem, the hard evidence indicates that teens exposed to such treatments, on average, subsequently get into *more* trouble than do those not given the "scared straight" treatment (Petrosino et al., 2003).

4. **Could bias contaminate the conclusion?** Critical thinkers know the conditions under which biases are likely to occur and can recognize common types of bias we will examine in this chapter. For example, they would question whether medical researchers who are involved in assessing new drugs can truly remain unbiased if they are receiving money from the companies whose drugs they are testing (McCook, 2006).

The form of bias most applicable to our "scared straight" example is **emotional bias:** People not only fear crime and criminals but also are often in favor of harsh treatments for criminal behavior, as evidenced by the recent spate of "three strikes" laws (which mandate a lifetime in prison after three felony convictions). Accordingly, the "scared straight" approach may appeal to people simply because of its harshness. Also, people with a loved one who has gotten into some trouble may be especially vulnerable to promises of easy reform: Their desire for help can interfere with clear thinking.

Another common form of bias is **confirmation bias,** the all-too-human tendency to remember events that confirm our beliefs and ignore or forget contradictory evidence (Halpern, 2002; Nickerson, 1998). For example, confirmation bias explains why people persist in their beliefs that astrology works: They remember the predictions that seemed accurate and forget the ones that missed the mark. Confirmation bias also explains why gamblers have better recollections for their wins than for their losses, or why we persist in thinking a particular object is our lucky charm. Amazingly, recent research reveals this bias may be partly biological in nature. In a study done before a recent presidential election, people listened to their favorite politicians making statements that contradicted themselves. Upon hearing the contradictory statement, brain circuits associated with reasoning in the listeners suddenly shut down, while brain regions most involved with emotion remained active (Shermer, 2006; Westen et al., 2006). It was as though the brain was saying, "I don't want to hear anything that conflicts with my beliefs." Thus, we may have to exert extra effort and diligence to overcome this bias.

5. **Does the reasoning avoid common fallacies?** We will study several common logical fallacies in this book, but the one most applicable to the "scared straight" example is the assumption that common sense is a substitute for scientific evidence. In fact,

---

anecdotal evidence   First-hand accounts that vividly describe the experiences of one or a few people, but may erroneously be assumed to be scientific evidence.

emotional bias   The tendency to make judgments based on attitudes and feelings, rather than on the basis of a rational analysis of the evidence.

confirmation bias   The tendency to attend to evidence that complements and confirms our beliefs or expectations, while ignoring evidence that does not.

You may have seen the "scared straight" issue parodied on the TV show *Saturday Night Live.*

in many cases there exists common sense to support both sides of an issue. For example, we hear that "Birds of a feather flock together"—but we also hear that "Opposites attract." Similarly, we are told that "The early bird gets the worm," but aren't we also cautioned that "Haste makes waste?" Which, then, is true? Only an examination of the evidence can reliably provide the answer. Stay tuned later in this chapter, and in Chapter 6, for other common fallacies that derail critical thinking.

6. **Does the issue require multiple perspectives?** The "scared straight" intervention makes the simplistic assumption that fear of punishment is the best deterrent to delinquency, so inducing fear will prevent delinquency. A more sophisticated view sees delinquency as a complex problem that demands scrutiny from several perspectives. Psychologists, for example, may look at delinquency from the standpoints of learning, social influence, or personality traits. Economists would be interested in the financial incentives for delinquency. And sociologists would focus on such things as gangs, poverty, and community structures. Surely such a multifaceted problem will require a more complex solution than a threatening program.

Thinking Critically about the Chapter Problem How would you apply these critical thinking guidelines to the chapter-opening problem about whether sugar makes children hyperactive? First, consider the source: Is the mother of an 8-year-old an expert on biological effects of sugar? Assuming she is not, you'd have to wonder if the source of her belief is a reliable one or if she is just repeating some "common sense" she's often heard but never questioned. Second, examine the evidence: Have scientific tests been conducted to measure the effects of sugar on children? Third, could any biases be at work? For example, if we *expect* children to be hyperactive after consuming sugar, that is likely what we will observe. Fourth, is the claimant avoiding common fallacies in reasoning? In this case, even if we can prove that kids who consume more sugar are more hyperactive, we can't be sure that sugar is the cause: Alternatively, perhaps kids who are already hyperactive eat more sugar as a means of maintaining their high need for activity. Finally, we should recognize that there are probably other reasons kids get excited at parties. We will explore some of these competing perspectives in the second section of this chapter.

Do It Yourself!   PSYCHOLOGICAL SCIENCE OR PSYCHOBABBLE?

Now, let's put a sampling of your psychological beliefs to the test. Some of the following statements are true, and some are false. Don't worry if you get a few—or all—of the items wrong: You will have lots of company. The point is that what so-called common sense teaches us about psychological processes may not withstand the scrutiny of a scientific test. Mark each of the following statements as "true" or "false." (The answers are given at the end.)

1. _____ It is a myth that most people use only about 10% of their brains.

2. _____ During your most vivid dreams, your body may be paralyzed.

3. _____ Psychological stress can cause physical illness.

4. _____ The color red exists only as a sensation in the brain. There is no "red" in the world outside the brain.

5. _____ Bipolar (manic–depressive) disorder is caused by a conflict in the unconscious mind.

6. _____ The newborn child's mind is essentially a "blank slate" on which everything he or she will know must be "written" (learned) by experience.

7. _____ Everything that happens to us leaves a permanent record in memory.

8. _____ You were born with all the brain cells that you will ever have.

9. _____ Intelligence is a nearly pure genetic trait that is fixed at the same level throughout a person's life.

10. _____ Polygraph ("lie detector") devices are remarkably accurate in detecting physical responses that, in the eye of a trained examiner, reliably indicate when a suspect is lying.

Answers The first four items are true; the rest are false. Here are some brief explanations for each item; you will find more detail in the chapters indicated in parentheses. **1.** True: This is a myth. We use all parts of our brains every day. (See Chapter 2, "Biopsychology, Neuroscience, and Human Nature.") **2.** True: During our most vivid dreams, which occur during rapid eye movement sleep (REM), the voluntary muscles in our body are paralyzed, with the exception of those controlling our eyes. (See Chapter 8, "States of Consciousness.") **3.** True: The link between mind and body can make you sick when you are under chronic stress. (See Chapter 14, "From Stress to Health and Well-Being.") **4.** True: Strange as it may seem, all sensations of color are created in the brain itself. Light waves do have different *frequencies,* but they have no color. The brain interprets the various frequencies of light as different colors. (See Chapter 3, "Sensation and Perception.") **5.** False: There is no evidence at all that unconscious conflicts play a role in bipolar disorder. Instead, the evidence suggests a strong biochemical component. The disorder usually responds well to certain drugs, hinting that it involves faulty brain chemistry. Research also suggests that this faulty chemistry may have a genetic basis. (See Chapter 12, "Psychological Disorders," and Chapter 13, "Therapies for Psychological Disorders.") **6.** False: Far from being a "blank slate," the newborn child has a large repertoire of built-in abilities and protective reflexes. The "blank slate" myth also ignores the child's genetic potential. (See Chapter 7, "Development over the Lifespan.") **7.** False: Although many details of our lives are remembered, there is no evidence that memory records all the details of our lives. In fact, we have good reason to believe that most of the information around us never reaches memory and that what does reach memory often becomes distorted. (See Chapter 5, "Memory.") **8.** False: Contrary to what scientists thought just a few years ago, some parts of the brain continue to create new cells throughout life. (See Chapter 2, "Biopsychology, Neuroscience, and Human Nature.") **9.** False: Intelligence is the result of both heredity and environment. Because it depends, in part, on environment, your level of intelligence (as measured by an IQ test) can change throughout your life. (See Chapter 6, "Thinking and Intelligence.") **10.** False: Even the most expert polygrapher can incorrectly classify a truth-teller as a liar or fail to identify someone who is lying. Objective evidence supporting the accuracy of lie detectors is meager. (See Chapter 9, "Motivation and Emotion.")

[PSYCHOLOGY MATTERS]

Using Psychology to Learn Psychology

Map the Concepts at MyPsychLab

Throughout this book, we show you how to use psychology to learn psychology. For example, we have built in learning tools to help you construct a mental map (sometimes called a *cognitive map* or *concept map*) of every chapter, which is guaranteed to make your studying of psychology easier. Among the most important are the numbered Key Questions and Core Concepts. And in MyPsychLab, you will find a tool specially designed to help you to construct concept maps of each chapter.

The Key Questions, which act as the main headings in each chapter, give you a "heads up" by signaling what to watch for as you read. For example, Key Question 1.1 for this section of the chapter asked, **WHAT IS PSYCHOLOGY—AND WHAT IS IT** NOT? This tells you this section will define psychology and make some distinctions between psychology and other fields with which it may be confused or overlap. You are much more likely to remember new concepts if you approach them with an appropriate Key Question in mind (Glaser, 1990). You can also use the Key Question to check your understanding of each section before an exam. If you have a study partner, try asking each other to give detailed answers to the Key Questions.

Think of Core Concepts as brief answers to the Key Questions. (In fact, each one is numbered to match its Key Question.) In other words, a Core Concept highlights the central idea in each section—much like a preview at the movies. Recognize, though, that a Core Concept is not a complete answer but rather a capsule summary of ideas to be fleshed out. For example, the Core Concept for this section says:

> **Psychology is a broad field with many specialties, but fundamentally, psychology is the science of behavior and mental processes.**

This alerts you to the two important ideas in this section: *(1) psychology studies both the mind and behavior,* and *(2) there is a variety of specialties within psychology.* Knowing these overarching themes will help you find the important ideas and organize them in your mind.

After you have constructed the foundation of your mental map with the overarching themes, fill in the details using the boldfaced terms in that section so your map shows how each term fits into the theme. For example, can you explain the difference between applied, experimental, and teaching psychologists? Between psychology, psychiatry, and pseudo-psychology?

In summary, then, Key Questions and Core Concepts lead you to the big ideas in the chapter and provide a framework for the various concepts in that chapter. They will help you step back from the details to see meaningful patterns—as the saying goes—to distinguish the forest from the trees (and consequently, to understand how all the trees fit into the forest).

Check Your Understanding

✓ **Study** and **Review** at **MyPsychLab**

1. **RECALL:** In what way is modern psychology's scope broader than the Greek concept of *psyche*?

2. **RECALL:** Name two types of *applied* psychologists.

3. **TRUE OR FALSE:** Most psychologists are therapists.

4. **APPLICATION:** Which critical thinking questions discussed in this section would be most applicable to the argument that harsher sentences are the best way of dealing with crime because "punishment is the only language that criminals understand"?

5. **UNDERSTANDING THE CORE CONCEPT:** How is psychology different from psychiatry and other disciplines that deal with people?

Answers 1. Modern psychology studies behavior as well as the mind. **2.** There are many sorts of applied psychologists. The ones mentioned in this chapter are I/O psychologists, sports psychologists, school psychologists, clinical and counseling psychologists, forensic psychologists, and environmental psychologists. **3.** False. **4.** Probably the most applicable for this claim would be these: "What is the evidence?" and "Could bias contaminate the conclusion?" But we wouldn't disagree with any other questions you may have listed because, just as with the "scared straight" issue, they could all apply to a critical analysis of the claim. **5.** Psychology is a broader field, covering all aspects of behavior and mental processes.

1.2 KEY QUESTION
What Are Psychology's Six Main Perspectives?

The shape of modern psychology has been molded by its history, which dates back some 25 centuries to the Greek philosophers Socrates, Plato, and Aristotle. These sages not only speculated about consciousness and madness; they also knew that emotions could distort thinking and that our perceptions are merely interpretations of the external world. Even today, people would probably agree with many of these ancient conjectures—and so would modern psychology.

The Greeks, however, get only partial credit for laying the foundations of psychology. At roughly the same time, Asian and African societies were developing their own psychological ideas. In Asia, followers of yoga and Buddhism were exploring consciousness, which they attempted to control with meditation. Meanwhile, in Africa, other explanations for personality and mental disorders were emerging from traditional spiritual beliefs (Berry et al., 1992). Based on these *folk psychologies,* shamans (healers) developed therapies rivaling the effectiveness of treatments used in psychology and psychiatry today (Lambo, 1978). It was, however, the Greek tradition and, later, the Church that most influenced the winding developmental path of Western psychology as a science.

What role did the Church play in shaping the study of psychology? During medieval centuries, for example, clerics actively suppressed inquiry into human nature, partly in an attempt to discourage interest in the "world of the flesh." For medieval Christians, the human mind and soul were inseparable and—like the mind of God—presented a mystery that mortals should never try to solve.

Change of this entrenched viewpoint did not come easily. It took a series of radical new ideas, spaced over several hundred years, to break the medieval mindset and lay the intellectual foundation for modern psychology—which brings us to our Core Concept for this section:

> ## Core Concept 1.2
>
> **Six main viewpoints dominate modern psychology—the biological, cognitive, behavioral, whole-person, developmental, and sociocultural perspectives—each of which grew out of radical new concepts about mind and behavior.**

As we examine these perspectives, you will see that each viewpoint offers its own unique explanation for human behavior. Taken together, they comprise psychology's multiple perspectives, each of which will become an important tool in your "psychology toolbox" for understanding human behavior. To help you see for yourself how useful these perspectives can be, we will apply each one to a problem with which many students struggle: procrastination. Let's begin with the biological perspective.

Separation of Mind and Body and the Modern Biological Perspective

The 17th-century philosopher René Descartes *(Day-CART)* proposed the first radical new concept that eventually led to modern psychology: *a distinction between the spiritual mind and the physical body.* The genius of Descartes' insight was that it allowed the Church to keep the mind off limits for scientific inquiry, while simultaneously permitting the study of human sensations and behaviors because they were based on physical activity in the nervous system. His proposal fit well with exciting new discoveries about biology, in which scientists had just learned how the sense organs of animals convert stimulation into nerve impulses and muscular responses. Such discoveries, when combined with Descartes' separation of mind and body, allowed scientists to demonstrate that biological processes, rather than mysterious spiritual forces, caused sensations and simple reflexive behaviors.

The Modern Biological Perspective Four hundred years later, Descartes' revolutionary perspective provides the basis for the modern **biological perspective**. No longer constrained by the dictates of the medieval Church, however, modern biological psychologists have rejoined mind and body (although they leave issues of the soul to religion), and now view the mind as a product of the brain.

In this current view, our personalities, preferences, behavior patterns, and abilities all stem from our physical makeup. Accordingly, biological psychologists search for the causes of our behavior in the brain, the nervous system, the endocrine (hormone) system, and the genes. Procrastination, from this perspective, may result from a certain type of brain chemistry (Liu, 2004), which could be inherited. While they don't deny the value of other perspectives on mind and behavior, biological psychologists aim to learn as much as possible about the physical underpinnings of psychological processes.

biological perspective   The psychological perspective that searches for the causes of behavior in the functioning of genes, the brain and nervous system, and the endocrine (hormone) system.

Two Variations on the Biological Theme As you might imagine, the biological view has strong roots in medicine and biological science. In fact, the emerging field of **neuroscience** combines biological psychology with biology, neurology, and other disciplines interested in brain processes. Thanks to spectacular advances in computers and brain-imaging techniques, neuroscience is a hot area of research. Among their achievements, neuroscientists have learned how damage to certain parts of the brain can destroy specific abilities, such as speech, social skills, or memory. And, as we will see in Chapter 8, they now use brain wave patterns to open up the hidden world of sleep and dreams.

Another important variant of biological psychology sprouted recently from ideas proposed by Charles Darwin some 150 years ago. This new **evolutionary psychology** holds that much human behavior arises from inherited tendencies, and it has gained a substantial boost from the recent surge of genetics research. In the evolutionary view, our genetic makeup—underlying our most deeply ingrained behaviors—was shaped by conditions our remote ancestors faced thousands of years ago.

According to evolutionary psychology, environmental forces have pruned the human family tree, favoring the survival and reproduction of individuals with the most adaptive mental and physical characteristics. Darwin called this process *natural selection*. Through it, the physical characteristics of our species have evolved (changed) in the direction of characteristics that gave the fittest organisms a competitive advantage.

Some proponents of evolutionary psychology have made highly controversial claims. In their view, even the most undesirable human behaviors, such as warfare, rape, and infanticide, may have grown out of biological tendencies that once helped humans adapt and survive (Buss, 2008). This approach also proposes controversial biological explanations for certain gender differences—why, for instance, men typically have more sexual partners than do women. Stay tuned for more of this controversy in our discussion of sexuality in Chapter 9.

neuroscience The field devoted to understanding how the brain creates thoughts, feelings, motives, consciousness, memories, and other mental processes.

evolutionary psychology A relatively new specialty in psychology that sees behavior and mental processes in terms of their genetic adaptations for survival and reproduction.

The Founding of Scientific Psychology and the Modern Cognitive Perspective

Another radical idea that shaped the early science of psychology came from chemistry, where scientists had developed the famous *periodic table* after noticing patterns in properties of the chemical elements. At one stroke, the periodic table made the relationships among the elements clear. Wilhelm Wundt, a German scientist (who, incidentally,

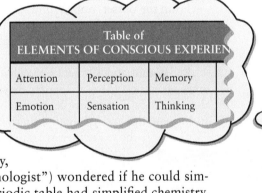

became the first person to call himself a "psychologist") wondered if he could simplify the human psyche in the same way the periodic table had simplified chemistry. Perhaps he could discover "the elements of conscious experience"! Although Wundt never realized his dream of a periodic table for the mind, he did have this breakthrough insight: *The methods of science used to objectively measure and study the natural world, such as in chemistry or physics, could be used to study the mind and body as well.*

Introspecting for the Elements of Conscious Experience "Please press the button as soon as you see the light," Professor Wundt might have said, as he readied to record the *reaction time* between the light stimulus and a student's response. Such simple yet concrete experiments were common fare in 1879 in the world's first psychology laboratory at the University of Leipzig. There, Wundt and his students also performed studies in which trained volunteers described their sensory and emotional responses to various stimuli, using a technique called **introspection**. These were history's first psychology experiments: studies of what Wundt and his students proposed to be the basic "elements" of consciousness, including sensation and perception, memory, attention, emotion, thinking, learning, and language. All our mental activity, they asserted, consists of different combinations of these basic processes.

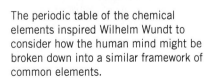

The periodic table of the chemical elements inspired Wilhelm Wundt to consider how the human mind might be broken down into a similar framework of common elements.

introspection The process of reporting on one's own conscious mental experiences.

Do It Yourself! A DEMONSTRATION FROM GESTALT PSYCHOLOGY

FIGURE 1.2
Takete or Maluma?

Without reading further, decide quickly which one of the two figures above (see Figure 1.2) you would name "Takete" and which you would call "Maluma." You might want to see if your friends give the same answer.

According to an early 20th-century group of German psychologists, known as the *Gestalt psychologists,* the names you give to these figures may reflect the associations wired into your brain. Indeed, most people think that the soft-sounding term *Maluma* is more appropriate for the rounded left-hand figure, while the sharp-sounding term *Takete* better fits the pointy figure on the right (Köhler, 1947). This was just one of many simple tests they developed in their quest to understand how we perceive our world.

For such demonstrations, the Gestalt psychologists borrowed Wundt's method of introspection, but they objected to his emphasis on the parts, or "elements," of consciousness. Instead, the Gestalt psychologists sought to understand how we construct "perceptual wholes," or *Gestalts.* How do we, for example, form the perception of a face from its component lines, shapes, colors, and textures? Their ultimate goal was even grander: They believed that understanding perception would lead them to an understanding of how the brain creates perceptions. You will get to know the Gestalt psychologists better in Chapter 3, when we take an in-depth look at sensation and perception.

---

structuralism A historical school of psychology devoted to uncovering the basic structures that make up mind and thought. Structuralists sought the "elements" of conscious experience.

Wundt's Legacy: Structuralism Wundt's pupil, Edward Bradford Titchener, brought the quest for the elements of consciousness to America, where Titchener began calling it **structuralism**. Titchener's term was fitting, because his goal—like that of Wundt—was to reveal the most basic "structures" or components of the mind (Fancher, 1979). So, even though Wundt never used the term, he is considered the father of structuralism.

From the outset, both Wundt and Titchener became magnets for critics. Objections especially targeted the introspective method as being too subjective. After all, said the critics, how can we judge the accuracy of people's descriptions of their thoughts and feelings?

But Wundt and Titchener have had the last laugh. Even though psychologists sometimes view their ideas as quaint, they still rely on updated versions of the old structuralist methods. For example, you will see introspection at work when we study sleep and dreaming, and you can experience it firsthand in the upcoming *Do It Yourself!*

functionalism A historical school of psychology that believed mental processes could best be understood in terms of their adaptive purpose and function.

box. Further, we can guess that Wundt and Titchener, if they were alive today, would still be laughing for one more reason: The topics they first identified and explored can be found as chapter headings in every introductory psychology text—including this one.

Cognitive psychologist Elizabeth Loftus has done pioneering studies showing the fallibility of memory and eyewitness testimony.

James and the Function of Mind and Behavior One of Wundt's most vocal critics, the American psychologist William James, argued that the German's approach was far too narrow. (James also said it was boring—which didn't help his already strained relationship with Wundt.) Psychology should include the *function* of consciousness, not just its *structure*, James argued. Appropriately, his brand of psychology led to a "school"[2] that became known as **functionalism** (Fancher, 1979).

James and his followers found Charles Darwin's ideas far more interesting than Wundt's. Like Darwin, James had a deep interest in emotion that included its relation to the body and behavior (not just as an element of consciousness, as in Wundt's system). He also liked

---

[2]The term *school* refers to a group of thinkers who share the same core beliefs.

Do It Yourself! AN INTROSPECTIVE LOOK AT THE NECKER CUBE

The cube in Figure 1.3A will trick your eye—or, more accurately, it will trick your brain. Look at the cube for a few moments, and suddenly it will seem to change perspectives. For a time it may seem as if you were viewing the cube from the upper right (see Figure 1.3B). Then, abruptly, it will shift and appear as though you were seeing it from the lower left (see Figure 1.3C).

It may take a little time for the cube to shift the first time. But once you see it change, you won't be able to prevent it from alternating back and forth, seemingly at random. Try showing the cube to a few friends and asking them what they see. Do they see it shifting perspectives, as you do?

This phenomenon was not discovered by a psychologist. Rather, Louis Necker, a Swiss geologist, first noticed it nearly 200 years ago while looking at cube-shaped crystals under a microscope. Necker's amazing cube illustrates two important points.

First, it illustrates the much-maligned process of *introspection*, pioneered by Wundt and his students. You will note that the only way we can demonstrate that the **Necker cube** changes perspectives in our minds is by introspection: having people look at the cube and report what they see. And why is this important to psychology? Only the most hard-core behaviorists would deny that something happens mentally within a person looking at the cube. In fact, the Necker cube demonstrates that we add meaning to our sensations—a process called *perception*, which will be a main focus of Chapter 3.

The second important point is this: The Necker cube can serve as a metaphor for the multiple perspectives in psychology. Just as there is no single right way to see the cube, there is no single perspective in psychology that gives us the whole "truth" about behavior and mental

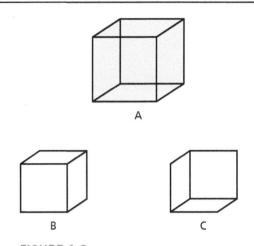

FIGURE 1.3

Different Perspectives of the Necker Cube

processes. Put another way, if we are to understand psychology fully, we must alternately shift our viewpoints among multiple perspectives.

Darwin's emphasis on organisms *adapting* to their environments. James therefore proposed that psychology should explain how people adapt—or fail to adapt—to the real world outside the laboratory.

The functionalists, then, became the first *applied* psychologists—examining how psychology could be used to improve human life. James himself wrote extensively on the development of learned "habits," the psychology of religion, and teaching. He is also thought to be the first American professor ever to ask for student evaluations (Fancher, 1979). His follower, John Dewey, founded the "progressive education" movement, which emphasized learning by *doing* rather than by merely listening to lectures and memorizing facts.

Introspection was the point on which structuralism and functionalism agreed. Ironically, their point of agreement was also their greatest point of vulnerability: The introspective method was subjective, leaving them vulnerable to criticism that their versions of psychology were not really scientific. Overcoming this problem took more than half a century and the cooperation of experts from several disciplines who came together to form the *cognitive perspective*.

The Modern Cognitive Perspective The development of the computer—which became the new metaphor for the mind—gave psychology an irresistible push toward a new synthesis: the modern **cognitive perspective.** Following in the tradition of its structuralist, functionalist, and Gestalt ancestors, this perspective emphasizes *cognition,* or mental activity, such as perceptions, interpretations, expectations, beliefs, and memories. From this viewpoint, a person's thoughts and actions are the result of the unique cognitive pattern of perceptions and interpretations of her experiences.

Today, however, the cognitive perspective boasts more objective methods of observation than its forebears, thanks to stunning advancements in brain-imaging techniques that allow scientists to view the brain as it engages in various mental processes.

Necker cube An ambiguous two-dimensional figure of a cube that can be seen from different perspectives: The Necker cube is used here to illustrate the notion that there is no single "right way" to view psychological processes.

cognitive perspective Another of the main psychological viewpoints distinguished by an emphasis on mental processes, such as learning, memory, perception, and thinking, as forms of information processing.

CONNECTION CHAPTER 2

Brain scanning methods such as CT, PET, MRI, and fMRI use advanced computer technology to see into the brain without opening the skull (p. 64).

behaviorism   A historical school (as well as a modern perspective) that has sought to make psychology an objective science by focusing only on behavior—to the exclusion of mental processes.

How would cognitive psychologists explain procrastination? First, they might point out that procrastinators often underestimate how long a project might take—illustrating the role of cognitive expectations in our behavior patterns. Also, procrastinators may be victims of confirmation bias if they remember the times they previously procrastinated yet completed a project on time, while forgetting the deadlines they missed. Finally, people who put things off until the last minute may not interpret their behavior as a problem—perhaps they tell themselves they do their best work under pressure. In all these ways, cognitive psychology sheds light on the internal thinking processes that influence procrastination and other human behaviors.

The Behavioral Perspective: Focusing on Observable Behavior

Early in the 1900s, a particularly radical and feisty group, known as the *behaviorists,* made a name for themselves by disagreeing with nearly everyone. Most famously, they proposed the idea that the mind should not be part of psychology at all! John B. Watson, an early leader of the behaviorist movement, argued that a truly objective science of psychology should deal solely with observable events: physical *stimuli* from the environment and the organism's overt *responses*. **Behaviorism**, said Watson, is the science of *behavior* and the measurable environmental conditions that influence it (refer to Table 1.1).

Why did behaviorists reject mental processes—such as introspection—as a viable area of scientific study? B. F. Skinner, another influential behaviorist, may have best summarized this perspective when he suggested that the seductive concept of "mind"

TABLE 1.1 **Psychology's Six Perspectives**

Perspective	What Determines Behavior?	Sources
Biological perspective	The brain, nervous system, endocrine system (hormones), and genes.	Rene Descartes
Cognitive perspective	A person's unique pattern of perceptions, interpretations, expectations, beliefs, and memories.	Wilhelm Wundt and William James
Behavioral perspective	The stimuli in our environment, and the previous consequences of our behaviors.	John Watson and B.F. Skinner
Whole-person perspective	*Psychodynamic:* Processes in our unconscious mind.	Sigmund Freud
	Humanistic: Our innate needs to grow, and to fulfill our best possible potential.	Carl Rogers and Abraham Maslow
	Trait and temperament: Unique personality characteristics that are consistent over time and across situations.	Ancient Greeks
Developmental perspective	The interaction of heredity and environment, which unfolds in predictable patterns through the lifespan.	Mary Ainsworth, Jean Piaget
Sociocultural perspective	The power of the situation. Social and cultural influences can overpower the influence of all other factors in determining behavior.	Stanley Milgram, Philip Zimbardo

has led psychology in circles. The mind, he said, is something so subjective that it cannot even be proved to exist (Skinner, 1990). (Think about it: Can you prove you have a mind?) As Skinner noted wryly, "The crucial age-old mistake is the belief that . . . what we feel as we behave is the cause of our behaving" (Skinner, 1989, p. 17). Thus, for the behaviorists, a person's thoughts or emotions became irrelevant—it was only behavior that could be reliably observed and measured. So, for example, behaviorists examined whether a young child would learn to avoid a harmless white rat if the rat was paired with a sudden loud sound. Importantly, the behaviorists refrained from making any subjective assumptions about what the outward behavior (avoidance) represented internally (such as fear).

We can summarize the radical new idea that drove behaviorism this way: *Psychology should be limited to the study of observable behavior and the environmental stimuli that shape behavior.* This **behavioral perspective** called attention especially to the way our actions are modified by their consequences, as when a child is praised for saying "Thank you" or an adult is rewarded for good job performance with a pay raise. The behaviorists contributed greatly to our detailed understanding of environmental forces that impact all kinds of human learning, and have also given us powerful strategies for changing behavior by altering the environment (Alferink, 2005; Roediger, 2004). We will examine these ideas more closely in Chapter 4.

How do you think behaviorists, with their emphasis on reward and punishment, might explain procrastination? Consider the rewards reaped from putting off something you don't want to do: Instead of the dreaded work, you likely spend the time doing something you enjoy, which is instantly gratifying. Then, when you tackle the problem at the last minute, you get rewarded by the feeling of success when you manage to pull it off and get it done just in the nick of time! Is it any wonder why procrastination is a difficult behavior to change? Fortunately, in Chapter 4, you will learn some effective strategies offered by these same behaviorists for overcoming this troublesome pattern.

Strict behaviorists, such as B. F. Skinner, believe that psychology should focus on the laws that govern behavior—that is, on the relations between stimuli (S) and responses (R)—rather than on the subjective processes of the mind.

behavioral perspective A psychological viewpoint that finds the source of our actions in environmental stimuli, rather than in inner mental processes.

The Whole-Person Perspectives: Psychodynamic, Humanistic, and Trait and Temperament Psychology

As the 20th century dawned, a new challenge to Wundt and structuralism came from the Viennese physician Sigmund Freud and his disciples, who were developing a method of treating mental disorders based on yet another radical idea: *Personality and mental disorders arise mainly from processes in the unconscious mind, outside of our awareness* (refer to Table 1.1). Although Freud was not the first to suggest that we are unaware of some mental processes, neither structuralism nor functionalism had imagined that unconscious processes could dominate the personality and cause mental disorders. Moreover, Freud's *psychoanalytic theory* aimed to explain the *whole person*, not just certain components (such as attention, perception, memory, behavior, or emotion), as other schools of psychology had done. His goal was to explain every aspect of mind and behavior in a single, grand theory.

Psychodynamic Psychology Freud could be a difficult mentor, provoking many of his followers to break ranks and develop their own theories. We use the term *psychodynamic* to refer both to Freud's ideas and to all these other *neo-Freudian* formulations that arose from Freud's notion that the mind (psyche), especially the unconscious mind, is a reservoir of energy (dynamics) for the personality. This energy, says **psychodynamic psychology**, is what motivates us.

psychodynamic psychology A clinical approach emphasizing the understanding of mental disorders in terms of unconscious needs, desires, memories, and conflicts.

This cartoon illustrates the Freudian slip, which suggests that thoughts or feelings we try to hide from others will sometimes accidentally find their way into our speech.

The first and best-known representative of the psychodynamic approach is, of course, Sigmund Freud, whose system is called **psychoanalysis.** Originally conceived as a medical technique for treating mental disorders, psychoanalysts emphasize the analysis of dreams, slips of the tongue (the so-called Freudian slip), and a technique called *free association* to gather clues to the unconscious conflicts and "unacceptable" desires thought to be censored by consciousness. For example, psychoanalysts might interpret a person's pattern of self-defeating behavior—such as procrastination—as motivated by an unconscious fear of failure.

Like Freud, most psychoanalysts today are physicians with a specialty in psychiatry and advanced training in Freudian methods. (And now, as promised, you know the difference between a *psychologist* and a *psychoanalyst.*) But these practitioners are not the only ones aspiring to explain the whole person. Two other groups share an interest in a global understanding of the personality, *humanistic psychology* and *trait and temperament psychology.* Here, we group all three under the heading **whole-person perspectives.**

Humanistic Psychology   Reacting to the psychoanalytic emphasis on sinister forces in the unconscious, **humanistic psychology** took a different tack. Their radical new idea was *an emphasis on the positive side of our nature that included human ability, growth, and potential* (refer to Table 1.1). Led by the likes of Abraham Maslow and Carl Rogers, they offered a model of human nature that proposed innate needs for growth and goodness, and also emphasized the free will people can exercise to make choices affecting their lives and growth (Kendler, 2005).

In the humanistic view, your self-concept and self-esteem have a huge influence on your thoughts, emotions, and actions, all of which ultimately impact development of your potential. Like psychodynamic psychology, humanistic psychology has had a major impact on the practice of counseling and psychotherapy.

Trait and Temperament Psychology   The ancient Greeks, who anticipated so many modern ideas, proclaimed that personality is ruled by four body *humors* (fluids): blood, phlegm, melancholer, and yellow bile. Depending on which humor was dominant, an individual's personality might be sanguine (dominated by blood), slow and deliberate (phlegm), melancholy (melancholer), or angry and aggressive (yellow bile).

We no longer buy into the ancient Greek typology, of course. But their notion of *personality traits* lives on in modern times as **trait and temperament psychology.** The fundamental idea distinguishing this group says: *Differences among people arise from differences in persistent characteristics and internal dispositions called* traits *and* temperaments (refer to Table 1.1).

psychoanalysis   An approach to psychology based on Sigmund Freud's assertions, which emphasize unconscious processes. The term is used to refer broadly both to Freud's psychoanalytic theory and to his psychoanalytic treatment method.

whole-person perspectives   A group of psychological perspectives that take a global view of the person: Included are *psychodynamic psychology, humanistic psychology,* and *trait and temperament psychology.*

humanistic psychology   A clinical approach emphasizing human ability, growth, potential, and free will.

CONNECTION CHAPTER 10

People's personalities differ on five major trait dimensions, cleverly called the *Big Five* (p. 423).

trait and temperament psychology   A psychological perspective that views behavior and personality as the products of enduring psychological characteristics.

You have probably heard of such traits as *introversion* and *extraversion,* which seem to be fundamental characteristics of human nature. Other traits psychologists have identified in people all over the world include a sense of anxiety or well-being, openness to new experiences, agreeableness, and conscientiousness. We will examine these "Big Five" personality traits (as well as the other whole-person theories) more closely in Chapter 10. Some psychologists also propose that we differ on an even more fundamental level called *temperament,* thought to account for the different dispositions observed among newborn babies (and among adults as well).

Trait and temperament psychologists might explain procrastination in terms of the extent to which a person possesses the trait of conscientiousness. So, for example, a person who is high in conscientiousness—in other words, takes commitments very seriously—would be less likely to procrastinate. The individual who habitually puts things off, yet doesn't get stressed at missed deadlines, would be labeled low on conscientiousness and in possession of an easy temperament (thus explaining the low stress). All these individual characteristics would be presumed to be at least partly biological in nature and would be expected to be fairly consistent over time and across situations.

The Developmental Perspective: Changes Arising from Nature and Nurture

Change may be the only constant in our lives. According to the **developmental perspective,** psychological change results from the interaction between the *heredity* written in our genes and the influence of our *environment* (see Table 1.1). But which counts most heavily: *nature* (heredity) or *nurture* (environment)? As we have seen, biological psychologists emphasize nature, while behaviorists emphasize nurture. Developmental psychology is where the two forces meet.

developmental perspective   One of the six main psychological viewpoints, distinguished by its emphasis on nature and nurture and on predictable changes that occur across the lifespan.

The big idea that defines the developmental perspective is this: *People change in predictable ways as the influences of heredity and environment unfold over time.* In other words, humans think and act differently at different times of their lives. Physically, development can be seen in such predictable processes as growth, puberty, and menopause. Psychologically, development includes the acquisition of language, logical thinking, and the assumption of different roles at different times of life. Developmental psychologists, then, might not be surprised by the teen who procrastinates. On the contrary, they may see it as normal behavior at that age, given that teens are still learning how to juggle multiple responsibilities and accurately estimate how long things take to complete—all while simultaneously coping with their changing bodies and social worlds.

In the past, much of the research in developmental psychology has focused on children—in part because they change so rapidly and in rather predictable ways. Developmental psychologists are increasing their scrutiny of teens and adults, however, as we discover how developmental processes continue throughout our lives. In Chapter 7, we will explore some common patterns of psychological change seen across the entire lifespan, from conception to old age. The developmental theme will appear elsewhere throughout this text, too, because development affects all our psychological processes, from biology to social interaction.

The Sociocultural Perspective: The Individual in Context

Who could deny that people exert powerful influences on each other? The **sociocultural perspective** places the idea of *social influence* center stage. From this viewpoint, *social psychologists* probe the mysteries of liking, loving, prejudice, aggression, obedience, and conformity. In addition, many have become interested in how these social processes vary from one *culture* to another (refer to Table 1.1).

sociocultural perspective   A main psychological viewpoint emphasizing the importance of social interaction, social learning, and culture in explaining human behavior.

culture   A complex blend of language, beliefs, customs, values, and traditions developed by a group of people and shared with others in the same environment.

cross-cultural psychologists   Those who work in this specialty are interested in how psychological processes may differ among people of different cultures.

Dr. Phil Zimbardo, one of your authors, is a social psychologist who studies the "power of the situation" in controlling our behavior. You will see how strongly social situations affect our behavior when you read about his Stanford Prison Experiment in Chapter 11.

Culture, a complex blend of human language, beliefs, customs, values, and traditions, exerts profound influences on all of us. We can see culture in action not only as we compare people of one continent to those of another but also by comparing people, for example, in the California–Mexican culture of San Diego and the Scandinavian-based culture of Minnesota. Psychology's earlier blindness to culture was due, in part, to the beginnings of scientific psychology in Europe and North America, where most psychologists lived and worked under similar cultural conditions (Lonner & Malpass, 1994; Segall et al., 1998). Today the perspective has broadened: Less than half of the world's half-million psychologists live and work in the United States, and interest in psychology is growing in countries outside of Europe and North America (Pawlik & d'Ydewalle, 1996; Rosenzweig, 1992, 1999). Still, much of our psychological knowledge has a North American/European flavor. Recognizing this bias, **cross-cultural psychologists** have begun the long task of reexamining the "laws" of psychology across cultural and ethnic boundaries (Cole, 2006).

Proponents of the sociocultural view do not, of course, deny the effects of heredity or learning or even of unconscious processes. Rather, they bring to psychology a powerful additional concept: *the power of the situation.* From this viewpoint, then, *the social and cultural situation in which the person is embedded can sometimes overpower all other factors that influence behavior.* For example, certain cultures place greater emphasis on meeting deadlines, which would in turn influence the behavior (such as procrastination) of an individual in that culture. What situational or cultural forces have, in your own past, interfered with your timely attention to a project?

Together, then, these six perspectives all play key roles in developing a holistic understanding of human behavior. As we have seen with our example of procrastination, many perspectives can reasonably applied to any single behavior—and rarely is just one perspective sufficient to adequately explain the behavior. (We hasten to add, however, that explanations for a behavior are not intended as justifications for it. Instead, they function well as clues for overcoming a behavior when it is problematic, or for understanding behaviors in others.)

To summarize the perspectives we have just covered, please have a look at Figure 1.4. There you will find a thumbnail overview of the main viewpoints that make up the spectrum of modern psychology.

The Changing Face of Psychology

Modern psychology is a field in flux. In recent decades, the biological, cognitive, and developmental perspectives have become dominant. And increasingly, adherents of once-conflicting perspectives are making connections and joining forces: We now see such new and strange hybrid psychologists as "cognitive behaviorists" or "evolutionary developmentalists." At the same time, nearly all specialties within psychology seem eager to make a connection with neuroscience, which is rapidly becoming one of the pillars of the field.

We also call your attention to a noteworthy shift in the proportion of psychologists who are women and members of minority groups. Ethnic minorities—especially Asians, African Americans, and Latinos—are becoming psychologists in increasing numbers (Kohout, 2001). Even more striking is the new majority status of women in psychology. In 1906, only 12 percent of American psychologists listed were women, according to a listing in *American Men of Science* (named with no irony intended). By 1921, the proportion had risen above 20 percent. And now, women receive more than two-thirds of the new doctorates awarded in the field each year (Cynkar, 2007; Kohout, 2001).

Although psychology has always included a higher proportion of women than any of the other sciences, women have often found gender biases blocking their career paths

Cross-cultural psychologists, such as this researcher in Kenya, furnish important data for checking the validity of psychological knowledge.

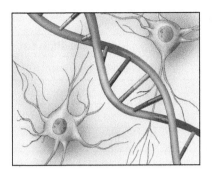

The Biological Perspective focuses on:
- nervous system
- endocrine system
- genetics
- physical characteristics

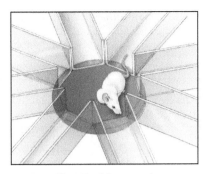

The Behavioral Perspective focuses on:
- learning
- control of behavior by the environment
- stimuli and responses—but not mental processes

The Developmental Perspective focuses on:
- changes in psychological functioning across the life span
- heredity and environment

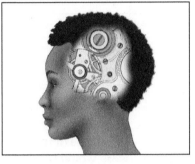

The Cognitive Perspective focuses on:
- mental processes, such as thought, learning, memory, and perception
- the mind as a computer-like "machine"
- how emotion and motivation influence thought and perception ("hot cognition")

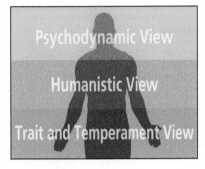

The Whole-Person Perspective includes:
- the *Psychodynamic View*, which emphasizes unconscious motivation and mental disorder
- the *Humanistic View*, which emphasizes mental health and human potential
- the *Trait and Temperament View*, which emphasizes personality characteristics and individual differences

The Sociocultural Perspective focuses on:
- social influences on behavior and mental processes
- how individuals function in groups
- cultural differences

FIGURE 1.4

Summary of Psychology's Six Main Perspectives

Do It Yourself! APPLYING PSYCHOLOGY'S PERSPECTIVES

The six perspectives in psychology can be one of the most useful tools you take away from this class. How? By applying them to behaviors of interest in your own life, you can become more sophisticated and more accurate in your interpretations of why people do what they do. Why do some people commit acts of terror or violence? What causes infidelity in romantic relationships? What makes a person feel anxious when speaking in public? Why do people smoke cigarettes? Consider one of these questions, or create one of your own. Can you explain how at least four of psychology's perspectives might explain that behavior? If so, you are well on your way to understanding the importance of multiple perspectives in the field of psychology.

TABLE 1.2 A Sampling of Women's Contributions to Psychology

	Research Area	Institutional Affiliation
Mary Ainsworth	Infant attachment	University of Toronto
Mary Calkins	Memory, psychology of the self	Wellesley College
Christine Ladd Franklin	Logic and color vision	Johns Hopkins University
Carol Gilligan	Gender studies, moral development	Harvard University
Julia Gulliver	Dreams and the subconscious self	Rockford University
Diane Halpern	Critical thinking, gender differences	University of Cincinnati
Elizabeth Loftus	False memory	Stanford University
Eleanor Maccoby	Developmental psychology, effects of divorce on children	University of Michigan
Lillien Martin	Psychophysics	Wellesley College
Christina Maslach	Burnout and job stress	Stanford University
Anna McKeag	Pain	Bardwell School
Sandra Scarr	Intelligence	Harvard University
Margaret Washburn	Perception	Vassar College

(Furumoto & Scarborough, 1986). For example, G. Stanley Hall, one of the pioneers of American psychology, notoriously asserted that academic work would ruin a woman's health and cause deterioration of her reproductive organs. Nevertheless, as early as 1905, the American Psychological Association elected its first female president, Mary Whiton Calkins. See Table 1.2 for a sampling of other important contributions made by women to the field of psychology.

[PSYCHOLOGY MATTERS]

Psychology as a Major

Becoming a fully fledged psychologist requires substantial training beyond the bachelor's degree. In graduate school, the psychology student takes advanced classes in one or more specialized areas while developing general skills as a scholar and researcher. On completion of the program, the student receives a master's or doctor's degree, typically a PhD (Doctor of Philosophy), a PsyD (Doctor of Psychology), or an EdD (Doctor of Education).

Satisfying careers are available, however, at various levels of education in psychology, although the widest range of choices is available to holders of a doctorate (Smith, 2002b). In most states, a license to practice psychology requires a doctorate plus a supervised internship. Most college and university teaching or research jobs in psychology also require a doctorate.

A master's degree, typically requiring two years of study beyond the bachelor's level, may qualify you for employment as a psychology instructor at the high school level or as an applied psychologist in certain specialties, such as counseling. Master's-level psychologists are common in human service agencies, as well as in private practice (although many states do not allow them to advertise themselves as "psychologists").

Holders of associate's degrees and bachelor's degrees in psychology or related human services fields may find jobs as psychological aides and technicians in agencies, hospitals, nursing homes, and rehabilitation centers. A bachelor's degree in psychology, coupled with training in business or education, can also lead to interesting careers in personnel management or education.

Further information about job prospects and salary levels for psychologists is available online in the U.S. Department of Labor's *Occupational Outlook Handbook* (2011–2012 edition) at www.bls.gov/oco/home.htm. You might also check out the American Psychological Association's career pages at www.apa.org/careers/resources/index.aspx.

Check Your Understanding

✓●—[Study and **Review** at **MyPsychLab**

1. **RECALL:** René Descartes made a science of psychology possible when he suggested that _____.

2. **APPLICATION:** "The differences between men and women are mainly the result of different survival and reproduction issues faced by the two sexes." Which of the main viewpoints in psychology would this statement represent?

3. **APPLICATION:** If you were a teacher trying to understand how students learn, which of the following perspectives would be most helpful?
   a. the cognitive view
   b. the psychodynamic view
   c. structuralism
   d. the trait and temperament view

4. **RECALL:** To which of the structuralists' and functionalists' ideas did the behaviorists object?

5. **RECALL:** Which of the whole-person views focuses on understanding the unconscious mind?

6. **APPLICATION:** "Soldiers may sometimes perform heroic acts, not so much because they have heroic personality traits but because they are in a *situation* that encourages heroic behavior." Which perspective is this observation most consistent with?

7. **APPLICATION:** If you wanted to tell whether a friend had experienced a perceptual shift while viewing the Necker cube, you would have to use the method of _____, which was pioneered by Wundt and the structuralists.

8. **UNDERSTANDING THE CORE CONCEPT:** Which of the following sets of factors are all associated with the perspective indicated?
   a. memory, personality, environment: the behavioral perspective
   b. mental health, mental disorder, mental imagery: the trait and temperament perspective
   c. heredity, environment, predictable changes throughout the lifespan: the developmental perspective
   d. neuroscience, evolutionary psychology, genetics: the cognitive perspective

....

Answers 1. sensations and behaviors are the result of activity in the nervous system. **2.** The biological perspective—in particular the viewpoint of evolutionary psychology **3.** a **4.** They particularly objected to the concept of the *mind* as an object of scientific study. They also objected to introspection as a subjective and therefore unscientific method. **5.** The psychodynamic view, especially psychoanalysis **6.** The sociocultural perspective **7.** introspection **8.** c.

┌─1.3 **KEY QUESTION**
└──── How Do Psychologists Develop New Knowledge?

Earlier in this chapter, we saw how Descartes' radical new idea separating the spiritual mind from the physical body enabled scientists to start identifying biological bases for behaviors, thus challenging the pseudoscientific "common sense" that attributed certain behaviors to mysterious spiritual forces. Today, psychology continues to dispute the unfounded claims of pseudoscience, which range from palm reading to psychic predictions to use of crystals to heal physical ailments.

What makes psychology different from these pseudopsychological approaches to understanding people? Not one of them has survived trial by the *scientific method*, which is a way of testing ideas against observations. Instead, pseudo-psychology is based on hope, confirmation bias, anecdote—and human gullibility.

You might think this an arrogant view for psychologists to take. Why can't we make room for many different ways of understanding people? In fact, we do. Psychologists welcome sociologists, anthropologists, psychiatrists, and other scientists as partners in the enterprise of understanding people. We reject only those approaches that mislead people by claiming to have "evidence" that is, in truth, only anecdotes and testimonials.

What makes psychology a real science, then, is the *method*. As our Core Concept for this section says:

> **Core Concept 1.3**
>
> **Psychologists, like all other scientists, use the scientific method to test their ideas empirically.**

scientific method   A four-step process for empirical investigation of a hypothesis under conditions designed to control biases and subjective judgments.

empirical investigation   An approach to research that relies on sensory experience and observation as research data.

theory   A testable explanation for a set of facts or observations. In science, a theory is not just speculation or a guess.

What is this marvelous method? Simply put, the **scientific method** is a way of putting ideas to an objective pass–fail test. The essential feature of this test is **empirical investigation**, the collection of objective information by means of careful measurements based on direct experience. From empirical investigations, psychological science ultimately seeks to develop comprehensive explanations for behavior and mental processes. In science, we call these explanations *theories*—a commonly misunderstood word.

"It's only a theory," people may say. But to a scientist, *theory* means something special. In brief, a scientific **theory** is a testable explanation for a broad set of facts or observations (Allen, 1995; Kukla, 1989). Obviously, this definition differs from the way people customarily use the term. In everyday language, *theory* can mean wild speculation or a mere hunch—an idea that has no evidence to support it. But to a scientist, a good theory has two attractive attributes: (a) the power to explain the facts and (b) the ability to be tested. Examples of well-supported theories include Einstein's theory of relativity, the germ theory of disease, and Darwin's theory of natural selection. And as you will see throughout this text, psychology has many well-supported theories too. But what are the essential steps involved in testing a theory?

Four Steps in the Scientific Method

Testing any idea scientifically requires four basic steps that we can illustrate by applying them to our problem examining the effects of sugar on children's activity (see Figure 1.5). All scientists follow essentially the same steps, no matter whether their field is psychology, biology, chemistry, astronomy, or any other scientific pursuit. Thus, it is the *method* that makes these fields scientific, not their subject matter.

hypothesis   A statement predicting the outcome of a scientific study; a statement predicting the relationship among variables in a study.

Develop a Hypothesis   The scientific method first requires a specific testable idea or prediction, called a **hypothesis**. The term literally means "little theory" because it often represents only one piece of a larger theoretical explanation. For example, a hypothesis predicting that introverted people are attracted to extraverted people might be part of a theory tying together all the components of romantic attraction. Alternatively, a hypothesis can just be an interesting idea that piques our curiosity—as in our study of the effects of sugar on children.

To be testable, a hypothesis must be potentially *falsifiable*—that is, stated in such a way that it can be shown to be either correct or incorrect. Let's illustrate how this works with the following hypothesis: *Sugar causes children to become hyperactive*. We could test it by having children consume sugar and then observing their activity level. If we find no increase, the hypothesis is falsified. The hypothesis would *not* be falsifiable if we merely stated a value judgment—for example, that sugar is "bad" for children. Science does not aim to make value judgments and cannot answer questions that can't be tested empirically. See Table 1.3 for examples of other questions science cannot answer.

operational definitions   Objective descriptions of concepts involved in a scientific study. Operational definitions may restate concepts to be studied in behavioral terms (e.g., fear may be operationally defined as moving away from a stimulus). Operational definitions also specify the procedures used to produce and measure important variables under investigation (e.g., "attraction" may be measured by the amount of time one person spends looking at another).

Next, the scientist must consider precisely how the hypothesis will be tested. This means defining all aspects of the study in concrete terms called **operational definitions**. The following examples could serve as operational definitions for our study.

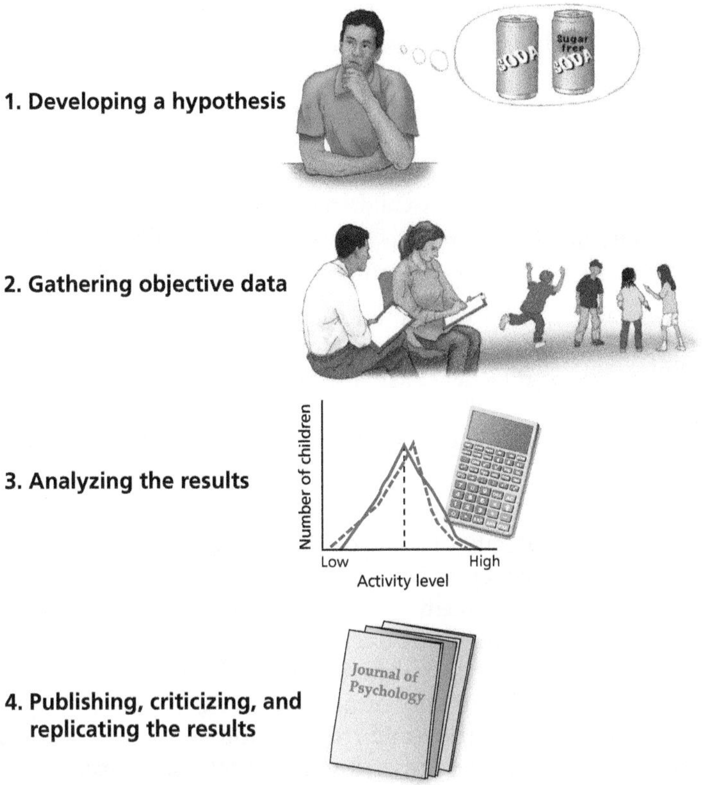
1. Developing a hypothesis
SODA
Sugar free SODA
2. Gathering objective data
3. Analyzing the results
Number of children
Low
High
Activity level
4. Publishing, criticizing, and replicating the results
Journal of Psychology

FIGURE 1.5
Four Steps in the Scientific Method

- *Operational definition of "children."* We can't test all the children in the world, of course. So, our operational definition of "children" might be all the third graders in one class at a nearby elementary school.
- *Operational definition of "sugar."* Likewise, we could define what we mean by "sugar" as the amount of sugar in a commercial soft drink. If we decide, for example, to use 7Up as our sugar source, we could operationally define "sugar" as the 38 grams available in one can of 7Up. (Using a noncaffeinated beverage, such as 7Up, avoids the possibly confounding effects of caffeine on the children's behavior.)

TABLE 1.3 What Questions Can the Scientific Method *Not* Answer?

The scientific method is not appropriate for answering questions that cannot be put to an objective, empirical test. Here are some examples of such issues:

Topic	Question
Ethics	Should scientists do research with animals?
Values	Which culture has the best attitude toward work and leisure?
Morality	Is abortion morally right or wrong?
Preferences	Is rap music better than blues?
Aesthetics	Was Picasso more creative than Van Gogh?
Existential issues	What is the meaning of life?
Religion	Does God exist?
Law	What should be the speed limit on interstate highways?

Although science can help us understand such issues, the answers ultimately must be settled by logic, faith, legislation, consensus, or other means that lie beyond the scope of the scientific method.

- *Operational definition of hyperactive.* This will be a bit more complicated. Suppose we have specially trained observers who will rate each child's behavior on the following 5-point scale:

passive		moderately active		very active
1	2	3	4	5

So, if our study specifies giving some children a sugar-sweetened drink and others the same drink containing artificial sweetener, we can operationally define "hyperactive" as a significantly higher average activity rating for the group getting the sugared drink.

With our hypothesis and operational definitions in hand, we have taken the first step in our scientific study. Next, we test our hypothesis. (The great failing of pseudosciences like astrology or fortunetelling is they never actually take this step of testing their assertions.)

Collect Objective Data   This is where we begin our empirical investigation. Literally, *empirical* means "experience based"—as contrasted with speculation based solely on hope, authority, faith, or "common sense." This literal definition can be misleading, however, if we mistakenly classify one person's experience as "empirical." Regardless of how powerful one person's experience might be, it remains merely a testimonial or an anecdote that needs to be verified under the controlled conditions of scientific research. As we discussed in the Critical Thinking section earlier in this chapter, it would be risky to assume one person's experiences would be true for others.

Investigating a question *empirically* means collecting evidence carefully and systematically, using one of several tried-and-true methods we will examine in depth in the next section. Such methods are designed to avoid false conclusions caused by our expectations, biases, and prejudices. Having done so, the **data** we obtain can be applied, or *generalized*, to a larger group of people with more confidence.

data   Pieces of information, especially information gathered by a researcher to be used in testing a hypothesis. (Singular: datum.)

Analyze the Results and Accept or Reject the Hypothesis   Once we have collected our data, we then analyze it using some type of mathematical or statistical formula. If you hate math, though, fear not: Detailed explanations of statistical procedures are beyond the scope of this book—in fact, advanced psychology students take entire courses on statistical methods! In our experiment, however, the statistical analysis will be relatively straightforward, because we merely want to know whether scores for the children receiving sugar are higher than those taking the sugar-free drink. If so, we can declare that our hypothesis has been supported. If not, we will reject it. Either way, we have learned something. You can find a statistical appendix for this text online at www.mypsychlab.com.

Publish, Criticize, and Replicate the Results   The final step in the scientific method exposes a completed study to the scrutiny and criticism of the scientific community by publishing it in a professional journal, making a presentation at a professional meeting, or—occasionally—writing a book. Then the researchers wait for the critics to respond.

If colleagues find the study interesting and important—and especially if it challenges other research or a widely held theory—critics may look for flaws in the research design: Did the experimenters choose the participants properly? Were the statistical analyses done correctly? Could other factors account for the results? Alternatively, they may decide to check the study by *replicating* it. To **replicate** the experiment, they would redo it themselves to see if they get the same results.

replicate   In research, this refers to doing a study over to see whether the same results are obtained. As a control for bias, replication is often done by someone other than the researcher who performed the original study.

In fact, our study of the effects of sugar on children is a simplified replication of research done previously by Mark Wolraich and his colleagues (1995). Their study lasted three weeks and compared one group of children who ate a high-sugar diet with another group given a low-sugar diet with artificial sweeteners. Contrary to folk wisdom, the researchers found no differences between the groups in behavior or cognitive (mental) function. So, if our study were to find a "sugar high" effect, it would contradict the Wolraich findings, and you can be sure it would receive careful scrutiny and criticism.

Criticism also occurs behind the scientific scenes to filter out poorly conceived or executed research prior to publication. Journal editors and book publishers (including the publishers of this book) routinely seek opinions of expert reviewers. As a result, authors usually receive helpful, if sometimes painful, suggestions for revision. Only when a hypothesis has cleared all these hurdles will editors put it in print and scholars tentatively accept it as scientific "truth."

We should emphasize, however, that scientific findings are always tentative. As long as they stand, they stand in jeopardy from a new study that requires a new interpretation or sends earlier work to the academic scrap heap. Consequently, the results of the Wolraich sugar study could be eventually replaced by better, more definitive knowledge. Obviously, then, the scientific method is an imperfect system, but it is the best method ever developed for testing ideas about the natural world. As such, it represents one of humankind's greatest intellectual achievements.

Five Types of Psychological Research

The scientific method, then, provides much greater credibility for ideas than does mere anecdote or pseudoscience. Within this method, there are several specific ways a researcher can collect objective data. Each has unique advantages, as well as limitations. One key step in conducting good research, then, is choosing the method best suited to your particular hypothesis and resources.

Experiments Like the word *theory*, the term **experiment** also has a very specific meaning in science. Contrary to everyday usage of the term to refer to any type of formal or informal test, the scientific use of the word applies to a particular set of procedures for collecting information under highly controlled conditions. As a result of its careful design, an experiment is the only type of research method we will discuss here that can reliably determine a cause–effect relationship. Thus, if a hypothesis is worded in a manner that suggests cause and effect—as ours does in stating that sugar *causes* hyperactivity in children—then the experiment is the best option. Let's see how our sugar study can determine cause and effect.

> **experiment** A kind of research in which the researcher controls all the conditions and directly manipulates the conditions, including the independent variable.

In the most basic experimental design, the researcher varies only one factor, known as a *variable,* and keeps all other conditions of the experiment under constant control—the same for all participants. Scientists call that one variable the **independent variable** because it operates independently of everything else in the study. In our sugar study, we hypothesized that sugar causes hyperactivity, so sugar/no sugar is our independent variable. By giving some children sugar and others a sugar substitute, and keeping all other conditions constant, we are manipulating the independent variable. Because all other aspects of the experiment are held constant, we can say that the independent variable is the *cause* of any experimental effects we observe.

> **independent variable** A stimulus condition so named because the experimenter changes it independently of all the other carefully controlled experimental conditions.

Likewise, the **dependent variable** is the outcome variable, or what we hypothesize to be the *effect*. In other words, any experimental effects we observe depend on the *in*dependent variable that we have introduced. In our sugar experiment, then, the dependent variable is the children's activity level. If the group receiving the sugar is later observed to be more active, we can be sure it was the sugar that caused the hyperactivity, because it was the only difference between the two groups. ◉➤

> **dependent variable** The measured outcome of a study; the responses of the subjects in a study.

> ◉➤ **Simulate** the **Experiment**
> Distinguishing Independent and Dependent Variables at
> **MyPsychLab**

Before going any further, we should clarify two other important terms used to identify our participants. Those receiving the treatment of interest (in our study, the high-sugar drink) are said to be in the *experimental condition*. Individuals exposed to the experimental condition, then, make up the **experimental group**. Meanwhile, those in the **control group** enter the *control condition,* where they do *not* receive the special treatment. (In our study, the control group will get the artificially sweetened drink.) Thus, the control group serves as a standard against which to compare those in the experimental group.

> **experimental group** Participants in an experiment who are exposed to the treatment of interest.

> **control group** Participants who are used as a comparison for the experimental group. The control group is not given the special treatment of interest.

How do we decide which participants will be placed into each group? The easy way to divide them up would be to let the children (or their parents) decide, based on their own preferences. The problem with that, however, is there could be some difference between children whose parents let them drink sugared drinks and those whose parents do not. Perhaps, for example, parents who allow their children to drink sugared drinks are more relaxed about rules in general, which could result in those same kids being rowdier in their play—which would confound our results. Similarly, it wouldn't do to put all the girls

random assignment   A process used to assign individuals to various experimental conditions by chance alone.

in one group and all the boys in the other. Why not? There could be gender differences in their physical reactions to sugar. In addition, one sex might be better than the other at controlling their reactions. These pre-existing differences could impact our outcome.

The best solution is to use **random assignment**, by which participants are assigned to each group purely by chance. One way to do this would be to list the children alphabetically and then assign alternating names to the experimental and control groups. In this way, random assignment minimizes any pre-existing differences between the two groups. This, in turn, assures that any differences in activity level are truly due to sugar rather than to some other factor such as sex or parenting style.

In summary, the experimental method is the gold standard for finding cause-and-effect relationships. It does so by isolating the variable of interest (the independent variable) and holding all other conditions of the experiment constant. Random assignment to experimental and control groups is used to minimize pre-existing differences between the groups so we can be more confident that differences in the outcome (the dependent variable) are due to the effects of the independent variable and nothing else.

Given the power of the experiment to find cause and effect, why do we need other methods? For one reason, not all hypotheses aim to find cause and effect—some merely wish to describe certain populations, such as determining what personality traits are common among psychology students. For another, ethical considerations prevent us from conducting certain kinds of experimental studies, notably those which might potentially harm participants. In such instances, then, one of the following research methods is a better or more practical choice.

Correlational Studies   In addition to the considerations described above, there is yet another factor that influences a researcher's choice of method: Due to practical or ethical considerations, sometimes scientists cannot gain enough control over the situation to allow them to conduct a true experiment. Suppose, for example, you wanted to test the hypothesis that children who ingest lead-based paint run an increased risk of learning disabilities. (Lead-based paint is common in older homes, especially in low-income urban housing.) You couldn't do an experiment, because an experiment would require you to manipulate the independent variable—which in this case would mean giving toxic material (lead) to a group of children. Obviously, this would be harmful and unethical.

correlational study   A form of research in which the relationship between variables is studied, but without the experimental manipulation of an independent variable. Correlational studies cannot determine cause-and-effect relationships.

Fortunately, you can find a way around the problem—but at the expense of some control over the research conditions. The solution takes the form of a **correlational study.** In correlational research you, in effect, look for a "natural experiment" that has already occurred by chance in the real world. So, in a correlational study on the effects of ingesting lead-based paint, you might look for a group of children who had already been exposed to lead paint. Then you would compare them to another group who had not been exposed. As a further control, you should try to match the groups so they are comparable in every conceivable respect (such as age, family income, and gender)—except in their exposure to lead-based paint.

The big drawback of a correlational study is that you can never be sure the groups are completely comparable, because you did not randomly assign people to experimental groups or manipulate the independent variable. In fact, the groups may differ on some important variables (such as access to health care or nutrition) that you could have overlooked. Thus, even if you observe more learning disabilities among children who were exposed to lead-based paint, you cannot conclude with certainty that exposure to the paint *caused* the disabilities. The most you can say is that lead-based paint is *correlated* (associated) with learning disabilities. This is, however, still useful, as it narrows the search for links to learning disabilities. In addition, a series of solid correlational findings sometimes pave the road to an experimental study, as we will discuss in the following text. Many research findings reported in the media are likely to be from correlational studies, rather than experimental ones, so let's take a closer look at what these findings mean and how we can accurately interpret them.

positive correlation   A correlation indicating that the variables change simultaneously in the same direction: As one grows larger or smaller, the other grows or shrinks in a parallel way.

Three Types of Correlations   If two variables show a pattern in which they vary in the same direction (as one variable increases, so does the other), we say they have a **positive correlation.** For example, we predicted a positive correlation in our hypothesis that children exposed to lead-based paint are at higher risk for learning disabilities. But when one variable decreases as the other increases, this is called a **negative correlation.** You would probably find a negative correlation between the amount of alcohol consumed by college students and their grade-point averages (as college students increase their consumption of alcohol, their grade-point averages decrease). Finally, if the variables have *no relationship* at all, there is a **zero correlation,** which is what you might expect between height and GPA, for example (see Figure 1.6).

Researchers usually express the degree of correlation as a number that can range from as low as –1.0 (reflecting a strong negative correlation) to a positive number as high as +1.0 (indicating a strong positive correlation). It is important to note that *a correlation can show a strong relationship even when it is negative.* (Note: Professors often ask test questions about this!) Suppose we find a correlation of –0.7 between anxiety and time spent studying. In other words, this is a negative correlation indicating more anxiety is correlated with less studying. Even though this is a negative correlation, it shows a *stronger* relationship than the positive correlation of +0.4 that is found, for example, between SAT scores and grades.

Interpreting Correlational Findings   One of the most common errors in critical thinking occurs when correlational findings are misinterpreted as cause-and-effect findings. For example, some years ago, research identified a positive correlation between children's self-esteem and their performance in school. Did that mean high self-esteem caused kids to do better in school? *Not necessarily—and to conclude otherwise is a critical thinking error!* While that notion certainly fits our "common sense" ideas about the benefits of self-esteem, without conducting an experiment, manipulating the independent variable (self-esteem), and randomly assigning students to experimental and control conditions, we cannot be sure what the causal factor is. Scientists often put the general principle this way: *Correlation does not necessarily mean causation.* ✳

In fact, any time you see a correlational finding, you must consider three possible interpretations for the finding:

- *A causes B.* If "A" refers to the first variable mentioned—in this case, self-esteem— and "B" refers to the second variable (grades), this interpretation recognizes that self-esteem may indeed influence a student's grades in school. That is, however, only one possibility.

- *B causes A.* It could also be the case that grades in school influence self-esteem—in other words, that our initial assumption about causality was backwards. If you think about it, couldn't it also be possible that students who do well in school feel

negative correlation   A correlation indicating that the variables change simultaneously in opposite directions: As one becomes larger, the other gets smaller.

zero correlation   When two variables have no relationship to each other.

✳─[Explore the Concept Correlations Do Not Show Causation at MyPsychLab

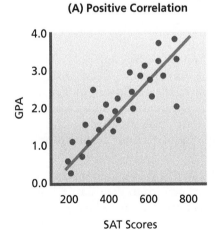
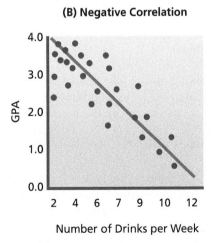
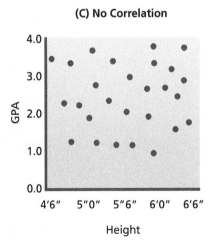

FIGURE 1.6

Three Types of Correlation

The graphs illustrate the three main types of correlation, with data points for 27 individuals. **(A)** shows a *positive correlation* between SAT scores and GPA; **(B)** shows a *negative correlation* between alcohol consumption and GPA; and **(C)** shows *no correlation* between height and GPA.

better about themselves as a result? If that were true, grades in school (rather than self-esteem) would be the driving force of the correlation.

- *C causes both A and B.* Yet a third possibility must also be recognized in contemplating correlational findings: What if a different variable (C)—something not measured in the study—was actually the driving force behind the observed relationship? In this example, what might influence a student's school performance *and* his or her self-esteem? Perhaps more time spent with parents helps a child succeed in school and also improves the child's self-esteem. In that case, we would be mistaken to assume that grades and self-esteem were related causally—instead, they just appeared that way due to lack of attention to the true source of both.

The important thing to remember is that without a true experiment, speculation about cause is just that: speculation—and potentially dangerous speculation at that. This danger was powerfully illustrated by the very findings we have discussed here: In the wake of correlational studies showing a relationship between self-esteem and grades, millions of dollars were spent nationwide on programs training teachers to help improve students' self-esteem, with the mistaken assumption that higher self-esteem would in turn raise students' grades. Did it work? No. On the contrary, follow-up experimental research discovered that getting good grades is one causal component in high self-esteem, providing support for the B causes A explanation given previously. Moreover, it turns out that self-control (in this case, an example of a C variable) promotes both self-esteem and school performance (Baumeister, 2003). Even trained researchers and lawmakers can make mistakes when "common sense" biases their accurate interpretations of research.

survey A technique used in descriptive research, typically involving seeking people's responses to a prepared set of verbal or written items.

Surveys   Which type of learning do students prefer: listening to lectures, reading material on their own, or participating in hands-on activities? If you want to know the answer to this question, you don't need to perform an experiment or a correlational study. Instead, you can simply ask students what they like using a **survey**, which is a popular and effective method of determining people's attitudes, preferences, or other characteristics.

Widely used by political pollsters and marketing consultants (as well as by many researchers in psychology and sociology), surveys typically ask people for their responses to a prepared set of questions. The biggest advantage of the survey method is its ability to gather data from large numbers of respondents relatively quickly and inexpensively, such as through Internet surveys. This easy access to many people is also the source of the survey's biggest disadvantage: its vulnerability to a variety of biases.

What are some common biases in conducting or interpreting results of a survey? *Social desirability bias* refers to respondents' tendency to answer questions in ways that are socially or politically correct (Schwarz, 1999). Other biases can stem from *wording of the questions* (Are they clear? Do they use emotionally charged words to elicit a particular type of response?), the *sample* (How well do the respondents represent the general population?), and the *survey conditions* (Is the survey anonymous? Are people completing it in a setting that might bias their responses?)

If care is taken to avoid these biases, surveys can be very useful—but only when the hypothesis can be legitimately studied with a survey. Examining the effects of sugar on children's activity level by asking parents if they've noticed their children behaving more actively after consuming sugar, for example, would reveal parents' opinions about sugar and hyperactivity—but opinions do not empirically test the relationship in which we are interested. Thus, it would not be an appropriate choice for solving our chapter problem.

naturalistic observation A form of descriptive research involving behavioral assessment of people or animals in their natural surroundings.

Naturalistic Observations   In her classic studies showing that chimpanzees have a complex, tool-making culture, Jane Goodall observed chimps in their natural jungle environment. Likewise, when psychological researchers want to know how people act in their natural surroundings (as contrasted with the artificial conditions of a laboratory), they use the same method of **naturalistic observation**. This approach is a good choice for studying child-rearing practices, shopping habits, or how people flirt in public. Thus, the setting for a naturalistic observation could be as varied as a home, a shopping mall, a restaurant, or a remote wilderness.

As you might guess, naturalistic observations are made under far less controlled conditions than are experiments because the researcher merely observes and records behaviors, rather than manipulating the environment. The best naturalistic observations, however, follow a carefully thought-out plan. Thus, such concerns as expectancy bias can be minimized by use of systematic procedures for observation and data collection and by careful training of observers.

The advantage of naturalistic observation is that you see the behaviors as they naturally occur, which often reveals insights not found in a laboratory setting. In some situations, it is also more cost effective to use the natural environment rather than try to reconstruct one in the lab. The disadvantages include the lack of control over the environment, which prohibits causal conclusions, as well as the time-consuming and expensive nature of a well-designed naturalistic study.

Jane Goodall used the method of naturalistic observation to study chimpanzee behavior.

Case Studies   How might you study what shaped comedian Stephen Colbert's sense of humor? You can't conduct any type of empirical research, because (for better or worse) you have only one Stephen Colbert. In situations such as this, researchers must rely on the **case study,** a unique type of research method that focuses in depth on only one or a few individuals, usually with rare problems or unusual talents. For example, in his book, *Creating Minds,* Howard Gardner (1993) used the case study method to explore the thought processes of several highly creative individuals, including Einstein, Picasso, and Freud. Therapists who use case studies to develop theories about mental disorder sometimes call this the *clinical method.* By either name, the disadvantages of this approach lie in its subjectivity, its small sample size, and the lack of control over variables that could affect the individuals under study. These limitations severely restrict the researcher's ability to draw conclusions that can be generalized or applied with confidence to other individuals. Nevertheless, the case study can sometimes give us valuable information that could be obtained in no other way.

case study   Research involving a single individual (or, at most, a few individuals).

Controlling Biases in Psychological Research

Assisted suicide. Abortion. Capital punishment. Do you have strong feelings and opinions on any of these issues? Emotion-laden topics can bring out biases that make critical thinking difficult, as we have seen. The possibility of bias, then, poses problems for psychologists interested in studying such issues as child abuse, gender differences, or the effects of racial prejudice—topics that may interest them precisely because of their own strong opinions. Left uncontrolled, researcher biases can affect the ways they design a study, collect the data, and interpret the results. Let's take a look at two forms of bias that require special vigilance in research.

Emotional bias, which we discussed earlier in connection with critical thinking, involves an individual's cherished beliefs, strong preferences, unquestioned assumptions, or personal prejudices. Often these are not obvious to the individual who has such biases. For example, in his book *Even the Rat Was White,* psychologist Robert Guthrie (1998) points out the bias in the long psychological tradition of research on college students—who were most often White—without realizing they were introducing bias with their sample-selection procedures. This practice limited the applicability of the research results to people of color. Fortunately, the scientific method, with its openness to peer criticism and replication, provides a powerful counterbalance to an experimenter's emotional bias. Still, scientists would prefer to identify and control their biases before potentially erroneous conclusions hit print.

Expectancy bias can also affect scientists' conclusions when they observe only what they *expect* to observe. (You can see a close kinship here with *confirmation bias,* also discussed earlier.) Expectancy bias revealed itself in, for example, a notable study in which psychology students trained rats to perform behaviors such as pressing a lever to obtain food (Rosenthal & Lawson, 1964). The experimenters told some students their rats were especially bright; other students heard their rats were slow learners. (In fact,

expectancy bias   The researcher allowing his or her expectations to affect the outcome of a study.

In his book *Even the Rat Was White,* Robert Guthrie called attention to the neglect of contributions by African Americans in psychology.

the experimenters had randomly selected both groups of rats from the same litters.) Sure enough, the students' data showed that rats believed to be bright outperformed their supposedly duller littermates—in accord with the students' expectations. How could this be? Apparently, rats perform better for an enthusiastic audience! Follow-up questionnaires showed that students with the "bright" rats were "more enthusiastic, encouraging, pleasant, and interested in their rat's performance."

Not only can these sources of bias lead to erroneous conclusions, they can also produce expensive or even dangerous consequences. Imagine that you are a psychologist working for a pharmaceutical company that wants you to test a new drug. With millions of dollars riding on the outcome, you may not be thinking with complete objectivity—despite your most sincere efforts. And what about the doctors who will prescribe the drug to patients in your study? Surely they will have high hopes for the drug, as will their patients. And so the stage is set for expectancy bias to creep covertly into the study.

Fortunately, scientists have developed a strategy for controlling expectancy bias by keeping participants in the research experimentally "blind," or uninformed, about whether they are getting the real treatment or a **placebo** (a sham "drug" or fake treatment with no medical value). Even better is the **double-blind study**, which keeps *both* participants and experimenters unaware of which group is receiving which treatment. In a double-blind drug study, then, neither researchers nor participants would know (until the end of the study) who was getting the new drug and who was getting the placebo. This scientific trick controls for experimenters' expectations by assuring that experimenters will not inadvertently treat the experimental group differently from the control group. And it controls for expectations of those receiving the experimental treatment, because they are also "blind" to which group they have been assigned.

As you can imagine, expectancy bias could affect the response of the children in our sugar study. Similarly, expectations of the observers could color their judgments. To prevent this, we should ensure that neither the children nor the observers nor the teachers know which children received each condition.

Ethical Issues in Psychological Research

Research also can involve serious ethical issues, such as the possibility of people being hurt or unduly distressed. No researcher would want this to happen, yet the issues are not always clear. Is it ethical, for example, in an experiment on aggression, to deliberately provoke people by insulting them? What degree of stress is too high a price to pay for the knowledge gained from the experiment? Such ethical issues raise difficult but important questions, and not all psychologists would answer them in exactly the same way.

To provide some guidelines for researchers, the American Psychological Association (APA) publishes *Ethical Principles of Psychologists and Code of Conduct* (2002a). This document not only deals with the ethical obligation to shield research participants from potentially harmful procedures, but it also warns researchers that information acquired about people during a study must be held confidential (Knapp & VandeCreek, 2003; Smith, 2003a, b).

Informed Consent One important ethical guideline involves gaining **informed consent**, which ensures that our participants are willingly engaging in our research. In our sugar study, for example, we might explain to parents and the teacher the broad outline of the experiment like this:

> We propose to examine the supposed effect of sugar on children's activity level. To do so, we have planned a simple study of the children in your child's third-grade classroom—subject to the permission of their parents. The procedure calls for dividing the children into two groups: At lunchtime, one group will be given a commercial soft drink (7Up) sweetened with sugar, while the other group will be given the same drink sweetened with artificial sweetener (Diet 7Up). The children will not be told to which groups they have been assigned. For the rest of the school day, specially trained observers will rate the children's activity level. Once averaged, ratings will show whether the group receiving

CONNECTION CHAPTER 3

For many people, the brain responds to placebos in much the same way that it responds to pain-relieving drugs (p. 110).

placebo *(pla-SEE-bo)* Substance that appears to be a drug but is not. Placebos are often referred to as "sugar pills" because they might contain only sugar, rather than a real drug.

double-blind study An experimental procedure in which both researchers and participants are uninformed about the nature of the independent variable being administered.

informed consent Insures that research participants are informed of the procedures of the research, as well as any potential dangers involved, so they may opt out if desired.

the sugar-sweetened drink was more active than the other group. We will share the results with you at the end of the study.

Deception The use of *deception* poses an especially knotty problem for researchers in psychology. As discussed above, the *Ethical Principles* document states that, under most circumstances, participation in research should be voluntary and informed, so volunteers are told what challenges they will face and have a real opportunity to opt out of the study. But the issue can be more complicated than it first appears. What if you are interested in the "good Samaritan" problem: the conditions under which people will help a stranger in distress? If you tell people you have contrived a phony emergency situation and ask them whether they are willing to help, you will spoil the very effect you are trying to study. Consequently, the guidelines do allow for deception under some conditions, provided no substantial risks are likely to accrue to the participants.

You might well ask, "Who judges the risks?" Most places where research is done now have watchdog committees, called *institutional review boards* (IRBs), that examine all studies proposed to be carried out within an institution, such as a college, university, or clinic. Further, when a researcher uses deception, the APA guidelines require that participants be informed of the deception as soon as possible without compromising the study's research goals. Thus, participants are *debriefed* after the study to make sure they suffer no lasting ill effects. Despite these precautions, some psychologists stand opposed to the use of deception in any form of psychological research (Baumrind, 1985; Ortmann & Hertwig, 1997).

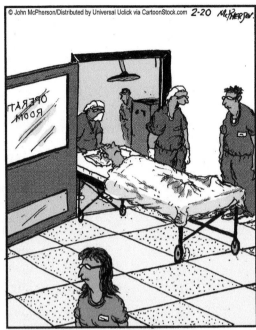

"It was a placebo surgery. I cut him open and just stitched him back up. I guarantee his phantom chest pains will be gone."

Animal Studies Another long-standing ethical issue surrounds the use of laboratory animals, such as rats, pigeons, and monkeys. Animals make attractive research subjects because of the relative simplicity of their nervous systems and the ease with which large numbers of individuals can be maintained under controlled conditions. Animals also have served as alternatives to humans when a procedure was deemed risky or outright harmful, such as implanting electrodes in the brain to study its parts.

With such concerns in mind nearly 100 years ago, officers of the American Psychological Association established a Committee on Precautions in Animal Experimentation, which wrote guidelines for animal research (Dewsbury, 1990). More recently, the APA's *Ethical Principles* document reiterated the experimenter's obligation to provide decent living conditions for research animals and to weigh any discomfort caused them against the value of the information sought in the research. Additional safeguards appear in a 1985 federal law that regulates animal research (Novak & Suomi, 1988).

Recent years have seen a renewal of concern about the use of animals as research subjects. When the research involves painful or damaging procedures, such as brain surgery, electrode implants, or pain studies, people become especially uneasy. Some feel that limitations should be more stringent, especially on studies using chimpanzees or other human-like animals. Others believe that limitations or outright bans should apply to all animal research, including studies of simple animals such as sea slugs (often used in neurological studies). While many psychologists support animal research under the APA guidelines, the issue remains a contested one (Bird, 2005; Plous, 1996).

[PSYCHOLOGY MATTERS]

The Perils of Pseudo-Psychology

Now that we understand the importance of the scientific method in determining the credibility of claims we hear in the news, let's look at a few serious problems that have resulted from failures to follow this reliable system carefully.

In 1949, the Nobel Prize in medicine went to the inventor of the "lobotomy," which at the time was a crude brain operation that disconnected the frontal lobes from the rest of the brain. Originally intended as a treatment for severe mental disorders, the operation led instead to thousands of permanently brain-injured patients. The procedure had no careful scientific basis, yet it became popular because people who *wanted* it to work didn't ask critical questions. Emotional bias (in this case, the desire to cure people with severe mental illnesses) promoted blind faith instead of clear-eyed scrutiny. As a result, people failed to examine the evidence objectively.

For a modern example of pseudo-psychology's harmful effects, we offer the widespread belief that positive thoughts can cure dire diseases such as cancer. What could possibly be wrong with that idea? For one thing, the evidence doesn't support the notion that a person's state of mind significantly impacts the chances of recovery from a serious physical illness (Cassileth et al., 1985; Coyne et al., 2007). For another, the attitude-can-make-you-well belief can lead to "blaming the victim," or assuming a patient didn't get well because his or her attitude was not sufficiently optimistic (Angell, 1985). And finally, for patients suffering from severe illness, the lure of positive thinking certainly presents a less painful and traumatic solution than does surgery, chemotherapy, or other medical procedures. Thus, their fear of the pain and suffering of proven medical treatment may bias them to put their faith in positive thinking instead of the more scientifically valid course of treatment.

Throughout this text, we aim to help you improve your own scientific thinking by identifying and countering your own critical thinking errors. We will emphasize critical thinking in three ways. One involves the problem presented at the beginning of each chapter: By applying the new knowledge you develop as you work your way through the chapter, you can solve the problem. The second is through the way we have integrated our six critical thinking guidelines, introduced in the first section of this chapter, into discussions of controversial issues in each chapter. In so doing, we hope you will become more accustomed to routinely using these guidelines to think through other controversial issues you encounter in your life. And, third, we have highlighted a special section at the end of each chapter, entitled "Critical Thinking Applied." In these features, we model the critical thinking process as we consider a current issue related to the chapter topic—for instance, in this chapter we explore a popular treatment for autism. After reading each of these special sections, we challenge you to follow our lead in critically thinking about some issue of particular interest to you in that area. You can maximize your gain from this class by choosing topics especially relevant to yourself, whether it be improving your memory, getting better sleep, or eliminating problem behaviors such as procrastination. As you will see, Psychology Matters!

Check Your Understanding

✓ Study and Review at MyPsychLab

1. **RECALL:** What is the difference between a scientific theory and a mere opinion?

2. **APPLICATION:** Which of the following could be an operational definition of "fear"?

   a. an intense feeling of terror and dread when thinking about some threatening situation

   b. panic

   c. a desire to avoid something

   d. moving away from a stimulus

3. **ANALYSIS:** Identify the only form of research that can determine cause and effect. Why is this so?

4. **ANALYSIS:** Why would an experimenter randomly assign participants to different experimental conditions?

5. **ANALYSIS:** Which one of the following correlations shows the strongest relationship between two variables?

   a. +0.4

   b. +0.38

   c. −0.7

   d. 0.05

6. **ANALYSIS:** What would be a good method for controlling expectancy bias in research on a new drug for depression?

7. **RECALL:** Why does research using deception pose an ethical problem?

8. **UNDERSTANDING THE CORE CONCEPT:** What do scientists mean by *empirical observation?*

Answers 1. A scientific theory is a testable explanation for available facts or observations. An opinion is not necessarily testable, nor can it generally explain all the relevant information. **2.** d. (because it is the only one phrased in terms of behaviors that can be observed objectively) **3.** Only the experiment can determine cause and effect, because it is the only method that manipulates the independent variable. **4.** Random assignment helps ensure that the experimental and control groups are comparable. **5.** c. **6.** A double-blind study, because it controls for the expectations of both the experimenters and the participants who receive the drug. **7.** Deception involves a conflict with the principle that participants in research should give their informed consent. (Deception is, however, permitted under certain circumstances specified in the Ethical Principles document.) **8.** Empirical observation requires making careful measurements based on direct experience.

CRITICAL THINKING APPLIED

Facilitated Communication

Autism is a developmental disorder that can cause severe impairments in attention, cognition, communication, and social functioning. In the most extreme forms, persons with autism often seem encapsulated in their own worlds, disconnected from people around them. Consequently, working with them can sometimes be quite discouraging for parents and teachers alike. It is no wonder, then, that a technique known as *facilitated communication* was heralded as a dramatic breakthrough in the treatment of autism.

Facilitated communication rests on the belief that untapped language abilities lie hidden by the mask of autism. Proponents of this technique use a trained *facilitator* to see through the mask by helping the person with autism answer questions by pointing to letters on a letter board or keyboard. (You can see how this is done in the accompanying photo.) Parents and teachers welcomed the initial enthusiastic reports on facilitated communication. But would those reports withstand the scrutiny of science?

What Are the Critical Issues?

On its face, the claim that a person with autism is, somehow, ready but unable to communicate is quite appealing to anyone personally involved in the issue—after all, communication is a basic element of human relationships. But many psychologists remained skeptical. What critical thinking questions did they ask?

Is the Claim Reasonable or Extreme? The notion that a simple pointing technique could break through the barrier of autism sounded too good to be true, said critics. Indeed, such extreme claims are typically a cue for critical thinkers to examine the claim and the evidence more closely. Testimonials, no matter how powerful, are no substitute for empirical evidence.

What Is the Evidence? Sure enough, evidence from scientific studies showed that, when the facilitator knew the questions, the child with autism would appear to give sensible answers. But when "blinders" were applied—by hiding the questions from the facilitator—the responses were inaccurate or nonsensical (American Psychological Association, 2003d; Lilienfeld, 2007).

Could Bias Contaminate the Conclusion? The evidence above reveals one form of bias you may have already suspected: The helper was—consciously or unconsciously—guiding the child's hand to produce the messages. This expectancy bias became apparent when erroneous responses emerged under conditions where the facilitator didn't know the question. Confirmation bias and emotional biases were undoubtedly at work,

Autism A developmental disorder marked by disabilities in language, social interaction, and the ability to understand another person's state of mind.

When skeptical psychologists tested the claims for facilitated communication, they found that it wasn't the autistic children who were responsible for the messages.

too: Parents and teachers, desperate for an effective treatment, uncritically accepted the anecdotal reports of success.

What Conclusions Can We Draw?

Sadly, although facilitated communication had extended hope to beleaguered parents and teachers, a scientific look presented a picture showing how uncritical belief could create consequences far worse than false hopes. More effective treatments were delayed, and moreover, parents blamed themselves when their children did not respond to the treatment as expected (Levine et al., 1994). Worst of all were the false accusations of sexual abuse based on messages thought to have come from children with autism (Bicklen, 1990; Heckler, 1994). The research left little doubt, however, that these messages had originated wholly in the minds of the facilitators. In light of such findings, the American Psychological Association (2003b) denounced facilitated communication as a failure and relegated it to the junk pile of ineffective therapies.

What lessons about critical thinking can you, as a student of psychology, take away from the facilitated communication fiasco? We hope you will develop a skeptical attitude about reports of extraordinary new treatments, dramatic psychological breakthroughs, and products that claim to help you develop untapped potential. And we hope you will always pause to ask: What is the evidence? Could the claims be merely the result of people's expectations? Perhaps the big lesson to be learned is this: No matter how much you want to believe, and no matter how many anecdotes and testimonials you have, there is no substitute for empirical evidence.

Do It Yourself!   CHALLENGING YOUR OWN PSEUDOSCIENTIFIC BELIEFS

By now, you probably recognize that everyone—even well-trained scientists—risks falling prey to biases and pseudoscience. Thus, we hope you will accept that you, too, are vulnerable to these errors in logic. Here, we list several popular beliefs that—yes, you guessed it—do not hold up to scientific scrutiny. Choose one that you tend to believe and use the Internet to find reports of scientific studies of the belief.

Then identify at least two of the critical thinking guidelines that you violated when you believed that myth to be true. Then, share your findings with your classmates.

Popular Pseudoscientific Myths

Crime rates increase when the moon is full.

Venting anger is healthy.

Abused children become abusive adults.

Most people repress traumatic memories.

If you believe in yourself, you can do anything (or, Visualize success and you'll achieve it).

People who join cults are weak-minded or lack intelligence.

If you're depressed, think happy thoughts and you'll feel better.

CHAPTER SUMMARY

((•─[**Listen** to an audio file of your chapter at **MyPsychLab**

PROBLEM: How would psychology test the claim that sugar makes children hyperactive?

- Psychologists would use the *scientific method* to test this claim.

- In a *controlled experiment*—designed to show cause-and-effect—children would be assigned *randomly* to an *experimental group* or a *control group* and given a drink with sugar or a sugar substitute.

- Using a *double-blind* procedure to control for *experimenter bias* and the *placebo effect*, observers would rate each child's activity level.

- Analyzing the resulting *data* would show whether or not the *hypothesis* had been supported. If children who received the sugared drink were more active, we could conclude that sugar does make children hyperactive.

1.1   What Is Psychology—and What Is It *Not?*

[**Core Concept 1.1 Psychology is a broad field with many specialties, but fundamentally, psychology is the science of behavior and mental processes.**]

All psychologists are concerned with some aspect of behavior and mental processes. Unlike the pseudosciences, scientific **psychology** demands solid evidence to back up its claims. Within psychology, there are many specialties that fall within three broad areas. **Experimental psychologists** primarily do research but often teach as well. Those who are primarily **teachers of psychology** work in a variety of settings, including colleges, universities, and high schools. **Applied psychologists** practice many specialties, such as industrial/organizational, sports, school, rehabilitation, clinical and counseling, forensic, and environmental psychology. In contrast with psychology, **psychiatry** is a medical specialty that deals exclusively with mental disorders.

In the media, much of what appears to be psychology is actually **pseudo-psychology**. Noticing the difference requires development of **critical thinking skills**—which this book organizes around six questions to ask when confronting new claims that purport to be scientifically based:

- What is the source?
- Is the claim reasonable or extreme?
- What is the evidence?
- Could bias contaminate the conclusion?
- Does the reasoning avoid common fallacies?
- Does the issue require multiple perspectives?

anecdotal evidence (p. 8)
applied psychologists (p. 5)
confirmation bias (p. 8)
critical thinking skills (p. 7)
emotional bias (p. 8)
experimental psychologists (p. 5)
pseudo-psychology (p. 7)
psychiatry (p. 6)
psychology (p. 4)
teachers of psychology (p. 5)

1.2 What Are Psychology's Six Main Perspectives?

[**Core Concept 1.2** Six main viewpoints dominate modern psychology—the biological, cognitive, behavioral, whole-person, developmental, and sociocultural perspectives—each of which grew out of radical new concepts about mind and behavior.]

Psychology's roots stretch back to the ancient Greeks. Several hundred years ago, René Descartes helped the study of the mind to become scientific, based on his assertion that sensations and behaviors are linked to activity in the nervous system—a step that ultimately led to the modern **biological perspective**, which looks for the causes of behavior in physical processes such as brain function and genetics. Biological psychology itself has developed in two directions: the fields of **neuroscience** and **evolutionary psychology.**

The formal beginning of psychology as a science, however, is traced to the establishment by Wundt of the first psychological laboratory in 1879. Wundt's psychology, which American psychologists morphed into **structuralism**, advocated understanding mental processes such as consciousness by investigating their contents and structure. Another early school of psychology, known as **functionalism**, argued that mental processes are best understood in terms of their adaptive purposes and functions. Both were criticized for the use of **introspection**, which some psychologists found too subjective. Nevertheless, elements of these schools can be found in the modern **cognitive perspective**, with its interest in learning, memory, sensation, perception, language, and thinking and its emphasis on information processing.

The **behavioral perspective** emerged around 1900, rejecting the introspective method and mentalistic explanations, choosing instead to analyze behavior in terms of observable stimuli and responses. Proponents of **behaviorism**, such as John Watson and B. F. Skinner, have exerted a powerful influence on modern psychology with their demands for objective methods, insights into the nature of learning, and effective techniques for management of undesirable behavior.

Three rather different viewpoints make up the **whole-person perspective**, which takes a global view of the individual. Sigmund Freud's psychoanalytic approach, with its focus on mental disorder and unconscious processes, led to **psychoanalysis** and modern **psychodynamic psychology.** In contrast, **humanistic psychology**, led by Abraham Maslow and Carl Rogers, emphasizes the positive side of human nature. Meanwhile, **trait and temperament psychology** sees people in terms of their persistent characteristics and dispositions.

The **developmental perspective** calls attention to mental and behavioral changes that occur predictably throughout the lifespan. Such changes result from the interaction of heredity and environment. Alternatively, the **sociocultural perspective** argues that each individual is influenced by other people and by the culture in which they are all embedded.

Modern psychology has changed rapidly over the past decades as the biological, cognitive, and developmental perspectives have become dominant. At the same time, adherents of different perspectives are joining forces. Another major change involves the increasing number of women and minority-group members entering the field.

While careers in psychology are available at various educational levels, becoming a fully fledged psychologist requires a doctorate. Those with less than a doctorate work in various applied specialties as aides, teachers, and counselors.

behavioral perspective (p. 17)
behaviorism (p. 16)
biological perspective (p. 12)
cognitive perspective (p. 15)
cross-cultural psychologists (p. 20)
culture (p. 20)
developmental perspective (p. 19)
evolutionary psychology (p. 13)
functionalism (p. 14)
humanistic psychology (p. 18)
introspection (p. 13)
Necker cube (p. 15)
neuroscience (p. 13)
psychoanalysis (p. 18)
psychodynamic psychology (p. 17)
sociocultural perspective (p. 19)
structuralism (p. 14)
trait and temperament psychology (p. 18)
whole-person perspectives (p. 18)

1.3 How Do Psychologists Develop New Knowledge?

[**Core Concept 1.3** Psychologists, like all other scientists, use the scientific method to test their ideas empirically.]

Psychology differs from the pseudosciences in that it employs the scientific method to test its ideas empirically. The **scientific method** relies on testable **theories** and falsifiable **hypotheses.**

Research utilizing this scientific method can employ **experiments, correlational studies, surveys, naturalistic observations,** and **case studies.** Each method differs in the amount of control the researcher has over the conditions being investigated. Researchers can fall prey to **expectancy bias.** One way scientists control for bias in their studies is the double-blind method. Using the experimental method in large and well-controlled double-blind studies, researchers have failed to find evidence that links sugar to hyperactivity in children.

Psychologists follow a code of ethics, established by the American Psychological Association, for the humane treatment of subjects. Still, some areas of disagreement remain. These especially involve the use of deception and the use of animals as experimental subjects.

Despite widespread acceptance of the scientific method, pseudo-psychological claims abound. Unchecked, pseudo-psychology can have harmful effects, as seen in the use of the lobotomy.

case study (p. 31)
control group (p. 27)
correlational study (p. 28)
data (p. 26)
dependent variable (p. 27)
double-blind study (p. 32)
empirical investigation (p. 24)

expectancy bias (p. 31)
experiment (p. 27)
experimental group (p. 27)
hypothesis (p. 24)
independent variable (p. 27)
informed consent (p. 32)
naturalistic observation (p. 30)
negative correlation (p. 29)
operational definitions (p. 24)
placebo (p. 32)
positive correlation (p. 28)
random assignment (p. 28)
replicate (p. 26)
scientific method (p. 24)
survey (p. 30)
theory (p. 24)
zero correlation (p. 29)

CRITICAL THINKING APPLIED

Facilitated Communication

A form of therapy known as facilitated communication was originally touted as a revolutionary new method of communicating with persons with autism. Upon closer inspection, however, experimental studies revealed that reports of success were skewed by expectancy bias. As a result, facilitated communication was denounced by the American Psychological Association.

DISCOVERING PSYCHOLOGY **VIEWING GUIDE**

Watch the following videos by logging into MyPsychLab (www.mypsychlab.com). After you have watched the videos, answer the questions that follow.

PROGRAM 1: **PAST, PRESENT, AND PROMISE**

PROGRAM 2: **UNDERSTANDING RESEARCH**

Program Review

1. What is the best definition of psychology?
   a. the scientific study of how people interact in social groups
   b. the philosophy explaining the relation between brain and mind
   c. the scientific study of the behavior of individuals and of their mental processes
   d. the knowledge used to predict how virtually any organism will behave under specified conditions

2. What is the main goal of psychological research?
   a. to cure mental illness
   b. to find the biological bases of the behavior of organisms
   c. to predict and, in some cases, control behavior
   d. to provide valid legal testimony

3. Who founded the first psychology laboratory in the United States?
   a. Wilhelm Wundt
   b. William James
   c. G. Stanley Hall
   d. Sigmund Freud

4. Which of the following is desirable in research?
   a. having the control and experimental conditions differ on several variables
   b. interpreting correlation as implying causality
   c. systematic manipulation of the variable(s) of interest
   d. using samples of participants who are more capable than the population you want to draw conclusions about

5. What is the main reason the results of research studies are published?
   a. so researchers can prove they earned their money
   b. so other researchers can try to replicate the work
   c. so the general public can understand the importance of spending money on research
   d. so attempts at fraud and trickery are detected

6. Why does the placebo effect work?
   a. because researchers believe it does
   b. because participants believe in the power of the placebo
   c. because human beings prefer feeling they are in control
   d. because it is part of the scientific method

7. What is the purpose of a double-blind procedure?
   a. to test more than one variable at a time
   b. to repeat the results of previously published work
   c. to define a hypothesis clearly before it is tested
   d. to eliminate experimenter bias

8. A prediction of how two or more variables are likely to be related is called a
   a. theory.
   b. conclusion.
   c. hypothesis.
   d. correlation.

9. Why would other scientists want to replicate an experiment that has already been done?
   a. to have their names associated with a well-known phenomenon
   b. to gain a high-odds, low-risk publication
   c. to ensure that the phenomenon under study is real and reliable
   d. to calibrate their equipment with that of another laboratory

10. The reactions of the boys and the girls to the teacher in the *Candid Camera* episode were essentially similar. Professor Zimbardo attributes this reaction to
    a. how easily adolescents become embarrassed.
    b. how an attractive teacher violates expectations.
    c. the way sexual titillation makes people act.
    d. the need people have to hide their real reactions.

11. The amygdala is an area of the brain that processes
    a. sound.
    b. social status.
    c. faces.
    d. emotion.

12. What assumption underlies the use of reaction times to study prejudice indirectly?
    a. People of different ethnic backgrounds are quicker intellectually than people of other ethnicities.
    b. Concepts that are associated more strongly in memory are verified more quickly.
    c. Prejudice can't be studied in any other way.
    d. People respond to emotional memories more slowly than emotionless memories.

2 Biopsychology, Neuroscience, and Human *Nature*

CHAPTER PROBLEM What does Jill Bolte Taylor's experience teach us about how our brain is organized and about its amazing ability to adapt?

CRITICAL THINKING APPLIED Left Brain versus Right Brain

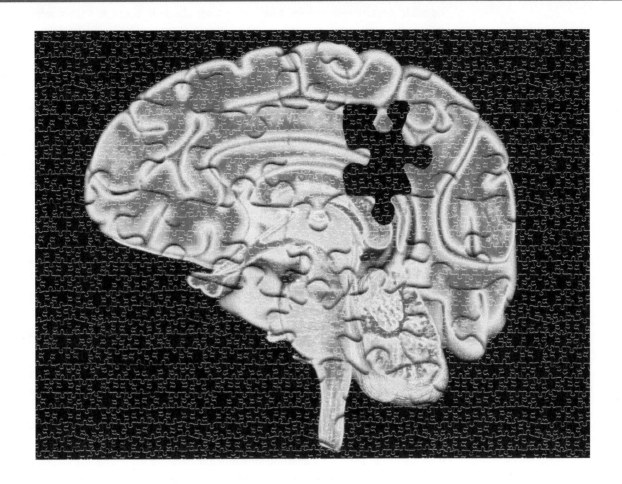

"I WAS LIVING LARGE," SAYS DR. JILL BOLTE TAYLOR, ALSO KNOWN AS THE *Singing Scientist* (Taylor, 2009, p. xiv). At age 37, the Harvard Medical School brain anatomist had won prestigious awards and was recognized nationwide for her breakthrough research on the brain's involvement in mental illness. Then, on a cold December morning, her life abruptly changed.

When Jill first awoke that fateful day, she noticed a painful pounding in her head that felt like a severe headache. As she tried to go about her normal morning routine, however, she began to notice odd changes in her body and her mind. Stepping into the shower became a focused effort in coordination. Her body felt strange; the sound of the water was a deafening roar, and the overhead light seared her eyes. As she tried to think rationally and figure out what was happening, she couldn't keep her thoughts on track. Instead, she found herself irresistibly distracted by a newfound fascination with the movement of her body parts. "As I held my hands up in front of my face and wiggled my fingers, I was simultaneously perplexed and intrigued. Wow, what a strange and amazing thing I am . . . I was both fascinated and humbled by how hard my little cells worked, moment by moment . . . I felt ethereal" (pp. 42–43). Then, her right arm became paralyzed, and suddenly she knew: "Oh my gosh, I'm having a stroke!"—followed immediately by something perhaps only a brain scientist would consider at a time like that, "Wow, this is so cool!" (p. 44).

Over the next few hours, Jill struggled with figuring out how to get help. She was no longer aware that calling 911 would bring emergency treatment, nor could she recognize the numbers on a telephone keypad. When—after spending a full hour figuring out how to call for help—she finally reached a coworker, she discovered that not only did she not understand his words, he could not understand hers: She had lost her ability to speak and to understand language. Fortunately, her coworker recognized her voice, but the several hours it took for Jill to get to a hospital took a profound toll on her brain. She could not sit up or walk without assistance. She could hear, but sounds were merely noise; she could not make sense out of them. She could see but could not distinguish color or determine whether a crack in the sidewalk was dangerous. She could not communicate with others. She didn't even recognize her own mother. The massive stroke she had suffered spilled blood throughout the left side of her brain, creating a toxic environment for millions of brain cells.

Remarkably, though, Jill recovered. Despite the extensive damage to her brain, she has returned to her career as a neuroanatomist, teaching at Indiana University School of Medicine and traveling as a national spokesperson for the Harvard Brain Bank. She water skis, plays guitar, and creates works of art that are uniquely representative of her experiences: anatomically correct stained glass brains. On the outside, observers see no signs of the traumatic brain injury she survived. On the inside, however, Jill is not the same person. Her injury and recovery rewired her brain, and with the rewiring came a different perspective on life and different personality traits. "I may look like me, and I may sound like me, but I'm different now, and I had to accept that," she states with grace and conviction. "I believe [Einstein] got it right when he said, 'I must be willing to give up what I am in order to become what I will be'" (p. 185).

PROBLEM: **What does Jill's experience teach us about how our brain is organized and about its amazing ability to adapt?**

What do we know about the human brain? In simplest terms, it is about the size of a grapefruit, it weighs about 3 pounds, and it has a pinkish-gray and wrinkled surface. But such bald facts offer no hint of the brain's amazing structure and capabilities. Some 100 billion *neurons* (nerve cells), each connecting with up to 10,000 other neurons, make the human brain the most complex structure known. Our largest computers seem primitive by comparison.

At birth, you actually had far more neurons than you do now. Many of them have been pruned away, probably from disuse in the first few years of your life. (Don't worry. It happens to everyone!) In adolescence, the number stabilizes and then remains essentially the same throughout adulthood as some cells die and others develop on a daily basis (Gage, 2003).

As for its capabilities, the human brain uses its vast nerve circuitry to regulate all our body functions, control our behavior, generate our emotions and desires, and process the experiences of a lifetime. Most of this activity operates unconsciously behind the scenes—much like the electronics in your TV. Yet when disease, drugs, or accidents destroy brain cells, the biological basis of the human mind becomes starkly apparent. Then we realize the critical role of biology in human sensation and perception, learning and memory, passion and pain, reason—and even madness.

Most remarkable of all, perhaps, the human brain has the ability to think about itself. This fact fascinates specialists in **biopsychology,** who work in a rapidly growing field that lies at the intersection of biology, behavior, and mental processes. Biopsychologists often collaborate with cognitive psychologists, biologists, computer scientists, chemists, neurologists, linguists, and others interested in the connection between brain and mind. The result is a vibrant interdisciplinary field known as *neuroscience* (Kandel & Squire, 2000).

Looking at mind and behavior from this *biological perspective* has produced many practical applications. For example, we now know that certain parts of the brain control sleep patterns—with the result that we now have effective treatments for a number of formerly untreatable sleep disorders. Likewise, the effects of certain psychoactive drugs, such as cocaine, heroin, and methamphetamine, make sense now that we

biopsychology   The specialty in psychology that studies the interaction of biology, behavior, and mental processes.

CONNECTION CHAPTER 1

Neuroscience grew out of the biological perspective in psychology, which looks for physiological explanations for human behavior and mental processes (p. 13).

understand how these drugs interact with chemicals produced by the brain. And, as we will see, recent discoveries involving mirror neurons, the genetic code for human life, brain implants, and the biological basis of memory promise many more benefits for people who live with brain disease.

We begin our exploration of biopsychology and neuroscience at the most basic level—by considering the twin domains of *genetics* and *evolution,* both of which have shaped our bodies and minds. Then we will examine the *endocrine system* and the *nervous system,* the two communication channels carrying messages throughout the body. Finally, we will focus on the brain itself. By reading this chapter, you will come to understand how Jill Bolte Taylor recovered from the massive damage to her brain, yet became an essentially different person. More importantly, you will learn how biological processes shape your every thought, feeling, and action.

2.1 KEY QUESTION
How Are Genes and Behavior Linked?

Just as fish have an inborn knack for swimming and most birds are built for flight, we humans also have *innate* (inborn) abilities. At birth, the human brain emerges already "programmed" for language, social interaction, self-preservation, and many other functions—as we can readily see in the interaction between babies and their caregivers. Babies "know," for example, how to search for the breast, how to communicate rather effectively through coos and cries and, surprisingly, how to imitate a person sticking out her tongue. We'll look more closely at the menu of innate human behaviors in our discussion of human development (Chapter 7), but for now, this is the question: How did such potential come to be woven into the brain's fabric?

The scientific answer rests on the concept of **evolution**, the process by which succeeding generations of organisms change as they adapt to changing environments. We can observe evolution in action on a microscopic level, when an antibiotic fails to work on a strain of bacteria that has evolved a resistance. When it comes to larger and more complex organisms, change occurs over much longer periods of time as these organisms adapt to changing climates, predators, diseases, and food supplies. In our own species, for example, change has favored large brains suited to language, complex problem solving, and social interaction.

Our Core Concept for this section makes this evolutionary process the link between genetics and behavior.

> **evolution** The gradual process of biological change that occurs in a species as it adapts to its environment.

> ### Core Concept 2.1
> **Evolution has fundamentally shaped psychological processes because it favors genetic variations that produce adaptive behavior.**

Our explanation of evolution begins in this section with the story of Charles Darwin, who gave the idea of evolutionary change to the world. Following that, we will build on Darwin's insight with a look at *genetics,* which involves the molecular machinery that makes evolution work—and ultimately influences all our thoughts and behaviors.

Evolution and Natural Selection

Although he trained for careers in both medicine and the ministry, Charles Darwin's greatest love was nature. He was thrilled, then, when in 1831 (with help from his botany professor) he landed a job as a "gentleman companion" aboard the *Beagle* (Phelan, 2009), a British research vessel surveying the coastline of South America. Darwin quickly became seasick, however, which made being on the ship unbearable, so he spent as much time as possible on land. Following his passion, he began studying the native species, collecting numerous specimens and keeping detailed records of the unusual life-forms he found. Struck by the similarities among the various animals and plants he studied, Darwin wondered if they could possibly be related to each other, and furthermore, if all creatures, including humans, might share a common ancestry.

He knew this notion flew in the face of accepted scholarship, as well as the religious doctrine of creationism. So, in his famous book, *On the Origin of Species* (1859), Darwin carefully made the case for the evolution of life. And controversial it was. The essential features of his argument, however, withstood withering attacks, and eventually his theory of evolution created a fundamental change in the way people saw their relationship to other living things (Keynes, 2002; Mayr, 2000).

The Evidence That Convinced Darwin What was the evidence that led Darwin to his radical conclusion about the evolution of organisms? Again and again on the voyage, he observed organisms exquisitely adapted to their environments: flowers that attracted certain insects, birds with beaks perfectly suited to cracking certain types of seeds. But he also observed *variation* among individuals within a species—just as some humans are taller than others or have better eyesight (Weiner, 1994). It occurred to Darwin that such variations could give one individual an advantage over others in the struggle for survival and reproduction. This, then, suggested a mechanism for evolution: a "weeding out" process he called **natural selection**. By means of natural selection, those individuals best adapted to their environment are more likely to flourish and reproduce; the poorly adapted tend to leave fewer offspring, and their line may die out. (You may have heard this described as *survival of the fittest,* a term Darwin disliked.) Through natural selection, then, a species gradually changes as it adapts to the demands of its environment.

natural selection   The driving force behind evolution by which the environment "selects" the fittest organisms.

Application to Psychology This process of adaptation and evolution helps us make sense of many observations we make in psychology. For example, human *phobias* (extreme and incapacitating fears) most often involve stimuli that signaled danger to our ancestors, such as snakes, heights, and lightning (Hersen & Thomas, 2005). In the same way, the fact that we spend about a third of our lives asleep makes sense in evolutionary terms: Sleep kept our ancestors out of trouble in the dark. Evolution also explains our innate preferences and distastes, such as the attractiveness of sweets and fatty foods (good sources of valuable calories for our ancestors) and a dislike for bitter-tasting substances (often signaling poisons).

Evolution is, of course, an emotionally loaded term and, as a result, many people have a distorted understanding of its real meaning. For example, some believe that Darwin's theory says humans "come from monkeys." But neither Darwin nor any other evolutionary scientist has ever said that. Rather, they say people and monkeys had a common ancestor millions of years ago—a big difference. Evolutionary theory says that, over time, the two species have diverged, each developing different sets of adaptive traits. For humans, this meant developing a big brain adapted for language (Buss et al., 1998).

We should be clear that the basic principles of evolution, while still controversial in some quarters, have been accepted by virtually all scientists for more than a century. That said, we should also note that evolutionary theory is a controversial newcomer to psychology. It is not that psychologists dispute Darwin—most do not. To its credit, evolutionary psychology may provide an elegant solution to the *nature–nurture* debate, which we learned about in Chapter 1, by its premise that behavior evolves from the interaction of heredity and environmental demands (Yee, 1995). Some worry, however, that recognition of a prominent genetic role in behavior may raise the question of whether genetics absolves us of our responsibility for troublesome behaviors such as aggression or addiction—a question to which evolutionary psychologists resoundingly reply, "No!" (Hagen, 2004).

In later chapters, we will discuss specific evolutionary theories that have been advanced to explain aggression, jealousy, sexual orientation, physical attraction and mate selection, parenting, cooperation, temperament, morality, and (always a psychological hot potato) gender differences. But for now, let us turn our attention to genetics and the biological underpinnings of heredity and evolutionary change.

More than 98 percent of our genetic material is also found in chimpanzees (Pennisi, 2007). This supports Darwin's idea that humans and apes had a common ancestor.

Genetics and Inheritance

In principle, the genetic code is quite simple. Much as the microscopic pits in a CD encode information that can become pictures or music, your *genes* encode molecular information that can become inherited traits. Consider your own unique combination of physical characteristics. Your height, facial features, and hair color, for example, all stem from the encoded genetic "blueprint" inherited from your parents and inscribed in every cell in your body. Likewise, genetics influences psychological characteristics, including your basic temperament, tendency to fears, and certain behavior patterns (Pinker, 2002).

Yet, even under the influence of heredity, you are a unique individual, different from either of your parents. One source of your uniqueness lies in your experience: the environment in which you grew up—distinct in time and, perhaps, in place from that of your parents. Another source of difference between you and either of your parents arises from the random combination of traits, both physical and psychological, each parent passed on to you from past generations in their own family lines. (It is important to note you do not inherit copies of *all* your father's and mother's genes. Rather, you get half of each, randomly shuffled.) This hybrid inheritance produced your unique **genotype**, the genetic pattern that makes you different from anyone else on earth. Still, as different as people may seem, 99.9 percent of human genetic material is the same (Marks, 2004).

If the genotype is the "blueprint," then the resulting structure is the **phenotype**. All your physical characteristics make up your phenotype, including not only your visible traits (for instance, the shape of your nose or the number of freckles you have) but also "hidden" biological traits, such as the chemistry and "wiring" of your brain. In fact, any *observable* characteristic is part of the phenotype—so the phenotype includes *behavior*. We should quickly point out that, while the phenotype is based in biology, it is not completely determined by heredity. Heredity never acts alone but always in partnership with the environment, which includes such biological influences as nutrition, disease, stress, and experiences that leave a lasting mark in the form of learning. The environment even plays a role before our birth, such as when poor medical care results in a birth defect.

Now, with these ideas about heredity, environment, genotypes, and phenotypes fresh in mind, let's turn to the details of heredity and individual variation that were yet to be discovered in Darwin's time.

CONNECTION CHAPTER 10

Infants differ in their tendency to be shy or outgoing, which is believed to be an aspect of *temperament* with a strong biological basis (p. 421).

genotype An organism's genetic makeup.

phenotype An organism's observable physical and behavioral characteristics.

Chromosomes, Genes, and DNA The blockbuster film *Jurassic Park* and its sequels relied on a clever twist of plot in which scientists recovered the genetic code for dinosaurs and created an island full of reptilian horrors. The stories, of course, are science

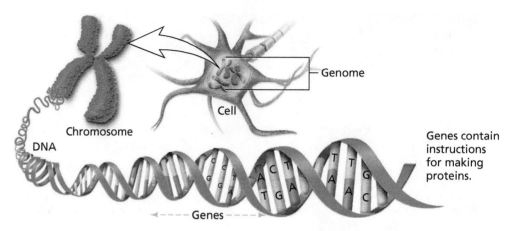

Cell

Genome

Chromosome

DNA

Genes contain instructions for making proteins.

Genes

FIGURE 2.1

DNA, Genes, and Chromosomes

A chromosome is composed mainly of a tightly coiled strand of DNA, an incredibly long molecule. Each chromosome contains thousands of genes, along with instructions for the "when" and "how" of gene expression, which together represent the organism's genome. Genes themselves are segments of DNA. Each gene contains instructions, coded in the four-nucleotide alphabet, for making a protein. The Human Genome Project has identified the sequence of nucleotides in all 23 pairs of our chromosomes.

genome   The complete set of genetic information contained within a cell.

DNA (deoxyribonucleic acid)   A long, complex molecule that encodes genetic characteristics.

gene   Segment of a chromosome that encodes the directions for the inherited physical and mental characteristics of an organism. Genes are the functional units of a chromosome.

chromosome   Tightly coiled threadlike structure along which the genes are organized, like beads on a necklace. Chromosomes consist primarily of DNA.

Read about How DNA Works at MyPsychLab

sex chromosomes   The X and Y chromosomes that determine our physical sex characteristics.

fiction, yet the films rest on an important scientific fact: Every cell in the body carries a complete set of biological instructions, known as a **genome,** for building the organism. For humans, these instructions are spelled out in 23 pairs of *chromosomes,* which, under a high-powered microscope, look like tiny twisted threads. Zooming in for an even closer look, we find that each chromosome consists of a long and tightly coiled chain of **DNA (deoxyribonucleic acid),** a molecule especially well suited for storing biological information (see Figure 2.1).

Genes are the "words" that make up each organism's instruction manual. Encoded in short segments of DNA, each gene contributes to the operation of an organism by specifying a single protein. Thousands of such proteins, in turn, serve as the building blocks for the organism's physical characteristics (part of the phenotype) and the regulation of the body's internal operations. Genes, because they differ slightly from one individual to another, provide the biological source for the variation that caught Darwin's attention.

Like the string of words in this paragraph, genes occur in sequence on the **chromosomes.** But chromosomes are much more than strings of genes. Like paragraphs, they also contain "punctuation" that indicates where each gene begins and ends, along with commands specifying how and when the genes will be expressed (Gibbs, 2003). Sometimes, however, these commands are wrong, or the genes themselves have defects. The resulting errors in gene expression can cause physical and developmental problems, such as cerebral palsy and mental retardation.

On a still smaller scale, genes are composed of even tinier molecular units called *nucleotides* that serve as individual "letters" in the genetic "words." Instead of a 26-letter alphabet, the genetic code uses just four nucleotides. Consequently, a particular gene may require hundreds of nucleotides strung together in a unique pattern to specify a particular protein. You can see why, then, the Human Genome Project is so exciting to scientists: It mapped the complete nucleotide pattern for all of the approximately 30,000 genes in the human organism, including multiple variations of patterns on each gene to account for individual differences! Results offer great hope for better understanding and treatment of physical and psychological disorders.

Of the 46 chromosomes (23 pairs), two warrant special mention: the **sex chromosomes.** Named X and Y for their shapes, these chromosomes carry genetic encoding for a male or female phenotype. We all inherit one X chromosome from our biological mothers.

In addition, we receive either an X or a Y from our biological fathers. When they pair up, two X chromosomes (XX) contain the code for femaleness, while an XY pair codes for maleness. In this sense, then, the chromosome we get from our fathers—either an X or a Y—determines our biological sex.

Genetic Explanations for Psychological Processes Most of our discussion of heredity and genetics could apply equally to fruit flies and butterflies, hollyhocks and humans. All organisms follow the same basic laws of heredity. The differences among species arise, then, from different genetic "words"—the genes themselves—"spelled" with the same four letters (nucleotides) of life's universal four-letter alphabet.

And what does all this have to do with psychology? Simply put, genes influence our psychological characteristics just as they do our physical traits. In later chapters, we will explore how genes affect such diverse human attributes as intelligence, personality, mental disorders, reading and language disabilities, and (perhaps) sexual orientation. Even our fears can have some genetic basis (Hariri et al., 2002). But, because genetic psychology is still a field in its infancy, we don't yet know exactly how or to what extent specific genes are involved in most psychological processes (Rutter, 2006).

It is also important to note that multiple genes, rather than just one, are thought to be involved in most disorders (Plomin, 2000). In only a few cases can we hold a single gene responsible for a specific psychological disorder. For example, just one abnormal gene has been linked to a rare pattern of impulsive violence found in several members of a Dutch family (Brunner et al., 1993). Experts expect that multiple genes contribute to most other conditions such as schizophrenia, a severe mental disorder, and Alzheimer's disease, a form of dementia. (St. George-Hyslop, 2000).

So, does this mean that heredity determines our psychological destiny? Will you grow up to be like your Uncle Henry? Not to worry. Although you may share many of his genes, your heredity never acts alone. Heredity and environment always work together to influence our behavior and mental processes (Pinker, 2002). Jill Bolte Taylor's intelligence, for example, has a genetic component (her mother went to Harvard and her father has a doctoral degree) but was further nurtured in her childhood environment and educational opportunities. Her ability to overcome the challenges of her severe medical condition, construct a new life, and go on to become one of *Time Magazine's* 100 Most Influential People in the World (2008) illustrates her creativity, a trait she attributes to her father—but also undoubtedly enhanced by her training as a scientist.

Even identical twins, who share the same genotype, display individual differences in appearance and personality that result from their distinct experiences, such as exposure to different people, places, chemicals, and diseases. Moreover, studies show that when one identical twin acquires a psychological disorder known to have a genetic basis (schizophrenia, for example), the other does not necessarily develop the same disorder. The takeaway message is this: *Never attribute psychological characteristics to genetics alone* (Ehrlich, 2000a, b; Mauron, 2001).

A final example of the interaction between heredity and environment—and one of the rays of hope from biopsychology—can be seen in a condition called *Down syndrome*. Associated with an extra chromosome 21, this disorder includes impaired physical development as well as mental retardation. Only a few years ago, people with Down syndrome faced bleak and unproductive lives, shut away in institutions where they depended almost wholly on others to fulfill their basic needs. Now, a better understanding of the disorder, along with a deeper appreciation for the interaction between genetics and environment, has changed that outlook. Although no cure has been found, today we know that people with Down syndrome are capable of considerable learning despite their genetic impairment. With special life skills training, those with Down syndrome learn to care for themselves, work, and establish some personal independence. In this way, environmental factors can powerfully shape genetic dispositions.

"Race" and Human Variation Certain features of skin color and other physical characteristics are more (or less) common among people who trace their ancestry to the same part of the world. Tropical ancestry is often associated with darker skin,

CONNECTION CHAPTER 9

The evidence suggests that sexual orientation is determined—at least in part—by heredity (p. 385).

CONNECTION CHAPTER 12

Schizophrenia is a psychotic disorder that affects about 1 out of 100 persons (p. 537).

which affords some protection from the sun, and lighter skin frequently identifies people from high latitudes, which receive less sun. While we commonly speak of "race" in terms of these superficial characteristics, biologists tell us there are no physical characteristics that divide people cleanly into distinct "racial" groups. We are all one species.

In reality, physical characteristics of the so-called "races" blend seamlessly one into another. There is no physical characteristic that reliably distinguishes the brain of a person of one geographic region, skin color, or ethnic origin from that of another. Inside the skull are many physical differences—even some gender differences—but no race-based differences. We should think of "race," therefore, as a socially defined term rather than a biological one. Alternatively, the concept of *culture* is a far better explanation for most—perhaps all—of the group differences important to psychologists (Cohen, 1998).

Just because race is not a precise biological concept, however, doesn't mean its social meaning is unimportant. On the contrary, race as a socially defined category can exert powerful influences on behavior. We will see, for example, that social conceptions of race influence expectations and prejudices. Please keep this notion in mind when we look at studies in which people who identify with different racial or ethnic groups are compared, for example, on intelligence and academic achievement (Eberhardt & Randall, 1997; Hirschfeld, 1996).

[PSYCHOLOGY MATTERS]

Choosing Your Children's Genes

Scientists already have the ability to control and alter the genetics of animals, like Dolly, the late and famous fatherless sheep, cloned from one of her mother's cells in 1996. Since that time, a variety of animals from cats to cattle have been cloned, though the success rate is just 1 to 2 percent of attempts (American Medical Association, 2010). But what about the prospects for genetic manipulation in people? Thanks to scientists working on the Human Genome Project, we are getting a glimpse of the genetic instructions that make us human. We now know the sequence of nucleotides on all the human chromosomes (Pennisi, 2001).

Psychologists expect this information to teach us something about the genetic basis for human differences in abilities, emotions, and resistance to stress (Kosslyn et al., 2002). High on the list will be disorders that affect millions: cancer, heart disease, autism, and depression. But not all the promise of human genetics lies in the future. We can already sample fetal cells and search for certain genetic problems, such as Down syndrome, Tay-Sachs disease, and sickle-cell anemia. And while many people support genetic testing, others wonder if technology is advancing faster than our ability to address the ethical issues it presents.

One such technique, known as pre-implantation genetic diagnosis (PGD), was developed to help couples decrease the risk of passing on a serious genetic disorder to an unborn child. By testing the fetus or embryo at a very early stage, reproductive scientists can ensure a genetically healthy fetus. Since its introduction in 1990, however, use of PGD has broadened. The United States and some other countries now allow use of PGD for sex selection: Almost half the clinics that offer PGD also offer parents the option to choose whether they will have a boy or a girl (Adams, 2010). Moreover, "savior siblings" are being engineered, so parents who have a child with a life-threatening disease (such as leukemia) can birth a sibling with the right bone marrow to save the ill child (Marcotty, 2010). And, most recently, a fertility clinic in Los Angeles announced its plans to offer genetic selection for physical traits such as height, hair color, and skin color (Naik, 2009). (Interestingly, the clinic retracted its offer after receiving a letter of objection from the Vatican.) But what will be the price of this technology? 📖

Undoubtedly, parents in this brave new genetic world will want their children to be smart and good looking—but by what standards will intelligence and looks be judged? And will everyone be able to place an order for their children's genes—or only the very wealthy? You can be certain the problems we face will be simultaneously biological, psychological, political, and ethical (Patenaude et al., 2002).

📖💻 **Read** about Choosing Your Own Children's Genes at **MyPsychLab**

CONNECTION CHAPTER 6 ➤

While intelligence is influenced by heredity, the relative contributions of nature and nurture are hotly debated (p. 251).

Already, psychologists provide guidance about how genetic knowledge can best be applied (Bronheim, 2000), particularly in helping people assess genetic risks in connection with family planning. We invite you to grapple with these issues by answering the following questions:

- If you could select three genetic traits for your children, which ones would you select?

- If a biological child of yours had a life-threatening illness, would you attempt to conceive a "savior sibling?" Why or why not? What circumstances or conditions would affect your decision?

- If you knew you might carry a gene responsible for a serious medical or behavioral disorder, would you want to be tested before having children? And would it be fair for a prospective partner to require you to be tested before conceiving children? Would it be fair for the state to make such a requirement?

These questions, of course, have no "right" answers; but your answers will help you define your stand on some of the most important issues we will face in this century. In considering them, think about how the critical thinking guidelines from Chapter 1 might affect your responses. For instance, to what degree might your own emotional bias color your reaction to these questions?

Check Your Understanding

✓ Study and Review at MyPsychLab

1. **RECALL:** Explain how natural selection increases certain genetic characteristics within a population of organisms.

2. **APPLICATION:** Name one of your own characteristics that is part of your phenotype.

3. **RECALL:** Which of the following statements expresses the correct relationship?

    a. Genes are made of chromosomes.
    b. DNA is made of chromosomes.
    c. Nucleotides are made of genes.
    d. Genes are made of DNA.

4. **ANALYSIS:** In purely evolutionary terms, which would be a measure of your success as an organism?

    a. your intellectual accomplishments
    b. the length of your life
    c. the number of children you have
    d. the contributions you make to the happiness of humanity

5. **UNDERSTANDING THE CORE CONCEPT:** Behavior consistently found in a species is likely to have a genetic basis that evolved because the behavior was adaptive. Name a common human behavior that illustrates this concept.

Answers 1. Natural selection relies on genetic variation among individuals within a population (or group) of organisms. Those best adapted to the environment have a survival and reproduction advantage, leaving more offspring than others. Over generations, these adaptive characteristics increase within the population. **2.** Your observable physical and behavioral characteristics, such as height and weight or the way you speak, make up your phenotype. **3.** d **4.** c **5.** Language, social interaction, self-preservation, basic parenting, "instincts," feeding in newborns—all have been influenced by evolution.

2.2 KEY QUESTION
How Does the Body Communicate Internally?

Imagine this: You are driving on a winding mountain road, and suddenly a car comes directly at you. At the last instant, you and the other driver swerve in opposite directions. Your heart pounds—and keeps pounding for several minutes after the danger has passed. Externally, you have avoided a potentially fatal accident. Internally, your body has responded to two kinds of messages from its two communication systems.

One is the fast-acting *nervous system,* with its extensive network of nerve cells carrying messages in pulses of electrical and chemical energy throughout the body.

This first-responder network comes quickly to your rescue in an emergency, carrying orders that accelerate your heart and tense your muscles for action. The other communication network, the slower-acting *endocrine system,* sends follow-up messages that support and sustain the response initiated by the nervous system. To do this, the endocrine glands, including the pituitary, thyroid, adrenals, and gonads, use chemical messengers we call *hormones.*

The two internal message systems cooperate not only in stressful situations but also in happier circumstances of high arousal, as when you receive an unexpected "A" on a test or meet someone especially attractive. The endocrine system and nervous system also work together during states of low arousal to keep vital body functions operating smoothly. Managing this cooperation between the endocrine system and the nervous system is the body's chief executive, the brain—which brings us to our Core Concept:

Core Concept 2.2

The brain coordinates the body's two communications systems, the nervous system and the endocrine system, which use similar chemical processes to communicate with targets throughout the body.

Why is this notion important for your understanding of psychology? For one thing, these two communication systems are the biological bedrock for all our thoughts, emotions, and behaviors. Another reason for studying the biology behind the body's internal communications is that it can help us understand how drugs, such as caffeine, alcohol, ecstasy, and Prozac, can change the chemistry of the mind. Finally, it will help you understand many common brain-based conditions, such as stroke, multiple sclerosis, and depression.

Our overview of the body's dual communication systems first spotlights the building block of the nervous system: the *neuron.* Next, we will see how networks of neurons work together as modular components of the greater network of the *nervous system* that extends throughout the body. Then we will shift our attention to the *endocrine system,* a group of glands that operates together and in parallel with the nervous system—also throughout the body.

The Neuron: Building Block of the Nervous System

neuron   Cell specialized to receive and transmit information to other cells in the body—also called a *nerve cell.* Bundles of many neurons are called *nerves.*

Like transistors in a computer, *neurons* or *nerve cells* are the fundamental processing units in the brain. In simplest terms, a **neuron** is merely a cell specialized to receive, process, and transmit information to other cells. And neurons do that very efficiently: A typical nerve cell may receive messages from a thousand others and, within a fraction of a second, decide to "fire," passing the message along at speeds up to 300 feet per second to another thousand neurons—or sometimes as many as 10,000 (Pinel, 2005).

Types of Neurons While neurons vary in shape and size, all have essentially the same structure, and all send messages in essentially the same way. Nevertheless, biopsychologists distinguish three major classes of neurons according to their location and function: *sensory neurons, motor neurons,* and *interneurons* (see Figure 2.2). **Sensory neurons,** or *afferent neurons,* act like one-way streets that carry traffic from the sense organs *toward* the brain. Accordingly, afferent neurons treat the brain to all your sensory experience, including vision, hearing, taste, touch, smell, pain, and balance. For example, when you test the water temperature in the shower with your hand, afferent neurons carry the message toward the brain.

sensory neuron   A nerve cell that carries messages *toward* the central nervous system from sense receptors; also called *afferent neurons.*

motor neuron   A nerve cell that carries messages *away* from the central nervous system toward the muscles and glands; also called *efferent neurons.*

In contrast, **motor neurons,** or *efferent neurons,* form the one-way routes that transport messages *away* from the brain and spinal cord to the muscles, organs, and glands. Motor neurons, therefore, carry the instructions for all our actions. So, in

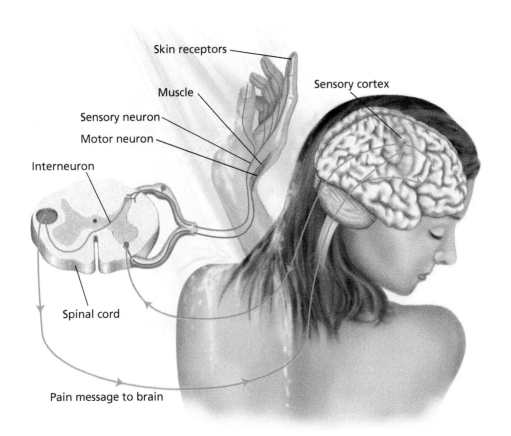

FIGURE 2.2

Sensory Neurons, Motor Neurons, and Interneurons

Information about the water temperature in the shower is carried by thousands of *sensory neurons* (afferent neurons) from the sense organs to the central nervous system. In this case, the message enters the spinal cord and is relayed by *interneurons* to the brain. There, the information is assessed and a response is initiated ("Turn the water temperature down!"). These instructions are sent to the muscles by means of *motor neurons* (efferent neurons). Large bundles of the message-carrying fibers from these neurons are called *nerves*.

our shower example, the motor neurons deliver the message that tells your hand just how much to move the shower control knob. ⓒ➤

Sensory and motor neurons rarely communicate directly with each other, except in the simplest of reflexive circuits. Instead, they usually rely on the go-between **interneurons** (also shown in Figure 2.2), which make up most of the billions of cells in the brain and spinal cord. Interneurons relay messages from sensory neurons to other interneurons or to motor neurons, sometimes in complex pathways. In fact, the brain itself is largely a network of intricately connected interneurons. To see how fast these neural circuits work, try the demonstration in the accompanying *Do It Yourself!* box.

How Neurons Work A look at Figure 2.3 will help you visualize the neuron's main components. The "receiver" parts, which accept most incoming messages, consist of finely branched fibers called **dendrites**. These dendritic fibers extend outward from the cell body, where they act like a net, collecting messages received from other neurons or by direct stimulation of the sense organs (e.g., the eyes, ears, or skin).

ⓒ➤ **Simulate** the **Experiment** Nerve Impulse and Afferent and Efferent Neurons at **MyPsychLab**

interneuron A nerve cell that relays messages between nerve cells, especially in the brain and spinal cord.

dendrite Branched fiber that extends outward from the cell body and carries information into the neuron.

Do It Yourself! **NEURAL MESSAGES AND REACTION TIME**

For only a dollar, you can find out how long it takes for the brain to process information and initiate a response.

Hold a crisp dollar bill by the middle of the short side so that it dangles downward. Have a friend put his or her thumb and index fingers on opposite sides and about an inch away from the center of the bill. Instruct your friend to pinch the

thumb and fingers together, and attempt to catch the bill when you drop it.

If you drop the bill without warning (being careful not to signal your intentions), your friend's brain will not be able to process the information rapidly enough to get a response to the hand before the dollar bill has dropped safely away.

What does this demonstrate? The time it takes to respond reflects the time it takes for the sensory nervous system to take in the information, for the brain to process it, and for the motor system to produce a response. All this involves millions of neurons; and, even though they respond quickly, their responses do take time.

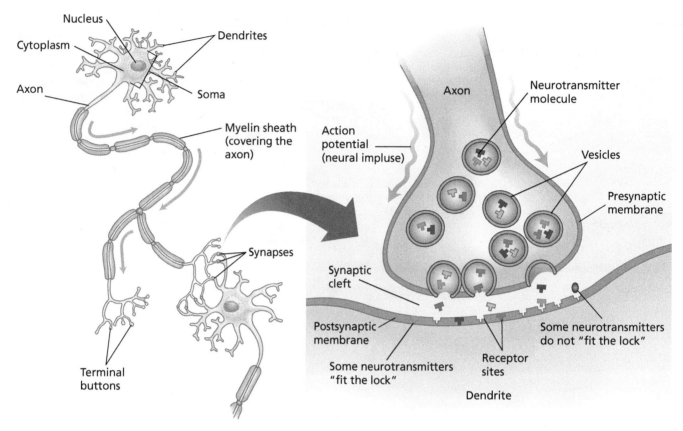

FIGURE 2.3

Structure and Function of the Neuron

A typical neuron receives thousands of messages at a time through its *dendrites* and *soma* (cell body). When the soma becomes sufficiently aroused, its own message is then passed to the *axon*, which transmits it by means of an *action potential* to the cell's *terminal buttons*. There, tiny vesicles containing *neurotransmitters* rupture and release their contents into the *synapse* (synaptic cleft). Appropriately shaped transmitter molecules arriving at the postsynaptic membrane can dock at *receptors*, where they stimulate the receiving cell. Excessive transmitters are taken back into the "sending" neuron by means of *reuptake*.

soma   The part of a cell (such as a neuron) containing the nucleus, which includes the chromosomes; also called the *cell body*.

axon   In a nerve cell, an extended fiber that conducts information from the soma to the terminal buttons. Information travels along the axon in the form of an electric charge called the *action potential.*

resting potential   The electrical charge of the axon in its inactive state, when the neuron is ready to "fire."

action potential   The nerve impulse caused by a change in the electrical charge across the cell membrane of the axon. When the neuron "fires," this charge travels down the axon and causes neurotransmitters to be released by the terminal buttons.

Dendrites then pass their messages on to the central part of the neuron, called the *cell body* or **soma**. Not only does the soma house the cell's chromosomes, it also conducts on-the-spot evaluation of the hundreds (or sometimes thousands) of messages received by the cell, often simultaneously. Making the assessment even more complex, some of these messages received by the neuron are *excitatory* (saying, in effect, "Fire!") and some are *inhibitory* ("Don't fire!"). The "decision" made by the soma depends on its overall level of arousal—which depends, in turn, on the sum of the incoming messages.

When excitation triumphs over inhibition, the neuron initiates a message of its own and sends it along a single "transmitter" fiber known as the **axon**. These axons vary tremendously in length. In a college basketball player, axons connecting the spinal cord with the toes can be more than 3 feet long, while at the other extreme, axons of interneurons in the brain may span only a tiny fraction of an inch.

The Action Potential   When arousal in the cell body reaches a critical level, it triggers an electrical impulse in the axon—like the electronic flash of a camera—and, as we said, the cell "fires." Much like a battery, the axon gets the electrical energy it needs to fire from charged chemicals called *ions*. In its normal, resting state—appropriately called the **resting potential**—the ions inside the axon have a negative electrical charge. But this negative state is easily upset. When the cell body becomes excited, it triggers a cascade of events, known as the **action potential**, that temporarily reverses the charge and causes an electrical signal to race along the axon (see Figure 2.3).

How does the electrical charge reverse itself? During the action potential, tiny pores open in a small area of the axon's membrane adjacent to the soma, allowing a rapid influx of positive ions. Almost immediately, the internal charge in that part of the axon changes from negative to positive. (We're talking 1/1000 of a second here.) Then, like a row of falling dominoes, these changes in the cell membrane progress down the axon. The result is an electrical signal that races from the soma toward the axon ending. There's no halfway about this action potential: Either the axon "fires" or it doesn't. Neuroscientists call this the **all-or-none principle.** Incidentally, when this process careens out of control, with very large numbers of neurons becoming hypersensitive and firing too easily, the result can be an epileptic seizure.

Then, almost immediately after firing, the cell's "ion pump" flushes out the positively charged ions and restores the neuron to its resting potential, ready to fire again. Incredibly, the whole complex cycle may take less than a hundredth of a second. It is an amazing performance—and that is not the end of the process. Information carried by the action potential must still traverse a tiny gap before reaching another cell. ✳

Synaptic Transmission Despite their close proximity to each other, nerve cells do not actually meet. A microscopic gap, called a **synapse,** lies between them, acting as an electrical insulator (see Figure 2.3). This *synaptic gap* (or *synaptic cleft*) prevents the charge from jumping directly from the axon to the next cell in the circuit (Dermietzel, 2006). Instead, the neuron must first stimulate tiny bulblike structures called **terminal buttons** located at the ends of the axon. Then, in a remarkable sequence of events known as **synaptic transmission,** the electrical message morphs into a chemical message that flows across the synaptic cleft and on to the next neuron. Let's examine that process more closely.

Neurotransmitters When the electrical impulse arrives at the terminal buttons, tiny bubblelike *vesicles* (sacs) inside them burst and release their chemical contents, known as **neurotransmitters,** into the synapse. These neurotransmitters then attempt to ferry the neural message across the gap to the next neuron in the chain (again, see Figure 2.3).

What do we mean by "attempt"? This is where the process gets a bit more complicated—partly because there are dozens of different neurotransmitters, each of which has a different chemical structure, and partly because each ruptured vesicle releases about 5,000 neurotransmitter molecules into the synapse (Kandel & Squire, 2000)! So, in order for the neural message to be passed along, there must be a receptor site on a nearby neuron that is an exact match to the shape of one of the neurotransmitters. (Remember learning in your basic science class what different molecules look like?) When there is a match, the neurotransmitter fits into the receptor site, much as a key fits into a lock. This lock-and-key process then stimulates the receiving neuron, which passes the message onward.

What happens to neurotransmitters that don't find a matching receptor site? Through a process called **reuptake,** many of them are drawn back into vesicles. Others are broken down by specially matched enzymes, rather like a chemical cleanser that removes unwanted substances from your clothing or carpet. Learning about these dual processes has proven useful in research aimed at developing treatments for a variety of disorders. For example, certain drugs—such as the well-known Prozac and its numerous chemical cousins—interfere with the reuptake process for a neurotransmitter called serotonin, which you may have heard is related to depression. By inhibiting the reuptake process for serotonin, the chemical remains available in the synapse longer, which increases the odds it will be picked up by a matching receptor site and utilized. Other drugs, such as Aricept, used to treat Alzheimer's disease, interfere with the work of the cleanup enzyme for acetylcholine (another neurotransmitter), which has the same result as reuptake inhibitors: It ultimately leaves more of the chemical available for use (National Institute on Aging, 2010). Table 2.1 describes several neurotransmitters found especially relevant to psychological functioning. We will also talk more about neurotransmitters and their relation to drug action in the upcoming *Psychology Matters* at the end of this section.

all-or-none principle   Refers to the fact that the action potential in the axon occurs either completely or not at all.

✳ Explore the Concept The Action Potential at MyPsychLab

synapse   The microscopic gap that serves as a communications link between neurons. Synapses also occur between neurons and the muscles or glands they serve.

terminal buttons   Tiny bulblike structures at the end of the axon that contain neurotransmitters that carry the neuron's message into the synapse.

synaptic transmission   The relaying of information across the synapse by means of chemical neurotransmitters.

neurotransmitter   Chemical messenger that relays neural messages across the synapse. Many neurotransmitters are also hormones.

reuptake   The process by which unused neurotransmitters are drawn back into the vesicles of their originating neuron

TABLE 2.1   Seven Important Neurotransmitters

Neurotransmitter	Normal Function	Problems Associated with Imbalance	Substances That Affect the Action of This Neurotransmitter
Dopamine	A transmitter used in brain circuits that produces sensations of pleasure and reward Used by CNS neurons involved in voluntary movement	Schizophrenia Parkinson's disease	Cocaine Amphetamine Methylphenidate (Ritalin) Alcohol
Serotonin	Regulates sleep and dreaming, mood, pain, aggression, appetite, and sexual behavior	Depression Certain anxiety disorders Obsessive–compulsive disorder	Fluoxetine (Prozac) Hallucinogenics (e.g., LSD)
Norepinephrine	Used by neurons in autonomic nervous system and by neurons in almost every region of the brain Controls heart rate, sleep, stress, sexual responsiveness, vigilance, and appetite	High blood pressure Depression	Tricyclic antidepressants Beta-blockers
Acetylcholine	The primary neurotransmitter used by efferent neurons carrying messages from the CNS Also involved in some kinds of learning and memory	Certain muscular disorders Alzheimer's disease	Nicotine Black widow spider venom Botulism toxin Curare Atropine Barbiturates
GABA	The most prevalent inhibitory neurotransmitter in neurons of the CNS	Anxiety Epilepsy	"Minor" tranquilizers (e.g., Valium, Librium) Alcohol
Glutamate	The primary excitatory neurotransmitter in the CNS Involved in learning and memory	Release of excessive glutamate apparently causes brain damage after stroke	PCP ("angel dust")
Endorphins	Pleasurable sensations and control of pain	Lowered levels resulting from opiate addiction	Opiates: opium, heroin, morphine, methadone

Synchronous Firing   Over the past decade, neuroscientists have discovered that some neurons—a small minority—don't play by the customary rules of synaptic transmission. That is, instead of using neurotransmitters to send messages across the synapse, they forego the chemical messages and communicate directly through electrical connections (Bullock et al., 2005; Dermietzel, 2006). Scientists have found these exceptional neurons with electrical synapses concentrated in special parts of the brain that orchestrate synchronized activity in a large number of other neurons, such as those involved in the coordinated beating of the heart. These synchronized bursts may also underlie the greatest mystery of all in the brain: how the brain combines input from many different modules into a single sensation, idea, or action.

Plasticity   Regardless of the communication method—electrical or chemical—neurons have the ability to *change*. One of our most extraordinary capabilities, **plasticity,** allows our brain to adapt or modify itself as the result of experience (Holloway, 2003; Kandel & Squire, 2000). For example, when we learn something new, dendrites can actually grow, and new synapses can be formed, both of which help create new connections with different neurons. And although earlier research focused on the brain's plasticity in our early years of life, newer studies find plasticity in the adult brain as well (Chklovskii et al., 2004).

Thus, plasticity helps account for the brain's ability to compensate for injury, such as when Jill Bolte Taylor's massive stroke wiped out a significant portion of one side of her brain, taking with it her language abilities, mathematical reasoning, and analytical skills. With the help of her mother and a team of rehabilitation experts, she slowly re-learned those skills—thanks to her brain's ability to create brand new connections to compensate for what was lost. Plasticity, then, enables the brain to continually be restructured and "reprogrammed," both in function and in physical structure, by experience (LeDoux, 2002).

Plasticity accounts for much of our human ability to adapt to our experiences—for better or for worse. For example, as a violin player gains expertise, the motor area of the brain linked to the fingers of the left hand becomes larger (Juliano, 1998). Likewise, the brain dedicates more neural real estate to the index finger used by a blind Braille reader (Elbert et al., 1995; LeDoux, 1996). On the other hand, plasticity also allows traumatic experiences to alter the brain's emotional responsiveness in ways that can interfere with everyday functioning (Arnsten, 1998). Thus, brain cells of soldiers who experience combat or of people who have been sexually assaulted can become rewired to be more sensitive to cues that could, in a similar situation, help protect them from harm. In everyday, nonthreatening circumstances, however, this same hair-trigger responsiveness can cause them to overreact to mild stressors—or even to simple unexpected surprises.

Brain Implants   Plasticity, of course, cannot compensate for injuries that are too extensive. Driven by this problem, neuroscientists are experimenting with computer chips implanted in the brain, hoping to restore some motor control in paralyzed patients. In one remarkable case, a 26-year-old paralyzed male received such a chip as an implant in his motor cortex. By merely thinking about movement, he learned to send signals from his brain to a computer, controlling a cursor by thought, much as he might have used a computer's mouse by hand. In this cerebral way, he could play video games, draw circles, operate a TV set, and even move a robotic hand—all of which his paralysis would have made impossible without the implant (Dunn, 2006; Hochberg et al., 2006).

Glial Cells: A Support Group for Neurons   Interwoven among the brain's vast network of neurons is an even greater number of *glial cells,* once thought to "glue" the neurons together. (In fact, the name comes from the Greek word for "glue.") Now, however, we know that glial cells provide structural support for neurons and also help form new synapses during learning (Fields, 2004; Gallo & Chittajallu, 2001). In addition, **glial cells** form the *myelin sheath,* a fatty insulation covering many axons in the brain and spinal cord. Like the casing on an electrical cable, the myelin sheath on a neuron insulates and protects the cell. It also helps speed the conduction of impulses along the axon (refer to Figure 2.3). Certain diseases, such as multiple sclerosis (MS), attack the myelin sheath, resulting in poor conduction of nerve impulses. That deficiency accounts for the variety of symptoms faced by persons with MS, ranging from difficulty with motor movement to sensory deficit to impairments in cognitive functioning (National Institutes of Health, 2010).

plasticity   The nervous system's ability to adapt or change as the result of experience. Plasticity may also help the nervous system adapt to physical damage.

CONNECTION CHAPTER 14

Extremely traumatic experiences can cause *posttraumatic stress disorder,* which can produce physical changes in the brain (p. 605).

glial cell   One of the cells that provide structural support for neurons. Glial cells also provide an insulating covering (the myelin sheath) of the axon for some neurons, which facilitates the electrical impulse.

So there you have the two main building blocks of the nervous system: *neurons,* with their amazing plasticity, and the supportive *glial cells,* which protect the neurons and help propagate neural messages. But, wondrous as these individual components are, in the big picture of behavior and mental processes, a single cell doesn't do very much. It takes millions of neurons flashing their electrochemical signals in synchronized waves back and forth through the incredibly complex neural networks in your brain to produce thoughts, sensations, and feelings. Similarly, all your actions arise from waves of nerve impulses delivered to your muscles, glands, and organs through the nervous system. It is to this larger picture—the nervous system—that we now turn our attention.

The Nervous System

If you could observe a neural message as it moves from stimulus to response, you would see it flow seamlessly from one part of the nervous system to another. The signal might begin, for example, in the eyes, then travel to the brain for extensive processing, and finally reemerge from the brain as a message instructing the muscles to respond. In fact, the **nervous system**, consisting of all the nerve cells in the body, functions as a single, complex, and interconnected unit. Nevertheless, we find it convenient to distinguish among divisions of the nervous system based on their location and the type of processing they do. The most basic distinction recognizes two major divisions: the *central nervous system* and the *peripheral nervous system* (see Figure 2.4).

nervous system   The entire network of neurons in the body, including the central nervous system, the peripheral nervous system, and their subdivisions.

The Central Nervous System   Composed of the *brain* and *spinal cord,* the **central nervous system (CNS)** serves as the body's "command central." The brain, filling roughly a third of the skull, makes complex decisions, coordinates our body functions, and initiates most of our behaviors. The spinal cord, playing a supportive role, serves as a sort of neural cable, connecting the brain with parts of the peripheral sensory and motor systems.

central nervous system (CNS)   The brain and the spinal cord.

Reflexes   The spinal cord has another job too. It takes charge of simple, swift **reflexes**—responses that do not require brain power, such as the reflex your physician elicits with

reflex   Simple unlearned response triggered by stimuli—such as the knee-jerk reflex set off by tapping the tendon just below your kneecap.

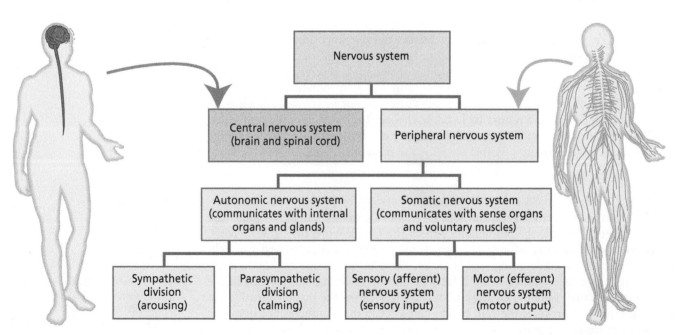

FIGURE 2.4

Organization of the Nervous System

This figure shows the major divisions of the nervous system. The figure on the left shows the *central nervous system,* while the figure on the right shows the *peripheral nervous system.*

a tap on the knee. We know that the brain is not involved in these simple reflexes, because a person whose spinal cord has been severed doesn't sense the pain—but may still be able to withdraw a limb reflexively from a painful stimulus. *Voluntary* movements, however, do require the brain. That's why damage to nerves in the spinal cord can produce paralysis of the limbs or trunk. The extent of paralysis depends on the location of the damage: The higher the site of damage, the greater the extent of the paralysis.

Contralateral Pathways   Significantly, most sensory and motor pathways carrying messages between the brain and the rest of the body are **contralateral**—that is, they cross over to the opposite side in the spinal cord or the brain stem. The result is that each side of the brain communicates primarily with the opposite side of the body or the environment. This fact is important in understanding how damage to one side of the brain often results in disabilities on the opposite side of the body (see Figure 2.5). Jill Bolte Taylor's stroke, for example, was in the left side of her brain, but it was her right arm that became paralyzed during the event.

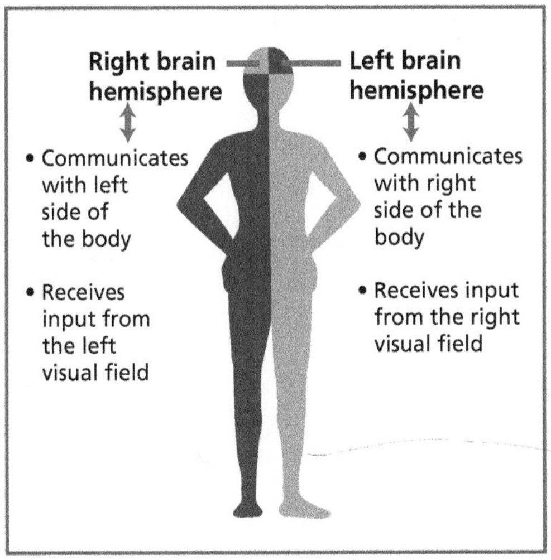

The Peripheral Nervous System   Also playing a supportive role, the **peripheral nervous system (PNS)** connects the central nervous system with the rest of the body through bundles of sensory and motor axons called *nerves*. The many branches of the PNS carry messages between the brain and the sense organs, the internal organs, and the muscles. In this role, the peripheral nervous system carries incoming messages telling your brain about the sights, sounds, tastes, smells, and textures of the world. Likewise, it carries outgoing signals telling your body's muscles and glands how to respond.

You might think of the PNS as a pick-up-and-delivery service for the central nervous system. If, for example, an aggressive dog approaches you, your PNS picks up the auditory information (barking, growling, snarling) and visual information (bared teeth, hair standing up on the neck) for delivery to the brain. Quickly, perceptual and emotional circuits in the brain assess the situation (Danger!) and communicate with other circuits, dispatching orders for a hasty retreat. The PNS then delivers those orders to mobilize your heart, lungs, legs, and other body parts needed to respond to the emergency. It does this through its two major divisions, the *somatic nervous system* and the *autonomic nervous system*. One deals primarily with our external world, the other with our internal responses. (A few moments spent studying Figure 2.4 will help you understand these divisions and subdivisions.)

The Somatic Division of the PNS   Think of the **somatic nervous system** as the brain's communications link with the outside world. Its sensory component connects the sense organs to the brain, and its motor component links the CNS with the skeletal muscles that control voluntary movements. So, for example, when you see a slice of pizza, the visual image is carried to the brain by the somatic division's *afferent* (sensory) system. Then, if all goes well, the *efferent* (motor) system sends instructions to muscles that propel the pizza on just the right trajectory into your open mouth.

The Autonomic Division of the PNS   The other major division of the PNS takes over once the pizza starts down your throat and into the province of the **autonomic nervous system** (*autonomic* means self-regulating or independent). This network carries signals that regulate our internal organs as they perform such jobs as digestion, respiration, heart rate, and arousal. And it does so unconsciously—without our having to think about it. The autonomic nervous system also works when you are asleep. Even during anesthesia, autonomic activity sustains our most basic vital functions.

And—wouldn't you know?—biopsychologists further divide the autonomic nervous system into two subparts: the *sympathetic* and *parasympathetic divisions* (as shown in Figure 2.6). The **sympathetic division** arouses the heart, lungs, and other organs in stressful or emergency situations, when our responses must be quick and powerfully energized. Often called the "fight-or-flight" system, the sympathetic division carries messages that help us respond quickly to a threat either by attacking

FIGURE 2.5

Contralateral Connections

For most sensory and motor functions, each side of the brain communicates with the opposite side of the body. (This is known as *contralateral* communication.)

contralateral pathways   Sensory and motor pathways between the brain and the rest of the body cross over to the opposite side en route, so messages from the right side of the body are processed by the left side of the brain and vice versa.

peripheral nervous system (PNS)   All parts of the nervous system lying outside the central nervous system. The peripheral nervous system includes the autonomic and somatic nervous systems.

somatic nervous system   A division of the peripheral nervous system that carries sensory information to the central nervous system and also sends voluntary messages to the body's skeletal muscles.

autonomic nervous system   The portion of the peripheral nervous system that sends communications between the central nervous system and the internal organs and glands.

sympathetic division   The part of the autonomic nervous system that sends messages to internal organs and glands that help us respond to stressful and emergency situations.

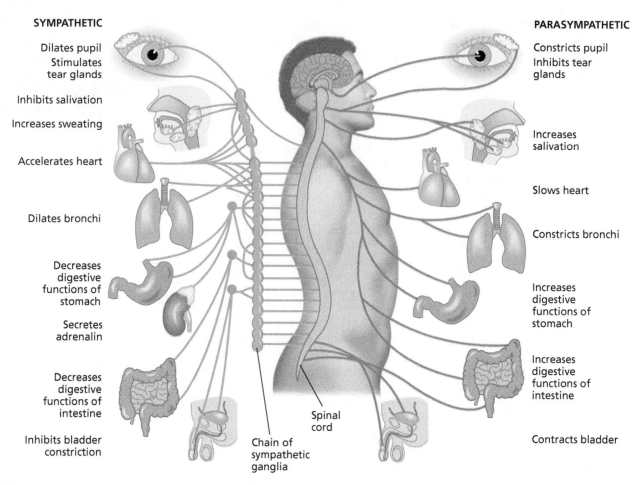

SYMPATHETIC

Dilates pupil
Stimulates tear glands

Inhibits salivation

Increases sweating

Accelerates heart

Dilates bronchi

Decreases digestive functions of stomach

Secretes adrenalin

Decreases digestive functions of intestine

Inhibits bladder constriction

Spinal cord

Chain of sympathetic ganglia

PARASYMPATHETIC

Constricts pupil
Inhibits tear glands

Increases salivation

Slows heart

Constricts bronchi

Increases digestive functions of stomach

Increases digestive functions of intestine

Contracts bladder

FIGURE 2.6

Divisions of the Autonomic Nervous System

The *sympathetic nervous system* (at left) regulates internal processes and behavior in stressful situations. On their way to and from the spinal cord, sympathetic nerve fibers make connections with specialized neural clusters called *ganglia*. The *parasympathetic nervous system* (at right) regulates day-to-day internal processes and behavior.

parasympathetic division   The part of the autonomic nervous system that monitors the routine operations of the internal organs and returns the body to calmer functioning after arousal by the sympathetic division.

endocrine system   The hormone system—the body's chemical messenger system, including the endocrine glands: pituitary, thyroid, parathyroid, adrenals, pancreas, ovaries, and testes.

or fleeing. The sympathetic system also creates the tension and arousal you feel during an exciting movie or first date. Perhaps you can recall how the sympathetic division of your autonomic nervous system made you feel during your last oral presentation. Was it hard to breathe? Were your palms sweaty? Did your stomach feel queasy? All these are sympathetic division functions.

The **parasympathetic division** does just the opposite: It applies the neural brakes, returning the body to a calm and collected state. But even though it has an opposing action, the parasympathetic division works cooperatively with the sympathetic system, like two children on a teeter-totter. Figure 2.6 shows the most important connections made by these two autonomic divisions.

Now, having completed our whirlwind tour of the nervous system, we return our attention briefly to its partner in internal communication, the *endocrine system*.

The Endocrine System

Perhaps you never thought of the bloodstream as a carrier of *information*, along with oxygen, nutrients, and wastes. Yet blood-borne information, in the form of *hormones*, serves as the communication channel among the glands of the **endocrine system**, shown in Figure 2.7. (*Endocrine* comes from the Greek *endo* for "within" and *krinein* for "secrete.")

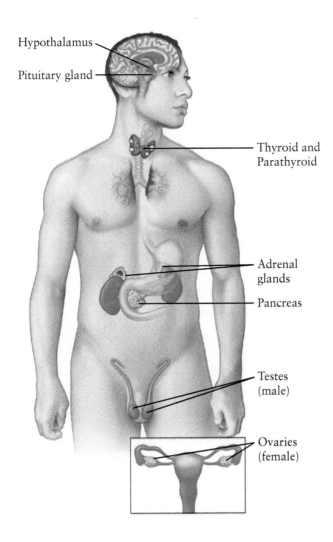

Hypothalamus

Pituitary gland

Thyroid and
Parathyroid

Adrenal
glands

Pancreas

Testes
(male)

Ovaries
(female)

FIGURE 2.7

Endocrine Glands

The pituitary gland is the "master gland" regulating the endocrine glands, whose locations are shown here. The pituitary gland is itself under control of the hypothalamus, an important structure that regulates many basic functions of the body.

Playing much the same role as neurotransmitters in the nervous system, **hormones** carry messages that influence not only body functions but also behaviors and emotions (Damasio, 2003; LeDoux, 2002). For example, hormones from the pituitary stimulate body growth. Hormones from the ovaries and testes influence sexual development and sexual responses. Hormones from the adrenals produce the arousal accompanying fear. And hormones from the thyroid control metabolism (rate of energy use). Once secreted into the blood by an endocrine gland, hormones circulate throughout the body until delivered to their targets, which may include not only other endocrine glands but also muscles and organs. Table 2.2 outlines the major endocrine glands and the body systems they regulate.

hormones Chemical messengers used by the endocrine system. Many hormones also serve as neurotransmitters in the nervous system.

How Does the Endocrine System Respond in a Crisis? Under normal (unaroused) conditions, the endocrine system works in parallel with the parasympathetic nervous system to sustain our basic body processes. But in a crisis, it shifts into a different mode, in support of the sympathetic nervous system. So, when you encounter a stressor or an emergency (such as the speeding car headed toward you), the hormone *epinephrine* (sometimes called *adrenalin*) is released into the bloodstream, sustaining the body's "fight or flight" reaction. In this way, the endocrine system finishes what your sympathetic nervous system started by keeping your heart pounding and your muscles tense, ready for action.

Later in the text, we will see what happens when this stressful state gets out of control. For example, people who have stressful jobs or unhappy relationships may develop a chronically elevated level of stress hormones in their blood, keeping them in a prolonged state of arousal. The price your mind and body pay for this extended arousal can be dear.

CONNECTION CHAPTER 14

Prolonged stress messages can produce physical and mental disorders by means of the *general adaptation syndrome* (p. 615).

TABLE 2.2 **Hormonal Functions of Major Endocrine Glands**

These Endocrine Glands . . .	Produce Hormones That Regulate. . .
Anterior pituitary	Ovaries and testes
	Breast milk production
	Metabolism
	Reactions to stress
Posterior pituitary	Conservation of water in the body
	Breast milk secretion
	Uterus contractions
Thyroid	Metabolism
	Physical growth and development
Parathyroid	Calcium levels in the body
Pancreas	Glucose (sugar) metabolism
Adrenal glands	Fight-or-flight response
	Metabolism
	Sexual desire (especially in women)
Ovaries	Development of female sexual characteristics
	Production of ova (eggs)
Testes	Development of male sexual characteristics
	Sperm production
	Sexual desire (in men)

pituitary gland   The "master gland" that produces hormones influencing the secretions of all other endocrine glands, as well as a hormone that influences growth. The pituitary is attached to the brain's hypothalamus, from which it takes its orders.

What Controls the Endocrine System?   At the base of your brain, a "master gland," called the **pituitary gland,** oversees all these endocrine responses (see Figure 2.7). It does so by sending out hormone signals of its own through the blood to other endocrine glands throughout the body. But the pituitary itself is really only a midlevel manager. It takes orders, in turn, from the brain—in particular from a small region to which it is attached: the *hypothalamus,* a brain component about which we will have more to say in a moment.

For now, we want to emphasize the notion that the peripheral nervous system and the endocrine system provide parallel means of communication, coordinated by their link in the brain. Ultimately, the brain decides which messages will be sent through both networks. We will next turn our attention to the master "nerve center" that makes these decisions—the brain—right after exploring how the concepts we just covered can explain the effects of psychoactive drugs.

[PSYCHOLOGY MATTERS]

How Psychoactive Drugs Affect the Nervous System

The mind-altering effects of marijuana, LSD, cocaine, methamphetamines, and sedatives attract millions of users. Millions more jolt their brains awake with the caffeine of their morning coffee, tea, or energy drink and the nicotine in an accompanying cigarette; at night they may attempt to reverse their arousal with the depressant effects of alcohol and sleeping pills. How do these seductive substances

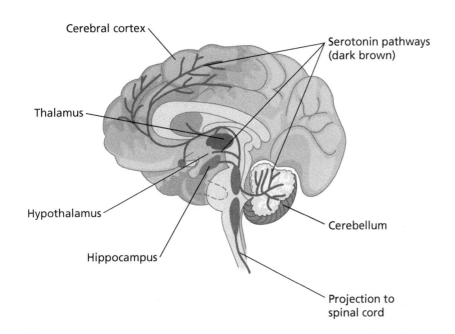

Cerebral cortex

Serotonin pathways
(dark brown)

Thalamus

Hypothalamus

Cerebellum

Hippocampus

Projection to
spinal cord

FIGURE 2.8

Serotonin Pathways in the Brain

Each neurotransmitter is associated with certain neural pathways in the brain. In this cross-section of the brain, you see the main pathways for serotonin. Drugs that stimulate or inhibit serotonin will selectively affect the brain regions shown in this diagram.

achieve their effects? The answer involves the ability of *psychoactive drugs* to enhance or inhibit natural chemical processes in our brains.

Agonists and Antagonists

The ecstasy and the agony of psychoactive drugs come mainly from their interactions with neurotransmitters. Some impersonate neurotransmitters by mimicking their effects in the brain. Other drugs act less directly by enhancing or dampening the effects of neurotransmitters. Those that enhance or mimic neurotransmitters are called **agonists.** Nicotine, for example, is an agonist because it acts like the neurotransmitter acetylcholine (refer to Table 2.1). This has the effect of "turning up the volume" in the acetylcholine pathways (the acetylcholine-using bundles of nerve cells controlling the muscles and connecting certain parts of the brain). Similarly, the well-known antidepressant Prozac (fluoxetine) acts as an agonist in the brain's serotonin pathways, where it makes more serotonin available (see Figure 2.8).

In contrast, **antagonists** are chemicals that dampen or inhibit the effects of neurotransmitters. Some drugs used to treat schizophrenia are antagonists because they interfere with the neurotransmitter dopamine—effectively "turning the volume down" and thus reducing the stimulation contributing to symptoms of delusions and hallucinations (Nairne, 2009). So-called beta blockers, often used to manage heart conditions, act as antagonists against both epinephrine and norepinephrine, thereby counteracting the effects of stress. In general, agonists facilitate and antagonists inhibit messages in parts of the nervous system using that transmitter.

Why Side Effects?

What causes drugs' unwanted side effects? The answer to that question involves an important principle about the brain's design. The brain contains many bundles of neurons—**neural pathways**—that interconnect its components, much as rail lines connect major cities. Moreover, each pathway employs only certain neurotransmitters—like rail lines allowing only certain companies to use their tracks. This fact allows a drug affecting a particular transmitter to target specific parts of the brain. Unfortunately for the drug takers, different pathways may employ the same neurotransmitter for widely different functions. Thus, the brain's multiple serotonin pathways connect with brain structures that affect not only mood but also sleep, appetite, and cognition, much as a railroad has lines that connect with different many cities. Because of these multiple serotonin pathways, taking Prozac (or one of its chemical cousins with other brand names) may treat depression but, at the same time, affect sleep patterns, appetite, and thinking. In fact, no psychoactive drug exists that acts like a "magic bullet," only striking one precise target in the brain without causing collateral effects.

agonists Drugs or other chemicals that enhance or mimic the effects of neurotransmitters.

antagonists Drugs or other chemicals that inhibit the effects of neurotransmitters.

neural pathways Bundles of nerve cells that follow generally the same route and employ the same neurotransmitter.

Check Your Understanding

✓•⟦Study and Review at MyPsychLab⟧

1. **RECALL:** Of the body's two main communication systems, the _____ is faster, while the _____ sends longer-lasting messages.

2. **APPLICATION:** You are touring a haunted house at Halloween, when suddenly you hear a blood-curdling scream right behind you. The _____ division of your autonomic nervous system quickly increases your heart rate. As you recover, the _____division slows your heart rate to normal.

3. **RECALL:** Explain how a neural message is carried across the synapse.

4. **RECALL:** Which gland takes orders from the brain but exerts control over the rest of the endocrine system?

5. **RECALL:** Make a sketch of two connecting neurons, indicating the locations of the dendrites, soma, axon, myelin sheath, terminal buttons, and synapse. Which part of the neuron sends messages by means of a brief electric charge?

6. **UNDERSTANDING THE CORE CONCEPT:** The chemical messengers in the brain are called _____, while in the endocrine system they are called _____.

Answers 1. nervous system/endocrine system **2.** sympathetic/parasympathetic **3.** When the electrical impulse arrives at the axon ending, neurotransmitters are released into the synapse. Some lodge in receptor sites on the opposite side of the synapse, where they stimulate the receiving neuron. **4.** The pituitary gland **5.** Your diagram should be similar to the one on the left side in Figure 2.3. The burst of electric energy (the action potential) occurs in the axon. **6.** neurotransmitters/hormones.

⌐2.3 KEY QUESTION
└── How Does the Brain Produce Behavior and Mental Processes?

Author Phil Zimbardo with the skull of Phineas Gage.

In September 1848, a 25-year-old American railroad worker named Phineas Gage sustained a serious head injury when a charge of blasting powder drove an iron rod into his face, up through the front of his brain, and out through the top of his head. (See accompanying photo.) Amazingly, Gage recovered from this injury and lived another 12 years—but as a psychologically changed man (Fleischman, 2002; Macmillan, 2000). Those who knew him remarked that Gage, once a dependable and likeable crew boss, had become an irresponsible and rowdy ruffian. "Gage was no longer Gage," remarked his former companions (Damasio, 1994, p. 8). We cannot help but wonder: Had the site of his injury—the front of his brain—been the home of Phineas Gage's "old self"? Further, the story of Gage's transformation sounds rather similar to Jill Bolte Taylor's assertion that, since her stroke, she is no longer "the same person." What could explain these changes?

These stories raise a larger question: What is the connection between mind and body? Humans have, of course, long recognized the existence of such a link—although they didn't always know the brain to be the organ of the mind. Even today we might speak, as they did in Shakespeare's time, of "giving one's heart" to another or of "not having the stomach" for something when describing revulsion—even though we now know that love doesn't really flow from the heart, nor disgust from the digestive system, but that all emotions, desires, and thoughts originate in the brain. (Apparently, this news hasn't reached songwriters, who have yet to pen a lyric proclaiming, "I love you with all of my brain.")

At last, neuroscientists have begun unraveling the deep mysteries of this complex organ of the mind. We now see the brain as a collection of distinct modules that work together like the components of a computer. This new understanding of the brain becomes the Core Concept for this final section of the chapter:

[**Core Concept 2.3**

The brain is composed of many specialized modules that work together to create mind and behavior.]

As you study the brain, you will find that each of its modular components has its own responsibilities (Cohen & Tong, 2001). Some process sensations, such as vision and hearing. Some regulate our emotional lives. Some contribute to memory. Some generate speech and other behaviors. What's the point? The specialized parts of the brain act like members of a championship team: each doing a particular job yet working smoothly together. Happily, many of these modules perform their tasks automatically and without conscious direction—as when you simultaneously walk, digest your breakfast, breathe, and carry on a conversation. But, when something goes awry with one or more of the brain's components, as it does in a stroke or as happened to Phineas Gage, the biological basis of thought or behavior comes to the fore.

Let's begin the story of the brain by exploring how neuroscientists go about opening the windows on its inner workings.

Windows on the Brain

Isolated within the protective skull, the brain can never actually touch velvet, taste chocolate, have sex, or see the blue of the sky. It only knows the outside world second-hand, through changing patterns of electrochemical activity in the peripheral nervous system, the brain's link with the world outside. To communicate within the body, the brain must rely on the neural and endocrine pathways that carry its messages to and from the muscles, organs, and glands throughout the body.

But what would you see if you could peer beneath the bony skull and behold the brain? Its wrinkled surface, rather like a giant walnut, tells us little about the brain's internal structure or function. For that, technology—such as *EEG, electrical stimulation,* and various types of *brain scans*—has opened new windows on the brain.

Sensing Brain Waves with the EEG For nearly one hundred years, neuroscientists have used the **electroencephalograph (or EEG)** to record weak voltage patterns called *brain waves,* sensed by electrodes pasted on the scalp. Much as city lights indicate which parts of town are most "alive" at night, the EEG senses which parts of the brain are most active. The EEG can identify, for example, regions involved in moving the hand or processing a visual image. It can also reveal abnormal waves caused by brain malfunctions, such as *epilepsy* (a seizure disorder that arises from an electrical "storm" in the brain). You can see the sort of information provided by the EEG in Figure 2.9A.

Useful as it is, however, the EEG is not very precise, indiscriminately recording the brain's electrical activity in a large region near the electrode. Because there may be

electroencephalograph (EEG) A device for recording brain waves, typically by electrodes placed on the scalp. The record produced is known as an electroencephalogram (also called an EEG).

CONNECTION CHAPTER 8

Sleep researchers use *brain waves,* recorded by the EEG, to identify REM sleep, which is characterized by dreaming (p. 335).

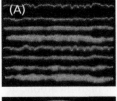
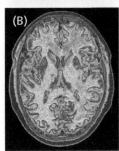
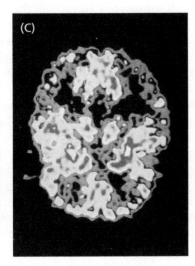
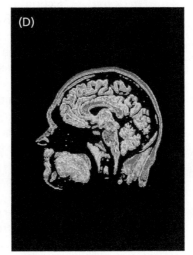
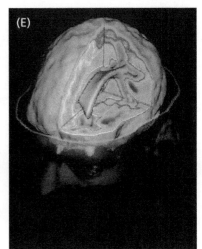

FIGURE 2.9

Windows on the Mind

Images from brain-scanning devices. **(A)** EEG; **(B)** CT scan; **(C)** PET; **(D)** MRI; and **(E)** fMRI. Each scanning and recording device has strengths and weaknesses.

fewer than a dozen electrodes used, the EEG does not paint a detailed electrical picture of the brain. Rather, it produces a coarse, moment-to-moment summary of electrical activity in millions of neurons—making it all the more amazing that we can sometimes read the traces of mental processes in an EEG record.

Mapping the Brain with Electric Probes The next step forward in understanding the brain came about half a century ago, when the great Canadian neurologist Wilder Penfield opened another window on the brain by "mapping" its pinkish-gray surface. During brain surgery, using a pen-shaped electric probe, Penfield stimulated patients' exposed brains with a gentle electric current and recorded the responses. (His patients were kept awake, but under local anesthesia, so they felt no pain.)

This was not just an experiment born out of curiosity. As a surgeon, Penfield needed to identify the exact boundaries of diseased brain areas to avoid removing healthy tissue. In the process, he found the brain's surface had distinct regions with distinct functions. Stimulating a certain spot might cause the left hand to move; another site might produce a sensation, such as a flash of light. Stimulating still other sites occasionally provoked a memory from childhood (Penfield, 1959; Penfield & Baldwin, 1952). Later, other scientists followed his lead and probed structures deeper in the brain. There they found that electrical stimulation could set off elaborate sequences of behavior or emotions. The overall conclusion from such work is unmistakable: Each region of the brain has its own specific functions.

Computerized Brain Scans During the past few decades, increasingly detailed views of the brain have emerged through sophisticated procedures collectively known as *brain scans.* Some types of scans make images with X-rays, others use radioactive tracers, and still others use magnetic fields. As a result, scientists can now make vivid pictures of brain structures without opening the skull. In medicine, brain scans help neurosurgeons locate brain abnormalities such as tumors or stroke-related damage. And in psychology, images obtained from brain scans can reveal where our thoughts and feelings are processed. How? Depending on the scanning method used, specific regions of the brain may "light up" when, for example, a person reads, speaks, solves problems, or feels certain emotions (Raichle, 1994).

The most common brain-scanning methods currently employed are *CT, PET, MRI,* and *fMRI:*

CT scanning, or computerized tomography, creates digital images of the brain from X-rays passed through the brain at various angles, as though it were being sliced like a tomato. By means of sophisticated computer analysis, this form of tomography (from the Greek *tomos,* "section") reveals soft-tissue structures of the brain that X-rays alone cannot show (see Figure 2.9B). CT scans produce good three-dimensional images and are relatively inexpensive; the downside is they employ X-rays, which can be harmful in high doses. CT scans are often used in hospitals for assessing traumatic brain injuries.

PET scanning, or positron emission tomography, shows brain *activity* (rather than just brain *structure*). One common PET technique does this by sensing low-level radioactive glucose (sugar), which concentrates in the brain's most active circuits. Areas of high metabolic activity show up brightly colored on the image (see Figure 2.9C). Thus, researchers can use PET scans to show which parts are more active or less active during a particular task.

MRI, or magnetic resonance imaging, uses brief, powerful pulses of magnetic energy to create highly detailed pictures of the structure of the brain (see Figure 2.9D). The MRI technique makes exceptionally clear, three-dimensional images, without the use of X-rays, which favors its use in research despite its higher cost.

fMRI, or functional magnetic resonance imaging, is a newer technique that records both brain *activity* and *structure,* thus offering the advantages of both PET and MRI (Alper, 1993; Collins, 2001). By monitoring the blood and oxygen flow in the brain, it distinguishes more active brain cells from less active ones. Thus, fMRI lets neuroscientists determine which parts of the brain are at work during various mental activities, much the same as PET, only with the more detailed images of MRI (see Figure 2.9E).

Which Scanning Method Is Best? Each type of brain scan has its particular strengths and weaknesses. For example, both PET and fMRI show which parts of the

CT scanning, or **computerized tomography** A computerized imaging technique that uses X-rays passed through the brain at various angles and then combined into an image.

PET scanning, or **positron emission tomography** An imaging technique that relies on the detection of radioactive sugar consumed by active brain cells.

MRI, or **magnetic resonance imaging** An imaging technique that relies on cells' responses in a high-intensity magnetic field.

fMRI, or **functional magnetic resonance imaging** A newer form of magnetic resonance imaging that records both brain structure and brain activity.

brain are active during a particular task, such as talking, looking at a picture, or solving a problem. Standard MRI excels at distinguishing the fine details of brain structure. But none of these methods can detect processes that occur only briefly, such as a shift in attention or a startle response. To capture such short-lived "conversations" among brain cells requires the EEG—which, unfortunately, is limited in its detail (Raichle, 1994). Currently, no single scanning technique gives biopsychologists a perfectly clear "window" on all the brain's activity.

Three Layers of the Brain

What we see through these windows also depends on the brain we are examining. Birds and reptiles manage to make a living with a brain that consists of little more than a stalk that regulates the most basic life processes and instinctual responses. Our own more complex brains arise from essentially the same stalk, called the **brain stem**. From an evolutionary perspective, then, this is the part of the brain with the longest ancestry and most basic functions. On top of that stalk, we and our mammalian cousins have evolved two more layers, known as the *limbic system* and the *cerebrum*, that give us greatly expanded brain powers (see Figure 2.10).

brain stem The most primitive of the brain's three major layers. It includes the medulla, pons, and the reticular formation.

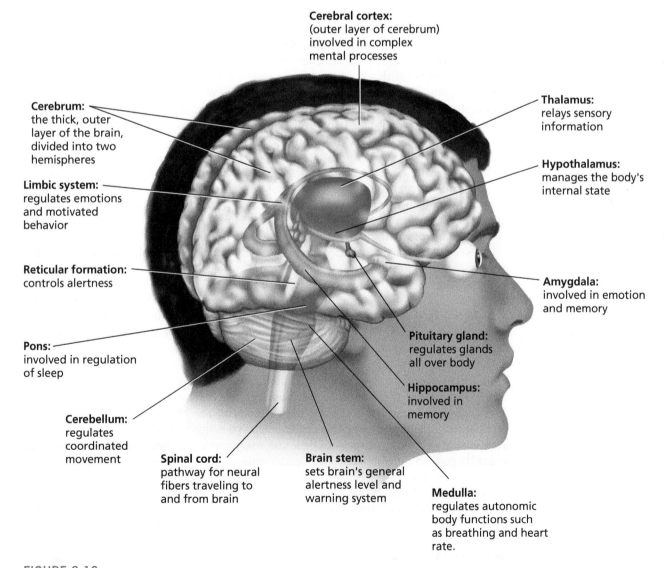

Cerebral cortex:
(outer layer of cerebrum)
involved in complex
mental processes

Cerebrum:
the thick, outer
layer of the brain,
divided into two
hemispheres

Limbic system:
regulates emotions
and motivated
behavior

Reticular formation:
controls alertness

Pons:
involved in regulation
of sleep

Cerebellum:
regulates
coordinated
movement

Spinal cord:
pathway for neural
fibers traveling to
and from brain

Brain stem:
sets brain's general
alertness level and
warning system

Thalamus:
relays sensory
information

Hypothalamus:
manages the body's
internal state

Amygdala:
involved in emotion
and memory

Pituitary gland:
regulates glands
all over body

Hippocampus:
involved in
memory

Medulla:
regulates autonomic
body functions such
as breathing and heart
rate.

FIGURE 2.10

Major Structures of the Brain

From an evolutionary perspective, the brain stem and cerebellum represent the oldest part of the brain; the limbic system evolved next; and the cerebral cortex is the most recent achievement in brain evolution.

The Brain Stem and Its Neighbors If you have ever fought to stay awake in class, you have struggled with your brain stem. Most of the time, however, it does its life-sustaining jobs less obviously and less obnoxiously. We can infer one of the brain stem's tasks from its location, linking the spinal cord with the rest of the brain. In this position, it serves as a conduit for nerve pathways carrying messages up and down the spinal corridor between the body and the brain. This is also where many sensory and motor pathways between the brain and our sense organs and skeletal muscles cross over to the opposite side, thus connecting each side of the brain to the opposite side of the body.

More than just a conduit, the brain stem also links together several important information-processing regions, three of which are contained in the brain stem itself (the *medulla,* the *pons,* and the *reticular formation*) and two that are adjacent (the *thalamus* and the *cerebellum*) (Pinel, 2005). From an evolutionary standpoint, all these are ancient structures found in the brains of creatures as diverse as penguins, pandas, pythons, porcupines, and people. You can see their specific locations in Figure 2.10.

The **medulla,** appearing as a bulge in the brain stem, regulates basic body functions, which include breathing, blood pressure, and heart rate. It operates on "automatic pilot"—without conscious awareness—to keep our internal organs operating. An even bigger bulge called the **pons** (meaning *bridge*) appears just above the medulla, where it houses nerve circuits that regulate the sleep and dreaming cycle. True to its name, the pons also acts as a "bridge" that connects the brain stem to the *cerebellum,* a structure involved in making coordinated movements.

The **reticular formation,** running through the center of everything, is a pencil-shaped bundle of nerve cells that forms the brain stem's core. One of the reticular formation's jobs is keeping the brain awake and alert. Others include monitoring the incoming stream of sensory information and directing attention to novel or important messages. And—don't blame your professor—it is the reticular formation you struggle with when you become drowsy in class.

The **thalamus,** a pair of football-shaped bodies perched atop the brain stem, receives nerve fibers from the reticular formation. Technically part of the cerebral hemispheres, not the brain stem, the thalamus acts like the central processing chip in a computer, directing the brain's incoming and outgoing sensory and motor traffic. Accordingly, it receives information from all the senses (except smell) and distributes this information to appropriate processing circuits throughout the brain.

The **cerebellum,** tucked under the back of the cerebral hemispheres and behind the brain stem, looks very much like a mini-brain—in fact, its name comes from the Latin for "little brain." Although not counted as part of the brain stem by many anatomists, the cerebellum enables our motor coordination and balance (Spencer et al., 2003; Wickelgren, 1998b). It is your cerebellum that allows you to run down a flight of stairs without being conscious of the precise movements of your feet. The cerebellum also helps us keep a series of events in order, as we do when listening to the sequence of notes in a melody (Bower & Parsons, 2003). Finally, the cerebellum gets involved in a basic form of learning that involves habitual responses we perform on cue—as when you learn to wince at the sound of the dentist's drill (Hazeltine & Ivry, 2002).

Taken together, these modules associated with the brain stem control the most basic functions of movement and of life itself. Note, again, that much of their work is automatic, functioning largely outside our awareness. The next two layers, however, assert themselves more obviously in consciousness.

The Limbic System: Emotions, Memories, and More We're sorry to report that your pet canary or goldfish doesn't have the emotional equipment that we mammals possess. You see, only mammals have a fully developed **limbic system,** a diverse collection of structures that wraps around the thalamus deep inside the cerebral hemispheres (see Figure 2.11). Together, these ram's-horn-shaped structures give us greatly enhanced capacity for emotions and memory, faculties that offer the huge advantage of mental flexibility. Because we have limbic systems, we don't have to rely solely on instincts and reflexes that dominate the behavior of simpler creatures.

---

medulla   A brain-stem structure that controls breathing and heart rate. The sensory and motor pathways connecting the brain to the body cross in the medulla.

pons   A brain-stem structure that regulates brain activity during sleep and dreaming. The name *pons* derives from the Latin word for "bridge."

reticular formation   A pencil-shaped structure forming the core of the brain stem. The reticular formation arouses the cortex to keep the brain alert and attentive to new stimulation.

thalamus   The brain's central "relay station," situated just atop the brain stem. Nearly all the messages going into or out of the brain pass through the thalamus.

CONNECTION CHAPTER 3

The sense of smell has a unique ability to evoke memories (p. 106).

cerebellum   The "little brain" attached to the brain stem. The cerebellum is responsible for coordinated movements.

limbic system   The middle layer of the brain, involved in emotion and memory. The limbic system includes the hippocampus, amygdala, hypothalamus, and other structures.

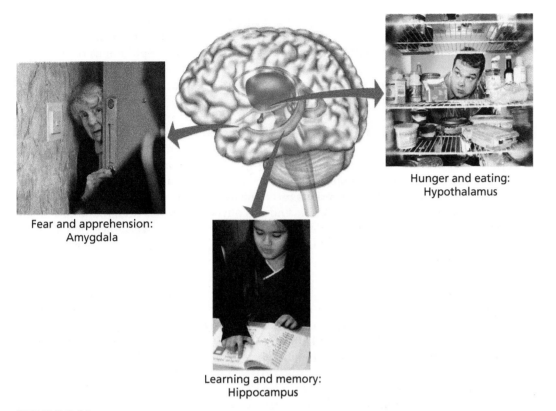

Fear and apprehension:
Amygdala

Hunger and eating:
Hypothalamus

Learning and memory:
Hippocampus

FIGURE 2.11

The Limbic System

The structures of the limbic system are involved with motivation, emotion, and certain memory processes.

The limbic system houses other modules as well, regulating such important processes as hunger, thirst, and body temperature. Overall, the limbic system is the brain's command post for emotions, motives, memory, and maintenance of a balanced condition within the body. Let's examine each of its modules and their corresponding functions in detail.

The Hippocampus and Memory   The **hippocampus** enables our memory system. (Actually, the brain has one hippocampus on each side, giving us two *hippocampi* [see Figure 2.10]). One of its jobs is to help us remember the location of objects, such as where you left your car in a large parking lot (Squire, 2007). And it appears to actually grow with experience, as suggested by a study of London cab drivers that found them to have larger hippocampi than people who didn't drive taxis, with more experienced cabbies having the largest hippocampi of all (Maguire et al., 2003).

In addition to its role in spatial memory, the hippocampus plays a key role in memory storage, as evidenced by the tragic story of H. M. (referred to by his initials to protect his privacy). In 1953, when he was in his early 20s, H. M. underwent a radical and experimental brain operation intended to treat frequent seizures that threatened his life (Hilts, 1995). The surgery removed most of the hippocampus on both sides of his brain and succeeded in reducing the frequency of his seizures. Unfortunately, the surgery also produced an unforeseen and disastrous side effect: After the operation, new experiences disappeared from H. M.'s memory almost as soon as they occurred, although his memory for details of his life prior to the surgery remained intact. For the rest of his life, when he tried to remember the years since 1953, H. M. drew a blank and was even unable to recognize his daily caregivers. In fact, he continued to believe he was living in 1953 right up until his death in 2008. This story, along with corroborating research, indicates that—although the hippocampus is not the storage location for memory—it is critically involved in creating new memories as we experience life.

hippocampus   A component of the limbic system, involved in establishing long-term memories.

amygdala   A limbic system structure involved in memory and emotion, particularly fear and aggression. Pronounced *a-MIG-da-la*.

The Amygdala and Emotion   Another limbic structure, the **amygdala**, takes its name from its shape: *amygdala* means "almond" in Greek. Like many other brain structures, there are actually two amygdalas, one extending in front of the hippocampus on each side (see Figure 2.10).

In a classic experiment designed to find out what the amygdala does, Heinrich Klüver and Paul Bucy (1939) surgically snipped the connections to the amygdala on both sides of the brain in normally foul-tempered rhesus monkeys. Postsurgically, the beasts became so docile and easy to handle that even Klüver and Bucy were surprised, demonstrating the amygdala's role in fear and aggression. More recent studies also note that the amygdala—perhaps aided by its close proximity to the hippocampus—uses memories to aid in emotional responses (Roozendaal et al., 2009), as when a person who was previously in a serious car accident overreacts to a minor threat (such as brief tailgating) from another driver. And this tiny structure has been found to activate in both men and women (although to a greater degree in men) when they view sexually arousing images (Hamann, 2005), illustrating its role in positive emotions as well as negative ones.

Pleasure and the Limbic System   In addition to the amygdala and hippocampus, the limbic system contains several so-called pleasure centers that create good feelings when aroused by electrical stimulation or by addictive drugs like cocaine, methamphetamine, and heroin (Olds & Fobes, 1981; Pinel, 2005). But you don't have to take drugs to stimulate these limbic pleasure circuits. Sex will do it too. So will eating, drinking, or exciting activities, such as riding a roller coaster. Even rich chocolate can arouse these rewarding brain circuits (Small et al., 2001).

Reward circuits also participate in our response to humor. For most people, having a brain scan is not a pleasant experience—largely because of the cramped spaces and strange, loud noises made by the machine. But by telling jokes during the fMRI scan, researchers got a few laughs from volunteers with their heads in the scanner. And, sure enough, for those who thought the jokes were funny, parts of the brain's reward circuitry "lit up" (Goel & Dolan, 2001; Watson et al., 2007).

hypothalamus   A limbic structure that serves as the brain's blood-testing laboratory, constantly monitoring the blood to determine the condition of the body.

CONNECTION CHAPTER 9

The *hypothalamus* contains important control circuits for several basic motives and drives, such as hunger and thirst (p. 377).

The Hypothalamus and Control over Motivation   In passing, we have already met the **hypothalamus**, the limbic structure responsible for maintaining the body in a stable, balanced condition, partly by initiating endocrine system messages (refer to Figure 2.10). Rich with blood vessels as well as neurons, the hypothalamus serves as your brain's blood-analysis laboratory. By constantly monitoring the blood, it detects small changes in body temperature, fluid levels, and nutrients. When it detects an imbalance (too much or too little water, for example), the hypothalamus immediately responds with orders aimed at restoring balance.

The hypothalamus makes its influence felt in other ways as well. Although much of its work occurs outside of consciousness, the hypothalamus sends neural messages to "higher" processing areas in the brain, making us aware of its needs (hunger, for example). It also controls our internal organs through its influence on the pituitary gland, attached to the underside of the hypothalamus at the base of the brain. Thus, the hypothalamus serves as the link between the nervous system and the endocrine system, through which it regulates emotional arousal and stress. Finally, the hypothalamus plays a role in our emotions by hosting some of the brain's reward circuits, especially those that generate the feel-good emotions associated with gratifying the hunger, thirst, and sex drives.

cerebral hemispheres   The large symmetrical halves of the brain located atop the brain stem.

corpus callosum   The band of nerve cells connecting and enabling communication between the two cerebral hemispheres.

The Cerebral Cortex: The Brain's Thinking Cap   When you look at a whole human brain, you mostly see the bulging **cerebral hemispheres**—a little bigger than your two fists held together. You may also notice they are connected by a band of fibers, known as the **corpus callosum**, through which the two hemispheres communicate with each other. The nearly symmetrical hemispheres form a thick cap (known as the *cerebrum*) that accounts for two-thirds of the brain's total mass and protects most of the limbic system. The hemispheres' thin outer layer, the **cerebral cortex**, with its distinctive folded and wrinkled surface, allows billions of cells to squeeze into the tight quarters inside your skull. Flattened out, the cortical surface would cover an area roughly the size of a newspaper page. But because of its convoluted surface, only about a third of the cortex is visible when the brain is exposed. For what it's worth: Women's brains have more folding and wrinkling than do men's, while, as we have seen, men's brains are slightly larger than women's, on the average (Luders et al., 2004). And what does this cerebral cortex do? The locus of our most awesome mental powers, it processes all our sensations, stores memories, and makes decisions—among many other functions, which we will consider in our discussion of its lobes in the following text.

Although we humans take pride in our big brains, it turns out ours are not the biggest on the planet. All large animals have large brains—a fact more closely related to body size than to intelligence. Nor is the wrinkled cortex a distinctively human trait. Again, all large animals have highly convoluted cortexes. If this bothers your self-esteem, take comfort in the fact that we do have more massive cortexes for our body weight than do other big-brained creatures. Although no one is sure exactly how or why the brain became so large in our species (Buss, 2008; Pennisi, 2006), comparisons with other animals show that human uniqueness lies more in the way our brains function than in size.

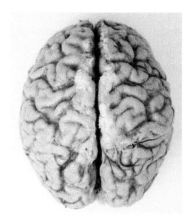

The cerebral hemispheres of the human brain.

cerebral cortex The thin gray matter covering the cerebral hemispheres, consisting of a ¼-inch layer dense with cell bodies of neurons. The cerebral cortex carries on the major portion of our "higher" mental processing, including thinking and perceiving.

Lobes of the Cerebral Cortex

In the late 1700s, the famous Austrian physician Franz Joseph Gall threw his considerable scientific weight behind the idea that specific regions of the brain control specific mental faculties, such as hearing, speech, movement, vision, and memory. Unfortunately, he carried this sensible idea to extremes: In his theory of *phrenology*, Gall claimed that the brain also had regions devoted to such traits as spirituality, hope, benevolence, friendship, destructiveness, and cautiousness. Moreover, he asserted that these traits could be detected as bumps on the skull, the "reading" of which became a minor scam industry.

Gall's ideas captured the public's attention and became enormously popular, even though his theory was mostly wrong. But he was absolutely right on one important point: his doctrine of *localization of function*, the notion that *different parts of the brain perform different tasks*. Discoveries in modern neuroscience have helped us correct Gall's picture of the cerebral cortex. As we discuss the geography of the cortex, please keep in mind that, while the lobes are convenient features, the functions we will ascribe to each do not always respect their precise boundaries.

The Frontal Lobes Your choice of major, your plans for the summer, and your ability to juggle your classes, your job, and your personal life all depend heavily on the cortical regions at the front of your brain, aptly named the **frontal lobes** (you have one in each hemisphere) (see Figure 2.12). Here, especially in the foremost region, known as the *prefrontal cortex*, we find circuitry for our most advanced mental functions, such as decision making, goal setting and follow-through, and anticipating future events (Miller, 2006a). The biological underpinnings of personality, temperament, and our sense of "self" seem to have important components here, too, as the case of Phineas Gage first suggested (Bower, 2006c).

At the back of the frontal lobe lies a special strip of cortex capable of taking action on our thoughts. Known as the **motor cortex**, this patch of brain takes its name from its main function: controlling the body's motor movement by sending messages to motor nerves and on to voluntary muscles. As you can see in Figure 2.13, the motor cortex contains an upside-down map of the body, represented by the *homunculus* (the distorted "little man" in the figure). A closer look at the motor homunculus shows that it exaggerates certain parts of the body, indicating that the brain allots a larger amount of cortex to body parts requiring more fine-tuned motor control such as the lips, tongue, and hands. Perhaps the most exaggerated areas represent the fingers (especially the thumb), reflecting the importance of manipulating objects. Another large area connects to facial muscles, used in expressions of emotion. Please remember, however, that

frontal lobes Cortical regions at the front of the brain that are especially involved in movement and in thinking.

motor cortex A narrow vertical strip of cortex in the frontal lobes lying just in front of the central fissure; controls voluntary movement.

FIGURE 2.12

The Four Lobes of the Cerebral Cortex

Each of the two hemispheres of the cerebral cortex has four lobes. Different sensory and motor functions have been associated with specific parts of each lobe, as shown here.

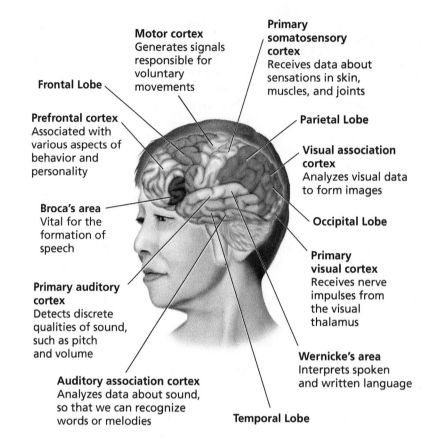

Motor cortex
Generates signals responsible for voluntary movements

Primary somatosensory cortex
Receives data about sensations in skin, muscles, and joints

Frontal Lobe

Prefrontal cortex
Associated with various aspects of behavior and personality

Parietal Lobe

Visual association cortex
Analyzes visual data to form images

Broca's area
Vital for the formation of speech

Occipital Lobe

Primary visual cortex
Receives nerve impulses from the visual thalamus

Primary auditory cortex
Detects discrete qualities of sound, such as pitch and volume

Wernicke's area
Interprets spoken and written language

Auditory association cortex
Analyzes data about sound, so that we can recognize words or melodies

Temporal Lobe

commands from the motor cortex on one side of the brain control muscles on the opposite side of the body. So a wink of your left eye originates in your right motor cortex, while the left motor cortex can wink your right eye.

Mirror Neurons Discovered in the Frontal Lobes   Recently, neuroscientists discovered a new class of neurons, called *mirror neurons,* scattered throughout the brain but especially in motor areas of the frontal lobes. These **mirror neurons** appear to fire when we observe another person performing some action, such as waving, drinking from a cup, or wincing in pain—just as if we had performed the same act ourselves. In effect, we may do and feel what we see in others—but in the privacy of our own minds (Dobbs, 2006a).

What could be their purpose? For one thing, mirror neurons may help children mimic—and therefore learn—language. What's more, these specialized cells may form part of a brain network enabling us to anticipate other people's intentions, says Italian neuroscientist Giacomo Rizzolatti, one of the discoverers of mirror neurons (Rizzolatti et al., 2006). Because they connect with the brain's emotional circuitry, mirror neurons may allow us to "mirror" other people's emotions in our minds. From an evolutionary perspective, observing and imitating others is a fundamental human characteristic, so mirror neurons could even turn out to be a biological basis of culture. Finally, some researchers believe deficits in the mirror system may underlie disorders, such as autism, that involve difficulties in imitation and in understanding others' feelings and intentions (Ramachandran & Oberman, 2006).

Although the discovery of mirror neurons has ignited great excitement in the field of brain science, let's take a moment to think critically about what research has actually found, versus what may—at this point, at least—be mere speculation. One caution centers around a common fallacy we discussed in Chapter 1: *the assumption of causation when only correlational data exist.* Just because our own motor cortex, for example, activates when we see another person engaging in a motor activity, we cannot conclude that our observation caused our corresponding

mirror neuron   A recently discovered class of neuron that fires in response to ("mirroring") observation of another person's actions or emotions.

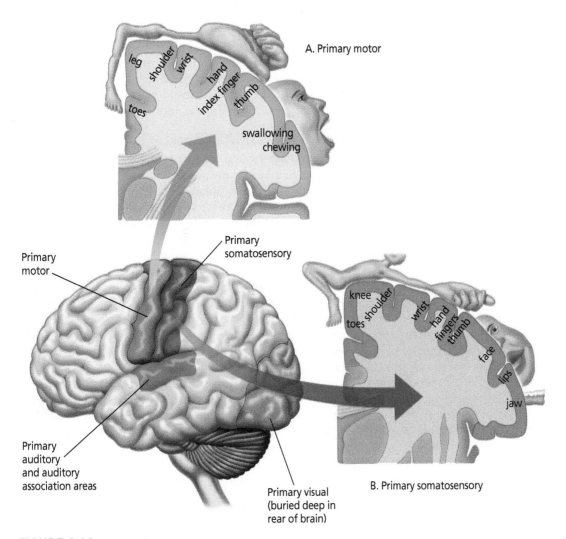

A. Primary motor

leg
shoulder
wrist
hand
index finger
thumb
toes
swallowing
chewing

Primary motor

Primary somatosensory

Primary auditory and auditory association areas

Primary visual (buried deep in rear of brain)

knee
shoulder
toes
wrist
hand
fingers
thumb
face
lips
jaw

B. Primary somatosensory

FIGURE 2.13

The Motor Cortex and the Somatosensory Cortex

Actions of the body's voluntary muscles are controlled by the *motor cortex* in the frontal lobe. The *somatosensory cortex* in the parietal lobe processes information about temperature, touch, body position, and pain. This diagram shows the proportion of tissue devoted to various activities or sensitivities in each cortex.

neural activity (Hickok, 2009). Thus, it would be premature—and dangerous—to assume that the lack of imitation sometimes found in autism, for example, was caused by mirror neuron deficit or dysfunction.

Second, and perhaps even more important, is the notion that mirror neuron activity implies the observer understands the meaning and intent of the action. For example, if you see Mary grasp a cup, you might infer from the way she grasps it that she intends to drink from it (rather than, say, give it to someone else). Mirror neuron enthusiasts have assumed this type of action-understanding comes with the mirror neuron package, so to speak—in other words, that mirror neuron activity promotes deeper understanding of the person's motives and actions, leading to conclusions that mirror neurons underlie empathy and social understanding. But research outside the area of mirror neurons clearly shows that understanding others' motivations can occur outside a mirror neuron system, in part as the result of analytical thinking skills (Hickok, 2010; Keysers, 2010).

In summary, then, while the discovery of mirror neuron circuitry is definitely exciting and may indeed prove to be a promising advance in understanding human thought, emotion, and behavior, we must remind ourselves that extraordinary claims require extraordinary evidence—and curb our enthusiasm a little in the meantime.

The Left Frontal Lobe's Role in Speech   In most people, the left frontal lobe has another important function: the production of speech (see Figure 2.12). First discovered in the mid-1800s by French neurologist Paul Broca, damage to this specialized region—aptly named *Broca's area*—can leave a person without the ability to talk. Surprisingly, though, the ability to understand speech lies elsewhere in the brain. As you might have guessed, Jill Bolte Taylor's stroke damaged Broca's area in her brain, which explains why she lost her ability to construct language.

The Parietal Lobes   To the rear of each frontal lobe lie two large patches of cortex that specialize in sensation (see Figure 2.12). These **parietal lobes** allow us to sense the warmth of a hot bath, the smoothness of silk, the poke of a rude elbow, and the gentleness of a caress. A special parietal strip, known as the **somatosensory cortex**, mirrors the adjacent strip of motor cortex we found in the frontal lobe. This somatosensory cortex has two main functions. First, it serves as the primary processing area for the sensations of touch, temperature, pain, and pressure from all over the body (Graziano et al., 2000; Helmuth, 2000). Second, it relates this information to a mental map of the body to help us locate the source of these sensations (refer to Figure 2.13).

Other maps in the parietal lobes keep track of the position of body parts, so they prevent you from biting your tongue or stepping on your own toes. And, when your leg "goes to sleep" and you can't feel anything but a tingling sensation, you have temporarily interrupted messages from the nerve cells that carry sensory information to body maps in the parietal lobe.

Besides processing sensation and keeping track of body parts, the right parietal lobes help us locate, in three-dimensional space, the positions of external objects detected by our senses. This helps us navigate through our day, from getting out of bed and finding our way into the shower to dressing ourselves, getting ourselves to school or work, and so on. Meanwhile, the left hemisphere's parietal lobe has its own special talents. It specializes in mathematical reasoning and locating the source of speech sounds, as when someone calls your name. It also works with the temporal lobe to extract meaning from speech and writing.

The Temporal Lobes   When the phone rings or a horn honks, the sound registers in your **temporal lobes**, on the lower side of each cerebral hemisphere (see Figure 2.12). There, the *auditory cortex* helps you make sense of sounds.

But the temporal lobes take responsibility for more than just hearing. In most people, a specialized section in the left auditory cortex (where it merges into the lower parietal lobe), known as *Wernicke's area*, helps process the meaning of language. When Jill Bolte Taylor phoned her coworker for help during her stroke, she could hear his words, but they sounded like gibberish to her. "Oh my gosh, he sounds like a golden retriever!" she thought (Taylor, 2009, p. 56). This was due to the damage underway in Wernicke's area of her brain. And it doesn't seem to matter if the language is spoken or signed: Research with hearing-impaired individuals finds that they recruit this same area in understanding sign language (Neville et al., 1998).

And that's not all. Portions of the temporal lobes "subcontract" from the visual cortex the work of recognizing faces. Other temporal regions work with the hippocampus on the important task of storing long-term memories. There is even a distinct patch of temporal cortex dedicated to perception of the human body (Kanwisher, 2006; Tsao, 2006). Finally, the right temporal lobe plays a significant role in interpreting the emotional tone of language—which explains why the gentle tone of her coworker's voice reassured Jill that he would bring help, despite her inability to understand his words (Taylor, 2009).

The Occipital Lobes   Have you ever "seen stars" after a hard bump to your head? If so, that visual sensation likely resulted from stimulation to your **occipital lobes** at the back of your brain (see Figure 2.12). Under more normal circumstances, the occipital lobes receive messages relayed from the eyes. There, the **visual cortex** constructs ongoing images of the world around us.

parietal lobes   Cortical areas lying toward the back and top of the brain; involved in touch sensation and in perceiving spatial relationships (the relationships of objects in space).

somatosensory cortex   A strip of the parietal lobe lying just behind the central fissure. The somatosensory cortex is involved with sensations of touch.

temporal lobes   Cortical lobes that process sounds, including speech. The temporal lobes are probably involved in storing long-term memories.

occipital lobes   The cortical regions at the back of the brain that house the visual cortex.

visual cortex   The visual processing areas of cortex in the occipital and temporal lobes.

To create pictures of the outside world, the brain divides up the incoming visual input and sends it to separate cortical areas for the processing of color, movement, shape, and shading—as we will see in more detail in Chapter 3. But the occipital lobes don't do all this work alone. As we noted previously, they coordinate with adjacent areas in the parietal lobes to locate objects in space. They also work with temporal regions to produce visual memories (Ishai & Sagi, 1995; Miyashita, 1995). To complete the picture, we should note that congenitally blind people recruit the visual cortex to help them read Braille (Amedi et al., 2005; Barach, 2003).

The Association Cortex In accomplishing its magnificent feats of multitasking, our brain relies both on the "primary processing areas" of the cortex as well as the "association areas" of the cortex. The **association cortex**, named for the belief that complex thinking relies upon associating ideas with each other, actually constitutes more than half of the cerebral cortex. But before these associations are made, specific areas of the cortex must process the raw data streaming in from the sense organs: For example, the primary visual cortex processes raw visual stimulation, such as the letters in a word and whether any are capitalized. Then the association area takes over to interpret the meaning of the message, such as perceiving the whole of the word or sentence. Thus, diverse parts of the association cortex, throughout our lobes, interpret sensations, lay plans, make decisions, and prepare us for action—precisely the mental powers in which we humans excel and that distinguish us from other animals.

association cortex Cortical regions throughout the brain that combine information from various other parts of the brain.

The Cooperative Brain No single part of the brain, however, takes sole responsibility for emotion, memory, personality, or any other complex psychological characteristic: There are no single "brain centers" for any of our major faculties. Rather, every mental and behavioral process involves the coordination and cooperation of many brain networks, each an expert at some highly specialized task (Damasio, 2003; LeDoux, 2002). For example, when you do something as simple as answer a ringing telephone, you hear it in your temporal lobes, interpret its meaning with the help of the frontal lobes, visually locate it with your occipital and parietal lobes, initiate grasping the phone on the orders of your frontal and parietal lobes, and engage in thoughtful conversation, again using frontal and temporal lobe circuitry. And the cortex cannot do its work without communicating with circuits lying deep beneath the surface: the limbic system, thalamus, brain stem, cerebellum, and other structures.

Clearly, the brain usually manages to "put it all together" in a coordinated effort to understand and respond to the world. Exactly *how* it does so is not clear to neuroscientists—and, in fact, constitutes one of the biggest mysteries of modern psychology. Some clues have appeared in recent work, however. Constantly active, even when we are asleep, our brains produce pulses of coordinated waves sweeping over the cortex that are thought, somehow, to coordinate activity in far-flung brain regions (Buzsáki, 2006). All these busy neural networks work in elegant coordination with each other in work and in play, in waking and sleeping, from conception to death—and mostly without our awareness.

CONNECTION CHAPTER 3

The puzzle of how the brain "puts it all together" is known as *the binding problem* (p. 113).

Cerebral Dominance

Throughout our discussion of various brain structures and their associated functions, we have made some distinctions between functions in the left and right hemispheres. We know, for example, that a person with injury to the right hemisphere would probably not experience language difficulties but could have trouble with spatial orientation—for example, feeling lost in a familiar place or unable to complete a simple jigsaw puzzle. This tendency for each hemisphere to take the lead in different tasks is called **cerebral dominance**, an often-exaggerated concept. While it is true that some processes are more under the control of the left hemisphere and others are predominantly right-hemisphere tasks, *both hemispheres continually work together to produce our thoughts, feelings, and behaviors*—courtesy of

cerebral dominance The tendency of each brain hemisphere to exert control over different functions, such as language or perception of spatial relationships.

the corpus callosum and its role in communication between the hemispheres. With that in mind, what differences are there between the hemispheres?

Language and Communication As we have seen, the left hemisphere usually dominates language functions, although both sides of the brain get involved to some extent. Typically, the left side is more active in manufacturing and processing the "what," or *content,* of speech. The right hemisphere, by contrast, interprets the *emotional tone* of speech (Vingerhoets et al., 2003), as we noted in the case of Jill's stroke. The right hemisphere also takes the lead in interpreting others' emotional responses and their nonverbal communication signals. As for our own emotions, the control of *negative* emotions, such as fear and anger, usually stems from the right frontal lobe, while the left frontal lobe typically regulates *positive* emotions such as joy (Davidson, 2000b).

Different Processing Styles Thus, the two hemispheres don't generally compete with each other. Rather, they make different contributions to the same task. In the lingo of neuroscience, the two hemispheres have different but complimentary *processing styles.* For example, the left hemisphere groups objects analytically and verbally—as by similarity in function (*knife* with *spoon*)—while the right hemisphere might match things by form or visual pattern—as in matching *coin* to *clock,* which are both round objects (Gazzaniga, 1970; Sperry, 1968, 1982). In general, we can describe the left hemisphere's processing style as more *analytic* and *sequential*, while the right hemisphere interprets experience more *holistically, emotionally,* and *spatially* (Reuter-Lorenz & Miller, 1998). In a normally functioning brain, the two styles complement each other, combining to produce a multifaceted perspective of the world.

In the wake of damage to the brain, though—such as Jill's stroke—the different processing styles may become starkly apparent. In Jill's case, she relied more on linear thinking during the first part of her life: "I spent a lifetime of thirty-seven years being enthusiastically committed to do-do-doing lots of stuff at a very fast pace" (Taylor, 2009, p. 70). The radical shift in her perception caused by the damage to her left hemisphere was noticeable right away, when she found herself incapable of keeping her thoughts on track while trying to plan how to get help. The step-by-step, time-oriented thinking she had taken for granted had vanished, and in its place a completely different perspective of herself and the world emerged. "I felt no rush to do anything (p. 71)," she marvels, as she remembers her joy in feeling connected to everything around her, in being exquisitely tuned to others' emotions, in taking time to ponder things, and in the deep inner peace that came with her new view of the world that emphasized the right brain's perspective.

If that description sounds like words a person might use to describe a religious or spiritual experience, neurological studies from the University of Pennsylvania may tell us why. Researchers conducted sophisticated brain scans on people who were meditating and found that in peak meditative states, activity in the left association cortex—the area that makes us aware of our body's physical boundaries—declined sharply. Thus, the self-transcendence reported by expert meditators, as well as Jill Taylor's similar feeling of being "one with the universe," appear to have a biological basis: When blood flow to that region of the left hemisphere slows down, our awareness of ourselves as separate and distinct organisms fades (Newberg et al., 2001a). In addition, decreased activity in the left parietal lobe, also noted in studies of meditators, correlates with an altered awareness of one's body in relation to space (Newberg et al., 2001b).

Some People Are Different—But That's Normal Just to complicate your picture of cerebral dominance, dominance patterns are not always the same from one person to another. Research demonstrating this fact uses a technique called *transcranial magnetic stimulation* (TMS) to deliver powerful magnetic pulses through the skull and into the brain. There, the magnetic fields interfere with the brain's electrical activity, temporarily disabling the targeted region without causing permanent damage. Surprisingly, when the left-side language areas receive TMS, language abilities in some people—mostly left-handers—remain unaffected. In general, these studies show that about one

CONNECTION CHAPTER 9

Emotional intelligence includes the ability to perceive and understand others' emotions (p. 396).

in ten individuals process language primarily on the *right* side of the brain. Another one in ten—again, mostly left-handers—have language functions distributed equally on both sides of the brain (Knecht et al., 2002).

Male and Female Brains In a culture where bigger is often seen as better, the undeniable fact that men (on average) have slightly larger brains than do women has caused heated debate. The real question, of course, is: What is the meaning of the size differential? Most neuroscientists think it is simply related to the male's larger body size—and not of much other importance (Brannon, 2008).

Within the brain, certain structures exhibit sex differences too. A part of the hypothalamus commonly believed to be associated with sexual behavior and, perhaps, gender identity, is larger in males than in females. Some studies have suggested that male brains are more *lateralized,* while females tend to distribute abilities, such as language, across both hemispheres, although findings in this area are mixed (Sommer et al., 2004). If true, however, the difference in lateralization may explain why women are more likely than men to recover speech after a stroke. Other than that, what advantage the difference in lateralization may have is unclear.

At present, no one has nailed down any psychological difference that can be attributed with certainty to physical differences between the brains of males and females. The research continues, but we suggest interpreting new claims with a liberal dose of critical thinking, being especially wary of bias that may influence the way results are interpreted. In fact, we will help you do just that in the Critical Thinking: Applied section at the end of this chapter.

The Strange and Fascinating Case of the Split Brain Imagine what your world might be like if your two hemispheres could *not* communicate—if your brain were, somehow, "split" in two. Would you be, literally, "of two minds"? (See Figure 2.14.) This is not an idle question, because there *are* people with "split brains," the result of a last-resort surgical procedure used to treat a rare condition of almost continuous epileptic seizures. Before their surgery, these patients produced abnormal electrical bursts of brain waves that seemed to "echo" back and forth between the hemispheres, quickly building into a seizure—much as feedback through a microphone generates a loud screeching noise. So the idea was to cut the corpus callosum—severing the connection between the hemispheres—and thereby prevent the seizure from raging out of control. But was there a psychological price? Curiously, split-brain patients appear mentally and behaviorally unaffected by this extreme procedure under all but the most unusual conditions.

Those unusual conditions involve clever tests contrived by Nobel Prize winner Roger Sperry (1968) and his colleague Michael Gazzaniga (2005). For example, when holding a ball in the left hand (without being able to see it), as shown in

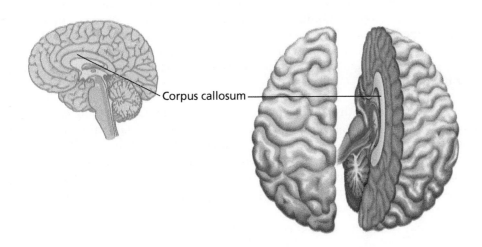

Corpus callosum

FIGURE 2.14

The Corpus Callosum

Only the corpus callosum is severed when the brain is "split." This medical procedure prevents communication between the cerebral hemispheres. Surprisingly, split-brain patients act like people with normal brains under most conditions. Special laboratory tests, however, reveal a duality of consciousness in the split brain.

FIGURE 2.15

Testing a Split-Brain Patient

Split-brain patients can name unseen objects placed in the right hand, but when an object is placed in the left hand, they cannot name it. Why?

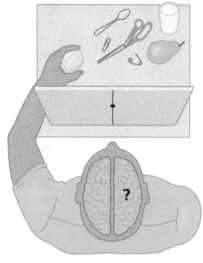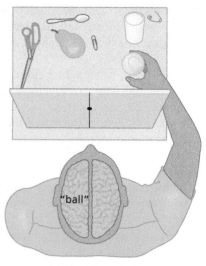

could *not* identify verbally   could identify verbally

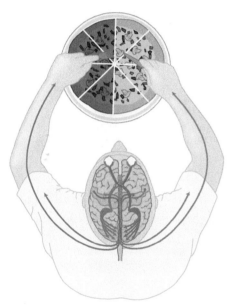

FIGURE 2.16

The Neural Pathways from the Eyes to the Visual Cortex

There are two things to notice in this illustration in which the person is looking at the center of the pizza. First, the information from the left side of the retina in each eye (which is the left visual field) corresponds to the right side of the pizza. Conversely, the right visual field senses the left side of the pizza. (This happens because the lens of the eye reverses the image.) Second, please notice that the optic nerves of both eyes join together at the *optic chiasm*, where information from the left sides of both retinas are routed to the left visual cortex, while images from the right sides of both retinas are routed to the right visual cortex. As a result, everything a person sees on the right gets processed in the left hemisphere's visual cortex, while the right visual cortex processes everything to the left of the point on which the eyes are fixed.

Figure 2.15, their split-brain patients could not identify it by touch, yet they had no trouble doing so when the ball was transferred to the right hand. In another test, split-brain patients said they saw nothing when an image of a spoon flashed briefly on the left side of the visual field. Yet, they could reach around a visual barrier with the right hand and easily pick the spoon out of an array of other objects.

How can we explain these odd findings? Let's see if we can use what we have learned in this chapter to solve this peculiar puzzle.

- First, remember that the corpus callosum enables communication between the hemispheres—so, when it is severed, each hemisphere must process information on its own. This explains, also, why split-brain patients can simultaneously draw a circle with one hand and a square with the other (a near-impossible task for those with intact brains. If you don't believe us, just try it!)

- Because the sensory pathways cross over to the opposite side as they ascend to the cortex, each side of the body communicates with the opposite side of the brain. So, each hemisphere perceives touch sensation from the hand on the opposite side of the body.

- Language is usually a left-hemisphere function. This, when combined with the contralateral sensory pathways, explains why these patients could name objects when they were processed in the left hemisphere. When sensory messages came in from the right visual field or the right hand (such as holding the ball in the right hand), the message crossed over to the left hemisphere, which—thanks to its language abilities—could name the object. Conversely, objects seen in the left visual field or felt in the left hand crossed over to the right hemisphere for processing, where—because the right hemisphere cannot produce speech—patients could not name the object. They could, however, identify it by touch.

In another study with a similar patient, Gazzaniga found something else remarkable. He began with images of paintings by an artist named Giuseppe Arcimboldo, famous for painting faces made entirely of figures, such as fruit, books, fish, and other objects (see the accompanying photo). Would the patient's left hemisphere's perception of the painting differ from his right hemisphere's view of it? (If you enjoy a challenge, try to remember something we discussed a few pages back that may help you figure out the answer before reading on.)

When the images were flashed briefly to his right visual field (and thus processed in his left hemisphere), he recognized only the objects in the image (such as fruit or books)—he did not "see" a face. When shown to his left visual field, however, the processing style of his right hemisphere enabled his recognition of a human face. This finding supports other research indicating a special ability for facial recognition in the right hemisphere (*The Man with Two Brains*, 1997). Clearly, both hemispheres play important roles in human abilities.

Two Consciousnesses   Such cerebral antics point to the most interesting finding in Sperry and Gazzaniga's work: the *duality of consciousness* observed in split-brain patients. When the two hemispheres received different information, it was as if the patient were two separate individuals. One patient told how his left hand would unzip his pants or unbutton his shirt at most inappropriate times, especially when he felt stressed. Another reported his misbehaving left hand turning off the television in the middle of a program he had been watching (Joseph, 1988). Why? Sperry theorized that the right hemisphere—which has little language ability, but which controls the left hand—was merely trying to find a way to communicate by getting attention any way it could (Sperry, 1964).

We must, however, be cautious about generalizing such findings from split-brain patients to individuals with normal brains. Gazzaniga (1998a, b) suggests we think of the human mind as neither a single nor a dual entity but rather as a *confederation of minds,* each specialized to process a specific kind of information. For most people, then, the corpus callosum serves as a connecting pathway that helps our confederation of minds share information. And so we come full circle to the Core Concept we encountered at the beginning of this section: The brain is composed of many specialized modules that work together to create mind and behavior (Baynes et al., 1998; Strauss, 1998).

A painting by Arcimboldo, who painted faces made of fruits, flowers, and books, and other figures. Gazzaniga used Arcimboldo's paintings to show how the two hemispheres process facial images differently.

What's It to *You*?   Nearly everybody knows someone who has suffered brain damage from an accident, a stroke, or a tumor. Your new knowledge of the brain and behavior will help you understand the problems such people face. And if you know what abilities have been lost or altered, you can usually make a good guess as to which part of the brain sustained the damage—especially if you bear in mind three simple principles:

1. Each side of the brain communicates with the opposite side of the body. Thus, if symptoms appear on one side of the body, it is likely that the other side of the brain was damaged (see Figure 2.17).
2. For most people, speech is mainly a left-hemisphere function.
3. Each lobe has special functions:

   - The occipital lobe specializes in vision;
   - The temporal lobe specializes in hearing, memory, and face recognition;
   - The parietal lobe specializes in locating sensations in space, including the surface of the body;
   - The frontal lobe specializes in motor movement, the production of speech, and certain higher mental functions that we often call "thinking" or "intelligence."

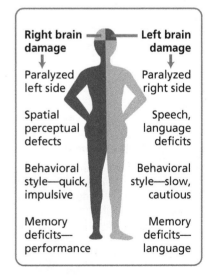

FIGURE 2.17

Contralateral Effects of Damage to the Cerebral Hemispheres

Here's how one of your authors (Bob) applied his knowledge of the brain:

I hadn't noticed Dad dragging the toe of his right foot ever so slightly as he walked. But my Mom noticed it on their nightly tour of the neighborhood, when he wasn't keeping up with her brisk pace. I just figured he was slowing down a bit in his later years.

Dad, too, casually dismissed his symptom, but Mom was persistent. She scheduled an appointment with the doctor. In turn, the doctor scheduled a brain scan that showed a remarkably large mass—a tumor—on the left side of Dad's brain. You can see what the neurologist saw in Figure 2.18—an image taken ear-to-ear through the head.

When I saw the pictures, I knew immediately what was happening. The tumor was located in an area that would interfere with tracking the position of the foot. I knew that each side of the brain communicates with the opposite side of the body—so it made sense that the tumor showing so clearly on the left side of Dad's brain (right side of the image) was affecting communications with his right foot.

The neurologist also told us that the diseased tissue was not in the brain itself. Rather, it was in the saclike layers surrounding the brain and spinal cord. That was good news, in an otherwise bleak report. Still, the mass was growing and putting pressure on the brain. The recommendation was surgery—which occurred after an anxious wait of a few weeks.

During this difficult time, I remember feeling grateful for my professional training. As a psychologist, I knew something about the brain, its disorders, and treatments. This allowed me to shift perspectives—from son to psychologist and back again. It helped me deal with the emotions that rose to the surface when I thought about the struggle for the organ of my father's mind.

Sadly, the operation did not produce the miraculous cure for which we had hoped. Although brain surgery is performed safely on thousands of patients each year—many of whom receive immense benefits in the quality and lengths of their lives—one has to remember that it is a procedure usually done on very

FIGURE 2.18

MRI Image of a Brain Tumor

This image, showing a side-to-side section toward the back of the head, reveals a large mass on the left side of the brain in a region involved with tracking the position of the right foot. Visible at the bottom is a cross-section of the cerebellum. Also visible are the folds in the cerebral cortex covering the brain. Near the center, you can see two of the brain's ventricles (hollow spaces filled with cerebrospinal fluid), which are often enlarged, as they are here, in Alzheimer's disease. The scan is of the father of one of your authors.

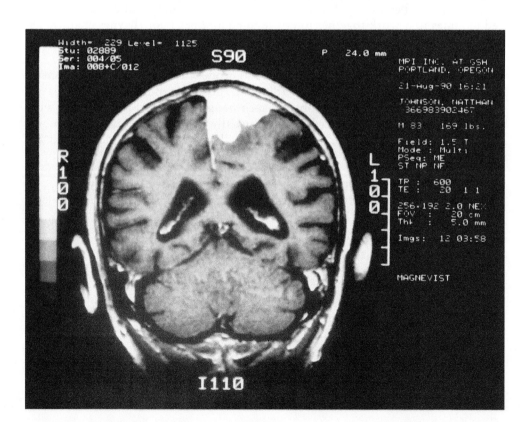

sick people. In fact, the operation did give Dad some time with us that he may otherwise not have had.

[PSYCHOLOGY MATTERS]

Using Psychology to Learn Psychology

The old idea that we use only 10 percent of our brains is nonsense that probably came from a time when neuroscientists hadn't figured out the functions of many cortical areas. Now we know that every part of the brain has a specific function, and they all get used every day. Therefore, simply finding a way to engage *more* of the brain is not the royal road to increased brainpower.

Have neuroscientists found anything you can use to improve your memory, especially for concepts you are learning in your classes? The fact that we employ many different regions of the cerebral cortex in learning and memory may be among their most practical discoveries (Kandel & Squire, 2000). Accordingly, if you can bring more of this cerebral circuitry to bear on your studies (about biopsychology, for example), your brain will develop a wider web of memories.

Reading the material in this book will help you form verbal (language) memories, parts of which involve circuits in the temporal cortex. Taking notes brings the motor cortex of the frontal lobes into play, adding a "motor memory" component to your study. Studying the accompanying photos, charts, and drawings adds visual and spatial memory components in the occipital and parietal lobes. Listening actively to your professor's lectures and discussing the material with a study partner will engage the auditory regions of the temporal cortex and create still more memory traces. Finally, anticipating questions that may appear on the exam will involve regions of the frontal lobes in your learning process.

In general, the more ways you can engage with the material—the more sensory and motor channels you can employ—the more memory components you will build in your brain's circuitry. As a result, you will have more ways of accessing what you have learned when you need to remember the material.

Check Your Understanding

✓•⌐Study and Review at MyPsychLab

1. **APPLICATION:** Suppose you are a neuroscientist interested in comparing what parts of the brain are most active when people are driving and talking on a cell phone. Which imaging technique would be best for your research?

2. **RECALL:** Name the three main layers of the human brain discussed in the text: _____, _____, and _____.

3. **APPLICATION:** An fMRI or a PET scan would show activity in a person's _____ during an emotional response.

4. **RECALL:** Make a sketch showing the four lobes of the cerebral cortex. Indicate the main functions of each lobe and which hemisphere controls language in most people. Which hemisphere controls the left hand?

5. **ANALYSIS:** A split-brain patient would have trouble using his _____ hand to select the object flashed on the left side of the screen. (*Hints:* Which hemisphere controls each hand? Which hemisphere processes information from the left side of the visual field?)

6. **UNDERSTANDING THE CORE CONCEPT:** The brain is composed of many specialized and interconnected modules that work together to create mind and behavior. Can you name at least two specialized parts of the brain that are known to work together?

Answers 1. fMRI would be best, because it not only gives detailed three-dimensional images but also shows different activity levels in different parts of the brain. The driving task, however, would have to be modified so it could be performed while in the fMRI machine. **2.** The brain stem and cerebellum, the limbic system, the cerebrum **3.** limbic system **4.** See the location of the four lobes in Figure 2.12. The left hemisphere controls language, and the right hemisphere controls your left hand. **5.** right **6.** Examples include the interaction of regions in the four lobes of the cerebral cortex when answering the phone. There are many other examples mentioned in this section.

CRITICAL THINKING APPLIED

Left Brain versus Right Brain

Would you rather solve a math problem or create a painting? Write an essay on an academic topic or invent a fictional story? According to pop science, the way you answer questions like this reveals whether you are a "left-brain" person or a "right-brain" person. Furthermore, the same sources often then encourage you to use that information to choose a career. Is there any truth to these claims?

The split-brain studies and discovery that the two sides of the brain process information differently have certainly captured public interest. Press reports claiming the left hemisphere is logical and the right hemisphere is emotional might easily lead to the mistaken conclusion that your friend Jamal, a guy with an analytic bent, lives mostly in his left hemisphere, while his wife Barb, more sensitive to people's emotions, filters her experience mainly through the right side of her brain.

Knowing a fad when they see it, pseudoscientists have developed workshops to help plodding analytical types get into their "right minds." Before you jump on this particular bandwagon, though, let's dig a little deeper.

What Are the Critical Issues?

The idea that people fall neatly into one category or another has popular appeal, but do the facts bear this out? Recent findings in neuroscience should be able to tell us how the left and right brain interact and whether people really are right- or left-brained.

Is the Claim Reasonable or Extreme?   As we have seen in this chapter, the notion that we rely on one side of the brain, largely to the exclusion of the other, is an exaggeration. Rather, we use both sides, in coordination with each other, all the time. As we often find in extreme claims, the "left brain vs. right brain" issue has oversimplified the scientific findings of hemispheric differences: People rarely fit neatly into one of two dichotomous categories. This serves as a good example of how honest findings (such as the work reported in this chapter on the differences between the hemispheres) often become wildly exaggerated by the time they reach the popular news media. We should always digest these reports with a healthy dose of skepticism and look closely at the evidence.

What Is the Evidence?   As we have seen, the two hemispheres have somewhat different *processing styles,* but the actual differences between the two hemispheres do not outweigh their similarities (Banich, 1998; Trope et al., 1992). Most important—and what the right-brain/left-brain faddists overlook—is that the two hemispheres of the intact brain cooperate with each other, each making its own complementary contribution to our mental lives (see Figure 2.17).

Could Bias Contaminate the Conclusion?   Two biases come easily to mind as we consider this issue. First—as we mentioned earlier—some businesses have made fortunes "selling" this idea, which creates an obvious bias if these same businesses are trying to convince you of its veracity. Emotional bias is likely present as well. After all, we humans like to classify things and people into categories: It appeals to our sense of order and soothes our need to resolve complex issues. Small wonder, then, that we often latch on to typologies that purport to explain human nature, characteristics, and behavior.

What Conclusions Can We Draw?

Unless you have a split brain, you bring the abilities of both sides of your brain to bear on everything you do. Why, then, do people have such obvious differences in the way they approach the same tasks? Some people *do* seem to approach things in a more analytical, logical fashion; others operate from a more intuitive and emotional perspective. But now that you know something of how the brain works, you understand that we cannot account for these differences simply by suggesting people employ one side of their brain or the other. Even split-brain patients use both sides of their brains! A better explanation involves different combinations of experience and brain physiology. People are different because of different combinations of nature and nurture—not because they use opposite sides of the brain.

Do It Yourself! USING BOTH SIDES OF YOUR BRAIN

Think of something you enjoy doing—it might be playing a particular sport or making music, cooking or having dinner with friends, studying or shopping, or whatever strikes your fancy. Now, imagine doing it for a couple of hours and all the minute details of what would likely occur in that period of time. Make a note of some of them and then try to identify which parts of the activity might be led by your left hemisphere and which parts of the activity are more likely coordinated by your right hemisphere. (Hint: Besides all the examples included earlier in the chapter, we have listed some in Figure 2.19.)

Chances are, in any pursuit, you'll see how involved both hemispheres need to be in order for you to fully engage in the experience. And because of that, you stand as living proof that you are neither "left-brained" nor "right-brained," but a beautifully coordinated example of "whole-brained!"

Left hemisphere

- Regulation of positive emotions
- Control of muscles used in speech
- Control of sequence of movements
- Spontaneous speaking and writing
- Memory for words and numbers
- Understanding speech and writing

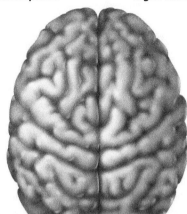

Right hemisphere

- Regulation of negative emotions
- Responses to simple commands
- Memory for shapes and music
- Interpreting spatial relationships and visual images
- Recognition of faces

FIGURE 2.19

Specialization of the Cerebral Hemispheres

While each hemisphere communicates with the opposite side of the body, the hemispheres each specialize in controlling different functions. For most people, the left hemisphere specializes in speech and other functions performed in sequence (such as walking, throwing, and reading). The right hemisphere specializes in synthesis: gathering many pieces of information and synthesizing it as a unified whole (as in recognizing faces or shapes).

CHAPTER SUMMARY

((•—[Listen to an audio file of your chapter at **MyPsychLab**

CHAPTER PROBLEM: What does Jill Bolte Taylor's experience teach us about how our brain is organized and about its amazing ability to adapt?

- Our brain communicates through *contralateral pathways*, so that sensory information from one side of the body is processed by the opposite *cerebral hemisphere*.

- Brain *plasticity* allows us to regain or rewire functions lost due to damage or trauma.

- Our brain is composed of a group of specialized structures, each of which performs certain tasks, but which all work together to produce thought, behavior, and emotion.

2.1 How Are Genes and Behavior Linked?

Core Concept 2.1 Evolution has fundamentally shaped psychological processes because it favors genetic variations that produce adaptive behavior.

Charles Darwin's theory of evolution explains behavior as the result of **natural selection.** Variation among individuals and competition for resources lead to survival of the most adaptive behavior as well as the fittest physical features. This principle underlies human behavior as well as that of other animals.

Genetics has clarified the biological basis for natural selection and inheritance. Our **chromosomes** contain thousands of **genes,** carrying traits inherited from our parents. Each gene consists of a **DNA** segment that encodes for a protein. Proteins, in turn, serve as the building blocks for the organism's structure and function, including the functioning of the brain. While a draft of the human genome has been completed, we do not yet know precisely how specific genes influence behavior and mental processes. Genetic research is nearing the point at which we may alter our genetic makeup or select certain genetic traits for our children. This new knowledge brings with it ethical choices that humans have never had to face before.

2.2   How Does the Body Communicate Internally?

> **Core Concept 2.2** **The brain coordinates the body's two communications systems, the nervous system and the endocrine system, which use similar chemical messengers to communicate with targets throughout the body.**

The body's two communication systems are the **nervous system** and the **endocrine system**. **Neurons** receive messages by means of stimulation of the **dendrites** and **soma**. When sufficiently aroused, a neuron generates an **action potential** along the **axon**. **Neurotransmitter** chemicals relay the message to receptors on cells across the **synapse**. The nervous system has two main divisions: the **central nervous system** and the **peripheral nervous system**. The peripheral nervous system, in turn, comprises the **somatic nervous system** (further divided into sensory and motor pathways) and the **autonomic nervous system**, which communicates with internal organs and glands. The **sympathetic division** of the autonomic nervous system is most active under stress, while the **parasympathetic division** attempts to maintain the body in a calmer state. The glands of the slower endocrine system also communicate with cells around the body by secreting **hormones** into the bloodstream. Endocrine system activity is controlled by the **pituitary gland**, attached to the base of the brain, where it receives orders from the hypothalamus. Psychoactive drugs affect the nervous system by influencing the effects of neurotransmitters by acting as **agonists** or **antagonists**. Unfortunately for people taking psychoactive drugs, many neural pathways in the brain may employ the same neurotransmitter, causing unwanted side effects.

2.3   How Does the Brain Produce Behavior and Mental Processes?

> **Core Concept 2.3** **The brain is composed of many specialized modules that work together to create mind and behavior.**

In modern times, researchers have opened windows on the brain, using the **EEG** to sense the brain's electrical activity. In recent years, computer technology has led to brain-scanning techniques, such as **CT, PET, MRI,** and **fMRI**—each having its advantages and disadvantages. We can conceive of the brain as being organized in three integrated layers. The **brain stem** and associated structures (including the **medulla, reticular formation, pons, thalamus,** and **cerebellum**) control many vital body functions, along with influencing alertness and motor movement. The **limbic system** (including the **hippocampus, amygdala,** and **hypothalamus**) plays a vital role in motivation, emotion, and memory. The **cerebral cortex** contains highly specialized modules. Its **frontal lobes** control motor functions, including speech, and higher mental functions. The **parietal lobes** specialize in sensation, especially the senses of touch and body position, as well as the understanding of speech. The **occipital lobes** deal exclusively with vision, while the **temporal lobes** have multiple roles involved in face recognition, hearing, and smell. Even though the functions of the brain are highly localized within specific modules, they normally work seamlessly together: Every mental and behavioral process involves the coordination and cooperation of many brain networks. The **association cortex** integrates the multitude of raw data into a coherent perception. While the two hemispheres are more similar than different, they are each equipped with specialties. Language, analytical thinking, and positive emotions are regulated primarily by circuits in the left hemisphere. The right hemisphere specializes in spatial interpretation, visual and musical memory, and negative emotions. The two hemispheres communicate across the **corpus callosum**. If the hemispheres are surgically severed, as when the corpus callosum is cut in split-brain patients, a duality of consciousness emerges. Because each side of the body has sensory and motor links to the opposite side of the brain, a split-brain patient who "sees" an object in only one hemisphere of the brain will only be able to locate that object by touch using the hand linked to the same hemisphere.

amygdala (p. 68)
association cortex (p. 73)
brain stem (p. 65)
cerebellum (p. 66)
cerebral cortex (p. 69)
cerebral dominance (p. 73)
cerebral hemispheres (p. 68)
corpus callosum (p. 68)

CT scanning or computerized tomography (p. 64)
electroencephalograph (EEG) (p. 63)
fMRI or functional magnetic resonance imaging (p. 64)
frontal lobes (p. 69)
hippocampus (p. 67)
hypothalamus (p. 68)
limbic system (p. 66)
medulla (p. 66)
mirror neuron (p. 70)
motor cortex (p. 69)
MRI or magnetic resonance imaging (p. 64)
occipital lobes (p. 72)
parietal lobes (p. 72)
PET scanning or positron emission tomography (p. 64)
pons (p. 66)
reticular formation (p. 66)
somatosensory cortex (p. 72)
temporal lobes (p. 72)
thalamus (p. 66)
visual cortex (p. 72)

CRITICAL THINKING APPLIED

Left Brain versus Right Brain

Pop science dichotomizes people into left-brained and right-brained people, based on whether they tend to be more analytical or intuitive. A closer look at the evidence for *hemispheric specialization*, however, reveals that this dichotomy is wildly oversimplied.

DISCOVERING PSYCHOLOGY **VIEWING GUIDE**

Watch the following videos by logging into MyPsychLab (www.mypsychlab.com). After you have watched the videos, answer the questions that follow.

PROGRAM 3: **THE BEHAVING BRAIN**

PROGRAM 4: **THE RESPONSIVE BRAIN**

PROGRAM 25: **COGNITIVE NEUROSCIENCE**

Program Review

1. What section of a nerve cell receives incoming information?
   a. axon
   b. terminal button
   c. synapse
   d. dendrite

2. In general, neuroscientists are interested in the
   a. brain mechanisms underlying normal and abnormal behavior.
   b. biological consequences of stress on the body.
   c. comparison of neurons with other types of cells.
   d. computer simulation of intelligence.

3. Which section of the brain coordinates body movement and maintains equilibrium?
   a. brain stem
   b. cerebellum
   c. hippocampus
   d. cerebrum

4. Which brain structure is most closely involved with emotion?
   a. cortex   c. limbic system
   b. brain stem   d. cerebellum

5. Which method of probing the brain produces actual pictures of the brain's inner workings?
   a. autopsies   c. brain imaging
   b. lesioning   d. electroencephalograms

6. Research related to acetylcholine may someday help people who
   a. have Alzheimer's disease.
   b. have Parkinson's disease.
   c. suffer spinal cord trauma.
   d. suffer from depression.

7. When we say the relationship between the brain and behavior is reciprocal, we mean that
   a. the brain controls behavior, but behavior can modify the brain.
   b. behavior determines what the brain will think about.
   c. the brain and behavior operate as separate systems with no interconnection.
   d. the brain alters behavior as it learns more about the world.

8. Which of the following is true about how neurons communicate with each other?
   a. All neuronal communication is excitatory.
   b. Neurons communicate with each other by sending electrical discharges across the connecting synapse.
   c. Neurons of any given type can communicate only with other neurons of the same type.
   d. The sum of excitatory and inhibitory signals to a neuron determines whether and how strongly it will respond.

9. Which part of the brain controls breathing?
   a. cerebellum   c. hypothalamus
   b. brain stem   d. limbic system

10. The cerebrum
    a. consists of two hemispheres connected by the corpus callosum.
    b. relays sensory impulses to the higher perceptual centers.
    c. releases seven different hormones to the pituitary gland.
    d. controls temperature and blood pressure.

11. After a rod was shot through Phineas Gage's skull, what psychological system was most strongly disrupted?
    a. his emotional responses
    b. his ability to sleep and wake
    c. his language comprehension
    d. his ability to count

12. Which of the following does not provide information about the structure of the brain?
    a. CAT   c. MRI
    b. EEG   d. fMRI

13. Which of the following provides the highest temporal and spatial resolution in brain imaging?
    a. ERP   c. PET
    b. MRI   d. fMRI

14. Stimuli that pass through the right eye are processed by
    a. the left side of the brain.
    b. the front of the brain.
    c. the right side of the brain.
    d. the brain stem.

15. The process of learning how to read shows that the brain is plastic. What does this mean?
    a. The brain is rigid in what it is designed to do.
    b. Learning how to read reorganizes the brain.
    c. The brain cannot be damaged simply by attempting new mental feats.
    d. The brain can be damaged when it attempts new mental feats.

16. If a scientist was studying the effects of endorphins on the body, the scientist would be likely to look at a participant's
    a. memory.
    b. mood.
    c. ability to learn new material.
    d. motivation to compete in sports.

17. What is the relationship between the results of Saul Schanberg's research and that of Tiffany Field?
    a. Their results are contradictory.
    b. The results of Schanberg's research led to Field's research.
    c. Their results show similar phenomena in different species.
    d. Their results are essentially unrelated.

18. What physical change did Mark Rosenzweig's team note when it studied rats raised in an enriched environment?
    a. a thicker cortex
    b. more neurons
    c. fewer neurotransmitters
    d. no physical changes were noted, only functional changes

19. A scientist who uses the methodologies of brain science to examine animal behavior in natural habitats is a
    a. naturalist.
    b. bioecologist.
    c. neuroethologist.
    d. cerebroetymologist.

20. With respect to the neurochemistry of the brain, all of these are true, *except* that
    a. scopolamine blocks the establishment of long-term memories.
    b. opioid peptides are naturally occurring chemicals in the brain.
    c. physosstigmine is responsible for information transmission in the perceptual pathways.
    d. endorphins play a major role in pleasure and pain experiences.

3

Sensation and Perception

CHAPTER PROBLEM Is there any way to tell whether the world we "see" in our minds is the same as the external world—and whether we see things as most others do?

CRITICAL THINKING APPLIED Subliminal Perception and Subliminal Persuasion

CAN YOU IMAGINE WHAT YOUR WORLD WOULD BE LIKE IF YOU COULD NO LONGER see colors—but merely black, white, and gray? Such a bizarre sensory loss befell Jonathan I., a 65-year-old New Yorker, following an automobile accident. Details of his case appear in neurologist Oliver Sacks's 1995 book, *An Anthropologist on Mars*. The accident caused damage to a region in Jonathan's brain that processes color information. At first, he also experienced amnesia for reading letters of the alphabet, which all seemed like a jumble of nonsensical markings. But, after five days, his inability to read disappeared. His loss of color vision, however, persisted as a permanent condition, known as *cerebral achromatopsia* (pronounced *ay-kroma-TOP-see-a*). Curiously, Jonathan also lost his memory for colors: He could no longer imagine, for instance, what "red" once looked like.

As you might expect, Jonathan became depressed by this turn in his life. And the problem was aggravated by his occupation. You see, Jonathan was a painter who had based his livelihood on representing his visual images of the world in vivid colors. Now this whole world of color was gone. Everything was drab—all "molded in lead." When he looked at his own paintings now, paintings that had seemed bursting with special meaning and emotional associations, all he could see were unfamiliar and meaningless objects on canvas.

Still, Jonathan's story has a more or less happy ending, one that reveals much about the resilience of the human spirit. Jonathan became a "night person," traveling and working at night and socializing with other night people. (As we will see in this chapter, good color vision depends on bright illumination such as daylight; most people's color vision is not as acute in the dark of night.) He also became aware that what remained of his vision was remarkably good, enabling him to read license plates from four blocks away at night. Jonathan began to reinterpret his "loss" as a "gift" in which he was no longer distracted by color so that he could now focus his work more intensely on shape, form, and content. Finally, he switched to painting only in black and white. Critics acclaimed his "new phase" as a success. He has also become a skilled sculptor, which he had never attempted before his accident. So, as Jonathan's world of color died, a new world of "pure forms" was born in his perception of the people, objects, and events in his environment.

What lessons can we learn from Jonathan's experience? His unusual sensory loss tells us that our picture of the world around us depends on an elaborate sensory system that processes incoming information. In other words, we don't experience the world directly, but instead through a series of "filters" that we call our *senses.* By examining such cases of sensory loss, psychologists have learned much about how the sensory processing system works. And, on a more personal level, case studies like Jonathan's allow us momentarily to slip outside our own experience to see more clearly how resilient humans can be in the face of catastrophic loss.

But Jonathan's case also raises some deeper issues. Many conditions can produce the inability to see colors: abnormalities in the eyes, the optic nerve, or the brain can interfere with vision and, specifically, with the ability to see colors, as Jonathan's case illustrates. But do colors exist in the world outside us—or is it possible that color is a creation of our brains?

At first, such a question may seem absurd. But let's look a little deeper. Yes, we will argue that color—and, in fact, all sensation—is a creation of the brain. But perhaps the more profound issue is this:

PROBLEM: Is there any way to tell whether the world we "see" in our minds is the same as the external world—and whether we see things as most others do?

This chapter will show you how psychologists have addressed such questions. The chapter also takes us the next logical step beyond our introduction to the brain to a consideration of how information from the outside world gets into the brain and how the brain makes sense of it.

Although the very private processes that connect us with the outside world extend deep into the brain, we will begin our chapter at the surface—at the sense organs. This is the territory of *sensory psychology.* We will define **sensation** simply as the process by which a stimulated receptor (such as the eyes or ears) creates a pattern of neural messages that represent the stimulus in the brain, giving rise to our initial experience of the stimulus. An important idea to remember is that sensation involves converting stimulation (such as a pinprick, a sound, or a flash of light) into a form the brain can understand (neural signals)—much as a cell phone converts an electronic signal into sound waves you can hear.

Psychologists who study sensation do so primarily from a biological perspective. As you will see, they have found that all our sense organs are, in some very basic ways, much alike. All the sense organs transform physical stimulation (such as light waves or sound waves) into the neural impulses that give us sensations (such as the experience of light or sound). In this chapter, you will also learn about the biological and psychological bases for color, odor, sound, texture, and taste. By the end of our excursion, you will know why tomatoes and limes have different hues, why a pinprick feels different from a caress, and why seeing doesn't always give us an accurate basis for believing.

Happily, under most conditions, our sensory experience is highly reliable. So when you catch sight of a friend, the sensation usually registers clearly, immediately,

sensation   The process by which stimulation of a sensory receptor produces neural impulses that the brain interprets as a sound, a visual image, an odor, a taste, a pain, or other sensory image. Sensation represents the first series of steps in processing of incoming information.

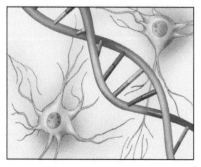

Psychologists study sensation primarily from a biological perspective.

and accurately. Yet, we humans do have our sensory limitations—just as other creatures do. In fact, we lack the acute senses so remarkable in many other species: the vision of hawks, the hearing of bats, the sense of smell of rodents, or the sensitivity to magnetic fields found in migratory birds. So do we humans excel at anything? Yes. Our species has evolved the sensory equipment that enables us to process a wider range and variety of sensory input than any other.

But sensation is only half the story. Our ultimate destination in this chapter lies, beyond mere sensation, in the amazing realm of *perception*. There we will uncover the psychological processes that attach meaning and personal significance to the sensory messages entering our brains. *Perceptual psychology* will help you understand how we assemble a series of tones into a familiar melody or a collage of shapes and shadings into a familiar face. More generally, we will define **perception** as a mental process that elaborates and assigns meaning to the incoming sensory patterns. Thus, *perception creates an interpretation of sensation*. Perception gives answers to such questions as: What do I see—a tomato? Is the sound I hear a church bell or a doorbell? Does the face belong to someone I know? Until quite recently, the study of perception was primarily the province of psychologists using the cognitive perspective. Now that brain scans have opened new "windows" on perceptual processes in the brain, neuroscientists have joined them in the quest to find biological explanations for perception.

As you can see, the boundary of sensation blurs into that of perception. Perception is essentially an interpretation and elaboration of sensation. Seen in these terms, sensation refers just to the initial steps in the processing of a stimulus. It is to these first sensory steps that we now turn our attention.

Human senses do not detect the earth's magnetic fields that migratory birds use for navigation.

perception A process that makes sensory patterns meaningful. It is perception that makes these words meaningful, rather than just a string of visual patterns. To make this happen, perception draws heavily on memory, motivation, emotion, and other psychological processes.

3.1 KEY QUESTION
How Does Stimulation Become Sensation?

A thunderstorm is approaching, and you feel the electric charge in the air make the hair stand up on your neck. Lightning flashes, and a split second later, you hear the thunderclap. It was close by, and you smell the ozone left in the wake of the bolt as it sizzled through the air. Your senses are warning you of danger.

Our senses have other adaptive functions, too. They aid our survival by directing us toward certain stimuli, such as tasty foods, which provide nourishment. Our senses also help us locate mates, seek shelter, and recognize our friends. Incidentally, our senses also give us the opportunity to find pleasure in music, art, athletics, food, and sex.

How do our senses accomplish all this? The complete answer is complex, but it involves one elegantly simple idea that applies across the sensory landscape: Our sensory impressions of the world involve *neural representations* of stimuli—not the actual stimuli themselves. The Core Concept puts it this way:

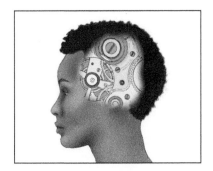

Until recently, psychologists studied perception primarily from a cognitive perspective.

Core Concept 3.1

The brain senses the world indirectly because the sense organs convert stimulation into the language of the nervous system: neural messages.

The brain never receives stimulation directly from the outside world. Its experience of a tomato is not the same as the tomato itself—although we usually assume that the two are identical. Neither can the brain receive light from a sunset, reach out and touch velvet, or inhale the fragrance of a rose. It must always rely on secondhand

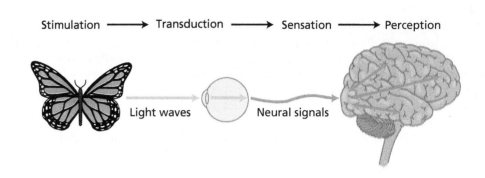

Stimulation ⟶ Transduction ⟶ Sensation ⟶ Perception

Light waves   Neural signals

FIGURE 3.1

Stimulation Becomes Perception

For visual stimulation to become meaningful perception, it must undergo several transformations. First, physical stimulation (light waves from the butterfly) is transduced by the eye, where information about the wavelength and intensity of the light is coded into neural signals. Second, the neural messages travel to the sensory cortex of the brain, where they become sensations of color, brightness, form, and movement. Finally, the process of perception interprets these sensations by making connections with memories, expectations, emotions, and motives in other parts of the brain. Similar processes operate on the information taken in by the other senses.

information from the go-between sensory system, which delivers only a coded neural message, out of which the brain must create its own experience (see Figure 3.1). Just as you cannot receive phone messages without a telephone receiver to convert the electronic energy into sound you can hear, your brain also needs its sensory system to convert the stimuli from the outside world into neural signals that it can comprehend.

To understand more deeply how the world's stimulation becomes the brain's sensation, we need to think about three attributes common to all the senses: *transduction, sensory adaptation,* and *thresholds*. They determine which stimuli will actually become sensation, what the quality and impact of that sensation will be, and whether it grabs our interest. These attributes determine, for example, whether a tomato actually registers in the sensory system strongly enough to enter our awareness, what its color and form appear to be, and how strongly it bids for our attention.

Transduction: Changing Stimulation to Sensation

It may seem incredible that basic sensations, such as the redness and flavor of our tomato—or the colors Jonathan could see before his accident—are entirely creations of the sense organs and brain. But remember that all sensory communication with the brain flows through neurons in the form of neural signals: Neurons cannot transmit light or sound waves or any other external stimulus. Accordingly, none of the light bouncing off the tomato ever actually reaches the brain. In fact, incoming light only travels as far as the back of the eyes. There the information it contains is converted to neural messages. Likewise, the chemicals that signal taste make their way only as far as the tongue, not all the way to the brain.

In all the sense organs, it is the job of the *sensory receptors,* such as the eyes and ears, to convert incoming stimulus information into electrochemical signals—neural activity—the only language the brain understands. As Jonathan I.'s case suggests, sensations, such as "red" or "sweet" or "cold," occur only when the neural signal reaches the cerebral cortex. The whole process seems so immediate and direct that it fools us into assuming that the sensation of redness is characteristic of a tomato or the sensation of cold is a characteristic of ice cream. But they are not! (You can discover how light is not necessary for sensations of light with the demonstration in the *Do It Yourself!* box, "Phosphenes Show That Your Brain Creates Sensations.")

Psychologists use the term **transduction** for the sensory process that converts the information carried by a physical stimulus, such as light or sound waves, into the form of neural messages. Transduction begins when a sensory neuron detects a physical stimulus (such as the sound wave made by a vibrating guitar string). When the appropriate stimulus reaches a sense organ, it activates specialized neurons, called *receptors,* that respond by converting their excitation into a nerve signal. This happens in much the same way that a bar-code reader (which is, after all, merely an electronic receptor) converts the series of lines on a frozen pizza box into an electronic signal that a computer can match with a price.

In our own sensory system, neural impulses carry the codes of sensory events in a form that can be further processed by the brain. To get to its destination, this information-carrying signal travels from the receptor cells along a *sensory pathway*—usually by way

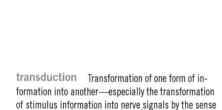

transduction   Transformation of one form of information into another—especially the transformation of stimulus information into nerve signals by the sense organs. As a result of transduction, the brain interprets the incoming light waves from a ripe tomato as red.

Do It Yourself! PHOSPHENES SHOW THAT YOUR BRAIN CREATES SENSATIONS

One of the simplest concepts in perceptual psychology is among the most difficult for most people to grasp: The brain and its sensory systems create the colors, sounds, tastes, odors, textures, and pains that you sense. You can demonstrate this to yourself in the following way.

Close your eyes and press gently with your finger on the inside corner of one eye. On the opposite side of your visual field, you will "see" a pattern caused by the pressure of your finger—not by light. These light sensations are *phosphenes,* visual images caused by fooling your visual system with pressure, which stimulates the optic nerve in much the same way light does. Direct electrical stimulation of the occipital lobe, sometimes done during brain surgery, can have the same

effect. This shows that light waves are not absolutely necessary for the sensation of light. The sensory experience of light, therefore, must be a creation of the brain rather than a property of objects in the external world.

Phosphenes may have some practical value, too. Several laboratories are working on ways to use phosphenes, created by stimulation sent from a TV camera to the occipital cortex to create visual sensations for people who have lost their sight (Wickelgren, 2006). Another promising approach under development involves replacing a section of the retina with an electronic microchip (Boahen, 2005; Liu et al., 2000). We hasten to add, however, that this technology is in its infancy (Cohen, 2002; U.S. Department of Energy Office of Science, 2011).

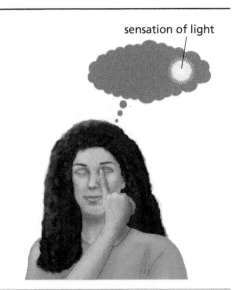

sensation of light

---

of the thalamus and on to specialized sensory processing areas in the brain. From the coded neural impulses arriving from these pathways, the brain then extracts information about the basic qualities of the stimulus, such as its intensity and direction. Please keep in mind, however, that the stimulus itself terminates in the receptor: The only thing that flows into the nervous system is *information* carried by the neural impulse.

Let's return now to the problem we set out at the beginning of the chapter: How could we tell whether the world we "see" in our minds is the same as the external world—and whether we see the world as others do? The idea of transduction gives us part of the answer. Because we do *not* see (or hear, or smell . . .) the external world directly, what we sense is an electrochemical rendition of the world created by the sensory receptors and the brain. To give an analogy: Just as digital photography changes a scene first into electronic signals and then into drops of ink on a piece of paper, so the process of sensation changes the world into a pattern of neural impulses realized in the brain.

Thresholds: The Boundaries of Sensation

What is the weakest stimulus an organism can detect? How dim can a light be and still be visible? How soft can music be and still be heard? These questions refer to the **absolute threshold** for different types of stimulation, which is the minimum amount of physical energy needed to produce a sensory experience. In the laboratory, a psychologist would define this operationally as the intensity at which the stimulus is detected accurately half of the time over many trials. This threshold will also vary from one person to another. So if you point out a faint star to a friend who says he cannot see it, the star's light is above your absolute threshold (you can see it) but below that of your friend (who cannot).

A faint stimulus does not abruptly become detectable as its intensity increases. Because of the fuzzy boundary between detection and nondetection, a person's absolute threshold is not absolute! In fact, it varies continually with our mental alertness and physical condition. Experiments designed to determine thresholds for various types of stimulation were among the earliest studies done by psychologists—who called this line of inquiry *psychophysics.* Table 3.1 shows some typical absolute threshold levels for several familiar natural stimuli.

We can illustrate another kind of threshold with the following imaginary experiment. Suppose you are relaxing by watching television on the one night you don't need

absolute threshold The amount of stimulation necessary for a stimulus to be detected. In practice, this means that the presence or absence of a stimulus is detected correctly half the time over many trials.

CONNECTION CHAPTER 1

An *operational definition* describes a concept in terms of the operations required to produce, observe, or measure it (p. 24).

TABLE 3.1 Approximate Sensory Thresholds of Five Senses

Sense	Detection Threshold
Sight	A candle flame at 30 miles on a clear, dark night
Hearing	The tick of a watch 20 feet away in a quiet room
Smell	One drop of perfume diffused throughout a three-room apartment
Taste	One teaspoon of sugar in 2 gallons of water
Touch	A bee's wing falling on the cheek from 1 centimeter above

difference threshold   The smallest amount by which a stimulus can be changed and the difference be detected half the time.

to study, while a roommate busily prepares for an early morning exam. Your roommate asks you to "turn it down a little" to eliminate the distraction. You feel that you should make some effort to comply but really wish to leave the volume as it is. What is the least amount you can lower the volume to prove your good intentions to your roommate while still keeping the sound clearly audible? Your ability to make judgments like this one depends on your **difference threshold** (also called the *just noticeable difference* or *JND*), the smallest physical difference between two stimuli that a person can reliably detect 50 percent of the time.

If you turn down the volume as little as possible, your roommate might complain, "I don't hear any difference." By this, your roommate probably means that the change in volume does not match his or her difference threshold. By gradually lowering the volume until your roommate says "when," you will be able to find the difference threshold that keeps the peace in your relationship.

Investigation of the difference thresholds across the senses has yielded some interesting insights into how human stimulus detection works. It turns out that *the JND is always large when the stimulus intensity is high and small when the stimulus intensity is low.* Psychologists refer to this idea—that the size of the JND is proportional to the intensity of the stimulus—as **Weber's law.** And what does Weber's law tell us about adjusting the TV volume? If you have the volume turned up very high, you will have to turn it down a lot to make the difference noticeable. On the other hand, if you already have the volume set to a very low level, a small adjustment will probably be noticeable enough for your roommate. The same principle operates across all our senses. Knowing this, you might guess that a weight lifter would notice the difference when small amounts are added to light weights, but it would take a much larger addition to be noticeable with heavy weights.

Weber's law   The concept that the size of a JND is proportional to the intensity of the stimulus; the JND is large when the stimulus intensity is high and small when the stimulus intensity is low.

What does all this mean for our understanding of human sensation? The general principle is this: We are built to detect *changes* in stimulation and *relationships* among stimuli. You can see how this works in the box, *Do It Yourself! An Enlightening Demonstration of Sensory Relationships.*

Do It Yourself!   **AN ENLIGHTENING DEMONSTRATION OF SENSORY RELATIONSHIPS**

In this simple demonstration, you will see how detection of change in brightness is relative, not absolute. Find a three-way lamp equipped with a bulb having equal wattage increments, such as a 50-100-150-watt bulb. (Wattage is closely related to brightness.) Then, in a dark room, switch the light on to 50 watts, which will seem like a *huge* increase in brightness relative to the dark. Next, turn the switch to change

from 50 to 100 watts: This will also seem like a large increase—but not so much as it did when you originally turned on the light in the dark. Finally, switch from 100 to 150 watts. Why does this last 50-watt increase, from 100 to 150 watts, appear only slightly brighter?

Your visual system does not give you an *absolute* sensation of brightness; rather, it provides information about the *relative*

change. That is, it compares the stimulus change to the background stimulation, translating the jump from 100 to 150 watts as a mere 50 percent increase (50 watts added to 100) compared to the earlier 100 percent increase (50 watts added to 50). This illustrates how your visual system computes sensory relationships rather than absolutes—and it is essentially the same with your other senses.

Signal Detection Theory

A deeper understanding of absolute and difference thresholds comes from *signal detection theory* (Green & Swets, 1966). Originally developed for engineering electronic sensors, signal detection theory uses the same concepts to explain both the electronic sensing of stimuli by devices, such as your TV set, and by the human senses, such as vision and hearing.

According to **signal detection theory**, sensation depends on the *characteristics of the stimulus*, the *background stimulation*, and the *detector*. Thus, how well you receive a stimulus, such as a professor's lecture, depends on the presence of competing stimuli in the background—the clacking keys of a nearby laptop or intrusive fantasies about a classmate. It will also depend on the condition of your "detector"—your brain—and, perhaps, whether it has been aroused by a strong cup of coffee or dulled by drugs or lack of sleep.

Signal detection theory also helps us understand why thresholds vary—why, for example, you might notice a certain sound one time and not the next. The classical theory of thresholds ignored the effects of the perceiver's physical condition, judgments, or biases. Thus, in classical psychophysics (as the study of stimulation, thresholds, and sensory experience was called before signal-detection theory came along), if a signal were intense enough to exceed one's absolute threshold, it would be sensed; if below the threshold, it would be missed. In the view of modern signal detection theory, sensation is not a simple yes-or-no experience but a *probability* that the signal will be detected and processed accurately.

So, what does signal detection theory offer psychology that was missing in classical psychophysics? One factor is the variability in human judgment. Another involves the conditions in which the signal occurs. Signal detection theory recognizes that the observer, whose physical and mental status is always in flux, must compare a sensory experience with ever-changing expectations and biological conditions. When something "goes bump in the night" after you have gone to bed, you must decide whether it is the cat, an intruder, or just your imagination. But what you decide it is depends on factors such as the keenness of your hearing and what you expect to hear, as well as other noises in the background. By taking into account the variable conditions that affect detection of a stimulus, signal detection theory provides a more accurate portrayal of sensation than did classical psychophysics.

signal detection theory Explains how we detect "signals," consisting of stimulation affecting our eyes, ears, nose, skin, and other sense organs. Signal detection theory says that sensation is a judgment the sensory system makes about incoming stimulation. Often, it occurs outside of consciousness. In contrast to older theories from psychophysics, signal detection theory takes observer characteristics into account.

Signal detection theory says that the background stimulation would make it less likely for you to hear someone calling your name on a busy downtown street than in a quiet park.

[PSYCHOLOGY MATTERS]

Sensory Adaptation

If you have ever jumped into a cool pool on a hot day, you know that sensation is critically influenced by *change*. In fact, a main role of our stimulus detectors is to announce changes in the external world—a flash of light, a splash of water, a clap of thunder, the approach of a lion, the prick of a pin, or the burst of flavor from a dollop of salsa. Thus, our sense organs are *change detectors*. Their receptors specialize in gathering information about new and changing events.

The great quantity of incoming sensation would quickly overwhelm us, if not for the ability of our sensory systems to adapt. **Sensory adaptation** is the diminishing responsiveness of sensory systems to prolonged stimulation, as when you adapt to the feel of swimming in cool water. In fact, any unchanging stimulation usually shifts into the background of our awareness unless it is quite intense or painful. On the other hand, any change in stimulation (as when a doorbell rings) will immediately draw your attention.

Incidentally, sensory adaptation accounts for the background music often played in stores being so forgettable: It has been deliberately selected and filtered to remove

sensory adaptation Loss of responsiveness in receptor cells after stimulation has remained unchanged for a while, as when a swimmer becomes adapted to the temperature of the water.

any large changes in volume or pitch that might distract attention from the merchandise. (On the other hand, do you see why it's not a good idea to listen to your favorite music while studying?)

Check Your Understanding

✓● Study and Review at MyPsychLab

1. **RECALL:** The sensory pathways carry information from _____ to _____.

2. **RECALL:** Why do sensory psychologists use the standard of *the amount of stimulation that your sensory system can detect about half the time* for identifying the absolute threshold?

3. **APPLICATION:** Which one would involve sensory adaptation?

   a. The odor of food cooking is more noticeable when you enter the house than after you have been there a while.

   b. The flavor of a spicy salsa on your taco seems hot by comparison with the blandness of the sour cream.

   c. You are unaware of a stimulus flashed on the screen at 1/100 of a second.

   d. You prefer the feel of silk to the feel of velvet.

4. **RECALL:** What is the psychological process that adds *meaning* to information obtained by the sensory system?

5. **UNDERSTANDING THE CORE CONCEPT:** Use the concept of *transduction* to explain why the brain never directly senses the outside world.

Answers 1. The sense organs; the brain. **2.** The amount of stimulation that we can detect is not fixed. Rather, it varies depending on ever-changing factors such as our level of arousal, distractions, fatigue, and motivation. **3.** a **4.** Perception **5.** The senses transduce stimulation from the external world into the form of neural impulses, which is the only form of information that the brain can use. Therefore, the brain does not deal directly with light, sound, odors, and other stimuli but only with information that has been changed (transduced) into neural messages.

3.2 **KEY QUESTION**
— How Are the Senses Alike? How Are They Different?

Vision, hearing, smell, taste, touch, pain, body position: In certain ways, all these senses are the same. We have seen that they all transduce stimulus energy into neural impulses. They are all more sensitive to change than to constant stimulation. And they all provide us information about the world—information that has survival value. But how are they *different?* With the exception of pain, each sense taps a different form of stimulus energy, and each sends the information it extracts to a different part of the brain. These contrasting ideas lead us to the Core Concept of this section:

> **Core Concept 3.2**
>
> **The senses all operate in much the same way, but each extracts different information and sends it to its own specialized processing region in the brain.**

As a result, *different sensations occur because different areas of the brain become activated.* Whether you hear a bell or see a bell depends ultimately on which part of the brain receives stimulation. We will explore how this all works by looking at each of the senses in turn. First, we will explore the visual system—the best understood of the senses—to discover how it transduces light waves into visual sensations of color and brightness.

Vision: How the Nervous System Processes Light

Animals with good vision have an enormous biological advantage. This fact has exerted evolutionary pressure to make vision the most complex, best-developed, and important sense for humans and most other highly mobile creatures. Good vision helps us detect desired targets, threats, and changes in our physical environment and to adapt our behavior accordingly. So, how does the visual system accomplish this?

The Anatomy of Visual Sensation You might think of the eye as a sort of "video camera" that the brain uses to make motion pictures of the world (see Figure 3.2). Like a camera, the eye gathers light through a lens, focuses it, and forms an image in the *retina* at the back of the eye. The lens, incidentally, turns the image left to right and upside down. (Because vision is so important, this visual reversal may have influenced the very structure of the brain, which, you will remember, tends to maintain this reversal in its sensory processing regions. Thus, most information from the sense organs crosses over to the opposite side of the brain. Likewise, "maps" of the body in the brain's sensory areas are typically reversed and inverted.)

But while a digital camera simply forms an electronic image, the eye forms an image that gets extensive further processing in the brain. The unique characteristic of the eye—what makes the eye different from other sense organs—lies in its ability to extract the information from light waves, which are simply a form of electromagnetic energy. The eye, then, *transduces* the characteristics of light into neural signals that the brain can process. This transduction happens in the **retina**, the light-sensitive layer of cells at the back of the eye that acts much like the light-sensitive chip in a digital camera.

And, as with a camera, things can go wrong. For example, the lenses of those who are "nearsighted" focus images short of (in front of) the retina; in those who are "farsighted," the focal point extends behind the retina. Either way, images are not sharp without corrective lenses.

The real work in the retina is performed by light-sensitive cells known as **photoreceptors**, which operate much like the tiny pixel receptors in a digital camera. These photoreceptors consist of two different types of specialized neurons—the *rods* and *cones* that absorb light energy and respond by creating neural impulses (see Figure 3.3). But why are there two sorts of photoreceptors?

Because we function sometimes in near darkness and sometimes in bright light, we have evolved two types of processors involving two distinct receptor cell types named for their shapes. The 125 million tiny **rods** "see in the dark"—that is, they detect low

retina   The thin light-sensitive layer at the back of the eyeball. The retina contains millions of photoreceptors and other nerve cells.

photoreceptors   Light-sensitive cells (neurons) in the retina that convert light energy to neural impulses. The photoreceptors are as far as light gets into the visual system.

rods   Photoreceptors in the retina that are especially sensitive to dim light but not to colors. Strange as it may seem, they are rod-shaped.

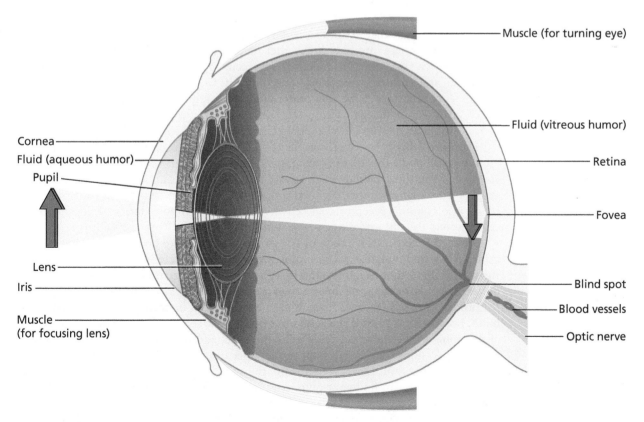

Cornea
Fluid (aqueous humor)
Pupil
Lens
Iris
Muscle (for focusing lens)

Muscle (for turning eye)
Fluid (vitreous humor)
Retina
Fovea
Blind spot
Blood vessels
Optic nerve

FIGURE 3.2
Structures of the Human Eye

FIGURE 3.3

Transduction of Light in the Retina

This simplified diagram shows the pathways that connect three layers of nerve cells in the retina. Incoming light passes through the ganglion cells and bipolar cells first before striking the photoreceptors at the back of the eyeball. Once stimulated, the rods and cones then transmit information to the bipolar cells (note that one bipolar cell combines information from several receptor cells). The bipolar cells then transmit neural impulses to the ganglion cells. Impulses travel from the ganglia to the brain via axons that make up the optic nerve.

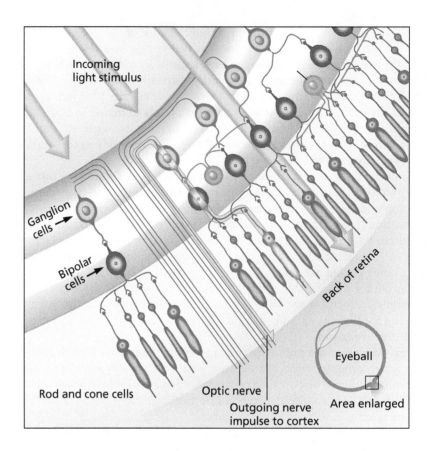

cones   Photoreceptors in the retina that are especially sensitive to colors but not to dim light. You may have guessed that the cones are cone-shaped.

fovea   The tiny area of sharpest vision in the retina.

optic nerve   The bundle of neurons that carries visual information from the retina to the brain.

blind spot   The point where the optic nerve exits the eye and where there are no photoreceptors. Any stimulus that falls on this area cannot be seen.

intensities of light at night, though they cannot make the fine distinctions that give rise to our sensations of color. Rod cells enable you to find a seat in a darkened movie theater.

Making the fine distinctions necessary for color vision is the job of the seven million **cones** that come into play in brighter light. Each cone is specialized to detect the light waves we sense either as blue, red, or green. In good light, then, we can use these cones to distinguish ripe tomatoes (sensed as red) from unripe ones (sensed as green). The cones concentrate in the very center of the retina, in a small region called the **fovea,** which gives us our sharpest vision. With movements of our eyeballs, we use the fovea to scan whatever interests us visually—the features of a face or, perhaps, a flower.

There are other types of cells in the retina that do not respond directly to light. The *bipolar cells* handle the job of collecting impulses from many photoreceptors (rods and cones) and shuttling them on to the *ganglion cells,* much as an airline hub collects passengers from many regional airports and shuttles them on to other destinations. The retina also contains receptor cells sensitive to edges and boundaries of objects; other cells respond to light and shadow and motion (Werblin & Roska, 2007).

Bundled together, the axons of the ganglion cells make up the **optic nerve,** which transports visual information from the eye to the brain (refer to Figures 3.2 and 3.3). Again, it is important to understand that the optic nerve carries no light—only patterns of nerve impulses conveying *information* derived from the incoming light.

Just as strangely, there is a small area of the retina in each eye where everyone is blind, because that part of the retina has no photoreceptors. This **blind spot** is located at the point where the optic nerve exits each eye, and the result is a gap in the visual field. You do not experience blindness there because what one eye misses is registered by the other eye, and the brain "fills in" the spot with information that matches the background. You can find your own blind spot by following the instructions in the *Do It Yourself!* box.

We should clarify that the visual impairment we call *blindness* can have many causes, which are usually unrelated to the blind spot. Blindness can result, for example, from damage to the retina, cataracts that make the lens opaque, damage to the optic nerve, or from damage to the visual processing areas in the brain.

Do It Yourself!   FIND YOUR BLIND SPOT

The "blind spot" occurs at the place on the retina where the neurons from the retina bunch together to exit the eyeball and form the optic nerve. There are no light-sensitive cells at this point on the retina. Consequently, you are "blind" in this small region of your visual field. The following demonstrations will help you determine where this blind spot occurs in your visual field.

Demonstration 1

Hold the text at arm's length, close your right eye, and fix your left eye on the "bank" figure. Keep your right eye closed and bring the book slowly closer. When it is about 10 to 12 inches away and the dollar sign is in your blind spot, the dollar sign will disappear—but you will not see a

"hole" in your visual field. Instead, your visual system "fills in" the missing area with information from the white background. You have "lost" your money!

Demonstration 2

To convince yourself that the brain fills in the missing part of the visual field with appropriate background, close your right eye

again and focus on the cross in the lower part of the figure. Once again, keeping the right eye closed, bring the book closer to you as you focus your left eye on the cross. This time, the gap in the line will disappear and will be filled in with a continuation of the line on either side. This shows that what you see in your blind spot may not really exist!

Bank

Processing Visual Sensation in the Brain We *look* with our eyes, but we *see* with the brain. That is, a special brain area called the *visual cortex* creates visual images from the information imported from the eyes through the optic nerve (see Figure 3.4). There in the visual cortex, the brain begins working its magic by transforming the incoming neural impulses into visual sensations of color, form, boundary, and

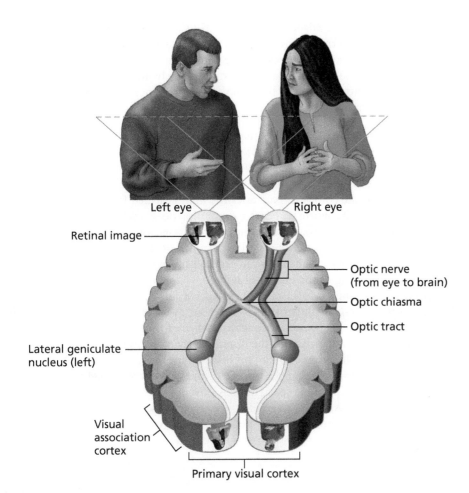

Left eye   Right eye
Retinal image
Optic nerve (from eye to brain)
Optic chiasma
Optic tract
Lateral geniculate nucleus (left)
Visual association cortex
Primary visual cortex

FIGURE 3.4

How Visual Stimulation Goes from the Eyes to the Brain

Light from objects in the visual field projects images on the retinas of the eyes. Please note two important things. First, the lens of the eye reverses the image on the retina—so the image of the man falls on the right side of the retina, and the image of the woman falls on the left. Second, the visual system splits the retinal image coming from each eye so that part of the image coming from each eye crosses over to the opposite side of the brain. (Note how branches of the optic pathway cross at the *optic chiasma*.) As a result, objects appearing in the *left* part of the visual field *of both eyes* (the man, in this diagram) are sent to the *right* hemisphere's visual cortex for processing, while objects in the *right* side of the visual field *of both eyes* (the woman, in this diagram) are sent to the *left* visual cortex. In general, the right hemisphere "sees" the left visual field, while the left hemisphere "sees" the right visual field.

Source: Frisby, J. P. (1980). *Seeing: Illusion, brain and mind*. New York: Oxford University Press. Copyright © 1979. Reprinted by permission of J. P. Frisby.

TABLE 3.2 Visual Stimulation Becomes Sensation

Color and brightness are the psychological counterparts of the wavelength and intensity of a light wave. Wavelength and intensity are physical characteristics of light waves, while color and brightness are psychological characteristics that exist only in the brain.

Physical Stimulation	Psychological Sensation
Wavelength	Color
Intensity (amplitude)	Brightness

CONNECTION CHAPTER 2

Note that part of the visual pathway of each eye crosses over to the cortex on the opposite side of the brain. This produced some of the bizarre responses that we saw in the tests of *split-brain* patients (p. 75).

brightness   A psychological sensation caused by the intensity (amplitude) of light waves.

color   Also called *hue*. Color is not a property of things in the external world. Rather, it is a *psychological sensation* created in the brain from information obtained by the eyes from the wavelengths of visible light.

electromagnetic spectrum   The entire range of electromagnetic energy, including radio waves, X-rays, microwaves, and visible light.

visible spectrum   The tiny part of the electromagnetic spectrum to which our eyes are sensitive. The visible spectrum of other creatures may be slightly different from our own.

movement. Amazingly, the visual cortex also manages to take the two-dimensional patterns from each eye and assemble them into our three-dimensional world of depth (Barinaga, 1998; Dobbins et al., 1998). With further processing, the cortex ultimately combines these visual sensations with memories, motives, emotions, and sensations of body position and touch to create a representation of the visual world that fits our current concerns and interests (de Gelder, 2000; Vuilleumier & Huang, 2009). These associations explain why, for example, you feel so strongly attracted by displays of appetizing foods if you go grocery shopping when you are hungry.

Let's return for a moment to the chapter problem and to the question, Do we "see" the world as others do? As far as sensation is concerned, we will find that the answer is a qualified "yes." That is, different people have essentially the same sensory apparatus (with the exceptions of a few individuals who, like Jonathan, cannot distinguish colors or who have other sensory deficits). Therefore, it is reasonable to assume that most people *sense* colors, sounds, textures, odors, and tastes in much the same way—although, as we will see, they do not necessarily *perceive* them in the same way. To see what we mean, let's start with the visual sensation of *brightness*.

How the Visual System Creates Brightness   Sensations of **brightness** come from the intensity or *amplitude* of light, determined by how much light reaches the retina (see Table 3.2). Bright light, as from the sun, involves a more intense light wave, which creates much neural activity in the retina, while relatively dim light, as from the moon, produces relatively little retinal activity. Ultimately, the brain senses brightness by the volume of neural activity it receives from the eyes.

How the Visual System Creates Color   You may have been surprised to learn that a flower or a ripe tomato, itself, has no **color**, or *hue*. Physical objects seen in bright light seem to have the marvelous property of being awash with color; but, as we have noted, the red tomatoes, yellow flowers, green trees, blue oceans, and multihued rainbows are, in themselves, actually quite colorless. Nor does the light reflected from these objects have color. Despite the way the world appears to us, color does not exist outside the brain because color is a *sensation* that the brain creates based on the wavelength of light striking our eyes. Thus, color exists only in the mind of the viewer—a *psychological* property of our sensory experience. To understand more fully how this happens, you must first know something of the nature of light.

The eyes detect the special form of energy that we call *visible light*. Physicists tell us that this light is pure energy—fundamentally the same as radio waves, microwaves, infrared light, ultraviolet light, X-rays, and cosmic rays. All are forms of *electromagnetic energy*. These waves differ in their wavelength (the distance they travel in making one wave cycle) as they vibrate in space, like ripples on a pond (see Figure 3.5). The light we see occupies but a tiny segment somewhere near the middle of the vast **electromagnetic spectrum**. Our only access to this electromagnetic spectrum lies through a small visual "window" called the **visible spectrum**. Because we have no biological receptors sensitive to the other portions of the electromagnetic spectrum, we must detect these waves through devices, such as radios and TVs, that convert the energy into signals we can use.

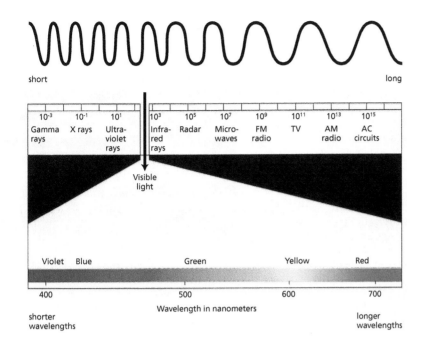

FIGURE 3.5

The Electromagnetic Spectrum

The only difference between visible light and other forms of electromagnetic energy is *wavelength*. The receptors in our eyes are sensitive to only a tiny portion of the electromagnetic spectrum.

Source: Sekuler, R., & Blake, R. (1994). *Perception*, 3rd ed. New York: McGraw-Hill. Copyright © 1994. Reprinted by permission of McGraw-Hill.

Within the narrow visible spectrum, light waves of different wavelengths give rise to our sensations of different colors. Longer waves make us see a tomato as red, and medium-length waves give rise to the sensations of yellow and green we see in lemons and limes. The shorter waves from a clear sky stimulate sensations of blue. Thus, the eye extracts information from the wavelength of light, and the brain uses that information to construct the sensations we see as colors (see Table 3.2).

Remarkably, our visual experiences of color, form, position, and depth are based on processing the stream of visual sensory information in different parts of the cortex. Colors themselves are realized in a specialized area, where humans are capable of discriminating among about five million different hues. It was damage in this part of the cortex that shut down Jonathan's ability to see colors. Other nearby cortical areas take responsibility for processing information about boundaries, shapes, and movements.

trichromatic theory The idea that colors are sensed by three different types of cones sensitive to light in the red, blue, and green wavelengths. The trichromatic (three-color) theory explains the earliest stage of color sensation. In honor of its originators, this is sometimes called the Young-Helmholtz theory.

opponent-process theory The idea that cells in the visual system process colors in complementary pairs, such as red or green or as yellow or blue. The opponent-process theory explains color sensation from the bipolar cells onward in the visual system.

afterimages Sensations that linger after the stimulus is removed. Most visual afterimages are *negative afterimages*, which appear in reversed colors.

Two Ways of Sensing Colors Even though color is realized in the cortex, color processing begins in the retina. There, three different types of cones sense different parts of the visible spectrum—light waves that we sense as red, green, and blue. This three-receptor explanation for color vision is known as the **trichromatic theory**, and for a time it was considered to account for color vision completely. We now know that the trichromatic theory best explains the initial stages of color vision in the cone cells.

Another explanation, called the **opponent-process theory**, better explains negative **afterimages** (see the *Do It Yourself!* box), phenomena that involve *opponent*, or complementary, colors. According to the opponent-process theory, the visual system processes colors, from the bipolar cells onward, in complementary pairs: red-green or yellow-blue. Thus, the sensation of a certain color, such as red, inhibits, or interferes with, the sensation of its complement, green. Taken together, the two theories explain two different aspects of color vision involving the retina and visual pathways. While all that may sound complicated, here is the take-home message: *The trichromatic theory explains color processing in the cones of the retina, while the opponent-process theory explains what happens in the bipolar cells and beyond.*

Color Blindness Not everyone sees colors in the same way, because some people are born with a deficiency in distinguishing colors. The incidence varies among

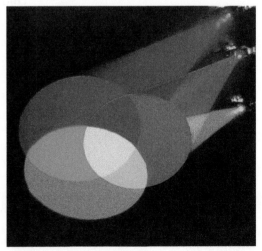

The combination of any two primary colors of light yields the complement of a third color. The combination of all three wavelengths produces white light. (The mixture of pigments, as in print, works differently, because pigments are made to absorb some wavelengths of light falling on them.)

Do It Yourself!   THE AMAZING AFTERIMAGE

After you stare at a colored object for a while, ganglion cells in your retina will become fatigued, causing an interesting visual effect. When you shift your gaze to a blank, white surface, you can "see" the object in complementary colors—as a visual afterimage. The "phantom flag" demonstration will show you how this works.

Stare at the dot in the center of the green, black, and orange flag for at least 30 seconds. Take care to hold your eyes steady and not to let them scan over the image during this time. Then quickly shift your gaze to the center of a sheet of white paper or to a light-colored blank wall. What do you see? Have your friends try this, too. Do they see the same afterimage?

(The effect may not be the same for people who are color blind.)

Afterimages may be negative or positive. Positive afterimages are caused by a continuation of the receptor and neural processes following stimulation. They are brief. An example of positive afterimages occurs when you see the trail of a sparkler twirled by a Fourth of July reveler. Negative afterimages are the opposite or the reverse of the original experience, as in the flag example. They last longer. Negative afterimages operate according to the *opponent-process theory* of color vision, which involves ganglion cells in the retina and the optic

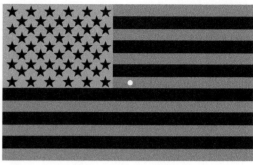

nerve. Apparently, in a negative afterimage, the fatigue in these cells produces sensations of a complementary color when they are exposed to white light.

---

color blindness   Typically a genetic disorder (although sometimes the result of trauma, as in the case of Jonathan) that prevents an individual from discriminating certain colors. The most common form is red–green color blindness.

racial groups (highest in Whites and lowest in Blacks). Overall about 8 percent of males in the United States are affected. Women rarely have the condition.

At the extreme, complete **color blindness** is the total inability to distinguish colors. More commonly, people merely have a color weakness that causes minor problems in distinguishing colors, especially under low-light conditions. People with one form of color weakness can't distinguish pale colors, such as pink or tan. Most color weakness or blindness, however, involves a problem in distinguishing red from green, especially at weak saturations. Those who confuse yellows and blues are rare, about one or two people per thousand. Rarest of all are those who see no color at all but see only variations in brightness. In fact, only about 500 cases of this total color blindness have ever been reported—including Jonathan I., whom we met at the beginning of this chapter. To find out whether you have a deficiency in color vision, look at Figure 3.6. If you see the number 29 in the dot pattern, your color vision is probably normal. If you see something else, you are probably at least partially color blind.

Hearing: If a Tree Falls in the Forest . . .

Imagine how your world would change if your ability to hear were suddenly diminished. You would quickly realize that hearing, like vision, provides you with the ability to locate objects in space, such as the source of a voice calling your name. In fact, hearing may be even more important than vision in orienting us toward distant events. We often hear things, such as footsteps coming up behind us, before we see the source of the sounds. Hearing may also tell us of events that we cannot see, including speech, music, or an approaching car.

But there is more to hearing than its function. Accordingly, we will look a little deeper to learn *how* we hear. In the next few pages, we will review what sensory psychologists have discovered about how sound waves are produced, how they are sensed, and how these sensations of sound are interpreted.

The Physics of Sound: How Sound Waves Are Produced   If Hollywood gave us an honest portrayal of exploding spaceships or planets, there would be absolutely no sound! In space, there is no air or other medium to carry sound waves, so if you were a witness to an exploding star, the experience would be eerily silent. On Earth, the energy of exploding objects, such as firecrackers, transfers to the surrounding medium—usually

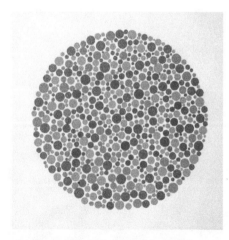

FIGURE 3.6

The Ishihara Color Blindness Test

Someone who cannot discriminate between red and green hues will not be able to identify the number hidden in the figure. What do you see? If you see the number 29 in the dot pattern, your color vision is probably normal.

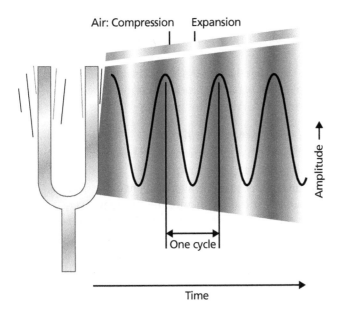

FIGURE 3.7

Sound Waves

Sound waves produced by the vibration of a tuning fork create waves of compressed and expanded air. The pitch that we hear depends on the *frequency* of the wave (the number of cycles per second). High pitches are the result of high-frequency waves. The *amplitude* or strength of a sound wave depends on how strongly the air is affected by the vibrations. In this diagram, amplitude is represented by the height of the graph.

air—in the form of sound waves. Essentially the same thing happens with rapidly vibrating objects, such as guitar strings, bells, and vocal cords, as the vibrations push the molecules of air back and forth. The resulting changes in pressure spread outward in the form of sound waves that can travel 1,100 feet per second.

The purest tones are made by a tuning fork (see Figure 3.7). When struck with a mallet, a tuning fork produces an extremely clean sound wave that has only two characteristics, *frequency* and *amplitude*. These are the two physical properties of any sound wave that determine how it will be sensed by the brain. **Frequency** refers to the number of vibrations or cycles the wave completes in a given amount of time, which in turn determines the highness or lowness of a sound (the *pitch*). Frequency is usually expressed in *cycles per second (cps)* or *hertz (Hz)*. **Amplitude** measures the physical strength of the sound wave (shown in graphs as the height of the wave); it is defined in units of sound pressure or energy. When you turn down the volume on your music system, you are decreasing the amplitude of the sound waves emerging from the speakers or ear buds.

frequency The number of cycles completed by a wave in a second.

amplitude The physical strength of a wave. This is shown on graphs as the height of the wave.

Sensing Sounds: How We Hear Sound Waves Much like vision, the psychological sensation of sound requires that waves be transduced into neural impulses and sent to the brain. This happens in four steps:

1. **Airborne sound waves are relayed to the inner ear.** In this initial transformation, vibrating waves of air enter the outer ear (also called the *pinna*) and move through the ear canal to the *eardrum,* or **tympanic membrane** (see Figure 3.8). This tightly stretched sheet of tissue transmits the vibrations to three tiny bones in the

tympanic membrane The eardrum.

FIGURE 3.8

Structures of the Human Ear

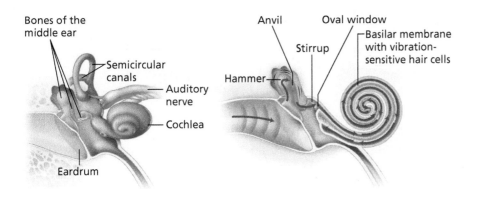

Sound waves are channeled by the outer ear *(pinna)* through the external canal, causing the tympanic membrane to vibrate. The vibration activates the tiny bones in the middle ear (*hammer, anvil,* and *stirrup*). These mechanical vibrations pass from the oval window to the cochlea, where they set an internal fluid in motion. The fluid movement stimulates tiny hair cells along the basilar membrane, inside the cochlea, to transmit neural impulses from the ear to the brain along the auditory nerve.

cochlea The primary organ of hearing; a coiled tube in the inner ear, where sound waves are transduced into nerve messages.

middle ear: the *hammer, anvil,* and *stirrup,* named for their shapes. These bones pass the vibrations on to the primary organ of hearing, the **cochlea**, located in the inner ear.

2. **The cochlea focuses the vibrations on the basilar membrane.** Here in the cochlea, the formerly airborne sound wave becomes "seaborne," because the coiled tube of the cochlea is filled with fluid. As the bony stirrup vibrates against the *oval window* at the base of the cochlea, the vibrations set the fluid into wave motion, much as a submarine sends a sonar "ping" through the water. As the fluid wave spreads through the cochlea, it causes vibration in the **basilar membrane**, a thin strip of hairy tissue running through the cochlea.

basilar membrane A thin strip of tissue sensitive to vibrations in the cochlea. The basilar membrane contains hair cells connected to neurons. When a sound wave causes the hair cells to vibrate, the associated neurons become excited. As a result, the sound waves are converted (transduced) into nerve activity.

3. **The basilar membrane converts the vibrations into neural messages.** The swaying of tiny hair cells on the vibrating basilar membrane stimulates sensory nerve endings connected to the hair cells. The excited neurons, then, transform the mechanical vibrations of the basilar membrane into neural activity.

4. **Finally, the neural messages travel to the auditory cortex in the brain.** Neural signals leave the cochlea in a bundle of neurons called the *auditory nerve*. The neurons from the two ears meet in the brain stem, which passes the auditory information to both sides of the brain. Ultimately, the signals arrive in the *auditory cortex* for higher-order processing.

CONNECTION CHAPTER 2

◄ The brain's primary auditory cortex lies in the *temporal lobes* (p. 72).

If the auditory system seems complicated, you might think of it as a sensory "relay team." Sound waves are first funneled in by the outer ear, then handed off from the eardrum to bones in the middle ear. These bones then hand off their mechanical vibrations to the cochlea and basilar membrane in the inner ear, where they finally become neural signals, which are, in turn, passed along to the brain. This series of steps transforms commonplace vibrations into experiences as exquisite and varied as music, doorbells, whispers, and shouts—and psychology lectures.

Psychological Qualities of Sound: How We Distinguish One Sound from Another No matter where they come from, sound waves—like light waves—have only two *physical* characteristics: *frequency* and *amplitude*. In the following discussion, we will show you how the brain converts these two characteristics into three *psychological sensations: pitch, loudness,* and *timbre.*

Sensations of Pitch A sound wave's *frequency* determines the highness or lowness of a sound—a quality known as **pitch**. High frequencies produce high-pitched sounds, and low frequencies produce low-pitched sounds, as you see in Table 3.3. As with light, our sensitivity to sound spans only a limited range of the sound waves that occur in nature. The range of human auditory sensitivity extends from frequencies as low as about 20 cps (the lowest range of a subwoofer in a good sound system) to frequencies as high

pitch A sensory characteristic of sound produced by the *frequency* of the sound wave.

TABLE 3.3 Auditory Stimulation Becomes Sensation

Pitch and loudness are the psychological counterparts of the frequency and amplitude (intensity) of a sound wave. Frequency and amplitude are characteristics of the physical sound wave, while sensations of pitch and loudness exist only in the brain. In addition, sound waves can be complex combinations of simpler waves. Psychologically, we experience this complexity as *timbre.* Compare this table with Table 3.2 for vision.

Physical stimulation	Waveform	Psychological sensation
Amplitude (intensity)	Loud Soft	Loudness
Frequency (wavelength)	Low High	Pitch
Complexity	Pure Complex	Timbre

would be hopelessly uncoordinated. (You have probably had just this experience when you tried to walk on a leg that had "gone to sleep.") The physical mechanisms that keep track of body position, movement, and balance actually consist of two different systems, the *vestibular sense* and the *kinesthetic sense.*

The **vestibular sense** is the body position sense that orients us with respect to gravity. It tells us the posture of our bodies—whether straight, leaning, reclining, or upside down. The vestibular sense also tells us when we are moving or how our motion is changing. The receptors for this information are tiny hairs (much like those we found in the basilar membrane) in the *semicircular canals* of the inner ear (refer to Figure 3.8). These hairs respond to our movements by detecting corresponding movements in the fluid of the semicircular canals. Disorders of this sense can cause extreme dizziness and disorientation.

The **kinesthetic sense**, the other sense of body position and movement, keeps track of body parts relative to each other. Your kinesthetic sense makes you aware of crossing your legs, for example, and tells you which hand is closer to your cell phone when it rings. Kinesthesis provides constant sensory feedback about what the muscles in your body are doing during motor activities, such as whether to continue reaching for your cup of coffee or to stop before you knock it over (Turvey, 1996).

Receptors for kinesthesis reside in the joints, muscles, and tendons. These receptors, as well as those for the vestibular sense, connect to processing regions in the brain's parietal lobes—which help us make a sensory "map" of the spatial relationship among objects and events. This processing usually happens automatically and effortlessly, outside of conscious awareness, except when we are deliberately learning the movements for a new physical skill, such as swinging a golf club or playing a musical instrument.

Smell Smell serves a protective function by sensing the odor of possibly dangerous food or, for some animals, the scent of a predator. We humans seem to use the sense of smell primarily in conjunction with taste to locate and identify calorie-dense foods, avoid tainted foods, and, it seems, to identify potential mates—a fact capitalized on by the perfume and cologne industry (Benson, 2002; Martins et al., 2005; Miller & Maner, 2010).

Many animals take the sense of smell a step farther by exploiting it for communication. For example, insects such as ants and termites and vertebrates such as dogs and cats communicate with each other by secreting and detecting odorous signals called **pheromones**—especially to signal not only sexual receptivity but also danger, territorial boundaries, food sources, and family members. It appears that the human use of the sense of smell is much more limited.

The Biology of Olfaction Biologically, the sense of smell, or **olfaction**, begins with chemical events in the nose. There, odors (in the form of airborne chemical molecules) interact with receptor proteins associated with specialized nerve cells (Axel, 1995; Turin, 2006). These cells, incidentally, are the body's only nerve cells that come in direct contact with the outside environment.

Odor molecules can be complex and varied. For example, freshly brewed coffee owes its aroma to as many as 600 volatile compounds (Wilson & Stevenson, 2006). More broadly, scientists have cataloged at least 1,500 different odor-producing molecules (Zimmer, 2010). Exactly how the nose makes sense of this cacophony of odors is not completely understood, but we do know that nasal receptors sense the shape of odor molecules (Foley & Matlin, 2010).

We also know that the nose's receptor cells transduce information about the stimulus and convey it to the brain's *olfactory bulbs,* located on the underside of the brain just below the frontal lobes (see Figure 3.11). There, our sensations of smell are initially processed and then passed on to many other parts of the brain (Mori et al., 1999). Unlike all the other senses, smell signals are *not* relayed through the thalamus, suggesting that smell has very ancient evolutionary roots.

vestibular sense The sense of body orientation with respect to gravity. The vestibular sense is closely associated with the inner ear and, in fact, is carried to the brain on a branch of the auditory nerve.

kinesthetic sense The sense of body position and movement of body parts relative to each other (also called *kinesthesis*)

Gymnasts and dancers rely on their vestibular and kinesthetic senses to give them information about the position and movement of their bodies.

pheromones Chemical signals released by organisms to communicate with other members of their species. Pheromones are often used by animals as sexual attractants. It is unclear whether or not humans employ pheromones.

olfaction The sense of smell.

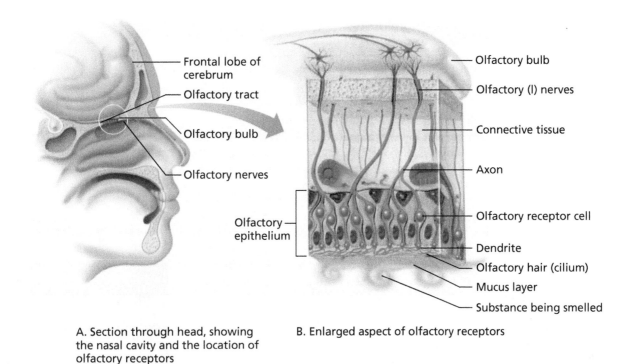

A. Section through head, showing the nasal cavity and the location of olfactory receptors

B. Enlarged aspect of olfactory receptors

FIGURE 3.11

Receptors for Smell

Source: Zimbardo, P. G., & Gerrig, R. J. (1999). *Psychology and life,* 15th ed. Boston, MA: Allyn and Bacon. © 1999 by Pearson Education. Reprinted by permission of the publisher.

The Psychology of Smell   Olfaction has an intimate connection with both emotion and memory. This may explain why the olfactory bulbs lie very close to, and communicate directly with, structures in the limbic system and temporal lobes that are associated with emotion and memory. Therefore, it is not surprising that both psychologists and writers have noticed that certain smells can evoke emotion-laden memories, sometimes of otherwise-forgotten events (Dingfelder, 2004a). If you think about it for a moment, you can probably recall a vivid memory "image" of the aroma associated with a favorite food—perhaps fresh bread or a spicy dish—from your childhood.

Taste   Like smell, taste is a sense based on chemistry. But the similarity doesn't end there: The senses of taste and smell have a close and cooperative working relationship—so many of the subtle distinctions you may think of as flavors really come from odors. (Much of the "taste" of an onion is odor, not flavor. And when you have a cold, you'll notice that food seems tasteless because your nasal passages are blocked.)

gustation   The sense of taste, from the same word root as "gusto;" also called the *gustatory sense.*

Most people know that our sense of taste, or **gustation**, involves four primary qualities or dimensions: sweet, sour, bitter, and salty. Less well known, however, is a fifth taste called *umami* (Chaudhari et al., 2000). Umami is the savory flavor found in protein-rich foods, such as meat, seafood, and cheese. It is also associated with monosodium glutamate (MSG), often used in Asian cuisine.

The taste receptor cells, located in the *taste buds* on the top and side of the tongue, sample flavors from food and drink as they pass by on the way to the stomach. These taste receptors cluster in small mucous-membrane projections called *papillae,* shown in Figure 3.12. Each is especially sensitive to molecules of a particular shape.

Moving beyond the receptors on the tongue, a specialized nerve "hotline" carries nothing but taste messages to specialized regions of the cortex. There, tastes are realized in the parietal lobe's somatosensory area. Conveniently, this region lies next to the patch of cortex that receives touch stimulation from the face (Gadsby, 2000).

Developmental Changes in Taste   Infants have heightened taste sensitivity, which is why babies universally cringe at the bitter taste of lemon. This supersensitivity, however, decreases with age. As a result, many elderly people complain that food has lost its

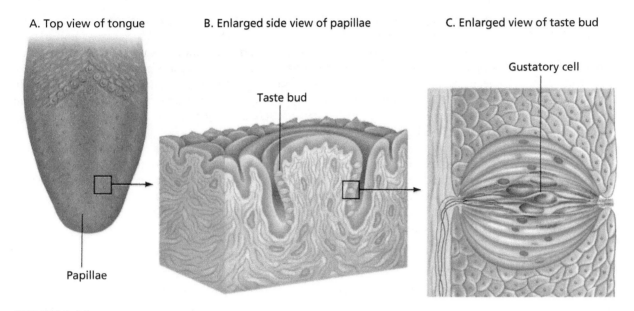

A. Top view of tongue   B. Enlarged side view of papillae   C. Enlarged view of taste bud

Gustatory cell

Taste bud

Papillae

FIGURE 3.12

Receptors for Taste

(A) Taste buds are clustered in papillae on the upper side of the tongue; **(B)** an enlarged view with individual papillae and taste buds visible; **(C)** one of the taste buds enlarged.

taste—which really means that they have lost much of their sensory ability to detect differences in the taste and smell of food. Compounding this effect, taste receptors can be easily damaged by alcohol, smoke, acids, or hot foods. Fortunately, we frequently replace our gustatory receptors—as we do our smell receptors. Because of this constant renewal, the taste system boasts the most resistance to permanent damage of all our senses, and a total loss of taste is extremely rare (Bartoshuk, 1990).

Supertasters   Individuals of any age vary in their sensitivity to taste sensations, a function of the density of papillae on the tongue (Bartoshuk, 2000, 2009; Bartoshuk et al., 1994). Those with the most taste buds are *supertasters* who live in a "neon" taste world relative to the rest of us—which accounts for their distaste for certain foods, such as broccoli or "diet" drinks, in which they detect a disturbingly bitter flavor (Duenwald, 2005). Is there any advantage to being a supertaster? Taste expert Linda Bartoshuk (1993) speculates that, because most poisons are bitter, supertasters have a survival advantage.

Such differences also speak to the problem with which we began the chapter—in particular, the question of whether different people sense the world in the same way. Bartoshuk's research suggests that, to the extent that the sense receptors exhibit some variation from one person to another, so does our sensory experience of the world. This variability is not so bizarre as to make one person's sensation of sweet the same as another person's sensation of sour. Rather, the variations observed involve simply the *intensity* of taste sensations, such as the bitter detected by supertasters. One big unknown, according to Bartoshuk, is whether people differ in their sensitivities to different taste sensations: for example, whether a person could be a supertaster for bitter while having only normal sensations for sweet or salt (personal communication, January 4, 2011).

On the other hand, taste researchers have detected differences in taste *preferences* between supertasters and those with normal taste sensations. In particular, supertasters more often report disliking foods that they find too sweet or too fatty. Although the significance of this remains to be determined, researchers have observed that supertasters, on the average, weigh less than their nonsupertasting counterparts (Bartoshuk, 2000).

The Skin Senses Consider the skin's remarkable versatility: It protects us against surface injury, holds in body fluids, and helps regulate body temperature. The skin also contains nerve endings that, when stimulated, produce sensations of touch, pain,

skin senses   Sensory systems for processing touch, warmth, cold, texture, and pain.

warmth, and cold. Like several other senses, these **skin senses** are connected to the somatosensory cortex located in the brain's parietal lobes.

The skin's sensitivity to stimulation varies tremendously over the body, depending in part on the number of receptors in each area. For example, we are ten times more accurate in sensing stimulation on our fingertips than stimulation on our backs. In general, our sensitivity is greatest where we need it most—on our face, tongue, and hands. Precise sensory feedback from these parts of the body permits effective eating, speaking, and grasping.

One important aspect of skin sensitivity—touch—plays a central role in human relationships. Through touch, we communicate our desire to give or receive comfort, support, and love (Fisher, 1992; Harlow, 1965). Touch also serves as a primary stimulus for sexual arousal in humans. And it is essential for healthy mental and physical development; the lack of touch stimulation can stunt mental and motor development (Anand & Scalzo, 2000).

Synesthesia: Sensations across the Senses

synesthesia   The mixing of sensations across sensory modalities, as in tasting shapes or seeing colors associated with numbers.

A small minority of otherwise "normal" people have a condition called **synesthesia**, which allows them to sense their worlds across sensory domains. Some actually taste shapes—so that pears may taste "round" and grapefruit "pointy" (Cytowic, 1993). Other synesthetes associate days of the week with colors—so that Wednesday may be "green" and Thursday may be "red." Their defining characteristic involves sensory experience that links one sense with another.

Through clever experiments, V. S. Ramachandran and his colleagues have shown that the cross-sensory sensations reported in synesthesia are real, not just metaphors (Ramachandran & Hubbard, 2001). You can take one of their tests in the accompanying *Do It Yourself!* box. Research also shows that this ability runs in families, so it probably has a genetic component.

What causes synesthesia? Apparently it can involve communication between different brain areas that process different sensations—often regions that lie close to each other in the cortex. Brain imaging studies implicate a cortical area called the *TPO*, lying at the junction of the *t*emporal, *p*arietal, and *o*ccipital lobes (Ramachandran & Hubbard, 2003). This region simultaneously processes information coming from many pathways. We all have some neural connections among these areas, theorizes Ramachandran, but synesthetes seem to have more than most.

The condition occurs slightly more often in highly creative people, Ramachandran notes. And it may account for the "auras" purportedly seen around people by some mystics (Holden, 2004). But perhaps we all have some cross-sensory abilities in us, which may be why we resonate with Shakespeare's famous metaphor in *Romeo and Juliet*, "It is the east, and Juliet is the sun." We know that he was not speaking literally, of course. Rather we understand that, for Romeo—and so for us—Juliet is linked, across our senses, with light, warmth, and sensory pleasure (Ramachandran & Hirstein, 1999).

Do It Yourself! A SYNESTHESIA TEST

Most people will not have any trouble seeing the 5 while staring at the cross (left), although the 5 becomes indistinct when surrounded by other numbers (right). If you are a synesthete who associates colors with numbers, however, you may be able to identify the 5 in the figure on the right because it appears as a blotch of the color associated with that number. (Adapted from Ramachandran & Hubbard, 2003.)

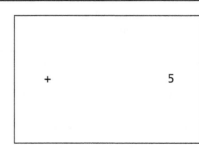
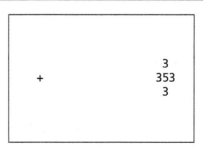

[PSYCHOLOGY MATTERS]

The Sense and Experience of Pain

If you have severe pain, nothing else matters. A wound or a toothache can dominate all other sensations. And if you are among the one-third of Americans who suffer from persistent or recurring pain, the experience can be debilitating and can sometimes even lead to suicide. Yet, pain is also part of your body's adaptive mechanism that makes you respond to conditions that threaten damage to your body.

Unlike other sensations, pain can arise from intense stimulation of various kinds, such as a very loud sound, heavy pressure, a pinprick, or an extremely bright light. But pain is not merely the result of stimulation. It is also affected by our moods and expectations, as you know if you were ever anxious about going to the dentist (Koyama et al., 2005).

Pain Receptors

In the skin, several types of specialized nerve cells, called *nociceptors,* sense painful stimuli and send their unpleasant messages to the central nervous system. Some nociceptors are most sensitive to heat, while others respond mainly to pressure, chemical trauma, or other tissue injury (Foley & Matlin, 2010). There are even specialized nociceptors for the sensation of itching—itself a type of pain (Gieler & Walter, 2008).

A Pain in the Brain

Even though they may seem to emanate from far-flung parts of the body, we actually feel painful sensations in the brain. There are two distinct regions that have primary roles in processing incoming pain messages (Foley & Matlin, 2010; Porreca & Price, 2009). One, involving a pathway terminating in the parietal lobe, registers the location, intensity, and the sharpness or dullness of pain. The other, a group of structures deep in the frontal cortex and in the limbic system, registers just how unpleasant the painful sensation is. People with damage to this second region may notice a painful stimulus but report that it does not feel unpleasant.

Phantom Limbs

One intriguing puzzle about pain concerns the mysterious sensations often experienced by people who have lost an arm or leg—a condition known as a *phantom limb*. In such cases, the amputee feels sensations—sometimes quite painful ones—that seem to come from the missing body part (Ramachandran & Blakeslee, 1998). Neurological studies show that the phantom limb sensations do not originate in damaged nerves in the sensory pathways. Nor are they purely imaginary. Rather, they arise in the brain itself—perhaps the result of the brain generating sensation when none comes from the missing limb (Dingfelder, 2007). The odd phenomenon of phantom limbs teaches us that understanding pain requires understanding not only painful sensations but also mechanisms in the brain that both process and inhibit pain.

The Gate-Control Theory

No one has yet developed a theory that explains everything about pain, but Melzack and Wall's (1965, 1983) **gate-control theory** explains a lot. In particular, it explains why pain can sometimes be blocked or facilitated "top-down" by our mental state. The "gate" itself involves special interneurons that can open or close the pain pathway running up the spinal cord toward the brain. Closing the gate interferes with the transmission of pain messages in the spinal pathway.

gate-control theory An explanation for pain control that proposes we have a neural "gate" that can, under some circumstances, block incoming pain signals.

What can close the gate? Messages from nonpain nerve fibers, such as those involved in touch, can inhibit pain transmission. This explains why you vigorously shake your hand when you hit your finger with a hammer. Just as important, messages from the brain can also close the gate. This is how opiate drugs, such as morphine, work—by initiating a cascade of inhibitory messages that travel downward to block incoming pain messages.

The gate on the pain pathway can also be opened and closed, such as hypnosis or the distraction of important events. (See Fields, 2009.) We have long known that people's interpretations of events affect whether or not stimuli are perceived as painful (Turk, 1994). For example, soldiers and athletes may suffer severe injuries that cause little pain until the excitement of the battle or contest is over. And as we will see in a moment, this mind–body effect on pain is evident in the action of *placebos* or other sham treatments.

Dealing with Pain

Wouldn't it be nice to banish the experience of pain altogether? In reality, such a condition can be deadly. People with congenital insensitivity to pain do not feel what is hurting them, and their bodies often become scarred and their limbs deformed from injuries they could have avoided if their brains were able to warn them of danger. Because of their failure to notice and respond to tissue-damaging stimuli, these people tend to die young (Manfredi et al., 1981).

In general, pain serves as an essential defense signal: It warns us of potential harm, and it helps us to survive in hostile environments and to get treatment for sickness and injury. Sometimes, however, chronic pain seems to be a disease in itself, with neurons in the pain pathways becoming hypersensitive, amplifying normal sensory stimulation into pain messages (Watkins & Maier, 2003). Research also suggests that chronic pain may, at least sometimes, arise from genes that get "turned on" in nerve-damaged tissue (Marx, 2004).

Analgesics

What can you do if you are in pain? Analgesic drugs, ranging from over-the-counter remedies such as aspirin and ibuprofen to prescription narcotics such as morphine, are widely used and effective. These act in a variety of ways. Morphine suppresses pain messages in the spinal cord and the brain; aspirin interferes with a chemical signal produced by damaged tissue (Basbaum & Julius, 2006; Carlson, 2007). Those using pain-killing drugs should be aware of unwanted side effects, such as digestive tract or liver damage and even addiction. But studies have shown that if you must use narcotics to control severe pain, the possibility of your becoming addicted is far less than it would be if you were using narcotics recreationally (Melzack, 1990).

Psychological Techniques for Pain Control

Many people can also learn to control pain by psychological techniques, such as hypnosis, relaxation, and thought-distraction procedures (Brown, 1998). For instance, a child receiving a shot at the doctor's office might be asked to take a series of deep breaths and look away. You also may be among those for whom pain can also be modified by **placebos**, mock drugs made to appear as real drugs. For example, a placebo may be an injection of mild saline solution (salt water) or a pill made of sugar. Such fake drugs are routinely given to a control group in tests of new pain drugs. Their effectiveness, of course, involves the people's *belief* that they are getting real medicine (Niemi, 2009; Wager, 2005; Wager et al., 2004). It is important to note, however, that the brain's response to a placebo is much the same as that of pain-relieving drugs: closing the spinal gate. Because this **placebo effect** is common, any drug deemed effective must prove itself stronger than a placebo.

How do placebos produce their effects? Apparently, the expectation of pain relief is enough to cause the brain to release painkilling endorphins. We believe this is so because brain scans show that essentially the same pain-suppression areas "light up" when patients take placebos or analgesic drugs (Petrovic et al., 2002). Further, we find that individuals who respond to placebos report that their pain increases when they take the endorphin-blocking drug *naltrexone* (Fields, 1978; Fields & Levine, 1984).

Surprisingly, the placebo effect doesn't necessarily require a placebo! In a controlled experiment, Dr. Fabrizio Benedetti and his colleagues (2005) showed that the physician's bedside manner, even without a painkilling drug, can suppress pain. For psychologists, this is an important discovery, demonstrating that the psychosocial context itself can have a therapeutic effect (Guterman, 2005).

placebo   Substance that appears to be a drug but is not. Placebos are often referred to as "sugar pills" because they might contain only sugar rather than a real drug.

placebo effect   A response to a placebo (a fake drug) caused by the belief that it is a real drug.

Controlling *Psychological* Pain with Analgesics

In another surprising development, psychologist C. Nathan DeWall and his colleagues (2010) have found that acetaminophen (the pain reliever in Tylenol) can lessen the psychological pain of social rejection. Volunteers who took acetaminophen, as compared with those taking placebos, reported far fewer feelings of social rejection in everyday life. And in a follow-up experimental study involving a computer game rigged to make players feel social rejection, fMRI scans showed that acetaminophen reduced activity in brain areas associated with social rejection and also with physical pain. What makes this research interesting is the suggestion that both physical and psychological hurts involve some of the same pain mechanisms in the brain.

Pain Tolerance

The threshold of pain varies enormously from person to person. Some people always demand Novocain from their dentist, while others may prefer dental work without the added hassle of an injection. And in the laboratory, one study found that electric shocks had to be eight times more powerful to produce painful sensations in their least-sensitive subjects as compared with their most-sensitive subjects (Rollman & Harris, 1987). Another experiment found that brain scans of people who are highly sensitive to pain show greater activation of the thalamus and the anterior cingulate cortex than in scans of those with greater pain tolerance (Coghill et al., 2003). At least part of this variation has a genetic basis (Couzin, 2006).

We should be clear on this point: There is no evidence of genetic differences in sensitivity to pain among different ethnic or racial groups, although many reports suggest that *culture* does affect how people interpret pain and respond to painful stimulation. For example, Western women often report that childbirth is an excruciatingly painful experience, while women in some cultures routinely give birth with little indication of distress. Severely wounded soldiers, too, typically need less pain medication than do civilians with comparable injuries—perhaps because of the "culture of bravery" instilled in soldiers or because a soldier knows that a wound represents a ticket out of the combat zone.

Readers should be cautioned, however, that much of the literature on cultural differences in response to pain relies far more on anecdotes than on controlled studies. Further, the scientific work that does exist in this area has frequently come to conflicting conclusions (Foster, 2006). Perhaps one of the most important influences to emerge from this work involves poverty and access to health care: Poor people are much less likely to seek medical attention until pain becomes severe.

Check Your Understanding

✔— Study and Review at MyPsychLab

1. **RECALL:** Name the two types of photoreceptors and indicate what sort of stimulation they detect.

2. **RECALL:** The *wavelength* of light causes sensations of _____, while the *intensity* of light causes sensations of _____.

   a. motion/shape
   b. color/brightness
   c. primary colors/secondary colors
   d. depth/color

3. **RECALL:** The *frequency theory* best explains how we hear _____ sounds, while the *place theory* best explains how we hear _____ sounds.

4. **SYNTHESIS:** What do all of the following senses have in common: vision, hearing, taste, smell, hearing, pain, equilibrium, and body position?

5. **RECALL:** Studies of painful phantom limbs show that the phantom pain originates in _____

   a. the brain.
   b. nerve cells damaged from the amputation.
   c. the imagination.
   d. ascending pathways in the spinal cord.

6. **UNDERSTANDING THE CORE CONCEPT:** Explain why different senses give us different sensations.

Answers 1. The rods are better than the cones for detecting objects in dim light. The cones give us high-resolution color vision in relatively bright light. **2.** b (color/brightness) **3.** low-pitched/high-pitched **4.** Each of these senses transduces physical stimulation into neural activity, and each responds more to change than to constant stimulation. **5.** a (the brain) **6.** The different sensations occur because the sensory information is processed by different parts of the brain.

FIGURE 3.13

Who Is This?

Perceptual processes help us recognize people and objects by matching the stimulus to images in memory.

percept   The meaningful product of perception—often an image that has been associated with concepts, memories of events, emotions, and motives.

what pathway   A neural pathway, projecting from the primary visual cortex to the temporal lobe, which involves identifying objects.

where pathway   A neural pathway that projects visual information to the parietal lobe; responsible for locating objects in space.

blindsight   The ability to locate objects despite damage to the visual system making it impossible for a person consciously to see and identify objects. Blindsight is thought to involve unconscious visual processing in the where pathway.

feature detectors   Cells in the cortex that specialize in extracting certain features of a stimulus.

3.3 KEY QUESTION
What Is the Relationship between Sensation and Perception?

We have described how sensory signals are transduced and transmitted to specific regions of your brain for further processing as visual images, pain, odors, and other sensations. Then what? You enlist your brain's perceptual machinery to attach *meaning* to the incoming sensory information. Does a bitter taste mean poison? Does a red flag mean danger? Does a smile signify a friendly overture? The Core Concept of this section emphasizes this perceptual elaboration of sensory information:

> **Core Concept 3.3**
>
> Perception brings *meaning* to sensation, so perception produces an interpretation of the world, not a perfect representation of it.

In brief, we might say that the task of perception is to organize sensation into stable, meaningful *percepts*. A **percept**, then, is not just a sensation but the associated meaning as well. As we describe this complex perceptual process, we will first consider how our perceptual apparatus usually manages to give us a reasonably accurate and useful image of the world. Then we will look at some illusions and other instances in which perception apparently fails spectacularly. Finally, we will examine two theories that attempt to capture the most fundamental principles at work behind these perceptual successes and failures.

Perceptual Processing: Finding Meaning in Sensation

How does the sensory image of a person (such as the individual pictured in Figure 3.13) become the percept of someone you recognize? That is, how does mere sensation become an elaborate and meaningful perception? Let's begin with two visual pathways that help us identify objects and locate them in space: the *what* pathway and the *where* pathway.

The What and Where Pathways in the Brain   The primary visual cortex, at the back of the brain, splits visual information into two interconnected streams (Fariva, 2009; Goodale & Milner, 1992). One stream, which flows mainly to the temporal lobe, extracts information about an object's color and shape. This **what pathway** allows us to determine *what* objects are. The other stream, the **where pathway**, projects to the parietal lobe, which determines an object's location. Evidence suggests that other senses, such as touch and hearing, also have *what* and *where* streams that interact with those in the visual system (Rauschecker & Tian, 2000).

Curiously, we are conscious of information in the *what* pathway but not necessarily in the *where* pathway. This fact explains a curious phenomenon known as **blindsight**, a condition that occurs in some people with damage to the *what* pathway—damage that makes them visually unaware of objects around them. Yet if the *where* pathway is intact, blindsight patients may be able to step over objects in their path or reach out and touch objects that they claim not to see (Ramachandran & Rogers-Ramachandran, 2008). In this way, persons with blindsight are much like a sophisticated robot that can sense and react to objects around it even though it lacks the ability to represent them in consciousness.

Feature Detectors   The deeper information travels into the brain along the *what* and *where* pathways, the more specialized processing becomes. Ultimately, specialized groups of cells in the visual pathways extract very specific stimulus features, such as an object's length, slant, color, boundary, location, and movement (Kandel & Squire, 2000). Perceptual psychologists call these cells **feature detectors**.

We know about feature detectors from animal experiments and also from cases like Jonathan's, in which brain injury or disease selectively robs an individual of the ability to detect certain features, such as colors or shapes. There is even a part of the temporal lobe—near the occipital cortex—with feature detectors that are especially sensitive to features of the human face (Carpenter, 1999).

Despite our extensive knowledge of feature detectors, we still don't know exactly how the brain manages to combine (or "bind") the multiple features it detects into a single percept of, say, a face. Psychologists call this puzzle the **binding problem,** and it may be the deepest mystery of perceptual psychology (Kandel & Squire, 2000).

We do have one tantalizing piece of this perceptual puzzle: Neuroscientists have discovered that the brain synchronizes the firing patterns in different groups of neurons that have each detected different features of the same object—much as an orchestra conductor determines the tempo at which all members of the ensemble will play a musical piece (Buzsáki, 2006). But just how this synchronization is involved in "binding" these features together remains a mystery.

Many viewers report that the flowers in Claude Monet's floral paintings, such as *Coquelicots*, produce a shimmering or moving sensation. Neuroscientists believe this occurs because the colors of the flowers have the same level of brightness as the colors in the surrounding field—and so are difficult for the colorblind "where" pathway to locate precisely in space (Dingfelder, 2010).

Top-Down and Bottom-Up Processing

Forming a percept also seems to involve imposing a pattern on sensation. This involves two complementary processes that psychologists call *top-down processing* and *bottom-up processing.* In **top-down processing,** our goals, past experience, knowledge, expectations, memory, motivations, or cultural background guide our perceptions of objects—or events (see Nelson, 1993). Trying to find your car keys in a cluttered room requires top-down processing. So does searching for Waldo in the popular children's series *Where's Waldo?* And if you skip lunch to go grocery shopping, top-down hunger signals will probably make you notice all the snack foods in the store.

In **bottom-up processing,** the characteristics of the stimulus (rather than a concept in our minds) exert a strong influence on our perceptions. Bottom-up processing relies heavily on the brain's feature detectors to sense these stimulus characteristics: Is it moving? What color is it? Is it loud, sweet, painful, pleasant smelling, wet, hot…? You are doing bottom-up processing when you notice a moving fish in an aquarium, a hot pepper in a stir-fry, or a loud noise in the middle of the night.

Thus, bottom-up processing involves sending sensory data into the system through receptors and sending it "upward" to the cortex, where a basic analysis, involving the feature detectors, is first performed to determine the characteristics of the stimulus. Psychologists also refer to this as *stimulus-driven processing* because the resulting percept is determined, or "driven," by stimulus features. By contrast, top-down processing flows in the opposite direction, with the percept being driven by some concept in the cortex—at the "top" of the brain. Because this sort of thinking relies heavily on concepts in the perceiver's own mind, it is also known as *conceptually driven processing.*

Perceptual Constancies

We can illustrate another aspect of perception with yet another example of top-down processing. Suppose that you are looking at a door, such as the one pictured in Figure 3.14A. You "know" that the door is rectangular, even though your sensory image of it is distorted when you are not looking at it straight-on. Your brain automatically corrects the sensory distortion so that you perceive the door as being rectangular, as in Figure 3.14B.

This ability to see an object as being the same shape from different angles or distances is just one example of a **perceptual constancy.** In fact, there are many kinds of perceptual constancies. These include *color constancy,* which allows us to see a flower as being the same color in the reddish light of sunset as in the white glare of midday. *Size constancy* allows us to perceive a person as the same size at different distances and also serves as a strong cue for depth perception. And it was *shape constancy* that allowed us to see the door as remaining rectangular from different angles. Together, these constancies help us identify and track objects in a changing world.

binding problem Refers to the process used by the brain to combine (or "bind") the results of many sensory operations into a single percept. This occurs, for example, when sensations of color, shape, boundary, and texture are combined to produce the percept of a person's face. No one knows exactly how the brain does this. Thus, the binding problem is one of the major unsolved mysteries in psychology.

top-down processing Perceptual analysis that emphasizes the perceiver's expectations, concept memories, and other cognitive factors, rather than being driven by the characteristics of the stimulus. "Top" refers to a mental set in the brain—which stands at the "top" of the perceptual processing system.

bottom-up processing Perceptual analysis that emphasizes characteristics of the stimulus, rather than our concepts and expectations. "Bottom" refers to the stimulus, which occurs at step one of perceptual processing.

perceptual constancy The ability to recognize the same object as remaining "constant" under different conditions, such as changes in illumination, distance, or location.

(A)   (B)

FIGURE 3.14

A Door by Any Other Shape Is Still a Door

(A) A door seen from an angle presents the eye with a distorted rect-angle image. **(B)** The brain perceives the door as rectangular.

inattentional blindness   A failure to notice changes occurring in one's visual field, apparently caused by narrowing the focus of one's attention.

change blindness   A perceptual failure to notice that a visual scene has changed from the way it had appeared previously. Unlike inattentional blindness, change blindness requires comparing a current scene to one from the past, stored in memory.

illusion   You have experienced an illusion when you have a demonstrably incorrect perception of a stimulus pattern, especially one that also fools others who are observing the same stimulus. (If no one else sees it the way you do, you could be having a *hallucination.* We'll take that term up in a later chapter on mental disorder.)

FIGURE 3.15

An Ambiguous Picture

What is depicted here? The difficulty in seeing the figure lies in its similarity to the background.

Inattentional Blindness and Change Blindness Some-times we don't notice things that occur right in front of our noses—particularly if they are unexpected and we haven't focused our attention on them. While driving, you may not notice a car unexpectedly shifting lanes. Psychologists call this **inattentional blindness** (Beck et al., 2004; Greer, 2004a). Magicians rely on it for many of their tricks (Sanders, 2009). They also rely on **change blindness**, a related phe-nomenon in which we fail to notice that something is dif-ferent now than it was before, as when a friend changes hair color or shaves a mustache (Martinez-Conde & Macknik, 2008).

We *do* notice changes that we anticipate, such as a red light turning to green. But laboratory studies show that many people don't notice when, in a series of photographs of the same scene, a red light is replaced by a stop sign. One way this may cause trouble in the world outside the laboratory is that people underestimate the extent to which they can be affected by change blindness. This probably occurs because our perceptual systems and our attention have limits on the amount of information they can process, so our expectations coming from the "top down" cause us to overlook the unexpected.

Perceptual Ambiguity and Distortion

A primary goal of perception is to get an accurate "fix" on the world—to recognize friends, foes, opportunities, and dangers. Survival sometimes depends on accurately perceiving the environment, but the environment is not always easy to "read." We can illustrate this difficulty with the photo of black and white splotches in Figure 3.15. What is it? When you eventually extract the stimulus figure from the back-ground, you will see it as a Dalmatian dog walking toward the upper left with its head down. The dog is hard to find because it blends so easily with the background. The same problem occurs when you try to single out a voice against the background of a noisy party.

But it is not just the inability to find an image that causes perceptual problems. Sometimes our perceptions can be wildly inaccurate because we misinterpret an image—as happens with sensory and perceptual *illusions.*

What Illusions Tell Us about Sensation and Perception When your mind deceives you by interpreting a stimulus pattern incor-rectly, you are experiencing an **illusion.** Such illusions can help us understand some fundamental properties of sensation and perception—particularly the discrepancy between our percepts and external reality (Cohen & Girgus, 1973).

Let's first examine a remarkable bottom-up illusion that works at the level of sensation: the black-and-white Hermann grid (see Figure 3.16). As you stare at the center of the grid, note how dark, fuzzy spots appear at the intersections of the white bars. But when you focus on an intersection, the spot vanishes. Why? The answer lies in the way receptor cells in your visual pathways interact with each other. The firing of certain cells that are sensitive to light–dark boundaries inhibits the activity of adjacent cells that would otherwise detect the white grid lines. This inhibiting process makes you sense darker regions—the

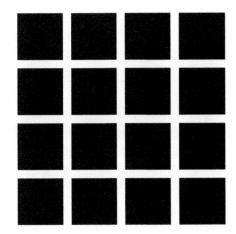

FIGURE 3.16

The Hermann Grid

Why do faint gray dots appear at the intersections of the grid? The illusion, which operates at the sensory level, is explained in the text.

Source: Levine, M. W., & Shefner, J. (2000). *Fundamentals of sensation & perception*. New York: Oxford University Press. Reprinted by permission of Michael W. Levine.

A.

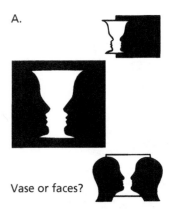

Vase or faces?

B.

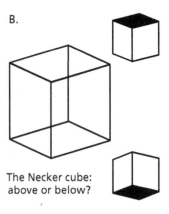

The Necker cube: above or below?

FIGURE 3.17

Perceptual Illusions

These ambiguous figures are illusions of perceptual interpretation.

ambiguous figures   Images that can be interpreted in more than one way. There is no "right" way to see an ambiguous figure.

grayish areas—at the white intersections just outside your focus. Even though you know (top-down) that the squares in the Hermann grid are black and the lines are white, this knowledge cannot overcome the illusion, which operates at a more basic, sensory level.

To study illusions at the level of perception, psychologists often employ **ambiguous figures**—stimulus patterns that can be interpreted (top-down) in two or more distinct ways, as in Figures 3.17A and 3.17B. There you see that both the vase/faces figure and the Necker cube are designed to confound your interpretations, not just your sensations. Each suggests two conflicting meanings: Once you have seen both, your perception will cycle back and forth between them as you look at the figure. Studies suggest that these alternating interpretations may involve the shifting of perceptual control between the left and right hemispheres of the brain (Gibbs, 2001).

Another dramatic illusion, recently discovered, appears in Figure 3.18. Although it is hard to believe, the squares marked A and B are the same shade of gray. Proof appears in the right-hand image, where the vertical bars are also the same gray shade. Why are we fooled by this illusion? Perceptual psychologists respond that the effect derives from *color and brightness constancy:* our ability to see an object as essentially unchanged under different lighting conditions, from the bright noon sun to near darkness (Gilchrist, 2006). Under normal conditions, this prevents us from being misled by shadows.

Figure 3.19 shows several other illusions that operate primarily at the level of perceptual interpretation. All are compelling, and all are controversial—particularly the Müller–Lyer illusion, which has intrigued psychologists for more than 100 years. Disregarding the arrowheads, which of the two horizontal lines in this figure appears longer? If you measure them, you will see that the horizontal lines are exactly the same length. What is the explanation? Answers to that question have

FIGURE 3.18

The Checkerboard Illusion

Appearances are deceiving: Squares A and B are actually the same shade of gray, as you can see on the right by comparing the squares with the vertical bars. The text explains why this occurs.

Source: Adelson, E. H. (2010). Checkershadow illusion. Retrieved from http://persci.mit.edu/gallery/checkershadow. © 1995, Edward H. Adelson.

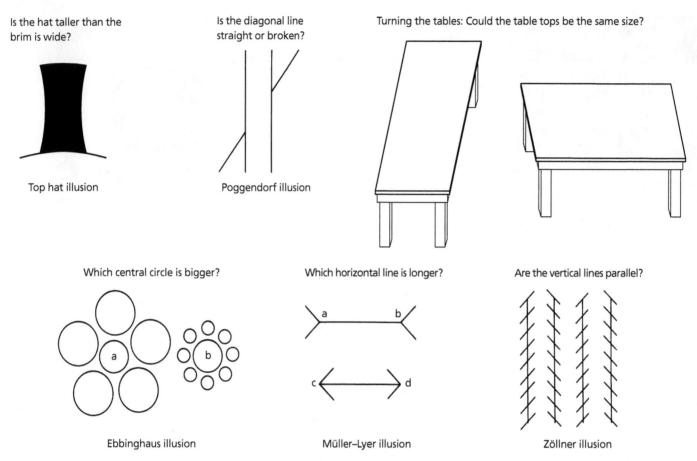

Is the hat taller than the brim is wide?

Top hat illusion

Is the diagonal line straight or broken?

Poggendorf illusion

Turning the tables: Could the table tops be the same size?

Which central circle is bigger?

Ebbinghaus illusion

Which horizontal line is longer?

Müller–Lyer illusion

Are the vertical lines parallel?

Zöllner illusion

FIGURE 3.19

Six Illusions to Tease Your Brain

Each of these illusions involves a bad "bet" made by your brain. What explanations can you give for the distortion of reality that each of these illusions produces? Are they caused by nature or nurture? The table illusion was originally developed by Roger N. Shepard and presented in his 1990 book *Mind Sights* (Freeman).

been offered in well over a thousand published studies, and psychologists still don't know for sure.

One popular theory, combining both top-down and bottom-up factors, has gathered some support. It suggests that we unconsciously interpret the Müller–Lyer figures as three-dimensional objects. So instead of arrowheads, we see the ends as angles that project toward or away from us like the inside and outside corners of a building or a room, as in Figure 3.20 The inside corner seems to recede in the distance, while the outside corner appears to extend toward us. Therefore, we judge the outside corner to be closer—and shorter. Why? When two objects make the same-size image on the retina and we judge one to be farther away than the other, we assume that the more distant one is larger.

Illusions in the Context of Culture   But what if you had grown up in a culture with no square-cornered buildings? Would you still see one line as longer than the other in the Müller–Lyer? In other words, do you have to *learn* to see the illusion, or is it "hard wired" into your brain? One way to answer such questions is through cross-cultural research. With this in mind, Richard Gregory (1977) went to South Africa to study a group of people known as the Zulus, who live in what he called a "circular culture." Aesthetically, people in that culture prefer curves to straight lines and square corners: Their round huts have round doors and windows; they till

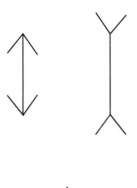

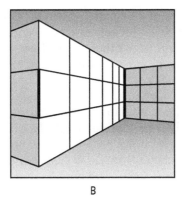

A   B

FIGURE 3.20
The Müller-Lyer Illusion

One explanation for the Müller-Lyer illusion says that your brain thinks it is seeing the inside and outside corners of a building in perspective.

their fields along sweeping curved lines, using curved plows; the children's toys lack straight lines.

So what happened when Gregory showed them the Müller–Lyer? Most saw the lines as nearly the same length. This suggests that the Müller–Lyer illusion is learned. A number of other studies support Gregory's conclusion that people who live in "carpentered" environments—where buildings are built with straight sides and 90-degree angles—are more susceptible to the illusion than those who (like the Zulus) live in "noncarpentered" worlds (Segall et al., 1999).

Applying the Lessons of Illusions Several prominent modern artists, fascinated with the visual experiences created by ambiguity, have used perceptual illusion as a central artistic feature of their work. Consider the two examples of art shown here. *Gestalt-Rugo* by Victor Vasarely (see Figure 3.21) produces depth reversals like those in the Necker cube, with corners that alternately project and recede. In *Sky and Water* by M. C. Escher (see Figure 3.22), you can see birds and fishes only through the process of figure–ground reversal, much like the vase/faces illusion we encountered earlier (see Figure 3.17). The effect of these paintings on us underscores the function of human perception to make sense of the world and to fix on the best interpretation we can make.

To interpret such illusions, we draw on our personal experiences, learning, and motivation. Knowing this, those who understand the principles of perception often can control illusions to achieve desired effects far beyond the world of painting. Architects and interior designers, for example, create illusions that make spaces seem larger or smaller than they really are. They may, for example, make a small apartment appear more spacious when it is painted in light colors and sparsely furnished. Similarly, set and lighting designers in movies and theatrical productions purposely create visual illusions on film and on stage. So, too, do many of us make everyday use of illusion in our choices of cosmetics and clothing (Dackman, 1986). Light-colored clothing and horizontal stripes can make our bodies seem larger, while dark-colored clothing and vertical stripes can make our bodies seem slimmer. In such ways, we use illusions to distort "reality" and make our lives more pleasant.

Theoretical Explanations for Perception

The fact that most people perceive most illusions and ambiguous figures in essentially the same way suggests that fundamental perceptual principles are at work. But what are these principles? To find some answers, we will examine two influential theories that explain how we form our perceptions: *Gestalt theory* and *learning-based inference.*

Although these two approaches may seem contradictory at first, they really emphasize complementary influences on perception. The Gestalt theory emphasizes how we organize incoming stimulation into meaningful perceptual patterns—because of the

FIGURE 3.21
Victor Vasarely's *Gestalt-Rugo*

FIGURE 3.22
M. C. Escher's *Sky and Water*

CONNECTION **CHAPTER 1**

The *nature–nurture* issue centers on the relative importance of heredity and environment (p. 44).

Gestalt psychology   From a German word (pronounced *gush-TAWLT*) that means "whole" or "form" or "configuration." (A Gestalt is also a *percept*.) The Gestalt psychologists believed that much of perception is shaped by innate factors built into the brain.

((•─ **Listen** to the **Podcast** Gestalt Principles at Work at **MyPsychLab**

figure   The part of a pattern that commands attention. The figure stands out against the ground.

ground   The part of a pattern that does not command attention; the background.

way our brains are innately "wired." On the other hand, learning-based inference emphasizes learned influences on perception, including the power of expectations, context, and culture. In other words, Gestalt theory emphasizes *nature,* and learning-based inference emphasizes *nurture.*

Perceptual Organization: The Gestalt Theory   You may have noticed that a series of blinking lights, perhaps on a theater marquee, can create the illusion of motion where there really is no motion. Similarly, there appears to be a white triangle in the *Do It Yourself!* box on this page—but there really is no white triangle. And, as we have seen, the Necker cube seems to flip back and forth between two alternative perspectives—but, of course, the flipping is all in your mind.

About 100 years ago, such perceptual tricks captured the interest of a group of German psychologists, who argued that the brain is innately wired to perceive not just stimuli but also *patterns* in stimulation (Sharps & Wertheimer, 2000). They called such a pattern a *Gestalt,* the German word for "perceptual pattern" or "configuration." Thus, from the raw material of stimulation, the brain forms a perceptual whole that is more than the mere sum of its sensory parts (Prinzmetal, 1995; Rock & Palmer, 1990). This perspective became known as **Gestalt psychology.**

The Gestaltists liked to point out that we perceive a square as a single figure rather than merely as four individual lines. Similarly, when you hear a familiar song, you do not focus on the individual notes. Rather, your brain extracts the melody, which is your perception of the overall *pattern* of notes. Such examples, the Gestalt psychologists argued, show that we always attempt to organize sensory information into meaningful patterns, the most basic elements of which are already present in our brains at birth. Because this approach has been so influential, we will examine some of the Gestalt discoveries in more detail. ((•

Figure and Ground   One of the most basic of perceptual processes identified by Gestalt psychology divides our perceptual experience into *figure* and *ground*. A **figure** is simply a pattern or image that grabs our attention. As we noted, psychologists sometimes call this a *Gestalt.* Everything else becomes **ground**, the backdrop against which we perceive

---

Do It Yourself!   **FIGURE OBSCURES GROUND**

The tendency to perceive a figure as being in front of a ground is strong. It is so strong, in fact, that you can even get this effect when the perceived figure doesn't actually exist! You can demonstrate this with an examination of the accompanying figure. (See also Ramachandran & Rogers-Ramachandran, 2010.) You probably perceive a fir-tree shape against a ground of red circles on a white surface. But, of course, there is no fir-tree figure printed on the page; the figure consists only of three solid red shapes and a black-line base. You perceive the illusory white triangle in front because the wedge-shaped cuts in the red circles seem to be the corners of a solid white triangle. To see an illusory six-pointed star, look at part B. Here, the nonexistent "top" triangle appears to blot out parts of red circles and a black-lined triangle, when

in fact none of these is depicted as complete figures. Again, this demonstrates that we prefer to see the figure as an

object that obscures the ground behind it. (That's why we often call the ground a "*back*ground.")

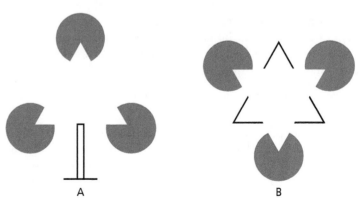

A   B

Subjective Contours
(A) A subjective fir tree; **(B)** a subjective six-pointed star.

the figure. A melody becomes a figure heard against a background of complex harmonies, and a spicy chunk of pepperoni becomes the figure against the ground of cheese, sauce, and bread that makes up a pizza. Visually, a figure could be a bright flashing sign or a word on the background of a page. And in the ambiguous faces/vase seen in Figure 3.17A, figure and ground reverse when the faces and vase alternately "pop out" as figure.

Closure: Filling in the Blanks   Our minds seem built to abhor a gap, as you saw in the *Do It Yourself!* above. Note especially the illusory white triangle—superimposed on red circles and black lines. Moreover, you will note that you have mentally divided the white area into two regions, the triangle and the background. Where this division occurs, you perceive *subjective contours:* boundaries that exist not in the stimulus but only in the subjective experience of your mind.

Your perception of these illusory triangles demonstrates a second powerful organizing process identified by the Gestalt psychologists. **Closure** makes you see incomplete figures as wholes by supplying the missing segments, filling in gaps, and making inferences about potentially hidden objects. So when you see a face peeking around a corner, your mind automatically fills in the hidden parts of the face and body. In general, humans have a natural tendency to perceive stimuli as complete and balanced even when pieces are missing. (Does this ring a _____ with you?) Closure is also responsible for filling in your "blind spot," as you saw on page 97.

In the foregoing demonstrations, we have seen how the perception of subjective contours and closure derives from the brain's ability to create percepts out of incomplete stimulation. Now let us turn to the perceptual laws that explain how we group the stimulus elements that are actually present in Gestalts.

The Gestalt Laws of Perceptual Grouping   It's easy to see a school of fish as a single unit—as a Gestalt. But why? And how do we mentally combine hundreds of notes together and perceive them as a single melody? How do we combine the elements of color, shadow, form, texture, and boundary into the percept of a friend's face? And why have thousands of people reported seeing "flying saucers" or the face of Jesus in the scorch marks on a tortilla? That is, how do we pull together in our minds the separate stimulus elements that seem to "belong" together? This is the *binding problem* again: one of the most fundamental problems in psychology. As we will see, the Gestalt psychologists made great strides in this area, even though the processes by which perceptual organization works are still debated today (Palmer, 2002).

In the heyday of Gestalt psychology, of course, there were no MRIs or PET scans. Modern neuroscience didn't exist. Hence, Gestalt psychologists like Max Wertheimer (1923) had to focus on the problem of perceptual organization in a different way—with

closure   The Gestalt principle that identifies the tendency to fill in gaps in figures and to see incomplete figures as complete.

A. Similarity

B. Proximity

C. Continuity

FIGURE 3.23

Gestalt Laws of Perceptual Grouping

Because of *similarity*, in **(A)**, you most easily see the *X*s grouped together, while *O*s form a separate Gestalt. So columns group together more easily than rows. The rows, made up of dissimilar elements, do not form patterns so easily. In **(B)**, *proximity* makes dissimilar elements easily group together when they are near each other. In **(C)**, even though the lines cut each other into many discontinuous segments, *continuity* makes it easier to see just two lines—each of which appears to be continuous as a single line cutting through the figure.

laws of perceptual grouping   The Gestalt principles of similarity, proximity, continuity, and common fate. These "laws" suggest how our brains prefer to group stimulus elements together to form a percept (Gestalt).

law of similarity   The Gestalt principle that we tend to group similar objects together in our perceptions.

law of proximity   The Gestalt principle that we tend to group objects together when they are near each other. *Proximity* means "nearness."

FIGURE 3.24

A Bird in the . . .

We usually see what we expect to see—not what is really there. Look again.

Quickly scan this photo. Then look away and describe as much as you recall. Next, turn to page 124 to learn what you may or may not have seen.

arrays of simple figures, such as you see in Figure 3.23. By varying a single factor and observing how it affected the way people perceived the structure of the array, Wertheimer was able to formulate a set of **laws of perceptual grouping**, which he inferred were built into the neural fabric of the brain.

According to Wertheimer's **law of similarity**, we group things together that have a similar look (or sound, or feel, and so on). So in Figure 3.23A, you see that the Xs and Os form distinct columns, rather than rows, because of similarity. Likewise, when you watch a football game, you use the colors of the uniforms to group the players into two teams because of similarity, even when they are mixed together during a play. You can also hear the law of similarity echoed in the old proverb "Birds of a feather flock together," which is a commentary not only on avian behavior but also on the assumptions we make about perceptual grouping. Any such tendency to perceive things as belonging together because they share common features reflects the law of similarity.

Now, suppose that, on one drowsy morning, you mistakenly put on two different-colored socks because they were together in the drawer and you assumed that they were a pair. Your mistake was merely Wertheimer's **law of proximity** (nearness) at work. The proximity principle says that we tend to group things together that are near each other, as you can see in the pairings of the Xs with the Os in Figure 3.23B. On the level of social perception, your parents were invoking the law of proximity when they cautioned you, "You're known by the company you keep."

We can see the Gestalt **law of continuity** in Figure 3.23C, where the straight line appears as a single, continuous line, even though the curved line repeatedly cuts through it. In general, the law of continuity says that we prefer smoothly connected and continuous figures to disjointed ones. Continuity also operates in the realm of social perception, where we commonly make the assumption of continuity in the personality of an individual whom we haven't seen for some time. So, despite interruptions in our contact with that person, we will expect to find continuity—to find him or her to be essentially the same person we knew earlier.

There is yet another form of perceptual grouping—one that we cannot illustrate in the pages of a book because it involves motion. But you can easily conjure up your own image that exemplifies the **law of common fate:** Imagine a school of fish, a gaggle of geese, or a uniformed marching band. When visual elements (the individual fish, geese, or band members) are moving together, you perceive them as a single Gestalt.

According to the Gestalt perspective, then, each of these examples of perceptual grouping illustrates the profound idea that our perceptions reflect innate patterns in the brain. These inborn mental processes, in a top-down fashion, determine the organization of the individual parts of the percept, just as mountains and valleys determine the course of a river. Moreover, the Gestalt psychologists suggested, the laws of perceptual grouping exemplify a more general principle known as the **law of Prägnanz** ("meaningfulness"). This principle states that we perceive the simplest pattern possible—the percept requiring the least mental effort. The most general of all the Gestalt principles, Prägnanz (pronounced *PRAYG-nonce*) has also been called the *minimum principle of perception*. The law of Prägnanz is what makes proofreading so hard to do, as you will find when you examine Figure 3.24.

Learning-Based Inference: The *Nurture* of Perception In 1866, Hermann von Helmholtz pointed out the important role of *learning* (or *nurture*) in perception. His theory of **learning-based inference** emphasized how people use prior learning to interpret new sensory information. Based on experience, then, the observer makes *inferences*—guesses or predictions—about what the sensations mean. This theory explains, for example, why you assume a birthday party is in progress when you see lighted candles on a cake: You have *learned* to associate cakes, candles, and birthdays.

Ordinarily, such perceptual inferences are fairly accurate. On the other hand, we have seen that confusing sensations and ambiguous arrangements can create perceptual illusions and erroneous conclusions. Our perceptual interpretations are, in effect, hypotheses about our sensations. For example, even babies come to expect that faces will have certain features in fixed arrangements (pair of eyes above nose, mouth below nose, etc.). In fact, our expectations about faces in their usual configuration are so thoroughly ingrained that we fail to "see" facial patterns that violate our expectations, particularly when they appear in an unfamiliar orientation. When you look at the two inverted portraits of Beyoncé (Figure 3.25), do you detect any important differences between them? Turn the book upside down for a surprise.

What, according to the theory of learning-based inference, determines how successful we will be in forming an accurate percept? The most important factors include the *context,* our *expectations,* and our *perceptual set.* We will see that each of these involves a way of narrowing our search of the vast store of concepts in long-term memory.

Context and Expectations Once you identify a context, you form expectations about what persons, objects, and events you are likely to experience (Biederman, 1989). To see what we mean, take a look at the following:

THE CAT

It says THE CAT, right? Now look again at the middle letter of each word. Physically, these two letters are exactly the same, yet you perceived the first as an *H* and the second as an *A.* Why? Clearly, your perception was affected by what you know about words in English. The context provided by *T__E* makes an *H* highly likely and an *A* unlikely, whereas the reverse is true of the context of *C__T* (Selfridge, 1955).

Here's a more real-world example: You have probably had difficulty recognizing people you know in situations where you didn't expect to see them, such as in a different city or a new social group. The problem, of course, is not that they looked different but that the context was unusual: You didn't *expect* them to be there. Thus, perceptual identification depends on context and expectations as well as on an object's physical properties.

Perceptual Set Another way learning serves as a platform from which context and expectation exert an influence on perception involves **perceptual set**—which is closely related to expectation. Under the influence of perceptual set, we have a readiness to notice and respond to certain stimulus cues—like a sprinter anticipating the starter's pistol. In general, perceptual set involves a focused alertness for a particular stimulus in a given context. For example, a new mother is set to hear the cries of her child. Likewise, if you drive a sporty red car, you probably know how the highway patrol has a perceptual set to notice speeding sporty red cars.

Often, a perceptual set leads you to transform an ambiguous stimulus into the one you were expecting. To experience this yourself, read quickly through the series of words that follow in both rows:

FOX; OWL; SNAKE; TURKEY; SWAN; D?CK

BOB; RAY; DAVE; BILL; TOM; D?CK

Notice how the words in the two rows lead you to read D?CK differently in each row. The meanings of the words read prior to the ambiguous stimulus create a perceptual

FIGURE 3.25

Two Perspectives on Beyoncé

Although one of these photos clearly has been altered, they look similar when viewed this way. However, turn the book upside down and look again.

law of continuity The Gestalt principle that we prefer perceptions of connected and continuous figures to disconnected and disjointed ones.

law of common fate The Gestalt principle that we tend to group similar objects together that share a common motion or destination.

law of Prägnanz The most general Gestalt principle, which states that the simplest organization, requiring the least cognitive effort, will emerge as the figure. *Prägnanz* shares a common root with *pregnant,* and so it carries the idea of a "fully developed figure." That is, our perceptual system prefers to see a fully developed Gestalt, such as a complete circle—as opposed to a broken circle.

learning-based inference The view that perception is primarily shaped by learning (or experience), rather than by innate factors.

perceptual set Readiness to detect a particular stimulus in a given context—as when a person who is afraid interprets an unfamiliar sound as a threat.

Do It Yourself! YOU SEE WHAT YOU'RE SET TO SEE

Labels create a context that can impose a perceptual set for an ambiguous figure. Have a friend look carefully at the picture of the "young woman" in image **(A)** of the accompanying figure, and have another friend examine the "old woman" in image **(B).** (Cover the other pictures while they do this.) Then have them look together at image **(C).** What do they see? Each will probably see something different, even though it's the same stimulus pattern. Prior exposure to the picture with a specific label will usually affect a person's perception of the ambiguous figure.

(A) A Young Woman

(B) An Old Woman

(C) Now what do you see?

set. Words that refer to animals create a perceptual set that influences you to read D?CK as "DUCK." Names create a perceptual set leading you to see D?CK as DICK. Yet another illustration of perceptual set appears in the *Do It Yourself!* box "You See What You're Set to See."

Cultural Influences on Perception Which of the following three items go together: chicken, cow, grass? If you are American, you are likely to group chicken and cow, because they are both animals. But if you are Chinese, you are more likely to put the latter two together, because cows eat grass. In general, says cross-cultural psychologist Richard Nisbett, Americans tend to put items in categories by abstract type rather than by relationship or function (Winerman, 2006d).

Nisbett and his colleagues have also found that East Asians typically perceive in a more holistic fashion than do Americans (Nisbett, 2003; Nisbett & Norenzayan, 2002). That is, the Asians pay more attention to, and can later recall more detail about, the context than do Americans. (This is true, incidentally, even if the American is of Chinese ancestry.) Specifically, when looking at a scene, people raised in America tend to spend more time scanning the "figure," while those raised in China usually focus more on details of the "ground" (Chua et al., 2005). "The Americans are more zoom and the East Asians are more panoramic," says neuroscientist Denise Park (Goldberg, 2008). Such distinctions are now even showing up as subtle differences on scans comparing brain activity of Asians and Americans on simple perceptual judgment tasks (Hedden et al., 2008).

Cross-cultural psychologists have pointed to still other cultural differences in perception (Segall et al., 1999). Consider, for example, the famous Ponzo illusion, based on linear perspective depth cues (see Figure 3.26). In your opinion, which bar is longer: the one on top (marked A) or the one on the bottom (marked B)? In actuality, both bars are the same length. (If you've developed a skeptical scientific attitude, you'll measure them!) Research shows, however, that responses to these figures depend strongly on culture-related experiences. Most readers of this book will report that the top bar appears longer than the bottom bar, yet people from some cultural backgrounds are not so easily fooled.

Why the difference? The world you have grown up in probably included many structures featuring parallel lines that seemed to converge in the distance: railroad tracks, long buildings, highways, and tunnels. Such experiences leave you vulnerable to images, such as the Ponzo illusion, in which cues for size and distance are unreliable.

But what about people from cultures where individuals have had far less experience with this cue for distance? Research on this issue has been carried

FIGURE 3.26

The Ponzo Illusion

The two white bars superimposed on the railroad track are actually identical in length. Because A appears farther away than B, we perceive it as longer.

out on the Pacific island of Guam, where there are no Ponzolike railroad tracks (Brislin, 1974, 1993). There, too, the roads are so winding that people have few opportunities to see roadsides "converge" in the distance. People who have spent their entire lives on Guam, then, presumably have fewer opportunities to learn the strong perceptual cue that converging lines indicate distance.

And, sure enough—just as researchers had predicted—people who had lived all their lives on Guam were less influenced by the Ponzo illusion than were respondents from the mainland United States. That is, they were less likely to report that the top line in the figure was longer. These results strongly support the argument that people's experiences affect their perceptions—as Helmholz had theorized. 📖

📖 **Read** about Cultural Differences in Interpretation of Symbols at **MyPsychLab**

Depth Perception: Nature or Nurture? Now that we have looked at two contrasting approaches to perception—Gestalt theory, which emphasizes nature, and learning-based inference, which emphasizes nurture—let's see how each explains a classic problem in psychology: depth perception. Are we born with the ability to perceive depth, or must we learn it? Let's look at the evidence.

Bower (1971) found evidence of depth perception in infants only 2 weeks old. By fitting his subjects with 3-D goggles, Bower produced powerful virtual reality images of a ball moving about in space. When the ball image suddenly appeared to move directly toward the infant's face, the reaction was increased heart rate and obvious anxiety. This suggests that some ability for depth perception is probably inborn or heavily influenced by genetic programming that unfolds in the course of early development.

Although depth perception appears early in human development, the idea of being cautious when there is danger of falling seems to develop later in infancy. In a famous demonstration, psychologists Eleanor Gibson and Richard Walk placed infants on a Plexiglas-topped table that appeared to drop off sharply on one end. (See the accompanying photo.) Reactions to the *visual cliff* occurred mainly in infants older than 6 months—old enough to crawl. Most readily crawled across the "shallow" side of the table, but they were reluctant to go over the "edge" of the visual cliff—indicating not only that they could perceive depth but also that they associated the drop-off with danger (Gibson & Walk, 1960). Developmental psychologists believe that crawling and depth perception are linked in that crawling helps infants develop their understanding of the three-dimensional world.

Digging deeper into the problem of depth perception, we find that our sense of depth or distance relies on multiple cues. We can group these depth cues in two categories, either *binocular cues* or *monocular cues.*

Apprehension about the "visual cliff" shows that infants make use of distance clues. This ability develops at about the same time an infant is learning to crawl.

Binocular Cues Certain depth cues, the **binocular cues,** depend on the use of two eyes. You can demonstrate this to yourself: Hold one finger about 6 inches from your eyes and look at it. Now move it about a foot farther away. Do you feel the change in your eye muscles as you focus at different distances? This feeling serves as one of the main cues for depth perception when looking at objects that are relatively close. The term for this, *binocular convergence,* suggests how the lines of vision from each eye converge at different angles on objects at different distances.

A related binocular depth cue, *retinal disparity,* arises from the difference in perspectives of the two eyes. To see how this works, again hold a finger about 12 inches from your face and look at it alternately with one eye and then with the other. Notice how you see a different view of your finger with each eye. Because we see greater disparity when looking at nearby objects than we do when viewing distant objects, these image differences coming from each eye provide us with depth information.

We can't say for sure whether the binocular cues are innate or learned. What we can say is that they rely heavily on our biology: a sense of eye muscle movement and the physically different images on the two retinas. The monocular cues, however, present a very different picture.

binocular cues Information taken in by both eyes that aids in depth perception, including binocular convergence and retinal disparity.

Did you see a woman committing suicide in the photo on page 120? Most people have difficulty identifying the falling woman in the center of the photo because of the confusing background and because they have no perceptual schema that makes them expect to see a person positioned horizontally in midair.

monocular cues   Information about depth that relies on the input of just one eye—includes relative size, light and shadow, interposition, relative motion, and atmospheric perspective.

Haze, fog, or air pollution makes distant objects less distinct, creating atmospheric perspective, which acts as a distance cue. Even the air itself provides a cue for distance by giving far-away objects a bluish cast.

Monocular Cues for Depth Perception   Not all cues for depth perception require both eyes. A one-eyed pilot we know, who manages to perceive depth well enough to maneuver the airplane safely during takeoffs and landings, is proof that one-eye cues convey a great deal of depth information. Here are some of the **monocular cues** that a one-eyed pilot (or a two-eyed pilot, for that matter) could learn to use while flying:

- If two objects that are assumed to be the same size cast different-sized images on the retina, observers usually judge them to lie at different distances. So a pilot flying low can learn to use the *relative size* of familiar objects on the ground as a cue for depth and distance. Because of this cue, automakers who install wide-angle rear-view mirrors always inscribe the warning on them, "Objects in the mirror are closer than they appear."

- If you have ever looked down a long, straight railroad track, you know that the parallel rails seem to come together in the distance—as we saw in the Ponzo illusion (p. 122). Likewise, a pilot approaching a runway for landing sees the runway as being much wider at the near end than at the far end. Both examples illustrate how *linear perspective,* the apparent convergence of parallel lines, can serve as a depth cue.

- Lighter-colored objects seem closer to us, and darker objects seem farther away. Thus, *light and shadow* work together as a distance cue. You will notice this the next time you drive your car at night with the headlights on: Objects that reflect the most light appear to be nearer than more dimly lit objects in the distance.

- We assume that closer objects will cut off our vision of more distant objects behind them, a distance cue known as *interposition.* So we know that partially hidden objects are more distant than the objects that hide them. You can see this effect right in front of you now, as your book partially obscures the background, which you judge to be farther away.

- As you move, objects at different distances appear to move through your field of vision at a different rate or with a different *relative motion.* Look for this one from your car window. Notice how the power poles or fence posts along the roadside appear to move by at great speed, while more distant objects stay in your field of view longer, appearing to move by more slowly. With this cue, student pilots learn to set up a glide path to landing by adjusting their descent so that the end of the runway appears to stay at a fixed spot on the windshield while more distant points appear to move upward and nearer objects seem to move downward.

- Haze or fog makes objects in the distance look fuzzy, less distinct, or invisible, creating another learned distance cue called *atmospheric perspective.* In the accompanying photo, you can see that more distant buildings lack clarity through the Los Angeles smog. At familiar airports, most pilots have identified a landmark three miles away. If they cannot see the landmark, they know that they must fly by relying on instruments.

So which of the two theories about perception that we have been discussing—Helmholtz's learning theory or the Gestaltists' innate theory—best accounts for depth perception? Both of them! That is, depth and distance perception—indeed, all our perceptual processes—show the influence of both nature and nurture.

Seeing and Believing

If you assume, as most people do, that your senses give you an accurate and undistorted picture of the outside world, you are mistaken (Segall et al., 1990). We hope that the illusions presented in this chapter will help make the point. We also hope that the chapter has helped you realize that people see the world through the filter of their own perceptions—and that marketing and politics depend on manipulating our perceptions (think iPhones, Droids, and Blackberries).

Magicians are also experts in manipulating perceptions—and so perceptual scientists are making them partners in perceptual research (Hyman, 1989; Martinez-Conde & Macknik, 2008; Sanders, 2009). The results include discoveries about change blindness, inattentional blindness, and brain modules involved in both attention and perception.

Unlike magicians, however, perceptual scientists are happy to reveal how sensation and perception play tricks on us all. (Incidentally, a magician friend of ours warns that smart people are the easiest ones to fool. So watch out!)

We hope that this chapter has shaken your faith in your senses and perceptions . . . just a bit. To drive the point home, consider this statement (which, unfortunately, was printed backward):

.rat eht saw tac ehT

Please turn it around in your mind: What does it say? At first most people see a sensible sentence that says, "The cat saw the rat." But take another look. The difficulty lies in the power of expectations to shape your interpretation of stimulation.

This demonstration illustrates once again that we don't merely sense the world as it is; we perceive it. The goal of the process by which stimulation becomes sensation and, finally, perception is to find meaning in our experience. But it is well to remember that we impose our own meanings on sensory experience.

Differences in the ways we interpret our experiences explain why two people can look at the same sunset, the same presidential candidates, or the same religions and perceive them so differently. Perceptual differences make us unique individuals. An old Spanish proverb makes the point elegantly:

Most of us assume that our senses give us an accurate picture of the world. This helps magicians like Lance Burton fool us with perceptual illusions.

En este mundo traidor	In this treacherous world
No hay verdad ni mentira;	There is neither truth nor lie;
Todo es según el color	All is according to the color
Del cristál con que se mira.	Of the lens through which we spy.

With this proverb in mind, let's return one more time to the problem with which we began the chapter—and in particular to the question of whether the world looks (feels, tastes, smells . . .) the same to different people. We have every reason to suspect that we all (with some variation) *sense* the world in roughly the same way. But because we attach different *meanings* to our sensations, it is clear that people *perceive* the world in many different ways—with, perhaps, as many differences as there are people. 📖

Read about Extrasensory Perception at **MyPsychLab**

[PSYCHOLOGY MATTERS]

Using Psychology to Learn Psychology

One of the most mistaken notions about studying and learning is that students should set aside a certain amount of time for study every day. This is not to suggest that you shouldn't study regularly. Rather, it is to say that you shouldn't focus on merely putting in your time. So where should you place your emphasis? (And what does this have to do with perceptual psychology?)

Recall the concept of *Gestalt*, the idea of the meaningful pattern, discussed earlier in this chapter. The Gestalt psychologists taught that we have an innate tendency to understand our world in terms of meaningful patterns. Applied to your studying, this means that your emphasis should be on finding meaningful patterns—Gestalts—in your course work.

In this chapter, for example, you will find that your authors have helped you by dividing the material into three major sections. You can think of each section as a conceptual Gestalt built around a Core Concept that ties it together and gives it meaning. We suggest that you organize your study of psychology around one of these meaningful units of material. That is, identify a major section of your book and study that until it makes sense.

To be more specific, you might spend an hour or two working on the first section of this chapter, where you would not only read the material but also connect each boldfaced term to the Core Concept. For example, what does the *difference threshold* have to do with the idea that the brain senses the world through neural messages? (Sample brief answer: The brain is geared to detect *changes* or *differences* that are conveyed to it in the form of neural

subliminal perception The process by which a stimulus that is below the awareness threshold can be sensed and interpreted outside of consciousness.

impulses.) We suggest that you do the same thing with each of the other boldfaced terms in the chapter. The result will be a deeper understanding of the material. In perceptual terms, you will be constructing a meaningful pattern—a Gestalt—around the Core Concept.

You can do that only by focusing on meaningful units of material rather than on the clock.

Check Your Understanding

✓●─ Study and **Review** at **MyPsychLab**

1. **APPLICATION:** Give an example, from your own experience, of top-down processing.

2. **RECALL:** Our brains have specialized cells, known as _____ _____, dedicated to identifying stimulus properties such as length, slant, color, and boundary.

3. **RECALL:** What do perceptual constancies do for us?

4. **RECALL:** What two basic perceptual properties seem to reverse or alternate in the faces/vase image (in Figure 3.17A)?

5. **APPLICATION:** When two close friends are talking, other people may not be able to follow their conversation because it has

many gaps that the friends can mentally fill in from their shared experience. Which Gestalt principle is illustrated by the friends' ability to fill in these conversational gaps?

6. **UNDERSTANDING THE CORE CONCEPT:** Which of the following best illustrates the idea that perception is not an exact internal copy of the world?
   - **a.** the sound of a familiar tune
   - **b.** the Ponzo illusion
   - **c.** a bright light
   - **d.** jumping in response to a pinprick

Answers 1. Your example should involve perception based on expectations, motives, emotions, or mental images—such as seeing a friend's face in a crowd or making sense of an unexpected sound in the house at night. **2.** feature detectors **3.** Perceptual constancies allow us to identify and track objects under a variety of conditions, such as changes in illumination or perspective. **4.** Figure and ground **5.** Closure **6.** b—because of all the choices listed, the Ponzo illusion involves the most extensive perceptual interpretation.

CRITICAL THINKING APPLIED

Subliminal Perception and Subliminal Persuasion

Could extremely weak stimulation—stimulation that you don't even notice—affect your attitudes, opinions, or behavior? We know that the brain does a lot of information processing outside of awareness. So the notion that your sensory system can operate below the level of awareness is the basis for the industry that sells "subliminal" recordings touted as remedies for obesity, shoplifting, smoking, and low self-esteem. The same notion also feeds the fear that certain musical groups imbed hidden messages in their recordings or that advertisers may be using subliminal messages to influence our buying habits and, perhaps, our votes (Vokey, 2002).

What Are the Critical Issues?

People are always hoping for a bit of magic. But before you put your money in the mail for that subliminal weight-loss CD, let's identify what exactly we're talking about—and what we're *not* talking about. If subliminal persuasion works as claimed, then it must work on *groups* of people—a mass audience—rather

than just on individuals. It also means that a persuasive message can change the behavior of large numbers of people, even though no one is aware of the message. The issue is *not* whether sensory and perceptual processing can occur outside of awareness. The issue is whether subliminal messages can effect a substantial change in people's attitudes, opinions, and behaviors.

Fame, Fortune, Fraud, and Subliminal Perception   There is always a possibility of fraud when fortune or fame is involved, which is certainly the case with claims of amazing powers—such as persuasion through **subliminal perception**. This should cue us to ask: What is the source of claims that subliminal persuasion techniques work? That question leads us to an advertising executive, one James Vicary, who dramatically announced to the press some years ago that he had discovered an irresistible sales technique, now known as "subliminal advertising." Vicary said that his method consisted of projecting very brief messages on the screen of a movie theater, urging the audience to "Drink Coke" and "Buy popcorn." He claimed that the ads presented ideas so fleetingly that the conscious mind could not perceive them—yet, he said, the messages would still lodge in the unconscious mind, where they would work on the viewers' desires unnoticed. Vicary also boasted that sales of Coca-Cola and popcorn had soared at a New Jersey theater where he tested the technique.

The public was both fascinated and outraged. Subliminal advertising became the subject of intense debate. People worried that they were being manipulated by powerful psychological forces without their consent. As a result, laws were proposed to quash the practice. But aside from the hysteria, was there any real cause for concern? To answer that question, we must ask: What is the evidence?

Examining the Evidence   Let's first see what the psychological science of perceptual thresholds can tell us. As you will recall, a *threshold* refers to the minimum amount of stimulation necessary to trigger a response. The word *subliminal* means "below the threshold" (*limen* = threshold). In the language of perceptual psychology, *subliminal* more specifically refers to stimuli lying near the absolute threshold. Such stimuli may, in fact, be strong enough to affect the sense organs and to enter the sensory system without causing conscious awareness of the stimulus. But the real question is this: Can subliminal stimuli in this range influence our thoughts and behavior?

Several studies have found that subliminal words flashed briefly on a screen (for less than 1/100 second) can "prime" a person's later responses (Merikle & Reingold, 1990). For example, can you fill in the following blanks to make a word?

SN _ _ _ EL

If you had been subliminally primed by a brief presentation of the appropriate word or picture, it would be more likely that you would have found the right answer, even though you were not aware of the priming stimulus. So does the fact that subliminal stimulation can affect our responses on such tasks mean that subliminal persuasion really works?

Of course, priming doesn't *always* work: It merely increases the chances of getting the "right" answer. The answer to the problem, by the way, is "snorkel." And were you aware that we were priming you with the photo, to the right, of a snorkeler? If you were, it just goes to show that sometimes people *do* realize when they are being primed.

What Conclusions Can We Draw?

Apparently people do perceive stimuli below the absolute threshold, under circumstances such as the demonstration above (Greenwald et al., 1996; Reber, 1993). Under very carefully controlled conditions, subliminal perception is a fact. But here is the problem for would-be subliminal advertisers who would attempt to influence us in the uncontrolled world outside the laboratory: Different people have thresholds at different levels. So what might be *sub*liminal for me could well be *supra*liminal (above the threshold) for you.

Consequently, the would-be subliminal advertiser runs the risk that some in the audience will notice—and perhaps be angry about—a stimulus aimed slightly below the average person's threshold. In fact, *no controlled research has ever shown that subliminal messages delivered to a mass audience can influence people's buying habits or voting patterns.*

And what about those subliminal recordings that some stores play to prevent shoplifting? Again, no reputable study has ever demonstrated their effectiveness. A more likely explanation for any decrease in shoplifting attributed to these messages lies in increased vigilance from employees who know that management is worried about shoplifting. The same goes for the tapes that claim to help you quit smoking, lose weight, become wildly creative, or achieve other dozens of elusive dreams. In a comprehensive study of subliminal self-help techniques, the U.S. Army found all to be without foundation (Druckman & Bjork, 1991). The simplest explanation for reports of success lies in the purchasers' expectations and in the need to prove that they did not spend their money foolishly. And finally, to take the rest of the worry out of subliminal persuasion, you should know one more bit of evidence. James Vicary eventually admitted that his claims for subliminal advertising were a hoax (Druckman & Bjork, 1991).

So, using our previous SNORKEL example, could you use what you know about the Gestalt principle of closure to get theatergoers to think about popcorn?

This photo carries a subliminal message, explained in the text.

CHAPTER SUMMARY

((•—[Listen to an audio file of your chapter at **MyPsychLab**

CHAPTER PROBLEM: Is there any way to tell whether the world we "see" in our minds is the same as the external world—and whether we see things as most others do?

- Different people probably have similar *sensations* in response to a stimulus because their sense organs and parts of the brain they use in sensation are similar.

- People differ, however, in their *perceptions*, because they draw on different experiences to interpret their sensations.

- The brain does not sense the external world directly. The sense organs *transduce* stimulation and deliver stimulus information to the brain in the form of neural impulses. Our sensory experiences are, therefore, what the brain creates from the information delivered in these neural impulses.

3.1 How Does Stimulation Become Sensation?

[Core Concept 3.1 **The brain senses the world indirectly because the sense organs convert stimulation into the language of the nervous system: neural messages.**]

The most fundamental step in sensation involves the **transduction** by the sense organs of physical stimuli into neural messages, which are sent onward in the sensory pathways to the appropriate part of the brain for further processing. Not all stimuli become sensations, because some fall below the **absolute threshold**. Further, changes in stimulation are noticed only if they exceed the **difference threshold**. Classical psychophysics focused on identifying thresholds for sensations and for just-noticeable differences, but a newer approach, called **signal detection theory**, explains sensation as a process involving context, physical sensitivity, and judgment. We should consider our senses to be *change detectors*. But because they accommodate to unchanging stimulation, we become less and less aware of constant stimulation.

absolute threshold (p. 91)
difference threshold (p. 92)
perception (p. 89)
sensation (p. 88)
sensory adaptation (p. 93)
signal detection theory (p. 93)
transduction (p. 90)
Weber's law (p. 92)

3.2 How Are the Senses Alike? How Are They Different?

[Core Concept 3.2 **The senses all operate in much the same way, but each extracts different information and sends it to its own specialized sensory processing region in the brain.**]

All the senses involve transduction of physical stimuli into nerve impulses. Thus, our sensations are not properties of the original stimulus, but rather are creations of the brain. In vision, **photoreceptors** in the retina transduce light waves into neural codes, which retain **frequency** and **amplitude** information. This visual information is then transmitted by the optic nerve to the brain's occipital lobe, which converts the neural signals into sensations of **color** and **brightness**. Both the **trichromatic theory** and the **opponent process theory** are required to explain how visual sensations are extracted. Vision makes use of only a tiny "window" in the electromagnetic spectrum.

In the ear, sound waves in the air are transduced into neural energy in the **cochlea** and then sent on to the brain's temporal lobes, where frequency and amplitude information are converted to sensations of **pitch, loudness,** and **timbre.**

Other senses include position and movement (the **vestibular** and **kinesthetic senses**), smell, taste, the **skin senses** (touch, pressure, and temperature), and pain. Like vision and hearing, these other senses are especially attuned to detect changes in stimulation. Further, all sensations are carried to the brain by neural impulses, but we experience different sensations because the impulses are processed by different sensory regions of the brain. In some people, sensations cross sensory domains. Studies suggest that **synesthesia** involves communication between sensory areas of the brain that lie close together. This seems to occur more often in highly creative people.

The experience of pain can be the result of intense stimulation in any of several sensory pathways. While we don't completely understand pain, the **gate-control theory** explains how pain can be suppressed by competing sensations or other mental processes. Similarly, the ideal *analgesic*—one without unwanted side effects—has not been discovered, although the **placebo effect** works exceptionally well for some people.

3.3 What Is the Relationship between Sensation and Perception?

[Core Concept 3.3 **Perception brings meaning to sensation, so perception produces an interpretation of the world, not a perfect representation of it.**]

Psychologists define perception as the stage at which meaning is attached to sensation. Visual identification of objects involves **feature detectors** in the **what pathway** that projects to the temporal lobe. The **where pathway**, projecting to the parietal lobe, involves the location of objects in space. The disorder known as **blindsight** occurs because the where pathway can operate outside of consciousness. We also derive meaning from **bottom-up** stimulus cues picked up by feature detectors and from **top-down** processes, especially those involving expectations. What remains unclear is how the brain manages to combine the output of many sensory circuits into a single percept: This is called the **binding problem**. By studying such perceptual phenomena as **illusions, perceptual constancies, change blindness,** and **inattentional blindness**, researchers can learn about the factors that influence and distort the construction of perceptions. Illusions demonstrate that perception does not necessarily form an accurate representation of the outside world.

Perception has been explained by theories that differ in their emphasis on the role of innate brain processes versus learning—nature versus nurture. **Gestalt psychology** emphasizes innate factors that help us organize stimulation into meaningful patterns. In particular, the Gestaltists have described the processes that help us distinguish **figure** from **ground**, to identify contours and apply **closure**, and to group stimuli according to **similarity, proximity, continuity,** and **common fate**. Some aspects of *depth perception*, such as *retinal disparity* and *convergence*, may be innate as well. The theory of **learning-based inference** also correctly points out that perception is influenced by experience, such as

context, **perceptual set**, and *culture*. Many aspects of depth perception, such as *relative motion, linear perspective,* and *atmospheric perspective,* seem to be learned.

Despite all we know about sensation and perception, many people uncritically accept the evidence of their senses (and perceptions) at face value. This allows magicians, politicians, and marketers an opening through which they can manipulate our perceptions and, ultimately, our behavior.

CRITICAL THINKING APPLIED

Subliminal Perception and Subliminal Persuasion

Subliminal messages, in the form of *priming*, have been shown to affect an individual's responses on simple tasks under carefully controlled conditions. Yet, despite advertising claims to the contrary, there is no evidence that techniques of **subliminal persuasion** are effective in persuading a mass audience to change their attitudes or behaviors.

DISCOVERING PSYCHOLOGY **VIEWING GUIDE**

Watch the following video by logging into MyPsychLab (www.mypsychlab.com).
After you have watched the video, answer the questions that follow.

PROGRAM 7: **SENSATION AND PERCEPTION**

Program Review

1. Imagine that a teaspoon of sugar is dissolved in 2 gallons of water. Rita can detect this level of sweetness at least half the time. This level is called the
   a. distal stimulus.
   b. perceptual constant.
   c. response bias.
   d. absolute threshold.

2. What is the job of a receptor?
   a. to transmit a neural impulse
   b. to connect new information with old information
   c. to detect a type of physical energy
   d. to receive an impulse from the brain

3. In what area of the brain is the visual cortex located?
   a. in the front
   b. in the middle
   c. in the back
   d. under the brain stem

4. What is the function of the thalamus in visual processing?
   a. It relays information to the cortex.
   b. It rotates the retinal image.
   c. It converts light energy to a neural impulse.
   d. It makes sense of the proximal stimulus.

5. David Hubel discusses the visual pathway and the response to a line. The program shows an experiment in which the response to a moving line changed dramatically with changes in the line's
   a. thickness.
   b. color.
   c. speed.
   d. orientation.

6. Misha Pavel used computer graphics to study how
   a. we process visual information.
   b. rods differ from cones in function.
   c. we combine information from different senses.
   d. physical energy is transduced in the visual system.

7. Imagine that a baseball player puts on special glasses that shift his visual field up 10 degrees. When he wears these glasses, the player sees everything higher than it actually is. After some practice, the player can hit with the glasses on. What will happen when the player first tries to hit with the glasses off?
   a. He will think that the ball is lower than it is.
   b. He will think that the ball is higher than it is.
   c. He will accurately perceive the ball's position.
   d. It is impossible to predict an individual's reaction in this situation.

8. Imagine that a small dog is walking toward you. As the dog gets closer, the image it casts on your retina
   a. gets larger.
   b. gets darker.
   c. gets smaller.
   d. stays exactly the same size.

9. Imagine the same small dog walking toward you. You know that the dog's size is unchanged as it draws nearer. A psychologist would attribute this to
   a. perceptual constancy.
   b. visual paradoxes.
   c. contrast effects.
   d. threshold differences.

10. Which of the following best illustrates that perception is an active process?
    a. bottom-up processing
    b. motion parallax
    c. top-down processing
    d. parietal senses

11. The program shows a drawing that can be seen as a rat or as a man. People were more likely to identify the drawing as a man if they
    a. were men themselves.
    b. had just seen pictures of people.
    c. were afraid of rats.
    d. looked at the picture holistically rather than analytically.

12. Where is the proximal stimulus found?
    a. in the outside world
    b. on the retina
    c. in the occipital lobe
    d. in the thalamus

13. How is visual information processed by the brain?
    a. It's processed by the parietal lobe, which relays the information to the temporal lobe.
    b. It's processed entirely within the frontal lobe.
    c. It's processed by the occipital lobe, which projects to the thalamus, which projects to a succession of areas in the cortex.
    d. If the information is abstract, it's processed by the cortex; if it's concrete, it's processed by the thalamus.

14. Which of the following is true about the proximal stimulus in visual perception?

    a. It's identical to the distal stimulus because the retina produces a faithful reproduction of the perceptual world.

    b. It's upside-down, flat, distorted, and obscured by blood vessels.

    c. It's black and white and consists of very sparse information about horizontal and vertical edges.

    d. It contains information about the degree of convergence of the two eyes.

15. Which of the following is an example of pure top-down processing (i.e., requires no bottom-up processing)?

    a. hallucinating

    b. understanding someone else's speech when honking horns are obscuring individual sounds

    c. perceiving a circular color patch that has been painted onto a canvas

    d. enjoying a melody

16. Which sensory information is *not* paired with the cortical lobe that is primarily responsible for processing it?

    a. visual information, occipital lobe

    b. speech, frontal lobe

    c. body senses, parietal lobe

    d. hearing, central sulcus lobe

17. When your eyes are shut, you cannot

    a. hallucinate.

    b. use contextual information from other senses to make inferences about what's there.

    c. transform a distal visual stimulus into a proximal stimulus.

    d. experience perceptual constancy.

18. The researcher David Hubel is best known for

    a. mapping visual receptor cells.

    b. discovering subjective contours.

    c. identifying the neural pathways by which body sensations occur.

    d. realizing that hearing and smell originate from the same brain area.

19. The primary reason why psychologists study illusions is because

    a. they help in identifying areas of the cortex that have been damaged.

    b. they serve as good "public relations" material for curious novices.

    c. they help in categorizing people into good and bad perceivers.

    d. they help in understanding how perception normally works.

20. The shrinking-square illusion demonstrated by Misha Pavel relies on processing of which kinds of feature?

    a. edges and corners

    b. color and texture

    c. torque and angular momentum

    d. density gradients and motion

4 Learning and Human *Nurture*

CHAPTER PROBLEM Assuming Sabra's fear of flying was a response she had learned, could it also be treated by learning? If so, how?

CRITICAL THINKING APPLIED Do Different People Have Different "Learning Styles"?

N 1924, JOHN WATSON BOASTED, "GIVE ME A DOZEN HEALTHY INFANTS, well-formed, and my own specified world to bring them up in and I'll guarantee to take any one at random and train him to become any type of specialist I might select—doctor, lawyer, artist, merchant-chief, and, yes, even beggar-man and thief, regardless of his talents, penchants, tendencies, abilities, vocations, and race of his ancestors." Decades later, the assumption behind Watson's lofty claim became the bedrock on which the community called Walden Two was built: *Nurture* trumps *nature.* Or, to put it another way: Environment carries far more weight than heredity in determining our behavior.

At Walden Two, residents can enter any sort of profession that interests them. In their leisure time, they can do whatever they like: attend concerts, lie on the grass, read, or perhaps drink coffee with friends. They have no crime, no drug problems, and no greedy politicians. In exchange for this happy lifestyle, community members must earn four "labor credits" each day, doing work needed by the community. (That's about 4 hours' work—fewer hours for unpleasant tasks, such as cleaning sewers, but more for the easiest work, perhaps pruning the roses.) Following Watson's vision, the founder of Walden Two, a psychologist named Frasier, believed people could have happy, fulfilling lives in an environment psychologically engineered to reward people for making socially beneficial choices. To reap these benefits, all a community must do is change the way it deals out rewards.

Where was this community built? Only in the mind of behaviorist B. F. Skinner. You see, *Walden Two* is a novel written by Skinner (1948) to promote his ideas on better living through behavioral psychology. But so alluring was the picture he painted of this mythical miniature society that many real-world communes sprang up, using *Walden Two* as the blueprint.

None of the real communities based on *Walden Two* ran so smoothly as the one in Skinner's mind. Yet at least one such group, Twin Oaks, located in Virginia, thrives after more than 40 years—but not without substantial modifications to Skinner's vision (Kincade, 1973). In fact, you can visit this group electronically through its website at www.twinoaks.org/index.html (Twin Oaks, 2007).

Nor was behaviorism's fate exactly as Skinner had envisioned it. Although the behaviorist perspective dominated psychology during much of the 20th century, its fortunes fell as cognitive psychology grew in prominence. But what remains is behaviorism's substantial legacy, including impressive theories of behavioral learning and a valuable set of therapeutic tools for treating learned disorders—such as fears and phobias. To illustrate what behaviorism has given us, consider the problem that confronted Sabra.

A newly minted college graduate, Sabra landed a dream job at an advertising firm in San Francisco. The work was interesting and challenging, and she enjoyed her new colleagues. The only problem was that her supervisor had asked her to attend an upcoming conference in Hawaii—and take an extra few days of vacation there at the company's expense. Why was that a problem? Sabra had a fear of flying.

PROBLEM: **Assuming Sabra's fear of flying was a response she had learned, could it also be treated by learning? If so, how?**

A common stereotype of psychological treatment involves "reliving" traumatic experiences that supposedly caused fear or some other symptom. Behavioral learning therapy, however, works differently. It focuses on the here and now instead of the past: The therapist acts like a coach, teaching the client new responses to replace old problem behaviors. So, as you consider how Sabra's fear might be treated, you might think along the following lines:

- What problematic behaviors would we expect to see in people like Sabra who are afraid of flying?
- What behaviors could Sabra learn to replace her fearful behavior?
- How could these new behaviors be taught?

While the solution to Sabra's problem involves learning, it's not the sort of hit-the-books learning that usually comes to mind for college students. Psychologists define the concept of **learning** broadly, as *a process through which experience produces a lasting change in behavior or mental processes.* According to this definition, then, Sabra's "flight training" would be learning—just as taking golf lessons or reading this text is a learning experience.

To avoid confusion, two parts of our definition need elaboration. First, we underscore the idea that learning involves a *lasting change.* Suppose you go to your doctor's office and get a particularly painful injection, during which the sight of the needle becomes associated with pain. The result: The next time you need a shot, and every time thereafter, you wince when you first see the needle. This persistent change in responding involves learning. In contrast, a simple, reflexive reaction, such as jumping when you hear an unexpected loud noise, does *not* qualify as learning because it produces no lasting change—nothing more than a fleeting reaction, even though it does entail a change in behavior.

Second, learning affects *behavior* or *mental processes.* In the doctor's office example above, it is easy to see how learning affects behavior. But mental processes are more difficult to observe. How could you tell, for example, whether a laboratory rat had simply learned the behaviors required to negotiate a maze (turn right, then left, then right . . .) or whether it was following some sort of mental image of the maze, much as you would follow a road map? (And why should we care what, if anything, was on a rat's mind?) Let's venture a little deeper into our definition of learning by considering the controversy surrounding mental processes.

learning   A lasting change in behavior or mental processes that results from experience.

Behavioral Learning versus Cognitive Learning The problem of observing mental events, whether in rats or in people, underlies a long-running controversy between behaviorists and cognitive psychologists that threads through this entire chapter. For more than 100 years, behaviorists maintained that psychology could be a true science only if it disregarded subjective mental processes and focused solely on observable stimuli and responses. On the other side of the issue, cognitive psychologists contend that the behavioral view is far too limiting and that understanding learning requires us to make inferences about hidden mental processes. In the following pages, we will see that both sides in this dispute have made important contributions to our knowledge.

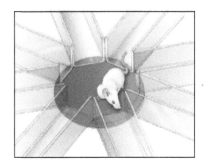

The behavioral perspective says that many abnormal behaviors are *learned*.

Learning versus Instincts So, what does learning—either behavioral or cognitive—do for us? Nearly all human activity, from working to playing to interacting with family and friends, involves some form of learning. Without learning, we would have no human language. We wouldn't know who our family or friends were. We would have no memory of our past or goals for our future. And without learning, we would be forced to rely on simple reflexes and a limited repertoire of innate behaviors, sometimes known as "instincts."

In contrast with learning, instinctive behavior is heavily influenced by genetic programming, as we see in bird migrations or animal mating rituals. In humans, however, behavior is much more influenced by learning than by instincts. For us, learning provides greater flexibility to adapt quickly to changing situations and new environments. In this sense, then, learning represents an evolutionary advance over instincts.

This giant leatherback turtle "instinctively" returns to its birthplace each year to nest. Although this behavior is heavily influenced by genetics, environmental cues such as tidal patterns play a role as well. Thus, scientists usually shun the term *instinct*, preferring the term *species-typical behavior*.

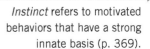

CONNECTION CHAPTER 9

Instinct refers to motivated behaviors that have a strong innate basis (p. 369).

Simple and Complex Forms of Learning Some forms of learning are quite simple. For example, if you live near a busy street, you may learn to ignore the sound of the traffic. This sort of learning, known as **habituation**, involves learning *not to respond* to stimulation. Habituation occurs in all animals that have nervous systems, from insects and worms to people. It helps you focus on important stimuli while ignoring stimuli that need no attention, such as the feel of the chair you are sitting on or the sound of the air conditioning in the background.

Another relatively simple form of learning is our general preference for familiar stimuli as contrasted with novel stimuli. This **mere exposure effxect** occurs regardless of whether the stimulus was associated with something pleasurable, or we were even aware of the stimulus. The mere exposure effect probably accounts for the effectiveness of much advertising (Zajonc, 1968, 2001). It also helps explain our attraction to people we see often at work or school and for songs we have heard at least a few times.

Other kinds of learning can be more complex. One type involves learning a connection between two stimuli—as when you associate a certain scent with a particular person who wears that fragrance. Another occurs when we associate our actions with rewarding or punishing consequences, such as a reprimand from the boss or an A from a professor. The initial sections of the chapter will emphasize these two especially important forms of **behavioral learning**, which we will call *classical conditioning* and *operant conditioning*.

In the third section of the chapter, we shift our focus from external behavior to internal mental processes. There, our look at *cognitive learning* will consider how sudden "flashes of insight" and imitative behavior require theories that go beyond behavioral learning to explain how we solve problems or why children imitate behavior for which they see other people being rewarded. We will also discuss acquisition of concepts, the most complex form of learning and, notably, the sort of learning you do in your college classes. We will close the chapter on a practical note by considering how to use the psychology of learning to help you study more effectively—and enjoy it.

Now, let's begin—with a form of behavioral learning that accounts for many of your own likes and dislikes: *classical conditioning.*

habituation Learning not to respond to the repeated presentation of a stimulus.

mere exposure effect A learned preference for stimuli to which we have been previously exposed.

behavioral learning Forms of learning, such as classical conditioning and operant conditioning, that can be described in terms of stimuli and responses.

4.1 KEY QUESTION
What Sort of Learning Does Classical Conditioning Explain?

CONNECTION CHAPTER 1

Structuralism and *functionalism* were two of the early "schools" of psychology (p. 14).

Ivan Pavlov (1849–1936) would have been insulted had you called him a psychologist. In fact, this Russian physiologist had only contempt for the structuralist and functionalist psychology of his time, which he saw as hopelessly mired in speculation about subjective mental life (Todes, 1997). Pavlov and the hundreds of student researchers who passed through his research "factory" were famous for their work on the digestive system—for which Pavlov eventually snared a Nobel prize (Fancher, 1979; Kimble, 1991).

Unexpectedly, however, their experiments on salivation (the first step in digestion) went awry, sending Pavlov and his crew on a detour into the psychology of learning—a detour that occupied Pavlov for the rest of his life. The problem they encountered was that their experimental animals began salivating even *before* food was put in their mouths (Dewsbury, 1997), which—from a biological perspective—was inexplicable, as salivation normally occurs only *after* food enters the mouth. Yet, in Pavlov's animals, saliva would start flowing when they merely saw the food or they heard the footsteps of the lab assistant bringing the food.

This response was a puzzle. What could be the biological function of salivating before receiving food? When Pavlov and his associates turned their attention to understanding these "psychic secretions," they made a series of discoveries that would forever change the course of psychology (Pavlov, 1928; Todes, 1997). Quite by accident, they had stumbled upon an objective model of learning that could be manipulated in the laboratory to tease out the connections among stimuli and responses. This discovery, now known as **classical conditioning**, forms the Core Concept of this section:

classical conditioning   A form of behavioral learning in which a previously neutral stimulus acquires the power to elicit the same innate reflex produced by another stimulus.

> ### Core Concept 4.1
>
> **Classical conditioning is a basic form of learning in which a stimulus that produces an innate reflex becomes associated with a previously neutral stimulus, which then acquires the power to elicit essentially the same response.**

In the following pages, we will see that classical conditioning accounts for some important behavior patterns found not only in animals but also in people. By means of classical conditioning, organisms learn about cues that help them anticipate and avoid danger, as well as cues alerting them to food, sexual opportunity, and other conditions that promote survival. First, however, let's examine the fundamental features Pavlov identified in classical conditioning.

To study classical conditioning, Pavlov (in the center of the photo) placed his dogs in a restraining apparatus. The dogs were then presented with a *neutral stimulus*, such as a tone. Through its association with food, the neutral stimulus became a *conditioned stimulus* eliciting salivation.

The Essentials of Classical Conditioning

Pavlov's work on learning focused on manipulating simple, automatic responses known as *reflexes* (Windholz, 1997). Salivation and eye blinks are examples of such reflexes, which commonly result from stimuli that have biological significance: The blinking reflex, for example, protects the eyes; the salivation reflex aids digestion.

Pavlov's great discovery was that his dogs could associate these reflexive responses with *new* stimuli—*neutral stimuli* that had previously produced no response (such as the sound of the lab assistant's footsteps). Thus, they could *learn* the connection between a reflex and a new stimulus. For example, Pavlov found he could teach a dog to salivate upon hearing a certain sound, such as the tone produced by striking a tuning fork or a bell. You have experienced the same sort of learning if your mouth waters when you read the menu in a restaurant.

To understand how these "conditioned reflexes" worked, Pavlov's team employed a simple experimental strategy. They first placed an untrained dog in a harness and set up a vial to capture the animal's saliva. Then, at intervals, they sounded a tone, after which they gave the dog a bit of food. At first, the dog salivated only after receiving the food—demonstrating a normal, biological reflex. But gradually, over a number of trials pairing the tone with the food, the dog began to salivate in response to the tone alone. Pavlov and his students had discovered that a **neutral stimulus** (one without any reflex-provoking power, such as a tone or a light), when paired with a natural reflex-producing stimulus (such as food), will by itself begin to elicit a learned response (salivation) similar to the original reflex. In humans, classical conditioning is the learning process that makes us associate romance with flowers or chocolate.

Figure 4.1 illustrates the main features of Pavlov's classical conditioning procedure. At first glance, the terms may seem a bit overwhelming. Nevertheless, you will find it immensely helpful to study them carefully now so they will come to mind easily later—when we analyze complicated, real-life learning situations, as in the acquisition and treatment of fears, phobias, and food aversions.

Acquisition Classical conditioning always involves an **unconditioned stimulus (UCS)**, a stimulus that automatically—that is, without conditioning—provokes a reflexive response. Pavlov used food as the UCS because it reliably produced the salivation reflex.

neutral stimulus Any stimulus that produces no conditioned response prior to learning. When it is brought into a conditioning experiment, the researcher will call it a conditioned stimulus (CS). The assumption is that some conditioning occurs after even one pairing of the CS and UCS.

unconditioned stimulus (UCS) In classical conditioning, UCS is the stimulus that elicits an unconditioned response.

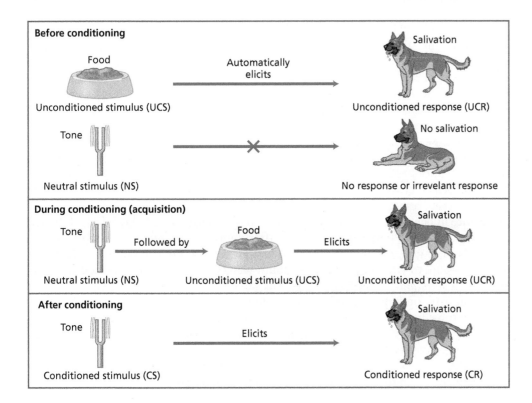

FIGURE 4.1

Basic Features of Classical Conditioning

Before conditioning, the food (UCS) naturally elicits salivation (UCR). A tone from a tuning fork is a neutral stimulus (NS) and has no effect. During conditioning (the acquisition phase), the tone (NS) is paired with the food (UCS), which continues to elicit the salivation response (UCR). Through its association with the food, the previously neutral tone becomes a conditioned stimulus (CS), gradually producing a stronger and stronger salivation response (CR).

Source: Zimbardo, P.G., & Gerrig, R. J.. (1999). *Psychology and Life,* 15th ed. Boston, MA: Allyn and Bacon. Copyright © 1999 by Pearson Education. Reprinted by permission of the publisher.

unconditioned response (UCR)   In classical conditioning, the response elicited by an unconditioned stimulus without prior learning.

acquisition   The initial learning stage in classical conditioning, during which the conditioned response comes to be elicited by the conditioned stimulus.

conditioned stimulus (CS)   In classical conditioning, a previously neutral stimulus that comes to elicit the conditioned response. Customarily, in a conditioning experiment, the neutral stimulus is called a conditioned stimulus when it is first paired with an unconditioned stimulus (UCS).

conditioned response (CR)   In classical conditioning, a response elicited by a previously neutral stimulus that has become associated with the unconditioned stimulus.

In the language of classical conditioning, then, this is called an *unconditioned reflex* or, more commonly, an **unconditioned response (UCR)**. It is important to realize that the UCS–UCR connection is "wired in" and so involves no learning. His dogs didn't have to learn to salivate when they received food, just as you don't have to learn to cry out when you feel pain: Both are unconditioned responses.

Acquisition, the initial learning stage in classical conditioning, pairs a new stimulus—a neutral stimulus (NS)—with the unconditioned stimulus. Typically, after several trials, the neutral stimulus (the tone produced by a tuning fork, for example) will elicit essentially the same response as does the UCS. So, in Pavlov's experiments, when the sound alone began to produce salivation, this formerly neutral stimulus became a **conditioned stimulus (CS)**. Although this response to the conditioned stimulus is essentially the same as the response originally produced by the unconditioned stimulus, we now refer to it as the **conditioned response (CR)**—because it is occurring as a result of conditioning, or learning. The same thing may have happened to you in grade school, when your mouth watered (a conditioned response) at the sound of the lunch bell (a conditioned stimulus).

In conditioning, as in telling a joke, timing is critical. In most cases, the CS and UCS must occur *contiguously* (close together in time) so the organism can make the appropriate connection during acquisition. The range of time intervals between the CS and UCS that produces the best conditioning depends on the type of response being conditioned. For motor responses, such as eye blinks, a short interval of one second or less is best. For visceral responses, such as heart rate and salivation, longer intervals of five to 15 seconds work best. Conditioned fear optimally requires even longer intervals of many seconds or even minutes between the CS and the UCS. Taste aversions, we will see, can develop even after several hours' delay. (These time differentials probably have survival value. For example, in the case of taste aversions, rats seem to be genetically programmed to eat small amounts of an unfamiliar food and, if they don't get sick, return to the food after a few hours.)

These, then, are the building blocks of classical conditioning: the UCS, UCR, NS (which becomes the CS), CR, and the timing that connects them. Why did it take Pavlov three decades and 532 experiments to study such a simple phenomenon? There was more to classical conditioning than first met Pavlov's eyes. Along with *acquisition,* he also discovered *extinction, spontaneous recovery, generalization,* and *discrimination*—which we will now explore.

Extinction and Spontaneous Recovery   As a result of your grade-school experience with lunch bells, would your mouth still water at the sound of a school bell in your neighborhood today? In other words, do conditioned responses remain permanently in your behavioral repertoire? The good news, based on experiments by Pavlov's group, suggests they do not. Conditioned salivation responses in Pavlov's dogs were easily eliminated by withholding the UCS (food) over several trials in which the CS (the tone) was presented alone. In the language of classical conditioning, we call this **extinction (in classical conditioning)**. It occurs when a conditioned response disappears after repeated presentations of the CS without the UCS. Figure 4.2 shows how the conditioned response (salivation) becomes weaker and weaker during extinction trials. So, after years of hearing bells that were not immediately followed by food, we would not expect your mouth-watering response upon hearing a bell today. Extinction, then, is of considerable importance in behavioral therapies for fears and phobias, such as Sabra's fear of flying.

Now for the bad news: Imagine that, after many years, you are visiting your old grade school to give a presentation to the first graders. While you are there, the lunch bell rings—and, to your surprise, your mouth waters. Why? The conditioned response has made a *spontaneous recovery*. Much the same thing happened with Pavlov's dogs: Some time after undergoing extinction training, they would salivate again when they heard the tone. In technical terms, this **spontaneous recovery** occurs when *the CR reappears after extinction and after a period without exposure to the CS*. Happily, when spontaneous recovery happens, the conditioned response nearly always reappears at a lower intensity, as you can see in Figure 4.2. In practice, then, the CR can gradually be eliminated, although this may require several extinction sessions.

extinction (in classical conditioning)   The weakening of a conditioned response in the absence of an unconditioned stimulus.

CONNECTION CHAPTER 13

➤

Behavioral therapies are based on classical conditioning and operant conditioning (p. 568).

spontaneous recovery   The unexpected reappearance of an extinguished conditioned response after a time delay.

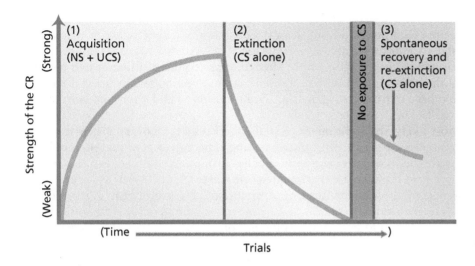

FIGURE 4.2

**Acquisition, Extinct[...]
Spontaneous Recov[...]**

(1) During acquisition (NS + UCS), [...] strength of the CR increases rapidly, after which the NS becomes the CS. (2) During extinction, when the UCS no longer follows the CS, the strength of the CR drops to zero. (3) After extinction, the CR may occasionally reappear, even when the UCS is still not presented; only the CS alone occurs. This reappearance of the CR is called "spontaneous recovery."

Source: Zimbardo, P.G., & Gerrig, R. J. (1999). *Psychology and Life,* 15th ed. Boston, MA: Allyn and Bacon. Copyright © 1999 by Pearson Education. Reprinted by permission of the publisher.

Generalization Now, switching to a visual CS, suppose you have developed a fear of spiders. Most likely, you will probably respond the same way to spiders of all sizes and markings. We call this **stimulus generalization:** giving a conditioned response to stimuli that are similar to the CS. Pavlov demonstrated stimulus generalization in his laboratory by showing that a well-trained dog would salivate in response to a tone of a slightly different pitch from the one used during conditioning. As you would expect, the closer the new sound was to the original, the stronger the response.

In everyday life, we see stimulus generalization when people acquire fears as a result of traumatic events. So a person who was bitten by a dog may develop a fear of all dogs rather than fearing only the specific dog responsible for the attack. Likewise, stimulus generalization accounts for an allergy sufferer's sneeze upon seeing a paper flower. In short, by means of stimulus generalization, we learn to give old responses in new situations.

stimulus generalization The extension of a learned response to stimuli that are similar to the conditioned stimulus.

Discrimination Learning As a child, you may have learned to salivate at the sound of the lunch bell, but—thanks to *stimulus discrimination*—your mouth probably didn't water when the doorbell rang. Much the opposite of stimulus generalization, **stimulus discrimination** occurs when an organism learns to respond to one stimulus but not to stimuli that are similar. Pavlov and his students demonstrated this when they taught dogs to distinguish between two tones of different frequencies. Once again, their procedure was simple: One tone was followed by food while another was not. Over a series of trials, the dogs gradually learned to discriminate between the tones, evidenced in salivation elicited by one tone and not the other. Beyond the laboratory, stimulus discrimination is the concept that underlies advertising campaigns aimed at conditioning us to discriminate between particular brands, as in the perennial battle between Pepsi and Coke. ✳

stimulus discrimination Learning to respond to a particular stimulus but not to stimuli that are similar.

Explore the Concept Stimulus Generalization and Stimulus Discrimination at MyPsychLab

Applications of Classical Conditioning

The beauty of classical conditioning is that it offers a simple explanation for many behaviors, from cravings to aversions. Moreover, it gives us the tools for eliminating unwanted human behaviors—although Pavlov himself never attempted any therapeutic applications. Instead, it fell to the American behaviorist, John Watson, to apply classical conditioning techniques to human problems.

The Notorious Case of Little Albert More than 90 years ago, John Watson and Rosalie Rayner first demonstrated conditioned fear in a human (Brewer, 1991; Fancher, 1979). In an experiment that would be considered unethical today, Watson and Rayner (1920/2000) conditioned an infant named Albert to react fearfully to

John Watson and Rosalie Rayner conditioned Little Albert to fear furry objects like this Santa Claus mask (*Discovering Psychology*, 1990). For years, no one knew what had become of Little Albert after the research. Archival records recently revealed that, sadly, Douglass Merritte—the boy known as Little Albert—died just a few years later from acquired hydrocephalus (Beck, et al., 2009).

CONNECTION CHAPTER 2

The *autonomic nervous system* regulates the internal organs (p. 57).

a white laboratory rat. They created the fear response by repeatedly presenting the rat, paired with the loud sound of a steel bar struck with a mallet, which acted as an aversive UCS. It took only seven trials for "Little Albert" to react with distress at the appearance of the rat (CS) alone. After Albert's response to the rat had become well established, Watson and Rayner showed that his aversion readily generalized from the rat to other furry objects, such as a Santa Claus mask and a fur coat worn by Watson (Harris, 1979).

Most likely, the experiment caused Albert only temporary distress, because his fear response extinguished rapidly, making it necessary for Watson and Raynor to renew the fear conditioning periodically. In fact, the need to recondition Albert nearly ended the whole experiment when Watson and Rayner were attempting to generalize the child's fear to a dog, a rabbit, and a sealskin coat. Watson decided to "freshen the reaction to the rat" by again striking the steel bar. The noise startled the dog, which began to bark, frightening not only Little Albert but both experimenters (Harris, 1979).

Unlike Little Albert's short-lived aversion to furry objects, some fears learned under highly stressful conditions can persist for years (LeDoux, 1996). During World War II, the Navy used a gong sounding at the rate of 100 rings a minute as a call to battle stations. For combat personnel aboard ship, this sound became strongly associated with danger—a CS for emotional arousal. The persistent effect of this association was shown in a study conducted 15 years after the war, when Navy combat veterans still gave a strong autonomic reaction to the old "call to battle stations" (Edwards & Acker, 1962).

Like those veterans, any of us can retain a readiness to respond to old emotional cues. Fortunately, however, classical conditioning also provides tools for eliminating troublesome conditioned fears (Wolpe & Plaud, 1997). One strategy combines extinction of the conditioned fear response with *counterconditioning*, a therapy that teaches a relaxation response to the CS. This approach has been particularly effective in dealing with phobias. As you may be thinking, we ought to consider counterconditioning as part of the treatment plan to help Sabra conquer her fear of flying.

Conditioned Food Aversions All three of your authors have had bad experiences with specific foods. Phil got sick after eating pork and beans in the grade school lunchroom, Bob became ill after a childhood overdose of olives, and Vivian became queasy after eating chicken salad (formerly one of her favorite meals). In all three cases, we associated our distress with the distinctive sight, smell, and taste of the food—which, for years afterward, was enough to cause feelings of nausea.

Unpleasant as it is, learning to avoid a food associated with illness has survival value. That's why humans and other animals readily form an association between illness and food—much more readily than between illness and a nonfood stimulus, such as a light or a tone. For example, nothing else present in your authors' environments during their bad food experiences became associated with nausea. Phil didn't become wary of the trays his school lunches were served on, Bob didn't develop a reaction to the highchair in which he developed his olive antipathy, and Vivian didn't avoid the friends who were dining with her when she ate the treacherous meal. It was solely the foods that became effective conditioned stimuli.

John Garcia and Robert Koelling (1966) first recognized this highly selective CS–UCS connection when they noticed rats wouldn't drink from water bottles in the chambers where they had previously been made nauseous by radiation. Could the rats be associating the taste of the water in those bottles with being sick? Subsequent experiments confirmed their suspicions and led to yet another important discovery. Rats readily learned an association between flavored water and illness, yet the rats could *not* be conditioned to associate flavored water with the pain of an electric shock delivered through a grid on the floor of the test chamber. This makes good sense from an evolutionary perspective, because illness can easily result from drinking (or eating) poisonous substances but rarely occurs following a sharp pain to the feet. Similarly, rats easily learned to fear bright lights and noise when they preceded an electric shock—but could *not* learn to connect those light and sound cues with subsequent illness. Such observations suggest that organisms have an inborn preparedness to associate certain stimuli with certain consequences, while other CS–UCS combinations are highly resistant to learning.

Biological Predispositions: A Challenge to Pavlov A major insight resulting from the Garcia and Koelling experiments is that conditioned aversions involve both nature and nurture. That is, the tendency to develop taste aversions appears to be "wired in" as part of our biological nature rather than purely learned. It is this biological basis for taste aversions that prompts psychologists to question some aspects of Pavlov's original theory of classical conditioning (Rescorla & Wagner, 1972).

Biological predispositions may also impact the timing involved in acquiring a conditioned aversion. For example, food aversions can develop even when the time interval between eating and illness extends over several hours—as compared with just a few seconds in Pavlov's experiments. Again, this suggests that in food aversions, we are not dealing with a simple classically conditioned response as Pavlov understood it but, instead, with a response based as much in nature (biology) as in nurture (learning).

And such biological predispositions go far beyond taste and food aversions. Psychologists now believe that many common fears and phobias arise from *genetic preparedness,* built into us from our ancestral past, disposing us to learn fears of harmful objects: snakes, spiders, blood, lightning, heights, and closed spaces. Likewise, anxiety about mutilation or other bodily harm can contribute to fears of seemingly modern objects or situations, such as injections, dentistry, or flying.

Real-World Applications of Classical Conditioning Examples of the impact of classical conditioning on human and on animal behavior abound. One clever experiment by John Garcia and his colleagues demonstrated how aversive conditioning can dissuade wild coyotes from attacking sheep. They did so by wrapping toxic lamb burgers in sheepskins and stashing them on sheep ranches: When roaming coyotes found and ate these meaty morsels, they became sick and—as predicted—developed a distaste for lamb meat. The result was a whopping 30 to 50 percent reduction in sheep attacks! So powerful was this aversion that, when captured and placed in a cage with a sheep, the coyotes would not get close to it. Some even vomited at the sight of a sheep (Garcia, 1990). Unfortunately, this type of conditioning does not appear to extend to sheep ranchers' behavior: Despite the success of these experiments in natural predator control, scientists have been unable to get the ranchers to use this method. Apparently, sheep ranchers have a strong aversion to feeding lamb to coyotes!

A conditioned taste aversion can make a coyote stop killing sheep.

Need help getting to sleep, studying, or getting yourself to the gym? A little classical conditioning might help: Try finding positive stimuli to associate with each of those activities. For example, experts recommend keeping your sleeping area quiet and peaceful at all times of the day and night so you learn to associate it with relaxation. Similarly, creating for yourself a specific study space that offers a comfortable chair, pleasant aromas or tastes, or other sensations that positively stimulate you will help you associate those positive stimuli with studying—especially if you allow yourself exposure to these particular stimuli only when you study. And the same principles apply to your efforts to exercise more: If you listen to your favorite music only while working out, chances are you'll start getting that pumped-up, "feels good to exercise" feeling when you hear it—and then you can use it as a stimulus to get yourself to the gym!

What is the big lesson coming out of all this work on classical conditioning? *Conditioning involves both nature and nurture.* That is, conditioning depends not only on the learned relationship among stimuli and responses but also on the way an organism is genetically attuned to certain stimuli in its environment (Barker et al., 1978; Dickinson, 2001). What any organism can—and cannot—learn in a given setting is to some extent a product of its evolutionary history (Garcia, 1993). And that is a concept that Pavlov never understood.

[PSYCHOLOGY MATTERS]

Taste Aversions and Chemotherapy

Imagine that your friend Jena is about to undergo her first round of chemotherapy, just to make sure any stray cells from the tumor found in her breast will be destroyed. To her surprise, the nurse enters the lab, not with the expected syringe, but with a dish of licorice-flavored ice cream. "Is this a new kind of therapy?" she asks. The nurse replies that it is, indeed, explaining that most patients who undergo chemotherapy experience nausea, which can make them "go off their feed" and quit eating, just when their body needs nourishment to fight the disease. "But," says the nurse, "We have found a way around the problem. If we give patients an unusual food before their chemotherapy, they usually develop an aversion only to that food." She continues, "Did you ever hear of Pavlov's dogs?"

Conditioned food aversions make evolutionary sense, as we have seen, because they helped our ancestors avoid poisonous foods. As is the case with some of our other evolutionary baggage, such ancient aversions can cause modern problems. People undergoing chemotherapy often develop aversions to normal foods in their diets to such an extent that they become malnourished. The aversions are nothing more than conditioned responses in which food (the CS) becomes associated with nausea. Chemotherapy personnel trained in classical conditioning use their knowledge to prevent the development of aversions to nutritive foods by arranging for meals to be withheld just before chemotherapy. And, as in Jena's case, they also present a "scapegoat" stimulus. By consuming candies or ice cream with unusual flavors before treatment, patients develop taste aversions only to those special flavors. For some patients, this practical solution to problems with chemotherapy may make the difference between life and death (Bernstein, 1988, 1991).

Check Your Understanding

✓●[Study and Review at MyPsychLab

1. **APPLICATION:** Give an example of classical conditioning from your everyday life and identify the UCS, UCR, NS (which becomes the CS), and CR.

2. **RECALL:** Before a response, such as salivation, becomes a conditioned response, it is a(n) _____.

3. **APPLICATION:** If you learned to fear electrical outlets after getting a painful shock, what would be the CS?

4. **UNDERSTANDING THE CORE CONCEPT:** Which one of the following could be an *unconditioned* stimulus (UCS) involved in classical conditioning?

   a. food
   b. a flashing light
   c. music
   d. money

....

Answers 1. Everyday examples of classical conditioning involve learning taste aversions (such as a dislike for olives) or fears (such as a fear of going to the dentist), as well as responses developed through association with positive stimuli. For example, if you develop feelings of contentment from the smell of your grandmother's house, the UCS is your grandmother's house, the UCR the contentment you feel when you are with her, the NS the smell of her house, which becomes the CS when you learn to associate it with her (after visiting her at her house several times). **2.** innate reflex or UCR **3.** The electrical outlet **4.** a—because it is the only one that produces an innate reflexive response (UCR).

┌─4.2 KEY QUESTION
└──── How Do We Learn New Behaviors By Operant Conditioning?

With classical conditioning, you can teach a dog to salivate, but you can't teach it to sit up or roll over. Why? Salivation is a passive, involuntary reflex, while sitting up and rolling over are much more complex responses that we usually think of as voluntary. To a behavioral psychologist, however, such "voluntary" behaviors are really controlled by *rewards* and *punishments*. And because rewards and punishments play no role in classical conditioning, another important form of learning must be at work. Psychologists call it *operant conditioning*. (An *operant,* incidentally, is an observable behavior that an organism uses to "operate" in, or have an effect on, the environment. Thus, if you are reading this book to get a good grade on the next test, reading is an operant behavior.) You might also think of **operant conditioning** as a form of learning in which the *consequences* of behavior can encourage behavior change. The Core Concept of this section puts the idea this way:

> **Core Concept 4.2**
>
> **In operant conditioning, the consequences of behavior, such as rewards and punishments, influence the probability that the behavior will occur again.**

Common rewarding consequences include money, praise, food, or high grades—all of which can encourage the behavior they follow. By contrast, punishments such as pain, loss of privileges, or low grades can discourage the behavior they follow.

As you will see, the theory of operant conditioning is an important one for at least two reasons. First, operant conditioning accounts for a much wider spectrum of behavior than does classical conditioning. And second, it explains *new and voluntary* behaviors—not just reflexive behaviors.

Skinner's Radical Behaviorism

The founding father of operant conditioning, American psychologist B. F. Skinner (1904–1990), based his whole career on the idea that the most powerful influences on behavior are its *consequences:* what happens immediately after the behavior. Actually, it wasn't Skinner's idea originally. He borrowed the notion of behavior being controlled by rewards and punishments from another American psychologist, Edward Thorndike, who demonstrated how hungry animals would work diligently to solve a problem by trial and error to obtain a food reward. Gradually, on succeeding trials, erroneous responses were eliminated and effective responses were "stamped in." Thorndike called this the **law of effect** (see Figure 4.3). The idea was that an animal's behavior leads to pleasant or unpleasant results that influence whether the animal will try those behaviors again.

The first thing Skinner did with Thorndike's psychology, however, was to rid it of subjective and unscientific speculation about the organism's feelings, intentions, or goals. What an animal "wanted" or the "pleasure" it felt was not important for an objective understanding of the animal's behavior. As a radical behaviorist, Skinner refused to consider what happens in an organism's mind, because such speculation cannot be verified by observation—and studying anything not directly observable threatened the scientific credibility of the fledgling field of psychology. For example, eating can be observed, but we cannot observe the inner experiences of hunger, the desire for food, or pleasure at eating.

The Power of Reinforcement

Skinner's passionate commitment to the establishment of behaviorism as a legitimate science permeated his work. For example, while we often speak of "reward" in casual conversation, Skinner preferred the more objective term **reinforcer**. Why so concerned over terminology? Skinner objected to the term *reward* on the grounds that rewards

operant conditioning   A form of behavioral learning in which the probability of a response is changed by its consequences—that is, by the stimuli that follow the response.

law of effect   The idea that responses that produced desirable results would be learned or "stamped" into the organism.

reinforcer   A condition (involving either the presentation or removal of a stimulus) that occurs after a response and strengthens that response.

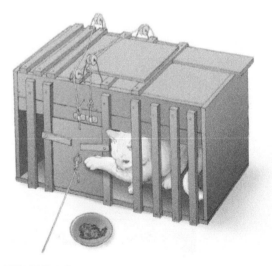

FIGURE 4.3

A Thorndike Puzzle Box

Unlike Pavlov's dogs, Thorndike's cats faced a problem requiring some kind of voluntary action on their part: how to open the door in the puzzle box to get a food reward lying just outside. To solve this problem, the animals used *trial-and-error learning,* rather than simple reflexive responses. At first, their responses seemed random, but gradually they eliminated ineffective behaviors. And when the effects of their behavior were desirable (that is, when the door finally opened and the animals got the food), they used this strategy on subsequent trials. This change in behavior based on consequences of previous trials is called the *law of effect.* Much the same trial-and-error learning occurs when you learn a skill, such as shooting a basketball.

positive reinforcement   A stimulus presented after a response and increasing the probability of that response happening again.

negative reinforcement   The removal of an unpleasant or aversive stimulus, contingent on a particular behavior. Contrast with *punishment.*

operant chamber   A boxlike apparatus that can be programmed to deliver reinforcers and punishers contingent on an animal's behavior. The operant chamber is often called a "Skinner box."

imply pleasure on the part of the recipient, which in turn assumes knowledge of the organism's inner experience—which was forbidden territory. Reinforcers, on the other hand, act on the behavior (rather than the organism's mind), which *is* directly observable (Winn, 2001). So Skinner defined a reinforcer as any stimulus that *follows* and *strengthens* a response. Food, money, and sex serve this function for most peoples; so do attention, praise, or a smile. All these are examples of **positive reinforcement,** which strengthens a response by occurring after the response and making the behavior more likely to occur again.

Most people know about positive reinforcement, of course, but fewer people understand the other main way to strengthen operant responses: the reinforcement of behavior by the *removal* of an unpleasant or aversive stimulus. Psychologists call this **negative reinforcement.** (The word *negative* here is used in the mathematical sense of *subtract* or *remove,* while *positive* means *add* or *apply.* Please be careful not to make the common mistake of confusing negative reinforcement with punishment: Instead, remember that reinforcement always *strengthens* behavior, whereas punishment—which we'll discuss shortly—weakens it.) So using an umbrella to avoid getting wet during a downpour is a behavior learned and maintained by negative reinforcement. That is, you use the umbrella to avoid or remove an unpleasant stimulus (getting wet). Likewise, when you buckle your seat belt to stop the annoying sound of the seat-belt buzzer in your car, you are receiving negative reinforcement. And taking a few minutes right now to highlight the distinction between negative reinforcement and punishment in your notes will help you avoid the unpleasant consequence of missing that question on the exam—providing yet another example of the power of negative reinforcement to strengthen behavior!

Reinforcing Technology: The "Skinner Box"   One of B. F. Skinner's (1956) innovations was a simple device for studying the effects of reinforcers on laboratory animals: a box with a lever an animal could press to obtain food. He called this device an **operant chamber.** (Nearly everyone else called it a "Skinner box," a term he detested.) Over the years, thousands of psychologists have used the apparatus to study operant conditioning.

The virtue of the operant chamber lay in its capacity to control the timing and frequency of reinforcement, factors that exert important influences on behavior, as you will soon see. Moreover, the Skinner box could be programmed to conduct experiments at any time of day—even when the researcher was home in bed.

Contingencies of Reinforcement   The timing and frequency of reinforcement determines its effect on behavior. So while grade reports delivered two or three times a year may reinforce college and university students for their studying, such a schedule has little effect on their day-to-day study habits. Many professors realize this, of course,

In this cartoon, the child was positively reinforced for crying by being allowed to sleep with mom and dad. Ironically, this is negative reinforcement for the parents, as they are letting the child sleep in their bed in order to avoid being disturbed by a crying baby.

Source: Hi & Lois © King Features Syndicate.

and schedule exams and assignments to award grades periodically throughout their courses. In this way, they encourage continual studying rather than one big push at the end of the semester. But that's not always enough.

Whether we're talking about college students, Fortune 500 CEOs, or laboratory rats, any plan to influence operant learning requires careful consideration of the timing and frequency of rewards. How often will they receive reinforcement? How much work must they do to earn a reinforcer? Will they be reinforced for every response or only after a certain number of responses? We will consider these questions below in our discussion of **reinforcement contingencies**, involving the many possible ways of associating responses and reinforcers. And stay alert for the *Psychology Matters* at the end of this section, where we will give you some tips for applying these principles to your own studying.

Continuous versus Intermittent Reinforcement Suppose you want to teach your dog a trick—say, sitting on command. It would be a good idea to begin the training program with a reward for every correct response. Psychologists call this **continuous reinforcement**. It's a useful tactic early in the learning process, because rewarding every correct response and ignoring the incorrect ones provide quick and clear feedback about which responses are desired. In addition, continuous reinforcement is useful for **shaping** complex new behaviors. Shaping, often used in animal training, involves the deliberate use of rewards (and sometimes punishments) to encourage better and better approximations of the desired behavior. (You have experienced shaping in school, as a teacher taught you to read, write, or play a musical instrument by gradually setting

B. F. Skinner is shown reinforcing the animal's behavior in an operant chamber or "Skinner box." The apparatus allows the experimenter to control all the stimuli in the animal's environment.

reinforcement contingencies   Relationships between a response and the changes in stimulation that follow the response.

continuous reinforcement   A type of reinforcement schedule by which all correct responses are reinforced.

shaping   An operant learning technique in which a new behavior is produced by reinforcing responses that are similar to the desired response.

Just to set the record straight, we'd like to mention a bit of trivia about the "baby tender" crib that Skinner devised for his daughter, Deborah (Benjamin & Nielsen-Gammon, 1999). It consisted of an enclosed, temperature-controlled box that unfortunately bore a superficial resemblance to the operant chambers used in his experiments. The public learned about the "baby tender" from an article by Skinner in the magazine *Ladies' Home Journal*. The story took on a life of its own, and, years later, stories arose about Deborah Skinner's supposed psychotic breakdown, lawsuits against her father, and eventual suicide—none of which were true. In fact, Deborah grew up to be a well-adjusted individual who loved her parents.

Shaping was undoubtedly used to get the dolphins to jump this high: They were likely reinforced gradually for higher and higher jumps until they eventually only received reinforcement for the highest jump.

intermittent reinforcement   A type of reinforcement schedule by which some, but not all, correct responses are reinforced; also called partial reinforcement.

extinction (in operant conditioning)   A process by which a response that has been learned is weakened by the absence or removal of reinforcement. (Compare with *extinction in classical conditioning*.)

schedule of reinforcement   A program specifying the frequency and timing of reinforcements.

ratio schedule   A program by which reinforcement depends on the number of correct responses.

interval schedule   A program by which reinforcement depends on the time interval elapsed since the last reinforcement.

fixed ratio (FR) schedule   A program by which reinforcement is contingent on a certain, unvarying number of responses.

higher standards.) By means of shaping, the teacher can continually "raise the bar" or increase the performance level required for earning a reward. This tells the learner when performance has improved. In general, then, we can say that *continuous reinforcement is a good strategy for shaping new behaviors.*

Continuous reinforcement does have some drawbacks. For one thing, failure to reward a correct response on one trial could easily be misinterpreted as a signal that the response was not correct. Consistency, then, is key to its success. Another drawback of continuous reinforcement occurs after the reinforcer has been earned many times: once the learner becomes satiated, the reinforcer loses its power to motivate. For example, if someone were training you to shoot free throws by rewarding you with a big candy bar after each successful attempt, the first candy bar might be highly rewarding, but after you have had several, the reward value dissipates.

Happily, once the desired behavior becomes well established (for example, when your dog has learned to sit), the demands of the situation change. The learner no longer needs rewards to discriminate a correct response from an incorrect one. It's time to shift to **intermittent reinforcement** (also called *partial reinforcement*), the rewarding of some, but not all, correct responses. A less frequent schedule of reinforcement—perhaps, after every third correct response—still serves as an incentive for your dog to sit on command, while helping to avoid satiation. In general, whether we're dealing with people or animals, *intermittent reinforcement is the most efficient way to maintain behaviors that have already been learned* (Robbins, 1971; Terry, 2000). As a practical matter, the transition to intermittent reinforcement can be made easier by mixing in social reinforcement ("Good dog!") with more tangible rewards (food, for example).

A big advantage of intermittent reinforcement is its resistance to *extinction*. The operant version of **extinction (in operant conditioning)** occurs when reinforcement is withheld, as when a gambler stops playing a slot machine that never pays off. Why do responses strengthened by intermittent reinforcement resist extinction better than do continuously rewarded responses? Imagine two gamblers and two slot machines. One machine inexplicably pays off on every trial, and another, more typical, machine pays on an unpredictable, intermittent schedule. Now, suppose both devices suddenly stop paying. Which gambler will catch on first? The one who has been rewarded for each push of the button (continuous reinforcement) will quickly notice the change, while the gambler who has won only occasionally (on partial reinforcement) may continue playing unrewarded for a long while.

Schedules of Reinforcement   Now that we have convinced you of the power of intermittent reinforcement, you should know it occurs in two main forms or **schedules of reinforcement.** One, the **ratio schedule**, rewards after a certain *number of responses.* The other, known as an **interval schedule**, reinforces after a certain *time interval.* Let's look at the advantages and disadvantages of each. As you read this section, refer frequently to Figure 4.4, which provides a visual summary of the results of each type of reinforcement.

Ratio Schedules   Suppose you own a business and pay your employees based on the amount of work they perform: You are maintaining them on a *ratio schedule* of reinforcement. That is, ratio schedules occur when rewards depend on the *number of correct responses* (see Figure 4.4). Psychologists make a further distinction between two subtypes of ratio schedules, *fixed ratio* and *variable ratio* schedules.

Fixed ratio (FR) schedules commonly occur in industry, when workers are paid on a piecework basis—a certain amount of pay for a certain amount of production. So if you own a tire factory and pay each worker a dollar for every five tires produced, you are using a fixed ratio schedule. Under this scheme, the amount of work (the number of responses) needed for a reward remains constant, but the faster people work, the more money they get. Not surprisingly, management likes FR schedules because the rate of responding is usually high (Terry, 2000; Whyte, 1972), or, in other words, it keeps people working quickly. Retail establishments also use fixed ratio schedules when, for example, you receive a free pizza after buying ten pizzas from your local pizza shop—which keeps you coming back to the same place for your next pizza.

Variable ratio (VR) schedules are less predictable. Telemarketers work on a VR schedule, because they never know how many calls they must make before they get the next sale, which acts as a reinforcer for the caller. Slot machine players also respond on a variable ratio schedule, never knowing when the machine will pay off. In both cases, continually changing the requirements for reinforcement keeps responses coming at a high rate—so high, in fact, that the VR schedule usually produces more responding than any other reinforcement schedule. In a demonstration of just how powerful a VR schedule could be, Skinner showed that a hungry pigeon would peck a disk 12,000 times an hour for rewards given, on the average, for every 110 pecks (Skinner, 1953)!

Interval Schedules   Time is of the essence on an interval schedule. That is, with an interval schedule, reinforcement depends on responses made within a certain *time period* (rather than on the total number of responses given) (see Figure 4.4). Psychologists distinguish the same two kinds of interval schedules as ratio schedules: *fixed interval* and *variable interval* schedules.

Fixed interval (FI) schedules commonly occur in the work world, where they may appear as a periodic paycheck or praise from the boss at a monthly staff meeting. A student who studies for a weekly quiz is also on a fixed interval schedule. In all such cases, the interval does not vary, so the time period between rewards remains constant. You may have already guessed that fixed interval reinforcement usually results in a comparatively low response rate. Ironically, this is the schedule most widely adopted by business. Even a rat in a Skinner box programmed for a fixed interval schedule soon learns it must produce only a limited amount of work during the interval to get its reward. Pressing the lever more often than required to get the food reward is just wasted energy. Thus, both rats and humans on fixed interval schedules may display only modest productivity until near the end of the interval, when the response rate increases rapidly. (Think of college students facing a term paper deadline.) Graphically, in Figure 4.4, you can see the "scalloped" pattern of behavior that results from this flurry of activity near the end of each interval.

Variable interval (VI) schedules are, perhaps, the most unpredictable of all. On a VI schedule, the time interval between rewards (or punishments) varies. The resulting rate of responding can be high, although not usually as high as for the VR schedule. (Think about it this way: You control the frequency of reward on the ratio schedule, because the faster you work, the sooner you reach the magic number required for the reward. On interval schedules, though, no matter how slowly or quickly you work, you cannot make time pass any faster: Until the specified amount of time has passed, you will not receive your reward.) For a pigeon or a rat in a Skinner box, the variable interval schedule may be a 30-second interval now, three minutes next, and a one-minute wait later. In the classroom, pop quizzes exemplify a VI schedule, as do random visits by the boss or drug tests on the job. And watch for responses typical of a VI schedule while waiting for an elevator: Because the delay between pressing the call button and the arrival of the elevator varies each time, some of your companions will press the button multiple times—much like pigeons in a Skinner box—as if more responses within an unpredictable time interval could control the elevator's arrival.

Primary and Secondary Reinforcers   You can easily see why stimuli that fulfill basic biological needs or desires provide reinforcement: Food reinforces a hungry animal, and water reinforces a thirsty one. Similarly, the opportunity for sex becomes a reinforcer for a sexually aroused organism. Psychologists call such stimuli **primary reinforcers.**

But money or grades provide a different sort of reinforcement: You can't eat them or drink them. Nor do they directly satisfy any physical need. So why do such things reinforce behavior so powerfully? Neutral stimuli, such as money or grades, acquire a reinforcing effect by association with primary reinforcers and so become **conditioned reinforcers or secondary reinforcers** for operant responses. The same thing happens with praise, smiles of approval, gold stars, "reward cards" used by merchants, and various

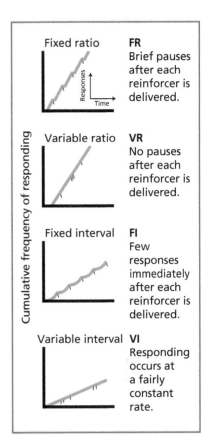

FIGURE 4.4

Reinforcement Schedules

The graphs show typical patterns of responding produced by four different schedules of reinforcement. (The hash marks indicate when reinforcement is delivered.) Notice that the steeper angle of the top two graphs shows how the ratio schedules usually produce more responses over a given period of time than do the interval schedules.

variable ratio (VR) schedule   A reinforcement program by which the number of responses required for a reinforcement varies from trial to trial.

fixed interval (FI) schedule   A program by which reinforcement is contingent upon a certain, fixed time period.

variable interval (VI) schedule   A program by which the time period between reinforcements varies from trial to trial.

primary reinforcer   A reinforcer, such as food or sex, that has an innate basis because of its biological value to an organism.

conditioned reinforcer or secondary reinforcer   A stimulus, such as money or tokens, that acquires its reinforcing power by a learned association with primary reinforcers.

kinds of status symbols. In fact, virtually any stimulus can become a secondary or conditioned reinforcer by being associated with a primary reinforcer. With strong conditioning, secondary reinforcers such as money, status, or awards can even become ends in themselves.

CONNECTION CHAPTER 9

The brain's reward system provides greater rewards for sweet and fatty foods, a preference that evolved from our ancestors' need for calorie-dense food to sustain them through times when food was scarce (p. 377).

instinctive drift   The tendency of an organism's innate (instinctive) responses to interfere with learned behavior.

token economy   A therapeutic method, based on operant conditioning, by which individuals are rewarded with tokens, which act as secondary reinforcers. The tokens can be redeemed for a variety of rewards and privileges.

Premack principle   The concept, developed by David Premack, that a more-preferred activity can be used to reinforce a less-preferred activity.

Piggy Banks and Token Economies The distinction between primary and secondary reinforcers brings up a more subtle point: Just as we saw in classical conditioning, operant conditioning is not pure learning, but it is built on a biological base; hence our "wired-in" preferences for certain reinforcers—to which "junk" food manufacturers pander with their sweet and fatty treats.

To illustrate the power of biology in operant conditioning, we offer the story of Keller and Marian Breland, two students of Skinner's who went into the animal training business, but encountered some unexpected trouble with their trained pigs. As you may know, pigs are very smart animals. Thus, the Brelands had no difficulty teaching them to pick up round wooden tokens and deposit them in a "piggy bank." The problem was that, over a period of weeks, these porcine subjects reverted to piggish behavior: They would repeatedly drop the token, root at it, pick it up and toss it in the air, and root it some more. This happened in pig after trained pig. Why? Because rooting is instinctive behavior for pigs. The Brelands (1961) found similar patterns in critters as diverse as raccoons, chickens, whales, and cows, and coined the term **instinctive drift** to describe this tendency for innate response tendencies to interfere with learned behavior. No wonder, then, people can't make their cats stop scratching the furniture—or can't altogether avoid the temptation of junk food.

Happily, psychologists have had better luck using tokens with people than with pigs. Mental institutions, for example, have tapped the power of conditioned reinforcers by setting up so-called *token economies* to encourage desirable and healthy patient behaviors. Under a **token economy**, staff may reinforce grooming or taking medication with plastic tokens. Patients soon learn they can exchange the tokens for highly desired rewards and privileges (Ayllon & Azrin, 1965; Holden, 1978). Alongside other forms of therapy, token economies help mental patients learn strategies for acting effectively in the world (Kazdin, 1994).

Preferred Activities as Reinforcers: The Premack Principle The opportunity to perform desirable activities can reinforce behavior just as effectively as food or drink or other primary reinforcers. For example, people who exercise regularly might use a daily run or fitness class as a reward for getting other tasks done. Likewise, teachers have found that young children will learn to sit still if such behavior is reinforced with the opportunity to run around and make noise later (Homme et al., 1963).

The principle at work here says the opportunity to engage in a preferred activity (active, noisy play) can be used to reinforce a less-preferred behavior (sitting still and listening to the teacher). Psychologists call this the **Premack principle**, after its discoverer. David Premack (1965) first demonstrated this concept in thirsty rats, which would spend more time running in an exercise wheel if the running were followed by an opportunity to drink. Conversely, another group of rats that were exercise deprived, but not thirsty, would increase the amount they drank if drinking were followed by a chance to run in the wheel. In exactly the same way, then, parents can use the Premack principle to get children to make the bed or do the dishes if the task is followed by the opportunity to play with friends. What preferred activity can you use to reinforce yourself for studying?

Reinforcement Across Cultures The laws of operant learning apply to all creatures with a brain. The biological mechanism underlying reinforcement is, apparently, much the same across species. On the other hand, exactly what serves as a reinforcer varies widely. Experience suggests that food for a hungry organism and water for a thirsty one will act as reinforcers because they satisfy basic needs related to survival. But what any particular individual will choose to satisfy those needs may depend as much on learning as on survival instincts—especially in humans, where secondary reinforcement is so important. For us, culture plays an especially powerful role in determining what will act as reinforcers. So while people in some cultures would find eating a cricket reinforcing, most people of Euro-American ancestry would not. Similarly, disposing of a noisy cricket might seem both sensible and rewarding to a Baptist, yet aversive to a Buddhist. And, just to underscore our point, we note that watching a game of cricket would most likely be rewarding to a British cricket fan—although punishingly dull to most Americans.

So culture shapes preferences in reinforcement, but reinforcement also shapes culture. When you first walk down a street in a foreign city, all the differences that catch your eye are merely different ways people have found to seek reinforcement or avoid punishment. A temple houses cultural attempts to seek rewards from a deity. Clothing may reflect attempts to seek a reinforcing mate or to feel comfortable in the climate. And a culture's cuisine evolves from learning to survive on the native plant and animal resources. In this sense, then, culture is a set of behaviors originally learned by operant conditioning and shared by a group of people.

Entomophagy is the practice of eating insects as food, which people in some cultures find reinforcing.

The Problem of Punishment

Punishment as a means of influencing behavior poses several difficulties, as schoolteachers and prison wardens will attest. Ideally, we might think of **punishment** as the opposite of reinforcement: an *aversive* consequence used to *weaken* the behavior it follows. And like reinforcement, punishment comes in two main forms. **Positive punishment** requires *application of an aversive stimulus*—as, when you touch a hot plate, the painful consequence reduces the likelihood of you repeating that behavior. The other main form of punishment, **negative punishment**, results from the *removal of a reinforcer*—as when parents take away a misbehaving teen's car keys. (You can see, then, that the terms *positive* and *negative*, when applied to punishment, operate the same way they do when applied to reinforcement: Positive punishment adds something, and negative punishment takes something away.) Technically, however—and this is one of the problems of punishment—an aversive stimulus is punishing only if it actually weakens the behavior it follows. In this sense, then, spankings or speeding tickets may or may not be punishment, depending on the results.

punishment An aversive consequence which, occurring after a response, diminishes the strength of that response. (Contrast with *negative reinforcement*.)

positive punishment The application of an aversive stimulus after a response.

negative punishment The removal of an attractive stimulus after a response.

Punishment versus Negative Reinforcement You have probably noted that punishment and negative reinforcement both involve unpleasant stimuli. How can you distinguish between the two? Let's see how punishment and negative reinforcement differ, using the following examples (see Figure 4.5). Suppose an animal in a

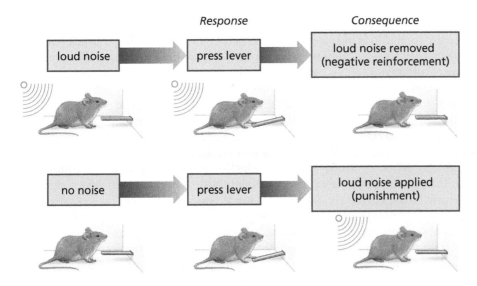

	Response	*Consequence*
loud noise	press lever	loud noise removed (negative reinforcement)
no noise	press lever	loud noise applied (punishment)

FIGURE 4.5

Negative Reinforcement and Punishment Compared

TABLE 4.1 **Four Kinds of Consequences**

		Apply (add) Stimulus (positive)	Remove (subtract) Stimulus (negative)
What is the effect of the stimulus (consequence) on behavior?	The probability of the behavior increases.	**Positive reinforcement** Example: An employee gets a bonus for good work (and continues to work hard).	**Negative reinforcement** Example: You take aspirin for your headache, and the headache vanishes (so you take aspirin the next time you have a headache).
	The probability of the behavior decreases.	**Positive punishment** Example: A speeder gets a traffic ticket (and drives away more slowly).	**Negative punishment** Example: A child who has stayed out late misses dinner (and comes home early next time).

Three important points to keep in mind as you study this table:
1. "Positive" and "negative" mean that a stimulus (consequence) has been added (presented) or subtracted (removed). These terms have nothing to do with "good" or "bad, pleasurable or painful."
2. We can often predict what effect a particular consequence will have, but the only way to know for sure whether it will be a reinforcer or a punisher is to observe its effect on behavior. For example, although we might guess that a spanking would punish a child, the attention might actually serve as a reinforcer to strengthen the unwanted behavior.
3. From a cognitive viewpoint, we can see that reinforcement consists of the presentation of a pleasant stimulus or the removal of an unpleasant one. Similarly, punishment entails the presentation of an unpleasant stimulus or the removal of a pleasant one.

Skinner box can turn off a loud, unpleasant noise by pressing a lever. This response produces negative reinforcement. Now compare that with the other animal in Figure 4.5 for which the loud noise serves as a punishment for pressing the lever.

The main point is this: Punishment and negative reinforcement lead to opposite effects on behavior (Baum, 1994). Punishment *decreases* a behavior or reduces its probability of recurring. In contrast, negative reinforcement—like positive reinforcement—always *increases* a response's probability of occurring again. And don't forget the descriptors *positive* and *negative* mean "add" and "remove." Thus, both positive reinforcement and positive punishment involve administering or "adding" a stimulus. On the other hand, negative reinforcement and negative punishment always involve withholding or removing a stimulus. For a concise summary of the distinctions between positive and negative reinforcement and punishment, please see Table 4.1.

Uses and Abuses of Punishment Many societies rely heavily on punishment and the threat of punishment to keep people "in line." We fine people, spank them, and give them bad grades, parking tickets, and disapproving looks. Around the world and throughout history, cultures have ritually engaged in shunning, stoning, flogging, imprisonment, and a veritable smorgasbord of creative methods of execution in attempts to deter unacceptable behavior. Currently, American jails and prisons contain more than 2 million people, while the United States currently maintains one in every 32 of its citizens in jail or prison or on probation or parole (Bureau of Justice Statistics, 2009).

Why do we use punishment so often? For one, it can sometimes produce an immediate change in behavior—which, incidentally, reinforces the punisher. For another, punishers may feel satisfaction by delivering the punishment, sensing they are "settling a score," "getting even," or making the other person "pay." This is why we speak of revenge as being "sweet," a sentiment that seems to underlie public attitudes toward the punishment of lawbreakers (Carlsmith, 2006).

But punishment—especially the sort of punishment involving pain, humiliation, or imprisonment—usually doesn't work as well in the long run (American Psychological Association, 2002b). Punished children may continue to misbehave; reprimanded employees may sabotage efforts to meet production goals. And people still commit crimes around the world, despite a variety of harsh punishment tactics. So why is punishment so difficult to use effectively? There are several reasons.

First, *punishment—unlike reinforcement—must be administered consistently.* Drivers will observe the speed limit when they know the highway patrol is watching; Andre will refrain from hitting his little brother when a parent is within earshot; and you will probably give up your wallet to a mugger who points a gun at you. But the power of punishment to suppress behavior usually disappears when the threat of punishment is removed (Skinner, 1953). If punishment is unlikely, it does not act as a deterrent—and in most cases, it is impossible to administer punishment consistently. Intermittent punishment is far less effective than punishment delivered after every undesired response: In fact, *not punishing* an occurrence of unwanted behavior can have the effect of rewarding it—as when a supervisor overlooks the late arrival of an employee. In general, you can be certain of controlling someone's behavior through punishment or threat of punishment only if you can control the environment all the time. Such total control is rarely feasible.

Second, *the lure of rewards may make the possibility of punishment seem worth the price.* This may be one factor impacting drug dealing—when the possibility of making a large amount of money outweighs the possibility of prison time (Levitt & Dubner, 2005). And, in a different way, the push-pull of punishment and rewards also affects dieters, when the short-term attraction of food may overpower the unwanted long-term consequences of weight gain. So if you attempt to control someone's behavior through punishment, you may fail if you do not control the rewards as well.

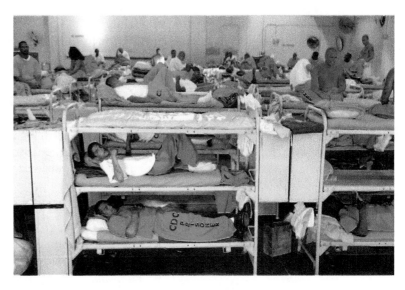

Prison riots and other aggressive behavior may result from highly punitive conditions.

Third, *punishment triggers escape or aggression.* When punished, an organism's survival instinct prompts it to flee from or otherwise avoid further punishment. And if escape is blocked, aggression can result. Corner a wounded animal, and it may savagely attack you. Put two rats in a Skinner box with an electrified floor grid, and the rats will attack each other (Ulrich & Azrin, 1962). Put humans in a harsh prison environment, and they may riot—or, if they are prison guards, they may abuse the prisoners (Zimbardo, 2004b, 2007).

Further, in a punitive environment, whether it be a prison, a school, or a home, people learn that punishment and aggression are legitimate means of influencing others. The punishment–aggression link also explains why abusing parents so often come from abusive families, and why aggressive delinquents frequently come from homes where aggressive behavior is commonplace (Golden, 2000). Unfortunately, the well-documented relationship between punishment and aggression remains widely unknown to the general public.

Here's a fourth reason why punishment is so often ineffective: *Punishment makes the learner fearful or apprehensive, which inhibits learning new and more desirable responses.* Unable to escape punishment, an organism may eventually give up its attempts at flight or fight and surrender to an overwhelming feeling of hopelessness. This passive acceptance of a punitive fate produces a behavior pattern called *learned helplessness* (Overmier & Seligman, 1967). In people, this reaction can produce the mental disorder known as depression (Terry, 2000).

If you want to produce a constructive change in attitudes and behavior, learned helplessness and depression are undesirable outcomes. The same goes for aggression and escape. And, perhaps most importantly, *punishment fails to teach learners what to do differently*, because it focuses attention on what *not* to do. All of these outcomes interfere with new learning. By contrast, individuals who have not been punished feel much freer to experiment with new behaviors.

Yet a fifth reason why punitive measures may fail: *Punishment is often applied unequally*, even though that violates our standards of fair and equal treatment. For example, parents and teachers punish boys more often than girls (Lytton & Romney, 1991). Then, too, children (especially grade school children) receive more physical punishment than do adults. And, to give one more example, our schools—and probably our society at large—more often punish members of minority groups than members of the majority (Hyman, 1996).

CONNECTION CHAPTER 11

In the Stanford Prison Experiment, the behavior of normal, healthy college men changed drastically after just a few days in a simulated prison environment (p. 500).

CONNECTION CHAPTER 14

Learned helplessness was originally found in dogs that, when repeatedly unable to escape shocks in their cages, eventually gave up and stopped trying. Learned helplessness has been documented widely in humans, including abused and discouraged children, battered wives, and prisoners of war (p. 624).

Does Punishment Ever Work? In limited circumstances, punishment can work remarkably well. For example, punishment can halt the self-destructive behavior of children with autism, who may injure themselves severely in some cases by banging their heads or chewing the flesh off their fingers. A mild electric shock or a splash of cold water in the face can quickly stop such unwanted behavior, although effects may be temporary (Holmes, 2001). It can also be combined effectively with reinforcement—as when students receive good grades for studying and failing grades for neglecting their work.

Punishment is also more likely to be successful if it involves a *logical consequence:* a consequence closely related to the undesirable behavior—as contrasted with an *un*related punishment, such as spanking or grounding. So, if a child leaves a toy truck on the stairs, a logical consequence might be to lose the toy for a week. To give another example, a logical consequence of coming home late for dinner is getting a cold dinner.

Rather than a purely punitive approach to misbehavior, research supports the combination of logical consequences, extinction, and the rewarding of desirable alternative responses. When you do decide to use punishment, it should meet the following conditions:

- *Punishment should be swift*—that is, immediate. Any delay will impair its effectiveness, so "You'll get spanked when your father gets home" is a poor punishment strategy.
- *Punishment should be consistent*—administered every time the unwanted response occurs. When bad behavior goes unpunished, the effect can actually be rewarding.
- *Punishment should be limited in duration and intensity*—meaningful enough to stop the behavior but appropriate enough to "make the punishment fit the crime."
- *Punishment should clearly target the behavior* and be a *logical consequence of the behavior* rather than an attack on character of the person (humiliation, sarcasm, or verbal abuse) or physical pain.
- *Punishment should be limited to the situation in which the response occurred.*
- *Punishment should not give mixed messages* to the punished person (such as, "You are not permitted to hit others, but I am allowed to hit you").
- *The most effective punishment is usually negative punishment,* such as loss of privileges, rather than the application of unpleasant stimuli such as a spanking.

A Checklist for Modifying Operant Behavior

Think of someone whose behavior you would like to change. For the sake of illustration, let's consider your niece Maddy's temper tantrums, which seem to be occurring with greater frequency—sometimes even when you take her out in public. Operant conditioning offers a selection of tools that can help: positive reinforcement on a variety of schedules, plus negative reinforcement, extinction, and punishment.

- Since *positive reinforcement* is always good bet, identify and encourage a desirable behavior in place of the unwanted behavior. The most effective parents and teachers often do this by shifting the child's attention to some other reinforcing activity. When taking her to the grocery store, for example, involve her in simple choices between, say, the green apples or the red ones. This keeps her interested, which will help prevent a temper tantrum, and also gives you an opportunity to provide positive reinforcement for her help ("Good idea, Maddy—I like the red ones, too!") And don't overlook the Premack principle, which lets Maddy do something she enjoys if she behaves for a certain period of time. (Incidentally, this is where *shaping* comes into play: To be effective, you must set goals for Maddy that are within her reach, so she can achieve them and reap the benefits of positive reinforcement. So, you might aim for just 20 minutes of good behavior at first, then—after she has achieved it and been rewarded—gradually work up to longer and longer periods of time.) Use continuous reinforcement at first, then scale back to a combination of intermittent reinforcement schedules to keep her tantrum free.
- *Negative reinforcement* can be useful too. If, for example, one of Maddy's household chores is taking out the trash, tell her you'll do it for her if she can play nicely with her sister (with no temper tantrums) that afternoon. That way, she avoids something she'd rather not do, which reinforces her for good behavior. You may have enjoyed negative reinforcement yourself if you've had a professor who let you opt out of the final exam if your other exam scores were high enough or skip a homework assignment if you'd achieved some other important goal in the class.

There are less effective applications of negative reinforcement, however. For example, parents commonly use nagging to try to get their children to, say, clean their rooms. In this scenario, parents nag until the room gets cleaned—thus, the child cleans the room to stop or to avoid the nagging. While this may get the job done, it's generally not pleasant for anyone. Instead, behaviorists recommend parents create positive reinforcers to provide incentives for the kids to clean their rooms. By offering meaningful rewards or using the Premack principle to encourage desired behaviors, you accomplish the same behavioral change without the tension that typically accompanies nagging or other aversive stimuli.

- *Extinction* guarantees a solution, but only if you control all the reinforcers. In Maddy's case, extinction comes from not giving in to the temper tantrum and not giving her what she wants. Instead, you simply allow the tantrum to burn itself out. This can be a challenge, since it means you must suffer through the tantrum, maybe even feeling embarrassed if she's throwing the tantrum in public. (Have you ever wondered why children seem intuitively to pick the most public places for such displays? Perhaps because they quickly learn they will be "rewarded" with candy or attention from an exasperated parent who just wants them to stop—which is another misuse of negative reinforcement!) Another problem with extinction, however, is that it may take a while, so extinction is not a good option if the subject is engaging in dangerous behavior, such as playing in a busy street.

- *Punishment* may be tempting, but we have seen that it usually produces unwanted effects, such as aggression or escape. In addition, punishment often damages the relationship between the punisher and the person being punished and is difficult to employ with unfailing consistency. If you do decide to punish Maddy for her tantrums, make it a logical consequence, such as a "time out" in her room if she is acting up at home—and doing so swiftly, but without undue harshness.

The best approach—often recommended by child psychologists—combines several tactics. In Maddy's case, this might involve both reinforcing her desirable behaviors and using extinction or logical consequences on her undesirable ones. We encourage you to try these strategies for yourself the next time you are dealing with someone whose behavior is undesirable. And remember: The behavior you may want to change could be your own!

Operant and Classical Conditioning Compared

Now that we have examined the main features of operant and classical conditioning, let's compare them side by side. As you can see in Table 4.2, the *consequences* of behavior—especially rewards and punishments—distinguish operant conditioning different from classical conditioning. But note this point of potential confusion: As the example in Figure 4.6 shows, food acts as a reward in operant conditioning, but in

TABLE 4.2 Classical and Operant Conditioning Compared

Classical Conditioning	Operant Conditioning
Behavior is controlled by stimuli that *precede* the response (by the CS and UCS).	Behavior is controlled by consequences (rewards, punishments, and the like) that *follow* the response.
No reward or punishment is involved (although pleasant and aversive stimuli may be used).	Often involves reward (reinforcement) or punishment.
Through conditioning, a new stimulus (the CS) comes to produce "old" (reflexive) behavior.	Through conditioning, a new stimulus (a reinforcer) produces new behavior.
Extinction is produced by withholding the UCS.	Extinction is produced by withholding reinforcement.
Learner is passive (responds reflexively): Responses are involuntary. That is, behavior is *elicited* by stimulation.	Learner is active (operant behavior): Responses are voluntary. That is, behavior is *emitted* by the organism.

FIGURE 4.6

The Same Stimulus Plays Different Roles in Classical Conditioning and Operant Conditioning

The same stimulus (food) can play vastly different roles, depending on which type of conditioning is involved. In classical conditioning, it can be the UCS, while in operant conditioning it can serve as a reinforcer for operant behavior. Note also that classical conditioning involves the association of two stimuli that occur *before* the response. Operant conditioning involves a reinforcing (rewarding) or punishing stimulus that occurs *after* the response.

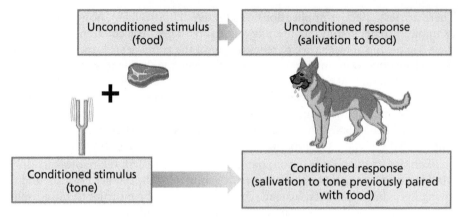

Classical Conditioning

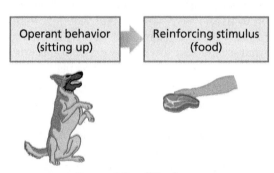

Operant Conditioning

classical conditioning, food is an unconditioned stimulus. The important thing to note is that in classical conditioning the food comes *before* the response—and therefore it cannot serve as a reward.

Because classical conditioning and operant conditioning differ in the order in which the stimulus and response occur, classically conditioned behavior is largely a response to *past stimulation*. (Think of Pavlov's dogs salivating after hearing a bell.) Operant behavior aims to attain some *future* reinforcement or avoid a punishment. (Think of a dog sitting to get a food reward.) To say it another way, operant conditioning requires a stimulus that follows the response, whereas classical conditioning ends with the response (see Figure 4.7).

FIGURE 4.7

Classical and Operant Conditioning Can Work Together

A response originally learned through classical conditioning can be maintained and strengthened by operant reinforcement.

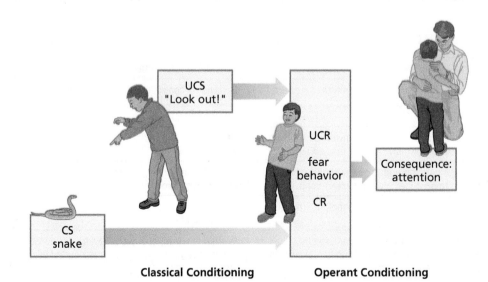

Classical Conditioning   **Operant Conditioning**

In this cartoon, Pavlov's dog is illustrating voluntary behavior (operant conditioning) by drooling in order to make Pavlov write in his little book.

Another difference between the two types of conditioning is the kinds of behaviors they target. Operant conditioning encourages *new behaviors*—whether they be making beds, going to work, developing healthy eating habits, or studying for an exam. Classical conditioning, on the other hand, emphasizes eliciting *old responses to new stimuli*— such as salivating at the sound of a bell or flinching at the sound of a dentist's drill.

You may have also noticed that extinction works in slightly different ways in the two forms of learning. In classical conditioning, extinction requires withholding the unconditioned stimulus. In operant conditioning, extinction results from withholding the reinforcer.

Operant conditioning and classical conditioning differ in several other important ways, as you saw in Table 4.2 (page 153). For one, operant behavior is not based on an automatic reflex action, as was the dog's salivation or Little Albert's crying. Accordingly, operant behavior seems more "voluntary"—more under the control of the responder. To paraphrase a proverb: You can stimulate a dog to salivation (a reflex), but you can't make it eat (an operant behavior).

But don't make the mistake of thinking that classical and operant conditioning are competing explanations for learning. They can be complementary. In fact, responses originally learned by classical conditioning will often be maintained later by operant conditioning. How? Consider a snake phobia. Suppose the fear of snakes was originally learned by classical conditioning when a snake (CS) was paired with a frightening UCS (someone yelling, "Look out!"). Once the phobic response is established, it could be maintained and strengthened by operant conditioning, as when bystanders give attention (positive reinforcement) to the fearful person (see Figure 4.7).

[PSYCHOLOGY MATTERS]

Using Psychology to Learn Psychology

You may have tried the Premack principle to encourage yourself to study more, perhaps by saving TV time or a trip to the refrigerator until your homework was done. It works for some people, but if it doesn't work for you, try making the studying itself more enjoyable and more reinforcing.

For most of us, getting together with people we like is reinforcing, regardless of the activity. So, make some (not all) of your studying a social activity. That is, schedule a time when you and another classmate or two can get together to identify and discuss important concepts, and try to predict what will be on the next test.

And don't focus just on vocabulary. Rather, try to discover the big picture—the overall meaning of each section of the chapter. The Core Concepts are a good place to start. Then you can discuss with your friends how the details fit in with the Core Concepts. You will most likely find that the social pressure of an upcoming study group (serving as an intermittent reinforcer) will help motivate you to get your reading done and identify murky points. When you get together for your group study session, you will discover that explaining what you have learned strengthens your own understanding. In this way, you reap the benefits of a series of reinforcements: time with friends, enhanced learning, and better performance on the exam.

Check Your Understanding

✓ **Study** and **Review** at **MyPsychLab**

1. **APPLICATION:** Give an example of a response a pet dog or cat might learn that could be explained by Thorndike's *law of effect*.

2. **APPLICATION:** Give an example of *negative reinforcement* from your own life.

3. **APPLICATION:** Suppose you have taught your dog to roll over for the reward of a dog biscuit. Which schedule of reinforcement would keep your dog responding the longest time?

   a. continuous reinforcement
   b. intermittent reinforcement
   c. negative reinforcement
   d. noncontingent reinforcement

4. **RECALL:** Give an example of something that serves as a conditioned reinforcer for most people.

5. **APPLICATION & ANALYSIS:** Suppose you are trying to teach Stevie not to hit his sister. What operant techniques would you use? Also, explain why extinction would not be wise in this case.

6. **UNDERSTANDING THE CORE CONCEPT:** What is a feature of operant conditioning that distinguishes it from classical conditioning?

Answers 1. Any response that was learned by being rewarded—such as sitting up for a food reward or scratching at the door to be let into the house—involves Thorndike's law of effect. **2.** Negative reinforcement occurs any time your behavior causes an unpleasant stimulus to stop bothering you. Examples include taking aspirin to stop a pain, going to the dentist for a toothache, or doing your chores to stop a roommate from nagging you. **3.** b **4.** Money is probably the most common example. **5.** The best approach is probably some combination of reinforcing alternative responses and "time out" for hitting behavior. Under extinction alone, Stevie would still continue to hit his sister for a period of time until the behavior is extinguished, which might inflict hardship on the sister. **6.** In operant conditioning, learning depends on stimuli that occur after the response. These stimuli include rewards and punishments. By contrast, classical conditioning focuses on stimuli that occur before the response.

4.3 KEY QUESTION
How Does Cognitive Psychology Explain Learning?

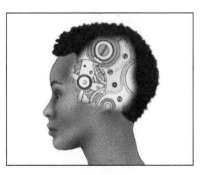

The cognitive perspective says that our *cognitions* can affect our mental health— or our mental disorders.

According to biologist J. D. Watson's (1968) account in *The Double Helix*, he and Francis Crick cracked the genetic code one day in a flash of insight following months of trial and error. You may have had a similarly sudden, if less famous, insight when solving a problem of your own. Such events present difficulties for strict behaviorists, because they obviously involve learning but are hard to explain in terms of Pavlovian or Skinnerian conditioning.

Many psychologists believe that an entirely different process, called *cognitive learning,* is responsible for such flashes of insight. From a cognitive perspective, learning does not always show itself immediately in behavior. Instead, learning can be reflected in mental activity alone—as the Core Concept for this section says:

Core Concept 4.3

According to cognitive psychology, some forms of learning must be explained as changes in mental processes rather than as changes in behavior alone.

Let's see how cognitive psychologists have approached this task of examining the covert mental processes behind learning. To do so, we first take you on a trip to the Canary Islands, off the coast of northern Africa.

Insight Learning: Köhler in the Canaries with Chimps

Isolated on the island of Tenerife during World War I, Gestalt psychologist Wolfgang Köhler *(KER-ler)* had time to think long and hard about learning. Disenchanted with the behaviorists' explanation for learning, Köhler sought to develop his own theories. To his way of thinking, psychology had to recognize mental processes as an essential component of learning, even though mental events had been spurned as subjective speculation by the behaviorists. To press his point, Köhler took advantage of a primate research facility constructed by the German government on Tenerife. There, he contrived experiments designed to reveal cognitive learning in observable behavior (Sharps & Wertheimer, 2000; Sherrill, 1991).

In a series of famous studies, Köhler showed that chimps could learn to solve complex problems, not just by trial and error (an explanation favored by behaviorists) but by "flashes of insight" that combined simpler responses learned previously. One such experiment involved Sultan, a chimp that had learned to pile up boxes and scramble on top of them to reach fruit suspended high in his cage, and to use sticks to obtain fruit that was just out of reach. When Köhler presented Sultan with a novel situation that combined the two problems—with fruit suspended even higher in the air—the chimp first attacked it unsuccessfully with sticks in trial-and-error fashion. Then, in apparent frustration, Sultan threw the sticks away, kicked the wall, and sat down. According to Köhler's report, the animal then scratched his head and began to stare at some boxes nearby. After a time of apparent "thinking," he suddenly jumped up and dragged a box and a stick underneath the fruit, climbed on the box, and knocked down his prize with the stick.

Remarkably, Sultan had never before seen or used such a combination of responses. This behavior, Köhler argued, was evidence that animals were not just mindlessly using conditioned responses but were learning by *insight:* by reorganizing their *perceptions*

The ruins of Köhler's old laboratory, known as La Casa Amarilla (the Yellow House), can still be seen near the town of Puerto de La Cruz. You can see a satellite view of it using the following coordinates in Google Earth: latitude 28° 24′52.23″ N and longitude 16° 31′47.93″ W. If you enjoy historical mysteries, you might read *A Whisper of Expionage,* a book exploring the possibility that Köhler was not only studying chimpanzee behavior but also spying on Allied shipping from his laboratory's vantage point on the coast of Tenerife during World War I (Ley, 1990).

CONNECTION CHAPTER 3

Gestalt psychology is best known for its work on perception (p. 118).

The sort of learning displayed by Köhler's chimps defied explanation by the behaviorists—in terms of classical conditioning and operant conditioning. Here, you see Sultan, Köhler's smartest animal, solving the problem of getting the bananas suspended out of reach by stacking the boxes and climbing on top of them. Köhler claimed that Sultan's behavior demonstrated insight learning.

of problems. He ventured that such behavior shows how apes, like humans, learn to solve problems by suddenly perceiving familiar objects in new forms or relationships—a decidedly mental process rather than a merely behavioral one. He called this **insight learning** (Köhler, 1925). Insight learning, said Köhler, results from an abrupt reorganization of the way a situation is perceived.

Behaviorism had no convincing explanation for Köhler's demonstration. Neither classical nor operant conditioning could account for Sultan's behavior in stimulus–response terms. Thus, the feats of Köhler's chimps demanded the cognitive explanation of perceptual reorganization.

Cognitive Maps: Tolman Finds Out What's on a Rat's Mind

Not long after Köhler's experiments with chimpanzees, the rats in Edward Tolman's lab at Berkeley also began behaving in ways that flew in the face of accepted behavioral doctrine. They would run through laboratory mazes as if following a mental "map" of the maze, rather than mindlessly executing a series of learned behaviors. Let's see how Tolman managed to demonstrate these "mindful" responses.

Mental Images—Not Behaviors If you have ever walked through your house in the dark, you have some idea what Tolman meant by "cognitive map." Technically, a **cognitive map** is a mental image an organism uses to navigate through a familiar environment. But could a simple-minded creature like a rat have such complex mental imagery? And, if so, how could the existence of these cognitive maps be demonstrated? A cognitive map, Tolman argued, was the only way to account for a rat quickly selecting an alternative route in a maze when the preferred path to the goal is blocked. In fact, rats will often select the shortest detour around a barrier, even though taking that particular route was never previously reinforced. Rather than blindly exploring different parts of the maze through trial and error (as behavioral theory would predict), Tolman's rats behaved as if they had a mental representation of the maze. (Figure 4.8 shows the arrangement of such a maze.)

In further support of his claim that learning was *mental,* not purely behavioral, Tolman offered another experiment: After his rats had learned to run a maze, he flooded it with water and showed that the rats were quite capable of swimming through

---

insight learning   A form of cognitive learning, originally described by the Gestalt psychologists, in which problem solving occurs by means of a sudden reorganization of perceptions.

cognitive map   In Tolman's work, a cognitive map was a mental representation of a maze or other physical space. Psychologists often use the term *cognitive map* more broadly to include an understanding of connections among concepts. Thus, a cognitive map can represent either a physical or a mental "space."

FIGURE 4.8

Using Cognitive Maps in Maze Learning

Rats used in this experiment preferred the direct path (Path 1) when it was open. When it was blocked at A, they preferred Path 2. When Path 2 was blocked at B, the rats usually chose Path 3. Their behavior indicated that they had a cognitive map of the best route to the food box.

Source: Tolman, E. C. & Honzik, C. H. (December 1930). Degrees of hunger, reward and nonreward, and maze learning in rats. *University of California Publication of Psychology,* 4(16).

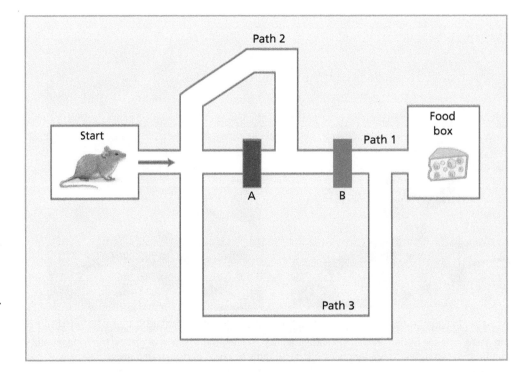

the maze. Again, this demonstrated what the animals had learned was a *concept*, not just behaviors. Instead of learning merely a sequence of right and left turns, Tolman argued, they had acquired a more abstract mental representation of the maze's spatial layout (Tolman & Honzik, 1930; Tolman et al., 1946).

Learning without Reinforcement In yet another study that attacked the very foundations of behaviorism, Tolman (1948) allowed his rats to wander freely about a maze for several hours. During this time, the rats received no rewards at all—they simply explored the maze. Yet, despite the lack of reinforcement, which behaviorists supposed to be essential for maze learning, the rats later learned to run the maze for a food reward more quickly than did other rats that had never seen the maze. Obviously, they had learned the maze during the exploratory period, even though no hint of learning could be seen in their behavior at the time. Tolman called this *latent learning*.

The Significance of Tolman's Work As with Köhler's experiments, what made Tolman's work both significant and provocative was its challenge to the prevailing views of Pavlov, Watson, and other behaviorists. While Tolman accepted the idea that psychologists must study observable behavior, he showed that simple associations between stimuli and responses could not explain the behavior observed in his experiments. Tolman's *cognitive* explanations, therefore, presented a provocative challenge to behaviorism (Gleitman, 1991).

Subsequent experiments on cognitive maps in rats, chimpanzees, and humans have broadly supported Tolman's work (Olton, 1992). More recently, brain imaging has pointed to the hippocampus as a structure involved in "drawing" the cognitive map in the brain (Jacobs & Schenk, 2003). So it seems clear that Tolman was on target: Organisms learn the spatial layout of their environments by exploration and do so even if they are not reinforced for exploring. From an evolutionary perspective, the ability to make cognitive maps would be highly adaptive in animals that must forage for food (Kamil et al., 1987).

In the following section, we shall see that Albert Bandura followed in Tolman's footsteps by toppling yet another pillar of behaviorism: the idea that rewards and punishments act only on the individual receiving them. Bandura proposed that rewards and punishments can be effective even if we merely see someone else get them. (This is why casinos make such a fuss over jackpot winners.) Bandura's work, then, suggests the consequences of behavior can operate indirectly, through *observation*. Let's see how he demonstrated this idea.

Observational Learning: Bandura's Challenge to Behaviorism

Does observing violent behavior make viewers more likely to become violent? A classic study by Albert Bandura suggests that it does—at least in the children he invited to his lab for a simple experiment. All it took to bring out aggressive behavior in these children was watching adults appearing to enjoy punching, hitting, and kicking an inflated plastic clown (a BoBo doll). When later given the opportunity, children who had seen the adult models showed far more aggressive behavior toward the doll than did children in a control condition who had not observed the aggressive models (Bandura et al., 1963). Subsequent studies have shown similar results: Children will imitate aggressive behaviors they have seen on television or in video games, exhibiting up to seven times more aggressive acts than children in a control condition—even when the models are merely cartoon characters (Anderson et al., 2007; Boyatzis et al., 1995).

Learning by Observation and Imitation An important implication of Bandura's BoBo doll study is that learning by observation and imitation can affect our behavior in new situations—when we have no personal experience. Thus, learning can occur not only by direct experience but also by watching the behavior of another person or *model*. If the model's actions appear successful—that is, if the model seems to find it reinforcing—we may behave in the same way. In this way, learning by observation and imitation is an extension of operant conditioning, by which we observe someone else getting rewards but act as though we had also received a reward. 👁

CONNECTION CHAPTER 6

A concept is a mental category we use to organize our thinking. In Tolman's experiments, his rats demonstrated learning of the concept of a maze (p. 216).

In the BoBo doll experiment, a boy and girl imitate the aggressive behavior that they have seen from an adult.

👁 **Watch** the **Video** Bandura's BoBo Doll Experiment at **MyPsychLab**

observational learning   A form of cognitive learning in which new responses are acquired after watching others' behavior and the consequences of their behavior.

Psychologists call this *social learning* or **observational learning.** It accounts for children learning aggressive behavior by imitating aggressive role models who are perceived as successful or admirable or who seem to be enjoying themselves. Observational learning also explains how people learn athletic skills, how to drive a car, and how to behave with friends and then shift roles in a job interview. And it illuminates changes in clothing fashions and the rapid spread of slang expressions.

Observational learning occurs in nonhuman species, too, as when a mother cat teaches her kittens how to hunt. One study demonstrated that even a creature as simple-brained as the octopus can learn from watching the behavior of other octopi (Fiorito & Scotto, 1992). Not to be outdone, a clever bowerbird in an Australian national park achieved notoriety through observational learning by fooling tourists with its imitation of a cell phone ringing (Winters, 2002).

Effects of Media Violence   As you might have guessed, much of the research on observational learning has focused on the impact of violence in film and video (Huesmann et al., 2003). Predictably, the issue is a controversial one, because much of the evidence is *correlational* (Anderson & Bushman, 2002). That evidence makes a credible case, based on more than 50 studies showing that observing violence is associated with violent behavior. But does observing violence *cause* violent behavior? Or is it the other way around: Could it be that violent people are drawn to violent films and videos?

CONNECTION CHAPTER 1

Only an *experimental* study can determine cause and effect (p. 27).

Thanks to more than 100 *experimental* studies, experts now know that observing violence truly does increase the likelihood of violent behavior (Huesmann & Moise, 1996; Primavera & Heron, 1996). In fact, the link between viewing violent media and subsequent behavior aggression is stronger than the link between lead-based paint and children's IQ, and is nearly as strong as the link between cigarette smoking and cancer (Bushman & Anderson, 2001). Viewers of media violence also show less emotional arousal and distress when they subsequently observe violent acts—a habituation-like condition known as *psychic numbing* (Murray & Kippax, 1979). Psychologist Elliot Aronson argues that extensive media violence is one factor contributing to violent tragedies, such as the Columbine High School shootings (Aronson, 2000).

Not all imitation is harmful, of course. Thanks to imitation, we also learn about charitable behavior, comforting others in distress, and driving on the legal side of the road. In general, people learn much—both prosocial (helping) and antisocial (hurting) behaviors—through observation of others. This capacity to learn from watching enables us to acquire behaviors efficiently, without going through tedious trial and error. So while observational learning is a factor in violent behavior, it also enables us to learn socially useful behaviors by profiting from the mistakes and successes of others.

Observational Learning Applied to Social Problems Around the Globe   Television is one of the most powerful sources of observational learning—and not only of the undesirable sort we have just noted. Here at home, the long-running children's program, *Sesame Street,* uses such well-loved characters as Big Bird and Cookie Monster to teach language, arithmetic, and courtesy through observational learning. And in Mexico, TV executive Miguel Sabido has deliberately drawn on Bandura's work in creating the popular soap opera *Ven Conmigo* (*Come with Me*), which focuses on a group of people who connect through a literacy class. After the initial season, enrollment in adult literacy classes in the broadcast area shot up to nine times the level in the previous year (Smith, 2002b).

The idea was taken up by a nonprofit group, Populations Communications International, which has promoted it worldwide. As a result, television dramas are now aimed not only at literacy but at promoting women's rights, safe sex, and preventing HIV and unwanted pregnancies. Such programs are wildly popular, reaching large numbers of devoted fans in dozens of countries and regions around the world, including Latin American, Africa, South and East Asia, the Middle East, the Caribbean, and the Philippines. In China, observers learn about the value of girls; in Tanzania, they learn that AIDS is transmitted by people, not by mosquitoes; and in India, the programs question the practice of child marriages. In the Caribbean, soap operas now promote responsible environmental practices.

Does it work? Very well, say professors Arvind Singhal and Everett Rogers (2002), who are currently gathering data on such projects. Because of a soap opera broadcast in

India, a whole village signed a letter promising to stop the practice of child marriages. Similarly, Tanzanians now increasingly approve of family planning. And in rural villages in India, the enrollment of girls in school has risen between ten and 38 percent. Overall, it appears that television can be a means of producing positive social change and act as a conduit for psychological research to make a significant difference in people's lives.

Brain Mechanisms and Learning

What do we know about the biology behind learning? On the level of neurons, learning apparently involves physical changes that strengthen the synapses in groups of nerve cells—a process called **long-term potentiation** (Antonova et al., 2001; Kandel, 2000). Initially, neurons in various brain areas involved in a learning task work very hard—for example, as a person learns the location of various objects, cells in the visual and parietal cortex may fire rapidly. But as learning progresses, the connections among the different cortical regions become stronger and the firing pattern becomes less intense (Büchel et al., 1999).

In operant conditioning, the brain's reward circuitry comes into play, especially in parts of the frontal cortex and the limbic system, rich in dopamine receptors (O'Doherty et al., 2004; Roesch & Olson, 2004). Many experts now believe the brain uses this circuitry to identify the rewards that are the essence of positive reinforcement (Fiorillo et al., 2003; Shizgal & Avanitogiannis, 2003). The limbic system also helps us remember strong emotions, such as fear, so often associated with classical conditioning (Miller, 2004). And in the next chapter, when we talk about memory, you will learn about other parts of the brain involved in learning.

The Brain on Extinction While it is important for our survival to remember emotion-laden events, it's also important to *forget* associations that turn out to be irrelevant. So just as wild animals need to forget about a water hole that has run dry, you must learn to deal with changes in school schedules or traffic laws. These examples involve *extinction* of responses learned previously. Neuroscientists have found that extinction occurs when certain neurotransmitters, including glutamate and norepinephrine, block memories (Miller, 2004; Travis, 2004).

Discoveries such as these have stimulated the search for drugs that could accomplish something previously only seen in futuristic movies: blocking the emotional trauma associated with certain events, such as combat experiences, violent crimes, and horrific accidents. And recent research boasts early success (Brunet et al., 2007; Kindt et al., 2009). In both animals and humans, experimenters have successfully eliminated the emotional arousal associated with typical memories of such traumatic events. And while this remarkable discovery holds great potential for survivors of violent crime, war, accidents, and natural disasters, ethical questions remain about future directions in this rapidly advancing field.

Linking Behavioral Learning with Cognitive Learning Neuroscience has found evidence in the brain to support both the behaviorist and the cognitive explanations for learning. Specifically, there may be two separate brain circuits for learning: one for simple stimulus–response learning and one for more complex tasks (Kandel & Hawkins, 1992). The simpler circuit seems responsible for the sort of "mindless" learning that occurs when a dog drools at the sound of a bell or when a person acquires a motor skill, such as riding a bike or kicking a soccer ball. This kind of learning occurs relatively slowly and improves with repetition over many trials. Significantly, classical conditioning and much of operant learning fit this description. By contrast, the second type of learning circuit seems responsible for more complex forms of learning requiring conscious processing: concept formation, insight learning, observational learning, and memory for specific events. If further research verifies that this division reflects a fundamental distinction in the nervous system, we will be able to say that those on the behavioral and cognitive extremes were both (partly) right. They were talking about fundamentally different ways the brain learns (see Figure 4.3) (Clark & Squire, 1998; Jog et al., 1999).

Billboards, television programs, and other media campaigns can be effective tools for promoting social change.

long-term potentiation A biological process involving physical changes that strengthen the synapses in groups of nerve cells that is believed to be the neural basis of learning.

Although scientists have discovered experimental methods of blocking the emotional trauma associated with memories of a traumatic event, the notion of a machine that can selectively delete memories (as in the film *Eternal Sunshine of the Spotless Mind*) will likely remain farfetched.

TABLE 4.3 Behavioral Learning and Cognitive Learning Compared

Behavioral Learning	Cognitive Learning
Focus is on observable events (stimuli and responses) only.	Inferences are made about mental processes that are not directly observable.
Learning consists of associations among stimuli and responses.	Learning as information processing: The learner seeks useful information from stimuli.
Main forms of learning are habituation, classical conditioning, and operant (instrumental) conditioning.	Learning also involves insight, observational learning, cognitive maps, and other more complex forms of learning.
Developed as a rebellion against the subjective methods of structuralism and functionalism: Behaviorism became the dominant perspective for much of the 20th century.	Developed as a rebellion against the narrow perspective of behaviorism: Cognitive psychology became the dominant perspective at the end of the 20th century.
Big names include Pavlov, Thorndike, Watson, and Skinner.	Big names include Köhler, Tolman, and Bandura.

Observational Learning and Mirror Neurons People obviously learn from their observations of others, as we saw in Bandura's BoBo doll studies. Similarly, if you see someone at the dinner table take a bite and grimace with disgust, you will be reluctant to taste the same dish. But the mystery has always been to understand how our brains respond to somebody else's rewards or punishments. The recent discovery of mirror neurons suggests a neurological basis for observational learning. It may be that the "mirror cells" in our brains are finely tuned to help us mirror other people's sense of being rewarded or punished by activating the same circuits in our own brains (Jaffe, 2007). Watch the news for further developments.

CONNECTION CHAPTER 2

Mirror neurons help us imitate other people's behavior (p. 70).

"Higher" Cognitive Learning

It now seems clear that much of the complex and abstract learning required in college classes is fundamentally different from the learning that Pavlov, Watson, and Skinner studied. Acquiring knowledge about the field of psychology, for example, involves building mental images, assimilating concepts, and pondering ways they can be related. It's not that behavioral conditioning isn't involved in human learning—after all, students do work for grades and salivate when they see a pizza—but principles of behavioral learning don't tell the whole story of "higher" cognitive learning.

The following chapters will take us deeper into this realm of cognitive learning, where we will discuss memory, thinking, concept formation, problem solving, and intelligence. There, you will learn more about mental structures that underlie cognition. The challenge we will face is exactly the one behaviorists were hoping to avoid: In studying cognition, we must make inferences about processes we cannot measure directly. We will find, however, that cognitive psychologists have developed very clever methods for obtaining objective data on which to base their inferences. The newest of these—coming fully online in the last decade or so—is brain imaging, which, as we will see, has brought psychologists very close to an objective glimpse at private mental processes.

But before we move on to these topics in the next chapter, let's return to the problem with which we began the chapter: Sabra's fear of flying.

[PSYCHOLOGY MATTERS]

Fear of Flying Revisited

Which kind of learning—operant conditioning or classical conditioning—do you suppose lay behind Sabra's aversion to flying? Although we may never know exactly what caused her fear in the first place, we can guess that both forms of conditioning were involved. Fears commonly arise through direct experience involving classical conditioning. Alternatively, fears can be learned through observational learning, perhaps from a fearful parent or peer. And once the fear has been learned, operant conditioning can maintain it, because people are rewarded by avoiding the feared object.

These assumptions have led some airlines to experiment with a hybrid treatment known as *cognitive-behavioral therapy*, aimed at helping people overcome their fear of flying. Happily, Sabra located one of these programs a few weeks before the conference started. She contacted the airline and signed up for three weekend sessions to be held at a nearby airport.

Through cognitive-behavioral therapy, Sabra learned new ways of thinking about the experience of flying. Gradual exposure to flying, called *desensitization* (a form of extinction), also helped to banish her fearful responses.

She arrived at the appointed time, full of expectations and apprehensions. Would the therapist probe her childhood experiences and fantasies? Would she have to take tranquilizers? Or would she have to undergo some sort of terrifying treatment, such as flying upside down in a small airplane?

Her worst expectations turned out to be unfounded. The treatment sessions were organized by a behavioral psychologist who gathered the nine participants in a small conference room. He began by saying that such fears are learned—much as you might learn to cringe when you hear a dentist's drill. But because it is not important how such fears originated, this fear-of-flying program would focus on the present, not the past, he said. Sabra began to feel more relaxed.

The conditioning-based therapy program combined several learning strategies. A classical conditioning component would involve extinction of her fear through gradual exposure to the experience of flying. Operant conditioning would play a role through social reinforcement from the therapist and other members of the group. In addition, a cognitive component would involve learning more about how airplanes work.

After a brief overview of the process they would experience over the next three weeks, the group took a tour of the airport, including the cabin of a passenger jet parked on the Tarmac. Then they went back to the conference room to learn about how a pilot controls an airplane and about the physical forces that keep it in the air. The group also watched some videos involving routine flights in a commercial jet. All in all, this first session went smoothly, and everyone seemed much more at ease than when they started.

The second weekend began with more classroom discussion. Then, the class went back into the airliner, where they took seats and went through a series of re-laxation exercises designed to extinguish the participants' fears and to learn a new and more relaxed response to the experience of being in an airplane. This training included deep breathing and progressive relaxation of specific muscle groups all over the body. When everyone in the group reported feeling relaxed, they again watched videos of flight on the plane's TV monitors. This was followed by more relaxation exercises. The final activity for the second weekend involved starting the engines and going through the preflight routine—all the way up to takeoff . . . and more relaxation exercises.

The final weekend session was almost identical to the previous one. The only difference was that "graduation" involved an actual flight—a 20-minute trip out over the local countryside and back to the airport. It was, of course, voluntary, but only one of the nine people in the class chose not to go. Sabra went, but not without some anxiety. The therapist, however, encouraged the group to focus on the relax-ation exercises they had learned rather than on their feelings of fear. To the amaze-ment of all who participated, these learning-based techniques helped them through the flight exercise without losing control of their emotional responses. Although no one's fear had vanished completely, everyone on board was able to bring it under control.

The happiest result was that Sabra was able to go to her meeting in Hawaii—where, by the way, she had a productive conference and a wonderful time. For our purposes we should also note that she has flown several times since then. Each trip gets a little easier, she says—just as the psychology of learning would predict.

Check Your Understanding

1. **ANALYSIS:** Why was *insight* rather than *trial and error* the best explanation for Sultan's solution to the problem of reaching the food reward?

2. **RECALL:** What evidence did Tolman have that his rats had developed cognitive maps of a maze?

3. **APPLICATION:** If you were going to use Bandura's findings in developing a program to prevent violence among middle school children, you might

   a. have children watch videos of children who are responding constructively to aggressive acts on the playground.

   b. punish children who are aggressive and reward those who are not aggressive.

   c. have children punch a BoBo doll to "get the aggression out of their system."

   d. punish children for aggressive acts performed at school.

4. **APPLICATION:** Mirror neurons seem to explain how observational learning works. So, looking at your answer to the previous question: What would the observers' mirror neurons be responding to?

5. **UNDERSTANDING THE CORE CONCEPT:** Pick one experiment described in this section of the chapter, and discuss why it is difficult to explain in purely behavioral terms.

Answers 1. Sultan had apparently given up on active trial-and-error attempts to solve the problem. Yet, after a period of inactivity, he abruptly found the solution, which involved piling the boxes so he could climb on them and reach the fruit. Köhler argued that Sultan had achieved the solution mentally, through insight. **2.** When their usual path was blocked, Tolman's rats would usually take the shortest alternative path to the goal. **3.** a **4.** The mirror neurons in the observers would be responding to the behavior of the children who are responding constructively to aggressive acts. **5.** All of the following are difficult to explain behaviorally because each challenges a basic principle of operant or classical conditioning: Köhler's experiments on insight learning (learning = a reorganization of perceptions), Tolman's "cognitive map" experiments (evidence that animals learn concepts rather than specific behaviors), and Bandura's studies of observational learning (children learn behaviors for which other people are rewarded).

CRITICAL THINKING APPLIED

Do Different People Have Different "Learning Styles"?

Without a doubt, people differ in the ways they approach learning. As you can see by observing your classmates, everyone brings a different set of interests, abilities, temperamental factors, developmental levels, social experiences, and emotions to bear on learning tasks. But can we say these differences constitute distinct "learning styles"? For example, are some people "visual learners" who need to *see* the material rather than hearing it, as, perhaps, an "auditory learner" must do?

Educators have been drawn to the concept of learning styles in the hope of encouraging learning by tailoring instruction to a student's learning style. The excitement about learning styles has, in turn, led to a proliferation of learning-style inventories, each aiming to diagnose how a student learns best, with implications for how to tailor a teaching environment to fit each learner. Perhaps you have taken one such test. But is all this buzz based on fact or fantasy?

What Are the Critical Issues?

From a critical perspective, the principal issue centers on the meaning of "learning styles." The term may seem intuitively clear—but does it mean the same thing to everyone? And are learning styles really *requirements* or mere *preferences* for learning? In other words, if you are a "visual learner," to what extent does this truly impact your ability to learn when visuals are not available? And are learning styles unchangeable (like eye color), or can people adjust their approach to learning to fit the demands of the subject matter (say, literature, psychology, dentistry, or music)?

What Is the Source?   Unfortunately, most of the publications on learning styles come from sources that have not performed the controlled studies needed to support their claims (Stahl, 1999). Rather, the "research" they say supports their claims is largely unpublished and thus has not be scrutinized by other scientists. As we learned in Chapter 1, publishing and critiquing studies and their results is a key step in the scientific method. Avoiding this requirement may be a warning sign that the claimant has fallen prey to one or more types of bias and thus lacks credibility.

What Is the Evidence?   One problem we encounter in examining the evidence for learning styles is that, even among learning-style enthusiasts, we find no agreed-upon list of distinct learning styles. Although educators commonly talk about "verbal learners," "visual learners," and "kinesthetic (movement) learners," some inventories also claim to assess some combination of the following styles: tactile (touch), logical, social, solitary, active/reflective, sensing/intuitive, thinking/feeling, judging/perceiving, sequential/global. This widespread disagreement regarding even the basic categories of "learning styles" should be a clue to the critical thinker that claims may be based on mere speculation and common sense rather than true scientific findings.

A second red flag we see when we examine the evidence is the scarcity of findings to support any relationship between a person's learning style and his or her actual learning. In fact, most advocates of learning styles have little supporting data for their claim that people with different scores learn the same material in different ways. In fact, the research we have shows that matching a teaching environment to a person's purported learning style has little to no effect on his or her achievement. Thus, a more accurate interpretation of learning styles may be that they reflect preferences in learning rather than requirements for learning (Krätzig & Arbuthnott, 2006).

There is, however, one scientific study that does show evidence for impact of certain learning styles on achievement. An ambitious program developed by cognitive psychologists Robert Sternberg and Elena Grigorenko first measured students' abilities for logical, creative, and practical thinking—arguably, three distinct forms of "intelligence" (Sternberg, 1994; Sternberg & Grigorenko, 1997). Then students in an introductory psychology course were divided into groups that received instruction emphasizing the form of intelligence on which they had scored highest. (A control group of students was deliberately mismatched.) Tests at the end of the course indicated that students did best when the teaching emphasis matched their intellectual style.

What was different about the Sternberg and Grigorenko study? In addition to the fact that their results did show better student achievement when the teaching style matched their intellectual profile—in terms of logical, creative, and practical thinking—they used a randomized, double-blind experimental method to test their hypothesis. Notably, most other "learning style assessments" fail to employ such rigorous and reliable scientific procedures.

Does the Issue Require Multiple Perspectives?

If learning styles do exist, could a cross-cultural perspective help us understand them (Winerman, 2006b)? Studies by Nisbett et al. (2003) have shown that Asians and Americans often perceive the world quite differently, with Americans focusing on central objects and Asians taking in a scene more globally. (The difference is cultural, not physiological: Americans of Asian ancestry perceive in essentially the same way as do other Americans.) To illustrate the difference in these two styles of "seeing," look at the image of the tiger against a jungle background on this page. Nisbett's group found that the typical American spends more mental energy on putting prominent elements of the scene—the tiger—into logical categories, while Asians usually pay more attention to the context and background—the jungle.

Culture can also influence the way people approach classroom learning. For example, Americans generally believe that academic success is the result of innate intelligence, while East Asians emphasize discipline and hard work (Li, 2005). Which belief system would you guess might encourage most children to do well in school?

The lines on this image, used by Nisbett's team, show one individual's eye movements when scanning the scene. Americans spent more time looking at the tiger and other prominent objects in the picture, whereas Asians spent more time scanning details of the context and background.

Other cultural differences can play a role in academic achievement as well, says Korean-born psychologist Heejung Kim. After struggling with classes that required group discussion, which was rare in her Korean educational experience, Kim (2002) decided to look for differences between the ways Asians and Americans approach academic tasks. As she predicted, when Asian and American college students were given problems to solve, the Americans usually benefited from talking over the problems with each other, while such discussion often inhibited problem solving by Asian students.

We note, however, that these cultural differences are not part of the current debate regarding "learning styles" and thus have not been included in any of the learning styles inventories marketed by a variety of organizations. We mention them here, however, to show that ideas currently based on popular opinion (such as the impact of learning styles on performance) stand to gain credibility by accepting criticism from the scientific community and using it to seek improvements in their theories. In this case, advocates of learning styles might do well to conduct controlled tests to investigate whether some of these cultural differences might result in actual performance differences and, if so, create categories of learning styles that truly reflect empirical differences.

What Conclusions Can We Draw?

In general, while we best be cautious about most claims regarding learning styles, we should remain open to new developments that may emerge from cross-cultural research and from work on Sternberg's three-intelligences theory. Beyond that, we should acknowledge that interest in learning styles has encouraged teachers and professors to present material in a variety of ways in their classes—including media, demonstrations, and various "active learning" techniques. Further, available research suggests everyone learns better when the same material can be approached in more than one way—both visual and verbal, as well as through hands-on learning (McKeachie, 1990, 1997, 1999).

But back to our main point: We recommend caution when interpreting results of tests that purport to identify your learning style. Beware of people who tell you that you are a visual learner, a reflective learner, or some other type: Just because you prefer images to words, for example, does not mean that you should avoid reading and just look at the pictures. This sort of thinking erroneously suggests that each person learns in only one way. It also erroneously suggests that the way we learn is fixed and unchanging. Instead, we need to learn how to adapt the way we learn to the type of material to be learned: You wouldn't learn about music in exactly the same way you would learn about math. Learning involves an interaction of many factors: the learner, the material, the medium in which the material is presented, the organization of the presentation, the personalities of the teacher and learner, and the environment in which learning takes place, to name a few. And your college experience presents a wonderful opportunity to learn to think in new and unaccustomed ways.

Do It Yourself! ADAPTING YOURSELF TO BETTER LEARNING

Most students would like to improve their performance in one or more classes. Rather than wasting time with the pseudoscience of learning styles, try applying the bona fide principles of classical and operant conditioning to a plan designed specifically to help you achieve your goal. Using the various principles you have learned so far in this chapter, design your own behavior change program.

First, identify a specific behavior. Instead of setting a broad goal, such as getting a better grade, make your goal specific—reading eight textbook pages per day, completing the "As You Read Practice Activities" in MyPsychLab, or reviewing your class notes each day. Then identify at least five ways you can encourage the new behavior based on the principles of classical and operant conditioning. For starters, you might identify one feeling or biological stimulus you want to associate with the desired behavior and figure out a way to achieve that with classical conditioning. Then, you'll definitely want to identify one or two reinforcers you can use—continuously at first. Next, decide what schedules of reinforcement you will implement once you have begun to shape the behavior successfully, and—based on that—write down how often you will receive a reinforcer and what it will be. For best results, use a variety of reinforcers on a variety of schedules to keep yourself responding well. Then get started! Keep track of your progress, and make adjustments as needed.

CHAPTER SUMMARY

((•─[**Listen** to an audio file of your chapter at **MyPsychLab**

CHAPTER PROBLEM: **Assuming Sabra's fear of flying was a response she had learned, could it also be treated by learning? If so, how?**

- *Classical conditioning* played one role in Sabra overcoming her fear of flying. By creating positive associations with the experience of flying, Sabra underwent a combination of *extinction* and *counter-conditioning*.

- *Operant conditioning* helped Sabra overcome her fear of flying through *shaping*—providing positive reinforcement for each

successive step toward flying in an airplane. The effectiveness of the treatment provided *negative reinforcement* by removing the anxiety and fear she had previously associated with flying.

- *Cognitive learning* added instruction about some of the aeronautical aspects of flying, thus helping Sabra develop a mental understanding of how airplanes work, as well as *observational* learning during which Sabra observed calm passengers takng a flight.

4.1 What Sort of Learning Does Classical Conditioning Explain?

> **Core Concept 4.1 Classical conditioning is a basic form of learning in which a stimulus that produces an innate reflex becomes associated with a previously neutral stimulus, which then acquires the power to elicit essentially the same response.**

Learning produces lasting changes in behavior or mental processes, giving us an advantage over organisms that rely more heavily on **reflexes** and **instincts**. Some forms of learning, such as **habituation**, are quite simple, while others, such as classical conditioning, operant conditioning, and cognitive learning, are more complex.

The earliest learning research focused on **classical conditioning**, beginning with Ivan Pavlov's discovery that **conditioned stimuli** (after being paired with **unconditioned stimuli**) could elicit reflexive responses. His experiments on dogs showed how **conditioned responses** could be **acquired** and **extinguished** and undergo **spontaneous recovery** in laboratory animals. He also demonstrated **stimulus generalization** and discrimination learning. John Watson extended Pavlov's work to people, notably in his famous experiment on the conditioning of fear in Little Albert. More recent work, particularly studies of taste aversions, suggests, however, that classical conditioning is not a simple stimulus–response learning process but also has a biological component. In general, classical conditioning affects basic, survival-oriented responses. Therapeutic applications of Pavlovian learning include the prevention of harmful food aversions in chemotherapy patients.

acquisition (p. 138)
behavioral learning (p. 135)
classical conditioning (p. 136)

conditioned response (CR) (p. 138)
conditioned stimulus (CS) (p. 138)
extinction (in classical conditioning) (p. 138)
habituation (p. 135)
learning (p. 134)
mere exposure effect (p. 135)
neutral stimulus (p. 137)
spontaneous recovery (p. 138)
stimulus discrimination (p. 139)
stimulus generalization (p. 139)
unconditioned response (UCR) (p. 138)
unconditioned stimulus (UCS) (p. 137)

4.2 How Do We Learn New Behaviors By Operant Conditioning?

[**Core Concept 4.2** In operant conditioning, the consequences of behavior, such as rewards and punishments, influence the probability that the behavior will occur again.]

A more active form of learning, called **instrumental conditioning**, was first explored by Edward Thorndike, who established the **law of effect** based on his study of trial-and-error learning. B. F. Skinner expanded Thorndike's work, now called **operant conditioning**, to explain how responses are influenced by their environmental consequences. His work identified and assessed various consequences, including **positive** and **negative reinforcement**, **punishment**, and an operant form of **extinction**. The power of operant conditioning involves producing new responses. To learn how this works, Skinner and others examined **continuous reinforcement** as well as several kinds of **intermittent reinforcement contingencies**, including **FR, VR, FI,** and **VI schedules**. As for punishment, research has shown it is more difficult to use than reinforcement because it has several undesirable side effects. There are, however, alternatives,

including operant extinction and rewarding of alternative responses, application of the **Premack principle**, and prompting and shaping new behaviors. These techniques have found practical use in controlling behavior in schools and other institutions, as well as in behavioral therapy for controlling fears and phobias.

conditioned reinforcer or secondary reinforcer (p. 147)
continuous reinforcement (p. 145)
extinction (in operant conditioning) (p. 146)
fixed interval (FI) schedules (p. 147)
fixed ratio (FR) schedules (p. 146)
instinctive drift (p. 148)
intermittent reinforcement (p. 146)
interval schedule (p. 146)
law of effect (p. 143)
negative punishment (p. 149)
negative reinforcement (p. 144)
operant chamber (p. 144)
operant conditioning (p. 143)
positive punishment (p. 149)

positive reinforcement (p. 144)
Premack principle (p. 148)
primary reinforcer (p. 147)
punishment (p. 149)
ratio schedule (p. 146)
reinforcement contingencies (p. 145)
reinforcer (p. 143)
schedule of reinforcement (p. 146)
shaping (p. 145)
token economy (p. 148)
variable interval (VI) schedule (p. 147)
variable ratio (VR) schedule (p. 147)

4.3 How Does Cognitive Psychology Explain Learning?

[**Core Concept 4.3** According to cognitive psychology, some forms of learning must be explained as changes in mental processes rather than as changes in behavior alone.]

Much research now suggests that learning is not just a process that links stimuli and responses: Learning is also cognitive. This was shown in Köhler's work on insight learning in chimpanzees, in Tolman's studies of cognitive maps in rats, and in Bandura's research on observational learning and imitation in humans—particularly the effect of observing aggressive models, which

spawned many studies on media violence and, recently, applications dealing with social problems, such as the spread of AIDS. All this cognitive research demonstrates that learning does not necessarily involve changes in behavior, nor does it require reinforcement. In the past three decades, cognitive scientists have reinterpreted behavioral learning, especially operant and classical conditioning, in cognitive terms, as well as searched for the neural basis of learning.

cognitive map (p. 158)
insight learning (p. 158)
long-term potentiation (p. 161)
observational learning (p. 160)

CRITICAL THINKING APPLIED

Do Different People Have Different "Learning Styles"?

Media attention on so-called learning styles continues to encourage learners to focus on learning in ways that match their learning style. Empirical evidence to support this notion, however, is sparse. Nor is there general agreement on a specific set of learning styles. A critical thinking approach suggests that people have learning *preferences*, but they can learn to adapt their approach to different kinds of material.

DISCOVERING PSYCHOLOGY **VIEWING GUIDE**

Watch the following video by logging into MyPsychLab (www.mypsychlab.com). After you have watched the video, answer the questions that follow.

PROGRAM 8: **LEARNING**

Program Review

1. Which of the following is an example of a fixed-action pattern?
   a. a fish leaping at bait that looks like a fly
   b. a flock of birds migrating in winter
   c. a person blinking when something gets in her eye
   d. a chimpanzee solving a problem using insight

2. What is the basic purpose of learning?
   a. to improve one's genes
   b. to understand the world one lives in
   c. to find food more successfully
   d. to adapt to changing circumstances

3. How have psychologists traditionally studied learning?
   a. in classrooms with children as participants
   b. in classrooms with college students as participants
   c. in laboratories with humans as participants
   d. in laboratories with nonhuman animals as participants

4. In his work, Pavlov found that a metronome could produce salivation in dogs because
   a. it signaled that food would arrive.
   b. it was the dogs' normal reaction to a metronome.
   c. it was on while the dogs ate.
   d. it extinguished the dogs' original response.

5. What is learned in classical conditioning?
   a. a relationship between an action and its consequence
   b. a relationship between two stimulus events
   c. a relationship between two response events
   d. classical conditioning does not involve learning

6. What point is Professor Zimbardo making when he says "Relax" while firing a pistol?
   a. There are fixed reactions to verbal stimuli.
   b. The acquisition process is reversed during extinction.
   c. Any stimulus can come to elicit any reaction.
   d. Unconditioned stimuli are frequently negative.

7. What point does Ader and Cohen's research on taste aversion in rats make about classical conditioning?
   a. It can be extinguished easily.
   b. It takes many conditioning trials to be effective.
   c. It is powerful enough to suppress the immune system.
   d. It tends to be more effective than instrumental conditioning.

8. What is Thorndike's law of effect?
   a. Learning is controlled by its consequences.
   b. Every action has an equal and opposite reaction.
   c. Effects are more easily changed than causes.
   d. A conditioned stimulus comes to have the same effect as an unconditioned stimulus.

9. According to John B. Watson, any behavior, even strong emotion, could be explained by the power of
   a. instinct.   c. innate ideas.
   b. inherited traits.   d. conditioning.

10. In Watson's work with Little Albert, why was Albert afraid of the Santa Claus mask?
    a. He had been classically conditioned with the mask.
    b. The mask was an unconditioned stimulus creating fear.
    c. He generalized his learned fear of the rat.
    d. Instrumental conditioning created a fear of strangers.

11. What was the point of the Skinner box?
    a. It kept animals safe.
    b. It provided a simple, highly controlled environment.
    c. It set up a classical conditioning situation.
    d. It allowed psychologists to use computers for research.

12. Skinner found that the rate at which a pigeon pecked at a target varied directly with
    a. the conditioned stimulus.
    b. the conditioned response.
    c. the operant antecedents.
    d. the reinforcing consequences.

13. Imagine a behavior therapist is treating a person who fears going out into public places. What would the therapist be likely to focus on?
    a. the conditioning experience that created the fear
    b. the deeper problems that the fear is a symptom of
    c. providing positive consequences for going out
    d. reinforcing the patient's desire to overcome the fear

14. When should the conditioned stimulus be presented in order to optimally produce classical conditioning?
    a. just before the unconditioned stimulus
    b. simultaneously with the unconditioned response
    c. just after the unconditioned stimulus
    d. just after the conditioned response

15. Operant conditioning can be used to achieve all of the following, *except*
    a. teaching dogs to assist the handicapped.
    b. teaching English grammar to infants.
    c. teaching self-control to someone who is trying to quit smoking.
    d. increasing productivity among factory workers.

16. Which psychologist has argued that in order to understand and control behavior, one has to consider both the reinforcements acting on the selected behavior and the reinforcements acting on the alternatives?
    a. E. Thorndike
    b. J. Watson
    c. B. F. Skinner
    d. H. Rachlin

17. If given a choice between an immediate small reinforcer and a delayed larger reinforcer, an untrained pigeon will
    a. select the immediate small one.
    b. select the delayed larger one.
    c. experiment and alternate across trials.
    d. not show any signs of perceiving the difference.

18. In order to produce extinction of a classically conditioned behavior, an experimenter would
    a. reward the behavior.
    b. pair the behavior with negative reinforcement.
    c. present the conditioned stimulus in the absence of the unconditioned stimulus.
    d. model the behavior for the organism.

19. In Pavlov's early work, bell is to food as
    a. unconditioned response is to conditioned response.
    b. conditioned stimulus is to unconditioned stimulus.
    c. unconditioned response is to conditioned stimulus.
    d. conditioned stimulus is to conditioned response.

20. Howard Rachlin has discovered that animals can be taught self-control through
    a. reinforcement.
    b. operant conditioning.
    c. instrumental conditioning.
    d. all of the above.

5

Memory

CHAPTER PROBLEM How can our knowledge about memory help us evaluate claims of recovered memories?

CRITICAL THINKING APPLIED The Recovered Memory Controversy

DOES MEMORY MAKE AN ACCURATE AND INDELIBLE RECORD OF OUR PAST? OR IS it like a footprint in the sand, shifting with time and circumstance? In fact, the truth about memory encompasses both of those extremes. Memory can be highly malleable—yet many of our memories are quite accurate. The challenge lies in knowing when to rely on memory and when to question it, as the following cases will illustrate.

CASE 1 Twelve-year-old Donna began to suffer severe migraine headaches that left her sleepless and depressed. Concerned, her parents, Judee and Dan, sought help for her. Over the next year, Donna was passed from one therapist to another, ending up with a psychiatric social worker who specialized in treatment of child abuse. It was to that therapist that Donna disclosed—for the first time—having been sexually molested at the age of 3 by a neighbor. The therapist concluded that memories of the assault, buried in her mind for so long, were probably responsible for some of Donna's current problems, so she continued to probe for details and other possible instances of sexual abuse.

Eventually, the therapist asked her to bring in a family photo album, which included a photo of Donna, taken at age 2 or 3, wearing only underpants. The therapist suggested this might be evidence that Donna's father had a sexual interest in her and, possibly, had molested her. More-over, the therapist contacted the authorities, who began an investigation (ABC News, 1995).

For two years, Donna felt intense pressure to blame her father, but consistently denied he had molested her. Finally, amid increasing confusion about her childhood memories, she began to believe she suffered from "repressed memory syndrome" and that her father had abused her repeatedly during her childhood. Eventually, Donna was hospitalized. While in the hospital, she was placed on medication, hypnotized repeatedly, and diagnosed with *multiple personality disorder* (now called *dissociative identity disorder*).

As for her father, Dan was arrested and tried on charges of abuse based solely on his daughter's recovered memory. When his two-week trial ended in a hung jury, Dan went free. Shortly after the trial, Donna moved to another state with a foster family. In new surroundings and far away from the system that had supported her story, she began to believe her memories were false. Eventually, her doctor recommended she be sent back to her family, where they began the slow process of rebuilding broken relationships and trust.

CASE 2 Ross is a college professor who entered therapy because he was unhappy with his life. Describing his condition, he said, "I felt somehow adrift, as if some anchor in my life had been raised. I had doubts about my marriage, my job, everything" (Schacter, 1996, p. 249). Then, some months after entering therapy, he had a dream that left him with a strong sense of unease about a certain camp counselor he had known as a youth. Over the next few hours, that sense of unease gradually became a vivid recollection of the counselor molesting him. From that point on, Ross became obsessed with the memory, finally hiring a private detective, who helped him track down the counselor in a small Oregon town. After numerous attempts to talk with the counselor by telephone, Ross at last made contact and taped the phone conversation. The counselor admitted molesting Ross, as well as several other boys at the camp. Strangely, Ross claimed he had simply not thought about the abuse for years—until he entered therapy.

PROBLEM: **How can our knowledge about memory help us evaluate claims of recovered memories?**

Keep in mind there is no sure way to "prove a negative." That is, without some independent evidence, no one could ever prove conclusively that abuse or some other apparently long-forgotten event did *not* occur. Instead, we must weigh claims against our understanding of memory. In particular, we need answers to the following questions:

- Does memory make an accurate record of everything we experience?
- Are traumatic experiences, such as those of sexual abuse, likely to be *repressed* (blocked from consciousness), as Sigmund Freud taught? Or are we more likely to *remember* our most emotional experiences, both good and bad?
- How reliable are memories of experiences from early childhood?
- How easily can memories be changed by suggestion, as when a therapist or police officer might suggest that sexual abuse occurred?
- Are vivid memories more accurate than ordinary, less-distinct memories?

You will find answers to these questions, and many more, in this chapter. Let's begin with the most fundamental question of all.

5.1 KEY QUESTION
What Is Memory?

Undoubtedly, memory does play tricks on us. Our best defense against those tricks is an understanding of how memory works. So let's begin building that understanding with a definition: Cognitive psychologists view **memory** as a system that encodes, stores, and retrieves information—a definition, by the way, that applies equally to an organism or a computer. Unlike a computer's memory, however, we humans have a *cognitive* memory system that selectively takes information from the senses and converts it into meaningful patterns that we store and access later as needed. These memory patterns, then, form the raw material for thought and behavior, which in turn enables you to recognize a friend's face, ride a bicycle, recollect a trip to

memory Any system—human, animal, or machine—that encodes, stores, and retrieves information.

Disneyland, and (if all goes well) recall the concepts you need during a test. More generally, our Core Concept characterizes memory this way:

> ## Core Concept 5.1
>
> **Human memory is an information processing system that works constructively to encode, store, and retrieve information.**

And how is memory related to *learning,* the topic of the last chapter? Learning and memory are different sides of the same coin. You might think of memory as the cognitive system that processes, encodes, and stores the information we learn, then later allows us to retrieve it. In other words, memory enables learning. So this chapter is really an extension of our discussion of cognitive learning in the last section of Chapter 4. The focus here, however, will be on more complex *human* learning and memory, as contrasted with the simpler forms of animal learning and conditioning we emphasized earlier.

Metaphors for Memory

We often use metaphors to help us understand complicated things. One such metaphor compares human memory to a library or a storehouse, emphasizing the ability of memory to hold large amounts of information (Haberlandt, 1999). Another, compares memory to a computer. Some metaphors for memory, however, are misleading. That's certainly the case with the "video recorder" metaphor for memory, which implies that human memory makes a complete and accurate record of everything we experience.

Experiments clearly show this video-recorder metaphor is wrong. And, especially in some cases of "recovered memories," believing in the unfailing accuracy of memory can be dangerously wrong. Instead, human memory is an *interpretive* system that takes in information and, much like an artist, discards certain details and organizes the rest into meaningful patterns. As a result, our memories represent our unique *perceptions* of events rather than being accurate or objective representations of the events themselves.

Simply put, then, we don't technically retrieve memories—in truth, we *reconstruct* them. We start with fragments of memory—like pieces of a jigsaw puzzle. Then, from these fragments, we reconstruct the incident (or idea, emotion, or image) by filling in the blanks *as we remember it,* rather than the way it actually was. Most of the time this works well enough that you don't realize just how much of remembrance is actually reconstruction.

A look at Figure 5.1 should convince you of this reconstructive process. Which image is the most accurate portrayal of a penny? Unless you are a coin collector, you probably pay little attention to the details of these familiar objects. So, when retrieving the image of a penny, you automatically fill in the gaps and missing details—without realizing how much of the memory image you are actually creating.

Some memories are sketchier than others. In general, psychologists have found we make the most complete and accurate memory records for:

- Information on which we have *focused our attention,* such as a friend's words against a background of other conversations
- Information in which we are *interested,* such as the plot of a favorite movie
- Information that *arouses us emotionally,* such as an especially enjoyable or painful experience (unless the material also brings our biases into play, as when we are in a heated discussion with a loved one)
- Information that *connects with previous experience,* such as a news item about the musician whose concert you attended last week
- Information that we *rehearse,* such as material reviewed before an exam

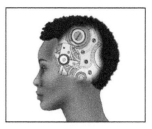

The cognitive perspective says that our *cognitions* can affect our mental health—or our mental disorders.

CONNECTION CHAPTER 1

Cognitive psychology is one of the six main perspectives in psychology (p. 16).

FIGURE 5.1

The Penny Test

Which of these images is an accurate portrayal of a penny?

Source: Nickerson, R., & Adams, M. (1979). Long-term memory for a common object. *Cognitive Psychology, 11*(1), 287–307. Copyright © 1979. Reprinted by permission of Elsevier.

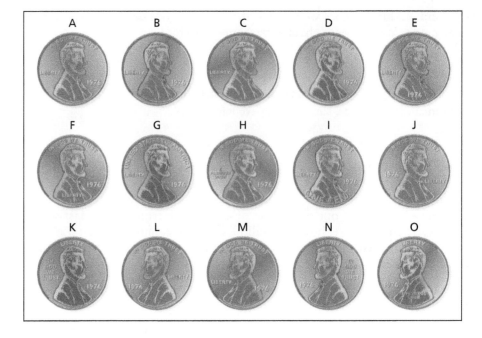

information-processing model   A cognitive understanding of memory, emphasizing how information is changed when it is encoded, stored, and retrieved.

encoding   The first of the three basic tasks of memory, involving the modification of information to fit the preferred format for the memory system.

The rest of the chapter will unfold this cognitive approach to memory, known as the **information-processing model**. It emphasizes the systematic changes information undergoes on its way to becoming a permanent memory—quite different from the naïve video recorder model. The information-processing model also emphasizes that memory is *functional*—that is, it performs useful functions for us. The most basic of these, we will see below, are the *encoding, storage,* and *retrieval* of information.

Memory's Three Basic Tasks

In simplest terms, human memory takes essentially meaningless sensory information (such as the sounds of your professor's voice) and changes it into meaningful patterns (words, sentences, and concepts) you can store and use later. To do so, memory must first *encode* the incoming sensory information in a useful format.

Encoding first requires that you *select* some stimulus event from the vast array of inputs assaulting your senses and make a preliminary classification of that stimulus. Is it a sound, visual image, odor, taste, or pain? Next you *identify* the distinctive features of that input. If it's a sound, is it loud, soft, or harsh? Does it fit some pattern, such as a car horn, a melody, a voice? Is it a sound you have heard before? Finally, you mentally tag, or *label*, an experience to make it meaningful. ("It's Dr. Johnson. He's my psychology professor!")

Often, encoding is so automatic and rapid that we have no awareness of the process. For example, you can probably recall what you had for breakfast this morning, even though you didn't deliberately try to make the experience "stick" in your mind. Emotionally charged experiences, such as an angry exchange with a colleague, are even more likely to lodge in memory without any effort to encode them (Dolan, 2002).

On the other hand, memories for concepts, such as the basic principles of psychology, usually require a deliberate encoding effort to establish a usable memory. In a process called *elaboration*, you attempt to connect a new concept with existing information in memory. One way to do this is to link the new material to personal, concrete examples, as when you associated the term *negative reinforcement* with the removal of pain when you take an aspirin. (As an aid to elaboration, this text deliberately provides many such examples that, we hope, will help you connect new concepts with your own experiences.) In fact, failure to elaborate is a common cause of memory errors: If you didn't know the answer to the Penny Test, for example, you probably never paid close attention to the configuration of a penny, and thus never really encoded it to begin with. (The correct answer, by the way, is A.)

Storage, the second essential memory task, involves the retention of encoded material over time. But it's not a simple process. As we get deeper into the workings of memory, you will learn that memory consists of three parts, or *stages,* each of which stores memories for different lengths of time and in different forms. The trick of getting difficult-to-remember material into long-term storage, then, is to recode the information in the way long-term memory "likes" it before the time clock runs out. For example, while listening to a lecture, you may have just a few seconds to encode a pattern or meaning in the sound of your professor's voice before new information comes along and the old information is lost.

Retrieval, the third basic memory task, is the payoff for your earlier efforts in encoding and storage. When you have a properly encoded memory, it takes only a split second for a good cue to access the information, bring it to consciousness, or, in some cases, to influence your behavior at an unconscious level. (Let's test the ability of your conscious retrieval machinery: Can you remember which of the three memory tasks occurs just before *storage?*)

Alas, retrieval doesn't always go well, because the human memory system—marvelous as it is—sometimes makes errors, distorts information, or even fails us completely. In the last section of the chapter, we will take a close look at these problems, which memory expert Daniel Schacter (1996) calls the "seven sins of memory."[1] The good news is you can combat memory's "sins" with a few simple techniques that you will also learn about in the following pages.

[PSYCHOLOGY MATTERS]

Would You Want a "Photographic" Memory?

Suppose your memory were so vivid and accurate you could "read" paragraphs of this book from memory during your next exam. Such was the power of a 23-year-old woman tested by Charles Stromeyer and Joseph Psotka (1970). One of the amazing things she could do was to look at the meaningless configuration of dots in the left-hand pattern in the *Do It Yourself!* box and combine it mentally with the right-hand image. The result was the combined pattern shown in Figure 5.2. (Did you see the number "63" before you looked at the solution?) Wouldn't it be great to have such a "photographic" memory? Not entirely, it turns out.

The technical term for "photographic memory" is **eidetic imagery.** Psychologists prefer this term because eidetic images differ in many important respects from images made by a camera (Haber, 1969, 1980; Searleman, 2007). For example, a photographic image renders everything in minute detail, while an eidetic image portrays the most interesting and meaningful parts of the scene most accurately and is subject to the same kind of distortions found in "normal" memories.

Eidetic memories also differ in several respects from typical human memory images. For one thing, *eidetikers* describe their memory images as having the vividness of the original experience (Neisser, 1967). For another, eidetic images are visualized as being "outside the head" rather than inside—in the "mind's eye." (Yet, unlike a person who is hallucinating, eidetikers recognize these images as *mental* images.) Further, an eidetic image can last for several minutes—even for days, in some cases. For example, the woman tested by Stromeyer and Psotka could pass the dot-combining test even when she saw the two patterns 24 hours apart. But, remarkable as this is, the persistence of eidetic images can be a curse. Eidetikers report that their vivid imagery sometimes clutters their minds and interferes with other things they want to think about (Hunter, 1964).

storage The second of the three basic tasks of memory, involving the retention of encoded material over time.

retrieval The third basic task of memory, involving the location and recovery of information from memory.

eidetic imagery An especially clear and persistent form of memory that is quite rare; sometimes known as "photographic memory."

---

[1] Schacter's "seven sins" of memory are a pun on the famous seven sins of medieval times. You can remember them by the acronym WASPLEG, which refers to *W*rath, *A*varice, *S*loth, *P*ride, *L*ust, *E*nvy, and *G*luttony.

Do It Yourself!   **A TEST OF EIDETIC IMAGERY**

Look at the dot pattern on the left in the figure for a few moments and try to fix it in your memory. With that image in mind, look at the dot pattern on the right. Try to put the two sets of dots together by recalling the first pattern while looking at the second one. If you are the rare individual who can mentally combine the two patterns, you will see something not apparent in either image alone. Difficult? No problem if you have eidetic imagery—but impossible for the rest of us. If you want to see the combined images, but can't combine them in your memory, look at Figure 5.2.

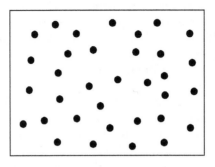 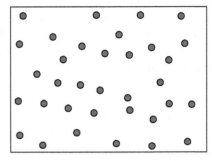

A Test of Eidetic Imagery

People with good eidetic imagery can mentally combine these two images to see something that appears in neither one alone.

CONNECTION CHAPTER 7

In Piaget's theory, the concrete operational stage, typically beginning around age 6 to 7, marks the transition from magical thinking to logical thinking (p. 285).

Eidetic imagery appears most commonly in children and only rarely in adults. One estimate suggests that up to five percent of children show some eidetic ability—although in most instances it's not good enough to pass the dot-combining test (Gray & Gummerman, 1975). And, in case you were wondering, there are no gender differences in eidetic memory: Boys and girls alike seem to have similar likelihoods of possessing the ability (Searleman, 2007). While no one knows why eidetic imagery tends to disappear in adults, it may follow some sort of developmental sequence—like losing one's baby teeth. Possibly its disappearance is related to the emphasis placed on logical thought that typically comes with the beginning of formal education, and dovetails with a change in children's thinking styles.

Case studies also suggest a connection between the decline of eidetic imagery and the development of language skills: Eidetikers report that eidetic images are strongest when they remain mere images; describing an eidetic image in words makes it fade from memory, and eidetikers learn to exploit this fact to control their intrusive imagery (Haber, 1969, 1970). Research in forensic psychology has found that, for ordinary people (noneidetikers) as well, giving verbal descriptions of suspects' faces interferes with later memories for those faces. Likewise, trying to describe other hard-to-verbalize perceptions, such as a voice or the taste of a wine, impairs most people's abilities to recall those perceptions later (Bower, 2003; Dodson et al., 1997).

A study from Nigeria further supports the idea that loss of eidetic ability may result from conflict between language skills and visual imagery: Eidetic imagery was found to be common not only among Ibo children but also among illiterate adults of the tribe who were living in rural villages. Although many of these adults could correctly draw details of images seen earlier, members of the same tribe who had moved to the city and learned to read showed little eidetic ability (Doob, 1964).

Whatever eidetic memory may be, it is clearly rare—so rare, in fact, that some psychologists have questioned its existence (Crowder, 1992). The few existing studies of "photographic memory" have portrayed it as different from everyday memory, as we have seen. Truthfully, however, we know relatively little about the phenomenon, and few psychologists are currently studying it.

Eidetic imagery presents not only a practical problem for those rare individuals who possess it but also a theoretical problem for cognitive psychologists. If eidetic imagery exists, is a known component of memory responsible? On the other hand, if it proves to be a unique form of memory, how does it fit with the widely accepted three-stage model of memory—which we will discuss next?

Check Your Understanding

✓•—⌈Study and Review at MyPsychLab

1. **ANALYSIS:** What is a major objection to the "video recorder" model of human memory?

2. **RECALL:** What are the three essential tasks of memory?

3. **ANALYSIS:** Suppose you have just adopted a new cat. You note her unique markings so you can recognize her among other cats in the neighborhood. What would a cognitive psychologist call this process of identifying the distinctive features of your cat?

4. **UNDERSTANDING THE CORE CONCEPT:** Which of the following memory systems reconstructs material during retrieval?

   a. computer memory

   b. human memory

   c. video recorder memory

   d. information recorded in a book

Answers 1. Unlike a video recorder, which makes an accurate and detailed record, memory stores an interpretation of experience. **2.** Encoding, storage, and retrieval. **3.** Encoding. **4.** b

5.2 KEY QUESTION
—— How Do We Form Memories?

If information in a lecture is to become part of your permanent memory, it must be processed in three sequential stages: first in *sensory memory,* then in *working memory*, and finally in *long-term memory.* The three stages work like an assembly line to convert a flow of incoming stimuli into meaningful patterns you can store and later reconstruct. This three-stage model, originally developed by Richard Atkinson and Richard Shiffrin (1968), is now widely accepted—with some elaborations and modifications. Figure 5.3 shows how information flows through the three stages. (Caution: Don't get these three *stages* confused with the three basic *tasks* of memory we covered earlier.)

Sensory memory, the most fleeting of the three stages, typically holds sights, sounds, smells, textures, and other sensory impressions for a maximum of a few seconds. Although sensory memory usually operates on an unconscious level, you can see its effects in the fading luminous trail made by a moving flashlight or a twirling Fourth-of-July sparkler. You can also hear the effects of fading sensory memories in the blending of one note into another as you listen to a melody. In general, these short-lived images allow us to maintain incoming sensory information just long enough for it to be screened for importance by working memory.

Working memory, the second stage of processing, selectively takes information from the sensory registers and makes connections with items already in long-term storage. (It is this connection we mean when we say, "That rings a bell!") Working memory holds information for up to 20 to 30 seconds (Nairne, 2003), making it a useful buffer for temporarily holding a name you have just heard or following directions someone has just given you. Originally, psychologists called this stage *short-term memory (STM),* reflecting the notion that this was merely a short-term, passive storage bin. Research has discovered, however, there are multiple active mental processes working at lightning speed to process information in this stage—hence the newer term *working memory.*

Long-term memory (LTM), the final stage of processing, receives information from working memory and can store it for long periods—sometimes for a lifetime. Information in

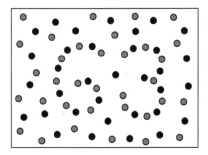

FIGURE 5.2

What an Eidetiker Sees

The combined images from the *Do It Yourself!* box form a number pattern.

Source: Klatzky, R. (1980). *Human Memory: Structures and Processes.* San Francisco: W. H. Freeman and Company. Copyright © 1975, 1980 by W. H. Freeman and Company. Used with permission.

sensory memory   The first of three memory stages, preserving brief sensory impressions of stimuli.

working memory   The second of three memory stages, and the one most limited in capacity. It preserves recently perceived events or experiences for less than a minute without rehearsal.

long-term memory (LTM)   The third of three memory stages, with the largest capacity and longest duration; LTM stores material organized according to meaning.

FIGURE 5.3

The Three Stages of Memory (simplified)

Memory is generally thought to be divided into three stages of processing. Everything that eventually goes into long-term storage must first be processed by sensory memory and working memory.

Like the trail of light from these sparklers, sensory memory holds incoming sensory information for just a brief moment.

long-term memory includes all our knowledge about the world, from an image of your mother's face to the lyrics to your favorite song and the year that Wilhelm Wundt established the first psychology laboratory. (Do you remember the year from Chapter 1?)

Our Core Concept captures the three stages in brief:

Core Concept 5.2

Each of the three memory stages encodes and stores memories in a different way, but they work together to transform sensory experience into a lasting record that has a pattern or meaning.

Our focus in this section will be on the unique contributions each stage makes to the final memory product (see Table 5.1). More specifically, we will look at each stage in terms of its storage *capacity,* its *duration* (how long it retains information), its *structure and function,* and its *biological basis.*

The First Stage: Sensory Memory

Your senses take in far more information than you can possibly use. While reading this book, they serve up all the words on the page, sounds in the room, the feel of your clothes on your skin, the temperature of the air, the slightly hungry feeling in your stomach. . . . How does the brain deal with this multitude of sensory input?

It's the job of sensory memory to hold the barrage of incoming sensation just long enough for your brain to scan it and decide which stream of information needs attention. But just how much information can sensory memory hold? Cognitive psychologist George Sperling answered this question by devising one of psychology's simplest and most clever experiments.

TABLE 5.1 The Three Stages of Memory Compared

	Sensory Memory	**Working Memory**	**Long-Term Memory**
Function	Briefly holds information awaiting entry into working memory	Involved in control of attention Attaches meaning to stimulation Makes associations among ideas and events	Long-term storage of information
Encoding	Sensory images: no meaningful encoding	Encodes information (especially by meaning) to make it acceptable for long-term storage	Stores information in meaningful mental categories
Storage capacity	12–16 items	7 ± 2 chunks	Unlimited
Duration	From 1/4 second to a few seconds	About 20 seconds unless repeatedly rehearsed	Unlimited
Structure	A separate sensory register for each sense	Central executive Phonological loop Sketchpad Episodic buffer	Procedural memory and declarative memory (further subdivided into semantic and episodic memory)
Biological basis	Sensory pathways	Involves the hippocampus and frontal lobes	Involves various parts of the cerebral cortex

The Capacity and Duration of Sensory Memory Sperling demonstrated that sensory memory can hold far more information than ever reaches consciousness. He first asked people to remember, as best they could, an array of letters flashed on a screen for a fraction of a second. (You might try glancing briefly at the array below and then trying to recall as many as you can.)

D J B W
X H G N
C L Y K

Not surprisingly, most people could remember only three or four items from a fraction-of-a-second exposure.

But, Sperling wondered, could it be possible that far more information than these three or four items entered a temporary memory buffer but vanished before it could be reported? To test this conjecture, he modified the experimental task as follows. Immediately after the array of letters flashed on the screen, an auditory cue signaled which row of letters to report: A high-pitched tone indicated the top row, a medium tone the middle row, and a low tone meant the bottom row. Thus, immediately after seeing the brief image and hearing a beep, respondents were to report items *from only one row,* rather than items from the whole array.

Under this *partial report* condition, most people achieved almost perfect accuracy—no matter which row was signaled. That is, Sperling's volunteers could accurately report *any single row,* but *not all rows.* This result suggested that the actual storage capacity of sensory memory can be 12 or more items—even though all but three or four items usually disappear from sensory memory before they can enter consciousness (Sperling, 1960, 1963).

Would it be better if our sensory memories lasted longer so we would have more time to scan them? Probably not. With new information constantly flowing in, old information needs to disappear quickly, lest the system become overloaded. We are built so that sensory memories last just long enough to dissolve into one another and give us a sense of flow and continuity in our experience. Fortunately, they do not usually last long enough to interfere with new sensory impressions.

The Structure and Function of Sensory Memory You might think of sensory memory as a sort of mental movie screen, where images are projected fleetingly and then disappear. In fact, this blending of images in sensory memory gives us the impression of motion in a "motion picture"—which is really just a rapid series of still images.

But not all sensory memory consists of visual images. We have a separate *sensory register* for each sense, with each register holding a different kind of sensory information, as shown in Figure 5.4. The register for vision, called *iconic memory,* stores the encoded light patterns experienced as visual images. Similarly, the sensory memory for hearing, known as *echoic memory,* holds encoded auditory stimuli.

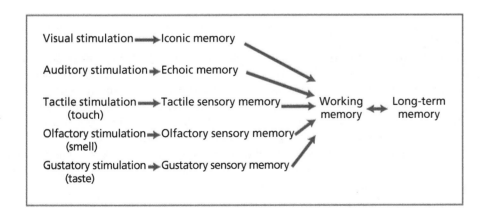

FIGURE 5.4

Multiple Sensory Stores

We have a separate sensory memory for each of our sensory pathways. All feed into working memory.

Please note that images in sensory memory have no meaning attached to them—just as digital images have no meaning to a camera. It's the job of sensory memory simply to store the images briefly. It's in the next stage, working memory, where we add meaning to sensation.

The Biological Basis of Sensory Memory The biology of sensory memory appears to be relatively simple. In this initial stage, memory images take the form of neural activity in the sense organs and their pathways to the brain. Thus, sensory memory consists of the rapidly fading trace of stimulation in our sensory systems (Bower, 2000b; Glanz, 1998). Working memory then "reads" these fading sensory traces and decides which ones will gain admittance into the spotlight of attention and which will be ignored and disappear.

The Second Stage: Working Memory

In the second stage of processing, working memory serves as the temporary storage site for a new name you just heard or for the first part of this sentence while you read the remainder. More broadly, working memory is the processor of conscious experience, including information coming from sensory memory, as well as information being retrieved from long-term memory (Jonides et al., 2005). Everything entering consciousness does so through working memory.

Moreover, working memory provides a mental "work space" where we sort and encode information before adding it to more permanent storage (Shiffrin, 1993). In doing so, it makes experiences meaningful by blending them with information from long-term memory. To give a concrete example: Working memory is the register into which you retrieve the information you learned in yesterday's class as you review for tomorrow's test.

You might think of working memory, then, as the "central processing chip" for the entire memory system. In this role, it typically holds information for 20–30 seconds—far longer than sensory memory. If you make a special effort to rehearse the material, information can remain active even longer, as when you repeat a new phone number to yourself before putting it into your phone's contact list. It is also the mental work space in which we consciously mull over ideas and images pulled from long-term storage in the process we call thinking. In all these roles, then, working memory is not only the center of mental action but also the liaison among other components of memory.

The Capacity and Duration of Working Memory Psychologist George Miller (1956) famously suggested that the "magic number" of this second stage of memory was 7±2. What he meant was that the storage component of working memory holds about seven items—a fact that caused lots of distress when phone companies began requiring callers to add an area code to the old seven-digit phone number. Working memory's storage capacity does vary slightly from person to person, so you may want to assess how much yours can hold by trying the test in the *Do It Yourself!* box.

When we overload working memory, earlier items usually drop away to accommodate more recent ones. Yet, when working memory fills up with information demanding attention, we can fail to notice new information streaming into our senses. That's why, in the opinion of many experts, this limited capacity of working memory makes it unsafe to use your cell phone while driving (Wickelgren, 2001). In fact, research finds we only process about 50 percent of incoming sensory information when we are concurrently driving and talking on a cell phone—even when the driver is using a hands-free set. And one in four auto accidents result from driving while using a cell phone (National Safety Council, 2010).

Do It Yourself! FINDING YOUR WORKING MEMORY CAPACITY

Look at the following list of numbers and scan the four-digit number, the first number on the list. Don't try to memorize it. Just read it quickly; then look away from the page and try to recall the number. If you remember it correctly, go on to the next longer number, continuing down the list until you begin to make mistakes. How many digits are in the longest number that you can squeeze into your working memory?

7 4 8 5
3 6 2 1 8
4 7 9 1 0 3
2 3 8 4 9 7 1
3 6 8 9 1 7 5 6
7 4 7 2 1 0 3 2 4
8 2 3 0 1 3 8 4 7 6

The result is your digit span, or your working (short-term) memory capacity for digits. Studies show that, under ideal testing conditions, most people can remember five to nine digits. If you remembered more, you may have been using special "chunking" techniques.

Note that working memory's meager storage capacity is significantly smaller than that of sensory memory. In fact, working memory has the smallest capacity of the three memory stages. This constraint, combined with its limited duration, makes working memory the information "bottleneck" of the memory system (see Figure 5.5). These twin problems of limited capacity and short duration present special obstacles for students trying to process and remember large amounts of information from a lecture or textbook. Fortunately, there are ways to work around these difficulties, as we will see.

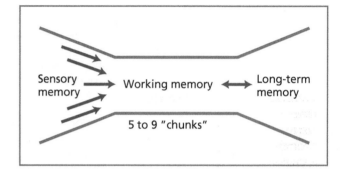

FIGURE 5.5

The Working Memory Bottleneck

Caught in the middle, with a much smaller capacity than sensory and long-term memories, working memory becomes an information bottleneck in the memory system. As a result, much incoming information from sensory memory is lost.

Chunks and Chunking In memory, a *chunk* is any pattern or meaningful unit of information. It might be a single letter or number, a name, or even a concept. For example, the letters P-H-I-L could constitute four chunks. However, you probably recognize this sequence as a name (in fact, the name of one of your authors), so you can combine the four letters into a single chunk. Thus, **chunking** helps you get more material into the seven slots of working memory.

The phone companies capitalized on chunking years ago. When they originally grouped the seven digits of a phone number (e.g., 6735201) into two shorter strings of numbers (673-5201), they helped us collapse seven separate items into two chunks—and now, with the addition of the area code conveniently chunked as well, we have only one additional thing to remember. The government uses the same chunking principle to help us remember our nine-digit Social Security numbers.

chunking Organizing pieces of information into a smaller number of meaningful units (or chunks)—a process that frees up space in working memory.

The Role of Rehearsal Imagine you are ordering pizza, and you ask your roommates what toppings they want. To keep their list in your working memory while you call the pizza place, you might repeat it to yourself over and over. This technique is called **maintenance rehearsal**, and it serves us well for maintaining information temporarily in consciousness by preventing competing inputs from crowding it out. But repetition is not an efficient way to transfer information to long-term memory, even though people often attempt to do so. So using this strategy to try to learn material for a test won't work very well.

A better strategy is **elaborative rehearsal**. With this method, information is not merely repeated but is actively connected to knowledge already stored. One way to do this is to associate a new idea with something it logically brings to mind for you. When you read about echoic memory, for example, did you think "that makes sense, since echoes have to do with sound?" Another way is to think of personal examples of concepts. In the last chapter, perhaps you came up with examples of positive reinforcement, negative reinforcement, and classical conditioning from your own life; if you did, we'll bet those concepts were easier to remember when you were tested on them.

maintenance rehearsal A working-memory process in which information is merely repeated or reviewed to keep it from fading while in working memory. Maintenance rehearsal involves no active elaboration.

elaborative rehearsal A working-memory process in which information is consciously reviewed and actively related to information already in LTM.

One caution about elaborative rehearsal: Make sure you have your facts straight before creating a web of connections for them! If, for example, you erroneously believe that memory is like a video recorder and think for a moment about how that makes sense, you are reinforcing a false memory. Likewise, if the therapist treating Donna (at the beginning of this chapter) told her to imagine situations where her Dad may have had opportunities to molest her, merely imagining those events could help create false memories (Loftus, 1997a; Zaragoza et al., 2011).

The Structure and Function of Working Memory When we introduced you to the concept of working memory at the beginning of this section, we said its name reflected the active nature of this stage of the memory process. So what are the activities working memory engages in? Currently, researchers Allen Baddeley and his colleagues believe there are four: the central executive, the phonological loop, the sketchpad, and an episodic buffer (Baddeley, 2000; Baddeley & Hitch, 1974). Let's take a closer look at each one (see Figure 5.6).

The Central Executive The information clearinghouse for working memory, the *central executive,* directs your attention to important input from both sensory memory and long-term memory and interfaces with the brain's voluntary (conscious) response system. Even now, as you sit reading this text, the central executive in your working memory is helping you decide whether to attend to these words or to other stimuli flowing in from your other senses, along with thoughts from long-term memory.

Acoustic Encoding: The Phonological Loop When you read words like "whirr," "pop," "cuckoo," and "splash," you can hear in your mind the sounds they describe. This **acoustic encoding** also happens with words that don't have imitative sounds. That is, working memory converts all the words we encounter into the sounds of our spoken language and shuttles them into its phonological loop—whether the words come through our eyes, as

acoustic encoding The conversion of information, especially semantic information, to sound patterns in working memory.

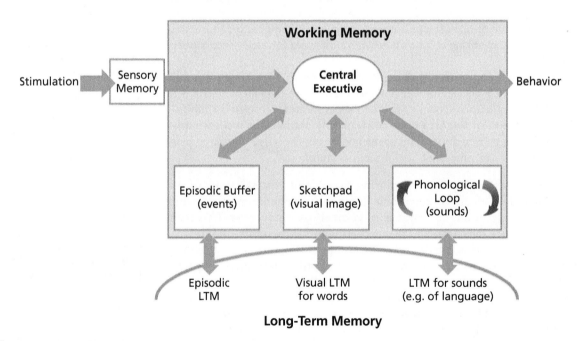

FIGURE 5.6

A Model of Working Memory

Atkinson and Shiffrin's original model divided memory into three stages. Events must first be processed by sensory memory and short-term memory (now called *working memory*) before they finally go into long-term memory storage—from which they can later be retrieved back into working memory. Baddeley's (2003) updated version of working memory includes a *central executive* that directs attention, a *sketchpad* for visual and spatial information, a *phonological loop* for sounds, and an *episodic buffer* that can combine many kinds of information into memories of events. This drawing includes all of these refinements to the original model of working memory.

Source: Baddeley, A. (2000). The episodic buffer: A new component of working memory? *Trends in Cognitive Sciences, 4,* 417–423.

in reading, or our ears, as in listening to speech (Baddeley, 2001). There, working memory maintains the verbal patterns in an acoustic (sound) form as they are processed.

Acoustic encoding can create its own brand of memory errors. When people recall lists of letters they have just seen, their mistakes often involve confusions of letters that have similar *sounds*—such as D and T—rather than letters with a similar *appearance*—such as E and F (Conrad, 1964). Mistakes aside, however, acoustic encoding has its advantages, particularly in learning and using language (Baddeley et al., 1998; Schacter, 1999).

Visual and Spatial Encoding: The Sketchpad   Serving much the same function for visual and spatial information, working memory's *sketchpad* encodes visual images and mental representations of objects in space. It holds the visual images you mentally rummage through when you're trying to remember where you left your car keys. It also holds the mental map you follow from home to class. Neurological evidence suggests that the sketchpad requires coordination among several brain systems, including the frontal and occipital lobes.

Binding Information Together: The Episodic Buffer   The most recent addition to Baddeley's model of working memory, the *episodic buffer* appears to bind the various pieces of information in working memory into a coherent episode. When planning a series of errands, for instance, we have to first identify all the places we need to go, then organize them into a logical route based on location, and finally calculate about how long the entire trip will take. So we have all the locations swimming around in our working memory as we mentally map them out, and various amounts of time associated with each one as we consider what we need to accomplish at each place. The episodic buffer acts as the temporary storage facility for these various pieces of our puzzle as we work it out. It also enables us to remember story lines of movies and other events, as it provides a place to organize the visual, spatial, phonological, and chronological aspects into a single memorable episode (Baddeley, 2003).

Levels of Processing in Working Memory   Here's an important tip: The more connections you can make in working memory between new information and knowledge you already have, the more likely you are to remember it later. Obviously this requires interaction between working memory and long-term memory. According to the **levels-of-processing theory** proposed by Fergus Craik and Robert Lockhart (1972), "deeper" processing—establishing more connections with long-term memories—makes new information more meaningful and more memorable. A famous experiment will illustrate this point.

Craik and Tulving (1975) had volunteers examine a list of 60 common words presented on a screen one at a time. As each word appeared, experimenters asked questions designed to influence how deeply each word was processed. For example, when BEAR appeared on the screen, the experimenters would ask one of three questions: "Is it in capital letters?" "Does it rhyme with *chair*?" "Is it an animal?" Craik and Tulving theorized that merely thinking about capital letters would not require processing the word as deeply as would comparing its sound with that of another word. But the deepest level of processing, they predicted, would occur when some aspect of the word's *meaning* was analyzed, as when they asked whether BEAR was an animal. Thus, they predicted that items processed more deeply would leave more robust traces in memory. And, sure enough, when participants were later asked to pick the original 60 words out of a larger list of 180, they remembered the deeply processed words the best, as the graph in Figure 5.7 shows. You can apply this strategy to your studying: Deeper processing of new information will help you develop stronger memories of the material.

The Biological Basis of Working Memory   Although some details remain unclear, working memory probably holds information in the form of messages flashed repeatedly in nerve circuits. Brain imaging implicates brain regions in

levels-of-processing theory   The explanation for the fact that information that is more thoroughly connected to meaningful items in long-term memory (more "deeply" processed) will be remembered better.

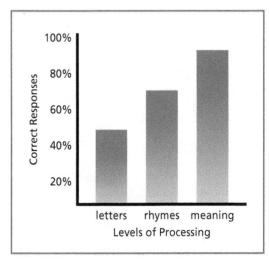

FIGURE 5.7

Results of Levels-of-Processing Experiment

In the Craik and Tulving (1975) experiment, words that were processed more deeply (for meaning) were remembered better than words examined for rhymes or for target letters.

the frontal cortex (Beardsley, 1997b; Smith, 2000), which in turn project to all sensory parts of the brain and areas known to be involved in long-term storage. Brain imaging also suggests the frontal lobes house some anatomically distinct "executive processes" that focus attention on information in short-term storage (Smith & Jonides, 1999). Together, these brain modules direct attention, set priorities, make plans, update the contents of working memory, and monitor the time sequence of events.

The Third Stage: Long-Term Memory

Can you remember who discovered classical conditioning? Can you ride a bicycle? How many birthdays have you had? Such information, along with everything else you know, is stored in your long-term memory (LTM), the last of the three memory stages.

Given the vast amount of data stored in LTM, it is a marvel that we can so easily gain access to so much of it. Remarkably, if someone asks your name, you don't have to rummage through a lifetime of information to find the answer. The method behind the marvel involves a special feature of long-term memory: Words and concepts are encoded by their meanings. This connects them, in turn, with other items that have similar meanings. Accordingly, you might picture LTM as a huge web of interconnected associations. As a result, good retrieval cues (stimuli that prompt the activation of a long-term memory) can navigate though the web and help you quickly locate the item you want amid all the data stored there.

The Capacity and Duration of Long-Term Memory   How much information can long-term memory hold? As far as we know, it has unlimited storage capacity. (No one has yet maxed it out, so you don't have to conserve memory by cutting back on your studying.) LTM can store the information of a lifetime: all the experiences, events, information, emotions, skills, words, categories, rules, and judgments that have been transferred from working memory. Thus, your LTM contains your total knowledge of the world and of yourself. This makes long-term memory the clear champion in both duration and storage capacity among the three stages of memory. But how does LTM manage to have unlimited capacity? That's another unsolved mystery of memory. Perhaps we might conceive of LTM as a sort of mental "scaffold," so the more associations you make, the more information it can hold.

The Structure and Function of Long-Term Memory   With a broad overview of LTM in mind, let's look at some of the details of its two main components. One, a register for the things we know how to *do,* is called *procedural memory.* The other, which stores information we can *describe*—facts we know and experiences we remember—is called *declarative memory.* We know that procedural and declarative memory are distinct because brain-damaged patients may lose one but not the other (as we will see).

Procedural Memory   We call on **procedural memory** when riding a bicycle, tying shoelaces, or playing a musical instrument. Indeed, we use procedural memory to store the mental directions, or "procedures," for all our well-practiced skills (Schacter, 1996). Much of procedural memory operates outside of awareness: Only during the early phases of training, when we must concentrate on every move we make, must we think consciously about the details of our performance. Later, after the skill is thoroughly learned, it operates largely beyond the fringes of awareness, as when a concert pianist performs a piece without consciously recalling the individual notes. (Figure 5.8 should help you clarify the relationship between the two major components of long-term memory.)

Declarative Memory   We use **declarative memory** to store facts, impressions, and events. Recalling the major perspectives in psychology or your most memorable vacation depends on declarative memory. In contrast with procedural memory, using declarative

procedural memory   A division of LTM that stores memories for how things are done.

Procedural memory allows experts like Oregon quarterback Darron Thomas to perform complex tasks automatically, without consciously recalling all the details.

declarative memory   A division of LTM that stores explicit information; also known as *fact memory.* Declarative memory has two subdivisions, episodic memory and semantic memory.

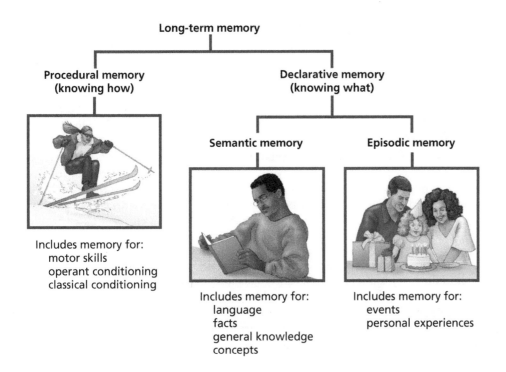

FIGURE 5.8
Components of Long-Term Memory

Declarative memory involves knowing specific information—knowing "what." It stores facts, personal experiences, language, concepts—things about which we might say, "I remember!" *Procedural memory* involves knowing "how"—particularly motor skills and behavioral learning.

memory typically requires conscious mental effort, as you see when people roll their eyes or make facial gestures while trying to recall facts or experiences.

To complicate matters, declarative memory itself has two major subdivisions, *episodic memory* and *semantic memory*. One deals with the rich detail of personal experiences (your first kiss), while the other simply stores information, without an "I-remember-when" context—information like the multiplication tables or the capital of your state.

Episodic memory stores your memories of events, or "episodes," in your life. It also stores *temporal coding* (or time tags) to identify *when* the event occurred and *context coding* that indicates *where* it took place. For example, you store memories of your recent vacation or of an unhappy love affair in episodic memory, along with codes for where and when these episodes occurred. In this way, episodic memory acts as your internal diary or *autobiographical memory*. You consult it when someone says, "Where were you on New Year's Eve?" or "What did you do in class last Tuesday?"

Semantic memory is the other division of declarative memory. (Refer to Figure 5.8 if this is becoming confusing.) It stores the basic meanings of words and concepts. Usually, semantic memory retains no information about the time and place in which its contents were acquired. Thus, you keep the meaning of *cat* in semantic memory—but probably not a recollection of the occasion on which you first learned the meaning of *cat*. In this respect, semantic memory more closely resembles an encyclopedia or a database than an autobiography. It stores a vast quantity of facts about names, faces, grammar, history, music, manners, scientific principles, and religious beliefs. All the facts and concepts you know are stored there, and you consult its registry when someone asks you, "Who was the third president?" or "What are the two major divisions of declarative memory?"

Schemas   When you attend a class, have dinner at a restaurant, make a phone call, or go to a birthday party, you know what to expect, because each of these events involves familiar scenarios. Cognitive psychologists call them **schemas**: clusters of knowledge in semantic memory that give us a context for understanding events (Squire, 2007). The exact contents of our schemas depend, of course, on culture and personal experience, but the point is that we invoke schemas to make new experiences meaningful.

episodic memory   A subdivision of declarative memory that stores personal events or "episodes."

semantic memory   A subdivision of declarative memory that stores general knowledge, including the meanings of words and concepts.

On the TV show *Are You Smarter Than a 5th Grader?*, host Jeff Foxworthy's questions call for facts stored in semantic memory.

schema   Cluster of related information that represents ideas or concepts in semantic memory. Schemas provide a context for understanding objects and events.

Schemas allow us quick access to information. So if someone says "birthday party," you can immediately draw on information that tells you what you might expect to be associated with a birthday party, such as eating cake and ice cream, singing "Happy Birthday," and opening presents. Just as important, when you invoke your "birthday party" schema, you don't have to sort through irrelevant knowledge in your memory—such as information contained in your "attending class" schema or your "dinner at a restaurant" schema. See for yourself how helpful schemas can be in the *Do It Yourself* box on this page.

Schemas, then, can be an aid to declarative long-term memory when they help us make sense out of new information by giving us a ready-made framework for it. On the other hand, they frequently lead us astray when it comes to details—as you may have realized in the *Do It Yourself* box. The problem is that we aren't usually aware of those memory errors when we make them. We will have a closer look at problems resulting from schema bias in the last part of this chapter.

Early Memories   Most people have difficulty remembering events that happened before their third birthday, a phenomenon called **childhood amnesia**. This suggests that younger children have limited episodic memory ability. Learning clearly occurs, however, long before age 3, probably from the moment of birth. We see this in a baby who learns to recognize a parent's face or in a toddler learning language. Thus, we know that very young children have, at least, a semantic memory and a procedural memory.

childhood amnesia   The inability to remember events during the first two or three years of life.

Until recently, psychologists thought childhood amnesia occurs because young children's brains have not yet formed neural connections required for episodic memory. Now, however, we know that the brain has begun to create necessary circuits by the end of the first year of life. For example, cognitive scientists have found children as young as 9 months showing some signs of episodic memory in the ability to imitate behaviors they have observed after a delay (Bauer et al., 2003). So why can't you remember your first birthday party? Part of the answer probably involves rudimentary language skills (for verbal encoding of memories), the lack of a sense of self (necessary as a reference point, but which doesn't develop until about age 2), and the lack of the complex schemas older children and adults use to help them remember.

Culture also influences people's early memories. For example, the earliest memories of Maori New Zealanders go back to 2.5 years, while Korean adults rarely remember anything before the age of 4. The difference seems to depend on how much the culture encourages children to tell detailed stories about their lives. "High elaborative" parents

Do It Yourself! HOW SCHEMAS IMPACT MEMORY

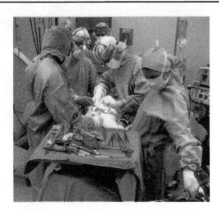

Read the following passage carefully:

Chief Resident Jones adjusted his face mask while anxiously surveying a pale figure secured to the long gleaming table before him. One swift stroke of his small, sharp instrument and a thin red line appeared. Then the eager young assistant carefully extended the opening as another aide pushed aside glistening surface fat so that the vital parts were laid bare. Everyone stared in horror at the ugly growth too large for removal. He now knew it was pointless to continue.

Now, without looking back, please complete the following exercise. Circle below the words that appeared in the passage:

patient   scalpel   blood   tumor
cancer   nurse   disease surgery

In the original study, most of the subjects who read this passage circled the words *patient, scalpel,* and *tumor.* Did you? However, none of the words were there! Interpreting the story as a medical story made it more understandable, but also resulted in inaccurate recall (Lachman et al., 1979). Once the subjects had related the story to their schema for hospital surgery, they "remembered" labels from their schema that were not present in what they had read. So while schemas help us organize information, they also create ample opportunity for errors in encoding and retrieval—which may create false memories, as we unconsciously modify information to make it more consistent with our schema-based expectations.

spend a lot of time encouraging children to talk about their daily experiences. This seems to strengthen early memories, enabling them to persist into adulthood (Leichtman, 2006; Winerman, 2005a).

The Biological Basis of Long-Term Memory Scientists have searched for the **engram,** the biological basis of long-term memory, for more than a century. One of their tactics involves looking for neural circuitry the brain uses to forge memories. Another approach goes to the level of synapses, looking for biochemical changes that might represent the physical *memory trace* within nerve cells. A tragic figure known as H. M., whom we met in Chapter 2, represents the first of these two approaches.

Clues from the Case of H. M. As a young man in 1953, H. M. lost most of his ability to form new memories—the result of an experimental brain operation performed as a last-ditch effort to treat his frequent epileptic seizures (Corkin, 2002; Hilts, 1995). From that point on, he was almost completely unable to create new memories of events in his life. So profound was his memory impairment that he never even learned to recognize the people who cared for him in the decades after his surgery.

Remarkably, H. M.'s memory for events prior to the operation remained normal, even as new experiences slipped away before he could store them in LTM. He knew nothing of the 9/11 attacks, the moon landings, or the computer revolution. He couldn't remember what he had for breakfast or the name of a visitor who left two minutes before. Ironically, one of the few things he was able to retain was that he had a memory problem. Even so, he was mildly surprised to see an aging face in the mirror, expecting the younger man he had been in 1953 (Milner et al., 1968; Rosenzweig, 1992). Yet, throughout his long ordeal, he maintained generally good spirits and worked willingly with psychologist Brenda Milner, whom he never could recognize, even after working with her for years.

H. M.'s medical record listed his condition as **anterograde amnesia**—which means a disability in forming new memories. To put the problem in cognitive terms, H. M. had a severe impairment in his ability to transfer new concepts and experiences from working memory to long-term memory (Scoville & Milner, 1957). From a biological perspective, the cause was removal of the hippocampus and amygdala on both sides of his brain (see Figure 5.9).

What did we learn from H. M.? Again speaking biologically, he taught us that the hippocampus and amygdala are crucial to laying down *new* declarative memories, although they seem to have no role in retrieving *old* (well-remembered) memories (Bechara et al., 1995; Wirth et al., 2003). Further, as we will see in a moment, H. M.'s case helped us understand the distinction between *procedural* memories and *declarative* memories. Remarkably, H. M. remained upbeat about his condition—even joking

New Zealand Maoris often remember events from when they were $2^1/_2$ years old—probably because their culture encourages children to tell stories about their lives.

engram The physical changes in the brain associated with a memory. It is also known as the *memory trace.*

Imagine if you looked into a mirror expecting to see a young version of yourself but instead saw yourself aged 30 or 40 years. This is what happened with H.M.

anterograde amnesia The inability to form new memories (as opposed to retrograde amnesia, which involves the inability to remember information previously stored in memory).

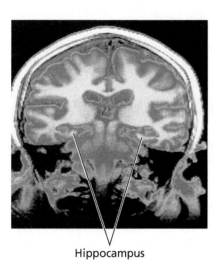

Hippocampus

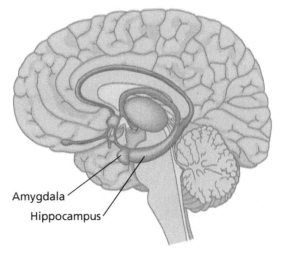

Amygdala
Hippocampus

FIGURE 5.9

The Hippocampus and Amygdala

The hippocampus and amygdala were surgically removed from both sides of H. M.'s brain. To help yourself visualize where these structures lie, compare the drawing with the MRI image. The MRI shows the brain in cross section, with a slice through the hippocampus visible on each side.

about his inability to remember—although, ironically, the removal of his amygdalas may have contributed to his positive disposition (Corkin, 2002).

Parts of the Brain Associated with Long-Term Memory   In the last two decades, neuroscientists have added much to the picture H. M. gave us of human memory. We now know the hippocampus (see Figure 5.9) is implicated in Alzheimer's disease, which also involves loss of ability to make new declarative memories. Neuroscientists have also discovered that the hippocampus's neural neighbor, the amygdala, processes memories that have strong emotional associations (Bechara et al., 1995). These emotional associations, it seems, act as an aid for quick access and retrieval (Dolan, 2002). The amygdala, then, plays a role in the persistent and troubling memories reported by soldiers and others who have experienced violent assaults. In some cases, these memories can be so disturbing that they constitute a condition known as *posttraumatic stress disorder*. Importantly, this same biological basis of emotional memories contributes to the lasting quality of most traumatic memories. ◉

Are memories, then, stored in the hippocampus and the amygdala? No. Memories for events and information (declarative memories) are actually stored throughout the cerebral cortex, with various pieces of a memory each stored in the part of the cortex that initially processed that particular sensory signal. So, for example, the memory of the great vacation you had at the beach last summer would have the visual components of the memory in your visual cortex, the sounds in the auditory cortex, the smells in the olfactory bulb, the sequence of events in the frontal lobes, and so forth. And, if you learned how to surf while you were there, that memory would be linked to the cerebellum and the motor cortex—just like other procedural memories that involve body movements and muscle memory.

How, you might wonder, do all these memory fragments get put back together properly? (In other words, how does the surfing memory end up with the other beach memories, rather than being misfiled with memories of your last visit to the dentist?) While the technical details of this fantastic feat remain a mystery to neuroscientists, we do know one part of the brain that plays a starring role. In the process known as memory **consolidation**, memories gradually become more permanent with the help of the hippocampus. Essentially, each time we retrieve a new declarative memory, pieces of that memory from all over the brain come together in the hippocampus, which somehow sorts through them and re-assembles the relevant ones into a coherent memory. Each time, the neural pathway for that particular memory becomes stronger, so eventually the memory doesn't need the hippocampus to bind it together. At that point, any single piece of the memory (for example, the smell of the ocean) is enough to produce the entire memory.

Understanding more about memory storage and consolidation reveals why H. M. could not form new declarative memories—without hippocampi, his brain was missing the hardware needed for these projects. It also explains why his ability to form new procedural memories remained intact—as these memories do not involve the hippocampus. And, for those of us with intact hippocampi, researchers report that new experiences consolidate much more rapidly if they are associated with existing memory schemas (Squire, 2007; Tse et al., 2007). For you, that might mean connecting what you learned about the hippocampus in Chapter 2 with the new information about its role in consolidation that you are learning here.

Memories, Neurons, and Synapses   A standard plot in soap operas and movies depicts a person who develops *amnesia* (loss of memory) after a blow or injury to the head. But does research support this soap-opera neuroscience? At the level of individual neurons, memories form initially as fragile chemical traces at the synapse and consolidate into more permanent synaptic changes over time. During this consolidation process, memories are especially vulnerable to interference by new experience, certain drugs, or a blow to the head (Doyère et al., 2007). The diagnosis, in the event of significant memory loss, would be **retrograde amnesia** or loss of prior memory. (Note that retrograde amnesia is the opposite of H. M.'s problem, *anterograde* amnesia, which was the inability to form *new* memories.)

◉—**Watch** the **Video** What Happens with Alzheimer's at **MyPsychLab**

CONNECTION CHAPTER 14 ➤

Lasting biological changes may occur in the brains of individuals with posttraumatic stress disorder (p. 605).

consolidation   The process by which short-term memories become long-term memories over a period of time.

retrograde amnesia   The inability to remember information previously stored in memory. (Contrast with anterograde amnesia.)

Memories can be strengthened, as well as weakened, during consolidation—especially by a person's emotional state. Research shows, however, that positive and negative emotions have vastly different effects on attention and therefore on memory. If you are happy, you tend to look at situations broadly and remember the "big picture." But if you are being robbed at gunpoint, you will most likely attend to the gun while paying less attention to details of the robber's appearance. In general, we can say that emotional arousal accounts for our most vivid memories, but not our most precise ones: The scope of happy memories tends to be larger, as negative emotions tend to restrict the focus of our memories (Dingfelder, 2005; Levine & Bluck, 2004).

Before leaving this section, we should note that from an evolutionary perspective, emotion plays a highly adaptive role in memory. If you survive a frightening encounter with a bear, for example, you are likely to remember to avoid bears in the future. For this, we can thank the amygdala, as well as emotion-related chemicals such as epinephrine (adrenalin) and certain stress hormones. Together, they enhance memory for emotion-laden experiences via the "supercharged" emotional associations they create (McGaugh, 2000).

[PSYCHOLOGY MATTERS]

"Flashbulb" Memories: Where Were You When . . . ?

The closest most people will come to having a "photographic memory" is a **flashbulb memory,** an exceptionally clear recollection of an important and emotion-packed event (Brown & Kulik, 1977). You probably harbor several such memories: a graduation, a tragic accident, a death, a big victory. It feels as though you made a flash picture in your mind of the striking scene. (The term was coined in the days when flash photography required a "flashbulb" for each picture.) The defining feature of a flashbulb memory is the source of the memory (Davidson et al., 2005): vivid images of where the individuals were at the time they received the news, what they were doing, and the emotions they felt.

flashbulb memory   A clear and vivid long-term memory of an especially meaningful and emotional event.

Many people form flashbulb memories of emotionally charged events in the news, such as the death of Michael Jackson, the September 11 attacks, or the election of Barack Obama as president (Pillemer, 1984; Schmolck et al., 2000). Cognitive psychologists take advantage of these naturally occurring opportunities for research, and in this case, use them to find the answer to this important question: Does the emotionally charged nature of flashbulb memories affect their accuracy?

One study at Duke University collected students' memories of the September 11 attacks the day after the event (Talarico & Rubin, 2003). Researchers also gathered memories of a normal, everyday event from the same participants. Thirty-two weeks later, participants' memories were tested for accuracy. The result? On average, flashbulb memories were no more accurate than everyday memories—both types of memories declined in accuracy over time. Importantly, however, participants' confidence in the flashbulb memories was quite high: Students were more confident about the accuracy of their flashbulb memories than their everyday memories, but it was false confidence. Significantly, confidence level for the flashbulb memories correlated with the initial level of emotional arousal during the flashbulb event. Other studies have corroborated the notion that emotional arousal increases the vividness of the memory—but not necessarily the accuracy of the memory.

Do you remember where you were and how you felt when Barack Obama won the 2008 Presidential Election? Chances are, your flashbulb memory is not as accurate as you think it is.

How do we make sense of these findings, given the strong evidence that exists for enhanced recollection of personal emotional events? First, we must note that flashbulb memories are rarely the same as a memory of personal involvement in a traumatic event. Flashbulb memories are often of publicly known, widely shared events—on an individual level, we may not have personal involvement in the situation. Thus, the public event is likely to be all over the news, discussed widely, and retold frequently. And in these frequent tellings, by many different people, details are likely to become distorted.

As the saying goes, then, the devil may be in the details. Flashbulb memory studies reveal that certain vivid details are often remembered with great accuracy, but also—especially over time—other, equally vivid details fail the accuracy test. One study of Israeli students, in the wake of the assassination of Prime Minister Itzhak Rabin, found that only about two-thirds of vividly reported memories were still accurate after 11 months (Nachson & Zelig, 2003)—although confidence in the erroneous memories remained high. As we noted earlier, traumatic events narrow the scope of our attention; thus, we encode only certain details and later fill in that sketch—quite unconsciously—with details we have heard from others or details that fit our schema for the event.

Even though this creates the potential for memory errors, the mistaking of confidence for accuracy may serve an adaptive purpose. Evolutionary psychologists suggest that, in times of stress, the ability to make a quick and confident decision might make the difference between life and death (Poldrack et al., 2008). In that way as well, the devil may truly be in the details.

Check Your Understanding

✔—[Study and Review at MyPsychLab

1. **RECALL:** Which part of memory has the smallest capacity? (That is, which part of memory is considered the "bottleneck" in the memory system?)

2. **RECALL:** Which part of long-term memory stores autobiographical information?

3. **RECALL:** To get material into permanent storage, it must be made meaningful while it is in _____.

4. **APPLICATION:** As you study vocabulary in this text, which of the following methods would result in the deepest level of processing?

a. learning the definition given in the marginal glossary

b. marking each term with a highlighter each time it occurs in a sentence in the text

c. thinking of an example of each term

d. having a friend read a definition, with you having to identify the term in question form, as on the TV show *Jeopardy*

5. **UNDERSTANDING THE CORE CONCEPT:** As the information in this book passes from one stage of your memory to the next, the information becomes more _____.

Answers 1. Working memory **2.** Episodic memory **3.** working memory **4.** c **5.** meaningful and associated with other information in LTM

5.3 KEY QUESTION
How Do We Retrieve Memories?

Memory can play several surprising tricks during retrieval. One involves the possibility of retrieving a memory you didn't know you had—which tells us some memories can be successfully encoded and stored without full awareness. Another quirk involves our confidence in recollections—as we saw in flashbulb memories. Our Core Concept summarizes the retrieval process this way:

[
Core Concept 5.3

Whether memories are implicit or explicit, successful retrieval depends on how they were encoded and how they are cued.
]

Implicit and Explicit Memory

We begin our exploration of retrieval with another lesson from H. M. You may recall that he retained the ability to learn new motor skills, even though he lost most of his ability to remember facts and events. For example, H. M. learned the difficult skill of mirror writing—writing while looking at his hands in a mirror (Milner et al., 1968; Raymond, 1989). In fact, his *procedural* memory for motor tasks was quite normal, even though he couldn't remember learning these skills and didn't even know he knew them.

But you don't have to have brain damage like H. M. to have memories of which you are unaware. A normal memory has disconnected islands of information too. For more than 100 years, psychologists have realized that people with no memory defects can know something without knowing they know it. Psychologist Daniel Schacter (1992, 1996) calls this **implicit memory**: memory that can affect your behavior without coming into full awareness. By contrast, **explicit memory** requires conscious awareness.

Procedural memories are often implicit, as when golfers remember how to swing a club without thinking about how to move their bodies. Likewise, H. M.'s mirror writing was an implicit memory. But implicit memories are not limited to procedural memory—nor is explicit memory the same as declarative memory. Information in your semantic store can be either *explicit* (such as in remembering the material you have studied for a test) or *implicit* (such as knowing the color of the building in which your psychology class is held). The general rule is this: A memory is implicit if it can affect behavior or mental processes without becoming conscious. Explicit memories, on the other hand, always involve consciousness during storage and retrieval.

In striking new studies, Skotko et al. (2004) found that H. M. could learn some new semantic material through implicit channels—that is, even though he didn't know he learned it. To do this, Skotko's group exploited H. M.'s favorite pastime of doing crossword puzzles. They devised crosswords that linked new information with knowledge H. M. had at the time of his operation: For example, H. M. knew that polio was a dreaded disease, but the polio vaccine was not discovered until after his surgery, so he had no knowledge of it. Yet by working on a specially designed crossword puzzle over a five-day period, H. M. learned to respond correctly to the item, "childhood disease successfully treated by Salk vaccine." Similarly, he was able to learn that Jacqueline Kennedy, wife of assassinated President John Kennedy, subsequently became Jacqueline Onassis. This technique, then, showed that H. M.'s problem was primarily one of explicit memory. 📖

implicit memory   A memory that was not deliberately learned or of which you have no conscious awareness.

explicit memory   Memory that has been processed with attention and can be consciously recalled.

Retrieval Cues

For accurate retrieval, both implicit and explicit memories require good cues. You have some understanding of such cues if you've ever used search terms in Google or another Internet search engine: Make a poor choice of terms, and you come up either with nothing or with Internet garbage. Long-term memory works much the same way, where a successful search requires good mental **retrieval cues** (the "search terms" used to recover a memory). Sometimes the only retrieval cue required to reactivate a long-dormant experience is a certain odor, such as the smell of fresh-baked cookies you associated with visiting Grandma's house. Other times, the retrieval cue might be an emotion, as when a person struggling with depression gets caught in a maelstrom of depressing memories. In our story of Ross at the beginning of the chapter, something in his dream may have served as a retrieval cue for the memory he had long forgotten.

On the other hand, some memories—especially semantic ones—are not so easily cued. During a test, for example, you may draw a blank if the wording of a question doesn't match the way you framed the material in your mind as you were studying. In other words, your memory may fail if the question isn't a good retrieval cue. In general, whether a retrieval cue is effective depends on the type of memory being sought and the web of associations in which the memory is embedded. The take-home lesson here? The more extensive your web of associations, the greater the chance of retrieving the information. Let's examine ways you can use this information to your advantage.

Read H.M.'s Obituary from *The New York Times* at **MyPsychLab**

retrieval cue   Stimulus used to bring a memory to consciousness or to cue a behavior.

Retrieving Implicit Memories by Priming   A quirk of implicit memory landed former Beatle George Harrison in court (Schacter, 1996). Lawyers for a singing group known as the Chiffons claimed the melody in Harrison's song "My Sweet Lord" was nearly identical to that of the Chiffon classic "He's So Fine." Harrison denied that he deliberately borrowed the melody, but conceded he had heard the Chiffons's tune prior to writing his own. The court agreed, stating that Harrison's borrowing was a product of "subconscious memory." Everyday life abounds with similar experiences, says Daniel Schacter (1996). You may have proposed an idea to a friend and had it rejected, but weeks later your friend excitedly proposed the same idea to you, as if it were entirely new.

In such real-life situations it can be hard to say what prompts an implicit memory to surface. Psychologists have, however, developed ways to "prime" implicit memories in the lab (Schacter, 1996). To illustrate, imagine you have volunteered for a memory experiment. First, you are shown a list of words for several seconds:

assassin, octopus, avocado, mystery, sheriff, climate

Then, an hour later, the experimenter asks you to examine another list and indicate which items you recognize from the earlier list: twilight, assassin, dinosaur, and mystery. That task is easy for you. But then the experimenter shows you some words with missing letters and asks you to fill in the blanks:

c h _ _ _ _ n k, o _ t _ _ u s, _ o g _ y _ _ _, _ l _ m _ t e

It is likely that answers for two of these pop readily into mind, *octopus* and *climate*. But chances are that you will be less successful with the other two words, *chipmunk* and *bogeyman*. This difference is due to **priming**, the procedure of providing cues that stimulate memories without awareness. Because you had been primed with the words *octopus* and *climate,* they more easily "popped out" in your consciousness than did words that had not been primed.

Retrieving Explicit Memories Anything stored in LTM must be "filed" according to its pattern or meaning. Consequently, the best way to add material to long-term memory is to associate it, while in working memory, with material already stored in LTM. We have called that process *elaborative rehearsal.* Encoding many such connections by elaborative rehearsal gives you more ways of accessing the information, much as a town with many access roads can be approached from many directions.

Meaningful Organization   One way of retrieving information from explicit memory involves getting the general idea or *gist* of an event, rather than a memory of the event as it actually occurred. Suppose you hear the sentence, "The book was returned to the library by Mary." Later, when asked if you heard the sentence, "Mary returned the book to the library," you may indeed mistakenly remember having heard the second sentence. This happens because we tend to remember the meaning or sense of the words—the **gist**—rather than the exact words themselves.

If you'll forgive us for repeating ourselves, we want to underscore the practical consequences of LTM being organized by meaning. *Storing new information in LTM usually requires that you make the information meaningful while it is in working memory.* This means that you must associate new information with things you already know. Sometimes it is important to remember all the details accurately (as in memorizing a mathematical formula), while at other times the important thing is to remember the gist (as when you read the case study of H. M.). In attempting to remember the gist, it is especially important to think of personal examples of the concepts and ideas you want to remember. (Are you getting into the habit of identifying personal examples of chapter concepts yet?)

Recall and Recognition   Explicit memories can be cued in two primary ways. One involves the kinds of retrieval cues used on essay tests; the other involves cues found on multiple choice tests. Essay tests require **recall** or retrieving a memory with minimal retrieval cues. That is, on an essay test, you must create an answer almost entirely from memory, with the help of only minimal cues from a question such as, "What are the two ways to cue explicit memories?"

CONNECTION CHAPTER 8

Priming is also a technique for studying nonconscious processes (p. 329).

priming   A technique for cuing implicit memories by providing cues that stimulate a memory without awareness of the connection between the cue and the retrieved memory.

gist   (pronounced *JIST*) The sense or meaning, as contrasted with the exact details.

recall   A retrieval method in which one must reproduce previously presented information.

Recognition, on another hand, is the method required by multiple-choice tests. In a recognition task, you merely identify whether a stimulus has been previously experienced. Normally, recognition is less demanding than recall because the cues are much more complete. Incidentally, the reason people say, "I'm terrible with names, but I never forget a face," is because recall (names) is usually tougher than recognition (faces).

The police use recognition when they ask an eyewitness to identify a suspect in a lineup. The witness is required only to match an image from memory (the crime) against a present stimulus (a suspect in the lineup). And what would be a comparable recall task? A witness working with a police artist to make a drawing of a suspect must recall, entirely from memory, the suspect's facial characteristics.

Of course, recognizing a previously recognized stimulus doesn't necessarily mean that stimulus matches the current context. We run into this problem on multiple-choice exams when several options offer concepts we have learned, but only one of them is a match to the particular question. Similarly, suspects have been falsely identified in police lineups by eyewitnesses if, for example, police have shown the eyewitness books of mug shots that include one or more of the suspects in the lineup. In these cases, eyewitnesses can mistakenly identify a suspect because they recognize him from the mug shot book rather than the actual crime (Weiner et al., 2003). Thus, although recognition generally produces more memories than recall, it also is more likely to produce false positives—or, in this case, false memories.

Other Factors Affecting Retrieval

We have seen that the ability to retrieve information from explicit declarative memory depends on whether the information was encoded and elaborated to make it meaningful. You won't be surprised to learn that alertness, stress level, drugs, and general knowledge also affect retrieval. Less well known, however, are the following, which relate to the context in which you encoded a memory and also the context in which you are remembering.

Encoding Specificity The more closely retrieval cues match the form in which the information was encoded, the better they will cue the appropriate memory. For example, perhaps you saw your psychology professor at the grocery store, but needed a moment to recognize who she or he was because the context didn't cue you to think "psychology professor." On the other hand, talking to a childhood friend may have cued a flood of memories you hadn't thought about for years. These two experiences illustrate the **encoding specificity principle**, which says successful recall depends on how well retrieval cues match cues present when the memory was encoded.

So, one important thing you can do in studying for exams is to anticipate what retrieval cues are likely to be on the test and organize your learning around those probable cues. Students who merely read the material and hope for the best may have trouble. In fact, this is such a common problem that psychologist Robert Bjork (2000) has suggested teachers introduce "desirable difficulties" into their courses to encourage students to encode the material in multiple ways. What are desirable difficulties? Bjork argues that by giving students assignments that require them to interact with the material in many different ways—projects, papers, problems, and presentations—professors help students build a greater web of associations into which a memory is embedded—and the more connections there are, the easier it becomes to cue a memory. If your own professor doesn't do this, what can you do to create more associations with the concepts you are learning?

Mood and Memory Information processing isn't just about facts and events; it's also about emotions and moods. We use the expressions "feeling blue" and "looking at the world through rose-colored glasses" to acknowledge that moods bias our perceptions. Likewise, our moods can also affect what we remember, a phenomenon called **mood-congruent memory.** If you have ever had an episode of uncontrollable giggling, you know how a euphoric mood can trigger one silly thought after another. And at

recognition A retrieval method in which one must identify present stimuli as having been previously presented.

encoding specificity principle The doctrine that memory is encoded and stored with specific cues related to the context in which it was formed. The more closely the retrieval cues match the form in which the information was encoded, the better it will be remembered.

mood-congruent memory A memory process that selectively retrieves memories that match (are congruent with) one's mood.

Because mood affects memory, people with depression may remember and report more negative symptoms to a physician. As a result, their treatment may differ from that given to patients with the same condition who do not have depression.

prospective memory   The aspect of memory that enables one to remember to take some action in the future—as remembering a doctor's appointment.

the other end of the mood spectrum, people with depression often report that all their thoughts have a melancholy aspect. In this way, depression can perpetuate itself through retrieval of depressing memories (Sakaki, 2007).

Not just a laboratory curiosity, mood-congruent memory can also have important health implications. Says memory researcher Gordon Bower, "Doctors assess what to do with you based on your complaints and how much you complain" (McCarthy, 1991). Because people with depression are likely to emphasize their medical symptoms, they may receive different treatment from that dispensed to more upbeat individuals with the same disease. This, says Bower, means physicians must learn to take a person's psychological state into consideration when deciding on a diagnosis and a course of therapy.

Prospective Memory   One of the most common memory tasks involves remembering to perform some action at a future time—such as keeping a doctor's appointment, going to lunch with a friend, or setting out the garbage cans on the appointed day. Psychologists call this **prospective memory**. Surprisingly, this important process of remembering to remember has received relatively little study. We do know a failure in prospective memory can have consequences that range from merely inconvenient and embarrassing to horrific:

> After a change in his usual routine, an adoring father forgot to turn toward the day care center and instead drove his usual route to work at the university. Several hours later, his infant son, who had been quietly asleep in the back seat, was dead (Einstein & McDaniel, 2005, p. 286).

How could such a terrible thing happen? The father probably became distracted from his intended task and fell into his customary routine. In situations like this, when people have to remember to deviate from their usual routine, they typically rely on *continuous monitoring,* which means trying to keep the intended action in mind. Continuous monitoring, however, can be easily derailed by distraction or habit. So if you find yourself in that situation, your best bet is to use a reliable prompt—which for the father may have meant placing his briefcase in the backseat with his child. Another good technique involves thinking of a specific cue you expect to encounter just before the required task. The father, for example, might have visualized a prominent landmark he would see just before the turn off his usual route and then focused on that landmark as a memory cue.

The Washington Monument is an example of a tapered stone object that is topped by a pyramid-shaped point. Can you recall the name for such objects? Or is it "on the tip of your tongue"?

TOT phenomenon   The inability to recall a word, while knowing that it is in memory. People often describe this frustrating experience as having the word "on the tip of the tongue."

[PSYCHOLOGY MATTERS]

On the Tip of Your Tongue

Answer as many of the following questions as you can:

- What is the North American equivalent of the reindeer?
- What do artists call the board on which they mix paints?
- What is the name for a tall, four-sided stone monument with a point at the top of its shaft?
- What instrument do navigators use to determine latitude by sighting on the stars?
- What is the name of a sheath used to contain a sword or dagger?
- What is the name of a small Chinese boat usually propelled with a single oar or pole?

If this demonstration works as expected, you couldn't remember all the answers, but you had a strong sense you had them somewhere in memory. You might say that the answer was "on the tip of your tongue." Appropriately enough, psychologists refer to this near-miss memory as the **TOT phenomenon** (Brown, 1991). Surveys show that most people have a "tip-of-the-tongue" (TOT) experience about once a week. Among those who watch *Jeopardy*, it may occur even more frequently. And, according to a recent study, deaf persons who use sign language sometimes have a "tip of the fingers" (TOF) experience in which they are sure they know a word but cannot quite retrieve the sign (Thompson et al., 2005). Obviously, then, some fundamental memory process underlies both the TOT and the TOF phenomena.

The most common TOT experiences center on names of personal acquaintances, names of famous persons, and familiar objects (Brown, 1991). About half the time, target words finally do pop into mind, usually within about one agonizing minute (Brown & McNeill, 1966).

What accounts for the TOT phenomenon? One possibility—often exploited in laboratory studies—involves inadequate context cues. This is probably what made you stumble on some of the items above: We did not give you enough context to activate the schema associated with the correct answer.

Another possibility involves *interference:* when another memory blocks access or retrieval, as when you were thinking of Jan when you unexpectedly meet Jill (Schacter, 1999). And, even though you were unable to recall some of the correct words in our demonstration of TOT (caribou, palette, obelisk, sextant, scabbard, sampan), you may have spotted the right answer in a recognition format. It's also likely that some features of the sought-for words abruptly popped to mind ("I know it begins with an *s!*"), even though the words themselves eluded you. So the TOT phenomenon occurs during a recall attempt when there is a weak match between retrieval cues and the encoding of the word in long-term memory.

And we'll bet you can't name all seven dwarfs.

Check Your Understanding

✓ Study and Review at MyPsychLab

1. **APPLICATION:** Remembering names is usually harder than remembering faces because names require _____, while faces merely require _____.

2. **APPLICATION:** At a high school class reunion, you are likely to experience a flood of memories that would be unlikely to come to mind under other circumstances. What memory process explains this?

3. **APPLICATION:** Give an example of mood-congruent memory.

4. **APPLICATION:** Give an example of a situation that would require prospective memory.

5. **RECALL:** A person experiencing the TOT phenomenon is unable to _____ a specific word.

   a. recognize   c. recall
   b. encode   d. process

6. **UNDERSTANDING THE CORE CONCEPT:** An implicit memory may be activated by priming, and an explicit memory may be activated by a recognizable stimulus. In either case, a psychologist would say that these memories are being

   a. cued.   c. encoded.
   b. recognized.   d. chunked.

Answers 1. recall/recognition **2.** Encoding specificity **3.** Good examples involve situations in which people who are feeling a strong emotion or mood selectively remember experiences associated with that mood. Thus, during a physical exam, a depressed person might report more unpleasant physical symptoms would than a happy person. **4.** Prospective memory involves having to remember to perform some action at a time in the future, such as taking medicine tonight, stopping at the grocery store on the way home, or calling one's parents next Friday evening. **5.** c **6.** a

---

5.4 KEY QUESTION
Why Does Memory Sometimes Fail Us?

We forget appointments and anniversaries. During a test you can't remember the terms you studied the night before. Or a familiar name seems just out of your mental reach. Yet, ironically, we sometimes cannot rid memory of an unhappy event. Why does memory play these tricks on us—making us remember what we would rather forget and forget what we want to remember?

According to memory expert Daniel Schacter, the culprit is what he terms the "seven sins" of memory: *transience, absent-mindedness, blocking, misattribution, suggestibility, bias,* and *unwanted persistence* (Schacter, 1999, 2001). Further, he claims these seven problems are really consequences of some very useful features of human memory. From an evolutionary perspective, these features stood our ancestors in good stead, so they are preserved in our own memory systems. Our Core Concept puts this notion more succinctly:

> ## Core Concept 5.4
>
> **Most of our memory problems arise from memory's "seven sins"— which are really by-products of otherwise adaptive features of human memory.**

While examining the "seven sins," we will consider such everyday memory problems as forgetting where you left your keys or the inability to forget an unpleasant experience. We will also explore strategies for improving memory by overcoming some of Schacter's "seven sins"—with special emphasis on how certain memory techniques can improve your studying. We begin with the frustration of fading memories.

Transience: Fading Memories Cause Forgetting

How would you do on a rigorous test of the course work you took a year ago? We thought so—because unused memories seem to weaken with time. Although no one has directly observed a human memory trace fade and disappear, much circumstantial evidence points to this **transience**, or impermanence, of long-term memory—the first of Schacter's "sins."

Ebbinghaus and the Forgetting Curve

In a classic study of transience, pioneering psychologist Hermann Ebbinghaus (1908/1973) first learned lists of *nonsense syllables* (such as POV, KEB, FIC, and RUZ) and tried to recall them over varying time intervals. This worked well over short periods, up to a few days. But to measure memory after long delays of weeks or months, when recall had failed completely, Ebbinghaus had to invent another method: He measured the number of trials required to *relearn* the original list. Because it generally took fewer trials to relearn a list than to learn it originally, the difference indicated a "savings" that could serve as a measure of memory. (If the original learning required ten trials and relearning required seven trials, the savings was 30 percent.) By using the *savings method,* Ebbinghaus could trace memory over long periods of time. The curve obtained from combining data from many experiments appears in Figure 5.10 and represents one of Ebbinghaus's most important discoveries: *For relatively meaningless material, we have a rapid initial loss of memory followed by a declining rate of loss.* Subsequent research shows that this **forgetting curve** captures the pattern of transience by which we forget much of the verbal material we learn.

Modern psychologists have built on Ebbinghaus's work but now have more interest in how we remember *meaningful* material, such as information you read in this book. Meaningful memories seem to fade too—though, fortunately, not as rapidly as Ebbinghaus's nonsense syllables. Current research sometimes uses brain scanning techniques, such as fMRI and PET, to visualize the diminishing brain activity that characterizes forgetting (Schacter, 1996, 1999).

Not all memories, however, follow the classic forgetting curve. We often retain well-used motor skills, for example, substantially intact in procedural memory for many years, even without practice—"just like riding a bicycle." Memory for foreign languages learned, but not used for a long period of time, also seems to remain relatively intact (subject to less forgetting than Ebbinghaus predicted) for as long as 50 years

transience   The impermanence of a long-term memory. Transience is based on the idea that long-term memories gradually fade in strength over time.

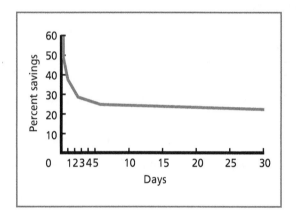

FIGURE 5.10

Ebbinghaus's Forgetting Curve

Ebbinghaus's forgetting curve shows that the savings demonstrated by relearning drops rapidly and reaches a plateau, below which little more is forgotten.

Source: Zimbardo, P. G., & Gerrig, R. J. (1999). *Psychology and Life,* 15th ed. Boston, MA: Allyn and Bacon. Copyright © 1999 by Pearson Education. Reprinted by permission of the publisher.

forgetting curve   A graph plotting the amount of retention and forgetting over time for a certain batch of material, such as a list of nonsense syllables. The typical forgetting curve is steep at first, becoming flatter as time goes on.

CONNECTION CHAPTER 2

fMRI and PET are brain scanning techniques that form images of especially active regions in the brain (p. 64).

(Bahrick, 1984). Similarly, recognition of high-school classmates' names and faces remains about 90 percent accurate even up to 45 years (although recall-based memory tasks show much lower retention; Bahrick, Bahrick, & Wittlinger, 1975). What accounts for less transience in these areas? We'll reveal the answer to that question near the end of the chapter in our discussion of study tips.

Interference One common cause of transience comes from *interference*—when one item prevents us from forming a robust memory for another item. This often occurs when you attempt to learn two conflicting things in succession, such as if you had a French class followed by a Spanish class.

What causes interference? Three main factors top the list:

1. **The more similar the two sets of material to be learned, the greater the likelihood of interference.** So French and Spanish classes are more likely to interfere with each other than are, say, psychology and accounting.

2. **Meaningless material is more vulnerable to interference than meaningful material.** Because LTM is organized by meaning, you will have more trouble remembering two locker combinations than you will two news bulletins. (The exception occurs when you experience a direct conflict in meaning, as when two news bulletins seem to be telling you conflicting things.)

3. **Emotional material can be an especially powerful cause of interference.** So if you broke up with your true love last night, you will probably forget what your literature professor says in class today.

Interference commonly arises when an old habit gets in the way of learning a new response, as we saw in the case of the father who forgot to stop at the day care center. Interference can also happen when people switch from one word-processing program to another. And, of course, interference accounts for the legendary problem old dogs have in learning new tricks. Everyday life offers many more examples, but interference theory groups them in two main categories, *proactive interference* and *retroactive interference*.

Proactive Interference When an old memory disrupts the learning and remembering of new information, **proactive interference** is the culprit. An example of proactive interference occurs every January when we have trouble remembering to write the correct date on our checks. *Pro-* means "forward," so in proactive interference, old memories act forward in time to block your attempts at new learning.

proactive interference A cause of forgetting by which previously stored information prevents learning and remembering new information.

Retroactive Interference When the opposite happens—when new information prevents your remembering older information—we can blame forgetting on **retroactive interference**. *Retro-* means "backward"; the newer material reaches back into your memory to push old material out of memory (see Figure 5.11). In a computer, retroactive interference occurs when you save a new document in place of an old one. Much the same thing happens in your own memory when you meet two new people in succession, and the second name causes you to forget the first one.

retroactive interference A cause of forgetting by which newly learned information prevents retrieval of previously stored material.

The Serial Position Effect Have you ever noticed that the first and last parts of a poem or vocabulary list are usually easier to learn and remember than the middle portion? In general, the *primacy effect* refers to the relative ease of remembering the first items in a series, while the *recency effect* refers to the strength of memory for the most recent items. Together, with diminished memory for the middle portion, we term this the **serial position effect**. So when you are introduced to several people in succession, you are more likely to remember the names of those you met first and last than those you met in between. (That's assuming other factors are equal, such as the commonness of their names, distinctiveness of their appearance, and their personalities.)

How does interference theory explain the serial position effect? Unlike the material at the ends of the poem or list, the part in the middle is exposed to a double dose of interference—both retroactively and proactively. That is, the middle receives interference

serial position effect A form of interference related to the sequence in which information is presented. Generally, items in the middle of the sequence are less well remembered than items presented first or last.

FIGURE 5.11

Two Types of Interference

In proactive interference, earlier learning (Spanish) interferes with memory for later information (French). In retroactive interference, new information (French) interferes with memory for information learned earlier (Spanish).

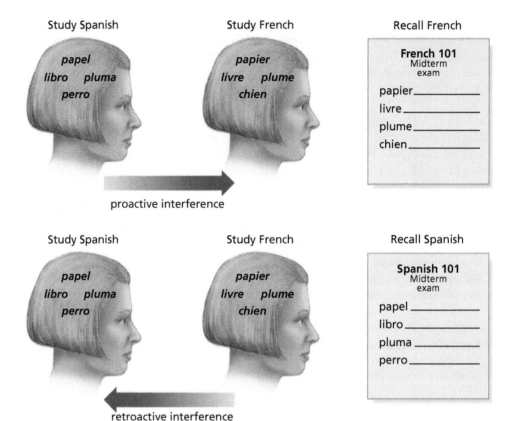

Study Spanish · Study French · Recall French

papel
libro   pluma
perro

papier
livre   plume
chien

French 101
Midterm exam

papier_____
livre_____
plume_____
chien_____

proactive interference

Study Spanish · Study French · Recall Spanish

papel
libro   pluma
perro

papier
livre   plume
chien

Spanish 101
Midterm exam

papel_____
libro_____
pluma_____
perro_____

retroactive interference

absent-mindedness Forgetting caused by lapses in attention.

Misplacing your car keys results from a shift in attention. Which of the seven "sins" does this represent?

blocking Forgetting that occurs when an item in memory cannot be accessed or retrieved. Blocking is caused by interference.

from both directions, while material at either end gets interference from only one side. So, in view of the serial position effect, perhaps it would be helpful to pay special attention to the material in the middle of this chapter.

Absent-Mindedness: Lapses of Attention Cause Forgetting

When you misplace your car keys or forget an anniversary, you have had an episode of **absent-mindedness**, the second "sin" of memory. It's not that the memory has disappeared from your brain circuits. Rather, you have suffered a retrieval failure caused by shifting your attention elsewhere. In the case of a forgotten anniversary, the attention problem occurred on the retrieval end—when you were concentrating on something that took your attention away from the upcoming anniversary. As for the car keys, your attentive shift probably occurred during the original encoding—when you weren't paying attention to where you laid them. This form of absent-mindedness often comes from listening to music or watching TV while studying.

This kind of encoding error was also at work in the "depth of processing" experiments we discussed earlier: People who encoded information shallowly ("Does the word contain an *e*?") were less able to recall the target word than those who encoded it deeply ("Is it an animal?"). Yet another example can be found in demonstrations of *change blindness:* In one study, participants viewed a movie clip in which one actor who was asking directions was replaced by another actor while they were briefly hidden by two men carrying a door in front of them. Amazingly, fewer than half the viewers noticed the change (Simons & Levin, 1998). Much the same thing may happen to you in the magic trick demonstration in Figure 5.12.

Blocking: Access Problems

Blocking, the third "sin" of memory, occurs when we lose access to information, such as when you see familiar people in new surroundings and can't remember their names. The most thoroughly studied form of blocking, however, involves the maddening TOT

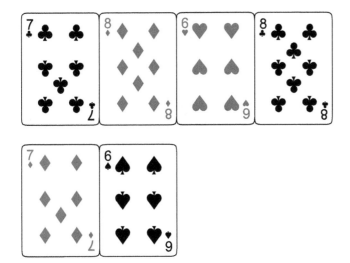

FIGURE 5.12A
The "Magic of Memory"

Pick one of the cards. Stare at it intently for at least 15 seconds, being careful not to shift your gaze to the other cards. Then turn the page.

experience: when you *know you know* the name for something but can't retrieve it. As we saw earlier, the TOT phenomenon often results from poor context cues that fail to activate the necessary memory schema.

Stress, too, can produce blocking, perhaps through failure to sustain one's focus of attention. Similarly, distraction can cause blocking on prospective memory tasks, such as remembering to perform a certain action at a certain time. Age plays a role, too, with blocking increasing as one grows older.

Misattribution: Memories in the Wrong Context

All three "sins" discussed so far make memories unavailable in one way or another. But these are not the only kinds of memory problems we experience. For example, we sometimes retrieve memories but associate them with the wrong time, place, or person. Schacter (1999) calls this **misattribution**, a problem that stems from the reconstructive nature of long-term memory. In the penny demonstration at the beginning of the chapter, you learned that we commonly retrieve incomplete memories and fill in the blanks to make them meaningful to us. This paves the way for mistakes that arise from connecting information with the wrong, but oh-so-sensible, context.

misattribution A memory fault that occurs when memories are retrieved but are associated with the wrong time, place, or person.

Here's an example of misattribution: Psychologist Donald Thompson was accused of rape based on a victim's detailed, but mistaken, description of her assailant (Thompson, 1988). Fortunately for Thompson, his alibi was indisputable. When the crime occurred, he was being interviewed live on television—about memory distortions. The victim, it turned out, had been watching the interview just before she was raped and, in the stress of the experience, misattributed the assault to Thompson, recalling his face instead of the face of her assailant.

Misattribution can also prompt people to mistakenly believe that other people's ideas are their own. This sort of misattribution occurs when a person hears an idea and keeps it in memory, forgetting its source. Unintentional plagiarism comes from this form of misattribution, as we saw earlier in the case of George Harrison of the Beatles.

Yet another type of misattribution can cause people to remember something they did not experience at all. Such was the case with volunteers who were asked to remember a set of words associated with a particular theme: *door, glass, pane, shade, ledge, sill, house, open, curtain, frame, view, breeze, sash, screen,* and *shutter.* Under these conditions, many later remembered *window,* even though that word was not on the list (Roediger & McDermott, 1995, 2000). This result again shows the power of context cues in determining the content of memory. And it demonstrates yet again how people tend to create and retrieve memories based on meaning.

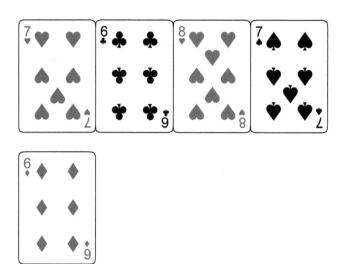

suggestibility The process of memory distortion as the result of deliberate or inadvertent suggestion.

misinformation effect The distortion of memory by suggestion or misinformation.

👁 **Watch** the **Video** Memory: Elizabeth Loftus at **MyPsychLab**

Suggestibility: External Cues Distort or Create Memories

Suggestion can also distort or even create memories, a possibility of particular concern to the courts. Attorneys or law enforcement officers interviewing witnesses may make suggestions about the facts of a case—either deliberately or unintentionally—that could alter a witness's memory. Such concerns about **suggestibility** prompted Elizabeth Loftus and John Palmer to find out just how easily eyewitness memories could be distorted.

Memory Distortion Participants in the Loftus and Palmer study first watched a film of two cars colliding. Then the experimenters asked them to estimate how fast the cars had been moving (Loftus, 1979, 1984; Loftus & Palmer, 1973). Half the witnesses were asked, "How fast were the cars going when they *smashed* into each other?" Their estimates, it turned out, were about 25 percent higher than those given by respondents asked, "How fast were the cars going when they *hit* each other?" This distortion of memory caused by misinformation has been dubbed, appropriately, the **misinformation effect.**

Clearly, the Loftus and Palmer study showed that memories can be distorted and embellished by even the most subtle cues and suggestions. But memories can also be *created* by similar methods. And it can be done without an individual's awareness. 👁

Fabricated Memories The famed developmental psychologist, Jean Piaget (1962), described a vivid memory of a traumatic event from his own early childhood:

> One of my first memories would date, if it were true, from my second year. I can still see, most clearly, the following scene in which I believed until I was about fifteen. I was sitting in my pram, which my nurse was pushing in the Champs Elysées [in Paris], when a man tried to kidnap me. I was held in by the strap fastened round me while my nurse bravely tried to stand between me and the thief. She received various scratches, and I can still see vaguely those on her face . . . (pp. 187–188).

Piaget's nurse described the alleged attack in vivid detail and was given an expensive watch from his parents as a token of thanks for her bravery. However, years later, the former nurse sent a letter to Piaget's family confessing the story had been fabricated and returning the watch. From this, Piaget (1962) concluded:

> I, therefore, must have heard, as a child, the account of this story, which my parents believed, and projected into the past in the form of a visual memory (Piaget, 1962, p. 188).

Are we all susceptible to creating false memories such as the one Piaget described? To find out, Elizabeth Loftus and her colleagues decided to do an experiment. They first contacted parents of a group of college students, obtaining lists of childhood events, which the students were then asked if they remembered. But embedded in those lists were plausible events that never happened, such as being lost in a shopping mall, spilling the punch bowl at a wedding, meeting Bugs Bunny at Disneyland (impossible because Bugs is not a Disney character), or experiencing a visit by a clown at a birthday party (Loftus, 2003a). After repeated recall attempts over a period of several days, about one-fourth of the students claimed to remember the bogus events. All that was required were some credible suggestions. (This experiment may remind you of Donna's case, with which we began our chapter: Repeated suggestions by the therapist led to Donna's fabricated memory.)

New research suggests that doctored photographs can also create false memories, perhaps even more powerfully than the stories used by Loftus and her colleagues. For example, in a variation of the lost-in-the-mall technique, adults viewed altered photographs purporting to show them riding in a hot air balloon. After seeing the photos several times over a period of two weeks, half the participants "remembered" details about the fictitious balloon ride (Wade et al., 2002). Even in this age of digital cameras and image-altering software, people don't always stop to question whether a photograph may have been modified (Garry & Gerrie, 2005).

Factors Affecting the Accuracy of Eyewitnesses So to what extent can we rely on eyewitness testimony? Obviously, it is possible in laboratory experiments to distinguish false memories from true ones. But what about real-life situations in which people claim to have recovered long-forgotten memories?

As we saw in our second case at the beginning of the chapter, Ross's recollection was independently verified by the confession of a camp counselor, but such objective evidence doesn't always materialize. In such cases, the best we can do is look for evidence of suggestion that may have produced the memory—as we see in false-memory experiments. If suggestion has occurred, a healthy dose of skepticism is warranted, unless objective evidence appears. Specifically, we should beware of eyewitness reports tainted by the following factors (Kassin, 2001):

The way mug shots are presented can bias the recollections of witnesses. Realizing this, the U.S. Department of Justice has published guidelines for interrogating eyewitnesses.

- *Leading questions* ("How fast were the cars going when they *smashed* into each other?") can influence witnesses' recollections. But such questions have less effect if witnesses are forewarned that interrogations can create memory bias.
- *The passage of substantial amounts of time,* which allows the original memory to fade, makes people more likely to misremember information.
- *Repeated retrieval:* Each time a memory is retrieved, it is reconstructed and then restored (much like a computer document that is retrieved, modified, and saved), increasing the chances of error.
- *The age of the witness:* Younger children and older adults may be especially susceptible to influence by misinformation.
- *Unwarranted confidence:* Confidence in a memory is not a sign of an accurate memory. In fact, misinformed individuals can actually come to believe the misinformation in which they feel confident.

Based on such concerns, the U.S. Department of Justice (1999) has published national guidelines for gathering eyewitness testimony, available on its website.

Bias: Beliefs, Attitudes, and Opinions Distort Memories

The sixth memory "sin," which Schacter calls *bias,* refers to the influence of personal beliefs, attitudes, and experiences on memory. Lots of domestic arguments of the "Did not! Did too!" variety owe their spirited exchanges to bias. While it's easier to see another person's biases than our own, here are two common forms you should especially guard against.

expectancy bias   The unconscious tendency to remember events as being congruent with our expectations.

Expectancy Bias   An unconscious tendency to remember events as being congruent with our expectations produces **expectancy bias**. To illustrate, suppose you are among a group of volunteers for an experiment in which you read a story about the relationship between Bob and Margie, a couple who plan to get married. Part of the story reveals that Bob doesn't want children, and he is worried about how Margie will react to that. When he does tell her, Margie is shocked, because she desperately wants children. To your surprise, you are informed after reading the story that, contrary to your expectations, Bob and Margie did get married. Meanwhile, another group of volunteers reads the same story but are told the couple ended their relationship. Other than the ending, will people in those two groups remember the Bob and Margie story differently?

In a laboratory experiment using this same story, those who heard the unexpected ending (the condition in which Bob and Margie decided to get married) gave the most erroneous reports. Why? Because of their expectancy biases, they recalled distorted information that made the outcome fit their initial expectations (Schacter, 1999; Spiro, 1980). One person, for example, "remembered" that Bob and Margie had separated but decided their love could overcome their differences. Another related that the couple had decided on adoption as a compromise. When something happens that violates our expectations, then, we may unconsciously skew the information so it better fits our pre-existing notions.

self-consistency bias   The commonly held idea that we are more consistent in our attitudes, opinions, and beliefs than we actually are.

Self-Consistency Bias   People abhor the thought of being inconsistent, even though research suggests that they are kidding themselves. This Schacter calls the **self-consistency bias**. For example, studies have found people to be far less consistent than they realized in their support for political candidates, as well as on political issues such as the equality of women, aid to minority groups, and the legalization of marijuana (Levine, 1997; Marcus, 1986).

Of particular interest for the study of memory, self-consistency bias can affect the content of our memories (Levine & Safer, 2002). One study interviewed dating couples twice, two months apart, and found memories about the relationship changed based on how well the relationship had progressed over the two-month interval. Importantly, though, participants generally did not recognize their inconsistencies. Those whose relationships had improved remembered their initial evaluations of their partners as more positive than they actually were, while those whose relationships had declined had the opposite response (Scharfe & Bartholomew, 1998). In this study, as well as many others involving attitudes, beliefs, opinions, or emotions, we see that our biases act as a sort of distorted mirror in which our memories are reflected—but without our awareness that our memories had been altered.

Persistence: When We Can't Forget

persistence   A memory problem in which unwanted memories cannot be put out of mind.

The seventh "sin" of memory, **persistence**, reminds us that memory sometimes works all too well. We all experience this occasionally, when a persistent thought, image, or melody cycles over and over in our minds. Thankfully, such intrusive memories are usually short lived. They can become a problem, though, when accompanied by intense negative emotions. At the extreme, the persistence of memories for unpleasant events creates a downward emotional spiral whereby people suffering from *depression* can't stop ruminating about unhappy events or traumas in their lives. Similarly, patients with *phobias* may become obsessed by fearful memories about snakes, dogs, crowds, spiders, or lightning. All of this underscores the powerful role that emotion plays in memory.

CONNECTION CHAPTER 12 ▶

People with *phobias* have extreme and unreasonable fears of specific objects or situations (p. 532).

The Advantages of the "Seven Sins" of Memory

Despite the grief they cause us, the "seven sins" arise from adaptive features of memory, argues Daniel Schacter (1999). Thus, transience—maddening as it is to the student taking a test—actually prevents the memory system from being overwhelmed by information it no longer needs. Similarly, blocking is useful when it allows only the most relevant information—information most strongly associated with present cues—to come to mind. These processes, then, help prevent us from a flood of unwanted and distracting memories.

Absent-mindedness, too, is the by-product of the useful ability to shift our attention. Similarly, misattributions, biases, and suggestibility result from a memory system built to focus on *meaning* and discard details: The alternative would be a computer-like memory filled with information at the expense of understanding. And, finally, we can see that the "sin" of persistence is really a feature of a memory system responsive to emotional experiences, particularly those involving dangerous situations. In general, then, the picture that emerges of memory's "failures" is also a picture of a system well adapted to conditions people have faced for thousands of years.

Improving Your Memory with Mnemonics

One way to improve your memory is to develop a tool kit of mental strategies known as *mnemonics* (pronounced *ni-MON-ix,* from the Greek word meaning "remember"). **Mnemonic strategies** help you encode new information by associating it with information already in long-term memory. To illustrate, we will take a detailed look at two mnemonic strategies, the *method of loci* and *natural language mediators,* both of which are especially useful for remembering lists. Then we will offer tips to help with the common problem of remembering names.

mnemonic strategy Technique for improving memory, especially by making connections between new material and information already present in long-term memory.

The Method of Loci Dating back to the ancient Greeks, the **method of loci** (pronounced *LOW-sye,* from *locus* or "place"), is literally one of the oldest tricks in this book. Greek orators originally devised the method of loci to help remember the major points of their speeches.

To illustrate, imagine a familiar sequence of places, such as the bed, desk, and chairs in your room. Then, using the method of loci, mentally move from place to place in the room, and as you go imagine putting one item from your list in each place. To retrieve the series, you merely take another mental tour, examining the places you used earlier. There you will "see" the item you put in each place. To remember a grocery list, for example, you might mentally picture a can of *tuna* on your bed, *shampoo* spilled on your desktop, and a box of *eggs* open on a chair. Bizarre or unconventional image combinations are usually easier to remember—so a can of tuna in your bedroom will make a more memorable image than tuna in your kitchen (Bower, 1972).

It's worth noting, by the way, that visual imagery is one of the most effective forms of encoding: You can easily remember things by associating them with vivid, distinctive mental pictures. In fact, you could remember your grocery list by using visual imagery alone. Simply combine the mental images of tuna, shampoo, and eggs in a bizarre but memorable way. So, you might picture a tuna floating on an enormous fried egg in a sea of foamy shampoo. Or you might imagine a celebrity you dislike eating tuna from the can, hair covered with shampoo suds, while you throw eggs at her.

method of loci A mnemonic technique that involves associating items on a list with a sequence of familiar physical locations.

Natural Language Mediators Memory aids called **natural language mediators** associate meaningful word patterns with new information to be remembered. Using this method to remember a grocery list, you would make up a story. Using the same list as before (tuna, shampoo, and eggs), the story might link the items this way: "The cat discovers I'm out of *tuna* so she interrupts me while I'm using the *shampoo* and meows to *egg* me on." (OK, we know it's hokey—but it works!) Similarly, advertisers know that rhyming slogans and rhythmic musical jingles make it easier for customers to remember their products and brand names (you may even have one stuck in your head now!). The chances are that a teacher in your past used a simple rhyme to help you remember a spelling rule ("*I* before *E* except after *C*") or the number of days in each month ("Thirty days has September . . . "). In a physics class, you may have used a natural language mediator in the form of an *acronym*—a word made up of initials—to learn the colors of the visible spectrum in their correct order: "Roy G. Biv" for red, orange, yellow, green, blue, indigo, violet.

natural language mediator Word associated with new information to be remembered.

Mnemonic strategies help us remember things by making them meaningful. Here, Wangari Maathai, the Nobel Peace Prize laureate from Kenya, tries her hand at learning the Chinese character for "tree"—which bears a resemblance to a stylized tree. Many Chinese and Japanese characters originally were drawings of the objects they represented.

whole method The mnemonic strategy of first approaching the material to be learned "as a whole," forming an impression of the overall meaning of the material. The details are later associated with this overall impression.

distributed learning A technique whereby the learner spaces learning sessions over time rather than trying to learn the material all in one study period.

Remembering Names The inability to remember people's names is one of the most common complaints about memory. So how could you use the power of association to remember names? In the first place, know that remembering names doesn't happen automatically. People who do it well work at it by making deliberate associations between a name and some characteristic of the person—the more unusual the association, the better.

Suppose, for example, you have just met us, the authors of this text, at a psychological convention. You might visualize Bob's face framed in a big *O,* taken from the middle of his name. To remember Vivian, think of her as "Vivacious Vivian," the liveliest person at the convention. And, as for Phil, you might visualize putting a hose in Phil's mouth and "fill"-ing him with water. (While unusual associations may be easier to remember than mundane ones, it is best not to tell people about the mnemonic you have devised to remember their names.)

In general, use of mnemonics teaches us that memory is flexible, personal, and creative. It also teaches us that *memory ultimately works by meaningful associations.* With this knowledge and a little experimentation, you can devise techniques for encoding and retrieval that work well for you, based on your own personal associations and, perhaps, on your own sense of humor.

[PSYCHOLOGY MATTERS]

Using Psychology to Learn Psychology

Mnemonic strategies designed for learning names or memorizing lists of unrelated items won't help much with the material you need to learn in your psychology class. There, the important material consists of concepts—often abstract concepts, such as "operant conditioning" or "retroactive interference"—ideas you need to understand rather than merely memorize. Such material calls for strategies geared both to concept learning and to avoiding the two memory "sins" feared most by college students, *transience* and *blocking.* Let's see what advice cognitive psychologists have for students trying to avoid these two quirks of memory.

Studying to Avoid Transience

- *Make the material personally meaningful.* Many studies have shown that memories remain stronger when they are meaningful, rather than just a collection of facts and definitions (Baddeley, 1998; Haberlandt, 1999). One good strategy for doing this is the **whole method**, a technique often used by actors who must learn a script in a short time. With this approach, begin by getting an overview of all the material—the "big picture" into which details can be assimilated. Suppose, for example, you have a test on this chapter next week. Using the whole method, you would read through the chapter outline and summary, along with all the Key Questions and Core Concepts on the chapter opening page, before beginning to read the details of the chapter. This approach erects a mental framework on which you can hang the details of encoding, interference, retrieval, and other memory topics.

- *Spread your learning out over time.* Next, use **distributed learning** to resist transience. In other words, study your psychology repeatedly and at frequent intervals rather than trying to learn it all at once in a single "cram" session (called *massed learning*). Distributed learning not only avoids the lowered efficiency of massed learning, which causes fatigue, but also strengthens memories in the process of consolidation. One study found that students who studied in two separate sessions, rather than just one, doubled the amount of information they learned in a given amount of time and also increased their understanding of the material (Bahrick et al., 1993). Distributed learning also results in longer retention of material (Schmidt & Bjork, 1992). And it helps us understand why we have enhanced memory capabilities for names and faces of high school friends even decades later: We likely accessed that information frequently while in high school—the equivalent of distributed learning.

- *Take active steps to minimize interference.* You can't avoid interference altogether, but you can avoid studying for another class after your review session for tomorrow's psychology test. And you can make sure you understand all the material and have cleared up any confusing points well before you go to the test. If, for example, you are not sure of the difference between *declarative memory* and *semantic memory,* discuss this with your instructor—before the day of the test.

Studying to Avoid Blocking on the Test

The strategies above will help you get to the test with a strong memory for what you need to know. To really do well on the test, though, you must also avoid blocking, the inability to retrieve what you have in memory. To help you achieve this, we suggest some techniques that apply two more ideas you learned in this chapter, *elaborative rehearsal* and *encoding specificity:*

- *Review and elaborate on the material.* Students often think that, just because they read the material once and understood it, they will remember it. With complex concepts and ideas, though, you need to review what you have learned several times. And your review should not be mindless and passive—merely looking at the words in the book. Instead, use *elaborative rehearsal.* One of the best ways of doing this when studying for a test is to create your own examples of the concepts. So, as you study about proactive interference, think of an example from your own experience. Also, review and rehearse mnemonics you may have created for some of the material, such as acronyms or vivid mental images of concepts. By adding associations to the material, you create more ways to access it when you need it.

- *Test yourself with retrieval cues you expect to see on the examination.* By using the principle of *encoding specificity,* you can learn the material in ways most likely to be cued by the questions on the test. This is often easier to do with a friend studying for the same test, ideally a few days before the exam, but after you have already prepared and feel ready. Your purpose, at this point, will not be to learn new material but to practice what you've learned as you anticipate the most likely test items. Does your professor prefer essay questions? Short-answer questions? Multiple choice? Try to think of and answer questions of the type most likely to appear on the test.

All these study strategies are based on well-established principles of learning and memory. Studying this way may sound like a lot of work—and it is. But the results will be worth the mental effort.

Check Your Understanding

1. **ANALYSIS:** What happens to memory over time, as described by Ebbinghaus's forgetting curve?

2. **APPLICATION:** Which kind of forgetting is involved when the sociology I studied yesterday makes it more difficult to learn and remember the psychology I am studying today?

3. **RECALL:** Describe at least three ways you can apply what you have learned in this chapter to improve your studying and memory.

4. **RECALL:** Which of the seven "sins" of memory was responsible for Piaget's fabricated memory of an attempted kidnapping?

5. **UNDERSTANDING THE CORE CONCEPT:** Which of the "sins" of memory probably helps us avoid dangerous situations we have encountered before?

Answers 1. *We forget rapidly at first and then more slowly as time goes on.* **2.** Proactive interference **3.** Elaborative rehearsal, distributed learning, and creating a variety of memory cues for each concept. **4.** Suggestibility **5.** Persistence

CRITICAL THINKING APPLIED

The Recovered Memory Controversy

Let's return now to the case studies with which we began the chapter. All involved claims of recovered memories: Ross's memory of molestation by a camp counselor was clearly accurate, and Donna's memory of abuse by her father was eventually repudiated. So where does that leave us when we hear about other such claims?

What Are the Critical Issues?

The controversy centers on the accuracy of claims of recovered memories—*not* on the reality of sexual abuse. Is it possible that recovered memories could be false? If so, we must decide how to judge their accuracy, especially memories of traumatic events.

Is the Claim Reasonable or Extreme?   Let's begin by asking: Is the notion of recovered memories of sexual abuse reasonable or outrageous? That is, does it fit with what we know both about memory and about sexual abuse? Let's see what the evidence can tell us.

We need to emphasize that sexual abuse of children *does* occur and poses a serious problem. How widespread is it? While estimates vary considerably, it appears that 4 to 20 percent of children in the United States have experienced at least one incident of sexual abuse (McAnulty & Burnette, 2004; Terry & Tallon, 2004). Accurate figures are difficult to obtain, of course, because people can be reluctant to discuss these experiences. And *if* it is true that sexual abuse can be blocked out of consciousness for long periods, the actual numbers could be higher.

We should also note that most claims of sexual abuse do *not* involve "recovered" memories. In general, we have no reason to doubt people who say they have been molested and have always remembered. The controversy centers on memories said to have been "recovered" after having been forgotten for months or even years.

What Is the Evidence?   The general public harbors a strong but unfounded belief that the most common response to trauma is *repression,* the blocking of memories in the unconscious, as first described by Sigmund Freud. But, in fact, most people who have traumatic experiences remember them vividly, rather than forgetting them (McNally et al., 2003). Unwelcome remembering of disturbing experiences is precisely the problem in posttraumatic stress disorder (PTSD). How, then, can we account for the fact that a portion of cases in almost every research study in this area includes some reports of repression (Greenhoot et al., 2008)?

Until recently, psychologists were at a loss to answer this question. But now, University of California psychologist Gail Goodwin and her colleagues (2010) may have found the answer.

A series of studies has revealed striking evidence that children with an avoidant attachment style—or a general lack of trust in their environment and the principal people in it (see Chapter 7)—are less likely to mentally process an abusive event when it occurs, resulting in less likelihood of a memory being encoded and stored in long-term memory. For these individuals, the end result may indeed be what has historically been termed "repression."

Could Bias Contaminate the Conclusion?   We have seen that memory does not make a complete record of our experiences. Nor is it always accurate. Of special relevance to the recovered memory controversy is research we discussed earlier in the chapter, showing that memories can rather easily be modified or even created by suggestion. As a result, participants not only report false memories but begin to believe them (Bruck & Ceci, 2004). Such experiments should make us skeptical of memories recovered during therapy or interrogation involving suggestive techniques. Memory expert Elizabeth Loftus argues that therapists who assume that most mental problems stem from childhood sexual abuse commonly use suggestive practices, although she does not say how widespread the problem might be (Loftus, 2003a, b). And in the book *Making Monsters,* social psychologist Richard Ofshe and his coauthor describe how clients can unknowingly tailor their recollections to fit their therapists' expectations. He adds that "therapists often encourage patients to redefine their life histories based on the new pseudomemories and, by doing so, redefine their most basic understanding of their families and themselves" (Ofshe & Watters, 1994, p. 6).

We are *not* saying that all, or even most, therapists use suggestive techniques to probe for memories of sexual abuse, although some certainly do (Poole et al., 1995). Nevertheless, patients should be wary of therapists who go "fishing" for repressed memories of early sexual experiences using such techniques as hypnosis, dream analysis, and suggestive questioning. No evidence exists in support of these methods for the recovery of accurate memories.

Another source of suggestion that pops up in a surprisingly large proportion of recovered memory cases is a book: *The Courage to Heal.* This book argues that forgotten memories of incest and abuse may lie behind people's feelings of powerlessness, inadequacy, vulnerability, and a long list of other unpleasant thoughts and emotions (Bass & Davis, 1988). The authors state, "If you . . . have a feeling that something abusive happened to you, it probably did" (pp. 21–22). None of these assertions, however, rests on anything more solid than speculation. Thus, say memory experts Elizabeth Loftus and Katherine Ketcham (1994), it seems likely that *The Courage to Heal* has contributed to many false memories of sexual abuse.

We should also note that the issue of recovered memories is both complex and charged with emotion—a situation ripe for emotional bias. Not only does the issue of sexual abuse strike many people close to home, but none of us wants to turn our back on those who believe they have been victims of sexual abuse. Yet what we know about memory tells us that we should not accept long-forgotten traumatic memories without corroborating evidence.

Does the Reasoning Avoid Common Fallacies? When we observe associations between things, we have a natural tendency to suspect that one might cause the other—as we associate overeating with gaining weight or spending time in the sun with a sunburn. Most of the time this logic serves us well, but occasionally it leads us to the wrong conclusions—as when we conclude that a chill causes a cold or that eating sweets causes a "sugar high." Experts call this the post hoc fallacy: *Post hoc* literally means "after the fact," and the idea is that looking back at events occurring in succession (e.g., sugar followed by excitement), we may erroneously conclude that the first event is the cause of the second.

How could the post hoc fallacy contribute to the "recovered memory" controversy? When people "look back" in their memories and find a memory (accurate or not) of abuse that seems to be associated with their current unhappiness, they assume the abusive event (again, whether real or erroneously remembered) is the cause of their current mental state. But, as we have seen, this conclusion may be faulty. Ironically, this can reinforce one's belief in the memory—through confirmation bias.

What Conclusions Can We Draw?

So, where does this leave us? Weigh the evidence yourself on a case-by-case basis, mindful of the possibility that emotional biases can affect your thinking. Keep in mind the following points as well:

- Sexual abuse of children *does* occur and is more prevalent than most professionals suspected just a generation ago (McAnulty & Burnette, 2004).
- On the other hand, memories cued by suggestion, as from therapists or police officers, are particularly vulnerable to distortion and fabrication (Loftus, 2003a). So, without independent evidence, there is no way to tell whether a recovered memory is true or false.
- Remember that people can feel just as certain about false memories as accurate ones.
- Although traumatic events can be forgotten and later recalled, they are much more likely to form persistent and intrusive memories that people cannot forget. Nevertheless, cases such as that of Ross show us that recovered memories of abuse can be true.
- Early memories, especially those of incidents that may have happened in infancy, are likely to be fantasies or misattributions. As we have seen, episodic memories of events before age 3 are rare (Schacter, 1996).
- One should be more suspicious of claims for memories that have been "repressed" and then "recovered" years later than for memories that have always been available to consciousness.

Do It Yourself! **FINDING OUT MORE ABOUT ISSUES IN REPORTS OF REPRESSED MEMORIES**

In this discussion, you may have noticed names of two researchers who are especially prominent in the area memory and false memories: Elizabeth Loftus and Gail Goodman. Find a recent article (published in the past year) by one of these authors, read it, and identify three main points the article makes that add to what you learned in this chapter.

CHAPTER SUMMARY

to an audio file of your chapter

CHAPTER PROBLEM: How can our knowledge about memory help us evaluate claims of recovered memories?

- Evidence clearly shows that most people form powerful memories of traumatic events, rather than repressing them.
- Up to one-third of the population has been demonstrated by research to be susceptible to relatively easy formation of

false memories. Thus, suggestive questioning techniques by therapists or other authority figures may inadvertently lead a person to create false memories that are in accordance with a therapist's suggestion.

- People with an avoidant attachment style have been found by researchers to be more likely to suppress traumatic memories than people with other attachment styles.

5.1 What Is Memory?

[**Core Concept 5.1** Human memory is an information processing system that works constructively to encode, store, and retrieve information.]

Human memory, like any **memory** system, involves three important tasks: **encoding, storage,** and **retrieval**. Although many people believe that memory makes a complete and accurate record, cognitive psychologists see human memory as an information processing system that interprets, distorts, and reconstructs information. **Eidetic imagery,** however, is a rare and poorly understood form of memory that produces especially vivid and persistent memories that may interfere with thought. It is not clear how eidetic memory fits with the widely accepted three-stage model of memory.

eidetic imagery (p. 175)
encoding (p. 174)
information-processing model (p. 174)
memory (p. 172)
retrieval (p. 175)
storage (p. 175)

5.2 How Do We Form Memories?

[**Core Concept 5.2** Each of the three memory stages encodes and stores memories in a different way, but they work together to transform sensory experience into a lasting record that has a pattern or meaning.]

The memory system is composed of three distinct stages: *sensory memory, working memory,* and *long-term memory.* The three stages work together sequentially to convert incoming sensory information into useful patterns or concepts that can be stored and retrieved when needed later.

Sensory memory holds 12 to 16 visual items for up to just a second or two, making use of the sensory pathways. A separate sensory register for each sense holds material just long enough for important information to be selected for further processing.

Working memory, which has the smallest storage capacity of the three stages and a duration of 20 to 30 seconds, draws information from sensory memory and long-term memory and processes it consciously. Theorists have proposed at least four components of working memory: a *central executive,* a *phonological loop,* a *sketchpad,* and an *episodic buffer.* We can cope with its limited duration and capacity by **chunking** and **rehearsal.** The biological basis of working memory is not clear, but it is believed to involve actively firing nerve circuits, probably in the frontal cortex.

Long-term memory has apparently unlimited storage capacity and duration. It has two main partitions, **declarative memory** (for facts and events) and **procedural memory** (for perceptual and motor skills). Declarative memory can be further divided into **episodic memory** and **semantic memory.** Semantic information is encoded, stored, and retrieved according to the meaning and context of the material. The case of H. M. showed that the hippocampus is involved in transferring information to long-term memory. Other research has found long-term memories associated with relatively permanent changes at the synaptic level.

Flashbulb memories are common in highly emotional experiences. While most people have a great deal of confidence in such vivid memories, studies have shown these memories are no more accurate than everyday memories.

acoustic encoding (p. 182)
anterograde amnesia (p. 187)
childhood amnesia (p. 186)
chunking (p. 181)
consolidation (p. 188)
declarative memory (p. 184)
elaborative rehearsal (p. 181)
engram (p. 187)
episodic memory (p. 185)
flashbulb memory (p. 189)
levels-of-processing theory (p. 183)
long-term memory (LTM) (p. 177)
maintenance rehearsal (p. 181)
procedural memory (p. 184)
retrograde amnesia (p. 188)
schema (p. 185)
semantic memory (p. 185)
sensory memory (p. 177)
working memory (p. 177)

5.3 How Do We Retrieve Memories?

[**Core Concept 5.3** Whether memories are implicit or explicit, successful retrieval depends on how they were encoded and how they are cued.]

H. M.'s case also demonstrated that information can be stored as **explicit** or **implicit** memories. The success of a memory search depends, in part, on the **retrieval cues.** Implicit memories can be cued by **priming.** Explicit memories can be cued by various **recall** or **recognition** tasks, although some tasks require remembering the **gist** rather than exact details. The accuracy of memory retrieval also depends on **encoding specificity** and **mood.** Relatively little is known about the conditions required for successful **prospective memory.** When there is a poor match between retrieval cues and the encoding, we may experience the **TOT phenomenon.**

5.4 Why Does Memory Sometimes Fail Us?

[Core Concept 5.4 **Most of our memory problems arise from memory's "seven sins"—which are really by-products of otherwise adaptive features of human memory.**]

Memory failures involve the "seven sins" of memory. These include forgetting, resulting from weakening memory traces **(transience)**, lapses of attention **(absent-mindedness)**, and inability to retrieve a memory **(blocking)**. Some forgetting can be attributed to a cause of transience known as **interference**. Memory can also fail when recollections are altered through **misattribution, suggestibility,** and **bias**. An important example involves eyewitness memories, which are subject to distortion. Suggestibility can also produce false memories that seem believable to the rememberer. The final "sin" of **persistence** occurs when unwanted memories linger in memory even when we would like to forget them.

The "seven sins" of memory, however, are by-products of a memory system that is well suited to solving problems of day-to-day living. Some of these problems can be overcome by **mnemonic strategies,** such as the **method of loci, natural**

language mediators, and other associative methods. The learning of concepts, however, requires special strategies geared to learning the *gist* of the material and to avoiding the two memory "sins" of transience and blocking.

CRITICAL THINKING APPLIED

The Recovered Memory Controversy

Most people mistakenly believe that traumatic memories are subject to repression and can later be recovered accurately through hypnosis or other techniques. Evidence indicates that not only do most people NOT repress traumatic memories, suggestive techniques can actually enable creation of false memories.

DISCOVERING PSYCHOLOGY **VIEWING GUIDE**

Watch the following video by logging into MyPsychLab (www.mypsychlab.com).
After you have watched the video, answer the questions that follow.

PROGRAM 9: **REMEMBERING AND FORGETTING**

Program Review

1. What pattern of remembering emerged in Hermann Ebbinghaus's research?
   a. Loss occurred at a steady rate.
   b. A small initial loss was followed by no further loss.
   c. There was no initial loss, but then there was a gradual decline.
   d. A sharp initial loss was followed by a gradual decline.

2. The way psychologists thought about and studied memory was changed by the invention of
   a. television.
   b. electroconvulsive shock therapy.
   c. the computer.
   d. the electron microscope.

3. What do we mean when we say that memories must be encoded?
   a. They must be taken from storage to be used.
   b. They must be put in a form the brain can register.
   c. They must be transferred from one network to another.
   d. They must be put in a passive storehouse.

4. About how many items can be held in short-term memory?
   a. three
   b. seven
   c. 11
   d. an unlimited number

5. Imagine you had a string of 20 one-digit numbers to remember. The best way to accomplish the task, which requires increasing the capacity of short-term memory, is through the technique of
   a. selective attention.
   b. peg words.
   c. rehearsing.
   d. chunking.

6. According to Gordon Bower, what is an important feature of good mnemonic systems?
   a. There is a dovetailing between storage and retrieval.
   b. The acoustic element is more important than the visual.
   c. The learner is strongly motivated to remember.
   d. Short-term memory is bypassed in favor of long-term memory.

7. According to Sigmund Freud, what is the purpose of repression?
   a. to protect the memory from encoding too much material
   b. to preserve the individual's self-esteem
   c. to activate networks of associations
   d. to fit new information into existing schemas

8. In an experiment, people spent a few minutes in an office. They were then asked to recall what they had seen. They were most likely to recall objects that
   a. fit into their existing schema of an office.
   b. carried little emotional content.
   c. were unusual within that particular context.
   d. related to objects they owned themselves.

9. The paintings Franco Magnani made of an Italian town were distorted mainly by
   a. repression, causing some features to be left out.
   b. a child's perspective.
   c. sensory gating, changing colors.
   d. false memories of items that were not really there.

10. What was Karl Lashley's goal in teaching rats how to negotiate mazes and then removing part of their cortexes?
    a. finding out how much tissue was necessary for learning to occur
    b. determining whether memory was localized in one area of the brain
    c. discovering how much tissue loss led to memory loss
    d. finding out whether conditioned responses could be eradicated

11. What has Richard Thompson found in his work with rabbits conditioned to a tone before an air puff?
    a. Rabbits learn the response more slowly after lesioning.
    b. Eyelid conditioning involves several brain areas.
    c. The memory of the response can be removed by lesioning.
    d. Once the response is learned, the memory is permanent, despite lesioning.

12. Patients with Alzheimer's disease find it almost impossible to produce
    a. unconditioned responses.
    b. conditioned stimuli.
    c. conditioned responses.
    d. unconditioned stimuli.

13. The best way to keep items in short-term memory for an indefinite length of time is to
    a. chunk.
    b. create context dependence.
    c. use the peg-word system.
    d. rehearse.

14. Long-term memory is organized as a
    a. complex network of associations.
    b. serial list.
    c. set of visual images.
    d. jumble of individual memories with no clear organizational scheme.

15. You remember a list of unrelated words by associating them, one at a time, with images of a bun, a shoe, a tree, a door, a hive, sticks, Heaven, a gate, a line, and a hen. What mnemonic technique are you using?
    a. method of loci
    b. peg-word
    c. link
    d. digit conversion

16. What did Karl Lashley conclude about the engram?
    a. It is localized in the brain stem.
    b. It is localized in the right hemisphere only.
    c. It is localized in the left hemisphere only.
    d. Complex memories cannot be pinpointed within the brain.

17. Long-term memories appear to be stored in the
    a. cortex.   c. hippocampus.
    b. occipital lobe. d. parietal lobe.

18. How has Diana Woodruff-Pak utilized Richard Thompson's work on eyeblink conditioning?
    a. as a precursor to early-onset dementia
    b. as a predictor of musical genius
    c. as a mechanism for growing brain cells in intact animals
    d. as a tool for training long-term visual memories

19. Which neurotransmitter(s) is/are disrupted in Alzheimer's patients?
    a. scopolamine
    b. acetylcholine
    c. both of the above
    d. none of the above

20. Alzheimer's disease is associated with the loss of
    a. memory.   c. life itself.
    b. personality. d. all of the above.

6 Thinking and Intelligence

FOLLOW YOUR PASSIONS AND YOU, TOO, MAY BECOME A MULTIMILLIONAIRE. At least that's what happened to Sergey Brin and Larry Page, graduate students in computer science at Stanford University. Both were deeply interested in finding a quicker way to search the Internet and extract specific information from its abundance of informational riches.

It was January of 1996, and both Brin and Page had some creative ideas about how to search the Web more efficiently than existing search engines could. After combining forces, the first thing this duo did was to build a computer in Larry's dorm room, equipping it with as much memory as they could afford.

The first-generation search engine to come out of their collaboration was BackRub, so called because it could identify and follow "back links" to discover which websites were listing a particular page—giving them an index of how valuable users had found a site to be. And, while their search engine performed well, Brin and Page couldn't get any of the big computer companies or existing Internet entrepreneurs to buy their design. So they started their own business—with a little financial help from their family and friends. One friend of a Stanford faculty member saw so much promise in their enterprise that he wrote them a check for $100,000. The check sat in a drawer in Page's desk for two weeks because they hadn't yet set up a company that could cash the check.

In most respects, Brin and Page's search engine worked like any other Web-searching software. It sent out electronic "spiders" that crawl across Web pages, looking for important terms and listing them in an index, along with their Web addresses. It also followed links on the Web pages it scanned (both forward and backward) and listed more terms. The secret ingredient for their success remains as closely guarded as the formula for Coca-Cola. It involves the way results are ranked for presentation to the user. More often than not, it manages to put the sites users want most near the top of a list that can include millions of possible sources. Thus, the software is designed to serve as the link between a concept in the user's mind and billions of words on the Web. In other words, Brin and Page had to organize their search engine to "think" as much as possible like a person—which is what this chapter is about.

The public seemed to like their search engine. In fact, the public liked it far better than did the big companies that had turned it down. And over the next decade, it became "the little engine that could." First, it outgrew Page's dorm room and—in the great tradition of American inventors and rock bands—into a garage. Today, it has offices spread throughout the United States and 36 other countries, with more than 20,000 employees. It also has a reputation as the most comprehensive of search engines, indexing key words from billions of Web pages. Every day, it processes hundreds of millions of search requests. Things got so busy that Brin and Page had to take a leave from graduate school to run the company—which they renamed after the term mathematicians use for the number 1 followed by 100 zeros. They called it Google.

In some respects, Brin and Page are like other legendary pioneers in the computer field: the two Steves, Jobs and Wozniak, who started Apple Computers in a garage, and Bill Gates who, with his friend Paul Allen, launched Microsoft on a shoestring. All could be called "geniuses," a term that frames our initial problem for this chapter:

PROBLEM: **What produces "genius," and to what extent are the people we call "geniuses" different from others?**

As we consider this problem, here are some additional questions worth pondering:

- Thomas Edison once said that genius is 1 percent inspiration, 99 percent perspiration. If so, does that mean genius is mainly a matter of high motivation rather than aptitude or talent?

- Is genius a product mainly of nature or of nurture?

- Do geniuses think differently from the rest of us? Or do they just use the same thought processes more effectively?

- Could Einstein (for example), whose specialty was physics, have been a genius in painting or literature or medicine if he had chosen to do so? That is, are there different kinds of genius? And is the potential for genius specific to a particular field?

We will address all these questions in the following pages. But first, let's return to Google and the computer metaphor for the human mind, as we begin our inquiry into thinking and intelligence.

Despite its phenomenal success, Google is only a pale imitation of the human mind. Sure, it can scan its memory, amassed from up to one trillion Web pages, and return over one billion links on, say, the term "search engine" in about a half second. But ask it what food to serve at a birthday party, and it will merely serve up (at this writing) 49,800,000 links to the terms "birthday" and "party" and "food." Unlike most human minds, Google and its network of supportive hardware is clueless. So is the computer on your desk. Computers just don't index information by *meaning*.

Nevertheless, computers in the hands of cognitive scientists can be powerful tools for studying how we think—for three reasons. First, these scientists use computers in brain imaging studies, which have shown the brain to be a system of interrelated processing modules, as we have seen. Second, researchers use computer simulations that attempt to model human thought processes. And third, while they haven't yet made a computer function exactly like a brain, cognitive scientists have adopted the computer as a metaphor for the brain, as a processor of information.

This **computer metaphor**—the brain as an information processor—suggests that thinking is nothing more, or less, than information processing. The information we use in thought can come from raw data we receive from our senses, but it can also come from meaningful

computer metaphor   The idea that the brain is an information-processing organ that operates, in some ways, like a computer.

concepts in long-term memory. As you can see, then, the psychology of thinking deals with the same processes we discussed in connection with learning and memory.

To be sure, the computer metaphor is not perfect. Computers can't deal with meaning. And, as we will see, they are not very good at abstract thought or humor (although they are *very* good at transmitting the millions of jokes shared on e-mail each day). Consequently, some psychologists encourage moving beyond the computer metaphor to talk about the sort of modular, parallel information processing that we now know the brain really does when it thinks. Evolutionary psychologists, for example, suggest the brain is more like a Swiss Army knife—an all-purpose tool that can adapt to many uses, with a variety of specialized components for particular functions. Nevertheless, the computer metaphor is a good place to begin our thinking about thought.

In the first two sections of this chapter, we will focus on the processes underlying thought, especially in decision making and problem solving. This discussion will examine the building blocks of thought: *concepts, images, schemas,* and *scripts.* Our excursion into thinking will also give us the opportunity to return for a closer look at that mysterious quality known as "genius."

In the second half of the chapter, we will turn to the form of thinking we call *intelligence.* There you will learn about IQ tests, conflicting perspectives on what intelligence really is, and what it means to say that IQ is "heritable." In the *Using Psychology to Learn Psychology* feature, you will learn how to apply the knowledge in this chapter to become an expert in psychology—or any other field you choose. Finally, our Critical Thinking Application will look at the controversial issue of gender differences in thought.

Watson, an IBM computer capable of responding to human language, bested two top-winning Jeopardy contestants in 2011. While this technology is a great leap forward in artificial intelligence, critics argue that rapid computational skills should not be confused with a true understanding of meaning.

6.1 KEY QUESTION
What Are the Components of Thought?

Solving a math problem, deciding what to do Friday night, and indulging a private fantasy all require *thinking.* We can conceive of thinking as a complex act of *cognition*—information processing in the brain—by which we deal with our world of ideas, feelings, desires, and experience. Our Core Concept notes that this information can come from within and from without, but it always involves some form of mental representation:

> ### Core Concept 6.1
> **Thinking is a cognitive process in which the brain uses information from the senses, emotions, and memory to create and manipulate mental representations such as concepts, images, schemas, and scripts.**

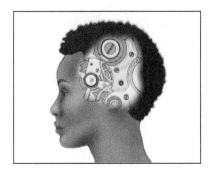

The cognitive perspective focuses on *mental processes* as the primary key to human behavior.

These mental representations, then, serve as the building blocks of cognition, while thinking organizes them in meaningful ways. The ultimate results are the higher thought processes we call reasoning, imagining, judging, deciding, problem solving, expertise, creativity, and—sometimes—genius.

Concepts

Have you ever visited a new place only to feel like you had been there before? Or had a conversation with someone and felt the experience was uncannily familiar? If so, you have experienced a phenomenon known as *déjà vu* (from the French for "seen before"). The term refers to the strange sense that your present experience matches a previous experience, even though you cannot retrieve the explicit memory. This feeling reflects the brain's ability to treat new stimuli as instances of familiar categories, even if the stimuli are slightly different from anything it has encountered before. Why is that important? Imagine what life would be like if, every time we started a new class in school, for example, we couldn't access any of our previous school experiences, so we had to start from scratch to figure out what to do, how to study, and what the point of school even was. This ability to assimilate experiences, objects, or ideas into familiar mental categories—and take the same action toward them or give them the same label—is one of the most basic attributes of thinking organisms (Mervis & Rosch, 1981).

concepts   Mental groupings of similar objects, ideas, or experiences.

natural concepts   Mental representations of objects and events drawn from our direct experience.

prototype   An ideal or most representative example of a conceptual category.

artificial concepts   Concepts defined by rules, such as word definitions and mathematical formulas.

The mental categories we form in this way are known as **concepts**. We use them as the building blocks of thinking because they help us organize our knowledge (Goldman-Rakic, 1992). Concepts can represent classes of objects such as "chair" or "food," living organisms such as "birds" or "buffaloes," or events like "birthday parties." They may also represent properties (such as "red" or "large"), abstractions (such as "truth" or "love"), relations (such as "smarter than"), procedures (such as how to tie your shoes), or intentions (such as the intention to break into a conversation) (Smith & Medin, 1981). But because concepts are mental structures, we cannot observe them directly. For the cognitive scientist, this means inferring concepts from their influence on behavior or on brain activity. For example, you cannot be sure another person shares your concept of "fun," but you can observe whether he or she responds the same way you do to stimuli you interpret as "fun."

Your natural concept of "bird" involves a prototype that is probably more like an eagle than a penguin. Hence, you would likely classify an eagle as a bird faster than you would a penguin. Biology majors, however, may also have an artificial concept of "bird" that works equally well for both.

Two Kinds of Concepts   Everyone conceptualizes the world in a unique way, so our concepts define who we are. Yet, behind this individual uniqueness lie similarities in the ways we all form concepts. In particular, we all distinguish between *natural concepts* and *artificial concepts* (Medin et al., 2000).

Natural concepts are imprecise mental categories that develop out of our everyday experiences in the world. You possess a natural concept of "bird" based on your experiences with birds, which in turn invokes a mental **prototype**, a generic image representing a typical bird from your experience (Hunt, 1989). To determine whether an object is a bird or not, you mentally compare it to your bird prototype—and the closer it matches, the quicker you can make your decision. Most people take less time to recognize an eagle as a bird than a penguin, for example (Rips, 1997). Our personal prototypes encompass all kinds of natural concepts, including friendship, intimacy, and sex. And, for all these, one person's prototype might differ from that of someone else, which can create the basis for misunderstanding in our relationships. Natural concepts are sometimes called "fuzzy concepts" because of their imprecision (Kosko & Isaka, 1993).

By comparison, **artificial concepts** are defined by a set of rules or characteristics, such as dictionary definitions or mathematical formulas. The definition of "rectangle" is an example. Artificial concepts represent precisely defined ideas or abstractions rather than actual objects in the world. So, if you are a zoology major, you may also have an artificial concept of "bird," which defines it as a "feathered biped." In fact, most of the concepts you learn in school are artificial concepts—such as "cognitive psychology," and even the concept of "concept"!

concept hierarchies   Levels of concepts, from most general to most specific, in which a more general level includes more specific concepts—as the concept of "animal" includes "dog," "giraffe," and "butterfly."

Concept Hierarchies   We organize much of our declarative memory into **concept hierarchies**, arranged from general to specific, as illustrated in Figure 6.1. For most people, the broad category of "animal" has several subcategories, such as "bird" and "fish," which are divided, in turn, into specific forms, such as "canary," "ostrich," "shark," and "salmon." The "animal" category may itself be a subcategory of the still larger category of "living beings." Also, we can often link each category to a variety of other concepts: For example, some birds are edible, some are endangered, and some are national symbols. In this way, our concept hierarchies are often intricate webs of concepts and associations.

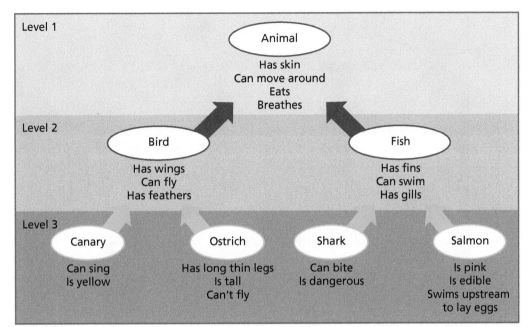

FIGURE 6.1

Hierarchically Organized Structure of Concepts

Culture, Concepts, and Thought Concepts can carry vastly different meanings in different cultures. For example, the concepts of "democracy" and "freedom," so dear to Americans, may have the connotation of chaos, excess, and rudeness in parts of Asia and the Middle East.

Americans also differ from many Asians in the ways they deal with conflicting ideas and contradictions (Peng & Nisbett, 1999). We can see this in the way the Chinese have dealt with the conflicting ideologies of capitalism and communism by allowing elements of both to flourish in their economy, an approach many Americans find difficult to understand. The Chinese culture encourages thinkers to keep opposing perspectives in mind and seek a "middle way," while American culture tends toward thinking in more polarized "either-or" terms—capitalism *or* communism.

Another big cultural difference involves the use of logic: Many cultures do not value the use of logical reasoning as much as do Europeans and North Americans (Bower, 2000a; Nisbett et al., 2001). Some seek "truth" by comparing new ideas with the wisdom of sacred writings, such as the Koran, the Bible, or the Upanishads. Even in the United States, many people place higher value on qualities variously known as "common sense," which refers to thinking based on experience rather than on logic.

What is the lesson to be learned from these cultural differences? While there are some universal principles of thought that cut across cultures, they involve very basic processes, such as the fact that everyone forms concepts. But when it comes to *how* they form concepts or the *meaning* they attach to them, we should be cautious about assuming that others think as we do.

Imagery and Cognitive Maps

We think in words, but we also think in pictures, spatial relationships, and other sensory images. Taking a moment to think of a friend's face, your favorite song, or the smell of warm cookies makes this obvious. Visual imagery adds complexity and richness to our thinking, as do images that involve the other senses (sound, taste, smell, and touch). Thinking with sensory imagery can be useful when solving problems in which relationships can be conveyed more clearly in an image than in words. That is why texts such as this one often encourage visual thinking by using pictures, diagrams, and charts. In fact, in MyPsychLab, you will find a concept mapping tool you can use to map the concepts in every chapter—thus illuminating your understanding of them both individually and in relation to each other.

Map the **Concepts** at **MyPsychLab**

FIGURE 6.2
Chicagocentric View of the World

How does this student's sketch compare with your view of the world?

Source: Solso, R. L. (1998). *Cognitive Psychology.* Boston, MA: Allyn and Bacon. Copyright © 1998 by Pearson Education. Reprinted by permission of the publisher.

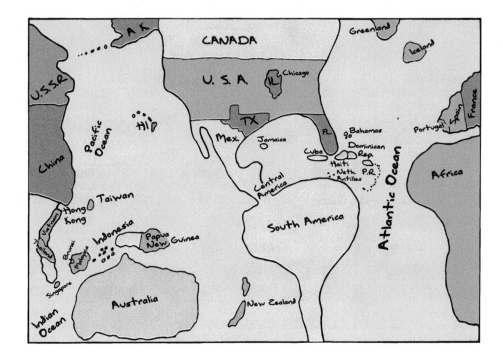

CONNECTION CHAPTER 4

Learning theorist Edward C. Tolman suggested that we form cognitive maps of our environment, which we use to guide our actions toward desired goals (p. 158).

A cognitive representation of physical space is a special form of visual concept called a *cognitive map.* Cognitive maps help you get to your psychology class, and enable you to give a friend directions to a nearby theater or deli. By using cognitive maps, people can move through their homes with their eyes closed or go to familiar destinations even when their usual routes are blocked. As you can see in Figures 6.2 and 6.3, though, people's cognitive maps can be vastly different. Just like other elements of thinking, they are based on our unique perceptions.

Thought and the Brain

Developments in brain imaging have allowed cognitive researchers to begin mapping the mind itself (Ashby & Waldron, 2000). Scientists can now connect certain thoughts, such as "dog" or "pencil," with specific electrical wave patterns in the brain (Garnsey, 1993; Osterhout & Holcomb, 1992). They do this by repeatedly presenting a stimulus (such as the word *dog* flashed on a screen) to a volunteer "wired" to record the brain's electrical responses. While the brain waves on just one trial may show no clear pattern, a computer can average many brain wave responses to a single, repeated stimulus (such as a tone or a visual image), eliminating the random background "noise" of the brain and isolating the unique brain wave pattern evoked by that stimulus (Kotchoubey, 2002).

Other methods tell us which parts of the brain switch on and off while we think. With PET scans, MRI, and fMRI, neuroscientists have identified brain regions that become active during various mental tasks. Two broad conclusions have come from this work. First, *thinking is an activity involving widely distributed areas of the brain—not just a single "thinking center."* Second, *neuroscientists now see the brain as a community of highly specialized modules, each of which deals with different components of thought* (Cree & McRae, 2003). Moreover, the brain generates many of the images used in thought with the same circuitry it uses for sensation. Thus, visual imagery drawn from memory activates the visual cortex, while auditory memories engage the auditory cortex (Behrmann, 2000). And thinking with language may involve different regions, depending on the topic. One brain-imaging study found that most jokes tickle us mainly in the language-processing areas of the cortex, while sound-alike puns activate the brain's sound-processing circuits as well (Goel & Dolan, 2001). In general, the picture of thought coming out of this work reveals thinking as a process composed of many modules acting in concert.

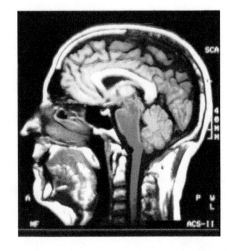

This MRI scan shows how many different parts of the brain can be active simultaneously.

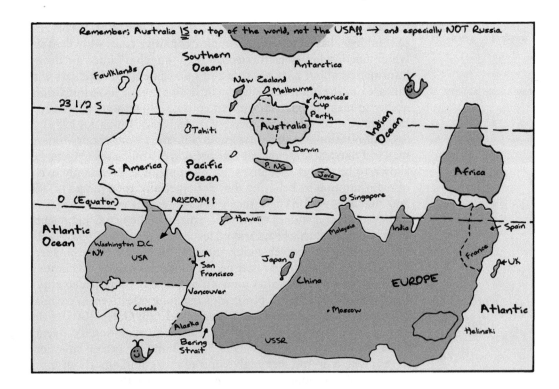

FIGURE 6.3

Australiocentric View of the World

Now who's "down under"? It probably would not occur to most Americans to draw a map "upside down" like this one drawn by an Australian student, placing Australia near the center of the world.

The maps we carry in our minds mirror the view of the world that we have developed from the perspective of our own culture. The maps you see here and in the previous figure came from a study aimed at understanding how nearly 4,000 students from 71 cities in 49 countries visualize the world. The majority of maps had a Eurocentric world view: Europe was placed in the center of the map and the other countries were arranged around it—probably due to the dominance for many centuries of Eurocentric maps in geography books. But the study also yielded many interesting culture-biased maps, such as the one by a Chicago student in Figure 6.2 and this one by an Australian student. American students, incidentally, performed especially poorly on this task, often misplacing countries. Students from the former Soviet Union and Hungary made the most accurately detailed maps (Saarinen, 1987).

Source: Solso, R. L. (1998). *Cognitive Psychology*. Boston, MA: Allyn and Bacon. Copyright © 1998 by Pearson Education. Reprinted by permission of the publisher.

The frontal lobes of the brain play an especially important role in coordinating mental activity as we make decisions and solve problems (Helmuth, 2003a; Koechlin et al., 2003). To do so, the prefrontal cortex (in the frontal lobes, just above your eyes) performs three different tasks: keeping track of the *episode* (the situation in which we find ourselves), understanding the *context* (the meaning of the situation), and responding to a specific *stimulus* in the situation. Here's how it works. Suppose you are driving to school, and you pass a dog on the side of the road that appears to have been hit by another car. The dog is clearly still alive but can't seem to walk (the stimulus). What do you do? If it were your neighborhood, and you recognized the dog, you would most likely stop and help, perhaps by finding the dog's owner or taking the dog to a vet. But what if you didn't live in that neighborhood and you didn't know the dog? Or what if you had an exam in the class you were trying to get to, and stopping to help might make you late—or even miss the exam? What if you were afraid of dogs? These different contexts would figure into your decision, all in just a few seconds. From a neuroscience perspective, the interesting thing is that all these tasks are performed by different combinations of brain modules that work together in seamless synchronicity. It's an impressive and sophisticated system.

Intuition

Psychologists have long known that when people make decisions—even about buying a house or selecting a spouse—they sometimes make quick judgments based on feelings as well as reason (Gladwell, 2005; Myers, 2002). This emotional component of thinking—like many other complex cognitive tasks—involves the prefrontal cortex, which unconsciously factors emotional "hunches" into our decisions in the form of information about past rewards and punishments. Individuals with severe damage to this area of the brain may display little emotion or have impairments in **intuition**—the ability to make judgments without consciously reasoning. As a result, they frequently make unwise choices when faced with decisions (Damasio, 1994).

intuition   The ability to make judgments without consciously reasoning.

But intuition is not always right. Sometimes our intuitive snap judgments, which may feel like truth, are merely our prejudices and biases (Myers, 2002). That has been shown to be true of executives, for example, who commonly overestimate the power of their intuition by believing they are especially good judges of other people's abilities and character. Accordingly, they often rely exclusively on in-person interviews for hiring, even though studies show they usually make better judgments when factoring in objective data, such as educational levels and test scores (Dawes, 2001).

Sometimes, however, quick intuitive judgments can be surprisingly on target. Dr. Nalini Ambady found that people make remarkably accurate judgments of a person's personality traits after viewing only a six-second video clip. Similarly, students' quick judgments about a professor's teaching effectiveness correlate highly with end-of-course ratings (Ambady & Rosenthal, 1993; Greer, 2005). Princeton psychologist Daniel Kahneman suggests that intuition is an evolutionary invention that helped our ancestors make snap judgments in difficult and dangerous situations (2003).

So, where do the seemingly contradictory findings about intuition leave us? The accuracy of our intuition may depend on, for one thing, the context in which we use it. In general, our "instincts" about personality are often correct—but, notes psychologist Frank Bernieri, the serial killer Ted Bundy made a good first impression, demonstrating that we do make occasional mistakes (Winerman, 2005c). When we "intuitively" make statistical or numerical judgments, however, we are much more likely to be wrong, says Kahneman. (How many English words end with *r*? Or how likely is it that I will be killed by a terrorist?) We will examine some reasons for these particular errors in the next few pages.

In addition to context, our intuition may also be more reliable in complex situations when time is limited: In those situations, our conscious processing skills—located in our working memory—simply may not be capable of handling the complexity or the number of factors that need to be quickly weighed. (Do you remember the "magic number" of working memory?) Here's an example: Participants in an experiment were asked to choose the best of four apartments after reading a list of a dozen factors about each one. The descriptions were designed to be both numerous and complex, including both positive features ("it's in a nice area") and negative ones ("the landlord is troublesome"). There were three experimental conditions: Some participants had to choose right away, some were given several minutes to think carefully before choosing, and some, after reading the information, were distracted for several minutes by a tedious task before choosing. (It was this third condition that aimed to assess pure intuition, because there was no opportunity for analysis.) The results were provocative. Participants in the distracted (intuitive) group were far better at choosing the most desirable apartment than either of the other groups (Dijksterhuis, 2004). Thus, in complex situations involving time pressures or distractions, our intuition may be a better guide than an incomplete attempt at logical analysis.

When time is not short, however, expertise does make a difference, as shown in a study that compared experienced college students to novices in dealing with typical college problems (Pretz, 2008). Yale seniors solved problems more effectively when they thought through a problem than when they simply followed their intuition. Conversely, freshmen had more success with intuition. Researchers theorize that, when a person has the expertise necessary to analyze a situation, intuition may impede clear thinking. In the absence of experience, though, intuition trumps a clumsy attempt at analysis.

The bottom line is this: It is important to recognize when we are making intuitive judgments and to consider the context, the time available, and our expertise in that area. We must also be mindful that intuition can be wrong: As we saw in our discussion of memory, confidence is not a reliable indicator of accuracy. For psychologists, the task that lies ahead may be to help us learn to use intuition more accurately (Haslam, 2007). As one researcher suggests, in many situations, the best solution may be to assess the facts, then hand them over to our unconscious. In that way, we may learn to balance our use of analysis and intuition (Dijksterhuis, 2004).

[PSYCHOLOGY MATTERS]

Schemas and Scripts Help You Know What to Expect

Much of your knowledge is stored in your brain as *schemas* (Oden, 1987): clusters of related concepts that provide a framework for thinking about objects, events, ideas, or even emotions. So you probably have schemas that represent "school," "Internet," "vacation," "music," and "fear." Let's look at some important ways that these schemas are used.

Expectations

Schemas are one of the attributes that Google and other search engines lack, so they have no real understanding of "birthday" or "psychology" or "nonfat mocha." But for us, schemas provide contexts and expectations about the features likely to be found when you encounter familiar people, situations, images, and ideas (Baldwin, 1992). For example, to an airline passenger, the word *terminal* probably conjures up a schema that includes scenes of crowds, long corridors, and airplanes. For a heart attack victim, however, the schema for *terminal* might include feelings of anxiety and thoughts of death. And for an auto mechanic, *terminal* might mean a connection for a battery cable.

Making Inferences

New information, which is often incomplete or ambiguous, makes more sense when you can relate it to existing knowledge in your stored schemas. So schemas enable you to make inferences about missing information. Consider this statement:

Tanya was upset to discover, on opening the basket, that she'd forgotten the salt.

With no further information, what can you infer about this event? *Salt* implies that the basket is a picnic basket containing food. The fact that Tanya is upset that the salt is missing suggests that the food in the basket is food that is usually salted, such as hard-boiled eggs or vegetables. You automatically know what other foods might be included and, equally important, what definitely is not: Everything in the world that is larger than a picnic basket and anything that would be inappropriate to take on a picnic—from a boa constrictor to bronze-plated baby shoes. Thus, the body of information you now have has been organized around a "picnic-basket" schema. So by relating the statement about Tanya to your schema, the statement gains meaning.

In a practical application of schema theory, researchers taught low-achieving math students to classify word problems into a few different types. For example, one type involved a "change" schema. The students learned that all "change" problems involve a story, such as this one: "Rudy had three pennies, and his mother gave him four more. How many does he now have?" They also learned common strategies for solving "change" problems. After several months of schema-based instruction, test results showed these students had made tremendous gains in their math scores—enough to move into the "above average" ranks (Jitendra et al., 2007). Classifying problems by schema helped them gain access to effective strategies for solutions.

Schemas and Humor

Schemas also serve as the foundation for much of our humor (Dingfelder, 2006). We often find things funny when they invoke two or more incongruous or incompatible schemas at once. Consider this joke:

A horse walks into a bar, and the bartender says, "Why the long face?"

CONNECTION CHAPTER 7

Piaget said that cognitive development involves changes in *schemas* (p. 282).

University of Chicago social psychologist Joshua Correll created a video game with images like this one to test respondents' stereotypes. In the game, participants had less than a second to decide if the person in the image was carrying a gun, a wallet, or a cell-phone, and press a button to shoot or not to shoot. Mistakes followed a clear pattern: Unarmed blacks were more likely than unarmed whites to be shot, demonstrating the power of schemas and expectations in our thought processes. Follow-up research indicated that police officers made fewer mistakes than civilians, and—for all participants—practicing the game improved accuracy, indicating that schemas can be revised with conscious effort.

This brief (and possibly lame) joke features multiple incongruous schemas, including (a) our knowledge that horses don't frequent bars and (b) the confusion over the horse's long nose and the "long face" as a metaphor for sadness.

Not everything we find incongruous is funny, however. A person being struck by a car on the sidewalk is not humorous. Generally, if the conflicting frames of reference involve threat or if the situation holds a cherished belief up to ridicule, we won't find it funny. If, however, schemas in a joke demean someone whom we consider threatening, we may well find it humorous. This accounts for much humor that we call racist, sexist, or political.

Scripts as Event Schemas

We have schemas not only about objects and events but also about persons, roles, and ourselves. These schemas help us decide what to expect or how people should behave in specific circumstances. An *event schema* or **script** consists of knowledge about sequences of interrelated, specific events and actions expected to occur in a certain way in particular settings (Baldwin, 1992). We have scripts for going to a restaurant, taking a vacation, listening to a lecture, going on a first date, and even making love. Conflict can arise, however, when your script differs from that of someone else in your world.

script A cluster of knowledge about sequences of events and actions expected to occur in particular settings.

Cultural Influences on Scripts

Scripts in other cultures may differ substantially from ours. For example, American women living in conservative Arab countries often report that many behaviors they take for granted at home—such as walking unescorted in public, wearing clothing showing their faces and legs, or driving a car—are considered scandalously inappropriate by citizens of their host country. To maintain good relations, many women change their behaviors to accommodate local customs. Similarly, Americans expect visitors from other countries to conform to their preferred ways, such as tipping servers 15 to 20 percent at a restaurant—far more than is customary in many other countries.

The cultural diversity of scripts around the world is the result of each culture's unique schema for viewing the world, which includes its values. We tend to feel comfortable with others who share our scripts because we see things the same way and know what to expect (Abelson, 1981; Schank & Abelson, 1977). Unfortunately, our discomfort with unfamiliar scripts can sometimes create divides, as when people say, "I tried to interact, but it was so awkward that I don't want to try again" (Brislin, 1993). In our increasingly multicultural world, understanding the power of scripts and schemas can help us be more open to others' scripts and more resilient in trying new ways to bridge the gaps—after all, variety is, they say, the spice of life.

Check Your Understanding

✔●─ Study and Review at **MyPsychLab**

1. **APPLICATION:** A dictionary definition would be an example of which kind of concept?

2. **APPLICATION:** Give an example of a concept hierarchy.

3. **APPLICATION:** Give an example of a script.

4. **UNDERSTANDING THE CORE CONCEPT:** All of the following are components of thought, except

   a. concepts.
   b. images.
   c. schemas.
   d. stimuli.

Answers 1. An artificial concept. **2.** Our example is animal, mammal, dog, cocker spaniel. Any such series forms a concept hierarchy, provided each category includes the one that follows. Another example would be food, Italian food, pasta, spaghetti. **3.** Knowing how to check out a book at the library is an example of a script. So is any other procedure, such as knowing how to study for a test or how to boil an egg. **4.** d

What Abilities Do Good Thinkers Possess?

The popularity of lotteries and casino games, in which chances of winning are small, shows us that human thought is not always logical. Instead, we might say thinking is *psycho*logical—which has some advantages. Departures from logic allow us to fantasize, daydream, act creatively, react unconsciously, respond emotionally, and generate new ideas.

We are, of course, capable of careful reasoning. After all, our species did invent that most logical of devices, the computer. Still, the psychology of thinking teaches us we should not always expect people to behave in a strictly logical manner. This ability to think *psycho*logically enhances our ability to solve problems. And, as we will see, good thinkers also know how to use effective thinking strategies and how to avoid ineffective or misleading strategies. We will also see that *psycho*logical thinking is more useful than mere logic because it helps us make decisions rapidly in a changing world that usually furnishes us incomplete information. Our Core Concept puts all this in more technical language:

> ## Core Concept 6.2
>
> **Good thinkers not only have a repertoire of effective strategies, called algorithms and heuristics, they also know how to avoid common impediments to problem solving and decision making.**

Problem Solving

Sergey Brin and Larry Page can certainly be called effective problem solvers. Likewise, artists, inventors, Nobel Prize winners, great presidents, successful business executives, world-class athletes, and high-achieving college students must be effective problem solvers. What strategies do they use? No matter what their field, most successful problem solvers share certain characteristics. They, of course, possess the requisite knowledge for solving the problems they face. In addition, they are skilled at (a) *identifying the problem* and (b) *selecting a strategy* to attack the problem. In the next few pages, we will examine these two skills with the aid of some examples.

Identifying the Problem A good problem solver learns to consider all relevant possibilities without leaping to conclusions prematurely. Suppose you are driving along the freeway and your car suddenly begins sputtering and then quits. As you coast to the shoulder, you notice the gas gauge says "empty." What do you do? Your action in this predicament depends on the problem you think you are solving. If you assume you are out of fuel, you may hike to the nearest service station for a gallon of gas. But you may be disappointed. By representing the problem as "out of gas," you may fail to notice a loose battery cable that interrupts the supply of electricity both to the spark plugs and to the gas gauge. The good problem solver considers all possibilities before committing to one solution.

Selecting a Strategy The second ingredient of successful problem solving requires selecting a strategy that fits the problem at hand (Wickelgren, 1974). For simple problems, a trial-and-error approach will do—as when you search in the dark for the key to your front door. More difficult problems require more efficient methods. Problems in specialized fields, such as engineering or medicine, may require not only specialized knowledge but also special procedures or formulas known as *algorithms*. In addition, expert problem solvers have a repertoire of more intuitive, but less precise, strategies called *heuristics*. Let's look more closely at both of these methods.

algorithms   Problem-solving procedures or formulas that guarantee a correct outcome, if correctly applied.

Algorithms   Whether you are a psychology student or a rocket scientist, selecting the right algorithms will guarantee correct solutions for many of your problems. What are these never-fail strategies? **Algorithms** are nothing more than formulas or procedures, like those you learned in science and math classes. They can help you solve particular kinds of problems for which you have all the necessary information. For example, you can use algorithms to balance your checkbook, figure your gas mileage, calculate your grade-point average, and make a call on your cell phone. If applied correctly, an algorithm always works because you merely follow a step-by-step procedure that leads directly from the problem to the solution.

Despite their usefulness, however, algorithms will not solve every problem you face. Problems involving subjective values or having too many unknowns (Will you be happier with a red car or a white car? Which is the best airline to take to Denver?) and problems that are just too complex for a formula (How can you get a promotion? What will the fish bite on today?) do not lend themselves to the use of algorithms. That is why we also need the more intuitive and flexible strategies called *heuristics*.

heuristics   Cognitive strategies or "rules of thumb" used as shortcuts to solve complex mental tasks. Unlike algorithms, heuristics do not guarantee a correct solution.

Heuristics   Everyone makes a collection of heuristics while going through life. Examples: "Don't keep bananas in the refrigerator." "If it doesn't work, see if it's plugged in." "Feed a cold and starve a fever" (or is it the other way around?). **Heuristics** are simple, basic rules—so-called "rules of thumb" that help us cut through the confusion of complicated situations. Unlike algorithms, heuristics do not guarantee a correct solution, but they often start us off in the right direction. Some heuristics require special knowledge, such as training in medicine or physics or psychology. Other heuristics, such as those you will learn in the following paragraphs, are more widely applicable—and well worth remembering.

Some Useful Heuristic Strategies   Here are three essential heuristics that should be in every problem solver's tool kit. They require no specialized knowledge, yet they can help in a wide variety of puzzling situations. The common element shared by all three involves approaching the problem from a different perspective.

Working Backward   Some problems, such as the maze seen in Figure 6.4, baffle us because they present so many possibilities we don't know where to start. A good way to attack this sort of puzzle is by beginning at the end and *working backward*. (Who says we must always begin at the beginning?) This strategy can eliminate some of the dead ends we would otherwise encounter by trial and error. In general, working backward offers an excellent strategy for problems in which the goal is clearly specified, such as mazes or certain math problems. In the larger world, police officers and investigators often work backward to solve crimes. By starting at the scene of the crime—where the event "ended"—and gathering information based on evidence and witness statements, the potential pool of suspects is narrowed down considerably. With fingerprints and sketches of the assailant in hand, investigators can focus their efforts accordingly, working backward as they follow clues to the origin (Lesgold, 1988).

Searching for Analogies   If a new problem is similar to one you have faced before, you may be able to employ a strategy you learned previously. The trick is to recognize the similarity, or *analogy*, between the new problem and the old one (Medin & Ross, 1992). For example, if you are an experienced cold-weather driver, you use this strategy to decide whether to install tire chains on a snowy day: "Is the snow as deep as it

FIGURE 6.4

Working Backward

Mazes and math problems often lend themselves to the heuristic of working backward. Try solving this maze, as the mouse must do, by starting at what would normally be the finish (in the center) and working backward to the start.

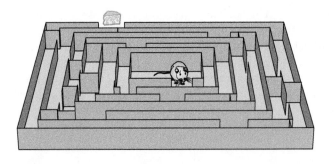

was last time I needed chains?" Even very complex problems may yield to this strategy. The cracking of the genetic code was assisted by the analogy of the DNA molecule being shaped like a spiral staircase.

Breaking a Big Problem into Smaller Problems   Are you facing a huge problem, such as an extensive term paper or a messy house? The best strategy may be to break the big problem into smaller, more manageable steps, often called *subgoals*. In writing a paper, for example, you might break the problem into the steps of selecting a topic, doing your library and Internet research, outlining the paper, writing the first draft, and revising the paper. In this way, you begin to organize the work and develop a plan for each part of the problem. Tackling the problem in a step-by-step fashion makes big problems seem more manageable. In fact, the Wright brothers deliberately used this heuristic to break down their problem of powered human flight into its components. By using a series of kites, gliders, and models, they studied the component problems of lift, stability, power, and directional control. Later, they put their discoveries together to solve the larger problem of powered human flight (Bradshaw, 1992).

Obstacles to Problem Solving   Having a good repertoire of strategies is essential to successful problem solving, but people often get stuck when they latch onto an ineffective strategy and won't let go. For this reason, problem solvers must learn to recognize obstacles that demand a new approach. Here are some of the most troublesome obstacles problem solvers face.

Mental Set   Have you ever studied for a new class the same way you studied effectively for a previous class—but in the new class, your old study methods didn't work at all, and as a result you did poorly on an exam? If so, psychologists would say you had an inappropriate **mental set**—the tendency to respond to a new problem in the same way you approached a similar problem previously. You "set" your mind on a strategy, but chose the wrong analogy, schema, or algorithm. You can see for yourself another type of mental set in the *Do It Yourself!* box on this page.

The rapid advance of technology offers us many opportunities to get stuck in mental sets—and an equal number of opportunities to practice overcoming them. Most of your professors, for example, probably delight in having broad Internet access to virtually unlimited sources of academic information: Their mental sets for preparing a new lecture may no longer include trips to the library, since they can access almost anything online. And if you've ever thought, "Oh, no, now I can't turn in my paper on time!" when your printer died the morning the paper was due, your obsolete mental set may have interfered with your recognition of an alternate solution: that you could save the paper on a flash drive and print it out at school instead.

mental set   The tendency to respond to a new problem in the manner used for a previous problem.

CONNECTION   CHAPTER 4

Kohler's chimp, Sultan, demonstrated the limitations of mental set when he, at first, couldn't figure out a way to reach a banana high above him—because previous strategies he had used successfully didn't work. Sultan's case also illustrates what is often a solution to the mental set barrier: *insight*, which often occurs spontaneously when we mentally step back from the problem in hopes of seeing it from a novel perspective (p. 157).

Do It Yourself! **OVERCOMING MENTAL SETS**

Each of the groups of letters in the columns below is a common but scrambled word. See if you can unscramble them:

nelin	frsca	raspe	tnsai
ensce	peshe	klsta	epslo
sdlen	nitra	nolem	naoce
lecam	macre	dlsco	tesle
slfal	elwha	hsfle	maste
dlchi	ytpar	naorg	egran
neque	htmou	egsta	eltab

Check your answers against the key on page 227.

Most people, whether they realize it or not, eventually solve the scrambled word problem with an algorithm by rearranging the order of the letters in all the words in the same way, using the formula 3-4-5-2-1. Thus,

n e l i n   becomes   l i n e n
1 2 3 4 5   3 4 5 2 1

Notice, however, that by using that *algorithm*, your answers for the last two columns won't agree with the "correct" ones given on page 227. The *mental* set you developed while working on the first two columns prevented you from seeing there is more than one answer for the last 14 items. The lesson of this demonstration is that a mental set can make you limit your options without realizing you have done so. While a mental set may produce results, you should occasionally stop to ask yourself whether you have slipped into a rut that prevents your seeing another answer. (Now, can you find some other possible answers to the scrambled words in the last two columns?)

functional fixedness   The inability to perceive a new use for an object associated with a different purpose; a form of mental set.

◄ **CONNECTION** CHAPTER 5

Compare functional fixedness with *proactive interference* (p. 197).

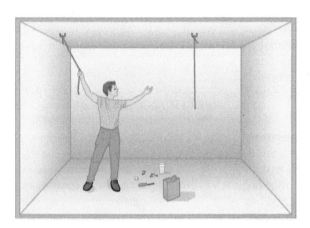

FIGURE 6.5

The Two-String Problem

How could you tie the two strings together using only the objects found in the room?

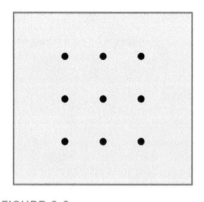

FIGURE 6.6

The Nine-Dot Problem

Can you connect all nine dots with four connecting straight lines without lifting your pencil from the paper?

Source: Adapted from Wickelgren, W. A. (1974). *Can you solve it? How to solve mathematical problems: elements of a theory of problems and problem solving.* San Francisco: W. H. Freeman. Copyright © 1974 by W. H. Freeman and Company. Reprinted by permission of Dover Publications.

Functional Fixedness   A special sort of mental set occurs when you think you need a screwdriver but don't realize you could tighten the bolt with a dime. Psychologists call this **functional fixedness**. Under this condition, the function of a familiar object becomes so set, or fixed, in your mind that you cannot see a new function for it. To illustrate, consider this classic problem:

Your psychology professor has offered you $5 if you can tie together two strings dangling from the ceiling without pulling them down (see Figure 6.5). But when you grab the end of one string and pull it toward the other one, you find that you cannot quite reach the other string. The only objects available to you in the room are on the floor in the corner: a Ping-Pong ball, five screws, a screwdriver, a glass of water, and a paper bag. How can you reach both strings at once and tie them together?

If you want to figure this out for yourself, don't read this paragraph until you've tried to solve the problem. In this problem, you may have had functional fixedness with regard to the screwdriver. Did you realize that you could use the screwdriver as a pendulum weight to swing one of the strings toward you?

Self-Imposed Limitations   We can be our own worst enemies when we impose unnecessary limitations on ourselves. The classic nine-dot problem in Figure 6.6 illustrates this neatly. To solve it, you must connect all nine dots with no more than four connecting straight lines—and without lifting your pencil from the paper. The instructions allow you to cross a line, but you may not retrace a line.

Hint: Most people who confront this problem impose an unnecessary restriction on themselves by assuming they cannot draw lines beyond the square made by the dots. Literally, they don't "think outside the box." Figure 6.7 gives two possible correct answers. Translating this into personal terms, we find many instances in which people impose unnecessary restrictions on themselves. Students may assume that they have no talent for math or science—thereby eliminating the possibility of a technical career. Or because of gender stereotypes, a man may never consider he could be a secretary or a grade school teacher, and a woman may assume she must be a nurse rather than a doctor. What real-life problems are you working on in which you have imposed unnecessary limitations on yourself?

Other Obstacles   There are many other obstacles to problem solving that we will simply mention rather than discuss in detail. These include lack of specific knowledge required by the problem, lack of interest, low self-esteem, fatigue, and drugs (even legal drugs such as cold medicines or sleeping pills). Arousal and its accompanying stress create another stumbling block for would-be problem solvers. When you study emotion and motivation later in this book, you will see there is an optimum arousal level for any task, be it basketball, brain surgery, or bartending. Beyond that critical point, further arousal causes performance to deteriorate. Thus, moderate levels of arousal actually facilitate everyday problem solving, but high stress levels can make problem solving impossible.

In general, we humans are thinkers who readily jump to conclusions, based on our knowledge but also biased by our knowledge—as well as our motives, emotions, and perceptions. In view of this, it is surprising that our thinking so often serves us well in day-to-day life. Yet, from another perspective it makes perfect sense; most of our problem-solving efforts draw on past experience to make predictions about future rewards or punishments. This, of course, is exactly what operant conditioning is all about—which suggests this mode of thinking is a fundamental part of our nature. Many of the "flaws" in our reasoning abilities, such as mental sets, are actually adaptive (but necessarily imperfect) strategies that help us apply previous experience to solve new problems.

Judging and Making Decisions

Whether you are a student, professor, or corporate president, you make decisions every day. "How much time do I need to study tonight?" "What grade does this paper deserve?" "How much should I invest?" Each decision is the solution to a problem—for which there may not be a clear answer, but instead requires judgment. Unfortunately, especially for those who have not studied the psychology of decision making, judgment can be clouded by emotions and biases that interfere with critical thinking. Let's examine the most common of these causes of poor judgment.

Confirmation Bias Suppose Tony has strong feelings about raising children: "Spare the rod and spoil the child," he says. How do you suppose Tony will deal with the news that punishment can actually encourage aggressive behavior? Chances are *confirmation bias* will cause him to ignore or find fault with information that doesn't fit his opinions while seeking and remembering information with which he agrees. He may tell tales of spoiled children who didn't get punishment for their transgressions or of upstanding adults, like himself, who owe their fine character to harsh discipline. A great deal of evidence shows the confirmation bias is a powerful and all-too-human tendency (Aronson, 2004; Nickerson, 1998). In fact, we all act like Tony sometimes, especially when we hold strong opinions.

Hindsight Bias A friend tells you he wrecked his car when he was texting while driving. "I can't believe it," he says, "It was just for a few seconds!" Your reply? "You should have known not to text when you're driving—haven't you read the studies that show you're almost guaranteed to get in an accident eventually?" Besides being an insensitive friend, you are guilty of the **hindsight bias**, sometimes called the "I-knew-it-all-along effect" (Fischhoff, 1975; Hawkins & Hastie, 1990). Just as guilty of hindsight bias are the Monday morning quarterbacks who know what play should have been called at the crucial point in yesterday's big game. This form of distorted thinking appears after an event has occurred and people overestimate their ability to have predicted it. Examples in the news abounded after 9/11, after the Arizona shooting of Congresswoman Gabrielle Giffords, and after every election.

The problem with hindsight bias is that it impedes our ability to learn from our mistakes: After all, anytime we're sure we "knew it all along," we are ignoring an opportunity to improve our judgment next time by recognizing our errors this time. A recent study of international investment bankers found hindsight bias coloring bankers' recollections of their accuracy in predicting stock prices—and the bankers most guilty of the bias also earned the fewest performance bonuses, indicating a correlation between a tendency for hindsight bias and for poor performance (Biais & Weber, 2009). In other words, being swayed by hindsight bias may increase our chances of repeating the same mistake.

> **CONNECTION CHAPTER 1**
>
> *Confirmation bias* makes us pay attention to events that confirm our beliefs and ignore evidence that contradicts them (p. 8).

hindsight bias The tendency, after learning about an event, to "second guess" or believe that one could have predicted the event in advance.

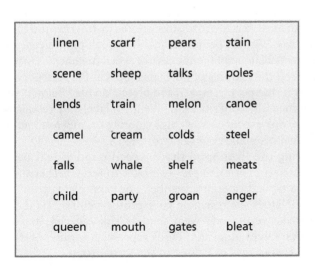

linen	scarf	pears	stain
scene	sheep	talks	poles
lends	train	melon	canoe
camel	cream	colds	steel
falls	whale	shelf	meats
child	party	groan	anger
queen	mouth	gates	bleat

Unscrambled Words (from page 225)

The words you found to solve the scrambled word problem may not jibe with the ones listed here—especially the third and fourth columns. Most people, whether they are aware of it or not, develop an *algorithm* as they work on the first two columns. While the formula will work on all the words, it becomes a *mental set* that interferes with the problem solver's ability to see alternative solutions for the words in the last two columns.

FIGURE 6.7

Two Solutions to the Nine-Dot Problem

Source: Adapted from Wickelgren, W. A. (1974).
Can you solve it? *How to solve mathematical
problems: elements of a theory of problems and
problem solving.* San Francisco: W. H. Freeman.
Copyright © 1974 by W. H. Freeman and Company.
Reprinted by permission of Dover Publications.

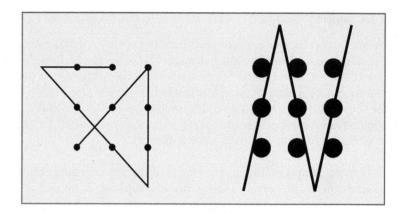

Anchoring Bias Ask a few of your friends, one at a time, to give a quick, off-the-top-of-the-head guess at the answer to the following simple math problem:

$$1 \times 2 \times 3 \times 4 \times 5 \times 6 \times 7 \times 8 = ?$$

Make them give you an estimate without actually doing the calculation; give them only about five seconds to think about it. Then, pose the problem in reverse to some other friends:

$$8 \times 7 \times 6 \times 5 \times 4 \times 3 \times 2 \times 1 = ?$$

Are the results different for the two groups?

Nobody will give precisely the right answer, of course, but it's likely that your friends will respond as volunteers did in Daniel Kahneman and Amos Tversky's (2000) experiment. It turns out the answers to such questions, where people usually don't have a good "ballpark" answer, depend on whether the problem begins with larger or smaller numbers. Those who saw the first problem gave a lower estimate than did those given the second problem. In Kahneman and Tversky's study, the average answer for the first group was 512, while the average for the second group was 2,250. Apparently, their "first impression"—larger or smaller numbers at the beginning of the problem—biased their responses. Incidentally, the correct answer (40,320) was larger than either group had imagined.

Kahneman and Tversky have explained the difference between the two groups on the basis of an **anchoring bias**. That is, people apparently use this flawed heuristic to "anchor" their thinking to the higher or lower numbers that appear at the beginning of the problem. The anchoring bias can affect our real-world decisions, as those who sell automobiles and real estate know well: What we ultimately decide to pay for a car or a house depends on the price and condition of the first item we are shown.

anchoring bias A faulty heuristic caused by basing (anchoring) an estimate on a completely irrelevant quantity.

Representativeness Bias If you assume blondes are mentally challenged or ministers are prudish or math professors are nerdish, your judgment is clouded by **representativeness bias**. Why do people succumb to such prejudices? Mere convenience: The representativeness bias simplifies the task of social judgment. Once something is "categorized," it shares all the features of other members in that category. The fallacy in this heuristic, of course, is that people, events, and objects do not "belong" to categories simply because we find it mentally convenient to give them labels. By relying on category memberships to organize our experiences, we risk ignoring or underestimating the tremendous diversity of individual cases and complexity of people.

When estimating the likelihood that a specific individual belongs to a certain category—"vegetarian," for example—we look to see whether the person possesses features found in a typical category member. For example, is your new acquaintance, Holly, a vegetarian? Does she resemble your prototype of a "typical" vegetarian? Perhaps you believe most vegetarians wear sandals, ride bicycles, and support liberal social causes. If so, you might judge that Holly represents enough of the characteristics of your concept of "vegetarians" to belong to the same group.

representativeness bias A faulty heuristic strategy based on the presumption that, once people or events are categorized, they share all the features of other members in that category.

But such an analysis is not entirely reasonable. Although some—perhaps many—vegetarians wear sandals, ride bicycles, and hold liberal views, the opposite may not be true: Because vegetarians are a minority group in the general population, it is unlikely that any particular individual who supports liberal social causes, wears sandals, and rides a bicycle is also vegetarian. That is, by ignoring the **base rate information**—the probability of a characteristic occurring in the general population—you have drawn an erroneous conclusion. While your representativeness bias—judging Holly by what seems to be her "type"—may not have dire consequences in this case, the same error underlies the more serious stereotypes and prejudices that result when people classify others solely on the basis of group membership.

base rate information   The probability of a characteristic occurring in the general population.

Availability Bias   Which is riskier: Traveling by car or by plane? Statistically, you are far more likely to be killed in an auto accident than in a plane crash, and most of us know this in our rational brains. Yet, why do we fear flying more than driving? The **availability bias** reflects our tendency to judge probabilities of events by how readily examples come to mind, and media coverage of plane crashes takes center stage with its vivid images—even though you are far more likely to die crossing the street than in a plane crash (Bailey, 2006). The same bias makes some people more wary of a shark bite than a dog bite, and more afraid of a terrorist attack than a heart attack. Similarly, people who watch a lot of violent crime on television judge their chances of being murdered or mugged as being much higher than do people who watch little television (Singer et al., 1984).

availability bias   A faulty heuristic strategy that estimates probabilities based on the availability of vivid mental images of the event.

The Tyranny of Choice   Not all decision problems stem from faulty heuristics; they can also come from outside factors. To illustrate: Have you ever had trouble deciding among a bewildering array of choices—perhaps in buying a car, a computer, or even a tube of toothpaste? Too many choices can interfere with effective decision making, sometimes to the point of immobilizing us. For example, when Sheena Sethi-Iyengar and her colleagues (2004) studied the choices employees made concerning matching contributions to retirement funds, they found that too many alternatives could, in effect, make people throw away free money. If employers offered to match employees' contributions and give them only two alternatives, 75 percent elected to participate. But when allowed to select among 59 possibilities, the participation rate fell to 60 percent. Apparently, some people just gave up. Psychologist Barry Schwartz (2004) calls this the **tyranny of choice.**

tyranny of choice   The impairment of effective decision making when confronted with an overwhelming number of choices.

Schwartz says the tyranny of choice can create stress, especially for those who feel compelled to make the "correct" decision or get the very "best buy." The antidote, he says, is "satisficing" rather than "maximizing." Satisficers, says Schwartz, scan their options until they find one that is merely "good enough," while maximizers stress themselves out by trying to make certain they have made the very best choice—perhaps getting caught in "analysis paralysis" and not making a decision at all.

Shoppers face the tyranny of choice when they must decide among similar products. Psychologist Barry Schwartz suggests quickly settling on one that is "good enough" rather than wasting time on "maximizing" a choice of little importance.

Decision Making and Critical Thinking   Much of the foregoing discussion should have a familiar ring, because it involves critical thinking. In fact, one of the critical thinking questions we pose in this book concerns biases, such as confirmation bias, anchoring bias, and availability bias. In other words, critical thinkers are alert to these common obstacles to problem solving.

In addition, we can now add a few more items to the list of critical-thinking skills we discussed in previous chapters. Specifically, the critical thinker should know how to identify a problem, select a strategy, and apply the most common algorithms and heuristic strategies. Critical thinkers also know about the various biases common in judgment and decision-making, and work to overcome them. All these skills can help you take your thinking to the next level: to become an expert—or even a creative genius.

Becoming a Creative Genius

Everyone would agree that Einstein was a creative genius. So were Aristotle and Bach. And we can make a case that Brin and Page, the Google guys, are geniuses, too. But what about your Aunt Elisa, who does watercolors? Such questions illustrate

creativity   A mental process that produces novel responses that contribute to the solutions of problems.

There was no question but that Albert Einstein was bright. He also had an independent streak, a sense of humor, an intense interest in the complex problem of gravity, and a willingness to restructure the problem. And he sought the stimulation of other physicists. But he probably did not use thought processes that were altogether different from those used by other thinkers.

experts   Individuals who possess well-organized funds of knowledge, including the effective problem-solving strategies, in a field.

aptitudes   Innate potentialities (as contrasted with abilities acquired by learning).

the big problem in creativity research: Experts cannot agree on an exact definition of **creativity**. Most, however, would go along with the slightly fuzzy notion that creativity is a process that produces novel responses to the solutions of problems. Most would also agree that a "genius" is someone whose insight and creativity are greater than those of ordinary folk. As with the idea of creativity, the boundary for genius is not well defined.

Let's follow the lead of psychologist Robert Weisberg, whose view of "genius" departs from the commonly held assumption that geniuses are completely different from the rest of us. In brief, he argues that geniuses are merely good problem solvers who also possess certain helpful—but entirely human—characteristics.

Creative Genius as Not So Superhuman   Here's how Weisberg (1986) characterized most people's assumptions about the quality we call "genius":

> Our society holds a very romantic view about the origins of creative achievements. . . .This is the genius view, and at its core is the belief that creative achievements come about through great leaps of imagination which occur because creative individuals are capable of extraordinary thought processes. In addition to their intellectual capacities, creative individuals are assumed to possess extraordinary personality characteristics which also play a role in bringing about creative leaps. These intellectual and personality characteristics are what is called "genius," and they are brought forth as the explanation for great creative achievements (p. 1).

But, according to Weisberg and some other scholars in this area (Bink & Marsh, 2000), there is surprisingly little evidence supporting this view. In fact, the notion that creative geniuses are a breed apart may actually discourage creativity by making people feel that real creativity lies out of their reach. A more productive view, suggests Weisberg, portrays the thinking of people we call geniuses as "ordinary thought processes in ordinary individuals" (p. 11). What produces extraordinary creativity, he says, is extensive knowledge, high motivation, and certain personality characteristics—not superhuman talents.

Knowledge and Understanding   Everyone agrees with Weisberg on one point: The most highly creative individuals have *expertise* or highly developed knowledge in their fields (Ericsson et al., 2006). In fact, you cannot become highly creative without first becoming an **expert**: having extensive and organized knowledge of the field in which you will make your creative contribution. But such mastery is not easily achieved, because it requires a high level of motivation to sustain years of intense training and practice. Studies indicate that about ten years of work, or 10,000 hours, are required to become fully competent in virtually any field, whether it be skiing, sculpture, singing, or psychology (Ericsson et al., 1993; Gladwell, 2008). Oh, yes, and this rule also applies to the field of computing, as in the case of Google founders Brin and Page. Meanwhile, such factors as time pressures or an overly critical supervisor, teacher, or parent can suppress the creative flow (Amabile et al., 2002).

Aptitudes, Personality Characteristics, and Creativity   In opposition to Weisberg, psychologist Howard Gardner (1993) argues that the extraordinary creativity we see in the work of Freud, Einstein, Picasso, and others results not only from expertise and motivation but also from certain patterns of abilities and personality characteristics. Highly creative individuals, he says, have **aptitudes**—largely innate potentialities—specific to certain domains. (These potentialities, of course, must be developed by intensive study and practice.) Freud, for example, had a special facility for creating with words and understanding people; Einstein was remarkably good at logic and spatial relationships; and Picasso's creativity arose from a combination of aptitudes comprising spatial relationships and interpersonal perceptiveness.

In addition to aptitudes, creative people usually possess a common cluster of personality traits, including the following (Barron & Harrington, 1981; Csikszentmihalyi, 1996):

- **Independence.** Highly creative people can resist social pressures to conform to conventional ways of thinking, at least in their area of creative interest (Amabile, 1983, 1987; Sternberg, 2001). That is, they have the confidence to strike out on their own. Because of this, perhaps, some creative people describe themselves as loners.

- **Intense interest in a problem.** Highly creative individuals must also have an all-consuming interest in their creative subject matter (Amabile, 2001), always tinkering, often just in their minds, with problems that fascinate them (Weisberg, 1986). External motivators, such as money or a Nobel Prize, may be attractive, but their main motivators are internal. Otherwise they could not sustain the long-term interest necessary for an original contribution.

- **Willingness to restructure the problem.** Highly creative people not only grapple with problems but often question the way a problem is presented (Sternberg, 2001). (Recall our earlier discussion about identifying the problem.) For example, students from the School of the Art Institute of Chicago who later became the most successful artists among their class members had one striking characteristic in common: They were always changing and redefining the assignments given by their instructors (Getzels & Csikszentmihalyi, 1976).

- **Preference for complexity.** Creative people seem drawn to complexity—to what may appear messy or chaotic to others. Moreover, they revel in the challenge of looking for simplicity in complexity. Thus, highly creative people may be attracted to the largest, most difficult, and most complex problems in their fields (Sternberg & Lubart, 1992).

- **A need for stimulating interaction.** Creativity of the highest order almost always grows out of an interaction of highly creative individuals. Early in their careers, creative people usually find a mentor—a teacher who brings them up to speed in their chosen field. Highly creative individuals may surpass their mentors and then seek additional stimulation from others like themselves. Often, this means leaving behind family and former friends (Gardner, 1993).

What is the take-home message? Those who have looked closely at creativity agree on two main points. First, creativity requires well-developed knowledge—often growing out of aptitudes—in the field in which the creative contribution will be made. Second, high-level creativity requires certain personal characteristics, such as independence and motivation to sustain an interest over a very long period of time. This combination of qualities, then, may be your formula for becoming a creative genius.

The Role of Intelligence in Creativity Is a high IQ necessary for one's creativity or to be a genius? The answer is a bit complicated. Low intelligence inhibits creativity—although we will see there are some special cases, known as *savants,* who may have a highly developed skill despite their mental handicaps. On the other end of the IQ spectrum, we find that having high intelligence does not necessarily produce creativity: There are lots of very bright people who never create anything that could be called groundbreaking or highly original and insightful. Thus, intelligence and creativity are distinct abilities. We can find plodding, unimaginative persons at all IQ levels, and we can find highly creative persons with only average IQ scores.

Robert Sternberg (2001) argues that creativity lies a step beyond IQ. In his view, creativity requires a decision to go against the expectations of the crowd. This makes creativity potentially achievable for anyone who chooses to adopt a creative attitude. Most people will not do so, he says, for a variety of reasons, including an unwillingness to take the necessary risks.

But we are, again, getting ahead of ourselves. To understand more deeply how creativity and intelligence are different, it will be helpful to know what intelligence is and how it is measured . . . coming up in a couple of pages.

[PSYCHOLOGY MATTERS]

Using Psychology to Learn Psychology

Obviously, *experts* are people who know a lot about a particular subject. Unlike a novice, an expert confronting a problem does not have to start from scratch. Experts often see a solution quickly because they have seen many similar problems before. That is, they are especially good at finding analogies.

Their secret lies in the way their knowledge is organized (Ericsson et al., 2006; Ross, 2006). Characteristically, the novice possesses knowledge that is both limited and unorganized, while experts have extensive knowledge organized into elaborate "chunks" and schemas. We can see this quite clearly in a famous study of world-class chess players.

Master chess players are better able than novices to remember common patterns of pieces on a chess board, indicating that they use chunking to remember familiar patterns. Incidentally, can you remember how many hours or years experience it generally takes for a person to become a master in chess—or any other area?

A Study of Chess Experts

Dutch psychologist Adriaan de Groot found some striking differences when he compared how well a group of grand master chess players and another group of merely "good" players could remember a chess problem. When allowed five seconds to view a configuration of pieces as they might appear on a chessboard during a match, grand masters could reproduce the pattern far more accurately than those with less proficiency (de Groot, 1965). Does that mean the grand masters had better visual memories? No. When confronted with a random pattern of pieces on the chess board—a pattern that would never happen in a match—grand masters did no better than the others. This suggests the experts were better able to draw on familiar patterns in memory (schemas, really), rather than trying to recall individual pieces and positions.

Expertise as Organized Knowledge

How do experts organize their knowledge? There is no easy formula. Through study and practice, they develop both a fund of knowledge to apply to a problem and a familiarity with the field's common problems and solutions. That is, they know not only the facts but also how the facts are interrelated and used (Bédard & Chi, 1992). Aside from facts and specific skills they must learn, would-be-experts must also acquire a repertoire of heuristics, or "tricks of the trade," unique to their field of expertise. These heuristics help them find solutions more quickly, without having to follow so many blind leads (Gentner & Stevens, 1983; Simon, 1992).

Practice versus Talent

Are experts born, or is expertise learned? The highest levels of skilled performance requiring speed and accuracy of movement, as in athletics or music, seems to depend, in part, on native ability (Ackerman, 2007; Simonton, 2001). Expertise in a field requiring the mastery of a body of knowledge (think psychology, medicine, or medieval literature) requires considerable study. There is evidence that people have differing aptitudes for performing at the highest levels in any given field, but it is impossible to predict in advance who has the requisite ability for a particular endeavor. At this point, the important variables seem to be motivation and practice—much as we saw with creativity (Ericsson & Charness, 1994).

Eventually, perhaps, the theories of multiple intelligences we will study later in this chapter can give us some practical assistance. But for now, especially if you are at the beginning of your college career, the best advice is to explore as many fields as you can to find out where your passions lie. You are much more likely to work long and hard on something you love.

So, How Do You Become an Expert?

A supportive environment, with good teachers and mentors, helps (Barab & Plucker, 2002). Beyond that, it's study and practice! But don't just focus on the details. Learn the important schemas and problem-solving strategies in your chosen field too.

What does this suggest for your learning of psychology and other disciplines? You can take the first steps in developing your expertise in any subject by attending to the way your professor and your text organize the information they present (Gonzalvo et al., 1994). Consider such questions as the following:

- What terms does your psychology professor mention over and over? These might be such concepts as "cognitive science," "behaviorism," "developmental," or "theoretical perspectives." For you they may be, at first, unfamiliar and abstract, but for the professor they may represent the core of the course. Make sure you know what they mean and why they are important.

- What concepts does the course syllabus emphasize? What terms are associated with the main topics?

- Around what concepts is the textbook organized? You may be able to discern this quickly by looking at the table of contents. Alternatively, authors may lay out the organizing points in the preface. (In this book, we have attempted to help you identify the organizing principles of each chapter in the form of Core Concepts.)

Identifying the organizing principles for the course will simplify your studying. This makes sense, of course, in light of what you learned earlier about memory. Long-term memory (as you will remember!) is organized by meaningful associations. Accordingly, when you have a simple and effective way of organizing material, you create a framework to help you store and retain it in long-term memory.

Check Your Understanding

✔●─Study and Review at MyPsychLab

1. **APPLICATION:** From your own experience, give an example of an algorithm.

2. **RECALL:** Good problem solvers often use "tricks of the trade" or "rules of thumb" known as _____.

3. **APPLICATION:** Which one of the following would be an example of the confirmation bias at work?
   a. Mary ignores negative information about her favorite political candidate.
   b. Aaron agrees with Joel's taste in music.
   c. Natasha refuses to eat a food she dislikes.
   d. Bill buys a new RV even though his wife was opposed to the purchase.

4. **RECALL:** List four personality characteristics commonly found in highly creative people.

5. **UNDERSTANDING THE CORE CONCEPT:** Heuristic strategies show that our thinking is often based on
   a. logic rather than emotion.
   b. experience rather than logic.
   c. trial and error rather than algorithms.
   d. creativity rather than genius.

Answers 1. The mathematical formula for finding the area of a triangle is an example of an algorithm—as is any formula or procedure that always gives the correct answer. **2.** heuristics **3.** a **4.** Any four of the following are correct: independence, intense interest in a problem (high motivational level), willingness to restructure problems, preference for complexity, need for stimulating interaction. **5.** b

6.3 KEY QUESTION
How Is Intelligence Measured?

Psychologists have long been fascinated by the ways in which people differ in their abilities to reason, solve problems, and think creatively. The assessment of individual differences, however, did not begin with modern psychology. Historical records show that sophisticated mental testing methods were used in ancient China. More than 2,000 years ago, the Chinese employed a program of civil service testing that required government officials to demonstrate their competence every third year at an oral examination. Later, applicants were required to pass written civil service tests to assess their knowledge of law, the military, agriculture, and geography. British diplomats and missionaries assigned to China in the early 1800s described the selection procedures so admiringly that the British, and later the Americans, adopted modified versions of China's system for the selection of civil service personnel (Wiggins, 1973).

Unlike the historical Chinese, however, modern Americans seem to be more interested in how "smart" people are, as opposed to how much they have learned. It is interest in this sort of "native ability" that spurred development of intelligence testing as we know it today. But, despite the long history of mental testing and the widespread use of intelligence tests in our society, the exact meaning of the term *intelligence* is still disputed (Neisser et al., 1996). Still, most psychologists would probably agree with the general definition we provided at the beginning of the chapter—that **intelligence** is the mental capacity to acquire knowledge, reason, and solve problems effectively. They would also agree that a complete picture of an individual's intelligence must be obtained from measurements across a variety of tasks. They disagree, however, on exactly what mental abilities constitute intelligence and whether they are many or few in number.

Everyone does acknowledge that intelligence is a relative term. That is, an individual's level of intelligence must be defined in relation to the same abilities in a comparison group, usually of the same age range. Everyone also agrees that intelligence is a *hypothetical construct:* a characteristic that is not directly observable but must be inferred from behavior. In practice, this means that intelligence is measured from an individual's responses on an intelligence test. The individual's scores are then compared to those of a reference group. Exactly what these tests should assess is the source of much controversy—and the focus of this section of the chapter.

intelligence The mental capacity to acquire knowledge, reason, and solve problems effectively.

> **Core Concept 6.3**
>
> **Intelligence testing has a history of controversy, but most psychologists now view intelligence as a normally distributed trait that can be measured by performance on a variety of tasks.**

On the original Binet-Simon test, a child was asked to perform tasks such as the following:

- Name various common objects (such as a clock or a cat) shown in pictures.
- Repeat a 15-word sentence given by the examiner.
- Give a word that rhymes with one given by the examiner.
- Imitate gestures (such as pointing to an object).
- Comply with simple commands (such as moving a block from one location to another).
- Explain the differences between two common objects.
- Use three words (given by the examiner) in a sentence.
- Define abstract terms (such as "friendship").

FIGURE 6.8

Sample Items from the First Binet-Simon Test

We begin our survey of intelligence and intelligence testing by introducing you to the founders of intelligence testing.

Binet and Simon Invent a School Abilities Test

Alfred Binet *(Bi-NAY)* and his colleague Théodore Simon stepped into history in 1904. At that time, a new law required all French children to attend school, and the government needed a means of identifying those who needed remedial help. Binet and Simon were asked to design a test for this purpose. They responded with 30 problems sampling a variety of abilities necessary for school (see Figure 6.8). The new approach was a success: It did, indeed, predict which children could or could not handle normal schoolwork.

Four important features distinguish the Binet-Simon approach (Binet, 1911):

1. They interpreted scores on their test as an estimate of current performance and not as a measure of innate intelligence.

2. They wanted test scores used to identify children who needed special help, not merely to categorize or label them as bright or dull.

3. They emphasized that training and opportunity could affect intelligence and wanted to pinpoint areas of performance in which special education could help certain children identified by their test.

4. They constructed the test *empirically*—based on how children were observed to perform—rather than tying the test to a particular theory of intelligence.

Binet and Simon assessed French children of various ages with this test and first computed an average score for children at each age. Then, they compared each child's performance to the averages for children of various ages The result of that comparison yielded a score for each individual child, expressed in terms of **mental age (MA)**: the average age at which individuals achieve a particular score. So, for example, when a child's score was the same as the average score for a group of 5-year-olds, the child was said to have a mental age of 5, regardless of his or her **chronological age (CA)**, the number of years since birth. Binet and Simon determined that students most needing remedial help were those whose MA was two years behind their CA.

mental age (MA)   The average age at which normal (average) individuals achieve a particular score.

chronological age (CA)   The number of years since the individual's birth.

American Psychologists Borrow Binet and Simon's Idea

Less than a decade after the French began testing school children, American psychologists imported the Binet-Simon test of school abilities and changed it into the form we now call the *IQ test*. They did this by modifying the scoring procedure, expanding the test's content, and obtaining scores from a large normative group of people, including adults. Soon "intelligence testing" was widely accepted as a technique by which Americans were defining themselves—and each other.

The Appeal of Intelligence Testing in America   Why did intelligence tests become so popular in the United States? Three forces changing the face of the country in the early 20th century conspired to make intelligence testing seem like an orderly way out of turmoil and uncertainty. First, the United States was experiencing an unprecedented wave of immigration resulting from global economic, social, and political crises. Second, new laws requiring universal education—schooling for all children—were flooding schools with students. And third, when World War I began, the military needed a way of assessing and classifying new recruits. Together, these events created a need to assess large numbers of people (Chapman, 1988). Intelligence was seen not only as a means of bringing order to the turbulence of rapid social change but also as an inexpensive and democratic way to separate those who could benefit from education or military leadership training from those who could not.

One consequence of the large-scale group-testing program in America was that the public came to accept the idea that intelligence tests could accurately differentiate people in terms of their mental abilities. This acceptance soon led to widespread use of tests in schools and industry. Another, more unfortunate, consequence was that the tests reinforced prevailing prejudices. Specifically, Army reports suggested that differences in test scores were linked to race and country of origin (Yerkes, 1921). Of course, the same statistics could have been used to demonstrate that environmental disadvantages limit the full development of people's intellectual abilities. Instead, immigrants with limited facility in English (the only language in which the tests were given) or even little understanding of how to take such tests were labeled as "morons," "idiots," and "imbeciles" (terms used at the time to specify different degrees of mental retardation).

While these problems are obvious to us now (with the help of hindsight), at the time they were obscured by the fact that the tests accomplished what most people wanted: They were simple to administer and provided a means of assessing and classifying people according to their scores. Any awareness of bias or unfair treatment was likely suppressed by emotional bias. As a result, the public generally perceived the tests as objective and democratic.

The Stanford-Binet Intelligence Scale   The most respected of the new American tests of intelligence came from the laboratory of Stanford University professor Lewis Terman. He adapted the Binet-Simon test for U.S. school children by standardizing its administration and its age-level norms. The result was the Stanford-Binet Intelligence Scale (Terman, 1916), which soon became the standard by which other measures of intelligence were judged. Because it had to be administered individually, Terman's test was less economical than the group tests. Nevertheless, it was better suited for spotting learning problems. Even more importantly, the Stanford-Binet test was designed both for children and adults.

With his new test, Terman introduced the concept of the **intelligence quotient (IQ)**, a term coined originally by German psychologist William Stern in 1914. The IQ was the ratio of mental age (MA) to chronological age (CA), multiplied by 100 (to eliminate decimals):

$$IQ = \frac{\text{Mental Age}}{\text{Chronological Age}} \times 100$$

> **intelligence quotient (IQ)**   A numerical score on an intelligence test, originally computed by dividing the person's mental age by chronological age and multiplying by 100.

Please follow us through the IQ equation with these examples: Consider a child with a chronological age of 8 years, whose test scores reveal a mental age of 10. Dividing the child's mental age by chronological age (MA/CA = 10/8) gives 1.25. Multiplying that result by 100, we obtain an IQ of 125. In contrast, another 8-year-old child who performs at the level of an average 6-year-old (MA = 6) has an IQ of 6/8 × 100 = 75, according to Terman's formula. Those whose mental age is the same as their chronological age have IQs of 100, which is considered to be the average or "normal" IQ.

Within a short time, the new Stanford-Binet test became a popular instrument in clinical psychology, psychiatry, and educational counseling. With the publication of his test, Terman also promoted his belief that intelligence is largely innate and measurable. The message, then, was that an IQ score reflected something fundamental and unchanging about people.

Although the Stanford-Binet became the "gold standard" of intelligence testing, it had its critics. The loudest objection was that it employed an inconsistent concept of intelligence because it measured different mental abilities at different ages. For example, 2- to 4-year-olds were tested on their ability to manipulate objects, whereas adults were tested almost exclusively on verbal items. Test makers heeded these criticisms, and, as the scientific understanding of intelligence increased, psychologists found it increasingly important to measure multiple intellectual abilities at all age levels. A modern revision of the Stanford-Binet now provides separate scores for several mental skills.

Problems with the IQ Formula

An inherent problem in calculating IQ scores became apparent as soon as psychologists began to use their formula with adults. Here's what happens: By the mid- to late teenage years, gains in mental age scores usually level off as people develop mentally in many different directions. Consequently, mental growth, as measured by a test, appears to slow down. As a result, Terman's formula for computing IQs makes normal children appear to become adults with mental retardation—at least as far as their test scores are concerned! Note what happens to the average 30-year-old's score if mental age, as measured by a test, stays at the same level as it was at age 15:

$$IQ = \frac{\text{Mental Age}}{\text{Chronological Age}} = \frac{15}{30} \times 100 = 50$$

Psychologists quickly realized this paints an erroneous picture of adult mental abilities. People do not grow less intelligent as they become adults (although their children sometimes think so). Rather, adults develop in different directions, which IQ scores do not necessarily reflect. Prudently, psychologists decided to abandon the original IQ formula and seek another means of calculating IQs. Their solution was similar to the familiar practice of "grading on the curve." This famous curve demands some explanation.

Calculating IQs "on the Curve"

Behind the new method for calculating IQ lay the assumption that intelligence is *normally distributed*. That is, intelligence is assumed to be spread through the population in varying degrees so that only a few people fall into the high or low ranges, while most cluster around a central average. In this respect, intelligence is presumed to be like many physical traits, including height, weight, and shoe size. If you were to measure any of these variables in a large number of people, you would probably get a set of scores that follow the same "curve" teachers use when they grade "on the curve." Let us take women's heights as an example.

Imagine you have randomly selected a large number of adult women and arranged them in single-file columns according to their heights (everybody 5′ tall in one column, 5′1″ in the next, 5′2″ in the next, and so on). You would find most of the women standing in the columns near the group's average height (see Figure 6.9). Only a few would be in the columns containing extremely tall women or extremely short women. We could easily describe the number of women at each height by a curve that follows the boundary of each column. We call this bell-shaped curve a **normal distribution (or normal curve)**.

Applying this same concept to intelligence, psychologists find that IQ scores (like the women's heights we considered above) fit a normal distribution (see Figure 6.10). More precisely, when IQ tests are given to large numbers of individuals, the scores of those at each age level are normally distributed. (Adults are placed in a group of their

normal distribution (or normal curve) A bell-shaped curve describing the spread of a characteristic throughout a population.

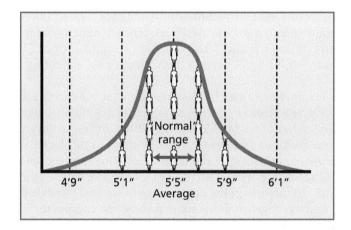

FIGURE 6.9

An (Imaginary) Normal Distribution of Women's Heights

The level of the curve at any point reflects the number of women with that height.

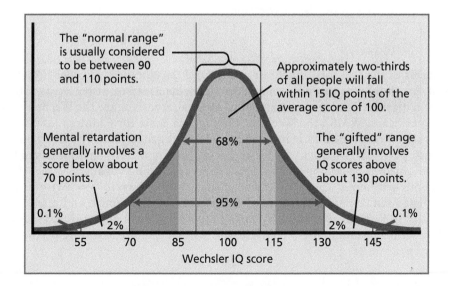

FIGURE 6.10

The Normal Distribution of IQ Scores among a Large Sample

Intelligence tests are usually designed to make the scores fit a normal distribution, with an average of 100. Within that distribution, the normal range of IQs typically spans scores of about 90 to 110—or about fifty percent of the population. The "gifted" and the "mentally retarded" ranges at opposite ends together account for less than five percent of the population.

normal range Scores falling near the middle of a normal distribution. The normal range of IQ scores is about 90–110 and includes about 50 percent of the population.

own, regardless of age, and the distribution of their scores also fits the bell-shaped curve.) Instead of using the old IQ formula, IQs are now determined from tables that indicate where test scores fall on the normal curve. The scores are statistically adjusted so the average for each age group is set at 100. Scores near the middle of the distribution (usually between 90 and 110) are considered to be in the **normal range**, which includes approximately 50 percent of the population (see Figure 6.11). At the extreme ends of the distribution, scores below 70 are often said to be in the *mentally retarded range,* while those above 130 are sometimes said to indicate *giftedness.*

Thus, IQ scores are no longer calculated by dividing mental age by chronological age. The concept of a ratio expressed as a multiple of 100 (a percentage-like number that is easy to understand) is retained, however. This solves the problem of calculating adult IQs by comparing adults with adults.

But one more problem has surfaced—and remains unsolved. Much to everyone's chagrin, James Flynn noticed the average IQ score has gradually increased, at the rate of about three points per decade, ever since the tests were invented—a fact obscured by "renorming" the tests every few years to keep the average IQ at 100 (Flynn, 1987). If taken at face value, this *Flynn effect* would mean that a person in the average range in your great-grandparents' time might be considered to have mental retardation today! Flynn, along with most other observers, believes such a conclusion is absurd. What, then, explains the effect (Flynn, 2003; Neisser et al., 1996)?

The gradual increase probably results from a combination of factors, including better test-taking skills, greater complexity and mental stimulation in society (everything from movies to games to computers to cell phones), more schooling, and better nutrition. Flynn (2007) himself points out that different components of intelligence have accelerated at different rates (with vocabulary, for example, hardly budging at all), so part of the IQ gain can be explained by societies valuing and encouraging factors that contribute to intelligence. For example, one question asks, "How are a dog and a rabbit alike?" A century ago, says Flynn, the answer would have been culture-specific: "You use dogs to hunt rabbits." Now, he notes, the correct answer would be "They are both mammals," reflecting better abstract thinking skills.

The Flynn effect, however, may be slowing down, at least in developed countries. Since the mid-1990s, test scores in European samples have stabilized and in some cases even declined somewhat (Teasdale & Owen, 2008). In lesser-developed countries, however, IQ scores continue to increase (Colom et al., 2007; Daley et al., 2003). At the same time, close examination of the Flynn effect since its beginning indicates the average rise in IQ score is generally a result of significant increases in the lower-end scores—but little or no increase in the upper range of scores (Teasdale & Owen, 1987). Putting all these findings together leads some theorists to suggest the Flynn effect may really be a mark of better *equality* in access to education, nutrition, and cognitive stimulation. If that is true, we may see a narrowing of the IQ gap between developed and developing countries in the decades to come.

IQ Testing Today

The success of the Stanford-Binet test encouraged development of other IQ tests. As a result, psychologists can now choose from a wide array of instruments for measuring intelligence. The most prominent of these alternatives are the Wechsler Adult Intelligence Scale (WAIS), the Wechsler Intelligence Scale for Children (WISC), and the Wechsler Preschool and Primary Scale of Intelligence (WPPSI). With these instruments, psychologist David Wechsler offers a family of tests that measures many skills presumed to be components of intelligence, including vocabulary, verbal comprehension, arithmetic ability, similarities (the ability to state how two things are alike), digit span (repeating a series of digits after the examiner), and block design (the ability to reproduce designs by fitting together blocks with colored sides). As our Core Concept noted, these tests measure intelligence by assessing performance on a variety of tasks.

Do It Yourself! SAMPLE IQ TEST ITEMS

Try your hand at the following items adapted from group tests of intelligence. Some of the items are more challenging than others. You will find the correct answers at the end.

VOCABULARY: Select the best definition for each word:

1. **viable**
   a. traveled
   b. capable of living
   c. V-shaped
   d. can be bent

2. **imminent**
   a. defenseless
   b. expensive
   c. impending
   d. notorious

ANALOGIES: Examine the relationship between the first two words. Then, find an answer that has the same relationship with the word in bold letters:

3. Washington: Lincoln
   July:
   a. January
   b. April
   c. May
   d. October

4. ocean: canoe
   verse:
   a. poem
   b. pen
   c. water
   d. serve

SIMILARITIES: Which letter on the right belongs to the same category as the one on the left?

5. **J   A M S Z T**
6. **A   S D U V X**

SEQUENCES: Choose the answer that best completes the sequence:

7. a z b y c x d?
   e   s   u   w   f
8. 1 3 6 10 15?
   16   18   21   27   128

MATHEMATICAL REASONING

9. Portland and Seattle are actually 150 miles apart, but on a map they are 2 inches apart. If Chicago and Norfolk are 5 inches apart on the same map, what is the actual distance between those two cities?
   a. 125 miles
   b. 250 miles
   c. 375 miles
   d. 525 miles

Answers 1. b **2.** c **3.** d (October comes after July) **4.** d (verse and serve have the same letters) **5.** S (the only one with a curve in it) **6.** U (the only vowel) **7.** W **8.** 21 **9.** c

---

Like the Stanford-Binet, the Wechsler tests are *individual* tests. That is, they are given to one person at a time. Also available are *group* tests of intelligence that can be administered to large numbers of students simultaneously. Unlike the Stanford-Binet and Wechsler tests, group tests consist of paper-and-pencil measures, involving booklets of questions and machine-scored answer sheets. The convenience of group tests—although not as precise as individual tests—has made IQ testing, along with other forms of academic assessment, widespread. It is quite likely you have taken such tests several times as you passed through grades 1 to 12, perhaps without realizing what they were. The items in the *Do It Yourself!* box are similar to items in many of these commonly used group tests of mental abilities.

What are IQ tests used for today? An IQ score assumes almost overwhelming importance in determining whether a child has "mental retardation" or is "gifted"—concepts we will examine more closely in the next Psychology Matters feature. Aside from those uses, IQ tests figure most prominently in the diagnosis of learning disabilities. The problem with that, says Dr. Jack Naglieri, is that IQ scores don't tell us much about which intervention strategies are likely to be effective with a given child (Benson, 2003a). To remedy this, Naglieri and others are developing tests that place less emphasis on a single number, such as IQ, and more on classifying people in ways that suggest helping strategies, such as identifying reading problems, perceptual problems, or attention disorders.

[PSYCHOLOGY MATTERS]

What Can You Do for an Exceptional Child?

As we have noted, mental retardation and giftedness lie at opposite ends of the intelligence spectrum. As traditionally conceived, **mental retardation** occupies the IQ range below 70—taking in scores achieved by approximately 2 percent of the population. Arbitrarily, **giftedness** begins 30 points above average, at 130 points, comprising another

mental retardation   Often conceived as representing the lower 2 percent of the IQ range, commencing about 30 points below average (below about 70 points). More sophisticated definitions also take into account an individual's level of social functioning and other abilities.

giftedness   Often conceived as representing the upper 2 percent of the IQ range, commencing about 30 points above average (at about 130 IQ points).

2 percent of the population. Bearing in mind all we have learned about limitations of IQ tests, let's take a brief look at these two categories.

Mental Retardation

The most current view of mental retardation deemphasizes IQ scores by focusing on practical abilities to get along in the world (Robinson et al., 2000). In fact, the American Association of Mental Retardation now offers a definition of mental retardation that does not even mention an IQ cutoff score. According to this new perspective, mental retardation involves "significantly subaverage intellectual functioning" that becomes apparent before age 18. It also involves limitations in at least two of the following areas: "communication, self-care, home living, social skills, community use, self-direction, health and safety, functional academics, leisure and work" (Turkington, 1993, p. 26).

Causes of Mental Retardation

CONNECTION CHAPTER 2

Down syndrome produces both physical symptoms and mental retardation; it arises from a chromosomal defect (p. 47).

Mental retardation has many causes (Daily et al., 2000; Scott & Carran, 1987). Some, such as Down syndrome, are known to be genetic because we can point to a specific genetically controlled defect. Some causes are purely environmental, as in *fetal alcohol syndrome,* which involves brain damage incurred before birth, resulting from maternal abuse of alcohol during pregnancy. Other environmental causes include postnatal accidents that damage the cognitive regions of the brain, or conditions of deprivation or neglect that fail to give the developing child experiences needed for intellectual growth. Some cases have no known cause.

Dealing with Mental Retardation

We have no cures, although research has found preventive measures for certain types of mental retardation. For example, a simple test performed routinely on newborn babies can identify a hidden genetic disorder known as PKU. If detected early, mental retardation usually associated with PKU can be prevented by a special diet. More generally, genetic counseling, pregnancy care services, and education of new parents are other preventive strategies (Scott & Carran, 1987).

Aside from prevention, special education programs help those with mental retardation learn vocational and independent living skills. Meanwhile, biological scientists hope one day to treat genetically based forms of mental retardation with therapies just now being conceived. For example, genetic treatment may involve splicing a healthy gene into a benign virus to "infect" all the cells of a person with mental retardation and replace the defective gene. At present, genetic treatments for certain physical diseases are in experimental phases and are at least a few years away in the treatment of mental retardation.

The Special Olympics offers children with mental retardation (and others with disabilities) an opportunity to capitalize on their abilities and to build self-esteem.

For now, what can you do if you have a child with mental retardation? Because the nervous system is so immature at birth and so much physical and mental development occurs during the first years of life, early interventions will have the greatest payoffs. Psychological approaches involving sensory stimulation and social interaction can be enormously important. With the benefit of an optimal educational program, gains of up to 15 IQ points are possible (Robinson et al., 2000).

In fact, an enriched environment may be just as helpful to a child with mental retardation as it is to a gifted child. Teams of special education teachers, speech therapists, educational psychologists, physicians, and other specialists can devise programs teaching persons with mental retardation to capitalize on the abilities they have, rather than being held prisoner of their disabilities (Schroeder et al., 1987). Behavior modification programs have been especially successful. As a result, many citizens with mental retardation have learned to care for themselves and acquired vocational skills enabling them to live independently (Landesman & Butterfield, 1987).

CONNECTION CHAPTER 13

Behavior modification therapies are based on behavioral learning principles derived from operant and classical conditioning (p. 568).

Giftedness

At the other end of the intelligence spectrum are the "gifted," with especially high IQs, typically defined as being in the top 1 or 2 percent of the population (Robinson et al.,

2000). But does a high IQ give its owner an advantage in life? A long look at gifted individuals suggests that it does.

Terman's Studies of Giftedness

The most extensive study of gifted individuals began in 1921 under the direction of Lewis Terman, the same person who brought Binet and Simon's IQ test to the United States (Leslie, 2000). From a large pool of children tested in California schools, Terman selected 1,528 children who scored near the top of the IQ range. His longitudinal research program followed these children as they went through school and into adulthood. Periodically through their lives, Terman retested them and gathered information on their achievements and adjustment patterns. The resulting decades of data revealed much about the nature of giftedness. Almost uniformly, Terman's gifted children excelled in school—as one might expect from the strong correlation between IQ and academic achievement. Terman also remarked on the good health and happiness of children in his sample, although newer evidence suggests that highly gifted children are susceptible to certain physical and psychological disorders (Winner, 2000).

As they moved into adulthood, the gifted group continued on the path of success. An unusually high number of scientists, writers, and professionals emerged from its ranks. Together they published more than 2,000 scientific articles, patented 235 inventions, and wrote 92 books. By middle age, more than 86 percent of the men in Terman's sample had entered high-status professions (Terman & Oden, 1959).

Yet, for all their achievements, no one in this high-IQ sample achieved the level of an Einstein, a Picasso, or a Martha Graham. Nor did a high IQ guarantee wealth or stature. In fact, many from Terman's sample led ordinary, undistinguished lives. The most visibly successful seemed to have, in addition to their high IQs, extraordinary motivation and someone at home or at school who was especially encouraging to them (Goleman, 1980; Oden, 1968)—some of the same characteristics found to be markers of "genius."

Dealing with Giftedness

Imagine you are the parent of a child with a very high IQ score, say 145. Which of the following would be the best course of action?

- Enroll your child in special after-school classes.
- Hire a tutor to help the child with his or her homework.
- Send the child to a private school.
- Do nothing special.

What do experts say? Don't rush out to enroll your child in special classes or provide other "help" because of his or her IQ score (Csikszentmihalyi et al., 1993; Wong & Csikszentmihalyi, 1991). Parents can destroy the spark of curiosity by pushing a child toward goals that do not hold the child's interest. Chances are you have already provided an environment in which your child's native ability could thrive. So do not make any rash and radical changes.

Above all, avoid making the child feel different because of his or her unusual abilities and high IQ score. In part because of the personality traits common in gifted children—especially a tendency to spend time alone, working on their interests—they are already more likely than other children to suffer social and emotional disorders (Winner, 2000). Nor should you feel smug about your genetic contribution to your child's intellect. Remember that intelligence involves a nature–nurture interaction—and, besides, IQ tests sample only a small fraction of human abilities. Other people's kids may have equally amazing abilities in untested regions of their intellects. In fact, many gifted individuals go unrecognized by schools because their outstanding talent shows up primarily in art or music—domains in which formal abilities testing is rarely done.

Remember, also, that a high IQ is no guarantee of high motivation, high creativity, or success in life. All it guarantees is an intellectual opportunity.

So, what should you do with a bright child? Nothing special that you would not have done before you knew his or her IQ score.

Check Your Understanding

✓● Study and Review at MyPsychLab

1. **RECALL:** One of Binet's great ideas was the concept of *mental age*, which he defined as _____.

2. **APPLICATION:** You tested a 12-year-old child and found a mental age of 15. Using the original IQ formula, what is her IQ?

3. **RECALL:** A problem with the original IQ formula is that it gave a distorted picture of the intellectual abilities of

   a. adults.
   b. children.
   c. persons with mental retardation.
   d. gifted students.

4. **UNDERSTANDING THE CORE CONCEPT:** If intelligence is a normally distributed characteristic, in what part of the distribution would you expect to find most people's scores on a test of intelligence?

Answers 1. the average age at which individuals achieve a particular score. Or, in different words, mental age is determined by the average score achieved by individuals of a particular chronological age. **2.** 125. **3.** a **4.** Near the middle of the distribution

6.4 KEY QUESTION
— Is Intelligence One or Many Abilities?

savant syndrome   Found in individuals having a remarkable talent (such as the ability to determine the day of the week for any given date) even though they are mentally slow in other domains.

People who show aptitude in one area—language, for example—often score high on tests of other domains as well, such as mathematics or spatial relationships. This fact argues for the idea of a single, general intellectual ability. But there are some glaring exceptions, such as persons with **savant syndrome**. These rare individuals have a remarkable, but limited, talent, such as the ability to multiply numbers quickly in their heads or determine the day of the week for any given date, even though they are mentally slow in other ways (Treffert & Wallace, 2002). Typically, they also show symptoms of autism (Winner, 2000), as you may have seen in Dustin Hoffman's classic portrayal of one such person in the film *Rain Man*. Such cases raise a serious question about the whole concept of a single, general intelligence factor. Obviously, there is no simple solution to the question of one or many intelligences. Different psychologists have dealt with the issue in different ways, as our Core Concept suggests:

Core Concept 6.4

Some psychologists believe that intelligence comprises one general factor, *g*, while others believe that intelligence is a collection of distinct abilities.

We will first examine this issue from the viewpoint of psychologists in the *psychometric tradition*: those who have been interested in developing tests to measure mental abilities. Following that, we will look at intelligence from the standpoint of cognitive psychologists, who bring a fresh perspective to the problem.

Psychometric Theories of Intelligence

Psychometrics is the field of "mental measurements." It is the psychological specialty that has given us most of our IQ tests, achievement tests, personality tests, the SAT, and a variety of other assessment instruments. Many pioneers in psychology, including Alfred Binet and Lewis Terman, carved their professional niches with contributions to psychometrics. Yet another famous figure in this field was Charles Spearman, a psychologist best known for his work suggesting that intelligence is a single factor.

Spearman's *g* Factor By the 1920s, there were many tests of intelligence available, and British psychologist Charles Spearman (1927) found that individuals' scores on different tests tend to be highly correlated; in other words, those who score high on one test also generally score high on others. These correlations, he said, point to a single, common factor of general intelligence underlying performance across all intellectual domains. Spearman did not deny that some people have outstanding talents or deficits in certain areas. But, he said, these individual differences should not blind us to a single *general intelligence* factor at work behind all our mental activity. Spearman called this general intellectual ability the ***g* factor**. He assumed this general factor is innate, and most psychologists at the time agreed with him (Tyler, 1988). More current studies also find strong support for a *g* factor (Johnson et al., 2008), as well as evidence of a significant innate component (Haworth et al., 2010).

Neuroscientists find some support for Spearman's theory, too. Various tests of *g* all point to certain regions of the brain, especially in the frontal lobes (Duncan et al., 2000; Haier et al., 2004). Could these be the loci of *g*? Although some neuroscientists think so, others believe this explanation oversimplifies both the nature of intelligence and of the brain (McArdle et al., 2002; Sternberg, 1999, 2000). In general, psychologists accept the existence of a *g* factor but debate the parameters and meaning of what it actually measures.

g factor   A general ability, proposed by Spearman, as the main factor underlying all intelligent mental activity.

Cattell's Fluid and Crystallized Intelligence Using sophisticated mathematical techniques, Raymond Cattell (1963) determined that general intelligence can be broken down into two relatively independent components he called *crystallized* and *fluid* *intelligence*. **Crystallized intelligence**, said Cattell, consists of the knowledge a person has acquired, plus the ability to access that knowledge. Thus, crystallized intelligence relates to the person's ability to store and retrieve information from semantic memory. It is measured by tests of vocabulary, arithmetic, and general information. In contrast, Cattell proposed **fluid intelligence** as the ability to see complex relationships and solve problems—abilities that involve algorithms and heuristics, which we discussed earlier in this chapter. Fluid intelligence is often measured by tests of block design and spatial visualization, tests that do not rely on the individual possessing certain "crystallized" background information to solve a problem. For Cattell, both types of intelligence were essential to adaptive living.

crystallized intelligence   The knowledge a person has acquired, plus the ability to access that knowledge.

CONNECTION CHAPTER 5

Much of our general knowledge is stored in *semantic memory*, a partition of long-term memory (p. 185).

fluid intelligence   The ability to see complex relationships and solve problems.

Cognitive Theories of Intelligence

Late in the 20th century, when the cognitive perspective emerged as a major force in psychology, it produced some radical new ideas about intelligence. In brief, the cognitive view of intelligence went well beyond the emphasis on vocabulary, logic, problem solving, and other skills previously measured to predict school success (see Table 6.1). Intelligence, said cognitive psychologists, includes cognitive processes underlying success in many areas of life—not just school (Sternberg, 2000)—and thus is much broader than the psychometric notion of intelligence. Instead of asking, "How smart are you?" cognitive theories ask, "How are you smart?" We will focus on the two most prominent of these cognitive theories.

Sternberg's Triarchic Theory You may know someone who seems to have plenty of "book smarts" but is not very successful in life, perhaps because they don't get along well with others or deal effectively with unexpected events. Psychologist Robert Sternberg says they lack **practical intelligence**: the ability to cope with people and events in their environment. Practical intelligence is sometimes called "street smarts," although it applies just as well at home, on the job, or at school as it does on the street. At its core is the ability to adapt to your environment, to shape an environment to suit your needs, or to find an environment in which you can thrive. Self-awareness, or knowledge of your strengths and limitations, is an important component of practical intelligence.

In contrast with practical intelligence, Sternberg calls the abilities measured by most IQ tests **analytical intelligence**, relying on problem solving, rational judgment, and

practical intelligence   According to Sternberg, the ability to cope with the environment; sometimes called "street smarts."

analytical intelligence   According to Sternberg, the ability measured by most IQ tests; includes the ability to analyze problems and find correct answers.

TABLE 6.1 Theories of Intelligence Compared

Spearman	Cattell	Sternberg	Gardner
	Crystallized intelligence		
g factor	Fluid intelligence	Analytical intelligence	Naturalistic intelligence
			Logical–mathematical intelligence
		Creative intelligence	Linguistic intelligence
			Spatial intelligence
			Musical intelligence
			Bodily–kinesthetic intelligence
		Practical intelligence	Interpersonal intelligence
			Intrapersonal intelligence

Note: Different theorists see intelligence as having different components, as shown in the columns of this table. The rows show roughly comparable components of intelligence described by various theories (although the reader should be aware that the correspondences are not exact). For example, Sternberg's practical intelligence is similar to Gardner's two components, called interpersonal intelligence and intrapersonal intelligence, while Spearman's *g* ignores these abilities.

the ability to compare and contrast ideas. Your grades in college are likely to be closely related to this logical reasoning ability.

Creative intelligence, Sternberg's third type of intelligence, helps people develop new ideas and see new relationships among concepts. Creative intelligence is what Picasso used to develop the form of painting called *Cubism* and what Einstein used to formulate his theory of relativity. It is also the form of intelligence Sternberg used to develop his new theory of intelligence.

Sternberg's three-part formulation is often called the **triarchic theory** of intelligence, because it combines three (*tri* = three) different kinds of intelligence. For Sternberg, each of these abilities—practical intelligence, analytical intelligence, and creative intelligence—is relatively independent of the others. That is, a person's ability in one of the three areas doesn't necessarily predict his or her intelligence in the other two. Each represents a different dimension for describing and evaluating human performance. This theory suggests it is inaccurate to think of a single IQ score as summarizing all that is important or valuable about people's mental abilities (Sternberg, 1999; Sternberg et al., 1995).

Recently, Sternberg and his colleagues (2003) put forth an additional element of intelligence—namely, **wisdom.** For Sternberg, wisdom involves using one's intelligence, whether it be analytical, practical, or creative, toward a common good rather than a selfish pursuit. For example, a car salesman who convinces a buyer to purchase a defective car may demonstrate practical intelligence, but not wisdom. Only by promoting wisdom can we achieve the societal goals that most people desire, says Sternberg. And research indicates he may be right, in at least one respect: Studies show that wisdom is one predictor of well-being in later life (Bianchi, 1994; Hartman, 2000). 👁

Gardner's Multiple Intelligences Like Sternberg, Harvard psychologist Howard Gardner views traditional IQ tests as limited measures of human mental abilities. But Gardner argues we have at least eight separate mental abilities, which he calls **multiple intelligences** (Ellison, 1984; Gardner, 1983, 1999a, 1999b):

1. **Linguistic intelligence.** Often measured on traditional IQ tests by vocabulary tests and tests of reading comprehension
2. **Logical-mathematical intelligence.** Also measured on most IQ tests with analogies, math problems, and logic problems

---

creative intelligence   According to Sternberg, the form of intelligence that helps people see new relationships among concepts; involves insight and creativity.

triarchic theory   The term for Sternberg's theory of intelligence; so called because it combines three ("tri-") main forms of intelligence.

wisdom   According to Sternberg, using one's intelligence toward a common good rather than a selfish pursuit.

👁—Watch the **Video** Robert Sternberg on Intelligence at **MyPsychLab**

multiple intelligences   A term used to refer to Gardner's theory, which proposes that there are eight (or more) forms of intelligence.

3. **Spatial intelligence.** The ability to form and manipulate mental images of objects and to think about their relationships in space

4. **Musical intelligence.** The ability to perform, compose, and appreciate musical patterns, including patterns of rhythms and pitches

5. **Bodily-kinesthetic intelligence.** The ability for controlled movement and coordination, such as that needed by an athlete or a surgeon

6. **Naturalistic intelligence.** The ability to classify living things as members of diverse groups (e.g., dogs, petunias, bacteria) and recognize subtle changes in one's environment

7. **Interpersonal intelligence.** The ability to understand other people's intentions, emotions, motives, and actions, as well as to work effectively with others

8. **Intrapersonal intelligence.** The ability to know oneself, to develop a satisfactory sense of identity, and to regulate one's life

Each of these intelligences arises from a separate module in the brain, Gardner claims. The latter two, interpersonal and intrapersonal intelligence, are similar to a capacity some psychologists call *emotional intelligence* (sometimes referred to as "EQ"). People who are high in emotional intelligence are good at "reading" other people's emotional states, as well as being especially aware of their own emotional responses.

Assessing Cognitive Theories of Intelligence. Perhaps the major contribution of the cognitive theories to our study of intelligence is their culturally inclusive value system: For cognitive theorists, there are many ways to excel, and one way is not necessarily superior to others. This notion has broad appeal. The challenge for these theories, though, lies in assessment: How can we reliably measure creative, practical, or interpersonal intelligence?

In an impressive project that was itself both creative and practical, Sternberg and his associates developed supplemental questions for SAT tests designed to measure creative and practical intelligences (Sternberg, 2007). Students wrote, for example, a story to go with the title *The Octopus's Sneakers,* or created a caption for an untitled comic strip, to measure creative intelligence. A variety of verbal and nonverbal problems—such as how to respond if you ask a professor for a letter of recommendation but the professor appears not to recognize you—aimed to assess practical intelligence. Sternberg's team scored the questions using originality, appropriateness to the context, and engagement to assess creative intelligence, with feasibility and suitability to the context as evaluators of practical intelligence. The results? Not only did the new tests prove to be valid measures of creativity and practical intelligence, they greatly increased colleges' ability to predict freshmen success. They also reduced ethnic group differences in college admissions, as the diversity of test questions was better able to identify cultural variations in demonstration of intelligence (Sternberg et al., 2006)—which is precisely the angle on intelligence we will examine next.

Cultural Definitions of Intelligence

Both Sternberg and Gardner see all components of intelligence as equally important. Yet the value of each is also culturally determined, according to what is needed by, useful to, and prized by a given society. If you lived in a Pacific island culture, for example, which would matter more: your SAT scores or your ability to navigate a boat on the open ocean? With such examples, cross-cultural psychologists have called our attention to the notion that "intelligence" can have quite different meanings in different cultures (Sternberg, 2000, 2004). In fact, many languages have no word at all for intelligence as we conceive of it: the mental processes associated with logic, vocabulary, mathematical ability, abstract thought, and academic success (Matsumoto, 1996).

African Concepts of Intelligence In rural Kenya, Sternberg found that children with the greatest practical intelligence skills actually scored lower on traditional IQ

CONNECTION CHAPTER 9

Emotional intelligence involves the ability to understand and use emotions effectively (p. 400).

The popular TV show *Survivor* emphasizes practical intelligence. This scene is from the "Redemption Island" episode in Nicaragua.

tests that measure academic success. "In Kenya," says Sternberg, "good grades don't get you anywhere. You're better off getting an apprenticeship or learning to mine or fish—those will allow you to support a family" (Winerman, 2005b). Consequently, the kids with the best minds don't learn academic skills but concentrate instead on practical skills that will get them ahead in life.

The Western assumption that intelligence is associated with school success and quick solutions to problems is not universal. The Buganda people in Uganda, for example, associate intelligence with slow and thoughtful responses. Yet another view is found among the Djerma-Sonhai in Niger (West Africa), who see intelligence as a combination of social skills and good memory. And for the Chinese, intelligence involves, among other things, extensive knowledge, determination, social responsibility, and ability for imitation.

A Native American Concept of Intelligence John Berry (1992) extensively studied mental abilities considered valuable among Native Americans. He began by asking

For this Native American teacher and her student, "intelligence" may have a different meaning from that used by Anglo Americans. In the Cree culture, intelligence involves wisdom and respect for others.

adult volunteers among the Cree in northern Ontario to provide him with Cree words that describe aspects of thinking, starting with examples like "smart" or "intelligent." The most frequent responses translate roughly to "wise, thinks hard, and thinks carefully."

Although Cree children attend schools introduced by the dominant Anglo (English-European) culture, the Cree themselves make a distinction between "school" intelligence and the "good thinking" valued in the Cree culture that seems to center on being respectful. As one respondent explained, intelligence "is being respectful in the Indian sense. You need to really know the other person and respect them for what they are" (Berry, 1992, p. 79). This attitude of respect for others is widespread in Native American cultures.

One term Berry's respondents offered as an example of the opposite of intelligence translates as "lives like a White." This refers disparagingly to behaviors the Cree have observed among some Anglo people. The Cree define "lives like a White" as a combination of being "stupid" and having "backwards knowledge." A "stupid" person does not know the necessary skills for survival and does not learn by respecting and listening to elders. One who has "backwards knowledge" disrupts relationships, creating disharmony, instead of encouraging smooth interactions with others. Such disruption is not necessarily intentional or malicious. For example, an English teacher may ask Cree students to write an essay to persuade others to change certain behaviors. However, in Cree culture, the concept of "persuading" interferes with the traditional Cree value of "accepting others as they are." By encouraging such questioning of elders and traditions—a common practice in Anglo education—the teacher promotes disruption, which may be a path to "wisdom" in Anglo culture but is "backward" in Cree views of intelligence.

As you can see from these examples, different cultures have different notions of intelligence. To understand and cooperate with people of diverse heritages, perhaps the most "intelligent" behavior is to resist the impulse to impose our own definition of "intelligence" on others.

The Question of Animal Intelligence

Animals can be taught to perform amazing tricks, as anyone who has ever been to the circus can attest. In the wild, packs of wolves, prides of lions, and pods of killer whales commonly cooperate in making a kill and in raising their young. Even your cat may act with skill and cunning as she herds you toward the kitchen in apparent hope of being fed. But do these feats demonstrate true thinking and intelligence, or merely operant conditioning—the ability to learn from previous consequences—as demonstrated by Thorndike's cats in their escapes from his "puzzle boxes"? 📖

Historically, scientists dismissed the idea of animal cognition as simple trained-animal tricks in disguise—until startling new reports began trickling in from scientists like Jane Goodall. Risking her career—and her life—in the jungles of Tanzania, Goodall spent 30 years watching and recording the behavior of wild chimpanzees (1986). And her gamble paid off handsomely. To give just one example from her long list of discoveries, Goodall reported that chimps strip leaves from twigs and use them to extract tasty morsels from a termite nest. Why was that amazing? She had discovered chimpanzees could make and use tools—an ability requiring forethought and planning, previously believed to set humans apart from the rest of the animal kingdom. Goodall's work, then, raised the provocative question of human uniqueness.

What Abilities Make Humans Unique? If not tool making, what distinctive cognitive abilities might we humans possess? One possibility is a **theory of mind**: the ability to know that our own thoughts may differ from someone else's thoughts. For example, a poker player uses a theory of mind when bluffing. So does a child who lies about raiding the cookie jar. But recent animal research shows the lowly Western scrub jay (a relative of the crow) may also have a theory of mind: When a scrub jay sees another bird watching while it is hiding a grub for a later meal, the jay will return later and re-hide the grub in another location (Dally et al., 2005). So much for human-only theory of mind conjecture!

Perhaps, then, it is *language* that distinguishes humans from animals. But alas for human pride! Animal behaviorist Karl Von Fritsch (1974) showed that a honeybee discovering a new source of nectar uses a language consisting of a "waggle dance," performed along a wall inside the hive, that conveys the direction and distance of the food. Other scientists point out that many animals use distinctive sounds to communicate different "ideas," such as the approach of a predator. But such animal communications have a limited repertoire: Do they qualify as true language? 📖

Language of the Apes One step toward the answer to that question came from researchers Allen and Beatrix Gardner (1969), who taught a chimpanzee named Washoe language skills previously thought to be impossible in nonhuman animals. By "adopting" Washoe when she was just 10 months old and raising her in an environment similar to that of a human child, the Gardners taught Washoe to communicate using American Sign Language (Dewsbury, 1996). By age 5, Washoe could sign some 160 words, and what's more, put them together in "sentences," as when she would declare, "Me Washoe"

📖 **Read** about Thorndike's Cats and Tolman's Rats at **MyPsychLab**

theory of mind   An awareness that other people's behavior may be influenced by beliefs, desires, and emotions that differ from one's own.

CONNECTION CHAPTER 7 ➤

Theory of mind is thought to underlie our human ability to form effective social relationships (p. 287).

📖 **Read** about Theory of Mind in Other Animals at **MyPsychLab**

Kanzi, a bonobo at the Great Ape Trust, not only communicates effectively with researcher Sue Savage-Rumbaugh, but reportedly is quite skilled at the video game Pac-Man, and also enjoys roasting marshmallows.

or request, "Please tickle more." She could even create novel signs in unfamiliar situations, as when she first saw a swan and signed "water bird." And, quite remarkably, she demonstrated emotional intelligence as well: When one of her caretakers, who had missed work for a time following a miscarriage, explained her absence to Washoe by signing, "My baby died," Washoe reportedly looked deep into the caretaker's eyes, then slowly and carefully signed "Cry," touching her cheek. Later that day, when it was time for the caretaker to leave, Washoe resisted, signing "Please person hug" (Fouts, 1997).

A parade of other primates followed in Washoe's footsteps by communicating with sign language, with plastic tokens of various shapes, and even with computers. Some outstripped Washoe by achieving vocabularies of up to 500 words (Savage-Rumbaugh, 1990) and responding to human vocal language in addition to sign language (Rumbaugh & Savage-Rumbaugh, 1994). A bonobo named Kanzi has an impressive language repertoire that includes concept words like *tomorrow* and *from*, as well as some elements of grammar, such as appropriate use of *–ing* and *–ed* to signal tense. When asked "Are you ready to play?" after a visitor who had promised to play with Kanzi finally showed up, Kanzi responded, "Past ready" (Kluger, 2010)—perhaps demonstrating a sense of wry humor in addition to language prowess. And a gorilla named Koko has been caught signing lies (Patterson & Linden, 1981), and even "swearing" at her handler in ASL, making the signs for "dirty toilet." At this point, then, most psychologists are convinced that primates can learn at least the rudiments of human language, perhaps at the level of a 2½-year-old human.

Channels of communication have also opened to a variety of other species. Dolphins have been taught to interpret and respond to complex strings of gestures and sounds. An African gray parrot, who answered to the name of Alex, could not only speak but count up to six objects and understand concepts such as size, giving the correct answers to questions such as "Which one is bigger?" And, not to be outdone, a border collie named Chaser knows the names of more than 1,000 toys and can also classify them by function and shape (Viegas, 2011).

What Are the Lessons of Research on Animal Language and Intelligence?

Without doubt, animals are capable of intelligent behavior, and all but the strictest of behaviorists would acknowledge that many animals are capable of cognition. And these abilities serve them well: Most animals are exquisitely adapted to a particular biological niche, which makes them intelligent in ways that aid their survival. When language is viewed as an adaptive function of a species, animals excel at it—in a manner that suits their species, not ours. Prairie dogs and meerkats signal each other differently in response to different predators; dolphins and whales use sounds and body language to effectively communicate desires to play, hunt, and mate; and even the lowly squid send messages to each other via changes in color and shape. In all these ways, animals communicate effectively, demonstrating species-specific intelligence.

The study of language and problem solving in nonhuman animals has pulled us down from our self-constructed pedestal by demonstrating that other creatures are capable of using what humans define as language at a surprising level of sophistication. Those who worry about maintaining feelings of species superiority, however, can take comfort in the knowledge that human language displays far more grammatical structure and productivity than do languages of other animals—but, to some extent, even that finding may reflect our limited ability to accurately measure animal language. As our research methods evolve, so does our understanding: One species of monkeys in the wild has recently been found to use syntax, a higher-order marker of language defined as the ability to combine units of language (such as sounds or words) in different ways to signal different meanings—much like humans distinguish between "Jesse groomed the dog," and "The dog groomed Jesse" (Outtara et al., 2009). And Chaser the border collie reportedly understands the distinction between nouns and verbs. Although human language abilities have certainly allowed us to grapple with abstract problems far greater than those in the animal world, we must acknowledge the human-centric nature of our perspective and be mindful of the limitations of both our perspective and our methods.

[PSYCHOLOGY MATTERS]

Test Scores and the Self-Fulfilling Prophecy

If you have ever been called "slow," "shy," "plain," "bossy," or "uncoordinated," you know, firsthand, the powerful effect labels and expectations can have. Such labels can influence not only people's beliefs but also their outcomes. Research in psychology sheds light on this fascinating process.

Expectations Influence Student Performance

In Chapter 1, you learned about the power of expectancy bias: Students who were told that they had "smart" rats treated their rats with more enthusiasm and encouragement than did the students who were told their rats were "slow learners," and the differences actually influenced rats' performance on tasks such as maze running. Robert Rosenthal and Lenore Jacobson, the researchers who led that study, wondered if teachers' expectations could similarly affect students' performance.

To find out, they gave grade school teachers erroneous information about the academic potential of about 20 percent of their students (approximately five in each classroom). Specifically, teachers were told some students had been identified by a standardized test as "bloomers" who would blossom academically during the coming year. In fact, testing had revealed no such thing; the "bloomers" had been randomly selected by the experimenters.

Knowing what happened with the rats, you might guess what happened in the classroom. Children whom teachers expected to blossom did exactly that. Further research identified four factors that made the difference (Harris & Rosenthal, 1986): Teachers unknowingly created a more encouraging climate for the students they expected to "bloom," gave them more differentiated feedback and more opportunities to demonstrate their knowledge, and also challenged them with more difficult work. Teachers rated these children as more curious and having more potential for success in life than other children. They also saw these children as happier, more interesting, better adjusted, more affectionate, and needing less social approval. Significantly, at the end of the year, the "bloomers" (who were really just randomly chosen children) made greater gains in IQ points than did students who did not get special treatment. The gains were especially pronounced among first and second graders. Rosenthal and Jacobson call this effect a **self-fulfilling prophecy.** You can see it operating anywhere that people live up to the expectations of others—or of themselves.

self-fulfilling prophecy   Observations or behaviors that result primarily from expectations.

What happened to the other children in these same classrooms—did any of them gain IQ points as well? Tests showed they did, although not as many as "bloomers." But an unexpected, and disturbing, negative correlation surfaced: The more IQ points gained by the students *not* expected to bloom, the less interesting and well-adjusted they were rated by their teachers. Based on that, Rosenthal (2002) cautions that unexpected intellectual growth may create negative responses from others in the environment—a possibility he suggests is worthy of further exploration.

The Self-Fulfilling Prophecy: Beyond the Classroom

Extending the pioneering work of Robert Rosenthal, social psychologists have carried their investigations out of the classroom to find self-fulfilling prophecies in other environments. In the workplace, positive expectations of employees have been found to raise productivity significantly; in the military, positive expectations raise performance to even greater levels than those observed in the private sector (Kierein & Gold, 2000). In jury trials, judges seem to deliver instructions to the jury differently when the judge thinks the suspect is guilty than when the judge perceives innocence—a difference that increases the likelihood of the defendant being found guilty by more than 30 percent (Rosenthal, 2002). And one randomized, double-blind study in a nursing home found that when caregivers had higher expectations, depression rates among patients decreased (Learman et al., 1990). Clearly, expectations from others can exert a powerful psychological influence on our own beliefs and even our outcomes.

Check Your Understanding

✓•─[Study and Review at MyPsychLab

1. **APPLICATION:** In Cattell's theory, the ability to use algorithms and heuristics would be called _____ intelligence.

2. **APPLICATION:** A friend tells you he has found a way to improve his grades by stopping by his psychology professor's office once a week to ask questions about the reading. In Sternberg's triarchic theory, which kind of intelligence is this?

3. **RECALL:** Name one of Gardner's eight intelligences that is also measured on standard IQ tests.

4. **RECALL:** Why does a self-fulfilling prophecy come true?

5. **UNDERSTANDING THE CORE CONCEPT:** Sternberg, Gardner, and others maintain that there are multiple intelligences. What is the position taken by Spearman and others on the opposite side of this argument?

Answers 1. fluid **2.** Practical intelligence **3.** Either linguistic intelligence or logical–mathematical intelligence would be correct. (Some intelligence tests also assess spatial intelligence.) **4.** Expectations: We frequently observe what we expect to see, even when our expectations are erroneous. So if we expect someone to be smart (obnoxious, stupid, pleasant, lazy, and so on), the chances are good that this "prophecy" will fulfill itself. **5.** Although they do not deny that different abilities exist, Spearman and others have argued intelligence involves a single general, or *g*, factor underlying all these special abilities.

6.5 KEY QUESTION
── How Do Psychologists Explain IQ Differences Among Groups?

While we find the full range of IQ scores in every ethnic group, we also find IQ differences among groups (Rushton & Jensen, 2005). In the United States, Americans of Asian extraction score higher, on average, than do Euro-Americans. Hispanics, African Americans, and Native Americans—again, on average—score lower. And we find group differences based on social class as well: Children from middle-income homes score higher on IQ tests than those from low-income homes (Jensen & Figueroa, 1975; Oakland & Glutting, 1990). Nobody disputes that these differences exist. What experts disagree about are the causes of these IQ discrepancies. As we will see, that disagreement is another example of the nature–nurture controversy. Our Core Concept describes the issue this way:

> ### Core Concept 6.5
>
> **While most psychologists agree that both heredity and environment affect intelligence, they disagree on the source of IQ differences among racial and social groups.**

The controversy over the source of intelligence is potentially of great importance for people's lives—and a politically hot issue. And when race becomes involved, such issues become even hotter. Never mind that the concept of distinct human "races" has no precise biological meaning, but rather a social one (Cooper, 2005; Sternberg et al., 2005).

If we assume intelligence is primarily the result of innate (hereditary) factors, we will likely conclude it is fixed and unchangeable. For some, this easily leads to the conclusion that a group (usually a racial group) with low IQ scores must be innately inferior and, perhaps, should be treated as second-class citizens. On the other hand, if we conclude that intelligence is shaped largely by experience (environment), we are more likely to make a range of educational opportunities available for everyone and to view people of all ethnic, cultural, and economic groups as equals. Either way, our conclusion may become a self-fulfilling prophecy.

In actuality, neither the hereditarian nor the environmentalist view is completely right. Repeatedly in this text, we have seen that psychologists now recognize the roles of both heredity and environment in all our behavior and mental processes. But there is more to the issue of group differences than this. In this section, we will add an important complication to the heredity–environment interaction: While each *individual's* intelligence is determined, in part, by heredity, this fact does not mean that IQ differences *among groups* have some biological basis. On the contrary, many psychologists have argued that group differences are totally environmental—although this, too, is disputed, as our Core Concept suggests. Historically, the naturists' side of the IQ question has received most attention—but what does research reveal today?

Intelligence and the Politics of Immigration

In the early 1900s, Henry Goddard, an influential psychologist who believed that intelligence is a hereditary trait, proposed all immigrants undergo tests in order to exclude those found to be "mentally defective" (Strickland, 2000). In 1924, Congress passed legislation to limit immigration of groups and nationalities "proven" to be of inferior intellect—based largely on Goddard's data. Among the groups restricted were Jews, Italians, and Russians. What Goddard and the U.S. Congress ignored was that the tests were given in English—often to people with little familiarity with the English language and the culture in which the tests were conceived. No wonder many of these immigrants received low scores!

At Ellis Island, this customs official attaches labels to the coats of this German family.

Today we are more aware of the shortcomings of intelligence tests. We also know that, while heredity has an effect on an individual's intelligence, experience does too. And we know that Goddard used faulty reasoning when he concluded that heredity accounts for group differences in intelligence. To understand how heredity could affect individual differences but not group differences, let us look first at evidence supporting the hereditarian and environmentalist arguments.

What Evidence Shows That Intelligence Is Influenced by Heredity?

Many lines of research indicate a hereditary influence on intelligence. Studies comparing IQ scores of identical twins with fraternal twins and other siblings show a strong genetic correlation. The gold standard for differentiating the effects of heredity and environment involves looking at children raised by adoptive parents and, in rare cases, twins separated at birth. Such studies reveal that IQs are more closely correlated between children and their biological parents than between children and adoptive parents (Plomin & DeFries, 1998). Work coming out of the Human Genome Project also supports the notion that intelligence has a genetic component, most likely involving the interaction of many genes (Chorney et al., 1998). The trend is clear: The closer the genetic relationship—from cousins to siblings to twins—the closer the relationship of IQ scores, as Table 6.2 shows. In fact, studies of twins and adopted children reveal genetic influences on a whole range of attributes as diverse as heart functioning (Brown, 1990), personality traits (Tellegen et al., 1988), hypnotizability (Morgan et al., 1970), and intelligence (Sternberg et al., 2005).

While psychologists agree that heredity plays an important part in determining an individual's IQ scores, they also agree that it remains difficult to estimate the relative weights of heredity and environment (Sternberg et al., 2005). One reason for this is that children who live in the same family setting do not necessarily share precisely the same psychological environment. First-born children, for example, are treated differently from the youngest. You probably are aware of this fact if you have siblings.

TABLE 6.2 Correlation of IQ Scores with Genetic Relationship

Genetic Relationship	Correlation between IQ Scores
Identical Twins	
Reared together	0.86
Reared apart	0.72
Fraternal Twins	
Reared together	0.60
Siblings	
Reared together	0.47
Reared apart	0.24
Parent/Child	0.40
Foster Parent/Child	0.31
Cousins	0.15

A correlation shows the degree of association between variables—in this case, between the IQs of pairs of individuals. The closer to 1.0, the closer the connection. For example, we can see that the IQ scores of identical twins reared together are more closely correlated (0.86) than the IQs of mere siblings reared together (0.47). The data strongly suggest a genetic component that contributes to intelligence.

Source: Bouchard & McGue. (2003). Familial studies of intelligence: A review. *Science, 212,* 1055–1059. Adapted with permission from AAAS.

What Evidence Shows That Intelligence Is Influenced by Environment?

The evidence for environment influences on intellectual development is persuasive too. For example, in a longitudinal study of 110 children from impoverished homes (Farah et al., 2008), researchers assessed children on both language ability and memory (two important aspects of intelligence). They also evaluated the children's home environments on two factors: (a) How stimulating were they? (judged by the child's access to such things as books and musical instruments) and (b) How nurturing were they? (rated according to observations of positive emotional climate, along with attention and praise given by parents). What the study revealed was a combination of the expected and the unexpected:

- A stimulating environment was strongly associated with language ability but not with memory.
- A nurturing environment was associated with memory but not with language ability.

How can we explain these results? The relationship between parental nurturing and memory mirrors results of animal studies showing that nurturing reduces stress—and since production of stress hormones interferes with memory, it makes sense nurturing might improve memory. The expected connection between environmental stimulation and language ability reinforced results from numerous other studies showing the positive impact of a rich environment on cognitive development. ◉

Watch the **Video** Piano Lessons and Development at **MyPsychLab**

Environmental effects surface even when we look for genetic effects: We find greater similarities of IQ among people who have been reared together than those reared apart. And, in laboratory animals, a stimulus-enriched habitat early in life results in a more complex, complete development of brain cells and cortical regions. The superior performance of these animals on a range of tasks persists through life. In other experiments, we find that young monkeys who are trained to solve problems and also offered companionship from other monkeys display more active curiosity and higher intelligence than those reared without this environmental stimulation.

Such findings hint that we might boost intellectual functioning of human infants by enriching their environments. Indeed, we will see that early intervention programs can raise children's IQ scores (Barlow, 2008). Moreover, the amount of schooling children receive correlates well with their IQ scores (Ceci & Williams, 1997). Even in adulthood, environmental factors, such as the cognitive complexity and intellectual demands of one's job, can influence mental abilities throughout life (Dixon et al., 1985).

Recently, William Dickens and James Flynn (2006) reported the first evidence that the IQ gap between Euro-Americans and African Americans is narrowing—indicating that environment rather than heredity is the cause of the difference. Citing data from large groups on four different IQ tests over the past three decades, they find the gap has narrowed by up to 50 percent—which translates into nearly eight IQ points (Krakovsky, 2007.) There is more evidence for the environmental side of the nature–nurture debate about intelligence, but to understand it, we must pause to explore an important—and often misunderstood—concept: *heritability*.

Heritability (not *Heredity*) and Group Differences

We see, then, that intelligence has a hereditary component. But, just because intelligence can be influenced by heredity—perhaps even a substantial amount—does not mean the environment has no impact (Dickens & Flynn, 2001; Neisser et al., 1996). Moreover, the influence of heredity on individual intelligence does not mean that heredity accounts for differences we observe *between* groups. To understand why this is so, we need to distinguish *heredity* from another important term: *heritability*. Specifically, **heritability** refers to the amount of trait variation within a group that can be attributed to genetic differences.

To illustrate, suppose we examine a group of children all raised in an intellectually stimulating environment, with devoted parents who spent lots of time interacting with them and reading to them—things we know improve intellectual abilities. Among these children, we would find variation in intellectual abilities. Because their environments were essentially the same, however, we could attribute much of the differences in their IQ scores to the effects of heredity. Thus, we could say that *in this group, IQ has high heritability*.

In contrast, suppose we examine a group of children raised in conditions of neglect—given mere custodial care in an orphanage, with no intellectual stimulation from their caregivers. We would most likely find little variance among these children's IQ scores because they are all intellectually stunted. *For this group, IQ would have low heritability*—in other words, the genetic contribution to their IQ was minimized, because the poor environment limited development of their genetic potential.

So the IQ differences between the two groups would be real. But—and this is the important part—*our observations tell us nothing about genetic differences (if any) between the groups*. For all we know, they could have the same genetic potential. Because the environments were so different, we cannot determine what role genetics may have played in the differences between their IQ scores.

Because people are exposed to different cultural traditions and experience different levels of wealth or discrimination, we have no way to evaluate what proportion of differences *between* groups should be attributed to heredity or to environment. To reiterate: *Heritability is a concept that refers to within-group differences, not between-group differences*. Thus, it is important to realize that *we can speak of heritable differences only within a group of individuals who have shared essentially the same environment* (Sternberg et al., 2005).

Another point is worth repeating as well: Biologists, including those working on the Human Genome Project, have determined that "race" is not a valid biological concept (Cooper, 2005; Sternberg et al., 2005). There are no biological boundaries defining different races. Even if we use a social definition, where people define their own racial group, differences between the gene pools of people who claim to be of different racial groups are very small compared to genetic differences among individual members of the same group (Bamshad & Olson, 2003). For all these reasons, then, evidence does not support the notion of genetic differences producing IQ discrepancies we observe among "racial" groups.

The Jensen Controversy Despite the concerns we just cited, some psychologists remain unconvinced that environment can account for group differences in IQ (Nisbett,

heritability The amount of trait variation within a group raised under the same conditions that can be attributed to genetic differences. Heritability tells us nothing about between-group differences.

In the top photo, children are learning in a stimulating environment; thus, because their environment maximized the potential for all of them, we could attribute their individual differences in IQ to their heredity. For these children, IQ would have high heritability.

In the lower photo of children at an impoverished Albanian orphanage, the lack of intellectual stimulation would result in lower IQs for all the children. Thus, since their genetic potential was limited by their impoverished environment, we would say their IQ had low heritability.

2005; Rushton & Jensen, 2005). In the 1960s, for example, Harvard psychologist Arthur Jensen (1969) contended that racial differences in IQ have a substantial genetic basis. We can boost IQ scores to some extent, said Jensen, by helping the poor and disadvantaged, but there are limits imposed by heredity.

In support of his thesis, Jensen cited several studies showing a strong influence of heredity on IQ. He also presented a complex statistical argument showing only weak environmental effects on IQ and achievement. Then, turning his attention to government programs attempting to give extra help to disadvantaged Black children, Jensen claimed that, while most had shown some positive effects, none had erased the racial differences in performance. What remained must be a genetic difference in abilities, he maintained.

Over the next five years, more than 100 published articles responded to Jensen's challenge. In what became a heated debate, critics pointed out several factors Jensen minimized or ignored, including the effects of racism, lower teacher expectations for Black children, lack of opportunity, low self-esteem, and a White, middle-class bias built into IQ and achievement tests (Neisser, 1997; Neisser et al., 1996). While Jensen holds to his original position (Jensen, 1998, 2000), many psychologists now agree that a combination of environmental factors can explain the differences on which Jensen built his case. Let us now look at some of the post-Jensen discoveries, beginning with a study of children whose environment had been altered by adoption.

The Scarr and Weinberg Adoption Study A monumental study by Sandra Scarr and Richard Weinberg (1967, 1978) confronted the issue head-on by comparing 115 Black and White children who were adopted into similar home environments in Minnesota. Their research utilized educational records and IQ test scores from both the biological families and the adoptive families. For both groups of children, the biological parents had average IQ scores (near 100), while the adoptive parents' IQs were somewhat higher, averaging above 115.

What did Scarr and Weinberg find when they reexamined the IQ scores of these two groups of adoptees in late adolescence? There were no differences! Both the Black group and the White group of adoptees had scores that averaged about 110—significantly higher than their biological parents, though not quite as high as their adoptive parents. Such results testify to a powerful effect of the environment on IQ. The results also contradict Jensen's claim that group differences are genetic.

Social Class and IQ Research on the relationship between social class and IQ shows similar environmental effects. Socioeconomic class (as reflected in an individual's financial status and lifestyle) clearly correlates with IQ: Affluence is associated with higher IQ scores, while groups with the lowest average IQ scores experience the greatest degree of poverty, illiteracy, and hopelessness. Supporters of the environmental position claim that racism and discrimination initially landed many minorities in impoverished neighborhoods, and these same factors continue to keep them there today.

How does social class affect IQ? The relationship is not a simple one: The negative effects of growing up in a disadvantaged home far outweigh the benefits of growing up in a wealthy family (Turkheimer et al., 2003). In fact, poverty creates circumstances that limit individual potential in many ways, particularly in terms of nutrition, health care, and education (Brown & Pollitt, 1996; Neisser et al., 1996). Poverty also means less-adequate health care, so it should not surprise you that researchers have linked poor health during pregnancy and low birth weight to low mental ability in children. Research also shows a significant proportion of children with low IQs adversely affected by "environmental insults," such as living in homes with lead-based paint chips peeling from walls, causing toxic lead exposure in children who ingest this material (Needleman et al., 1990). And poverty also means less of other factors known to promote intellectual development, such as good nutrition and access to books and computers. Job schedules leaving parents little time to stimulate a child's intellect correlate with poverty as well, and can be detrimental to performance on tasks such as those demanded by IQ tests (for example, vocabulary or sentence comprehension).

Poverty has other crippling effects too. In most parts of the United States, public schools are funded by revenue from local property taxes. Thus, wealthy neighborhoods can provide bigger and better school facilities and amenities, while poorer districts may suffer from crowding, physically deteriorating structures, threats to personal safety, poorly prepared teachers, and lack of access to computers. In such environments, even children with the aptitude to learn may find it difficult to rise above their circumstances. Proponents of the view that environment has a strong influence on intelligence usually support equal-opportunity legislation, better schools, and intervention programs that help disadvantaged children build self-confidence and learn skills necessary to succeed in school (Tirozzi & Uro, 1997).

Head Start: A Successful Intervention Program   One such intervention program is *Head Start,* originally implemented some 40 years ago to provide educational enrichment for disadvantaged children. It grew from the assumption that many children from deprived families need an intellectual boost to prepare them for school. The program is intended to head off problems on several fronts by serving children's physical and mental needs with nutritional and medical support, plus a year or two of preschool education. Wisely, Head Start also involves parents in making policy, planning programs, working in classrooms, and learning about parenting and child development. Head Start centers around the country currently serve about 900,000 children yearly (U.S. Department of Health and Human Services, 2010)—estimated to be 40 percent of the number who need it (Ripple et al., 1999).

Does it work? Again, there is some controversy (Jensen, 1969; Kantrowitz, 1992), although a great deal of research suggests that Head Start does help disadvantaged children get ready for school (Garces et al., 2002; Ripple & Zigler, 2003). Children enrolled in the program score higher on IQ tests and have higher school achievement during early grades than a matched control group who received no such intervention (Zigler & Styfco, 1994). More important, their head start lasts. Although differences between Head Start children and control group kids diminish over time, the effects persist into adolescence. Among other things, Head Start children are less likely to be placed in special education classes, less likely to fail a grade, more likely to graduate from high school, and less likely to have trouble with the law.

Despite the positive effects of Head Start, newer research indicates programs such as this may not start early enough. Most children in Head Start are preschoolers, but educational intervention starting in the first months of life can raise infants' scores on intelligence tests by as much as 30 percent compared to control groups (Ramey & Ramey, 1998a, 1998b; Wickelgren, 1999). Although gains may diminish with time, especially if supportive programs are withdrawn, significant differences remain when intervention starts in infancy. Clearly, then, the earlier a child is immersed in an enriched environment, the stronger the effects.

Children in Head Start programs develop higher IQs and perform better in school than do children from similar environments who do not attend Head Start programs.

Test Biases and Culture-Fair Tests   Still, other forces influence IQ scores and contribute to group differences, including problems with the IQ tests themselves. Many psychologists have argued that IQ test questions have built-in biases toward a middle- or upper-class background—biases that favor the White child (Helms, 1992). For an opposing view, however, that holds that test bias does *not* contribute to group differences in IQ scores, see Jensen (2000) and Reynolds (2000).

One source of possible bias stems from the fact that most IQ tests rely heavily on vocabulary level. This gives a big advantage to children who have been read to and who are encouraged to read. We can see a related bias in a well-known IQ test that asks for a definition of *opulent* (rich), a term one is far less likely to hear in a poor household. To their credit, however, test makers are working hard to rid their tests of items that discriminate against people of minority cultural backgrounds (Benson, 2003a).

Noted psychologist Janet Helms (1992) points out another possible flaw in current IQ testing: It "assumes that White-American culture defines the most intellectually rich environment" (p. 1086). Seldom do we ask how well White children learn the norms of other cultures—which is a provocative and quite reasonable question. According to Helms, why should the Caucasian American norm be the standard by which everyone else is judged?

Psychologists realize that a culture-free test of ability or achievement is an impossibility. Nevertheless, most agree we should strive for *culture-fair* tests that minimize cultural biases as much as possible. So, for example, attempts are being made to develop non-verbal intelligence tests involving mazes and the manipulation of shapes as a means of overcoming test bias based on the test being constructed in a person's nonnative language.

Given the importance of reducing discrimination, what criticisms could possibly be leveled at the goal of culture-fair tests? First, not all minority groups do poorly on traditional intelligence tests. For example, we have seen that Asian Americans often do better than Americans of European ancestry (Sue & Okazaki, 1990). Second, culture-fair tests do a poorer job than traditional IQ tests of predicting academic success: Because they de-emphasize verbal skills, they fail to assess one of the more important components of school performance (Aiken, 1987; Humphreys, 1988).

The Bell Curve: **Another Hereditarian Offensive**   The dispute over causes of racial differences in IQ flared again in 1994. At issue was a book, *The Bell Curve: Intelligence and Class Structure in American Life,* by Richard Herrnstein and Charles Murray. The name echoes the bell-shaped "normal distribution" of IQ scores (see shape of the graph in Figure 6.10 on page 237). Herrnstein and Murray argued that racial differences in IQ have a strong genetic basis. If these innate differences were accepted, the nation could move on to more enlightened and humane social policies, they said. Critics immediately identified not only a racist bias but pointed to questionable science at the core of *The Bell Curve.*

How is *The Bell Curve*'s argument flawed? The answer will be familiar to you by now: While there is no doubt that heredity influences individual intelligence, Herrnstein and Murray, like hereditarians before them, offered no proof that differences *between groups* exposed to different environments have a hereditary basis (Coughlin, 1994; Fraser, 1995). Further, much of the "evidence" they offer is suspect (Kamin, 1994). One study cited by Herrnstein and Murray claimed to document the low IQs of Black Africans, but it relied on tests given in English—a language in which the Zulu subjects of the study were not fluent (Kamin, 1995). The test used in that study also assumed subjects were familiar with electrical appliances found in urban middle-class homes (rather than Zulu villages) and equipment, such as microscopes, not typically found in Zulu schools.

Compounding the problems in their analysis of the evidence, Herrnstein and Murray commit another critical thinking error we have emphasized in this text: They confuse correlation with causation. In fact, the Herrnstein and Murray argument is just as plausible when turned around: Poverty and all the social and economic disadvantages that go with it could just as well be important causes—rather than results—of low IQ scores.

Despite its flaws, *The Bell Curve* struck a chord with many Americans. It resonates with the preference for simple genetic "causes" for behavior rather than more complex explanations. But not every culture places such emphasis on genetic causes. We can see a different perspective in a study that asked Americans and Asians to account for a child's academic success: American respondents emphasized "innate ability," whereas Asian respondents emphasized the importance of "studying hard" (Stevenson et al., 1993). Thus, the idea that individual and group differences in performance have an innate basis is a widespread belief in American culture. Interestingly, however, Stanford professor Carol Dweck's (2007/2008) work shows that when parents and teachers adopt an approach similar to the Asian view, their children are more interested in school, learn more, and achieve higher grades.

[PSYCHOLOGY MATTERS]

Stereotype Threat

Can you get smarter? Or is your IQ a fixed number? As we have seen, many people believe their "smarts" is a given. But, as Shakespeare once observed, there's the rub: If you think your intelligence is fixed, you will probably live up to your expectations. This is, of course, the expectancy bias and the self-fulfilling prophecy at work.

Psychologists have argued that members of some groups harbor low expectations about the abilities of everyone in their group. These expectations, as you might guess, can adversely affect IQ scores, especially when people are reminded of the stereotype (Schwartz, 1997). Psychologist Claude Steele calls this **stereotype threat** and has amassed a lot of evidence of its negative effect on many members of minority groups, particularly in academic situations (Steele, 1997; Steele et al., 2002). One study found that merely being asked to identify their race resulted in lower scores for minority students on a test of academic abilities (Steele, 1997). In another study, a group of Black women taking an IQ test were told that White women usually do better on the test. As a result of this stereotype threat, these Black women received scores that averaged a full 10 points lower than a comparison group who were told that Black women usually receive high scores (Thomas, 1991).

Stereotype threat is not necessarily a racial or ethnic issue. We find it also in the domain of gender, where girls may learn to feel inferior in science and math, or boys may be taught they have lesser verbal skills. Stereotype threat can also intimidate older persons who worry about memory failure or that as "old dogs" they cannot learn "new tricks." Anyone who believes he or she is part of an inferior group is vulnerable to these feelings of anxiety, intimidation, and inferiority.

Is there a way to combat stereotype threat? Social psychologist Joshua Aronson and his colleagues (2001) found that grades improved for college students who were encouraged to think of intelligence as being influenced by experience and expectations rather than as a fixed trait. The grades of African American students actually rose more than those of White students and those in a control group. Apparently, those who may have felt themselves targets of stereotype threat reaped the most benefits from this program.

stereotype threat   An expectation of being judged by the standard of a negative stereotype. Such expectations can adversely affect performance.

CONNECTION CHAPTER 11

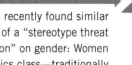

Aronson recently found similar effects of a "stereotype threat intervention" on gender: Women in a physics class—traditionally a male-dominated field—who completed a short affirmation statement of their personal values performed better in the class than a matched set of women in a control group (p. 497).

New research on stereotype threat indicates that inferior performance by women and men in non-traditional fields, as well as by racial minorities in non-traditional fields, may be overcome when stereotypes are eliminated or countered.

Check Your Understanding

✓ **Study** and **Review** at **MyPsychLab**

1. **RECALL:** Did Goddard's view of intelligence place more emphasis on nature (heredity) or nurture (environment)?

2. **ANALYSIS:** What is the position taken by most modern psychologists with regard to intelligence and the heredity–environment issue?

3. **APPLICATION:** Cite one piece of evidence showing that intelligence is influenced by heredity and one piece of evidence that intelligence is influenced by the environment.

4. **RECALL:** Put the words *between* and *within* in the appropriate places in the following statement: Heritability may account for

differences _____ groups but not for differences _____ groups.

5. **APPLICATION:** Give an example of the conditions under which you would you expect stereotype threat to occur.

6. **UNDERSTANDING THE CORE CONCEPT:** Although everyone agrees that heredity produces differences in intelligence among individuals, there is no evidence that it accounts for differences among _____ .

Answers 1. Goddard, along with most early American psychologists interested in intelligence, believed heredity was the most powerful influence on intelligence. **2.** Neither heredity nor environment acts alone: Intelligence involves an interaction of heredity and environmental factors. **3.** Evidence for hereditary influence includes twin studies and correlations of IQs among biological relatives. Evidence for environmental influence includes comparison of siblings reared together versus those reared apart, and the correlation of IQ scores with amount of schooling, and the recent narrowing of the racial IQ gap. **4.** within; between. **5.** Stereotype threat occurs any time people have low expectations of the group to which they belong, especially when they are reminded of those expectations. One example involves women who believe they have low aptitude for math and who are taking a math class, particularly if the teacher raises the issue of gender differences in math. **6.** racial or ethnic groups

CRITICAL THINKING APPLIED

The Question of Gender Differences

In June 2006, Dr. Larry Summers, the president of Harvard University, lost his job, in part because he opined that factors other than socialization—most notably innate intellectual differences—may account for the undisputed fact that men outnumber women in most scientific fields. (Psychology, incidentally, is an exception!) So, what is really going on? A look at the evidence requires some interpretation—based on your critical thinking skills.

What Are the Critical Issues?

It's the nature–nurture controversy: Are the undisputed gender differences we see the result of different ways men and women are socialized? Are they the result of prejudice, discrimination, and lack of opportunity for women who go into science? Or are they the result of different ways that men's and women's brains process information?

Could Bias Contaminate the Conclusion?   Certainly, the first thing that comes to mind is the possibility of bias—on both sides of the issue. In addition to potential problems of "political correctness," we all have a vested interest in making sure our gender doesn't come off looking less smart than the other.

Beyond bias, we should be willing to judge the evidence on its merits and, perhaps, be willing to look at the issue from multiple perspectives. After all, it may be that both sides have a piece of the truth.

What is the Evidence from the "Nurture" Perspective?
After an extensive review of the literature on gender, Janet Shibley Hyde (2007) points out that men and women are far more similar than different on nearly all dimensions studied—a view she calls the *gender similarities hypothesis*. Similarities include such diverse characteristics as mathematical ability, problem solving, reading comprehension, leadership effectiveness, and moral reasoning. But there are a few exceptions, most of which won't surprise you. These include greater male aggression, acceptance of casual sex, and throwing velocity— differences she allows may have biological roots. In general, however, Hyde favors an explanation that emphasizes the different ways that males and females are socialized. One factor may be the whole set of expectations (and limitations) society offers girls as they are growing up. Hyde says the few physical differences between men and women "are important mainly because they are amplified by cultural beliefs and roles."

Further, Hyde cautions, many people tend to believe that any male–female differences we may find in the brains of men and women are "hard wired" and unchangeable. Instead, she urges us to see such differences as rooted in the brain's *plasticity,* by which the very fabric of the brain is altered by experience. In fact, brains seem to be changing: The number of women entering scientific fields has surged dramatically in the last decade, with women now making up, for example, half of the graduating classes at U.S. medical schools (Halpern et al., 2007/2008).

What Is the Evidence from the "Nature" Perspective?
Taking quite a different approach, Roy Baumeister (2007) calls our attention to a different set of facts. He notes that men, as a group, are more *variable* and *extreme* than women—with more men lying at the opposite poles of virtually all mental and behavioral dimensions. Men, he says, seem to outnumber women among both the biggest losers and the biggest winners. Thus, we find more men than women in prisons and homeless shelters and among those with mental retardation—as well as among jazz musicians, scientists (except in psychology), members of Congress, and people whom we call "geniuses." If men go to extremes more than women, says Baumeister, we would find these gender differences, *and yet the averages could be the same.*

Baumeister is quick to point out that he doesn't see one gender as being better than the other—merely that evolution selected different traits in men and women. In general, he says, cultures give the highest payoffs to men who take risks and have the most extreme skills. These extremists, the risk-takers, are also the ones who tend to have the most children, who perpetuate the trend. The situation is quite different for women, Baumeister argues. The evolutionary pressures for women have emphasized playing it safer than men do—which is the smart thing when your opportunities for leaving offspring are biologically much more limited than are men's.

What Conclusions Can We Draw?

Which side to believe? As we noted earlier, both sides may have part of the truth. Both agree that gender differences in abilities are small. Baumeister suggests the gender differences have more to do with motivation (particularly the male willingness to take risks) than with ability, while Hyde maintains the differences are mainly cultural and, therefore, can be shaped. You will have to decide the issue for yourself, but we urge you, as a critical thinker, to be mindful of your own biases. In the end, this issue may have to be seen from multiple perspectives—rather like the changing views of the Necker cube.

Do It Yourself! RATIONAL THINKING ABOUT GENDER DIFFERENCES

Do you remember your favorite toys and games when you were a child? Name two or three of them, and consider how those early preferences might have been influenced by your environment.

For example, did you receive encouragement that guided you toward (or away from) certain games, toys, or activities? Were there opportunities in your school or neighborhood targeted primarily at one gender, to the exclusion of the other? In what ways did these environmental forces shape your preferences—both then and now?

How does your consideration of early influences on your own gender development influence your thinking about the effects of nature and nurture in gender differences?

CHAPTER SUMMARY

((•—[**Listen** to an audio file of your chapter at **MyPsychLab**

CHAPTER PROBLEM: What produces "genius," and to what extent are the people we call "geniuses" different from others?

- Although most people think geniuses are different from ordinary people, little evidence exists to support this view.

- Research indicates that "geniuses" are people with ordinary thought processes who have high degrees of motivation,

extensive knowledge in their field, and certain personality characteristics.

- In addition to those listed above, key components in the formula for becoming a genius include seeking out an area for which you have high aptitude and great enjoyment and then spending a minimum of 10,000 hours developing expertise in that area.

6.1 What Are the Components of Thought?

> **Core Concept 6.1** Thinking is a cognitive process in which the brain uses information from the senses, emotions, and memory to create and manipulate mental representations such as concepts, images, schemas, and scripts.

Cognitive scientists often use the **computer metaphor** to conceive of the brain as an information-processing organ. Thinking is a mental process that forms new mental representations by transforming available information coming from various sources, including the senses, emotions, and memory. **Natural concepts** and **artificial concepts** are building blocks of thinking; they are formed by identifying properties that are common to a class of objects or ideas. Concepts are often arranged in *hierarchies*, ranging from general to specific, but the way they are organized varies across cultures.

Other mental structures that guide thinking include **schemas**, **scripts**, visual imagery, and cognitive maps.

Neuroscientists use brain imaging techniques to study the connections between thought processes and the brain—particularly the frontal lobes. At the same time, other scientists have emphasized the role of emotions in thinking, especially in **intuition**. Schemas and scripts assume special importance in understanding thought because they are mental structures that organize concepts, helping us make sense of new information and events—and underlie a sense of humor. Our schemas and scripts are influenced by culture.

artificial concepts (p. 216)
computer metaphor (p. 214)
concept hierarchies (p. 216)
concepts (p. 216)
intuition (p. 220)
natural concepts (p. 216)
prototype (p. 216)
script (p. 222)

6.2 What Abilities Do Good Thinkers Possess?

[Core Concept 6.2 **Good thinkers not only have a repertoire of effective strategies, called algorithms and heuristics, they also know how to avoid the common impediments to problem solving and decision making.**]

Two of the most crucial thinking skills involve *identifying the problem* and *selecting a problem-solving strategy*. Useful strategies include **algorithms**, which produce a single correct answer, and **heuristics**, or "rules of thumb." Among the most useful heuristics are *working backward, searching for analogies,* and *breaking a bigger problem into smaller problems.* Common obstacles to problem solving include **mental set, functional fixedness,** and *self-imposed limitations.*

Judgment and *decision making* can be flawed by biases and faulty heuristics. These include the *confirmation bias,* **hindsight bias, anchoring bias, representativeness bias,** and **availability bias.** Judgment can also be affected by factors outside the person, such as the **tyranny of choice.** In general,

good decision makers are those who use good critical thinking skills.

People who are often called "creative geniuses" are highly motivated **experts** who often have a certain cluster of traits, such as independence and a need for stimulating interaction. They appear, however, to use ordinary thinking processes, although the role of natural talent is a subject of dispute.

algorithms (p. 224)
anchoring bias (p. 228)
aptitudes (p. 230)
availability bias (p. 229)
base rate information (p. 229)
creativity (p. 230)
experts (p. 230)
functional fixedness (p. 226)
heuristics (p. 224)
hindsight bias (p. 227)
mental set (p. 225)
representativeness bias (p. 228)
tyranny of choice (p. 229)

6.3 How Is Intelligence Measured?

[Core Concept 6.3 **Intelligence testing has a history of controversy, but most psychologists now view intelligence as a normally distributed trait that can be measured by performance on a variety of tasks.**]

The measurement of *intelligence* is both common and controversial. Assessment of mental ability has an ancient human history but was not based on scientific practice until the 20th century. In 1904, Binet and Simon developed the first workable test of intelligence, based on the assumption that education can modify intellectual performance.

In America, IQ testing became widespread for the assessment of Army recruits, immigrants, and schoolchildren. The original

IQ calculation was abandoned in favor of standard scores based on the **normal distribution.** Today, IQ tests come in both individual and group forms. They are typically used to diagnose learning disabilities and to assess whether a child is eligible for special education classes. In particular, IQ scores are a key ingredient in identifying **mental retardation** and **giftedness,** which are often seen as occupying the extremes of the IQ distribution.

chronological age (CA) (p. 235)
giftedness (p. 239)
intelligence (p. 234)
intelligence quotient (IQ) (p. 236)
mental age (MA) (p. 235)
mental retardation (p. 239)
normal distribution (or normal curve) (p. 237)
normal range (p. 238)

6.4 Is Intelligence One or Many Abilities?

[Core Concept 6.4 **Some psychologists believe that intelligence comprises one general factor, g, while others believe that intelligence is a collection of distinct abilities.**]

Among the first *psychometric theories* of intelligence, Spearman's analysis emphasized a single, common factor known as *g.* Later, Cattell separated *g* into two components: **fluid intelligence** and **crystallized intelligence.** Modern cognitive psychologists conceive of intelligence as a combination of several abilities.

In particular, Gardner and Sternberg have taken the lead in extending the definition of intelligence beyond school-related tasks. Sternberg's **triarchic theory** proposes **analytic, creative,** and **practical intelligences,** while Gardner's theory of **multiple intelligences** has claimed eight components of intelligence. Meanwhile, cross-cultural psychologists have shown that "intelligence" has different meanings in different cultures. A century of research shows that animals, too, are capable of intelligent behavior, as in chimpanzees that make tools and use language. Recent work also shows that some animals may have a **theory of mind.**

In the United States, much emphasis is placed on mental tests. In such a climate, however, a big danger lies in test scores becoming mere labels that influence people's behavior through the **self-fulfilling prophecy.**

analytical intelligence (p. 243)
creative intelligence (p. 244)
crystallized intelligence (p. 243)
fluid intelligence (p. 243)
***g* factor** (p. 243)

multiple intelligences (p. 244)
practical intelligence (p. 243)
savant syndrome (p. 242)
self-fulfilling prophecy (p. 249)
theory of mind (p. 247)
triarchic theory (p. 244)
wisdom (p. 244)

6.5 How Do Psychologists Explain IQ Differences among Groups?

[**Core Concept 6.5** While most psychologists agree that both heredity and environment affect intelligence, they disagree on the source of IQ differences among racial and social groups.]

Hereditarian arguments maintain that intelligence is substantially influenced by genetics, a belief endorsed at one time by the U.S. government, which used IQ tests to restrict immigration early in the 20th century. *Environmental* approaches argue that intelligence can be dramatically shaped by influences such as health, economics, and education. While most psychologists now agree that intelligence is *heritable,* they also know that **heritability** refers to variation within a group and does not imply that between-group differences are the result of hereditary factors.

The dispute over the nature and nurture of group differences in intelligence flared again in 1969, when Jensen argued that the evidence favored a strong genetic influence. This argument was echoed in the 1994 book *The Bell Curve.* Critics have pointed out that much of the research cited by those taking the extreme hereditarian position is flawed. In addition, intelligence testing itself may be biased in favor of those with particular language and cultural experiences. Hereditarian claims, however, have stimulated much research, such as Scarr and Weinberg's research on adopted children and follow-up studies of the Head Start program. This research suggests that the racial and class differences in IQ scores can be attributed to environmental differences and to the influence of low expectations and negative stereotypes, as found in stereotype threat.

heritability (p. 253)
stereotype threat (p. 257)

CRITICAL THINKING APPLIED

The Question of Gender Differences

While the topic of gender differences remains hotly contested, supporters of both sides of the issue agree that the differences—compared to the similarities—are quite small and may be influenced by both nature and nurture.

DISCOVERING PSYCHOLOGY **VIEWING GUIDE**

Watch the following videos by logging into MyPsychLab (www.mypsychlab.com).
After you have watched the videos, answer the questions that follow.

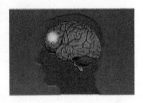

PROGRAM 10: **COGNITIVE PROCESSES**

PROGRAM 11: **JUDGMENT AND DECISION MAKING**

PROGRAM 16: **TESTING AND INTELLIGENCE**

Program Review

1. Michael Posner's work on brain imaging showed
   a. major differences between the brains of young and old adults, with cognitive processes more localized in brains of the elderly.
   b. that blood flow decreases in the brain as thinking becomes more efficient.
   c. that electrical stimulation of the brain can enhance performance on logic puzzles reliably.
   d. that patterns of brain activity differ in predictable ways when people see words versus read them aloud versus name the function of the objects to which they refer.

2. A cognitive psychologist would be most interested in which one of the following issues?
   a. how you decide which answer is correct for this question
   b. how pain stimuli are processed
   c. maturation of the efferent system
   d. how to distinguish mania from schizophrenia

3. What is one's prototype of a tree most likely to be similar to?
   a. a maple tree
   b. a palm tree
   c. a Christmas tree
   d. a dead tree

4. According to the program, why do people assume that Montreal is farther north than Seattle?
   a. because we have learned it
   b. because we are less familiar with Montreal than with Seattle
   c. because Canada is north of the United States in our mental maps
   d. because we are not good at making such judgments

5. What is one way in which human problem solving appears to be quite different from the way computers solve problems?
   a. Humans can solve problems that don't involve numbers.
   b. Humans are more logical in their approach to problems.
   c. Humans have trouble when content is unfamiliar.
   d. Humans are less likely to be misled by bias.

6. What is a cognitive illusion?
   a. a mental map that we can scan for information
   b. a biased mental strategy
   c. a concept formed on the basis of a perceptual illusion
   d. a decision motivated by emotion

7. How did Freud explain the fact that human beings sometimes make irrational decisions?
   a. They are driven by primitive needs.
   b. They are influenced by the emotions of the crowd.

c. They are basing their decisions on availability.

d. They are using standard human mental processes.

8. Why would smokers be likely to underestimate the chance of developing lung cancer?

a. They do not dread the disease.

b. It is an unfamiliar risk.

c. It is not representative.

d. It represents a delayed consequence.

9. Irving Janis studied how the decision to invade Cuba was made during the Kennedy administration. What advice does Janis offer to promote better decision making?

a. Encourage groupthink by team-building exercises.

b. Appoint one group member to play devil's advocate.

c. Restrict the size of the group.

d. Assume that silence means consent on the part of all group members.

10. How does cognitive dissonance make us feel?

a. We are so uncomfortable that we try to reduce the dissonance.

b. We enjoy it so much that we actively seek dissonance.

c. Our reaction to dissonance depends largely on personality.

d. It creates boredom, which we try to overcome.

11. You read the following sentences: "Mary heard the ice cream truck. She remembered her birthday money and ran into the house." What allowed you to understand how these sentences are related?

a. a cognitive illusion

b. reasoning by analogy

c. a schema

d. the anchoring heuristic

12. According to Robert Glaser, intelligence is

a. a skill and can be developed.

b. genetically determined.

c. a myth.

d. no higher in humans than it is in chimpanzees and bonobos.

13. Greg is visiting a foreign country that is known for its current political unrest, and he has seen news reports over the past week about tourists being kidnapped. Although his chances of being killed in a car accident during his vacation are higher than his chances of being killed by terrorists, he believes the opposite. What cognitive process is behind his error?

a. representativeness heuristic

b. availability heuristic

c. anchoring and adjustment heuristic

d. framing heuristic

14. What is the goal of psychological assessment?

a. to derive a theory of human cognition

b. to see how people vary in ability, behavior, and personality

c. to measure the stages of growth in intellectual abilities

d. to diagnose psychological problems

15. What was Binet's aim in developing a measure of intelligence?

a. to identify children in need of special help

b. to show that intelligence was innate

c. to weed out inferior children

d. to provide an empirical basis for a theory of intelligence

16. What formula did Terman create to express intelligence?

a. $MA/CA = IQ$

b. $MA \times CA = IQ$

c. $CA/MA \times 100 = IQ$

d. $MA/CA \times 100 = IQ$

17. The attempt by neuroscientists to find biologically based measures of intelligence rests on the assumption that intelligence involves

a. multiple factors.

b. cultural learning.

c. speed of adaptation.

d. high excitability.

18. The growing practice of "teaching for tests" creates the possibility of

a. lessened ecological validity (i.e., the test doesn't tell us how the subject might perform in the real world).

b. eliminating stereotype threat.

c. lowered reliability.

d. eliminating genetic influences on intelligence.

19. Standardized intelligence tests typically

a. overvalue verbal ability.

b. give too much value to creative problem solving.

c. are biased to give exceptionally high scores to people from other cultures.

d. are the best available predictors of life success.

20. What we have learned about intelligence over the years is that it is not

a. complex.

b. influenced by environment.

c. a singular process.

d. culturally defined.

7

Development Over the Lifespan

CHAPTER PROBLEM Do the amazing accounts of similarities in twins reared apart indicate we are primarily a product of our genes? Or do genetics and environment work together to influence growth and development over the lifespan?

CRITICAL THINKING APPLIED The Mozart Effect

WHAT COULD GRAB MEDIA INTEREST MORE THAN A STORY OF TWINS separated at birth and reunited as adults? Many such tales have emerged from psychologist Thomas Bouchard's famous twin-study project at the University of Minnesota. But what really attracts journalists are reports of uncanny similarities between identical twins raised by different parents, taught by different teachers, influenced by different peers and siblings, and sometimes even raised in different cultures.

Take, for example, the "Jim Twins." Separated just a few weeks after they were born, identical twins Jim Springer and Jim Lewis were adopted separately and raised apart. Yet something drove them on parallel paths, even though those paths didn't cross again for 39 years. At their reunion, the "Jim twins" discovered some remarkable similarities in their habits, preferences, and experiences. Some examples:

- They achieved nearly identical scores on tests of personality, intelligence, attitudes, and interests.
- Medically, both have mildly high blood pressure and have had spells that they mistakenly thought were heart attacks; both have had vasectomies; both suffer from migraine headaches.
- Both chain-smoke Salem cigarettes and drink Miller Lite beer.
- Both had been indifferent students: Jim Lewis dropped out in the tenth grade, while Jim Springer managed to graduate from high school.

- Both had been married twice, and both of their first wives were named Linda. Both of their second wives were named Betty. Both men leave love notes around the house.
- Lewis had three sons, including one named James Alan. Springer had three daughters, plus a son named James Allan.
- Both had owned dogs named Toy.
- Both drive Chevrolets, chew their fingernails, like stock-car racing, and dislike baseball.
- Both had been sheriff's deputies.
- Both do woodworking as a hobby. Lewis likes to make miniature picnic tables, and Springer makes miniature rocking chairs. Both had built white benches around trees in their yards.

When he first read about the two Jims in a newspaper, Bouchard knew their case presented a rare opportunity to study the relative effects of heredity and environment and how they unfold over time in the process we call development (Holden, 1980a,b; Lykken et al., 1992). The Jims agreed to participate and thus became the first of some 115 pairs of reunited twins (plus four sets of reared-apart triplets) to be studied over the next 20 years at the University of Minnesota.

Another remarkable pair, Oskar Stör and Jack Yufe, was also separated at birth, and from that point on their lives went in almost unbelievably different directions. Stör was raised by his grandmother in Czechoslovakia and attended a Nazi-run school during World War II, while Yufe was taken to Trinidad and raised as a Jew by his biological father. Oskar is now married, a strong union man, and a devoted skier, while Jack is separated, a businessman, and a self-styled workaholic. Still, alongside these huge differences, researchers found some striking similarities in seemingly trivial behavior patterns. Both twins wear neatly clipped moustaches; both read magazines from back to front; both have a habit of storing rubber bands on their wrists; both flush the toilet before using it; both like to dunk buttered toast in coffee; and both think it is funny to sneeze loudly in public.

PROBLEM: Do the amazing accounts of similarities in twins reared apart indicate we are primarily a product of our genes? Or do genetics and environment work together to influence growth and development over the lifespan?

As compelling as these stories are, we must interpret them with care (Phelps et al., 1997). Let's begin that interpretation by putting on our critical thinking caps and asking some important questions:

- Are these twin stories representative of all twins reared apart, or are they exceptional cases?
- When we notice striking similarities between biological relatives—whether they be twins, siblings, or parent–child relationships—what factors other than genetics might account for these similarities?
- Are there methods by which we can reliably tease out the differences between the genetic contributions and the influences of the environment to make an accurate determination of the relative contribution of each?

These fascinating questions are just part of what we'll explore in our study of human development across the lifespan. Broadly speaking, **developmental psychology** is the psychology of growth, change, and consistency from conception to death. It asks how thinking, feeling, and behavior change through infancy, childhood, adolescence, and adulthood. It examines these changes from multiple perspectives—physical, emotional, cognitive, and sociocultural. *The primary questions for developmental psychologists, then, are these: How do individuals predictably change throughout the lifespan, and what roles do heredity and environment play in these changes?*

developmental psychology   The psychological specialty that studies how organisms grow and change over time as the result of biological and environmental influences.

This issue of heredity and environment is important, so let's take a closer look at it. Psychologists call this the **nature–nurture issue**: As you know from Chapters 2 and 4, *nature* refers to the contribution of our heredity, whereas *nurture* refers to the role of our environment. In earlier years, the nature–nurture question was an either-or question, but modern researchers have a more sophisticated understanding of this complex issue (Bronfenbrenner & Ceci, 1994; Dannefer & Perlmutter, 1990). Today, the nature–nurture issue recognizes that both nature and nurture play a role in almost all aspects of human behavior, and it now questions (1) what the relative weight of each of these factors is and (2) how the two factors might interact to ultimately produce a given characteristic.

What do we mean by interact? Simply put, *nature–nurture interaction* means we are all born with certain predispositions (*nature*) that, if exposed to the proper experiences in our environment (*nurture*), can reach their full potential. If you are good at, say, math or music, your ability is really the result of a combination of genetic potential and experience. Heredity establishes your potential, but experience determines if and how your potential will be realized. To put it yet another way: Nature proposes, and nurture disposes.

Still, we may ask, "Which of our traits does heredity affect most? And which are most heavily influenced by learning or other environmental factors (such as disease or nutrition)?" More and more information is available to help answer these questions, and we will explore this puzzle throughout this chapter. We must, however, be cautious in our interpretation of these findings. For example, we know that in the genetic disorder known as Down syndrome, biology has a very strong influence. In this condition, the output of abnormal chromosomes leads to mental retardation—and there is no cure. But there is hazard in knowing this: Parents or teachers of children with such disorders may erroneously conclude that biology determines the child's destiny and give up hope. By focusing on the genetic side of the disorder, they may overlook effective learning-based treatments that can measurably improve the living skills of individuals with this disorder.

Mindful of such dangers, psychologists have nonetheless forged ahead in the study of hereditary and environmental contributions to thought and behavior. To do so, they have invented several clever methods for weighing the effects of nature and nurture. **Twin studies** represent one such method. The work of Thomas Bouchard, for example, offers some tantalizing clues about the relative contribution of nature and nurture: In this type of situation, any similarities between the two are likely a result of shared heredity, since they did not share a common environment growing up. This type of twin set, however, is a scarce resource. Far more common are twin sets raised together, and fortunately, psychologists have figured out how to learn from these twins as well. Because *identical twins* have essentially the same genotype and *fraternal twins* have (on the average) only 50 percent of their genes in common, hereditary effects show up more strongly in identical twins. (In studies comparing these two twin types, the fraternal twins serve as a sort of control group.) Such studies have given us valuable information on the role of genetics in a variety of mental and behavioral disorders, including alcoholism, Alzheimer's disease, schizophrenia, depression, and autism (Muhle, 2004; Plomin et al., 1994).

Another method used to measure the effects of heredity and environment involves **adoption studies**. If you adopted a baby, whom would he or she resemble most as an adult: you, or the biological parents? Researchers in adoption studies compare the characteristics of adopted children with those of their biological and adoptive family members. Similarities with the biological family point to the effects of nature, while similarities with the adoptive family suggest the influence of nurture. This work, in concert with twin studies, has revealed genetic contributions to a variety of psychological characteristics such as intelligence, sexual orientation, temperament, and impulsive behavior—all of which we will learn about in more detail in the pages to come (Alanko, et al., 2010; Bouchard, 1994; Dabbs, 2000).

nature–nurture issue The long-standing discussion over the relative importance of nature (heredity) and nurture (environment) in their influence on behavior and mental processes.

Harry Potter is a good illustration of the nature–nurture interaction. Born to pure-bloods (parents with magical powers) but raised by muggles (people without magical abilities), his own magic didn't flourish until he entered the magic-supporting environment of Hogwarts School.

twin study A means of separating the effects of nature and nurture by which investigators may compare identical twins to fraternal twins or compare twins separated early in life and raised in different environments.

CONNECTION CHAPTER 1

The control group in a study serves as a standard against which other groups can be compared (p. 27).

adoption study A method of separating the effect of nature and nurture by which investigators compare characteristics of adopted children with those of individuals in their biological and adoptive families.

7.1 KEY QUESTION
What Innate Abilities Does the Infant Possess?

People used to think babies began life as a "blank slate"—with an empty brain and no abilities. In modern times, however, that picture has changed. We now see that newborns possess a remarkable set of abilities acquired through their genes. They are adept at locating food and avoiding potential harm, and their social nature facilitates their survival as well. We focus on these inborn or **innate abilities** in the Core Concept for this section:

innate ability   Capability of an infant that is inborn or biologically based.

> ### Core Concept 7.1
>
> Newborns have innate abilities for finding nourishment, avoiding harmful situations, and interacting with others—all of which are genetically designed to facilitate survival.

To be sure, the newborn's capabilities are limited, but they are effective enough to promote survival. You arrived in the world already "knowing," for example, how to get nourishment by suckling, how to raise your hands to shield your eyes from bright light, and how to get attention by cooing and crying. Still, it is helpful to think of the newborn's basic abilities as a sort of scaffold to which new and more complex abilities are added as the child grows and develops.

To explain where these abilities come from and how they develop, we will organize our discussion around three important developmental periods: the *prenatal period,* the newborn or *neonatal period,* and *infancy.* You will notice that, in each phase, development builds on the abilities and structures laid down earlier.

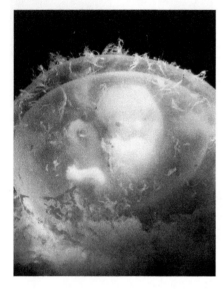

As the brain grows in the developing embryo, it forms as many as 250,000 new neurons per minute.

prenatal period   The developmental period before birth.

Prenatal Development

The **prenatal period** is a time of furious developmental activity between conception and birth that readies the organism for life on its own outside the womb. Development typically occurs over the span of nine months and is divided into three phases: the germinal, embryonic, and fetal stages.

zygote   A fertilized egg.

embryo   In humans, the name for the developing organism during the first 8 weeks after conception.

Three Phases of Prenatal Development   Shortly after conception, the fertilized egg, also known as a **zygote**, begins to grow through cell division. During this *germinal phase,* one cell becomes two; two become four; and when the number reaches about 150—a mere week or so after conception—the zygote implants itself in the lining of the uterus. At this point, it (along with cells that will form the *placenta* and other supportive structures) becomes an **embryo**. It is now connected to the mother's body and thus affected by anything she eats or drinks or to which she is otherwise exposed.

During the *embryonic phase,* the genetic plan determines how all the organs that will ultimately be part of the newborn start to form. In a process known as differentiation, the embryo's cells begin to specialize as components of particular organ systems. (Before differentiation, certain cells in the embryo, known as embryonic stem cells, are capable of forming into any organ of the body.) One example of differentiation is the development of anatomical sex: If the embryo's genetic plan contains two X chromosomes, the child will be female, but if it contains an X and a Y chromosome, a male will develop.

Read about an Embryo's Beginning at **MyPsychLab**

After the eighth week, the developing embryo is called a **fetus**. In the *fetal stage,* spontaneous movements and basic reflexes begin to appear. For example, as early as 14 weeks, some babies can be seen on ultrasound to curve their hands around something that comes in contact with their palm (Sparling et al., 1999). This is the beginning of the grasping reflex, and it has adaptive significance. By the 16th week, the brain is fully formed and the fetus can feel pain (Anand & Hickey, 1987). The baby can hear sounds from outside the womb by the 27th week, enabling the ability to recognize certain sounds and rhythms shortly after birth. The brain will continue to develop, growing

fetus   In humans, the term for the developing organism between the embryonic stage and birth.

new neurons at an amazing rate of up to 250,000 per minute. At birth, the newborn's brain contains some 100 billion neurons (Dowling, 1992).

Teratogens: Prenatal Toxins During prenatal development, the **placenta** is the organ that surrounds the embryo/fetus. It serves as a conduit between mother and child, letting nutrients in and waste out, and it can also screen out some—but not all—potentially harmful substances. Some toxic substances, called **teratogens**, still get in and can cause irreparable damage. Teratogens include viruses (such as HIV, the AIDS virus), certain drugs and other chemicals, and even some herbs. Among the most common teratogens are nicotine and alcohol.

Fetal alcohol syndrome (FAS) can occur in children of mothers who drink alcohol during pregnancy. A leading cause of mental retardation, FAS may also cause babies to have poor motor coordination, impaired attention, and hyperactivity. Mothers who consume one or more drinks per day risk fetal alcohol exposure, which has been found to impair development of language ability, memory, learning, and a host of other cognitive and physical functions (Office of the Surgeon General, 2005). Furthermore, a series of studies at the University of Pittsburgh indicates that even minimal exposure—in some cases fewer than five drinks per week—can result in lower IQ and significantly retarded physical development: At age 14, children who had been exposed to even light alcohol consumption in utero weighed on average 16 pounds less than children whose mothers had abstained from alcohol during pregnancy (Day, 2002; Willford, 2006).

Exposure to nicotine, as well as some commonly taken herbs and supplements, can also damage the developing fetus. Women who smoke during pregnancy are more likely to have children with lower birth weight, learning deficits, and ADHD (Button et al., 2005). Maternal smoking is also associated with greater risk of sudden infant death syndrome (SIDS; Bruin et al., 2007). Even some popular herbal remedies and supplements, such as gingko and ginseng, have been found to have detrimental effects on a developing fetus (Chan et al., 2003; Dugoua et al., 2006). ◉

The Neonatal Period: Abilities of the Newborn Child

By the time a newborn arrives in the world, then, a great deal of neural and sensory development has already taken place. (The term **neonatal period** refers to the first month after birth.) This current understanding of the newborn's sensory awareness is a far cry from the "great blooming, buzzing confusion" experts once thought characterized the newborn's world (James, 1950/1890). Indeed, more recent research has revealed that newborns have all five senses working, as well as a variety of behavioral reflexes they use to respond to and manipulate their environment. Together, these many abilities effectively help newborns survive and thrive in their environment.

Sensory Abilities in the Newborn What exactly can newborns do with their senses? For one thing, they can respond to taste: the sweeter the fluid, the more continuously and forcefully an infant will suck (Lipsitt et al., 1976). For another, they smile when they smell banana essence, and they prefer salted to unsalted cereal (Bernstein, 1990; Harris et al., 1990). They recoil, however, from the taste of lemon or shrimp and the smell of rotten eggs. And, as early as 12 hours after birth, they show distinct signs of pleasure at the taste of sugar water or vanilla. All these responses are part of the newborn's ability to seek healthy nourishment—as the Core Concept for this section suggests.

Just as heredity biases newborns' tastes, it also programs a preference for human faces to most other visual patterns (Fantz, 1963). Even their neonatal nearsightedness helps: Their optimal focus of about 12 inches is ideally suited for looking at faces. By just a few days after birth, neonates recognize their mother's face. Their distance vision, however, is poor, with a visual acuity of about 20/500 (which means that they can discriminate at 20 feet stimuli that most older children can see clearly at 500 feet). These immature systems develop very rapidly (Banks & Bennett, 1988), however, and by about seven weeks, infants' visual pathways and motor coordination enable them to maintain eye contact with a caregiver—an important element in establishing a relationship.

placenta The organ interface between the embryo or fetus and the mother. The placenta separates the bloodstreams, but it allows the exchange of nutrients and waste products.

teratogen Substances from the environment, including viruses, drugs, and other chemicals, that can damage the developing organism during the prenatal period.

fetal alcohol syndrome (FAS) A set of physical and mental problems seen in children whose mothers drink excessive amounts of alcohol during pregnancy.

◉ **Watch** the **Video** The Effects of Prenatal Smoking on Children's Development at **MyPsychLab**

neonatal period In humans, the neonatal (newborn) period extends through the first month after birth.

What else can newborns do with their senses? Although they can see colors, their ability to differentiate colors, such as red from orange from blue, becomes dramatically better a month or two after birth (Teller, 1998). They also prefer to look at objects with a high degree of contrast, such as checkerboards, or target shapes. By 3 months, babies can perceive depth and are well on their way to enjoying the visual abilities of adults. Moreover, it may surprise you to know that infants seem to possess some basic mathematical ability. In one clever study, infants watched dolls being put into and taken out of a display case. When the display case subsequently contained a number of dolls inconsistent with what the infants had observed, they gazed longer at that case, indicating greater interest in an unexpected outcome—as if they were trying to figure out something that didn't make sense (Wynn, 1992, 1995). Such core knowledge serves as the foundation for the later development of more complex skills, such as those required for arithmetic (Spelke, 2000).

Newborns also have strong auditory preferences, preferring human voices over other sounds, and the sounds and rhythms of their own language to nonnative languages (Goodwyn & Acredolo, 2000). Before assuming these preferences genetic, though, we must recall that the developing fetus can hear sounds from outside the womb during the last few months in utero. Thus, an alternate interpretation is that these auditory preferences result from prior exposure to human voices in their native language. To test whether these preferences are genetic or environmental, one study had expectant mothers read *The Cat in the Hat* aloud twice a day for the last six weeks of their pregnancy; then, after the babies were born, the researchers played audiotapes of the mothers reading that story as well as a different story. The findings? Babies expressed an overwhelming preference for the sound of the familiar story being read over the sound of a different story. Neonates also display greater attraction to female voices than to those of men, and within a few weeks of birth they begin to recognize their mothers' voice (Carpenter, 1973; DeCasper & Spence, 1986). Thus, nurture—by way of prior experience—may be the driving force behind these newborn auditory preferences.

Read about Newborns and Their Preferences at **MyPsychLab**

Social Abilities   Have you ever noticed that if you stick your tongue out at a baby, he will stick his tongue out back at you? This delightful game reveals just one of many behaviors newborns and infants will mimic. While in the past, some child development experts wondered if this reflected an in-depth cognitive understanding of the other person's behavior, the recent discovery of *mirror neurons* offers a more likely explanation. **Mimicry** of a variety of behaviors, like other innate abilities we have discussed, helps the infant survive and thrive in the environment.

As the foregoing discussion suggests, infants are built for social interaction. In fact, they not only respond to, but also interact with, their caregivers from the moment of birth. Film studies of this interaction reveal an amazing degree of **synchronicity:** close coordination between the gazing, vocalizing, touching, and smiling of infants and mothers or other caregivers (Martin, 1981). And while babies respond and learn, they also send out their own messages to those willing to listen to and love them. The result of this interaction is seen in studies showing how the expressions of mothers and infants are coordinated (Fogel, 1991). So, a 3-month-old infant may laugh when her mother laughs and frown or cry in response to her display of negative emotion (Tronick et al., 1980). These early interactions, the combined result of nature (mirror neurons) and nurture (positive reinforcement gained from mimicry), form the basis for the later development of empathy.

Innate Reflexes   Aside from their sensory abilities and mimicry, babies are born with a remarkable set of **innate reflexes** providing a biological platform for later development. Among these reflexes, the *postural reflex* allows babies to sit with support, and the *grasping reflex* enables them to cling to a caregiver. The *rooting reflex* is apparent when newborns turn their heads toward anything that strokes their cheeks—a nipple or a finger—and begin to suck it. And if you have ever noticed that when you hold a baby upright over a solid surface, her legs will lift up as if she were marching, you've

---

CONNECTION CHAPTER 2

Although research on mirror neurons is still in the early stages, we do know that when we see a person performing some kind of action, our own brain activates in the same region as if we were performing the action ourselves (p. 70).

mimicry   The imitation of other people's behaviors.

synchronicity   The close coordination between the gazing, vocalizing, touching, and smiling of infants and caregivers.

innate reflex   Reflexive response present at birth.

witnessed the *stepping reflex,* which helps prepare a baby to walk. There are also a number of reflexes that act as built-in safety features to help them avoid or escape from loud noises, bright lights, and painful stimuli. And in their cooing, smiling, and crying, babies have perhaps their most effective tools for building social relationships. All of this, of course, makes much evolutionary sense because these abilities are highly adaptive and promote survival.

Infancy: Building on the Neonatal Blueprint

Following the neonatal period, the child enters **infancy,** a period that lasts until about 18 months of age—the time when speech begins to become better developed. (The Latin root *infans* means "incapable of speech.") It is a time of rapid, genetically programmed growth and still-heavy reliance on the repertoire of reflexes and "instinctive" behaviors that we discussed earlier. All of these abilities arise from a nervous system that continues to develop at a breathtaking pace.

Neural Development While the prenatal brain focused on producing new brain cells, many of the neurons are not fully connected to each other at birth. Stimulation from the environment assumes an important role in creating and consolidating connections. Each time an infant is exposed to a new stimulus, dendrites and axons actually grow and branch out to facilitate connections between the neurons involved in that experience (Kolb, 1989). The more frequently the fledgling neural connections are utilized, the more permanent they become. In other words, "neurons that fire together, wire together" (Courchesne et al., 1994).

Sensitive Periods The early years are the most fertile time for brain development in many areas, including language and emotional intelligence. In fact, in some domains—such as hearing and vision—stimulation must occur during a specific "window of opportunity," or the ability will not develop normally (Lewis & Maurer, 2005; Trainor, 2005). This is called a **sensitive period** in development. Evidence for sensitive periods comes from, for example, a study of adults who were born profoundly deaf. Some of them learned American Sign Language (ASL) early in life, whereas others didn't learn it until much later. Those who didn't learn ASL—their first learned language—until adolescence or adulthood never reached the level of competency with the language as did children who learned it in early childhood (Mayberry, 1991; Singleton & Newport, 2004). You might feel some connection to this finding if you ever tried to learn a new language as an adult—it was probably far more difficult than it would have been if you'd learned it as a child!

Brain Development As the dendrites and axons grow and connect, the total mass of neural tissue in the brain increases rapidly—by 50 percent in the first two years. By 4 years of age, it nearly doubles its birth size. For the next ten years, the types of experiences the infant is exposed to will largely determine which regions and functions of the brain become most developed. The genetic program (along with physical limitations imposed by the size of the skull) does not allow the tremendous growth of brain circuitry to continue indefinitely, however. By about 11 years of age, unused connections begin to be trimmed away in a process called **synaptic pruning.** Notably, this process does not destroy the neurons themselves but instead returns them to an uncommitted state, awaiting a role in future development (Johnson, 1998).

Maturation and Development Sitting, crawling, and walking—like the growth of the brain, the growth spurt of puberty, and the onset of menopause—all occur on their own biological time schedules. Psychologists use the term **maturation** for the unfolding of these genetically programmed processes of growth and development over time. When organisms are raised under adequate environmental conditions, their maturation follows a predictable pattern. In humans, maturation generates all the sequences and patterns of behavior seen in Figure 7.1.

infancy   In humans, infancy spans the time between the end of the neonatal period and the establishment of language—usually at about 18 months to 2 years.

CONNECTION CHAPTER 9

Instinct is a common but imprecise term for behaviors that have a strong genetic basis (p. 369).

sensitive period   A span of time during which the organism is especially responsive to stimuli of a particular sort. Organisms may have sensitive periods for exposure to certain hormones or chemicals; similarly, they may have sensitive periods for learning language or receiving the visual stimulation necessary for normal development of vision.

synaptic pruning   The process of trimming unused brain connections, making neurons available for future development.

maturation   The process by which the genetic program manifests itself over time.

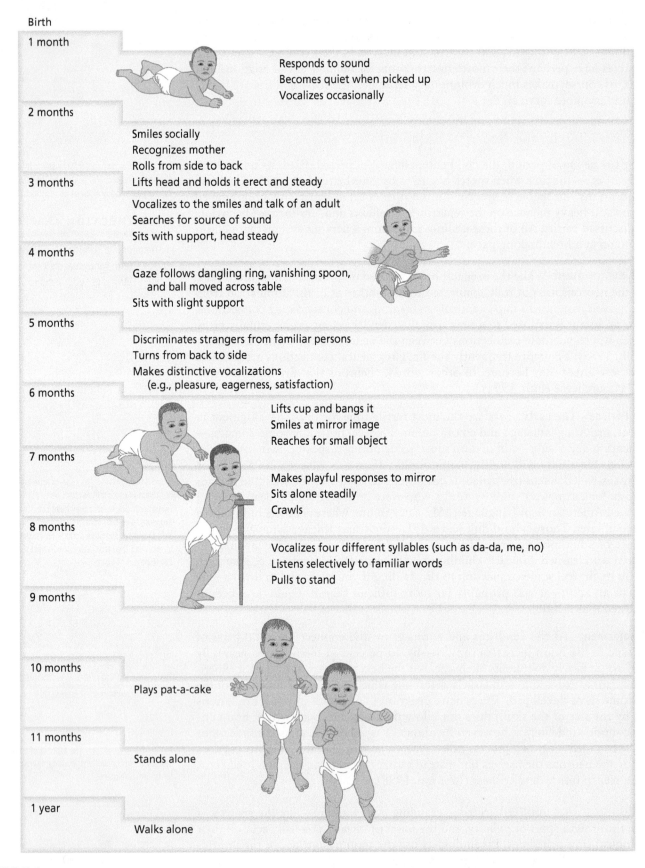

Birth

1 month
Responds to sound
Becomes quiet when picked up
Vocalizes occasionally

2 months

Smiles socially
Recognizes mother
Rolls from side to back
3 months
Lifts head and holds it erect and steady

Vocalizes to the smiles and talk of an adult
Searches for source of sound
Sits with support, head steady

4 months

Gaze follows dangling ring, vanishing spoon,
    and ball moved across table
Sits with slight support

5 months

Discriminates strangers from familiar persons
Turns from back to side
Makes distinctive vocalizations
    (e.g., pleasure, eagerness, satisfaction)
6 months

Lifts cup and bangs it
Smiles at mirror image
Reaches for small object

7 months

Makes playful responses to mirror
Sits alone steadily
Crawls

8 months

Vocalizes four different syllables (such as da-da, me, no)
Listens selectively to familiar words
Pulls to stand

9 months

10 months

Plays pat-a-cake

11 months

Stands alone

1 year

Walks alone

FIGURE 7.1

Maturational Timetable for Motor Control

This figure shows average ages at which each behavior is performed. There are considerable individual differences in the *rate* of development, so the time at which each response occurs is variable. Most infants, however, closely follow the *sequence* of development outlined here.

We must, however, keep in mind the role of the environment and its interaction with our hereditary nature. While maturation dictates the general time frame in which an individual becomes biologically ready for a new phase, the environment can speed up or slow down the exact time of development. Prominent biologist Edward Wilson (1998, 2004) describes this principle as a **genetic leash.** Because of the genetic leash, a child without special training learns to walk following a time-ordered pattern typical of all physically capable members of our species (see Figure 7.1). Indeed, in the Hopi culture where children are carried in cradle boards, walking occurs on a similar schedule (Dennis & Dennis, 1940). Children who receive special training, though, can learn to walk up to several months earlier, a finding illustrated in several African cultures who make a habit of bouncing babies on their feet, which speeds development of their leg muscles and motor control (Gardiner et al., 1998). And at the other extreme, children in Iranian orphanages who received little human contact and little opportunity to leave their cribs were significantly slower in learning to walk (Dennis, 1960).

The concept of the genetic leash will remain useful as we continue to study various patterns of human development. It eloquently illustrates the inescapable interaction between nature and nurture that is so fundamental to understanding how and why individuals develop as they do. We will see examples of this interaction throughout our study of language and cognitive development, social development, moral development, and emotional development—and moreover, in all major stages of the human lifespan.

Contact Comfort   As infants develop greater sensory and motor abilities through both nature and nurture, they rely on caregivers to provide the necessary stimulation. One type of stimulation we haven't yet discussed is the importance of touch. In the first half of the 19th century, many experts assumed infants sought physical contact with their caregivers only as a means to an end—with the end being food or nourishment. Beyond providing the necessary nourishment, these "cupboard theory" proponents argued, infants derived no further benefit from physical contact. Psychologists Harry and Margaret Harlow disagreed (Harlow, 1965; Harlow & Harlow, 1966) and tested their theory using infant monkeys separated from their mothers at birth. The Harlows placed orphaned baby monkeys in cages where they had access to two artificial surrogate mothers. One was a simple wire figure that provided milk through a nipple—a "cupboard," but little else. The other was a cloth-covered figure providing no milk but offering abundant stimulation from its soft terry-cloth cover. The results? Despite the nourishment provided by the wire model, the baby monkeys spent little time with it, preferring instead to remain nestled to the cloth mother. Moreover, when the infant monkeys were frightened, they sought comfort by clinging to the cloth figure. They also used it as a base of operations when exploring new situations. With these observations, then, the Harlows were able to show that infant monkeys become attached to and prefer a "mother" figure that provides **contact comfort,** the stimulation and reassurance derived from physical touch.

Human infants need contact comfort too. Since the Harlow's groundbreaking study, we have learned that physical contact promotes the release of pleasure-inducing endorphins. And touch stimulates physical development as well. University of Miami developmental psychologist Tiffany Field first experimented with massage on premature babies in 1986 and found that daily massage resulted in faster weight gain. Since Field's landmark study, further research has revealed a wide array of benefits associated with touch, including faster intellectual development, improved digestive tract functioning, improved circulation, and decreased production of stress hormones. Dovetailing with studies highlighting the benefits of touch is research documenting negative outcomes in children who are abused or neglected (Glaser, 2003). Clearly, a close, interactive relationship with loving adults is a child's first step toward healthy physical growth and normal socialization (Blum, 2002; Sapolsky, 2002).

genetic leash   Edward Wilson's term for the constraints placed on development by heredity.

One of Harlow's monkeys, clinging to the artificial terrycloth mother that provided contact comfort. Next to it, you can also see the wire mother that provided milk but no contact comfort.

contact comfort   Stimulation and reassurance derived from the physical touch of a caregiver.

attachment   The enduring socio-emotional relationship between a child and a parent or other regular caregiver.

imprinting   A primitive form of learning in which some young animals follow and form an attachment to the first moving object they see and hear.

Watch the Video *Attachment in Infants* at **MyPsychLab**

secure attachment   The attachment style of children who are relaxed and comfortable with their caregivers and tolerant of strangers and new experiences—as contrasted with children who are *insecurely attached.*

separation anxiety   A common pattern of distress seen in young children when separated from their caregivers.

anxious-ambivalent attachment   One of two primary response patterns seen in insecurely attached children in which a child wants contact with the caregiver, shows excessive distress when separated from the caregiver, and proves difficult to console even when reunited.

avoidant attachment   One of two primary response patterns seen in insecurely attached children in which a child shows no interest in contact with the caregiver and displays neither distress when separated from the caregiver nor happiness when reunited.

Attachment   Psychologists refer to the establishment of a close emotional relationship between a child and a parent figure as **attachment**. This relationship is especially important because it lays the foundation for other close relationships that follow throughout a person's lifetime (Cassidy & Shaver, 2008).

Attachment appears to occur instinctively in many species, although it is not necessarily limited to the infant's interactions with the biological parents. One striking example occurs in **imprinting**, the powerful attraction of infants of some species (notably in birds) to the first moving object or individual they see. A baby chick hatched by a mother duck will form an attachment to its surrogate mother—even though it is a chicken, not a duck. The imprinted chick will even follow its duck-mother right up to the water's edge when she and her ducklings go for a swim. (This scientific concept was illustrated in Hans Christian Andersen's story "The Ugly Duckling.") Thus, the imprinting tendency is an innate predisposition, although the organism's environment and experience determine what form it will take.

In humans, research on contact comfort provided early evidence of the physical need for attachment. Building on the Harlows' work with monkeys, psychologist John Bowlby (1969, 1973) suggested human attachment is innate, begins as early as the first few weeks, and functions as a survival strategy for infants. From an evolutionary perspective, it stands to reason that infants who stay close to their caregivers would be less vulnerable to threats from the environment. One study found, for example, that when mothers left the room, their 2- to 4-month-old babies' skin temperature dropped, a sign of emotional distress (Mizukami et al., 1990). In these youngsters, skin temperature dropped even more when a stranger replaced the mother. In contrast, skin temperature remained steady if the mother stayed in the room—even if the stranger was present. Apparently, children only a few months old rely on their caretakers as a "safe place," even before they can indicate attachment by walking or crawling (Bee, 1994).

Attachment Styles   Have you ever noticed, though, that children seem to differ in their types of attachment? Some children seem comfortable with strangers when their primary caregiver is present, while others appear clingy and fearful. Still others seem to care very little who is present. Developmental psychologist Mary Ainsworth not only noticed those patterns but also spent a career studying the various forms attachment takes in humans. To do so, she developed an innovative laboratory procedure called the "Strange Situation," which continues to be used today as the standard for measuring attachment.

What is this clever procedure? The Strange Situation involves putting young children and their primary caregiver into a series of interactions—sometimes together, sometimes separated, and sometimes with a stranger. Researchers then observe how the child responds to these various situations (Ainsworth, 1989; Lamb, 1999). Using such methods in a variety of cultures, Ainsworth found that children's responses fell into two main categories, reflecting either **secure attachment** or insecure attachment. *Securely attached* children were relaxed and comfortable with their caregivers and tolerant of or even interested in strangers and new experiences. When separated from their caregivers, they became upset—which, from 6 to 30 months, is a normal behavior called **separation anxiety**—but calmed down immediately on the caregiver's return and resumed their normal activities. They seemed to perceive their caregivers as a "secure base" from which to explore the world, confident the caregiver would be available to help if needed.

Insecurely attached children could be divided into two categories: *anxious-ambivalent* and *avoidant*. The **anxious-ambivalent** children wanted contact with their caregivers but cried with fear and anger when separated from them and proved difficult to console even when reunited. They clung anxiously to their caregivers when a stranger approached and were uncomfortable exploring new situations. Conversely, the **avoidant** children weren't interested in contact, displaying no distress when separated from their caregivers and no particular happiness when reunited. Overall, some 65 percent of American children develop secure attachment, while about 20 percent are avoidant, and 15 percent are anxious-ambivalent (Berk, 2007).

Do It Yourself! WHAT'S YOUR ATTACHMENT STYLE?

Identify which one of the following three self-descriptions you most agree with (adapted from Shaver & Hazan, 1994):

1. I am somewhat uncomfortable being close to others; I find it difficult to trust them completely, difficult to allow myself to depend on them. I am nervous when anyone gets too close, and love partners often want me to be more intimate than I feel comfortable being.

2. I find that others are reluctant to get as close as I would like. I often worry that my partner doesn't really love me or won't want to stay with me. I want to get very close to my partner, and this sometimes scares people away.

3. I find it relatively easy to get close to others and am comfortable depending on them. I don't often worry about being abandoned or about someone getting too close to me.

What Your Choice Means We realize that it is probably obvious to you which of the statements above is "best." Nevertheless, just considering the alternatives should help you understand attachment styles—and, perhaps, yourself—a little better. Here's our interpretation: If you selected the first statement, you agreed with the attitude that reflects an avoidant, insecure attachment. This style was chosen by 25 percent of Shaver and Hazan's respondent sample. The second statement reflects an anxious-ambivalent, insecure attachment style, selected by 20 percent of the sample. The third statement reflects a secure attachment style, the most common pattern identified, accounting for 55 percent of respondents (Shaver & Hazan, 1994).

What do these styles signify for later life? Through interviews, observations, and questionnaires, researchers have identified several consequences of attachment style, secure or insecure, in adulthood (Ainsworth, 1989; Collins & Read, 1990; Hazan & Shaver, 1990; Kirkpatrick & Shaver, 1992; Shaver & Hazan, 1993, 1994; Simpson, 1990):

- **Secure individuals** have more positive self-concepts and believe that most other people are good natured and well intentioned. They see their personal relationships as trustworthy and satisfying.

- Secure respondents are satisfied with their job security, coworkers, income, and work activity. They put a higher value on relationships than on work and derive their greatest pleasure from connections to others.

- Insecure, anxious-ambivalent persons report emotional extremes and jealousy. They feel unappreciated, insecure, and unlikely to win professional advancement. They make less money than those with other attachment styles, working more for approval and recognition than financial gain. They fantasize about succeeding but often slack off after receiving praise.

- Avoidant people fear intimacy and expect their relationships to fail. They place a higher value on work than on relationships and generally like their work and job security. They follow a workaholic pattern, but (not surprisingly) they are dissatisfied with their coworkers.

- Secure individuals tend to choose as partners others who are secure. After breakups, avoidant individuals claim to be less bothered by the loss of the relationship, although this may be a defensive claim, with distress showing up in other ways (e.g., physical symptoms).

Attachment has become a very hot topic over the past decade, as a burgeoning body of research indicates that patterns established in infancy affect a variety of childhood and adult behaviors, including aggression, friendships, job satisfaction, relationship choices, and intimacy experiences (Berk, 2004; Gomez & McLaren, 2007). But what causes a child to develop a particular attachment style? For many years, nurture was presumed to be the culprit: Specifically, it was thought that good parents produced securely attached children, while inconsistent parenting produced anxious-ambivalent children, and neglectful parenting led to avoidant attachment.

Today, though, most researchers recognize that nature and nurture interact in the development of attachment style. Infant temperament, for example, which is largely genetic, influences how easy or difficult it is to be responsive to an infant. It is not surprising, then, that one study found that babies who were fussier in the first few days of life were more likely to have an anxious-ambivalent attachment style one year later (Miyake, 1993). This seems quite logical, as most parents would have more difficulty consistently "reading" the signals from a temperamental baby than with an easy baby, thus creating an interaction effect between infant temperament and parenting style.

Culture and Attachment Before making up your mind about which attachment style is "best," though, consider the important factor of culture. Did you assume, like many Americans do, that secure attachment is the ideal? On the contrary, German families prefer avoidant attachment, as it promotes greater self-sufficiency, while Japanese parents rarely leave their children unattended, fostering greater dependence and an accompanying anxious-ambivalent attachment style (Grossman et al., 1985; Miyake et al., 1985). Like many qualities, then, the judgment of which is "ideal" depends heavily on the prevailing values of the culture.

Long-Term Effects of Attachment And attachment isn't just for kids. As children grow up and become adults, they no longer restrict their attachment to their primary caregiver: They gradually widen their attachments to include other family members, friends, teachers, coworkers, and others in their community. Evidence suggests the primary attachment relationship, though, continues to serve as a working model for later important relationships. In other words, whatever the child learns to expect in that first caregiver relationship becomes the lens through which later relationships are perceived and interpreted. Securely attached children are likely to be well adjusted and interact easily with others, whereas anxious-ambivalent children often turn into suspicious adults, and avoidantly attached children are least likely to form close emotional bonds with others.

We should emphasize, however, that—powerful as attachment is—individuals who lack healthy attachments in infancy and childhood are not necessarily doomed to failure in life. While attachment problems are good predictors of later problems with social relationships, many people succeed in overcoming attachment difficulties (Kagan, 1996, 1998). Healthy relationships, later in childhood or even in adulthood, can "reset" the working model. With such caveats in mind, we now invite you to take the quiz in the *Do It Yourself!* box, "What's Your Attachment Style?"

Psychosocial Development: Trust versus Mistrust The large body of research on attachment dovetails nicely with the first stage in one of the major lifespan theories of development. Erik Erikson (1902–1994) was a prominent psychoanalyst who believed that, on an unconscious level, we form basic beliefs about ourselves and our relationship to our social world as we go through life. These basic beliefs influence our development through the choices we make in our relationships. Furthermore, Erikson thought each of these basic beliefs developed out of a crisis (which could be resolved successfully or remain unresolved) at a critical period in our development. Thus, he characterized each of the eight **psychosocial stages** in his developmental theory as a choice between two opposing beliefs, such as *trust versus mistrust,* the first developmental problem of our lives (see Table 7.1).

Erikson theorized that, in the first 18 months of life, the major developmental task facing the infant is to develop a sense of **trust** in the world. As we have seen, infants who develop a secure attachment style see the world as an interesting place, full of new experiences to explore. With the knowledge of a primary caregiver as a "safe base" from which to explore, these infants become prepared to develop into children (and later into adults) who are comfortable in new situations and possess an adventurous and resilient spirit to help them through life. Children who do not develop this will experience difficulties navigating through later developmental challenges, as the issue of trust remains unresolved and acts as a barrier between the individual and the social world. To put it more simply, infants who do not develop a basic sense of trust in their social world will have trouble forming and maintaining satisfactory relationships. In this way, the basic unconscious assumption of trust fosters the choice to trust others, whereas a basic assumption of mistrust promotes suspicion.

While Erikson's theory has its critics, the criticism revolves primarily around whether his eight stages occur in their prescribed order for everyone or whether they can be experienced at different times for different people (based at least in part on cultural norms). Critics also note Erikson's work was based primarily on his own clinical observations rather than rigorous scientific methods. Remarkably, though, many of his observations have since been supported by methodologically sound research. And his was the first theory of human development to encompass the entire lifespan: Previous theories were interested only in the first 12 to 17 years

psychosocial stage In Erikson's theory, the developmental stages refer to eight major challenges that appear successively across the lifespan, which require an individual to rethink his or her goals, as well as relationships with others.

trust The major developmental goal during the first 18 months of life. According to Erikson's theory, the child must choose between trusting or not trusting others.

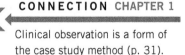

CONNECTION CHAPTER 1

Clinical observation is a form of the case study method (p. 31).

TABLE 7.1 Erikson's Psychosocial Stages

Age/Period (approximate)	Principal Challenge	Adequate Resolution	Inadequate Resolution
0–1½ years	Trust vs. mistrust	Basic sense of safety, security; ability to rely on forces outside oneself	Insecurity, anxiety
1½–3 years	Autonomy vs. shame or self-doubt	Perception of self as agent; capable of controlling one's own body and making things happen	Feelings of inadequacy about self-control, control of events
3–6 years	Initiative vs. guilt	Confidence in oneself as being able to initiate, create	Feelings of guilt over one's limitations or inabilities
6 years to puberty	Industry vs. inferiority	Perceived competence in basic social and intellectual skills; self-acceptance	Lack of self-confidence; feelings of failure
Adolescence	Identity vs. role confusion	Comfortable sense of self as a person, both unique and socially accepted	Sense of self as fragmented, shifting, unclear sense of self
Early adulthood	Intimacy vs. isolation	Capacity for closeness and commitment to another	Feeling of loneliness, separation; denial of intimacy needs
Middle adulthood	Generativity vs. stagnation	Focus of concern beyond oneself, to family, society, future generations	Self-indulgent concerns; lack of future orientation
Late adulthood	Ego-integrity vs. despair	Sense of wholeness; basic satisfaction with life	Feelings of futility, disappointment

of life, with the misguided notion that, once you got through adolescence, you were fully and permanently developed! For these reasons, Erikson's theory remains prominent today in the study of human development. We will return to his theory, and explore the other seven stages he proposed, in later sections of this chapter.

[PSYCHOLOGY MATTERS]

Not Just Fun and Games: The Role of Child's Play in Life Success

Now that we understand that both nature and nurture influence our outcomes in life, let's illustrate their interaction by examining a psychological trait of utmost importance to having success in life: **self-control**. This ability to restrain our impulses and make effective choices often requires us to delay instant gratification in pursuit of longer range success. An ever-growing body of research finds low self-control to be a strong predictor of delinquency and criminal behavior, while higher self-control is linked to a variety of positive outcomes—including happier relationships, higher grades, better self-esteem, secure attachment, and less alcohol abuse (Tangney et al., 2004). Even when the effects of intelligence and social class—two

self-control The ability to delay instant gratification in pursuit of longer-range positive outcomes.

CONNECTION CHAPTER 9

Impulse control, as seen in the classic "marshmallow test," is a key element of emotional intelligence (p. 401).

Unstructured, make-believe play helps children develop executive function, self-regulation, and self-control.

executive function   Cognitive abilities in the frontal lobes necessary for complex thinking, planning, and goal-directed behavior

other strong predictors of success—are accounted for, self-control remains one of the strongest predictors of these important life outcomes (Moffitt et al., 2011). Clearly, then, self-control is important—so how do we get it?

Nature—or our genetic inheritance—sets the stage for our baseline ability to manage our emotions and control our impulses. Evidence for this is found in twin studies that shows, for example, identical twins are much more alike in impulsivity than fraternal twins (Vernon et al., 2008). Notably, however, the genetic contribution to this trait appears to account for only about 40 percent of it—leaving ample room for environmental contributions.

Given what we learned in Chapter 2 about brain development and plasticity, it stands to reason that the sooner we nurture self-control, the better our chances of developing it. Parents can teach children to manage their impulses in a variety of simple ways, such as picking up their toys before going outside, finishing homework before getting television time, or eating all their vegetables in order to get dessert. Clear, consistent rules help children learn to manage their worlds and provide guidelines for achieving their goals. At school, teachers in some programs wear a double-sided cue card around their neck, showing a green side when children are behaving well, but flipping it over to the red side as a cue to a child acting irresponsibly. In this way, children get instant and palatable feedback, which helps them learn to manage their emotions and make positive choices—thus enabling environmental influences to stretch the "genetic leash" of impulse control.

Rules and structure, however, can go too far. A growing number of child psychologists are expressing concern at the way childhood play has evolved in past decades (Berk, 2002). Compared to kids in previous generations, today's child engages in much more supervised and structured playtime, such as league sports, leaving less time for imaginative, make-believe play. Why does that matter? Improvisational play requires more thinking, planning, creativity, and self-management on the child's part than does structured play—and these are precisely the skills that help develop a child's **executive function** or the frontal lobe areas in our brains linked to goal attainment and self-regulation. Studies show that kids who engage in more imaginative play with their peers learn executive functions sooner, resulting in greater cooperation with peers, more participation and responsibility in assigned tasks, and better social skills (Elias & Berk, 2002).

What's more, imaginative play helps build vocabulary. Young children playing doctor, for example, use bigger words than they otherwise would, such as "injection" or "thermometer." Preschoolers playing "airport" were overheard telling another "passenger" that her bottle exceeded the 3-ounce liquid limit (Bartlett, 2011). Psychologist Laura Berk notes that for kids to regulate themselves and their games, they need to engage in "private speech," talking themselves through each phase in planning and carrying out the game. As a result, they gain not only language skills but also cognitive flexibility and self-control.

The evolution of play styles has another effect, powerfully demonstrated in a replication study comparing 21st-century children to kids in the 1940s. Among other things, kids aged 3, 5, and 7 were asked to stand still for a period of time. Seventy years ago, 5-year-olds could stand still for about three minutes, and 7-year-olds could do so as long as they needed to. In the current study, however, 5-year-olds couldn't stand still at all, and 7-year-olds managed to follow instructions for about three minutes—equal to that of 5-year-olds in the 1940s study (Spiegel, 2008).

While modern life certainly offers a variety of advantages to children, enhanced self-control does not appear to be one of them. And "nature" doesn't evolve so fast as to explain the changes. Thus, given what research tells us about the connection between self-regulation and life success in a broad array of areas, parents and teachers may do well to focus more efforts on creating environments that help kids develop this important ability.

Check Your Understanding

✓○ Study and Review at MyPsychLab

1. **RECALL:** "Nature" refers to the effects of _____, and "nurture" refers to the effects of _____.

2. **APPLICATION:** You are a psychologist working in a pediatric hospital. According to research by Tiffany Fields, which of the following should staff do to promote healthy development in the newborns?

   a. Talk to them.
   b. Touch them.
   c. Make eye contact.
   d. Sing to them.

3. **ANALYSIS:** What factors influence the type of attachment style an infant develops?

4. **RECALL:** Which of the following are teratogens? (Choose all that apply)

   a. alcohol
   b. nicotine
   c. prenatal vitamins
   d. ginseng

5. **UNDERSTANDING THE CORE CONCEPT:** Describe three ways that the infant comes into the world prepared to survive and thrive.

Answers 1. genetics or heredity; the environment **2.** b **3.** Infant temperament and the consistency and responsiveness of the caregiver **4.** a, b, and d **5.** Infants have an array of behavioral reflexes, sensory abilities, and social abilities (such as mimicry) that promote adaptation to their environments.

7.2 KEY QUESTION
What Are the Developmental Tasks of Childhood?

Three of the greatest accomplishments of your life include acquiring your native language, forming relationships with important people in your life, and developing your ability to think and reason. Each of these serves as the basis for further development later in life. And we will see that, as children work through these tasks, they undergo profound psychological changes resulting from both their genetic code and their environment. Here's how our Core Concept states the main idea of this section:

Core Concept 7.2

Nature and nurture work together to help children master important developmental tasks, especially in the areas of language acquisition, cognitive development, and development of social relationships.

Developmental differences between children and adults are huge, but the differences in language, thought, and socialization are not simply the result of adults' greater experience or store of information. The differences between children and adults also involve the unfolding of crucial maturational processes. In other words, children's abilities are a result of not only their learning but also their unique level of brain development. Let us first explore these processes at work in the development of language.

How Children Acquire Language

One of the defining characteristics of humans is the use of complex language—our ability to communicate through spoken and written words and gestures. From a developmental perspective, human language acquisition is awe inspiring: Newborn children know no words at all, yet in only a few years, virtually all become fluent speakers of any language they hear spoken regularly—or see, in the case of gestural languages such as American Sign Language. What makes them such adept language learners? Developmental specialists believe human infants possess innate abilities geared specifically for this task (Pinker, 1994, 2006).

Language Structures in the Brain

Do children learn language primarily by mimicking the sounds and/or signs they hear or see in their environment? According to one prominent theory, mimicry accounts for only part of their learning. An elegant biological foundation underlies the practice children get imitating others—a foundation that enables much more rapid development of language than mere imitation would allow. That foundation is an inborn mental structure that psycholinguist Noam Chomsky (1965, 1977) calls a **language acquisition device (LAD)**. Breaking new ground in our understanding of language development, Chomsky proposed that humans are born with a sort of mental software program that helps children acquire the vocabulary, grammar, and rules of the language to which they are exposed. Many experts agree (Hauser et al., 2002). Further, research based on the Human Genome Project provides evidence that the foundations of language are, in part, genetic (Liegeois et al., 2001).

In Chomsky's theory, the LAD, or "mental software program," contains some very basic rules common to all human languages. One such rule might be the distinction between nouns (for names of things) and verbs (for actions). These innate rules, Chomsky suggests, make it easier for children to discover patterns in languages to which they are exposed. Additional evidence for Chomsky's theory comes from the fact that children worldwide learn their native languages in very similar stages at very similar times. A logical hypothesis for explaining this pattern would be that children possess inborn "programs" for language development that automatically run at certain times in the child's life.

Despite the widespread agreement that humans possess an innate ability to acquire language, we cannot ignore the role of the environment. Although infants are born with the ability to produce all the sounds in the approximately 4,000 languages spoken on our planet, by about 6 months of age they seem to have zeroed in on the dominant language in their environment. The months spent hearing these sounds combine with their own experiments at verbalization to refine their efforts, and they lose the ability to produce sounds that are not part of their own language. Children being raised in a Japanese-speaking culture, for example, lose the ability to distinguish between the sounds made by the letters *R* and *L,* as the letter *L* is not part of the Japanese language (Iverson et al., 2003).

Such cultural variations in the specifics of children's language development suggest that the built-in capacity for language is not a rigid device, but rather a set of "listening rules" or guidelines for perceiving language (Bee, 1994; Slobin, 1985a, b). Babies pay attention to the sounds and rhythms of the sound strings they hear others speak (or in sign language, see), especially the beginnings, endings, and stressed syllables. Relying on their built-in "listening guides," young children can quickly deduce the patterns and rules for producing their own speech. These observations underscore the notion that the LAD is flexible, enabling ready adaptation to dominant language in the young child's environment (Goldin-Meadow & Mylander, 1990; Meier, 1991).

Acquiring Vocabulary and Grammar

So, inborn abilities lay the foundation for learning language, but how do children learn the specific words and structure of their particular language? In fact, they are practicing earlier than you probably realized. By 4 months of age, for example, babies are **babbling**: making repetitive syllables such as "mamamama." And babbling isn't just baby talk—it is the infant beginning to experiment with the building blocks of his or her language. Interestingly, deaf babies raised in a sign-language environment start babbling at just the same time—but with their hands, mimicking repetitive syllables from ASL (Pettito & Marentette, 1991). Babbling develops rapidly, and by about their first birthday, babies enter the one-word stage and are speaking full words. They are also learning new words quite rapidly; you might notice the "naming explosion," when children seem to delight in their efforts to point to objects and name them. By age 2, children enter the two-word stage, which tremendously increases the range of meanings they can convey. At that point, the average child has a vocabulary of nearly 1,000 different words (Huttenlocher et al., 1991). That number burgeons to an astounding 10,000 words by age 6 (Anglin, 1993, 1995). Over the next several years, the pace of vocabulary acquisition accelerates even more,

language acquisition device (LAD) A biologically organized mental structure in the brain that facilitates the learning of language because (according to Chomsky) it is innately programmed with some of the fundamental rules of grammar.

babbling The production of repetitive syllables, characteristic of the early stages of language acquisition.

as you can see in Figure 7.2, with the average child gaining about 50,000 new words in that short time span.

Practice Makes Perfect Even though the rapid development of language seems driven largely by a genetic timetable, the role of culture and the environment impact the degree and the pace at which children learn language. Like many learning tasks, the frequency of practice makes a difference. Mothers generally talk more with their young daughters than with their young sons (Leaper et al., 1998). Even more pronounced is the difference between children raised in low- versus middle-SES households (the term *SES* refers to socioeconomic status, which is a composite indicator of income and education level). Parents in low-SES households read to their children an average of just 25 hours between the ages of 1 and 5—compared to a whopping 1,000 hours in the middle-SES group (Neuman, 2003). These differences in early learning are evident in findings that girls and middle-SES children begin kindergarten with more advanced verbal skills than boys and children from low-income SES families (Ready et al., 2005).

Grammar Turns Vocabulary into Language Even if you have a limited vocabulary, you can combine the same words in different sequences to convey a rich variety of meanings. For example, "I saw him chasing a dog" and "I saw a dog chasing him" both use exactly the same words, but switching the order of the words *him* and *dog* yields completely different meanings. **Grammar** makes this possible: It is a language's set of rules about combining and ordering words to make understandable sentences (Naigles, 1990; Naigles & Kako, 1993). Different languages may use considerably different rules about grammatical combinations. In Japanese, for example, the verb always comes last, while English is much more lax about verb position. And if you speak Spanish, you may know that while English speakers would say "the blue house," in Spanish the color name would come after the noun (*la casa azul*).

First Sentences In their early two- and three-word sentences, children produce **telegraphic speech:** short, simple sequences of nouns and verbs without plurals, tenses, or function words like *the* and *of*. For example, "Ball hit Evie cry" is telegraphic speech. To develop the ability to make full sentences, children must learn to use other forms of speech, such as modifiers (adjectives and adverbs) and articles (the, those), and they must learn how to put words together grammatically. In English, this means recognizing and producing the familiar subject-verb-object order, as in "The lamb followed Mary."

Finally, as children's language ability develops, they become skilled in using **morphemes,** the individual meaningful units that make up words. For example, the word "unmarried," has three morphemes: "un," "marry," and "ed." Similarly, "subcategories" has three: "sub," "category," and "es." Morphemes can mark verbs to show tense (walked, walking) and mark nouns to show possession (Maria's, the people's) and plurality (foxes, children). (Can you identify the number of morphemes in each of those examples?) Often, however, children make mistakes because they do not know the rule or they apply an inappropriate one (Marcus, 1996). One common error, known as *overregularization,* applies a rule too widely and creates incorrect forms. For example, after learning to make past tense verb forms by adding -d or -ed, children may apply this "rule" even to its exceptions, the irregular verbs, creating such nonwords as *hitted* and *breaked.* Learning to add -s or -es to make plurals, children may apply the rule to irregular nouns, as in *foots* or *mouses.*

Other Language Skills To communicate effectively, words and the grammatical rules for combining them are only the beginning: children also need to learn the *social rules of conversation.* They must learn how to join a discussion, how to take turns talking and listening, and how to make contributions that are relevant. Adult speakers use body language, intonation, and facial expressions to enhance their communication. They also respond to feedback they get from listeners and are often able to take the perspective of the listener. Children must master these skills to become successful communicators, which in turn enables them to become part of a human language community.

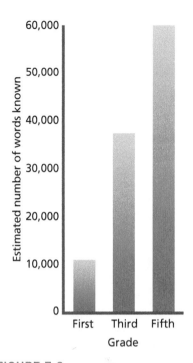

FIGURE 7.2

Growth in Grade School Children's Vocabulary

The number of words in a child's vocabulary increases rapidly during the grade school years—an even faster rate of increase than during the preschool years. The chart shows total vocabulary, including words that a child can use (production vocabulary) and words that a child can understand (comprehension vocabulary). These data were reported in 1995 by J. M. Anglin of the University of Waterloo, Ontario, Canada.

grammar The rules of a language, specifying how to use the elements of language and word order to produce understandable sentences.

telegraphic speech Short, simple sequences of nouns and verbs without plurals, tenses, or function words like *the* and *of*—somewhat like the language once used in telegrams.

morpheme A meaningful unit of language that makes up words. Some whole words are morphemes (example: *word*); other morphemes include grammatical components that alter a word's meaning (examples: *-ed, -ing,* and *un-*).

As they grow older, children also learn to express abstract meanings, especially as their thoughts extend beyond the physical world and into their psychological world. For example, after the age of 2, children begin to use words such as *dream, forget, pretend, believe, guess,* and *hope* as they talk about internal states (Shatz et al., 1983). They also use words such as *happy, sad,* and *angry* to refer to emotional states. Later, after further cognitive advances, we will explore in the next section, they understand and use highly abstract words such as *truth, justice,* and *idea*.

What is the major point that stands out amid the complexities of language acquisition? It is part of our Core Concept: *Language is a major developmental task of childhood—for which children are exquisitely prepared.* And the way they acquire and use language suggests that these early steps on the path to adulthood involve a combination of learning and innate processes that unfold on their own developmental timetables.

Cognitive Development: Piaget's Theory

If you have ever known a toddler going through the naming explosion, you have seen that children have an insatiable appetite for labeling things they know. Behind this labeling is their emerging ability for thinking, perceiving, and remembering. The next few pages will focus on how these mental abilities emerge: a process called **cognitive development**, which is the second of the three main developmental tasks of childhood identified in our Core Concept.

Psychologists interested in cognitive development ask such questions as: *When do children realize that objects still exist even when they can't see them? Do they know it is possible to hold ideas that aren't true? Can they understand that people have desires and dreams, but objects do not?* Developmental psychologists investigate not only what children think but also how they think, as illustrated in the pioneering work of Swiss psychologist Jean Piaget. For nearly 50 years, Piaget observed children's intellectual development and formulated his observations into a comprehensive theory.

Piaget began this quest to understand the child's mind by carefully observing the behavior of his own three children. His methods were simple: He would pose problems to them, observe their responses, slightly alter the situations, and once again observe their responses. Piaget paid special attention to the developmental transitions and changes in his children's thinking, reasoning, and problem solving. This focus led to a **stage theory** of development, which emphasized Piaget's view that people undergo distinctive revolutions in their thought processes, producing four discrete *stages* that emerge as they move through childhood and adolescence. We will see below that three key ideas distinguish Piaget's approach: (1) *schemas,* (2) the interaction of *assimilation* and *accommodation,* and (3) the *stages of cognitive development.*

Schemas To illustrate the concept of schemas, think of some four-legged animals. Now think of some that are friendly. Then think of one that barks. You might have started by imagining elephants, tigers, cats, and dogs (all four-legged), then narrowed your choices down to cats and dogs (four-legged and friendly), and finally to just dogs (which bark). You could do this easily because you have developed mental structures that enable you to interpret concepts and events. Piaget termed such mental structures **schemas**. We have schemas for concepts, such as "dog" and "development." We have schemas for actions, such as "eating with chopsticks," or "studying." We also have schemas for solving problems, such as "finding the area of a circle" or "dealing with a crying baby." In general, schemas are mental frameworks that guide thinking. According to Piaget, they are also the building blocks of development. Schemas form and change as we develop and organize our knowledge to deal with new experiences and predict future events. As you read this, you are building a schema about schemas!

Assimilation and Accommodation In Piaget's system, two dynamic processes underlie all cognitive growth: assimilation and accommodation. **Assimilation** is a mental process that incorporates new information into existing schemas. So a baby who knows how to grasp a rattle will apply the same strategy to grab onto a sparkly piece of jewelry

cognitive development The global term for the development of thought processes from childhood through adulthood.

stage theory An explanation of development that emphasizes distinctive or rather abrupt changes. A stage theory of cognitive development, then, emphasizes revolutionary changes in thought processes.

CONNECTION CHAPTER 6

Schemas are knowledge clusters or general conceptual frameworks that provide expectations about topics, events, objects, people, and situations in one's life (p. 221).

schema In Piaget's theory, a mental structure or program that guides a developing child's thought.

assimilation A mental process that incorporates new information into existing schemas.

worn by his caregiver. Likewise, an older child whose family has a pet canary might use assimilation during a trip to the zoo when she learns that a large parrot or flamingo is also a bird. You, too, experience assimilation when you read about a favorite actor's new film or learn to use an updated version of a particular program on your computer. Essentially, when we assimilate, we are broadening an existing schema by integrating new information into it.

By contrast, we use **accommodation** when new information does not fit neatly into an existing schema. Accommodation is the process of restructuring or modifying schemas to accommodate the new information. Thus, a child who has learned to grasp rattles and jewelry may have trouble trying to grasp a large ball the same way. Similarly, if the child on her first trip to the zoo encounters a bat, she will have to create a new schema for "bat," since it is a creature with wings but is not a bird. Adults experience accommodation of their mental schemas too. For example, the Internet has caused widespread accommodation in the schemas people use to conceptualize shopping and communicating. As a student, you may sometimes need to modify your schema for studying when strategies that used to work for you no longer result in the grades you desire.

Accommodation can also help you adapt to different customs and cultures. For example, communication rules vary among different cultures, even in the United States. If your schema for communicating includes a polite pause after one speaker finishes and another begins, you might not be able to get a word in edgewise if you find yourself in a group whose schema embraces interrupting and "talking over" each other. In our increasingly multicultural world, accommodation can be a very effective strategy in adapting to new environments.

For Piaget, cognitive development results from the continual interweaving of assimilation and accommodation. Through these two processes, the individual's behavior and knowledge become less dependent on concrete external reality and increasingly reliant on internal thought. In general, assimilation makes new information fit our existing views of the world, and accommodation changes our views to fit new information.

Piaget's Stages of Cognitive Development Now that we understand schemas and how they are affected by new information, let's examine the four revolutionary changes Piaget observed in children's perception of the world as they develop. He described these changes as stages of cognitive growth: the *sensorimotor stage* (infancy), the *preoperational stage* (early childhood), the *concrete operational stage* (middle childhood), and the *formal operational stage* (adolescence). At each stage, distinct thinking styles emerge as the child progresses from sensory reaction to logical thought. It is important to note that the maturation process dictates that all children progress through the four stages in the same sequence. Due to the interaction of heredity and environment, though, some children pass more quickly through a given stage than others. A child in an education-rich environment, for example, will master the cognitive tasks of each stage more rapidly than one with limited educational opportunities.

The Sensorimotor Stage (Birth to about Age 2) We have seen that children enter the world equipped with many innate sensory abilities and reflexive behaviors, such as recognizing familiar sounds and the grasping and sucking reflexes. According to Piaget, children in the **sensorimotor stage** explore the world primarily through these senses and motor actions. For example, they learn to coordinate the information they are receiving from their senses with their motor abilities, such as learning to swivel their head to see something behind them, and then to crawl or walk toward it if they desire the object. Piaget called this **sensorimotor intelligence.**

During this rapidly evolving stage of development, babies work toward the major achievement of this stage: **object permanence**, which begins at about 8 months. Prior to that time, you might have noticed babies will not look for a toy or other object that disappears. Piaget interpreted this behavior to mean they did not understand that the object still existed when they could no longer see it. In other words, it was "out

An infant finds that the sucking reflex works just as well with a bottle as with a breast and, thus, assimilates when she adds sucking a bottle to her existing schema for sucking.

accommodation A mental process that modifies schemas in order to include (or accommodate) new information.

A child who knows that small creatures with wings are birds uses accommodation when he learns that this winged creature is not a bird, but a butterfly.

sensorimotor stage The first stage in Piaget's theory, during which the child relies heavily on innate motor responses to stimuli.

sensorimotor intelligence Piaget's term for the infant's approach to the world, relying on relatively simple physical (motor) responses to sensory experience.

object permanence The knowledge that objects exist independently of one's own actions or awareness.

of sight, out of mind." Beginning around 8 months, though, if you show an infant a toy and then let her see you hide it under, say, a blanket, she will look for it under the blanket. What's more, she will reliably do this even with a delay of a minute or more between the hiding and the seeking. This demonstrates the beginning of the understanding of object permanence. Over the next several months, infants develop the ability to seek something after increasingly longer delays and also become more successful at finding objects hidden in different locations than they were the first time (Moore & Meltzoff, 2004).

Object permanence, then, helps us understand separation anxiety, which we briefly discussed earlier in this chapter. As anyone who has cared for an infant has surely noticed, infants typically become quite upset when you leave—which makes perfect sense in the early stages of object permanence. After all, they don't yet understand you will come back at some point. Instead, when you leave the room, you cease to exist. Imagine how frightening that would be for an infant! Once object permanence is completely mastered, marking the end of the sensorimotor stage, a child understands that someone or something still exists, even when they can't see it. As a result, most children grow out of separation anxiety by about age 2.

Concurrently with these accomplishments, infants are learning **goal-directed behavior**, as evidenced by their experiments with various objects. For example, a child who drops a spoon might be very interested in the clatter it makes as it bounces off a tile floor and want to repeat the action over and over again. What may seem annoying to an onlooker with sensitive hearing is really just the infant delighting in exercising some control over his world!

The emergence of object permanence, combined with an infant's increasing experiments with goal-directed behavior, provide substantial evidence that infants are beginning to form **mental representations** of objects and to recognize their own relation to the world. This mental imagery empowers a child's thinking and problem solving. Imitative behaviors that, early in infancy, were confined to the immediate present situation will show up after increasing delays in time, in what is the beginning of *observational learning*. By 6 months, infants will imitate behaviors they saw the previous day, and during the second year, they can retain and imitate images of previously seen behaviors for as long as a month (Klein & Meltzoff, 1999). These achievements of the sensorimotor stage propel the toddler into the next stage: the preoperational stage.

The Preoperational Stage (from about 2 to 7 Years of Age) The cognitive advances in the next developmental stage, the **preoperational stage**, grow out of the ability to represent objects mentally. After noting rapid development during the sensorimotor stage, Piaget seems to have seen the preoperational stage as a sort of transition stage between the sensorimotor stage and the third stage (the concrete operational stage). In his observations, this was a period in which symbolic abilities that emerged in the sensorimotor stage expanded and consolidated. As such, he described the primary features of this stage as limitations in a child's thinking, rather than advances. Let's consider some of those features.

- **Egocentrism** causes children to see the world only in terms of themselves and their own position. Further, they assume that others see the world in the same way they do. (We hasten to add that Piaget did not intend egocentrism to be interpreted as selfishness, but rather as a limited perspective on the world.) Piaget discovered this through an experiment he called the "three mountains task" (see Figure 7.3). ◉

    So, when you are talking to a preoperational child on the phone, she may simply nod in response to a question you ask (without saying anything), not realizing you can't see her nodding. Another charming example of egocentrism is the child who covers his eyes and then thinks no one can see him! As a result of this egocentrism, Piaget thought preoperational children were not yet able to fully empathize with others or take others' points of view. This is one aspect of Piaget's theory that has been challenged, a point we will elaborate on shortly.

goal-directed behavior An ability that emerges during the sensorimotor period by which infants develop the ability to keep a simple goal in mind as they pursue it.

mental representation The ability to form internal images of objects and events.

preoperational stage The second stage in Piaget's theory, marked by well-developed mental representation and the use of language.

egocentrism In Piaget's theory, the inability to realize that there are other viewpoints beside one's own.

◉— **Watch** the **Video** The Preschool Years: Egocentrism at **MyPsychLab**

- **Animistic thinking** involves the belief that inanimate objects have life and mental processes, just as people do. This is when we see children having a tea party with their teddy bears, putting a Band-Aid on a doll that has fallen and hit the ground, or worrying that trimming a tree might hurt it.

- **Centration** occurs when a child focuses his attention too narrowly, missing out on other important information. That is, the child can "center" on only one bit of information at a time. As a result, the child will not understand the "big picture" of an event or problem. So, for example, a thirsty child may insist on drinking a "big glass" of juice, preferring a tall narrow container to a short wide one that in truth holds an equal amount. In the preoperational child's mind, the height of the glass is mistakenly assumed to hold more juice, and the bigger width of the other glass is not noticed (see Figure 7.4). (See the *Do It Yourself!* box on page 286.)

- **Irreversibility** is the inability to think through a series of events or steps involved in solving a problem and then to reverse course, returning to the mental starting point. In short, preoperational children lack the mental trial-and-error ability of older children to do and then undo an act in their minds. For example, Sam might see Maria spill a box of raisins on the table and—because the raisins are spread out over a large area—think, "Wow! Maria has lots more raisins than I have in my little box." But preoperational Sam cannot mentally reverse the process and think, "If she put them all back in the box, it would look like the same amount I have in mine." This inability represents the biggest obstacle to logical thinking in the preoperational child.

While we might see these as limitations, it is important to recognize what developments are taking place during this time. Children are experimenting with their newly acquired ability to use mental representations, and in the process they are often highly creative. We see this creativity in the animism they display and in other make-believe games that are a central feature of the preoperational stage. In fact, it can be argued that, when creativity in problem solving declines in the next stage, the decline is not just a gain but in some ways also a loss.

The Concrete Operational Stage (from about 7 to about 11 Years of Age) In the next stage, children break through the barrier of irreversibility to understand, for the first time, that many things stay essentially the same even when their superficial appearance changes. In this **concrete operational stage**, they can understand that a short, wide glass can hold as much juice as a tall, narrow one or that the spilled raisins that came out of the box must fit back into the box. In mastering **conservation**, the problems that defeated the preoperational child now yield to a new understanding of the way volume is conserved. Similarly, they now understand that a string of red beads is not longer than an identical string of blue beads, even though the red beads are stretched out in a line while the blue beads lie in a small pile. They realize the beads look different in their grouping, but this does not mean they are different in number.

FIGURE 7.3

Piaget's Three-Mountain Task

In Piaget's Three Mountain task, a child is shown a figure of three mountains. One mountain has a red cross at the top, one has a small house, and the third is snow-capped. On the other side of the figure (across the table from the child) sits a doll. When asked which mountain view the doll has, the preoperational child typically thinks the doll's view is the same as the child's own view. Piaget used this task to illustrate egocentrism or the inability to understand that others' perspectives may differ from our own.

Source: Berk, L. E. (2007). *Development through the lifespan*. 4th ed. Boston, MA: Allyn and Bacon. Copyright © 2007 by Pearson Education. Reprinted by permission of the publisher.

animistic thinking A preoperational mode of thought in which inanimate objects are imagined to have life and mental processes.

irreversibility The inability, in the preoperational child, to think through a series of events or mental operations and then mentally reverse the steps.

centration A preoperational thought pattern involving the inability to take into account more than one factor at a time.

conservation The understanding that the physical properties of an object or substance do not change when appearances change but nothing is added or taken away.

concrete operational stage The third of Piaget's stages, when a child understands conservation but still is incapable of abstract thought.

"Do they have the same amount of water or a different amount?"   "Now watch what I do" (pouring).   "Do they have the same amount of water or a different amount?"

FIGURE 7.4

Conservation of Liquid Task

Preoperational thinkers cannot understand that the amount of liquid remains the same when poured into a different-sized container. Mastery of this conservation task marks the transition to the concrete operational stage

Do It Yourself!   PLAYING WITH CHILDREN—PIAGETIAN STYLE

If you have access to a child, you can try out some of the problems Piaget posed for his children to study their thinking. For example, with a preoperational or concrete operational child, it's always fun to give a conservation problem that involves pouring liquid from a tall, narrow container into a short, wide one. Begin by pouring the same amounts into two identical vessels, such as glass measuring cups. Get the child to agree that you are starting with the same amount in each. Then pour the liquid from one vessel into a shallow pan. Ask the child, "Does one of these have more than the other, or are they both the same?" Then see if your child's responses fit with Piaget's observations.

Piaget found that the concrete operational child—one who understands conservation—will know that the volume of liquid remains the same, regardless of the shape of the container. The preoperational child will think that the shallow pan has less because the liquid does not come up as high on the container. This shows that the younger child does not know that volume is conserved, regardless of the shape of the container. Piaget claimed that it also showed that the younger child cannot reason about both height and width simultaneously.

---

mental operation   Solving a problem by manipulating images in one's mind.

Along with the ability to understand conservation, children at this stage have another wondrous new ability. They now can solve problems by manipulating concepts entirely in their minds: That is, they can perform **mental operations**. This allows concrete operational children to think things through before taking action. As a result, they may be less impulsive. They are also less gullible, giving up many "magical" notions, such as the belief in Santa Claus or the Tooth Fairy, that they now believe to be impossible.

Using their ability for performing mental operations, concrete operational children begin to use simple reasoning to solve problems. The symbols they use in reasoning are, however, still mainly symbols for concrete objects and events, not abstractions. The limitations of their concrete thinking reveal themselves in the familiar game of "20 Questions," the goal of which is to determine the identity of an object by asking the fewest possible yes/no questions of the person who thinks up the object. A child in this stage usually makes a series of specific guesses about what the object is ("Is it a bird?" "Is it a cat?"), rather than asking higher-level questions that more efficiently narrow down the possibilities for the correct answer ("Does it fly?" "Does it have fur?").

We will save our discussion of Piaget's final stage of cognitive development—the formal operational stage—for our discussion of adolescence. For now, suffice it to say that the final stage involves the development of abstract thought. Table 7.2 summarizes Piaget's four stages.

Beyond Piaget: Contemporary Perspectives on Cognitive Development Most psychologists accept the broad picture Piaget painted of development (Beilin, 1992; Lourenço & Machado, 1996). However, researchers have shown that children are,

TABLE 7.2 Piaget's Stages of Cognitive Development

Stage (Ages)	Characteristics and Major Accomplishments
Sensorimotor (approximately 0–2 years)	Children explore the world through their senses and motor abilities. Object permanence and goal-directed behavior emerge, along with the beginning of symbolic thought.
Preoperational (approximately 2–7 years)	Children's thought is characterized by egocentrism, animistic thinking, centration, and irreversibility. Symbolic thought continues to develop.
Concrete operations (approximately 7–11 years)	Children have mastered conservation and develop the ability to perform mental operations with images of concrete, tangible objects.
Formal operations (approximately 12+ years)	Teens and adults in this stage develop ability for abstract reasoning and hypothetical thought.

in some ways, more intellectually sophisticated at each stage than Piaget believed (Munakata et al., 1997).

Hints of Abilities Appear Earlier Than Piaget Thought   The limitations Piaget observed in the sensorimotor and preoperational stages can sometimes be mastered by children still in these age ranges. Object permanence is one example: The beginning of mental representation occurs as early as 4 months of age rather than in the second year, as Piaget thought. Children at that age shown "possible" and "impossible" events do not show surprise when viewing the possible event, but do show surprise upon seeing the "impossible" event (Baillargeon & DeVos, 1991; see Figure 7.5).

Researchers have also found, in contrast with Piaget's notion of centration, that by age 3 or 4, children understand that the unseen insides of objects (such as the inside of an egg, a rubber ball, or a dog) are not necessarily identical to their external appearances (Gelman & Wellman, 1991). And contrary to Piaget's claims about animistic thinking, 3- to 5-year-old children, when pressed to do so, are consistently able to distinguish between real and purely mental (imaginary) entities (Wellman & Estes, 1986). Finally, regarding egocentrism, by age 4 children can often see others' perspectives, as illustrated by the fact that they use simpler language and shorter words when talking with 2-year-olds than they do with older children or adults (Gelman & Shatz, 1978). Overall, Piaget's observations regarding the sequence of stages are accurate, but children today seem to develop some cognitive skills at a more accelerated pace than Piaget believed.

A Theory of Mind   These cognitive advances signal development of a **theory of mind**, which is an understanding that others may have beliefs, desires, and emotions different from one's own and that these mental states underlie their behavior (Frith & Frith, 1999). Your theory of mind underlies your expectations about how people will act in certain situations—such as when given a gift or when spoken to angrily. Importantly, it includes recognition that our expectations about others' actions may have to be adjusted based on what we know about the individual in question. This understanding of others' mental worlds facilitates empathy for others, enables deception, and increases our chance of making sound judgments about people when it counts.

theory of mind   An awareness that other people's behavior may be influenced by beliefs, desires, and emotions that differ from one's own.

Recent evidence indicates these abilities may begin as early as 6 months of age—which dovetails with recent findings on object permanence discussed in the previous section. At that age, one study discovered that infants could reliably distinguish between a helpful character and a harmful character and unfailingly chose the helpful character as a playmate (Hamlin et al., 2007). The cognitive milestones of the

Test Events

Possible event	Possible event	Impossible event
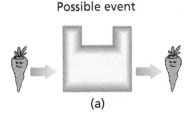	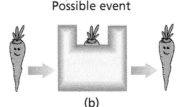	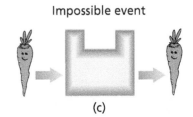
(a)	(b)	(c)

FIGURE 7.5

Testing Infants for Object Permanence

In this innovative test of object permanence, infants are shown a series of "possible" and "impossible" events. In **(a)**, a short carrot approaches a screen with a window at the top, then moves behind the screen, and finally emerges from the other side of the screen. In **(b)**, a tall carrot does the same thing. The top of the short carrot is *not* visible through the window as it passes (because it is shorter than the window), but the top of the taller carrot *is* visible as it passes the window. Because both of these scenarios are logical, they represent the "possible" events. In **(c)**, a tall carrot approaches and passes behind the screen, but this time the carrot top is *not* visible through the window (as it should be). Three- to 4-month-old infants gaze longer at this "impossible" scenario than they do at the "possible" events, indicating what may be the beginnings of object permanence.

Source: Adapted from Fig. 1, Baillargeon, R., & DeVos, J., 1991, Object permanence in young infants: further evidence. *Child Development, 62,* p. 1230. © The Society for Research in Child Development.

sensorimotor and preoperational stages facilitate further development of this initial accomplishment; and, by 5 years of age, children cross-culturally seem to understand that others' perceptions of the world may differ from their own (Callaghan et al., 2005).

Stages or Waves?   A second criticism of Piaget's theory questions his notion of the stages as abrupt transitions. Newer research suggests the transitions between one stage and another are more continuous than Piaget's theory implies. Psychologist Robert Siegler suggests a new metaphor for development (Siegler, 1994). Instead of the abrupt changes implied by stage theories, he proposes we think of "waves." The **wave metaphor**, he says, better fits both the scientific data and our everyday experience, which shows the variability of children's behavior. For example, during a single day, a child may use several different strategies to solve the same linguistic problem: "I ate," "I eated," and "I ated." This is not the pattern we would find if a child were making a sudden leap from one stage to another. Instead, says Siegler, this is a pattern of overlapping developmental waves, where each wave can be thought of as the ebb and flow in the strength of a cognitive strategy (Azar, 1995).

The Importance of Culture in Learning   Russian psychologist Lev Vygotsky (1934, 1987) emphasized the importance of cultural values and practices in a child's cognitive development, including the role of communication in learning. For Vygotsky, cognitive development was really the mental mastery of the rules and norms of a culture, transmitted via social interaction. Vygotsky's work, supported by others in more recent years (Conner & Cross, 2003; Rogoff, 2003), demonstrates how adults and other "experts" can help children develop their cognitive abilities more rapidly using a process called **scaffolding.** Just as a wood and steel scaffold provides support for the construction of buildings, cognitive scaffolding creates a support structure for constructing knowledge. By paying close attention to a child's current skill level, parents or teachers can tailor their instruction to that child by attaching each new lesson to something the child already knows. Vygotsky further identified the need for new challenges to be a bit beyond the child's current learning, but reachable with a little help, and not so far out of reach as to set the child up to fail. This *zone of proximal development* provides an important guideline for the parent or teacher in creating a learning plan for the child.

Social and Emotional Development

Our health, happiness, and even our survival depend on forming meaningful, effective relationships in the family, with peers—and, later in life, on the job. As children, we begin the long process of learning the rules our society follows for social and political interactions. Children must also learn to monitor their own feelings and behavior and to understand those of others. This process of social and emotional development is one of the most important developmental tasks of childhood, and it relies on both nature and nurture.

Temperament   One powerful influence on the way children interact with the world is their **temperament.** Psychologists use the term *temperament* for an individual's inherited, "wired-in" pattern of personality and behavior. Harvard researcher Jerome Kagan, who has studied temperament in thousands of children, observed that about 20 percent of children are born with tendencies toward shyness, while about 40 percent are born predisposed to boldness (Kagan, 1998). Shy babies, in the face of unfamiliar situations, become upset or withdrawn and are likely to try to avoid the situation. Bold babies, on the other hand, are more sociable and likely to react with interest to new situations.

Brain-imaging studies indicate these differences are physiological: Shy babies have more active amygdalas than do bold babies (Schwartz et al., 2003). These active amygdalas set in motion a series of physiological responses to stress, such as higher heart rate, release of stress hormones, and greater skin temperature changes in response to new situations. Thus, the shy children are physiologically wired to be more sensitive

---

wave metaphor   A way of conceptualizing cognitive development as occurring more gradually—in "waves"—rather than abruptly, as the stage theory suggests.

scaffolding   A teaching strategy which emphasizes the role of help from others in providing support for a person's learning.

temperament   An individual's characteristic manner of behavior or reaction—assumed to have a strong genetic basis.

CONNECTION CHAPTER 2

The amygdala, a part of the limbic system, is especially involved in the emotions of fear and aggression (p. 68).

to change and stress than their bold, sensation-seeking counterparts. This sensitivity may promote an advantage in interpersonal relations, however. Child development researcher Grazyna Kochanska (2009) suggests that fearfulness in children plays an important role in the child's moral development, fostering awareness of the consequences for wrongdoings—including empathy for the victim. Children who exhibit normal fearfulness are more likely to feel guilty after committing an offense, and that guilt helps serve as a deterrent later to repeated wrongdoings. ⊙

While basic temperaments can be recognized almost at birth, they are not written in stone (Kagan, 1996). From very early on, the environment interacts with these genetic tendencies, so that parenting styles and other aspects of a child's experience can modify the way temperament expresses itself. Oftentimes, people are less likely to engage and be playful with a shy baby, which will accentuate the child's initial disposition. On the other hand, if a shy baby's parents recognize the child's withdrawal and gently play with her and encourage her to interact, the child will become more outgoing than her temperament would otherwise have predicted. And a bold child reared by bold parents will certainly experience and respond to the world differently than will a bold child reared by timid or fearful parents. Thus, children are capable of learning a variety of responses to the world within their hereditary temperamental range—as long as people in their environment teach them.

Temperament is remarkably stable over time; that is, your temperament at birth is generally similar to your temperament throughout childhood, adolescence, and adulthood. While environmental influences can modify a temperament somewhat, the genetic leash limits the extent of change. Thus, it is important to note that no temperament is ideal for all situations. We should "remember that in a complex society like ours, each temperamental type can find its adaptive niche" (Kagan, quoted in Gallagher, 1994, p. 47). Much of our individual life success is linked to our ability to find an environment that capitalizes on our strengths.

Socialization Through interaction with your parents, peers, and others, you learned how to get along with people, a developmental task called **socialization**. Socialization, however, doesn't just happen in childhood. It is the lifelong process of shaping an individual's behavior patterns, values, standards, skills, attitudes, and motives to conform to those considered desirable in a particular society (Hetherington & Parke, 1975). Institutions such as family, schools, and the media exert pressure on the child to adopt socially approved values. Socialization of gender roles is one example: Boys and girls are often taught different ways of behaving and interacting. Leisure-time choices, such as television and peers, have heavy influences as well. An increasing number of preschool children are shaped also by their experiences in day care. And one other influence is of supreme importance: parenting styles.

Four Parenting Styles and Their Effects Most approaches to child rearing fall into one of four distinct parenting styles found in families all over the world (Baumrind, 1967, 1971; Russell et al., 2002). (As you read about these, you might try to imagine how you may have turned out differently if your parents had used one of the other approaches.) **Authoritarian parents** often live by the slogan, "Spare the rod and spoil the child." They demand conformity and obedience and tolerate little discussion of rules, which they enforce with punishment or threats of punishment. In an alternative approach, **authoritative parents** can be demanding, too. They have high expectations of their children, which they enforce with consequences. But unlike authoritarian parents, they combine high standards with warmth and respect for the child's views: They are quite willing to listen to a child's ideas and feelings and often encourage a democratic family atmosphere. Authoritative parents usually place a heavy emphasis on reasoning and explaining to help children learn to anticipate the consequences of their behavior.

Taking a third approach, **permissive parents** set few rules and allow children to make their own decisions. Like authoritative parents, they are caring and communicative, but permissive parents give most decision-making responsibility to their children. Permissive parents believe children can learn better from the consequences of their own

⊙ **Watch** the **Video** Temperament at **MyPsychLab**

socialization   The lifelong process of shaping an individual's behavior patterns, values, standards, skills, attitudes, and motives to conform to those regarded as desirable in a particular society.

authoritarian parent   One of the four parenting styles, characterized by demands for conformity and obedience, with little tolerance for discussion of rules, which the parent enforces with punishment or threats of punishment.

authoritative parent   One of the four parenting styles, characterized by high expectations of the children, which the parent enforces with consequences rather than punitive actions. Authoritative parents combine high standards with warmth and respect for the child's views.

permissive parent   One of the four parenting styles, characterized by setting few rules and allowing children to make their own decisions. While they may be caring and communicative, permissive parents give most decision-making responsibility to their children.

TABLE 7.3 **Features of the Four Parenting Styles**

Style	Emotional Involvement	Authority	Autonomy
Authoritarian	Parent is cold and rejecting; frequently degrades the child.	Parent is highly demanding; may use coercion by yelling, commanding, criticizing, and reliance on punishment.	Parent makes most decisions for the child; rarely listens to child's viewpoint.
Authoritative	Parent is warm, attentive, and sensitive to child's needs and interests.	Parent makes reasonable demands for the child's maturity level; explains and enforces rules.	Parent permits child to make decisions in accord with developmental readiness; listens to child's viewpoint.
Permissive	Parent is warm, but may spoil the child.	Parent makes few or no demands—often out of misplaced concern for child's self-esteem.	Parent permits child to make decisions before the child is ready.
Uninvolved	Parent is emotionally detached, withdrawn, and inattentive.	Parent makes few or no demands—often lacking in interest or expectations for the child.	Parent is indifferent to child's decisions and point of view.

Source: Berk, L. E. (2004). *Development through the lifespan*, 3rd ed. Boston, MA: Allyn & Bacon. Copyright © 2004 by Pearson Education. Published and reprinted by permission of Allyn & Bacon, Boston, MA.

uninvolved parent One of the four parenting styles, characterized by indifference or rejection, sometimes to the point of neglect or abuse.

actions than they can from following rules set by their parents. Finally, **uninvolved parents** tend to be either indifferent or rejecting, sometimes to the point of neglect or abuse (Maccoby & Martin, 1983). Typically, parents in this group lead such stress-filled lives that they have little time or energy for their children (see Table 7.3).

You can probably guess the usual outcomes of these different parenting styles. Research shows children with authoritative parents tend to be confident, self-reliant, and enthusiastic. Overall, these children are happier, less troublesome, and more successful. Those with permissive or uninvolved parents are typically less mature, more impulsive, more dependent, and more demanding. Children with authoritarian parents tend to be anxious and insecure. In fact, in some cases, authoritarian parenting may be a risk factor for antisocial behavior. A groundbreaking new study examined the combined effects of parenting style and attachment style on children's outcomes. The findings? In insecurely attached children, authoritarian parenting increased their risk of later antisocial behavior. Securely attached children, on the other hand, were able to tolerate authoritarian parenting without become oppositional. Researchers suggest that secure attachment may serve a protective role, leading the child to interpret the parent's harsher parenting behaviors as benevolent rather than threatening—as an insecurely attached child might (Kochanska et al., 2009).

Thinking back to our earlier discussion of attachment, these findings shouldn't be surprising. Generally speaking, authoritative parents take a more involved, interactive role in their children's lives—forming a stronger social–emotional attachment—than do the other three types of parents. This lays a strong foundation for prosocial behavior in the developing child.

Much of the early research on parenting styles was conducted in middle-class Western cultures. Can we expect the same findings elsewhere? Recent studies reveal that culture does play a role in parenting styles and parenting effectiveness, but not in the way you might think. Chinese, Hispanic, and Asian Pacific Island parents all tend to engage in stricter parenting than many Western parents and, from a distance, may resemble the authoritarian parenting style. A closer look, however, reveals that these same parents typically combine their strict rules and demands for respect with a great deal of warmth—especially from fathers. When this combination is present, children exhibit the same positive outcomes seen in Western children with authoritative parents (Berk, 2007). And in the United States, low-SES African American families exert high degrees of control over their children with positive results: These children do better in school and with peers than their counterparts who do not receive strict parenting (Taylor, Hinton, & Wilson, 1995).

Effects of Day Care   As working parents increasingly rely on day care for their children, many people are asking the following question: How necessary is it to have a full-time caregiver? The question is an urgent one in many countries, including the United States, where more than 60 percent of women with children under 6 years of age work outside the home, and more children are cared for by paid providers than by relatives (U.S. Department of Health and Human Services, 2009).

The research on this issue sends mixed messages. First, the good news: Most children thrive in day care. Both intellectually and socially, they do as well as—sometimes better than—children raised at home by a full-time parent. Now, the bad news: Poor-quality day care experiences can influence children to be aggressive, depressed, or otherwise maladjusted. Fortunately, ongoing nationwide studies of child care indicate that the overwhelming majority of day care centers do a fine job (Bower, 1996; NICHD Early Child Care Research Network, 2003, 2007).

As important as day care is in our society, it is comforting to note that having alternative caregivers does not in itself cause psychological problems. Rather, difficulties appear most often in poorly staffed centers where large numbers of children get little attention from only a few adults (Howes et al., 1988; NICHD Early Child Care Research Network, 2000). Another source of difficulty results from the unfortunate fact that children who are placed in the poorest quality day care programs are most often from the poorest, most disorganized, and most highly stressed families. Developmental psychologist Laura Berk (2004) concludes that this volatile combination of inadequate day care and family pressure places some children at high risk for emotional and behavioral problems. Yet, she says, using this evidence to curtail day care services would be mistaken, because forcing a parent on a marginal income to stay home may expose children to an even greater level of risk.

All this means that day care is, in itself, neither good nor bad. It is the quality of care, whether given by a parent or a paid provider, that makes all the difference. Development expert Sandra Scarr (1998) says:

> There is an extraordinary international consensus among child-care researchers and practitioners about what quality child care is: It is warm, supportive interactions with adults in a safe, healthy, and stimulating environment, where early education and trusting relationships combine to support individual children's physical, emotional, social, and intellectual development . . . (p. 102).

Leisure Influences   Children and adolescents in the United States and other industrialized countries have much more free time than do children elsewhere in the world. In nonindustrialized societies, children average some six hours a day working at some sort of chores or labor. By comparison, the typical American child spends less than one-half hour at such tasks. On the other hand, American children spend more time (on the average) doing schoolwork than did children in years past—although not as much as their foreign counterparts in other industrialized countries. Overall, though, the amount of free time available to U.S. children has increased dramatically over the last several generations (Larson, 2001). On average, American children today spend between 40 and 50 percent of their waking hours in discretionary activity.

Children and teens in the United States spend less time studying than do their counterparts in other industrialized countries—a finding thought to be related to U.S. students' lower scores on standardized tests.

What do children and teens do with all this leisure time? Almost seven hours per day (averaged to include weekends) is spent with media: A majority of that time is spent watching television, with an additional two hours a day on the computer and playing video games (Kaiser Foundation, 2005). Reading for pleasure is moderately popular; it is more so for girls than boys, though, and declines for both sexes as children grow into adolescence (Nippold et al., 2005). Time spent playing decreases as a child ages, becoming replaced largely by media-oriented activities, which are often engaged in with friends as well. Overall, kids and teens spend twice as much time with media as they do with friends and family combined, and six times more than they spend in physical activity, reading, or doing homework.

What impact do these leisure-time activities have on a child's development? Research findings are mixed. Time with friends is associated with well-being at all ages (Rawlins, 1992) and may be especially important in adolescence. Playing sports, which kids and teens do for just over an hour a day on average, has obvious benefits for health, as well as—depending on the sport and the environment—leadership, cooperation, and motivation. The effects of television, a topic of close scrutiny over the past few decades, seem to depend primarily on the type of programming being viewed. Educational television, which accounts for about 25 percent of children's television viewing, has a positive impact on literacy and cognitive development (Linebarger et. al., 2004). Heavy viewing of entertainment television, on the other hand, is a strong predictor of later deficiency in reading ability for young children (Ennemoser & Schneider, 2007). And the hundreds of studies examining the impact of viewing violent television leave no doubt that it increases aggressive behavior in viewers (Strasburger, 1995). Moreover, viewing any kind of entertainment television prior to the age of the 3 is powerfully linked to attention problems later in childhood (Zimmerman & Christakis, 2007). We will examine the mechanics of this association in the *Psychology Matters* feature on ADHD at the end of this section.

Playing video games with violent content affects aggression in a manner similar to that of watching violent television. In addition, research shows that violent video games decrease players' sensitivity to real-world violence (Carnagey et al., 2007) and also decrease prosocial (helping) behavior (Anderson & Bushman, 2001). On the other hand, frequent video-gaming appears to improve visual–spatial processing (Green & Bavelier, 2007). And not all video games are violent. Educational video games can improve critical thinking and learning in a variety of subjects ranging from social studies to math. Once again, the message seems clear: The content matters more than the medium itself.

CONNECTION CHAPTER 4

Habituation occurs when we become desensitized to a repeated stimulus so that it no longer produces the initial response (p. 135).

Gender Differences in Socialization   Anyone watching young boys and girls playing will notice gender differences in their social interaction. The sexes usually prefer to segregate themselves—a pattern that holds across cultures (Maccoby, 1998, 2000). In their play, boys are typically more aggressive than girls, although there are certainly exceptions. Girls tend to organize themselves into small, cooperative groups. By contrast, boys often form larger groups with a hierarchical structure or "pecking order." In these groups, individual boys continually compete for higher ranking positions. They frequently resort to aggressive tactics, such as hitting, shoving, and verbal threats. Gender differences are noticeable in choices of leisure activities as well. Boys are more likely to play sports or computer games with their leisure time than girls are, whereas girls watch more television (Cherney & London, 2006).

Evolutionary psychologists believe these gender differences have an innate basis (Buss, 1999), which may be related, in part, to gender differences in testosterone levels (Dabbs, 2000). This does not mean, of course, that environmental factors, such as parenting styles and peer influences, make no difference. Social-cognitive theorists like Kay Bussey and Albert Bandura (1999) remind us that children also learn gender roles and gender-related behaviors, such as aggressiveness, competitiveness, or cooperation, from their social environments and role models.

Psychosocial Development in Childhood: Erikson's Stages In the first section of this chapter, we introduced you to Erikson's theory of lifespan development and examined his first stage of trust versus mistrust. In childhood, individuals progress through three more of Erikson's stages, each time encountering a new "crossroad" and developing another key component in their schemas about themselves and their relation to the world. What do these stages reveal about what the social world looks like through a child's eyes?

Autonomy versus Shame or Self-Doubt In the second stage, which runs from about 18 months to 3 years of age, toddlers are rapidly learning to walk and talk. This increasing level of interaction with the world is laden with opportunities to directly influence outcomes. To develop a sense of independence or **autonomy**—the main developmental task in this stage—children need freedom (and sometimes encouragement) to try to do things on their own when appropriate. Too much restriction or criticism can lead to self-doubt, whereas harsh demands made too early, such as attempting toilet training before the child is ready, can lead to shame and discourage efforts to persevere in mastering new tasks; hence the name for this stage, *autonomy versus shame or self-doubt*. Children who enter this stage with a general sense of trust in the world are more likely to successfully develop autonomy than children who did not master the first stage.

Although Erikson didn't address the role of temperament in psychosocial development, we should point out its influence: We would expect shy children to need more gentle encouragement than bold children. Thus, although a nurturing and supportive environment is key to development of autonomy, nature plays a role as well.

Initiative versus Guilt Once a child develops trust and autonomy, the third challenge is to cultivate **initiative**, or the ability to initiate activities oneself, rather than merely responding to others. During the preschool years, autonomous children will become more purposeful, wanting to choose what to wear, what to eat, or how to spend their time. The danger at this stage comes from overcontrolling adults, who may demand an impossible degree of self-control ("Why can't you sit still?"), which can result in the child feeling overcome by inadequacy and guilt. The term for this stage reflects these two alternatives: *initiative versus guilt*. Caregivers' responses to self-initiated activities either encourage or discourage the freedom and self-confidence needed for the next stage.

Industry versus Inferiority Children who successfully master Erikson's first three stages enter elementary school ready to develop their skills and competencies in a more systematic way. From ages 6 to 12, school activities and sports offer arenas for learning more complex intellectual and motor skills, while peer interaction offers the chance to develop social skills. Successful efforts in these pursuits lead to feelings of competence, which Erikson called **industry**. Nurturing and supportive parenting at this stage helps children reflect on their experiences, learning from both their successes and failures and also recognizing that some failures are inevitable. On the other hand, children with overly demanding or disengaged parents may have trouble seeing their failures in perspective and ultimately develop a sense of inferiority. Likewise, youngsters who had trouble with one or more of the earlier stages may become discouraged spectators rather than performers, leading also to feelings of inferiority rather than competence. The term for this stage, therefore, is *industry versus inferiority*.

In summary, we have seen how development of language, cognitive skills, and social competencies all interact during the rapid growth and changes of childhood. Individual gains in each of these areas progress on a general biological timetable, but the pace and nature of the gains are heavily influenced by our environment. In the next section, we will see how these achievements of childhood lay the foundation for another period of rapid changes: the world of adolescence.

autonomy In Erikson's theory, autonomy is the major developmental task of the second stage in childhood. Achieving autonomy involves developing a sense of independence, as opposed to being plagued by *self-doubt*.

initiative In Erikson's theory, initiative is the major developmental task in the third stage of childhood. Initiative is characterized by the ability to initiate activities oneself, rather than merely responding to others or feeling *guilt* at not measuring up to other's expectations.

industry Erikson's term for a sense of confidence that characterizes the main goal of the fourth developmental stage in childhood. Children who do not develop industry (confidence) will slip into a self-perception of *inferiority*.

[PSYCHOLOGY MATTERS]

The Puzzle of ADHD

attention-deficit hyperactivity disorder (ADHD) A psychological disorder involving poor impulse control, difficulty concentrating on a task for a sustained period of time, high distractibility, and excessive activity.

Attention-deficit hyperactivity disorder (ADHD), is a psychological disorder found in 3 to 5 percent of school-age children in America, with cross-cultural prevalence similar at about 5 percent (Faraone et al., 2003). Symptoms of ADHD include poor impulse control, difficulty concentrating on a task for a sustained period of time, high distractibility, and excessive activity. In boys, these symptoms often manifest themselves in disruptive behavior—such as the boy who frequently jumps out of his seat in class, blurts out answers, or interrupts a conversation. In girls, however—who comprise only about 20 percent of ADHD diagnoses—the disorder more often looks like lack of organization or a tendency to lose things. In both boys and girls, these difficulties bleed over into multiple domains, often resulting in poor academic performance and unstable peer relationships. In fact, the impact of symptoms on multiple domains in life is a key criterion for diagnosis of ADHD and necessary to distinguish true ADHD from commonly occurring symptoms of stressful lives or features of normal childhood development. The disorder seems to follow a predictable developmental path, with symptoms appearing in the early childhood years and, in roughly 50 percent of cases, spontaneously fading away as the child enters adolescence. Nonetheless, some individuals continue to exhibit symptoms of ADHD throughout adulthood.

CONNECTION CHAPTER 12

ADHD is classified as one of several developmental disorders—a category that also includes autism and dyslexia (p. 542).

ADHD has received quite a bit of public attention in recent years, and as a result, most people know something about it. As is often the case, though, the layperson's knowledge of a psychological disorder may rely on media reports, Hollywood portrayals, and the words of a well-meaning (but sometimes misinformed) friend or even teacher—and consequently isn't as factual as he or she thinks it is. And overconfidence in one's knowledge about something medical or psychological sometimes leads to self-diagnosis, which may or may not be accurate. Given the increasing numbers of our students who report having symptoms of ADHD, we think it's important to set the record straight about what ADHD is, what we know about its causes, and what research tells us about effective treatments.

What Causes ADHD?

Research to determine the causes of ADHD is in the early stages, although twin studies and other heritability research point to a strong genetic component. From a nurture perspective, prenatal exposure to nicotine and alcohol have been found to increase incidence of ADHD. And while some theories of environmental causes—such as a diet too high in sugar—have been debunked, recent research has revealed some provocative findings. As we know, the first few years of life are a time when the brain is developing synaptic connections at a furious pace. A recent longitudinal study with a nationally representative sample now provides strong evidence that viewing noneducational television prior to the age of 3 predicts attention deficits later in childhood (Zimmerman & Christakis, 2007). What's more, the culprit wasn't only violent television—even nonviolent entertainment programs and DVDs produced this effect. Researchers suggest it is the fast-paced movement of entertainment programming driving the finding: In other words, watching programs that quickly and frequently switch from one scene to another—during a time when brain connections are forming—limits the brain's opportunities to create pathways for more extended focus and concentration. Instead, it trains the brain to seek rapid changes in stimulation. It's easy to see how this sets a child up for problems with attention span later in life. This also explains why viewing similar amounts of educational television (which moves more slowly) did not increase incidence of attention deficits later in childhood. The study controlled for other factors that may influence development of attention deficits, such as family environment, parenting style, and cognitive stimulation. According to a companion study, 90 percent of children under 24 months regularly watch television, and half of what they view is entertainment television (Zimmerman et al., 2007).

Physiologically, how does an ADHD brain differ from a "normal" brain? One important difference has to do with the neurotransmitter dopamine, active when a person is engaged in an interesting task. People with ADHD seem to receive fewer and/or weaker dopamine bursts, which correlates with less engagement and long-term interest in a task. And while earlier research indicated that ADHD brains were smaller than non-ADHD brains, newer research reveals that ADHD brains develop normally and achieve normal size; they simply take a few years longer to do so in the cortical regions. The prefrontal cortex is slowest to develop in ADHD brains—up to five years later than non-ADHD brains—which fits with ADHD patients' difficulties staying focused on a multistep task requiring planning and follow-through. Interestingly, the motor cortex actually develops faster than normal in ADHD brains, which researchers suggest might explain the hyperactivity feature of ADHD (Shaw et al., 2007). Overall, the finding that ADHD brains develop normally, albeit more slowly, may explain why some children with ADHD seem to "grow out of it" sometime in adolescence—but still leaves a puzzle as to why some do not.

How Can ADHD Be Treated?

Both medication and psychological treatments can be effective in treating ADHD, but optimal treatment varies considerably among individuals. Some do very well on medication, but careful monitoring and management by a physician with expertise in ADHD is highly recommended to match each patient with the right medication and dosage for that individual. Also, findings suggest periodic "trial withdrawals" to determine whether a child still needs medication (Swanson et al., 2007a)—of course, trial withdrawals must be conducted with the close supervision of the prescribing physician.

Alternatively, behavioral therapy helps children with ADHD learn to control some of their problematic behaviors and replace them with more effective behaviors—for example, learning to recognize an impulse and count to 10 before acting on it. Parents and other family members are crucial partners in effective behavioral therapy. Parents can set clear expectations and use principles of operant conditioning to help shape the child's behavior, one step at a time. All members of the family can help provide redirection when the child loses focus and reinforcement for each success. As with any type of behavior modification program, though, consistency is important, which means the family must prioritize the time and attention necessary for treatment to be effective—which can be a challenge when a family is already juggling multiple tasks and priorities.

Behavioral therapy is the treatment of choice for very young children (for whom medication is not recommended). Also, it may be the best initial treatment for someone who has recently developed symptoms of ADHD; then, if it does not improve symptoms, medication may be added to the treatment plan. Indeed, one recent national study found that, for many, a combination of medication and behavior treatment works best (MTA Cooperative Group, 1999).

In closing, we offer a few notes of caution. First, although studies to date do not show any serious long-term effects of ADHD medication, it may be too soon to know for sure. We do know that children not taking ADHD medication grow about an inch taller, on average, than those who have taken medication such as Ritalin (Swanson et al., 2007). Also, families and teachers should keep in mind the power of labeling. When we label someone as having ADHD, especially without a valid diagnosis, we run the risk of the individual developing an identity consistent with the symptoms of ADHD, habits that later may be hard to overcome—even if the individual's brain no longer fits the ADHD profile. Finally, a recent article offers what may be a more balanced perspective on the disorder:

> [We must] remember that ADHD children possess many positive traits. They tend to be free-spirited, inquisitive, energetic and funny, as well as intelligent and creative. Their behavior is often spontaneous, helpful and sensitive. Many ADHD children are talented multitaskers, last-minute specialists and improvisationalists. Parents and educators should encourage these strengths and let their children know whenever possible that these qualities are highly valued (Rothenberger & Banaschewski, 2007).

CONNECTION CHAPTER 4

Behavioral psychology examines how we learn by association and by reward and punishment (p. 135).

Check Your Understanding

✓•─ **Study** and **Review** at **MyPsychLab**

1. **ANALYSIS:** Is the human ability for language innate or learned? Explain your answer.

2. **MATCHING:** Match the ability/limitation with the Piagetian stage at which it becomes an important characteristic of thinking:

   a. conservation
   b. egocentrism
   c. object permanence

      1. sensorimotor stage
      2. preoperational stage
      3. concrete operational stage

3. **APPLICATION:** Imagine that you are a family counselor. What parenting style would you encourage parents to adopt in order to promote confidence and self-reliance in their children?

4. **ANALYSIS:** According to research cited in this section, what is the best advice you can give parents about whether their children should watch television and play video games?

5. **UNDERSTANDING THE CORE CONCEPT:** Which is most important for healthy development in childhood: nature or nurture?

Answers 1. We are born with specialized structures in our brain especially designed for language, but environmental factors—such as frequency of exposure to language and the specific language spoken or signed in the environment—determine the pace and type of language that develops. Thus, it is both innate and learned. **2.** a = 3; b = 2; c = 1 **3.** Authoritative **4.** Educational television promotes literacy and cognitive development, but viewing of entertainment television predicts later reading deficiencies in young children and is also linked to development of ADHD. Violent television increases aggression in viewers. Violent video games do the same and also decrease sensitivity to real-world violence and reduce the likelihood of prosocial behavior. Educational video games can improve critical thinking and learning. **5.** Nature and nurture both play critical roles in healthy development.

7.3 KEY QUESTION
─ What Changes Mark the Transition of Adolescence?

Were all your developmental tasks finished by the time you entered *adolescence* (or, in plain English, were you "all grown up")? Most early theorists thought so. After that, they assumed, the psyche was set for life and would undergo few important changes. Modern research disputes these older views. Today's psychologists agree that we have a remarkable capacity for developmental change throughout our lifespan (Kagan, 1996, 1998). Again, in adolescence, the big changes lie in three important areas—as our Core Concept says:

> **Core Concept 7.3**
>
> **Adolescence offers new developmental challenges growing out of physical changes, cognitive changes, and socioemotional pressures.**

When does adolescence begin? Or, to put the question more personally, what event first made you think of yourself as an adolescent? Chances are it had something to do with your sexual maturation, such as a first menstrual period or a nocturnal ejaculation. Psychologists mark the beginning of **adolescence** at the onset of puberty, when sexual maturity (the ability to reproduce) is attained. Besides sexual maturity, what else happens during adolescence? And when does adolescence end and adulthood begin?

adolescence   In industrial societies, a developmental period beginning at puberty and ending (less clearly) at adulthood.

Adolescence and Culture

Variations among cultures compound the difficulty of specifying the span of adolescence. Although the physical changes that take place at this stage are universal, the social and psychological dimensions of adolescence depend heavily on cultural context. For example, if you enter your teen years in a society that celebrates puberty as the entry to adulthood and rewards you with power to make responsible choices, you will have a very different experience than someone whose culture dismisses teenagers as confused and potentially dangerous troublemakers.

Can you imagine becoming an "adult" around age 13? In most nonindustrial societies, that is the norm: There is not an adolescent stage as we know it. Instead, children in these societies move directly into adulthood with **rites of passage**. These rituals usually take place about the time of puberty and serve as public acknowledgment of the transition from childhood to adulthood. Rites of passage vary widely among cultures, from extremely painful rituals to periods of instruction on sexual and cultural practices or periods of seclusion involving survival ordeals. For example, in some tribal groups, a young person takes a meditative journey alone or submits to symbolic scarring or circumcision surrounded by friends and family. Once individuals have completed the passage, there is no ambiguity about their status: They are adults, and ties to their childhood have been severed.

Our own culture has some transition rituals, but the meanings are less well defined, and as a result, they do not provide clear markers for the beginning of adolescent or adult status. Qualifying for a driver's license is one such rite of passage for many middle-class teens in America. Another, which you might recall, is high school graduation. Mexican American girls may celebrate *quinceañeras,* and Jewish American teens may celebrate bat mitzvahs or bar mitzvahs. All of these provide a young person with an added measure of freedom and independence not available to children, but none are necessarily aligned with the transition into or out of adolescence.

Although many issues loom large in adolescence, we will focus on the most important developmental tasks confronting adolescents in the United States and the industrialized Western world. The central task of this period is establishing one's identity. That complex process includes coming to terms with physical maturity, achieving a new level of cognitive development, redefining social roles and emotional issues, dealing with sexual opportunities and pressures, and the development of moral standards. We begin with the physical changes marking the end of childhood and the onset of adolescence.

Physical Maturation in Adolescence

One of the first signs of approaching adolescence is the pubescent growth spurt. **Puberty,** or sexual maturity, for boys begins with increasing size of the testicles, while for girls typically begins with the development of breasts. Sprouting of pubic hair generally follows for both sexes, along with growth of external genitalia. This process generally commences around age 10 or 11 for girls, and about two years later for boys. Puberty peaks with the production of live sperm in boys, (usually at about age 14 in the United States), and **menarche,** or the onset of menstruation, in girls (usually between ages 11 and 14; Slyper, 2006).

Do you recall becoming more aware of your appearance during adolescence? Dramatic physical changes and heightened emphasis on peer acceptance—especially acceptance by sexually attractive peers—intensify concern with one's **body image.** Boys and girls alike often judge themselves harshly by the standards they think other people may be applying to them. And, unfair as it may be, physical attractiveness does influence the way people think about each other (Hatfield & Rapson, 1993). Thus, one of the most formidable tasks of adolescence involves coming to terms with one's physical self by developing a realistic—yet accepting—body image. This image is dependent not only on measurable features, such as height and weight, but also on perceptions of other people's assessments and on cultural standards of physical beauty. And the age at which teens go through puberty has an impact on their body image: boys who mature earlier than their peers generally have a positive body image, whereas early-maturing girls often have a negative body image. These girls also report more bullying from peers (Downing & Bellis, 2009).

And note other gender differences: Approximately 44 percent of American adolescent girls and 23 percent of boys claimed they have "frequently felt ugly and unattractive." Similar data have been found across many cultures (Offer et al., 1981, 1988). Physical

rite of passage Social ritual that marks the transition between developmental stages, especially between childhood and adulthood.

puberty The onset of sexual maturity.

menarche The onset of menstruation.

body image An individual's perception of and feelings about their physical appearance.

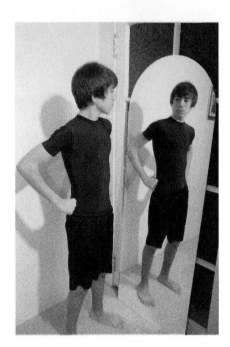

Body image—for boys and girls alike—becomes especially important in the teenage years.

Watch the Video Adolescent Sexuality at **MyPsychLab**

sexual orientation   The direction of one's sexual interests (usually for individuals of the same sex, the opposite sex, or both sexes).

appearance is clearly one of the biggest concerns among adolescents (Perkins & Lerner, 1995). Girls' self-concepts are particularly tied to perceptions of their physical attractiveness, while boys seem more concerned with their physical prowess, athletic ability, and effectiveness in achieving goals (Lerner et al., 1976; Wade, 1991). In general, girls and women are more dissatisfied with their weight and shape than are males, and they experience more conflict about food and eating (Rolls et al., 1991). One study found that 56 percent of teenage girls had gone on diets because they thought themselves too heavy—when in reality, most of them were within a normal weight range (Patton et al., 1997). These differences probably mirror a preoccupation with female beauty and male strength—an inevitable source of concern because not all adolescents can embody the cultural ideals of attractiveness.

Culture, however, influences the relationship between body image and self-acceptance. For example, self-esteem of White adolescents is more tied to physical attractiveness than is that of Black adolescents—for both sexes (Wade, 1991). Yet, for teens in Hong Kong, while body fat is related to physical self-concept, it doesn't decrease global self-esteem at all. In fact, being too thin is perceived in a similar manner as being too fat, probably reflecting the Chinese cultural value on moderation, as well as greater acceptance of obesity than American culture (Marsh et al., 2007). But the spread of Western ideals is expanding the reach of powerful media images and their impact on teens' body images: Young women in both the Middle East and Japan are developing body-image problems at increasing rates (Chisuwa & O'Day, 2010; Thomas et al., 2010). Although adolescents seem to become more accepting of their appearances over time, the attainment of acceptable body images can be a difficult task.

Adolescent Sexuality

A new awareness of sexual feelings and impulses accompanies physical maturity. Not surprisingly, perhaps, a majority of American adolescent males and females report thinking about sex often (Offer et al., 1981). By age 17, about 40 percent of teens in the United States and Canada have had their first sexual experience, a figure that rises to about 75 percent by age 20 (Berk, 2007; Harvey & Spigner, 1995). Many of these teens, however, lack adequate knowledge or harbor misconceptions about sex and sexuality, and this lack of accurate knowledge creates a variety of problems ranging from STIs (sexually transmitted infections) to unwanted pregnancy to unsatisfactory sexual experiences. ⊙

Masturbation is the most common orgasmic expression of sexual impulses in adolescence (Wilson & Medora, 1990). By age 16, almost 90 percent of boys and 60 percent of girls in the United States report they have masturbated (Janus & Janus, 1993). But these figures are only estimates and could well be low. You can imagine the problems scientists face in trying to get good data on private sexual practices. Sex research typically involves surveys, which—even when anonymous, as most are—may not give a complete picture of behaviors often associated with shame and guilt.

Sexual orientation also begins to emerge in adolescence, with the majority of adolescents having a predominantly heterosexual orientation. Males and females, though, differ in reports of their first sexual experiences. For the vast majority of females, emotional involvement is an important ingredient of sexual attraction. In contrast, for most males, personal relationships appear to be less important than the sex act itself. In fact, the average male reports little emotional involvement with his first sexual partner (Miller & Simon, 1980; Sprecher et al., 1995).

The same cautions that apply to the data on masturbation also apply to the research on the prevalence of gay, lesbian, and bisexual orientations. Studies generally find that 8 to 12 percent of teens report having had sexual contact with a same-sex partner. Same-sex behavior, however, does not necessarily mean the individual considers him- or herself to be gay, lesbian, or even bisexual. Some experiment with same-sex activity yet think of themselves as heterosexual. For others, however, such experiences do fit with a gay, lesbian, or bisexual orientation. And about one in every eight teens say they are unsure of their primary sexual orientation (Faulkner & Cranston, 1998).

Sexual attraction toward the same sex or both sexes is difficult to resolve during adolescence, when individuals are intensely concerned with the conventions and norms of their society. While most gay and lesbian individuals first become aware of their sexual orientation in early adolescence, many may not attain self-acceptance of their sexual identities until their middle or late 20s or beyond (Newman & Muzzonigro, 1993). The time lag undoubtedly reflects the relative lack of social support for nontraditional sexual orientations and exemplifies the importance of society's role in all aspects of identity development.

Neural and Cognitive Development in Adolescence

Changes that began in the womb continue to occur in the adolescent brain (Spear, 2000). While early childhood is the most rapid period for development of neural connections, the frontal lobes of the brain continue to mature throughout adolescence and into young adulthood. What are the implications of this adolescent change in neurology?

Sexual orientation is an important element of identity.

Teens: Guided by Reason or Emotion? The frontal lobes, as you learned in Chapter 2, are necessary for rational thinking and judgment (among other things). The orbito-frontal cortex, in particular, helps us weigh the emotional component of a choice with a more rational evaluation of our long-term goals. It puts the brakes, so to speak, on the basic impulses driven by our amygdala. In adolescence, the amygdala is fully developed, but the frontal lobes (including the orbito-frontal cortex) are not. This imbalance in the pace of brain development means the teen brain is wired to react more emotionally than an adult (for whom both areas are developed) or a child (for whom neither area is developed). Teens' amygdalas send impulses their frontal cortices can't effectively process (McClure et al., 2004). Add to that the pubescent increases in estrogen and testosterone levels (Spear, 2000), and it's no wonder adolescents are prone to sensation-seeking and risk-taking behaviors.

Is this unique brain pattern of adolescence necessarily bad, though? As previously noted, adolescence is a time when individuals establish their identity, with the ultimate goal of becoming independent from the family unit. Perhaps the increased risk taking is a necessary component that helps teens explore and experiment in their environments. In other words, it may provide a biological basis for the courage necessary to go out on one's own. Further, the heightened emotional reactivity may aid in threat perception, helping the teen become quickly aware of dangers associated with new activities and thus promoting success and survival. The same brain patterns have, in fact, been observed in nonhuman species such as primates and rodents, suggesting that the neural development of adolescence may indeed serve an important evolutionary purpose (Casey et al., 2008).

The Brain Undergoes Major Pruning Earlier in this chapter, we noted the importance of sensitive periods for development of certain abilities, along with the pruning process that begins to occur around the time of adolescence (Kurth et al., 2010). The two concepts together underscored the importance of a rich environment in the early years of life, so neural pathways can form to support a wide variety of skills and abilities. By early adolescence, regions of the brain that haven't been adequately stimulated begin to be trimmed away in the process of synaptic pruning. As this occurs, the adolescent brain becomes gradually less adept at learning completely new things as opportunities for neural connections begin to diminish. On the plus side, this allows for enhanced development of stronger regions: Continued use of established connections increases the myelin of the neurons, which in turn enables faster functioning. On the minus side, though, plasticity is reduced and problematic behavior patterns or traits that have developed become more resistant to change or intervention. And if the pruning process goes awry, important connections may be lost, which could help explain the onset in late adolescence and early adulthood of disorders such as schizophrenia (Moskowitz, 2009).

By adolescence, then, behavior patterns developed in earlier years have strengthened considerably. Adolescence may represent the last fertile opportunity to intervene in the development of strong traits, be they athletic, artistic, linguistic, or psychopathic. For example, studies of various treatment programs for individuals with psychopathic traits such as callous and unemotional behavior show the highest rate of success among 4- to 6-year-olds, with moderate success among teen offenders and no measurable success among adults (Caldwell et al., 2007; Dadds & Fraser, 2006). Also, a twin study found that maintaining a high GPA could act as a buffer against development of antisocial behavior in the teen years, decreasing the impact of other genetic and environmental risk factors (Johnson et al., 2009).

Piaget's Final Stage: Formal Operational Thought Adolescence brings with it Piaget's final stage of cognitive growth, involving the ability for abstract and complex thought. In this **formal operational stage**, the individual begins to ponder introspective problems, such as how to become better accepted by peers. Teens also become capable of dealing with abstract and intangible issues, such as fairness, love, and reasons for existence. Essentially, they learn to deal with hypothetical problems rather than needing the concrete base of the previous stage. With these formal operational reasoning powers, adolescents and adults can now approach life's problems using more systematic thinking strategies. In the "20 Questions" game we mentioned earlier in the chapter, for example, they impose their own structures on the task, starting with broad categories and then formulating and testing hypotheses in light of their knowledge of categories and relationships. Their questioning moves from general categories ("Is it an animal?") to subcategories ("Does it fly?") and then to specific guesses ("Is it a bird?"; Bruner et al., 1966).

Current research, however, questions Piaget's notion that formal operational thought necessarily develops in adolescence. Some adults, it seems, never develop this capacity; instead, it appears dependent on education and experience. College-educated people are more likely to demonstrate formal operational thought, and in general, people are most skillful with abstractions and hypotheticals in their areas of expertise (Keating, 2004). Overall, development of this type of cognitive ability, more than any of Piaget's other cognitive tasks, appears highly reliant on cultural values and the environment.

formal operational stage The last of Piaget's stages, during which abstract thought appears.

Moral Development: Kohlberg's Theory

Is there a pattern in the development of our sense of right and wrong? The best-known psychological approach to moral development comes from the late Lawrence Kohlberg (1964, 1981), who based his theory on Piaget's view of cognitive development. After all, reasoned Kohlberg, moral thinking is just a special form of cognition. Mirroring Piaget's stages, each stage in Kohlberg's theory of moral reasoning is based on a different moral standard. Table 7.4 summarizes these stages.

What interested Kohlberg most were the ways people reason about moral problems, rather than what they might do when led into temptation (Alper, 1985; Kohlberg, 1968). Accordingly, Kohlberg probed people's moral thinking by presenting people with a series of *moral dilemmas,* such as this one:

In Europe a woman was near death from a very special kind of cancer. There was one drug that the doctors thought might save her. It was a form of radium that a druggist in the same town had recently discovered. The drug was expensive to make, but the druggist was charging ten times what the drug cost him to make. He paid $200 for the radium and charged $2000 for a small dose of the drug. The sick woman's husband, Heinz, went to everyone he knew to borrow the money, but he could only get together about $1000, which is half of what it cost. He told the druggist that his wife was dying and asked him to sell it cheaper or let him pay later. But the druggist said, "No, I discovered the drug, and I'm going to make money from it." So Heinz got desperate and broke into the man's

With their peers, adolescents refine their social skills and try out different social behaviors. Gradually, they define their social identities, the kind of people they choose to be, and the sorts of relationships they will pursue.

Are parents still important to the adolescent? The answer is an unequivocal yes. Parents who continue to monitor their teens' activities, and maintain open and healthy communication through these years, are most likely to see their teenagers successfully navigate the challenges of adolescence. A high-quality parent–child relationship remains the strongest predictor of adolescent mental health (Steinberg & Silk, 2002).

Erikson's Psychosocial Development in Adolescence   Erik Erikson noted the emergence of an independent self in adolescence and characterized it as the essential dilemma of adolescence. This search for **identity**, Erikson asserted, can be impeded by the confusion of playing many different roles for different audiences in an expanding social world. Thus, he called this stage *identity versus role confusion*. Resolving this *identity crisis* helps the individual develop a sense of a coherent self. Psychologist James Marcia suggests that, as teens seek their own identities, they may experience several different levels of identity development based on their degrees of *commitment* to an identity and the amount of *exploration* they have done (see Figure 7.6). While it is normal and healthy for one's identity to change throughout life, failure of the adolescent to find a satisfactory resolution for his or her identity issues may result in a self-concept that lacks a stable core. Resolution of this issue is both a personal process and a social experience (Erikson, 1963).

Is Adolescence a Period of Turmoil?   Problems with loneliness, depression, and shyness can also become significant during adolescence, which is one reason for the sharp increase in suicide among teenagers (Berk, 2004; U.S. Bureau of the Census, 2002). Studies of adolescent suicide show that the triggering experience for such a tragedy is often a shaming or humiliating event, such as failure in some achievement or a romantic rejection (Garland & Zigler, 1993). The intensity of a young person's social and personal motives, combined with the overactive emotional brain, can make it hard to keep perspective and recognize that even difficult times will pass and everyone makes mistakes.

But is adolescence inevitably a period of turmoil? It is a period in which individuals are likely to have conflicts with their parents, experience extremes of mood, and engage in risky behaviors (Arnett, 1999). For some, adolescence certainly presents overwhelming problems in relationships and in self-esteem. Yet for most teens, these years are not a time of anxiety and despair (Myers & Diener, 1995). While many parents anticipate that the relationship with their children will encounter a rocky road when the children enter adolescence, the more typical experience is relatively tranquil.

In adolescence, peer relationships take on increasing importance.

identity   In Erikson's theory, identity is a sense of who one is—a coherent self. Developing a sense of identity is the main goal of adolescence.

		Has the individual made a *commitment* to certain beliefs, values, and interests?	
		Yes	No
Has the individual thoroughly *explored* a variety of options regarding personal beliefs, values, and interests?	Yes	**Identity Achievement:** Commitment to personal identity as a result of significant exploration	**Identity Moratorium:** Actively exploring identity options prior to making identity commitment.
	No	**Identity Foreclosure:** Commitment to personal identity based on conformity to values of others (parents, peers, etc.), without having personally explored other options.	**Identity Diffusion:** Undeveloped identity, characterized by lack of interest in such matters, or indecision about them.

FIGURE 7.6

Marcia's Stages of Identity Development

In fact, the majority of adolescent youth say they feel close to their parents (Galambos, 1992). In general, those who have the least trouble are adolescents with authoritative parents—who are responsive and, at the same time, hold their children to high standards. Adolescents who have the most difficulty are more likely to come from homes where parenting is either permissive or authoritarian (Collins et al., 2000).

[PSYCHOLOGY MATTERS]

Using Psychology to Learn Psychology: Cognitive Development in College Students

Does your arrival at the formal operational stage, in the middle or high school years, signal the end of the cognitive line? Or will your thinking abilities continue to develop as you go on through college? If you are a returning student in your 30s, 40s, or beyond, will your cognitive development continue apace with your younger counterparts? A study by developmental psychologist William Perry suggests that your perspective on learning will change and mature as your college experience unfolds. This prediction is based on a sample of students Perry followed through their undergraduate years at Harvard and Radcliffe. He found that students' views of psychology and their other social science courses changed radically, as did their views of what they were there to learn (Perry, 1970, 1994).

At first, students in Perry's study had difficulty coming to grips with the diverse and conflicting viewpoints they encountered in their courses. For example, many confronted, for the first time, the idea that reasonable people can disagree—even about their most cherished "truths" concerning good and evil, God, nature, and human nature:

> A few seemed to find the notion of multiple frames of reference wholly unintelligible. Others responded with violent shock to their confrontation in dormitory chat sessions, or in their academic work, or both. Others experienced a joyful sense of liberation (Perry, 1970, p. 4).

In dealing with this academic culture shock, Perry's students passed through a series of distinct intellectual stages reminiscent of Piaget's stages. And, although they arrived at college at different levels of cognitive maturity and continued to develop at different rates, all progressed through the same intellectual stages in the same sequence. Here are some of the highlights of this intellectual journey:

- Students at first typically see college or university as a storehouse of information—a place to learn the Right Answers. Thus, they believe it is the professor's job to help students find these answers.

- Sooner or later, students discover an unexpected—perhaps shocking—diversity of opinion, even among the experts. At this stage, college students are likely to attribute conflicting opinions to confusion among poorly qualified experts.

- Eventually, students begin to accept diverse views as legitimate—but only in the fuzzy areas (such as psychology, other social sciences, and humanities) where experts haven't yet found the Right Answers. They decide that, in subjects where the Right Answers haven't been nailed down, professors grade them on "good expression" of their ideas.

- Next, some students (not all) discover that uncertainty and diversity of opinion are everywhere—not just in the social sciences and humanities. They typically solve this problem in their minds by dividing the academic world into two realms: (a) one in which Right Answers exist (even though they haven't all been discovered) and (b) another in which anyone's opinion is as good as anyone else's. Often, at this stage, they perceive math and the "hard" sciences as the realm of Right Answers, leaving the social sciences and humanities in the realm of opinion.

- Finally, the most mature students come to see that multiple perspectives exist and are valuable in all fields of study.

The students who achieve the final stage begin to see "truth" as tentative. They now realize knowledge is always building and changing—even in the "hard" sciences. And they realize a college education is not just learning an endless series of facts. Rather, it is learning how to think critically about the important questions and major concepts of a field. In this text, we have called them "Key Questions" and "Core Concepts."

Check Your Understanding

✓ Study and Review at MyPsychLab

1. **RECALL:** What is the major developmental task of adolescence, according to Erikson?

   a. puberty
   b. formal operational thought
   c. identity
   d. intimacy

2. **ANALYSIS:** You are watching a television program and see an interview with a psychologist who has written a new book entitled *The Teen Years: Face It, Parents—You Don't Matter Anymore!* Is this point of view accurate, according to research? Why or why not?

3. **RECALL:** About what percent of North American teens have had their first sexual experience by age 17?

   a. 20 percent
   b. 40 percent
   c. 60 percent
   d. 75 percent

4. **APPLICATION:** Your next-door neighbor is a teenage boy who recently got arrested for shoplifting. In talking about it, he says, "I realize now I shouldn't have done that. My parents are really mad at me, and my teachers think I'm a troublemaker." Which of Kohlberg's stages of moral development does this boy seem to be in?

5. **UNDERSTANDING THE CORE CONCEPT:** What three categories of changes lead to the challenges faced in adolescence?

Answers 1. c **2.** No, it is not accurate. Although peers become more influential in adolescence, parents still play a key role in their teens' healthy development. **3.** b **4.** Kohlberg's stage 3 **5.** Physical changes, cognitive changes, and socioemotional pressures

---

7.4 KEY QUESTION
What Developmental Challenges Do Adults Face?

The transition from adolescence to young adulthood is marked by decisions about advanced education, career, and intimate relationships. Making such decisions and adjusting to the consequences are major tasks of adulthood because they shape the course of adult psychological development. But development doesn't stop there. Continuing pressures of careers, families, and friends, along with the relentless physical maturation (and eventual decline) of the body, continually present new developmental challenges. In today's world, though, the traditional clock for aging has been set back, essentially "buying more time" for adults in all stages of adulthood. This revolution in aging is a key element in our Core Concept for this section:

> ### Core Concept 7.4
>
> **Nature and nurture continue to interact as we progress through a series of transitions in adulthood, with cultural norms about age combining with new technology to increase both the length and quality of life for many adults.**

A couple of points in our Core Concept should be noted before we examine adulthood in more depth. First, you have probably gathered from earlier sections of this chapter that stage theories—although very popular for describing human development—are often guilty of oversimplification. While the major developmental tasks and categories of leading stage theories, such as those proposed by Piaget, Kohlberg, and Erikson, are largely holding up to empirical scrutiny, psychologists now agree that development doesn't occur in rigid stages. Rather, it is a more continuous process, occurring in waves or spurts. In other words, then, the stage theories may have gotten the "what" correct, but the "when" is more fluid than they thought it was. At no time in the lifespan is this more true than in adult development. Research finds that healthy adults pass through a series of transitions as they progress from early through middle and into late adulthood. Successful passage through these transitions involves reflection and readjustment, which we will discuss over the next few pages.

A second point worth noting is the changing nature of adulthood in the Western world. Thanks to better health care and technology, people are living longer than ever before and often enjoying better health in their later years than previous generations. This, in turn, is changing adults' perceptions of the lifespan and its various ages and stages. Fewer adults feel compelled to marry or settle down in their early 20s, or to retire when they hit 65. We are seeing the beginning of a "revolution" in aging, spawned by both nature (the longer lifespan) and nurture (the ways our culture is adapting to the change).

This **revolution in aging** is prompting renewed attention to the study of adult development in psychological science. Although for many years we relied on theories based on clinical observation, we are now accumulating an increasing body of empirical research. Interestingly, much of this new research supports traditional clinical theories—but it also sheds new light on the processes of adulthood in the 21st century. To see how these developmental changes unfold, let's begin with personality—where we find some surprising agreement among otherwise diverse theories.

Freud taught that adult development is driven by two basic needs: love and work. Abraham Maslow (1970) described the critical needs as love and belonging, which, when satisfied, allow emergence of our needs for esteem and fulfillment. Other theorists divide the basic needs of adulthood into affiliation or social acceptance needs, achievement or competence needs, and power needs (McClelland, 1975, 1985; McClelland & Boyatzis, 1982). And in Erikson's theory, the early and middle adult years focus on needs for intimacy and "generativity." While all these theories offer important clues to healthy adulthood, what they all share is recognition of the need for human relationships. Because Erikson gave the most comprehensive account of adult development, we will use his theory as our framework, into which we will build recent empirical research that illuminates the course of adulthood today.

Early Adulthood: Explorations, Autonomy, and Intimacy

What are the developmental tasks of early adulthood? And perhaps a bigger question for 20-somethings is this: When exactly does adulthood begin? In our teen years, many of us look forward to the "freedom" of turning 18 and becoming a legal adult. But does psychological adulthood arrive at 18 as well?

Intimacy versus Isolation   Early adulthood, said Erikson, poses the challenge of establishing close relationships with other adults (look again at Table 7.1 on page 277). He described **intimacy** as the capacity to make a full commitment—sexual, emotional, and moral—to another person. Making intimate commitments requires compromising personal preferences, accepting responsibilities, and yielding some privacy and independence, but it also brings great rewards. To achieve intimacy, however, the individual must resolve the conflict between the need for closeness and the fear of vulnerability and risks such closeness can bring. Failure to successfully resolve this crisis leads to *isolation* and the inability to connect to others in meaningful ways.

For Erikson, the young adult must first consolidate a clear sense of identity (resolving the crisis of adolescence) before being able to cope successfully with the risks and benefits of adult intimacy. In essence, you must know who and what you are before you can successfully commit to love and share your life with someone else. However, the sequence from identity to intimacy Erikson described may not accurately

revolution in aging   A change in the way people think about aging in modern industrialized nations. This new perspective grows out of increased longevity, better health care, and more lifestyle choices available to older adults. It has also stimulated the psychological study of adult development.

CONNECTION CHAPTER 10

Personality theories aim to explain the whole person and focus on characteristics that remain relatively stable in an individual throughout his or her lifespan (p. 414).

intimacy   In Erikson's theory, the main developmental task of early adulthood, involving the capacity to make a full commitment—sexual, emotional, and moral—to another person.

reflect present-day realities. The trend in recent years has been for young adults to live together before marrying and to delay making contractual commitments to lifelong intimacy with one person. In addition, many individuals today struggle with identity issues (for example, career choices) at the same time they are trying to deal with intimacy issues. Life for young adults in the 21st century offers more choices and more complications than did the same period of life for the generation described by Erikson.

Emerging Adulthood: The In-Between Stage Psychologist Jeffrey Arnett (2000a, 2001), in recognition of the differences between adulthood today and in previous generations, proposes a transitional period to adulthood he calls **emerging adulthood.** This period encompasses the late teens through the 20s, a time during which many individuals in industrialized societies have passed through adolescence but do not yet perceive themselves to be adults. Whereas in earlier historical times, visible events such as marriage, the birth of the first child, and establishment in a career were perceived as the markers of entrance into adulthood, today's young people cite more opaque events, such as accepting personal responsibility for themselves and making independent decisions, as the important indicators of adulthood. And most emerging adults today report only partial progress toward these milestones of self-sufficiency (Arnett, 1997).

> **emerging adulthood**   A transition period between adolescence and adulthood.

Emerging adulthood is a time of exploration and experimentation in all areas. Late teens and 20-somethings are trying out different types of work, exploring alternative lifestyles and worldviews, and figuring out what kind of person is right for them romantically. As they do so, they are less predictable in their educational pursuits, choice of residences, and degree of financial responsibility than at any other time in their life. Almost half will move out of their parents' home and back in again during this period, and while 60 percent start taking college classes within one year of graduating from high school, only half of these students have completed four or more years by their late 20s (Bianchi & Spain, 1996; U.S. Bureau of the Census, 2011). Of those who do graduate from college, more are choosing graduate school than in previous generations (Mogelonsky, 1996). Young adults also take more risks than at any other time of their life—including adolescence. Rates of alcohol and substance abuse, reckless driving, and unprotected sex peak during these years (Arnett, 1992). These patterns of experimentation may be due to the absence of serious role responsibilities combined with freedom from parental supervision.

Did Erikson get it right, then, in his identification of the major tasks of adolescence and early adulthood? In general, he did. Although not widely noted, he observed that, in industrialized societies, young people seemed to enjoy what he called a prolonged period of adolescence during which role experimentation continued. This, indeed, is exactly what empirical research such as Arnett's is demonstrating today. And current studies indicate that, by about age 30, a majority of Westerners have married and had their first child, have made the transition from school to full-time work, and perceive themselves as having entered adulthood. Presumably, then, at this point they have achieved the intimacy that Erikson described as the major developmental task of early adulthood. Notably, young adults today also name intimacy, or personal relationships, as the key to a happy life (Arnett, 2000b), although many admit struggling to balance the competing needs of intimacy and autonomy. As we will see, this pursuit of an optimal balance of these two needs will continue to characterize later phases of adulthood.

Modern Approaches to Intimacy How, then, do today's adults achieve intimacy? Though 90 percent or more still marry, marriage often occurs more than once in an individual's life. The same pattern applies to gay and lesbian long-term relationships—whether they may legally marry in their state or not (Knox & Schact, 2008). In fact, about half of all U.S. marriages end in divorce (U.S. Bureau of the Census, 2002). Moreover, an increasing number of couples are cohabiting rather than getting married (Doyle, 2002b). The high divorce rate probably results, in part, from individuals seeking intimacy before they have resolved their own identities. Unrealistic expectations of each other and of what constitutes an ideal marriage and family structure contribute to divorce as well (Cleek & Pearson, 1985), as does our cultural priority on individual happiness. On the other hand, there is evidence that communication and affection between spouses is better than it was in earlier times, and that those who learn good communication skills substantially improve their chances of avoiding divorce (Caplow, 1982; Markman & Notarius, 1993).

In the 21st century, married people are more likely to see each other as partners and friends and less likely to feel constrained by society's expectations of a "husband" or "wife." Partners in **peer marriages** talk with and help each other in ways that work best for their relationship, irrespective of traditional ideas about the man being "boss" or the wife being responsible for "women's work" (Schwartz, 1994). The key to a fair and satisfying relationship is communication in which both partners feel able to openly express their hopes and fears (Klagsbrun, 1985). A mushrooming of knowledge on how good communication sustains relationships has helped our culture to view marriage as a worthwhile investment and see therapy as a valuable option for supporting such efforts (Gottman, 1994; Notarius, 1996). In brief, relating is no longer viewed as a set of skills that "comes naturally" with the establishment of intimacy. Instead, close relationships are seen as lifelong works in progress—worthwhile investments of time and energy whose quality can be improved with clearer self-understanding, effective conflict resolution, and good communication.

What makes for good communication and effective conflict resolution? Surprisingly, there is no correlation between the frequency of a couple's conflicts and the health of their relationship: Couples who disagree often are no more likely to divorce than couples with less frequent conflict. What does matter is the ratio of positive interactions to negative interactions, with the optimal balance found to be 5:1 (Gottman, 1995). In other words, regardless of how much conflict there is in a marriage, the marriage will be healthy if the couple has five times more positive than negative interactions with each other. And "positive interactions" don't have to be long romantic weekends or elaborate dates: small things such as a smile, a kiss, a compliment, or a thank-you all count. (A long romantic weekend or a great date would, then, presumably have quite a few positive interactions.) Negative interactions, on the other hand, can also be small—but pack a powerful punch—and include such behaviors as hostile sarcasm, name calling, a frustrated roll of the eyes, or an angry slam of the door. By maintaining a 5:1 ratio of positive to negative interactions, the couple is creating a supportive foundation that strengthens the relationship's immune system, so to speak. When conflict does arise, then, partners are less likely to take things personally or feel defensive, which allows the focus to remain on problem solving rather than blaming.

peer marriage   Marriage in which the couple see each other as partners and friends, as contrasted with the older stereotypic roles of "husband" and "wife."

This happy couple can expect a successful marriage if they maintain a 5:1 ratio of positive to negative interactions with each other.

The Challenges of Midlife: Complexity and Generativity

For many people, the concept of midlife conjures up thoughts of the dreaded midlife crisis and birthday cards poking fun at being "over the hill." Contrary to stereotypes of middle age, though, research finds middle adulthood to be a peak period of development in many respects. Cognitively, many adults in this age range have developed considerable skill in combining and integrating a variety of thinking styles, including reflection, analysis, and dialectical reasoning (which is the ability to compare and evaluate contradictory viewpoints; Baltes & Staudinger, 1993; King & Kitchener, 1994). They are also experts at integrating their cognitions and emotions, resulting in more thoughtful, deliberate, and reflective coping responses to stressful events (Diehl et al., 1996).

Taken together, these skills enable the midlife adult to juggle a variety of interests, which often include work, family, community, hobbies, and self-care. And indeed, this busy, complex lifestyle is what characterizes healthy midlife adults today. Psychologists Rosalind Barnett and Janet Hyde (2001) note that dual-career families are now the norm, with women receiving professional training at an unprecedented level. Hand in hand with this trend is greater fluidity among roles as worker and family member: Men less often define themselves only as workers and family providers, and women are less likely to define themselves solely as wives and mothers. For most people, these expanded roles provide a greater network of social support and an increased sense of well-being. In addition to greater diversity in roles, midlife adults today enjoy greater variety in their relationships, resources, and lifestyle than ever before (Moen & Wethington, 1999). This *complexity* is related to well-being in that complex individuals see life as a series of challenges, full of variety, that lead to growth (Ryff & Heincke, 1983). And, overall, adults over age 50 are less stressed, more happy, and less worried than younger individuals (Stone et. al,, 2010).

Generativity versus Stagnation According to Erikson, **generativity** is the major developmental task of middle adulthood. For those who successfully met the earlier challenges of identity and intimacy, generativity provides an opportunity to make a meaningful and lasting contribution to family, work, society, or future generations. Thus, people in this phase of life broaden their focus beyond self and partner, often by raising children, serving as volunteers in community service groups, or nurturing the next generation in some other way. Research confirms that adults who express a strong sense of being generative and productive also report high life satisfaction (McAdams et al., 1993). In contrast, those who have not resolved earlier crises of identity and intimacy may experience a "midlife crisis." Such people may question past choices, becoming cynical and stagnant or, at the other extreme, self-indulgent and reckless. The good news is—once again contrary to stereotypes of midlife—most people do not undergo a midlife crisis. What's more, the idea that adults become depressed and lose direction when their children "leave the nest" is also a myth (Clay, 2003a, b).

generativity The process of making a commitment beyond oneself to family, work, society, or future generations. In Erikson's theory, generativity is the developmental challenge of midlife.

Transitions What does happen for most adults in midlife is that they progress through a **transition** that involves redefining, or transformation, of a life role. Indeed, evidence indicates that adult life is characterized by a series of transitions, starting with the transition to adulthood and occurring perhaps every 15 to 20 years throughout adulthood (Levinson, 1986; Sugarman, 2001). Successful transitions typically involve a period of heightened self-reflection, which includes reappraisal of the current role, exploration of new possibilities offering a renewed sense of meaning, and the decision to let go of the old role and commit to the new one. Transitions may involve expected events such as getting married, having children, or retiring, or unexpected events such as a sudden illness, breakup, or loss of a job or loved one. In addition, events that were expected but did not occur—such as a job promotion that never materialized or a person who always wanted children but never had any—can prompt a transition. And finally, transitions can be gradual, as with a relationship or job that, over time, becomes less and less fulfilling, or a person who becomes increasingly self-confident: In any case, at some point the individual becomes aware of a critical difference, which propels him or her into the transition period.

transition A period of time during which an individual redefines or transforms a life role, goal, value, or lifestyle.

Given that our physical, cognitive, and emotional capabilities—as well as our social contexts—tend to evolve and change throughout our lives, transitions are a natural response to these shifts in our internal and external worlds. And there is accumulating evidence that adults who live the longest and healthiest lives are the ones who successfully navigate through these transitions and emerge from each one with a renewed sense of meaning and passion for life (Levinson, 1978, 1996; Ryff & Heidrich, 1997). Interestingly, transitions may sometimes involve a revisit to one of Erikson's earlier stages, such as a retooling of one's identity or the transformation of an intimate relationship. And, given what we know about complexity, we might predict that complex individuals—with their positive, challenge- and growth-oriented outlook—would be more likely to experience successful transitions.

In summary, the reality of middle adulthood in today's Western society is a far cry from the "over-the-hill" stereotype that still persists in some people's minds. Many midlife adults are energetic, forward-moving individuals who are making meaningful contributions to the world and enjoying the many opportunities available to them in love, work, and personal growth. And it appears to be generativity and complexity that fuel achievement of this healthy model of middle adulthood.

Engaging in new challenges is one of the keys to successful passage through the transitions of adulthood. This woman earned her Masters degree in Elementary Education at the age of 52.

Late Adulthood: The Age of Integrity

At the beginning of the 20th century, only 3 percent of the U.S. population was over 65. One hundred years later, that figure is about 13 percent. And as the Baby Boom generation reaches this age over the next few years, nearly one-fourth of our population will be in this oldest group.

By the year 2030, we will witness a profound demographic shift (change in population characteristics). By that time, more than 80 million Americans will be over 60 years of age. For the first time in history, the number of people in the 60-plus age group will outnumber those under 20 years of age. This will represent a dramatic reversal of all previous demographics and a potentially significant shift away from today's youth-oriented culture (Pifer & Bronte, 1986). Among the effects: Tattoos and body piercings will become common in nursing homes, and there will be far fewer people to pay Social Security and Medicare bills.

With drastic changes in our society's age distribution looming, it is more crucial than ever to understand the nature of aging as well as the abilities and needs of the elderly (Roush, 1996). And, on a personal level, it may be helpful to anticipate some of the developmental challenges your parents and grandparents are facing, as well as what you can expect in the last phase of your life.

From a biological perspective, aging typically means decline: Energy reserves are reduced, and cell machinery functions less efficiently. From a cognitive perspective, however, aging is no longer synonymous with decline (Qualls & Abeles, 2000). Many abilities, including expert skills and some aspects of memory, can actually improve with age (Azar, 1996; Krampe & Ericsson, 1996). A lifetime's accumulation of experience may finally culminate in wisdom—if the mind remains open and active. Activity, in fact—whether physical, social-emotional, or cognitive—seems to be key to healthy aging: The phrase "Use it or lose it!" applies to many aspects of late adulthood. Thus, theories of aging are models of balance or trade-offs: In old age, a person may lose energy reserves but gain an ability to control emotional experiences and thereby conserve energy (Baltes, 1987). And many of our negative assumptions about aging are related to our cultural values: Cultures that revere their elders have very different perspectives and expectations of aging. What are the tasks of aging, and what opportunities and limitations will we confront in our later years?

Ego-Integrity versus Despair According to Erikson, an increasing awareness of your own mortality and the changes in your body, behavior, and social roles sets the stage for late adulthood. Erikson called the crisis of this stage *ego-integrity versus despair*. **Ego-integrity**, the healthy end of this dimension, involves the ability to look back on life without regrets and to enjoy a sense of wholeness. It requires reflection on times both good and bad, with appreciation for what turned out well and acceptance of what did not. By now, you know that Erikson believed previous crises must have enjoyed successful resolutions in order to master new challenges, so you are probably considering how a well-developed identity, meaningful close relationships, and a sense of having contributed to the next generation would probably facilitate this type of reflection and acceptance. For those whose previous crises had unhealthy solutions, however, aspirations may remain unfulfilled, and these individuals may experience futility, despair, and self-deprecation. Sadly, they often then fail to resolve the crisis successfully at this final developmental stage.

Physical Changes Some of the most obvious changes that occur with age affect people's physical appearances and abilities. As we age, we can expect our skin to wrinkle, our hair to thin and gray, and our height to decrease an inch or two. Our hearts and lungs operate less efficiently, decreasing our physical stamina. We can also expect some of our senses to dull. More and more, however, modern life is finding older adults taking control of their bodies in ways that are reducing the deterioration long thought to be inevitable. Successful aging takes into consideration both individual potential and realistic limits (Baltes, 1993).

---

ego-integrity   In Erikson's theory, the developmental task of late adulthood—involving the ability to look back on life without regrets and to enjoy a sense of wholeness.

Read about Sensory Deficiencies in Aging at **MyPsychLab**

To what extent can older adults influence their physical aging? Continuing (or even beginning) a consistent program of physical exercise helps ward off some of the physical decline typically associated with aging. Aerobic activity such as walking or swimming improves cardiovascular functioning, and weight training improves blood flow and builds muscle mass, which in turn improves posture, balance, and the ability to physically manage everyday activities (such as grocery shopping or gardening). Even for individuals who have previously been sedentary, beginning an exercise program as late as age 80 results in measurable gains physically, emotionally, and even cognitively. Regular exercise provides better blood and oxygen flow to the brain, which in turn reduces deterioration of brain cells and improves attention (Colcombe et al., 2004). There is also evidence that exercise reduces incidence of Alzheimer's and other brain disorders (Marx, 2005).

Another myth about aging in Western culture is that elderly people cannot or should not be sexually active. Belief in this myth can be a greater obstacle than any physical limitations to experiencing satisfying sex in late adulthood. Although frequency and desire may decrease somewhat, there is no age, for either men or women, at which the capability for arousal or orgasm ceases. (This is particularly true now that drugs, such as the well-advertised Viagra, have enhanced erectile ability for millions of older men.) And while sex loses its reproductive functions in late adulthood, it doesn't lose its capacity for providing pleasure. Regular sex also enhances healthy aging because it provides arousal, aerobic exercise, fantasy, and social interaction (Ornstein & Sobel, 1989). Experience and creativity can compensate for physical changes or loss of physical stamina.

Cognitive Changes Older adults often fear that aging is inevitably accompanied by the loss of mental abilities. But is this fear justified? Certain parts of the brain, particularly the frontal lobes, do lose mass as we age, but there is little evidence this causes a general mental decline in healthy adults. On one hand, performance on tasks requiring imagination, such as vivid imagery strategies for memorizing, does seem to decline with age (Baltes & Kliegl, 1992). And people do acquire information more slowly by the time they are in their 70s and 80s. But on the other hand, the decline for the average person may not be as severe as folk wisdom assumes (Helmuth, 2003c). Brain-imaging studies reveal that older people's brains compensate for decline by processing information differently, bringing more regions into play (Cabeza, 2002; Helmuth, 2002). And, just like physical exercise prolongs physical health, mental exercise keeps aging brains working more effectively. Moreover, some abilities improve with age. Vocabulary, for example, is consistently better in older adults, as are social skills. And, with regard to skilled performance, musicians have been shown to improve well into their 90s (Krampe & Ericsson, 1996). Psychologists are now exploring age-related gains in wisdom, such as expertise in practical knowledge and life experience (Baltes, 1990). Finally, we note persistent evidence that physical exercise improves learning, memory, and other cognitive functions in older adults, along with new research showing that consumption of omega fatty acids can combine with physical exercise to produce exponential benefits to brain functioning and plasticity (Chodzko-Zajko et al., 2009; von Praag, 2009). The message is clear: More active elders enjoy better cognitive and better physical health.

What about memory? A common complaint among older adults is that their ability to remember things is not as good as it used to be. Most of these age-related memory difficulties appear in the part of the memory system associated with processing and storing new information (Poon, 1985); aging does not seem to diminish access to knowledge or events stored long ago. So an elderly person may have to ask the name of a new acquaintance several times before finally remembering it but has no trouble recalling the names of old friends. A more important concern might be that people explain memory loss differently depending on the age of the forgetful person. Using a double standard, younger adults attribute other young adults' memory failures to lack of effort but those of older adults to loss of ability (Parr & Siegert, 1993). We may also fall prey to confirmation bias: If we assume older people forget more, we will notice and remember when one does and chalk it up to age, whereas when a younger person forgets something, we either dismiss it or attribute it to something situational.

Older adults who pursue higher degrees of environmental stimulation tend to maintain higher levels of cognitive abilities.

Alzheimer's disease A degenerative brain disease, usually noticed first by its debilitating effects on memory.

Particularly worrisome to older people and those who love them is **Alzheimer's disease**, a degenerative disorder of the brain that produces diminished thinking abilities, memory problems and, ultimately, death. Alzheimer's disease is estimated to occur in about 10 percent of the population over the age of 65, with the incidence increasing with age to more than 50 percent in people beyond age 85 (National Institute on Aging, 2004). One of the early symptoms involves memory problems, causing many older persons to become anxious when they are unable to remember a name or an event—a difficulty to which they would have given little thought when younger. It is an especially frightening disorder because it can render people helpless, rob them of their ability to make new memories, and make them forget loved ones. New advances in Alzheimer's research, though, are making some promising headway into our understanding and treatment of this serious disorder. In fact, new tests can identify Alzheimer's disease with a remarkably high accuracy rate—years before symptoms even appear (DeMeyer et al., 2010). And although a cure has not yet been discovered, early diagnosis and treatment can now slow the progress of the disease, thus extending the quality of life of an individual with Alzheimer's disease.

Social and Emotional Changes The social and emotional state of older adults is another area rife with misconceptions and stereotypes of grumpy and isolated old folks. While it is true that an unfortunate consequence of living a long life is outliving some friends and family members, research finds older adults largely maintaining healthy emotions and social relationships. Stanford University professor Laura Carstensen notes that, as people age, they tend to engage in **selective social interaction**, maintaining only the most rewarding contacts for the investment of their physical and emotional energy (Carstensen, 1987, 1991; Lang & Carstensen, 1994). Maintaining even a single intimate relationship can markedly improve personal health, as can living with a beloved pet (Siegel, 1990).

selective social interaction Choosing to restrict the number of one's social contacts to those who are the most gratifying.

Older adults also seem to benefit from emotional systems that, in some ways, grow keener with age. One recent study found that older adults felt greater sadness than middle or younger adults when exposed to sad movie scenes (Seider et al., 2010). At the same time, though, older adults feel more positive emotions and fewer negative emotions than their younger counterparts (Mroczek, 2001). How do we reconcile these seemingly contradictory findings? According to Carstensen (1987, 1991), older adults manage their emotions by seeking out positive environments and avoiding the negative ones (Sanders, 2010). Moreover, they enjoy a broader perspective on their experiences, probably as a result of their assortment of life experiences. They are more likely to take disappointment in stride, bounce back from personal criticism, and focus on the positive. Overall, most older adults feel satisfied with life and enjoy fairly high levels of well-being (Charles & Carstensen, 2010).

How do older adults characterize well-being? In a series of interviews with middle-aged and older adults, Ryff (1989) found that both men and women defined well-being in terms of relationships with others: They strived to be caring, compassionate people and valued having a good social support network. The keys to well-being, according to these interviews, are accepting change, enjoying life, and cultivating a sense of humor.

Keys to Successful Aging What other strategies are effective in coping with aging? Older adults can remain both active and close to people by doing volunteer work in the community, traveling, joining clubs and classes, or spending time with grandchildren. Much research supports this notion of the need for close relationships with others. And it is the basis for one of the most practical applications you can take with you from this text: *Anything that isolates us from sources of social support—from a reliable network of friends and family—puts us at risk for a host of physical ills, mental problems, and even social pathologies.* We are social creatures, and we need each other's help and support to be effective and healthy (Basic Behavioral Science Task Force, 1996). In addition, we might learn lessons from other cultures where older citizens are respected and venerated for their wisdom. Before this happens, however, people must overcome stereotypes of the elderly as incapable and incompetent (Brewer et al., 1981).

Successful aging, then—much like success at any age—seems to consist of making the most of gains while minimizing the impact of losses (Schulz & Heckhausen, 1996). Additionally, it is helpful to realize that loss of specific abilities need not represent threats to one's sense of self. As one's physical and psychological resources change, so do one's goals (Carstensen & Freund, 1994). From this perspective, late adulthood is a time of increasing fulfillment. If you ask adults in midlife and beyond if they wanted to be 25 again, "you don't get a lot of takers," notes researcher Arthur Stone (Fields, 2010).

[PSYCHOLOGY MATTERS]

A Look Back at the Jim Twins and Your Own Development

Now that you have learned some key elements of human development over the lifespan, what conclusions can you draw about why each of us develops into the individuals we are? By now, you have enough knowledge about the interaction of genes and environment to know that neither, on its own, can account for a person's outcomes. Both play key roles, often at different stages of development. But can you apply what you've learned to your own outcomes? First, let's try our hand at explaining the Jim twins, whom we met in the introductory section of this chapter.

To see the twin pairs in a broader perspective, you need to know that they are "outliers"—extreme among the twins studied at Minnesota, even though they have received a lion's share of media coverage. Although Bouchard and his colleagues found many unexpected developmental similarities between individuals in all the twin pairs they studied, most were not nearly so much alike as Oskar and Jack or the Jims. Moreover, even Bouchard acknowledges that many of the similarities are just coincidences (The Mysteries, 1998). And while mere coincidence does not offer a dazzling explanation, the alternatives seem absurd. No one seriously suggests, for example, that the names of Betty and Linda could have been written into the genes of the two Jims or that heredity really specifies storing rubber bands on one's wrists.

The real story, then, is both less dramatic and more important: Identical twins do show remarkable similarities, but mainly in the characteristics you might expect: intelligence, temperament, gestures, posture, and pace of speech—all of which do make sense as genetically influenced traits. And the fact that fraternal twins and other siblings show fewer similarities also suggests that hereditary forces are at work in all of us, whether we are twins or not. Bouchard (1994) himself takes a rather extreme position, suggesting that heredity accounts for up to 80 percent of the similarities observed among identical twins (What We Learn, 1998). Critics aren't so sure.

What objections do critics raise concerning the twin studies Bouchard and others have been conducting? First, they note that, stunning as the similarities between identical twins may seem, the effects of the environment also show up in twin pairs. None of them displays behavior that is identical across the board. And the fact that twins reared together typically are more alike than those reared apart provides additional testimony to the effects of environment. Furthermore, the personalities of most twin pairs become less alike as they age, providing even greater evidence that the environment, as well as heredity, continues to shape development (McCartney et al., 1990).

We should note, too, that many of the twin pairs studied by Bouchard had been reunited for some time before he found them—an environmental condition that could easily accentuate, or even create, similarities. This was true, for example, of Oskar Stör and Jack Yufe, the Nazi and Jewish twins, who met five months before Bouchard got to them. In fact, says psychologist Leon Kamin, Bouchard's twins face strong incentives to exaggerate their similarities and minimize their differences to please the research team and to attract media attention (Horgan, 1993). (Since their story broke in the press, Stör and Yufe have hired agents, made paid appearances on TV, and sold their story to a Hollywood film producer.)

A third criticism points out that because identical twins look alike, people often treat them alike. This is an environmental factor that can account for many similarities in behavior. For example, attractive people generally are seen by others as more interesting and friendly, which in turn elicits friendliness from others—and ultimately leads to different outcomes than would be found in less attractive individuals, whether or not they have been raised together. The resulting similarity, then, can be due to environment as much as it is to heredity.

CONNECTION CHAPTER 1

Expectancy bias can distort perceptions and research findings (p. 31).

Finally, critics also remind us that scientists' hopes and expectations can influence their conclusions in this sort of research. Because Bouchard and other investigators of identical twins expect to find some hereditary influences, their attention will be drawn more to similarities than to differences. In fact, this is what most people do when they meet: Their conversation jumps from topic to topic until they discover common interests, attitudes, experiences, or activities.

So, is there any point of consensus about the twin studies and the effects of heredity and environment? Bouchard and his critics alike would agree that neither heredity nor environment ever acts alone to produce behavior or mental processes. They always interact. Thus, from a developmental perspective, heredity and environment work together to shape an individual throughout a person's life—in all the ways we have noted throughout this chapter.

Do It Yourself!   NATURE AND NURTURE IN YOUR OWN DEVELOPMENT

Consider one of your own traits—choose one that interests you, or that you are especially curious about.

1. Name and describe the trait, and give an example or two of how the trait shows up in your behavior and impacts your life.
2. Then, consider nature and nurture in your particular trait: First, discuss similarities you have noticed between you and your family members with

this trait. Remember, though, that if you shared an environment with these family members, similarities could be genetic (if your family is biologically related to you)—or learned.

3. Next, see what information you can find in the way of research to determine what portion of that particular trait is found to be genetic, and what portion is thought to be learned. (If you look in the index of

this book, you might find references to your trait in this book; if not, your professor will provide suggestions for references.)

4. Finally, summarize the findings you discover, then apply them to your own life by discussing your new thoughts about to what extent your trait is inherited, as well as ways you might have learned it from your environment.

Check Your Understanding

✓● Study and Review at MyPsychLab

1. **ANALYSIS:** How is emerging adulthood different than early adulthood?

2. **APPLICATION:** The couple who lives next door to you has a very successful marriage: They have been together more than 25 years, have raised three well-adjusted children, and spend a lot of time together doing things they both enjoy. When a friend of yours visits, though, and notices them arguing in the backyard—which they often seem to do—she asks you how they can have such a good marriage but argue so much. How can you explain that to her?

3. **RECALL:** What are the keys to successful middle adulthood?

4. **RECALL:** Describe at least two ways the phrase "Use it or lose it!" applies to healthy aging.

5. **UNDERSTANDING THE CORE CONCEPT:** Describe two factors that contribute to the current "revolution" in aging.

Answers 1. Emerging adulthood is a transitional period between adolescence and early adulthood, during which individuals in industrialized societies experiment with different roles, viewpoints, and relationships. **2.** They probably maintain a ratio of 5:1 positive to negative interactions. **3.** Generativity and complexity **4.** Older adults must keep physically and mentally active in order to keep their bodies and brains healthy. **5.** Technology is helping us stay healthier and live longer, and changing social norms are changing the Western perception of aging.

CRITICAL THINKING APPLIED

The Mozart Effect

Imagine this: You have just had your first child and are now the proud parent of what you are sure is the most amazing baby ever born (we aren't making fun of you—we all feel that way about our kids!). Like many parents, you want to offer your child every opportunity you can to help him (or her) reach full potential. So what would you do if you heard that listening to Mozart would make your baby smarter? In 1993, this provocative finding was announced by a pair of scientific researchers who, indeed, found that listening to Mozart boosted IQ scores (Rauscher et al., 1993). The report received widespread media coverage and gave birth to a host of innovations. Governors in at least two states instituted requirements to provide a Mozart CD to every newborn; websites sprang up that sold all things musical with promises of transforming the listener's "health, education, and well-being" (www.themozarteffect.com); and expectant mothers began to play Mozart to their unborn children via headphones on their tummies. Before jumping on the bandwagon, though, it might be wise to apply some critical thinking to this remarkable claim.

What Are the Critical Issues?

Could listening to Mozart really improve IQ? If the study appears valid, how does the new finding fit with other established findings about effects of music and about boosting intelligence? Would other types of music—classical or otherwise—have similar effects? And finally, if listening to a certain type of music really does boost IQ, can we be sure it is the music itself boosting the IQ, or could it be something else about the experience of listening to music that was driving the IQ gain? These are just a few of the questions that a good critical thinker might ask when first hearing this remarkable claim.

Extraordinary Claims Require Extraordinary Evidence   The first thing that might come to mind for you is the extreme nature of this assertion: The original study reported that IQ scores increased by 8 to 9 points after listening to just ten minutes of Mozart! Is there extraordinary evidence to support this *extraordinary claim?* An inspection of the *source* reveals the claimants are researchers at a respected university, which lends initial credibility to their assertion. What, then, is the nature of the *evidence?* First, the finding was indeed based on an empirical study rather than anecdotal evidence, so it passes that test. A second element of the evidence to examine is the sample: Who were the participants, and how well do they represent the population at large? In this case, participants were college students, which might give you pause. Would the findings necessarily apply to babies? Or could the effect be limited to people already at a certain level of cognitive development?

Does the Reasoning Avoid Common Fallacies?   One common fallacy is the correlation–causation issue. In this study, researchers used an experimental design with random assignment to groups, so the findings do appear causal rather than correlational in nature. Even when the findings of a study are valid, though, another common fallacy can occur when they are interpreted in a manner that oversimplifies or exaggerates the meaning of the findings. In this case, is it reasonable to conclude from the findings of this study that listening to Mozart boosts IQ?

Here's where it gets really interesting: A closer look at the findings reveals the IQ gain found in the study was only temporary and disappeared after about 15 minutes. And, second, the measure used to assess IQ (which by definition is a global measure) was actually a test of visual–spatial competence (which is just one specific element of IQ tests). To say that Mozart boosts intelligence is clearly an exaggeration of the actual findings.

What Conclusions Can We Draw?

In the years following the original study, more than 20 similar studies have been conducted and published in recognized scientific journals. While a few found evidence of what has become popularly known as "the Mozart effect," most did not (Steele et al., 1999). In fact, in-depth studies of the process reveal that the short-term boost in IQ score is more accurately a result of a slight increase in positive mood reported by most participants when listening to the particular Mozart composition used in many of the studies: *When mood was measured before and after listening to the music and statistically removed from the equation, the temporary IQ increase disappeared* (Thompson et al., 2001). What's more, other mildly positive experiences, such as listening to a story rather than sitting in silence for ten minutes, produce the same increase in mood and subsequently the same temporary IQ gain (Nantais & Schellenberg, 1999).

A more reasonable conclusion of these studies is that experiences that increase positive mood facilitate better visual–spatial reasoning while the mood remains elevated. This finding, contrary to the "Mozart effect" claim, is corroborated by other psychological research. Some studies, for example, have uncovered a relationship between positive mood and performance on cognitive tasks (Ashby et al., 1999; Kenealy, 1997). And listening to music that promotes happiness has been found to increase speed and productivity on a variety of tasks.

To be fair, it wasn't the original research report that exaggerated the findings or implied they would apply to babies, but media reports that proliferated in the wake of the research. Stanford University professor Chip Heath thinks he knows why: His analysis reveals that the original 1993 article received far more attention in newspaper stories than any other research report published around that time, and the greatest coverage in states with the lowest student test scores. "Problems attract solutions," says Heath, and Americans as a culture seem more obsessed with early childhood education than many other cultures worldwide (Krakovsky, 2005).

The anxiety noted by Heath, as we learned in Chapter 1, can breed *emotional bias*, which in turn can influence people to latch on to solutions that seem simple and promise grand results. Add to that findings from memory research indicating

that each time a story is told by one person to another, details become distorted—and can you imagine how many people read a newspaper article (which likely distorted the original finding), then told a friend, who told another friend, and so on? It's no wonder the myth of the Mozart effect took such a strong hold in our culture. And finally, the confirmation bias helps us understand why people still persist in believing the Mozart effect to be true, despite research reports and newspaper articles that have debunked it.

Do It Yourself! DEVELOPMENTAL ISSUES IN CYBERSPACE

Choose another example of a widely held belief about factors influencing development of children, adolescents, or adults. (For example, you might choose the controversy about autism and immunizations, the impact of sex education on sexual behavior, or a topic within this chapter you'd like to learn more about.) Then find three websites that claim to offer information about the topic—they can be pro, con, or a combination of both. Evaluate each website using our critical thinking guidelines.

CHAPTER SUMMARY

((•─[Listen to an audio file of your chapter at **MyPsychLab**

PROBLEM: Do the amazing accounts of similarities in twins reared apart indicate we are primarily a product of our genes? Or do genetics and environment work together to influence growth and development over the lifespan?

- Dramatic media stories, such as that of the Jim Twins, represent the most unusual cases of similarities among identical twins raised apart. Moreover, any two individuals reared in the same culture will most likely find some "amazing" coincidences in their beliefs, attitudes, experiences, or behaviors.

- Many of our physical characteristics are primarily genetic. Of our psychological characteristics, traits such as intelligence, temperament, and certain personality traits—currently known to be some of the most strongly genetically-influenced traits—can only be partly attributed to our genetic inheritance.

- Throughout our lives, from conception to death, our environments play a strong role in development of all our psychological characteristics.

7.1 What Innate Abilities Does the Infant Possess?

[Core Concept 7.1 **Newborns have innate abilities for finding nourishment, avoiding harmful situations, and interacting with others—all of which are genetically designed to facilitate survival.**]

From the moment of conception, genetics and the environment interact to influence early development. During the 9-month **prenatal period**, the fertilized egg **(zygote)** becomes an **embryo** and then a **fetus. Teratogens** are harmful substances taken in by the mother that can cause damage to the developing fetus. Development of sensory abilities and basic reflexes begins in the prenatal period, and at birth newborns prefer sweet tastes and familiar sounds and have visual abilities ideally suited for looking at faces. **Innate reflexes** such as grasping and sucking help them survive and thrive, as does their ability for **mimicry**. The newborn brain contains some 100 billion neurons.

Infancy spans the first 18 months of life. **Maturation** refers to the genetically programmed events and timeline of normal development, such as crawling before walking and babbling before language development. And while exposure to a rich variety of stimuli in the environment promotes optimal brain development and can speed up the "average" pace of development, the **genetic leash** limits the degree to which the environment plays a role.

Infants need human contact to survive and thrive, and their innate sensory abilities, reflexes, and mimicry promote development of social relationships. During infancy, they establish a close emotional relationship with their primary caregiver, which lays the foundation for the way they perceive and interact in close relationships later in their lives. This attachment style is either **secure, anxious-ambivalent,** or **avoidant,** and it is influenced by both the child's temperament and the responsiveness and accessibility of the primary caregiver. Erikson referred to this first stage of social development as **trust** versus mistrust. Cultural practices and preferences regarding attachment style vary, illustrating the role of the environment in development. The role of play also varies among different cultures and impacts development of children's **executive function.**

7.2 What Are the Developmental Tasks of Childhood?

[Core Concept 7.2 **Nature and nurture work together to help children master important developmental tasks, especially in the areas of language acquisition, cognitive development, and development of social relationships.**]

The rapid development of language ability is one of the most amazing developmental feats of early childhood. There is widespread agreement that we are born with innate mental structures that facilitate language development, which Chomsky called **language acquisition devices (LADs)**. While all normally developing infants will acquire language on a relatively predictable timeline—as long as they are exposed to language in their environment—the specific language they develop depends on the language(s) to which they are exposed and can be verbal or sign language. Frequency of exposure can also modify the pace of language development. Babbling begins at about 4 months of age and is the first step toward language development. **Grammar, telegraphic speech**, and use of **morphemes** follow in just a few years.

Cognitive development refers to the emergence of mental abilities such as thinking, perceiving, and remembering. Jean Piaget proposed the most influential model of cognitive development, which suggests that children progress through four distinct stages, each of which is characterized by identifiable changes in mental abilities. Throughout the stages, **schemas** form the mental frameworks for our understanding of concepts, and these schemas are modified by assimilation and accommodation as we acquire new information. The **sensorimotor stage** is characterized by the emergence of goal-directed behavior and object permanence, while the subsequent **preoperational stage** is marked by egocentrism, animistic thinking, centration, and irreversibility. Progression beyond the limitations of the preoperational stage marks the beginning of the **concrete operations stage**, during which children master conservation. Piaget's fourth stage doesn't begin until adolescence. Although many of Piaget's observations have withstood the test of time, today's researchers note that children progress more rapidly and less abruptly through the stages than Piaget believed. Vygotsky's theory of cognitive development notes the importance of culture in development and adds the concepts of **scaffolding** and a *zone of proximal development* to our understanding of how children's mental processes develop.

The third developmental task of childhood is development of social relationships. Our basic temperament, present at birth, plays a strong role in our socioemotional development; but, like most other abilities, it can be modified by support or challenges in our environment. **Socialization** refers to the process by which children learn the social rules and norms of their culture, and parenting style plays a significant role in socialization. Overall, the best child outcomes typically result from an **authoritative** parenting style. The influence of day care on development depends entirely on the quality of day care rather than the amount of time spent in day care. The influence of leisure activities, such as television and video games, depends on both the time spent in the activity as well as the type of program or game being viewed or played.

Erikson observed three major developmental stages during childhood. **Autonomy** can be encouraged by an optimal balance of freedom and support. **Initiative**, the goal of the third stage, is marked by increased choices and self-directed behavior. **Industry** can develop in the elementary school years when children are encouraged to develop their skills and abilities and learn to respond effectively to both successes and failures. Optimal development at each stage increases the chances for mastery of each successive stage.

7.3 What Changes Mark the Transition of Adolescence?

Core Concept 7.3 Adolescence offers new developmental challenges growing out of physical changes, cognitive changes, and socioemotional pressures.

Physically, **adolescence** begins with the onset of **puberty**. Psychologically, the meaning of adolescence varies culturally, as does the time at which adolescence is thought to end. In Western culture, the physical changes brought on by puberty often promote greater attention to physical appearance, which in some Western cultures is linked to self-esteem. Sexuality and **sexual orientation** begin to develop during adolescence, with almost half of North American teens having their first sexual experience by age 17.

Cognitively, adolescence is characterized by Piaget's **formal operational stage**, during which increasing ability for abstract thought develops—if cultural educational norms support

abstract thought. Moral thinking may also progress to higher levels. Risk taking increases during adolescence for Western teens, and although hormonal surges sometimes increase emotionality, most teens do not experience adolescence as a time of turmoil. While the influence of peers takes on greater importance than in the childhood years, a stable relationship with parents is a crucial factor in the successful transition through adolescence. The primary developmental task of this period, according to Erikson, is the development of a unique **identity**.

7.4 What Developmental Challenges Do Adults Face?

Core Concept 7.4 Nature and nurture continue to interact as we progress through a series of transitions in adulthood, and cultural norms about age combine with new technology to increase both the length and quality of life for many adults.

Adult development is a relatively new field of study and is receiving increased attention by psychologists as more adults live longer and healthier lives. Rather than perceiving adulthood as a series of concrete and well-defined stages, research indicates that well-developed adults progress through a series

of transitions throughout adulthood, each of which is marked by reflection on past years and growth into new directions.

According to Erikson, the major developmental task of *early adulthood* is the development of **intimacy**, characterized by a long-term commitment to an intimate partner. In previous generations, Westerners expected this to occur in a person's 20s, but in industrialized societies today, a transition period called **emerging adulthood** may precede intimacy and early adulthood. After the exploration and experimentation of emerging adulthood, most adults marry. Successful intimate relationships rely on effective communication and conflict resolution and on a 5:1 ratio of positive to negative interactions.

Contrary to popular belief, research indicates that midlife is a peak period of development in many respects. Middle adults' ability to integrate a variety of complex thinking skills facilitates a complex life that includes work, relationships, and healthy coping with stressful life events. Erikson saw the main developmental task of **middle adulthood** as **generativity,** which involves contributing to the next generation. Midlife crises are not experienced by most midlife adults, although those who have not resolved earlier developmental tasks successfully are more at risk for a midlife crisis.

Late adulthood, according to Erikson, is best navigated by the achievement of **ego-integrity** or the ability to accept both the successes and failures of one's past and present. Both cognitive and physical decline can—to some extent—be slowed significantly by regular physical and mental exercise. Moreover, some abilities, such as vocabulary and social skills, actually improve with age. Cultural norms also have an impact on aging and foster expectations of positive or negative changes along with it. Remaining active and engaged on all levels—physically, intellectually, and socially—is the most important key to healthy aging.

Alzheimer's disease (p. 312)
ego-integrity (p. 310)
emerging adulthood (p. 307)
generativity (p. 309)
intimacy (p. 306)
peer marriage (p. 308)
revolution in aging (p. 306)
selective social interaction (p. 312)
transition (p. 309)

CRITICAL THINKING APPLIED

The Mozart Effect

The notion that playing classical music for babies before birth will subsequently increase their IQ score has become a popular belief. But a closer look at the research indicates that the claim is wildly exaggerated. The gain in IQ score disappeared after just 15 minutes, and further testing revealed that it was actually positive mood that temporarily increased cognitive functioning.

DISCOVERING PSYCHOLOGY **VIEWING GUIDE**

Watch the following videos by logging into MyPsychLab (www.mypsychlab.com).
After you have watched the videos, answer the questions that follow.

PROGRAM 5: **THE DEVELOPING CHILD**

PROGRAM 6: **LANGUAGE DEVELOPMENT**

PROGRAM 17: **SEX AND GENDER**

PROGRAM 18: **MATURING AND AGING**

Program Review

1. Jean Piaget has studied how children think. According to Piaget, around what age does a child typically master the idea that the amount of a liquid remains the same when it is poured from one container to another container with a different shape?
   a. 2 years old
   c. 6 years old
   b. 4 years old
   d. 8 years old

2. A baby is shown an orange ball a dozen times in a row. How would you predict the baby would respond?
   a. The baby will make the same interested response each time.
   b. The baby will respond with less and less interest each time.
   c. The baby will respond with more and more interest each time.
   d. The baby will not be interested at any time.

3. The Wild Boy of Aveyron represents which important issue in developmental psychology?
   a. ethics in experimentation
   b. the relation of physical development to social development
   c. nature versus nurture
   d. interpretation of experimental data

4. At 1 month of age, babies
   a. are best described as "a blooming, buzzing confusion."
   b. prefer stimuli that are constant and don't vary.
   c. have not yet opened their eyes.
   d. prefer human faces over other visual stimuli.

5. Which of the following psychological characteristics appear(s) to have a genetic component?
   a. activity level
   b. tendency to be outgoing
   c. risk for some psychopathologies
   d. all of the above

6. What sounds do very young babies prefer?
   a. ocean sounds
   b. human voices
   c. other babies
   d. soft music

7. How does the development of language competence compare from culture to culture?

   a. It varies greatly.

   b. It is remarkably similar.

   c. Western cultures are similar to each other, whereas Eastern cultures are very different.

   d. This topic is just beginning to be explored by researchers.

8. Which of the following stages of communication consists of simple sentences that lack plurals, articles, and tenses, but tend to have the constituent words in the order appropriate to the child's native language?

   a. telegraphic speech

   b. babbling

   c. question asking

   d. ritualistic speech

9. According to research by Zella Lurin and Jeffrey Rubin, the difference in the language parents use to describe their newborn sons or daughters is primarily a reflection of

   a. actual physical differences in the newborns.

   b. differences in the way the newborns behave.

   c. the way the hospital staff responds to the babies.

   d. the parents' expectations coloring their perceptions.

10. The term *androgynous* would best apply to which of the following people?

   a. a macho man who participates in body-building competitions

   b. a dainty woman who belongs to a sewing club

   c. a young boy who never talks in class because he feels shy

   d. a male rock star who wears heavy makeup, long hair, and feminine clothing

11. Because of the way we socialize our children, men tend to experience more freedom to _____, whereas women tend to experience more freedom to _____.

   a. explore; criticize

   b. withdraw; invent

   c. discover; express themselves

   d. express themselves; explore

12. How has research on lifespan development changed our idea of human nature?

   a. We see development as a growth process of early life.

   b. We see that a longer lifespan creates problems for society.

   c. We view people as continuing to develop throughout life.

   d. We regard development as a hormonally based process.

13. According to Erikson, the young adult faces a conflict between

   a. isolation and intimacy.

   b. heterosexuality and homosexuality.

   c. autonomy and shame.

   d. wholeness and futility.

14. Assuming that a person remains healthy, what happens to the ability to derive sexual pleasure as one ages?

   a. It does not change.

   b. It gradually diminishes.

   c. It abruptly ceases.

   d. It depends on the availability of a suitable partner.

15. In which of the following areas do the elderly typically have an advantage over college students?

   a. The elderly are better able to climb stairs.

   b. The elderly generally have higher short-term memory capacity.

   c. The elderly are less lonely.

   d. The elderly have a more developed sense of humor.

8

States of Consciousness

CHAPTER PROBLEM How can psychologists objectively examine the worlds of dreaming and other subjective mental states?

CRITICAL THINKING APPLIED The Unconscious—Reconsidered

H AVE YOU EVER HAD A DREAM YOU ENJOYED SO MUCH THAT YOU
wanted to linger in bed so you could disappear back into it? On a hot June
morning in Phoenix, a housewife and mother of three awoke from just that sort
of dream.

In my dream, two people were having an intense conversation in a meadow in the woods.
One of these people was just your average girl. The other person was fantastically beautiful,
sparkly, and a vampire. They were discussing the difficulties inherent in the facts that (A) they
were falling in love with each other while (B) the vampire was particularly attracted to the scent
of her blood, and was having a difficult time restraining himself from killing her immediately
(Meyer, 2011).

Captivated by the intensely handsome young man in the dream and intrigued by the personalities and the dilemma of the couple, she began to write a story about them—a story that
quickly developed into the blockbuster series of books and movies called *Twilight*.

Stephenie Meyer was not the first to be inspired by a dream. From ancient times, dreams
have been regarded as sources of insight, creativity, and prophecy. We can see this, for example, in the Old Testament story of the Israelite Joseph, who interpreted Pharaoh's dreams of
fat and lean cattle as predicting first the years of plenty and then the years of famine that lay in
store for the Egyptian kingdom (Genesis, 41:i–vii).

In more modern times, English poet Samuel Taylor Coleridge attributed the imagery of his
poem "Kubla Khan" to a dream (possibly drug-induced) that he experienced after reading a biography of the famed Mongol warrior. Likewise, artists such as surrealist Salvador Dali found dreams
to be vivid sources of imagery. Composers as varied as Mozart, Beethoven, the Beatles, and

Sting have all credited their dreams with inspiring certain works. In the scientific world, chemist August Kekule's discovery of the structure of the benzene molecule was sparked by his dream of a snake rolled into a loop, grasping its own tail tucked in its mouth. Even the famous horror writer Stephen King claims to have harvested story ideas from his own childhood nightmares.

Why do we dream? Do dreams help us solve problems? Do they reflect the workings of the unconscious mind? Or are dreams just random mental "junk"—perhaps debris left over from the previous day? The difficulty in studying dreams with the methods of science is that these mental states are private experiences. No one else can experience your dreams directly. These issues, then, frame the problem on which we will focus in this chapter.

PROBLEM: **How can psychologists objectively examine the worlds of dreaming and other subjective mental states?**

Dreaming represents one of many states of consciousness possible for the human mind. Others include our familiar state of wakefulness and the less-familiar states of hypnosis, meditation, and the chemically altered states produced by psychoactive drugs—all of which we will study in this chapter. But that's not all. Behind these conscious states, much of the brain's work occurs offline—outside of awareness (Wallace & Fisher, 1999). This includes such mundane tasks as the retrieval of information from memory (What is seven times nine?), as well as the primitive operations occurring in the deep regions of the brain that control basic biological functions, such as blood pressure and body temperature. Somewhere between these extremes are parts of the mind that somehow deal with our once-conscious memories and gut-level responses, as varied as recollections of this morning's breakfast or your most embarrassing moment. As we will see, the nature of this netherworld of nonconscious ideas, feelings, desires, and images has been controversial ever since Freud suggested that dreams may reflect unrecognized and unconscious fears and desires. In this chapter, we will evaluate this claim, as well as others made for hidden levels of processing in the mind. To do so, we begin with the familiar state of consciousness that fills most of our waking hours.

CONNECTION CHAPTER 2

The *hypothalamus*, for example, unconsciously regulates several biological drives (p. 68).

8.1 KEY QUESTION
How Is Consciousness Related to Other Mental Processes?

What does it mean to be conscious? Is it alertness? Is it awareness, perhaps of oneself and of one's environment? Both these suggestions seem reasonable. But consider this: Discovery of the chemical transmission between neurons (rather than electrical transmission, as previously thought) came to physiologist Otto Loewi in a dream, from which he awoke and scribbled down his idea on paper next to his bed. He went back to sleep, but in the morning found he couldn't decipher his handwriting and could not remember the design of the experiment he had dreamed of. Fortunately, he had the same dream the next night, and this time he got out of bed immediately, raced to his lab, and tried the experiment—which set the stage for his Nobel Prize-winning contribution to medicine in 1936.

So here is the question: Was Loewi conscious when, in his sleep, he designed the revolutionary experiment? Although we generally assume that alertness is a prerequisite for clear thinking or problem solving—such as that which produced Loewi's idea—we don't typically think of sleeping or dreaming as a state of alertness, so we probably wouldn't say he was alert. Was he conscious when he wrote it down, only to find he could not read what he wrote the next morning? He was aware enough to reach for a pen and paper, and we generally assume we must be conscious for such goal-directed behavior. But if he was conscious when he wrote it down, why couldn't he make sense of it the next day?

This puzzling example illustrates the difficulty psychologists sometimes have in defining exactly what it means to be conscious. The problem is that consciousness is so subjective and elusive—like searching for the end of the rainbow (Damasio, 1999, 2000). The conundrum first presented itself when structuralists attempted to dissect conscious experience more than a century ago. As you will recall, they used a simple technique called *introspection*, asking people to report on their own conscious experience. The slippery, subjective nature of consciousness quickly became obvious to nearly everyone, and psychologists began to despair that science would never find a way to study objectively something so private as conscious experience. (Think about it: How could you prove that you have consciousness?)

The problem seemed so intractable that, early in the 20th century, the notorious and influential behaviorist John Watson declared the mind out of bounds for the young science of psychology. Mental processes were little more than by-products of our actions, he said. (You don't cry because you are sad; you are sad because some event makes you cry.) Under Watson's direction, psychology became simply the science of behavior. And so psychology not only lost its consciousness but also lost its mind!

The psychology of consciousness remained in limbo until the 1960s, when a coalition of cognitive psychologists, neuroscientists, and computer scientists brought it back to life (Gardner, 1985). They did so for two reasons. First, many psychological issues had surfaced that needed a better explanation than behaviorism could deliver: quirks of memory, perceptual illusions, and drug-induced states (which were very popular in the 1960s). The second reason for the reemergence of consciousness came from technology. Scientists were acquiring new tools—especially computers, which made brain scans possible. Computers also provided a model that could explain how the brain processes information.

The combination of new tools and unsolved problems, then, led to a multidisciplinary effort that became known as **cognitive neuroscience**. Attracting scientists from a variety of fields, cognitive neuroscience set out to unravel the mystery of how the brain processes information and creates conscious experience. From the perspective of cognitive neuroscience, the brain acts like a biological computing device with vast resources—among them 100 billion transistor-like neurons, each with thousands of interconnections—capable of creating the complex universe of imagination and experience we think of as consciousness (Chalmers, 1995).

The big picture that emerges is one of a conscious mind that can take on a variety of roles, as we will see. But the conscious mind must focus sequentially, first on one thing and then another, like a moving spotlight (Tononi & Edelman, 1998). Consciousness is not good at multitasking; so, if you try to drive while texting on your cell phone, you must shift your attention back and forth between tasks (Rubenstein et al., 2001; Strayer et al., 2003). Meanwhile, **nonconscious processes** have no such restriction and can work on many jobs at the same time—which is why you can walk, chew gum, and breathe simultaneously. In more technical terms, consciousness must process information *serially,* while nonconscious brain circuits can process many streams of information *in parallel.* This big picture, then, leads us to our core concept for this section:

Core Concept 8.1

The brain operates on many levels at once—both conscious and unconscious.

Let's get back to the question we posed at the beginning of this section: What exactly is consciousness? Thanks to advances in cognitive neuroscience, we now define **consciousness** not as a state of being but as the brain *process* that creates our mental representation of the world and our current thoughts. Identifying it as a process acknowledges that consciousness is dynamic and continual rather than static and concrete. And it is a process with links to other processes we have studied, including memory, learning, sensation, and perception.

CONNECTION CHAPTER 1

Wundt and the structuralists pioneered the use of *introspection* in their search for "the elements of conscious experience" (p. 14).

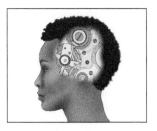

Although Freud used a psychodynamic perspective for his pioneering work on unconscious processes in his patients, it was the cognitive psychologists who showed that subjective mental states could be studied objectively with the tools of science.

cognitive neuroscience An interdisciplinary field involving cognitive psychology, neurology, biology, computer science, linguistics, and specialists from other fields who are interested in the connection between mental processes and the brain.

nonconscious process Any brain process that does not involve conscious processing, including both preconscious memories and unconscious processes.

consciousness The process by which the brain creates a mental model of our experience. The most common, or ordinary, consciousness occurs during wakefulness, although there are can be altered states of consciousness.

CONNECTION CHAPTER 5

◄————————

Working memory imposes a
limitation on consciousness
because it holds only about seven
"chunks" of information (p. 177).

CONNECTION CHAPTER 4

◄————————

Behavioral learning includes
operant conditioning and
classical conditioning (p. 135).

attention   A process by which consciousness
focuses on a single item or "chunk" in working memory.

For example, everything entering consciousness passes through working memory. When sensory stimulation gains our attention and passes from sensory memory into working memory, we become conscious of it. Thus, we can also say we are conscious of everything that enters working memory. Therefore, some psychologists have suggested working memory is actually the long-sought seat of consciousness (Engle; 2002; LeDoux, 1996).

Consciousness is also linked to learning. As you might recall from Chapter 4, cognitive learning and behavioral learning seem to involve different brain mechanisms. Most *cognitive learning* (such as your learning of the material in this chapter) relies on conscious processes. On the other hand, much *behavioral learning*, particularly classical conditioning—such as the acquisition of a phobic response—relies heavily on processes that can occur outside of consciousness.

Another process linked to consciousness is **attention**, a feature that makes one item stand out among others in consciousness—as when someone calls your name in a crowded room. Attention also enables you to follow the thread of a conversation against a background of other voices. (Psychologists call this *selective attention* or the *cocktail party phenomenon*.) Attention, in turn, is closely related to the dual processes of *sensation and perception*, which we studied in Chapter 3. There, you also read about *pain* perception—a mental process for which the link to consciousness is only partially known. Later in this chapter, we will explore how states of consciousness, such as hypnosis, may be effective in managing pain.

One last point about the role of consciousness is this: It helps you combine both reality and fantasy and creates a sort of ongoing "movie" in your head. For example, if you see a doughnut when you are hungry, working memory forms a conscious image of the doughnut (based on sensation and perception) and consults long-term memory, which—thanks to behavioral learning—associates the image with food and allows you to imagine eating it. In this way, consciousness relies on all the processes we have discussed. But exactly *how* the brain does this is perhaps psychology's greatest mystery. How do the patterns in the firing of billions of neurons become the conscious image of a doughnut—or of the words and ideas on this page?

Tools for Studying Consciousness

High-tech tools, such as the fMRI, PET, and EEG, have opened new windows to the brain that enable researchers to see which regions are active during various mental tasks. In other words, we can identify some of the "what" of consciousness: Although these imaging devices do not, of course, reveal the actual contents of conscious experience, they do indicate distinct groups of brain structures that "light up," for example, when we read, speak, or shift our attention (see Figure 8.1). The resulting images leave no doubt that conscious processing involves simultaneous activity in many brain circuits, especially in the cortex and pathways connecting the thalamus to the cortex. But, to glimpse the underlying mental processes—the "how" of consciousness—psychologists have devised other, even more ingenious, techniques. We will see many of these throughout this chapter and, in fact, throughout this book. For the moment, though, we will give you just two examples as previews of coming attractions.

Mental Rotation   A classic experiment by Roger Shepard and Jacqueline Metzler (1971) showed that it's not merely a metaphor when people speak of "turning things over" in their minds. Using drawings like those in Figure 8.2, Shepard and Metzler asked volunteers to decide whether the two images in each pair show the same object in different positions. They reasoned that, if the mind actually rotates images when comparing them, people would take longer to respond when the difference between the angles of the images in each pair is increased. And that is exactly what they found. If you try this experiment on your friends, it is likely that they, too, will respond more quickly to pair A—where the images have been rotated through a smaller angle—than to pairs B and C.

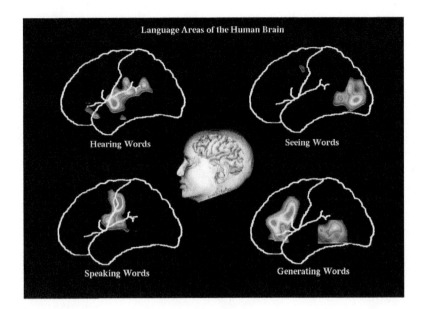

FIGURE 8.1

PET Scans of the Brain at Work

These PET scans show how distinct regions of the brain become active during different conscious tasks.

Zooming in with the Mind Another clever approach to the "how" of consciousness takes a different twist: Stephen Kosslyn found we can use our conscious minds to "zoom in," camera-like, on the details of our mental images. To demonstrate this, Kosslyn (1976) first asked people to think of objects, such as an elephant or a cat or a chair. Then he asked questions about details of the imagined object (for example, "Is it a black cat?" or "Does it have a long tail?"), recording how long it took for people to answer. He discovered that the smaller the detail he asked for, the longer subjects needed for a response. People required extra time, Kosslyn proposed, to make a closer examination of their mental images.

Both these experiments suggest we consciously manipulate our visual images. And we do so in much the same way that we might manipulate physical objects in the outside world (Kosslyn, 1983). You can try this yourself with the demonstration in the box on the next page, *Do It Yourself! Zooming in on Mental Images*. As we progress through the chapter, you will learn about other techniques used by neuroscientists to study consciousness and its allied mental processes. First, though, let's look more closely at some models of the mind.

Models of the Conscious and Nonconscious Minds

As psychologists have attempted to study and understand consciousness, several models have emerged that remain useful today. You might recall from Chapter 6 that searching for analogies can be a useful problem-solving strategy. Psychologists have employed a similar strategy in trying to nail down the essence of consciousness by searching for the best metaphor to represent this elusive concept. Let's look at a few of these models.

Freud's Levels of Consciousness Sigmund Freud originally suggested a notion many of us take for granted today: that our minds operate on several levels at once. The metaphor he developed as a model for consciousness compared it to the tip of an iceberg, suggesting a much larger presence beneath the surface. Freud saw this larger presence—the *unconscious*—as a reservoir of needs, desires, wishes, and traumatic memories. Moreover, he believed that processing in the unconscious—outside our awareness—could influence our conscious thoughts, feelings, dreams, fantasies, and actions. A large body of evidence now confirms Freud's insight that much of the mind lurks and works out of sight, beneath the level of awareness.

The Preconscious Psychologists often use Freud's term, the **preconscious**, in referring to memories of events (your birthday last year, for example) and facts (Salem is the

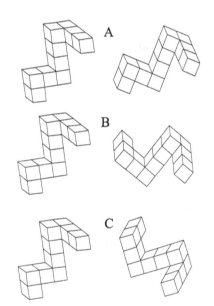

FIGURE 8.2

Figures for the Mental Rotation Experiment

These figures are similar to those used in Shepard and Metzler's mental rotation experiment. Results showed that people took longer to decide whether the images were the same or different as the images in each pair were rotated through greater angles. You might try your own test to verify their findings.

preconscious Freud's notion that the mind has a special unconscious storehouse for information not currently in consciousness but readily available to consciousness. Example: your telephone number is stored in the preconscious.

Do It Yourself! ZOOMING IN ON MENTAL IMAGES

Ask a friend to close his or her eyes and imagine a house. Then ask your friend to describe the color of the roof, the front door, and doorbell button. Using a watch or clock that displays seconds, record the amount of time it takes to get each answer. Based on Kosslyn's research, which item would you predict would require the longest response time? The shortest?

You will probably find that the smaller the detail you ask for, the longer it takes your friend to respond. Kosslyn interpreted this to mean that people need the extra time to "zoom in" on a mental image to resolve smaller features. In other words, we examine our mental images in the same way that we examine physical objects in the external world in order to perceive the "big picture" or the details.

capital of Oregon) that are not conscious but are readily accessible. These memories can cross over to consciousness with relative ease when something cues their recall. Otherwise, they lie in the background of the mind, just beyond the boundary of consciousness until needed. Thus, the preconscious, in the modern cognitive sense, is much the same as *long-term memory.*

Preconscious processing isn't restricted to the serial, one-thing-at-a-time limitation of consciousness. That is, it can search for information in many places at once—an ability called *parallel processing.* On the other hand, the preconscious lacks the ability consciousness has for deliberate thinking. You might think of the preconscious as a memory storehouse, where the stock is constantly rotated so that the most recently used and most emotionally loaded information is most easily accessed.

The Unconscious A dictionary might define the term *unconscious* as the absence of all consciousness, as in one who has fainted, become comatose, or is under anesthesia. Freud, however, defined the unconscious as a reservoir of primitive motives and threatening memories hidden from awareness. And cognitive psychologists have still another meaning for *unconscious* that refers to any sort of nonconscious process (including breathing, turning your head, etc.) produced in the brain. Pulling these notions together, we will define the **unconscious** as a broad term that refers to many levels of processing below the level of awareness. These can range from preconscious memory to brain activity that controls basic body functions to the processes that operate in the background when we form a perception, say, of a table or a comment made by a friend. Such unconscious processes can be subtle—perhaps leading, without our realization, to anxiety or depression (Kihlstrom, 1987).

You can get some idea of how unconscious processes can affect us if you think about how you often follow a familiar route to work or school without apparent thought—even when you are driving! Unconscious processing can also be studied in the laboratory, as you will see in the following demonstration. Try filling in the blanks to make a word from the following stem:

unconscious In classic Freudian theory, a part of the mind that houses emotional memories, desires, and feelings that would be threatening if brought to consciousness. Many modern cognitive psychologists, however, view the unconscious in less sinister terms, as including all nonconscious mental processes.

D E F — — —

Using a technique called *priming,* psychologists can influence the answers people give to such problems—without their being conscious that they were influenced. In the example just given, there are a number of possible ways to complete the word stem, including *defend, defeat, defect, defile, deform, defray,* and *defuse.* We don't know for sure what your answer was, but we did set you up to think of the word *define.* How? We deliberately "primed" your response by using the word *define* several times in the previous paragraph. (There is no certainty, of course, that you would respond as predicted—merely an increased probability.) With methods such as this, psychologists have a powerful tool for probing the interaction of conscious and unconscious processes.

James' Stream of Consciousness William James offered a different metaphor for consciousness, likening ordinary waking consciousness to a flowing stream carrying ever-changing sensations, perceptions, thoughts, memories, feelings, motives, and desires. This "stream of consciousness" includes awareness of ourselves and of stimulation from our environment. According to James, it can also include physical sensations from within, such as hunger, thirst, pain, and pleasure.

Part of James' theory was somewhat similar to Freud's distinction between the conscious and the preconscious. For James, consciousness had two levels: an area of focus, which included whatever we are attending closely to at any given time, and a peripheral consciousness encompassing the feelings and associations that give meaning and context to our focus. So, for example, when you attend the wedding of a friend, your focus is on the couple getting married and the guests with whom you are interacting. The feelings you have about the marriage, all the things you know about what led the couple to this pivotal moment in their lives, and whatever other memories the event triggers for you are all part of the peripheral conscious, like the supporting actors in a drama. In this way, we might use vision as another metaphor to describe James' model of consciousness: Like our peripheral vision, our peripheral consciousness is not the subject of our focus, but lends meaning and context to it.

The Modern Cognitive Perspective The final metaphor we offer for consciousness comes from cognitive psychology. The *computer metaphor* likens consciousness to the information and images that appear on a computer screen, while nonconscious processes are like the electronic activity behind the scenes, deep inside the computer. Most of the time, our nonconscious machinery quietly operates in parallel with consciousness, but occasionally a nonconscious motive or emotion becomes so strong it erupts into consciousness—as when a peculiar odor associated with an emotional memory suddenly brings that emotion to the forefront, or when a growing hunger drive bursts into awareness.

All these metaphors can help us grasp the nature of consciousness, and we will return to them periodically throughout the chapter as we develop our understanding of this fascinating process. Before leaving this section, though, let's ask one more important question: Why is consciousness important?

What Does Consciousness Do for Us?

At this moment, your consciousness is focused on these words, written in black letters on a white page. But the words don't stand alone. Like James suggested in his discussion of peripheral consciousness, the words also have meaning, which flows through consciousness as you read. You can, of course, shift the spotlight of your attention to something else—music in the background, perhaps—and, as you do so, the words on the page slip into the fringes of awareness. You may be moving your eyes across the page, but the meaning does not really register. (Every student has had this experience.)

Now, if we can have your attention again, we'd like to remind you that consciousness has many functions. Three especially important ones were illustrated by the scenario in the previous paragraph (Solso, 2001; Tononi & Edelman, 1998):

- **Consciousness restricts our attention.** Because consciousness processes information serially, it limits what you notice and think about. In this way, consciousness

CONNECTION CHAPTER 5

Psychologists use *priming* to study *implicit memory* (p. 192).

William James spoke of the "stream of consciousness," which portrayed consciousness as an active, ever-changing process. (Courtesy Susan Dupor.)

Both James and Freud theorized that we have two levels of consciousness. The focus of our consciousness, like the focus of our attention on the singer in the spotlight, takes center stage. Equally important, however, is what James called our peripheral conscious: Just as the band adds richness to the singer's performance, our peripheral consciousness adds rich contextual detail to our area of focus.

keeps your brain from being overwhelmed by stimulation. Unfortunately, the one-thing-at-a-time property of consciousness will not let you concentrate on what you are reading when you shift your attention to music playing in the background.

CONNECTION CHAPTER 3

Perception is the process of adding meaning to sensation (p. 89).

- **Consciousness provides a mental "meeting place,"** where sensation can *combine* with memory, emotions, motives, and a host of other psychological processes in the process we have called *perception*. Consciousness, then, is the canvas on which we customarily create a meaningful picture from the palette of stimulation offered by our internal and external worlds. This is the aspect of consciousness that links meaning to words on a page or connects the emotion of joy to the sight of an old friend's face. Indeed, neuroimaging research indicates that the essence of consciousness is to make linkages among different parts of the brain (Massimini et al., 2005). Consciousness, therefore, lies at the very heart of cognition.

- **Consciousness allows us to create a mental model of the world**—a model we can *manipulate* in our minds. Unlike simpler organisms, consciousness frees us from being prisoners of the moment: We don't just react reflexively to stimulation. Instead, we use a conscious model of our world that draws on memory and forethought, bringing both the past and the future into awareness. With this model, we can think and plan by manipulating our mental world to evaluate alternative responses and imagine how effective they will be. It is this feature of consciousness that, for example, helps you make associations between concepts in this text and your own experiences, or keeps you from being brutally honest with a friend wearing clothes you don't like.

These three features—*restriction, combination,* and *manipulation*—apply in varying degrees to all states of consciousness, whether dreaming, hypnosis, meditation, a drug-induced state, or our "normal" waking state. But what about the condition known as a coma: Where does it fit into our study of consciousness?

Coma and Related States

coma   An unconscious state, during which a person lacks the normal cycles of sleep and wakefulness, that usually lasts only a few days. The comatose state differs from the *minimally conscious state* and the *persistent vegetative state.*

The general public profoundly misunderstands what it means to be in a **coma**. This misunderstanding stems, in part, from a few highly publicized and emotional cases that provoked heated discussion about the ethics of discontinuing life support in severely brain-injured patients (Meyers, 2007). The flames are fanned, too, by reports of "miraculous" recoveries. So what are the facts?

Comas are not stable, long-term states. Rather, they usually last only a few days—up to about two weeks—after brain injury. In a comatose state, patients lack the normal cycles of sleep and wakefulness, their eyes usually remain closed, and they cannot be aroused. Those who improve transition to a *minimally conscious state,* during which they may have limited awareness and a functioning brain. Recovery is usually gradual (National Institute of Neurological Disorders and Stroke, 2007). Those who do not improve deteriorate into a *persistent vegetative state.* In this condition, they may open their eyes periodically, and they pass in and out of normal sleep cycles, but they have only minimal brain activity and basic reflexes. Chances for full recovery from a persistent vegetative state are slim.

But diagnosis of a persistent vegetative state is sometimes inaccurate, as the measurement of brain activity is not a perfect science. And such a mistake could potentially be fatal when the diagnosis is used to make decisions about whether or not to continue life support. Promising new brain imaging techniques are being discovered, however, that can more accurately identify the level of brain activity and awareness in patients who appear to be in persistent vegetative states. Advances in PET and MRI technology have recently enabled researchers to predict successfully which patients in persistent vegetative state would improve and transition into minimally conscious states (Owen et al., 2009). Stay tuned for further developments.

[PSYCHOLOGY MATTERS]

Using Psychology to Learn Psychology

Want to expand your consciousness? In the strictest sense, it is not really possible, because consciousness has a limited capacity. As we have noted, consciousness can focus on only one thing at a time. What can be expanded, however, is the access your consciousness has to information stored in your preconscious memory. Learning how to do that can be of tremendous help to students who need to absorb a large amount of information and to prove it on an exam.

You will, of course, have an advantage if you face an exam with your consciousness unimpaired by the massive sleep debt students sometimes incur in an "all-nighter" study session. No amount of caffeine can bring your sleep-deprived consciousness back to optimum functioning. Just as your teachers have always preached—and as you learned in Chapter 5—it is far better to spread your studying over several days or weeks than to try to learn everything at once. So there is your first tip to increasing your access to your preconscious!

Because of its severely limited capacity, you cannot possibly hold in consciousness everything you need to remember for an exam. The material must be stored, readily accessible but outside of consciousness, in preconscious long-term memory. The trick is to be able to bring it back into consciousness when needed. Here are some more strategies to help:

A good study partner can help you gain a deeper and stronger grasp of the concepts.

1. **Study for the gist.** Students sometimes think their professors ask "trick questions," although professors almost never do so intentionally. In reality, a good exam question will show whether students understand the meaning of a term—the *gist*—rather than having merely memorized a definition. A twofold study strategy can help you get the gist (pronounced *JIST*) of a concept. First, put the textbook or class definition into your own words. Second, think of an example from your own experience that illustrates the concept.

2. **Look for connections among concepts.** Once you have the gist of the concepts, you will probably also need to know how those concepts are related to each other. The professor may ask you to explain, for example, the relationship between *consciousness* and *preconsciousness*. Therefore, a good study strategy is to ask yourself how a new concept (e.g., *preconscious*) is related to other concepts learned previously (e.g., *conscious* or *unconscious*). As we noted in Chapter 6, the cognitive mapping tool in MyPsychLab can be a great asset to help you find connections between concepts.

Map the **Concepts** at **MyPsychLab**

3. **Anticipate the most likely cues.** Just because you "know" the material doesn't mean the exam questions will automatically prompt the release of the information from long-term memory back into consciousness. It pays, therefore, to spend some of your study time thinking about the kinds of questions your professor might ask. For example, you will learn in this chapter about the effects of various psychoactive drugs, but you could be stumped if the professor asks you to explain why alcohol is more like barbiturates than opiates. You can often anticipate such questions by noting what the professor emphasizes in lecture. It also helps to think of the kinds of questions that your professor is known to favor. (A study partner helps a lot with this.) Some of the most common essay questions begin with terms such as "Explain," "Evaluate," or "Compare and contrast."

In general, the relationship between consciousness and memory suggests that to learn the kind of material required in your college classes, you must actively process the material while it is in your consciousness. To do so effectively, you must make the material meaningful. This requires understanding it in your own words, with your own examples—thus making connections between new information and old information already in your memory. It also requires organizing information so you see how it is interconnected. And, finally, it requires anticipating the cues that will be used to bring it back to consciousness.

Check Your Understanding

✔●─Study and Review at MyPsychLab

1. **RECALL:** Why did behaviorist John Watson object to defining psychology as the science of consciousness?

2. **RECALL:** What technology would a cognitive neuroscientist be likely to use in studying consciousness?

3. **APPLICATION:** How would you sample the contents of another person's *preconscious* mind?

4. **UNDERSTANDING THE CORE CONCEPT:** Returning to the example at the beginning of this section, in which Otto Loewi

discovered the chemical nature of neural transmissions based on a dream: In what ways might Loewi's brain have been simultaneously operating on both conscious and unconscious levels? For example, how might the inability of his consciousness to parallel process have played a role in his messy handwriting as he attempted to remember the dream? Also, if he thought about the problem and the dream before going to bed the second night, how could the preconscious have helped him awaken when he had the dream the second time and jump out of bed?

Answers 1. Watson and other behaviorists argued that consciousness is a subjective mental state that cannot be studied with objective methods of science. **2.** Cognitive neuroscientists commonly use fMRI and other brain scanning techniques. **3.** Ask him or her to recall specific information from memory, such as a phone number or a concept that had been previously learned. **4.** Although we cannot know for sure, we might speculate something like this: Loewi's idea originated in his unconscious while dreaming; then, his consciousness attempted to take over when he awoke and thought to write it down. Because our conscious mind cannot parallel process, the restriction of his focus to the attempt to remember the dream may have interfered with his ability to legibly record the dream. Then, when the dream recurred the next night, the boundary between his preconscious and unconscious may have fluctuated as a result of thinking about the lost dream the second time before he went to bed that night—thus allowing his conscious mind to come to attention when he had the dream the second time and prompting him to jump out of bed and test it right away so as not to lose it again.

8.2 KEY QUESTION
What Cycles Occur in Everyday Consciousness?

If you are a "morning person," you are probably at your peak of alertness soon after you awaken. But this mental state doesn't last all day. Like most other people, you likely experience a period of mental lethargy in the afternoon—at which point you may join much of the Latin world and wisely take a siesta. Later, your alertness increases for a time, only to fade again during the evening hours. Punctuating this cycle may be periods of heightened focus and attention and periods of reverie, known as daydreams. Finally, whether you are a "morning" or "night" person, you eventually drift into that third of your life in which conscious contact with the outside world nearly ceases: sleep.

Psychologists have traced these cyclic changes in consciousness, looking for reliable patterns. Our Core Concept for this section of the chapter summarizes what they have found:

Core Concept 8.2

Consciousness fluctuates in cycles that correspond to our biological rhythms and to patterns of stimulation in our environment.

In this section, we focus primarily on the cyclic changes in consciousness involved in sleep and nocturnal dreaming. We begin, however, with another sort of "dreaming" that occurs while we are awake.

Daydreaming

daydreaming A common (and quite normal) variation of consciousness in which attention shifts to memories, expectations, desires, or fantasies and away from the immediate situation.

In the mildly altered state of consciousness we call **daydreaming**, attention turns inward to memories, expectations, and desires—often with vivid mental imagery (Roche & McConkey, 1990). Daydreaming occurs most often when people are alone, relaxed, engaged in a boring or routine task, or just about to fall asleep (Singer, 1966, 1975). But is daydreaming normal? You may be relieved to know that most people daydream every day. In fact, it is abnormal if you do not! On average, about 30 percent of our waking hours is spent daydreaming, with young adults reporting the most frequent and vivid daydreams. Both the incidence and the intensity of daydreams appear to decline significantly with increasing age (Giambra, 2000; Singer & McCraven, 1961).

Why Do We Daydream? A brain scan study by Malia Mason and her colleagues (2007) recently discovered that daydreaming may be inevitable. A complex web of regions in the brain, concentrated in the frontal and temporal lobes and dubbed the "brain default network," automatically activates when the brain is in a restful state, or not focused on something in the external environment. Activity in this network appears to be highest when people are daydreaming about future events or personal memories of the past or imagining how someone is feeling or thinking (Buckner et al, 2008). Thus, the brain seems wired to remain active, even at rest—a finding that will help us understand our nighttime dreams a little later in this section.

Is Daydreaming Helpful or Harmful? Daydreams can serve valuable, healthy functions (Klinger, 1987). They often dwell on practical and current concerns in our lives, such as classes, goals (trivial or significant), and interpersonal relationships. As we ruminate on these concerns, daydreaming can help us make plans and solve problems: for some people, this kind of daydreaming increases the chances of reaching their goals (Langens, 2003). Daydreams can also be a source of creative insight, rather like the flashes of intuition we discussed in Chapter 6. When faced with a difficult problem, occasional periods of mind-wandering can give our brains access to unconscious associations and possibilities that may provide that "Aha!" moment that reveals the perfect solution (Schooler et al., 1995).

Be careful about the timing of your daydreaming, though. New research indicates that daydreaming can interfere with memories of recently learned material. And the more distant the daydream from reality, the greater the effect: Students who daydreamed about an international vacation forgot more than students who dreamed about a local vacation (Delaney et al., 2010). This suggests that if you slip into daydreaming during an important study session, you risk forgetting some of what you just learned.

And we must include one more caution about daydreaming. Research coming out of the Harvard laboratory of Matthew Killingsworth and Dan Gilbert (2010) threatens one of our most common assumptions about daydreaming—the notion that daydreaming is a happy pursuit. A study of more than 2,000 adults of all ages used a specially created iPhone app to check in with participants at random times of the day. When their app chimed, participants answered a few quick questions about what they were doing, whether they were focused on it or not, and how happy they were. Findings revealed something that might surprise you: People were happiest when they were fully immersed and focused on a task—not when they were daydreaming. So, despite the fact that a wandering mind may be part of our brain's wiring system, it appears that an engaged mind is a happier mind.

How do daydreams compare with dreams of the night? No matter how realistic our fantasies may be, daydreams are rarely as vivid as our most colorful night dreams. Neither are they as mysterious—because they are more under our control. Nor do they occur, like night dreams, under the influence of biological cycles and the strange world that we call sleep. It is to this nighttime world that we now turn our attention.

Sleep: The Mysterious Third of Our Lives

If you live to be 90, you will have slept for nearly 30 years. But what is this mysterious mental state? Once the province of psychoanalysts, prophets, poets, and painters, the world of sleep is now a vibrant field of scientific study revealing that sleep is one of our natural biological cycles (Beardsley, 1996). We begin our exploration of this realm of altered consciousness with an examination of these cycles.

Circadian Rhythms All creatures are influenced by nature's cyclic changes, especially the daily pattern of light and darkness. Among the most important for us humans are those known as **circadian rhythms**, bodily patterns that repeat approximately every 24 hours. (Circadian comes from the Latin *circa* for "about" and *dies* for "a day.") Internal control of these recurring rhythms resides in our hypothalamus, where

circadian rhythm A physiological pattern that repeats approximately every 24 hours—such as the sleep–wakefulness cycle.

our "biological clock" sets the cadence of such functions as metabolism, heart rate, body temperature, and hormonal activity (Pinel, 2005). A group of cells in the hypothalamus known as the suprachiasmatic nucleus (SCN) receives input from the eyes, so it is especially sensitive to the light–dark cycles of day and night (Barinaga, 2002). From a biological perspective, then, the cycle of sleep and wakefulness is just another circadian rhythm.

For most of us, the normal sleep–wakefulness pattern is naturally a bit longer than a day. When living for long periods in environments with no time cues, most people settle into a circadian cycle closer to 25 hours. In a 24-hour world, however, our pattern becomes trained to readjust itself each day by our exposure to light and our habitual routines (Dement & Vaughan, 1999).

Circadian Rhythms Impact Travelers—and Everyone Else   The slightly-longer-than-24-hour timespan of our natural circadian cycle sheds light on the condition know as *jet lag*, with its symptoms of fatigue, irresistible sleepiness, and temporary cognitive deficits. When we fly from east to west, our bodies adapt fairly easily to the longer day in the new locale, since the lengthening of the day matches up with our natural tendency for a longer cycle. Arriving in Seattle from New York, for example, at 7 P.M., your body on New York time thinks it is 10 P.M. In this situation, most people can stay up a little later to fit in with the new time zone and awaken the next morning at an appropriate local time without taking a circadian-rhythm hit. Flying eastward is a different story, though, because you lose hours. Your 7 A.M. wake-up call—when your body thinks it is 4 A.M.—will likely be a rude awakening, and you will have trouble being functional. The loss of hours in your circadian cycle, then, creates greater jet lag than a gain—and for each hour lost, it can take your body about a day to recover. For this reason, experts recommend a variety of strategies to help yourself start adjusting to the new local time a few days before actually arriving.

Read about Tips for Managing Jet Lag at **MyPsychLab**

Even people who don't routinely jet around the world experience the effects of similar circadian shifts—often on a weekly basis. Here's why: Most of us tend to stay up later at night on weekends, when we don't have to get up for school or work the next morning. But research indicates that, for every hour you stay up later on the weekend, thus sleeping later the next morning, you are shifting your circadian rhythm forward in a manner that feels natural to our bodies. When Monday morning rolls around, then, and your alarm rings to wake you up, the surprise to your circadian cycle causes a condition known as the "Monday morning blues."

Is It Natural to Sleep Through the Night?   You may think of sleep as a process that occurs in an approximately eight-hour period, from the time you go to bed until your alarm wakes you in the morning. But that pattern is rather new in human history and limited mainly to people in industrialized countries. The "natural" human tendency is to sleep in a more fluid pattern, whenever one feels like it, in shorter periods during the day or longer stretches during the night (Bosveld, 2007; Warren, 2007). In rural villages throughout the world, sleepers will often wake up for an hour or two in the middle of the night and talk, play, have sex, or tend the fire—showing us just how malleable our sleep–wakefulness schedules can be.

Yet anything that cuts your sleep short or throws your internal clock off its biological schedule can affect how you feel and behave. Work schedules that shift from day to night are notorious for such effects (Dement & Vaughan, 1999; Moore-Ede, 1993)—although, like jet lag, symptoms are worse when shifts move backward in time than forward. And effects can be drastic: One study found that nurses with rotating shifts were twice as likely as those with regular shifts to fall asleep while driving to or from work, with double the risk of accident or error related to sleepiness on the job (Gold et al., 1992). Staying up all night studying for an exam will have similar consequences.

The Main Events of Sleep   Sleep was a mystery for most of human history—until late one night in 1952, when graduate student Eugene Aserinsky decided to record his sleeping son's brain waves and muscle movements of the eyes (Brown, 2003).

Almost one-third of workers in America report having fallen asleep on the job at least once in the past month, according to the National Sleep Foundation. Among shift workers—who, among other things, work in hospitals and air traffic control—that figure rises to over 50 percent.

The session proceeded uneventfully for about an hour and a half, with nothing but the slow rhythms of sleep appearing as tracks on the EEG. Then, suddenly, a flurry of eye movements appeared. The recording showed the boy's eyeballs darting back and forth as though he were watching a fast-changing scene. At the same time, brain wave patterns showed the boy was alert. Expecting to find his son awake and looking around, Aserinsky entered the bedroom and was surprised to see him fast asleep, lying quietly with his eyes closed. Intrigued, the researcher ran more volunteers through the same procedure and found similar patterns in all of them.

About every 90 minutes during sleep, we enter the state Aserinsky discovered. What we now call **REM sleep** is marked by fast brain waves and rapid eye movements (REM) beneath closed eyelids, lasting several minutes or longer and then abruptly ceasing (Aserinsky & Kleitman, 1953). The interim periods, without rapid eye movements, are known as **non-REM (NREM) sleep.**

What happens in the mind and brain during these two different phases of sleep? To find out, researchers awakened sleepers during either REM sleep or NREM sleep and asked them to describe their mental activity (Dement & Kleitman, 1957; McNamara et al., 2005). The NREM reports typically contained either brief descriptions of ordinary daily events or no mental activity at all. By contrast, REM reports were filled with vivid cognitions, featuring fanciful, bizarre scenes, often of an aggressive nature. In other words, rapid eye movements were a sign of dreaming.

Strangely, while the eyes dance during REM sleep, voluntary muscles in the rest of the body remain immobile, in a condition known as **sleep paralysis.** From an evolutionary perspective, this probably kept our ancestors from wandering out of their caves and into trouble while acting out their dreams. (In case you're wondering: Sleepwalking and sleep talking don't occur during REM sleep but in the deeper stages of NREM sleep.) We'll have much more to say about dreaming in a moment. For now, let's see how REM sleep fits with the other phases of sleep.

The Sleep Cycle Imagine you are a volunteer subject in a laboratory sleep experiment. Connected to EEG recording equipment, you get comfortable with the wires linking your body to the machinery and settle in for a night's snooze. While you are still awake and alert, the EEG shows your brain waves pulsing at a rate of about 14 cycles per second (cps). As you relax and become drowsy, they slow to about 8 to 12 cps. When you fall asleep, your brain waves register a cycle of activity much like the pattern in Figure 8.3—a cycle that repeats over and over through the night.

REM sleep   A stage of sleep that occurs approximately every 90 minutes, marked by bursts of rapid eye movements occurring under closed eyelids. REM sleep periods are associated with dreaming.

non-REM (NREM) sleep   The recurring periods, mainly associated with the deeper stages of sleep, when a sleeper is not showing rapid eye movements.

sleep paralysis   A condition in which a sleeper is unable to move any of the voluntary muscles except those controlling the eyes. Sleep paralysis normally occurs during REM sleep.

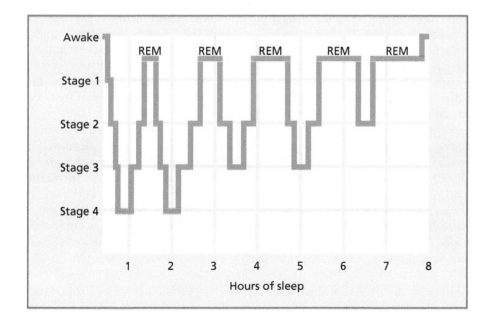

FIGURE 8.3

Stages of Sleep

In a typical night, the deepest sleep (Stages 3 and 4) occurs mainly in the first few hours. As the night progresses, the sleeper spends less time in Stages 3 and 4 and more time in REM.

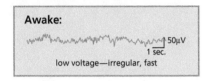

Awake:

low voltage—irregular, fast

Drowsy:

alpha waves (8–12 cps)

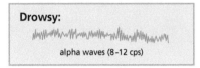

Stage 1:

theta waves (3–7 cps)

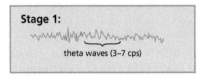

Stage 2:

Sleep spindle   K complex

(12–14 cps)

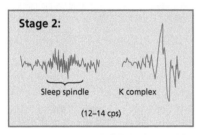

Stages 3 and 4:

delta waves (1/2–2 cps) >75 microvolts

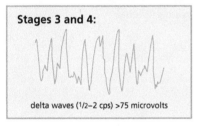

REM sleep:

Sawtooth   Sawtooth
waves   waves

low voltage—random, fast activity
with sawtooth waves

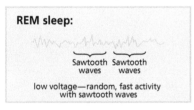

FIGURE 8.4

EEG Patterns in Stages of Sleep

REM rebound   A condition of increased REM sleep caused by REM-sleep deprivation.

A closer look at the recording of this cycle the next morning will show several distinct stages, each with a characteristic EEG signature (see Figure 8.4):

- In Stage 1 sleep, the EEG displays some slower (theta) activity, along with fast (beta) brain waves similar to those seen in the waking state.
- During Stage 2, the generally slower EEG is punctuated by sleep spindles—short bursts of fast electrical activity that reliably signal the end of Stage 1.
- In the following two stages (3 and 4), the sleeper enters a progressively deeper state of relaxed sleep. Heart rate and breathing slow down. Brain waves also slow dramatically, with delta waves appearing for the first time. The deepest point in the sleep cycle occurs in Stage 4, about a half hour after sleep onset.
- As Stage 4 ends, the electrical activity of the brain increases, and the sleeper climbs back up through the stages in reverse order.
- Rather than going into Stage 1 again, though, the sleeper begins to produce fast beta waves on the EEG, along with rapid eye movements—the sign of REM sleep. After about 10 minutes of REM, the sleeper slips back into Stage 2 and the entire cycle repeats itself, with each succeeding REM period getting longer and longer.

Over the course of an average night's sleep, most people travel through the stages of sleep four to six times. In each successive cycle, the amount of time spent in deep sleep (Stages 3 and 4) decreases, and the amount of time spent in REM sleep increases—so we may get up to an hour of REM at the end of a full sleep session. A look at Figure 8.3 will show you how this pattern plays out through a typical night's sleep. Please note the three most important features of normal sleep: (a) the 90-minute cycles, (b) the occurrence of deepest sleep near the beginning of the night, and (c) the increase in REM duration as sleep progresses.

What would happen if a person were deprived of REM for a whole night? Laboratory studies, waking sleepers up each time they slip into REM, reveal tiredness and irritability in these REM-deprived sleepers the next day. During the following night, they typically spend much more time in REM sleep than usual, a condition known as **REM rebound.** This observation suggests that REM sleep satisfies some kind of biological need. Sleep-deprived college students take note: Because we get most of our REM sleep during the last few cycles of the night, we inevitably suffer some REM deprivation and REM rebound if we cut our night's sleep short.

Why Do We Sleep? Sleep is so common among animals that it surely must have some essential function, but sleep scientists disagree on what that function is (Maquet, 2001; Rechtschaffen, 1998). There are several possibilities. Evolutionary psychology suggests sleep may have evolved to enable animals to conserve energy and stay out of harm's way at times when there was no need to forage for food or search for mates (Dement & Vaughan, 1999; Miller, 2007). These functions, then, are coordinated by the brain's circadian clock. Some experiments also show that sleep improves mental functioning, particularly memory and problem solving (Wagner et al., 2004).

Another function of sleep was poetically described by William Shakespeare, when he spoke of "sleep that knits up the ravelled sleave of care." Thus, sleep may have a restorative function for the body and mind. Some studies suggest that damaged brain cells get repaired during sleep; others find that sleep promotes formation of new neurons in the brain—while sleep deprivation inhibits this process (Siegel, 2003; Winerman, 2006b). Sleep and dreams may also help the brain to flush out the day's accumulation of unwanted and useless information—much like reformatting a computer disk (Crick & Mitchison, 1983). While progress has been made in learning how sleep actually restores us, a detailed picture still eludes sleep scientists (Winerman, 2006b).

The Need for Sleep How much sleep we need depends on several factors. Genetics, for one, sets the sleep requirements and individual variations of our circadian rhythms

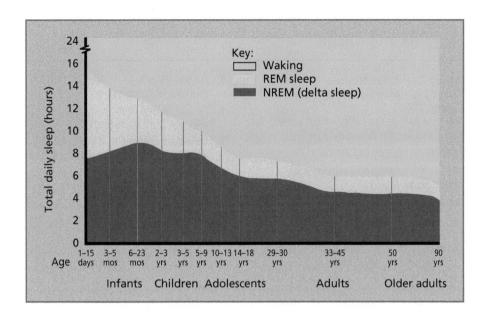

FIGURE 8.5
Patterns of Human Sleep Over a Lifetime

The graph shows changes with age in the total amounts of REM and NREM sleep and in the percentage of time spent in REM sleep. Note that, over the years, the amount of REM sleep decreases considerably, while NREM diminishes less sharply.

Source: From Roffwarg et al., Ontogenetic Development of the human sleep-dream cycl. *Science, 152,* 604–616. Reprinted with permission from AAAS.

(Barinaga, 1997b; Haimov & Lavie, 1996). Personal characteristics and habits are other factors. For example, people who sleep longer than average tend to be more artistic, creative, nervous, worrisome, and nonconforming, whereas short sleepers are generally more energetic and extroverted (Hartmann, 1973). And it is no surprise that our exercise habits influence the need for sleep. Strenuous physical activity during the day increases the amount of slow-wave sleep in Stage 4—although it has no effect on REM time (Horne, 1988).

From a developmental perspective, sleep duration and the shape of the sleep cycle change over a lifetime. As Figure 8.5 shows, newborns sleep about 16 hours per day, with half that time devoted to REM. During childhood, those numbers gradually decline, probably as a result of the maturing brain. Teens need more than nine hours' sleep per night, according to recent research, but get only about seven and a half (Carskadon, 2002), with about 20 percent REM. By old age, we sleep even less, with only 15 percent of sleep spent in REM. Find out whether you are getting enough sleep by answering the questions in the accompanying *Do It Yourself!* box.

Sleep Debt Wreaks Havoc Your mother was right: Most adults need to sleep about eight hours, or a bit more, to feel good and function efficiently. In the sleep laboratory, when volunteers are placed in a dark room and allowed to sleep without interruption and without reference to clocks, the average adult settles into a pattern that produces about eight and one-half hours of sleep each night. Yet most Americans get significantly less—night after night (Greer, 2004b; Maas, 1999). This creates a sleep shortage researcher William Dement calls a **sleep debt** (Dement & Vaughan, 1999).

People who pile up a chronic sleep debt usually don't realize it (Dement, 2000; Dement & Vaughan, 1999). They may be groggy when the alarm clock rouses them in the morning but fail to recognize it as a sign of a sleep debt because their circadian clocks nudge them into wakefulness over the next few hours. Afternoon drowsiness may be attributed to a big lunch—which, in truth, does not cause sleepiness. (It's the internal clock again.) They may also rationalize their struggle to stay awake in a meeting or class by telling themselves sleepiness is a normal response to boredom (Van Dongen et al., 2003). In fact, the normal response to boredom is restlessness—not sleepiness—unless one is sleep deprived.

Even when you have not had enough sleep, the clock in your brain can make you feel relatively alert at certain times of the day—usually late morning and late afternoon. But with a chronic sleep debt, you are never as alert and mentally efficient as you could be if the sleep debt were paid with a few good nights of sleep (Van Dongen et al., 2003). And it can affect your very life: Sleep deprivation is associated not only

CONNECTION CHAPTER 7

The brain continues to develop and also to prune excessive neurons throughout childhood and adolescence (p. 271).

sleep debt A sleep deficiency caused by not getting the amount of sleep required for optimal functioning.

Do It Yourself! HOW MUCH SLEEP DO YOU NEED?

Many college students operate in a chronic state of sleep deprivation. Because their schedules are crowded with study, work, and social events, students may convince themselves that they need only a few hours sleep each night. And, in fact, the average college student sleeps only about 6.8 hours a night (Hicks, 1990). Does too little sleep really make a difference in how well you perform in your classes? Psychologist Cheryl Spinweber (1990) has found that sleep-deprived undergraduates get lower grades than their counterparts who get enough sleep. Recent studies also suggest that sleep deprivation contributes to weight gain: People who sleep less than seven hours a night have high rates of obesity (Harder, 2006).

How can you tell if you need more sleep? Answer the following questions honestly:

1. Do you often feel sleepy in your classes?
2. Do you sleep late on weekends?
3. Do you usually get sleepy when you get bored?
4. Do you often fall asleep while reading or watching TV?
5. Do you usually fall asleep within five minutes of going to bed?
6. Do you awake in the morning feeling that you are not rested?
7. Would you oversleep if you did not use an alarm clock to drive you out of bed?

If you answered "Yes" to any of these questions, chances are that you are shorting yourself on sleep. You may also be paying the price in the quality of your learning and in your grades.

Drowsy driving accounts for 100,000 accidents each year, many of them fatalities.

with weight gain but also with a shortened lifespan (National Institute of Medicine, 2006). In addition, the sleep debt is sometimes "paid" with a tragedy—as in the 2010 crash of an airliner in India. All 158 people on board were killed when the pilot—who had fallen asleep at the controls for almost two hours and was too groggy to make sound judgments when he awoke just before landing—overshot the runway and the plane exploded into a ball of fire (Athrady, 2010).

Of special interest to students is this fact: Sleep deprivation has devastating effects on cognitive and motor functioning (Pilcher & Walters, 1997). According to William Dement, it "makes you stupid" (Dement & Vaughan, 1999, p. 231). Just how "stupid" was shown in a study that deprived one group of volunteers of sleep and gave another group enough alcohol to make them legally drunk (their blood alcohol content reached 0.1 percent). After 24 hours of sleep loss—like staying up all night studying for a test—the sleepy volunteers performed just like the intoxicated group on tests of thinking and coordination (Fletcher et al., 2003). What effects do you suppose chronic sleep deprivation, so common during medical internships and residencies, has on physician performance?[1]

Dreaming: The Pageants of the Night

Every night of your life, a spectacular series of events is staged in your dreams. What produces these fantastic cognitive spectacles? And what—if anything—do they mean? As we saw earlier, sleep scientists now know that dreams occur regularly throughout the night, most often in REM sleep. They also know which parts of the brain control dreaming—including, especially, parts of the brain stem. What remains most mysterious about this stage of sleep is *why* we dream.

The ancient Israelites interpreted dreams as messages from God. Their Egyptian contemporaries attempted to influence dreams by sleeping in temples dedicated to the god of dreaming, Serapis. In India, the sacred Vedas described the religious significance of dreams. Meanwhile, in China, dreaming held an element of risk. During a dream, the ancient Chinese believed the soul wandered about outside the body. For that reason, they were reluctant to awaken a sleeper hastily, lest the soul not find its way back to the body (Dement, 1980).

From the perspective of many African and Native American cultures, dreams are an extension of waking reality. Consequently, when traditional Cherokee Indians dreamed of snakebite, they received appropriate emergency treatment upon awakening. Likewise, when an African tribal chieftain dreamed of England, he ordered a set

---

[1]Further information on the hazards associated with sleep deprivation in physicians is available online from PubMed: www.pubmedcentral.nih.gov/articlerender.fcgi?artid=1200708.

of European clothes; and, when he appeared in the new togs, his friends congratulated him on making the trip (Dement, 1980).

In contrast with these folk theories, sleep scientists approach dreaming with this question: What biological function do dreams have? Most experts suspect dreams may be necessary for healthy brain functioning, although the evidence for that is not certain, as you will see in the following text (Siegel, 2003). And, most recently, researchers have been focusing on the cognitive functioning of dreams.

A closely related issue concerns the *meaning* of dreams. Evolutionary psychologists propose dreams may offer safe opportunities to rehearse ways of dealing with dangerous situations, but the evidence is iffy (Franklin & Zyphur, 2005). From a cognitive perspective, some experts see dreams as meaningful mental events, reflecting important events or fantasies in the dreamer's mental world. Other cognitive scientists are finding connections between dreaming and memory, and even propose that dreams help us construct meaning in our lives (Stickgold, 2011). But others argue dreams may have no meaning at all and are merely random brain activity during sleep. Let's look at all sides of this debate on the meaningfulness of dreams.

Dreams as Meaningful Events At the beginning of the 20th century, Sigmund Freud laid out the most complex and comprehensive theory of dreams and their meanings ever developed—a theory that has enjoyed enormous influence, despite lack of scientific evidence (Squier & Domhoff, 1998). In this view, dreams represent "the royal road to the unconscious," paved with clues to an individual's hidden mental life. For Freud, dream analysis became the cornerstone of psychoanalysis, as described in his classic book *The Interpretation of Dreams* (1900).

Freud's Theory of Dreams In psychoanalytic theory, dreams have two main functions: to guard sleep (by disguising disruptive thoughts with symbols) and to serve as sources of wish fulfillment. Freud believed dreams play their guardian role by relieving psychic tensions created during the day and serve their wish-fulfillment function by allowing the dreamer to work harmlessly through unconscious desires.

Freud made an important distinction between a dream's **manifest content**—the dream's story line—and the **latent content**—the (supposed) symbolic meaning of the dream. Psychoanalytic therapists, therefore, scrutinize the manifest content of their patients' dreams for clues relating to hidden motives and conflicts lurking in the unconscious. For example, clues relating to sexual conflicts might take the form of long rigid objects or containers that, in Freudian theory, symbolize the male and female genitals. Similarly, a departure or a journey may represent a death, loss, or a new beginning.

Must you be a trained psychoanalyst to understand dreams? Not necessarily. In some cases, the manifest content of our dreams has a fairly obvious connection to our waking lives—thus, the symbolism is only thinly disguised. For example, one study found that individuals depressed about divorce often had dreams about past relationships (Cartwright, 1984). By analyzing the patterns and content of your own dreams, you may be able to start to decode many of the images and actions you dream about (Hall, 1953/1966; Van de Castle, 1994). We must emphasize, however, there is little solid scientific support for Freudian interpretations of latent dream content.

Dreams Vary by Culture, Gender, and Age The influence of culture on dream content reveals itself in a variety of ways. For example, reports from the West African nation of Ghana tell us dreams in that region often feature attacks by cows (Barnouw, 1963). Americans frequently find themselves embarrassed by public nudity in their dreams, although such reports rarely occur in cultures where people customarily wear few clothes. Images of death appear more often in dreams of Mexican American college students than in dreams of Anglo American students, probably because concerns about death are a more important feature of life in Latin American cultures (Roll et al., 1974). In general, cross-cultural research lends support to Rosalind Cartwright's (1977) hypothesis that dreams reflect life events that are important to the dreamer.

manifest content The story line of a dream, taken at face value without interpretation.

latent content The symbolic meaning of objects and events in a dream. Latent content is usually an interpretation based on Freud's psychoanalytic theory or one of its variants. For example, the latent content of a dream involving clocks might involve fear of the menstrual cycle and, hence, of one's sexuality.

Death-related images appear more often in dreams of Mexican American college students than in those of Anglo-American college students. This probably occurs because death is more prominently a part of Mexican culture, as can be seen in this figure, used in the Day of the Dead celebration.

Sleep scientists now know that the content of dreams also varies by age and gender (Domhoff, 1996). Children are more likely to dream about animals than adults are, and the animals in their dreams are more likely to be large, threatening, and wild. In contrast, college students dream more often of small animals, pets, and tame creatures. This may mean children feel less in control of their world than adults do and thus see the world depicted in scarier imagery while they sleep (Van de Castle, 1983, 1994).

Women everywhere more commonly dream of children, while men more often dream of aggression, weapons, and tools (Murray, 1995). And American women may be more equal-opportunity dreamers than their male counterparts: In a sample of more than 1,800 dreams collected by dream researcher Calvin Hall, women dreamed about both men and women, while men more often dreamed about men—twice as often, in fact, as they dreamed about women. Hall also found that hostile interactions between characters outnumbered friendly exchanges, and that two-thirds of emotional dreams had a negative complexion, such as anger and sadness (Hall, 1951, 1984).

Dreams and Recent Experience Dream content frequently connects with recent experience and things we thought about during the previous day. But, strangely, if you deliberately try *not* to think about something, it is even more likely to pop up in your dreams (Wegner et al., 2004). So, if you have been worrying about your job all day—or trying to forget about it—you're likely to dream about work tonight, especially during your first REM period.

Typically, then, the first dream of the night connects with events of the previous day. Dreams in the second REM period (90 minutes later) often build on a theme that emerged during the first REM period. And so it goes through the night, like an evolving rumor passed from one person to another: The final dream that emerges may have a connection—but only a remote one—to events of the previous day. Because the last dream of the night is the one most likely to be remembered, we may not recognize the link with the previous day's events (Cartwright, 1977; Kiester, 1980).

Dreams and Memory Some of the most exciting research on dreams comes from cognitive neuroscience. For example, we now know that REM sleep plays an important role in memory consolidation. When students learned a difficult logic game, those who enjoyed a full night of REM sleep afterward performed better on the task the next day than did those deprived of postlearning REM (Smith, 2004). Indeed, the brain replenishes neurotransmitters in its memory networks during REM, notes sleep researcher James Maas. It may be that REM sleep helps weave new experiences into the fabric of old memories (Greer, 2004b).

Recent research suggests that NREM sleep also selectively reinforces certain kinds of memory, especially for facts and locations (Miller, 2007). In the lab of Harvard sleep scientist Bob Stickgold, students spent an hour working on a difficult three-dimensional maze problem on a computer, starting over repeatedly in new locations in the maze. One of their goals was to find and remember the location of a tree in the maze. Next, half the students took a nap while the other half engaged in quiet activity. Nappers were awakened from NREM sleep and questioned about their dreams. Nonnappers answered questions about their thoughts at the same intervals. Later, when students worked again on the maze problem, nappers who had dreamed about the maze found the tree more quickly than did other students in the study (Bower, 2010).

Dreams as Random Activity of the Brain Not everyone believes dream content is meaningful. In particular, **activation-synthesis theory** posits that dreams result when the sleeping brain tries to make sense of its own spontaneous bursts of activity (Leonard, 1998; Squier & Domhoff, 1998). In this view, dreams originate in periodic neural discharges emitted by the sleeping brain stem. As this energy sweeps over the cerebral cortex, the sleeper experiences impressions of sensation, memory, motivation, emotion, and movement (the "activation" part of the theory). Although the cortical activation

activation-synthesis theory The theory that dreams begin (are activated) with random electrical activation coming from the brain stem. The storyline of dreams are the brain's attempt to make sense of (to synthesize) this random activity.

is random, and the images it generates may not be logically connected, the brain tries to make sense of the stimulation it receives. To do so, it weaves a coherent story that pulls together the "messages" in these random electrical bursts (the "synthesis" part of the theory). A dream, then, could merely be the brain's way of making sense out of nonsense.

The original proponents of this theory, J. Allan Hobson and Robert McCarley (1977), based their argument on the idea that the brain needs constant stimulation to grow and develop. During sleep, the brain blocks out external stimulation, so REM sleep steps in to provide stimulation from within. Dream content, therefore, results from brain activation, not from unconscious wishes or other meaningful mental processes. While Hobson (1988, 2002) still claims the story line in our dreams is added as a "brainstorm afterthought," he does acknowledge that a dreamer's synthesis of the activations may nevertheless have some psychological meaning based on the influences of culture, gender, personality factors, and recent events.

Dreams as a Source of Creative Insights Even if Hobson and McCarley are right—that dreams have no special meaning other than an attempt by the brain to make sense out of nonsense—dreams could still be a source of creative ideas. In fact, it would be astonishing if we did not turn to such wild and sometimes wonderful scenes in the night for inspiration. As we have seen, writers, composers, and scientists have done just that.

"Dream explorer" Robert Moss (1996) cites 19th-century physiologist Herman von Helmholtz, who insisted that creative dreaming would result from doing three things: first, saturating yourself in a problem or issue that interests you; next, letting your creative ideas incubate by shifting attention to something relaxing and unrelated; and finally, allowing yourself time to experience illumination, a sudden flash of insight into the answer you seek.

Now, in the 21st century, empirical support is accumulating for this notion. In REM sleep, our brains seem primed to put ideas together in previously unconceived ways. When awakened from REM sleep and given word-association tasks, people produce more novel associations than when they are awake. And students studying complex math problems double their chances of finding novel solutions to the problem after a full night of sleep (Stickgold & Walker, 2004). It's as if our REMing brain is released from the boundaries of our waking sensibilities and uses the opportunity to try out new combinations of ideas—which is precisely the basis of creativity.

Sleep and dreaming have inspired many artists, as seen here in Rousseau's *Sleeping Gypsy.*

Read about Finding Your Creative Inspiration in Dreams at **MyPsychLab**

[PSYCHOLOGY MATTERS]

Sleep Disorders

Are you among the more than 100 million Americans who get insufficient or poor-quality sleep? Some of these sleep problems are job related. Among people who work night shifts, for example, more than half nod off at least once a week on the job. And it may be no coincidence that some of the world's most serious accidents—including the disastrous radiation emissions at the Three Mile Island and Chernobyl nuclear plants and the massive toxic chemical discharge at Bhopal—have occurred during late-evening hours when workers are likely to be programmed for sleep. Sleep experts speculate that many accidents occur because key personnel fail to function optimally as a result of insufficient sleep—as we noted earlier in the case of the 2010 plane crash in India (Dement & Vaughan, 1999).

Along with these job-related sleep problems, several clinical sleep disorders are studied in the labs of sleep researchers. Some are common, while others are both rare and bizarre. Some are relatively benign, and some are potentially life threatening. The single element tying them together is a disruption in one or more parts of the normal sleep cycle.

This student struggles with insomnia, a problem that has many different psychological, environmental, and biological causes. About one-third of all adults are plagued by this most common of sleep disorders.

insomnia   The most common of sleep disorders—involving insufficient sleep, the inability to fall asleep quickly, frequent arousals, or early awakenings.

Insomnia is usually the diagnosis when people feel dissatisfied with the amount of sleep they get. Its symptoms include chronic inability to fall asleep quickly, frequent arousals during sleep, or early-morning awakening. Insomnia sufferers number about one-third of all adults, making this the most common sleep disorder (Dement & Vaughan, 1999).

An occasional bout of sleeplessness is normal, especially when you have exciting or worrisome events on your mind. And don't worry: These incidents pose no special danger unless you try to treat the problem with barbiturates or over-the-counter "sleeping pills." These drugs disrupt the normal sleep cycle by cutting short REM sleep periods (Dement, 1980). As a result, they can actually aggravate the effects of insomnia by making the user feel less rested and more sleepy. A new generation of prescription drugs for the treatment of insomnia—the ones you see heavily advertised on TV—seems to avoid many of these problems, although long-term-use studies are still in progress. (Harder, 2005). And side effects such as rebound insomnia and morning grogginess still plague some users. An alternative is psychological treatment employing cognitive behavioral therapy, which has had remarkable success in helping people learn effective strategies for avoiding insomnia (Smith, 2001).

CONNECTION CHAPTER 13

Cognitive behavior therapy combines cognitive and behavioral techniques in treating psychological disorders (p. 571).

Incidentally, counting sheep won't help you break the insomnia barrier. Neither will some other boring mental task. Researchers at Oxford University have shown that it is better to imagine some soothing but complex scene, such as a waterfall. Counting one sheep after another apparently isn't interesting enough to keep the sleep-inhibiting worries of the day out of mind (Randerson, 2002). And there are a variety of ways you can control your own environment to promote a good night's sleep—visit the Read section in MyPsychLab for tips.

Read about Controlling Your Environment to Promote a Good Night's Sleep at **MyPsychLab**

sleep apnea   A respiratory disorder in which the person intermittently stops breathing many times while asleep.

Sleep apnea, another common disorder, often goes unnoticed, apparent only as daytime sleepiness and a sleep partner's complaints about snoring. But behind the curtain of the night, the cause lies in an abnormality of breathing. A person with sleep apnea actually stops breathing for up to a minute, as often as several hundred times each night! (In case you're concerned, the brief cessation of breathing a few times each hour during the night is normal.) Most commonly, this results from collapse of the airway in the throat when the sleeper's muscle tone relaxes. The result is the second major symptom of sleep apnea: frequent loud snoring, occurring each time the patient runs short of oxygen and tries mightily to get air through the collapsed airway (Seligson, 1994). As breathing stops and the sleeper's blood oxygen level plummets, the body's emergency system kicks into gear, causing distress hormones to course through the body. In the process, the sleeper awakens briefly, begins breathing again, and then falls back to sleep. Because most of this happens in deep sleep, there is usually no memory of the episode.

Failure to recognize the nature of the problem can cause those with sleep apnea—and their families and coworkers—to interpret unusual daytime behavior, such as inattention or falling asleep, as laziness or neglect. While this may be disruptive to relationships, sleep apnea can also have harmful biological effects that include damage to brain cells, along with elevated blood pressure that can impose dangerous levels of stress on the blood vessels and heart (Gami et al., 2005).

Occasional episodes of sleep apnea are likely to occur in premature infants, who may need physical stimulation to start breathing again. Further, any tendency toward sleep apnea can be aggravated by putting a young child to bed on his or her stomach. (Instead, sleep scientists strongly recommend "back to sleep.") Obviously, the problem can be lethal, and it is one possible cause of *sudden infant death syndrome* (SIDS). Until their underdeveloped respiratory systems mature, "preemies" must remain connected to breathing monitors while they sleep. In contrast, permanent breathing failure is not a strong concern for adults with sleep apnea, for whom treatment focuses on decreasing the hundreds of nightly apnea episodes. This is usually accomplished by using a device that pumps extra air into the lungs and keeps the airway open during sleep.

Night terrors, occurring primarily in children, pose no health threat—although they can be quite distressing. Typically, a night terror attack presents itself in the screaming of a terrified-looking child who is actually in Stage 4 sleep and very difficult to awaken. When finally alert, the child may still feel afraid but have no specific memory of what mental events caused the night terror. In fact, the whole experience is likely to be more memorable to beleaguered family members than to the child.

night terrors   Deep sleep episodes that seem to produce terror, although any terrifying mental experience (such as a dream) is usually forgotten on awakening. Night terrors occur mainly in children.

Unlike garden-variety nightmares, sleep-terror episodes occur in deep sleep rather than in REM sleep. In this respect, they are like sleepwalking, sleep talking, and bed wetting, which also occur in Stage 4. All these conditions seem to have a genetic component. In themselves, they pose no danger, although sleepwalkers can inadvertently climb out of upper-story windows or walk into a busy street—so it pays to take some precautions. (Incidentally, it's just a myth that waking a sleepwalker is dangerous.) In most cases, sleepwalking and night terrors diminish or disappear in adulthood, but if they pose persistent and chronic problems, the individual should be evaluated by a sleep specialist. Bed wetting can usually be ameliorated by a simple behavior modification procedure that employs a pad with a built-in alarm that sounds when damp.

Narcolepsy, one of the most unusual of sleep disorders, produces sudden daytime sleep attacks, often without warning. But these are no ordinary waves of drowsiness. So suddenly do these sleep attacks develop that narcolepsy sufferers have reported falling asleep while driving a car, climbing a ladder, or scuba diving under 20 feet of water. Narcoleptic sleep attacks may also be preceded by a sudden loss of muscle control, a condition known as *cataplexy.*

narcolepsy   A disorder of REM sleep, involving sleep-onset REM periods and sudden daytime REM-sleep attacks usually accompanied by cataplexy.

Strangely, anything exciting can trigger a narcoleptic episode. For example, these patients commonly report they fall asleep while laughing at a joke or even during sex. Obviously, narcolepsy can be dangerous—and not so good for intimate relationships, either.

Assembling the pieces of this puzzle, we find that narcolepsy is a disorder of REM sleep (Marschall, 2007). Specifically, a sleep recording will show that the narcolepsy victim has an abnormal sleep-onset REM period. That is, instead of waiting the usual 90 minutes to begin REM, the narcoleptic person enters REM as sleep begins. You may have already guessed that the accompanying cataplexy is simply REM sleep paralysis.

Studies of narcoleptic animals show that the disorder stems from a genetic problem affecting the sleep-control circuitry in the brain stem. Recent research implicates a diminished supply of *hypocretin,* a chemical produced in the hypothalamus (Harder, 2004; Marschall, 2007). So far, there is no cure, but certain drugs can diminish the frequency of both the sleep attacks and the cataplexy. Now that we know the cause is biological, narcoleptic patients are no longer sent to psychotherapy aimed at searching for the unconscious conflicts once assumed to underlie the disorder.

So, what should you do if you suspect that you have a sleep disorder, such as chronic insomnia, sleep apnea, or narcolepsy? An evaluation by a sleep expert is the place to start. Many hospitals have sleep disorder clinics to which your physician or clinical psychologist can refer you.

Check Your Understanding

✓●─ **Study** and **Review** at **MyPsychLab**

1. **RECALL:** What do brain scans tell us about the daydreaming brain?

2. **RECALL:** What muscular changes occur during REM sleep?

3. **RECALL:** Suppose you are working in a sleep laboratory, monitoring a subject's sleep recording during the night. As the night progresses, you would expect to see that

   a. sleep becomes deeper and deeper.
   b. REM periods become longer.
   c. Stage 3 and 4 sleep periods lengthen.
   d. dreaming becomes less frequent.

4. **RECALL:** According to the activation-synthesis theory, what causes our dreams?

5. **APPLICATION:** Which sleep disorder is marked by a REM period at the beginning of sleep?

6. **UNDERSTANDING THE CORE CONCEPT:** Our Core Concept states that consciousness changes in cycles that normally correspond to our biological rhythms and to the patterns of our environment. Give an example of a recurring mental state that illustrates this concept.

Answers 1. Brain scans suggest daydreaming is generated by activity in a "default network" of circuits in the brain that remains active during the restful waking state. **2.** Sleep paralysis affects all the voluntary muscles except those controlling eye movements. **3.** b **4.** According to the activation-synthesis theory, dreams are an attempt by the brain to make sense of random activity in the brain stem during sleep. **5.** Narcolepsy **6.** Sleep and dreaming are among the cyclic changes in consciousness.

┌─ **8.3 KEY QUESTION**
└────── **What Other Forms Can Consciousness Take?**

Children stand on their heads or spin around to make themselves dizzy. You may seek similar sensations from hair-raising theme-park rides or sky diving. But why do we do these strange things to ourselves? One view says "human beings are born with a drive to experience modes of awareness other than the normal waking one; from very young ages, children experiment with techniques to change consciousness" (Weil, 1977, p. 37). So sleep, dreams, fantasies, and thrilling experiences offer compelling alternatives to everyday conscious experience.

Psychological techniques, such as hypnosis and meditation, can alter consciousness too. So can drugs, which some people use to find the altered state of consciousness they seek. In this section, we will explore these variations on consciousness and find the theme that ties these altered states of consciousness together. Our Core Concept for this section puts it this way:

[
Core Concept 8.3

An altered state of consciousness occurs when some aspect of normal consciousness is modified by mental, behavioral, or chemical means.
]

This notion carries the important implication that altered states do not involve mysterious or paranormal phenomena that defy rational explanation. Rather, altered states are modifications of ordinary consciousness that we can study with the tools of science. Let's begin with what we know about hypnosis.

Hypnosis

The cartoon images have it wrong. Neither the hypnotist's eyes nor fingertips emit strange, mesmerizing rays that send subjects into a compliant stupor—nor does a dangling shiny bauble have the power to control people's minds. A more accurate picture would show the hypnotist making suggestions to promote concentration and relaxation (Barber, 1976, 1986). Soon the subject appears to be asleep, although he or she can hear suggestions and carry out requests. But this real-life depiction can be just as dramatic as the cartoon images: In some cases, the individual under hypnosis demonstrates amazing powers to ignore pain, remember long-forgotten details, and create hallucinations. But what mental processes make these things happen?

The term *hypnosis* derives from *Hypnos,* the Greek god of sleep. Yet EEG records tell us that ordinary sleep plays no role in hypnosis, even though hypnotized individuals may appear to be in a relaxed, sleeplike state. In fact, there is no unique EEG signature for hypnosis. Most authorities would define **hypnosis** as a state of awareness characterized by deep relaxation, heightened suggestibility, and focused attention.

When deeply hypnotized, some people respond to suggestion with dramatic changes in perception, memory, motivation, and sense of self-control (Orne, 1980). Stage hypnotists can make carefully selected volunteers quack like a duck or appear to enjoy the taste of a bitter lemon. Afterward, people often report they experienced heightened responsiveness to the hypnotist's suggestions and performed their behavior without intention or conscious effort. But are all people susceptible to hypnosis?

Hypnotizability Dramatic stage performances of hypnosis give the impression that hypnotic power lies with the hypnotist. But the real star is the person who is hypnotized. The hypnotist is more like an experienced guide showing the way. And some individuals can even learn to practice self-hypnosis, or autohypnosis, by inducing the hypnotic state through self-administered suggestions.

The single most important factor in achieving a hypnotic state is susceptibility. Experts call this *hypnotizability* and measure it by a person's responsiveness to standardized suggestions. Individuals differ in this susceptibility, varying from complete unresponsiveness to any suggestion to total responsiveness to virtually every suggestion. A highly hypnotizable person may respond to suggestions to move his or her arms, walk about, experience hallucinations, have amnesia for important memories, and become insensitive to painful stimuli. And, we should add, because hypnosis involves heightened suggestibility, any "recovered memories" obtained by this means are highly suspect.

Hypnotizability also depends on age. Among adults, only 10 to 15 percent are highly hypnotizable, while up to 85 percent of children fall into that category (Blakeslee, 2005). Figure 8.6 shows the percentage of college students who achieved various levels of hypnotizability the first time they were given a hypnotic induction test. For example, a hypnotist may test a new subject's acceptance of suggestion by saying, "Your right hand is lighter than air," and observing whether the subject allows his or her arm to float upward. High scorers are more likely than low scorers to experience pain relief, or hypnotic analgesia, and to respond to hypnotic suggestions for experiencing perceptual distortions.

Is Hypnosis a Distinct State of Consciousness? The experts disagree about the psychological mechanisms involved in hypnosis (Kirsch & Lynn, 1995, 1998). Some believe hypnosis is a distinct state of consciousness, quite separate from sleep or our normal waking state (Fromm & Shor, 1979). Others propose that hypnosis is simply suggestibility (Barber, 1979; Kirsch & Braffman, 2001). In this latter view, hypnotic subjects are not entranced but merely motivated to focus their attention and respond to suggestion. Yet, a third view argues that hypnosis is essentially a social process,

hypnosis   An induced state of awareness, usually characterized by heightened suggestibility, deep relaxation, and highly focused attention.

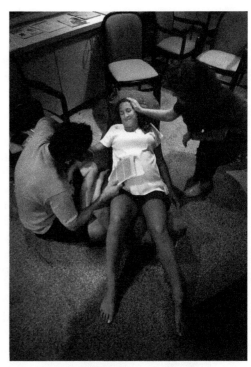

For many people, hypnosis can help control pain. Here, a woman is learning hypnotic techniques that she will use in natural childbirth.

CONNECTION CHAPTER 5

Studies in which false memories are created call into question "recovered" memories obtained as the result of any sort of prompting or suggestion (p. 206).

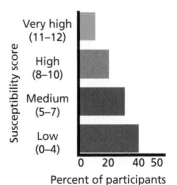

FIGURE 8.6

Level of Hypnosis Reached at First Induction

This graph shows the results achieved by 533 participants hypnotized for the first time. (Hypnotizability was measured by the 12-item Stanford Hypnotic Susceptibility Scale.)

involving role playing—in which people act as they believe a hypnotized person would, often to please the hypnotist (Sarbin & Coe, 1972). In support of this view, critics of hypnosis as an "altered state" note that people who have *not* been hypnotized can duplicate apparently amazing feats, such as becoming "human planks" suspended between two chairs.

An intriguing perspective, originally proposed by researcher Ernest Hilgard (1992), portrays hypnosis as a dissociated state, involving a "hidden observer" in the person's mind, operating in parallel with normal consciousness. Hilgard has shown that hypnotized individuals who say they feel no pain when their hand is placed in ice water will nevertheless respond affirmatively when told, "If some part of you does feel pain, please raise your right index finger." Hilgard believed that attention to the painful sensation was shifted to the hidden observer, leaving normal consciousness blissfully unaware.

Finally, a cognitive view proposes that hypnosis involves a shift in top-down processing—that is, thinking driven by expectations and mental imagery rather than by incoming stimulation. Thus, people are hypnotized because they want or expect to be, so they focus on expressing and achieving the responses the hypnotist tries to evoke. To test this idea, neuroscientist Amir Raz and his colleagues altered volunteers' top-down processing by means of hypnotic suggestions that they would "forget" how to read. Brain scans showed the suggestion temporarily inactivated the part of their brains that decodes words (Blakeslee, 2005; Raz et al., 2002).

In support of the idea that hypnosis creates profound top-down changes in the brain, another study suggested to deeply hypnotized patients they were touching uncomfortably warm metal. What happened? The parts of their brains associated with pain perception "lit up" in the same pattern found in brain scans of a control group who actually touched a 120-degree metal rod (Derbyshire et al., 2004; Winerman, 2006b).

Is there common ground among these perspectives? Perhaps all have a bit of the truth. It may be that hypnosis, like the normal waking state, can cover a whole range of dissociated states, intensified motives, shifted expectations, and social interactions.

Practical Uses of Hypnosis   Stage tricks aside, what is hypnosis good for? Because of its powerful influence on psychological and physical functions in some people, hypnosis is a useful tool for researchers studying the mind–body connection (Oakley, 2006). By using normal volunteers under hypnosis, an experimenter can induce temporary mental conditions, such as anxiety, depression, or hallucinations, instead of having to find individuals who already have these problems. For example, in one study of psychological issues associated with hearing loss, college students given the hypnotic suggestion to become deaf on cue reported feeling paranoid and excluded because they could not hear what other subjects were saying and assumed they were being deliberately whispered about and excluded (Zimbardo et al., 1981). ◉

Hypnosis can aid in psychological treatment too. For instance, it can be an effective tool in desensitizing people with phobias (fears) of heights or spiders. It can also be part of a relaxation training program designed to combat stress. In addition, therapists find it useful for eliminating unwanted behaviors, such as smoking, where a frequently used technique calls for planting posthypnotic suggestions to diminish a patient's cravings for nicotine (Barnier & McConkey, 1998; Kihlstrom, 1985). In the same way, a therapist can also induce the patient to forget events that occurred during or prior to the hypnotic session, an effect called *posthypnotic amnesia.*

Finally, hypnosis has a growing role in pain management, especially during procedures that would otherwise involve the risks of anesthesia (Nash, 2001; Patterson, 2004). For example, the Lamaze method of natural childbirth uses a hypnosis-like procedure as a primary means of pain control. It is important to note, however, that not everyone can be hypnotized deeply enough for effective pain relief (Callahan, 1997). Still, hypnosis alone allows some patients to undergo treatments that would otherwise cause excruciating pain (Finer, 1980), in some cases masking pain more effectively than acupuncture, aspirin, Valium, or even morphine (Stern et al., 1977). In randomized,

CONNECTION CHAPTER 12

In certain clinical disorders, known as *dissociated states*, part of the personality becomes disconnected from the rest of the personality. This is the defining feature of dissociative identity disorder—formerly called "multiple personality disorder" (p. 535).

The "human plank" is one of the earliest stage tricks used by performers pretending to hypnotize people.

◉—[**Watch** the **Video** Hypnosis at **MyPsychLab**

experimental studies, hypnosis has reduced pain across a wide variety of conditions, including women with metastatic breast cancer, patients with dental sensitivity, and survivors of physical trauma, just to name a few (Nash & Tasso, 2010; Patterson et al., 2010). Chronic pain conditions such as arthritis, fibromyalgia, and headaches have also been treated effectively with hypnosis (Patterson, 2010).

How does hypnosis produce pain relief? Hilgard's hidden-observer explanation is one possibility, although other scientists have taken a more biological approach to the problem. Currently there is no universally accepted explanation, although we can rule out one contender. Experiments have demonstrated that the opiate-like *endorphins*, which account for the pain-relieving property of placebos, are *not* responsible for hypnotic analgesia (Grevert & Goldstein, 1985). As you will recall, we considered another possibility, called the *gate-control theory*, in our discussion of pain (in Chapter 3). For now, we will accept hypnosis as a valuable tool about which much remains to be learned concerning the ways in which it alters consciousness.

Meditation

Many religions and traditional psychologies of Asian and Pacific cultures use forms of **meditation** to direct consciousness away from worldly concerns and temptations. Although the purpose of meditation varies, many practitioners seek some form of spiritual enlightenment and an increase in self-knowledge and well-being. Meditators use a variety of techniques but commonly begin by concentrating on a repetitive behavior (such as breathing), assuming certain body positions (yogic postures), and minimizing external stimulation. Meditation can last from just a few minutes to several hours.

Viewing meditation as an altered state of consciousness may reflect a particularly Western worldview, because Asian beliefs about the mind are typically different from those of Western cultures (Austin, 1998; Rosch, 1999). Buddhism, for example, teaches that the visible universe is an illusion of the senses. To become enlightened, a Buddhist aims to control bodily yearnings, to stop ordinary experiences of the senses and mind, and to see things in their truest light. Thus, in the Buddhist view, meditation more accurately captures reality.

In contrast with its long history in Asia and the Pacific, meditation has only recently been taken seriously by psychology as a subject for scientific study. Its spiritual aspects aside, early studies indicated meditating was in many ways like resting, because it reduced various signs of bodily arousal (Morrell, 1986). Newer studies, however, are finding a provocative array of changes in the brain associated with meditation—changes that, in turn, may affect empathy, self-awareness, attention, and stress.

What effects of meditation can be demonstrated objectively? Experienced meditators show changes in brain wave patterns, especially in frontal lobe activity, associated with positive emotions (Davidson et al., 2003; Kasamatsu & Hirai, 1966). Other studies link meditation with beneficial changes in blood pressure and stress hormones (Seeman et al., 2003). Research also finds that meditation produces relaxation and reduces anxiety, especially in people who live and work in stress-filled environments (Benson, 1975; van Dam, 1996)—although some research with control groups does not show meditation to be superior to other relaxation techniques (Toneatto & Nguyen, 2007). Meditation also seems to produce at least short-term gains in attention and problem solving (van den Hurk et al., 2010). And a first-of-its-kind study using MRI scans to study the brains of people before and after eight weeks of meditation training discovered what happens in the brain to explain these findings: The hippocampus, parts of the frontal lobes, and brain areas relevant to learning, memory, compassion, and attention all increased in size in the meditators as compared to a control group (Hölzel et al., 2011). Furthermore, the density of meditators' amygdalas decreased, providing a clue to the role of meditation in stress reduction.

The overall picture shows meditation to be an effective method for relaxing, reducing stress, disengaging from worldly concerns, and—possibly—improving cognitive function. It also produces health-promoting physical changes. And increasingly, practitioners in medicine and in psychology are seeking to understand it and try to harness it

CONNECTION CHAPTER 3

Endorphins are the body's own opiate-like substances (p. 110).

Meditation produces relaxation, changes in brain waves and density, lower blood pressure, a decrease in stress hormones, and perhaps new insights.

meditation A state of consciousness often induced by focusing on a repetitive behavior, assuming certain body positions, and minimizing external stimulation. Meditation may be intended to enhance self-knowledge, well-being, and spirituality.

for therapeutic purposes (Barinaga, 2003b). But whether meditation holds an advantage over other techniques—psychological, physical, and spiritual—awaits findings of future research.

Psychoactive Drug States

For millennia, humans have used alcohol, opium, cannabis, mescaline, coca, caffeine, and other drugs to alter their everyday perceptions of reality. Especially under stress, people throughout the world take drugs for pleasure, for relaxation, or just to avoid the cares of their daily lives. Some drugs, such as LSD, are taken in pursuit of hallucinations. Other drugs (alcohol is an example) can act as "social lubricants" to help people feel comfortable with each other. Still others are used by those seeking a euphoric "rush," a "buzz," a state of tranquility, or even stupor. What, if anything, do all these drugs have in common?

psychoactive drug Chemical that affects mental processes and behavior by its effect on the brain.

To some extent, all **psychoactive drugs** impair brain mechanisms that usually help us make decisions (Gazzaniga, 1998a). In addition, the most widely abused drugs, such as cocaine, heroin, cannabis, and methamphetamines, all stimulate the brain's "reward circuits." From an evolutionary perspective, our brains are built to find pleasure in many substances (such as the taste of sweet or fatty foods) that helped our ancestors survive and reproduce. Cocaine, heroin, and amphetamines trick the brain by exploiting these same mechanisms with strong, direct, and pleasurable signals that make our bodies "think" that these substances are good for us (Nesse & Berridge, 1997).

Trends in Drug Use Cultural trends influence drug-taking behavior. The United States saw this vividly during the 1960s and 1970s, when the country entered a period of casual experimentation with recreational drugs and other mind-altering techniques. Data from several sources, including emergency room visits, drug arrests, and surveys, indicate that overall illicit drug use has declined since the early 1990s. Today, while almost half of adults have tried drugs, only about 15 percent have used an illicit drug in the past year. Marijuana remains by far the most common, accounting for more than half of illicit drug use. Recreational use of prescription drugs (such as Vicodin and Oxycontin) accounts for about 30 percent, and cocaine and hallucinogens account for only about 10 percent each—which translates to about one person in 75 for the latter two. Alcohol and tobacco far outstrip illicit drugs in popularity, however: About two-thirds of adults in America drink alcoholic beverages, and one in four uses tobacco products (Substance Abuse and Mental Health Services Administration [SAMHSA], 2010).

Age of drug use varies as well, with peak use between the ages of 18 and 20. Usage declines steadily as age increases—with one curious exception: Recent data show that drug use among 50-somethings has more than doubled since 2002. Experts explain this aberration as a result of the influx of baby-boomers into this age range—a unique generation of Americans who came of age in a culture of drug use and apparently never gave it up (SAMHSA, 2009).

Among teens, use of some drugs is falling while use of others is on the rise (see Figure 8.7). Cigarette smoking is at its lowest point in 35 years. Alcohol use, including binge drinking, is decreasing as well, as is use of hallucinogens, cocaine, and methamphetamine. Use of MDMA (ecstasy), however, is increasing—especially among eighth and tenth graders—corresponding with a worrisome decline in teens' perception of risk associated with the drug. In 2010, one in 20 high school students used MDMA. Nonprescription use of Vicodin is even higher, with about one in ten high school students saying they've used it in the past month, often trading it and other prescription pills like Xanax and Oxycontin at "pharming" parties.

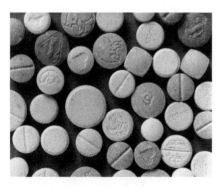

MDMA (commonly known as *ecstasy*) is marketed as a harmless, feel-good drug. Research shows serious side-effects, however—both short and long term—that many users don't know about.

Let us now have a closer look at the most commonly used and abused psychoactive drugs, grouping them in categories: *hallucinogens, opiates, depressants,* and *stimulants* (see Table 8.1). In general, all the drugs in each category have similar effects on the mind and brain.

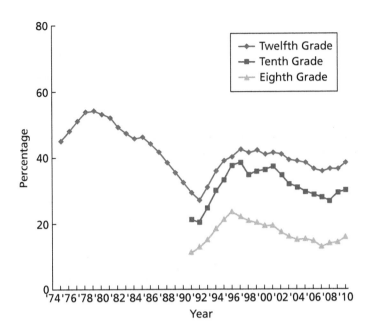

FIGURE 8.7

Trends in an Annual Use of Illicit Drug Use Index

This graph shows the percentage of teens reporting the use of illegal drugs.

Source: From the Monitoring the Future Study, University of Michigan. Reprinted by permission of the Inter-University Consortium for Political and Social Research.

TABLE 8.1 Characteristics of Psychoactive Drugs

Drug	Medical Uses	Common Effects Reported by Users
Opiates		
Morphine	Painkiller, cough suppressant	Euphoria ("rush"), tranquillity, drowsiness
Heroin	No medical uses in the United States	Euphoria, tranquillity, drowsiness (more powerful than morphine)
Codeine	Painkiller, cough suppressant	Euphoria, drowsiness, "silliness"
Methadone	Treatment of heroin addiction	Slow action prevents heroin craving
Hallucinogens		
Mescaline	None	Hallucinations, sensuality; similar to LSD but fewer reported emotional responses
Psilocybin	None	Well-being, perceptual distortions, less emotionally intense than LSD
LSD	None	Hallucinations, often emotional reactions
PCP	Veterinary anesthetic	Body image distortions, amnesia, unpredictable emotional reactions, dissociation (feeling of being cut off from one's environment)
Cannabis	Reduces nausea from chemotherapy; reduces pressure in the eye	Euphoria, time distortion, intensified sensory experience

(Continued)

TABLE 8.1 *(Continued)*

Drug	Medical Uses	Common Effects Reported by Users
Depressants and Antianxiety Drugs		
Barbiturates	Sedative, sleep, anticonvulsant, anesthetic	Relaxation, sedation, euphoria
Benzodiazepines	Antianxiety, sleep, anticonvulsant, sedative	Stress and anxiety reduction ("tranquilizing")
Rohypnol	None in United States (elsewhere: sedation, anxiety, anesthesia, and treatment of insomnia)	Same as other benzodiazepines, but longer lasting; also amnesia (hence its reputation as the "date-rape drug")
Alcohol	Antiseptic	Relaxation, well-being, cognitive and motor impairment
Stimulants		
Amphetamines	Weight control, ADHD, counteract anesthesia	Confidence, mental energy, alertness, hallucinations, paranoia
Methamphetamine	None	Same as other amphetamines, but more intense
MDMA (ecstasy)	None (originally an appetite suppressant)	Euphoria, hot flashes, perceptual distortions, excitement
Cocaine	Local anesthetic	Much the same as amphetamines, sexual arousal (except in chronic users), dramatic mood changes as effects wear off (irritability, depression)
Nicotine	Gum, patch for cessation of smoking	Stimulant effect, relaxation, concentration, reduces nicotine craving
Caffeine	Weight control, stimulant in acute respiratory failure, analgesia	Stimulant effect, increased alertness and concentration

hallucinogen A drug that creates hallucinations or alters perceptions of the external environment and inner awareness.

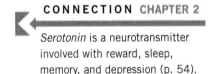

CONNECTION CHAPTER 2

Serotonin is a neurotransmitter involved with reward, sleep, memory, and depression (p. 54).

Hallucinogens The class of drugs known as **hallucinogens** produces changes in consciousness by altering perceptions, creating hallucinations, and blurring the boundary between the self and the external world. For example, an individual experiencing hallucinogenic effects might listen to music and suddenly feel he or she is producing the music or that the music is coming from within. Most hallucinogenic drugs act in the brain at specific receptor sites for the neurotransmitter serotonin (Jacobs, 1987).

Commonly used hallucinogens include *mescaline* (made from a type of cactus), *psilocybin* (from a mushroom), *LSD* or "acid," and *PCP* (also called phencyclidine or "angel dust"). Both LSD and PCP are synthetic drugs made in chemical laboratories. PCP was a favorite of young people who used hallucinogens until word got around that the intensity and duration of its effects were quite unpredictable. The drug produces a strange dissociative reaction in which the user feels disembodied or removed from parts of his or her personality. Users may become confused or insensitive to pain and, when using high doses, experience convulsions or even death.

Cannabis, or marijuana, derived from the hemp plant (used to make rope as well as dope), acts primarily as a hallucinogen. (Experts disagree to some extent on its classification, however, as it also has properties of stimulants and depressants.) Its active ingredient is *THC* (tetrahydrocannabinol), found in both the plant's dried leaves and flowers and in its solidified resin (hashish). Most commonly it is smoked, although it can also be eaten.

The experience obtained from ingesting THC depends on its dose. Small doses may create mild, pleasurable highs, and large doses can cause long hallucinogenic reactions. Unlike alcohol, its effects can last for many hours—long after users feel the drug's influence has ended. The pleasant effects include altered perception, sedation, pain relief, mild euphoria, and distortions of space and time—similar in some respects to the effects of heroin (Wickelgren, 1997). Depending on the social context and expectations, the effects can also be an unpleasant mixture of fear, anxiety, and confusion. In addition, cannabis often produces temporary failures in memory, as well as impairments in motor coordination. Those who work or drive under its influence suffer a higher risk of accidents—and those who attempt to study under its influence are likely to be wasting their time.

Some habitual cannabis users become psychologically addicted to its pleasurable effects, craving it so often that it interferes with other pursuits, including school or work. The potential for physical dependence on this drug, however, is lower than most other psychoactive substances (Grinspoon et al., 1997; Pinel, 2005). And, although controversial, cannabis also has medical uses, especially in treating nausea associated with chemotherapy and in reducing eye pressure associated with glaucoma.

What causes the mind-altering effects of this drug? In the brain, THC causes the release of dopamine, which suggests an effect on the brain's reward system (Carlson, 2007). Neuroscientists have discovered cannabis receptors in many other parts of the brain too (Nicoll & Alger, 2004; Wilson & Nicoll, 2002). This strongly suggests that the brain makes its own THC-like chemicals, which it uses to modulate information flow. Thus, marijuana and hashish seem to produce their mind-altering effects by exploiting the natural chemistry of the brain. Their interference with thinking and memory, then, is no wonder, because these receptors are particularly abundant in pathways involving these functions.

An evolutionary perspective suggests that the brain's own cannabis must have some beneficial function. Following this lead, a few neuroscientists are exploring just what the brain's "natural marijuana," more properly termed *endocannabinoids,* does for us. The hope is to eventually develop new therapies for a variety of human afflictions linked to brain areas that respond to THC, including circuits implicated in appetite, pain, nausea, and addiction. Thus, the research may lead to new treatments for obesity, chronic pain, the nausea produced by chemotherapy, and addiction by developing drugs to regulate the body's use of its own endocannabinoids (Marx, 2006; Nicoll & Alger, 2004).

Opiates Another class of drugs, known as **opiates**, includes *morphine, heroin,* and *codeine*—all made from the opium poppy. These are highly addictive drugs that suppress physical sensation and response to stimulation. As a result, some of them have found wide use in medicine, where they have particularly good analgesic (pain-relieving) properties and also serve as cough suppressants. (The only other medical use for opiates is in managing diarrhea.)

opiate Highly addictive drug, derived from opium, that can produce a profound sense of well-being and has strong pain-relieving properties.

Derived from morphine, heroin originally was developed in 19th-century Germany by the Bayer Company (of aspirin fame) but was abandoned because it is so highly addictive (more so than morphine). For the intravenous heroin user, however, the drug is attractive because, in the absence of pain, it gives a strong rush of pleasurable sensations. These feelings of euphoria supplant all worries and awareness of bodily needs, although—surprisingly—there are no major changes in cognitive abilities. Under heroin's influence, the user can usually converse normally and think clearly. Unfortunately, serious addiction is likely once a person begins to inject heroin for pleasure. To avoid the intense cravings and painful sensations of withdrawal, the addict must take the drug frequently—at least daily—making it a very expensive habit to maintain.

In recent years, several opiate-based drugs have come on the market, under brand names such as Oxycontin, Vicodin, Darvon, Percodan, and Demerol. Medically, they are effective painkillers, although their potential for addiction is high in chronic users. Unfortunately, because they produce the same feel-good effects as other opiates, they are also widely abused.

Like marijuana, opiates have special receptor sites in the brain. The discovery of these opiate receptors led to the realization that the brain makes its own opiates, the *endorphins,* which act as the body's natural analgesics or painkillers. This research stimulated a quest for drugs that have the same pain-fighting qualities as opiates but without their addictive properties. The hope is, so far, unfulfilled.

Methadone, a synthetic opiate, can be taken orally and therefore doesn't require injection. It has essentially the same euphoric, analgesic, and addictive effects as heroin but doesn't produce the same "rush" because the drug level in the brain increases slowly. This feature makes methadone useful as a substitute for heroin in drug treatment programs, in which the patient is switched to methadone and then gradually weaned from opiates altogether.

Paradoxically, patients who take opiates for pain control under medical supervision rarely become highly addicted. The reason for the difference in effects between the use of opiates for pleasure and for pain is unclear. It appears, however, the presence of pain causes opiates to affect parts of the brain other than the "reward centers" involved in pleasure. The practical point is this: There is little to fear from legitimate medical use of opiates for controlling pain (Melzack, 1990).

Depressants and Antianxiety Drugs The broad class of drugs that slows mental and physical activity by inhibiting activity in the central nervous system is collectively known as **depressants.** (Depressants don't necessarily make people feel clinically depressed, in the sense of "sad.") They include *barbiturates* (usually prescribed for sedation), *benzodiazepines* (antianxiety drugs), and *alcohol* (a social stimulant and nervous system depressant). In appropriate dosages, these drugs can relieve symptoms of pain or anxiety, but overuse or abuse is dangerous because they impair reflexes and judgment. They may also be addictive.

Barbiturates, commonly used in sleeping pills, can induce sleep. Unfortunately, they have the side effect of interfering with REM sleep. This leaves the user feeling groggy and at risk for severe REM rebound, filling sleep with unpleasant dreams. Worse yet, overdoses of barbiturates may cause loss of consciousness, sometimes to the point of coma and even death. Fatal reactions to barbiturates are made all the more likely because the lethal dose is relatively close to the dose required for inducing sleep or other desired effects. The chance of accidental overdose can be compounded by alcohol or other depressant drugs, which magnify the depressant action of barbiturates (Maisto et al., 1995).

Benzodiazepines (pronounced *BEN-zo-dye-AZ-a-peens*), commonly prescribed to treat anxiety, are safer than barbiturates and reduce anxiety without causing sleepiness or sedation. For this reason, physicians often call them "minor tranquilizers"—the best-known and most widely prescribed, which include Valium and Xanax.

While most benzodiazepines are relatively safe, they can be overused and abused. Overdoses produce poor muscle coordination, slurred speech, weakness, and irritability, while withdrawal symptoms include increased anxiety, muscle twitching, and sensitivity to sound and light. Significantly, benzodiazepines are almost never taken by recreational drug users because people who are not suffering from anxiety usually do not like their effects (Wesson et al., 1992).

Alcohol, another drug that acts as a brain depressant, was one of the first psychoactive substances used by humankind. Under its influence, people have a variety of reactions involving loosening of inhibitions. At first, this may seem like a contradiction: How can a depressant make people less inhibited? What actually happens is that alcohol depresses activity in the brain circuits that control self-monitoring of our thoughts and behavior. The result depends on the context and the personality of the imbiber, who may become more talkative or quiet, friendly or abusive, ebullient or, sometimes, psychologically depressed. Alcohol's effects also depend on whether other drugs, such as MDMA or Rohypnol (a form of benzodiazepine sometimes known as the "date-rape drug"), are being used simultaneously. Such drugs are believed by users to enhance social interaction and empathy, although their effects can easily spin out of control, especially in combination with alcohol (Gahlinger, 2004).

---

depressant   Drug that slows down mental and physical activity by inhibiting transmission of nerve impulses in the central nervous system.

CONNECTION CHAPTER 13

Benzodiazepines are used to treat anxiety-related problems such as *panic disorder* and *obsessive compulsive disorder* (p. 580).

Physically, alcohol in small doses can induce relaxation and even slightly improve an adult's reaction time. In just slightly larger amounts, it impairs co-ordination and mental processing—although sometimes drinkers believe their performance has been improved. Moreover, it is quite easy for alcohol to ac-cumulate in the system because the body may not metabolize it as fast as it is ingested. In general, the body breaks down alcohol at the rate of only 1 ounce per hour, and greater amounts consumed in short periods stay in the body and depress activity in the central nervous system. When the level of alcohol in the blood reaches a mere 0.1 percent (1/1000 of the blood), an individual experi-ences deficits in thinking, memory, and judgment, along with emotional instabil-ity and coordination problems. In some parts of the United States, this level of blood alcohol qualifies a driver as being legally drunk. (Most states, in fact, set a somewhat lower limit of 0.08 percent as the legal threshold for drunkenness.)

Physical dependence, tolerance, and addiction to alcohol may begin with social pressure and binge drinking—as seen in this student who readies himself to drink from an ice luge at a party.

Distillers, brewers, and wine makers spend millions of dollars annually promoting the social and personal benefits of alcoholic beverages. And, to be sure, many adults use alcohol prudently. Nevertheless, an estimated 5 to 10 percent of American adults who use alcohol drink to the extent that it harms their health, career, or family and social re-lationships. To some extent, the problem is rooted in our genes—but genetics is far from the whole answer (Nurnberger & Bierut, 2007). People also *learn* to abuse alcohol, often in response to social pressure. Eventually, physical dependence, tolerance, and addiction develop with prolonged heavy drinking—of the sort that often begins with binge drink-ing, common on college campuses. When the amount and frequency of drinking alcohol interferes with job or school performance, impairs social and family relationships, and creates serious health problems, the diagnosis of *alcoholism* is appropriate (see Julien, 2007; Vallee, 1998).

Abuse of alcohol is a significant problem for more than 17 million Americans (Adelson, 2006; Grant & Dawson, 2006). And alcoholism affects more than just the individual drinker. For example, alcohol ingested by a pregnant woman can affect the fetus and is a leading cause of mental retardation (Committee on Substance Abuse, 2000). Alcohol abuse affects other family members, too. Some 40 percent of Americans see the effects of alcohol abuse in their families (Vallee, 1998). The problem is especially prevalent among White males and young adults. Too often, the problem becomes a lethal one, because alcohol-related automobile accidents are the leading cause of death in the 15 to 25 age group.

stimulant A drug that arouses the central nervous system, speeding up mental and physical responses.

Stimulants In contrast with depressants, **stimulants** speed up central nervous system activity. The result is a boost in both mental and physical activity level, which is why long-distance truck drivers sometimes use them to stay awake behind the wheel. Par-adoxically, stimulants can also increase concentration and reduce activity level, par-ticularly in hyperactive children with attention-deficit/hyperactivity disorder (ADHD). Physicians also prescribe them for narcoleptic patients to prevent sleep attacks.

CONNECTION CHAPTER 7

ADHD is a relatively common disorder of attention span and behavior, usually diagnosed in children but sometimes found in adults (p. 294).

Recreational users of stimulants seek other effects: intense pleasurable sensations, increased self-confidence, and euphoria. *Cocaine,* in particular, packs what may be the most powerfully rewarding punch of any illegal drug (Landry, 1997). Crack, an espe-cially addictive form of cocaine, produces a swift, pleasurable high that also wears off quickly. Amphetamines (often called "speed") and related drugs have effects compa-rable to cocaine. Among these, a particularly notorious variant known as *methamphet-amine* came into widespread use during the 1990s. Use of "meth" can lead to severe health problems, including physical damage in the brain.

Still another stimulant, known as *MDMA* (often called "ecstasy"), has grown popular in "rave" culture, where it has a reputation for creating a feeling of euphoria and closeness to others (Thompson et al., 2007). It is also known for energizing users to dance for hours, sometimes leading to convulsions, death, and other unpleasant consequences (Gahlinger, 2004; Yacoubian et al., 2004). Ecstasy produces increased blood pressure and heart rate, hyperthermia (elevated temperature), and dehydration. Long-term use is also known to impair attention, learning, and memory, probably through impairment of serotonin-using neurons (Levinthal, 2008; Verbaten, 2003).

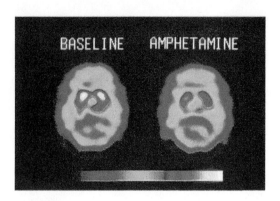

Brain changes during use of drugs can be seen on PET scan images. Much less activity is seen in the limbic system of the brain under the influence of amphetamines.

Stimulant drugs hold other dangers as well. Heavy amphetamine and cocaine users may experience frightening hallucinations and paranoid delusions—symptoms also associated with severe mental disorder. And these drugs can send users on an emotional roller coaster of euphoric highs and depressive lows, leading to an increase in frequency and dosage, quickly making the abuse of such drugs spiral out of control. Yet another danger accrues to "secondhand" users: Children exposed to cocaine in their mother's blood while in the womb are at increased risk for developing cognitive problems, emotional difficulties, and behavior-control disorders (Vogel, 1997).

Two other stimulants you may not even think of as psychoactive drugs are *caffeine* and *nicotine*—yet their effects on the brain are swift and powerful. Within ten minutes, two cups of strong coffee or tea deliver enough caffeine to have a measurable effect on the heart, blood circulation, and brain signals. Nicotine inhaled in tobacco smoke can have similar effects within just seconds. Both drugs are addictive, and both augment the effects of natural reward chemicals released by the brain. In this way, nicotine and caffeine tease the brain's reward pathways into responding as if using these substances were associated with something beneficial. Fortunately, in the case of caffeine, the negative effects are minor for most people. Further, caffeine has a built-in "braking" action that limits its intake because high dosages also produce uncomfortable anxiety-like feelings.

In contrast to caffeine, nicotine is a much more dangerous drug for two reasons: Nicotine is highly addictive, and it has been associated with a variety of health problems, including cancer, emphysema, and heart disease. In fact, the negative impact of smoking on health is greater than that of all other psychoactive drugs combined—including heroin, cocaine, and alcohol. According to the U.S. Public Health Service, smoking is the leading cause of preventable disease, carrying a human cost of about 438,000 deaths annually (Centers for Disease Control and Prevention, 2007). As a result, the American Medical Association has formally recommended that the U.S. Food and Drug Administration regard nicotine as a drug to be regulated.

The Altered States of Anesthesia   While anesthetics have come a long way in the 160 years since the discoveries of chloroform and ether, science has relatively little knowledge of how **general anesthetics** alter consciousness and suppress pain awareness (Orser, 2007). Although anesthetized people appear to "go to sleep," general anesthesia is quite different from sleep. Anesthesia involves none of the REM and NREM stages associated with sleep, even though it induces these sleep-like components: *sedation* (greatly reduced arousal), *unconsciousness* (lack of awareness and responsiveness), *immobility* (temporary paralysis), and *amnesia* (lack of recall for the period under the influence of the anesthetic). Strangely, these four components of anesthesia seem to be independent of one another. For example, conscious patients often carry on lively conversations as they "go under"—yet they rarely have a memory of these events.

One tentative theory suggests that anesthetics interrupt the process by which different parts of the brain work together, or "synchronize," thereby preventing consciousness. They may do so by mimicking or enhancing the action of GABA, one of the brain's main inhibitory neurotransmitters. In this respect, anesthetics may be just another group of psychoactive drugs that interfere with consciousness.

general anesthetic   Substance that suppresses consciousness and awareness of pain. Most anesthetics also produce sedation and immobility.

[PSYCHOLOGY MATTERS]

Dependence and Addiction

CONNECTION CHAPTER 2

Most psychoactive drugs mimic neurotransmitters or enhance or dampen their effects at the synapses (p. 53).

We have seen that psychoactive drugs alter the functioning of neurons in the brain and, as a consequence, temporarily change one's consciousness. The same may be true about the steroids used by some athletes (Adelson, 2005). Once in the brain, such drugs usually act on synapses to block or stimulate neural messages. In this way, drugs profoundly alter the brain's communication system, affecting perception, memory, mood, and behavior.

Significantly, a given dose of many psychoactive drugs has a weaker consciousness-altering effect with continued use. As a result, the user needs larger and larger dosages to achieve the same effect. This reduced effectiveness with repeated use of a drug is called **tolerance**. Hand-in-hand with tolerance goes **physical dependence**—a process in which the body adjusts to and comes to need the substance, in part because the production of neurotransmitters in the brain is affected by the frequent presence of the drug (Wickelgren, 1998c). A person with a physical dependence requires the drug in his or her body and may suffer unpleasant *withdrawal* symptoms if the drug is not present. Some scientists believe the desire to avoid withdrawal is as important as the pleasurable effects of drugs in producing *addiction* (Everitt & Robbins, 2005).

A person who develops tolerance to a highly addictive drug such as heroin becomes less sensitive to all sorts of natural reinforcers, including the pleasures of friendship, food, and everyday entertainment: The drug, in increasing dosages, becomes the only thing capable of providing pleasure (Helmuth, 2001a). **Addiction** is said to occur when the person continues to use a drug in the face of adverse effects on his or her health or life—often despite repeated attempts to stop.

Addiction is not all physical, however. When heroin addicts routinely "shoot up" in the same environment—say, in the bathroom—a *learned* response actually anticipates the drug and prepares the body for it. The result is that the addict can tolerate dosages that are larger than when drugs are injected at a novel location (Dingfelder, 2004b). Thus, overdoses may occur if the user attempts to shoot up with his or her "usual amount" in a novel location.

Withdrawal involves uncomfortable physical and mental symptoms that occur when drug use is discontinued. It can include physical trembling, perspiring, nausea, increased sensitivity to pain and, in the case of extreme alcohol withdrawal, even death. Although heroin and alcohol are the drugs that most commonly come to mind when we think of withdrawal symptoms, nicotine and caffeine, as well as certain sleeping pills and "tranquilizing" drugs, also cause unpleasant withdrawal symptoms.

Individuals may find themselves craving or hungering for a drug and its effects, even when they are not physically dependent—a condition known as **psychological dependence** or *psychological addiction*. This usually results from the powerfully rewarding effects they produce. Psychological dependence can occur with many drugs, including caffeine and nicotine, prescription medications, and over-the-counter drugs.

Addiction, whether biological or psychological, ultimately affects the brain (Nestler & Malenka, 2004). Consequently, in the view of many public health professionals, this makes both forms of addiction brain diseases (Leshner, 1997). On the other hand, the general public has been reluctant to view drug addicts as people who have an illness. Instead, the public often thinks of addicts as weak or bad individuals who should be punished (MacCoun, 1998).

What difference does it make whether we label addiction a "disease"? When addicts are seen as persons suffering from a disease, they are most logically placed in treatment programs. By contrast, when they are seen as persons with character defects, addicts are sent to prison for punishment—which does little to break the cycle of drug use, crime, and addiction.

Strange as it may seem, some experts argue that viewing addiction as a disease may also *interfere* with the effective treatment of drug addicts. How could this be? The disease model of addiction, with its emphasis on biological causes and medical treatment, does little to deal with the social and economic contexts in which addictions develop. This may explain why psychologically based programs that treat alcohol abuse as a behavioral problem may work better than medically based programs (Miller & Brown, 1997).

Treatment programs have an especially poor record with heroin addicts who learned their habits on the streets of the United States. In contrast, treatment was more successful with the thousands of veterans who became addicted to the heroin readily available to troops during the Vietnam war. What made the difference? The addicted veterans did not remain in the environment where they had become addicted—which

tolerance   The reduced effectiveness a drug has after repeated use.

physical dependence   A process by which the body adjusts to, and comes to need, a drug for its everyday functioning.

addiction   A condition in which a person continues to use a drug despite its adverse effects—often despite repeated attempts to discontinue using the drug. Addiction may be based on physical or psychological dependence.

withdrawal   A pattern of uncomfortable or painful physical symptoms and cravings experienced by the user when the level of drug is decreased or the drug is eliminated.

psychological dependence   A desire to obtain or use a drug, even though there is no physical dependence.

The line between substance use and abuse is easy to cross with addictive drugs, most of which act on the brain's "pleasure centers."

was the wartime culture of Vietnam. Instead, they returned home to an environment not usually supportive of a heroin habit. On the other hand, heroin users who become addicted at home tend to return, after treatment, to the same environment that originally led to their addiction.

Whether it be physical or psychological, a disease, or a character flaw, drug addiction poses many personal and social problems. Clearly, this is a field that has much room for new ideas and new research.

Check Your Understanding

✓● Study and Review at MyPsychLab

1. **RECALL:** What does evidence show concerning hypnosis as a distinct state of consciousness?

2. **RECALL:** What physical changes are associated with meditation?

3. **RECALL:** Psychoactive drugs usually create their effects by stimulating _____ in the brain.

4. **RECALL:** Most hallucinogens act on brain sites that involve the neurotransmitter _____.

5. **SYNTHESIS:** In what respect are opiates like cannabis?

6. **APPLICATION:** Which of the following groups of drugs have the opposite effects on the brain?

a. hallucinogens and stimulants
b. opiates and sedatives
c. stimulants and depressants
d. depressants and opiates

7. **RECALL:** Why do many psychologists object to the "disease model" of addiction?

8. **UNDERSTANDING THE CORE CONCEPT:** Altered states do not involve any mysterious or paranormal phenomena. Rather, they are modifications of ordinary consciousness we can study with the tools of science, because they are produced by _____, _____, and _____ changes in the person.

Answers 1. No solid evidence to date shows that hypnosis is a unique state of consciousness. **2.** Many physical changes occur with meditation, including changes in brain wave patterns, frontal lobe changes associated with positive emotions, beneficial changes in blood pressure and stress hormones and, over time, increased thickness of the brain's cortex. **3.** reward circuits (so-called "pleasure centers") **4.** serotonin **5.** Both have specific receptor sites in the brain. **6.** c **7.** The disease model tends to emphasize biological causes and medical treatment at the expense of recognizing the social and economic contexts in which addictions develop. **8.** mental; behavioral; physical changes in the person

---

CRITICAL THINKING APPLIED

The Unconscious—Reconsidered

As we have seen, the term *unconscious* can have many meanings. In Freud's psychoanalytic theory, for example, powerful unconscious forces actively work to block (or *repress*) traumatic memories and destructive urges (Freud, 1925). If allowed to break through into consciousness, these would cause extreme anxiety, Freud taught. In this view, then, the unconscious mind serves as a mental dungeon where terrible needs and threatening memories can be kept "locked up" outside of awareness.

Freud's ideas captivated artists and writers in the Western world. For example, Joseph Conrad's novel *Heart of Darkness* tells the story of one man's internal and unconscious struggle with his evil desires for power, destruction, and death. Unconscious desires can be sexual, as well, said Freud. What else could account for the dubious success of the titillating stories splashed so obviously across the pages of the tabloids and the screens of the "soaps"?

Freud also taught that we "forget" anniversaries because we have unconscious reservations about the relationship. He said we choose mates who are, on an unconscious level, substitutes for our fathers and mothers. And he gave us the concept of the "Freudian slip," which one wag defined as "saying one thing when you really mean your mother."

Freud, then, placed the *ego*—the rational decision-maker part of the mind—at the center of consciousness. There, he said, it assumes the responsibility of keeping the sexual and aggressive forces of the unconscious in check. But was he right? Or were Freud's ideas better as metaphors than as objective science?

What Are the Critical Issues?

Freud's theory can explain almost anything—and in very compelling language. He portrayed a mind perpetually locked in an internal struggle against itself. And we can see evidence all around us of the sexual and aggressive urges that loomed so important in his theory: in advertising, video games, movies, politics, and the ways people fight and flirt. So the issue is not whether sexual and aggressive urges influence human behavior, but whether these urges operate as Freud suggested: primarily at an unconscious level and in a mind continually in conflict with itself.

What Is the Source?　Without a doubt, Freud was a perceptive observer of people and a creative theorist, and his views have been enormously influential. But his genius and his influence don't necessarily make his views correct. For example, his seeming obsession with sex makes sense in the context of the rigid and "proper" culture of early-20th-century Europe, which frowned on public references to sexuality. (In some quarters, the term *leg* was considered inappropriate for mixed company.) From the perspective of 21st-century Europe and North America, however, with sexual content quite common in conversation and in the media, we have no reason to believe that sexual thoughts are mostly unconscious. If anything, many people seem consciously preoccupied with sex. This does not mean, of course, that the unconscious does not exist. But it does raise questions about the unconscious as Freud envisioned it.

Could Bias Contaminate the Conclusion?　Given the cultural constraints of his time, we should consider whether the seething sexual cauldron of desire that was the Freudian unconscious might be the result of biases in Freud's thinking—biases produced by the sexually uptight culture of which he was a part. Anytime there exist strong feelings toward something, emotional bias is a risk. Freud may have also been guilty of *confirmation bias*, finding evidence of the unconscious everywhere: in dreams, forgetting, slips of the tongue and other everyday errors, developmental stages of childhood, and mental disorders.

Does the Reasoning Avoid Common Fallacies?　Freud may have also committed a common logical fallacy known as *begging the question*, or assuming the very thing one is trying to prove. We suggest that Freud begs the question by assuming that unconscious conflict is the cause of all the mental phenomena he describes—from forgetting an anniversary to a fear of dogs to having a dream about flying. Why is this a logical fallacy? Because Freud's argument is also an attempt to prove the existence of a conflicted unconscious. He even suggested that resistance to his arguments is evidence of the unconscious at work! Such arguments are sometimes called *circular reasoning*.

And for our part, as critical thinkers, we must be careful not to commit the fallacy often described as "throwing the baby out with the bath water." That is, even if we find fault with some of Freud's notions, we do not need to reject the concept of an unconscious altogether. In fact, as you will see in the next chapter, the unconscious plays a huge role in our motivations and emotions.

What Conclusions Can We Draw?

We can question Freud and still respect his brilliance and his stature. After all, he developed an amazingly comprehensive and appealing theory of mind in the early days of the 20th century—long before brain scans and other tools of modern psychology were available. Almost certainly, some of his ideas had to be erroneous in light of newer knowledge. The important question, then, is whether Freud's concept of consciousness and the unconscious mind is still reasonable in view of the evidence psychology has accumulated since Freud's time.

In recent years, techniques such as brain scans and priming have made it possible to probe unconscious thought processes in ways never dreamed of by Freud (Kihlstrom, 1990; Kihlstrom et al., 1992). In the resulting picture, the unconscious—although quite expansive, as Freud imagined—does not appear so sinister as Freud portrayed it. In fact, it may have a much simpler structure than the complicated censoring and repressing system that Freud proposed (Greenwald, 1992).

Brain scans do provide support for some of Freud's broad notions, such as the idea that many parts of the brain can operate outside of consciousness. What Freud didn't know is how much of this activity is devoted to simple background tasks, such as maintaining body temperature and controlling hunger and thirst. Likewise, the brain performs a sort of "preconscious" screening on the incoming stream of sights, sounds, smells, and textures. This screening also provides a quick-and-dirty appraisal of events for their attractiveness or harmfulness (LeDoux, 1996). Such processing can even save your life, as when you react "without thinking" to a swerving car coming at you.

Ironically, then, the cognitive view of an unconscious that monitors, sorts, discards, and stores the flood of data we encounter may give the unconscious an even larger role than Freud originally conceived. But it is not the picture of a scheming and plotting unconscious, full of sinister urges that must be vented (Baumeister, 2005; Wilson, 2002). Rather, the less-than-conscious mind seems to work, for the most part, in concert with consciousness, rather than against it—although, when we discuss mental disorders, we will see that a fearful experience can sometimes leave a lasting mark on the unconscious screening process that is difficult to eradicate.

Do It Yourself!　**CULTURAL PERCEPTIONS OF CONSCIOUSNESS**

Do an Internet search on "drugs" and "cultural differences." What cultures allow consciousness-altering practices that your culture makes illegal? Conversely, are there cultures that ban consciousness-altering practices (such as drinking alcohol) that Western culture allows? How might the belief systems of the culture impact the altered states they support or prohibit?

CHAPTER SUMMARY

 ((•─[Listen** to an audio file of your chapter at **MyPsychLab**

CHAPTER PROBLEM: How can psychologists objectively examine the worlds of dreaming and other subjective mental states?

- Brain scanning technologies such as EEG, PET, MRI, and fMRI help scientists study subjective mental states.

- Using these technologies, combined with other scientific methods such as experiments, researchers have learned much about the nature of sleep. Hypnosis and meditation have only

recently begun to be studied scientifically, but early results show that these altered states of consciousness do produce some predictable changes in the brain.

- Psychoactive drugs also produce altered states of consciousness, which result from the effects of the particular drug on the brain's communication system and neurotransmitters.

8.1 How Is Consciousness Related to Other Mental Processes?

[Core Concept 8.1 **The brain operates on many levels at once—both conscious and unconscious.**]

Consciousness represents one of the major mysteries of psychology, both in its ordinary waking state and in its many *altered states*. Consciousness is a process linked to working memory, learning, and attention. Behaviorists rejected consciousness as a topic too subjective for scientific study, but **cognitive neuroscience** shows that scientific methods can be applied to consciousness using both psychological techniques and brain scanning technology.

Psychologists have used various metaphors for consciousness. Freud likened consciousness to an iceberg, in which the **unconscious** played a powerful role in motivation. James spoke of a "stream of consciousness". The modern cognitive perspective uses a computer metaphor. In addition to consciousness, the mind has many **nonconscious** modes that can operate outside awareness. These include the **preconscious** and various levels of unconscious processing. While consciousness is limited to serial processing, the mind can process information nonconsciously in parallel channels.

Consciousness involves at least three important factors: restricted **attention**, widespread connections among diverse areas of the brain, and a mental model of the world used in thinking. Comas are short-term states that transition into either a *minimally conscious state* or a *persistent vegetative state*. Measuring consciousness in **coma** patients is difficult and sometimes erroneous but is improving with advanced brain scanning techniques.

Because consciousness is limited, students using their knowledge of consciousness can employ study methods that facilitate the passage of information from consciousness into long-term memory so that it remains accessible to consciousness. All such techniques involve making the material meaningful.

attention (p. 326)
cognitive neuroscience (p. 325)
coma (p. 330)
consciousness (p. 325)
nonconscious process (p. 325)
preconscious (p. 327)
unconscious (p. 328)

8.2 What Cycles Occur in Everyday Consciousness?

[Core Concept 8.2 **Consciousness fluctuates in cycles that correspond to our biological rhythms and to the patterns of stimulation in our environment.**]

Consciousness shifts and changes in everyday life, commonly taking the form of daydreaming, sleep, and nocturnal dreams. **Daydreaming** is probably inevitable and is a function of the default status of the waking. Daydreaming can enhance problem solving and creative insight but can also interfere with memory and happiness.

Although the function of *sleep* is not altogether clear, everyone agrees that sleep and wakefulness are part of the **circadian rhythms**. Too little sleep incurs a **sleep debt**, which impairs mental functioning. Sleep researchers have revealed the features of the normal *sleep cycle*, including the four *stages of sleep*, as revealed by recordings of brain waves on the EEG. These sleep stages recur in 90-minute cycles, featuring both **REM** and **non-REM** periods. Over the course of the night, each ensuing sleep cycle involves less deep sleep and more REM sleep. The sleep cycle also changes dramatically with age. Most adults need at least 8 hours of sleep every night.

The function of *dreams* is also unclear, but they often occur in REM sleep, accompanied by **sleep paralysis**. Dreams have, however, always been a source of inspiration and creativity for humankind in cultures around the world. Among theories of dreams, Freud's has been the most influential—although it has little empirical support. Studies show that dreams vary by culture, gender, and age. Many theories suggest dreams are meaningful events, and research shows they often involve problems of the previous day; **activation-synthesis theory** claims

358

that dreams are essentially meaningless. Recent studies suggest that dreams may help in the consolidation of memory.

Abnormalities in the sleep cycle can produce various sleep disorders. **Narcolepsy** is a disorder of REM sleep, **insomnia** involves shortened sleep, and **sleep apnea** involves abnormalities in deep sleep. Other disorders of a less serious nature include **night terrors**, *sleep talking*, *bed wetting*, and *sleepwalking*.

activation-synthesis theory (p. 340)
circadian rhythm (p. 333)
daydreaming (p. 332)

insomnia (p. 342)
latent content (p. 339)
manifest content (p. 339)
narcolepsy (p. 343)
night terrors (p. 343)
non-REM (NREM) sleep (p. 335)
REM rebound (p. 336)
REM sleep (p. 335)
sleep apnea (p. 342)
sleep debt (p. 337)
sleep paralysis (p. 335)

8.3 What Other Forms Can Consciousness Take?

Core Concept 8.3 **An altered state of consciousness occurs when some aspect of normal consciousness is modified by mental, behavioral, or chemical means.**

Altered states of consciousness include hypnosis, meditation, and psychoactive drug states. **Hypnosis** remains especially puzzling as to whether it is a separate state of consciousness. Some scientists view it merely as a suggestible state; others see it as role playing or involving a "hidden observer." Cognitive psychologists have suggested it involves a shift in top-down processing. It is known to block pain, although it does not act like placebos. While hypnosis has many uses in therapy and research, one drawback is that not everyone can be deeply hypnotized.

Meditation has a long history in Asian and Pacific cultures but has only recently been studied by psychologists. Likewise, experts dispute whether meditation is a distinct state of consciousness, even though it has measurable effects on arousal and anxiety, as well as producing changes in brain waves, blood pressure, and stress hormones. Meditation has recently been found to improve brain functioning in several areas.

Most **psychoactive drugs** produce sensations of pleasure and well-being that make these drugs especially attractive and potentially addictive. **Hallucinogens** (such as cannabis, mescaline, psilocybin, LSD, and PCP) generally affect receptor sites for serotonin. Distinct receptor sites for THC and for the **opiates** (including morphine, heroin, codeine, and methadone) suggest that the brain makes its own version of these substances. **Depressants** (including barbiturates, benzodiazepines, and alcohol) act to inhibit communication within

the brain; many depressants are among the commonly abused drugs. Medically, **barbiturates** are often prescribed for their sleep-inducing properties, while **benzodiazepines** are used to treat anxiety. Most people use alcohol responsibly, although between 5 and 10 percent of American adults are problem drinkers. **Stimulants** (such as amphetamines, cocaine, and MDMA) are widely abused, although amphetamines are prescribed for ADHD. Caffeine and nicotine also act as stimulants. **General anesthetics** alter consciousness and suppress pain. Their effects are different from sleep. In general, they produce sedation, unconsciousness, immobility, and amnesia for events occurring during anesthesia.

Many psychoactive drugs can lead to **addiction**. One indication of this potential is increased **tolerance**; another is **physical dependence**, marked by **withdrawal symptoms**. Some drugs that are not physically addicting produce **psychological dependence**. Although addiction has been characterized as a *disease*, some psychologists believe that the disease model of addiction is shortsighted.

addiction (p. 355)
depressant (p. 352)
general anesthetic (p. 354)
hallucinogen (p. 350)
hypnosis (p. 345)
meditation (p. 347)
opiate (p. 351)
physical dependence (p. 355)
psychoactive drug (p. 348)
psychological dependence (p. 355)
stimulant (p. 353)
tolerance (p. 355)
withdrawal (p. 355)

CRITICAL THINKING APPLIED

The Unconscious—Reconsidered

Over 150 years ago, Freud proposed a model of the unconscious that remains widely referenced today. Modern technologies show that the unconscious exists and, in fact, is possibly even more expansive than Freud imagined. On the other hand, these same technologies reveal our unconscious processes to be far less sinister than Freud theorized.

DISCOVERING PSYCHOLOGY **VIEWING GUIDE**

Watch the following videos by logging into MyPsychLab (www.mypsychlab.com).
After you have watched the videos, answer the questions that follow.

PROGRAM 13: **THE MIND AWAKE AND ASLEEP**

PROGRAM 14: **THE MIND HIDDEN AND DIVIDED**

Program Review

1. Which of the following is an example of a circadian rhythm?
   a. eating three meals a day at approximately the same time
   b. experiencing alternate periods of REM and non-REM sleep
   c. having systematic changes in hormone levels during 24 hours
   d. having changes in fertility levels during a month

2. What is a positive function of daydreaming?
   a. It focuses attention on a task.
   b. It reduces demands made on the brain.
   c. It enables us to be mentally active when we are bored.
   d. It provides delta wave activity normally received only in sleep.

3. According to Freud, dreams are significant because they
   a. permit neurotransmitters to be regenerated.
   b. reveal unconscious fears and desires.
   c. forecast the future.
   d. supply a story line to patterns of electrical charges.

4. According to McCarley and Hobson, what is true about REM sleep?
   a. Adults spend more time in REM sleep than do infants.
   b. REM sleep is an unnecessary physiological function.
   c. The random burst of brain activity occurs first, followed by the dreamer's attempt to make sense of it.
   d. The subconscious expresses its deepest desires during REM sleep.

5. According to Freud, how do we feel when painful memories or unacceptable urges threaten to break into consciousness?
   a. relieved
   b. guilty
   c. sad
   d. anxious

6. What are Freudian slips thought to reveal?
   a. what we have dreamed about
   b. how we really feel
   c. who we would like to be transformed into
   d. why we make certain choices

7. What happens if a hypnotized person who expects to smell cologne actually smells ammonia?
   a. The ammonia smell wakes him from the trance.
   b. He recognizes the ammonia smell, but he remains hypnotized.
   c. He interprets the ammonia smell as a musky cologne.
   d. He overgeneralizes and finds that the cologne smells like ammonia.

8. All of the following appear to fluctuate based on circadian rhythm, except
   a. intelligence.
   b. hormone levels.
   c. blood pressure.
   d. body temperature.

9. Consciousness performs all of the following functions, except
   a. filtering sensory data.
   b. enabling us to respond flexibly.
   c. allowing us to have a sense of our own mortality.
   d. guiding performance of highly routinized actions.

10. What occurs about every 90 minutes throughout sleep?
    a. rapid eye movement
    b. rapid irregular changes in brain activity
    c. dreaming
    d. more than one of the above

11. How normal is it to experience alternate states of consciousness?

    a. It happens to most people, mainly in times of stress.

    b. It is something we all experience every day.

    c. It is rare and generally indicates a mental disorder.

    d. It is common in childhood and becomes rarer with age.

12. In the program, the part of the brain that is identified as the "interior decorator" imposing order on experience is the

    a. pons.

    b. hippocampus.

    c. limbic system.

    d. cerebral cortex.

13. Ernest Hartmann points out the logic behind Shakespeare's description of sleep. According to Hartmann, a major function of sleep is that it allows the brain to

    a. process material too threatening to be dealt with consciously.

    b. integrate the day's events with previously learned material.

    c. make plans for the day ahead.

    d. discharge a buildup of electrical activity.

14. Which part of the brain is responsible for conscious awareness?

    a. cerebral cortex

    b. brain stem

    c. limbic system

    d. hypothalamus

15. When societies around the world were studied, what proportion of them practiced some culturally patterned form of altering consciousness?

    a. practically none

    b. about a third

    c. about half

    d. the vast majority

16. Instances in which people believe they have remembered long-forgotten traumatic events are known as

    a. repression.

    b. suppression.

    c. recovered memories.

    d. fugue states.

17. Sigmund Freud is to the unconscious as _____ is to discovered memories.

    a. B. F. Skinner

    b. Jonathan Schooler

    c. Michael Gazzaniga

    d. Stephen LaBerge

18. According to Freud, normal people banish undesirable memories from their conscious minds through

    a. repression.

    b. projection.

    c. anterograde amnesia.

    d. hysteria.

19. Which topic related to human consciousness is conveyed by the story of Dr. Jekyll and Mr. Hyde?

    a. witchcraft

    b. hypnosis

    c. identity transformation

    d. sleep disorders

20. Communication between the two hemispheres of the brain is disrupted when

    a. a person is in deep meditation.

    b. a person is in deep Freudian denial.

    c. a person has just recovered an early memory.

    d. the corpus callosum is severed.

9 Motivation and Emotion

CHAPTER PROBLEM Motivation is largely an internal and subjective process: How can we determine what motivates people like Lance Armstrong to work so hard at becoming the best in the world at what they do?

CRITICAL THINKING APPLIED Do Lie Detectors Really Detect Lies?

W HAT MOTIVATES LANCE ARMSTRONG? THE WORLD'S BEST-KNOWN cyclist, Lance has seven times won his sport's premiere event, the Tour de France, a gruelling three-week bicycle race covering more than 2,000 miles. His mother Linda declared that he was always a competitive child—and one that often tested the boundaries, as well as her patience.

Did his competitive spirit originate in his tumultuous family life? When Lance was a baby, his father moved out, and his parents divorced. About three years later, his mother remarried a man named Armstrong, who adopted the boy and gave him his name. But it was always his mother who was the dominant figure in Lance's early years in Plano, Texas ("Lance Armstrong," 2010).

Despite having little money, his mother managed to buy Lance his first bicycle when he was seven. He loved the bike, but it was the Plano city swim team that gave him, at age 12, his first competitive athletic experiences. (Lance rode his bike 10 miles to swim practice in the morning and then cycled on to school. After school in the afternoon, he rode back to swim some more—after which he pedalled home.) At the peak of his swimming career, the young Armstrong won fourth at the state tournament in the 1500-meter freestyle.

Armstrong's focus shifted when, at age 13, he entered the Iron Kids Triathlon, an event that combined swimming with biking and running. He won easily. Three years later, he turned professional and soon triumphed in several national triathlon championships. Eventually Armstrong's achievements attracted the attention of scientists at the Cooper Institute for Aerobic Research, who found that his oxygen consumption during exercise was the highest they had ever recorded. Clearly, he was a specimen ideally suited for sustained aerobic exercise. So, was it Lance's natural athletic ability, plus a string of early successes, that kept him training and eventually pushed him onto the world stage?

In 1992, he decided to narrow his focus exclusively to bicycle racing. A spot on the U.S. Olympic team quickly led to a sponsorship by Motorola on the professional cycling tour. A string of increasingly prestigious victories followed—until the bad news came in 1996. At the age of 25, Armstrong, who was experiencing unexplained fatigue and pain while riding, received a diagnosis of advanced testicular cancer. Worse, tests showed that the disease had spread to his lungs and brain.

After consultations with doctors, he chose an aggressive regimen of surgery and chemotherapy, even though the doctors estimated his chances of survival at less than 40 percent. Two years later, when they said that somehow, he had beaten the odds, Lance was already training for a comeback.

And come back he did. In 1999, he won the first of his seven Tour de France titles. And in 2002, *Sports Illustrated* magazine named him Sportsman of the Year.

Shortly after he fell ill, he launched the Lance Armstrong Foundation, devoted to fighting cancer through national awareness programs and funding initiatives for new treatments. But what role did the disease play in his motivation to excel? His website quotes him as saying, "Cancer was the best thing that ever happened to me" ("Lance's Bio," 2010).

PROBLEM: **Motivation is largely an internal and subjective process: How can we determine what motivates people like Lance Armstrong to work so hard at becoming the best in the world at what they do?**

Throughout this chapter, we will use Lance Armstrong's case to illustrate the basic concepts involved in motivation and emotion. We begin by defining what we mean by motivation, followed by consideration of what motivates people to work—or, like Lance Armstrong, to log hours of gruelling training for the Tour de France. Is it for some external (*extrinsic*) reward, or is it done for personal (*intrinsic*) satisfaction?

9.1 KEY QUESTION
What Motivates Us?

In everyday conversation, we use many terms that refer to motivation: *drive, instinct, energy, purpose, goal, intensity, perseverance, desire, want,* and *need*. You will note that all these terms refer to internal psychological "forces" that presumably make us do what we do. But the fact that we cannot observe these internal forces is what makes the psychology of motivation so challenging.

Questions about motivation seldom arise when people behave predictably: getting up in the morning, answering the phone, stopping for red lights, or greeting their friends. On the other hand, we *do* wonder what motivates people whose behavior falls outside the bounds of the ordinary, such as those who seem obsessed with food or sex, those who gamble away their life savings, those who rob banks—and those celebrities who behave indiscreetly.

Yet another part of the problem of motivation involves motivating people. If you are also an employer, you probably want to motivate your employees to work hard. If you are a coach, you want to motivate your players to train hard so the team can win. But let's bring it closer to home: As a student, you probably also want to learn how to motivate yourself to study a bit more.

So, how do we go about understanding and controlling motivation? Let's begin with the basics, by defining what we mean by *motivation*.

> ### Core Concept 9.1
>
> **Motives are internal dispositions to act in certain ways, although they can be influenced by multiple factors, both internal and external.**

More broadly, the concept of **motivation** refers to all the processes involved in (a) *sensing a need or desire,* and then (b) *activating and guiding the organism* by selecting, directing, and sustaining the mental and physical activity aimed at meeting the need or desire; and finally, when the need is met, (c) *reducing the sensation of need.* Take thirst, for example: On a warm day, you may sense a biological need for fluids that causes you to feel thirsty. That feeling of thirst then focuses your behavior on getting something to drink. When you have drunk your fill, the uncomfortable sensation of thirst diminishes, and the motive fades into the background.

Sometimes, of course, students drink beer not to quench their thirst, but because their friends are drinking or because TV ads have primed them to associate beer drinking with fun. In this case, the need is said to be purely *psychological,* not a *biological* need. In fact, many of our motives involve a complex combination of biological and psychological needs, especially those involving our social interactions, emotions, and goals. Take, for example, the complex processes that underlie our motivation for work.

Why People Work: McClelland's Theory

Most people work to make money, of course. Psychologists refer to money and other incentives as *extrinsic motivators,* because they come from outside the person. In general, **extrinsic motivation** involves external stimuli that goad an organism to action. For students, grades are one of the most powerful extrinsic motivators. Other examples of extrinsic motivators include food, drink, praise, awards, and sex.

People can also have *intrinsic motives* for working—motives that arise from within the person. You are intrinsically motivated when you enjoy meeting a new challenge on the job. More generally, **intrinsic motivation** involves engaging in an activity—work or play—for its own sake, regardless of an external reward or threat. You just do it because it meets a psychological need. In short, an intrinsically motivated activity is its own reward.

So, how could we assess a person's motivation for work? Psychologist David McClelland (1958) suspected that the stories people would tell to describe a series of ambiguous pictures could reveal their motives—using the *Thematic Apperception Test (TAT),* developed by Henry Murray (1938). You can see one such picture in Figure 9.1, but before you read the caption, imagine what might be happening with the boy and the violin. Initially, McClelland rated the stories for what they described as the **need for achievement (n Ach),** defined as the desire to attain a difficult, but desired, goal.

Now read the caption for Figure 9.1 if you haven't already done so: It gives examples of how a high–*n Ach* individual and a low–*n Ach* individual might interpret the same picture. With these examples in mind, you can judge whether your own story is low or high in *n Ach.*

Indeed, McClelland found that certain characteristics distinguish people with a high need for achievement, as measured by the stories they told about ambiguous pictures. They not only work harder and become more successful at their work than those lower in achievement motivation, but they also show more persistence on difficult tasks (McClelland, 1987b; Schultz & Schultz, 2006). In school, those with high *n Ach* tend to get better grades (Raynor, 1970), perhaps because they also tend to have higher IQ scores (Harris, 2004). In their career paths, they take more competitive jobs (McClelland, 1965), assume more leadership roles, and earn more rapid promotions (Andrews, 1967). If they go into business, they are more successful than those with low *n Ach* (McClelland, 1987a, 1993).

I/O Psychology: Putting Achievement Motivation in Perspective Worker motivation is the domain of industrial/organizational (I/O) psychologists, who know that not everyone has a high need for achievement, nor does every job offer intrinsic challenges. At least two other motives propel us to work (McClelland, 1985). For some of us, work meets a *need for affiliation,* while for others work satisfies a *need for power.* (The need for power should not necessarily be construed as negative but rather in the more positive sense of wanting to plan projects and manage people to get a job done.) Given

motivation   Refers to all the processes involved in initiating, directing, and maintaining physical and psychological activities.

CONNECTION CHAPTER 4

Money can also be a *secondary reinforcer*, because it can be associated with things that satisfy more basic needs (p. 147).

extrinsic motivation   The desire to engage in an activity to achieve an external consequence, such as a reward.

intrinsic motivation   The desire to engage in an activity for its own sake rather than for some external consequence, such as a reward.

need for achievement (n Ach)   In McClelland's theory, a mental state that produces a psychological motive to excel or to reach some goal.

FIGURE 9.1

Alternative Interpretations of an Ambiguous Picture

Story Showing High *n Ach:* The boy has just finished his violin lesson. He's happy at his progress and is beginning to believe that all his sacrifices have been worthwhile. To become a concert violinist, he will have to give up much of his social life and practice for many hours each day. Although he knows he could make more money by going into his father's business, he is more interested in being a great violinist and giving people joy with his music. He renews his personal commitment to do all it takes to make it.
Story Showing Low *n Ach:* The boy is holding his brother's violin and wishing he could play it. But he knows it isn't worth the time, energy, and money for lessons. He feels sorry for his brother, who has given up all the fun things in life to practice, practice, practice. It would be great to wake up one day and be a top-notch musician, but it doesn't happen that way. The reality is boring practice, no fun, and the likelihood that he'll become just another guy playing a musical instrument in a small-town band.

According to McClelland, people have different patterns of motivation for work. Some are motivated by affiliation, some by power, and some by the need for achievement (*n Ach*). A good leader knows how to capitalize on each of these.

Misty Hyman (top) and Naoko Takahashi (bottom) have very different perspectives on their athletic achievements—perspectives that reflect their cultural differences.

these three needs for work—achievement, affiliation, and power—it becomes the manager's task to structure jobs so that workers simultaneously meet their own needs as well as the manager's goal for productivity. (Managers, themselves, are usually motivated both by the needs for achievement and power.)

There are, of course, other reasons why we work beyond achievement, affiliation, and power needs. As we have said, work is a way to make a living. It is also a means to a desired lifestyle. But most of all, work is wrapped up in a person's identity: I am a teacher, a surgeon, a farmer, a park ranger, and so on. We focus on achievement, affiliation, and power here because those are the motives that have received the most attention so far by psychologists.

Should you find yourself in a management position, here are some need-specific pointers that come out of the research on motivating employees:

- Give those high in *n Ach* tasks that challenge them, but with achievable goals. Even though high–*n Ach* employees are not primarily motivated by extrinsic rewards, you can use bonuses, praise, and recognition effectively with them as feedback for good performance.

- A cooperative, rather than competitive, environment is best for those high in the need for *affiliation*. Find opportunities for such employees to work with others in teams rather than at socially isolated workstations.

- For those high in *power*, give them the opportunity to manage projects or work teams. You can encourage power-oriented workers to become leaders who help their subordinates satisfy their own needs. Again—although power motivation can be purely self-serving—don't fall into the trap of thinking that the need for power is necessarily bad.

Satisfying people's needs should make them happier with their jobs and more motivated to work. I/O psychologists call this *job satisfaction*. But does job satisfaction actually lead to better employee performance? Studies show that higher job satisfaction indeed correlates with lower absenteeism, lower employee turnover, and increased productivity—all of which are reflected in increased profits for any business (Schultz & Schultz, 2006).

It is also worth noting that the need for achievement is not limited to work. It can also boost performance in art, science, literature—and in athletics. Let's explore two instructive cases in point.

A Cross-Cultural View of Achievement   When she won the Olympic gold medal in the women's 200-meter butterfly, American swimmer Misty Hyman said:

> I think I just stayed focused. It was time to show the world what I could do. I am just glad I was able to do it. I knew I could beat Suzy O'Neil, deep down in my heart I believed it, and I know this whole week the doubts kept creeping in, they were with me on the blocks, but I just said, "No, this is my night" (Neal, 2000).

Contrast that with Naoko Takahashi's explanation of why she won the women's marathon:

> Here is the best coach in the world, the best manager in the world, and all of the people who support me—all of these things were getting together and became a gold medal. So I think I didn't get it alone, not only by myself (Yamamoto, 2000).

As you can see from these distinctively different quotes, the American's perspective on achievement motivation reflects a distinctively Western bias. Americans tend to see achievement as the result of individual talent, determination, intelligence, or attitude. Much of the world, however, sees achievement differently—in a broader context, as a combination of personal, social, and emotional factors (Markus et al., 2006).

This observation fits with Harry Triandis's (1990) distinction between cultures that emphasize *individualism* or *collectivism*. Western cultures, including the United States,

Canada, Britain, and Western Europe, emphasize **individualism.** People growing up in these cultures learn to place a premium on individual performance. By contrast, says Triandis, the cultures of Latin America, Asia, Africa, and the Middle East often emphasize **collectivism,** which values group loyalty and subordination of self to the group. Even in the collectivist cultures of Japan, Hong Kong, and South Korea, where high values are placed on doing well in school and business, the overarching goal is not achieving individual honors but bringing honor to the family, team, or other group.

Without a cross-cultural perspective, it would be easy for Americans to jump to the erroneous conclusion that motivation for individual achievement is a "natural" part of the human makeup. But Triandis's insight suggests that *n Ach* has a strong cultural component. In collectivist cultures, the social context is considered just as important for achievement as are talent, intelligence, or other personal characteristics in individualistic cultures.

individualism   The view, common in the Euro-American world, that places a high value on individual achievement and distinction.

collectivism   The view, common in Asia, Africa, Latin America, and the Middle East, that values group loyalty and pride over individual distinction.

The Unexpected Effects of Rewards on Motivation

We have suggested that extrinsic rewards are among the many reasons people work. But what do you suppose would happen if people were given extrinsic rewards (praise, money, or other incentives) for leisure activities—rewards for doing things that they find *intrinsically* enjoyable? Would the reward make the activity more—or less—enjoyable? Would a reward affect motivation?

Overjustification   To find out, Mark Lepper and his colleagues (1973) performed a classic experiment using two groups of schoolchildren who enjoyed drawing pictures. One group agreed to draw pictures for a reward certificate, while a control group made drawings without any expectation of reward. Both groups made their drawings enthusiastically. Some days later, however, when given the opportunity to draw pictures again, without a reward, the previously rewarded children were much less enthusiastic about drawing than those who had not been rewarded. In fact, the group that had received no rewards were actually *more* interested in drawing than they had been the first time!

Lepper's group concluded that external reinforcement had squelched the internal motivation in the reward group, an effect they called **overjustification.** As a result of overjustification, they reasoned, the children's motivation had changed from intrinsic to extrinsic. Consequently, the children were less interested in making pictures in the absence of reward. It appears that a reward can sometimes take the fun out of doing something for the sheer pleasure of it.

overjustification   The process by which extrinsic (external) rewards can sometimes displace internal motivation, as when a child receives money for playing video games.

When Do Rewards Work?   But do rewards *always* have this overjustification effect? If they did, how could we explain the fact that many professionals both love their work and get paid for it? Subsequent experiments have made it clear that rewards can interfere with intrinsic motivation, but only under certain conditions (Covington, 2000; Eisenberger & Cameron, 1996).

Specifically, the overjustification effect occurs when a reward is given *without regard for quality of performance.* This explains what happened to the children who were given certificates for their drawings. The same thing can happen in the business world, when employees are given year-end bonuses regardless of the quality of their work or in the classroom when all students get As.

The lesson is this: Rewards can be used effectively to motivate people—but only if the rewards are given for a job well done, contingent on quality of performance, not as a bribe. In general, rewards can have three major effects on motivation, depending on the conditions:

- Rewards can be an effective way of motivating people *to do things they would not otherwise want to do*—such as mowing the lawn or taking out the garbage.

- Rewards can actually add to intrinsic motivation, *if given for good performance:* We saw this clearly in the case of Lance Armstrong.

- And, as we have also seen, rewards can *interfere* with intrinsic motivation, *if given without regard for the quality of the work*—as Lepper's study showed.

Overjustification occurs when extrinsic rewards for doing something enjoyable take the intrinsic fun out of the activity. It is likely that this person would not enjoy video games as much if he were paid for playing.

So, if a child doesn't like to practice the piano, wash the dishes, or do homework, no amount of reward is going to change her attitude. On the other hand, if she enjoys piano practice, you can feel free to give praise or a special treat for a job well done. Such rewards can make a motivated person even more motivated. Similarly, if you have disinterested employees, don't bother trying to motivate them with pay raises (unless, of course, the reason they're unmotivated is that you are paying them poorly). But when it is deserved, impromptu praise, an unexpected award, or some other small recognition may make good employees perform even better. The danger of rewards seems to occur only when the rewards are extrinsic and are given without regard to the level of performance.

So, how do you think professors should reward students in order to encourage their best work?

[PSYCHOLOGY MATTERS]

Using Psychology to Learn Psychology

flow In Csikszentmihalyi's theory, an intense focus on an activity accompanied by increased creativity and near-ecstatic feelings. Flow involves intrinsic motivation.

The world's greatest achievements in music, art, science, business, and countless other pursuits usually arise from intrinsically motivated people pursuing ideas or goals in which they are deeply interested. People achieve this state of mind when absorbed by some problem or activity that makes them lose track of time and become oblivious to events around them. Psychologist Mihaly Csikszentmihalyi (1990, 1998) calls this special state of mind **flow**. And although some people turn to drugs or alcohol to experience an artificial flow feeling, meaningful work produces far more satisfying and sustained flow experiences. Athletes, such as Lance Armstrong, could probably not endure their intense daily training regimens without entering the flow state.

What is the link with studying and learning? If you find yourself lacking in motivation to learn the material for a particular class, the extrinsic promise of eventual good grades may not be enough to prod you to study effectively tonight. You may, however, be able to trick yourself into developing intrinsic motivation and flow by posing this question: What do people who are specialists in this field find interesting? Among other things, the experts are fascinated by an unsolved mystery, a theoretical dispute, or the possibility of an exciting practical application. A psychologist, for example, might wonder: What motivates violent behavior? Or, how can we increase people's motivation to achieve? Once you find such an issue, try to discover what solutions have been proposed. In this way, you will share the mindset of those who are leaders in the field. And—who knows?—perhaps you will become fascinated too.

Check Your Understanding

✓—[**Study** and **Review** at **MyPsychLab**]

1. **RECALL:** Give four reasons why psychologists find the concept of *motivation* useful.

2. **APPLICATION:** Give an example of an *extrinsic* motivator that might induce a child to do her homework.

3. **RECALL:** McClelland theorized that some workers are motivated by *n Ach*, while others are motivated by needs for

   a. money and praise.
   b. affiliation and power.
   c. sex and aggression.
   d. intrinsic reinforcement.

4. **UNDERSTANDING THE CORE CONCEPT:** Motivation takes many forms, but all involve inferred mental processes that select and direct our

   a. cognitions.
   b. behaviors.
   c. sensations.
   d. emotions.

Answers 1. The concept of motivation (1) connects observable behavior to internal states, (2) accounts for variability in behavior, (3) explains perseverance despite adversity, and (4) relates biology to behavior. **2.** Any incentive, such as money, extra TV time, or a favorite food. (Threat of punishment could also be an intrinsic motivator, but probably wouldn't work as well.) **3.** b **4.** b

9.2 KEY QUESTION
How Are Our Motivational Priorities Determined?

Until recently, psychology had no comprehensive explanation or theory that successfully accounted for the whole range of motivation. Hunger seemed so different from the need for achievement. Fears often have roots hidden from consciousness. Most biological drives feel unpleasant, but sexual arousal is pleasurable. The result was that some psychologists concentrated on the most basic survival motives, such as hunger and thirst, while other psychologists tried to explain sex, affiliation, creativity, and a variety of other motives. No one, however, managed to put together a motivational "theory of everything" that could encompass all our motives and, at the same time, be consistent with real-world observations.

But now, a new contender has emerged that, many psychologists say, may be able to do it all.

> **Core Concept 9.2**
>
> **A new theory combining Maslow's hierarchy with evolutionary psychology solves some long-standing problems by suggesting that functional, proximal, and developmental factors set our motivational priorities.**

About a half-century ago, Abraham Maslow proposed one of the most influential ideas ever to come out of psychology: that different motives have different priorities, based on a *hierarchy of needs*. For example, a threat to one's life usually trumps thirst. But thirst takes priority over the needs for affiliation or respect. But what about the artist who, in the *flow* state, disregards the need for food or warmth, sometimes for days at a time? And what about those "instincts" that drive animal migrations and, perhaps, some human behaviors, such as nursing in newborn infants? Let's see how a new hierarchy of needs incorporates these concepts.

Instinct Theory

Since the early days of William James, psychologists have realized that all creatures, humans included, possess an inborn set of behaviors that promotes survival. According to **instinct theory**, these built-in behaviors account reasonably well for the regular cycles of animal activity, found in essentially the same form across a species. We see these cycles in bird migrations, in the mating rituals of antelope, and in the return of salmon to the streams in which they were hatched only to spawn and die after a journey of more than 1,000 miles.

Although such so-called "instinctive" behavior patterns do not depend heavily on learning, experience can modify them. Thus, we see a combination of instinctive behavior and learning when bees communicate the location of food to each other or a mother cat helps her kittens hone their hunting skills. Such examples show that "instincts" involve both a lot of nature (genetically determined) and a little nurture (learning).

Because the term *instinct* seemed to explain so much, it migrated quickly from the scientific vocabulary to the speech of everyday life. Unfortunately, it lost precision in the process. So we now speak casually of "maternal instincts" or of an athlete who "instinctively catches the ball" or of an agent who has an "instinct" for picking new talent. In fact, we use the term in so many ways that its meaning has become almost meaningless—a mere label rather than an explanation for behavior.

As a result, the term *instinct* has long since dropped out of favor among scientists (Deckers, 2001). Ethologists, who study animal behavior in natural habitats, now prefer the term **fixed-action patterns**, more narrowly defined as unlearned behavior patterns that are triggered by identifiable stimuli and that occur throughout a species. Examples

instinct theory   The now-outmoded view that certain behaviors are completely determined by innate factors. The instinct theory was flawed because it overlooked the effects of learning and because it employed instincts merely as labels rather than as explanations for behavior.

fixed-action patterns   Genetically based behaviors, seen across a species, that can be set off by a specific stimulus. The concept of *fixed-action patterns* has replaced the older notion of instinct.

of fixed-action patterns include not only the "instinctive" behaviors described earlier but also such diverse behaviors as nest building in birds, suckling responses in newborn mammals, and dominance displays in baboons.

Do instincts—perhaps in their new guise as fixed-action patterns—explain any part of human behavior? The question raises the nature–nurture controversy under a new name. Biology *does* seem to account for some human behaviors, such as nursing, that we see in newborns. But instincts or fixed-action patterns are not very useful in explaining the array of more complex behaviors found in people at work and play. For example, while we might speculate that the motivation of a hard-driving executive could involve some basic "killer" instinct, such an explanation is no better than attributing Lance Armstrong's success to a bicycle-riding instinct.

Drive Theory

The concept of *drive* originated as an alternative to instinct for explaining behavior with a strong biological basis, as in eating, drinking, and mating. Psychologists defined a **biological drive** as the state of energy or tension that moves an organism to meet a biological need (Woodworth, 1918). Thus, thirst drives an animal in need of water to drink. Likewise, a need for food arouses a hunger that drives organisms to eat. So, in **drive theory**, a biological **need** produces a drive state that, in turn, channels behavior toward meeting the need. When the need is satisfied, drive level subsides—a process called *drive reduction.* You have experienced drive reduction when you feel satisfied after a big meal or when you get in a warm bath after being chilled.

According to drive theory, what organisms seek is a balanced condition in the body, known as **homeostasis** (Hull, 1943, 1952). So, creatures that have an *un*balanced condition (caused, say, by lack of fluids) are driven to seek a homeostatic balance (by drinking). Similarly, we can understand hunger as an imbalance in the body's energy supply. It is this imbalance that drives, or motivates, a food-deprived animal to eat in order to restore a condition of equilibrium.

Unfortunately for drive theory, the story of motivation has proved not to be that simple. In particular, drive theory faltered when cognitive, social, and cultural forces were at work, as we will see later in our discussion of hunger. Moreover, drive theory cannot explain why, in the absence of any apparent deprivation or obvious needs, organisms sometimes act merely to *increase* stimulation. It is hard to imagine, for example, a basic need or a biological drive that could prompt people to go skiing or jump out of airplanes. Even at an animal level, laboratory rats that are hungry or thirsty and given opportunity to eat or drink in a new maze environment do not initially eat or drink. Rather, they explore the novel setting first: Curiosity trumps hunger and thirst (Zimbardo & Montgomery, 1957).

Cognitive psychologists also pointed out that biological drives could not explain behavior motivated by goals, such as getting a promotion at work or an A in psychology. Nor will drives explain why laboratory rats will cross an electrified grid merely to reach a novel environment to explore or why Lance Armstrong endured thousands of hours of grueling training to win glory. Psychologists call these *psychological motives.* In contrast to *biological drives,* psychological motives serve no immediate biological need but, rather, are strongly rooted in learning, incentives, threats, or social and cultural pressures. The human need for achievement is another good example of a psychological motive. Obviously, many motivated behaviors, especially in humans, can stem from a combination of biological and cognitive or environmental factors. We will see the practical side of the biological versus psychological distinction later when we dissect hunger, the quintessential example of a combined biological drive and psychological motive.

For these reasons, psychologists have concluded that drive theory holds some—but not all—answers to the riddle of motivation. Still, they have been reluctant to abandon the concept of *drive,* which has come to mean a biologically based motive that plays an important role in survival or reproduction. We now look on drive theory as a useful but incomplete theory of motivation.

biological drive   A motive, such as thirst, that is based primarily in biology. A *drive* is a state of tension that motivates an organism to satisfy a biological *need.*

drive theory   Developed as an alternative to instinct theory, drive theory explains motivation as a process in which a biological *need* produces a *drive* that moves an organism to meet the need. For most drives this process returns the organism to a balanced condition, known as *homeostasis.*

need   In drive theory, a need is a biological imbalance (such as dehydration) that threatens survival if the need is left unmet. Biological needs are believed to produce drives.

homeostasis   The body's tendency to maintain a biologically balanced condition, especially with regard to nutrients, water, and temperature.

According to drive theory, a need for fluids motivates (drives) us to drink. A homeostatic balance is reached when the need is satisfied.

Freud's Psychodynamic Theory

Sigmund Freud challenged the view that we know what motivates our own behavior. Instead, Freud proposed, most human motivation stems from the murky depths of the unconscious mind, which he called the *id*. There, he said, lurked two basic desires: *eros*, the erotic desire; and *thanatos*, the aggressive or destructive impulse. Virtually everything we do, said Freud, is based on one of these urges or on the maneuvers that the mind uses to keep these desires in check. To avoid mental problems, we must continually seek acceptable outlets for our sexual and aggressive needs. Freud believed that work, especially creative work, indirectly satisfied the sex drive, while aggressive acts like swearing and shouting or playing aggressive games serve as a psychologically safe outlet for our deeper destructive tendencies.

It is important to realize that Freud developed his ideas in the heyday of instinct theory, so eros and thanatos are often thought of as instincts. But it would oversimplify Freud's theory to think of it as just another instinct theory. He wasn't trying to explain the everyday, biologically based behaviors that we find in eating, drinking, mating, nursing, and sleeping. Rather, he was trying to explain the symptoms we find in mental disorders such as phobias or depression.

The new evolutionary theory of motivation borrows Freud's notion that two main motives underlie all we do. Evolutionary psychologists agree that just two fundamental motives underlie everything we do. But in place of sex and aggression, the new theory posits the Darwinian needs for survival and reproduction.

Modern-day psychologists also agree that Freud had put his finger on another important idea: Much mental activity, including motivation, *does* occur outside of consciousness. But, as we saw in Chapter 8, they stand divided on the details of the Freudian unconscious, a thread that will continue in the next chapter (Bornstein, 2001; Westen, 1998).

One more of Freud's ideas was also on target, according to the evolutionary theorists. Among the principal theories of motivation discussed in this chapter, Freud's is the only one that takes a *developmental* approach to motivation. That is, Freud taught that our motives undergo change as we move from childhood to adulthood. With maturity, he said, our sexual and aggressive desires become less conscious. We also develop more and more subtle and sophisticated ways of meeting our needs—particularly desires for sex and aggression—without getting into trouble (see Table 9.1).

TABLE 9.1 Theories of Motivation Compared

Theories	Emphasis	Examples
Instinct Theory	Biological processes that motivate behavior patterns specific to a species	bird migration, fish schooling
Drive Theory	Needs produce drives that motivate behavior until drives are reduced	hunger, thirst
Freud's Theory	Motivation arises from unconscious desires; developmental changes in these urges appear as we mature	sex, aggression
Maslow's Theory	Motives result from needs, which occur in a priority order (a needs hierarchy)	esteem needs, self-actualization
Evolutionary Theory	Priority of motives determined by functional, proximal, and developmental factors	Food odor (proximal stimulus) may raise the priority of hunger drive

Maslow's Hierarchy of Needs

What happens when you must choose between meeting a biological need and fulfilling a desire based on learning—as when you choose between sleeping and staying up all night to study for an exam? Abraham Maslow (1970) said that you usually act on your most pressing needs, which occur in a natural *hierarchy* or priority order, with biological needs taking precedence. Unlike the other theories of motivation we have considered, Maslow's perspective attempts to span the whole gamut of human motivation from biological drives to social motives to creativity (Nicholson, 2007).

Maslow's most memorable innovation, then, was his **hierarchy of needs**, which posited six classes of needs listed in priority order (see Figure 9.2). The "higher" needs exert their influence on behavior only when the more basic needs are satisfied:

hierarchy of needs   In Maslow's theory, the notion that needs occur in priority order, with the biological needs as the most basic.

- *Biological needs,* such as hunger and thirst, lie at the base of the hierarchy and must be satisfied before higher needs take over.
- *Safety needs* motivate us to avoid danger, but only when biological needs are reasonably well satisfied. Thus, a hungry animal may risk its physical safety for food until it gets its belly full, at which point the safety needs take over.
- *Love, attachment, and affiliation needs* energize us when we are no longer concerned about the more basic drives such as hunger, thirst, and safety. These "higher" needs make us want to affiliate with others, to love, and to be loved.
- *Esteem needs,* following next in the hierarchy, include the needs to like oneself, to see oneself as competent and effective, and to do what is necessary to earn the respect of oneself and others.
- *Self-actualization,* the "highest" need, but with the lowest priority, motivates us to seek the fullest development of our creative human potential. Self-actualizing persons are self-aware, self-accepting, socially responsive, spontaneous, and open to novelty and challenge.

CONNECTION CHAPTER 7

Note the similarity between *self-transcendence* and Erikson's notion of *generativity,* which involves making a contribution to family, work, society, or future generations (p. 309).

In his original formulation, Maslow put self-actualization at the peak of the needs hierarchy. But late in his life, Maslow suggested yet another highest order need, which he called *self-transcendence.* This he conceptualized as going beyond self-actualization, seeking to further some cause beyond the self (Koltko-Rivera, 2006). Satisfying this need could involve anything from volunteer work to absorption in religion, politics, music, or an intellectual pursuit. What distinguishes self-transcendence from self-actualization is its shift beyond personal pleasure or other egocentric benefits.

But how does Maslow's theory square with observation? It explains why we may neglect our friends or our career goals in favor of meeting pressing biological needs signaled by pain, thirst, sleepiness, or sexual desire. Yet—in contradiction to Maslow's theory—people may sometimes neglect their basic biological needs in favor of higher ones, as we might see in a father risking his life to rescue his child from a burning building. To Maslow's credit, he recognized these problems. Just as important, he called attention to the role of social motivation in our lives at a time when these motives were being neglected by psychology (Nicholson, 2007). As a result, a great body of work now demonstrates this need we have for relationships with others.

Critics point out that Maslow's theory also fails to explain other important human behaviors: why you might miss a meal when you are absorbed in an interesting book or why sensation seekers would pursue risky interests (such as rock climbing or auto racing) that override their safety needs. The theory also fails to explain the behavior of people who deliberately take their own lives. And it ignores the powerful sex drive.

Cross-cultural psychologists have also criticized Maslow's theory and other "self theories," noting that an emphasis on self-actualization applies primarily to individualistic cultures, which

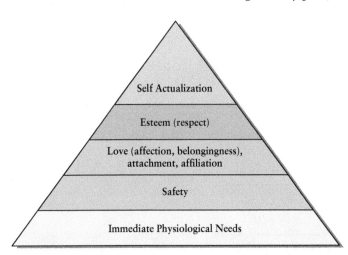

FIGURE 9.2
Maslow's Hierarchy of Needs

emphasize individual achievement (Gambrel & Cianci, 2003). In contrast, group-oriented (collectivistic) cultures emphasize success of the group rather than *self*-actualization (Shiraev & Levy, 2006). In fairness to Maslow, however, we should note that he recognized that there could be cultural differences in motivation (1943). And even the severest critics will acknowledge that, with all its flaws, Maslow's theory was an important step toward a comprehensive theory of motivation. 📖

📖—**Read** about Maslow's Influence at **MyPsychLab**

Putting It All Together: A New Hierarchy of Needs

In the face of such criticism, can we find something in Maslow's theory worth saving? Douglas Kenrick and his colleagues (2010) point to the idea of a *motivational hierarchy* as Maslow's singular great insight. But, they note, its major difficulty is that our motivational priorities are not rigidly fixed—as Maslow himself realized. Indeed, an individual may change motivational priorities from time to time. Nor do different people necessarily have the same motivational priorities. The solution, said Kenrick's group, is to understand that that we must view the needs hierarchy as fluid—subject to change by three sorts of influences, seen as what they call the *functional, proximal,* and *developmental levels of analysis*.

The **functional level of analysis** looks at the *function* of a motive, which (from an evolutionary perspective) relates to survival and reproductive success. Functional influences arrange our motives in a kind of "default" hierarchy, grounded in the basic needs, such as hunger and thirst. These needs motivate us to seek such things as food drink, warmth, and shelter, without which we could not live. Similarly, sexual motivation arises from the evolutionary mandate to propel one's genes into future generations. This need for sexual gratification and reproduction, then, gives rise to a whole range of social needs, including not only the physical urge for sex but also needs for affiliation, esteem, and parenting. These "higher" reproductive needs, however, generally have lower priority than the survival needs.

functional level of analysis Concerns the adaptive function of a motive in terms of the organism's survival and reproduction.

Proximal means "nearby"—so the **proximal level of analysis** focuses on immediate events, objects, incentives, and threats that influence motivation. For example, the aroma of freshly baked bread is a proximal stimulus that can suddenly arouse the hunger motive. Or imagine that you are at a theater enjoying a movie when someone yells, "Fire!" Your motivation suddenly shifts from relaxation and enjoyment of the movie to fear and self-preservation. In more formal terms, an important *proximal* stimulus can trigger a temporary modification in your usual motivational hierarchy.

proximal level of analysis Concerns stimuli in the organism's immediate environment, which can change motivational priorities. (In humans, *proximal* could also refer to things that the individual is thinking about.)

Your stage of life can also affect your motivational profile. Thus, the **developmental level of analysis** shows how the order in which motives appear changes throughout your life span. For example, hunger, thirst, and contact comfort held center stage when you were a baby, but you didn't give a whit about reproduction or about garnering the esteem of your peers. But, when you became a teenager, sexual motives and the need for social approval probably occupied a prominent place in your needs hierarchy, sometimes trumping even the biological hunger and thirst drives. Likewise, proximal cues may affect you differently at different developmental stages. So, you may be most sensitive to different proximal cues—for example to contact comfort when you are young or to a comely peer in your teens.

developmental level of analysis Concerns changes in the organism's developmental progress that might change motivational priorities, as when hormones heighten sexual interest in adolescence.

Less obvious are the evolutionary foundations for artistic creativity, athletic pursuits, stamp collecting, or any of a thousand other human pursuits. And this is where the new theory proposed by Kenrick and his group becomes controversial: They push self-actualization off the pinnacle of Maslow's hierarchy and replace it with needs for mating and parenting (which Maslow had neglected). All the productivity and creativity that Maslow thought of as self-actualization is really just a means to the real ends of reproduction and assuring the survival of one's genetic offspring. As you might expect, critics have raised objections (Ackerman & Bargh, 2010; Kesebir et al., 2010; Lyubomirsky & Boehm, 2010; Peterson & Park, 2010).

What Kenrick's group may have overlooked is the possibility that "higher" motives—including a need to be creative or to satisfy one's curiosity—may have become functionally independent of their evolutionary roots. Certainly, creative persons—famous

FIGURE 9.3
Evolutionary Psychology's Revision of Maslow's Hierarchy

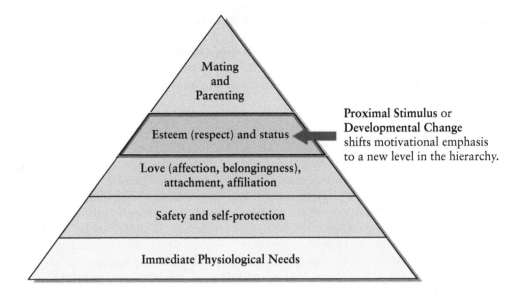

Proximal Stimulus or Developmental Change shifts motivational emphasis to a new level in the hierarchy.

Mating and Parenting

Esteem (respect) and status

Love (affection, belongingness), attachment, affiliation

Safety and self-protection

Immediate Physiological Needs

entertainers, for example—have an advantage in the mating game. Nevertheless, evolution may also have taken a shortcut by wiring our creative urges directly to our pleasure centers. If that is true—and it remains to be explored by researchers—people may pursue their interests just for the pure joy of doing so (Peterson & Park, 2010). This *intrinsic motivation* may have become functionally independent of its original biological aims.

Where does all this leave us? A consensus seems to be emerging on a few ideas that may bring some unity to the field of motivation at long last (Schaller et al., 2010). Most psychologists would likely agree that:

- Our motives have a "default" hierarchy or priority order that is essentially the same from person to person—much as Maslow described.
- This default hierarchy of motives must be understood in a functional or evolutionary context, with the most basic motives being related to survival, followed by motives related to reproduction and to survival of offspring.
- An individual's motivational hierarchy is not rigid but can be influenced by proximal stimuli and by the person's developmental level.

As we have noted, there remains some disagreement as to whether the "higher" motives (such as creativity) are always based on the reproductive urge or can instead become independent *intrinsic* motives.

What this new hybrid approach to motivation does for us, then, is to bring together Maslow's hierarchy and evolutionary psychology to make a big tent that can encompass motivation of all sorts—from hunger and thirst to affiliation, status, and creativity. All must be ultimately understood in terms of a hierarchy and in terms of their evolutionary roots. We still don't know precisely how the brain manages to arrange and rearrange the motivational hierarchy, but at last we may have a framework within which the theoretical details can be worked out.

[PSYCHOLOGY MATTERS]

Determining What Motivates Others

Where do you start when you want to know what motivates a person's behavior—perhaps someone who has been self-destructive or hurtful to you? We suggest caution before deciding that the source is some immutable personality trait. Instead, we recommend first looking for any external incentives or threats—extrinsic motivators—that might be at work. Many times, these will tell the whole story.

Beyond that, we suggest you consider social motivation. While Maslow emphasized social motives in his hierarchy of needs, he wasn't the first to suggest their importance in human behavior. Alfred Adler, a contemporary of Sigmund Freud, was arguably the first social psychologist (Ansbacher & Ansbacher, 1956). Adler taught that problem behavior often grows out of feelings of personal inadequacy and perceived social threats. The counterbalancing trend in the healthy personality is a goal or need for cooperation and the desire for acceptance by others. He called this *social interest.* Modern social psychologists combine the notions of social motivation with extrinsic incentives and threats in what they call the "power of the situation."

Applying these notions to Lance Armstrong, it is not a stretch to suspect that his motivation involves a highly competitive desire to win. But whether that is a "neurotic" goal growing out of deep feelings of inferiority, we do not have enough information to know. Should he ever seek psychological help, the therapist would certainly raise that question—to which Armstrong may or may not know the answer. 📖

Adler's ideas are much more complex than we can detail here. Suffice it to say that a person who feels threatened may respond defensively, with annoying behavior or aggression. If you are that person's parent, teacher, employer, or friend, the trick is not to respond in kind. Don't give attention to an attention getter. Don't respond aggressively to an aggressor. Don't try to "get even" with a vengeful person. And don't smother a withdrawn individual with pity. Instead, treat the person with respect—and an understanding of the social motives behind the unwanted behavior.

CONNECTION CHAPTER 11

For social psychologists, the *power of the situation* better explains human behavior than do personality traits (p. 462).

Read about Athletes and Performance Enhancing Drugs at **MyPsychLab**

Check Your Understanding

✓ **Study** and **Review** at **MyPsychLab**

1. **RECALL:** Why has the term *instinct* dropped out of favor with psychologists?

2. **ANALYSIS:** What is the role of *homeostasis* in drive theory?

3. **RECALL:** In Freud's theory, our basic motives are
   a. social.
   b. conscious.
   c. unconscious.
   d. established by evolutionary pressures.

4. **ANALYSIS:** Explain why self-actualization is characterized as the "highest" need, but with the lowest priority.

5. **UNDERSTANDING THE CORE CONCEPT:** The evolution-based modification of Maslow's hierarchy of needs suggests that our motivational priorities can change, depending primarily on
   a. our developmental level and proximal stimuli.
   b. our stress level and social status.
   c. our intellect and experience.
   d. peer pressure and social status.

Answers 1. *Instinct* has become an imprecise term that merely labels behavior rather than explaining it. **2.** *Homeostasis* refers to the equilibrium condition to which an organism tends to return after reducing a biological drive. **3.** c **4.** Self-actualization is at the top of the pyramid of Maslow's hierarchy—and in this sense is the "highest" of the needs. However, the needs lower in the hierarchy are more basic and so have higher priority than self-actualization. **5.** a

---

┌─9.3 **KEY QUESTION**
Where Do Hunger and Sex Fit into the Motivational Hierarchy?

In this section of the chapter, we focus on hunger and sex, two quite different motives that represent the twin forces that evolution has used to shape the human species: the drives to *survive* and *reproduce*. Everyone reading this book inherited the genes of ancestors who managed to do both. Here's the big idea around which this section is organized.

[
Core Concept 9.3

Although dissimilar in many respects, hunger and sex both have evolutionary origins, and each has an essential place in the motivational hierarchy.
]

Ultimately, our task is to show how an evolutionary new perspective on motivation manages to bring both of these motives together under one theoretical umbrella.

Hunger: A Homeostatic Drive *and* a Psychological Motive

You will probably survive if you don't have sex, but you will die if you don't eat. Unlike sex, hunger is one of our personal biological survival mechanisms (Rozin, 1996). When food is available, the hunger drive leads quite naturally to eating. Yet there is more to hunger than biology: It has social and cognitive foundations, too, as we will see in the *multiple-systems approach* to hunger and weight control (see Figure 9.4).

The Multiple-Systems Approach to Hunger Your brain generates hunger by combining biological and psychological information of many kinds, including your body's energy requirements and nutritional state, your food preferences, food cues in your environment, and cultural demands. For example, your readiness to eat a slice of bacon depends on factors such as your blood sugar level, how long it has been since you last ate, whether you like bacon, what time of day it is (breakfast?), whether a friend might be offering you a slice, and whether bacon is an acceptable food in your culture. Assembling all these data, the brain sends signals to neural, hormonal, organ, and muscle systems to start or stop bacon seeking and eating (DeAngelis, 2004b; Flier & Maratos-Flier, 2007). As you may have surmised, the multiple-systems approach is another way of saying that hunger operates at many

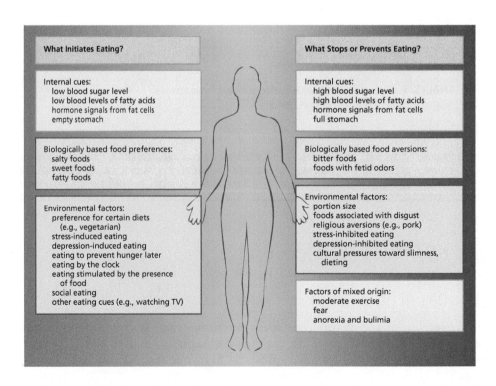

FIGURE 9.4

Multiple-Systems Model of Hunger and Eating

Hunger isn't just a matter of an empty stomach. The multiple-systems model combines all the known influences on hunger and eating.

levels of the motivational hierarchy, meeting many needs that do not necessarily stem from the biological hunger drive.

Biological Factors Affecting Hunger and Eating   In the brain, the stomach, the blood, and fat cells stored all over the body, a host of biological factors work to regulate hunger and eating behavior. Among the most important are these:

- **Brain mechanisms controlling hunger.** The hypothalamus is literally a "nerve center" for hunger, with one region activating feelings of hunger and another dampening hunger. But the hypothalamus does not operate alone. Other regions, particularly in the brain stem, work with the hypothalamus to monitor the status of blood sugar, nutrients in the gut, and fat stores, using a suite of receptors and chemical messengers (Flier, 2006).

- **Set point (homeostatic) mechanisms.** An internal biological "scale" continually assesses the body's fat stores and informs the central nervous system of the result. Whenever deposits stored in specialized fat cells fall below a certain level, or **set point**, signals trigger eating behavior—a homeostatic process. Research suggests that obesity may result when this homeostatic balance gets off kilter. Studies implicate certain chemicals (such as the hormone *ghrelin*) that signal hunger, along with others (such as *leptin*) that signal when the set point has been reached. Animals lacking leptin, for example, continue to eat even when not hungry (Grimm, 2007).

- **Sensors in the stomach.** Pressure detectors in the stomach signal fullness or a feeling of emptiness. These messages are sent to the brain, where they combine with information about blood nutrients and the status of the body's fat cells.

- **Reward system preferences.** The brain's reward system gives us preferences for sweet and high-fat foods. These preferences have a biological basis that evolved to steer our ancestors toward calorie-dense foods, enabling them to survive when food supplies were unpredictable. This tendency has been exploited in modern times by the manufacturers of sweet and fatty snack foods.

- **Exercise.** Physical activity also contributes to hunger and satiation. Extreme exercise provokes hunger, but studies show that moderate exercise actually suppresses appetite (Hill & Peters, 1998).

These biological hunger mechanisms operate at the most basic level of the needs hierarchy.

Psychological Factors Affecting Hunger and Eating   In addition to the biological mechanisms that regulate eating, our emotional state can encourage or discourage eating. For example, both humans and animals refrain from eating when they feel threatened. (These are some of the *proximal* factors that we discussed earlier.) Stress and depression can also affect appetite, although the effects are variable: Some people respond by eating more and some by eating less.

Learning plays a role too. Because we also associate certain situations with food, we may feel hungry regardless of our biological needs. This explains why you suddenly want to eat when you notice that the clock says lunchtime. It also explains why you snack while watching TV or dish up a second helping at Thanksgiving dinner.

Culture can have a huge effect too. This can be seen in societies, such as the United States, where media influences and social norms promote a thin body type. On the other hand, in Oceania, where larger figures are often considered more attractive, social norms promote heftier bodies (Newman, 2004).

While the ideal promoted in movies, magazines, and on TV is one of thinness, Americans receive a different message from commercials that encourage eating. That message, combined with an abundance of cheap, tasty junk food results in a growing obesity problem in a population obsessed with weight. Moreover, as the influence of U.S. culture becomes more global, American eating habits have become more universal, with the result that calorie-dense snacks and fast foods are making people fatter all over the world (Hébert, 2005; Popkin, 2007).

set point   Refers to the tendency of the body to maintain a certain level of body fat and body weight.

In the global economy, calorie-dense fast foods have become readily available, changing dietary habits and contributing to a worldwide epidemic of obesity.

anorexia nervosa   An eating disorder involving persistent loss of appetite that endangers an individual's health and stemming from emotional or psychological reasons rather than from organic causes.

bulimia nervosa   An eating disorder characterized by eating binges followed by "purges," induced by vomiting or laxatives; typically initiated as a weight-control measure.

CONNECTION CHAPTER 12

People with obsessive-compulsive disorder have persistent and intrusive thoughts and may also feel compelled to act out ritual behaviors (p. 533).

Eating Disorders Only rarely does the condition called *anorexia* (persistent lack of appetite) result from a physical disorder, such as shock, nausea, or an allergic reaction. More commonly, the cause has psychological roots—in which case the syndrome is called **anorexia nervosa**. "Nervous anorexia" typically manifests itself in extreme dieting. It can be so extreme, in fact, that the disorder posts the highest mortality rate of any recognized psychological condition (Agras et al., 2004; Park, 2007). In the following discussion, we will revert to common usage by calling the disorder simply *anorexia*.

What qualifies as anorexia? When a person weighs less than 85 percent of her desirable weight and still worries about being fat, anorexia is the likely diagnosis. People with anorexia may also face a problem called *bulimia* or **bulimia nervosa**, characterized by periods of binge eating followed by drastic purging measures, which may include vomiting, fasting, or using laxatives. In many cases, depression and obsessive-compulsive disorder further complicate the clinical picture.

Commonly, a person with anorexia acts as though she is unaware of her condition and continues dieting, ignoring other danger signs that may include cessation of menstruation, osteoporosis, bone fractures, and shrinkage of brain tissue. Over time, bulimic vomiting, done to purge the food she has eaten, results in damage to her esophagus, throat, and teeth caused by stomach acid.

What causes anorexia? A strong hint comes from the finding that most persons with the disorder are young females. Significantly, such eating disorders are most prevalent in Western cultures, particularly among middle- and upper-middle-class young women (Striegel-Moore & Bulik, 2007). Clearly, it is not a hunger disorder caused by lack of resources.

Those with anorexia commonly have histories of good behavior, as well as academic and social success, but they nevertheless starve themselves, hoping to become more acceptably thin and attractive (Keel & Klump, 2003). In an effort to lose imagined "excess" weight, the person with anorexia rigidly suppresses her appetite, feeling rewarded for such self-control when she does lose pounds and inches—but never feeling quite thin enough (see Figure 9.5).

Work focusing on genetic factors has complicated the assumption that social pressures cause anorexia and bulimia (Novotney, 2009; Striegel-Moore & Bulik, 2007). This makes sense from an evolutionary standpoint, says clinical psychologist Shan Guisinger (2003). She points out the hyperactivity often seen in individuals with anorexia—as opposed to the lethargy common in most starving persons—suggesting that hyperactivity under conditions of starvation may have been an advantage that motivated the ancestors of modern-day individuals with anorexia to leave famine-impoverished environments.

FIGURE 9.5

Women's Body Images

April Fallon and Paul Rozin (1985) asked female college students to give their current weight, their ideal weight, and the weight they believed men would consider ideal. The results show that the average woman felt that her current weight was significantly higher than her ideal weight—and higher than the weight she thought men would like. To make matters worse, women also see their bodies as looking larger than they actually are (Thompson, 1986). When men were asked to rate themselves on a similar questionnaire, Fallon and Rozin found no such discrepancies between ideal and actual weights. But, when asked what they saw as the ideal weight for women, they chose a higher weight than women did. No wonder women go on diets more often than men and are more likely to have a major eating disorder (Mintz & Betz, 1986; Striegel-Moore et al., 1993).

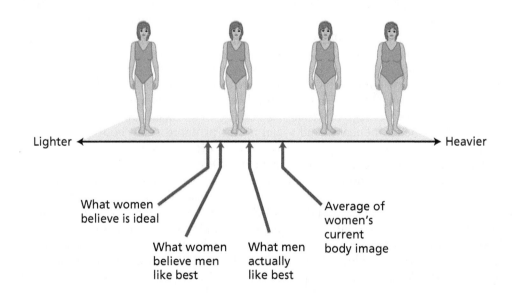

Lighter ← → Heavier

What women believe is ideal

What women believe men like best

What men actually like best

Average of women's current body image

All in all, it is beginning to appear that anorexia—like hunger itself—is a condition caused by multiple factors that stem from biology, cognition, and social pressures.

Obesity and Weight Control At the other extreme of weight control, the problem of obesity has grown at an alarming rate since the early 1980s, with the result that 65 percent of Americans are overweight and 30 percent are now classified as obese (DeAngelis, 2004b; Mann et al., 2007). The real problem, of course, is not obesity but the associated health risks for such problems as heart disease, stroke, and diabetes—although experts disagree on just how much of a problem this is among those who are only slightly overweight (Couzin, 2005; Gibbs, 2005). Unfortunately, the fundamental causes of this obesity epidemic are not well understood (Doyle, 2006).

No one in the field of obesity research believes that the condition results from the lack of "will power"—a simplistic and scientifically useless concept, as we will see in the next section (Friedman, 2003). Rather, most experts believe that obesity results from multiple factors. Prominent among them are poor diet, including super-size portions and an increasing prevalence of food high in fat and sugar. In one laboratory experiment, rats given a diet of sausage, Ho Hos, pound cake, bacon, and cheesecake lost the ability to control their eating and quickly became obese (Johnson & Kenny, 2010).

Genetics also have a role (Bell, 2010; DeAngelis, 2004a; Flier & Maratos-Flier, 2007), but so does activity level. For example, the long-term Nurses' Health Study showed that every two-hour increase in daily TV watching translated into a 23-percent increase in obesity among the nurses in the sample (Hu et al., 2003). Finally, one study suggests not getting enough sleep may trigger eating and a resulting weight gain, perhaps because the body mistakes sleepiness for hunger (Hasler et al., 2004).

From an evolutionary viewpoint, humans are still Stone Age creatures biologically adapted to deal with periods of feast and famine. So we tend to eat more than we need when food is abundant as a hedge against future periods of starvation. Unfortunately, this Stone-Age strategy is not well suited to life in a modern world—where most people in developed countries also have no need to expend energy running down game or digging roots. Nor are we well suited for a world of French fries, deep-dish pizzas, donuts, Snickers, and nachos, which appeal to our deeply ingrained tastes for salty, fatty, and sweet foods—which just happen to be rich in calories (Parker-Pope, 2009; Pinel et al., 2000).

The problem is also not lack of awareness. Americans, especially, seem obsessed by weight and weight loss, as a glance at the magazine headlines on the newsstand will show. At any given time, approximately three out of ten adult Americans say they are on some sort of weight-control diet (Gallup, 2010).

Yet, despite all we know about hunger and weight control, no one has yet discovered a weight-loss scheme that really works for most people. Notwithstanding nationally advertised claims, no diet, surgical procedure, drug, or other weight-loss gimmick has ever produced long-term weight loss for a majority of the people who have tried it. At this point, the best odds for most people lie in cognitive-behavioral therapies (Institute of Medicine, 2002; Rich, 2004). And for those struggling with weight, it is encouraging to know that some potentially effective weight-control chemicals are being tested as you read this, although it may be several years before anything both safe and effective comes to market (Flier & Maratos-Flier, 2007). In the meantime, experts suggest that the best pathway to long-term weight control involves maintaining a well-balanced diet, a program of moderate exercise and, if you want some extra help, cognitive-behavioral therapy.

The Problem of Will Power and Chocolate Cookies

Psychologists don't talk much about "will power," although the term can be heard in everyday conversation, where it usually refers to resisting food, drink, or some other temptation. In particular, psychologists don't like the archaic assumption of the "will" as a special faculty of the mind—a throwback to 19th-century phrenology. Thus, "will power" is like the term "instinct"—merely a label rather than an explanation. Psychologists also object to the term "will power" because it is often used as a moral judgment, suggesting that a person has a deficiency in character—a "weak will."

Alternatives to Will Power   Modern psychologists usually prefer terms such as *self-control* or *impulse control*—terms that carry less baggage and can be related to environmental influences and to known brain mechanisms. For example, we know that controlling one's eating is more difficult during the holiday season, with its abundance of food. Similarly, damage to parts of the limbic system is known to make control of eating more difficult.

Psychologists have also contrived devilish tests to measure impulse control. What have they found? To nobody's surprise, the ability to control one's impulses correlates with all sorts of positive outcomes, including better mental health, more effective coping skills, better relationships, and higher academic achievement. But such findings still leave the big question unanswered: What *is* self-control—or "will power"?

The Biology of Self-Control   A team of researchers at Florida State University seems to have placed the ability to resist temptation on a solid scientific footing (Gailliot et al., 2007). What they found is that self-control has a biological basis. And it also has a price.

The Florida group first placed undergraduate psychology students in one of several onerous situations in which they were asked to exercise self-control—such as resisting a tempting plate of warm, freshly baked chocolate cookies or watching a funny video clip without laughing. Then the researchers gave the students a second task, such as a scrambled-word problem or a hand–eye coordination test. A control group also performed the second task, but they were not first asked to stifle their laughter, nor were they exposed to plates of tempting cookies.

Before we go any further, see if you can predict who did better on the second task. Was it those in the experimental group, who had to resist their impulses? Or was it the control group, who had been allowed to indulge themselves?

You were right if you guessed that those who had to face down temptation (resisting the cookies or soberly watching the funny video) were *less* successful on the second task. Apparently self-control is a cognitive resource that, like physical stamina, can become temporarily depleted. And, surprisingly, self-control seems to have a physical presence in the blood, as well as in behavior. The study found that those who had been asked to control their urges had lower blood-sugar levels than those who had not restrained themselves. Because sugar (glucose) is an energy source for the body, the researchers speculate that exerting will power used up some of that energy, making people less efficient on the second task (Baumeister et al., 1998, 2007; Wargo, 2009).

But there is hope for those weak of will! A sugared drink not only brought blood glucose back up to its original level, but it brought the performance of the self-controllers back to the level of the indulgers. Apparently, what we call "will power" is based, at least in part, on the body's ready energy reserves.

So, should you have a cola and a candy bar to boost your "will" before the next psychology test? Probably not such a good idea, says Matthew Gaillot, leader of the Florida study—especially if you are trying to control your weight. Better, he says, to keep your energy level up with a diet that includes longer-lasting proteins or complex carbohydrates (Cynkar, 2007).

And some additional advice from a cognitive perspective: If you want to insure that you are mentally sharp, moderation is a better strategy than denial.

Sexual Motivation: An Urge You Can Live Without

No one enjoys being hungry or thirsty. But we can't say the same for sex: Unlike hunger or thirst, *arousal* of the sex drive can be pleasurable. And even though sexually aroused individuals may seek to reduce the tension by mating or other sexual activity, the sex drive is not homeostatic—again unlike hunger and thirst. That is, having sex does not return the body to an equilibrium condition. Moreover, sexual motivation can serve diverse goals, including pleasure, reproduction, and social bonding. In other words, sex—like hunger—is linked with diverse motives in the hierarchy.

In one other respect, sexual motivation has a kinship with hunger and thirst: It has its roots in survival. But even in this respect, sex is unique among biological drives because lack of sex poses no threat to the *individual's* survival. We can't live for long without food or water, but some people live their lives without sexual activity (although some would say that that's not really living!). Rather, sexual motivation involves the survival of the species, not the individual.

All the biological drives—sex included—exert such powerful influences on behavior that they have led to numerous social constraints and taboos, such as prohibitions on eating certain meats or drinking alcohol. In the realm of sexuality, we find extensive culture-specific rules and sanctions involving a wide variety of sexual practices. In fact, all societies regulate sexual activity, but the restrictions vary widely. For example, homosexuality has been historically suppressed in the United States and in Arab cultures, but it is widely accepted in many Asian and Pacific Island nations. Rules about marriage among relatives and exposure of genitals and breasts also vary from culture to culture.

Even the discussion of sex can become mired in taboo, misinformation, and embarrassment. Scientists who study human sexuality have felt intense social and political pressures, which show no signs of abating in the present. The result is that the scientific understanding of sexuality, which we will survey below, has been hard won.

Our cultural lessons and life experiences influence the meaning of sex in our lives.

The Scientific Study of Sexuality In the mid-20th century, a titillated public clamored to read the first major scientific study of human sexuality, based on interviews of some 17,000 Americans. In two notorious books—one on men and one on women—Alfred Kinsey and his colleagues (1948, 1953) revealed that certain behaviors (oral sex, for example) previously considered rare and even abnormal were actually quite widespread. While Kinsey's data are now more than 50 years old, his interviews continue to be considered an important source of information about human sexuality, especially since no one else has conducted such in-depth interviews of such a large and varied sample.

In the 1990s, another large survey of American sexuality was described in *The Social Organization of Sexuality: Sexual Practices in the United States* (Laumann et al., 1994) and in a smaller, more readable companion volume called *Sex in America* (see Table 9.2) (Michael et al., 1994). This project, known as the National Health and Social Life Survey (NHSLS), involved interviews of 3,432 adults, ages 18 to 59. While there were some built-in sources of bias (for example, only English-speaking persons were interviewed), the NHSLS managed to get a remarkable response rate: Of those recruited for the survey, 79 percent agreed to participate. When melded with other surveys taken since Kinsey's time, this study showed, among other things, a marked increase in the percentage of youth who are sexually active, along with a declining age at first intercourse (Wells & Twenge, 2005). A smaller but more recent survey, however, shows that the percentage of teens who say they are virgins has increased slightly in the past decade (Doyle, 2007). Estimates of homosexual and bisexual preferences have also risen moderately.

But sexuality is not controlled solely by social pressures. In a study comparing identical twins with fraternal twins, researchers have found that the age at which individuals first have sex is strongly influenced by genetics (Weiss, 2007). Because the same work also showed a genetic influence on the tendency to get in trouble with the law, the scientists speculate that the underlying factor may be a risk-taking tendency.

TABLE 9.2 Sexual Preferences and Behaviors of Adult Americans

Frequency of Intercourse	Not at All	A Few Times per Year	A Few Times per Month	Two or More Times per Week
Percentage of men	14	16	37	34
Percentage of women	10	18	36	37

Number of Sexual Partners Since Age 18	0	1	2–4	5–10	10–20	21+
Percentage of men	3	20	21	23	16	17
Percentage of women	3	31	31	20	6	3

Infidelity While Married	
Men	15.1%
Women	2.7%

Sexual Orientation	Males	Females
Heterosexual	96.9	98.6
Homosexual	2.0	0.9
Bisexual	0.8	0.5

Source: Adapted from Michael, R. T., Gagnon, J. H., Laumann, E. O., & Kolata, G. (1994). Sex *in America: A definitive survey.* New York: Little, Brown. Table based on survey of 3,432 scientifically selected adult respondents. There has not been a major survey of American sexual preferences and behaviors since 1994.

Masters and Johnson: Gender Similarities and the Physiology of Sex   Although Kinsey first shocked the nation's sexual sensibilities, it was William Masters and Virginia Johnson (1966, 1970, 1979) who really broke with tradition and taboo by bringing sex into their laboratory. Never before had scientists studied sex by directly observing and recording the responses of people engaging in sexual behavior of various sorts, including masturbation and intercourse. During these observational studies, Masters and Johnson discovered not what people *said* about sex but how people actually *reacted physically* during sex. In the wake of their daring departure from tradition, the study of human sexual behavior has become much more accepted as a legitimate field of scientific inquiry.

These observations revealed four phases of human sexual responding, which Masters and Johnson collectively called the **sexual response cycle** (see Figure 9.6). Here are the distinguishing events of each phase:

sexual response cycle   The four-stage sequence of arousal, plateau, orgasm, and resolution, occurring in both men and women.

- In the *excitement phase,* blood vessel changes in the pelvic region cause the clitoris to swell and the penis to become erect. Blood and other fluids also become congested in the testicles and vagina.
- During the *plateau phase,* a maximal level of arousal is reached. Rapid increases occur in heartbeat, respiration, blood pressure, glandular secretions, and muscle tension.
- Reaching the *orgasm phase,* males and females experience a very intense and pleasurable sense of release from the cumulative sexual tension. Orgasm, characterized by rhythmic genital contractions, culminates in ejaculation of semen in men and clitoral and vaginal sensations in women.
- During the *resolution phase,* the body gradually returns to its preexcitement state, as fluids dissipate from the sex organs. At the same time, blood pressure and heart rate, which had increased dramatically, drop to their customary levels.

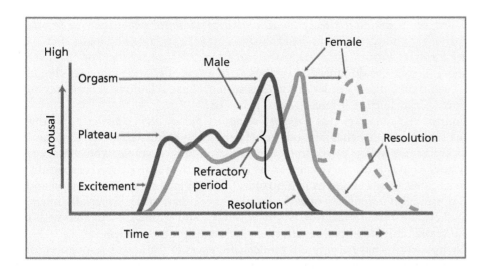

FIGURE 9.6
The Sexual Response Cycle

Note that the phases of sexual response in males and females have similar patterns. The primary differences are in the time it takes for males and females to reach each phase and in the greater likelihood that females will achieve multiple orgasms.

Source: Gagnon, J. H. (1977). *Human Sexualities.* Glenview, IL: Scott Foresman. Reprinted by permission of J. H. Gagnon.

Note also that Masters and Johnson focused on physiological arousal and responses. Accordingly, they paid relatively little attention to psychological aspects of sexuality, such as emotional responses or social pressures on sexual activity. Nevertheless, Masters and Johnson drew several newsworthy conclusions about the biology of sex:

- Men and women have remarkably similar patterns of biological response, regardless of the source of sexual arousal—whether it be intercourse or masturbation.

- Although the phases of the sexual response cycle are similar in the two sexes, women tend to respond more slowly but often remain aroused longer. This makes sense from a biological standpoint because the male is likely to ejaculate before the female loses interest.

- Many women can have multiple orgasms in a short time period, while men rarely do.

- Size of the genitals or other physical sex characteristics (such as vulva, breasts, and penis) is generally unrelated to any aspect of sexual performance (except, perhaps, attitudes about one's sexual capability).

Most important, perhaps, Masters and Johnson used their discoveries about sexual behavior to develop effective behavioral therapies for a variety of sexual disorders, including male erectile disorder (inability to achieve or maintain an erection), premature ejaculation, and female orgasmic disorder.

An Alternative View: Men and Women Differ in Their Sexuality   While Masters and Johnson called our attention to the similarities between men and women in the sexual response cycle, other researchers have focused on the differences. For example, Meredith Chivers and her colleagues (2007) have discovered that heterosexual women are aroused by a broader range of erotic stimuli than are heterosexual men. Moreover, gay men and lesbian women are more particular in their erotic tastes than were their heterosexual counterparts. Other researchers have looked deep in the brain, pinpointing the reward areas associated with orgasm—which can be as strong, for example, as the brain's response to heroin (Portner, 2008).

Ann Peplau (2003) has pointed out four especially important differences between men and women. First, she notes, *men show more interest in sex than do women*—on the average, of course. Men not only think about sex more often, but they are also more likely to attend to visual sexual stimuli. They also generally prefer to have sex more frequently than do women.

Second, *women are more likely than men to view sex in the context of a committed relationship*. That is, says Peplau, women are more likely to "romanticize" sexual desire as a longing for emotional intimacy, while men tend to see sex more as physical pleasure. As a result, women generally (both heterosexual and lesbian women) have a less permissive attitude toward casual sex than do men (including both gay and straight men).

CONNECTION CHAPTER 13

The behavior therapies focus on what people do rather than on what they think or feel. Such treatments are effective for a variety of problems, including not only sexual problems but also phobias and other anxiety disorders (p. 568).

Third, *sex is more likely to be linked with aggression for males than for females.* As you probably know, rape is almost exclusively an act committed by males. But even in milder forms, aggression is more a male than a female characteristic. For example, men are more likely to be domineering or abusive in a sexual relationship. (We should add that, even though these gender differences seem to have a biological basis, nothing in this fact excuses hurtful or forced sexual behavior.)

Fourth, Peplau argues that *women's sexuality has greater "plasticity."* By that she means that women's behaviors and beliefs are more readily shaped by cultural and social factors, as well as by the immediate situation. For example, women's sexual activity over time is far more variable in its frequency than men's. This is especially true when circumstances change, as in a divorce. Cultural factors, such as religion and cultural norms, also influence women's sexuality more than men's. Especially interesting is the fact that higher education is, for both men and women, correlated with more liberal sexual attitudes—but the effect is much stronger for women.

Neuroscientists have also found gender differences in the brain's responses (Portner, 2008). Specifically, during orgasm, many regions associated with emotional control in a woman's brain—unlike a man's—seem to fall silent. That response, suggest researcher Gert Holstege and her colleagues (2003), involves the dampening of anxiety responses that could otherwise inhibit orgasm.

Read about Sexual Cues and Sexual Scripts at **MyPsychLab**

CONNECTION CHAPTER 2

Natural selection is Darwin's term for the environmental conditions that favored the "survival of the fittest" (p. 44).

An Evolutionary Perspective on Sexuality The evolutionary perspective looks for the basis of sexual motivation in the pressures of natural selection. Accordingly, some observers (Buss, 2008) argue that selection pressures have produced different mating strategies and, therefore, different gender roles for men and women. (We are speaking of heterosexuals here, because the evolutionary aspects of homosexuality and bisexuality are unclear at this point.)

Biologically speaking, the goal of both sexes is to leave as many offspring as possible. Yet the potential physical costs of mating and parenting differ for males and females (Bjorklund & Shackelford, 1999). As a result, the sexes have evolved different—and sometimes conflicting—mating strategies, say evolutionary psychologists.

Females can produce only a few children over a lifetime, and they make a huge biological investment in pregnancy and a substantial commitment of time and energy in child rearing. Therefore, the best sexual strategy for females involves caution in mate selection. For males, however, the costs and benefits are much different because they cannot become pregnant—nor do they usually spend as much time with children as women do. For males, evolutionary theory says, the biggest payoff results from copulating as often as possible with mates who are in prime breeding condition. As a result, men tend to seek young and physically well-developed partners, while females may seek somewhat older mates who can offer resources, status, and protection for offspring. Not incidentally, these agendas often produce conflict, promiscuity, and sexual jealousy.

Although the evolutionary perspective may seem cold hearted in its view of sexual motivation, it *does* account for many gender differences in mating behaviors, such as the larger number of sexual partners typically reported by men than women (see Table 9.2 on page 382). Even so, biology does not prohibit the learning of alternative sex roles and scripts, nor does it explain the social and cultural pressures that cast men and women in different roles (Eagly & Wood, 1999). Moreover, evolutionary psychology does not explain why most people remain with their mates over extended periods of time (Hazan & Diamond, 2000) or why gay and lesbian relationships persist across cultures. A complete understanding of human sexual motivation, therefore, must include both its evolutionary roots and the many variations that occur through learning.

Sex, Hunger, and the Hierarchy of Needs

Maslow said almost nothing about sex. The new evolution-based needs hierarchy, however, corrects this omission. Kenrick's group still gives priority to hunger, thirst, and other survival needs at the base of the hierarchy. Sex and related motives follow at the "higher" levels: attachment, affiliation, belongingness, and parenting. But this doesn't mean that a pizza always wins over the opportunity for sex. As we have seen, the hierarchy is fluid, not rigid. In addition, hunger and sex are both biological drives *and* psychological motives. Because biological drives generally have priority over psychological motives, the attraction of sex can sometimes take precedence over eating—in which case proximal sex overpowers proximal pizza.

[PSYCHOLOGY MATTERS]

The What and Why of Sexual Orientation

Ever since Kinsey's first reports were published, we have known that human **sexual orientation** is a complex issue relating to sexual attraction, along with several other aspects of human relating, including our sexual behavior, desired intimate relationships, affiliation with gay or straight (or other) communities, and how we personally identify our sexual orientation (Herek et al., 2010).

Heterosexuality and homosexuality represent the two major forms of sexual orientation: A *heterosexual orientation* is to the opposite sex; a *homosexual orientation* is to the same sex. Another common variation is *bisexuality,* which refers to sexual interest in both males and females (Diamond, 2008). But to complicate matters, cross-cultural studies reveal considerable variability in sexual orientation. In parts of New Guinea, for example, the culture dictates that homosexual behavior is universal among young males, who then switch to a heterosexual orientation when they marry (Money, 1987). Among American adults, various estimates put the percentage of homosexuality at 1 to 9 percent, more or less, depending on whether homosexuality is defined as (a) feelings of attraction to persons of the same sex, (b) one's primary orientation or, (c) having *ever* engaged in same-sex erotic behavior (Diamond, 2007; Savin-Williams, 2006). As Table 9.2 (page 382) indicates, the incidence of homosexuality among females is about half that of males. Incidentally, homosexual behavior is quite common among animals—particularly bonobos (pigmy chimpanzees), who are genetically close relatives to humans (Driscoll, 2008).

Transsexualism refers to people who view themselves as persons of the sex opposite to their biological sex. Thus, a transsexual person with the phenotype of a male thinks of him/herself as a female. Such persons should not be confused with cross-dressers, who indulge in a sexual fetish known as *transvestism*. (Those who cross-dress for nonsexual reasons are not classified under transvestism.) It is also important to realize that none of these variations predicts sexual orientation. That is, knowing that a person is transsexual or a cross-dresser does not tell us whether he or she is gay, lesbian, bisexual, or straight (Devor, 1993).

Origins of Sexual Orientation

So, what does the available evidence tell us about the factors that determine sexual orientation? We know several things that are *not* involved. Speaking biologically, we know that sexual orientation in adults is *not* related to testosterone levels—although the issue of testosterone or estrogen influences on the fetus is still an open question (McAnulty & Burnette, 2004). From a social perspective, we also know that parenting styles or family configurations do *not* cause children to identify as straight or gay (Golombok & Tasker, 1996). Similarly, researchers have come up empty handed in their attempts to link human sexual orientation to early sexual experiences, such as molestation or other abuse.

Although much of the work has focused on biology, most experts have concluded that a combination of biological, environmental, and social factors are at play. To illustrate this research, let's look at a famous study of male identical twins. Richard Pillard

sexual orientation   One's erotic attraction toward members of the same sex (a homosexual orientation), the opposite sex (heterosexual orientation), or both sexes (a bisexual orientation).

The origins of sexual orientation are unclear, although some evidence points to biological factors. What is clear is that research on sexual orientation often generates controversy.

and Michael Bailey (1991) discovered that when one twin is homosexual, the chance of the other being homosexual is about 50 percent. This compares with an incidence of roughly 5 or 6 percent in the general population. The same study also found that the rate drops to 22 percent for fraternal twins and 11 percent for adoptive brothers of homosexuals. A later study of female twin pairs produced essentially the same results (Bower, 1992).

One of the more puzzling findings links sexual orientation in males (but not females) to birth order, specifically how many older brothers one has (Abrams, 2007; Blanchard, 2008; Bogaert, 2005). The more older brothers a boy has, the more likely he is to have a same-sex orientation. This effect occurs whether or not boys are raised with their biological brothers, according to a study of adopted versus biological brothers—a finding that apparently rules out environmental influences after birth (Bogaert, 2006). While no one knows what the causative factor is, some scientists believe that some aspect of the prenatal environment tips the balance one way or the other. (Bower, 2006a).

Again, research shows that social and environmental factors must also be taken into account. While few studies examine how adolescents develop a sexual orientation, some scholars theorize that social influences such as peers, the media, schools, and parenting can affect the direction of sexual development. Hyde and Jaffee (2000) reviewed numerous large studies that suggest adolescent girls who become heterosexual often develop their identities and social roles amidst messages that disparage homosexuality and promote heterosexuality.

Turning to the earlier preadolescent period, a longitudinal study of 182 children in fourth to eighth grade looked at the ways some children enter into a period of sexual questioning (Carver et al., 2004). Specifically, the researchers found that girls and boys who, for various reasons, question whether they will marry someone of the other sex and whether they will fulfill typical gender roles come to feel distressed about their competence in peer relationships (although this turmoil seems not to affect how much they are liked and accepted by their peers).

Research in this area remains controversial because of the strong feelings, political issues, and prejudices involved (Herek, 2000). Further, it has attracted scientific criticism because much of it is correlational—rather than experimental—so the data cannot establish cause and effect with certainty. Moreover, some observers object to this whole line of research, saying that gay men and lesbians should not feel pressured to justify their behavior by seeking a "cause" for it (Byne, 1995).

Not a Disorder

We should also note that, until the 1970s, the diagnostic manual of the American Psychiatric Association listed homosexuality as a mental disorder—a classification that has since been removed and repudiated by both psychologists and psychiatrists (Greenberg, 1997). Then, more recently, the American Psychological Association passed a resolution advising against therapies aimed at changing sexual orientation, on the grounds that they are ineffective, unnecessary, and potentially harmful (Munsey, 2009).

And what does the evidence say about sexual orientation and mental health? The message coming through numerous studies says that mental disorders and relationship problems occur in about the same proportion in heterosexuals and homosexuals (DeAngelis, 2002c; Kurdek, 2005). As we might expect, the only exception involves stress-related problems—e.g., anxiety and depression—associated with discrimination against homosexuals. The research also shows no differences in adjustment or development of children raised by heterosexual or homosexual parents (APA, 2010; Patterson, 2006).

So, where does this leave us in our understanding of sexual orientation? Attitudes toward minority forms of sexual orientation, such as homosexuality, differ sharply among cultures around the world, with Americans among the most divided on issues such as gay marriage. Most experts—but not all—would say that the research strongly supports some biological influence on sexual orientation. Just how biology might influence our behavior in the bedroom, however, remains a major puzzle and a topic for continuing research.

Check Your Understanding

✔●─Study and Review at MyPsychLab

1. **RECALL:** Describe the *multiple systems approach* to understanding hunger.

2. **RECALL:** Explain, from an evolutionary perspective, why obesity is becoming more prevalent in industrialized nations.

3. **RECALL:** From a biological perspective, in what respect is sex different from other biological drives, such as hunger and thirst?

4. **RECALL:** What are the four major differences between men's and women's sexuality, according to Peplau?

5. **ANALYSIS:** Why do psychologists avoid the term *will power?* What terms do they prefer instead?

6. **UNDERSTANDING THE CORE CONCEPT:** For which of the motives discussed in this section would biological factors be *least* important in accounting for the differences between one person and another?

   a. hunger
   b. thirst
   c. a *n Ach*
   d. sex

Answers 1. Because hunger has not only biological components but also cognitive, social, and cultural aspects, it must be understood as involving a complex interaction of factors. The multiple systems approach recognizes such factors as blood sugar and fat levels monitored by the hypothalamus, homeostatic feedback from fat cells, pressure and nutrient detectors in the stomach, reward systems in the brain, physical activity, emotional state, food-related stimuli, and social-cultural pressures. **2.** From an evolutionary standpoint, the human body evolved in an environment that required much more physical exertion than is required of most people in industrialized countries. This decrease in activity, along with an abundance of calorie-dense foods, has led to obesity. **3.** Sex is not a homeostatic drive, nor is it essential for the survival of the individual. **4.** Peplau says that (a) men show more interest in sex than do women, (b) women are more likely to view sex in the context of a committed relationship, (c) males are more likely to associate sex with aggression, and (d) women's sexuality has more plasticity than men's. **5.** The term *will power* suggests that it is a separate faculty of the mind, yet there is no evidence of a "will" that cannot be explained in more conventional terms that do not carry the baggage of a defect in character. Psychologists prefer to speak of "self-control" or "impulse control." **6.** c (because all the others involve biological drives).

─9.4 **KEY QUESTION**
── How Do Our Emotions Motivate Us?

One of the most pervasive misunderstandings about the human mind is the idea that emotion is the opposite of reason. Consider the case of Elliot. Once a model employee, he had let the quality of his work slip to the point that he finally lost his job. If anything, said his supervisors, Elliot had become almost too focused on the details of his work, yet he had trouble setting priorities. He often latched onto a small task, such as sorting a client's paperwork, and spent the whole afternoon on various classification schemes—never quite getting to the real job he had been assigned (Damasio, 1994).

His personal life also fell apart. A divorce was followed by a short marriage and another divorce. Several attempts at starting his own business involved glaringly flawed decisions that finally ate up all his savings.

Yet, surprisingly, in most respects Elliot seemed normal. He had a pleasant personality and an engaging sense of humor. He was obviously smart—well aware of important events, names, and dates. He understood the political and economic affairs of the day. In fact, examinations revealed nothing wrong with his movements, memory, perceptual abilities, language skills, intellect, or ability to learn.

Complaints of headaches led the family doctor to suspect that the changes in Elliot pointed to something wrong in his brain. Tests proved the suspicion correct, revealing a mass the size of a small orange that was pressing on the frontal lobes just above Elliot's eyes.

The tumor was removed, but not before it had damaged the frontal lobes in a pattern remarkably similar to that of the notorious Phineas Gage, whom you met in Chapter 2. But the effects in Elliot were more subtle than in Gage. As a psychologist who examined him said, "We might summarize Elliot's predicament as *to know but not to feel*" (Damasio, 1994, p. 45). His reasoning abilities were intact, but the damage to the circuitry of Elliot's frontal lobes disrupted his ability to use his emotions to establish priorities among the objects, events, and people in his life. In short, Elliot had been emotionally crippled. With a disruption in his ability to connect concepts and emotions, Elliot could not value one course of action over another.

So, what does Elliot's case tell us about the role of emotions in our thinking? What happened to Elliot, Phineas Gage, and others with similar problems makes it clear that emotion is a vital ingredient in thinking and, especially, in decision making (Forgas, 2008; Gray, 2004). In the remainder of this chapter, we will explore some discoveries about how the brain processes emotions and what these discoveries mean about the intimate connection between emotion and reason.

> ### Core Concept 9.4
>
> **Emotions are a special class of motives that help us attend to and respond to important (usually external) situations and communicate our intentions to others.**

How is emotion linked to motivation? Note that both words share a common root, *"mot-"* from the Latin *motus,* meaning "move." The psychology of emotion has retained this meaning by viewing emotion as a special sort of motivation directed outward. Emotions also increase our arousal, attach the values we call "feelings" to people, objects, and events that we judge important, and produce an approach or avoidance response. Let's look more closely at these components of emotion.

What Emotions Are Made Of

emotion　A four-part process that involves physiological arousal, subjective feelings, cognitive interpretation, and behavioral expression. Emotions help organisms deal with important external events.

In brief, every **emotion** has four main components: *physiological arousal, cognitive interpretation, subjective feelings,* and *behavioral expression.* We can illustrate with an example closer to home.

Suppose that you win a cool $50 million in the lottery. Chances are that the news will make you jump and shout, your heart race, and a wave of joy wash over your brain. Congratulations! You have just had an emotion! The *physiological arousal* component involves an alarm broadcast simultaneously throughout the autonomic nervous system and the endocrine system. The result is an extensive visceral response that includes your racing heart.

The second component of emotion, a *cognitive interpretation* of events and feelings, involves a conscious recognition and interpretation of the situation. Undoubtedly, you would interpret the news about your winning lottery ticket as good fortune. The same processes—both conscious and unconscious—can happen with unpleasant experiences too. (Think of a hungry bear chasing you.)

The *subjective feeling* component of your fear may come from several sources. One involves the brain sensing the body's current state of arousal. The other comes from memories of the body's state in similar situations in the past. There, the brain stores a sort of emotional "body-image" that Antonio Damasio (1994, 2003) calls a *somatic marker.* In response to the hungry bear, your brain retrieves a body-image memory of how you felt during past encounters with danger, including a racing heart, a cold sweat, and the feeling of running away.

The recently discovered "mirror neuron" system is yet another source of emotional feelings. These brain circuits activate to make you feel the somatic marker of an emotion when you see someone else's emotional state, as in a sad movie (Miller, 2006c; Niedenthal, 2007). In our hungry bear example, your mirror neurons may reflect the emotions of a companion who sees the bear before you do. Numerous studies support this conjecture, but one of the more interesting ones involved the positive emotions of romantically involved couples. When researchers looked at the simultaneous brain scans of such couples, they found that when one had an unpleasant experience, the other showed essentially the same changes in the emotion-related parts of the brain (Singer et al., 2004).

◄ **CONNECTION** CHAPTER 2

"Mirror neurons" allow us to understand others' behaviors, emotional states, and intentions (p. 70).

Finally, the fourth component of emotion produces an *expression of emotion in behavior*. So, when you learned of your lottery winnings, you probably smiled, gave a whoop of joy, and perhaps danced around the room as you babbled the news to your companions. Alternatively, the sight of a hungry bear most likely would activate the "fight-or-flight" response, as well as in emotion-laden facial expressions and vocalizations, such as crying, grimacing, or shouting.

And what functions do these emotional responses serve? Surely emotions must do more than just adding variety or "color" to our mental lives. Let's see.

What Emotions Do for Us

Whether they occur in humans, hyenas, cats, or kangaroos, emotions serve as arousal states that signal important events, such as a threat or the presence of a receptive mate. They also become etched in memory to help the organism recognize such situations quickly when they recur (Dolan, 2002; LeDoux, 1996; Lee, 2009). Thus, Lance Armstrong uses emotion in deciding when to overtake an opponent in a race. And our own ability to connect emotional memories to new situations accounts for emotions as diverse as the fear generated by a hungry bear, the joy produced by a winning lottery ticket, or an A on a term paper.

In general, emotions are either *positive* or *negative,* which leads to a tendency for *approach* or *avoidance* (Davidson et al., 2000). The "approach" emotions, such as delight and joy, are generally positive, and they make a person, object, or situation attractive (as when we find another person desirable). Brain scans suggest that these approach emotions involve the dopamine reward system. In contrast, most of the negative emotions, such as fear and disgust, are associated with rejection or avoidance (as when we fear going to the dentist). These avoidance emotions usually involve the amygdala.

Natural selection has shaped our emotions, which explains why they well up in situations that might affect our survival or reproductive success (Gross, 1998; Izard, 2007). For example, fear undoubtedly helped individuals in your family tree to avoid situations that could have made them a meal instead of an ancestor. Similarly, the emotion we call "love" may commit us to a family, which helps to continue our genetic line. Likewise, sexual jealousy can be seen as an emotion that evolved to deal with the biologically important problem of mate infidelity, which threatens the individual's chances of producing offspring (Buss & Schmitt, 1993). Humor, too, may have evolved to serve a social purpose, as we can surmise from the "in-jokes" and rampant laughter among people in tightly knit social groups (Ayan, 2009; Provine, 2004; Winerman, 2006d).

We glimpsed yet another important-but-little-known function of emotions in Elliot's story. You will recall that his tumor interfered not only with his ability to process emotion but also with his judgment. The cases of Elliot and others like him confirm that our emotions help us make decisions, because they attach values to the alternatives (De Martino et al., 2006; Miller, 2006a).

And where do emotions fit in the new evolution-based hierarchy? Obviously, many emotions relate to survival, as does the fear you might feel in our hungry-bear example. Other emotions relate to sexual arousal and reproduction, as in the attraction you feel to potential mate. The survival-related emotions, then, would operate near the bottom of the motivational pyramid, where they generally have a high priority. That leaves the sex- and affiliation-related emotions—attraction and love, for example—on the upper levels of the hierarchy, where they generally have lower priority than the survival-based motives.

Counting the Emotions

How many emotions are there? A long look in the dictionary turns up more than 500 emotional terms (Averill, 1980). Most experts, however, see a more limited number of *basic emotions*. Carroll Izard (2007) argues for six: interest, joy/happiness, sadness, anger, disgust, and fear. Paul Ekman's list contains seven: anger, disgust, fear, happiness, sadness, contempt, and surprise—based on the universally recognized facial

CONNECTION CHAPTER 2

The amygdala is a part of the limbic system that is particularly involved in fear (p. 68).

Sexual jealousy probably has an evolutionary basis because mate infidelity threatens the individual's chances of producing offspring.

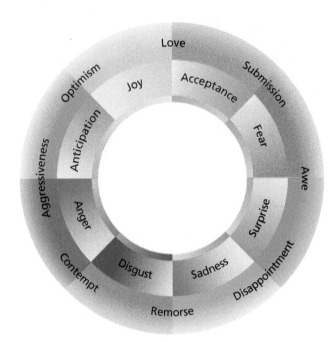

FIGURE 9.7
The Emotion Wheel

Robert Plutchik's emotion wheel arranges eight primary emotions on the inner ring of a circle of opposite emotions. Pairs of adjacent emotions can combine to form more complex emotions noted on the outer ring of the figure. For example, love is portrayed as a combination of joy and acceptance. Still other emotions, such as envy or regret (not shown), emerge from still other combinations of more basic emotions portrayed on the wheel.

Source: Plutchik, R. (1980, February) A language for the emotions. *Psychology Today*, 13(9), 68–78. Used with permission of *Psychology Today* © 2008.

display rules The permissible ways of displaying emotions in a particular society.

expressions he has studied. And Robert Plutchik (1980, 1984) has made a case for eight basic emotions that emerged from a mathematical analysis of people's ratings of a large number of emotional terms (see Figure 9.7). Recent work suggests that Plutchik's list could be expanded to include pride (Azar, 2006; Tracy & Robins, 2006). Even though different theorists approach the problem in different ways, their differences are relatively minor. The essential idea that we have a limited number of basic emotions with a larger number of *secondary emotions* involves blends of the more basic emotions.

Cultural Universals in Emotional Expression

You can usually tell when a friend is happy or angry by the look on her face or by her actions. This can be useful in deciding whether to spend Friday evening with her at the movies. More generally, communication through emotional expression aids our social interactions. But does raising the eyebrows and rounding the mouth convey the same message in Minneapolis as it does in Madagascar? Much research on emotional expression has centered on such questions.

According to Paul Ekman (2003), the leading authority on facial expression of emotions, people speak and understand the same basic "facial language" the world around. Ekman's group has demonstrated that humans share a built-in set of emotional expressions that testify to the common biological heritage of the human species. Smiles, for example, usually signal happiness, and frowns indicate sadness on the faces of people in such far-flung places as Argentina, Japan, Spain, Hungary, Poland, Sumatra, the United States, Vietnam, the jungles of New Guinea, and the native villages north of the Arctic Circle (Biehl et al., 1997).

But it may not surprise you to learn that gender can make a difference in what we read into other people's facial expressions. One study found a bias toward seeing anger in men's faces and happy expressions in women's faces (Becker et al., 2007). This finding makes sense from an evolutionary perspective, because angry men have always been a source of danger, while a happy woman's face may have signaled safety (Azar, 2007).

You can check your own skill at interpreting facial expressions by taking the quiz in the *Do It Yourself!* box on the next page. Ekman and his colleagues (1987) claim that people everywhere can recognize at least seven basic emotions: sadness, fear, anger, disgust, contempt, happiness, and surprise. Nevertheless, huge differences exist across cultures in both the context and intensity of emotional displays—because of so-called **display rules.** In many Asian cultures, for example, children are taught to control emotional responses—especially negative ones—while many American children are encouraged to express their feelings more openly (Smith et al., 2006). As a result, people are generally better at judging emotions of people from their own culture than in members of another cultural group (Elfenbein & Ambady, 2003).

Regardless of culture, babies express emotions almost at birth. In fact, a lusty cry is a sign of good health. And from their first days of life, babies display a small repertoire of facial expressions that communicate their feelings (Ganchrow et al., 1983). Likewise, the ability to read facial expressions develops early (but not so early as emotional expression). Very young children pay close attention to facial expressions, and by age 5 they nearly equal adults in their skill at reading emotions in people's faces (Nelson, 1987). New evidence, however, suggests that at least one of Ekman's "basic" emotional expressions doesn't come so easily. According to James Russell, children do not understand the facial expressions indicating disgust until about age 5, even though they use words to express disgust (such as "gross" and "yucky") much earlier (Bower, 2010; Russell & Widen, 2002).

All this work on facial expressions points to a biological underpinning for our abilities to express and interpret a basic set of human emotions. Moreover, as Charles

Do It Yourself! IDENTIFYING FACIAL EXPRESSIONS OF EMOTION

Take the facial emotion identification test to see how well you can identify each of the seven emotions that Ekman claims are culturally universal. Do not read the answers until you have matched each of the following pictures with one of these emotions: disgust, happiness, anger, sadness, surprise, fear, and contempt. Apparently, people everywhere in the world interpret these expressions in the same way. This tells us that certain facial expressions of emotion are probably rooted in our human genetic heritage.

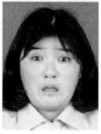

Answers The facial expressions are (top row from left) happiness, surprise, anger, disgust; (bottom row) fear, sadness, contempt.

Darwin pointed out more than a century ago, some emotional expressions cross species boundaries. Darwin especially noted the similarity of our own facial expressions of fear and rage to those of chimpanzees and wolves (Darwin, 1998/1862; Ekman, 1984).

But are *all* emotional expressions universal? Cross-cultural psychologists tell us that certain emotional responses carry different meanings in different cultures (Ekman, 1992, 1994; Ellsworth, 1994). These, therefore, must be learned rather than innate. For example, what emotion do you suppose might be conveyed by sticking out the tongue? For Americans, this might indicate disgust or fatigue, while in China it can signify surprise. Similarly, a grin on an American face may indicate joy, while on a Japanese face it may just as easily mean embarrassment. To give one more example, a somber expression and downcast eyes might indicate unhappiness to someone in a Euro-American culture, whereas it could be a sign of respect to many Asians. Clearly, culture influences emotional expression. ⊙▶

Simulate the **Experiment**
Recognizing Facial Expressions of Emotions at **MyPsychLab**

[PSYCHOLOGY MATTERS]

Gender Differences in Emotion Depend on Biology *and* Culture

You may have suspected that some emotional differences between males and females have a biological basis. This would explain, for example, why certain emotional disturbances, such as panic disorder and depression, occur more commonly in women. Biological differences may also explain why men show more anger and display more physiological signs of emotional arousal during interpersonal conflicts than do women (Fischer et al., 2004). Anger, of course, can lead to violence—and men commit most of the world's violent acts.

Some gender differences, however, may depend as much on culture as on biology. For instance, in the United States, males and females may learn quite different lessons about emotional control. Display rules dictate that men and boys show their anger (Fischer, 1993). Indeed, they may be rewarded for displays of anger and aggression.

On the other hand, they may also be punished for "weak" emotional displays such as crying, depression, and sadness (Gottman, 1994). At the same time, the pattern of reinforcement and punishment is reversed for females. Women and girls may receive encouragement for emotions that show vulnerability. But they may be punished for displaying emotions that suggest dominance (Fischer et al., 2004).

Despite these differences, neither sex is more emotionally expressive overall. Rather, cultures differ in emotional expression much more than do the sexes (Brannon, 2008; Wallbott et al., 1986). In Israel and Italy, for instance, men more often than women hide their feelings of sadness. The opposite holds true in Britain, Spain, Switzerland, and Germany, where women are more likely than men to hide sadness. In many collectivist cultures, as we have noted, both genders learn display rules to restrain all their emotional expressions. Overall, however, the differences among individuals overshadow the differences of either gender or culture.

Check Your Understanding

✓— Study and Review at **MyPsychLab**

1. **RECALL:** What are four main components of emotions?

2. **RECALL:** Name an emotion that is *not* one of the culturally universal emotions identified by Ekman's research.

3. **ANALYSIS:** Give an example that illustrates how *display rules* can modify the universal facial expressions of emotion.

4. **RECALL:** What differences in emotional expression of men and women seem to be heavily influenced by culture?

5. **UNDERSTANDING THE CORE CONCEPT:** What is the adaptive value of communicating our emotional states?

   a. to help us understand our own needs better

   b. to help us deceive others about our emotional states and get what we want

   c. to help us anticipate each other's responses and so to live more easily in groups

   d. to help us get rid of strong negative emotions, such as fear and anger

Answers 1. Four main components of emotions: physiological arousal, cognitive interpretation, subjective feelings, and behavioral expression **2.** Pride, optimism, jealousy, envy, anxiety—in fact, any emotion other than Ekman's seven universal emotions: sadness, fear, anger, disgust, contempt, happiness, and surprise **3.** Smiles may indicate happiness in some cultures and embarrassment in others. Other examples are mentioned in the section on display rules. **4.** Cultures often encourage men to show emotions related to anger, aggression, and dominance, while they encourage women to show emotions related to compliance and submission. **5.** c; our emotions convey our intentions to others.

9.5 KEY QUESTION
— What Processes Control Our Emotions?

Suppose that you are touring a haunted house at Halloween when a filmy figure startles you with ghostly "Boo!" Your emotional response is immediate. It may involve an outward reaction such as jumping, gasping, or screaming. At the same time, you respond internally with changes in your body chemistry, the function of your internal organs, and arousal in certain parts of your brain and autonomic nervous system. Moreover, gut-level emotional responses, such as an accelerated heartbeat, can persist long after you realize that you were really in no danger—after you realize that you were frightened merely by someone dressed in a sheet.

This suggests that emotion operates on both the conscious and unconscious levels. And that idea connects to one of the great recent discoveries in psychology: the existence of two emotion pathways in the brain. These dual pathways are the focus of the Core Concept for this section:

> ### Core Concept 9.5
>
> **Research has clarified the processes underlying both our conscious and unconscious emotional lives, shedding light on some old controversies.**

In the following pages, we will see how the young neuroscience of emotion has begun to identify the machinery that produces our emotions. The details have not yet become fully clear, but we do have a broad-brush picture of the emotion pathways in the brain and their connections throughout the body. So in this last section, we will first see how the two emotion pathways work. Then we will see how they have helped resolve some ancient disputes in the field. Finally, at the end of this section, we will turn to a practical application to learn how emotional arousal can affect our performance on an examination or in an athletic contest.

The Neuroscience of Emotion

People who suffer from intense fears of snakes or spiders usually know that their responses are irrational, yet they can't seem to conquer them. But how can a person to hold two such conflicting mindsets? The answer lies in the brain's two distinct emotion processing systems (LeDoux, 1996, 2000).

Emotions in the Unconscious   One emotion-processing system—the *fast response system*—operates mainly at an unconscious level, where it quickly screens incoming stimuli and helps us respond quickly to potentially dangerous events, even before they reach consciousness. This system, linked to *implicit memory,* acts as an early-warning defense that produces, for example, a near-instantaneous fright response to an unexpected loud noise (Helmuth, 2003b). It relies primarily on deep-brain circuitry that operates automatically, without requiring deliberate conscious control (see Figure 9.8).

The unconscious emotion circuits have a built-in sensitivity to certain stimuli, such as snakes and spiders, that posed threats throughout human history. This explains

CONNECTION CHAPTER 5

Implicit memories involve material of which we are unaware—but that can affect behavior (p. 191).

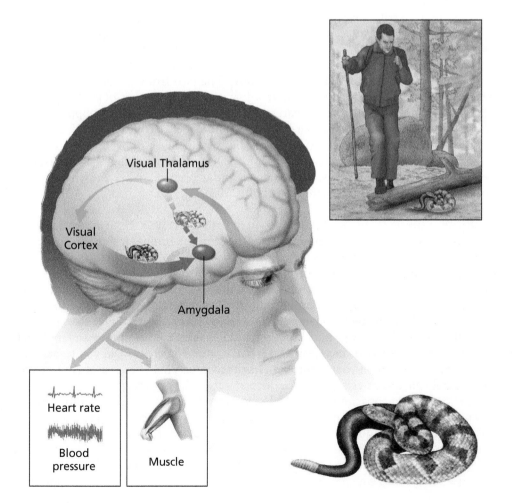

FIGURE 9.8
Two Emotion-Processing Pathways

Two emotion systems are at work when the hiker sees a snake. One is fast and unconscious; the other operates more slowly and consciously. The fast system routes incoming visual information through the visual thalamus to the amygdala (dotted pathway), which quickly initiates fear and avoidance responses—all occurring unconsciously. The slower pathway involves the visual cortex, which makes a more complete appraisal of the stimulus and also sends an emotional message to the amygdala and other lower brain structures. The result of this is a conscious perception of the situation and a conscious feeling of fear.

why fears of spiders and snakes are more common than fears of, say, electricity or automobiles, which now cause more deaths than do spiders and snakes but have only recently become dangers. Moreover, this quick-response system can easily learn new fears through classical conditioning.

You can see how this configuration of the fast response system could be adaptive, because it errs on the side of caution. Unfortunately, the fast response system is also a slow-to-forget system, making it hard to extinguish the anxieties and fears that, instead, can blossom into more serious problems known as *phobias*.

CONNECTION CHAPTER 12

Phobias are one form of anxiety disorder (p. 532).

Conscious Emotional Processing The other emotional system—the one that involves conscious processing—has links to *explicit memory* (LeDoux, 1996; Mather, 2007). Its responses are comparatively slow and considered. This is the system that makes our hiker become cautious in places likely to harbor snakes. Because the conscious system uses different brain circuits from those supporting unconscious emotional processing, your conscious view of events can differ significantly from the emotions roused by your unconscious. Thus, if you have a phobia, you can truly be of "two minds"—feeling fear, despite "knowing" that there is no sensible basis for the feeling.

The Cerebral Cortex's Role in Emotion The cerebral cortex—the outermost layer of brain tissue and our "thinking cap"—plays the starring role in the conscious emotion pathway, where it both interprets events and associates them with memories and feelings. As we have seen, emotional memories help us make decisions by attaching emotional values to the choices we face. It is this process at work when you ask yourself, "Do I want chocolate or strawberry?" or, "Do I want to save my money or buy a new stereo?"

We must add a caution here: Although emotion is an integral part of decision making, it does not necessarily guarantee the *right* decisions. Moreover, intense emotions can immobilize the organism, rendering measured decision making impossible (Pham, 2007). And, as we will see in our discussion of stress in the last chapter of this book, extreme or prolonged emotional responses can produce physical illness.

One other cortical quirk deserves mention: The two frontal lobes have complementary roles in controlling our emotions. Just as distinct patches of cortex produce different sensations, positive and negative emotions are associated with opposite hemispheres, an effect called **lateralization of emotion**. The evidence comes from EEG recordings of normal people's emotional reactions along with EEGs of people with damage to the right or left hemisphere (Davidson et al., 2000). In general, the right hemisphere specializes in negative emotions, such as anger and depression, while the left processes more positive, joyful emotions (Kosslyn et al., 2002).

lateralization of emotion   The two brain hemispheres process different various emotions. The left hemisphere apparently focuses on positive emotions (for example, happiness), while the right hemisphere deals primarily with negative emotions (such as anger).

Emotions Where the Cortex Meets the Limbic System Neuroscientists now think they know where emotion and reason meet in the brain—where the conscious emotion-processing pathway meets the limbic system. It's a small patch of brain with a big name: the *ventromedial prefrontal cortex (VMPFC)*. Located on the floor of the brain's frontal lobes, just behind the eyes, the VMPFC has extensive connections with both the amygdala and the hippocampus (Wagar & Thagard, 2006). There, like a recording technician combining inputs for a sound track, the VMPFC mixes external stimulation with the body's "gut" reaction and converts the result into an emotional memory: Was it positive or negative? Did it make your skin creep? Did you feel a lump in your throat? A knot in your stomach? Thanks to your VMPFC, most of your memories probably have such visceral associations attached.

The fast-and-unconscious emotional pathway also connects to the brain's limbic system, as you can see in Figure 9.8. Situated in the layer above the brain stem, the limbic structures undoubtedly evolved as control systems for behaviors used in attack, defense, and retreat: the "fight-or-flight" response (Caldwell, 1995; LeDoux, 1994, 1996). Evidence for this comes from lesioning (cutting) or electrically stimulating parts of the limbic system, which can produce dramatic changes in emotional responding.

Depending on which part of the limbic system is affected, tame animals may become killers, whereas prey and predators may become peaceful companions (Delgado, 1969).

Particularly well documented is the importance of the amygdala in the emotion of fear (LeDoux, 1996; Whalen, 1998; Winkielman et al., 2007). Like a guard dog, the amygdala stands alert for threats (Hamann et al., 2002; Helmuth, 2003a). As you can see in the figure, the amygdala receives messages from the quick-and-unconscious emotion-processing pathway as well as from the longer-and-slower conscious pathway.

The Autonomic Nervous System's Role in Emotion When you become emotionally aroused, the messages that you "take to heart" (and to your other internal organs) flash to their destinations through the autonomic nervous system (Levenson, 1992). It's the parasympathetic division that usually dominates in pleasant emotions. But when you are startled or when you experience some unpleasant emotion, the sympathetic division goes into action (see Table 9.3).

Suppose you are in an emergency. (A speeding car is coming directly at you!). Your brain alerts your body by means of messages carried along the nerves of the sympathetic system. Signals speeding along the sympathetic pathways direct the adrenal glands to release stress hormones. Other signals make your heart race and blood pressure rise. Simultaneously, the sympathetic system directs certain blood vessels to constrict, diverting energy to the voluntary muscles and away from the stomach and intestines. (This causes the feeling of a "knot" in your stomach.)

When the emergency passes, the parasympathetic division takes over, carrying instructions that counteract the emergency orders of a few moments earlier. You may, however, remain aroused for some time after experiencing a strong emotional activation because hormones continue to circulate in the bloodstream. If the emotion-provoking situation is prolonged (as when you work for a boss who hassles you every day), the sustained emergency response can sap your energy and cause both physical and mental problems.

Emotional Chemistry The body produces hundreds of chemicals, but among the most important for our emotions are the neurotransmitters serotonin, epinephrine (adrenalin), and norepinephrine. Serotonin is linked with feelings of depression. Epinephrine is the hormone that accompanies fear. Norepinephrine is more abundant in anger.

Steroid hormones (the same ones abused by some bodybuilders and other athletes) also exert a powerful influence on our emotions. In addition to their effects on muscles, steroids act on nerve cells, causing them to change their excitability. This is a normal part of the body's response to emergency situations. But when steroid drugs are ingested over extended periods, these potent chemicals have the effect of keeping the body (including the brain) in a continual emergency state. Brain circuits, especially

CONNECTION CHAPTER 2

The autonomic nervous system controls the internal organs along with many signs of emotional arousal (p. 57).

CONNECTION CHAPTER 13

Drugs that inhibit the reuptake of serotonin are often used to treat depression (p. 579).

TABLE 9.3 Responses Associated with Emotion

Component of Emotion	Type of Response	Example
Physiological arousal	Neural, hormonal, visceral, and muscular changes	Increased heart rate, blushing, becoming pale, sweating, rapid breathing
Subjective feelings	The private experience of one's internal affective state	Feelings of rage, sadness, happiness
Cognitive interpretation	Attaching meaning to the emotional experience by drawing on memory and perceptual processes	Blaming someone, perceiving a threat
Social/behavioral reactions	Expressing emotion through gestures, facial expressions, or other actions	Smiling, crying, screaming for help

CONNECTION CHAPTER 13

Cognitive-behavioral therapy focuses on changing both mental and behavioral responses (p. 571).

those associated with arousal, threat, stress, and strong emotions, remain in a state of heightened alert. The result can be "roid" rage or, sometimes, depression (Daly et al., 2003; Miller et al., 2002). You will learn much more about the effects of steroid hormones in our discussion of stress in Chapter 14.

Can you learn to control these responses? Yes—at least to some extent. Biofeedback and cognitive-behavioral therapy target just such responses associated with anxiety, fear, and anger. In the final section of this chapter, we will see how programs aimed at developing *emotional intelligence* can help people learn to control their emotional responses before they catapult out of control. In the meantime, let's see how a certain level of emotional arousal helps you achieve your best performance in athletics, on the job, and even during your next psychology exam.

Arousal, Performance, and the Inverted U

Athletes always want to be "up" for a game—but how far up should they be? Cheering sports fans might think that increased arousal will always improve performance—but that is not necessarily true. Too much arousal can make an athlete "choke" and cause performance to falter. The same is true when you take an examination. Up to a point, increasing levels of arousal can motivate you to study and to remember at exam time what you studied. Unfortunately, only slightly higher levels can cause test anxiety and poor performance.

This complex relationship between arousal and behavior has been studied both in laboratory animals and in humans under all sorts of conditions. For example, in experiments on learning, the curve plotting the performance of hungry rats working to get a food reward first rises and then later declines with increasing arousal. The same pattern holds for humans in a variety of circumstances, including neurosurgeons, truck drivers, and professional entertainers.

inverted U function   A term that describes the relationship between arousal and performance. Both low and high levels of arousal produce lower performance than does a moderate level of arousal.

Psychologists call this the **inverted U function** (so named because the graph resembles an upside-down letter U, as you can see in Figure 9.9). It suggests that either too little or too much arousal can impair performance. Think about it: How much pressure would you want your dentist or surgeon to feel? Which brings us to a second important point.

The optimum amount of arousal varies with the task. As you see in the figure, it takes more arousal to achieve peak performance on simple tasks or tasks in which responses have been thoroughly rehearsed (as in most sports) than it does on complex tasks or those that require much thinking and planning as the situation develops. So it should not surprise you that cheers and high levels of arousal are more likely to boost performance in basketball games than in brain surgery.

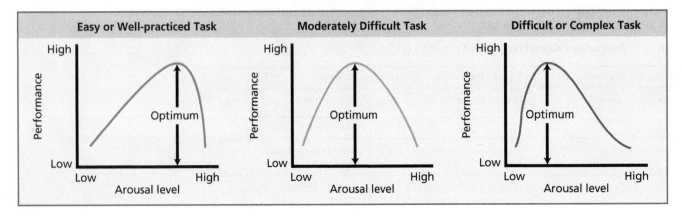

FIGURE 9.9
The Inverted U

Performance varies with arousal level and task difficulty. For easy or well-practiced tasks, a higher level of arousal increases performance effectiveness. However, for difficult or complex tasks, a lower level or arousal is optimal. A moderate level of arousal is generally best for tasks of moderate difficulty. These inverted U-shaped functions show that performance is poorest at both low and high extremes.

Finally, the amount of stimulation needed to produce optimal arousal also varies with the individual. In fact, some people seem to thrive on the thrill of dangerous sports, such as rock climbing and skydiving—activities that would produce immobilizing levels of arousal in most of us. Marvin Zuckerman (2004), who has studied people he calls **sensation seekers**, believes that such individuals have a biological need for high levels of stimulation. Frank Farley also refers to them as Big T (thrill-seeking) personalities, who he believes are prominent in sports, business, science, and art. Einstein was a Big T "mental personality," says Farley (Munsey, 2006). Research suggests that the underlying biology involves the brain's dopamine pathways (Bevins, 2001). You can test your own sensation-seeking tendencies with Zuckerman's scale, found in the *Do It Yourself!* box.

sensation seekers In Zuckerman's theory, individuals who have a biological need for higher levels of stimulation than do most other people.

Theories of Emotion: Resolving Some Old Issues

Let's return to our hungry bear: Suppose that you have the unlikely misfortune to encounter a this creature while on your way to class one morning. We will bet that you will experience the emotion of fear. But what internal process actually produces the *feeling* of fear? Does it come from the thought, "Uh-oh. I'm in danger"? Or does it

Do It Yourself!   ARE YOU A SENSATION SEEKER?

Different people seem to need different levels of emotional arousal. Marvin Zuckerman argues that "sensation seekers" have an unusually high need for stimulation that produces arousal. In addition to the need for thrills, sensation seekers may be impulsive, engage in risky behaviors, prefer new experiences, and be easily bored (Kohn et al., 1979; Malatesta et al., 1981; Zuckerman, 1974).

From your score on the Sensation Seeking Scale below, you can get a rough idea of your own level of sensation seeking. You may also want to give this scale to some of your friends. Do you suppose that most people choose friends who have sensation-seeking tendencies similar to their own? Wide differences in sensation-seeking tendencies may account for strain on close relationships when one person is reluctant to take the risks that the other actively seeks.

The Sensation-Seeking Scale

Choose A or B for each item, depending on which response better describes your preferences. The scoring key appears at the end.

1. A I would like a job that requires a lot of traveling.
   B I would prefer a job in one location.
2. A I am invigorated by a brisk, cold day.
   B I can't wait to get indoors on a cold day.
3. A I get bored seeing the same old faces.

B I like the comfortable familiarity of everyday friends.
4. A I would prefer living in an ideal society in which everyone is safe, secure, and happy.
   B I would have preferred living in the unsettled days of our history.
5. A I sometimes like to do things that are a little frightening.
   B A sensible person avoids activities that are dangerous.
6. A I would not like to be hypnotized.
   B I would like to have the experience of being hypnotized.
7. A The most important goal of life is to live it to the fullest and experience as much as possible.
   B The most important goal of life is to find peace and happiness.
8. A I would like to try parachute jumping.
   B I would never want to try jumping out of a plane, with or without a parachute.
9. A I enter cold water gradually, giving myself time to get used to it.
   B I like to dive or jump right into the ocean or a cold pool.
10. A When I go on a vacation, I prefer the comfort of a good room and bed.
    B When I go on a vacation, I prefer the change of camping out.
11. A I prefer people who are emotionally expressive even if they are a bit unstable.

B I prefer people who are calm and even tempered.
12. A A good painting should shock or jolt the senses.
    B A good painting should give one a feeling of peace and security.
13. A People who ride motorcycles must have some kind of unconscious need to hurt themselves.
    B I would like to drive or ride a motorcycle.

Key Each of the following answers earns one point: 1A, 2A, 3A, 4B, 5A, 6B, 7A, 8A, 9B, 10B, 11A, 12A, 13B. Compare your point total with the following norms for sensation seeking: **0–3**: Very low, **4–5**: Low, **6–9**: Average, **10–11**: High, **12–13**: Very high

Source: Zuckerman, M. (1978, February). The search for high sensation. *Psychology Today*, 12, 38–46. Reprinted by permission of Sussex Publishers, Inc.

Sensation seekers thrive on stimulation that might terrify others.

come from sensing your racing heart and wrenching gut? And, you may be wondering, why would anyone care where emotions come from?

In response to the last question: Psychologists have long argued over the relationship between emotion, cognition, and physical responses—not only out of intellectual curiosity but also because an understanding of emotion is a key to finding effective treatments for certain emotional problems, such as panic attacks and depression, as well as the everyday problems of anger, envy, and jealousy. Should we try to treat anger, for example, by targeting angry thoughts? Or should we focus on angry behaviors or, perhaps, the visceral responses that accompany rage?

Recent discoveries in neuroscience have helped us resolve some long-disputed issues surrounding the interaction of biology, cognition, and behavior in emotion (Forgas, 2008). Let's look briefly at the controversies and how new insights have begun to resolve them.

Do Our Feelings Come from Physical Responses? In the early days of psychology, just over a century ago, William James taught that physical sensations underlie our feelings. "We feel sorry because we cry, angry because we strike, afraid because we tremble," James said (1890/1950, p. 1006). As for your response to the bear, James argued that you would not run because you are afraid, but that *you would feel afraid because you run*. While this statement may appear absurd on its face, James was no fool. He knew that emotion was more than just feelings. What he was really saying was something quite sensible—that emotions require a *combination* of cognitions and physical sensations—and that the physical sensations were the feelings. In James' (1884) own words:

> Without the bodily states following on the perception [of the bear], the latter would be purely cognitive in form, pale, colourless, destitute of emotional warmth. We might then see the bear, and judge it best to run, receive the insult and deem it right to strike, but we could not actually *feel* afraid or angry (pp. 189–190).

This view, simultaneously proposed by Danish psychologist Carl Lange, became known as the **James–Lange theory.**

James–Lange theory The proposal that an emotion-provoking stimulus produces a physical response that, in turn, produces an emotion.

Or Do Our Feelings Come from Cognitions? Other scientists, notably Walter Cannon and Philip Bard, objected that physical changes in our behavior or our internal organs occur too slowly to account for split-second emotional reactions, such as those we feel in the face of danger. They also objected that our physical responses are not varied enough to account for the whole palate of human emotion. In their view, referred to as the **Cannon–Bard theory,** cognitive appraisal of a situation (the hungry bear again) simultaneously produces both the emotional feeling and the physical response.

Cannon–Bard theory The counterproposal that an emotional feeling and an internal physiological response occur at the same time: One is not the cause of the other. Both were believed to be the result of cognitive appraisal of the situation.

Which side was right? It turns out that each had part of the truth. On the one hand, modern neuroscience has confirmed that our physical state can influence our emotions—much as the James–Lange theory argued (LeDoux, 1996). In fact, you may have noted how your own physical state affects your emotions, as when you get edgy feelings after drinking too much coffee or become grumpy when hungry. In a similar fashion, psychoactive drugs, such as alcohol or nicotine or Prozac, influence the physical condition of the brain and hence alter our moods.

Other support for the James–Lange theory comes from the discovery that the brain maintains memories of physical states that are associated with events. These are the "somatic markers" we mentioned earlier (Damasio, 1994; Niedenthal, 2007). When you see the bear leaping toward you, your brain quickly conjures a body-memory of the physical response it had previously in another threatening situation. This *somatic-marker hypothesis*, then, effectively counters Walter Cannon's objection that physical changes in the body occur too slowly to cause our feelings—because the somatic marker of emotion resides in the brain itself.

On the other hand—and in support of the Cannon–Bard view—emotions can also be aroused by external cues detected either by the conscious or the unconscious emotional system. Thus, emotion can result from conscious thought (as when you fret over an exam) or from unconscious memories (as when you feel disgust at the sight of a food that had once made you sick). Incidentally, cognitive psychologists now believe that both depression and phobic reactions can result from conditioned responses of the unconscious emotional system.

When the Situation Gets Complicated: The Two-Factor Theory As we noted, you can make yourself emotional just by thinking, as any student with "test anxiety" will testify. The more you think about the dire consequences of failing a test, the more the anxiety builds. "Method" actors, like the late Marlon Brando, have long exploited this fact to make themselves feel real emotions on stage. They do so by recalling an incident from their own experience that produced the emotion they want to portray, such as grief, joy, or anger.

Stanley Schachter's (1971) **two-factor theory** adds an interesting twist to the role of cognition in emotion. His theory suggests that the emotions we feel depend on our appraisal of both (a) our internal *physical state* and (b) the *external situation* in which we find ourselves. Strange effects occur when these two factors conflict—as they did in the following classic study of emotion, which enterprising students may want to adopt in order to spice up their romantic lives.

An attractive female researcher positioned herself at the end of a footbridge and interviewed unsuspecting males who had just crossed. On one occasion she selected a safe, sturdy bridge; another time, a wobbly suspension bridge across a deep canyon—deliberately selected to elicit physical arousal. The researcher, pretending to be interested in the effects of scenery on creativity, asked the men to write brief stories about a picture. She also invited them to call her if they wanted more information about the study. As predicted, those men who had just crossed the wobbly bridge (and were, presumably, more physically aroused by the experience) wrote stories containing more sexual imagery than those who used the safer structure. And four times as many of them called the female researcher "to get more information"! Apparently, the men who had crossed the shaky bridge interpreted their increased arousal as emotional attraction to the female interviewer (Dutton & Aron, 1974).

Before you rush out to find the love of your life on a wobbly bridge, we must caution you, numerous attempts to test the two-factor theory have supported the two-factor theory only under certain conditions (Leventhal & Tomarken, 1986; Sinclair et al., 1994). What are the conditions under which we are likely to confound physical arousal with emotion? Normally, external events confirm what our biology tells us, without much need for elaborate interpretation—as when you feel disgust at smelling an unpleasant odor or joy at seeing an old friend. But what happens when we experience physical arousal from not-so-obvious sources, such as exercise, heat, or drugs? Misattribution, it seems, is most likely in a complex environment where many stimuli are competing for our attention, as in the bridge study. It is also likely in an environment where we have faulty information about our physical arousal, as when unsuspected caffeine in a soft drink makes us edgy (see Figure 9.10).

How Much Conscious Control Do We Have Over Our Emotions?

The ability to deal with emotions is important in many professions. Physicians, nurses, firefighters, and police officers, for example, must be able to comfort others yet maintain a "professional distance" when dealing with disability and death. Likewise, in many social situations, it can be desirable to mask or modify what you are feeling. If you dislike a professor, you might be wise not to show your true emotions. And if you have strong romantic feelings toward someone—more than he or she realizes—it might be safest to reveal the depth of your feelings gradually, lest you frighten the person away with too much too soon. Even in leisure activities like playing poker or

two-factor theory The idea that emotion results from the cognitive appraisal of both physical arousal (Factor #1) and an emotion-provoking stimulus (Factor #2).

The two-factor theory would predict that decaffeinated-coffee drinkers who accidentally drank coffee with caffeine could mistake the resulting physical arousal for an emotion. Could that be happening here?

During a break at the Western Psychological Association convention near Vancouver, British Columbia, psychologists Susan Horton and Bob Johnson (one of your authors) reenact the Dutton study of attraction on the Capilano Bridge, where the original study was performed.

Theories of Emotion

James–Lange Theory: Every emotion corresponds to a distinctive pattern of physiological arousal.

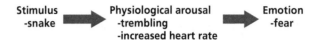

Cannon–Bard Theory: Emotions arise from a cognitive appraisal (interpretation) of the stimulus. (This theory was proposed as an alternative to the James–Lange theory because Cannon and Bard believed that emotions occur too quickly to be the result of physiological arousal, as the James–Lange theory asserted.)

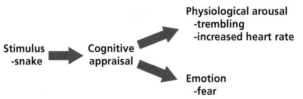

Schacter's Two-Factor Theory: Emotions arise from a cognitive interpretation of the stimulus *and* physiological arousal. Sometimes, however, the person attributes feelings of arousal to one stimulus (the snake), even though the arousal has really been caused by another stimulus—e.g., caffeine or, as in the Capilano Bridge study, having just crossed the swinging bridge. (Dutton & Eron, 1974).

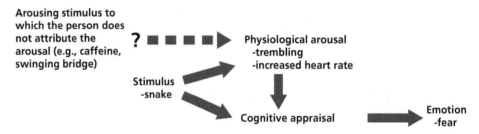

FIGURE 9.10

Theories of Emotion Compared

planning your next move in chess, you will be most successful if you keep your real feelings, beliefs, and intentions guarded. All of these examples testify that emotional control has an important role in our ability to interact with other people.

Developing Emotional Intelligence   Peter Salovey and John Mayer (1990) have suggested that it takes a certain sort of "smarts" to understand and control one's emotions. They called it **emotional intelligence.** More recently, Salovey and his colleague Daisy Grewal (2005) have emphasized four components of emotional intelligence:

emotional intelligence   The ability to understand and control emotional responses.

- **Perceiving emotions.** The ability to detect and decipher emotions in oneself and others
- **Using emotions.** The ability to harness one's emotions in the service of thinking and problem solving
- **Understanding emotions.** The ability to comprehend the complex relationships among emotions, such as the relationship between grief and anger or how two people can have different emotional reactions to the same event
- **Managing emotions.** The ability to regulate one's own emotions and influence those of others

An Army squad leader needs emotional intelligence to lead people under stressful conditions.

The Predictive Power of Emotional Intelligence   As Salovey and Grewal suggest, those with high emotional intelligence are not only tuned in to their own emotions and those of others, but they can also manage their negative feelings and curtail inappropriate expression of their impulses. The power of this ability can be seen in Stanford psychologist Walter Mischel's ingenious "marshmallow test."

> Just imagine you're four years old, and someone makes the following proposal: If you'll wait until after he runs an errand, you can have two marshmallows for a treat. If you can't wait until then, you can have only one—but you can have it right now (Goleman, 1995, pp. 80–81).

How did the children in this experiment respond to the temptation of the single marshmallow that sat before them, within reach? Goleman continues:

> Some four-year-olds were able to wait what must surely have seemed an endless fifteen to twenty minutes for the experimenter to return. To sustain themselves in their struggle they covered their eyes so they wouldn't have to stare at temptation, or rested their heads in their arms, talked to themselves, sang, played games with their hands and feet, even tried to go to sleep. These plucky preschoolers got the two-marshmallow reward. But others, more impulsive, grabbed the one marshmallow, almost always within seconds of the experimenter's leaving the room on his "errand" (Goleman, 1995, pp. 80–81).

When these same children were tracked down in adolescence, the amazing predictive power of the marshmallow test was revealed. As a group, those who had curbed their impulse to grab the single marshmallow were, as adolescents, better off on all counts. They had become more self-reliant, more effective in interpersonal relationships, better students, and better able to handle frustration and stress. By contrast, the children who had given in to temptation had adolescent lives marked by troubled relationships, shyness, stubbornness, and indecisiveness. They also were much more likely to hold low opinions of themselves, to mistrust others, and to be easily provoked by frustrations. In the academic sphere, they were more likely to be uninterested in school. Daniel Goleman (1995) notes that the marshmallow test also correlated clearly with SAT scores: Those who, as 4-year-olds, were able to delay gratification scored, on the average, 210 points higher than did their counterparts who had grabbed the single marshmallow years earlier.

The usefulness of the marshmallow test, of course, is limited to young children. But other, more sophisticated measures have been developed for use with older children and adults (see Figure 9.11). The Mayer-Salovey-Caruso Emotional Intelligence Test (MSCEIT), for example, predicts satisfaction with social relationships among college students, deviant behavior in male adolescents, marital satisfaction, and success on the job (Salovey & Grewal, 2005).

But, cautions John Mayer (1999), emotional intelligence is not a perfect predictor of success, happiness, and good relationships. Nor should we think of it as a replacement

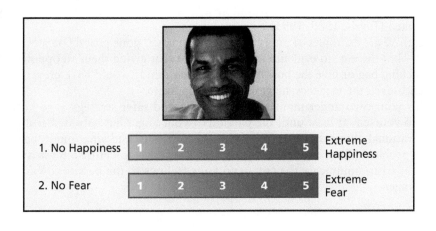

FIGURE 9.11
Sample Item from a Test of Emotional Intelligence

Shown is an item similar to those found on the Mayer-Salovey-Caruso Emotional Intelligence Test. Respondents are asked to click on the number on each scale that corresponds to the emotional state of the person shown in the photo.

Source: Salovey, P. & Grewel, D. (2005) The science of emotional intelligence. *Current Directions in Psychological Science, 14,* 283. Reprinted by permission of Blackwell Publishing.

for traditional IQ scores. Rather, says Mayer, emotional intelligence is merely another variable that can help us refine our understanding of behavior.

The Nature and Nurture of Emotional Intelligence   Is emotional intelligence a characteristic fixed by nature, or is it nurtured by experience? Indeed, studies show that severely maltreated children often have difficulty as adults in forming attachments and interpreting emotional expressions (Pollak, 2008).

But Goleman (1995) believes that learning can also have a positive effect. Based on programs already in place in visionary schools across the country, he has a plan for adding emotional training to the curriculum. The result, he believes, will bring improved relationships, increased self-respect, and even, perhaps, gains in academic achievement. The takeaway message, then, is that while emotions do sometimes slip out of control, we are not simply at their mercy. Emotional understanding and control are skills that can be acquired (Clifton & Myers, 2005).

Not so fast, say Matthew Lieberman and Robert Rosenthal (2001) in an article titled "Why Introverts Can't Always Tell Who Likes Them." Lieberman and Rosenthal suggest that emotional intelligence may be just another name for extraversion, a personality characteristic that has roots in biology as well as learning. Introverts, according to their study, are just not as good at sensing other people's emotions, especially in settings that require multitasking—and, Lieberman and Rosenthal suggest, perhaps they can never learn to be as sensitive as extraverts. The resolution of this issue remains uncertain at the moment.

Critics also point out that emotional control has a dark side. Just as some people get into trouble when they let their emotions—particularly negative emotions—go unchecked, others take emotional control to the opposite extreme. They become so guarded that they never convey affection, humor, or honest displeasure. Studies also show that overcontrolling emotions interferes with memory for emotionally charged events (Carpenter, 2000; Richards & Gross, 2000). Before we launch a program of encouraging emotional control, perhaps we should consider what such training may do to people who already overcontrol their emotions. In fact, research shows that emotionally healthy people know how both to control and to express their emotions—and when it is appropriate to do so (Bonanno et al., 2004).

Read about Keeping Anger Under Control at **MyPsychLab**

Let It Out: A Dangerous Myth   Experts agree that the public clings to some dangerous misinformation about venting anger, a process also known as *catharsis*. On television shows, for example, you can see people attacking and humiliating others, as if the public dumping of hostile feelings will somehow eliminate their anger. In fact, "getting it out of your system" is likely to bring only the most fleeting feeling of satisfaction. It's also likely to encourage more angry responses in the future.

While many people believe that "bottling up" emotions risks an uncontrollable emotional outburst, this belief is at odds with the truth. While expressing your anger can sometimes be helpful, merely giving vent to your rage usually just makes you more angry—even if you just punch the wall or throw your coffee mug. Moreover, studies show that such ventilation makes you more apt to react with anger the next time you are provoked (Tavris, 1989, 1995).

Sure, there are examples of angry workers who have "gone postal" on a murderous rampage—but there is no evidence at all to suggest that giving them an opportunity to hit a punching bag or give the boss "a piece of their mind" would have prevented such tragedies. In fact, the evidence suggests just the opposite.

As for your own anger management, a saner and safer strategy is to keep your feelings to yourself, at least until the passion of your anger has subsided and you can be more rational about the nature of your real complaint and what might be done to solve the problem (Tavris, 1989, 1995). Often, all it takes to defuse a tense and angry situation is to communicate the facts and your feelings to the person toward whom you feel anger.

[PSYCHOLOGY MATTERS]

Detecting Deception

How easy is it for people to conceal their emotions while telling a lie? You might think you can spot deception when someone fails to "look you in the eye" or fidgets nervously. If so, you could be setting yourself up to be duped. Most of us are poor lie detectors—or truth detectors, for that matter. One reason is that our social interactions usually occur in familiar situations, with people we know and trust, and where we pay little attention to nonverbal cues.

Experts who study deception find that these nonverbal cues are the best signs of deceit: A person who deliberately tries to hoodwink us may "leak" uncontrolled nonverbal signals of deception. Knowing how to read these cues could help you decide whether a huckster is lying to you, your physician might be holding back some bad news, or a politician is shading the truth. Keep in mind, however, that the studies of deception are based on probabilities, not certainties. None of this has yet reached the level of an exact science.

The real key to effective deception detection, say the experts, is observing a person's behavior over time. Without the chance for repeated observations, you are much less able to judge a person's honesty (Marsh, 1988). Still, we can offer some pointers for situations in which even a little help in deception detection might be better than none at all (Adelson, 2004; DePaulo et al., 2003):

- Some lies involve giving false information, as when a used-car salesperson is telling you that a junker is in good working order. In such cases, the effort to hide the truth requires some cognitive effort. This may result in heightened attention (evident in dilation of the pupils), longer pauses in speech (to choose words carefully), and more constrained movement and gesturing (in an attempt to avoid "giving away" the truth).

- Criminals sometimes confess to crimes for which they know the police have other evidence of guilt. In these cases, criminals may lie to minimize the extent of their involvement in the crime. Analysis of such taped confessions shows that the liar tends to repeat selectively the distorted or falsified details of the story (Dingfelder, 2004c).

- When a lie involves hiding one's true feelings of anger or exuberance—as a good poker player does when holding a straight flush—the liar may become physically and behaviorally more aroused and animated. This becomes evident in postural shifts, speech errors, nervous gestures (such as preening by touching or stroking the hair or face), and shrugging (as if to dismiss the lie).

- The face is easier to control than the body, so a deceiver may work on keeping a "poker face" but forget to restrain bodily clues. A smart deception detective might therefore concentrate on a speaker's body movements: Are they rhythmic? Are they calculated? Do the hands move freely or nervously?

- The eyes sometimes give deceivers away—especially when they're using the common social deception of trying to look happy or amused when they are not. While our attention may more naturally focus on a smile as an indicator of happiness or amusement, the mouth can be manipulated much more easily than the muscles around the eyes. Only in genuine grins do the eye muscles crinkle up the skin on either side of the eyes. You can test your ability to tell a real from a fake smile in the *Do It Yourself!* box below.

- Speaking of eyes, the ability to "look you straight in the eye" is, in fact, a reasonably good indicator of truth telling—but only when dealing with people who usually tell the truth. When they do lie, their amateurish efforts to deceive often show up in averted gaze, reduced blinking (indicating concentration of attention elsewhere), and less smiling. You may be fooled by a practiced liar who can look straight at you while telling complete fiction.

Do It Yourself! THE EYES HAVE IT

Can you tell if people are sincere when they smile at you? Smiles aren't made just with the mouth, but with the whole face, especially the eyes. A real smile is different from a fake one, primarily around the eyes. Specifically, when we feel genuine joy or mirth, the orbicularis occuli muscles wrinkle up the skin around the eyes.

With this in mind, take a look at these two pictures of smiling faces and see if you can tell which one is the real smile and which one is forced.

- Culture affects the way we distinguish truth from lies. Thus, people are more accurate in detecting liars among people in their own culture. For example, one study found that Jordanians are generally more animated than Americans when talking and that Americans may incorrectly perceive this as "nervousness" and judge the Jordanian to be lying (Bond & Atoum, 2000; Dingfelder, 2004c).

And what about *polygraph* machines—so-called "lie detectors" that are sometimes used by police interrogators and government security agencies? We will take a closer look at these devices in our *Critical Thinking Applied* section on the next page.

Check **Your Understanding**

✓—[**Study** and **Review** at **MyPsychLab**

1. **RECALL:** During emotional arousal, the _____ nervous system sends messages to the internal organs.

2. **APPLICATION:** Give an example of a situation in which a person would be likely to misattribute the source of arousal.

3. **RECALL:** The debate between William James and Walter Cannon over the nature of emotion involved the roles played by

   a. biology, cognition, and behavior.
   b. nature and nurture.
   c. learning, memory, and instincts.
   d. arousal and stress.

4. **RECALL:** Damasio's *somatic marker hypothesis* gives support for the James–Lange theory of emotion because

   a. it argues that emotions are purely psychological, not biological.
   b. it requires cognitive appraisal of all factors involved in emotion.
   c. it argues that physical responses involved in emotion are represented in the brain.
   d. it requires *no* cognitive appraisal of feelings.

5. **ANALYSIS:** The "marshmallow test" revealed emotional intelligence by measuring a child's

   a. self-control.
   b. ability to manipulate others.
   c. blood sugar level.
   d. interactions with other children under highly stressful conditions.

6. **APPLICATION:** Venting your anger on some safe object, such as a punching bag, is likely to

   a. help you get rid of your anger.
   b. make you more angry.
   c. have no effect.
   d. extinguish the aggressive impulse in your unconscious (fast) emotional pathway.

7. **UNDERSTANDING THE CORE CONCEPT:** Briefly describe the two emotion pathways that neuroscientists have discovered.

Answers 1. autonomic **2.** The "swinging bridge" study is the classic example, but others include unexpected physical changes that might occur when you are getting sick, becoming overheated or dehydrated, or mistakenly drinking a caffeinated beverage instead of one without caffeine. **3.** a **4.** c **5.** a **6.** b **7.** The fast pathway produces a near-immediate response and operates mainly at an unconscious level. The slower pathway involves the cerebral cortex and operates largely at the conscious level.

CRITICAL THINKING APPLIED

Do Lie Detectors Really Detect Lies?

The **polygraph** or "lie detector" test is based on the assumption that people will display physical signs of arousal when lying; so most polygraph machines make a record of the suspect's heart rate, breathing rate, perspiration, and blood pressure. Occasionally, voice-print analysis is also employed. Thus, the device really acts as an emotional arousal detector rather than a direct indicator of truth or lies. But does it work? Let's see how a polygraph examination is conducted.

Polygraphers typically employ several tricks of their trade. They may start the interview by persuading the subject that the machine is highly accurate. A common ploy is to ask a series of loaded questions designed to provoke obvious emotional reactions. For example, "Did you ever, in your life, take anything that did not belong to you?" In another favorite technique, the examiner uses a deceptive stimulation procedure, or "stim test," in which the subject draws a card from a "stacked" deck. Then, the examiner pretends to identify the card from the subject's polygraph responses (Kleinmuntz & Szucko, 1984).

When the actual interrogation begins, it will consist of an artistic mix of *relevant questions, irrelevant questions,* and *control questions.* The irrelevant questions ("Are you sitting down right now?") are designed to elicit truthful answers accompanied by a physical response consistent with truth telling. The control questions ("Did you ever lie to your parents?") are designed to elicit an anxious, emotionally aroused response pattern. Then, the examiner can compare the subject's responses to these two types of questions with responses to the relevant questions ("Did you steal the jewels?"). It is assumed that a guilty suspect will give a stronger response to these questions than to the irrelevant and control questions.

What Are the Critical Issues?

If you are unfamiliar with the controversy surrounding "lie detectors," you should inform yourself on the positions taken by both sides (not a bad approach to any issue!). A good way to begin is by typing "polygraph" into your favorite search engine. Your authors have done this and have searched the scientific literature, as well. Here's what we have turned up.

Is There a Possibility of Bias?
We think there is, and it comes in two forms—both on the "pro" side of the issue. A formidable polygraph industry has an economic interest in convincing the public that polygraph tests can, indeed, distinguish truth tellers from liars. A second form of bias comes from those obsessed by fear of crime and terrorism and who see humanity in stark black-and-white terms—as consisting of good people and evil people.

polygraph A device that records or graphs many ("poly") measures of physical arousal, such as heart rate, breathing, perspiration, and blood pressure. A polygraph is often called a "lie detector," even though it is really an arousal detector.

false positive Mistaken identification of a person as having a particular characteristic. In polygraphy, a false positive is an erroneous identification of a truthful person as being a liar.

Are There Logical Errors Involved?
We believe that proponents of the polygraph commit two types of logical error. The first involves pointing to individual cases in which they claim a "lie detector" test either revealed a liar or forced a confession from a reluctant suspect. This is nothing more than "proof by testimonial," as we see all the time in ads for "miracle" weight-loss products or engine-oil additives. The fact is that testimonials are no substitute for a controlled scientific test.

The other main logical error is *oversimplification.* By focusing on apparent successes, they may gloss over the failures—which, in the case of the polygraph, can be quite serious. As we will see, the polygraph failures can lead to a surprisingly large number of honest people being identified as liars.

What Is the Evidence?
Without a doubt, wrongdoers sometimes confess when confronted with polygraph evidence against them. Yet, critics have pointed out several problems with the polygraphic procedure that could easily land innocent people in prison and let the guilty walk free (Aftergood, 2000). For example, polygraph subjects know when they are suspects, so some will give heightened responses to the critical questions even when they are innocent. On the other hand, some people can give deceptive responses because they have learned to control or distort their emotional responses. To do so, they may employ simple physical movements, drugs, or biofeedback training—a procedure in which people are given moment-to-moment information on certain biological responses, such as perspiration or heart rate (Saxe et al., 1985). Either way, a polygraph examiner risks incorrectly identifying innocent people as guilty and failing to spot the liars.

Important statistical issues call the polygraph procedure into further question. Even if the examination were 95 percent accurate, a 5 percent error rate could lead to the misidentification of many innocent people as being guilty. To illustrate, imagine that your company arranges for all 500 of your employees to take a polygraph test to find out who has been stealing office supplies. Imagine also that only about 4 percent (20 out of 500 people) are really stealing, which is not an unreasonable estimate. If the lie detector test is 95 percent accurate, it will correctly spot 19 of these 20 thieves. But the test will also give 5 percent **false positives**, falsely fingering 5 percent of the innocent people. Of the 480 innocent employees, the polygraph will inaccurately implicate 24 as liars. That is, *you could end up with more people falsely accused of lying than people correctly accused of lying.* This was borne out in a field study of suspected criminals who were later either convicted or declared innocent. The polygraph results were no better than a random coin flip (Brett et al., 1986).

An equally serious concern with polygraphy is that there are no generally accepted standards either for administering a polygraph examination or for interpreting its results. Different examiners could conceivably come to different conclusions based on the same polygraph record.

What Conclusions Can We Draw?

For these reasons, the U.S. Congress has outlawed most uses of polygraph tests in job screening and in most areas of the government, except for high-security-risk positions. National Academies of Science (2003) has gone even further in a report saying that the polygraph is too crude to be useful for screening people to identify possible terrorists or other national security risks. Your authors agree.

As far as criminal investigations are concerned, we find a patchwork of laws on the admissibility of polygraph evidence among the states. Few have gone so far as imposing complete bans and 20 more allow such evidence only on agreement of both sides—although, in a few states, polygraph results are still routinely admissible in court (Gruben & Madsen, 2005). So where do you come down on the issue of using the polygraph in criminal cases? Does the fact that a "lie detector" test can sometimes force a confession from a suspect justify its use?

Alternative Approaches to Deception Detection

The reining-in of polygraph testing has spurred the development of alternative means of detecting dishonesty (Capps & Ryan, 2005; Lane, 2006). Much of this work has been devoted to paper-and-pencil instruments that are often called "integrity tests." How well do these instruments work? Not

very well, according to reports by the American Psychological Association and by the U.S. government's Office of Technology Assessment. In general, like the polygraph, these instruments seem to be more accurate than mere interviews, but they also suffer from a high false-positive rate.

More recently, researchers have turned to brain scanning techniques to see if they can catch liars (Ross, 2003). A certain brain wave pattern known as P300 has been linked with a variety of attention-getting cues, such as hearing one's name, but studies show it can also be evoked by fibbing. In addition, fMRI images show that lying activates all the brain areas involved in telling the truth, plus several more (Langleben et al., 2002). This suggests that lying is not something completely separate from the truth but an operation the liar must perform on the truth, says psychiatrist Daniel Langleben, all of which raises the concern that there is too much hype and too little solid evidence behind brain-scan-based lie detection (Gamer, 2009; Stix, 2008). In addition, some neuroscientists worry about the ethics of peering directly into people's brains to "read" the neural traces of their private thoughts (Pearson, 2006).

The potential advantage of these newer brain-scan techniques is that they bypass the anxiety-response pathway used by polygraphy. By registering neural activity, they get much closer to the person's actual thoughts. But how well do these alternative methods work? Not well enough for the police and the courts—yet.

Finally, Paul Ekman—the same one who studies universal facial expressions of emotion—has found that liars often display fleeting "microexpressions" and other nonverbal cues. In one study, Ekman and his colleague Maureen O'Sullivan found that some people are especially good at detecting deception, but they are a small minority. In their tests, most people perform at about the chance level. Still, Ekman and O'Sullivan hope to learn what those most skilled at detecting deception look for and teach that to police officers and other concerned with crime and security issues (Adelson, 2004).

Do It Yourself! THINKING CRITICALLY ABOUT POLYGRAPHY

A quick Web search, using such terms as *polygraph, lie,* and *lie detection,* will reveal hundreds of sites arguing either for or against the use of polygraph exams to identify lawbreakers, potential terrorists, or other security risks. Pick a site—either pro or con—and analyze it according to our six criteria for critical thinking:

1. The source is credible—either an expert on the subject or someone who relies on those with expertise.

2. The claim is reasonable—not extreme.

3. The claim is supported by scientifically sound evidence, not testimonials or anecdotes.

4. There is no reasonable suspicion of bias, such as self-interest, emotional bias, or confirmation bias.

5. The claim avoids common logical fallacies, such as selective use of the evidence (e.g., using only the data that support one's position, while ignoring the rest).

6. Does the source use multiple psychological perspectives when appropriate?

Additional resources to help you with this Thinking Critically exercise are available in MyPsychLab. See also "The Truth About Lie Detectors (aka Polygraph Tests)" on the American Psychological Association's website: /www.apa.org/research/action/polygraph.aspx.

CHAPTER SUMMARY

((•—Listen to an audio file of your chapter at **MyPsychLab**

CHAPTER PROBLEM: Motivation is largely an internal and subjective process: How can we determine what motivates people like Lance Armstrong to work so hard at becoming the best in the world at what they do?

- The subjective nature of motivation has forced psychologists to study the underlying processes indirectly, using a variety of methods, including animal studies, the *TAT*, and brain scans.

- Psychologists have identified many important influences on motivation, including culture, goals, unconscious processes, various biological factors, and social pressures. Rewards, both *intrinsic* and *extrinsic* are also important for world-class athletes like Lance Armstrong.

- One of the biggest questions involves the priorities we give to our motives—an issue that Maslow addressed in his famous *hierarchy of needs*. Recently, evolutionary psychologists have proposed an updated needs hierarchy. Many athletes, performers and artists apparently do much of their work in a state of *flow*—a mental state in which the person focuses on an intrinsically rewarding task to the exclusion of all other needs.

- Understanding motivation also requires understanding a person's emotions—because emotions are a class of motives aroused by persons, objects, and situations in the individual's external world. Emotions serve as the "values" we place on alternatives when we make choices and decisions.

9.1 What Motivates Us?

[Core Concept 9.1 **Motives are internal dispositions to act in certain ways, although they can be influenced by multiple factors, both internal and external.**]

The concept of **motivation** refers to inferred internal processes that select and direct behavior toward a goal. Motivation also helps explain behavior that cannot be explained by the circumstances alone. Psychologists find it useful to distinguish **intrinsic motivation** from **extrinsic motivation**.

David McClelland pioneered the study of the **need for achievement (n Ach)**, a motive important for I/O psychologists concerned about worker motivation and job satisfaction. The need for achievement also correlates with academic success and other accomplishments in life. But just as important as **n Ach** are the needs for power and affiliation, according to McClelland. Cross-cultural research also shows that societies vary in the intensity of their need for achievement,

depending on their tendencies toward **individualism** or **collectivism**.

Psychologists have found that extrinsic rewards can destroy motivation for intrinsically rewarding tasks through **overjustification**. This is not always the case, however, but rather when rewards are given without regard for the quality of performance.

Great achievements usually come from people in a state of **flow**. Those in a flow state are intrinsically motivated by some problem or activity. The use of drugs or alcohol to achieve an artificial flow feeling is not usually effective.

motivation (p. 365)
extrinsic motivation (p. 365)
intrinsic motivation (p. 365)
need for achievement (n Ach) (p. 365)
individualism (p. 367)
collectivism (p. 367)
overjustification (p. 367)
flow (p. 368)

9.2 How Are Our Motivational Priorities Determined?

[Core Concept 9.2 **A new theory combining Maslow's hierarchy with evolutionary psychology solves some long-standing problems by suggesting that functional, proximal, and developmental factors set our motivational priorities.**]

Psychology has no successful theory that accounts for all of human motivation. Psychologists have explained biologically based motivation in terms of **instinct theory, fixed-action patterns**, and **drive theory**, and **homeostasis**. Cognitive psychologists have emphasized **biological motives**. Freud called attention to **unconscious motivation** and taught that all our motives derive from unconscious sexual and aggressive desires.

None of these approaches successfully explains the full range of human motivation, however.

With his influential **hierarchy of needs**, Maslow attempted to explain the priorities in which human motives appear. Critics have, however, pointed out many exceptions to his hierarchy. Recently, evolutionary psychologists have proposed a revision of Maslow's theory suggesting that our "default" motivational priorities can change, depending on developmental factors and on important (proximal) stimuli.

In trying to understand another person's motivation, a good place to start is with extrinsic incentives and threats. In addition, Alfred Adler taught that social motives explain many problem behaviors. Social psychologists combine these notions under the heading of the *power of the situation*.

instinct theory (p. 369)
fixed action patterns (p. 369)

9.3   Where Do Hunger and Sex Fit into the Motivational Hierarchy?

[**Core Concept** 9.3 **Although dissimilar in many respects, hunger and sex both have evolutionary origins, and each has an essential place in the motivational hierarchy.**]

Hunger is both a biological drive and a psychological motive, best understood by a multiple-systems approach. Americans receive mixed messages from the media, promoting both thinness and calorie-dense foods, which may play a role in disorders such as obesity, **anorexia nervosa**, and **bulimia nervosa**. None of these problems is completely understood, although both social and biological factors are thought to be involved. The problem of obesity has become an epidemic in America and is rapidly being exported throughout the world. Many people seek to control their appetite and body weight, although no weight-loss scheme is effective for most people over the long run.

Will power is a common term in everyday language, although psychologists avoid it because it suggests a separate faculty of the mind. They prefer *impulse control* or *self-control*, terms that can be explained in terms of brain mechanisms and environmental influences. Recently, researchers have found that impulse control takes a cognitive toll and is reflected in blood sugar levels.

Unlike hunger and weight control, the sex drive is not homeostatic, even though sexual motivation is heavily influenced by biology, but learning also plays a role, especially in humans. Particularly since Kinsey's surveys, the scientific study of sexuality has caused controversy in America, even though survey research shows that, over the last half century, Americans have become more liberal in their sexual practices. Masters and Johnson were the first to do extensive studies of sexual behavior in the laboratory, finding that the **sexual response cycles** of men and women are similar. More recently, Peplau has emphasized differences in male and female sexuality. Those adhering to the evolutionary perspective argue that differences in male and female sexuality arise from conflicting mating strategies and from the large biological investment women have in pregnancy—both of which encourage more promiscuity in men.

As Maslow's hierarchy did, the new evolution-based hierarchy generally gives hunger priority over sex, although the hierarchy is fluid.

The greatest puzzle about sexuality centers on the origins of **sexual orientation**, especially the factors leading to heterosexuality, homosexuality, and bisexuality. Transsexualism and transvestism are not predictive of sexual orientation. Most experts agree that sexual orientation involves a combination of biological, environmental, and social factors, although much of the research has focused on biology. Since the 1970s, homosexuality has not been viewed as a disorder by psychologists and psychiatrists.

9.4   How Do Our Emotions Motivate Us?

[**Core Concept** 9.4 **Emotions are a special class of motives that help us attend to and respond to important (usually external) situations and communicate our intentions to others.**]

Emotion is a process involving four main components: physiological arousal, cognitive interpretation, subjective feelings, and behavioral expression. Emotions can also act as motives. From an evolutionary standpoint, they help us approach or avoid recurring stimuli that are important for survival and reproduction. Socially, emotional expressions serve to communicate feelings and intentions, apparently aided by "mirror neurons."

Most experts posit a limited number of *basic emotions* that, in combination, produce a larger number of *secondary emotions*. At least seven basic facial expressions of emotion are universally understood across cultures, although these can be modified by culture-specific **display rules**. These universal emotions are probably biologically based.

Some emotional differences between males and females have biological roots. This is seen in differential rates of certain emotional disorders, as well as more frequent displays of anger in men. On the other hand, cultural differences demonstrate that some gender differences in emotion are learned. Specifically, different cultures teach men and women different display rules about controlling emotional expression. Despite the differences, neither sex can be said to be more emotional than the other.

9.5 What Processes Control Our Emotions?

[Core Concept 9.5 **Research has clarified the processes underlying both our conscious and unconscious emotional lives, shedding light on some old controversies.**]

Neuroscience has revealed two distinct emotion systems in the brain. One, a fast-response system, operates mainly at an unconscious level and relies on deep limbic structures, especially the amygdala. The other involves conscious processing in the cortex. The pathways intersect in the *ventromedial prefrontal cortex.* Emotions also involve visceral changes in response to messages transmitted by the autonomic nervous system and the hormone system. In addition to the two emotion pathways, the two hemispheres have a **lateralization of emotion** by which each specializes in processing a different class of emotion.

The inverted U theory describes the complex relationship between emotional arousal and performance: Increasing arousal improves performance—but only up to a certain optimum level of arousal, which depends on the complexity of the task. **Sensation seekers** seem to have an especially high need for arousal.

Understanding how the two emotion systems work has begun to resolve some long-standing controversies involving the roles of cognition and physical responses in emotion. The **James–Lange theory** argued that physical sensations and physical responses produce emotional feelings. The opposing **Cannon–Bard theory** stated that our cognitive appraisal produces both emotions and the accompanying physical response. Stanley Schachter's **two-factor theory** suggested that emotions are the result of cognitive appraisal of both our internal physical state and the external situation. The research shows that all three viewpoints have a share in the truth.

Emotional intelligence, the ability to keep one's emotions from getting out of control, is vital for maintaining good social relationships. It is distinct from the abilities measured by traditional IQ tests. Increased emotional control can be achieved by learning, as demonstrated in anger management programs. Tests of emotional intelligence show that those who score highly tend to succeed in social situations.

Under some circumstances, the expression of anger without aggression can have positive results. The public, however, generally holds the dangerous misconception that it is always best to "vent" one's anger and "get it out of the system." Studies show that such venting often leads to the increased likelihood of aggression later.

lateralization of emotion (p. 394)
inverted U function (p. 396)
sensation seekers (p. 397)
James–Lange theory (p. 398)
Cannon–Bard theory (p. 398)
two-factor theory (p. 399)
emotional intelligence (p. 400)

CRITICAL THINKING APPLIED

Do Lie Detectors Really Detect Lies?

"Lie detectors" work on the assumption that people will show physical signs of arousal when lying. While polygraph examiners sometimes extract confessions when they convince suspects that the test can show them lying, the evidence does not indicate that the results are always reliable. Particularly troubling is that, under some circumstances, the polygraph test can identify more false positives than actual liars. Alternative approaches that use facial expressions or brain scans are being explored, but so far they have not been validated.

DISCOVERING PSYCHOLOGY **VIEWING GUIDE**

Watch the following video by logging into MyPsychLab (www.mypsychlab.com).
After you have watched the video, answer the questions that follow.

PROGRAM 12: **MOTIVATION AND EMOTION**

Program Review

1. What is the general term for all the physical and psychological processes that start behavior, maintain it, and stop it?
   a. explanatory style
   b. repression
   c. addiction
   d. motivation

2. Phoebe has a phobia regarding cats. What is her motivation?
   a. environmental arousal
   b. overwhelming fear
   c. repressed sexual satisfaction
   d. a need for attachment to others

3. What is the role of the pleasure–pain principle in motivation?
   a. We repress our pleasure in others' pain.
   b. We seek pleasure and avoid pain.
   c. We persist in doing things even when they are painful.
   d. We are more intensely motivated by pain than by pleasure.

4. Which activity most clearly involves a "reframing" of the tension between desire and restraint?
   a. eating before you feel hungry
   b. seeking pleasurable physical contact with others
   c. working long hours for an eventual goal
   d. getting angry at someone who interferes with your plans

5. Sigmund Freud thought there were two primary motivations. One of these is
   a. expressing aggression.
   b. seeking transcendence.
   c. fulfilling creativity.
   d. feeling secure.

6. Compared with Freud's view of human motivation, that of Abraham Maslow could be characterized as being more
   a. negative.   c. optimistic.
   b. hormonally based.   d. pathologically based.

7. Behaviors, such as male peacocks displaying their feathers or male rams fighting, are related to which part of sexual reproduction?
   a. providing a safe place for mating
   b. focusing the male's attention on mating
   c. selecting a partner with good genes
   d. mating at the correct time of year

8. In Norman Adler's research on mating behavior in rats, what is the function of the ten or so mountings?
   a. to trigger hormone production and uterine contractions in the female
   b. to warn off rival males
   c. to cause fertilization
   d. to impress the female

9. What kinds of emotions tend to be involved in romantic love?
   a. mainly intense, positive emotions
   b. mainly intense, negative emotions
   c. a mixture of intense and weak emotions that are mainly positive
   d. a mixture of positive and negative emotions that are intense

10. Charles Darwin cited the similarity of certain expressions of emotions as evidence that
    a. all species learn emotions.
    b. emotions are innate.
    c. emotions promote survival of the fittest.
    d. genetic variability is advantageous.

11. Pictures of happy and sad American workers are shown to U.S. college students and to Italian workers. Based on your knowledge of Paul Ekman's research, what would you predict about how well the groups would identify the emotions?
    a. Both groups will identify the emotions correctly.
    b. Only the Americans will identify the emotions correctly.
    c. Only the Italians will identify the emotions correctly.
    d. Neither group will identify the emotions correctly.

12. Theodore has an explanatory style that emphasizes the external, the unstable, and the specific. He makes a mistake at work that causes his boss to become very angry. Which statement is Theodore most likely to make to himself?

    a. "I always make such stupid mistakes."

    b. "I was just distracted by the noise outside."

    c. "All my life, people have always gotten so mad at me."

    d. "If I were a better person, this wouldn't have happened."

13. Why does Martin Seligman believe that it might be appropriate to help children who develop a pessimistic explanatory style?

    a. These children are unpleasant to be around.

    b. These children lack contact with reality.

    c. These children are at risk for depression.

    d. Other children who live with these children are likely to develop the same style.

14. What other outcome will a pessimistic explanatory style likely affect, according to Seligman?

    a. health

    b. artistic ability

    c. reasoning skills

    d. language competence

15. All of the following are possible origins of a pessimistic explanatory style, *except*

    a. assessments by important adults in our lives.

    b. the reality of our first major negative life event.

    c. our mother's pessimism level.

    d. our level of introversion/extraversion.

16. Which theorist is best known for positing a hierarchy of needs that humans strive to meet?

    a. Freud   c. Maslow

    b. Rogers   d. Seligman

17. Although motivation can lead to unpleasant states (e.g., hunger, frustration), it seems to have evolved because of its benefits to

    a. survival.   c. health.

    b. propagation of the species.   d. all of the above.

18. What has Robert Plutchik argued about emotions?

    a. There are three basic types of emotions: happiness, sadness, and anger.

    b. There are eight basic emotions, consisting of four pairs of opposites.

    c. Love is not a universal emotion; some cultures do not show signs of having it.

    d. Emotional experience is determined by physiology alone.

19. Four people have been obese for as long as they can remember. Their doctors tell all of them that their obesity is putting them at risk for several illnesses. Who is most likely to join a gym, go on a diet, and get in shape?

    a. Al, whose explanatory style includes an internal locus of control

    b. Bob, who has a pessimistic explanatory style

    c. Chuck, whose explanatory style includes an unstable locus of control

    d. Dwayne, who is depressed about his obesity

20. Wolves and squirrels are most likely to show which of the following in their mating patterns?

    a. romantic love

    b. competition by females for males

    c. competition by males for females

    d. a preference for mating in the autumn so that the offspring will be born during the winter

10 Personality: Theories of the Whole Person

	Core Concepts	Psychology Matters
10.1 What Forces Shape Our Personalities? Biology, Human Nature, and Personality The Effects of Nurture: Personality and the Environment The Effects of Nature: Dispositions and Mental Processes Social and Cultural Contributions to Personality	Personality is shaped by the combined forces of biological, situational, and mental processes—all embedded in a sociocultural and developmental context.	**Explaining Unusual People and Unusual Behavior** You don't need a theory of personality to explain why people do the expected.
10.2 What Persistent Patterns, or *Dispositions*, Make Up Our Personalities? Personality and Temperament Personality as a Composite of Traits	The *dispositional* theories all suggest a small set of personality characteristics, known as temperaments, traits, or types, that provide consistency to the individual's personality over time.	**Finding Your Type** When it comes to classifying personality according to types, a little caution may be in order.
10.3 How Do Mental *Processes* Help Shape Our Personalities? Psychodynamic Theories: Emphasis on Motivation and Mental Disorder Humanistic Theories: Emphasis on Human Potential and Mental Health Social-Cognitive Theories: Emphasis on Social Learning Current Trends: The Person in a Social System	While each of the *process* theories sees different forces at work in personality, all portray personality as the result of both internal mental processes and social interactions.	**Using Psychology to Learn Psychology** An external locus of control about grades poses danger for students.
10.4 What "Theories" Do People Use to Understand Themselves and Others? Implicit Personality Theories Self-Narratives: The Stories of Our Lives The Effects of Culture on Our Views of Personality	Our understanding of ourselves and others is based on implicit theories of personality and our own self-narratives—both of which are influenced by culture.	**The Personality of Time** Whether you live in the past, present, or future can have a big impact on your life.

CHAPTER PROBLEM What influences were at work to produce the unique behavioral patterns, high achievement motivation, and consistency over time and place that we see in the personality of Mary Calkins?

CRITICAL THINKING APPLIED The Person–Situation Controversy

DO YOU THINK OF YOURSELF AS UNIQUE? OR ARE YOU PRETTY MUCH the same as most other people? Are you able to predict pretty well what things you will or won't do in the coming year based on your sense of who you are and what you stand for? Do your friends and family see you as consistent and predictable in how you behave in different settings? Most people assume that how they usually behave is largely the function of a set of inner determinants, genes, character, and personality traits that, taken together, form their core self.

The idea that you are a distinct individual with a self that makes you different from everyone else is an assumption that we rarely question. But what most of us probably don't realize is that the concept of the self took root in psychology because of a woman who struggled all her life to be recognized as a competent scholar by an academic world that dismissed her because of her "unacceptable" gender (Calkins, 1906, 1930; DiFebo, 2002).

Mary Calkins came into psychology through the back door. Wellesley College, where she had been teaching languages, recognized her as an outstanding teacher and offered her a job in the emerging discipline of psychology, provided she could get some additional training—a practice not unusual at women's colleges at the time. But finding a graduate school that would take a woman was not easy in the late 1800s. Nevertheless, Harvard was a possibility, especially because the legendary William James (discussed in Chapter 1) wanted her to be his student.

There was only one obstacle: Harvard did not accept female students at that time. Its president, Charles Eliot, strongly believed in separate education for men and women but he relented under pressure from James and other members of the psychology department—only under the condition that Mary Calkins attend classes informally and not be eligible for a degree. (Harvard refused to award doctorates to women until 1963.)

Mary Whiton Calkins, the first woman to become president of the American Psychological Association, never received her PhD although she earned it.

personality   The psychological qualities that bring continuity to an individual's behavior in different situations and at different times.

CONNECTION CHAPTER 12

Multiple personality and *split personality* are older terms for dissociative identity disorder (p. 536).

By the spring of 1895, Calkins had finished her coursework and had completed ground-breaking research on memory, which became her doctoral dissertation, *Association: An Essay Analytic and Experimental*. The rebellious psychology faculty at Harvard held an unauthorized oral defense of her dissertation and petitioned the board of directors to award her a PhD. William James praised her performance as "the most brilliant examination for the PhD that we have had at Harvard." Nevertheless, the directors refused. An incensed William James told Calkins that Harvard's action was "enough to make dynamiters of you and all women" (Furumoto, 1979, p. 350).

Despite being denied the doctoral degree she had earned, Mary Calkins returned to Wellesley where, as promised, she was welcomed as a teacher of psychology. A productive scholar as well as a teacher, she eventually published more than 100 articles and books, including her best-selling text, *An Introduction to Psychology*. In 1902, she pointedly refused the consolation prize of a PhD from Radcliffe College, a women's institution associated with Harvard. And in 1905, she became the first woman president of the American Psychological Association.

Calkins's pattern of persistent motivation to learn and succeed despite the obstacles spanning her entire professional life illustrates the central idea of this chapter: **Personality** consists of all the psychological qualities and processes that bring continuity to an individual's behavior in different situations and across different times. It's a broad concept that we might also describe as the thread of consistency that runs through our lives (Cervone & Shoda, 1999). And should this thread of consistency break, it may leave a personality fraught with the inconsistencies that we see, for example, in personality disorders or more extreme mental impairments as in bipolar disorder, schizophrenia, and so-called "multiple personality" disorder.

The puzzle facing the psychologist interested in personality requires fitting together all the diverse pieces that make up the individual. It requires an integration of everything we have studied up until now—learning, perception, development, motivation, emotion, and all the rest—in the attempt to understand the individual as a unified whole. In Chapter 1, we named this the *whole-person perspective*.

In some respects, personality is pretty simple because we are all somewhat alike. We generally prefer pleasure to pain, we seek meaning in our lives, and we often judge ourselves by the standards set by the behavior of others. But beyond such obvious similarities, we are also unique individuals—each unlike anyone else. Just as there are no two fingerprints exactly alike among the billions of people worldwide, so too there are really not any two people exactly alike who are totally interchangeable—not even identical twins. So personality is also the psychology of *individual differences*—what makes us think, feel, and act differently from others in the same situation.

How does a psychologist go about making sense of personality? Let us illustrate using Mary Calkins as the subject of the problem around which this chapter is organized.

PROBLEM: What influences were at work to produce the unique behavioral patterns, high achievement motivation, and consistency over time and place that we see in the personality of Mary Calkins?

Was her personality shaped primarily by the people around her and events in her life? Those events were so often beyond her control that we must consider another possibility: that her courage and determination arose more from internal traits—from her basic makeup. That basic makeup includes her values, attitudes, work habits, and self-reinforcing tendencies. You may recognize these two broad alternatives as another variation on the basic nature–nurture question we have encountered earlier. The answer, of course, lies with both: Experience *and* innate factors shaped Mary Calkins's personality, just as they shape yours and ours.

In this chapter, we will examine several theoretical explanations for what personality is, how it develops, and how it functions. As we do so, you will find that some theories place more emphasis on nature and others on nurture. You will also find that particular theories are suited to dealing with particular kinds of personality issues. For example:

- If what you need is a snapshot of a person's current personality characteristics—as you might want if you were screening job applicants for your company—a theory of *temperaments, traits,* or *types* may be your best bet.

- If your goal is to understand someone as a developing, changing being—a friend who asks you for advice, perhaps—you will probably find one of the *psychodynamic, humanistic,* or *social-cognitive theories* of personality most helpful.

- If you are most interested in how people understand each other—as you might be if you were doing marriage counseling or conflict management—you will want to know the assumptions people make about each other. That is, you will want to know their *implicit theories of personality.*

- And, if you are wondering whether people understand each other in the same ways the world around, you will want to know about the *cross-cultural* work in personality that we have infused throughout the chapter.

We begin our exploration of personality now with an overview of the forces that have shaped us all.

10.1 KEY QUESTION
What Forces Shape Our Personalities?

Personality makes us not only human but also different from everyone else. Thus, we might think of personality as the "default settings" for our individually unique patterns of motives, emotions, and perceptions along with our learned schemas for understanding ourselves and our world (McAdams & Pals, 2006). *Personality* is also the collective term for the qualities that make us who we are. All of this, in turn, is embedded in the context of our culture, social relationships, and developmental level. In other words, virtually every aspect of our being comes together to form our personality (see Figure 10.1.). We can capture this idea in our Core Concept for this section.

Core Concept 10.1

Personality is shaped by the combined forces of biological, situational, and mental processes—all embedded in a sociocultural and developmental context.

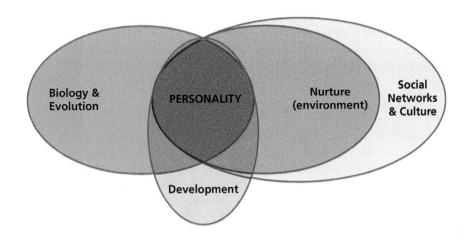

FIGURE 10.1

Personality as the Psychology of the Whole Person

We can think of personality as the intersection of all the psychological characteristics and processes that make us both human and, at the same time, different from everyone else.

Let's look at each of these elements of personality, beginning with an overview of the forces of biology and evolution.

Biology, Human Nature, and Personality

Put two laboratory rats in a cage and electrify the floor with repeated shocks, and the rats will attack each other. We can see much of the same behavior in humans, who lash out at any convenient target when they feel threatened. Thus, in the early 20th century, the number of lynchings of Blacks in the Southern United States rose and fell in a mirror-image response to the state of the economy—particularly the price of cotton. And in the 1930s, Nazi leader Adolph Hitler placed the blame for Germany's economic troubles on Jews, against whom he turned Germany into a racist Nazi state that embraced the Holocaust—the systematically orchestrated genocide of all European Jews.

These are all examples of what Sigmund Freud called *displacement of aggression*. Sometimes we call it *scapegoating*, after the ancient Hebrew ritual of symbolically transferring the sins of the tribe to a goat that was then driven out into the desert to die. Displacement was also what William James was talking about when he suggested that Harvard's refusal to give Mary Calkins the degree she earned was "enough to make dynamiters of you and all women." He meant female terrorists who would feel justified in using dynamite to blow up Harvard University, or at least its sexist male administration.

Nothing, of course, can justify mayhem, murder, or genocide—but perhaps we can explain these actions. According to David Barash (2007), human history is the story of those who responded to painful or threatening situations by striking at the nearest target. Those who did so had a clear evolutionary advantage over those who just sat and "took it" because they were less likely to be victims the next time around. They were also more likely to breed and pass along this tendency for aggression and displacement to their descendants.

Displacement of aggression is not the only human characteristic that seems to be built into our biology. As we noted earlier, most people prefer pleasure to pain—often sexual pleasure. The obvious human propensity for sex and aggression fits with Darwin's idea that we come from a long line of ancestors who were driven to survive and reproduce. Sigmund Freud, picking up this "survival of the fittest" notion, argued that everything we do arises from a sex-based survival "instinct" and an "instinct" for defense and aggression. Other theorists have proposed that personality is based on still other motives that undoubtedly have some basis in biology—particularly social motives. Much like ants and bees, they have pointed out, we humans are "social animals" too.

Which view is right? Modern neuroscience and evolutionary psychology suggest that the search for only a few basic urges behind all human behavior is misguided (McAdams & Pals, 2006). The emerging picture is a far messier one. We (that is, our brains) seem to be collections of "modules," each adapted to a different purpose—which may be the reason we have so many different motives, each operating by different rules, as we saw in the previous chapter. Sex, aggression, hunger, affiliation, thirst, and achievement—each is simultaneously a separate module in the brain but also a part of the collective entity we call "personality."

The Effects of Nurture: Personality and the Environment

Biology and evolution can't explain everything. Even the geneticists grudgingly admit that heredity accounts for only roughly half our characteristics (Robins, 2005). For example, a child whose parents both have schizophrenia, a largely genetically based mental disorder, is likely also to develop schizophrenia only 50 percent of the time. What accounts for the rest of the equation? The rest, broadly speaking, comes from the environment, which molds us according to the principles of behavioral conditioning, cognitive learning, and social psychology.

William James studied consciousness and was interested in how the mind functions to guide behavior.

CONNECTION CHAPTER 4

Environment often affects us through *operant conditioning* and *classical conditioning* (p. 135).

What environments make the most difference? Many personality theorists empha-size early childhood experiences: From this perspective, your own personality owes much to your parents, not just for their genes but also for the environment they gave you (assuming you were raised by your parents). At the extreme, children who receive essentially no human contact, as in those abandoned to custodial care in the worst of orphanages, emerge as stunted on virtually every measure of physical and mental well-being (Nelson et al., 2007; Spitz, 1946).

There is some dispute over just how persistent the family environment is as we come under the sway of adolescent peer pressures (Harris, 1995). Yet even birth order seems to influence personality throughout our lives, because the environment for each successive child in a family—from the oldest to the youngest—is different. Were you the first child? If so, you are more likely than your later-born siblings to end up in a career that requires use of your intellect and high achievement, says development theo-rist J. Frank Sulloway (1996). Or are you the youngest? Chances are that you are more likely to make people laugh than your more sober older siblings. A specific example underscores the point: In a study of more than 700 brothers who played professional baseball, Sulloway found that younger brothers were far more likely to take chances and risks, such as attempting to steal bases, than were their more conservative first-born siblings. In addition, the younger brothers were also more likely to be successful when they took such risks (Sulloway & Zweigenhaft, 2010). Incidentally, the high-achieving Mary Calkins, as the first-born of five children in her family, fits the pattern. (We should add that no one believes these patterns *always* hold true; they are merely statistical probabilities that hold on average.)

So important are environmental influences that personality psychologist Walter Mischel (2003) has suggested that they usually overwhelm all other effects—including any inborn traits. Just think how often during the day you simply respond to environmental dictates, from the ringing of your alarm clock to the commands of red traffic lights to the inquiry, "How are you?" So, is Mischel right? We will examine this issue, better known as the *person–situation controversy*, in the *Critical Thinking Applied* section at the end of the chapter.

The Effects of Nature: Dispositions and Mental Processes

Important as the environment is, we still must pass our experiences through a series of internal mental "filters" that represent core elements of personality. Suppose, for example, that you are an outgoing person—an *extravert*—who prefers to be with other people than to be more solitary. Your sister, however, prefers to spend more time alone practicing music and painting with watercolors. She would be classified as an *introvert*. You will interpret your experiences from your extraverted point of view. Party time! The introvert–extravert dimension exemplifies the *descriptive* approach to personality, focusing on an individual's relatively stable *personality characteristics* or **dispositions**. Others that we might call *process theories* go beyond description to explain personality in terms of the internal **personality processes** we have been studying throughout this text: motivation, perception, learning, and development, as well as conscious and unconscious processes. For a complete explanation of personality, we seem to need both the *disposi-tional theories* and *process theories* that we will encounter later in the chapter.

disposition   Relatively stable personality pattern, including temperaments, traits, and personality types.

personality process   The internal working of the personality, involving motivation, emotion, perception, and learning, as well as unconscious processes.

Social and Cultural Contributions to Personality

According to cross-cultural psychologist Juris Draguns (1979), the very concept of personality theory is a Western (Euro-American) invention. So it is not surprising that the most comprehensive and influential theories of personality were created by people trained in the framework of the Western social sciences, with a built-in bias toward individualism and a unique "self" (Guisinger & Blatt, 1994; Segall et al., 1999). Other cultures, however, address the problem of differences among people in their own ways. Most of these non-Western perspectives have originated in religion (Walsh, 1984). Hindus, for example, see personality as a union of opposing characteristics (Murphy & Murphy, 1968). The Chinese concept of complementary opposite forces, *yin* and *yang*, provides another variation on this same theme.

individualism   The view, common in the Euro-American world, that places a high value on individual achievement and distinction.

collectivism   The view, common in Asia, Africa, Latin America, and the Middle East, that values group loyalty and pride over individual distinction.

But what about the inverse problem? What influence does culture have on personality? We will see that, in a few respects, personality is much the same across cultures. That is, we can describe people all over the world in terms of just a few basic personality traits. For instance, people everywhere vary in their level of anxiety and in their tendency to be outgoing or introverted. But there are also components of personality on which cultures themselves exert huge differences. One example involves *individualism* versus *collectivism*. People in the United States and other Western countries tend to emphasize **individualism**, which rewards those who stand out from the crowd because of such characteristics as talent, intelligence, or athletic ability. In contrast, people in the more group-oriented cultures of Asia, Africa, Latin America, and the Middle East emphasize **collectivism**, which rewards people for fitting in with the group and promoting social harmony.

And *within* any culture, be it individualistic or collectivistic, social relationships have an enormous impact on personality—as we have noted in neglected children and in those forced to grow up in "tough" neighborhoods. To a large extent, who you are is determined by those with whom you interacted while growing up, including not just your parents but also your siblings, classmates, teachers, and anyone else with whom you had spent time interacting. Thus, your personality is, in part, a creation of other people—so, in the final section of this chapter, we will look more closely at just how these social and cultural factors shape our personalities. An interesting new issue to consider is the impact on you of your *Facebook* friends and contacts, with some of whom you may never have "face time."

Cross-Cultural Differences in Shyness   The interplay of culture and environmental learning is revealed when we examine differences in shyness between Asians and Israelis. Research has shown that in the United States, about 40 percent of adults considered themselves to be shy people (in 1970 to 1980), but that figure rose to about 60 percent among Asian-Americans and dropped to about 25 percent among Jewish-Americans (Zimbardo, 1977). Similar disparities were found when Chinese and Israelis were surveyed in their home countries.

Why such a striking difference in this universal trait of shyness? Interviews with parents, teachers, coaches, and children uncovered a simple causal factor: How each culture dealt with a child's successes and failures. In many Asian cultures, when a child or anyone tries a task and succeeds, who gets the credit? Answer: the grandparents, parents, teachers, coaches, and perhaps even Buddha get some credit in that belief system. But what if that child fails at a task, who gets the blame? Answer: All blame is heaped on the child. The resulting behavioral style becomes one of low risk taking, cautiousness, and minimizing personal visibility in general; in short, becoming a shy person. "A nail that sticks out will soon be hammered down" is a theme in those cultures that promotes modest reserve.

In Israel, the child who fails at an assigned task is greeted by everyone else fully ready to take the blame—for not feeding him enough, for not giving her sufficient training, for the unfairness of the competition, and more. But should the child succeed, the heavens open with endless praise. (The Yiddish term is *kvelling,* or making much ado, sometimes about nothing.) Thus, Israeli children are encouraged to take risks, to put both feet forward, to be outgoing because—their culture teaches them—there is nothing to lose and everything to gain. It's a recipe for antishyness, to be sure (Carducci & Zimbardo, 1995; Pines & Zimbardo, 1978).

[PSYCHOLOGY MATTERS]

Explaining Unusual People and Unusual Behavior

You don't need a theory of personality to explain why people generally get to work on time, sing along at concerts, or spend weekends with their family and friends. That is, you don't need a theory of personality to explain why people do what you would expect them to do, because in some situations, most of us do the same thing. But, when they behave in odd and unexpected ways, a personality theory comes in very handy. A good theory can help you understand interesting and unusual people, such as Mary Calkins, or those whom you read about in the newspaper—perhaps a serial killer, a politician embroiled in sex scandal, or the antics of a favorite movie star who is in and out of drug rehab seemingly every other week.

In early 2011, a 22-year-old man, Jared Loughner, shocked the nation by gunning down 19 citizens assembled in a public space in Tucson, Arizona, to meet and greet their Congresswoman, Gabrielle Giffords (Lacey & Herszenhorn, 2011). The senator survived a bullet shot into her head, but six others died. The disaster would have been even worse had the shooter been able to reload his automatic weapon and fire off another round of 31 bullets. Fortunately, he was prevented from doing so by the heroic actions of three people, a young man assisted by an elderly man and woman. What was wrong with the killer, and what was right with those heroes? The general public, as well as psychologists, wants to know the answers to those questions.

Tiger Woods, one of the world's most recognized personalities, was exposed as having sexual affairs with many women. His sexual obsession cost him his marriage and millions of dollars in alimony and lost endorsements, as well as public disgrace.

Going from this unknown person engaging in unusual behavior to a super well-known person also engaging behavior that was unusual for him, we have the case of golfing legend Tiger Woods. This seemingly happily married family man was publicly exposed as having engaged repeatedly in sexual escapades with many different "escorts." The scandal destroyed his marriage, seriously damaged his career, and cost him tens of millions of dollars in lost income from his sponsors. To understand the why of his transgression, we will need to turn to both personality and motivational psychology later on.

But which approach to personality is best? Unfortunately, we will see that none has the whole truth. Each theory we cover in this chapter can help you see people from a different angle, so you may need to use several perspectives to get the whole-person picture. To give you a preview of coming attractions, let's suppose that you are a counseling psychologist working at a college counseling center and a client, a young woman, tells you that she is contemplating suicide. How can your knowledge of personality help you understand her?

From a purely descriptive point of view, you might assess her personality *traits* and *temperament*. Is she conscientious? Is she outgoing or shy? Anxious? To find out, you might give her one of several personality "tests" that we will talk about in the next section of the chapter. Her profile of traits and temperament may suggest some form of psychological treatment or, perhaps, a more direct drug therapy.

If you decide on a psychological therapy, you will be working with the internal *processes* in her personality and, perhaps, social forces at work in her environment and culture. This is the territory originally staked out by Sigmund Freud and his supporters and, more recently, by experimental psychologists.

A *psychodynamic theory* would direct your focus toward her motives and emotions, some of which may be unconscious, that she does not recognize. Is she a hostile person who has turned her hostility on herself? Does she have some unfinished emotional business from an earlier developmental stage, such as guilt for angry feelings toward her parents? What is the nature of her social relationships?

In contrast, a *humanistic theory* would emphasize the exploration of her potentialities rather than of her deficiencies. What are her talents? Her hopes and desires? And what obstacles stand between her and her goals? A humanistic theory would also help you explore her unmet needs. Do her suicidal thoughts result from conscious feelings that she is alone, unloved, or not sufficiently respected?

A *social-cognitive theory,* with its emphasis on perception and learning, might suggest that her difficulty is in the way she interprets events. Does she always assume that her best efforts are not good enough? Does she believe that she can control the events in her life, or do external events control her? A cognitive approach might also alert you to the possibility that her suicidal thoughts reflect a suicidal role model—perhaps a friend, a family member, or, as in "copycat suicides," some celebrity who has recently committed suicide in a particular way.

All of these approaches to personality will be explored in detail later in the chapter. For now, here is the take-away message: No one theory has a complete answer to the problem of understanding why people do what they do. The trait and temperament theories can provide a descriptive snapshot of a person's characteristics, while the "process" theories (psychodynamic, humanistic, or social-cognitive theories) describe the forces that underlie those characteristics. And in most cases—whether they be heroes, villains, Tiger Woods, or the suicidal young woman we described—some combination of both is in order.

Check Your Understanding

✓●─[Study] and **Review** at **MyPsychLab**

1. **RECALL:** The fact that displacement of aggression is found in humans everywhere, as well as in animals, suggests that it is rooted in _____.

2. **APPLICATION:** Give an example that shows the influence of nurture on personality.

3. **ANALYSIS:** What is the distinction between trait and temperament theories and the *process* theories of personality?

4. **RECALL:** A person from a collectivist culture is more likely than one from an individualist culture to emphasize _____.

5. **UNDERSTANDING THE CORE CONCEPT:** What are the major factors that affect the formation of the personality?

Answers 1. our biological nature **2.** An example given in the text involves the influence of birth order on personality. There are many others, including, perhaps, examples from your own experience. And in the news we read of "child soldiers" who are caught in the civil wars of the world's poorest countries and are trained as hardened killers. **3.** The dispositional theories describe personality in terms of characteristics (traits, temperaments, or types), while the process theories describe personality in terms of internal processes (e.g., motivation, learning, or perception) and social interactions. **4.** the importance of the group and harmonious relationships within the group **5.** Personality is shaped by biology, the environment (situational pressures), mental processes, development, and the sociocultural context.

Hippocrates was an early contributor to the idea of a mind–body connection. One of his beliefs was that our individual temperament is driven by our predominant body fluid, or humor, and could be either sanguine, choleric, melancholic, or phlegmatic.

humors   Four body fluids—blood, phlegm, black bile, and yellow bile—that, according to an ancient theory, control personality by their relative abundance.

⌐10.2 KEY QUESTION
What Persistent Patterns, or *Dispositions*, Make Up Our Personalities?

Two thousand years before academic psychology appeared, people were classifying each other according to four *temperaments,* based on a theory proposed by the Greek physician Hippocrates *(Hip-POCK-rah-tees)*. A person's temperament, he suggested, resulted from the balance of the four **humors**, or fluids, secreted by the body (see Figure 10.2). A *sanguine,* or cheerful, person was characterized by strong, warm blood. A *choleric* temperament, marked by anger, came from yellow bile (called *choler*), believed to flow from the liver. Hippocrates thought that the spleen produced black bile, from which arose a *melancholic,* or depressed, temperament. Finally, if the body's dominant fluid is phlegm, or mucus, the person will have a *phlegmatic* temperament: cool, aloof, sluggish, and unemotional. Hippocrates' biology may have been a little off the mark, but his notion of temperaments established itself as "common sense." Even today, you will occasionally encounter his terms used to describe people's personalities.

In modern times, other personality classification systems have appeared. The most simplistic ones are just stereotypes: if fat, then jolly; if an engineer, then conservative; if female, then sympathetic. Obviously, these beliefs oversimplify the very complicated problem of understanding the patterns found in personality. Even you may be guilty of such oversimplifications if you think of people strictly according to categories and stereotypes: college major, gender, ethnicity, and qualities such as honesty, friendliness, or sense of humor.

Still, something in human nature and the cognitive tendency to simplify complexity seems to encourage us to group people into categories. So some personality theorists have sought to describe people in terms of just a few basic *temperaments:* global

The Humor Theory		
Humors	**Source**	**Temperament**
blood	heart	sanguine (cheerful)
choler (yellow bile)	liver	choleric (angry)
melancholer (black bile)	**spleen**	**melancholy (depressed)**
phlegm	brain	phlegmatic (sluggish)

FIGURE 10.2
The Humor Theory

dispositions of personality, such as "outgoing" or "shy," that have a strong biological basis. Others prefer to look for combinations of *traits,* which are generally thought of as multiple dimensions of personality, such as cautious versus reckless or friendly versus unfriendly, which are usually considered to be more influenced by experience (learning) than are temperaments. Still others classify people according to personality *types,* which are categories rather than dimensions: You either fit the pattern for a type or you do not. For example, if introversion is a *trait dimension,* then people can have degrees of introversion. On the other hand, if introversion is a *type,* then people are classified as either being introverted or not.

While each of these approaches is a bit different, our Core Concept indicates that they also have a common meeting ground:

Core Concept 10.2

The *dispositional* theories all suggest a small set of personality characteristics, known as temperaments, traits, or types, that provide consistency to the individual's personality over time.

Because the terms *temperament, trait,* and *type* overlap, we will follow the custom of placing them all under the generic heading of **dispositional theories.** But what makes such theories different from mere stereotypes—the conservative engineer, the macho male, or the blond bimbo? It's all in the science. A good temperament, trait, or type theory must have a solid scientific base. In that light, let's evaluate each of these approaches to personality, beginning with *temperament.*

Personality and Temperament

Psychologists define *temperament* as the biologically based personality dispositions that are usually apparent in early childhood and that establish the foundation of the personality and the mood of an individual's approach to life (Hogan et al., 1996; Mischel, 1993). When speaking of temperaments, psychologists are usually referring to one or two dominant and long-standing themes, such as shyness or moodiness, that characterize a person's personality, perhaps from birth. Modern psychology has, of course, abandoned the four humors theory of temperament, but it has retained its most basic concept: *Biological dispositions do affect our basic personalities.* In support of this view, psychologists can now point to structures in the brain that are known to regulate fundamental aspects of personality (LeDoux, 2002). You will recall, for example, the case of Phineas Gage, who received an accidental "lobotomy" and thereby demonstrated the role of the frontal lobes in regulating one's basic disposition—an observation confirmed by modern neuroscience.

Temperament from Transmitters? Biological psychologists now suspect that some individual differences in temperament also arise from the balance of chemicals in the

dispositional theory A general term that includes the temperament, trait, and type approaches to personality.

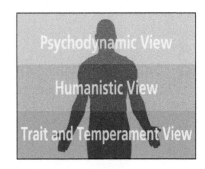

CONNECTION CHAPTER 2

Phineas Gage was a railroad worker who experienced an amazing consequence of an exploding metal rod shooting into and out of his skull. He survived, but his personality and basic response style changed dramatically to become more confrontational and emotional (p. 62).

Some shyness is inherited, and some is learned through personal experience and cultural norms.

brain, which may, in turn, have a genetic basis (Azar, 2002b; Sapolsky, 1992). In this sense, the theory of humors still lives but in a different guise: Modern biological psychology has replaced the humors with neurotransmitters. So, depression—which characterizes most suicidal people with suicidal thoughts—may result from an imbalance of certain transmitters. Likewise, anxiety, anger, and euphoria may each arise from other neurochemical patterns. As developmental psychologist Jerome Kagan says, "We all have the same neurotransmitters, but each of us has a slightly different mix" (Stavish, 1994, p. 7). That, says Kagan, is what accounts for many of the temperamental differences among people.

In fact, Kagan runs a fascinating research program focusing on the inherited basis of shyness (Kagan, et al. 2005; Kagan et al., 1994). This program has clearly demonstrated that, on their very first day, newborns in the nursery already differ in the degree to which they are responsive to stimulation. About 20 percent of all children are highly responsive and excitable, and 10 percent are extremely "inhibited." While approximately twice as many (35 to 40 percent) remain calm in response to new stimulation, another 10 percent can be seen as "bold." Over their first few months of life, these initial differences manifest themselves in temperamental differences: Many of the excitable, inhibited infants become shy and introverted, while the less excitable, more bold ones become extraverted. Although these tendencies change in some children, for most they persist over time, with the majority of children being classified with the same temperament in measurements taken over an 11-year interval. Kagan describes such effects as being due to "push of nature" in different directions.

Tempered With a Bit of Learning? On the other hand, we know that the percentage of shy college-age students—40 percent or more—is much higher than the percentage of these initially inhibited shy babies (Zimbardo, 1990). It is thus reasonable to assume that some shyness is inherited, while even more is learned through negative experiences in one's social life. It is also the case that if a child is withdrawn, startles easily, is unlikely to smile, and is fearful of both strangers and novelty, then that child will create an environment that is not friendly, playful, or supportive. Which baby would you pick up and play with more, an easily startled one or a smiling, outgoing one? This difference in social stimulation, in turn, pushes the inhibited child toward shyness and the bold child toward being a cheerleader. In this way, heredity and environment interact, with initially inherited characteristics becoming amplified—or perhaps muted—over time, because they produce social signals telling others to either approach and play or stay away.

So does biology determine your destiny? An inherited temperament may set the *range* of your responses to some life situations. However, temperament by itself does not fully determine your life experiences (Kagan & Snidman, 1998). Even among your biological relatives, your unique family position, experiences, and sense of self all combine to guarantee that your personality pattern is unlike that of anyone else in the known universe (Bouchard et al., 1990).

Personality as a Composite of Traits

traits Multiple stable personality characteristics that are presumed to exist within the individual and guide his or her thoughts and actions under various conditions.

If you were to describe a friend, you would probably use the language of *traits:* moody, cheerful, melancholy, enthusiastic, volatile, friendly, or smart. **Traits** are multiple, stable personality characteristics that are presumed to exist within the individual and guide his or her thoughts and actions under various conditions. We might think of traits as the product of hidden psychological processes—the way our motives, emotions, and cognitions are customarily expressed in behavior (Winter et al., 1998).

How do traits differ from temperament? Think of temperament as the foundation of personality, deeply rooted in our individual biological nature. Then think of traits as a multidimensional structure built on the foundation of temperament but also influenced by experience. Traits emerge from temperaments as nature is expanded by nurture.

The "Big Five" Traits: The Five-Factor Theory Trait theorists focus primarily on the motivational and emotional components of personality, excluding other attributes such as IQ and creativity. With the statistical tool of *factor analysis* (which helps them look for relationships, or common clusters, among personality test items), many investigators have identified five dominant personality factors. This perspective is known as the **five-factor theory.** Personality theorists often call these factors the *Big Five* (Carver & Scheier, 2008; John & Srivastava, 1999). As yet, we have no universally accepted names for these five factors, although the italicized terms in the list below are widely used.

You will note that, although we give each trait a single label, the Big Five traits are really *bipolar dimensions*—not to be confused with *bipolar disorders*. That is, they exist on a continuum, with most people falling somewhere between the extremes—near the middle of the continuum—on most of these dimensions. (In parentheses below, we list the name of the opposite end of the dimension for each trait.)

- *Openness to experience,* also called inquiring intellect, curiosity, independence (at the opposite pole: closed-mindedness, low curiosity, unimaginative)
- *Conscientiousness,* also called dependability, goal-directedness, perseverance, superego strength, prudence, or constraint (at the opposite pole: impulsiveness, carelessness, or irresponsibility)
- *Extraversion,* also called social adaptability, assertiveness, sociability, boldness, or self-confidence (at the opposite pole: introversion, shyness)
- *Agreeableness,* also called warmth and likeability, with those on this end of the continuum taking a prosocial approach to others (at the opposite pole: coldness, negativity, or antagonism)
- *Neuroticism,* also called anxiety or emotionality (at the opposite pole: emotional stability or emotional control)

Here's an aid to remembering these five trait dimensions: Think of the acronym *OCEAN,* standing for Openness, Conscientiousness, Extraversion, Agreeableness, and Neuroticism. ✳

As you ponder this five-factor theory, it is important to realize that no score is necessarily "good" or "bad." While U.S. culture tends to value extroversion over introversion, either one can be adaptive, depending on the social and cultural situation. Thus, introversion may be a desirable trait for a writer, while extraversion may be preferred in a sales manager. Similarly, we value conscientiousness, openness, agreeableness, and emotional stability, but scoring on the "lower" end of each of these isn't necessarily a bad thing. For example, for a creative person, the tendency to follow one's own beliefs and not be unduly swayed by others (lower agreeableness) is beneficial. Similarly, too much conscientiousness probably limits one's ability to take advantage of unexpected opportunities, and too much openness could lead a person to be a "Jack (or Jill) of all trades" and master of none. Rather than making judgments about what traits we "should" possess, it is better to capitalize on the traits we have and find an environment that offers the best fit with what we have going for us.

The five-factor theory greatly simplifies a formerly confusing picture. Although debate still continues about the details, a broad coalition of theorists has now concluded that we can describe people with reasonable accuracy on just these five dimensions—quite an achievement in view of the several hundred trait terms one can find listed in the dictionary (Allport & Odbert, 1936)! "The five-factor model has fulfilled its promise to bring order to a Babel of Taxonomies and instruments," according to some prominent personality theorists (Caprara & Cervone, 2000). Researchers have identified both genetic and environmental influences on the development of these individual differences in personality (Bourchard & McGue, 2003).

Significantly, the five-factor model also seems to have validity across cultures, with several large studies demonstrating that the five-factor model works in more than 50 cultures in Europe, Asia, Africa, and the Americas (McCrae et al., 2005; Schmitt et al., 2007). However, that broad conclusion must be tempered because most of these studies utilized university students as respondents, who are people more influenced by

five-factor theory A trait perspective suggesting that personality is composed of five fundamental personality dimensions (also known as the Big Five): openness to experience, conscientiousness, extraversion, agreeableness, and neuroticism.

Explore the *Concept* The Five Factor Model at **MyPsychLab**

	Strongly disagree	Disagree somewhat	Neither agree nor disagree	Agree somewhat	Strongly agree
1. I am a talkative person.	○	○	○	○	○
2. I often feel shy.	○	○	○	○	○
3. I am usually full of energy.	○	○	○	○	○
4. I worry a lot.	○	○	○	○	○
5. I am inventive.	○	○	○	○	○
6. I have no artistic interests.	○	○	○	○	○
7. I like new challenges and experiences.	○	○	○	○	○
8. I see myself as reliable.	○	○	○	○	○
9. I like to be with people.	○	○	○	○	○
10. I can remain calm in difficult situations.	○	○	○	○	○

FIGURE 10.3

Sample Five-Factor Personality Inventory Items

An instrument measuring the Big Five personality traits might ask you to indicate how much you agree or disagree with each statement by checking the circle under the appropriate point on the scale. There are no right or wrong answers.

European-American world views, and have not included cultural subgroups that may not fit the descriptors of this simplified model. Anthropologist Rick Shweder (1991) reminds us that in some cultures, people are defined not by their personal dispositions; instead, what matters are their social roles, position within the family structure, or goals.

Assessing Traits with Personality Inventories If you were a clinical or counseling psychologist, you might want to assess a client's personality on the five factors using a paper-and-pencil instrument such as the *NEO Personality Inventory* (or *NEO-PI*).[1] This simple but highly respected measure has been used to study personality stability across the lifespan and also the relationship of personality characteristics to physical health and various life events (see Figure 10.3).

If, however, you want an instrument that measures clinical traits—that is, signs of mental disorder—the *Minnesota Multiphasic Personality Inventory*, usually referred to as the **MMPI-2**, is a good bet. (The "2" means it is a revised form of the original *MMPI*.) Unlike the *NEO-PI*, the *MMPI-2* does not measure the Big Five personality dimensions. Rather, its ten clinical scales (shown in Table 10.1) were developed to assess serious mental problems such as depression, schizophrenia, and paranoia (Helmes & Reddon, 1993). Its 567 items deal with a variety of attitudes, habits, fears, preferences, physical health, beliefs, and general outlook. We won't compromise the actual test items, but here are some true–false statements similar to those on the *MMPI-2*:

MMPI-2   A widely used personality assessment instrument that gives scores on ten important clinical traits; also called the *Minnesota Multiphasic Personality Inventory.*

- I am often bothered by thoughts about sex.
- Sometimes I like to stir up some excitement.
- If people had not judged me unfairly, I would have been far more successful.

Respondents are asked to indicate whether each statement describes them, and their answers are compared against responses of people in clinical populations with known

---

[1]NEO stands for neuroticism, extraversion, and openness. Conscientiousness and agreeableness were added later, but the name, *NEO Personality Inventory,* was not changed.

TABLE 10.1 *MMPI-2* Clinical Scales

Hypochondriasis (Hs): Abnormal concern with bodily functions
Depression (D): Pessimism; hopelessness; slowing of action and thought
Conversion hysteria (Hy): Unconscious use of mental problems to avoid conflicts or responsibility
Psychopathic deviate (Pd): Disregard for social custom; shallow emotions; inability to profit from experience
Masculinity–femininity (Mf): Differences between men and women
Paranoia (Pa): Suspiciousness; delusions of grandeur or persecution
Psychasthenia (Pt): Obsessions; compulsions; fears; low self-esteem; guilt; indecisiveness
Schizophrenia (Sc): Bizarre, unusual thoughts or behavior; withdrawal; hallucinations; delusions
Hypomania (Ma): Emotional excitement; flight of ideas; overactivity
Social introversion (Si): Shyness; disinterest in others; insecurity

mental disorders of various kinds. Thus, the scoring is *empirically* based—that is, it is based on scientific data of comparisons of each individual's pattern of responding with the average, or base rate responses, of each of a number of different clinical populations. It is not just the reasonable opinion of the test maker.

People who take personality inventories such as the *MMPI-2* often agonize over their answers to particular questions, concerned that a "wrong" answer might lead to being diagnosed as mentally disturbed. Not to worry! Personality profiles derived from *MMPI-2* responses are *never* based on a single item—or even two or three. Rather, each item merely makes a weighted contribution to one or more of the many subscales.

Could you fake a good or bad score on the *MMPI-2?* Probably not. The test has four cleverly designed "lie" scales that signal something amiss when they pick up too many unusual responses. Here are some items similar to those on the lie scales:

- Sometimes I put off doing things I know I ought to do.
- On occasion, I have passed on some gossip.
- Once in a while, I find a dirty joke amusing.

Too many attempts to make yourself look good or bad will elevate your lie scale scores into the questionable range.

From a scientific standpoint, the *MMPI-2* and the *NEO-PI* are exemplary instruments—for two reasons. First, they have excellent **reliability**. This means that they provide consistent and stable scores. So, when a person takes the same test on two different occasions, the scores are likely to be much the same. In fact, any usable test must have good reliability; otherwise the scores would be erratic and undependable. If the individual has not changed from test time 1 to time 2, then her or his test scores should remain relatively constant. When the scores do change significantly, then it means something has intervened during those two time periods, which is affecting the individual's mental state or functioning. This is cause for an alert.

reliability An attribute of a psychological test that gives consistent results.

Second, the *MMPI-2* and the *NEO-PI* have good **validity**, which means that they actually measure what they were designed to measure—e.g., personality traits or signs of mental disturbance. The *MMPI-2* does a credible job, for example, of identifying individuals with depression or psychosis (Greene, 1991)—although it must be used with care in non-Western cultures because it is not clear that its validity holds when the instrument has been translated into other languages (Dana, 1993). Moreover, some observers suggest that some items may have culture-specific content (Golden & Figueroa, 2007). Clinicians should also exercise caution when giving personality inventories to members of ethnic minorities in the United States, because minority groups are not always well represented in the samples used in developing the test originally (Butcher & Williams, 1992; Graham, 1990).

validity An attribute of a psychological test that actually measures what it is being used to measure.

Evaluating the Temperament and Trait Theories   Several criticisms have been leveled at the temperament and trait theories and the tests they have spawned. For one, these theories give us a "snapshot" of personality—a picture that portrays personality as fixed and static rather than as a dynamic process that can undergo developmental changes depending on our experience. Another criticism says that they oversimplify our complex natures by describing personality on just a few dimensions. What would we gain, for example, by finding that Mary Calkins scored high on traits such as conscientiousness and dominance but low on agreeableness? While such judgments might validate our observations, labels leave out important details.

On the positive side, trait theories give us some ability to *predict* behavior in common situations, such as work settings—to select employees who are well suited to the job and to screen out those who might cause problems. Moreover, the Big Five traits really do predict most of the things that truly matter to most of us, including health, academic success, and success in our interpersonal relationships—and with accuracy comparable to that of many diagnostic tests used in medicine (Robins, 2005).

But in the end, trait theories suffer from one of the same problems as the old instinct theories. Both *describe* behavior with a label but do not *explain* it. For example, we can attribute depression to a depressive trait or an outgoing personality to extraversion without really understanding the behavior. In short, trait theories identify common traits, but they do not tell us much about their source or how traits interact (McAdams, 1992; Pervin, 1985). Moreover, because most people display a trait only to a moderate degree, we must ask how useful traits are for understanding all but the extreme cases.

Finally, with trait theory, we again encounter the problem of the *self-fulfilling prophecy*. When given trait labels, people may be influenced by the expectations implied by those labels, making it difficult for them to change undesirable behavior. A child labeled "shy," for example, may have to struggle against both the label and the trait.

CONNECTION CHAPTER 6

The original self-fulfilling prophecy in psychology involved an experiment in which students' academic performance was altered by manipulating teachers' expectations (p. 249).

personality type   Similar to a trait, but instead of being a *dimension*, a type is a *category* that is believed to represent a common cluster of personality characteristics.

Myers–Briggs Type Indicator (MBTI)   A widely used personality test based on Jungian types.

[PSYCHOLOGY MATTERS]

Finding Your Type

Do you fancy yourself an introvert or an extravert? Emotionally stable or excitable? Dependable or irresponsible? Modern trait theory assumes that you could fall anywhere between these extremes, while the older notion of **personality types** puts people in distinct categories. Which view—trait or type—more accurately captures human nature? To find out, let's perform a critical examination of the most widely used instrument for assessing personality types, the *Myers–Briggs Type Indicator (MBTI)*. Because the *Myers–Briggs* derives from the personality types found in Carl Jung's theory, this discussion will also serve as a bridge to the next section of the chapter, where we will study Jung's theory, as well as other classical theories of personality, in detail.

Uses of the *MBTI*

Chances are you have taken the *MBTI*, because it is given to some two million people each year, often at self-awareness workshops and team-building business seminars (Druckman & Bjork, 1991). In the business world, consultants commonly use the *MBTI* in management training sessions to convey the message that people have distinct personality patterns that suit them for specific kinds of jobs. In college counseling centers, students may be advised to select a career that fits with their personality type, as revealed on the *MBTI*. It also finds a use in relationship counseling, where couples are taught to accommodate to each other's personality types.

On the Myers–Briggs test, examinees answer a series of questions about how they make judgments, perceive the world, and relate to others (Myers & Myers, 1995). Based on these responses, a scoring system assigns an individual to a four-dimensional personality type, derived from the Jungian dimensions of Introversion–Extraversion, Thinking–Feeling, Sensation–Intuition, and Judgment–Perception. We will discuss these dimensions further in the next section of this chapter.

What Does Research on the *MBTI* Tell Us about Personality Types?

Remember that a *reliable* test gives consistent results, as when a person takes the same test repeatedly. Unfortunately, the reliability of the *MBTI* is questionable. One study, for example, found that fewer than half of those tested on the *MBTI* had the same type when retested 5 weeks later (McCarley & Carskadon, 1983). Another study found a change in at least one of the four type categories in about 75 percent of respondents (Druckman & Bjork, 1991). Such results certainly raise questions about the fundamental concept of "type."

A second issue concerns the *validity* of the *Myers–Briggs* test. We have said that a valid test actually measures what it is intended to measure. And again, the research on the *MBTI* gives a mixed picture (Druckman & Bjork, 1991). The data fail to show that the *MBTI* truly identifies distinct personality *types* (Furnham et al., 2003)—that a person is a sum of each of the four type designations. Instead, the test shows that people are distributed all along the introversion–extraversion continuum. This evidence is much more consistent with the concept of *traits*—that different people have different *degrees* of a characteristic—rather than the *type* notion of either having it or not.

As for identifying personality patterns associated with particular occupations, the evidence is also shaky. True enough, those who work with people in service professions—entertainers, counselors, managers, and those in sales—tend to score higher on extraversion. By comparison, librarians, computer specialists, and physicians number many introverts in their ranks. The danger lies, however, in turning averages into stereotypes. In fact, the data show a diversity of types within occupations. Further, we find a conspicuous lack of evidence documenting a relationship between personality type and occupational success: There is no basis for the idea that having a particular personality type makes you better suited for a particular career. Although proponents of the *MBTI* claim it to be useful in vocational counseling, a review of the literature by a team from the National Academy of Sciences found no relationship between personality type, as revealed by the *MBTI*, and performance on a particular job (Druckman & Bjork, 1991). This report has, however, been hotly disputed by users of the instrument (Pearman, 1991). But overall, we can say that the *Myers–Briggs Type Indicator* has not proven to have the validity or reliability needed as the basis for making important life decisions. The National Academy of Sciences Report concludes, "Lacking such evidence, it is a curiosity why the instrument is used so widely" (Druckman & Bjork, 1991, p. 99).

Check Your Understanding

✓ Study and Review at MyPsychLab

1. **RECALL:** Jerome Kagan has suggested that the biological basis for different temperaments may come from each person's unique mix of _____.

2. **APPLICATION:** A friend of yours always seems agitated and anxious, even when nothing in the circumstances would provoke such a response. Which one of the Big Five traits seems to describe this characteristic of your friend?

3. **RECALL:** The *MMPI-2* does not assess conventional personality traits. Instead, its 10 clinical scales assess _____.

4. **RECALL:** The limits to applying the big five trait scale to non-Western cultures may be due, in part, to differences in the importance of _____.

5. **ANALYSIS:** If you were using a *trait theory,* you would assess people _____; but if you were using a *type theory,* you would assess people _____.

a. clinically / experimentally
b. according to their behavior / according to their mental processes
c. on their positive characteristics / on their negative characteristics
d. on dimensions / in categories

6. **UNDERSTANDING THE CORE CONCEPT:** Temperament, trait, and type theories describe the differences among people in terms of _____ but not _____.

a. personality characteristics/personality processes
b. mental disorders/mental health
c. nature/nurture
d. conscious processes/unconscious processes

Answers 1. neurotransmitters **2.** Neuroticism **3.** tendencies toward serious mental problems **4.** social roles and family structure patterns **5.** d **6.** a

10.3 KEY QUESTION
Do Mental *Processes* Help Shape Our Personalities?

Tiger Woods is the most successful golfer of all time, as well as the highest paid professional athlete in the world, making as much as $90 million in 2010. His tournaments were avidly followed by throngs of adoring fans, and he was admired as a family man, close to his parents and to his beautiful wife and their two young children. All that changed dramatically when it was revealed in December 2009 that Tiger had been having numerous extramarital sexual affairs. His life fell apart, his wife divorced him, sponsors stopped endorsing him, and though he took time off from golf for several months, Tiger never returned to his old top-of-the-scoreboard game again. It has been estimated that his infidelities cost him up to $12 billion of lost income and alimony, not to mention loss of respect and social acceptance.

We will use the case of Tiger Woods, along with that of Mary Calkins, to illustrate various theories of personality throughout the rest of the chapter.

To understand the psychological forces underlying both Woods's and Calkins's traits, we turn to theories that look at the mental *processes* that actively shape people's personalities—as opposed to the static traits, types, and temperaments that we have been considering to this point. Specifically, we will consider three kinds of "process" theories: the *psychodynamic,* the *humanistic,* and the *cognitive theories.* What do they have in common? Our Core Concept says:

> ## Core Concept 10.3
>
> **While each of the *process* theories sees different forces at work in personality, all portray personality as the result of both internal mental processes and social interactions.**

psychodynamic theory   A group of theories that originated with Freud. All emphasize motivation—often unconscious motivation—and the influence of the past on the development of mental disorders.

humanistic theories   A group of personality theories that focus on human growth and potential rather than on mental disorder. All emphasize the functioning of the individual in the present rather than on the influence of past events.

social-cognitive theories   A group of theories that involve explanations of limited but important aspects of personality (e.g., locus of control). All grew out of experimental psychology.

Although the three viewpoints we will consider in this section of the chapter—the *psychodynamic, humanistic,* and *social-cognitive* theories—share some common ground, each emphasizes a different combination of factors. The **psychodynamic theories** call attention to motivation, especially unconscious motives, and the influence of past experiences on our mental health. **Humanistic theories** emphasize consciousness and our present, subjective reality: what we believe is important now and how we think of ourselves in relation to others. And the **social-cognitive theories** describe the influence of learning, perception, and social interaction on behavior.

Psychodynamic Theories: Emphasis on Motivation and Mental Disorder

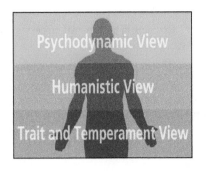

The psychodynamic approach originated in the late 1800s with a medical puzzle called *hysteria,* now known as *conversion disorder.* In patients with this condition, the physician sees physical symptoms such as a muscle weakness, loss of sensation in a part of the body, or even a paralysis—but no apparent physical cause, such as nerve damage. The psychological nature of hysteria finally became apparent when the French physician Jean Charcot (pronounced *Shar-COE*) demonstrated that he could make hysterical symptoms disappear by suggestion while his patients were in a hypnotic trance.

Freud and Psychoanalysis   Hearing of Charcot's work, the young and curious doctor Sigmund Freud (1856–1939) traveled to Paris to observe Charcot's renowned hypnotic demonstrations for himself. Inspired by what he saw, Freud returned to Vienna, resolving to try the hypnotic cure on his own patients. But to his dismay, Dr. Freud found that he could not hypnotize many of them deeply enough to duplicate Charcot's results. He did not know that people vary widely in their degree of *hypnotizability,* the ability to follow suggestions offered by a hypnotic agent. Moreover, even the ones who lost their symptoms under hypnosis usually regained them after the trance was lifted. Finally, a frustrated Freud resolved to find another way to understand and treat the

French physician Jean Charcot showed that he could temporarily eliminate symptoms of hysteria in patients who were hypnotized. Young Sigmund Freud found inspiration in Charcot's demonstrations.

mysterious illness. The result was the first comprehensive theory of personality—and still a standard by which all others are compared.

The new approach Freud created became known as **psychoanalysis** or **psychoanalytic theory.** Technically, *psychoanalytic theory* is the term for Freud's explanation of personality and mental disorder, while *psychoanalysis* refers to his system of treatment for mental disorder. In practice, however, it has always been difficult to separate Freud's theory from his therapeutic procedures. Thus the term *psychoanalysis* is often used to refer to both (Carver & Scheier, 2008).

As you study Freud's theory, you may find some points on which you agree and others on which you disagree. We recommend bringing all your critical thinking skills to bear, but at the same time, you should maintain a respect for Freud and the task he faced, more than 100 years ago, as the first great explainer of human personality.

The Freudian Unconscious   At center stage in personality, Freud placed the **unconscious,** the mind's hidden, seething cauldron of powerful impulses, instincts, motives, and conflicts that energize the personality. We normally have no awareness of this hidden psychic territory, said Freud, because its contents are so threatening and anxiety provoking that the conscious mind refuses to acknowledge its existence, even in the healthiest of us. Only by using the special techniques of psychoanalysis can a therapist find, for example, that a person who had been sexually molested in childhood still retains these aversive memories in the unconscious. We glimpse such memories when they attempt to escape from the unconscious, disguised perhaps as a dream or a slip of the tongue or as a symptom of mental disorder, such as depression or a phobia. So, mentally healthy or not, Freud maintained that we all go about our daily business without knowing the real hidden motives behind some of our behaviors.

Unconscious Drives and Instincts   Freud taught that the turbulent processes in the unconscious mind are fueled by psychological energy from our most basic and secret motives, drives, and desires—the mental equivalent of steam in a boiler. Psychoanalytic theory, then, explains how this mental "steam" is transformed and expressed in disguised form in our conscious thoughts and behavior.

The unconscious sex drive, which Freud named *Eros* after the Greek god of passionate love, could be expressed either directly through sexual activity or indirectly through such releases as joking, work, or creative pursuits. (Perhaps you had never thought of activities like dancing, drawing, cooking, studying, or body building as sexual acts—but Freud did!) The energy produced by Eros he termed **libido,** from the

psychoanalysis   A method of treating mental disorders that is based on Sigmund Freud's psychoanalytic theory. The goal of psychoanalysis is to release unacknowledged conflicts, urges, and memories from the unconscious. (In common usage, the term often refers broadly both to Freud's psychoanalytic theory and to his psychoanalytic treatment method.)

psychoanalytic theory   Freud's theory of personality and mental disorder.

unconscious   In Freudian theory, this is the psychic domain of which the individual is not aware but that is the storehouse of repressed impulses, drives, and conflicts unavailable to consciousness.

CONNECTION CHAPTER 5

False memory experiments by Elizabeth Loftus and others have raised serious questions about memories of abuse recovered during therapy (p. 200).

libido   The Freudian concept of psychic energy that drives individuals to experience sensual pleasure.

Sigmund Freud is seen here walking with his daughter Anna Freud, who later became a psychoanalyst in her own right.

id   The primitive, unconscious portion of the personality that houses the most basic drives and stores repressed memories.

superego   The mind's storehouse of values, including moral attitudes learned from parents and from society; roughly the same as the common notion of the conscience.

ego   The conscious, rational part of the personality, charged with keeping peace between the superego and the id.

psychosexual stages   Successive, instinctive developmental phases in which pleasure is associated with stimulation of different bodily areas at different times of life.

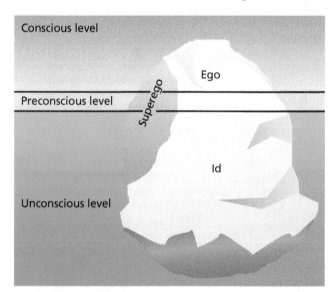

Conscious level

Preconscious level

Unconscious level

Ego

Superego

Id

FIGURE 10.4

Freud's Model of the Mind

In another famous metaphor, Freud likened the mind to an iceberg because only a small portion appears "above the surface"—in consciousness. Meanwhile, the vast unconscious mind lurks "beneath the surface" of our awareness.

Latin word for "lust." Libidinal energy, in turn, fuels or energizes the rest of the personality as a primitive life force.

But Eros and its libidinal energy did not explain everything that fascinated Freud. Specifically, it did not explain acts of human aggression and destruction. Nor did it explain the symptoms of the war veterans who continued to relive their wartime traumas in nightmares and hallucinations. Such misery could only be accounted for by another drive, which he named *Thanatos* (from the Greek word for "death"). Freud conceived of Thanatos as the unconscious "death instinct" that drives the aggressive and destructive acts that humans commit against each other and even against themselves. (Think of smoking, compulsive gambling, reckless driving, or drug abuse.)

The Structure of the Personality   Freud pictured the personality as a trinity composed of the *ego,* the *id,* and the *superego,* which together form a mind continually at war within itself. He believed that the sexual and aggressive forces of the id wage a continuing battle against the moralistic forces of the superego. The ever-practical ego serves as the moderator of this conflict. (Figure 10.4 represents the three parts of the personality pictorially.)

Freud conceived of the **id** as the primitive, unconscious reservoir that contains the basic motives, drives, and instinctive desires—including Eros and Thanatos—that energize all three parts of the personality. Like a child, the id always acts on impulse and pushes for immediate gratification—especially sexual, physical, and emotional pleasures—to be experienced here and now without concern for consequences.

By contrast, the superego serves as the mind's parental avatars—virtual "parents" living in the mind—in charge of values and morals learned from parents, teachers, other authority figures, and society. The **superego** corresponds roughly to our common notion of "conscience." It develops as the child forms an internal set of rules based on the external rules imposed by parents and other adults. And it is the inner voice of "shoulds" and "should nots." The superego also includes the *ego ideal,* an individual's view of the kind of person he or she should strive to become. Understandably, the superego frequently opposes id's desires, because the id wants to do only what feels good, while the superego insists on doing only what is right and moral.

Former President Jimmy Carter, a model of decorum, got in trouble for his honest confession in a *Playboy* interview, "I've looked on a lot of women with lust. I've committed adultery in my heart many times." In Freudian parlance, that was his *ego,* the conscious, rational portion of the mind, describing how it must resolve conflicts between desires of the id and moral ideals of the superego. The **ego,** like a referee, often must make decisions that satisfy no part of the personality completely, but it keeps the whole out of trouble. This enabled President Carter to sin only in his heart, but not in his Oval Office, unlike former President Clinton, whose ego was dominated by id or underwhelmed by superego. That was even more true with Tiger Woods, whose id ruled the roost as his superego was put on hold. In extreme instances, when pressures escalate to the point where the ego cannot find workable compromises to major conflicts, mental disorder may be triggered.

The Influence of Early Experience on Personality Development   As Freud talked with his patients about their pasts, he began to understand that personality follows a developmental pattern through childhood and into adulthood. He proposed that emerging sexual and aggressive drives propel the child through a series of **psychosexual stages.** In each stage, stimulation of specific body regions is associated with erotic pleasure.

In the *oral stage,* pleasure is associated with the mouth: suckling, crying, spewing. In the *anal stage,* pleasure comes from stimulating parts of the body associated with elimination. (This explains the pleasure young children get from sharing dirty words, like "shit.") Next, in the *phallic stage,* pleasure comes from "immature" sexual expression, such as masturbation. Finally, after a quiet period of *latency*, the adult *genital stage* brings maturity and mental well-being to those fortunate enough to resolve the conflicts of earlier stages.

Why such a seemingly bizarre theory of child development? Among the issues that Freud was trying to resolve with his theory of psychosexual development were those of gender identity and gender roles. Why, he wondered, do boys usually develop a masculine identity, even though most boys are raised primarily by their mothers? Why do boys and girls, as they become adults, most often develop a sexual attraction to the opposite sex? And why do some *not* follow this pattern?

Freud's answers to these questions were convoluted and, many psychologists would say, contrived. His psychodynamic perspective ignored the external influence of the different ways that boys and girls are socialized; it also ignored the possibility of differences in genetic programming, of which almost nothing was known in Freud's day. For boys, his solution was the **Oedipus complex**, an unconscious conflict that initially drives young males to feel an immature erotic attraction toward their mothers. (You may have heard a little boy say that he wants to marry his mother when he grows up.) As the boy goes through the stages of psychosexual development, resolution of the Oedipal conflict requires him to *displace* (shift) his emerging sexual desires away from his mother, directing them instead to females of his own age. At the same time, he develops an **identification** with his father. In a parallel fashion, Freud theorized that girls develop an attraction to their fathers and so become competitive with their mothers for his affection. This unconscious conflict among girls is known as the **Electra complex**, named after another important Greek figure.

Most psychologists today reject these Freudian assumptions about psychosexual development because they lack scientific support. It is important, however, to remember three things: First, we still don't fully understand how sexual attraction works. Second, Freudian concepts about psychosexual development—strange as they may seem—continue to have a wide impact outside psychology, particularly in literature, and notably so in current psychology in France. And finally, while Freud may have been wrong about the details of psychosexual development, he may have been right about the overall pattern and about the idea that children all progress through *stages of development* (Bower, 1998b) that is a central focus among many developmental psychologists.

For example, Freud may have been right in his assertion that certain difficulties early in life lead to **fixation** or arrested psychological development. An *oral stage* fixation, caused by a failure to throw off the dependency of the first year of life, may lead to dependency on others in later childhood and adulthood. We may also see an oral fixation, he said, in certain behaviors involving "oral tendencies," such as overeating, alcoholism, smoking, and talkativeness. Among these diverse problems, we find a common theme: using the mouth as the way to connect with what one needs or wants. Similarly, Freud presumed that fixation in the *anal stage* came from problems associated with the second year of life when toilet training is a big issue. Anal fixations, he said, can result in a stubborn, compulsive, stingy, or excessively neat pattern of behavior—all related to the theme of controlling one's body or life.

Ego Defenses   In dealing with conflict between the id's impulses and the superego's demand to deny them, Freud said that the ego calls upon a suite of **ego defense mechanisms**. All operate, he said, at the *preconscious level*—just beneath the surface of consciousness. So under mild pressure from the id we may rely, as President Carter did, on simple ego defenses, such as *fantasy* or *rationalization*. But if unconscious desires become too insistent, the ego may solve the problem by "putting a lid on the id"—that is, by sequestering both extreme desires and threatening memories deep in the unconscious mind. Freud called this **repression**. It is the most central of all ego defenses because it is assumed to influence much of our behavior and perceptions in disguised fashion. It can lead to dysfunctional sexual relationships as well as failures to relate openly to others who are symbolically similar to some repressed ideal or feared person.

During the phallic stage, said Freud, a child must resolve feelings of conflict and anxiety by identifying more closely with the same-sex parent.

Oedipus complex   According to Freud, a largely unconscious process whereby young males displace an erotic attraction toward their mother to females of their own age and, at the same time, identify with their fathers.

identification   The mental process by which an individual tries to become like another person, especially the same-sex parent.

Electra complex   Concept advanced by Carl Jung, highlighting a girl's psychosexual competition with mother for the father's love, which is resolved in psychoanalyitic theory when girl comes to identify with same sex adult; equivalent to Oedipus Complex in males.

CONNECTION CHAPTER 7

Recall our discussion of developmental stages as central to human development across the lifespan (p. 306).

fixation   Occurs when psychosexual development is arrested at an immature stage.

ego defense mechanism   A largely unconscious mental strategy employed to reduce the experience of conflict or anxiety.

repression   An unconscious process that excludes unacceptable thoughts and feelings from awareness and memory.

CONNECTION CHAPTER 8

Freud developed an elaborate system of dream interpretation (p. 339).

Repression can block access to feelings as well as memories. So a child might repress strong feelings of anger toward her father—which, if acted on, might incur severe punishment. Likewise, boys repress the erotic Oedipal feelings they have for their mothers. Once repressed, a feeling or a desire can no longer operate consciously. But, said Freud, it is not gone. At an unconscious level, repressed feelings, desires, and memories continue to influence behavior, but in less direct ways, perhaps disguised, as we have seen, in dreams, fantasies, or symptoms of mental disorder.

Always the keen observer of human behavior, Freud proposed many other ego defense mechanisms besides fantasy, rationalization, and repression. Here are some of the most important:

- **Denial.** "I don't have a problem." This defense avoids a difficult situation by simply denying that it exists. Denial is a defense frequently seen, for example, in people with drinking problems, people who have problems managing anger, and people who engage in risky behavior, such as casual, unprotected sex.

- **Rationalization.** A student who feels stressed by academic pressures may decide to cheat on a test, rationalizing it by saying that "everyone does it." People using this defense mechanism give socially acceptable reasons for actions that are really based on motives that they believe to be socially unacceptable.

- **Reaction formation.** We see reaction formation in people who, troubled by their own sexual desires, rail against "dirty books" in the city library or seek coercive laws regulating other people's sexual behavior. This ego defense mechanism occurs whenever people act exactly in opposition to their unconscious desires. Recently, a member of Congress who had long been openly attacking homosexuality as a sin was exposed playing footsies with another man in a public toilet. Such behavior is either an instance of reaction formation or blatant hypocrisy.

- **Displacement.** When your boss makes you angry, you may later displace your anger by yelling at your friend or pounding on the wall. More generally, displacement involves shifting your reaction from the real source of your distress to a safer individual or object.

- **Regression.** Under stress, some people hide; others cry, throw things, or even wet their pants. That is, they regress to an earlier developmental stage by adopting immature, juvenile behaviors that were effective ways of dealing with stress when they were younger.

- **Sublimation.** When sexual energies are bottled up, the person may seek more socially acceptable outlets by engaging in intense creative actions or in excessive work activities. Freud conjectured that sublimation was responsible for some of civilization's major advances. (Perhaps Tiger Woods's obsession with perfecting his golfing came at the expense of making time for engaging in youthful sexual explorations. Once having achieved super success in his work, he may have felt entitled to unleash his sexual desires.)

- **Projection.** When some personal attitudes or values cannot be fully accepted or owned up to, they can be directed outward as characteristics of others. Thus, a person in a committed relationship who is feeling attracted to someone else accuses his or her partner of cheating. Someone who cannot accept harboring prejudiced views toward some outgroup comes to see others as prejudiced, sexist, or racist, for example. More generally, people may use the defense of projection to misattribute their own unconscious desires and fears onto other people or objects.

This latter concept—projection—led to the development of projective tests, which have found extensive use in clinical psychology for evaluating personality and mental disorders. We take a brief detour at this point to introduce you to these projective techniques.

Projective Tests: Diagnosis via a Defense Mechanism   What do you see in Figure 10.5? The head of an insect? An MRI scan of the brain? Something else? Ambiguous images such as these are the basis for **projective tests** that psychodynamic clinicians employ to probe their patients' innermost feelings, motives, conflicts, and desires. The assumption is

projective test   *Personality assessment instrument, such as the Rorschach and TAT, which is based on Freud's ego defense mechanism of projection.*

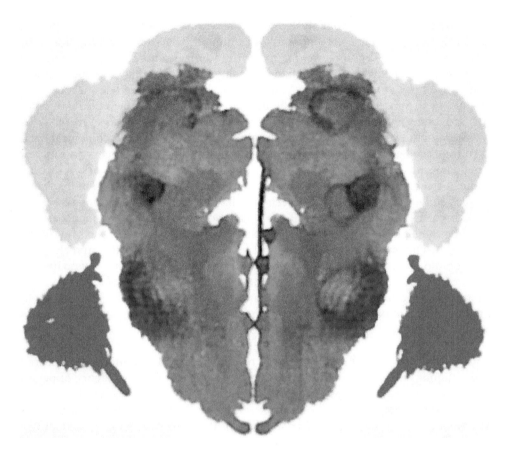

FIGURE 10.5

An Inkblot Similar to Those Used in the Rorschach Test

that troubled people will *project* their hidden motives and conflicts onto such images, much as people gazing at the clouds may see objects in them that fit their fantasies.

In the most famous of projective techniques, the ***Rorschach Inkblot Technique*** (pronounced *ROAR-shock*), the stimuli are merely symmetrical inkblots. The technique calls for showing the images one at a time and asking the respondent, "What do you see? What does this seem to be?" The examiner usually interprets responses psychoanalytically by noting how they might reflect unconscious sexual and aggressive impulses or repressed conflicts (Erdberg, 1990).

How well does the *Rorschach* work? It gets low marks from many psychologists because objective studies have been disappointing in the lack of consistency and accuracy in measuring individual differences in personality (Lilienfeld et al., 2010). Moreover, critics claim that the test is based on concepts such as unconscious motivation that are impossible to demonstrate objectively. Despite these criticisms, many clinicians have continued to champion the *Rorschach,* arguing that it can provide unique insights as part of a broader personality assessment (Hibbard, 2003).

By comparison, the ***Thematic Apperception Test (TAT)***, developed by Harvard psychologist Henry Murray, is a projective test that stands on somewhat firmer scientific ground, especially for assessing achievement motivation, as we saw in Chapter 9. The test consists of ambiguous pictures, like the one in Figure 10.6, for which respondents are instructed to generate a story, telling what the characters in the scenes are doing and thinking (present focus), what led up to each event (past focus), and how each situation might end (future focus). According to the projection hypothesis underlying the *TAT,* the respondent first perceives the elements in the picture and then *apperceives* (fills in) personal interpretations and explanations based on his or her own thoughts, feelings, and needs. The examiner then interprets the responses by looking for psychological themes, such as aggression, sexual needs, achievement motives, and relationships among people mentioned in the stories. (What do you imagine Tiger Woods's TAT story would have focused on prior to his sexual scandal?)

Rorschach Inkblot Technique   A projective test requiring subjects to describe what they see in a series of ten inkblots.

Thematic Apperception Test (TAT)   A projective test requiring subjects to make up stories that explain ambiguous pictures.

FIGURE 10.6

Images similar to this one are used in the *TAT* to elicit motivational themes from respondents.

psychic determinism   Freud's assumption that all our mental and behavioral responses are caused by unconscious traumas, desires, or conflicts.

Psychic Determinism   Psychoanalysis literally leaves nothing to accident. According to the principle of **psychic determinism**, all of human behavior is determined by our inner mental states—by unconscious memories, desires, and conflicts. Chance and coincidence do not exist in the Freudian dictionary. Inevitably, the way you feel unconsciously leaks out in your behavior. You just can't help it. You are late for a class you don't like or to a meeting with a snobby person, you forget someone's birthday, or you say, "'sad to meet you,' oh, I'm sorry, I meant 'glad to meet you,'" and so forth.

Accordingly, everything a person does potentially has a deep psychological meaning to the Freudian analyst. In therapy, mental symptoms such as fears and phobias are signs of unconscious difficulties that are to be uncovered and worked through. Similarly, the analyst may catch a glimpse of the unconscious at work in a so-called *Freudian slip*—when "accidental" speech or behavior belies an unconscious conflict or desire. Former President George W. Bush was famous for slips of the tongue, as when intending to emphasize how strongly his party felt about the family, he said instead, "Republicans understand the importance of *bondage* between a mother and child." Or, when a radio announcer was promoting Wonder Bread, extolling it in comparison to other brands, as "the best of breasts." (We hasten to add, in defense of anyone who has committed a speech blunder, that cognitive psychologists today believe that most slips of the tongue are mix-ups in the brain mechanisms we use to produce language and so have no relationship to unconscious intentions.)

Evaluating Freud's Work   Whatever your reaction to Freud, you must give him credit for developing the first and still, perhaps, the most comprehensive theory of personality, mental disorder, and psychotherapy. He did so at a time when we had no understanding of genetics and neurotransmitters, no particularly effective treatments for most mental disorders, and no understanding of the influences on gender identity or sexual development. His writing was so incisive and his arguments so compelling that he has had a greater impact than any other theorist on the way all of us think about personality and mental abnormality, whether we realize it or not. He gave us the unconscious, the concept of developmental stages, the notion of defense mechanisms, and the idea that behavior—and even our dreams—may have hidden meanings. Moreover, he made human sexuality a central theme in personal development and disordered functioning during a Victorian era where any mention of sex was taboo. Even among psychologists, who had largely rejected his ideas in recent years, Freud is enjoying renewed support as one of the keenest observers of human behavior who has ever lived (Solms, 2004). Again and again he saw in little things big antecedents or consequences. Freud was to Sherlock Holmes as a mind detective is to a homicide detective. Nearly everyone would agree that people *do* displace aggression, rationalize their behavior, and see their own shortcomings more easily in others than in themselves.

CONNECTION CHAPTER 1

Operational definitions are stated in objective, observable, and measurable terms (p. 24).

Freud as Unscientific   Nevertheless, Freud still plays to mixed reviews (Azar, 1997; McCullough, 2001). The biggest problem is that many of his concepts, such as "libido," "anal stage," or "repression," are vague, lacking clear operational definitions. In an earlier chapter, we saw this problem in the controversy over recovery of repressed memories. Without credible, independently verifiable evidence (which rarely exists), how could one ever determine whether a recovered memory had been truly repressed or was merely implanted by suggestion of a therapist or social worker or from reading media accounts? Such difficulties make psychoanalytic theory difficult to evaluate scientifically.[2]

Although Freud never bothered to build a careful scientific case for his observations, critics may have judged him too harshly on this count, argues Drew Westen (1998), one of Freud's staunch defenders. Researchers have validated many of his most fundamental insights, says Westen. Among these well-established notions:

---

[2]Because many of Freud's ideas are not testable, his psychoanalytic theory is not truly a *scientific* theory as we defined the term in Chapter 1. Here, we follow common usage, which nevertheless calls it a theory because it is such a comprehensive explanation for personality and mental disorder. It should be noted, however, that valiant efforts are being made to put Freud's concepts on a scientific footing (Cramer, 2000).

- Much of mental life *is* unconscious (although the unconscious may not operate exactly as Freud envisioned);
- People *can* have conflicts arising from conflicting motives (some conscious and some unconscious) that push them in different directions simultaneously;
- Stable personality patterns *do* begin to form in childhood—sometimes for better, sometimes for worse—in part as the result of childhood experiences.

Retrospective but Not Prospective　A second criticism says that Freudian theory is a seductive explanation for the past but a poor predictor of future responses. That is, it may be merely a clever example of *hindsight bias,* in which we have the illusion of seeing things more clearly in retrospect. And by overemphasizing the origins of behavior in childhood, psychoanalysis may compound the problem by directing attention away from the stressors of the present that may be the real causes of mental and behavioral disorders.

Gender Issues　A third criticism faults Freud for giving short shrift to women. Particularly aggravating is his portrayal of women as inevitably suffering from "penis envy." (He thought that women spent their lives unconsciously trying to make up for their biological deficit in this department.) A better explanation is that Freud's theory simply projects onto women his own attitudes and those of the male-centered world of his time.

Newer Views of the Unconscious　A final criticism claims that the unconscious mind is not as smart or purposeful as Freud believed (Loftus & Klinger, 1992). In this newer view, coming out of neuroscience research in emotion, the brain has parallel conscious and unconscious processing pathways, with the unconscious quick to detect emotion-provoking stimuli (think of your "gut" reaction to a shadowy figure approaching you on a dark street), while consciousness acts more deliberately and logically ("OK," you say to yourself. "Remain calm and act naturally, and maybe he won't sense that you are scared.") This new view of an unconscious emotional processing system is much less malign and turbulent than the unconscious filled with raging sexual desires and destructive death wishes that Freud had imagined (LeDoux, 1996).

CONNECTION CHAPTER 9

Emotion-provoking stimuli are processed in two parallel pathways in the brain (p. 394).

Freud's Appeal beyond Psychology　Despite these objections, Freud's ideas have found a receptive audience with the public at large (Adler, 2006). Much of his appeal may be explained by his graceful writing and by his emphasis on sexuality, a topic that grabs everyone's interest—as Freud well knew! As a result, Freudian images and symbols abound in the art and literature of the 20th century. His ideas have had an enormous influence on marketing as well. For example, advertisers make billions by associating products with sexy models, hinting that the products will bring sexual satisfaction to their owners. They also capitalize on Freud's destructive instinct by reminding us of threats to our happiness (social rejection, irregularity, untimely death) and then offering products and services to reduce our anxiety and restore hope. Perhaps Freud was right after all!

Sex sells cars and virtually everything in our culture by association of objects with sexy models.

How Would Freud Have Seen Mary Calkins?　Let us end our discussion of Freud by seeing whether his explanation of personality can give us a useful perspective on Mary Calkins. A psychoanalyst interpreting her sense of purpose and willingness to fight the system might look first to her childhood for experiences that may have shaped her personality.

The Calkins family was especially close (Furumoto, 1979). Mary's mother, Charlotte Calkins, suffered from deteriorating health, so Mary, as the eldest child, took over many of the duties of running the household—an especially interesting development in view of Freud's suggestion that girls compete with their mothers for their fathers' attention. For his part, Mary's father, the Reverend Wolcott Calkins, was a Congregationalist minister who placed a high value on education and personally tutored Mary at a time when education for women was not fashionable. Any sexual feelings she may have felt from this close association with her father would then get sublimated into Mary's intense work habits for the rest of her life.

Another decisive event, which caused Mary great distress, was the death of her younger sister. From a Freudian viewpoint, her sister's death may have produced a conflict based on unconscious feelings of *sibling rivalry* for the parents' affections. A Freudian analyst might suggest that, in her work, Calkins sublimated her sadness or, perhaps, her anger at the necessity of taking on mother's role and at the sexist prejudices she endured. As is usual with psychoanalysis, of course, these guesses are guided by hindsight—and cannot be either proved or disproved.

The Neo-Freudians   Freud was always a controversial and charismatic figure—an image he liked to promote (Sulloway, 1992). And although he attracted many followers, Freud tolerated no criticism from any of them concerning the basic principles of psychoanalysis. So, like rebellious children, several of Freud's equally strong-willed disciples broke away to establish their own systems of personality, mental disorder, and treatment. While these **neo-Freudians** (literally, "new Freudians") sometimes departed from Freud's theory, they always retained his *psychodynamic* emphasis. That is, they kept Freud's idea of personality as an emerging process driven by motivational energy—even as they disagreed about the specific motives that energize personality. And you may disagree too: Are our motives primarily sexual or social? Conscious or unconscious? Is personality determined by events in the past or by our goals for the future? Let's examine some of the divergent paths followed by these neo-Freudians.

Carl Jung: Extending the Unconscious   Freud attracted many disciples, but none was more famous than Carl Jung (pronounced *YOONG*), a member of the inner circle of colleagues who helped Freud develop and refine psychoanalytic theory during the first decade of the 1900s. For a time, Freud viewed the somewhat younger Jung as his "crown prince" and probable successor. But Freud's paternal attitude increasingly vexed Jung, who was developing radical theoretical ideas of his own (Carver & Scheier, 2008). Eventually this personality conflict—which Freud interpreted as Jung's unconscious wish to usurp his fatherly authority—caused a split in their relationship.

For Jung, the break with Freud centered on two issues. First, Jung thought that his mentor had overemphasized sexuality at the expense of other unconscious needs and desires that Jung saw at the heart of personality. In particular, he believed spirituality to be a fundamental human motive, coequal with sexuality. Moreover, he disputed the very structure of the unconscious mind. Jung's new and expanded vision of the unconscious is Jung's most famous innovation.

The Collective Unconscious   In place of the Freudian id, Jung installed a two-part unconscious, consisting of both a *personal unconscious* and a *collective unconscious*. While the Jungian **personal unconscious** spanned essentially the same territory as the Freudian id, its collective twin was another matter—and wholly a Jungian creation. He saw in the **collective unconscious** a reservoir for instinctive "memories" shared by people everywhere—in much the same way that humans share a common genetic code. These collective memories tie together countless generations of human history and give us the ancient images, called **archetypes**, that appear and reappear in art, literature, and folktales around the world (Jung, 1936/1959). For Jung, the causes of mental disorder include not only repressed traumas and conflicts in the personal unconscious but also failure to acknowledge the archetypes we find unacceptable in our collective unconscious.

Among these archetypal memories, Jung identified the *animus* and the *anima*, which represent the masculine and feminine sides of our personalities. Other archetypes give us the universal concepts of *mother, father, birth, death,* the *hero,* the *trickster, God,* and the *self*. On the darker side of the self lurks the *shadow* archetype, representing the destructive and aggressive tendencies (similar to Freud's Thanatos) that we don't want

neo-Freudian   Literally "new Freudian;" refers to theorists who broke with Freud but whose theories retain a psychodynamic aspect, especially a focus on motivation as the source of energy for the personality.

personal unconscious   Jung's term for that portion of the unconscious corresponding roughly to the Freudian id.

collective unconscious   Jung's addition to the unconscious, involving a reservoir for instinctive "memories," including the archetypes, which exist in all people.

archetype   One of the ancient memory images in the collective unconscious. Archetypes appear and reappear in art, literature, and folktales around the world.

Jungian archetypes abound in art, literature, and film. This photo, from *The Lord of the Rings,* shows Gandalf who embodies the archetype of magician or trickster. The same archetype is evoked by the coyote in Native American legends and by Merlin in the King Arthur legends.

TABLE 10.2 Jung's Opposing Tendencies in Personality

conscious ←——————————→	unconscious
extravert ←——————————→	introvert
rational ←——————————→	irrational
thinking ←——————————→	feeling
intuition ←——————————→	sensation
good ←——————————→	bad
masculine ←——————————→	feminine

to acknowledge in our personalities. You can recognize your own shadow archetype at work the next time you feel angry, hostile, envious, or jealous. From a Jungian perspective, we might wonder whether Tiger Woods was denying, even to himself, the shadow in his personality. 👁

Watch the **Video** Carl Jung: Unconscious at **MyPsychLab**

Personality Types Revisited   Jung's *principle of opposites* portrays each personality as a balance between opposing pairs of tendencies or dispositions, which you see in Table 10.2. Jung taught that most people tend to favor one or the other in each pair. The overall pattern of such tendencies, then, was termed a *personality type*, which Jung believed to be a stable and enduring aspect of the individual's personality.

The most famous of these pairs is **introversion** and **extraversion**. Extraverts turn attention outward, on external experience. As a result, extraverts are more in tune with people and things in the world around them than they are with their own inner needs. They tend to be outgoing and unaffected by self-consciousness. Introverts, by contrast, focus on inner experience—their own thoughts and feelings—which makes them seem more shy and less sociable. Jung believed that few people have all pairs of forces in perfect balance. Instead, one or another dominates, giving rise to personality types (Fadiman & Frager, 2001).

introversion   The Jungian dimension that focuses on inner experience—one's own thoughts and feelings—making the introvert less outgoing and sociable than the extravert.

extraversion   The Jungian personality dimension that involves turning one's attention outward, toward others.

Evaluating Jung's Work   Like Freud, Jung's influence is now most evident outside of psychology, particularly in literature and the popular press—again because they do not lend themselves to objective observation and testing. In two respects, however, Jung has had a big impact on psychological thinking. First, he challenged Freud and thereby opened the door to a spate of alternative personality theories. Second, his notion of *personality types,* and especially the concepts of *introversion* and *extraversion,* makes Jung not only a psychodynamic theorist but a pillar of the temperament/trait/type approach. And, as we noted earlier, his theory of types underlies the widely used (yet controversial) Myers-Briggs test.

Could Jung's theory give us a new perspective on Mary Calkins? He might have suspected that her determination to succeed in the male-dominated world of her day was energized by conflicts between the masculine and feminine sides of her nature, the animus and anima. Another Jungian possibility is that her mother's ill health, which caused her to relinquish much of the maternal role, made Mary deny her own maternal archetype—which may have been why she never married, and also why she was so willing to embrace the intense work schedule within a male-dominated world of academia.

Karen Horney: A Feminist Voice in Psychodynamic Psychology   Karen Horney *(HORN-eye)* and Anna Freud, Sigmund Freud's daughter, represent virtually the only feminine voices within the early decades of the psychoanalytic movement. In this role, Horney disputed the elder Freud's notion of the Oedipus complex and especially his assertion that women must suffer from *penis envy* (Horney, 1939). Instead, said Horney, women want the same opportunities and rights that men enjoy, and many

basic anxiety   An emotion, proposed by Karen Horney, that gives a sense of uncertainty and loneliness in a hostile world and can lead to maladjustment.

neurotic needs   Signs of neurosis in Horney's theory, the ten needs are normal desires carried to a neurotic extreme.

Psychoanalyst Karen Horney asserted that personality differences between men and women are largely the result of different social roles rather than unconscious urges or early childhood experiences. She believed that people are driven more by social motives than sexual motives.

personality differences between males and females result from learned social roles, not from unconscious urges. She also disputed Freud's contention that personality is determined mainly by early childhood experiences. For Horney, normal growth involves the full development of social relationships and of one's potential. This development, however, may be blocked by a sense of uncertainty and isolation that she called **basic anxiety.** It is this basic anxiety that can lead to adjustment problems and mental disorder.

Neurotic Needs   When basic anxiety gets out of control, people become *neurotic.* The neurotic person, said Horney (1942), suffers from "unconscious strivings developed in order to cope with life despite fears, helplessness, and isolation" (p. 40). These unconscious strivings manifest themselves in one or more **neurotic needs**, which are normal desires taken to extremes. You can see these neurotic needs listed in Table 10.3.

Horney also identified three common patterns of attitudes and behavior that people use to deal with basic anxiety: They move either *toward others, against others,* or *away from others.* Those who neurotically move *toward others* have a pathological need for constant reminders of love and approval. Such persons may need someone to help, to take care of, or for whom to "sacrifice" themselves. Alternatively, they may seek someone on whom they can become dependent. They may end up behaving passively and feeling victimized. In contrast, those who move *against others* earn power and respect by competing or attacking successfully, but they risk being feared and ending up "lonely at the top." Those who take the third route, moving *away from others* to protect themselves from imagined hurt and rejection, are likely to close themselves off from intimacy and support. "Better to be feared, than loved" is a theme of one of the Mafia gangsters in the movie *A Bronx Tale* that concisely depicts what Horney meant by dealing with basic anxiety with a personality style that moves *against* people.

What analysis would Horney have made of Mary Calkins? We suspect that she would have focused on Calkins's achievements, attempting to determine whether they were the result of a healthy drive to fulfill her potential or a neurotic need for power. Undoubtedly, Horney would have reminded us that society often praises these needs in men and punishes them in women. She would also have pointed out that much of Calkins's professional identity was shaped by having to deal with the male-centered academic world of her time. In that context, Calkins not only drew on the strength of a supportive family of her childhood but also the support of the all-female Wellesley faculty that became the "family" of her adulthood. From this point of view, it is likely that Horney may have seen in Calkins a robust and healthy personality caught in a difficult web of social constraints and contradictions.

Horney might have seen in Tiger Woods his ambivalence toward a dominating father who forced him to practice golf endlessly starting at a very young age and was perhaps aware of his "alleged womanizing." After his father's death in 2006, Tiger became all that his father seemed to want from him: to become a super star golfer and super womanizer.

TABLE 10.3 Horney's Ten Neurotic Needs

> 1. Need for affection and approval
> 2. Need for a partner and dread of being left alone
> 3. Need to restrict one's life and remain inconspicuous
> 4. Need for power and control over others
> 5. Need to exploit others
> 6. Need for recognition or prestige
> 7. Need for personal admiration
> 8. Need for personal achievement
> 9. Need for self-sufficiency and independence
> 10. Need for perfection and unassailability

Evaluating Horney's Work   Karen Horney's ideas were largely neglected early in her career (Monte, 1980). Then her 1967 book, *Feminine Psychology,* appeared at just the right time to elevate her among those seeking a feminist perspective within psychology and psychiatry (Horney, 1967). But, having attracted renewed interest, will Horney eventually slip again into oblivion? Her ideas suffer from the same flaw that plagues the other psychodynamic theories: a weak scientific foundation. It awaits someone to translate her concepts into operational terms that can be put to a scientific test. What should be evident to you even as a young student of psychology is that all these people were big-time thinkers, theorizing in grand fashion and abstractly about the nature of human nature. They were not oriented nor fully trained toward testing parts of their ideas as hypotheses relating independent to dependent variables in experimental paradigms.

Other Neo-Freudian Theorists   Sigmund Freud's revolutionary ideas attracted many others to the psychoanalytic movement—many of whom, like Carl Jung, Karen Horney, Erik Erikson, and Alfred Adler, also broke from Freud to develop their own ideas. For the most part, the post-Freudian theorists accepted the notions of psychic determinism and unconscious motivation. But they did not always agree with Freud on the details, especially about the sex and death instincts or the indelible nature of early life experiences. Broadly speaking, the neo-Freudians made several significant changes in the course of psychoanalysis:

- They put greater emphasis on ego functions, including ego defenses, development of the self, and conscious thought as the major components of the personality—whereas Freud focused primarily on the unconscious.
- They gave social variables (culture, family, and peers) an important role in shaping personality—whereas Freud focused mainly on instinctive urges and unconscious conflicts.
- They extended personality development beyond childhood to include the lifespan—whereas Freud focused mainly on early childhood experiences.

As we saw in Chapter 7, neo-Freudian Erik Erikson proposed an elaborate theory of personality development that unfolded in stages throughout the lifespan, a conjecture that has recently received support from psychologist Sanjay Srivastava and his team (2003) at the University of Oregon. Their data show that personality continues to change well into adulthood, with people in their 20s growing more conscientious and those in their 30s and beyond gaining as they age on measures of agreeableness, warmth, generosity, and helpfulness.

In such ways, then, the post-Freudians broke Freud's monopoly on personality theory and paved the way for the new ideas developed by the humanistic and cognitive theorists.

CONNECTION CHAPTER 7

Erikson's theory described the development of personality across the lifespan (p. 276).

Humanistic Theories: Emphasis on Human Potential and Mental Health

Neither Freud nor the neo-Freudians had much to say about those of us who are "normal." With an emphasis on internal conflict and mental disorder, they offered compelling explanations for mental disorders, but they largely failed to provide a usable theory of the healthy personality. And so the humanistic approach stepped in to fill that need for a bright-light view of human nature in place of the dark lenses of their theoretical predecessors.

Humanistic psychologists are optimistic on a grand scale. For them, personality is not driven by unconscious conflicts and defenses against anxiety but rather by positive needs to adapt, learn, grow, and thrive. They have retained the idea of motivation as a central component of personality, but they have accentuated the positive motives, such as love, esteem, and self-actualization. They see mental disorders as stemming from unhealthy *situations* rather than from unhealthy *individuals*. Once people are freed

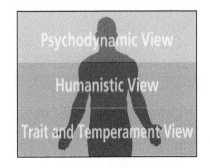

self-actualizing personality   A healthy individual who has met his or her basic needs and is free to be creative and fulfil his or her potentialities.

Maslow considered Eleanor Roosevelt to be a self-actualizing person.

▶ **CONNECTION** CHAPTER 9

Maslow's *hierarchy of needs* claims that motives occur in a priority order (p. 372).

Read about Maslow's Help in Founding Great Businesses at **MyPsychLab**

fully functioning person   Carl Rogers's term for a healthy, self-actualizing individual who has a self-concept that is both positive and congruent with reality.

phenomenal field   One's psychological reality, composed of one's perceptions and feelings.

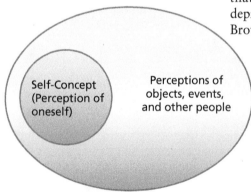

FIGURE 10.7
Rogers's Phenomenal Field

For Carl Rogers, what we perceive and feel is the only reality. The totality of all our feelings and perceptions he dubbed the *phenomenal field*. Note that the *self-concept* is a perception of oneself and therefore a part of the phenomenal field. In the *fully functioning person,* the self-concept is both positive and *congruent* with the feedback received from others.

from negative situations, such as negative self-evaluations ("I'm not smart") and abusive relationships or jobs and careers that are demeaning or debilitating, the innate tendency to be healthy should actively guide them to life-enhancing choices.

Abraham Maslow and the Healthy Personality   Abraham Maslow referred to the humanistic view as psychology's "third force," to contrast his ideas with the psychoanalytic and behaviorist movements that had dominated psychology during most of his lifetime. He was especially concerned by the Freudian fixation on mental disturbance and maladjustment. Instead, Maslow argued, we need a theory that describes mental health as something more than just the absence of illness. That theoretical need became his life's quest. He sought the ingredients of the healthy personality where no one had ever looked for them before: in people who had lived especially full and productive lives (Maslow, 1968, 1970, 1971).

Self-Actualizers   Maslow's subjects included the historical figures Abraham Lincoln and Thomas Jefferson, plus several persons of stature during his own lifetime: Albert Einstein, Albert Schweitzer, and Eleanor Roosevelt. In these individuals, Maslow found healthy personalities focused on goals beyond their own basic needs. Some, like Lincoln and Roosevelt, were oriented toward the needs of humanity. Others, like Einstein, were oriented toward understanding the natural world. Most became engaged in causes about which they felt deeply. Maslow called them all **self-actualizing personalities.** He characterized his self-actualizers as creative, full of good humor, and given to spontaneity—but, at the same time, accepting of their own limitations and those of others. In brief, self-actualizers are those who feel free to fulfill their potentialities. It is a state of being that we should aspire to become and embrace. 📖

Needs in a Hierarchy   Although Maslow was most interested in the healthy, self-actualizing personality, his theory of a *hierarchy of needs* also offers an explanation of maladjustment. As you will recall, Maslow proposed that our needs are arranged in a priority order, from the biological needs to needs for safety, love, esteem, and self-actualization. An unfulfilled "deficiency" need, such as a need for love or esteem, can produce maladjustment, while satisfaction of such needs allows the person to pursue interests that promote growth and fulfillment. Indeed, research shows that people who have low self-esteem may go through life feeling fearful, angry, or depressed, while those who are self-accepting lead far happier lives (Baumeister, 1993; Brown, 1991).

Carl Rogers's Fully Functioning Person   Unlike Maslow, Carl Rogers (1961) was a therapist who often worked with dysfunctional people rather than self-actualizers. Yet he did not overlook the healthy personality, which he called the **fully functioning person.** He described such an individual as having a self-concept that is both *positive* and *congruent* with reality. That is, the fully functioning person has high self-esteem, which is consistent (congruent) with the messages he or she receives from others who express their approval, friendship, and love. Negative experiences, such as loss of a job or rejection by a lover, can produce *incongruence,* a threat to one's self-esteem.

The Phenomenal Field: The Person's Reality   Rogers insisted that psychology recognize the importance of perceptions and feelings, which he called the **phenomenal field.** We respond only to this subjective experience, not to an objective reality. That is why a student's reaction to a grade depends entirely on her or his perception of the personal meaning of that letter grade. Receiving a C may shock a student who is used to receiving As but thrill one who has been failing: Both are reacting to their own subjective phenomenal fields. In Rogers's system, then, the phenomenal field is part of the personality, as a sort of filter for our experiences (see Figure 10.7). It contains our interpretations of both the external and internal worlds, and it also contains the *self,* the humanists' version of the Freudian ego.

Conditional versus Unconditional Relationships   Interestingly, Rogers himself had an unhappy and dysfunctional childhood, dominated by the rigid rules of his parents' strict religious beliefs. So restrictive was this environment that he once remarked that he felt "wicked" when he first tasted a bottle of soda pop without his parents' knowledge (Rogers, 1961). Later, from an adult perspective, Rogers concluded that children from homes like his, where parental love is *conditional* (dependent) on good behavior, may grow up with excessive anxiety and a strong sense of guilt that leads to low self-esteem and mental disorder. Instead of parental "guilt-mongers," he believed, we need people who can give us *unconditional positive regard*—love without conditions attached.

Unlike the psychodynamic theorists who focused on sinister motives, Rogers, Maslow, and other humanistic personality theorists including Rollo May (1966) believe that our most basic motives are for positive growth. In its healthiest form, self-actualization is a striving to realize one's potential—to develop fully one's capacities and talents. According to the humanistic theorists, this innate quest is a constructive, guiding force that moves each person toward positive behaviors and the enhancement of the self.

A Humanistic Perspective on Mary Calkins   A humanist trying to understand what drove Mary Calkins would probably begin by asking: How did she see her world—and herself? And what mattered to her? They would be especially interested in her strengths: her intelligence, her nurturing family background, and her supportive circle of colleagues at Wellesley and in the psychology group at Harvard. They would also note that Calkins worked all her life to make psychology the science of the self (by which she meant the whole person, not the fragmented and narrow approach of the structuralists or the "mindless" approach of the behaviorists of that era). In this respect, Mary Calkins might be considered one of the pioneers of humanistic psychology.

Evaluating the Humanistic Theories   The upbeat humanistic view of personality brought a welcome change for therapists who had wearied of the dark, pessimistic Freudian perspective, with its emphasis on unspeakable desires and repressed traumas. They liked the humanistic focus on making one's present and future life more palatable rather than dredging up painful memories of an unalterable past. They also liked its attention to mental health rather than mental disorder.

Are Humanistic Theories "Self"-Centered?   But not everyone jumped on the humanists' bandwagon. Many critics chided the humanists for their fuzzy concepts: What exactly is "self-actualization," they asked? Is it an inborn tendency, or is it created by one's culture? And, added the psychoanalysts, the humanistic emphasis on conscious experience does not recognize the power of the unconscious. Finally, cross-cultural psychologists criticized the humanists' emphasis on the self—as in *self*-concept, *self*-esteem, and *self*-actualization. This "self-centered" picture of personality, they noted, may merely be the viewpoint of observers looking through the lens of an individualistic Western culture that is alien to non-Western views where community and family are more vital than any selfhood (Heine et al., 1999).

We should be clear: No one denies the existence of a self within the personality—that is, some sort of process that distinguishes the individual from everything else. We all distinguish "me" from "thee." In fact, MRI and PET scans demonstrate the existence of specialized brain modules related to processing thoughts about the self (Heatherton et al., 2004). And even in the collectivistic cultures, the self exists, although the emphasis is on a self embedded in a social context. The real issue, then, is whether the self should be the centerpiece of personality or a side show.

Self-Esteem: Cause or Effect?   Recently, the whole popular notion of self-esteem as the essential ingredient for mental health has been brought under the lens of research and critical thinking . . . and surprisingly found questionable. Why is this important? Many programs designed to improve education, combat drug abuse, and discourage teen sex and violence are based on boosting self-esteem of adolescent students. Yet after a review of the research, psychologist Roy Baumeister et al. (2003) report that low

CONNECTION CHAPTER 1

Structuralism sought the "elements" of conscious experience (p. 14).

self-esteem causes none of these problems. In fact, studies show that bullies and drug users often have *high* self-esteem. So rather than focusing on high self-esteem as an end in itself, Baumeister and his colleagues urge promoting positive achievements and prosocial behaviors, with the expectation that self-esteem will follow in their wake.

Positive Psychology: The New Humanism?   In the past decade, a movement known as **positive psychology,** pioneered by psychologist Martin Seligman, was formed to pursue essentially the same goals established by the humanists. The difference is that those allied with positive psychology are more concerned than were most humanists about laying a scientific foundation for their theories, with greater precision for the specific terms in the lexicon that comprises human strengths and virtues (Peterson & Seligman, 2004). This ever-expanding "fourth force" has produced important work that we will see on happiness, social support, health, and well-being in Chapter 14. Even so, the positive psychology movement itself is limited as an all-purpose explanation of personality by its restricted focus on only the desirable aspects of human functioning. In a sense, it is similar to the Dalai Lama's emphasis on becoming a compassionate person, which is perhaps one of the noblest personal virtues, but fails to recognize its function in a world filled with evil of all kinds. That positive self-oriented compassion must be transformed into heroic *action* if it is to become a mechanism for social and political change (Dalai Lama, 2007).

So, is there an alternative view that overcomes the problems we have seen in the psychodynamic, humanistic, and the new positive psychology theories? Let's next consider the cognitive approach.

Author Phil Zimbardo being greeted by the Dalai Lama, prior to their public dialogue about the importance of compassion, as a personal virtue being transformed ino the civic virtue of heroic action in order to challenge evil in the world.

Social-Cognitive Theories: Emphasis on Social Learning

To understand why we must put up with those tamper-proof seals on pill bottles, we need to go back a few years to 1982, when someone (the case is still unsolved) slipped cyanide into a batch of Tylenol capsules. The result was seven deaths. And before manufacturers could get those pesky new seals in place, several copycat attempts to contaminate other drugs occurred. Sales of those drugs plummeted, so observers speculated that the motive—held maybe by competitors, not just psychopathic individuals—was to bankrupt certain drug companies.

The personality-related question is this: Can we explain these despicable acts entirely by looking at unconscious motives, selves being actualized, or perverted strengths and virtues? Social-cognitive theorists answer with a resounding, "No!" We must take learning into account—*social learning,* to be more precise. In fact, we must take into account the full range of psychological processes, including cognition, motivation, and emotion, as well as the environment (Cervone, 2004). Here, we will sample two of these approaches.

Observational Learning and Personality: Bandura's Theory   You don't have to yell "Fire!" in a crowded theater to know what would happen if you did. Stanford University's Albert Bandura maintains that we are driven not just by inner motivational forces or even by receiving external rewards and punishments but by our *expectations* of how our actions might gain us rewards or cost us pains. And many of those expectations, he notes, don't come from direct experience but rather from observing what happens to others (Bandura, 1986). Thus, a distinctive feature of the human personality is the ability to foresee the consequences of actions, particularly in learning what happens to others when they behave in certain ways.

Perhaps this is the most important contribution of Bandura's theory: the idea that we can learn *vicariously*—that is, from others. This *social learning,* or **observational learning,** is the process by which people learn new responses by watching each other's behavior and noting its consequences. That is, others act as *role models* that we either accept or reject, depending on whether they are rewarded or punished for their behavior. So, when Ramon sees Billy hit his brother and get punished for it, Ramon learns through observation that hitting is not a good strategy to adopt. But if he gets away with it or is praised for toughening up his kid brother, a different lesson is learned. Thus, through observational learning, Ramon can see what works and what does not work without having to go through trial and error for himself. In Bandura's view, then, personality is a collection of *learned* behavior patterns, many of which we have borrowed by observational learning.

As Bandura's theory suggests, children develop a clearer sense of identity by observing how men and women behave in their culture.

Through observational learning, children and adults acquire information about their social environment. Likewise, skills, attitudes, and beliefs may be acquired simply by noting what others do and the consequences that follow. In this way, children may learn to say "please" and "thank you," to be quiet in libraries, and to refrain from public nose picking. The down side, of course, is that bad habits can be acquired by observing negative role models, such as a relative with a fear of spiders, or by exposure to TV shows that seem to reward antisocial behaviors, like shooting people, abusing drugs, or putting poison in Tylenol capsules. The point is that people don't always have to try out behaviors themselves in order to learn from experience.

But, says Bandura, personality is not just a repertoire of learned behavior. Understanding the whole person means understanding the continued interaction among behavior, cognition, and the environment. He calls this **reciprocal determinism** (Bandura, 1981, 1999).

reciprocal determinism The process in which cognitions, behavior, and the environment mutually influence each other.

How does reciprocal determinism work in real life? If, for example, you like psychology, your interest (a cognition) will probably lead you to spend time in the psychology department on campus (an environment) interacting with students and faculty (social behavior) who share your interest. To the extent that you find this stimulating and rewarding, this activity will reciprocally strengthen your interest in psychology and encourage you to spend more time in the psychology department. Each of the three elements—behavior, cognition, and the environment—reinforces the others. You can see the simple but powerful relationship among these variables in Figure 10.8.

Locus of Control: Rotter's Theory Another cognitive psychologist, Julian Rotter (rhymes with *voter*) developed a hybrid theory that we first introduced to you in connection with motivation in Chapter 9. Rotter tells us that our behavior depends on our sense of personal power or **locus of control**. Perceived locus of control, then, acts as a sort of filter through which we see our experiences and as a motive for action or inaction. Thus, Rotter's theory is both a trait theory and a "process" theory that focuses on a single but important dimension of personality.

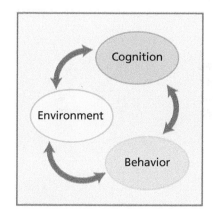

FIGURE 10.8

Reciprocal Determinism

In reciprocal determinism, the individual's cognitions, behavior, and the environment all interact.

locus of control An individual's sense of whether control over his or her life is internal or external.

To illustrate, we ask you this question: When you ride in a car, do you always use a seat belt, or do you think that being hurt or killed in an accident depends on when your "number comes up"? If you always use the belt and automatically click it every time you get into a car as driver or passenger, you probably have an *internal locus of control* because by doing so you are exerting some control over your fate. On the other hand, if you have a fatalistic feeling that you have no control over the events in your life, that whatever will be, will be, you probably don't buckle up (except to avoid being fined where it is illegal not to do so). In that case, you have an *external locus of control.*

Scores on Rotter's *Internal–External Locus of Control Scale* correlate with people's emotions and behavior in many situations (Rotter, 1990). For example, those with an internal locus of control are not only more likely to get good grades, but they also are more likely to exercise and watch their diets than are externals (Balch & Ross, 1975; Findley & Cooper, 1983). As you might expect, externals are more likely to be depressed (Benassi et al., 1988).

Many studies suggest that locus of control is an important characteristic of our personalities. That is, an internal or external disposition seems to be a reliable personality

Do It Yourself! FINDING YOUR LOCUS OF CONTROL

Julian Rotter (1966) has developed a test that assesses a person's sense of internal or external control over events. The test items consist of pairs of contrasting statements, and subjects must choose one statement with which they most agree from each pair. This format is called a forced-choice test. Unlike many other personality tests, the scoring for each item on Rotter's Internal–External Scale is transparent: The test-taker can easily tell in which direction most items are scored. Here are some items from a preliminary version of the test (Rotter, 1971).

You can see which direction you lean by counting up the number of statements with which you agreed in each column. Agreement with those in the left column suggests an internal locus of control.

1a. Promotions are earned through hard work and persistence.

2a. In my experience I have noticed that there is usually a direct connection between how hard I study and the grades I get.

3a. If one knows how to deal with people, they are really quite easily led.

4a. People like me can change the course of world affairs if we make ourselves heard.

5a. I am the master of my fate.

1b. Making a lot of money is largely a matter of getting the right breaks.

2b. Many times the reactions of teachers seem haphazard to me.

3b. I have little influence over the way other people behave.

4b. It is only wishful thinking to believe that one can really influence what happens in society at large.

5b. A great deal that happens to me is probably a matter of chance.

---

characteristic—although Rotter resists calling this a *trait* because he believes the term conveys the erroneous idea that internality–externality could be fixed and unchangeable. It is also quite likely that your own locus of control varies with different situations in your everyday life. If you are a good student, smart, and get good grades, you are internal in academic settings. But if you are overweight and come from a family where obesity is common, you are also likely to be external in restaurants and wherever tasty but unhealthy food is presented to you. You can capture the flavor of Rotter's Locus of Control Scale by following the instructions in the *Do It Yourself!* box.

Evaluating the Social-Cognitive Approach to Personality   Critics argue that the cognitive theories generally overemphasize rational information processing and overlook both emotion and unconscious processes as important components of personality. So for those who feel that emotions and motives are central to the functioning of human personality, the cognitive approaches to personality have a blind spot. However, because emotion and associated unconscious processes have assumed a greater role in cognitive psychology recently, we can anticipate a new generation of cognitive theories of personality that do take these aspects of personality into account (Mischel & Shoda, 1995).

The real strength of the social-cognitive theories is their foundation of solid psychological research—unlike most of the ideas proposed by the Freudians, neo-Freudians, and humanists. You will recall, for example, Bandura's famous Bobo doll experiment in observational learning, which we discussed in Chapter 4. The price paid for the social-cognitive theories, however, is that they are much less comprehensive than the old and grand theories of personality proposed by Freud and his successors. The payoff, however, has come in the form of both explanations and specific treatments for a number of mental disorders that often seem to involve observational learning, particularly anxiety-based disorders, such as phobias, and behavior disorders in children.

Finally, we might ask how a cognitive psychologist would explain Mary Calkins. One focus would be on how she interpreted the rewards and punishments she experienced in trying to complete her graduate work in psychology and how these interpretations shaped her behavior. A cognitive theorist might note that Calkins obviously had an internal locus of control that was part of a reciprocal interaction with the social support she received at home, at Wellesley, and from her mentors at Harvard—which, in turn, reinforced her determination and hard work. And, they might add, Mary Calkins became a role model for the women who came after her to study psychology.

CONNECTION CHAPTER 12

Other *anxiety disorders* include *panic disorder* and *obsessive-compulsive disorder* (p. 530).

Current Trends: The Person in a Social System

Gone are the days when Freud, Jung, Horney, and others were building the grand, sweeping theories of personality that attempted to explain everything we humans do. First the humanistic and later the cognitive theorists arose to point out blind spots in the older psychodynamic theories. Now the emphasis has shifted again, as psychologists have brought elements of the psychodynamic, humanistic, and cognitive perspectives together with new knowledge about the impact of culture, gender, and family dynamics. You should be especially aware of three important new trends in our thinking about personality.

In **family systems theory,** for example, the basic unit of analysis is not the individual but the family (Gilbert, 1992; Mones et al., 2007). This perspective holds that the ways people interacted first in their family and, later, in their peer groups shape personality. While Freud and others did recognize that parents influence children, the new emphasis is on *interaction*—on the ways that members of the family or the peer group influence each other. This has led to viewing people with psychological problems as individuals embedded in dysfunctional groups rather than as "sick" persons. This emphasis has also given us a new interpersonal language for personality. We often speak now of *codependence* (instead of *dependent* personalities) and *communication* (instead of mere talk). We also have a heightened awareness of relationships and process (the changes that occur as relationships develop).

family systems theory   A perspective on personality and treatment that emphasizes the family rather than the individual as the basic unit of analysis.

A second trend comes from psychology's increasing awareness of cultural differences, as more and more publications on personality come from psychologists around the world—not just from Europe and America (Quiñones-Vidal et al., 2004). Psychologist Stanley Sue (1991) also reminds us that our own society is becoming ethnically more diverse. No longer can we assume that everyone we meet shares the same cultural experience or the same values. This also means that psychologists must be sensitive to the role of cultural factors both in shaping personality and in contributing to the mental health and illness of ethnically and racially diverse people (Sue, 1983).

A third trend comes from an increasing appreciation of gender influences. While we do not know the weights to assign nature and nurture in our attempts to understand gender differences, we do know that males and females often perceive situations differently (Tavris, 1991). We have also seen that males tend to be more physically aggressive than females. And females tend to form close relationships in small, equal-status groups, while males tend to connect in larger groups (teams) organized hierarchically with leaders and followers.

Together, these three trends have enlarged our understanding of the forces that shape personality. The new emphasis is on diversity and group processes rather than on the traits and mental processes of individuals. As a result, the picture of personality has become much more complex—but it is becoming far more realistic.

[PSYCHOLOGY MATTERS]

Using Psychology to Learn Psychology

Although an internal or external locus of control can be a central feature of your personality, your perceived locus of control can also change from situation to situation. When you are speaking in front of a group, you may feel that the situation is beyond your control, yet when you are behind the wheel or on skis, you may feel that you are fully the master. And what about your education? Do you have a sense of internal or external control with regard to—say—your grade in psychology?

An external locus of control about grades poses a danger for the college student because college life is so full of distractions and temptations. If you believe that your grades are largely beyond your control, you can easily be driven by the enticements of the moment and let your studies slide. This attitude can, of course, become a self-fulfilling prophecy that ruins your grades not only in psychology but across the board.

The following questions will help you assess your own academic locus of control:

- On a test do you often find that, even when you know the material, anxiety wipes the information from your memory?
- Do you often know the material well but perceive that the test is unfair or covers material that the professor did not indicate would be on the test?
- Are you so easily distracted that you can never quite get around to studying?
- Do you believe that some people are born to be good students and some are not?
- Do you feel that you have no control over the grades you receive?
- Do you feel that you are not smart enough to cope with college-level work?
- Do you feel that success in college is largely a matter of playing up to the professors?

If you answered "yes" to several of these questions, then you probably have an external locus of control with respect to your college work—an attitude that can hamper your chances of college success. What can be done? Nothing—if you are completely convinced that your success in college is beyond your control. If, however, you are open to the idea of establishing more control over your college experience, here are a few suggestions:

- If you experience test anxiety, get help from your counseling center or learning resources center.
- Form a study group among friends taking the same classes, or find a tutor at your learning resources center.
- Talk to your professors individually: Ask them to give you some pointers on what they consider to be especially important in their classes. (But don't ask, "What's going to be on the test?")
- Go to your school's learning resources center, and get an assessment of your strengths and weaknesses and of your interest patterns. Then make a plan to correct your weaknesses (e.g., with tutoring or with remedial classes in your weak areas). At the same time, build on your strengths by selecting a major that capitalizes on your aptitudes and interests.

We would wish you good luck—but only an externalizer would want that!

Check Your Understanding

✓● Study and Review at MyPsychLab

1. **RECALL:** What was Sigmund Freud's greatest discovery—and the concept that distinguishes psychoanalysis from the humanistic and social-cognitive theories?

2. **APPLICATION:** Name a type of behavior that, according to the Freudians, is driven by Thanatos.

3. **RECALL:** What is the ego defense mechanism on which the *Rorschach* and *TAT* are based?

4. **APPLICATION:** If you react strongly to angry outbursts in others, you may be struggling with which Jungian archetype?

5. **RECALL:** In contrast with Freud, Karen Horney believed that the forces behind our behaviors are _____.

6. **RECALL:** The humanistic theorists were very different from the psychodynamic theorists because of their emphasis on _____.

7. **APPLICATION:** You try to understand people based on the role models they follow. Which kind of personality theorist are you?

8. **UNDERSTANDING THE CORE CONCEPT:** What do the psychodynamic, humanistic, and cognitive theories of personality have in common?

   a. They all view personality as largely unconscious.
   b. They all acknowledge the importance of internal mental processes.
   c. They all say that men and women have entirely different motives underlying their behaviors.
   d. They all have a strong basis in psychological research.

Answers 1. Most psychologists would say that it was Freud's discovery of unconscious mind. **2.** Any aggressive or destructive behavior would be correct. **3.** Projection **4.** The shadow archetype **5.** social **6.** the healthy personality and human potential **7.** A social-cognitive theorist **8.** b

⌐10.4 KEY QUESTION
What "Theories" Do People Use to Understand Themselves and Others?

We have seen how psychologists view personality. But how do ordinary people go about understanding each other? And how do they understand themselves? All of us regularly make assumptions—right or wrong—about other people's personalities as well as our own. You do so when you go on a date, apply for a job, or form your first impression of a professor or classmate. We might also wonder whether people in other cultures make the same assumptions about personality that we do. These issues are significant because the "folk theories," or *implicit personality theories,* that people use to understand people can support or undermine relationships among individuals—or even among nations. Our Core Concept says:

> ### Core Concept 10.4
> **Our understanding of ourselves and others is based on implicit theories of personality and our own self-narratives—both of which are influenced by culture.**

Let's look first at the implicit theories we use to understand others before moving on to consider how we understand ourselves.

Implicit Personality Theories

Think of someone who has been a role model for you. Now think of someone you can't stand to be around. In both cases, you associate those individuals with personal traits: honesty, reliability, sense of humor, generosity, outgoing attitude, aggressiveness, moodiness, pessimism, and so on. Even as a child, you had a rudimentary system for appraising personality. You tried to determine whether new acquaintances would be friend or foe; you worked out ways of dealing with your parents or teachers based on how you read their personalities.

In each case, your judgments were personality assessments reflecting your **implicit personality theory,** your personal explanation of personality that almost certainly relied on connecting people's behavior with the traits you attributed to them. Like the *implicit memories* we studied in Chapter 5, *implicit theories of personality* operate in the background, largely outside of our awareness, where they simplify the task of understanding other people (Fiske & Neuberg, 1990; Macrae et al., 1994).

Most of the time, implicit theories work well enough to make social relationships run smoothly—at least in familiar environments. While our expectations can easily miss the mark in unfamiliar cultures, in more familiar territory, our implicit theories of personality help us anticipate people's motives and behavior, allowing us to perform our work, buy our morning mochas, pass our courses, and interact with our friends. In some respects, our implicit theories may not be all that different from the five-factor theory. According to a study in which college students rated the personalities of other students they had observed but didn't know, their impressions agreed remarkably well with scores derived from the *Big Five Inventory* (Mehl et al., 2006). There was one interesting exception: Assertive or argumentative behavior was seen by the raters as a sign of emotional stability in men but as indicating emotional *instability* in women!

Implicit theories can have other blind spots too. They may err by relying on naive assumptions and stereotypes about traits and physical characteristics (Hochwalder, 1995). So hefty people may be assumed to be jolly or blondes a little short on intellect. Similarly, we may erroneously assume certain traits always go together—creativity and emotional instability, for example. So what implicit assumptions would you make about the personality of Tiger Woods knowing that he was one of the most highly visible and identifiable men in the world, who, to experience moments of pleasure, would risk everything if his adventures were ever made public?

implicit personality theory   A person's set of unquestioned assumptions about personality, used to simplify the task of understanding others.

Implicit theories may also give bad predictions when people's motives and feelings influence their judgment of others' personalities, as Freud suggested with his concept of *projection*. Accordingly, a person who is feeling angry, happy, or depressed may naïvely assume that other people are feeling the same way too.

Finally, people's implicit theories may conflict on the issue of whether personality traits are fixed or changeable. As you might expect, those believing in fixed traits are more likely to see others as stereotypes (e.g., "all Italians are alike") than are those whose implicit theories assumed the malleability of personality (Levy et al., 1998; Molden & Dweck, 2006). And consider the impact that either assumption—personality as fixed or changeable—could have on how parents raise their children, teachers respond to certain students, and coaches, trainers, and business leaders deal with success or failures of their players and personnel.

Carol Dweck (2006) has discovered in her 20 years of research on this issue that our **mindset** is not just a sideshow of personality; it is a major aspect of our entire mental world. It helps to shape our goals, influences whether we become optimistic or pessimistic about our future, and even whether we are likely to fulfill our potential. What happens when you, your parents, teachers, or coaches believe that any particular ability or talent is "*fixed*"—you have it or you do not? And say you and they believe you are one of the special ones who has IT. You are a musical protégé as a child, a super track star, or a gifted writer. With abilities "fixed by nature," you are entitled to succeed without having to break a sweat. So you are likely to work less hard, practice less, and then you even do well initially when the competition is rather low level. On the other side of aisle is the kid with the "*growth*" mind set: He and others in his corner share the view that any talent or ability is in a constant state of development and can improve only with intensive practice and hard work. Next, assume that both fail to meet some goal. The growth-mindset kid realizes it is essential to work harder and practice more hours to get ahead in contrast to the fixed-mindset kid who comes to feel inadequate, as less than advertised, as letting down all those who believed in her or his innate superiority. Popular author Malcolm Gladwell builds on such ideas in his bestseller, *Outliers* (2008), to inform us all that the single major difference between those youth who were praised as child protégés and succeeded versus those who failed to realize their assumed potential is 10,000 hours of practice!

Self-Narratives: The Stories of Our Lives

How do you respond when someone says, "Tell me about yourself"? You probably reply with a few sentences about where you are from, what you like to do with your leisure time, and what your occupational goals are. But what do you say when you ask yourself the same question? The "story" that you tell yourself about yourself is what psychologist Dan McAdams (2006) calls a **self-narrative.** He claims that the self-narrative is just as important a component of personality as are motives, emotions, or social relationships. The self-narrative is really a broader conception of the self-concept: It is the story of the self-concept over time. The self-narrative serves as the common thread that holds the elements of personality together, like beads on a necklace. And, says McAdams, our identity depends on keeping this narrative going throughout our lives, to give us a sense of unity and purpose.

Culture, of course, has a big effect on the self-narrative stories we *want* to tell ourselves. While McAdams hasn't yet done extensive cross-cultural research, he has identified a peculiarly important self-narrative in the American culture. He calls it the **redemptive self.** See if you recognize yourself in some elements of the redemptive self-narrative:

- You have always felt fortunate—not necessarily because of an economic advantage, but perhaps because you have a special talent or were singled out for special treatment by a teacher or other nurturing adult.

- At some point, you realized that other people are not so fortunate. Through no fault of their own, they experience suffering or disadvantage.

mindset   The extent to which one believes abilities and talents are fixed by nature or can change and grow through practice and that experience influences success that requires hard work and effort, and also one's reactions to failure.

self-narrative   The "stories" one tells about oneself. Self-narratives help people sense a thread of consistency through their personalities over time.

redemptive self   A common self-narrative identified by McAdams in generative Americans. The redemptive self involves a sense of being called to overcome obstacles in the effort to help others.

- Because you are advantaged and others are not, you feel a responsibility or a challenge to improve the lives of others in some way.

- Probably in childhood or adolescence, you developed a belief system, perhaps rooted in religion, although not necessarily so, that has since guided your actions, particularly in your efforts to help others.

- You meet unexpected obstacles and overcome them. You have negative experiences but learn and grow from them, and you see a future of continued growth and progress, despite the near certainty of daunting obstacles ahead.

Not everyone's self-narrative follows exactly this pattern, of course. But McAdams often finds a pattern like this in *generative* adults, a term originally used by developmental psychologist Erik Erikson to describe healthy, productive adults. More specifically, generativity refers to adults who are committed to something outside themselves—to the community and to the welfare of future generations. It remains to be seen what narratives characterize healthy adults in other cultures.

The Effects of Culture on Our Views of Personality

As we have seen, Westerners tend to put the *individual* or the *self* at the center of personality. While people the world over do make the assumption of a distinct self, much of the world—especially those in collectivist cultures—assumes that the self is embedded in a larger social network. They further assume that individuals cannot be understood in isolation from others with whom they have some sort of relationship—which brings us to cross-cultural researcher Harry Triandis.

Individualism, Collectivism, and Personality According to Triandis (1995), cultures differ most fundamentally on the dimension of *individualism* versus *collectivism*. For those raised in the Euro-American tradition, the individual is the basic unit of society, while those raised in many Asian and African cultures emphasize the family or other social groups. In collectivistic cultures, people tend to form identities that blend harmoniously with the group, and they expect that others are motivated to do the same. In individualistic cultures, people think of themselves as having a unique identity, independent of their social relationships (Pedersen, 1979). Thus, for Euro-Americans, the self is a whole, while for many Asians and Africans the self is only a part (Cohen & Gunz, 2002).

Most Asian cultures have a collectivist tradition that affirms the group, rather than the individual, as the fundamental social unit.

Let us be clear: Neither the individualistic nor the collectivistic approach is "better." Each has advantages and disadvantages from different perspectives. The collectivist cultures encourage group effort, typically for the benefit and glory of the group—often a work group or a family group. On the other hand, a person such as Mary Calkins, who challenged society's norms, would be more likely to thrive in an individualistic culture.

Many aspects of peoples' personalities and behavior derive from their culture's position on the individualism versus collectivism spectrum. So, in judging people, Americans and Europeans tend to make the **fundamental attribution error or FAE.** This bias is twofold in overestimating the causes of any behavior as primarily a function of dispositional factors—internal to the actor—while simultaneously underestimating the social-situational—external—factors. This misperception stems from the assumption that other people's actions, especially annoying, clumsy, inappropriate, or otherwise undesirable behaviors, result from their personalities rather than from the situation. If you come to your psychology class late, other students are likely to assume that you are a "late" or disorganized person—if you are at an American college or university. But if you arrived late to a psychology class in China or Japan, the students there would be more likely to assume that your behavior had some external cause, such as traffic problems. In general, the fundamental attribution error is less common in group-oriented, *collectivistic* cultures, such as are found in Latin American and Asia (Church et al., 2005; Lillard, 1997).

fundamental attribution error The dual tendency to overemphasize internal, dispositional causes and minimize external, situational pressures. The FAE is more common in individualistic cultures than in collectivistic cultures.

CONNECTION CHAPTER 11

To avoid the fundamental attribution error, social psychologists recommend first looking for a situational explanation for unusual behavior (p. 490).

CONNECTION CHAPTER 9

McClelland has found the
need for achievement to be an
important variable predicting
employee performance (p. 365).

Read about Other Cultural Differences
in Views of Personality at **MyPsychLab**

Cultures differ on other dimensions too. For example, when given the choice of competition or cooperation, individualistic Americans characteristically choose to compete (Aronson, 2004; Gallo & McClintock, 1965). And as we saw in Chapter 9, Americans, on the average, also score higher on measures of need for achievement than do people in collectivist cultures.

[PSYCHOLOGY MATTERS]

The Personality of Time

Life is filled with decisions, big ones and small ones, trivial and significant ones. Study or party with friends? One more beer before driving home or give keys to a responsible driver? Spend Saturday playing new video game or writing term paper? In one sense, your personality is composed of the sum of all the actions you take based on how you resolve those decisions. But what are the major influences on your decision-making process?

We can identify three ways most people go about making such decisions. Actually, they are embedded in one of three time zones. For some, the biggest influences come from stimulation in the immediate situation: sensory (smell, taste, look, feel), biological (arousal, hunger, tiredness), and social (what others are doing, saying, modeling). Decisions based primarily on such input are focused on the present, and when they are typical of a given person, we can call him or her *present-oriented*. Others faced with the same decisions look back to similar situations in the past and use those memories of what happened to do it again or not. Again, when this focus becomes typical for most decisions, that person can be considered *past-oriented*. Still others deal with that decisional matrix not by attending solely to the present or the past, because their focus is on the future consequences of their imagined actions. They do quick cost–benefit estimations and then act when rewards are greater than losses. We can consider such people who do so habitually to be *future-oriented*.

These subjective conceptions of time have powerful consequences on our values, judgments, decisions, and behaviors. And they do so nonconsciously, out of our awareness, because these temporal biases have been learned from childhood by many experiences such as cultural and social modeling, education, social class, religion, stability of family and nation, and more. Thus, for example, those most likely to develop a future time orientation are more educated, from industrialized nations, from Protestant backgrounds and stable families, and do not live near the equator (where the climate never changes so people live more in the present).

Such ideas were transformed into a series of 56 inventory items that college students replied to on five-point response measures according to how characteristic each

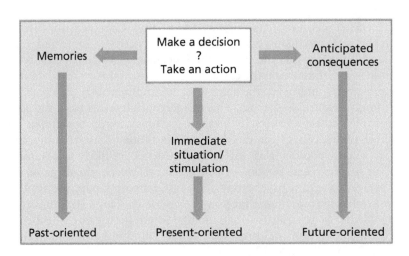

FIGURE 10.9
Conceptual Time Perspective Model

one was for them. The five time factors that emerged formed a resulting scale that was very reliable and also had high predictive validity, known as the Zimbardo Time Perspective Inventory or ZTPI (Boyd & Zimbardo, 2008; Zimbardo & Boyd, 1999).

The five time perspective factors and a typical scale item of each are:

Future: "Meeting tomorrow's deadlines and doing other necessary work comes before tonight's play."

Present-Hedonistic: "I believe that getting together with one's friends to party is one of life's important pleasures."

Present-Fatalistic: "It doesn't make sense to worry about the future, since there is nothing I can do about it anyway."

Past-Positive: "I prefer family rituals that are regularly repeated."

Past-Negative: "I think about the good things that I have missed out in my life."

(Note: To check out your own time perspective scores, complete the ZTPI on www. TheTimeParadox.com.)

When the scores on each of these factors were correlated with many standard personality test responses and other personally reported traits in a sample of more than 200 college students, the following major correlations emerged. (Recall that most results correlating any personality trait measures with other standard measures are usually in the range of 0.20 to 0.30 when you consider the robust correlations found with this new measure.)

Future: Conscientiousness, $r = +0.70$; Preference for Consistency, $r = +0.60$; but $r = -0.40$ for Sensation Seeking.

Present-Hedonistic: Novelty and Sensation Seeking, $r = +0.70$; but $r = -0.75$ for Ego Under Control.

Present-Fatalistic: Aggression, $r = +0.50$; Trait Anxiety, $r = +0.50$; Depression, $r = +0.45$; but $r = -0.70$ for Concern for Future Consequences.

Past-Positive: Happiness, $r = +0.40$; Self-Esteem, $r = +0.30$; but Trait Anxiety, $r = -0.30$, and $r = -0.20$ Aggression.

Past-Negative: Trait Anxiety, $r = +0.75$; Depression, $r = +0.70$; Aggression, $r = +0.60$; but Self-Esteem, $r = -0.60$, and Emotional Stability, $r = -0.55$.

> **CONNECTION** CHAPTER 1
>
> Correlations measure the strength of the relationship between two variables, with larger numbers such as 0.70 and −0.55 representing stronger associations than smaller correlations such as 0.20 and −0.10 (p. 29).

What does all this mean to you? Knowing how strong the relationships between these factors are, and also how many different patterns are seen in a group of functioning college students, you can apply these findings to your own habits to get a sense of what your own direction currently is. To be someone high on Present-Fatalism or Past-Negative is a sign of risk given the adverse nature of the traits and experiences related to each of these states. Obviously success in academia and business will depend on a healthy dose of Future orientation, but not to the point of becoming a nerdy workaholic who sacrifices friends, family, fun, and sleep for success. Present-Hedonism is essential in *moderation* to reward oneself for a task completed well, but in excess, it can become impulsive and addictive to whatever is the source of pleasure for the person, such as food, gambling, drugs, sex, or video games.

It is also important to highlight that robust relationship between being Future-Oriented and Conscientiousness. Why? Because Conscientiousness is the only personality trait directly linked to biological mortality: Conscientious people live at least 2 years longer at every age level than their less-conscientious peers and family members! This powerful finding is the conclusion from a recent meta-analysis of 20 independent studies with more than 9,000 individuals from six different nations that used a variety of different meanings for this construct (Kern & Friedman, 2008).

It is not a magical relationship with Future-Orientation, but why it occurs is obvious when we note that students who are high on the Future factor get regular medical and dental checkups, get cancer checks regularly, eat healthier foods, wear seat belts, drink less alcohol, smoke less, and do not engage in risky behaviors. Viola! Longer lives than those who do the opposite.

But Is Time Perspective a Personality Trait?   What do we have to add to the information presented thus far for you to answer this question, "yes it is, or likely it is"? How about determining whether the five time perspective factors are significantly related to each of the Big Five Factors in the NEO Personality Inventory (Costa & McCrae, 1992a)? A new dissertation from Lithuania has done just that for us with surprisingly supportive findings (Kairys, 2010).

This study tested more than 700 people comprising both genders in three different age groups: young (18–22); mid-aged (30–50); and older (60 and above). Thus, its findings are generalizable across age and gender in a large population from a European nation. The results? "Time perspective and personality traits in the Five Factor model are highly correlated, and such correlations are found when correlating similar personality traits between themselves" (Kairys, 2010, p. 22). Moreover, "time perspective is related to personality traits" and "it [time perspective] should belong to the domain of personality traits" (Kairys, 2010, 27, 28). What, specifically, were the relationships found between time perspective and the Big Five traits?

Conscientiousness is significantly and positively related to Future TP (time perspective).

Openness to Experience and Extraversion relate to Present-Hedonistic TP, which has low scores on Conscientiousness.

Neuroticism is positively related to Present-Fatalistic TP, as we might expect.

Extraversion and Agreeableness relate strongly to Past-Positive TP.

Finally, Neuroticism is positively related to Past-Negative TP, but this Past-Negative factor correlates negatively with both Extraversion and Conscientiousness.

It is important to note that no differences were found in the relationships between the time perspective factors and the personality traits across the three age groups, although hedonism decreases with age. Nevertheless, TP is relatively stable in the population over time.

We would like you to think more deeply about how you relate to time perspective and how your behavior might be under the influence of something you carry around in your head without knowing about it. Now that you are mindful of it, make it work for you to create a more optimal time perspective that enables you to shift time zones flexibly depending on the demands of each of life's situations you face. The alternative is to be a mindless slave of time, stuck in the past, locked into future overdrive, or endlessly idling in a present mode. Our advice: Carpe diem—but after exams are aced.

Check Your Understanding

✓●─[Study and Review at MyPsychLab

1. **APPLICATION:** Name a country that generally values the achievement of a team or group over that of the individual.

2. **RECALL:** In what important respect have people's implicit theories of personality been found to differ?

3. **RECALL:** What is the term that best describes the dynamic relationship between culture and personality?

4. **APPLICATION:** Give an example of the *fundamental attribution error*. In what cultures would you be likely to find people committing the fundamental attribution error?

5. **UNDERSTANDING THE CORE CONCEPT:** People's implicit personality theories involve

   a. negative, but not positive, characteristics.

   b. the assumptions that they make about each other's motives, intentions, and behaviors.

   c. assumptions about themselves that they want to hide from others.

   d. opinions that they privately hold about others but will not say openly.

Answers: 1. China, Japan, India, Mexico, or nearly any country in Asia, Latin America, or the Middle East **2.** People's implicit theories differ on whether personality traits are fixed or changeable. **3.** Interaction **4.** The fundamental attribution error (FAE) occurs when you attribute a person's behavior to an internal disposition rather than to external factors. So, for example, you would be committing the FAE when someone trips and drops his books and you attribute it to clumsiness. Research shows the FAE to be more common in individualistic cultures, such as the majority cultures in Europe and the United States. **5.** b

CRITICAL THINKING APPLIED

The Person–Situation Controversy

Cognitive theorist Walter Mischel dropped a scientific bomb-shell on the personality theorists with evidence suggesting that we behave far less consistently from one situation to another than most had assumed (1968, 1973, 2003). A person who is extraverted at a party can become shy and retiring in class; your "neurotic" friend may become a pillar of strength in a crisis. Like Rosalind in Shakespeare's *As You Like It,* one person can present different personalities in different situations and to different people. So, Mischel argued, knowledge of the *situation* is more important in predicting behavior than know-ing a person's traits. The ensuing tumult within the field has become known as the **person–situation controversy** (Pervin, 1985).

Mischel's argument challenged the very foundations of most personality theories. After all, if people do act incon-sistently in different situations, then what good is a theory of personality? Is there no continuity in personality? Crit-ics mounted withering attacks on Mischel's thesis, pointing out that his methods underestimated a thread of consistency across situations (Epstein, 1980). Bem and Allen (1974) have also pointed out that some people behave more consistently than others. Moreover, people are most consistent when oth-ers are watching (Kenrick & Stringfield, 1980) and when in familiar situations (Funder, 1983a, b; Funder & Ozer, 1983).

While the foundations of personality psychology were shuddering, the person–situation controversy gave a boost to social psychology, where psychologists had always ar-gued the *power of the situation.* As we will see in the next chapter, situations can turn normal college students into li-ars, lovers, or even cruel tormentors. But where does all this leave us in dealing with the person–situation controversy?

What Are the Critical Issues?

This is *not* an either-or dispute: It's not a question of whether traits *or* situations control behavior. Rather, it is a question of which has more influence and when it does. All sides of the person–situation debate agree that both the person and the situation have an effect. It's the degree of weighting of the person and the situation that is at issue.

There is a second issue too. How much does the power of personality traits vary from one situation to another? At the extreme, for a prisoner in solitary confinement, the situ-ation obviously has overwhelming importance. But the more important focus is on ordinary people in their everyday lives: How much power does the situation have vis-à-vis traits? It's not an easy question to answer.

People Are Inconsistent   If we look at the same person over time, we may find him or her reacting very differently to the

person–situation controversy   Debate over the relative contributions to understand-ing human behavior from personality processes, like traits, versus social psychological pro-cesses, like the power of situational variables.

same situation on different occasions. Consider: Do you *always* order the same thing when you go to your favorite restaurant? Or are you *always* cheerful with your friends? Psychologist William Fleeson urges us to think of personality traits as a sort of average of how the person customarily behaves. (Per-haps you are *usually* cheerful—on the average.)

Even more surprising was what researchers found when they monitored people as they moved from one situation to another. One study had volunteers carry small personal data assistant (PDA) devices and, several times a day, record their situation, their behavior, and their self-assessment on the Big Five traits. The discovery: People's self-described personality traits change as radically as their behavior when they move from one situation to another (Fleeson, 2004).

The lesson to be learned here is that the majority of fac-tors affecting behavior simply cannot be assigned to the person *or* the situation. Behavior seems to result from an *interaction* of trait and situational variables (Kenrick & Funder, 1988). In fact, Mischel has never suggested that we abandon theories of personality. Rather, he sees behavior as a function of the situation, the individual's *interpretation* of the situation, and the personality (Mischel, 1990, 2003; Mischel & Shoda, 1995).

It Also Depends on *What Kind of* Situation   It also makes a difference if the situation is familiar or novel. If familiar, then one's habitual ways of dealing with it are likely to be elicited and thus our knowledge of the person's personality will allow reasonably accurate predictions. However, in novel situations where old habits are not appropriate, individuals tend to look to others to define what is the appropriate way to behave, and situational forces submerge personality differences. In the next chapter on social psychology, remember this lesson when you are introduced to some of the most fascinating studies in psychology that shocked the world.

What Conclusions Can We Draw?

Which side of the person–situation debate is right? Both are. The difficulty was that that they were right about different things. According to personality psychologist William Fleeson (2004), traits help us understand behavior over long periods of time, when a thread of consistency can be seen in personality—as an individual's behavior converges on a personal average. Over shorter intervals, and especially in particular situations, a person's behavior can be highly variable, as we have seen. So, by taking a long view, the trait perspective is right, while on a moment-to-moment basis, the situation perspective wins.

But which side gets the most weight also depends on whether the situation is strong or weak, as Mischel has said. And to further complicate matters, we have to figure culture into the equation as part of the situation: Evidence has emerged that an individual's personality traits have more influence on behavior in individualistic cultures than in collectivistic cultures (Church et al., 2006). That makes sense, of course, when we think that an individualistic culture places high values on certain traits such as intelligence (as opposed to hard work). And it also makes sense in light of the finding that people in collectivist cultures are less susceptible to the fundamental attribution error—because they emphasize the power of the situation.

CHAPTER SUMMARY

(((•─[Listen to an audio file of your chapter at **MyPsychLab**

CHAPTER PROBLEM: What influences were at work to produce the unique behavioral patterns, high achievement motivation, and consistency over time and place that we see in the personality of Mary Calkins?

- Psychologists recognize the uniqueness of human personalities, yet seek to discover the common patterns between people in their traits, characters, and dispositional features based on genetic, biological, experiential, social, and cultural contributions.

- Psychodynamic theories, particularly Freud's theory, would emphasize early experiences—especially traumas—as well as relations among siblings and with parents. Horney and Jung would have focused on the societal pressures faced by women.

- Trait and temperament theories would look for enduring personality characteristics, such as openness, conscientiousness, and introversion. A major contribution in this domain of psychology has been the quantification of features of personality using a variety of assessment techniques to reveal individual differences in personality.

- Humanistic psychologists, such as Maslow, would focus on a person's goals, strengths, self-concept, and social relationships.

- Social-cognitive theorists would be interested in the person's locus of control. They would also assess the individual's interpretation of important experiences in life.

10.1 What Forces Shape Our Personalities?

[Core Concept 10.1 **Personality is shaped by the combined forces of biological, situational, and mental processes—all embedded in a sociocultural and developmental context.**]

We can think of **personality** as the "default settings" for our unique pattern of motives, emotions, and perceptions, along with our learned schemas for understanding ourselves and our world. Personality also has deep evolutionary roots, as seen in displacement of aggression. Neuroscience suggests that the biology of personality comprises a collection of brain modules, each adapted to a different purpose.

But personality also involves nurture—that is, learning driven by the environment, as seen in the effect of family position on personality. The person–situation controversy centers on the relative importance of situations (the environment) as compared with internal traits and mental processes.

The chapter makes an important distinction between personality characteristics, or **dispositions**, and **personality**

processes. We need both dispositional theories and process theories for a complete understanding of personality.

Cross-cultural psychologists have complicated the problem of personality by suggesting that personality may not be a universal concept and that Western cultures have a bias toward individualism and a unique self. In fact, all cultures have a tendency either to **individualism** or **collectivism**, both of which leave their imprint on personality. In any culture, however, an individual's personality is, in part, a creation of interactions with other people.

One does not need a theory of personality for explaining ordinary behavior. A good theory, however, is helpful for explaining unusual behavior and eccentric people. The most common theories can be grouped as follows: *dispositional theories* (trait and temperament theories) and *process theories* (psychodynamic theories, humanistic theories, and social-cognitive theories).

collectivism (p. 418)
dispositions (p. 417)
individualism (p. 418)
personality (p. 414)
personality processes (p. 417)

10.2 What Persistent Patterns, or *Dispositions,* Make Up Our Personalities?

> Core Concept 10.2 The *dispositional* theories all suggest a small set of personality characteristics, known as temperaments, traits, or types, that provide consistency to the individual's personality over time.

Temperament, trait, and type theories are descriptive approaches to personality with a long history stretching back to the humor theory of the ancient Greeks. Modern theories speak of types, traits, and temperaments. In this chapter, we group all three under the heading of **dispositional theories perspectives.**

Temperament refers to innate personality dispositions, which may be tied to factors in the brain and in the genes. Kagan's work has focused on the inhibited versus uninhibited dimension of temperament. By contrast, traits are thought of as multiple dimensions existing, to some degree, in each person's personality. Traits give personality consistency across situations and may be influenced by both heredity and learning. Many psychologists now agree on the Big Five traits, which seem to have validity across cultures. Trait assessment is the basis for many psychological tests: Some assess common traits, such as the Big Five, while others, such as the *MMPI-2,* assess clinical characteristics. Both the trait and temperament theories do a reasonably good job of describing and predicting behavior, but they offer no explanations for the underlying processes.

Type theory is exemplified in the controversial and widely used *MBTI,* based on Jung's personality typology. Research suggests that people's characteristics, as measured by the *MBTI* or other personality tests, do not fall into neat type categories but are more accurately conceived of on trait dimensions.

dispositional theories (p. 421)	personality type
five-factor theory (p. 423)	(p. 426)
humors (p. 420)	reliability (p. 425)
MMPI-2 (p. 424)	traits (p. 422)
Myers–Briggs Type Indicator	validity (p. 425)
(MBTI) (p. 426)	

10.3 How Do Mental *Processes* Help Shape Our Personalities?

> Core Concept 10.3 While each of the *process* theories sees different forces at work in personality, all portray personality as the result of both internal mental processes and social interactions.

The **psychodynamic, humanistic,** and **social-cognitive theories** all seek to explain the internal processes and social interactions that shape our personalities. Freud's **psychoanalytic theory** states that the personality arises out of **unconscious** desires, conflicts, and memories. None of our thoughts or behaviors happens by accident, according to the principle of **psychic determinism.** Early childhood experiences also have a strong influence on personality, as the child goes through predictable **psychosexual stages** in which conflicts are dealt with unconsciously. Freud believed that the personality consisted of three main structures, the **id** (the reservoir of unconscious desires), the **ego** (the largely conscious part of the mind), and the **superego** (which contains the conscience and the ego ideal). Part of the ego, involving the **ego defense mechanisms,** operates outside of consciousness. One of these defense mechanisms, projection, is the basis for widely used **projective tests,** including the *Rorschach* and the *TAT.*

Freud's theory has been extremely influential. Still, critics fault Freud's work for being scientifically unsound, a poor basis for prediction, and unfair to women. Modern psychology also suggests that the unconscious mind is less clever and purposeful than Freud believed.

Other psychodynamic theories, such as those proposed by Jung and Horney, also assume that personality is a dynamic process that involves strong and often-conflicting motives and emotions. Each of these **neo-Freudians,** however, emphasizes different aspects of personality. Jung proposed a **collective unconscious** populated by **archetypes.** He also proposed that people fall into certain personality types, characterized especially by tendencies to **introversion** and **extraversion.** Horney, on the other hand, emphasized conscious processes, **basic anxiety, neurotic needs,** and feminist issues in personality theory. Some other neo-Freudians, such as Erikson, also emphasized consciousness as well as lifelong personality development.

The humanistic theories, such as those of Maslow and Rogers, argue that people are naturally driven toward **self-actualization,** but this tendency can be suppressed by unhealthy conditions and perceptions. Maslow proposed a hierarchy of needs, suggesting that when the deficiency needs are met, a person is more likely to pursue self-actualization. Rogers taught that the **fully functioning person** has a positive self-concept that is congruent with reality, while mental disorder arises from incongruence. High self-esteem is more likely when a child comes from a family that provides unconditional positive regard.

The humanistic theories have had considerable impact on psychotherapy, but they have been criticized for being "self"-centered and lacking a strong scientific base. The social-cognitive theories, by contrast, do have a scientific basis, although they are much more limited in scope than are the psychodynamic and humanistic theories. Bandura's social-cognitive theory suggests that personality is shaped by **observational learning.** This occurs in an interaction of cognition, behavior, and the environment known as **reciprocal determinism.** According to Rotter's **locus-of-control theory,** those with an internal locus are more likely to feel they can control events in their lives than those who have an external locus of control.

Modern theories of personality, unlike those of Freud, Jung, Horney, and the other psychodynamic theorists, have not attempted to provide comprehensive explanations for all aspects of personality. In **family systems theory,** for example, emphasis has turned to the individual acting in a social environment. Other emphases include cultural influences on personality as well as an awareness of gender differences.

10.4 What "Theories" Do People Use to Understand Themselves and Others?

Core Concept 10.4 Our understanding of ourselves and others is based on implicit theories of personality and our own self-narratives—both of which are influenced by culture.

People everywhere deal with each other on the basis of their **implicit personality theories**, which simplify the task of understanding others. Implicit theories often use the same traits that the five-factor theory does, although some gender biases have been reported. Implicit theories also may rely on naïve assumptions, and they often differ on whether personality is fixed or changeable.

Moreover, cross-cultural psychologists have found that the assumptions people make about personality and behavior vary widely across cultures—depending especially on whether the culture emphasizes individualism or collectivism. Those in individualistic cultures are more prone to the **fundamental attribution error**. There are many other dimensions impinging on personality on which cultures differ, including social status, romantic love, expression of feelings, locus of control, and thinking versus feeling.

CRITICAL THINKING APPLIED

The Person–Situation Controversy

This ongoing controversy between personality psychologists and social psychologists focuses on the relative significance of what the person brings into a given behavioral setting, and what the situation brings out of that person when trying to understand any human action. As with the nature versus nurture controversy, both play important roles when they interact in shaping behavioral outcomes.

DISCOVERING PSYCHOLOGY **VIEWING GUIDE**

Watch the following video by logging into MyPsychLab (www.mypsychlab.com). After you have watched the video, answer the questions that follow.

PROGRAM 15: **THE SELF**

Program Review

1. What name did William James give to the part of the self that focuses on the images we create in the mind of others?
   a. the material self
   b. the spiritual self
   c. the social self
   d. the outer self

2. Gail is a toddler who is gradually separating from her mother. This process is called
   a. identification.
   b. individuation.
   c. self-presentation.
   d. self-consciousness.

3. In Freudian theory, the part of the person that acts as a police officer restraining drives and passions is called the
   a. superego.
   b. ego.
   c. id.
   d. libido.

4. Which statement reflects the humanistic view of the self, according to Carl Rogers?
   a. Our impulses are in constant conflict with society's demands.
   b. We have a capacity for self-direction and self-understanding.
   c. We form an image of ourselves that determines what we can do.
   d. Our views of ourselves are created by how people react to us.

5. When we characterize self-image as a schema, we mean that
   a. we use it to organize information about ourselves.
   b. other people see us in terms of the image we project.
   c. it is a good predictor of performance in specific situations.
   d. we rationalize our behavior to fit into an image.

6. In Albert Bandura's research, people were given the task of improving production at a model furniture factory. They performed best when they believed that performance
   a. depended on their intelligence.
   b. related mainly to how confident they felt.
   c. would be given a material reward.
   d. was based on learning an acquirable skill.

7. Which of the following behaviors signal low status in a status transaction?
   a. maintaining eye contact
   b. using complete sentences
   c. moving in slow, smooth way
   d. touching one's face or hair

8. According to the principles of behavioral confirmation, what reaction do people generally have to a person who is depressed?
   a. People sympathetically offer help to the person.
   b. People regard the person as inadequate.
   c. People act falsely cheerful to make the person happy.
   d. People treat a depressed person the same as anybody else.

9. What was referred to in the film as a type of psychological genocide?
   a. drugs
   b. falling emphasis on education
   c. prejudice
   d. immigration

10. What is the relevance of schemas to the self?
    a. We try to avoid schemas in constructing our sense of self.
    b. We organize our beliefs about ourselves in terms of schemas.
    c. Schemas are what makes us individuals.
    d. Schemas are always negative, since they underlie prejudice.

11. In Teresa Amabile's work on creativity, how did being in a competitive situation affect creativity?
    a. It reduced creativity.
    b. It increased creativity.
    c. Its effects varied depending on the person's innate creativity.
    d. There was no effect.

12. According to Hazel Markus, culture is what you
    a. think.
    b. see.
    c. do.
    d. hate.

13. The phrase "mutual constitution" refers to which two components, according to Hazel Markus?
    a. parent and child
    b. art and scholarship
    c. religion and society
    d. self and culture

14. In which culture are you most likely to find a definition of the person as a part of the group?
    a. Japanese
    b. American
    c. Portuguese
    d. Russian

15. The high rate of alcoholism among Native Americans was cited as an example of
    a. individualism.
    b. the psychological effects of prejudice.
    c. mutual constitution.
    d. striving for superiority.

16. According to William James, which part of the self serves as our inner witness to outside events?
    a. the material self
    b. the spiritual self
    c. the social self
    d. the outer self

17. Of the following psychologists, who is considered to be the least optimistic about the human condition?
    a. Freud
    b. Adler
    c. Rogers
    d. Maslow

18. Which of the following refers to how capable we believe we are of mastering challenges?
    a. self-efficacy
    b. self-handicapping
    c. confirmatory behavior
    d. status transaction

19. Teresa Amabile is to creativity as _____ is to behavioral confirmation.
    a. Alfred Adler
    b. Patricia Ryan
    c. Mark Snyder
    d. Albert Bandura

20. Who is credited as being responsible for psychology's return to the self?
    a. William James
    b. B. F. Skinner
    c. Patricia Ryan
    d. Carl Rogers

11

Social Psychology

CHAPTER PROBLEM What makes ordinary people willing to harm other people, as they did in Milgram's shocking experiment?

CRITICAL THINKING APPLIED Is Terrorism "a Senseless Act of Violence, Perpetrated by Crazy Fanatics"?

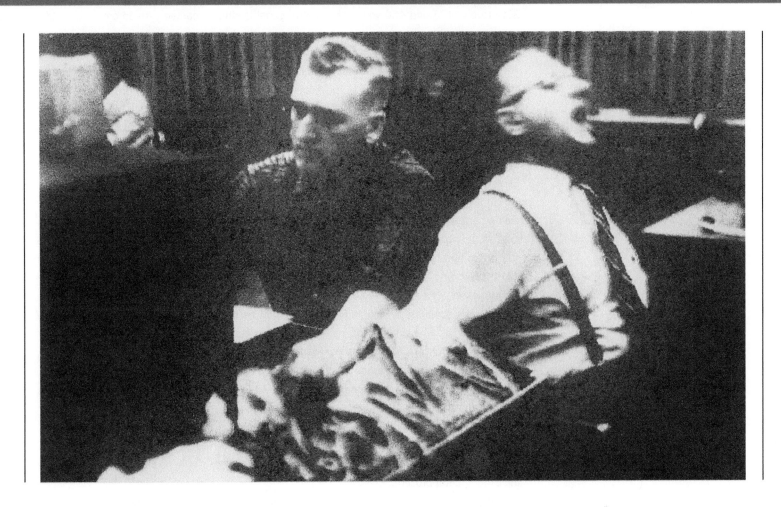

WHILE READING THE SUNDAY NEWSPAPER, BILL NOTICES THAT A prestigious university is recruiting adults to participate in a psychological study designed to help people improve their memory. He decides to volunteer for what seems like an interesting and worthwhile experiment, for which he will also get paid a small fee. On his arrival at the university's laboratory, Bill is greeted by the researcher and introduced to a second applicant named Douglas. The Experimenter, impressive in his laboratory coat, explains that the research study will test a new method of improving people's learning and memory—by punishing them for their errors. "We know that positive reinforcement for correct responding is a key to developing animal and human memory. We now want to test whether punishing someone for incorrect responses will have a similar effect," he says. The two men draw straws to determine who plays each role of Teacher and Learner; it does not seem to matter which man plays which role.

The task is straightforward: Bill will play the role of the "Teacher" and give Douglas, the "Learner," a set of word pairings to memorize in a given time period. Every time that the Learner provides the correct answer, the Teacher gives him a verbal reward, "Good" or "That's right." When wrong, the Teacher is to press a lever on the impressive-looking shock apparatus that delivers an immediate shock to punish the Learner.

The shock generator has 30 switches, starting from a low level of only 15 volts and increasing in intensity in 15-volt steps all the way up to 450 volts. The control panel indicates both the voltage level of each of the switches and a corresponding description of that level. For instance, the 25th level (375 volts) is labeled "Danger, Severe Shock," and at the 29th and

30th levels (435 and 450 volts), the control panel is simply marked with an ominous "XXX." The experimenter goes on to note that every time the Learner makes a mistake, the Teacher must press the next higher-level voltage switch.

The Learner is escorted into an adjacent room, where his arms are strapped down and an electrode is attached to his wrist. The shock generator in the next room will deliver the shocks to the Learner's wrist—if and when he makes any errors. Douglas mentions that he has a slight heart condition and hopes the shocks will not hurt him much. The Experimenter reassures him not to worry, that the shocks may become strong but will not cause any permanent damage. Bill administers the test material and communicates over the intercom to Douglas, while the Experimenter stands near him.

Initially, Douglas performs well, getting rewarding praise from Bill. However, he soon starts making errors, for which Bill immediately starts pressing those shock switches. As Douglas messes up more and more, the shock levels increase, and he complains that the shocks are starting to hurt. At 75 volts, he moans and groans; at 150 volts, the 10th level, Douglas has had enough and demands to be released from the experiment. Bill looks anxiously at the Experimenter, who nods that he must continue. As the shock levels increase in intensity, so do Douglas's screams, as well as his reminder that he has a heart condition. Bill is now really distressed: "Sir, who will be responsible if anything happens to that man?" The Experimenter dismisses his concern about personal responsibility by declaring, "I will be fully responsible, now continue your task, Teacher." More trials, more shocks, more screams from the next room. Bill hesitates, questioning whether he should go on, but the Experimenter insists that he has no choice but to do so.

At 300 volts, Douglas demands to be freed and complains louder about his heart condition. Bill has had enough; He verbally dissents, "I can't continue to hurt him, sir, I refuse to go on." The Experimenter calmly insists that Bill must continue because he has a contract to complete the experimental procedure.

Reluctantly, Bill continues to punish Douglas for his errors until he reaches the level of 330 volts. Bill hears a scream, a thud, and then silence from the shock chamber. "He is not responding; someone should go in there to see if he is all right." But the Experimenter remains impassive, telling Bill, "If the Learner doesn't answer in a reasonable time, consider it wrong because errors of omission (failing to respond) must be punished in the same way as errors of commission—that is The Rule you must obey."

As Bill continues to give the next shock level, there is no response from his pupil, Douglas. Bill complains louder that it doesn't make sense for him to continue under these circumstances. However, nothing he says sways the Experimenter to allow him to exit from this unexpectedly distressing situation. Instead, he is told to simply follow the rules because Bill's job as Teacher is to keep posing the test items and shocking the Learner's errors—even if it means going all the way up the scale to the full and final 450 volts.

How do you think *you* would act if you were in Bill's seat as the Teacher in this social memory experiment? At what shock level would you absolutely refuse to continue? Most of us believe that we would have verbally dissented, then disobeyed behaviorally, and just walked out. You would never sell out your morality for few dollars, would you?

This experiment was actually conducted by a young social psychologist named Stanley Milgram back in 1963 at Yale University in New Haven, Connecticut, where he was a new assistant professor. He tested more than 500 ordinary citizens from all walks of life (none were students) and discovered that two out of every three Teachers (65 percent) went all the way up to the maximum shock level of 450 volts. Most dissented along the way, but the *majority* obeyed the authority figure to deliver what they believed might be lethal levels of shock. (We should add that the Learner was actually a research confederate, trained to act like another middle-aged participant. He did not get shocked, but the teacher-subject believed he was.) You will read more about Milgram's experiment later in this chapter, but for now let's examine what this experiment tells us about human nature.

PROBLEM: **What makes ordinary people willing to harm other people, as they did in Milgram's shocking experiment?**

It is equally important to realize that although the majority obeyed fully, there was a minority who did refuse to give into this unjust authority. We then want to consider what makes people help others, come to the aid of the distressed, volunteer their time and services, and even act heroically?

Welcome to **social psychology,** the field that investigates how individuals affect each other. It may be a relief to hear that not all of social psychology brings such bad news about ourselves as does this experiment on obedience to authority. This exciting field of social psychology also explores the forces that bring people together for friendships and loving relationships, as well as for cooperation and conflict resolution. As you study social psychology in this chapter, you will learn how people's thoughts, feelings, perceptions, motives, and behavior are influenced by their interactions with others. Social psychologists try to understand behavior within its social context. Defined broadly, the **social context** includes the real, imagined, or symbolic presence of other people; the activities and interactions that take place among people; the settings in which behavior occurs; and the expectations and social norms governing behavior in a given setting (Sherif, 1981). Simply put, social psychologists study the person in her or his behavioral context. They are curious to discover the interrelationships between the person and the situation, how individual personality and character may affect behavior in social settings, and also how they are in turn influenced by factors in the social situation. Of course, such a focus includes investigating group behavior, such as teamwork and conformity, as well as group prejudice and terrorism. They believe that by understanding the processes and mechanisms that give rise to negative social behaviors, positive interventions can be developed to prevent or transform such actions.

Most of all, the obedience research underscores *the power of social situations to control human behavior.* This is a major theme to emerge from social psychological research of the past 50 years. In the first part of this chapter, you will see how seemingly minor features of social settings can have a huge impact on what we think and how we feel and act.

Yet as powerful as any situation can be, psychologists know that it is not only objective reality to which we respond. It is not just the physical size and shape and color of a room that might affect how we act when in it; rather, we respond to our subjective interpretation of the situation—to our personal *perception*—of what it means to us. Thus, the same physical setting can differ significantly from person to person, and it can change over time as we experience it differently. This, then, is the second important theme in social psychology: *the personal construction of a subjective social reality.* We must grasp this world of expectations and perceptions to understand the attractive forces at work in building friendships and romantic relationships as well as the repulsive forces underlying violence, prejudice, and discrimination.

In the third part of this chapter, we inquire *who or what creates various situations and maintains them,* such as prisons, gangs, cults, torture centers, but also positive settings, like your college, volunteer organizations, AAA, summer camps, and many other settings that have an impact on human behavior. Initially, we will focus on research that highlights the ways that *situations* matter in influencing how we think, feel, and act. Next, we expand our perspective to highlight the ways that *systems* matter in creating, maintaining, and justifying various life situations, for better or for worse. A classroom where bullying is taking place would be a *situation,* a behavioral context,

social psychology The branch of psychology that studies the effects of social variables and cognitions on individual behavior and social interactions.

social context The combination of (a) people, (b) the activities and interactions among people, (c) the setting in which behavior occurs, and (d) the expectations and social norms governing behavior in that setting.

whereas the *system* would be the school administration and its policies and procedures. We will also see how social psychologists have experimented with altering the situation to change subjective social reality that, in turn, helps to promote the human condition. That is a lofty goal of many social psychologists who are hard at work to help realize it in many domains.

We begin now with the first of these three themes, the power of the situation, and we are delighted to share with you what we consider to be some of the most interesting research in all of psychology.

11.1 KEY QUESTION
How Does the Social Situation Affect Our Behavior?

Imagine you find yourself in an interview for a great summer job, with the possibility of being hired as an intern at Google.com. During the interview, the interviewer tries to break the ice by telling an off-color sexual joke that you personally find a bit offensive. Do you let him know what you are feeling, or do you laugh? Afterward, he suggests that you go to lunch together in the company cafeteria. Because the lunch is free, do you go all out and order a full-course meal with some good wine, or a simpler, healthier one? Do you start the conversation or wait for him to direct it? Do you gulp down your favorite dessert before the soup that is less appealing to you? After you cut the meat, will you shift your fork from your left hand to your right hand as you put the food you cut into your mouth, or do you always keep the fork in your left hand?

Even in this simple social situation, there are many social and cultural rules governing what is appropriate and acceptable behavior. If you are like most people in an unfamiliar situation such as this, you will take your cues of what is the "right" thing to do from those around you. The interviewer essentially sets the table for the conversation, and you follow suit, as well as order the kind of meal he is having, and pretend to like his off-color joke. You want the job and therefore are more compliant than you might be otherwise. Europeans do not switch hands, as Americans do, when eating, a habit learned unconsciously in family settings by observing others, rarely being told to do so. Desserts, however desirable, come last in the eating sequence—that is part of a standard restaurant or home meal script.

The power of situations to dominate our personalities and override our history of learning, values, and beliefs is greatest when we are enmeshed in new settings. The more novel the situation, the less we rely on our past habitual ways of responding and call into action our usually automatic cognitive biases. We look to others to define for us what is necessary to behave in ways others will find acceptable and appropriate. But what is acceptable in your first visit to a church service or a funeral will be quite different from your first experience with fraternity hazing or at a rock concert. We will see that the pressures of these social situations can have powerful psychological effects, getting us to do things we might never do ordinarily—even immoral, unethical, and illegal actions.

Those pressures were operating on Bill when he was acting the role of "Teacher" in Milgram's obedience experiment, leading him to deliver extremely painful shocks to an innocent, likeable "Learner." Social roles, situational rules, how we are dressed, whether we are anonymous or highly visible, if we are in a competition, or the mere presence of others can all profoundly influence how we behave. Often, these subtle situational variables affect us in many ways even without our awareness. They may even guide our actions in mindless or stupid ways. Our Core Concept emphasizes this point:

Core Concept 11.1

We usually adapt our behavior to the demands of the social situation, and in new or ambiguous situations, we take our cues from the behavior of others in that setting.

In this section, we will explore the concept called *situationism* and the research that supports it. **Situationism** assumes that the external environment, or the behavioral context, can have both subtle and forceful effects on people's thoughts, feelings, and behaviors. Situationism is contrasted with *dispositionism*, the tendency to attribute behavior to internal factors such as genes, personality traits, and character qualities. **Dispositionism** is the tendency to look within the individual actor for explanations of why someone acted in a particular way. Social psychologists argue that such a tendency has limited our appreciation of the extent to which social situations offer the better explanation for that behavior. Of course, it is not a matter of either-or, but usually there is an *interaction* between dispositional tendencies and situational forces to shape the final behavior that we observe and want to understand. This Person × Situation interaction is at the core of both personality and social psychology, yet relatively little research has been done identifying the relative contributions of each factor in a given behavior in a particular social setting for specific kinds of individuals (Kihlstrom, 2011). Next, let's look more closely at the power of the situation to create mischief under the headings of conformity, obedience, mindless groupthink, and the failure to help others in distress.

situationism   The view that environmental conditions may influence people's behavior as much as or more than their personal dispositions do under some circumstances.

dispositionism   A psychological orientation that focuses primarily on the inner characteristics of individuals, such as personality dispositions, values, character, and genetic makeup. Contrasted with situationism, the focus is on external causes of behavior.

CONNECTION CHAPTER 10

The Person × Situation debate is still hot in both areas (p. 453).

Social Standards of Behavior

A job interview, such as the one described above for a job at Google, provides an example of situational influences on your behavior as you try to do "what is right" in front of your prospective employer, sometimes to do anything to get that prized job. You will also notice the power of the situation when you compare the way students talk to their friends versus their professors or how you act at family dinners versus watching favorite TV programs with your pals. Most people learn to size up their social circumstances and conform their behavior to situational demands. The responses most people make depend heavily on two factors, the *social roles* they play and *social norms* of the group. Let us look at both of these closely.

Social Roles and Social Norms How do you go about answering the basic question: Who are you? One answer might be: I am a college student, work part time at a store, firstborn in a big family, religious, a cyclist, rock musician, and good looking. Each of those descriptors becomes a *social role* you play in your personal life drama. People from a culture that is more focused on collective values than individual values might answer the "Who am I?" question with: I am a sister, a part of family X, of member or tribe Y. A **social role** is one of several socially defined patterns of behavior that are expected of persons in a given setting or group. The roles you assume may result from your interests, abilities, and goals—or they may be imposed on you by the group or by cultural, economic, or biological conditions beyond your control. In any case, social roles prescribe your behavior by making obvious what you should do, how you should do it, when, where, and why. Some roles are organized around our gender, such as women being more likely to be caregivers for children and the elderly. Other key roles are organized around family activities, such as planning vacations, taking out the trash, cooking, setting the table, repairing broken things, and so forth. Occupations are filled with many roles, such as receptionist, union organizer, manager, claims agent, technician, and more.

social role   A socially defined pattern of behavior that is expected of persons in a given setting or group.

The situations in which you live and function also determine the roles that are available to you and the behaviors others expect of you. Being a college student, for example, is a social role that carries certain implicit assumptions about attending classes, studying, and handing in papers before deadline. It also implies a certain degree of privilege, of usually not having to work full time, and of being interested in improving how your mind works and also having the luxury of time to explore your career options. In addition, the adoption of this role makes other roles less likely. Thus, your role as college student diminishes the chances that you will assume the role of homeless person, drug pusher, or witch doctor, for example. But more mature students might head their own family, hold full-time jobs, be returning veterans, or be social-political activists.

In addition to specific social roles that individuals enact, groups develop many "unwritten rules" for the ways that all members should act. Gangs may demand unquestioned obedience to their leader and a willingness to fight or kill anyone designated as the "enemy." Modern-day male executives in technology businesses usually do not wear ties and typically wear jeans to work, which would be the wrong attire in other business settings, such as selling insurance. Female Muslim students may wear veils to class (as a religious statement), and must do some in some cultures. Italians greet each other by kissing on the cheek in a fixed order, right then left, and in Poland, they add a third kiss for good measure. These expectations, called **social norms,** dictate socially appropriate attitudes and behaviors in particular behavioral settings. Social norms can be broad guidelines, such as ideas about which political or religious attitudes are considered acceptable. Social norms can also be quite specific, embodying standards of conduct such as being quiet in the library or shining your shoes for a job interview. Norms can guide conversation, as when they restrict discussion of sensitive or taboo subjects in the presence of certain company.

Some norms exist in unwritten rules that are built into various situations, such as when teachers are lecturing, students are expected to listen and not talk simultaneously. However, what about the norms governing your behavior in elevators? We bet you always face the front of the elevator and either stop talking to a friend or talk lower when others are there as well. Why? Where are those rules written? How did you learn them? What would happen if the next time you enter an elevator filled with other people, you face the rear? Try that little experiment and see how others react. (It is a classic demonstration first shown on TV's *Candid Camera* program in the 1960s.) Or try sitting down when everyone stands up for the national anthem. To know if a social norm is operating, just try to violate it and check out the reactions of others in that same setting. If they express distress of some kind, you know you broke a norm.

When a person joins a new group, such as a work group or a group of friends, there is always an adjustment period during which the individual tries to discover how best to fit in. Adjustment to a group typically involves discovering its social norms. Individuals experience this adjustment in two ways: by first noticing the *uniformities* and *regularities* in certain behaviors, and then by observing the *negative consequences* when someone violates a social norm.

For example, a new student in your school who carries books and notes in an attaché case will be seen as "out of it" if backpacks are in, and vice versa in other schools. The same is true of dress codes, which are rarely explicit but can guide how almost everyone dresses. Guys wearing baseball caps backward or sideways would have been laughed at a generation ago, before they were "in." The same is now true with athletes wearing diamond earrings or flashy tattoos. Also, elaborate handshake rituals among some guys have replaced the "old-fashioned" simple hand-in-hand shake.

Schemas and Scripts Recall the way in which we form schemas to help organize lots of information and for guiding our actions. A *schema* is a cluster of related concepts that provides a general conceptual framework for thinking about a topic, an event, an object, a person, or a situation in one's life. Once a schema is formed, it enables us to make predictions about what to expect in various settings. It is often upsetting when one of our schemas is violated and fails to predict the expected. Imagine going into a (non–fast food) restaurant, ordering your meal, and getting the bill before any food appears. Imagine that the waitperson brings the dessert first, then the main course, then the appetizer. Violation of expectation! Schemas become "shoulds" about how people ought to behave in certain settings; and when they do not, this provokes negative reactions, when we assume that person must be sharing our schema. The restaurant example involved a violation of an event schema or script. A **script** involves a person's knowledge about the *sequence* of events and behavioral actions that is expected of a particular social role in a given setting.

Social Norms Influence Students' Political Views Can the political views of faculty influence those of their students? Social psychologist Theodore Newcomb posed

social norms   A group's expectations regarding what is appropriate and acceptable for its members' attitudes and behaviors.

CONNECTION CHAPTER 4

Bandura demonstrated that we acquire many social behaviors through observational learning (p. 159).

CONNECTION CHAPTER 6

Schemas are cognitive structures that integrate knowledge and expectations about a topic or concept (p. 221).

script   Knowledge about the sequence of events and actions that is expected in a particular setting.

this question. The college: Vermont's Bennington College. The time: the 1930s. The students: women from wealthy, conservative homes with decidedly conservative values. The faculty: young, dynamic, and liberal. Bennington's campus culture had a prevailing norm of political and economic liberalism. The researcher wondered: Which forces most shape the attitudes of these students, their family's or their faculty's? His data showed that the immediately present norms of the campus won the war of influence against the remote norms of the family. In most women, their initial attitude of conservatism was transformed as they progressed through their college years, so that by their senior year, they had clearly converted to liberal thinking and causes (Newcomb, 1943). But was that shift in attitudes enduring?

Twenty years later, the social influence of the Bennington experience was still evident. Women who had graduated as liberals were still liberals; the minority who had resisted the prevailing liberal norm had remained conservative. This was accomplished in part by each of them marrying their "own kind" politically. Most of the women had married husbands with values similar to their own—either liberal or conservative—and created supportive new home environments that sustained those different ideologies. The liberal Bennington allegiance was evident some 30 years later in the 1960 presidential election, when 60 percent of the class Newcomb had investigated voted for liberal John Kennedy rather than conservative Richard Nixon—in contrast to less than 30 percent support for Kennedy among graduates of comparable colleges at that time (Newcomb et al., 1967).

Campus culture is not the only source of norms and group pressure, of course. One's workplace, neighborhood, religious group, and family all communicate standards for behavior—and threaten sanctions (such as firing, social rejection, or excommunication) for violating those norms. But a high school, college, or university environment can have a powerful impact on young people. This is especially true if they have had narrow life experiences and had not previously encountered attitudes radically different from their own. For example, new college students commonly adopt classmates' political opinions, as in the Bennington study, and also frequently take on religious beliefs of classmates, as well as attitudes about sex and alcohol (Prentice & Miller, 1993; Schroeder & Prentice, 1995).

Conformity

How powerful are these social pressures? We can see the effects of social pressure in people's moods, clothing styles, and leisure activities (Totterdell, 2000; Totterdell et al., 1998). This tendency to mimic other people is called the **chameleon effect**, after the animal that changes its skin color to blend into its varied environments (Chartrand & Bargh, 1999). We have seen how social pressure in political attitudes influenced Bennington College students. But can social influence be strong enough to make people follow a group norm that is clearly and objectively wrong? Could the power of that situation prove stronger than the evidence of your own eyes? Could a group of strangers get you to see the world through their distorted eyes? 👁

chameleon effect   The tendency to mimic other people, named after the animal that changes its skin color to fit into its varied environments.

👁 **Watch** the **Video** Conformity and Influence in Groups at **MyPsychLab**

The Asch Effect: A Minority of One in a Challenging Majority A receptionist shows the last-arriving participant into a waiting room, where conversation with six other volunteers reveals that they are all there for the same experiment. What the latest arrival does not know is that the other six are really confederates of the experimenter. Together, they have rehearsed an elaborate plan to exert social pressure on the one real participant.

Soon the experimenter enters and invites all seven into another room where they sit in a row of seven chairs facing an easel. On the easel, the group sees a stack of large cards, like the one in Figure 11.1, featuring four vertical lines. The task is to say which of the lines, A, B, or C, appears to be the same length as Standard line X. Casually, the experimenter starts to collect judgments from the group, beginning at the other end of the row from the one real subject. Everyone appears mildly bored at this apparently simple task.

FIGURE 11.1

Conformity in the Asch experiments

In this photo from Asch's study, the naive individual, number 6, displays obvious concern about the majority's erroneous judgment. At top right, you see a typical stimulus array. At top left, the graph illustrates conformity across 12 critical trials, when individuals were grouped with a unanimous majority or had the support of a single dissenting partner. (A lower percentage of correct estimates indicates a greater degree of conformity with the group's false judgment.)

Asch effect   A form of conformity in which a group majority influences individual judgments of unambiguous stimuli, as with line judgments.

conformity   The tendency for people to adopt the behaviors, attitudes, and opinions of other members of a group.

Everything goes smoothly until the third card comes up. On that card (see Figure 11.1), line B is obviously the correct answer—so the one naive participant cannot believe that the first person says "A." As a psychology student, our naive volunteer knows that different people perceive the world differently, which makes it easy to attribute this response to an individual perceptual deviation. Then the second person agrees: "A." When the third and the fourth persons also say "A," the naive volunteer begins to wonder, "Am *I* the one with the loose perceptual screw?" As the next to last to respond, his perception has been placed in conflict with the statements of all five people who have responded before. Squinting at the card again, he stammers, "Uh . . . 'A.'" The remaining respondent makes it unanimous.

As the experiment proceeds through the deck of 18 cards, the other participants sometimes give the "right" answer, but often they make an apparently incorrect judgment. Are they crazy? Shaken, our naive volunteer goes along with everyone else's "mistakes," rationalizing that it would be inappropriate to spoil the experiment by disagreeing.

What would you do under these circumstances? You may think that you would resist the pressure if you really had been in one of Asch's experiments. Perhaps so. In fact, almost two-thirds of the naive participants in Asch's original experiment actually withstood the group pressure to conform to the plainly erroneous judgments. But, one-third *did* conform.

Social psychologists call this the **Asch effect:** the powerful influence that a group exerts on the judgments of an individual. And Solomon Asch's experiment has become the classic illustration of **conformity**—the tendency for people to adopt the behavior and opinions presented by other group members. Even though individuals were judging matters of fact, not merely personal opinions, many caved in to conformity pressures.

This result encouraged Asch and others to tinker with the experimental conditions a bit, contriving circumstances under which fully *two*-thirds of his participants yielded to the majority. What are the conditions that researchers have found to encourage conformity?

- **Unanimity of the majority.** If everyone in the group agrees, they can exert a powerful social pressure. But if even one person defects from the majority, the spell is broken and yielding drops dramatically (Asch, 1940, 1955, 1956).

- **Size of the group.** In a group of only one or two other people, most subjects apparently feel little pressure to conform to the group's erroneous judgments. The pressure suddenly increases when confronting a group of three. Surprisingly, there is almost no difference in the conformity effect of a group of three and a group of 15.

- **Making a public commitment rather than a private one.** If you believe others in the group will not hear your responses, you are less likely to go along with them when you think they are incorrect (Deutsch & Gerard, 1955).

- **Ambiguity.** When the lines are nearly the same length—so that the correct answer is not crystal clear—people seem more prone to self-doubt and to conformity.

- **Makeup of the majority.** Consistent with the findings on self-esteem, more conformity occurs when the group has high status (Eagly, 1987) or is otherwise seen by the individual as being important. Incidentally, women are no more likely to conform to the group than are men, unless the task is a stereotypically male-oriented task, such as making judgments about the quality of power tools (Eagly & Carli, 1981).

- **Self-esteem.** As you might guess, people who place a low value on themselves are more likely to conform in the Asch experiment (Aronson, 1991).

- **Power of an ally.** We want to highlight one finding that can have personal relevance to you: the importance of even one person challenging the group's norm. Even in a large group, giving the person one ally who dissented from the majority opinion sharply reduced conformity (as shown in Figure 11.1). With such a "partner," nearly all subjects resisted the pressures to conform. This is one of the most positive take-away messages from this research. If you are willing to challenge the group openly, chances are you will influence others to join your rebellion. Even one hero can inspire others not to yield to the group pressure.

- **Independents.** Despite powerful pressures to yield, some individuals are able to resist and maintain their independence, standing their ground to "call 'em as they see 'em"—even to the point of deliberately giving a wrong answer when the group gives a correct one (Friend et al., 1990).

Numerous studies have revealed additional factors that influence conformity. (These experiments have included both females and males.) Specifically, a person is more likely to conform under the following circumstances:

- When a judgment task is difficult or ambiguous (Saltzstein & Sandberg, 1979)
- When the group members are perceived as especially competent
- When their responses are given publicly rather than privately
- When the group majority is unanimous—but once that unanimity is broken, the rate of conformity drops dramatically (Allen & Levine, 1969; Morris & Miller, 1975)

So now imagine you are about to vote openly in a group, as is common in clubs or on boards of directors. You will probably conform to the group majority if: (a) the issue being decided is complex or confusing, (b) others in the group seem to know what they are talking about, (c) you must vote by raising your hand instead of casting an anonymous ballot, (d) the entire group casting their votes before you all vote in a certain way, and especially if (e) the leader votes first.

Being informed about such conformity pressures should make you wiser about how you might go along with the group even when they are heading in a wrong or even immoral direction. Resisting such influence requires critical thinking and being mindful of what you have learned about the power of social forces.

In the Asch effect, people conform because of *normative influences,* wanting to be accepted, approved, liked, and not rejected by others. Another reason for conformity comes from *informational influences,* wanting to be correct and to understand the correct way to act in any given situation.

Clearly this poses ethical problems, when confederates of the researcher lie to fellow students about their perceptions. How could you do the basic Asch paradigm without deception? How about everyone views the lines wearing goggles; the real subject's goggles are just clear and show the lines as they are in reality, but the goggles of the majority of students are altered so that they all see the lines the same way, but distorted to make dissimilar size lines look the same as the standard. This technique has been used in a recent study with participants wearing glasses similar to those in 3D movies with polarizing filters (Mori & Arai, 2010). In that study, with 104 Japanese students tested in groups of four, where three wore the distorting glasses and the other wore a different, normal pair of glasses, Asch's conformity effect was obtained without deceptive confederates. However, the effect was found only for female students and with an even greater conformity percentage than in the original. But the majority, totally unlike Asch's original results with males, did not sway the males. Why do you think this gender difference might have happened?

Cultural Differences in Conformity   The Asch test has gone to several parts of the world, revealing remarkably similar results from most groups. The proportion of those who yield to group pressure (under Asch's original conditions) hovers around one-third in a wide variety of societies. The following table shows some typical results of such studies.

The consistency of these results hints that the same force is at work across different cultures. Nevertheless, some caution is in order. Participants in most of these investigations were college student volunteers, a fact that may make them different in many ways from other people in their own societies. A few studies have found exceptions to the apparent trend of consistency, and those exceptions pose interesting questions about conformity and culture. For example, among those from the Bantu culture in Rhodesia, 51 percent conformed on the Asch test. We can easily explain this result because this Bantu culture customarily exacts a heavy penalty for nonconformity to social customs. At the other extreme, German university students yielded to the group only 22 percent of the time. This very low percentage was unexpected, but it might be attributable to the age of the German sample, which was older than the other groups.

The most surprising results, however, may be the high level of *non*conformity among Japanese students. The casual observer of Japanese culture is usually struck by the conformity to group norms displayed by the Japanese. Yet in the Asch situation, participants yielded at the remarkably low rate of 25 percent—significantly less than the reputedly nonconformist Americans. Moreover, the Japanese subjects were especially high in *anticonformity*, a deliberate rejection of group norms: 34 percent gave deliberately *wrong* answers when the rest of the group gave correct responses! A possible explanation is that the Japanese culture of conformity may, in reality, be found

TABLE 11.1   Cross-Cultural Differences in Conformity in the Asch Situation

Country	Percentage Yielding on the Asch Test
Rhodesia	51%
Fiji	36%
Brazil	34%
United States	33%
Hong Kong	32%
Lebanon	31%
Japan	25%
Germany	22%

Source: Mann, L. (1980). Cross-cultural studies of small groups. In H. C. Triandis & R. Brislin (Eds.), *Handbook of cross-cultural psychology* (Vol. 5, pp. 155–209). Boston, MA: Allyn & Bacon.

only within the group to whom the individual Japanese person feels special allegiance. Thus, when Japanese students were presented with judgments made by a group of strangers, they felt little pressure to conform because it was not *their* group.

The Autokinetic Effect An early classic experiment, conducted by Turkish-American psychologist, Muzafer Sherif (1935), demonstrated how social influence can lead to internalization of a new norm. Participants were asked to judge the amount of movement of a spot of light that was actually stationary but appeared to move when viewed with no reference points in total darkness. This is a perceptual illusion known as the **autokinetic effect.** Originally, individual judgments varied widely. However, when the participants came together in a group consisting of strangers to state their judgments aloud, their estimates began to converge. They began to see the light move in the same direction and in similar amounts. Even more interesting was the final part of Sherif's study—when alone in the same darkened room after the group viewing, these participants continued to follow the group norm that had emerged when they were together. As in the Asch studies, the group influenced individuals' perceptions.

Moreover, once norms are established in a group, they tend to perpetuate themselves. In later research, these autokinetic group norms persisted even when tested a year later when the former participants were retested alone—without former group members witnessing the judgments (Rohrer et al., 1954). Norms can be transmitted from one generation of group members to the next and can continue to influence people's behavior long after the original group that created the norm no longer exists (Insko et al., 1980). How do we know that norms can have transgenerational influence? In autokinetic effect studies, researchers replaced one group member with a new one after each set of autokinetic trials until all the members of the group were new to the situation. The group's autokinetic norm remained true to the one handed down to them across several successive generations (Jacobs & Campbell, 1961). Do you see how this experiment captures the processes that allow real-life norms to be passed down across generations in businesses or political groups? Such norms come to be part of the corporate culture that dictates how its members should see the world in common ways—sometimes for better as in firms like Apple and Google, but sometimes for the worse, as in the corrupted Enron and Arthur Anderson Accounting firms. (We recommend viewing of the documentary film, *Inside Job*, 2011, to understand some of the social psychological forces that contributed to the financial meltdown in Wall Street and around the world.)

Conformity and Independence Light Up the Brain Differently New technology, not available in Asch's day, offers intriguing insights into the role of the brain in social conformity. When people conform, are they rationally deciding to go along with the group out of normative needs, or are they actually changing their perceptions and accepting the validity of the new, though erroneous, information provided by the group? A recent study (Berns et al., 2005) used advanced brain-scanning technology to answer this question. It also answers the question of whether the old Asch effect could work with the current generation of more sophisticated students. (A peek ahead says, "Yes.")

Using functional magnetic resonance imaging (fMRI), researchers can now peer into the active brain as a person engages in various tasks and detect which specific brain regions are energized as they carry out these tasks. Understanding what mental functions those brain regions control tells us what it means when they are activated by any given experimental task.

Here's how the study worked. Imagine that you are one of 32 volunteers recruited for a study of perception. You have to mentally rotate images of three-dimensional objects to determine if the objects are the same or different from a standard object. In the waiting room, you meet four other volunteers, with whom you begin to bond by practicing games on laptop computers, taking photos of one another, and chatting. They are really actors, "confederates" who will soon be faking their answers on the test trials so that they are in agreement with each other, but not with the correct responses that you generate. You are selected as the one to go into the scanner while the

autokinetic effect The perceived motion of a stationary dot of light in a totally dark room; used by Muzafir Sherif to study the formation of group norms.

CONNECTION CHAPTER 2

Neuroscientists use *brain scanning* as a technique for studying specific brain areas activated by different mental tasks (p. 64).

others outside look at the objects first as a group and then decide if they are same or different. The rest of the procedure follows Asch's original experiment with the actors giving false answers, while you have to decide to go along with the majority or with your perception.

As in Asch's experiments, you (as the typical subject) would have caved in to group pressure, on average giving the group's wrong answers 41 percent of the time. When you yielded to the group's erroneous judgment, your conformity would have been seen in the brain scan as changes in selected regions of the brain's cortex dedicated to vision and spatial awareness (specifically, activity increases in the right intraparietal sulcus). Surprisingly, there would be no changes in areas of the forebrain that deal with monitoring conflicts, planning, and other higher-order mental activities. On the other hand, if you made independent judgments that went against the group, then your brain lit up in the areas that are associated with emotional salience (the right amygdala and related regions). This means that resistance creates an emotional burden for those who maintain their independence—autonomy comes at a psychic cost.

The lead author of this research, neuroscientist Gregory Berns (2005), concludes, "We like to think that seeing is believing, but the study's findings show that seeing is believing what the group tells you to believe." This means that other people's views, when crystallized into a group consensus, can actually affect how we perceive important aspects of the external world, thus calling into question the nature of truth itself.

It is only by becoming aware of our vulnerability to social pressure that we can begin to build resistance to conformity when it is not in our best interest to yield to the mentality of the herd. One problem is that many people maintain an *illusion of personal invulnerability*—a "Not ME" syndrome. They assume that others may be susceptible to situational forces, but that they are different, special kind of folks who can resist such forces. Paradoxically, such a naïve view makes them more susceptible to influence agents because their guard is down, and they do not engage in mindful, critical analyses of situational forces acting on them.

It is also important to mention that this research using neurobiology techniques to study social psychological processes is becoming widespread in the field of social psychology and is known as **social neuroscience.** Social neuroscience is a new area of research that uses methodologies from brain sciences to investigate various types of social behavior, such as stereotyping in prejudice, attitudes, self-control, and emotional regulation (Azar, 2002a; Cacioppo & Brentson, 2005).

social neuroscience   An area of research that uses methodologies from brain sciences to investigate various types of social behavior, such as stereotyping in prejudice, attitudes, self-control, and emotional regulation.

Groupthink   Groups themselves can also be pressured to conform. This important social psychological process that encourages conformity in the thinking and decision making of individuals when they are in groups, like committees, has been termed **groupthink** by psychologist Irving Janis (1972; Janis & Mann, 1977). In groupthink, members of the group attempt to conform their opinions to what each believes to be the consensus of the group. This conformity bias leads the group to take actions each member might normally consider to be unwise. Five conditions likely to promote groupthink are:

groupthink   The term for the poor judgments and bad decisions made by members of groups that are overly influenced by perceived group consensus or the leader's point of view.

- Directive leadership, a dominant leader
- High group **cohesiveness,** with absence of dissenting views
- Lack of norms requiring methodical procedures for evidence collection/evaluation
- Homogeneity of members' social background and ideology
- High stress from external threats with low hope of a better solution than that of the group leader

cohesiveness   Solidarity, loyalty, and a sense of group membership.

CONNECTION CHAPTER 6

Our judgments and decisions are often affected by personal biases (p. 227).

This concept was first developed to help understand bad decisions made by the U.S. government regarding the bombing of Pearl Harbor in 1941, the Vietnam War, and especially the disastrous invasion of Cuba's Bay of Pigs. In that case, highly intelligent members of President John Kennedy's cabinet made a foolish decision to start an invasion against Cuba based on faulty reports by anti-Castro Cuban refugees. Later, others have cited groupthink as a factor that contributed to the faulty decisions in the space shuttle disasters and the bankruptcy of Enron Corporation. The 2003 decision by the Bush administration to wage preemptive war against Iraq was similarly based on several false beliefs among Bush's cabinet of otherwise smart advisors. They wanted to believe (their lie) that Saddam Hussein possessed nuclear weapons that he would deliver to Osama bin Laden to use in another terrorist attack on the United States (Schwartz & Wald, 2003).

The U.S. Senate Intelligence Committee investigating the justifications for the Iraq War cited groupthink as one of the processes involved in that decision. It is interesting to note the use of this social psychological concept in an official report of that government committee:

> The Intelligence Community (IC) has long struggled with the need for analysts to overcome analytic biases. . . . This bias that pervaded both the IC's analytic and collection communities represents "group think," a term coined by psychologist Irving Janis in the 1970's to describe a process in which a group can make bad or irrational decisions as each member of the group attempts to conform their opinions to what they believe to be the consensus of the group. IC personnel involved in the Iraq WMD issue demonstrated several aspects of groupthink: examining few alternatives, selective gathering of information, pressure to conform within the group or withhold criticism, and collective rationalization (U.S. Senate, 2004, p. 4).

Recently, the U.S. Directorate of Intelligence has found a way of minimizing the risk of groupthink by developing "Red Teams" whose task is to challenge all decisions with more reliable evidence. They insist on convergence of multiple sources of independent evidence to support all action-based decisions by government agencies. Former CIA Director Porter Goss has encouraged innovation and creativity in how the CIA approaches its mission. In a report outlining the new defenses against mindless groupthink, Goss said:

> The primary criticism was that our analysts were "too wedded to their assumptions" and that our tradecraft—the way we analyze a subject and communicate our findings—needed strengthening. . . . Above all, we seek to foster in each analyst a sense of individual initiative, responsibility and ownership, as well as the recognition that providing analysis vital to our national security requires challenging orthodoxy and constantly testing our assumptions. Mastering the fundamentals of tradecraft and building expertise are critical, but we also must aspire to a level of creativity and insight that allows us to look beyond the obvious and flag the unexpected. Only then can we truly fulfill our obligation to help protect the American people (Kringen, 2006).

Obedience to Authority

So far, we have seen how groups influence individuals. But the arrow of influence also points the other way: Certain individuals, such as charismatic leaders and authorities, can command the obedience of groups—even large masses of people. The ultimate demonstration of this effect was seen in the World War II era, with the emergence of Adolph Hitler in Germany and Benito Mussolini in Italy. These dictators transformed the rational citizens of whole nations into mindlessly loyal followers of a fascist ideology bent on world conquest. But the same was true in Cambodia in the 1970s where Pol Pot, the brutal dictator and leader of the Khmer Rouge, decided to eliminate social classes by forcing everyone to work on farms. Those likely to resist—the educated, intellectuals, and foreigners—were tortured, starved to death, and murdered. In a 4-year reign of terror, known as the Killing Fields of Cambodia, nearly 2 million people were killed.

Modern social psychology had its origins in this World War II wartime crucible of fear and prejudice. It was natural, then, that many of the early social psychologists

Unquestioning obedience to authority led more than 900 members of an American cult community in Jonestown to commit mass suicide under orders from their leader, the Reverend Jim Jones.

focused on the personalities of people drawn into fascist groups. Specifically, they looked for an authoritarian personality behind the fascist group mentality (Adorno et al., 1950). But that dispositional analysis failed to recognize the social, economic, historical, and political realities operating on those European populations at that time. To clarify this point, let us reflect for a moment on some more modern examples of unquestioning obedience to authority.

In 1978, a group of American citizens left California to relocate their Protestant religious order, called Peoples Temple, in the South American jungle of Guyana. There, following the orders of their charismatic leader, the Reverend Jim Jones, more than 900 members of the Peoples Temple willingly administered lethal doses of cyanide to hundreds of their children, then to their parents, and then to themselves. Those who refused were murdered by other members of this cult—by their friends.

Then, in 1993, 100 members of a religious sect joined their leader, David Koresh, in defying federal agents who had surrounded their compound. After a standoff of several weeks, the Branch Davidians set fire to their quarters rather than surrender. In the resulting conflagration, scores of men, women, and children perished. Four years later, the college-educated members of another group calling itself Heaven's Gate followed their leader's command to commit mass suicide in order to achieve a "higher plane" of being. And, on September 11, 2001, followers of Osama bin Laden weaponized American commercial airliners and piloted them into the Pentagon and the World Trade Center. In addition to murdering thousands of people, they knowingly committed suicide. And even more recently, scores of suicide bombers, both men and women, have blown themselves apart as "revolutionary martyrs" in the Palestinian campaign against Israel. Were these people mentally deranged, stupid, and totally strange creatures—unlike us? Are there any conditions under which you would blindly obey an order from a person you love and respect (or fear) to do such extreme deeds? Would you, for example, obey an authority figure that told you to electrocute a stranger? Of course, you are saying to yourself, "No way," "Not me," "I am not that kind of person." But think about what each of the people we have described above must have been thinking *before* they were caught up in their obedience trap—the same thing as you, probably.

Let's return to our opening story of Bill trapped in the experiment created by social psychologist Stanley Milgram (1965, 1974). His research revealed that the willingness of people to follow the orders of an authority, even potentially lethal ones, is not confined to a few extreme personalities or deranged individuals. This finding, along with certain ethical issues that the experiment raises, places Milgram's work at the center of one of the biggest controversies in psychology (Blass, 1996). We will look at more of the findings generated by that program of research on *obedience* and visit a series of follow-up studies that expand its relevance and applicability to everyday life settings and to recent media exploitation of this Milgram effect in French reality TV. But first, let's consider how some experts on human behavior failed to predict the high rate of obedience found in this research.

Milgram's Research Revisited Milgram described his experimental procedure to each of 40 psychiatrists and then asked them to estimate the percentage of American citizens who would go to each of the 30 levels in the experiment. On average, they predicted that fewer than 1 percent would go all the way to the end, that only sadists would engage in such sadistic behavior, and that most people would drop out at the tenth level of 150 volts.

They could not have been more wrong! These experts on human behavior were totally wrong for two reasons. (This dual tendency of overestimating person power and underestimating situation power is known as the *fundamental attribution error, FAE*.) First, they ignored all the situational determinants of behavior in the procedural

CONNECTION CHAPTER 10

In contrast to most personality theories focusing on *internal* processes as detriments of behavior, social psychology emphasizes the importance of the *external* social situation (p. 419).

description of the experiment. That is, they failed to recognize the significance of the authority power, the roles of Teacher and Learner, the rules, the diffusion of personal responsibility (when the experimenter claimed to the "Teacher" that he would be responsible for anything that might happen to the "Learner"), the definition of what were appropriate and expected behaviors by the Teacher, and the other social pressures toward obedience.

Second, their training in traditional psychiatry led them to rely too heavily on the dispositional perspective to understand unusual behavior—to look for explanations within the individual's personality makeup and not in the external behavioral context. Thus, their estimate of only 1 percent as blindly obedient to authority, as going all the way up to the maximum shock level of 450 volts, is a base rate against which we can assess what actually happened in this research.

Before examining the pattern of results, we need to add that Milgram wanted to show that his results were not due to the authority power of Yale University—which is what New Haven is all about. So he transplanted his laboratory to a rundown office building in downtown Bridgeport, Connecticut, and repeated the experiment as a project of a fictitious, private research firm with no apparent connection to Yale. There he tested another 500 ordinary citizens and added female participants as Teachers to the experimental mix. So what was the actual level of blind obedience to authority?

As with those tested at Yale, the majority of these Bridgeport participants obeyed fully: two out of every three (65 percent) went all the way up the maximum shock level of 450 volts! These "Teachers" shocked their "Learner" over and over again despite his increasingly desperate pleas to stop. This was as true of the young and old, men and women, well educated and less so, and across many occupations and careers.

Variations on an Obedience Theme Milgram carried out 19 different experiments—each one a different variation of the basic paradigm of: Experimenter/-Teacher/-Learner/-Memory Testing/-Errors Shocked. In each of these studies, he varied one social-psychological variable and observed its impact on the extent of obedience to the authority's pressure to continue to shock the Learner. He added women in one study, varied the physical proximity or remoteness of either the Experimenter-Teacher link or the Teacher-Learner link, had peers model rebellion or full obedience before the Teacher had his chance to begin, and added other social variations in each experiment.

As can be seen in Figure 11.2, the data for 16 of these variations clearly reveal the extreme pliability of human nature: Under some conditions, almost everyone could be totally obedient, while under other conditions, almost everyone could resist authority pressures. It all depends on how the social situation was constructed by the researcher and experienced by the participants. Milgram was able to demonstrate that compliance rates could soar to more than 90 percent of people administering the 450-volt maximum if others were seen obeying, or the obedience rate could be reduced to less than 10 percent by introducing just one crucial social variable of others rebelling into the compliance recipe.

The Milgram Obedience Experiment
The "shock generator" looked ominous but didn't actually deliver shocks to the "Learner" (middle photo), who was a confederate of the experimenter. The last photo shows the experimenter giving instructions to the "Teacher," who is seated in front of the shock generator.

FIGURE 11.2

Obedience in Milgram's Experiments

The graph shows a profile of weak or strong obedience effects across situational variations of Milgram's study of obedience to authority.

Source: Miller, A. G. (1986). *The Obedience Experiments: A Case Study of Controversy in the Social Sciences*. Westport, CT: Praeger Publishers. Copyright © 1986 by Praeger Publishers, Inc. Reproduced with permission of Greenwood Publishing Group, Inc., Westport, CT.

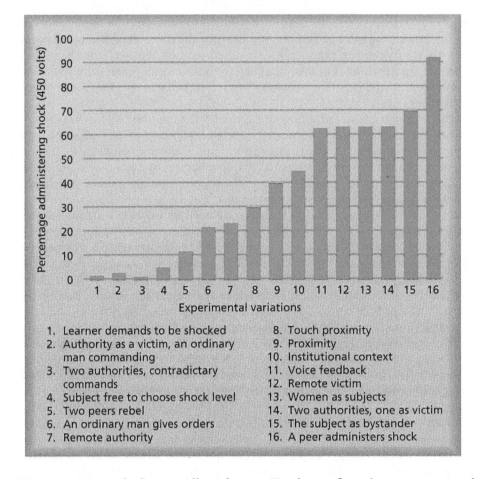

1. Learner demands to be shocked
2. Authority as a victim, an ordinary man commanding
3. Two authorities, contradictary commands
4. Subject free to choose shock level
5. Two peers rebel
6. An ordinary man gives orders
7. Remote authority
8. Touch proximity
9. Proximity
10. Institutional context
11. Voice feedback
12. Remote victim
13. Women as subjects
14. Two authorities, one as victim
15. The subject as bystander
16. A peer administers shock

Want maximum obedience? Allow the new Teacher to first observe someone else administering the final shock level. Want people to resist authority pressures? Provide social models of peers who rebel. Participants also refused to deliver the shocks if the Learner said he wanted to be shocked; that's masochistic, and they are not sadists! They also were reluctant to give high levels of shock when the Experimenter filled in as the Learner and they were supposed to shock him. They were more likely to shock when the Learner was remote than nearby. In each of the other variations on this diverse range of ordinary American citizens, of widely varying ages, occupations, and of both sexes, it was possible to elicit low, medium, or high levels of compliant obedience with a flick of the Situational Switch—as if one were simply turning a Human Nature Dial within their psyches. This large sample of a thousand ordinary citizens from such varied backgrounds makes the results of *Milgram's Obedience to Authority* studies among the most generalizable in all the social sciences.

Of course, no shocks were ever delivered to the Learner. The "victim" of the "shocks" was an accomplished actor who congenially chatted with his "Teacher" after the experiment and assured him he was fine and had never felt any shocks. All of his comments during the study had been recorded previously to standardize the procedure across the many trials and variations of the study. Moreover, the powerful authority figure in the gray lab coat was not a "real" authority, not Milgram himself, but a high school biology teacher! And, for all the "Teachers" knew, when once the Learner fell silent after the 330 volt shock, he may have been unconscious or dead—but in any case his memory could not be improved by further shocks. Nevertheless, hundreds of people mindlessly obeyed and continued doing as ordered even though it made no sense—had they thought rationally and critically about what they were doing. They should have realized that the study was not about improving the learner's memory; it was about *them* as reluctant punishing agents.

British author C. P. Snow reminds us, "When you think of the long and gloomy history of man, you will find more hideous crimes have been committed in the name of obedience than have been committed in the name of rebellion."

Such research, and the many replications that followed in countries around the world, challenges our conception that "good people" cannot be seduced into becoming perpetrators of evil. It suggests that the line between good and evil is not fixed and permanent but rather is sufficiently permeable to allow almost anyone to move across from one behavioral realm to the other. It all depends on the power of the new, unfamiliar situation they face and with which they most cope.

Heroic Defiance This concept of situational power faces one challenge, that of individual heroic defiance. **Heroes** are people who are able to resist situational forces that overwhelm their peers and remain true to their personal values. They are the "whistleblowers" who challenge corrupt or immoral systems by not going along with the company norm or institutional SOP, standard operating procedures.

An Army Reservist, Joe Darby, became one such hero when, in 2004, he exposed the horrendous abuses of prisoners by his buddies at Iraq's Abu Ghraib Prison. He did so by showing to a senior investigating officer a CD with the images of prisoner abuse taken by other MPs on the night shift. The officer then initiated an investigation that stopped those abuses, which had been going on for months.

But such "heroes" are often despised by their former colleagues and made to pay a high price for not being a silent "team player." Darby, for example, had to go into hiding under protective custody for 3 years, along with his wife and mother, because of death threats against him by soldiers in his battalion and by people in their hometown for humiliating the American military in exposing those photos of sadistic abuse of prisoners. After being released in 2007, Darby did finally receive a hero award at the Kennedy Center in Washington, DC.

Heroes come in all sizes and backgrounds. During the opening ceremonies of the 2008 Olympics in Beijing, China, a little boy was ushered in on the shoulders of Yao Ming, Houston Rockets' star basketball player. The boy, Lin Hao, was in his school in Szechuan province when a massive earthquake hit. He survived the collapse of the school roof, but most of the other students were killed. While escaping, he noticed two children struggling to get out from under the debris. He raced back to save them, and when asked why he risked his life in doing so, Lin's reply was that of a "duty hero." He said that he was the Hall Monitor, and it was his job to look after his classmates. Here is a fine example of transforming compassion into heroic action. A behavioral definition of heroism: a voluntary act on behalf of others in need, or in defense of a moral cause, with potential personal risk or cost, and without expectation of tangible reward. 📖

In February 2011, the world witnessed a remarkable event as hundreds of thousands of Egyptians, mostly young men and women, openly defied the repressive regime of their President Mubarak. They withstood counterattacks by his civilian supporters and brutal beatings by his initially loyal Army. However, this leaderless mass persisted for 18 days to demonstrate in the main Cairo square using social media technology to keep organized and focused, while Arab TV carried their call for freedom to television viewers around the globe. In the end, their collective heroism won the day, and hopefully the start of a new democratic nation in the Middle East that will be a model for Egypt's neighbor states.

Curiously, there is relatively little systematic research on heroes and heroism, especially compared to the abundance of research on the dark side of human nature, as revealed throughout this chapter. Why do you think that is so?

Cross-Cultural Tests of Milgram's Research

Because of its structural design and its detailed protocol, the basic Milgram obedience experiment encouraged replication by independent investigators in many countries. A recent comparative analysis was made of the rates of obedience across eight studies conducted in the United States and of nine replications in European, African, and Asian countries. There were comparably high levels of compliance by research volunteers in these different studies and nations. The majority obedience effect of a mean 61 percent found in the U.S. replications was matched by the 66 percent obedience

heroes People whose actions help others in emergencies or challenge unjust or corrupt systems, doing so without concern for reward or likely negative consequences for them by acting in deviant ways.

Would you risk your life to defy authority in defense of your beliefs, as this Chinese student did, defying a tank force coming to crush the student rebellion at Tiananmen Square?

📖●┤**Read** about the Heroic Imagination Project at **MyPsychLab**

A 9-year old Chinese boy acted heroically to save the lives of classmates in an earthquake. Here, Lin Hao is with Yao Ming during the opening ceremony of the 2008 Beijing Olympics.

Egyptian citizens successfully and peacefully deposed their dictator by acts of collective heroism despite violent attacks against them by the Army and the dictator's supporters.

found across all the other national samples. The range of obedience went from a low of 31 to a high of 91 percent in the U.S. studies, and from a low of 28 percent (Australia) to a high of 88 percent (South Africa) in the cross-national replications. There was also stability of obedience over decades of time as well as over place. There was no association between when a study was done (between 1963 and 1985) and degree of obedience (Blass, 2004).

Using a variation of the Milgram paradigm, researchers in Utrecht University, Holland, and in Palermo University, Sicily, found obedience rates comparable to those in some of Milgram's experimental variations. The situation they created was that of a coach who had to deliver increasingly critical feedback to his performer when he did poorly, allegedly to build resilience in performers. They had to deliver a series of graded hostile comments, as if they were their own, for each error. Critical feedback given to the Performer consisted of a graded series of increasingly negative comments on his performance and rude remarks about his lack of ability. For example, a mild criticism was "You are going bad . . .", a moderately negative feedback was "You are really ridiculous!", and an extremely negative feedback was "You are really the most stupid person I have ever seen!" Obedience to authority was determined as delivering the full set of 15 hostile comments. In one of the Utrecht studies, more than 90 percent of the students playing the role of coach went all the way (Meeus & Raaijmakers, 1986). In the Sicilian study using that same procedure, obedience was only 30 percent, but that was in a condition where coach and performer were in close proximity and the experimenter was in an adjacent room. That is exactly what Milgram found for those experimental variations (Bocchiaro & Zimbardo, 2008).

More than four decades after Milgram's research, a made-for-TV replication was conducted with college students at Santa Clara University, in California, by researcher Jerry Burger (2009). For ethical reasons, the study was terminated when the teachers pressed the 150-volt switch, the tenth level. Once again, the majority obeyed the dictates of the experiment and presumably would have been likely to continue onward and upward to the full 450 volts if that were possible.

In 2010, a television show in France staged the Milgram experiment for a live audience, who got to vote to shock or not to shock the victim in distress. Egged on by a glamorous presenter, cries of "punishment" from a studio audience and dramatic music, the overwhelming majority of the participants obeyed orders to continue delivering the shocks—despite the man's screams of agony and pleas for them to stop. The percentage giving maximum shock soared to 80 percent in what the producers term "The Game of Death"!

Why Do We Obey Authority? From the many variations Milgram conducted on his original study, we can conclude that people tended to be obedient under the following conditions (Milgram, 1965, 1974; Rosenhan, 1969):

- When a peer modeled obedience by complying with the authority figure's commands
- When the victim was remote from the Teacher and could not be seen or heard, thereby promoting a sense of anonymity
- When the Teacher was under direct surveillance of the authority figure so that he was aware of the authority's presence
- When the authority figure had higher status relative to the Teacher

What are the lessons to be learned? If you carefully review these conditions (refer back to Figure 11.2), you can see that the obedience effect results from situational variables and not personality variables. In fact, personality tests administered to the participants did not reveal any traits that differentiated those who obeyed from those who refused, nor did they identify any psychological disturbance or abnormality in the obedient punishers. These findings enable us to rule out individual personality as a variable in obedient behavior. Going beyond the experimental findings to applying

TABLE 11.2 Ten Steps Toward Evil—Getting Good People to Harm Others

Now imagine the opposite of each tactic to create the path to heroic behavior.

- Provide people with an ideology to justify beliefs for actions.
- Make people take a small first step toward a harmful act with a minor, trivial action and then gradually increase those small actions.
- Slowly transform a once-compassionate leader into a dictatorial figure.
- Provide people with vague and ever-changing rules.
- Relabel the situation's actors and their actions to legitimize the ideology.
- Provide people with social models of compliance.
- Allow verbal dissent but only if people continue to comply behaviorally with orders.
- Encourage dehumanizing the victim.
- Diffuse responsibility.
- Make exiting the situation difficult.

them to real-world settings, we can outline ten basic steps or processes that can seduce ordinary, even good, people to go down the slippery slope of evil, as seen in Table 11.2.

Some Real-World Extensions of the Milgram Obedience to Authority Paradigm

Let's look at blind obedience to authority in two real-life settings: the first, a study of nurses' willingness to follow a doctor's orders that were not legitimate, and the second, an actual incident in which store managers followed telephoned orders (from a pervert pretending to be a police officer) to violate the privacy of another employee.

Nurses Obey Doctor's Dangerous Orders If the relationship between teachers and students is one of power-based authority, how much more so is that between physicians and nurses? To find out, a team of doctors and nurses tested obedience in their authority system by determining whether nurses would follow or disobey an illegitimate request by an unknown physician in a real hospital setting (Hofling et al., 1966). Each of 22 nurses individually received a call from an unknown staff doctor who told her to administer a medication to his patient immediately, before he got to the hospital. His order doubled the maximum amount indicated as a high dose. When this dilemma was presented as a hypothetical scenario, 10 of 12 nurses in that hospital said they would refuse to obey because it violated hospital procedures (Krackow & Blass, 1995). However, the power of the situation took over on the hospital ward: Twenty-one of 22 nurses put to the test started to pour the medication (actually a fake drug) to administer to the patient—before the researcher stopped them from doing so. That solitary disobedient nurse should have been given a raise and a hero's medal!

The Fast-Food Restaurant Authority Hoax Another remarkable real-world illustration of the Milgram effect in action comes from a telephone hoax perpetrated in 68 fast-food restaurants across 32 states. Assistant store managers blindly followed the orders of a phone caller, pretending to be a police officer, who insisted that they strip search a young female employee he said had stolen property on her.

The alleged officer instructed the assistant manager to detain the employee in the back room, strip her naked, and search her extensively for the stolen goods. The caller insisted on being told in graphic detail what was happening, and all the while the video surveillance cameras were recording these remarkable events as they unfolded. In some cases, the abuse escalated to having her masturbate and perform sexual acts on a male assistant who was supposed to be guarding her (Wolfson, 2005).

One of the innocent victims of the Authority Hoax on the witness stand. She received a large settlement from the fast-food company where she worked and had been abused.

This bizarre authority-influence-in-absentia has seduced dozens of ordinary people in that situation to violate store policy, and presumably their own ethical and moral principles, to molest and humiliate honest young employees. In 2007, the perpetrator was uncovered—a former corrections officer—but freed for lack of direct evidence.

One reasonable reaction you might have to learning about this hoax is to focus on the dispositions of the victim and her assailants, as naïve, ignorant, gullible individuals. However, when we learn that this scam has been carried out successfully in a great many similar settings across many states, many different and fast-food restaurants, with dozens of assistant managers deceived, then our analysis must shift away from simply blaming the victims to recognizing the power of situational forces involved in this scenario. One of the assistant store managers warned reporters not to judge them so quickly because they couldn't predict what they might have done unless they experienced the same situation (Gibney, 2006). And it is the exact advice we give to you after reading this chapter and being aware of the fundamental attribution error.

The Bystander Problem: The Evil of Inaction

"Throughout history, it has been the inaction of those who could have acted; the indifference of those who should have known better; the silence of the voice of justice when it mattered most; that has made it possible for evil to triumph."
—Haile Selassie, Former Emperor of Ethiopia

Kitty Genovese, victim of brutality and bystander apathy

Harm doesn't always come from a hurtful act. It can also come from *inaction* when someone needs help. We can illustrate this fact with an event that stunned the nation and became a legend about the apparent callousness of human nature. On March 13, 1964, the *New York Times* reported that 38 citizens of Queens watched for more than half an hour as a man with a knife stalked and killed Kitty Genovese, one of their neighbors, in three separate attacks. The article said that the sound of the bystanders' voices and the sudden glow of their bedroom lights twice interrupted the assault, but each time the assailant returned and stabbed her again. According to the report, only one witness called the police—after the woman had been murdered.

The story of Kitty Genovese's murder dominated the news for days, as a shocked nation was served up media commentary that played on the angles of bystander apathy and the indifference of New Yorkers. Why didn't they help? Was it something about New York—or could the same thing happen anywhere?

A recent investigation of police records and other archival materials has found that the real story was different from the original *Times* report (Manning, Levine, & Collins, 2007). For one thing, there was no basis for the claim that 38 people witnessed the event. Further, most of the assault took place in an entry hall, out of view of neighbors. And, in fact, a few phone calls to the police *were* made during the attack. Remember also, at that time, there was no 911 emergency number to facilitate such calls. It was still a tragedy, of course, but not one that proved the people of New York to be the indifferent bystanders the original story made them out to be. For psychology, the important result of this Kitty Genovese incident was that it led to some important research on bystander intervention that focused on the *power of the situation*. Under what circumstances will people help—or not?

Sadly, the general issue of public apathy in failing to get involved in helping someone in distress is not limited in time or geography. In October 2009, after a school dance, at Richmond, California High School, a 15-year-old girl student was brutally gang raped by at least five men and boys, and also beaten over a 2-hour period. As many as a dozen people looked on and did nothing; none called 911 emergency on their cell phones; some are reported as having even been texting about this "event."

Contrived Emergencies Soon after the Kitty Genovese murder and the analysis in the press, two young social psychologists, Bibb Latané and John Darley, began a series of studies on the **bystander intervention problem**. These studies all ingeniously created laboratory analogues of the difficulties faced by bystanders in real emergency situations. In one such experiment, a college student, placed alone in a room with an intercom, was led to believe that he was communicating with one or more students in adjacent rooms. During a discussion about personal problems, this individual heard what sounded like another student having a seizure and gasping for help. During the "seizure," the bystander couldn't talk to the other students or find out what, if anything, they were doing about the emergency. The dependent variable was the speed with which he reported the emergency to the experimenter. The independent variable was the number of people he believed were in the discussion group with him.

It turned out that the speed of response by those in this situation depended on the number of bystanders they thought were present. The more people they believed to be listening in on the situation in other rooms, the slower they were to report the seizure, if they did so at all. As you can see in Figure 11.3, all those in a two-person situation intervened within 160 seconds, but only 60 percent of those who believed they were part of a large group ever informed the experimenter that another student was seriously ill (Latané & Darley, 1968).

Was it the *person* or the *situation*? Personality tests showed no significant relationship between particular personality characteristics of the participants and their speed or likelihood of intervening. The best predictor of bystander intervention was the situational variable of group size: that is, the number of other bystanders present. By way of explanation, Darley and Latané proposed that the likelihood of intervention decreases as the group increases in size because each person assumes that others will help, so he or she does not have to make that commitment. Individuals who perceive themselves as part of a large group of potential interveners

bystander intervention problem   Laboratory and field study analogues of the difficulties faced by bystanders in real emergency situations.

CONNECTION CHAPTER 1

The *independent variable* refers to the stimulus conditions or experimenter-varied conditions for different groups in an experiment, while the *dependent variable* is the measured outcome (p. 27).

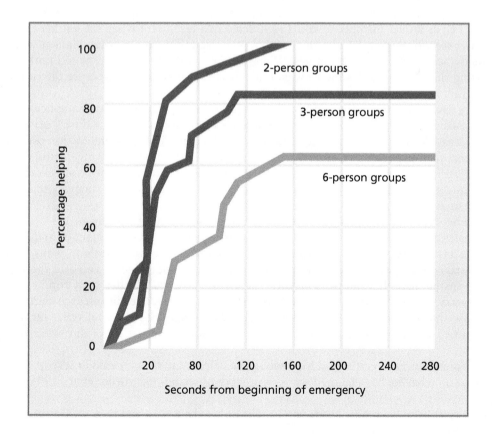

FIGURE 11.3

Bystander Intervention in an Emergency

The more people present in a crisis, the less likely it is that any one bystander will intervene. As this summary of research findings shows, bystanders act most quickly in two-person groupings.

Source: Darley, S. M. & Latané, B. (1968). Bystander intervention in emergencies: diffusion of responsibilities. *Journal of Personality & Social Psychology, 8* (4), pp. 377–384. Copyright © 1968 by the American Psychological Association.

diffusion of responsibility   Dilution or weakening of each group member's obligation to act when responsibility is perceived to be shared with all group members or accepted by the leader.

experience a **diffusion of responsibility**: a dilution or weakening of each group member's obligation to help, to become personally involved. You may have experienced moments of diffused responsibility if you have driven past a disabled car beside a busy highway because you believed "surely someone else" would stop and help—as you went on your way.

Another factor was undoubtedly also at work: *conformity*. As you will remember from our Core Concept and from Asch's studies of conformity, when people don't know what to do, they take their cues from others. The same thing occurred in the bystander studies, where those who failed to intervene were observing and conforming to the behavior of other people who were doing nothing. They allowed the absence of helping by others to *define the situation* for them as one in which the norm was that it was OK to be passively indifferent.

Does Training Encourage Helping?   Two studies suggest that the bystander problem can be countered with appropriate training. Ted Huston and his colleagues (1981) found no personality traits that distinguished people who had helped in actual emergency situations from those who had not. But they did find that helpers more often had had some medical, police, first-aid, or CPR training in dealing with emergency situations. And another study shows that even a psychology class lecture on the bystander problem can help (Beaman et al., 1978). Students had an opportunity to help a "victim" slumped in a doorway while walking by with a nonresponsive confederate of the experimenter. Those who had attended a lecture on bystander intervention were twice as likely to stop and attempt to help as those who had not received the lecture on helping. Education apparently can make a difference; we hope *you* will also use the lessons of this chapter in constructive ways.

Need Help? Ask for It!

To demonstrate the positive effects of situational power, social psychologist Tom Moriarity (1975) arranged two fascinating experiments. In the first study, New Yorkers watched as a thief snatched a woman's suitcase in a restaurant when she left her table. In the second, they watched a thief grab a portable radio from a beach blanket when the owner left it for a few minutes. What did these onlookers do? Some did nothing, letting the thief go on his merry way. But others did intervene. What were the conditions under which some helped and others did not?

In each experiment, the would-be theft victim (the experimenter's accomplice) had first asked the soon-to-be observer of the crime either "Do you have the time?" or "Will you please keep an eye on my bag (radio) while I'm gone?" The first interaction elicited no personal responsibility, and almost all of the bystanders stood by idly as the theft unfolded. However, of those who had agreed to watch the victim's property, almost every bystander intervened. They called for help, and some even tackled the runaway thief on the beach!

The encouraging message is that we can often convert apathy to action and transform callousness to kindness just by asking for it. The mere act of requesting a favor forges a special human bond that involves other people in ways that materially change the situation. It makes them feel responsible to you and thereby responsible for what happens in your shared social world. Under such conditions, ordinary people can become Good Samaritans. But we will see in research outlined below that the *situation* can make a theology student about to deliver a sermon about the Good Samaritan effect into a Bad Samaritan—if he or she were in a hurry.

Your chances of getting aid from would-be helpers can be increased in several ways based on what we have learned across a number of studies (Schroeder et al., 1995):

- **Ask for help.** Let others know you need it rather than assuming they realize your need or know what is required.

Do It Yourself! WHAT MAKES A SAMARITAN GOOD OR BAD?

Now that you know something about bystander intervention, let's see how good you are at picking the crucial variable out of a bystander situation inspired by the biblical tale of the Good Samaritan (see Luke 10:30–37). In the biblical account, several important people are too busy to help a stranger in distress. He is finally assisted by an outsider, a Samaritan, who takes the time to offer aid. Could the failure of the distressed individual's countrymen to help be due to character flaws or personal dispositions? Or was it determined by the situation?

Social psychologists decided to put students at the Princeton Theological Seminary into a similar situation. It was made all the more ironic because they thought that they were being evaluated on the quality of the sermons they were about to deliver on the parable of the Good Samaritan. Let's see what happened when these seminarians were given an opportunity to help someone in distress.

With sermon in hand, each was directed to a nearby building where the sermon was to be recorded. But as the student walked down an alley between the two buildings, he or she came upon a man slumped in a doorway, in obvious need of help. The student now had the chance to practice what he or she was about to preach. What would you guess was the crucial variable that predicted how likely a seminarian—ready to preach about the Good Samaritan—was to help a person in distress? Choose one:

- How religious the seminarian was (as rated by his classmates).
- How "neurotic" the seminarian was (as rated on the "Big Five" personality traits).
- How much of a hurry the seminarian was in.
- How old the seminarian was.

All of the dispositional variables (personal characteristics) of the seminarians were controlled by random assignment of subjects to three different conditions. Thus, we know that personality was not the determining factor. Rather, it was a situational variable: time. Before the seminarians left the briefing room to have their sermons recorded in a nearby building, each was told how much time he had to get to the studio. Some were assigned to a late condition in which they had to hurry to make the next session; others to an on-time condition in which they would make the next session just on time; and a third group to an early condition in which they had a few spare minutes before they would be recorded.

What were the results? Of those who were in a hurry, only 10 percent helped. Ninety percent failed to act as Good Samaritans! If they were on time, 45 percent helped the stranger. The greatest bystander intervention came from 63 percent of those who were not in any time bind (see Figure 11.4).

Remarkably, the manipulation of time urgency made those in the "late" condition six times less likely to help than those in the "early" condition. While fulfilling their obligation to hurry, these individuals appeared to have a single-minded purpose that blinded them to other events around them. Again, it was the power of the situation.

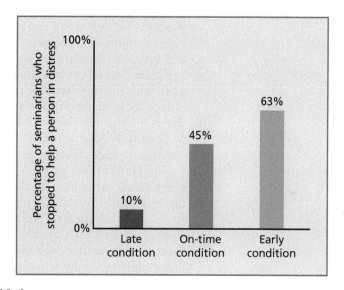

FIGURE 11.4

Results of the "Good Samaritan" Study

Even on their way to deliver the Good Samaritan Sermon, the vast majority of seminary students did not stop to help a distressed victim.

Source: Darley, J. M., & Batson, C. D. (1973). From Jerusalem to Jericho: A study of situational and dispositional variables in helping behavior. *Journal of Personality and Social Psychology, 27,* 100–108.

- **Reduce the ambiguity of the situation** by clearly explaining the problem and what should be done: "She's fainted! Call an ambulance right away," or "Someone broke into my house—call the police and give them this address!"
- **Identify specific individuals** so they do not diffuse responsibility with others present: "You, in the red shirt: Call 911!" or "Will the person in the blue Toyota please call for a tow truck right away?"

None of these tactics guarantees the safety of your person or possessions, of course. Nevertheless, they probably represent your best hope if you find yourself, alone in a crowd, facing a real emergency.

[PSYCHOLOGY MATTERS]

On Being "Shoe" at Yale U

When I (PGZ) arrived at Yale University to start my graduate career in the mid-1950s, I was dressed in all my South Bronx splendor—blue suede shoes, peg pants, long dangling key chain, big rolled collar, and other cool clothes. A month or two later, I was wearing chino pants, button-down shirts, and loafer-type shoes. I was not fully aware of the subtle social pressures to change my "taste" in apparel, but knew that I felt more "in" in those weird Yalie clothes than I had in my good old Bronx duds. But as a budding psychologist, I used my personal case study to motivate me to find out more about that unwritten dress code, one that everyone around the campus at that time was following as if a Marine drill instructor were ordering our total mindless compliance.

My interviews with seniors revealed that indeed there was a powerful dress code that the **in-group** formulated regularly to distinguish them from the mass of **out-group** pretenders. Every single item of clothing could be identified by those in the know as socially appropriate at that time for real Yale men to wear (it was all male at that time). I was informed that the underlying concept was termed "shoe." (Yale men of that era and earlier could be identified as wearing white buck shoes.) To be "shoe" was to be in, to be cool, to be with it, to be right on, and so forth. Not only was every bit of clothing indexed as to its degree of "shoeness," but so was everything else in that universe. Tennis, golf, and crew were shoe; basketball was not. Asking questions in lecture classes was not shoe; tailgating before football games was shoe, but only if done with the right style or panache. Of equal interest to me was the fact that shoe ratings changed periodically to keep outsiders from being mistaken as really true blue shoe. One year, the Yale senior ring was shoe to wear, the next year it might be unshoe; or handmade bow ties would become unshoe and clip-on bow ties would vault from low-shoe to high-shoe rating.

My team of informants helped me to form an index of the shoe strengths of every conceivable item of clothing that a Yale student might wear that year. With the help of my introductory psychology students, we went into the dormitories and found out what students from each college class actually had in their wardrobes. We then multiplied each of those items of clothing by their Shoe Index and averaged those ratings across each class from frosh to senior. Next, we separated out students' shoe scores by whether they had come from prep schools versus public high schools.

Three major significant results were obvious from our graphs of the quantification of shoeness at Yale:

1. Student wardrobes became ever more shoe as they progress from lowly frosh up to high-powered seniors.
2. Preppy frosh were much more shoe than were their classmates from public high schools.
3. Over the 4 years, the gap between prep schoolers and high schoolers diminished, so that by senior year they were almost equally shoe.

When Yale became coed in the next decade, this kind of "shoeness" became less apparent, went underground, and now may exist only in very modified forms. But let this be a lesson to you whatever school you are in: Much of what you think is the You in Your Taste is really the Them in social conformity pressures subtly imposed on you to be like Them in order to be liked by Them. All too often, we go along to get along (Zimbardo, 2008).

in-group   The group with which an individual identifies.

out-group   Those outside the group with which an individual identifies.

Check Your Understanding

1. **RECALL:** Which of the following would be a social role?

   a. prisoner
   b. ordering from a menu
   c. defying unjust authority
   d. all of the above

2. **RECALL:** In the Asch studies, which of the following produced a *decrease* in conformity?

   a. The task was seen as difficult or ambiguous.
   b. The subject had to respond publicly, rather than privately.
   c. The majority was not unanimous in its judgment.
   d. The group was very large.

3. **RECALL:** In Milgram's original study, about what proportion of the "teacher-subjects" gave the maximum shock?

   a. about two-thirds
   b. about 50 percent
   c. about 25 percent
   d. nearly all

4. **RECALL:** Although conformity is a social phenomenon, brain regions that are activated when someone conforms are different from those brain regions activated by resisting and being independent.

   True
   False

5. **APPLICATION:** What is the main difference between altruistic actions and heroic actions?

   a. voluntary nature of altruism
   b. altruism can be in groups; heroism is a solo action
   c. higher costs/risks in heroism
   d. none of the above

6. **APPLICATION:** If you were a victim in an emergency, what lessons from social psychology would you apply to get the help you need?

   a. Ask for it.
   b. Make your request specific.
   c. Engage particular individual observers.
   d. Do all of the above.

7. **UNDERSTANDING THE CORE CONCEPT:** What consequences does attempting to understand human behavior in terms of situational causes have for the personal responsibility of the actors involved?

   a. excuses them entirely
   b. limits their guilt if they murdered someone
   c. does not change personal responsibility and guilt, only severity of sentence
   d. forces the situation to be put on trial as well

Answers 1. a **2.** c **3.** a **4.** True **5.** c **6.** d **7.** c

---

11.2 KEY QUESTION
Constructing Social Reality: What Influences Our Judgments of Others?

Powerful as a social situation is, it doesn't account for everything that people do. For example, it does not account for the individual differences we see in people's choices of friends and romantic partners, nor does it account for their prejudices. To explain the patterns we find in social interaction, we must also look at cognitive processes. In the language of social psychology, we need to understand how we construct our **social reality**—our subjective interpretations of other people and of our relationships. Thus, the social reality we construct determines whom we find attractive, whom we find threatening, whom we seek out, and whom we avoid. This, then, leads us to the second lesson of social psychology, captured in our next Core Concept:

social reality An individual's subjective interpretation of other people and of one's relationships with them.

> ### Core Concept 11.2
> The judgments we make about others depend not only on their behavior but also on our interpretation of their actions within a social context.

We will illustrate how these cognitive factors operate by analyzing how they affect our attitudes toward other people. Let's start out by asking a simple question: What makes people like each other? That is, what produces interpersonal attraction?

Interpersonal Attraction

It is no surprise that we are attracted to people who have something to offer us (Brehm et al., 2002; Simpson & Harris, 1994). We tend to like those who give us gifts, agree with us, act friendly toward us, share our interests, entertain us, and help us in times of need—unless, of course, we suspect that their behavior is self-serving or hypocritical. Although we don't necessarily mind giving something back in the form of a social exchange, we shrink from relationships that merely take from us and offer nothing in return. In the best of relationships, as in a friendship, partnership, marriage, or business relationship, both parties receive rewards. You might consider whether this is true in your own relationships as we look at the reward theory of attraction next.

Reward Theory: We (Usually) Prefer Rewarding Relationships Most good relationships can be seen as an exchange of benefits (Batson, 1987; Clark et al., 1989). The benefits could be some combination of money and material possessions. Or the exchange might involve something intangible like praise, status, information, sex, or emotional support.

Social psychologist Elliot Aronson (2004) summarizes this in a **reward theory of attraction**, which says that attraction is a form of social learning. By looking at the social costs and benefits, claims Aronson, we can usually understand why people are attracted to each other. In brief, reward theory says that we like best those who give us maximum rewards at minimum cost. After we look at the evidence, we think you will agree that this theory explains (almost) everything about interpersonal attraction. Social psychologists have found four especially powerful sources of reward that predict interpersonal attraction: proximity, similarity, self-disclosure, and physical attractiveness. Most of us choose our friends, associates, and lovers because they offer some combination of these factors at a relatively low social cost.

Proximity An old saying advises, "Absence makes the heart grow fonder." Another contradicts with "Out of sight, out of mind." Which one is correct? Studies show that frequent sightings best predict our closest relationships and the people we see most often are the people who live and work nearest us (Simpson & Harris, 1994). In college dormitories, residents more often become close friends with the person who lives in the next room than they do with the person who lives two doors down (Priest & Sawyer, 1967). Residents of apartments make more friendships among people who live on the same floor than among those who live on other floors (Nahemow & Lawton, 1975). Those who live in neighborhoods more often become friends with the occupants of the house next door than with people living two houses away (Festinger et al., 1950). This **principle of proximity** (nearness) also accounts for the fact that many people end up married to the boy or girl next door (Ineichen, 1979). And it correctly predicts that people at work will make more friends among those with whom they have the most contact (Segal, 1974).

Although you don't have to like your neighbors, the proximity rule says that when two individuals are equally attractive, you are more likely to make friends with the nearest one: The rewards are equal, but the cost is less in terms of time and inconvenience (Gilbertson et al., 1998). Apparently, another old saying, that familiarity breeds contempt, should be revised in light of social psychological research: In fact, familiarity more often breeds friendship. Increased contact, itself, often increases peoples' liking for each other (Bornstein, 1989).

Similarity Do birds of a feather flock together, or do opposites attract? Which of these proverbs has the best research evidence to support it? People usually find it more rewarding to strike up a friendship with someone who shares their attitudes,

---

reward theory of attraction A social learning view that predicts we like best those who give us maximum rewards at minimum cost.

CONNECTION CHAPTER 4

Social learning involves expectations of rewards and punishments learned through social interactions and observation of others (p. 160).

principle of proximity The notion that people at work will make more friends among those who are nearby—with whom they have the most contact. *Proximity* means "nearness."

interests, values, and experiences than to bother with people who are disagreeable or merely different (Simpson & Harris, 1994). If two people have just discovered that they share tastes in music, politics, and attitudes toward education, they will probably hit it off because they have, in effect, exchanged compliments that reward each other for their tastes and attitudes (Byrne, 1969). The **similarity principle** also explains why teenagers are most likely to make friends among those who share their political and religious views, educational aspirations, and attitudes toward music, alcohol, and drugs (Kandel, 1978). Likewise, similarity accounts for the fact that most people find marriage partners of the same age, race, social status, attitudes, and values (Brehm, 1992; Hendrick & Hendrick, 1992). In general, similarity, like proximity, makes the hearts grow fonder. However, it is also true that over time, couples can also experience attitude realignment, as each of them gradually shifts views on various issues to be more closely aligned to those of their partner (Davis & Rusbult, 2001).

Self-Disclosure Good friends and lovers share intimate details about themselves (Sternberg, 1998). This practice of **self-disclosure** not only allows people to know each other more deeply, but it also sends signals of trust. It is as if I say, "Here is a piece of information that I want you to know about me, and I trust you not to hurt me with it." Friends and lovers usually find such exchanges highly rewarding. When you observe people exchanging confidences and details about their lives, you can predict that they are becoming more and more attracted to each other. Given that sharing personal disclosures comes after a sense of trust has been created in a relationship, it both takes time to reach this level of intimacy and is an index of that trust the disclosing person has in the other. Think about the people with whom you share secrets and those you never would. What underlies these acts of sharing or withholding secrets? The very act of telling someone that you want to share a secret with them automatically confers on them a special status in the relationship since secrets are by definition private and rare events.

Physical Attractiveness Yet another old saying tells us that beauty is only skin deep. Nevertheless, people usually find it more rewarding to associate with people they consider physically attractive than with those they consider to be plain or homely (Patzer, 1985). Fair or not, good looks are a real social asset. Potential employers, for example, prefer good-looking job candidates to plainer applicants (Cash & Janda, 1984). Looks also affect people's judgments of children. Attractive children are judged as happier and more competent than their peers (Eagly et al., 1991). Even babies judge people by their appearances. We know this because babies gaze longer at pictures of normal faces than at those of distorted faces (Langlois et al., 1987).

Most people are repelled by the idea that they might make judgments based only on looks. Indeed, when asked what they look for in a dating partner, college students rank physical attractiveness down toward the middle of the list. But what people say does not match what they do—at least as far as their first impressions go. Across many studies involving a variety of characteristics, including intelligence, sincerity, masculinity, femininity, and independence, it was *physical attractiveness* that overwhelmed everything else as the best predictor of how well a person would be liked after a first meeting (Aronson, 2004).

Other research shows that the principle of attractiveness applies equally to same-sex and opposite-sex relationships (Maruyama & Miller, 1975). Gender differences do exist, however. While both males and females are strongly influenced by physical attractiveness, men seem to be more influenced by looks than are women (Feingold, 1990).

These findings may come as bad news for the majority of us, who consider ourselves rather average-looking at best. But we can take some comfort in a study that suggests that people actually consider a composite of "average" features to be the most attractive. Investigators fed images of many students' faces into a computer program that manipulated the facial features to be more or less of an average combination of all features from the many different student portraits. Surprisingly, they found that

similarity principle The notion that people are attracted to those who are most similar to themselves on significant dimensions.

CONNECTION CHAPTER 3

The Gestalt principle of *similarity* refers to grouping stimulus objects that shared common perceptual features (p. 120).

self-disclosure The sharing of personal information and feelings with another person as part of the process of developing trust.

people usually liked best the images having features closest to the average size and shape (Rhodes et al., 1999).

Now some bad news for you exceptionally attractive readers: While we usually associate positive qualities with attractive individuals (Calvert, 1988), extreme attractiveness can also be a liability. Physically attractive people are seen as more poised, interesting, sociable, independent, exciting, sexual, intelligent, well adjusted, and successful, but they are also perceived as more vain and materialistic (Hassebrauck, 1988). A "double standard" also comes into play. For example, the public favors good-looking male politicians but disparages their attractive female counterparts (Sigelman et al., 1986). It is also double trouble to be shy and handsome or beautiful because others mistake those with a reserved demeanor as being cold, indifferent, or feeling superior.

These effects of physical attractiveness hint that reward, as powerful as it is, does not account for everything. We will see this more clearly in the next section, as we explore some important exceptions to the reward theory of attraction.

Exceptions to the Reward Theory of Attraction While the rules of proximity, similarity, self-disclosure, and physical attractiveness may explain a lot about interpersonal attraction, a casual look around reveals lots of relationships that don't seem especially rewarding. Why, for example, might a woman be attracted to a man who abuses her? Or why would a person want to join an organization that requires a difficult or degrading initiation ritual? Such relationships pose most interesting puzzles (Aronson, 2004). Could some people actually feel more attraction when they find that another person has less to offer them? Let's try to uncover the principles of social cognition operating behind some interesting exceptions to a reward theory of attraction.

Expectations and the Influence of Self-Esteem We have seen that reward theory predicts our attraction to good-looking people—and, to a lesser degree, those who are nearby, smart, self-disclosing, like-minded, and powerful. Yet you have probably observed that most people end up with friends and mates whom they judge to be of about their same level of overall desirability—the so-called **matching hypothesis** (Feingold, 1988; Harvey & Pauwels, 1999). How does this happen? Is our selection of associates the result of a sort of bargaining for the best we can get in the interpersonal marketplace?

Yes, says **expectancy-value theory.** People usually decide whether to pursue a relationship by weighing the value they see in another person (including such qualities as physical attractiveness, wit, interests, and intelligence) against their expectation of success in the relationship (Will the other person be attracted to me?). Most of us don't waste time on trying to connect with others who either seem "too good"—or "not good enough"—for what we think of our important attributes and values. We tend to seek a match that is harmonious with our self-definition, assuming it is reality based. Thus, we initiate relationships with the most attractive people we think will probably like us in return. In this sense, expectancy-value theory is not so much a competitor of reward theory as it is a refinement of it.

A new look at the matching hypothesis, however, took advantage of a popular online dating site and also laboratory studies to show that the matching hypothesis is more complicated than psychologists had thought (Taylor et al., 2011). Unexpectedly, physical attractiveness, by itself, was not a good predictor in these studies. Rather, the research showed that two more global factors need to be taken into account: *self-worth* (what people think of themselves) and *social desirability* (popularity). In general, participants in these online experiments tended to initiate contacts with those having similar self-worth and social desirability.

And what happened when they ventured "out of their league?" Men, more so than women, were successful in initiating contacts with persons rated at or above their own social desirability level. But woe to those who sought to play "out of their league" in physical attractiveness: More often than not, they were ignored when they initiated contacts with those (independently judged to be) more physically attractive than themselves.

Other research shows that people with low opinions of themselves tend to establish relationships with people who share their views, often with people who devalue them.

matching hypothesis The prediction that most people will find friends and mates that are perceived to be of about their same level of attractiveness.

expectancy-value theory A social psychology theory that states how people decide whether to pursue a relationship by weighing the potential value of the relationship against their expectation of success in establishing the relationship.

Not surprisingly, this can lead to dysfunctional relationships. Such individuals may actually feel a stronger commitment to a relationship when their partner thinks poorly of them than they do when the partner thinks well of them (Swann et al., 1992).

Similarly, those individuals who appear to be extremely competent can also be losers in the expectancy-value game. Why? Most of us keep such people at a distance, probably because we fear that they will be quick to reject our approaches. But, if you happen to be one of these stunningly superior people, do not despair: Social psychologists have found hope! When highly competent individuals commit minor blunders—spilling a drink or dropping a stack of papers—other people actually like them better, probably because blunders bring them down to everyone else's level and "normalize" them (Aronson et al., 1966, 1970). Don't count on this, however, unless you are so awesomely competent as to be unapproachable. The latté-in-the-lap trick only makes most of us look like klutzes, whom people like less.

Attraction and Dissonance *Semper fidelis,* says the Marine Corps motto: "Always faithful." Considering the discomforting experiences that people must endure to become Marines (grueling physical conditioning, loss of sleep, lack of privacy, being yelled at, suffering punishment for small infractions of rules), it may seem remarkable that recruits routinely develop so much loyalty to their organization. The same is true of more enduring loyalty to fraternities that practice hazing compared to college house plans that do not. Obviously, some powerfully attractive and interesting forces are at work.

Cognitive dissonance theory offers a compelling explanation for the mental adjustments that occur in people who voluntarily undergo unpleasant experiences (Festinger, 1957). The theory says that when people voluntarily act in ways that produce *psychological* discomfort or otherwise clash with their attitudes and values, they develop a highly motivating mental state called cognitive dissonance. Those who continue to smoke yet know the negative (lethal health) consequences of cigarette addiction experience dissonance, as do gamblers who continually lose but keep playing. The same holds true for people who find they are acting in ways that cause them to experience physical discomfort. Thus, our Marine recruits may feel cognitive dissonance when they find that they have volunteered for an experience that is far more punishing than they had imagined from the recruiting ads. And what is the psychological result?

According to cognitive dissonance theory, people are motivated to avoid the uncomfortable state of dissonance. If they find themselves experiencing cognitive dissonance, they attempt to reduce it in ways that are predictable, even if not always entirely logical. The two main ways of reducing dissonance are to change either one's behavior or one's cognitions. So, in civilian life, if the boss is abusive, you might avoid dissonance by simply finding another job. But in the case of a Marine recruit, changing jobs is not an option: It is too late to turn back once basic training has started. A recruit experiencing cognitive dissonance, therefore, is motivated to adjust his or her thinking. Most likely, the recruit will resolve the dissonance by rationalizing the experience ("It's tough, but it builds character!") and by developing a stronger loyalty to the organization ("Being a member of such an elite group is worth all the suffering!"). ◉

In general, cognitive dissonance theory says that when people's cognitions and actions are in conflict (a state of *dissonance*), they often reduce the conflict by changing their thinking, their attitudes and values, to fit their behavior. Why? People don't like to see themselves as being foolish or inconsistent. So, to explain their own behavior to themselves, people are motivated to change their attitudes, which are private, rather than their overt behavior, which is public. To do otherwise would threaten their self-esteem.

One qualification on this theory has recently come to light. In Japan, and, perhaps, in other parts of Asia, studies show that people have a lesser need to maintain high self-esteem than do North Americans (Bower, 1997a; Heine et al., 1999). As a result, cognitive dissonance was found to have less power to change attitudes among

Cognitive dissonance theory predicts that these recruits will increase their loyalty to the Marine Corps as a result of their basic training ordeal.

cognitive dissonance   A highly motivating state in which people have conflicting cognitions, especially when their voluntary actions conflict with their attitudes or values. Leon Festinger was its originator.

CONNECTION CHAPTER 9

Social psychologists view cognitive dissonance as a powerful *psychological motive* (p. 365).

◉ **Watch** the **Video** Cognitive Dissonance: Need to Justify Our Actions at **MyPsychLab**

CONNECTION CHAPTER 9

Collectivist cultures socialize
people to value the needs of the
group before the desires of the
individual (p. 367).

Japanese. Apparently, cognitive dissonance is yet another psychological process that operates differently in collectivist and individualistic cultures.

The Explanatory Power of Dissonance   Despite cultural variations, cognitive dissonance theory explains many things that people do to justify their behavior and thereby avoid dissonance. For example, it explains why smokers so often rationalize their habit. It explains why people who have put their efforts into a project, whether it be volunteering for the Red Cross or writing a letter of recommendation, become more committed to the cause as time goes on—to justify their effort. It also explains why, if you have just decided to buy a Toyota Prius, you will attend to new information supporting your choice (such as Prius commercials on TV), but you will tend to ignore dissonance-producing information (such as its higher price, or a Prius broken down alongside the freeway, or its massive recall for faulty acceleration).

Cognitive dissonance theory also helps us understand certain puzzling social relationships, such as a woman who is attracted to a man who abuses her. Her dissonance might be summed up in this thought: "Why am I staying with someone who hurts me?" Her powerful drive for self-justification may make her reduce the dissonance by focusing on his good points and minimizing the abuse. And, if she has low self-esteem, she may also tell herself that she deserved his abuse.

To put the matter in more general terms: Cognitive dissonance theory predicts that people are attracted to those for whom they believe they have suffered voluntarily. A general reward theory, by contrast, would never have predicted that outcome. Another vital contribution made by dissonance theorists is providing a theoretical framework for understanding why we all come to justify our foolish beliefs, bad decisions, and even hurtful acts against others—by justification and disowning personal responsibility for dissonance-generating decisions (Tavris & Aronson, 2007).

To sum up our discussion on interpersonal attraction: You will not usually go far wrong if you use a reward theory to understand why people are attracted to each other. People initiate social relationships because they expect some sort of benefit. It may be an outright reward, such as money or status or sex, or it may be an avoidance of some feared consequence, such as pain of social isolation or social rejection. (We will see in our chapter on health and stress that such rejection can cause significant biological impairments.)

But social psychology also shows that a simple reward theory cannot, by itself, account for all the subtlety of human social interaction. A more sophisticated and useful understanding of attraction must take into account such cognitive factors as expectations, self-esteem, and cognitive dissonance. That is, a complete theory must take into account the ways that we interpret our social environment. This notion of subjective interpretation also underlies other judgments that we make about people, those we love and those we hate.

CONNECTION CHAPTER 14

Stress can impact on our biological
functioning in many ways, for
better of for worse (p. 600).

Loving Relationships

Although people sometimes do terrible things to one another, the complexity and beauty of the human mind also enable people to be caring and loving. Liking and loving are essential for happiness (Kim & Hatfield, 2004). Further, the pleasures of attraction and love appear to be part of the very circuitry and chemistry of our brains (Bartels & Zeki, 2004).

How do we know when attraction becomes love? To a large extent, our culture tells us how. Each culture has certain common themes defining love—such as sexual arousal, attachment, concern for the other's welfare, and a willingness to make a commitment. But the idea of "love" can vary greatly from culture to culture (Sternberg, 1998).

There are also many kinds of love. The love that a parent has for a child differs from the love that longtime friends have for each other. Both differ from the commitment found, say, in a loving couple that have been married for 40 years. Yet, for many Americans, the term *love* brings to mind yet another form of attraction based on infatuation and sexual desire: **romantic love**, a temporary and highly emotional condition that generally fades after a few months (Hatfield et al., 1995; Hatfield & Rapson, 1998). But the American assumption that romantic love is the basis for a long-term intimate commitment is not universal. In many other cultures, marriage is seen as an economic bond or, perhaps, as a political relationship linking families. Indeed, a variety of cultures still promote "arranged marriages" where parents or even grandparents decide on the best match for the son or daughter that will enhance the status of the family in power or finances.

Psychologist Robert Sternberg (1998) has proposed an interesting view in his **triangular theory of love.** He says that love can have three components: passion (erotic attraction), intimacy (sharing feelings and confidences), and commitment (dedication to putting this relationship first in one's life). Various forms of love can be understood in terms of different combinations of these three components. Thus, Sternberg suggests that:

- *Romantic love* is high on passion and intimacy but low on commitment.
- *Liking* and *friendship* are characterized by intimacy but not by passion and commitment.
- *Infatuation* has a high level of passion, but it has not developed into intimacy or a committed relationship.
- *Complete love* (consummate love) involves all three: passion, intimacy, and commitment. *Companionate love* often follows the consummate kind with a dimming of the passion but often with greater intimacy and commitment.

The need to understand what strengthens and weakens loving relationships in our own culture has acquired some urgency because of the "divorce epidemic" in the United States (Brehm, 1992; Harvey & Pauwels, 1999). If current rates hold, approximately half of all today's first marriages—and up to 60 percent of second marriages—will end in divorce. Much research stimulated by concern about high divorce rates has focused on the effects of divorce on children (Ahrons, 1994). The negative effects are lessened when the divorce is amicable and former spouses coparent and do not denigrate each other to the children. Sometimes removing children from a conflict-ridden family setting, or one with an abusive parent, is clearly better for them.

In the past decade or so, however, research emphasis has shifted to the processes by which couples maintain loving relationships and the environments that challenge relationships (Berscheid, 1999). We now know, for example, that for a relationship to stay healthy and to thrive, both partners must see it as rewarding and equitable. As we saw in our discussion of reward theory, both must, over the long run, feel that they are getting something out of the relationship, not just giving. What they get—the rewards of the relationship—can involve many things, including adventure, status, laughter, mental stimulation, and material goods, as well as nurturance, love, and social support.

In addition, for a relationship to thrive, communication between partners must be open, ongoing, and mutually validating (Monaghan, 1999). Research shows that couples in lasting relationships have five times more positive interactions than negative ones—including exchanges of smiles, loving touches, laughter, and compliments (Gottman, 1994). Yet, because every relationship experiences an occasional communication breakdown, the partners must know how to deal with conflicts effectively. Conflicts must be faced early and resolved fairly and effectively. Ultimately, each partner must take responsibility for his or her own identity, self-esteem, and commitment to the relationship—rather than expect the partner to engage in mind reading or self-sacrifice.

This has been the briefest sampling from the growing social psychology of relationships. Such research has practical applications. Teachers familiar with research findings can now inform their students about the basic principles of healthy relationships. Therapists apply these principles in advising clients on how to communicate with partners, negotiate the terms of their relationships, and resolve inevitable conflicts. More immediately, as you yourself learn about the factors that influence how you perceive and relate to others, you should gain a greater sense of self-control and well-being in your own intimate connections with others (Harvey, 1996; Harvey et al., 1990).

romantic love A temporary and highly emotional condition based on infatuation and sexual desire.

triangular theory of love Developed by Robert Sternberg, a theory that describes various kinds of love in terms of three components: passion (erotic attraction), intimacy (sharing feelings and confidences), and commitment (dedication to putting this relationship first in one's life).

Is it love? Social psychologists have been exploring the psychology of the human heart, collecting and interpreting data about how people fall in love and strengthen their bonds of intimacy. Most recently, the emphasis has shifted to the factors that keep relationships together.

Long-Term Romantic Love   For too many couples who were initially hot for each other in romantic, passionate love, they've "lost that loving feeling." However, we can be encouraged by new research revealing that couples in long-term romantic love relationships can keep the flame burning hot, at least in their brains (Acevedo, Aron, Fisher, and Brown, 2011). Individual men and women who had been in such relationships for more than 20 years had their brains scanned in fMRI procedures under two different conditions. They viewed facial images of their partner, as well as comparison images of highly familiar acquaintances, close, long-term friends, or someone not familiar. The effects obtained were specific only to their intensely loved, long-term partner; for other images the brain patterns were random. Areas activated were in the parts of the brain associated with the dopamine-rich reward and basal ganglia system—similar to activation in new love. However, there is added cerebral arousal among these long-term lovers that involves brain systems that are also associated with maternal attachment and pair bonding.

CONNECTION CHAPTER 2

Neuroscience researchers use the technique of functional magnetic resonance imaging, fMRI, to "light up" brain regions activated by a person's thoughts, emotions, and perceptions while in the scanner (p. 64).

Making Cognitive Attributions

We are always trying to explain to ourselves why people do what they do. Suppose you are riding on a bus when a middle-aged woman with an armload of packages gets on. In the process of finding a seat, she drops everything on the floor as the bus starts up. How do you explain her behavior? Do you think of her as the victim of circumstances, or is she incompetent or eliciting sympathy so someone will give up a seat to her?

Social psychologists have found that we tend to attribute other people's actions and misfortunes to their personal traits rather than to situational forces, such as the unpredictable lurching of the bus. This helps explain why we often hear attributions of laziness or low intelligence to the poor or homeless rather than an externally imposed lack of opportunity (Zucker & Weiner, 1993). It also helps us understand why most commentators on the Kitty Genovese murder attributed the inaction of the bystanders to defects in character of those who did not help rather than to social influences on them (emergency 911 was not in effect at that time, so it was not clear who to call in emergencies; it was difficult to view the crime scene at night from high-story apartments, and so on). 👁

On the other side of the attributional coin, we find that people use the same process to explain each other's successes. So you may ascribe the success of a favorite singer, athlete, or family member to personal traits, such as exceptional talent or intense motivation. In doing so, we tend to ignore the effects of situational forces, such as the influence of family, coaches, a marketing blitz, long hours of practice, sacrifices, or just a "lucky break."

👁—Watch the **Video** Attribution at **MyPsychLab**

fundamental attribution error (FAE)   The dual tendency to overemphasize internal, dispositional causes and minimize external, situational pressures. The FAE is more common in individualistic cultures than in collectivistic cultures.

The Fundamental Attribution Error

The Fundamental Attribution Error   Psychologists refer to the **fundamental attribution error (FAE)** as the dual tendency to overemphasize personal traits (the rush to the dispositional) while minimizing situational influences. Recall our use of the FAE to explain the low estimates of psychiatrists when predicting the typical shock level of most American citizens in the Milgram obedience experiment. The FAE is not always an "error," of course. If the causes really are dispositional, the observer's guess is correct. So the FAE is best thought of as a *bias* rather than a mistake. However, the FAE is an error in the sense that an observer may overlook legitimate, situational explanations for another's actions. For example, if the car in front of you brakes suddenly so that you almost collide, your first impression may be that the other driver is at fault, a dispositional judgment. But what if the driver slowed down to avoid hitting a dog that ran into the road? Then the explanation for the near-accident would be situational, not dispositional. By reminding ourselves that circumstances may account for seemingly inexplicable actions, we are less likely to commit the FAE. As a general principle, we encourage you to practice *"attributional charity,"* which involves always trying first to find a situational explanation for strange or unusual behavior of others before blaming them with dispositional explanations. Blame the situation before rushing to blame the person. It can help you to change the situation for the better as well as avoid hurting the feelings of a friend or associate.

Despite its name, however, the fundamental attribution error is not as fundamental as psychologists at first thought. Cross-cultural research has suggested that it is more pervasive in individualistic cultures, as found in the United States or Canada, than in collectivist cultures, as found in Japan or China (Norenzayan & Nisbett, 2000). Even within the United States, urban children are more susceptible to the fundamental attribution error than are their country cousins (Lillard, 1999). Why do you think this is so?

Biased Thinking about Yourself Oddly, you probably judge yourself by two different standards, depending on whether you experience success or failure. When things go well, most people attribute their own success to internal factors, such as motivation, talent, or skill ("I am good at taking multiple-choice tests"). But when things go poorly, they attribute failure to external factors beyond their control ("The professor asked trick questions;" Smith & Ellsworth, 1987). Psychologists have dubbed this tendency the **self-serving bias** (Bradley, 1978; Fletcher & Ward, 1988). Self-serving biases are probably rooted in the need for self-esteem, a preference for interpretations that save face and cast our actions in the best possible light—both to ourselves and to others (Schlenker et al., 1990).

self-serving bias An attributional pattern in which one takes credit for success but denies responsibility for failure. (Compare with *fundamental attribution error*.)

Social pressures to excel as an individual make the self-serving bias, like the fundamental attribution error, more common in individualist cultures than in collectivist cultures (Markus & Kitayama, 1994). In addition, when trying to understand the behavior of others, we tend often to use dispositional explanations, finding things "in them" that might explain why they did this or that. However, when we are trying to figure out the reasons for our own actions, we tend to look to the situational factors acting on us, because we are more aware of them than in our judgments of others. If you believed that you would have defied the authority in the Milgram study and quit long before the 450-volt shock level, despite the evidence that the majority went all the way, a self-serving bias was at work to make you think of yourself as able to resist situational forces that overwhelmed others.

Universal Dimensions of Social Cognition: Warmth and Competence
Among the most basic social perceptions anyone makes are those of "others" as friend or foe, intending to do us good or ill, and able to enact those intentions or not. A large body of new research has established that perceived liking and respecting of others are the two universal dimensions of human social cognition, at both individual and group levels. People in all cultures differentiate each other by *liking* (assessed as warmth and trustworthiness) and by *respecting* (assessed as competence and efficiency). The warmth dimension is captured in traits that are related to perceived intent, including friendliness, helpfulness, sincerity, trustworthiness, and morality. By contrast, the competence dimension reflects those traits that are related to perceived ability, intelligence, skill, creativity, and efficacy (Fiske et al., 2007).

When these two dimensions are plotted on a graph, as in Figure 11.5, we see that four quadrants emerge: I. high warmth and low competence; II. high warmth and high competence; III. low warmth and low competence; and IV. low warmth and high competence. A large body of research reveals distinct emotions and behaviors that are associated with each of the social perceptions typical of the four quadrants (Fiske et al., 2007).

Can you think of at least three factors discussed so far in this chapter that might be motivating the helping behavior shown in this situation?

Those who are perceived to be high in warmth fall into quadrants I and II. But, as you will see, even though we are drawn to those in both groups because of their perceived warmth, we react to them quite differently depending on how we perceive their competence. For people that we view as fitting in quadrant I, we tend to feel pity and may actively seek to help them. (People frequently perceive the elderly and those with disabilities as falling into quadrant I.) The added perception of competence, however, produces quadrant II, containing those we like or admire—and with whom we want to associate. (This quadrant includes those with whom we identify or aspire to associate—perhaps pastors or rabbis, movie stars, sports heroes, or Bill Gates of Microsoft, and Mark Zuckerberg, founder of Facebook.)

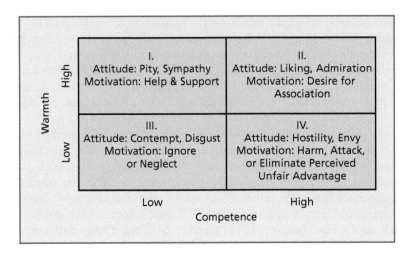

Now consider how we react to those we perceive as low in warmth. For those we pigeonhole in quadrant III—whom we perceive as being low in both warmth and competence—we feel disdain and a desire to avoid, ignore, or neglect them. (For many people, these would include members of some minority groups or welfare recipients.) But our most negative feelings are reserved for those we place in quadrant IV: people whom we perceive as privileged but somehow undeserving. For most of us, the occupants of quadrant IV provoke feelings of envy and the wish to "bring them down a notch or two"—perhaps even the desire to cause them harm. (Common examples might include politicians, lawyers, and the very rich.)

The authors of this research argue that group-based prejudices and stereotypes appear high on one of these two dimensions and low on the other, thereby creating ambivalent affect and volatile behavior that has the potential to endanger constructive intergroup relationships.

Cross-Cultural Research on the Need for Positive Self-Regard   Before moving on to the final section in our exploration of social psychology, it is important to consider a rather profound question about the self in relationship to others. Is it true that all people seek positive self-regard—that is, are all people motivated to possess, enhance, and maintain a positive self-concept? Is this a basic attribute of humankind? It would seem so if we consider what people around us do to enhance their self-esteem, the efforts made to be special, even through self-serving biases and personal affirmations. If we look around in North America, the answer might be different than if we look around in Japan.

Researchers have carefully examined both cultural contexts to identify how specific social environmental arrangements of their practices and institutions can promote and sustain the mentalities associated with self-regard. They have found that many aspects of life in North America lead both to an excessive focus on the self as an individual entity as well as encouraging motivation to regard one's self in positive ways, as special, unique, and entitled. This can be seen in ads, movies, songs, diaries, and many aspects of contemporary American culture. By contrast, what is more typical in Japanese culture is the development of a self-critical focus. Personal evaluation usually begins with a critique of the individual's performance or even lifestyle. That critical orientation is both self-effacing and humbling, thereby minimizing any tendency toward arrogance. However, its goal is to seek ways to improve one's attitudes and behaviors in constructive fashion, which satisfies both the individual's needs as well as that of the family, team, business, and the larger community. Such research is important in qualifying what appear to be universal aspects of human nature but are actually culturally specific (Heine et al., 1999).

Prejudice and Discrimination

While our attributions about others can be positive or negative, prejudice, as social psychologists use the term, always involves a negative judgment some people hold about other people. *Prejudice* can make an employer discriminate against women (or men) for a management job. It can make a teacher expect poor work from a minority student. And, in some places in the world, it has led to *genocide*, the systematic extermination of a group of people because of their racial or ethnic origins. We will define **prejudice** as negative attitudes, beliefs, and feelings toward an individual based solely on his or her membership in a particular group or category.

That category may be real, like gender or ethnicity, but it can also be created in the mind of the prejudiced person, such as considering some people as "poor white trash," or others as "left-wing liberals." Prejudice may be expressed as negative emotions (such as dislike or fear), negative attributions or stereotypes that justify the attitude, and/or attempts to avoid, control, dominate, or eliminate those in the target group. Prejudiced attitudes serve as extreme biasing filters that influence the way others are perceived and treated. Thus, prejudice exerts a powerful force for selectively processing, organizing, and remembering pertinent information about particular people. It is also pervasive; most people in most nations harbor prejudices of varying kinds, some conscious and some nonconscious (as new research is uncovering, to be treated later in this section).

Let's distinguish prejudice from *discrimination,* a related concept. While prejudice is an attitude, discrimination is a behavior. **Discrimination** can be defined as a negative *action* taken against an individual because of his or her group membership. Racial profiling, for example, is often considered a discriminatory procedure because it singles out individual people based solely on racial features. It can result in more arrests of minority members because police are more likely to confront them than majority members for their "suspicious behavior." But, while discrimination can arise from prejudice, we will see soon that this is not always the case. In this section, we will review the causes of prejudice, the role of dehumanization as a basic process in prejudice, and combating prejudice, and we will end with new research on stereotype threat. 👁

prejudice   A negative attitude toward an individual based solely on his or her membership in a particular group or category, often without any direct evidence.

discrimination   A negative action taken against an individual as a result of his or her group or categorical membership. It is the behavior that prejudice generates.

👁—**Watch** the **Video** about Prejudice at **MyPsychLab**

Causes of Prejudice   Prejudices can emerge from many sources (Allport, 1954; Aronson, 2004). Some we acquire at an early age. Some are defensive reactions when we feel threatened. Some are the result of conformity to social customs. And some help us distinguish strangers (and possible foes) from friends (Whitley, 1999). An understanding of these sources of prejudice will provide us with the foundation necessary for thinking about possible "cures," ways to combat these antisocial reactions. Here, we present five causes of prejudice that have been studied by social psychologists: *dissimilarity and social distance, economic competition, scapegoating, conformity to social norms,* and *media stereotyping.*

social distance   The perceived difference or similarity between oneself and another person.

Dissimilarity and Social Distance   If similarity breeds liking, then *dissimilarity* can breed disdain—and prejudice. So, if you wear baggy shorts, a baseball cap backwards, and a nose ring, it's a good bet that some middle-aged people from a traditional background would feel uncomfortable around you. They are likely to perceive you as a part of a social group that flaunts values and encourages "radical" behaviors quite distinct from those of their own group. Even small perceived differences in appearance can easily become fertile ground for the growth of prejudice.

What psychological principles are at work? When you perceive someone to be unlike the people in your in-group, you mentally place that person at a greater **social distance** than members of your own group. You are then less likely to view that individual as a social equal (Turner & Oakes, 1989). This inequality easily translates into inferiority, making it easier for you to treat members of an out-group with contempt. Historically, more powerful groups have discriminated against out-groups by withholding privileges, sending members of out-groups to different schools, making them sit in the back of the bus, forcing them into low-wage jobs, sending them to jail and into restrictive neighborhood ghettos, and otherwise violating their personal dignity.

Would your mother be pleased if you invited this teen to dinner in your home? If not, would that be a prejudice?

Economic Competition   A second cause of prejudice occurs in highly competitive situations, where one group wins economic benefits or jobs at the other group's expense, which can easily fan the flames of prejudice. For example, in the Pacific Northwest, where competition over old-growth forests threatens jobs and wildlife habitat, prejudice sets timber workers and environmentalists against each other. Likewise, surveys have found, for example, prejudice against Black Americans to be greatest among White groups poised at an economic level just above the Black American average—precisely the ones who would feel their jobs most threatened by Black Americans (Greeley & Sheatsley, 1971). It is often true that much prejudice exists not only down from those in privileged positions to those in minority positions but across minority groups, between recent immigrants from different countries, or when new immigrants threaten the financial security of established minorities.

This was the case in New York City's South Bronx area when, after World War II, thousands of migrants from Puerto Rico emigrated to that neighborhood (after a massive sugar crop failure and given free government airfare to the United States). They competed with Blacks living there and others coming back from war service for housing and low-level jobs. Researchers discovered high levels of antagonism and prejudice between these two minority groups, each struggling "to make it" in America and also coping with top-down prejudice against both of them by the majority White population (Zimbardo, 1953).

Scapegoating   To understand a third cause of prejudice, consider how the Hebrew priests of olden times performed a ritual that symbolically transferred the sins of the people to a goat—the *scapegoat*. The animal was then driven into the desert to carry its burden of guilt away from the community. The term *scapegoat* has been applied in modern times to an innocent person or group who receives blame when others feel threatened. On a large and horrifying scale, German Jews served as scapegoats for the Nazis in World War II. Hitler's propaganda program encouraged this by creating visual images of German Jews as totally different from the rest of the German population; such terrible images set them apart as the "faces of the enemy" (Keen, 1991). Such visual propaganda, that most nations use as a prelude to going to war, first creates an enemy that is hated by the general populace and then feared enough to want to destroy them or have one's son kill them as part of the army. This mentality is called the "hostile imagination" that creates a psychology of enmity—of instilling hatred of the "Other."

Scapegoating works most readily when the object of scorn is readily identifiable by skin color or some distinctive physical features or when media propaganda can create such differences in the minds of the dominant group (Sax, 2002). It also becomes more probable when conditions worsen in a neighborhood or a country, and people are seeking to blame someone for that change from the good old days to bad times.

Conformity to Social Norms   The source of discrimination and prejudice that is perhaps the most pervasive is an unthinking tendency to maintain conditions the way they are, even when those conditions involve unfair assumptions, prejudices, and customs. For example, in many offices, it is the norm for secretaries to be female and executives to be male. Only 18 percent of private corporations have women on their boards in the United States. That low percentage drops to 2 percent in Italy and less than 1 percent in Japan in 2008. In Arab nations, it would be rare to have any women in such positions unless they were relatives of the top executives. Because of this norm, it may be difficult for highly qualified women to break into the executive ranks, to breach the "glass ceiling" above them. We may find the same process where the norm says that nurses and lab technicians should be females and engineers and mathematicians should be males. When we see that most people in a given profession are of a particular gender or race, we assume that is the way of the world, the way the social order meant it to be, rather than considering the social and economic conditions that have made it that way. So when women note that most computer workers are males, they are likely to avoid taking computer science courses or going into such careers, which then become for "men only." The opposite is now true in psychology. The majority of students taking psychology courses, majoring in it, and going on in psychology careers are now women, a major gender reversal in the past decade. As our field becomes identified as

scapegoating   Blaming an innocent person or a group for one's own troubles and then discriminating against or abusing them.

Schoolchildren in Nazi Germany (1930s and 1940s) read textbooks describing Jews as inferior to the "Aryan race." Illustrations in those books also depicted Jewish children excluded from schools.

"women only," some psychologists worry that males will be even less likely to enter it, and salaries for all will decrease.

So we see, then, that a social norm develops for various reasons and it becomes the accepted standard of what is perceived as appropriate and "right." When that happens, behavioral discrimination itself can cause or reinforce prejudiced attitudes. Imagine that you were the male executive who discriminated against a woman applying for an executive position. Or imagine that you were the White bus driver in the 1950s South who routinely sent Black passengers to a special section in the back of the bus. In both cases, you were simply following the social norm of what others like you were all doing. However, you would have had to justify your own behavior to yourself and to others. And if you have just treated people as second-class citizens because of their gender or ethnicity, it will be difficult, perhaps impossible, for you to think of them as anything other than inferior beings (without having a severe attack of cognitive dissonance). In this way, your discriminatory behavior can cause or strengthen our prejudice attitudes. Because we are *rationalizing* creatures as much as *rational* ones, we endlessly justify our decisions and behavior to make them appear reasonable by generating "good reasons" for our bad behaviors (Tavris & Aronson, 2007).

Media Stereotypes   Our fifth cause of prejudice occurs when stereotyped images used to depict groups of people in film, in print, and on television reinforce prejudicial social norms. Such images are far from harmless, because people have learned many of their prejudices from the stereotypes they saw on TV and in books, movies, and magazines (Greenberg, 1986). On the other hand, images in the media can also change those norms. Until the Black Power movement gained media attention, Africans and African Americans were most often portrayed in movies and on TV as simple, slow, comic characters, perpetuating the "Sambo" image that many Whites held.

Fortunately, the most blatant racial stereotypes have disappeared from the national media in the past few decades. Media distortions still occur, of course, but they are subtler. Prime time features three times as many male as female characters (Aronson, 2004). Most are shown in professional and managerial positions, even though two-thirds of the U.S. workforce is employed in blue-collar and service jobs. The proportion of non-Whites and older persons who appear on TV is also much smaller than the general population. For viewers, the result is a biased picture of the world. This is where it becomes critical to have a variety of role models in the media that portray positions of influence and credibility to young people from those subgroups, such as women and ethnic/racial minority members as TV news anchors.

Dehumanization   The most powerful psychological process underlying prejudice, discrimination, and intergroup violence is *dehumanization*. It does so by causing some people to view others as less than human, even subhuman. **Dehumanization** can be defined as a psychological process that biases perception and cognitions of others in ways that deprive them of their humanity, rendering them totally dissimilar and worthless. It is the mechanism behind thinking of particular disliked other people as objects, as the enemy, as animals and insects. Just as a retinal cataract blurs one's visual field, dehumanization is like a "cortical cataract" that blinds the mind to any perceived similarity between Us and Them. Thinking about others as less than human means that one can suspend moral reasoning, empathy, compassion, and other processes that constrain hate and violence. It enables ordinary, even good, people to do bad, even evil deeds (Sherrer, 2008, Zimbardo, 2007).

A case in point of dehumanization in action occurred in 1994 in Rwanda, Africa. The Hutu government spread propaganda that the Tutsi people living there were the enemy of the Hutus; that they were insects, cockroaches, and had to be destroyed. Men armed with government-supplied machetes and women with clubs massacred 800,000 of their neighbors in 100 days (Hatzfeld, 2005). A powerful documentary of this dehumanization leading to genocide can be seen at www.pbs.org/wgbh/pages/frontline/shows/evil/.

Can such a complex psychological process be studied experimentally? Yes, indeed, and with a remarkably simple manipulation used by researcher Albert Bandura and his students (Bandura et al., 1975).

dehumanization   The psychological process of thinking about certain other people or groups as less than human, like feared or hated animals. A basic process in much prejudice and mass violence.

CONNECTION CHAPTER 10

Bandura pioneered the study of social models and observational learning (p. 442).

A small group of students from one college were supposed to be helping another group of students from a different local college to improve their decision-making skills. They were to provide standard problems to be solved collectively and then reward good solutions and punish bad ones. Punishment was via increasing levels of electric shock administered to the entire working group (no shocks were actually given; the participants only believed they were). The experimental manipulation consisted of the research assistant telling the experimenter that the students from the other school were ready to begin as the working group. Those who would do the shocking were randomly assigned to one of three conditions: Neutral, hearing only that the other students were ready; Dehumanizing, hearing that the other students seemed like "Animals," and Humanizing, hearing that the other students seemed like "Nice Guys." The results: Simply hearing others labeled "Animals" by a stranger and believing they were also college students was sufficient to induce the students in that condition to administer significantly more shock than in the Neutral condition, and increasingly so over the ten trials. The good news: Humanizing others resulted in significantly less punishment than in the control condition, where students had no information about those others. So sticks and stones may break your bones, but bad names and dehumanization might kill you.

Combating Prejudice   During the civil rights struggles of the 1950s and 1960s, educators believed that prejudice could be overcome through a gradual process of information campaigns and education. But experience provided no encouragement for this hope. In fact, these informational approaches are among the least effective tools for combating prejudice. The reason? Selective exposure! Prejudiced people (like everyone else) usually avoid information that conflicts with their view of the world, so they never watched or listened to those messages. Even for those who want to change their prejudiced attitudes, erasing the strong emotions and motivational foundations associated with long-standing prejudices is difficult with merely cognitively based informational messages (Devine & Zuwerink, 1994). The process is even more difficult for those who cherish their prejudices because their sense of self-worth is boosted by perceiving others as less worthy than them.

So, how can one attack the prejudices of people who do not want to listen to another viewpoint? Research in social psychology suggests several possibilities. Among them are the use of new role models, equal status contact, and (surprisingly) new legislation.

New Role Models   Former Secretary of State Condoleezza Rice, Hillary Clinton, Barack Obama, and many others serve as new role models in prestigious jobs and leadership positions where few of their race or gender have appeared before. These role models encourage people in these groups who might never have considered such careers. What we do not know much about, however, is the ability of role models to change the minds of people who are already prejudiced. It is likely that they are perceived as "exceptions to the rule"; but, as the exceptions increase, maybe the rule bends or changes. Role models may serve better to prevent prejudice than to cure it.

President Barack Obama and Supreme Court Judge Sonia Sotomayor are role models for minority youth from Black and Hispanic communities.

Equal Status Contact   Slave owners always had plenty of contact with their slaves, but they always managed to hang onto their prejudices. Obviously, mere contact with people from an out-group is not enough to erase in-group prejudices against them. Evidence, however, from integrated public housing (where the economic threat of lowered property values is not an issue) suggests that when people are placed together under conditions of equal status, where neither wields power over the other, the chances of developing understanding increase (Deutsch & Collins, 1951; Wilner et al., 1955). In an extensive review of all available literature, Tom Pettigrew (1998) found strong support for the power of equal-status contact to prevent and reduce prejudice among many different kinds of groups.

The Jigsaw Classroom   Although we said earlier that educational approaches to dealing with prejudice proved overly optimistic, one approach has been spectacularly successful. Social psychologist Elliott Aronson and his team showed that prejudice can be reduced in classrooms from grades 3 to 12 by substituting cooperative learning for the usual competitive style typical in traditional classrooms (Aronson, 1978; 1997). In Aronson's approach, the key is making each student an expert on one part of the lesson that all the other students in his or her group need for successful team performance. Every student becomes an integral part of the "jigsaw puzzle" that cannot be solved without their input. This strategy promotes active listening, group interaction, peer teaching, and enhanced appreciation of the value of students from minority groups who become equals in their knowledge of the new material that the rest of their team needs and comes to value. But how do we know that this approach actually reduces prejudice? Here is Aronson's response:

> Because we had randomly introduced the jigsaw intervention into some classrooms and not others, we were able to compare the progress of the jigsaw students with that of students in traditional classrooms. After only eight weeks there were clear differences, even though students spent only a small portion of their time in jigsaw groups. When tested objectively, jigsaw students expressed less prejudice and negative stereotyping, were more self-confident, and reported liking school better than children in traditional classrooms. Moreover, children in jigsaw classes were absent less often than were other students, and they showed greater academic improvement; poorer students in the jigsaw classroom scored significantly higher on objective exams than comparable students in traditional classes, while the good students continued to do as well as the good students in traditional classes (Aronson, 1978, p. 257).

Legislation   You can't legislate morality. Right? Wrong! One of the most convincing studies showing that the old cliché is wrong comes from an experiment done in the late 1940s, comparing the attitudes of White tenants toward Black tenants in public housing projects. In one project, White and Black occupants were assigned to different buildings; that is, the project was racially segregated. A second project mixed or integrated the two racial groups by assigning housing in the same buildings. Only in the racially integrated project did prejudicial attitudes sharply decrease (Deutsch & Collins, 1951). This result strongly suggests that rules requiring equal status contact can diminish prejudice.

This notion is reinforced by a larger social "experiment" that was done under far less controlled conditions. During the past 60 years, the United States has adopted laws abolishing racial discrimination. The consequences were sometimes violent, but prejudice and discrimination have gradually diminished. Nevertheless, evidence for a shift in prejudiced attitudes comes from polls showing that, initially, in the 1940s, fewer than 30 percent of White Americans favored desegregation. Yet that percentage has steadily climbed to well above 90 percent in this era (Aronson, 2004).

Because these changes in public opinion were not part of a carefully controlled experiment, we cannot say that the data prove that legislation has caused people's prejudices to diminish. Nevertheless, we can argue that the increased number of White Americans favoring desegregation is exactly what one might predict from cognitive dissonance theory: When the law requires people to act in a less discriminatory fashion, people have to justify their new behavior by softening their prejudiced attitudes. From this vantage point, it appears that legislation—when enforced—can affect prejudiced attitudes, after all. We now see that with dramatic changes in attitudes toward smoking and smokers following legal bans on smoking in many public venues.

Stereotype Threat   Who we think we are or how we think others see us may determine how we perform on various tests of ability. That principle emerges from a large body of research in this new area of social psychology, started by researcher Claude Steele, his colleagues, and students (Steele et al., 2002). **Stereotype threat** refers to the negative effect on performance that arises when an individual becomes aware that members of his or her group are expected to perform poorly in that domain. This research reveals that performance on both intellectual and athletic tasks is shaped by awareness of existing stereotypes about the groups to which one belongs. It happens even if the person does not believe the stereotype is true; what matters is that others do

stereotype threat   The negative effect on performance that arises when an individual becomes aware that members of his or her group are expected to perform poorly in that domain.

 **CONNECTION** CHAPTER 6

Stereotype threat has been shown to affect people's academic performance (p. 257).

and that the performer becomes aware that such a negative stereotype threatens his or her self-identity (Haslam et al., 2008).

So college women in a math course take a special math test and do as well as male students, unless they first have to check off the gender box: Female. When reminded of their gender, their performance becomes significantly poorer, confirming the stereotype about woman and math. Likewise, the stereotype of Blacks having lower IQ than Whites subconsciously creates anxiety that their performance will risk confirming this stereotype. That anxiety interferes with optimal cognitive processing and their positive self-identity, and they end up doing more poorly. Thus, making someone's identity salient, where a negative sterotype exists about its deficiency in some domain leads to diminished performance on a variety of tasks, from spatial reasoning to golf scores (see McGlone and Aronson, 2006; and Stone et al., 1996).

[PSYCHOLOGY MATTERS]

Stereotype Lift and Values Affirmations

The enhanced performance of a *reverse* stereotype—that makes you believe you are superior to another group on any dimension—is known as *"stereotype lift."* If Whites take a test they know to be evaluative of intellectual ability, or a test in which the negative stereotype of Blacks is made salient, they get a psychological edge from being on the upside of the negative stereotype and perform better (Walton & Cohen, 2003).

When people feel positively labeled with a stereotype, they also perform better, an effect known as "stereotype susceptibility." Accordingly, if Asian women taking a math test are required to focus on the fact that they are either woman or Asian, they do worse when reminded of their female status but better than the control condition of no identity focus when they are reminded of their Asian status (and the implicit stereotype of Asian math superiority). Again, here is stereotype lift at work. Thus, we can make stereotypes work for us as well as against our performance (Shih et al., 1999).

Could we use the notion of stereotype lift to counteract stereotype threat? Perhaps we encourage people to rediscover their best selves before tackling that challenging exam or course. How about having them affirm the values that matter most to them prior to being exposed to a course in which people like them often do not do well? More specifically, what would happen if women affirmed their values just prior to starting an introductory physics course, where typically the average grade for women is C level, while it is B for males? Such a study was conducted by Akira Miyake and his research team (Miyake et al., 2010), which confirmed that the gender gap in college science achievement could be reduced dramatically by a psychological intervention of values affirmation.

In this double-blind experiment, half of the male students ($n = 283$) and half of the females ($n = 116$) were randomly assigned to a writing exercise prior to the start of their introductory physics course that asked them to write about their most important values. To paraphrase the instructions: "Think about the things that are important to you. Perhaps you care about creativity, family relationships, your career, or having a sense of humor. Pick two or three of these values and write a few sentences about *why* they are important to you. You have fifteen minutes." For the Control condition, the other half of the students was told to think about their *least* important values and how they might relate to other people. The TAs who gave this writing exercise did not know it was related to the affirmation research, nor did any of the researchers know which students were assigned to the affirmation or control condition until the data were analyzed. Two types of data were used to evaluate the effectiveness of this values affirmation: Final grades, largely based on four exams, and a measure of understanding basic physics concepts, FMCE (force and motion conceptual evaluation). As can be seen in the graphed data in Figure 11.6, in the control group, men outperformed women by an average of 10 points, even when controlling for their prior achievement, but among the students who affirmed their own values, this gender gap nearly vanished. Those women who were self-affirmed got far more B grades, and far fewer got Cs. The same effect was found for the FMCE measure of understanding basic physics concepts.

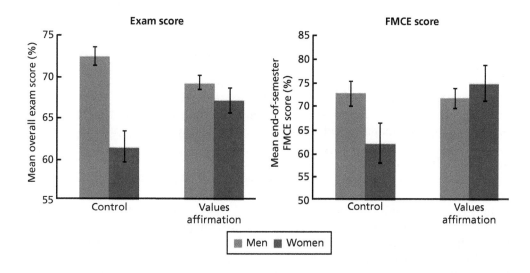

FIGURE 11.6

Values Affirmation Reduces Gender Gap in Physics Grades and Concept Knowledge

Thus, it is evident that a simple psychological intervention can have a major impact on the academic performance of women in the science subject of physics.

Geoffrey Cohen and colleagues established the power of values affirmations in earlier research with White and Black seventh graders, where Black students completing the exercise improved their grades significantly, and those who were low to moderate achievers beforehand improved the most (Cohen et al., 2006). There is even more good news: These gains can be sustained over several years with a few simple booster sessions where children write about a different value or delve more deeply into ones they had written about earlier (Cohen et al., 2009).

Check Your Understanding

✓•⎯Study and Review at MyPsychLab

1. **RECALL:** According to Aronson, we can explain almost everything about interpersonal attraction with a theory of

   a. love.
   c. genetic predispositions.
   b. rewards.
   d gender.

2. **RECALL:** Which of the following does the research say is most important in predicting initial attraction?

   a. physical attractiveness
   c. personality
   b. money
   d. nurturing qualities

3. **RECALL:** In trying to understand why Ron was late for an appointment, Jane blamed his lack of conscientiousness and ignored the facts of rush hour traffic and a major storm that hit town. Jane is guilty of

   a. the chameleon effect.
   b. the expectancy-value violation.
   c. scapegoating.
   d. fundamental attribution error.

4. **APPLICATION:** According to cognitive dissonance theory, which of the following would be the best strategy for getting people to like you?

   a. Give them presents.
   b. Show interest in their interests.
   c. Tell them that you like them.
   d. Persuade them to perform a difficult or unpleasant task for you.

5. **RECALL:** Prejudice is a(n) _____, while discrimination is a(n) _____ .

   a. behavior/attitude
   c. attitude/behavior
   b. instinct/choice
   d. stimulus/response

6. **RECALL:** The evidence suggests that one of the most effective techniques for eliminating racial prejudice has been

   a. education.
   c. legislation.
   b. threat and force.
   d. tax incentives.

7. **APPLICATION:** To reduce prejudice in a working group in a factory, which is the better strategy? (a) to make some usually discriminated-against workers feel special by giving them higher status or (b) create a jigsaw team in which they had special information to share with their group.

8. **UNDERSTANDING THE CORE CONCEPT:** Reward theory, expectancy-value theory, cognitive dissonance theory, and attribution theory all tell us that we respond not just to situations but to

   a. our cognitive interpretations.
   b. our social instincts.
   c. the intensity of the stimuli.
   d. our biological needs and drives.

Answers 1. b **2.** a **3.** d **4.** d **5.** c **6.** c **7.** b **8.** a

11.3 KEY QUESTION
How Do Systems Create Situations That Influence Behavior?

CONNECTION CHAPTER 13

Marriage counselors and family therapists often use a *systems* approach to understanding and resolving family conflicts (p. 567).

system power   Influences on behavior that come from top-down sources in the form of creating and maintaining various situations that in turn have an impact on actions of individuals in those behavioral contexts.

We spend most of our lives in various institutions—family, schools, hospitals, jobs, military, prison, elderly homes—and may end in a hospice. Each of these settings involves *systems* of management and control, explicit and implicit rules of conduct, and reward and punishment structures, and they come with a history, a culture, and a legal status. In many cases, it is **system power** that creates, maintains, and gives meaning and justification to a social situation. System power differs from social norms that come from within groups because this is top-down power to exercise control over groups and individuals. Although social psychologists have highlighted the influence of *situations* on behavior, as you have seen in this chapter, they have tended not to acknowledge the greater power that *systems* have to make those situations work as they do, sometimes for the better, but sometimes for the worse. This, then, leads us to the third lesson of social psychology, captured in our final Core Concept:

> ### Core Concept 11.3
> **Systems shape situations, which in turn affect behavior—and by understanding systems, we can learn how to change them and modify their influences on us.**

We will illustrate how system power can create a remarkably powerful social situation that affected the behavior of all within its behavioral context in research known as the **Stanford Prison Experiment.** Then, we will briefly examine other systems that have also generated abusive behavior, such as that in the Abu Ghraib prison in Iraq. Unfortunately, we do not have the space in this chapter to also illustrate in detail how network systems work for good causes. Here we are thinking about those involved in most nonviolent movements that train citizens in passive resistance, such as Gandhi in India, Martin Luther King, Jr. in the American civil rights struggle, and Nelson Mandela in opposing apartheid in South Africa. Similar system networks were critical for Christians who helped Jews escape the Nazi Holocaust.

Stanford Prison Experiment   Classic study of institutional power in directing normal, healthy college student volunteers playing randomly assigned roles of prisoners and guards to behave contrary to their dispositional tendencies, as cruel guards or pathological prisoners.

The Stanford Prison Experiment

On a summer Sunday in California, a siren shattered the serenity of college student Tommy Whitlow's morning. A city police car screeched to a halt in front of his home. Within minutes, Tommy was charged with a felony, informed of his constitutional rights, frisked, and handcuffed. After he was booked and fingerprinted at the city jail, Tommy was blindfolded and transported to the Stanford County Prison, where he was stripped and issued a smock-type uniform with an I.D. number on the front and back. Tommy became "Prisoner 8612." Eight other college students were also arrested and assigned numbers during that mass arrest by the local police.

The prison guards were anonymous in their khaki military uniforms, reflector sunglasses, and nameless identity as "Mr. Correctional Officer," but with symbols of power shown off in their big nightsticks, whistles, and handcuffs. To them, the powerless prisoners were nothing more than their worthless numbers.

The guards insisted that prisoners obey all of their many arbitrary rules without question or hesitation. Failure to do so led to losses of privileges. At first, privileges included opportunities to read, write, or talk to other inmates. Later, the slightest protest resulted in the loss of "privileges" of eating, sleeping, washing, or having visitors during visiting nights. Failure to obey rules also resulted in a variety of unpleasant tasks such as endless push-ups, jumping jacks, and number count-offs that lasted for hours on end. Each day saw an escalation of the level of hostile abuse by the guards against their prisoners: making them clean toilets with bare hands, doing push-ups while a guard stepped on the prisoner's back, spending long hours naked in solitary confinement, and finally engaging in degrading forms of sexual humiliation.

"Prisoner 8612" encountered some guards whose behavior toward him and the other prisoners was sadistic, taking apparent pleasure in cruelty; others were just tough and demanding; a few were not abusive. However, none of the few "good" guards ever challenged the extremely demeaning actions of the "perpetrators of evil."

Less than 36 hours after the mass arrest, "Prisoner 8612," who had become the ringleader of an aborted prisoner rebellion that morning, had to be released because of an extreme stress reaction of screaming, crying, rage, and depression. On successive days, three more prisoners developed similar stress-related symptoms. A fifth prisoner developed a psychosomatic rash all over his body when the parole board rejected his appeal, and he too was released from the Stanford County Jail.

Everyone in the prison, guard and prisoner alike, had been selected from a large pool of student volunteers. On the basis of extensive psychological tests and interviews, the volunteers had been judged as law-abiding, emotionally stable, physically healthy, and "normal-average" on all personality trait measures. In this mock prison experiment, assignment of participants to the independent variable treatment of "guard" or "prisoner" roles had been determined randomly. Thus, in the beginning, there were no systematic differences between the "ordinary" college males who were in the two different experimental roles of prisoner or guard. By the end of the study, there were no similarities between these two alien groups. The prisoners lived in the jail around the clock, and the guards worked standard 8-hour shifts.

As guards, students who had been pacifists and "nice guys" in their usual life settings behaved aggressively—sometimes even sadistically. As prisoners, psychologically stable students soon behaved pathologically, passively resigning themselves to their unexpected fate of learned helplessness. The power of the simulated prison situation had created a new social reality—a functionally real prison—in the minds of both the jailers and their captives. The situation became so powerfully disturbing that the researchers were forced to terminate the 2-week study after only 6 days.

Although Tommy Whitlow said he wouldn't want to go through it again, he valued the personal experience because he learned so much about himself and about human nature. Fortunately, he and the other students were basically healthy, and extensive debriefing showed that they readily bounced back from the prison experience. Follow-ups over many years revealed no lasting negative effects on these students. The participants had all learned an important lesson: Never underestimate the power of a bad situation to overwhelm the personalities and good upbringing of even the best and brightest among us, and of a system to create such situations (Zimbardo, 2007).

The basic results of this study were replicated in cross-cultural research in Australia (Lovibond et al., 1979). However, there was never the same degree of violence exhibited by the guards, perhaps because this study followed the cultural norm of everyone having afternoon teatime! For detailed information about this dramatic study and many related issues, see www.prisonexp.org.

Scenes from the Stanford Prison Experiment

Suppose you had been a subject in the Stanford Prison Experiment. Would you have been a good guard—or a sadist? Would you be a model compliant prisoner—or a rebel? Could you have resisted the pressures and stresses of these circumstances? It is a similar question raised about how you think you might have behaved if you were the "Teacher" in the Milgram obedience research—obey or defy? We'd all like to believe we would be good guards and heroic prisoners; we would never step across that line between good and evil. And, of course, we all believe that we would be able to keep things in perspective, knowing that it was "just an experiment," only role playing and not real. But the best bet is that most of us would react the same way as these participants did. This disturbing study raises many questions about how well we really know ourselves, our inner dispositional qualities, and how much we appreciate the subtle powers of external forces on us, the situational qualities. Obviously, it also raises ethical issues about whether such research should have ever been done or allowed to continue.

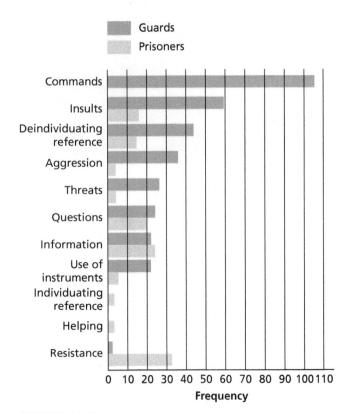

FIGURE 11.7

Guard and Prisoner Behavior

Source: Gerrig, R. J. & Zimbardo, P. G. (2008). *Psychology and Life.* 18th ed. Boston, MA: Allyn and Bacon. Copyright © 2008 by Pearson Education. Reprinted by permission of the publisher.

By the conclusion of the Stanford Prison Experiment, guards' and prisoners' behavior differed from each other in virtually every observable way (see Figure 11.7). Yet, it was only chance, in the form of random assignment, that had decided their roles—roles that had created status and power differences that were validated in the prison situation and supported by the system of prison authorities. No one taught the participants to play their roles. Without ever visiting real prisons, all the participants had earlier in their lives learned information about the interaction between the powerful and the powerless. A guard type is someone who limits the freedom of prisoner types to manage their behavior and make them behave more predictably. This task is aided by the use of coercive rules, which include explicit punishment for violations. Prisoners can only react to the social structure of a prisonlike setting created by those with power. Rebellion and compliance are the only options of the prisoners; the first choice results in punishment, while the second results in a loss of autonomy and dignity.

The student participants had already experienced such power differences in many of their previous social interactions in various systems of control: parent–child, teacher–student, doctor–patient, boss–worker, male–female. They merely refined and intensified their prior patterns of behavior for this particular setting. Each student could have played either role. Many students in the guard role reported being surprised at how easily they enjoyed controlling other people. The toughest guard recalled later for a TV documentary that the guards were like puppeteers pulling the strings of their prisoner-puppets—and "getting our jollies off" in the process. Just putting on the uniform was enough to transform them from passive college students into aggressive prison guards.

Milgram's obedience research and the Stanford Prison Experiment form bookends of much research, illustrating the power of situations over behavior. However, the obedience studies were about *individual* authority power, while the prison experiment is about the power of an institution, a *system* of domination. The guards maintained the situation of abuse, but so did the research team of psychologists; the police contributed to its reality, as did many others who visited the prison setting—a prison chaplain, a public defender, parents and friends on visiting nights, and civilians on the parole board.

Chains of System Command

Psychologists seek to understand behavior in order to promote prosocial forms and alter for the better antisocial aspects of behavior. Understanding why some people engage in "bad behaviors" does not excuse them; rather, it leads to new ideas about changing the causal influences on those behaviors. A full understanding of most complex human behavior should include an appreciation of the ways in which situational conditions are created and shaped by higher-order factors—*systems of power.* Systems, not just dispositions and situations, must be taken into account in order to understand complex behavior patterns.

Aberrant, illegal, or immoral behavior by individuals in service professions, such as policemen, corrections officers, or soldiers, or even in business settings, is typically labeled the misdeeds of "a few bad apples." The implication is they are a rare exception and must be set on one side of the impermeable line between evil and good, with the majority of good apples set on the other side. But who is making that distinction? Usually it is the guardians of the system—who want to isolate the problem to deflect attention and blame away from those at the top who may be responsible for creating impossible working conditions or for a lack of their oversight or supervision. Again the *bad apple-dispositional view* ignores the *bad apple barrel-situational view* and its potentially corrupting situational impact on those within it. A systems analysis focuses on the next step higher, on *the bad barrel makers-systemic view*, on those with the power to design the barrel. It is the "power elite," the barrel makers, often working behind the scenes, who arrange many of the conditions of life for the rest of us who must spend time in the variety of institutional settings they have constructed.

The Situation and the System at Abu Ghraib Prison   The world became aware of the abuses of Iraqi prisoners by American Military Police guards in **Abu Ghraib Prison** with the April 2004 televised exposure of horrific images that they had taken (see one such image on this page).

Immediately, the military chain of command dismissed it all as the work of a few rogue soldiers, while the president's chain of command likewise blamed it on a few bad apples. Both systems were quick to assert that it was not systemic, not occurring in other military prisons. However, investigative reporter Seymour Hersh (2004a) exposed the lie in that attribution with his analysis of the culpability of both of those systems of power, those chains of "irresponsible" command. The title of his May 5, 2004, article in *The New Yorker* was "Torture at Abu Ghraib. American soldiers brutalize Iraqis: How far up does the responsibility go?" His answer: all the way to the top of the military and civilian system of command (see also Hersh, 2004b).

A review of the dozen reports investigating these abuses, most written by generals and government officials, clearly highlights the situational influences on American Army Reserve soldiers from their impossible working conditions in the Abu Ghraib dungeon. What is now obvious is that these influences were made possible by systemic failures of military leadership and surveillance. In fact, these reports highlight many situational and system failures, as well as personal moral failures of the soldiers involved (Zimbardo, 2007). In sum, there were three processes interacting at Abu Ghraib: dispositional, situational, and systemic processes. Tragically, similar abuses in military prisons and other war zones have occurred before, during, and after the revelation of events at Abu Ghraib.

The Systems Lesson   The most important lesson to be learned from the Core Concept for this section is that *situations are created by systems*. Systems provide the institutional support, authority, and resources that allow situations to operate as they do. System power involves authorization or institutionalized permission to behave in prescribed ways or to forbid and punish actions that are disapproved. It provides the "higher authority" that gives validation to playing new roles, following new rules, and taking actions that would ordinarily be constrained by existing laws, norms, morals, and ethics. Such validation usually comes cloaked in the mantle of ideology. Ideology is a slogan or proposition that usually legitimizes whatever means are necessary to attain an ultimate goal. The programs, policies, and standard operating procedures that are developed to support an ideology become an essential component of the system. The system's procedures are considered reasonable and appropriate as the ideology comes to be accepted as sacred.

However, although all systems involve individuals at varying levels of power and status, most systems are not transparent, concealing much of their operation from outsiders. So even when a system is failing to meet its objectives and goals, as many failing educational or correctional systems are (as well as corporations that engage in corrupt practices), higher-ups are hidden from public scrutiny.

Nevertheless, to change undesirable behavior and promote more socially desirable behavior, it is *not* sufficient to continue to rely on the individualistic medical model of treating people (or disciplining) individuals for problem behavior when the situation might be a fault. And plans to improve situations must involve understanding and modifying the systems that create and maintain them. Instead, our call is for using a *public health model* that recognizes individual affliction and illness as the consequence of a vector of disease in society. *Prevention* rather than just treatment becomes the goal; inoculating against a virus prevents the spread of an epidemic. This should be as true for the evils of prejudice, violence, and bullying in our society as it is for viral infections.

Abu Ghraib Prison   Prison in Iraq made famous by revelation of photos taken by Army Reserve MP guards in the acts of humiliating and torturing prisoners.

One of the many photos taken by American Military Police guards at Abu Ghraib Prison in Iraq

Using Psychology to Understand the Abuses at Abu Ghraib Over a 3-month period, Military Police, Army Reservists, working the night shift at Tier 1-A in that dungeon, used some of the 1,000 prisoners detained there as their "playthings"—piling them naked in pyramids, hanging them upside down with women's panties over their heads, dragging them around the ground on dog leashes, and sexually degrading them in various ways. Tier 1-A was the interrogation center run by Military Intelligence, the CIA, and a civilian interrogator contractor. When the unexpected insurgency against the U.S. forces suddenly escalated, the chain of command needed "actionable intelligence" from these detainees. So the Military Police prison guards were given permission by higher-ups to "soften up" the prisoners, to prepare them for interrogation, to "take the gloves off."

Given that official permission for abuse, and with no senior officer ever providing oversight or surveillance of that night shift, all hell broke loose. However, the soldiers did not think what they were doing was wrong; one said it was only "fun and games." In fact, they documented these games with their own candid photographs of themselves with their abused prisoners in hundreds of horrific images.

One investigating committee was headed by James Schlesinger, former Secretary of Defense, and included generals and other high-ranking officials. The report notes the relevance of social psychological research and theory to the understanding of these abuses:

> The potential for abusive treatment of detainees during the Global War on Terrorism was entirely predictable based on a fundamental understanding of the principles of social psychology coupled with an awareness of numerous known environmental risk factors. . . . Findings from the field of social psychology suggest that the conditions of war and the dynamics of detainee operations carry inherent risks for human mistreatment, and therefore must be approached with great caution and careful planning and training.
>
> Such conditions neither excuse nor absolve the individuals who engaged in deliberate immoral or illegal behaviors [even though] certain conditions heightened the possibility of abusive treatment.

Schlesinger Report   Report issued by one of the official investigations of the Abu Ghraib Prison abuses, headed by James Schlesinger, former Secretary of Defense. It highlighted the social psychological factors that contributed to creating an abusive environment.

The ***Schlesinger Report*** boldly proclaims that the "landmark Stanford study provides a cautionary tale for all military detention operations." In contrasting the relatively benign environment of the Stanford Prison Experiment, the report makes evident that "in military detention operations, soldiers work under stressful combat conditions that are far from benign." The implication is that those combat conditions might be expected to generate even more extreme abuses of power by military police than were observed in our mock prison experiment. The *Schlesinger Report* concludes with a statement that underscores much of what we have presented in this chapter: "Psychologists have attempted to understand how and why individuals and groups who usually act humanely can sometimes act otherwise in certain circumstances." Among the concepts this report outlines to help explain why abusive behaviors occur among ordinarily humane individuals are deindividuation, dehumanization, enemy image, groupthink, moral disengagement, social facilitation, and other environmental factors.

There are fewer more direct statements that we are aware of that highlight the value of psychological theories and social psychological research than this official government report. The full report, and especially Appendix G, which is notable for students of psychology, can be found at: www.prisonexp.org/pdf/SchlesingerReport.pdf.

Preventing Bullying by Systemic Changes and Reframing

Bullying in school and in the workplace is primarily about some students and workers making life miserable for others by extreme teasing, threatening, physically abusing, and damaging personal reputations through lies and gossip. Most other students and coworkers who are neither bullies nor victim but bystanders aware of the problem yet usually ignore it or passively accept it (see Coloroso, 2008). The traditional method for dealing with bullies is to identify the culprits and punish them in various ways, moving them to other classes, schools, or jobs. This is likely to move the abusers and their abuse to different venues but not change them; often it makes them even angrier and vengeful. **Bullying** is defined as systematically and chronically inflicting physical hurt and/or psychological distress on one or more others, whether they are students in school or workers in the workplace.

In the 1990s, statistics on the prevalence of bullying revealed it was relatively low in Sweden, with an estimated 15 percent of all Swedish schoolchildren being bullied or admitting to being bullies themselves (Olweus, 1993). However, a more recent survey documented a dramatically higher prevalence in Britain with 73 percent of a British sample reporting being bullied, being the bully perpetrator, or having witnessed bullying directly (McLeod, 2008). This large-scale study included nearly 2,000 students, aged 12 through 19, across 14 schools. In a 2010 survey of 43,000 high school students in the United States, half said they've bullied someone in the past year, and nearly half said they'd been physically abused, teased, or taunted in a way that seriously upset them (Dalton, 2010). Among the negative fallout of bullying is shown in the estimated 160,000 students who have refused to go to school because of the possible physical and verbal aggression of their peers (as reported at www.nobully.com). 📖

bullying The act of tormenting others, in school classrooms or work settings, by one or more others, for personal, sadistic pleasure. It qualifies as a form of ordinary or everyday evil.

📖 **Read** about Preventing Bullying at **MyPsychLab**

What Does Bullying Look Like Today? Below are the most frequently experienced types:

- **Physical bullying:** Direct physical force is used to hurt someone else by hitting, pushing, shoving, kicking, pinching, or holding them down. Physical bullying also includes taking or breaking someone's belongings or stealing or extorting money.
- **Verbal bullying:** Use of words to hurt someone. This includes threatening, taunting, intimidating, insulting, sarcasm, name calling, teasing, slurs, graffiti, put-downs, and ridicule. It also includes hostile gestures such as making faces, staring, giving the evil eye, eye-rolling, and spitting.
- **Relational bullying:** Leaving someone out of a group or purposely excluding them, gossiping, teasing, whispering, and spreading rumors. It includes turning your back on someone else, giving them the silent treatment, ostracizing, or scapegoating.
- **Cyberbullying:** Use of cell-phones, text messages, e-mails, instant messages, web blogs, and postings to bully another student in any of the ways described above. Examples of cyberbullying are sending threatening or insulting messages by phone and e-mail and spreading destructive rumors that ruin the reputation of a fellow student or worker.
- **Harassment:** Offensive and possibly threatening behavior including the use of extreme verbal language, offensive questions or statements, stalking, physical force, or unwanted sexual advances. Sexual harassment is persistent and unwanted sexual advances, where the consequences of refusing could be harmful to the victim. Usually harassment is a repeated set of actions, but not always.

Bullying can occur just about everywhere: in any kind of school—poor or wealthy, public or private, single-sex or co-educational, conservative or progressive. It happens in or outside the classroom, in the workplace, and online. Boys and girls are equal targets of bullying. In most cases, boys bully other boys, and girls bully other girls. As Evelyn Field (2007), author of *Bully Blocking: Six Secrets to Help Children Deal with Teasing and Bullying*, explained:

> Bullying is a game where some children systematically abuse their power. Bullies can go on a shopping spree at the beginning of every year looking for suitable targets . . . Boys often use bullying tactics to make a reputation and girls do so to protect their reputation. Boys tend to be hunters who belong to large, hierarchical tribes. They typically bully openly and prefer physical bullying. They focus upon individual achievement and action, supported by their physical

prowess. They are less interested in teasing, exclusion and indirect bullying [tactics favored by girls] (pp. 7, 8).

Some argue that bullying is no worse than it used to be and kids today should just "suck it up," while others are convinced bullies are going too far. Recently bullying has become an international concern due to escalated violence and a number of teen suicides traced to cyberbullying. Though "technology is not radically changing what's happening, it's simply making what's happening far more visible," says social media researcher Danah Boyd (Leach, 2010); it is difficult to deny the impact the Internet has had on the bullying landscape. Because of the permeability and reach of the Net as well as anonymity of users, dehumanization has not only become easier, the impact has become greater and even lethal.

Prevention of bullying requires switching from the usual punishment model of bullies to a systemwide set of practices that give zero tolerance for bullying. The impetus for change must come top-down from school superintendents and principals, involving teachers and parents, and then enabling students themselves as agents of change (Kalman, 2008). Researcher Dan Olweus (1993) has used such a system change model in Sweden and other Scandinavian countries with considerable success. In the United States, students who seem "different," are more shy, have physical handicaps, and are gay or have alternative sexual orientations are bullied. "Actual or perceived sexual orientation is one of the most common reasons that students are harassed by their peers, second only to physical appearance," according to psychologist Peter Goldbaum (Novotney, 2008). At the core of new programs to combat and prevent bullying is developing curricula and practices from elementary school throughout all grades that promote respect for the dignity of individuals and for acceptance and tolerance of human diversity.

For bullying issues that can revolve around the target's image, your authors advocate changing the self-image and sense of helplessness of those individuals. They can learn to stop communicating through body language that they are vulnerable targets. They can be taught how to cultivate positive self-esteem, new body language, and effective social communication skills as well as ways to get more social support from their peers. In their book, *Stick Up For Yourself: Every Kid's Guide to Personal Power and Positive Self-Esteem*, Gershen Kaufman and his colleagues (1999) explain:

> Positive self-esteem is the single most important psychological skill we can develop in order to thrive in society. Having self-esteem means being proud of ourselves and experiencing that pride from within. Without self-esteem, kids doubt themselves, cave in to peer pressure, feel worthless or inferior . . . With self-esteem, kids feel secure inside themselves, are more willing to take positive risks, are more likely to take responsibility for their actions, can cope with life's changes and challenges, and are resilient in the face of rejection, disappointment, failure, and defeat (p. ii).

Note: Self-esteem should not be confused with arrogance, contempt, or a big ego. People who have positive self-esteem don't depend on what other people think of them because they are confident of their worth and happy in their own skins.

Historically, bullies were viewed as having various mental health deficiencies, but new research reveals a very different social dynamic is operating. Many people bully others as a means to climb the social hierarchy among their peers. Most bullying is occurring among students who are in the middle to upper ranges of social status in their schools. It is not happening at the highest or lowest status levels. A research team of sociologists followed approximately 3,700 U.S. students in grades 8 to 10 for one school year, identifying acts of social aggression and relating them to indices of social status (Faris & Felmlee, 2011). Each student was asked to list five students who had been mean to them or picked on them, with aggression defined as activities intending to cause harm or pain, physically or emotionally. Status was established as how central a student was in friendship networks where each student nominated his or her five best friends. Those with highest status have no need to bully anyone, and those with lowest status don't have the social power to pull off being aggressive.

[PSYCHOLOGY MATTERS]

Using Psychology to Learn Psychology

You may associate persuasion with advertising and politics, but persuasion does not stop there. It is woven into all human interaction—including the exchanges of ideas that occur in the classroom. There, your professors and fellow students will attempt to persuade you with reasoned arguments, and they will expect you to set out your points of view in the same fashion. But, aside from the open exchange of ideas and opinions, there are other, more subtle persuasive pressures of which you should be aware, says social psychologist Robert Cialdini (2001a). If you don't know about these, you run the risk of letting other people make up your mind for you. We will discuss three such subtle forms of influence that you will encounter in your college or university experience.

Social Validation

Although you may see a popular movie because your friends like it, going along with the crowd is a poor basis for judging the theories you encounter in your classes. Many of the world's discarded ideas were once accepted by nearly everyone. In psychology, these include the false notions that we use only 10 percent of our brain, that personality is determined by the first 2 years of life, and that IQ tests are a good measure of innate abilities. So, rather than accepting what you hear and read, questioning even the most widely held concepts is a good habit. In fact, most famous scientists have built their careers on challenging ideas that everyone else accepted.

Authority

The lectures you hear and the textbooks you read are full of authority figures. Every parenthetical reference in this text, for example, cites an authority. Most are given, in part, to persuade you that the argument being offered is credible. The problem, of course, is that ideas are not true merely because some authority says so. For example, just a few years ago, every introductory psychology text in print taught that no new neurons were created in the brain after birth. Now we know that the textbooks and the experts they cited were wrong. Real proof of such assertions, however, requires more objective evidence obtained by the scientific method—not just the declaration of an authority.

The Poison Parasite Argument

In advertising, a good way to undermine a competitor, says Cialdini, is with a message that calls into question the opponent's credibility. Then, to get people to remember what you have said, you can infect your opponent with a "parasite"—a mnemonic link that reminds people of your message every time they hear your opponent's pitch (Brookhart, 2001). A classic example involved antismoking ads that looked like Marlboro commercials, except that they featured a coughing, sickly "Marlboro Man." You may encounter the same sort of poison parasite argument in a lecture or a textbook that attempts to hold someone's ideas up to ridicule. That's not necessarily bad: In the academic world, weak ideas should perish. The sneaky, dishonest form of this technique, however, involves a misrepresentation or oversimplification of the opponent's arguments. The antidote is to be alert for ridicule and to check out the other side of the argument yourself.

The social psychology of persuasion, of course, involves much more than we have discussed here. A good place to look for more information is Cialdini's (2007) book *Influence: The Psychology of Persuasion*. Perhaps the most important idea is that some knowledge of persuasion can forearm you against the persuasive techniques you will encounter, both in and out of the classroom. When you know how effective persuaders operate—as "influence professionals," you are less likely to donate money to causes you don't care about, buy a car you don't really like, or accept a theory without examining the evidence critically.

Check Your Understanding

✓● Study and Review at MyPsychLab

1. **RECALL:** The Stanford prison experiment illustrates the power of _____ to influence people's behavior.

   a. personality   **c.** childhood experiences
   b. heredity   **d.** the situation

2. **RECALL:** What was the independent variable in the Stanford Prison Experiment?

   a. random assignment to prisoner or guard roles
   b. IQ level differences of those in the two roles
   c. cultural backgrounds of the volunteers
   d. all of the above

3. **RECALL:** The abuses perpetrated by the MPs at Abu Ghraib Prison were blamed entirely on the soldiers as symptoms of their being "bad apples." Who is *least* likely to make such a negative dispositional attribution?

   a. a social psychologist
   b. a trial lawyer for the prosecution
   c. military leaders
   d. civilian chain of command leaders

4. **UNDERSTANDING THE CORE CONCEPT:** If you wanted to stop bullying in your school, what would most likely be an effective strategy to follow?

   a. Punish the bully publicly.
   b. Teach the victim to fight back.
   c. Reward the bully for not bullying any victims.
   d. Change the entire school system to have zero tolerance for bullying.

Answers 1. d 2. a 3. a 4. d

CRITICAL THINKING APPLIED

Is Terrorism "a Senseless Act of Violence, Perpetrated by Crazy Fanatics"?

The terrorist attacks of September 11, 2001, and suicide bombings in Israel, Iraq, London, Madrid, and elsewhere around the world raise questions for which there are no easy answers. *Terrorism* is really about psychology. It typically involves a relatively small group of people working as a network who take dramatic, violent actions against a larger group with the intention of spreading fear of death among them and inducing anxiety and uncertainty about their government's ability to protect them. Terrorists do not want to conquer other nations' land, as in traditional wars, but to conquer the minds of their enemies by making them feel victimized and fearful of random attacks.

What Are the Critical Issues?

Global terrorism is an escalating threat that many nations must face in the coming years. Terrorists operate in networks that vary in their degree of organization, but they are not national states. A war against terrorism is an *asymmetrical war,* of nations against collectives of individuals, without uniforms or designated sovereign territories. Their tactics are hit and run, attacking at random times, amplifying the surprise value of their destructive power.

Some of the critical issues for you to consider include the following. How can a war against terrorism ever be "won"? What would winning actually look like if there were no one leader to surrender? Why is the best strategy for meeting this global challenge international cooperation and intelligence resource sharing rather than dominant nations acting unilaterally? What is the pipeline that is generating so many terrorists? In what sense can the threat of terrorism be reduced by "winning the hearts and minds" of young people who might be recruited by elders to join terrorist cells or be trained to become suicide bombers?

What Critical Thinking Questions Should We Ask?

The reasons for terrorist violence are many and complex. However, media sources of such claims try to simplify complexity and reduce ambiguity to simple frameworks. They often exaggerate fears for viewers and listeners. "If it bleeds, it leads," is a classic statement about what it takes to be the lead TV news item (see Breckenridge & Zimbardo, 2006, about mass-mediated fear). When they or the general public do not understand something, there is a readiness to label it "senseless." That only means it does not make sense to them or that there is no solid evidence for the motivations behind it. For example, vandalism has been called senseless until it becomes apparent that it is often done by have-nots who are trying to make an impact on society, a destructive, dramatic one when they are not able to make a more constructive one. As citizens and critical thinkers, we need to call for better information from our politicians, educators, journalists, and others who may try to assign easy answers to complex problems.

Is the Claim Reasonable or Extreme?   Obviously this is an extreme generalization and simplification of a complex social-political-cultural issue. Unfortunately, the easiest and most simplistic response is to demonize those who perpetrate evil deeds—but that is merely name calling, and we should resist it, not to excuse it but to learn what factors lead to such deeds. Mere name calling blinds us to the power of the situation to create aggression in ordinary people, as we have seen in the Milgram and Stanford Prison research. More important, it prevents us from dealing with the situations that nurture violence. Labeling others as "evil" or "pathological" usually prevents any attempt to understand the reasons for their actions, instead making them into objects of scorn or disdain. Again, it is a related mistake to think of violence and terrorism as "senseless." On the contrary, destructive deeds always make sense from the perpetrator's frame of reference. As Shakespeare's Hamlet said, there is "method" in madness: We must understand the method in the minds of potential terrorists if we are to deter them.

What Is the Evidence?   A summary of recent perspectives on what moves people to kill themselves and innocent bystanders is available in a thorough report by *New York Times* correspondent Sarah Kershaw (2010). Research has shown that aggressive behavior can be induced by situations that create prejudice, conformity, frustration, threat, or wounded pride (Aronson, 2004; Baumeister et al., 1996). There is no evidence that terrorists, even suicide bombers, are pathological. Rather, they are filled with anger and desire for revenge against what they perceive as injustice. They are often well educated, in stable relationships, and now likely to be from both sexes. In many cases, they become part of a systematic training program to learn the skills necessary to effectively destroy one's perceived enemy and accept being a martyr for a cause they believe is just (Merari, 2006).

The flammable combination of poverty, powerlessness, and hopelessness is the tinder that the September 11 attacks were intended to ignite, says Jonathan Lash (2001), president of the World Resources Institute in Washington, D.C. Much of the world lives in poverty and hunger and sees no way out. Ethnic hatred and wars aggravate their plight. Moreover, the number of people living in these miserable conditions is increasing, as most of the world's population explosion is occurring in poorer countries. And, to make matters more volatile, says Lash, a large proportion of these desperate people depend directly on resources that are rapidly being depleted: fisheries, forests, soils, and water resources. As a result, every day, thousands flee their traditional homelands and stream into the largest and poorest cities. Most are young—a result of the high birth rates in the Third World. Mr. Lash warns that urban slums, filled with restless, jobless young men, are "tinderboxes of anger and despair; easy recruiting grounds for bin Laden or those who may come after him" (p. 1789). We have seen this in recent violent riots in the slums outside Paris by young immigrants without jobs and educational opportunities.

Could Bias Contaminate the Conclusion?   Several biases are at work here: first, the dispositional bias of focusing on individual perpetrators and ignoring their behavioral context, the situation, and the system that gives shape and purpose to their actions; second, a simplification bias that reduces difficult, complex issues to simple terms that give an illusion of easy solutions. The reasoning behind making and accepting this assertion about terrorism and terrorists includes giving in to common fallacies, as we have seen. Combating it involves understanding the immediate causal contributions leading to becoming a terrorist as well as the broader systemic influences on such extreme decisions that individuals and groups make.

What Conclusions Can We Draw?

Understanding terrorism requires the combined insights of many perspectives—and not just those from psychology. Issues of money, power, resources, and ancient grudges must be considered as well. But—like it or not—many people in the world perceive the United States as the enemy. Understanding this perception—and dealing constructively with it—demands that Americans see the conflict from someone else's point of view: those who consider the United States to be the enemy.

We must also realize that terrorism does not always involve international conflict. Just consider the student shootings at Columbine High, Virginia Tech University, and the mass murders and wounding of innocent civilians as recently as early 2011 in Tucson, Arizona, along with thousands of racial/ethnic hate crimes, attacks against gays, and violence directed at abortion providers that have made news in recent years (Doyle, 2001). It would be a mistake to believe that terrorism is always an outside threat from foreigners: Even though some cultures are more violent than others, every culture can breed violent people who terrorize others (Moghaddam et al., 1993; Shiraev & Levy, 2001). Just remember that the bomber who blew up the Oklahoma City federal building and killed hundreds of innocent people was an American terrorist named Timothy McVeigh. The Ku Klux Klan was (is) a uniquely American terrorist organization acting in violent ways to instill fear and terror in Blacks and others they considered their enemy.

Supplementing Psychology with a Cross-Cultural and Historical Perspective   A complete picture of terrorism, however, necessitates taking perspectives that extend beyond psychology (Segall et al., 1999). When we expand our view of terrorism, we can see that long-standing hostilities arise from religious, ethnic, and racial prejudices and from poverty, powerlessness, and hopelessness. To arrive at this understanding, however, we must view terrorism from historical, economic, and political perspectives—again, not to excuse violent acts but to understand their origins. We cannot understand, for example, the tensions between Christianity and Islam without knowing about the 200-year war that the Western world calls the Crusades (1095 to 1291) or the fall of the six-centuries-old Ottoman Empire (1300 to 1922) at the end of World War I. Although such events may seem remote, they changed the trajectory of history, and their religious significance continues to fuel conflict in the Middle East today. The role of cultural values in terrorism is outlined in a recent issue of the American Psychological Association's *Monitor on Psychology* by reporter Tori DeAngelis (2009), in which she summarizes the views of Iranian-American psychologist Fathali Moghaddam (2007) and others.

Exercise: Creating a Terrorist Mindset   How might it be possible to create a class exercise that enables students to get a sense of what it feels like to adopt the mentality of a destructive terrorist? How about creating terrorist cells of all students in a course, each of which has the mission to blow up a building on the campus that they think should be destroyed. Well, not really flamed out, but symbolically destroyed.

Zimbardo did such a class exercise recently by dividing 100 students into 20 terrorist cells of five students in each. Their mission was to agree on a campus target building, justify its destruction, check out security, plan a time of attack, then post a 3-foot duct tape cross prominently on the target, poise in front of it for 5 minutes, record it in a photo or video, and if not arrested, they had succeeded as effective terrorists.

Of course, life is not that simple for terrorists because there are spies and counter-agents of the enemy. So in this demonstration, the students were informed that some cells might include spies—in fact, each of them had a fellow student instructed to be a spy—collecting hard data on the cell by means of concealed audio recordings or e-mails and similar tactics. That data were then turned over to the class TAs, who would use it to intercept the terrorist plans before they could be enacted. Half the cells effectively carried out their mission, half failed. When the students shared their plans with the rest of the class, the secret ingredient for success was paranoia and total suspicion of every other cell member

so that the whole group never met together but dealt with only one other at a time and did body searches for recording equipment. Those that were open and trusting got whacked by the "TA secret service agents."

Consider persuading your instructor to try this role-playing demonstration.

A Positive Endnote

We can think of no better way to end a chapter that focused mostly on the way good people go bad than to leave you with a wonderful statement about the unity of humankind and the need to respect our kinship with one another. It is from poet and preacher John Donne *(Meditations XV11):*

> All mankind is of one author, and is one volume; when one man dies, one chapter is not torn out of the book, but translated into a better language; and every chapter must be so translated. . . . As therefore the bell that rings to a sermon, calls not upon the preacher only, but upon the congregation to come: so this bell calls us all. . . . No man is an island, entire of itself . . . any man's death diminishes me, because I am involved in mankind; and therefore never send to know for whom the bell tolls; it tolls for thee.

So, when in doubt: Take the high moral road, be mindful of situational forces, be wary of potentially unjust authority, be sensitive to your need to "go along to get along with others," accept personal responsibility for your actions, keep your critical facilities activated, and adopt a heroic imagination that transforms your sense of compassion for others into heroic action that changes the world for the better.

CHAPTER SUMMARY

((•─[**Listen** to an audio file of your chapter at **MyPsychLab**

CHAPTER PROBLEM: What makes ordinary people willing to harm other people, as they did in Milgram's shocking experiment?

- Individual behavior is influenced by situational factors more than we recognize, for better or for worse, but awareness of how they operate can fortify us against their negative power.

- Situations are also personal mental constructions as each of creates subjective realities of the behavioral contexts around us, and of the people we deal with in loving or hateful relationships.

- Most psychologists have largely ignored systematic forces, but effective major behavioral change must include recognizing how systems create and justify situations, which in turn can come to exert power on our thinking, feeling and acting.

11.1   How Does the Social Situation Affect Our Behavior?

[**Core Concept 11.1** We usually adapt our behavior to the demands of the social situation, and in new or ambiguous situations, we take our cues from the behavior of others in that setting.]

Social psychologists study the behavior of individuals or groups in the context of particular situations. Much research in this area reveals how norms and social roles can be major sources of situational influence. The Asch studies demonstrated the powerful effect of the group to produce conformity, even when the group is clearly wrong. Another shocking demonstration of situational power came from Stanley Milgram's controversial experiments on obedience to authority. Situational influence can also lead to inaction: The bystander studies showed that individuals are inhibited by the number of bystanders, the ambiguity of the situation, and their resultant perception of their social role and responsibility. Groupthink occurs even in the highest level of government decision making, whereby smart people advocate actions that may be disastrous by mindlessly following the consensus of the group or its leader's opinion. Heroes are often ordinary people who take extraordinary action to help others or oppose evil activities. We usually adapt our behavior to the demands of the social situation, and in ambiguous situations, we take our cues from the behavior of others.

Asch effect (p. 466)
autokinetic effect (p. 469)
bystander intervention problem (p. 479)

chameleon effect (p. 465)
cohesiveness (p. 470)
conformity (p. 466)
diffusion of responsibility (p. 480)
dispositionism (p. 463)
groupthink (p. 470)
heroes (p. 475)
in-group (p. 482)
out-group (p. 482)
script (p. 464)
situationism (p. 463)
social neuroscience (p. 470)
social context (p. 461)
social norms (p. 464)
social psychology (p. 461)
social role (p. 463)

11.2 Constructing Social Reality: What Influences Our Judgments of Others?

[**Core Concept 11.2** The judgments we make about others depend not only on their behavior but also on our interpretation of their actions within a social context.]

The situation, by itself, does not determine behavior. Rather, it is our personal interpretation of the situation—our constructed social reality—that regulates behavior, including our social interactions. Usually we are attracted to relationships that we find rewarding, although there are exceptions, predicted by **expectancy-value theory** and **cognitive dissonance theory**. Attribution theory predicts that we will attribute other people's blunders to their traits or character (the **fundamental attribution error**) and our own to the situation (the **self-serving bias**), although this tendency depends on one's culture. Healthy, loving relationships also demonstrate the social construction of reality, because there are many kinds of love and many cultural variations in the understanding and practice of love.

Prejudice and discrimination also demonstrate how we construct our own social reality through such cognitive processes as the perception of social distance and threats, the influence of media stereotypes, **scapegoating**, and **dehumanization**.

We are all vulnerable to stereotype threat that can have a negative impact on our performance when we are made aware that we belong to a group that does poorly on certain tasks and tests.

The judgments we make about others depend not only on their behavior but also on our interpretation of their actions within a social context.

cognitive dissonance theory (p. 487)
dehumanization (p. 495)
discrimination (p. 493)
expectancy-value theory (p. 486)
fundamental attribution error (FAE) (p. 490)
matching hypothesis (p. 486)
prejudice (p. 493)
principle of proximity (p. 484)
reward theory of attraction (p. 484)
romantic love (p. 489)
scapegoating (p. 494)
self-disclosure (p. 485)
self-serving bias (p. 491)
similarity principle (p. 485)
social distance (p. 493)
social reality (p. 483)
stereotype threat (p. 497)
triangular theory of love (p. 489)

11.3 How Do Systems Create Situations That Influence Behavior?

[**Core Concept 11.3** Systems shape situations, which in turn affect behavior—and by understanding systems, we can learn how to change them and modify their influences around us.]

Many studies in social psychology—particularly those dealing with obedience and conformity—show that the power of the situation can pressure ordinary people to commit horrible acts, such as those of soldiers in Iraq's **Abu Ghraib Prison**. Understanding such complex behavior involves three levels of analysis: the individual's dispositions, the situation's forces, and the power of the system that creates and maintains specific situations.

The **Stanford Prison Experiment** put "good apples" in a "bad barrel" for nearly a week to test the dispositional versus situational explanations for the adverse outcomes. However, what has been ignored is the system that generates such bad barrels. Changing unacceptable behavior, such as **bullying**, discrimination, or terrorism, requires understanding how to modify systems of power and the situations they create and sustain, not just behavior modification of the individual actors.

Systems are complex structures embedded in a matrix of cultural, historical, economic, political, and legal subsystems that must be identified and changed if they generate illegal, immoral, or unethical behavior.

Abu Ghraib Prison (p. 503)
bullying (p. 505)
Schlesinger Report (p. 504)
Stanford Prison Experiment (p. 500)
system power (p. 500)

CRITICAL THINKING APPLIED

Is Terrorism "a Senseless Act of Violence, Perpetrated by Crazy Fanatics"?

Terrorism is a widespread global phenomenon likely to be a permanent feature of the threats posed to nations by networks of individuals in an asymmetrical war. It is important to understand terrorist acts as a psychological process as well as the political, cultural, economic and religious contributions to creating this new role of someone becoming a terrorist. One strategy of prevention is learning how to win the hearts of minds of potential terrorist recruits away from violence and toward becoming pro-social change agents to rectify wrongs in their communities and nations.

DISCOVERING PSYCHOLOGY **VIEWING GUIDE**

Watch the following videos by logging into MyPsychLab (www.mypsychlab.com). After you have watched the videos, answer the questions that follow.

PROGRAM 19: **THE POWER OF THE SITUATION**

PROGRAM 20: **CONSTRUCTING SOCIAL REALITY**

Program Review

1. What do social psychologists study?
   a. how people are influenced by other people
   b. how people act in different societies
   c. why some people are more socially successful than others
   d. what happens to isolated individuals

2. What precipitated Kurt Lewin's interest in leadership roles?
   a. the rise of social psychology
   b. the trial of Adolf Eichmann
   c. Hitler's ascent to power
   d. the creation of the United Nations after World War II

3. In Lewin's study, how did the boys behave when they had autocratic leaders?
   a. They had fun but got little accomplished.
   b. They were playful and did motivated, original work.

   c. They were hostile toward each other and got nothing done.
   d. They worked hard but acted aggressively toward each other.

4. In Solomon Asch's experiments, about what percent of participants went along with the group's obviously mistaken judgment at least once?
   a. 70 percent   c. 30 percent
   b. 50 percent   d. 90 percent

5. Before Stanley Milgram did his experiments on obedience, experts were asked to predict the results. The experts
   a. overestimated people's willingness to administer shocks.
   b. underestimated people's willingness to administer shocks.
   c. gave accurate estimates of people's behavior.
   d. believed most people would refuse to continue with the experiment.

6. Which light did Milgram's experiment shed on the behavior of citizens in Nazi Germany?

   a. Situational forces can bring about blind obedience.

   b. Personal traits of individuals are most important in determining behavior.

   c. Cultural factors unique to Germany account for the rise of the Nazis.

   d. Human beings enjoy being cruel when they have the opportunity.

7. Which statement most clearly reflects the fundamental attribution error?

   a. Everyone is entitled to good medical care.

   b. Ethical guidelines are essential to conducting responsible research.

   c. People who are unemployed are too lazy to work.

   d. Everyone who reads about the Milgram experiment is shocked by the results.

8. Why did the prison study conducted by Philip Zimbardo and his colleagues have to be called off?

   a. A review committee felt that it violated ethical guidelines.

   b. It consumed too much of the students' time.

   c. The main hypothesis was supported, so there was no need to continue.

   d. The situation that had been created was too dangerous to maintain.

9. How did Tom Moriarity get people on a beach to intervene during a robbery?

   a. by creating a human bond through a simple request

   b. by reminding people of their civic duty to turn in criminals

   c. by making the thief look less threatening

   d. by providing a model of responsible behavior

10. Which leadership style tends to produce hard work when the leader is watching but much less cooperation when the leader is absent?

    a. authoritative   c. democratic

    b. autocratic   d. laissez-faire

11. Typically, people who participated in Milgram's study

    a. appeared to relish the opportunity to hurt someone else.

    b. objected but still obeyed.

    c. refused to continue and successfully stopped the experiment.

    d. came to recruit others into shocking the learner.

12. Psychologists refer to the power to create subjective realities as the power of

    a. social reinforcement.   c. cognitive control.

    b. prejudice.   d. the Pygmalion effect.

13. When Jane Elliot divided her classroom of third graders into the inferior brown-eyed people and the superior blue-eyed students, what did she observe?

    a. The students were too young to understand what was expected.

    b. The students refused to behave badly toward their friends and classmates.

    c. The boys tended to go along with the categorization, but the girls did not.

    d. The blue-eyed students acted superior and were cruel to the brown-eyed students who acted inferior.

14. In the research carried out by Robert Rosenthal and Lenore Jacobson, what caused the performance of some students to improve dramatically?

    a. Teachers were led to expect such improvement and so changed the way they treated these students.

    b. These students performed exceptionally well on a special test designed to predict improved performance.

    c. Teachers gave these students higher grades because they knew the researchers were expecting the improvement.

    d. The students felt honored to be included in the experiment and, therefore, were motivated to improve.

15. Robert Rosenthal demonstrated the Pygmalion effect in the classroom by showing that teachers behave differently toward students for whom they have high expectations in all of the following ways, *except*

    a. by punishing them more for goofing off.

    b. by providing them with a warmer learning climate.

    c. by teaching more to them than to the other students.

    d. by providing more specific feedback when the student gives a wrong answer.

16. What happens to low-achieving students in the "jigsaw classroom"?

    a. They tend to fall further behind.

    b. They are given an opportunity to work at a lower level, thus increasing the chance of success.

    c. By becoming "experts," they improve their performance and their self-respect.

    d. By learning to compete more aggressively, they become more actively involved in their own learning.

17. When Robert Cialdini cites the example of the Hare Krishnas' behavior in giving people at airports a flower or other small gift, he is illustrating the principle of

    a. commitment.   c. scarcity.

    b. reciprocity.   d. consensus.

18. Salespeople might make use of the principle of scarcity by

    a. filling shelves up with a product and encouraging consumers to stock up.

    b. claiming they have a hard time ordering the product.

    c. imposing a deadline by which the consumer must make a decision.

    d. being difficult to get in touch with over the phone.

19. Nancy is participating in a bike-a-thon next month and is having a large group of friends over to her house in order to drum up sponsorships for the event. She is capitalizing on the principle of

    a. liking.   c. commitment.

    b. consensus.   d. authority.

20. An appropriate motto for the principle of consensus would be

    a. "I've reasoned it through."

    b. "I am doing it of my own free will."

    c. "It will be over quickly."

    d. "Everyone else is doing it."

12

Psychological Disorders

CHAPTER PROBLEM Is it possible to distinguish mental disorder from merely unusual behavior?
That is, are there specific signs that clearly indicate mental disorder?

CRITICAL THINKING APPLIED Insane Places Revisited—Another Look at the Rosenhan Study

THE VOLUNTEERS KNEW THEY WERE ON THEIR OWN. IF THEY MANAGED to get admitted to the hospital, the five men and three women knew that they would be treated as mental patients, not observers. None had ever been diagnosed with a mental illness, but perhaps they were not so "normal" after all: Would a normal person lie to get into such a place? In fact, all were collaborators in an experiment designed to find out whether normality would be recognized in a mental hospital.

The experimenter, David Rosenhan—himself one of the pseudopatients—suspected that terms such as *sanity, insanity, schizophrenia, mental illness,* and *abnormal* might have fuzzier boundaries than the psychiatric community believed. He also suspected that some of the "abnormal" behaviors seen in mental patients might originate in the abnormal atmosphere of the mental hospital rather than in the patients themselves. To test these ideas, Rosenhan and his collaborators decided to see how mental hospital staff members would deal with patients who were, in fact, not mentally ill. Could mental health professionals distinguish healthy people from those with mental disorders?

Individually, they applied for admission at different hospitals, complaining that they had recently heard voices that seemed to say "empty," "hollow," and "thud." Aside from this, they claimed no other symptoms. All used false names, and the four who were mental health professionals gave false occupations—but, apart from these minor fibs, they answered all questions truthfully. They even tried to act as normal as possible, although the prospect of entering the alien hospital environment made them feel anxious. They also worried about *not* being admitted and—worse yet—exposed as frauds. That concern vanished quickly, for all readily gained admittance at 12 different hospitals (some did it twice). All but one was diagnosed with *schizophrenia,* a major psychological disorder often accompanied by hearing imaginary voices.

After admission, the pseudopatients made no further claims that they heard voices or had any other abnormal symptoms. Indeed, all wanted to be on their best behavior to gain release as soon as possible. Their only apparent "deviance" involved taking notes on the experience—at first privately and later publicly, when they found that the staff paid little attention. The nursing records indicated that, when the staff did notice, they interpreted the note taking as part of the patient's illness. (One comment: "Patient engages in writing behavior.")

For the most part, the patients found themselves ignored by the staff—even when they asked for help or advice. But when the staff did interact with the patients, it was as though the patients were simply "cases," not persons. Consequently, it took an average of 19 days for the pseudopatients to convince the hospital staff that they were ready for discharge, despite the absence of abnormal symptoms. One unfortunate volunteer wasn't released for almost 2 months.

Two main findings from this classic study jarred the psychiatric community to its core. First, *no professional staff member at any of the hospitals ever realized that any of Rosenhan's pseudopatients was faking mental illness.* Of course, the staff may have assumed that the patients had been ill at the time of admission and had improved during their hospitalization. But that possibility did not let the professionals off Rosenhan's hook: Despite apparently normal behavior, not one pseudopatient was ever labeled as "normal" or "well" while in the hospital. And, on discharge, they were still seen as having schizophrenia—but "in remission."

Were the hospital staff members unskilled or unfeeling? Rosenhan didn't think so. He attributed their failure to perceive the pseudopatients' behavior as normal to being occupied with paperwork and other duties, leaving little time for observing and interacting with patients. The design of the psychiatric wards also contributed to the problem: Staff members spent most of their time in a glassed-in central office that patients called "the cage." As Rosenhan (1973a) said:

> It could be a mistake, and a very unfortunate one, to consider that what happened to us derived from malice or stupidity on the part of the staff. Quite the contrary, our overwhelming impression of them was of people who really cared, who were committed and who were uncommonly intelligent. Where they failed, as they sometimes did painfully, it would be more accurate to attribute those failures to the environment in which they, too, found themselves than to personal callousness. Their perceptions and behavior were controlled by the situation (p. 257).

CONNECTION CHAPTER 11

Social psychology has also emphasized the power of both the *situation* and the *system* to influence behavior (p. 463).

The mental hospital, then, became another example of a "sick" *system* that we discussed in the previous chapter.

Could it be that the pseudopatients also got caught up in the system and weren't behaving as normally as they believed? Rosenhan noted: *To everyone's surprise, the hospital patients readily detected the ruse, even though the professional staff did not.* The pseudopatients reported that the other patients regularly voiced their suspicions: "You're not crazy. You're a journalist or a professor. . . . You're checking up on the hospital." In his report of this experience, entitled "On Being Sane in Insane Places," Rosenhan (1973a) noted dryly: "The fact that the patients often recognized normality when staff did not raises important questions" (p. 252). You will hear the echo of these "important questions" as we critically examine the "medical model" of mental disorder.

One of those questions, then, is the problem that threads through this chapter:

PROBLEM: **Is it possible to distinguish mental disorder from merely unusual behavior? That is, are there specific signs that clearly indicate mental disorder?**

This chapter is organized around these two questions. As we discuss them, please note that Rosenhan did not dispute the existence of psychological disorders. Rather, he raised questions about clinical judgments made in the context of mental hospitals.

In fact, many people *do* experience the anguish of **psychopathology** (also called *mental disorder* or *mental illness*). According to the National Institute of Mental Health (NIMH, 2010b), more than 26 percent of the U.S. population—more than one in four Americans—are diagnosed with mental health problems in a given year. For one in 17, it will be a mental illness of serious proportions, such as major depression or schizophrenia. Over their lifespans, an estimated 46 percent of Americans will be diagnosed with some psychological disorder (Butcher et al., 2008). Again, Rosenhan was not suggesting that these conditions do not exist or do not exact a horrendous toll in human suffering—just that it can be difficult to distinguish normality from abnormality, particularly when we expect to see abnormality.

Rosenhan's pseudopatient study caused a tremendous flap, and many psychiatrists and clinical psychologists cried foul. Several ensuing responses in *Science,* the journal in which the study had been published, accused Rosenhan of slipshod research and of damaging the reputation of the mental health professions. Did they have a point? Was Rosenhan's study flawed? Or was it simply the cries of those who perceived Rosenhan's study as a personal attack? We will take a close look at these issues in the *Critical Thinking Applied* section at the end of the chapter. In the meantime, let's explore the problem of determining what mental disorder is and how it might be identified.

psychopathology Any pattern of emotions, behaviors, or thoughts inappropriate to the situation and leading to personal distress or the inability to achieve important goals. Other terms having essentially the same meaning include *mental illness, mental disorder,* and *psychological disorder.*

12.1 KEY QUESTION
What Is Psychological Disorder?

On the world stage, the picture of psychopathology is sobering. According to the World Health Organization, some 450 million people around the globe have mental disorders, with a large proportion living in poor countries that have no mental health care system (Miller, 2006d). Depression, for example, causes more disability among people aged 15 to 44 than any other condition except HIV/AIDS. In the United States, nearly half of all households have someone seeking treatment for a mental problem (Chamberlin, 2004).

Yet, as Rosenhan's study suggests, distinguishing "normal" from "abnormal" is not always a simple task. Consider, for example, how you would classify such eccentric personalities as Lady Gaga and Russell Brand. And what about a soldier who risks his or her life in combat: Is that "normal"? Or does a grief-stricken woman have a psychological disorder if she is unable to return to her normal routine 6 months after her husband has died?

Clinicians look for three classic symptoms of severe psychopathology: *hallucinations, delusions,* and *extreme affective disturbances.* **Hallucinations** are false sensory experiences, such as hearing nonexistent voices or "seeing things." You may recall that that Rosenhan's pseudopatients claimed to have hallucinations in the form of voices saying, "empty," "hollow," and "thud." By contrast, **delusions** involve troublesome irrational beliefs. For example, if you think you are the president of the United States (and you are not), or if you think people are out to "get" you (and they are not), you probably have a delusional disorder. The third classic symptom, **affective disturbances** are disorders of emotion or *affect.* Accordingly, a person who characteristically feels depressed, anxious, or manic may have an affective disorder.

Beyond such extreme signs of distress, the experts do not always agree. What qualifies as abnormal becomes a judgment call, a judgment made more difficult because no sharp boundary separates normal from abnormal thought and behavior. It may be helpful to think of psychological disorder as part of a continuum ranging from the absence of disorder to severe disorder, as shown in Table 12.1. The big idea here is that people with psychological disorders are not in a class by themselves. Rather, their disorders are an exaggeration of normal responses.

hallucination A false sensory experience that may suggest mental disorder. Hallucinations can have other causes, such as drugs or sensory isolation.

delusion An extreme disorder of thinking, involving persistent false beliefs. Delusions are the hallmark of paranoid disorders.

affective disturbances Disorders of emotion or mood.

TABLE 12.1　The Spectrum of Mental Disorder

Mental disorder occurs on a spectrum that ranges from the absence of signs of pathology to severe disturbances, such as are found in major depression or schizophrenia. The important point is that there is no sharp distinction that divides those with mental disorders from those who are "normal."

No Disorder	Mild Disorder	Moderate Disorder	Severe Disorder
Absence of signs of psychological disorder	Few signs of distress or other indicators of psychological disorder	Indicators of disorder are more pronounced and occur more frequently	Clear signs of psychological disorder, which dominate the person's life
Absence of behavior problems	Few behavior problems; responses usually appropriate to the situation	More distinct behavior problems; behavior is often inappropriate to the situation	Severe and frequent behavior problems; behavior is usually inappropriate to the situation
No problems with interpersonal relationships	Few difficulties with relationships	More frequent difficulties with relationships	Many poor relationships or lack of relationships with others

In this section of the chapter, we will focus on two contrasting views of psychopathology. One, coming to us from medicine, is sometimes called the "medical model." It portrays mental problems as akin to physical disorders: as sickness or disease. The other view, a psychological view, sees psychological disorders as the result of multiple factors that can involve both nature and nurture. As our Core Concept puts it:

Core Concept 12.1

The medical model views psychological disorders as "diseases," while the psychological view sees them as an interaction of biological, behavioral, cognitive, developmental, and social-cultural factors.

No matter how we conceptualize psychopathology, nearly everyone agrees that psychological disorder is common, touching the daily lives of millions. Mental disorder can be insidious, working its way into thoughts and feelings, diminishing its victims' emotional and physical well-being, along with personal and family relationships. And it can create an enormous financial burden through lost productivity, lost wages, and high costs of treatment. But, the way we think of psychopathology also has a consequence: As we will see, how we conceptualize psychopathology determines how we treat it—whether with drugs, charms, rituals, talk, torture, brain surgery, hospitalization, or commitment to an "insane asylum."

Changing Concepts of Psychological Disorder

In the ancient world, people assumed that supernatural powers were everywhere, accounting for good fortune, disease, and disaster. In this context, they perceived psychopathology as a sign that demons and spirits had taken possession of a person's mind and body (Sprock & Blashfield, 1991). If you had been living in this ancient world, your daily routine would have included rituals aimed at outwitting or placating these supernatural beings.

In about 400 B.C., the Greek physician Hippocrates took humanity's first step toward a scientific view of mental disorder by declaring that abnormal behavior has physical causes. As we saw in Chapter 10, Hippocrates taught his disciples to interpret the symptoms of psychopathology as an imbalance among four body fluids called "humors": blood, phlegm (mucus), black bile, and yellow bile. Those with an excess of black bile, for example, were inclined to melancholy or depression,

CONNECTION CHAPTER 10

Hippocrates' humor theory was a theory of temperaments (p. 420).

while those who had an abundance of blood were sanguine or warm-hearted. With this simple but revolutionary idea, Hippocrates incorporated mental disorders into medicine, and his view—that mental problems had natural, not supernatural, causes—influenced educated people in the Western world until the end of the Roman Empire.

In the Middle Ages, superstition eclipsed the Hippocratic model of mental disorder. Under the influence of the medieval Church, physicians and clergy reverted to the old ways of explaining abnormality in terms of demons and witchcraft. In these harsh times, the belief that Satan incited unusual behavior heaped fuel on the fires of the Inquisition. The "cure" involved attempts to drive out the demons that possessed the unfortunate victim's soul—literally, "beating the Devil" out of the supposedly possessed. As a result, thousands of mentally tormented people were tortured and executed all across Europe.

As late as 1692, the medieval view of mental disorder led frightened colonists in Massachusetts to convict and execute a number of their fellow citizens for witchcraft (Karlsen, 1998). What frightened them? A group of young girls had unexplained "fits" that neighbors interpreted as the result of witchcraft. A modern analysis of the witch trials has concluded that the girls were probably suffering from poisoning by a fungus growing on rye grain—the same fungus that produces the hallucinogenic drug LSD (Caporeal, 1976; Matossian, 1982, 1989).

A painting of the witchcraft trials held in Salem, Massachusetts, in 1692. Twenty people were executed before the hysteria subsided.

The Medical Model In the latter part of the 18th century, the "disease" view that had originated with Hippocrates re-emerged with the rise of science. The resulting **medical model** held that mental disorders are *diseases* of the mind that, like ordinary physical diseases, have objective causes and require specific treatments. People began to perceive individuals with psychological problems as sick (suffering from illness) rather than as immoral or demon-possessed.

medical model The view that mental disorders are diseases that, like ordinary physical diseases, have objective physical causes and require specific treatments.

And what a difference a new theory made! Treating mental *diseases* by torture and abuse made no sense. The new view of mental illness brought human reforms that called for placing the "insane" in protective "asylums." In this supportive atmosphere, many patients actually improved—even thrived—on rest, contemplation, and simple but useful work (Maher & Maher, 1985). Unfortunately, political pressures eventually turned the initially therapeutic asylums into overcrowded warehouses of neglected patients. ◉

Despite such problems, the revived medical model was unquestionably an improvement over the old demon model. Nevertheless, modern psychologists think that we are ready for yet another revolutionary change in perspective. In their view, the medical model has shortcomings of its own.

Psychologists argue that the assumption of "disease" leads to a doctor-knows-best approach, in which the therapist takes all the responsibility for diagnosing the illness and prescribing treatment. Under this "disease" assumption, the patient may become a passive recipient of medication and advice rather than an active participant in treatment. And, in fact, we see many mental patients today who are treated simply by the dispensing of pills. Psychologists believe that this attitude wrongly encourages dependency on the doctor, encourages unnecessary drug therapy, and does little to help the patient develop good coping skills and healthy behaviors.

Incidentally, a doctor-knows-best approach also makes mental illness a medical problem, taking responsibility (and business) away from psychologists and giving it to psychiatrists. Psychologists understandably bristle at the medical model's implication that their treatment of mental "diseases" should be done by physicians or under the supervision of physicians. In effect, the medical model assigns psychologists to second-class professional status. As you can see, ownership of the whole territory of psychological disorder is hotly contested.

◉—Watch the **Video** Asylum: A History of the Mental Institution in America at **MyPsychLab**

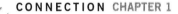

CONNECTION CHAPTER 1

Psychiatrists, but not psychologists, are trained in medicine (p. 6).

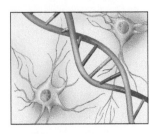

The *biological perspective* is one of several alternatives to the medical model. Others include the *behavioral perspective, cognitive perspective, social perspective,* and *developmental perspective.*

CONNECTION CHAPTER 4

Contingencies involve the timing and frequency of rewards and punishments (p. 144).

CONNECTION CHAPTER 10

Reciprocal determinism is a part of Bandura's social learning theory (p. 443).

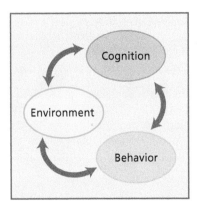

Reciprocal determinism is the process by which our cognitions, behaviors, and environments mutually influence each other.

Psychological Models What does psychology have to offer in place of the medical model? Most clinical psychologists have now turned to combinations of psychological perspectives that derive from *behaviorism, cognitive psychology, developmental psychology, social learning,* and *biological psychology.*

Psychological Alternatives to the Medical Model Modern psychologists agree with proponents of the medical model that biology can influence mental disorder. A *biological perspective* is certainly required to account for the genetic influences we see in schizophrenia, the anxiety disorders, mental retardation, and many other conditions. But psychological alternatives to the medical model also take into account behavioral, cognitive, developmental, and social-cultural factors that the medical perspective tends to neglect.

The *behavioral perspective* looks outward, emphasizing the influence of the environment. Thus, behavioral psychology tells us that many abnormal behaviors can be acquired in the same way that we learn healthy behaviors—through behavioral learning. This view helps us focus on the environmental conditions that maintain abnormal behaviors: rewards, punishments, and contingencies. For example, the behavioral perspective would suggest that a fear of public speaking could result from a humiliating public speaking experience and subsequent avoidance of any opportunity to develop and be reinforced for public speaking skills.

In contrast, the *cognitive perspective* looks inward, emphasizing mental processes, including thoughts, feelings, perceptions, and memory. Cognitive psychology focuses on such questions as these: Do people believe that they have control over their own lives (an *internal* or *external locus of control*)? How do they cope with threat and stress? Do they regularly experience troublesome emotions, such as depression or anxiety?

As we saw in the chapter on learning, social-learning theorists and others have built bridges that link these two perspectives. Both sides of that divide now acknowledge that cognition and behavior usually occur in a social context, requiring a *social perspective.* Through that lens, a psychologist might ask about a client's social support system, as well as social sources of stress on the job, at school, or from family and friends.

Albert Bandura typifies those who combine the social, behavioral, and cognitive perspectives: His concept of *reciprocal determinism* suggests that behavior, cognition, and social/environmental factors all mutually influence each other through social learning, behavioral learning, and cognitive learning. Thus, a fear of public speaking, for example, could have its origins in *social learning* when you heard people talk about "stage fright" and their anxiety about public speaking. Against that backdrop, then, you may have had an unpleasant *behavioral learning* experience in which people laughed at you while you were making a speech. That experience, in turn, could easily make you view yourself as "a poor public speaker"—as a result of *cognitive learning.* A result of this chain of social learning, behavioral learning, and cognitive learning—in which each step *reciprocally* reinforces the others—is the idea that public speaking is fear-producing experience.

Likewise, a *developmental perspective* looks for deviations from the expected pattern of biological and psychological development. Did the child begin to use language during the second year of life? Does the person have a functional *theory of mind* that allows her to understand other people's thoughts and intentions? Is emotional control appropriate to age? Such questions help the clinician identify and treat developmental disorders such as autism and mental retardation.

The Biopsychology of Mental Disorder Although most psychologists have reservations about the medical model, they do not deny the influence of biology on thought and behavior. An explosion of recent research in neuroscience confirms the role of the brain as a complex organ whose mental functions depend on a delicate balance of chemicals and neural circuits that are continually modified by our experiences. Genetic influences, brain injury, stress, and infection are still other factors that can tip the biological balance toward psychopathology (see Figure 12.1). Thus, modern biopsychology assumes that many mental disturbances involve not only cognitive, behavioral, developmental, and social-cultural factors but also the brain and nervous system (Insel, 2010).

On the heredity front, the Human Genome Project has specified the complete human genetic package. Many psychologists see this accomplishment as a ripe opportunity for specialists in behavioral genetics who are searching for genes associated with specific mental disorders (NIMH, 2003b). But the search won't be easy. So far, suspicious genetic abnormalities have been linked to schizophrenia, bipolar disorder, anxiety disorders, and autism, yet their exact roles in these conditions remain unclear. Most experts believe that such disorders are likely to result from multiple genes interacting with environmental factors, such as toxins, infections, or stressful events. Watch the news for further developments.

But let us be clear about the role of biology in mental disorder: Whatever neuroscience discovers in the future, biology will never account for everything. Our thoughts and behaviors are always a product of nature *and* nurture—biology *and* experience. And, as we will see in our discussion of stress, the way we think and feel can actually influence our biological being, including the very structure of the brain itself.

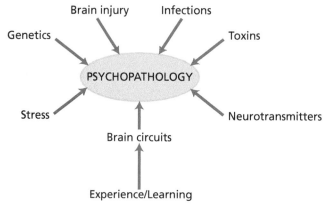

FIGURE 12.1

The Biopsychology of Mental Disorder

An explosion of research in neuroscience implicates a host of possible biological factors in psychopathology.

Source: Created by author

Indicators of Abnormality

While clinicians sometimes disagree about the *etiology* (causes) of psychological disorders, they usually agree broadly on the indicators, or signs, of abnormality (Rosenhan & Seligman, 1995). What are these indicators? Earlier we noted that hallucinations, delusions, and extreme affective disturbances are signs of severe mental disorder. But many psychological problems don't reveal themselves so obviously. Accordingly, clinicians also look for the following more subtle signs that can indicate psychological disturbances (see also Table 12.1):

- **Distress.** Does the individual show unusual or prolonged levels of unease or anxiety? Almost anyone will get nervous before an important test, but when one is so overwhelmed with unpleasant emotions that concentration for long periods becomes impossible, it becomes a sign of abnormality.

- **Maladaptiveness.** Does the person regularly act in ways that make others fearful or that interfere with his or her well-being? We can see this, for example, in someone who drinks so heavily that she or he cannot hold down a job or drive a car without endangering others.

- **Irrationality.** Does the person act or talk in ways that are irrational or even incomprehensible to others? A woman who converses with her long-dead sister, whose voice she hears in her head, is behaving irrationally. Likewise, behaviors or emotional responses that are inappropriate to the situation, such as laughing at the scene of a tragedy, show irrational loss of contact with one's social environment.

- **Unpredictability.** Does the individual behave erratically and inconsistently at different times or from one situation to another, as if experiencing a loss of control? For example, a child who suddenly bursts into tears or smashes his toys with no apparent provocation is behaving unpredictably. Similarly, an employer who treats her staff compassionately one day and abusively the next is acting unpredictably.

- **Unconventionality and undesirable behavior.** Does the person behave in ways that are statistically rare and violate social norms of what is legally or morally acceptable or desirable? Being merely "unusual" is not a sign of abnormality—so feel free to dye your hair red and green for Christmas. But if you decide to go beyond the bounds of social acceptability, say by painting yourself red and green and strolling naked in the mall at Christmastime, that would be considered a little abnormal.

Behaviors that make other people feel uncomfortable or threatened may be a sign of abnormality.

Is the presence of just one indicator enough to demonstrate abnormality? It's a judgment call. Clinicians feel more confidence in labeling behavior as "abnormal" when they see two or more signs of abnormality. (You will remember that the pseudopatients in Rosenhan's study presented only one symptom: hearing voices.) The more extreme and numerous the indicators, the more confident psychologists can be about identifying an abnormal condition. On the other hand, *none* of these criteria apply to *all* forms of disorder, as you will see.

While the presence of these indicators may suggest abnormality, the clinician still must decide which disorder it is. This can be difficult, because psychopathology takes many forms. Some diagnoses may have a familiar ring: *depression, phobia,* and *panic disorder.* You may be less well acquainted with others, such as *conversion disorder* or *borderline personality disorder.* In all, you will find some 300 specific varieties of psychopathology described in the *Diagnostic and Statistical Manual of Mental Disorders* (4th edition), known by clinicians and researchers as the *DSM-IV* ("DSM-four"). Even though it has a strong medical-model bias, mental health professionals of all backgrounds use this volume to diagnose psychopathology. So influential is this *DSM-IV* system that we will devote the entire middle portion of this chapter to an explanation of it.

A Caution to Readers

As you read about the symptoms of psychological disorder, you may begin to wonder about your own mental health. All students studying abnormal psychology face this hazard. To see what we mean, please answer the following questions, which are based on the indicators of abnormality discussed earlier:

1. Have you had periods of time when you felt "blue" for no apparent reason? (an indicator of *distress*)
2. Have you ever gone to a party on a night when you knew you should be studying? (an indicator of *maladaptiveness*)
3. Have you had an experience in which you thought you heard or saw something that wasn't really there? (an indicator of *irrationality*)
4. Have you had a flash of temper in which you said something that you later regretted? (an indicator of *unpredictability*)
5. Have you had unusual thoughts that you told no one about? (an indicator of *unconventionality*)
6. Have you made someone fearful or distressed because of something you said or did? (another indicator of *maladaptiveness*)

The fact is that almost everyone will answer "yes" to at least one—and perhaps all—of these questions. Yet this does not necessarily mean abnormality. Whether you are or anyone else is normal or abnormal is a matter of degree and frequency—and clinical judgment.

So, as we take a close look at specific psychological disorders in the next section of the chapter, you will most likely find some symptoms that you have experienced. So will your classmates. (A similar problem is common among medical students, who begin to notice that they, too, have symptoms of the physical diseases they learn about.) You should realize that *this is normal.* Another reason, of course, that you may see yourself in this chapter arises from the fact that no sharp line separates psychopathology from normalcy. Psychological disorders involve exaggerations of normal tendencies. We are not suggesting that concerns about psychological disorder should be taken lightly, however. If, after reading this chapter, you suspect that you may have a problem, you should discuss it with a professional.

[PSYCHOLOGY MATTERS]

The Plea of Insanity

Now, let's look at a closely related issue: the *plea of insanity.* What is your opinion: Does the insanity plea excuse criminal behavior and put thousands of dangerous people back on the streets? Let's take a critical look at the history and the facts.

In 1843, Daniel M'Naughten, a deranged woodcutter from Glasgow, Scotland, thought he had received "instructions from God" to kill the British prime minister, Robert Peel. Fortunately for Peel, this would-be assassin struck down his secretary by mistake. Apprehended and tried, M'Naughten was found "not guilty by reason of insanity." The court reasoned that M'Naughten's mental condition prevented him from knowing right from wrong. The public responded with outrage. Fast-forwarding 138 years, a similarly outraged public decried the modern-day insanity ruling involving John Hinckley, Jr., the young man who shot and wounded then-President Ronald Reagan. Such infamous cases have molded a low public opinion of the insanity defense. The citizenry blames psychologists and psychiatrists for clogging the courts with insanity pleas, allowing homicidal maniacs back on the streets, and letting criminals go to hospitals for "treatment" instead of prisons for punishment. But this public image of insanity rests on several mistaken assumptions.

For one, "insanity" appears nowhere among the *DSM-IV* listing of disorders recognized by psychologists and psychiatrists. Technically, **insanity** is neither a psychological nor psychiatric term. Rather, it is a *legal* term, which only a court—not psychologists or psychiatrists—can officially apply. By law in most states, insanity can include not only psychosis but also jealous rage, mental retardation, and a wide variety of other conditions in which a person might not be able to control his or her behavior or distinguish right from wrong (Mercado, 2006; Thio, 1995).

insanity A legal term, not a psychological or psychiatric one, referring to a person who is unable, because of a mental disorder or defect, to conform his or her behavior to the law.

So, why can we not simply abolish the laws that allow this technicality? The answer to that question turns on the definition of a crime. Legally, holding a person responsible for a crime requires that two criteria be met: (a) the person must have committed an *illegal act* (just wanting to commit a crime is not enough) and (b) the person must have *intentionally* done so. Merely wishing your boss dead is no crime (because you committed no illegal act). Neither is running over your boss accidentally when he steps in front of your moving car in the parking lot. But if you *plan* to run down the dastardly dude and then actually *do* so, you have committed an intentional and illegal act—and the courts can convict you of murder. From these examples, you can see why no one wants to give up the legal requirement of intent. But you can also see why an exception for intent leaves the door open for the controversial plea of insanity.

The plea of insanity is rare—and it is usually unsuccessful.

With these things in mind, take a moment to recall your estimate of the percentage of accused criminals who use the insanity plea. (See the accompanying *Do It Yourself!* box.) In reality, accused criminals use the insanity defense far less often than the public realizes. In actuality, it occurs in less than 1 percent of criminal cases, and of this tiny number, only a fraction are successful (Chiaccia, 2007), although we would note that it has been tried *unsuccessfully* in several famous murder cases, including those of David Birkowitz, Ted Bundy, Charles Manson, John Wayne Gacey, Jeffrey Dahmer, and Dan White (infamous for the "Twinkie defense," claiming that a diet of sugary foods had made him homicidal). To repeat: The insanity defense was not successful in any of those cases.

Still, the public has concern about abuses of the insanity plea. And the outcry has led several states to experiment with alternatives. One promising alternative would require separate verdicts on the *act* and the *intent*, allowing a jury to reach a verdict of "guilty but mentally ill" (Savitsky & Lindblom, 1986).

Do It Yourself! THE INSANITY PLEA: HOW BIG IS THE PROBLEM?

How often is the plea of insanity used? Before you read about the insanity defense in the next part of the chapter, try to guess the approximate percentage of accused criminals in the United States who use a plea of insanity in court: _____ percent. You will find the correct answer in the *Psychology Matters* section that follows. (An answer within 10 percent indicates that you have an exceptionally clear grasp of reality!)

Hint: Research shows that the public has an exaggerated impression of the problem.

Check Your Understanding

✓●─ **Study** and **Review** at **MyPsychLab**

1. **RECALL:** How did Rosenhan go about studying the way psychiatrists diagnose mental disorders?

2. **RECALL:** What are the three classic symptoms of severe mental disorder?

3. **ANALYSIS:** Consider the symptoms presented by the pseudopatients in Rosenhan's study. To what cause would their hallucinations have probably been attributed by (a) Hippocrates, (b) a physician or priest in the Middle Ages, and (c) a physician in the 1800s?

4. **RECALL:** Approximately how often do psychologists diagnose criminals as being insane? How often is the plea of insanity used in criminal cases in the United States?

5. **UNDERSTANDING THE CORE CONCEPT:** Give an example of what a psychologist might look for in attempting to understand a person's mental disorder—but that a psychiatrist using the "medical model" would probably *not* explore.

Answers 1. He arranged for mentally healthy volunteers to request admission to mental hospitals, based on the assertion that they had been hearing voices. Rosenhan interpreted their success (all were admitted) as an indicator that psychiatric diagnoses are not reliable. **2.** Hallucinations, delusions, and severe affective disturbances are the classic symptoms of severe mental disorder. **3.** (a) Hippocrates would have said that the hallucinations stemmed from a physical cause, most likely an imbalance in the four humors. (b) A medieval physician or priest would probably have attributed hallucinations to demon possession. (c) A physician in the 1800s would have attributed the symptoms to a disease—much as Hippocrates would have done. **4.** Psychologists do *not* diagnose people as sane or insane: Those are legal terms. In U.S. courts, the plea of insanity is used in less than 1 percent of criminal cases—most often unsuccessfully. **5.** A psychologist might look for many social, cognitive, and behavioral factors, such as the family environment (social), attention for disturbing behavior (behavioral), or locus of control (cognitive).

DSM-IV The fourth edition of the *Diagnostic and Statistical Manual of Mental Disorders,* published by the American Psychiatric Association; the most widely accepted psychiatric classification system in the United States.

┌12.2 KEY QUESTION
How Are Psychological Disorders Classified in the *DSM-IV?*

In much the same way a bookstore organizes its collection by themes (mystery, romance, etc.), the *Diagnostic and Statistical Manual of Mental Disorders* (4th ed.) brings order to the universe of psychopathology by placing some 300 mental disorders into just a few diagnostic categories. We will explore the most important of these categories in this chapter.

Usually called simply the **DSM-IV,** this manual represents the most widely used system for classifying psychopathology. It is important to note that the *DSM-IV* does *not* classify most disorders by *cause,* since the causes of most mental disorders remain either unknown or in dispute. Instead, as our Core Concept states:

[Core Concept 12.2

The *DSM-IV,* the most widely used system for classifying mental disorders, organizes them by their mental and behavioral symptoms.]

We will follow the lead of the *DSM-IV* in this chapter. But with more than 300 disorders described in that volume, it would be impossible to cover all of them here. Therefore, we will focus this chapter on those you are most likely to encounter either in daily life or in the study of psychopathology in more advanced courses.

Overview of the DSM-IV Classification System

The *DSM-IV* has two great virtues. First, it lays out specific criteria for diagnosing each of the 300+ mental disorders. And second, it gives practitioners a common language for the description of psychopathology. Even though the manual was developed primarily by psychiatrists, its terminology has been adopted by clinicians of all stripes, including psychiatrists, psychologists, and social workers. In addition, most health insurance companies use *DSM-IV* standards in determining what treatments they will pay for—a fact that gives this manual enormous economic clout.

The fourth edition of the *DSM*, published in 1994 and revised in 2000, brought with it some big changes, and the fifth edition, due in 2013, promises even more (American Psychiatric Association, 2010). In particular, the *DSM-IV* banished the term *neurosis* from the official language of psychiatry (although you will frequently hear the term used in more casual conversation). Originally, a **neurosis** or *neurotic disorder* was conceived of as a relatively common pattern of subjective distress or self-defeating behavior that did not show signs of brain abnormalities or grossly irrational thinking. In short, a "neurotic" was someone who might be unhappy or dissatisfied but not considered dangerously ill or out of touch with reality. In the *DSM-IV*, the term *neurosis* has been dropped. So, for example, "obsessive–compulsive neurosis" is now simply *obsessive–compulsive disorder.*

Similarly, **psychosis** was thought to differ from neurosis in both the quality and severity of symptoms. Clinicians no longer conceive of psychosis as a more severe form of neurosis but as a profoundly distinct condition. The *DSM-IV* now reserves the term *psychotic* mainly for disorders that involve loss of contact with reality, such as we see in schizophrenia.

As you may have surmised from its origins in psychiatry, the *DSM-IV* has close ties to the medical model of mental illness. Its language is the language of medicine—symptoms, syndromes, diagnoses, and diseases—and its final form is a curious mixture of science and tradition. (Note: It contains no diagnosis of "normal.")

Unlike early versions of the manual, which had a distinctly Freudian flavor, the *DSM-IV* manages, for the most part, to avoid endorsing theories of cause or treatment. It also differs from early versions of the *DSM* by giving extensive and specific descriptions of the symptoms of each disorder. So, while the *DSM-IV* has its critics, the need for a common language of psychological disorder has brought it wide acceptance. In fact, acceptance has been so wide that some critics complain of the "Americanization of mental illness"—the notion that the *DSM-IV* view of mental disorder assumes that mental disorders are the same the world around, regardless of culture (Watters, 2010).

neurosis Before the *DSM-IV*, this term was used as a label for subjective distress or self-defeating behavior that did not show signs of brain abnormalities or grossly irrational thinking.

psychosis A disorder involving profound disturbances in perception, rational thinking, or affect.

Five-Dimensional Diagnosis: The Multiaxial System

At the heart of the *DSM-IV* is a *multiaxial system* requiring assessment on five "axes," or dimensions of patient functioning. The primary diagnosis is usually on Axis I, which specifies the particular clinical disorder affecting the patient. Examples include major depression, panic disorder, and obsessive-compulsive disorder. Descriptions on the other four axes, then, typically describe the context in which the Axis I disorder occurs.

Axis II specifies any long-standing problems, such as the personality disorders and the developmental disorders. Likewise, a diagnosis on Axis III specifies any relevant medical problems, such as a stroke or dementia. Axis IV reminds the clinician to note any psychosocial or environmental issues that may affect the patient's functioning—issues such as divorce, death of a loved one, loss of a job, homelessness, legal problems, or exposure to a disaster. Finally, Axis V calls for an overall assessment of the patient on the Global Assessment of Functioning (GAF) Scale. This assessment may range from a high score of 100 (the total absence of symptoms) to a low of 1 (severe impairment that poses a danger to self or others).

Explore the **Concept** Axes of the DSM at **MyPsychLab**

The multiaxial system, therefore, gives the clinician a way to diagnose the patient's specific disorder and the context in which it occurs. In effect, it requires five separate diagnoses. Here's an example of a multiaxial diagnosis for a single patient:

Axis I	Major Depressive Disorder
Axis II	Narcissistic Personality Disorder
Axis III	Chronic lumbar pain, hypothyroidism
Axis IV	Recently divorced, unemployed
Axis V	GAF = 65

Controversy Surrounding the *DSM-IV*

Many clinicians have reservations about the *DSM-IV* system. For one thing, the *DSM-IV* classifies disorders by symptoms, not by underlying causes—as we have said. In fact, there are no objective laboratory-style tests for any of the primary disorders—so every *DSM-IV* diagnosis relies on subjective clinical judgment.

Another issue involves the "all-or-nothing" nature of a *DSM-IV* diagnosis: Many psychologists feel that mental disorders are not distinct categories. Instead, they see them as exaggerations of normal functioning. In this view, we all fall somewhere on the schizophrenic spectrum—and also on the spectra of autism, phobia, and paranoia.

And finally, many psychologists are uncomfortable with the idea of mental disorders being conceptualized as "diseases" and incorporated into the medical model. They believe that many mental disorders are not medical conditions at all but rather behavior patterns that have been *learned*. Some mental "illnesses" might even be a normal response to an abnormal environment.

Despite these points of dispute, most clinicians do use the *DSM-IV* system because it standardizes the criteria for diagnosing mental disorders. Moreover, it offers the only system accepted by most insurance companies in the United States—a powerful incentive for clinicians to go along with a framework widely acknowledged to be imperfect.

With these advantages and disadvantages in mind, then, let us now turn to a sampling of disorders described on Axes I and II of the *DSM-IV*. A look at the chart in the margin next to our discussion of each of the major diagnostic categories will give you an overview of the scheme the manual uses to classify these disorders. We begin with those that involve sustained extremes of emotion: the *mood disorders,* also known as *affective disorders.*

Mood Disorders

▶ **Mood Disorders:** Extremes of mood, from mania to depression

- Major depression
- Bipolar disorder

Who has never played on a losing team, fallen in love, or had some terrifying experience? Everyone experiences occasional strong, even unpleasant, emotional reactions. Emotional highs and lows are part of our everyday lives and a normal part of our interpretation of the world. However, when moods career out of control, soaring to extreme elation or plunging to deep depression, the diagnosis will probably be one of the **mood disorders.** The clinician will also suspect a mood disorder when an individual's emotions are consistently inappropriate to the situation. Here we will discuss the two best-known of these affective disturbances, *major depression* and *bipolar disorder.*

mood disorder   Abnormal disturbance in emotion or mood, including bipolar disorder and unipolar disorder. Mood disorders are also called affective disorders.

Major Depression

If you fail an important examination, lose a job, or lose a love, it is normal to feel depressed for a while. If a close friend dies, it is also normal to feel depressed. But if these feelings remain for weeks or months, long after the depressing event has passed, then you may have the clinically significant condition called **major depression** or *major depressive disorder*—among the commonest of all major mental disturbances.

major depression   A form of depression that does not alternate with mania.

Novelist William Styron (1990) wrote movingly about his own experience with severe depression: The pain he endured convinced him that clinical depression is much more than a bad mood. This sort of depression does not give way to periods of manic excitement or euphoria. Nor does it let its victims escape in sleep, because insomnia so commonly multiplies the suffering of depression (Harvey, 2008).

Incidence   Psychologist Martin Seligman (1973, 1975) has called depression the "common cold" of psychological problems. In the United States, it accounts for the majority of all mental hospital admissions. Depression is also the stuff of "the blues"—so common that it has produced a whole genre of music. And even if you have not, at some time, known major depression, chances are that you have experienced a milder form that clinicians call *dysthymia*. Even so, many clinicians believe depression, in both mild and severe forms, to be underdiagnosed and undertreated (Kessler et al., 2003; Robins et al., 1991).

The National Institute of Mental Health (NIMH) (2006) estimates that depression costs Americans about $83 billion each year, including the costs of hospitalization,

Do It Yourself! A DEPRESSION CHECK

Most people think that depression is marked by outward signs of sadness, such as weeping. But depression affects other aspects of thought and behavior, as well. For a quick check on your own tendencies to depression, please answer "yes" or "no" to each of the following questions:

1. Do you feel sad, hopeless, or guilty most of the time?

2. Do former friends avoid spending time with you? Or, do you feel you have lost interest in activities, events, and people around you?

3. Have you experienced any major change in appetite or body weight, though not from dieting?

4. Do you often feel restless or have difficulty sleeping, especially because of thoughts racing through your mind?

5. Do you feel more sluggish and fatigued than you ought to?

6. Do you spend excessive amounts of time sleeping?

7. Do you spend a lot of time "ruminating" about unhappy experiences you have had or mistakes you have made?

8. Have you been finding it increasingly difficult to think or concentrate?

9. Do you have recurrent thoughts of death or suicide?

10. Do you spend a great deal of time engaging in "escape" activities that help you avoid important issues in your life. (These might include excessive time spent playing video or computer games, reading, or alcohol consumption.)

This checklist is, of course, not a substitute for a clinical evaluation by a professional. While there is no "magic number" of items to which you must answer "yes" to qualify as depressed, if you answered "yes" to some of them and if you are concerned, you might want to seek a professional opinion. Remember that a diagnosis of depression is always a clinical judgment call, based on the signs listed in the *DSM-IV*. Essentially, the clinician will look at the pattern and the quality of your life, your feelings, and your behavior to determine whether or not they fit the *DSM-IV* criteria. Remember also that self-report is always subject to some bias. If you are concerned after considering the signs of depression in your life, we recommend an examination by a competent mental health professional.

therapy, and lost productivity. But the human cost cannot be measured in dollars. Countless people in the throes of depression may feel worthless, lack appetite, withdraw from friends and family, have difficulty sleeping, lose their jobs, and become agitated or lethargic. In severe cases, they may also have psychotic distortions of reality. You can give yourself a quick evaluation for signs of depression in the box, *Do It Yourself! A Depression Check*.

Most worrisome of all, suicide claims one in 50 people with depression (Bostwick & Pankratz, 2000). Significantly, a person with depression faces a significant risk of suicide both on the way down in a depressive episode and on the upswing. In fact, the risk of suicide is greater during these swings of mood than during the deepest phase of the depressive cycle. Why? Because, in the depths of depressive despair, a person may have no energy or will to do *anything*, much less carry out a plan for suicide. Other factors may compound the risk as well. Abuse of alcohol or other drugs, for example, multiplies the likelihood of suicide, as do poor impulse control, chronic physical diseases, and certain brain abnormalities (Ezzell, 2003; Springen, 2010).

Incidentally, your authors advise that a suicide threat always be taken seriously, even though you may think it is just a bid for attention—and even if you see no other signs of depression. But don't try to treat it yourself. You should direct any person who suggests he or she is thinking about suicide to a competent professional for help.

Cross-Cultural Comparisons   Studies reveal depression as the single most prevalent form of disability around the globe (Holden, 2000a), although the incidence of major depression varies widely, as Table 12.2 shows. In fairness, we should note a minority view holding that the diagnosis of depression is overused, because clinicians attach the label to people having a normal reaction to misfortune and because drug companies relentlessly push pills as the answer to life's unhappiness (Andrews & Thompson, 2009, 2010).

While some of the variation across cultures may be the result of differences in reporting depression and in readiness or reluctance to seek help for depression, other factors seem to be at work too. For example, the stresses of war have undoubtedly inflated the rate of depression in the Middle East (Thabet et al., 2004). And in Taiwan and Korea, the *low* rates of depression may reflect low rates of marital separation and

TABLE 12.2 Lifetime Risk of a Depressive Episode Lasting a Year or More

Taiwan	1.5%
Korea	2.9%
Puerto Rico	4.3%
United States	5.2%
Germany	9.2%
Canada	9.6%
New Zealand	11.6%
France	16.4%
Lebanon	19%

Source: Weissman, M. M., et al. (1996, July 24–31). Cross-national epidemiology of major depression and bipolar disorder. *Journal of the American Medical Association, 276*, 293–299.

divorce—factors known to be associated with high risk of depression in virtually all cultures.

Causes of Depression We have collected many pieces of the depression puzzle, but no one has managed to put them all together into a big picture that everyone likes. Some cases almost certainly have a genetic origin, because severe bouts with depression often run in families (Plomin et al., 1994). A few observers even suggest that a tendency for depression, at least in a mild form, may have even been adaptive in our evolutionary past because mild depression and worry helped people focus intently on problems that affected survival (Andrews & Thompson, 2009, 2010). And indeed, in people diagnosed with depression, we often find that they cannot take their minds off their troubles—a process called *rumination*.

Further indication of a biological basis for depression comes from the favorable response that many patients with depression have to drugs that affect the brain's neurotransmitters norepinephrine, serotonin, and dopamine (Ezzell, 2003). These antidepressant medicines also stimulate growth of new neurons in the hippocampus (Insel, 2007). This makes sense in light of studies showing that stress can both suppress the growth of neurons in the hippocampus *and* precipitate a depressive episode (Jacobs, 2004).

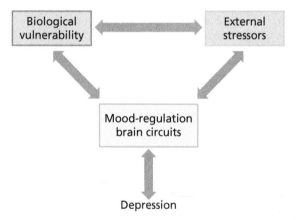

FIGURE 12.2

Mayberg's Model of Depression

In this view, depression results from an interplay of three major factors: (a) the brain's mood-regulating circuitry (including cortical, subcortical, and limbic system regions, and their neurotransmitters, (b) external stressors (including life events, physical trauma, and disease), and (c) biological vulnerability (including genetics and gender).

Source: Adaptation of Figure 1 from Mayberg, H. S. (2006). Defining neurocircuits in depression: strategies toward treatment selection based on neuroimaging phenotypes. *Psychiatric Annals, 36*(4), 259–268.

seasonal affective disorder (SAD) A form of depression believed to be caused by deprivation of sunlight.

CONNECTION CHAPTER 8

The "biological clock," located in the hypothalamus, regulates our circadian rhythms (p. 333).

Evidence also connects depression with lower brain wave activity in the left frontal lobe (Davidson, 1992a,b, 2000a; Robbins, 2000). And, in a few cases, depression may arise from viral infection (Bower, 1995b; Neimark, 2005). Such evidence leads some observers to view depression as a collection of disorders having a variety of causes and involving many parts of the brain (Kendler & Gardner, 1998).

Recently, neuroimaging has revealed a link between the amygdala and a part of the frontal lobes called *area 25*, located at the base of the frontal cortex, just over the roof of the mouth. In brains of those with depression, where many functions seem to slow down, area 25 paradoxically shows up on scans as "hot," says neuroscientist Helen Mayberg (Dobbs, 2006b; Insel, 2010; Mayberg, 2006, 2009). Moreover, successful therapies for depression—either drugs or psychotherapy—suppress activity in area 25. It's a puzzle. No one is sure exactly what area 25 is or exactly how it works, although Mayberg suspects that it acts as a sort of "switch" connecting the conscious "thinking" portions of the frontal lobes and the brain's unconscious "alarm system."

Mayberg also believes that area 25 does not act alone but rather interacts with a whole suite of brain modules that, together, produce depression. Thus, although Mayberg has fingered area 25, she says that we should not think of depression as a disorder of a particular region in the brain. Rather, it involves a malfunctioning *system* of structures in the cortex, subcortex, and limbic system, along with imbalances in the neurotransmitters serving these regions. She argues that depressive episodes occur when a person with a defect in this complex mood-regulating system encounters stress (see Figure 12.2).

Sunlight and Depression Adding to this rather confusing picture, clinicians have found that lack of sunlight can also initiate a special form of depression that appears during the dark winter months among people living in high latitudes (Insel, 2010; Lewy et al., 2006). You can see the relationship between light and depression in Figure 12.3.

Aptly named, this **seasonal affective disorder (SAD)** stems from low levels of the hormone melatonin, mediated by special light-sensitive cells—but not the rods and cones—in the retina. (Yes, some blind people do develop SAD!) Daily fluctuations in melatonin regulate our internal biological clocks (Steele & Johnson, 2009). Based on this knowledge, researchers have developed a simple and effective therapy to regulate the hormone by exposing those with SAD daily to bright artificial light. Therapists report that combining light therapy with cognitive-behavioral therapy or antidepressants works even better (DeAngelis, 2006).

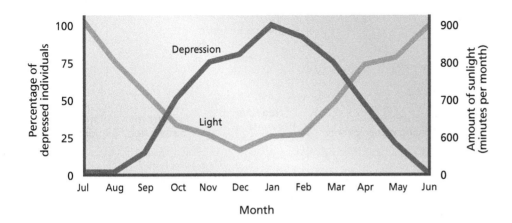

FIGURE 12.3

Relationship between Light and SAD

People who have seasonal affective disorder are most likely to experience symptoms of depression during months with shortened periods of sunlight.

Source: Based on Figure 1 from Rosenthal, N. E., Sack D. A., Gillen, J. C., Lewy, A. J., Goodwin, F. K., Davenport, Y., Mueller, P. S., Newsome, D. A., & Wehr, T. A. (1984). Seasonal affective disorder: a description of the syndrome and preliminary findings with light therapy. *Archives of General Psychiatry, 41,* pp. 72–80.

Psychological Factors   As with most other disorders, biology alone cannot entirely explain depression. We must also understand depression as a mental, social, and behavioral condition. Considerable evidence implicates stressful events, such as losing a job or the death of a loved one, as major factors in depression (Monroe & Reid, 2009). Low self-esteem and a pessimistic attitude can add fuel to a cycle of depressive thought patterns. Psychologists call this **rumination**, an incessant mental replay of depressive thoughts (Nolen-Hoeksema et al., 2008). While this whirlpool of depression may initially elicit attention and sympathy, it eventually turns people away, leaving the individual with depression isolated and even more depressed (see Figure 12.4).

Probably because of low self-esteem, depression-prone people are more likely to perpetuate the depression cycle by attributing negative events to their own personal flaws or external conditions that they feel helpless to change (Azar, 1994). Martin Seligman calls this **learned helplessness**. These negative self-attributions, then, feed the cycle of depression and despair (Coyne et al., 1991).

Who Becomes Depressed?   No one knows why women have higher depression rates than do men (Holden, 2005). According to Susan NolenHoeksema (2001), the difference may lie in the differing responses to sadness in men and women. When women experience sadness, she says, they tend to focus on the possible causes and consequences of their feelings. On the other hand, men attempt to distract themselves from feelings of depression, either by shifting their attention to something else or by doing something physical that will take their minds off their mood. This model suggests, then, that women ruminate more about their troubles, which increases their vulnerability to depression (Shea, 1998). Another possible source of the gender discrepancy in depression may involve norms that encourage women to seek help but discourage men from doing so. Thus, the differences we seen in the rates of depression may be, at least in part, due to gender differences in seeking help.

In addition to gender, age is also a factor in depression. According to NIMH (2010a), depression is more common among young adults than among those over 60. While the average age of onset is about 32 years of age, a large U.S. survey found that the likelihood of depression begins a sharp increase between 12 and 16 years (Hasin et al., 2005). The same study also found elevated rates of the disorder among Baby Boomers.

Bipolar Disorder   The other mood disorder we will consider involves extreme swings of mood, from periods of depression to times of extreme elation. Formerly known as *manic–depressive disorder,* the *DSM-IV* now lists the condition as **bipolar disorder.** The alternating periods of *mania* (excessive elation or manic excitement) and the profound sadness of depression represent the two "poles" of *bipolar.*

During the *manic phase,* the individual becomes euphoric, energetic, hyperactive, talkative, and emotionally wound tight like a spring. It is not unusual for people swept up in mania to spend their life savings on extravagant purchases or to have casual, unprotected sexual liaisons or to engage in other risky and frisky behaviors. When

rumination   A pernicious form of self-reflection in which a person repeatedly rethinks depressive thoughts and feelings.

learned helplessness   A condition in which depressed individuals learn to attribute negative events to their own personal flaws or external conditions that the person feels helpless to change. People with learned helplessness can be thought of as having an extreme form of *external locus of control.*

bipolar disorder   A mental abnormality involving swings of mood from mania to depression.

FIGURE 12.4

FIGURE 12.4

The Cognitive–Behavioral Cycle of Depression

As you follow Fred around the cycle, note how his depression feeds on itself.

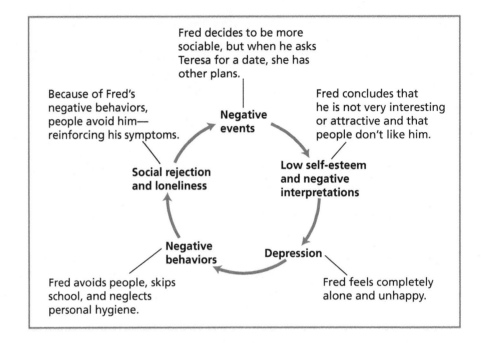

Fred decides to be more sociable, but when he asks Teresa for a date, she has other plans.

Because of Fred's negative behaviors, people avoid him—reinforcing his symptoms.

Negative events

Fred concludes that he is not very interesting or attractive and that people don't like him.

Social rejection and loneliness

Low self-esteem and negative interpretations

Negative behaviors

Depression

Fred avoids people, skips school, and neglects personal hygiene.

Fred feels completely alone and unhappy.

Dutch artist Vincent Van Gogh showed signs of bipolar disorder. This problem seems to have a high incidence among very creative people.

> **Anxiety Disorders:** Fear, anxiety, panic attacks
>
> • Generalized anxiety disorder
> • Panic disorder
> • Agoraphobia
> • Specific phobias
> • Obsessive–compulsive disorder

anxiety disorder   Mental problem characterized mainly by anxiety. Anxiety disorders include panic disorder, specific phobias, and obsessive–compulsive disorder.

the mania wanes, they then must deal with the damage they have created during their carefree and frenetic period. Soon, the *depressive phase* follows, bringing a dark wave of melancholy that sweeps over the mind. In this phase, the symptoms mimic those of major depression (also called "unipolar" depression). Biologically speaking, however, these two forms of depression differ: We know this because the antidepressant drugs that work well on major depression don't usually help victims of bipolar disorder—sometimes they even make it worse.

Research has established a genetic contribution, although the experts haven't yet pinpointed the exact genes involved (Bradbury, 2001). While only 2.6 percent of American adults have bipolar attacks, the disorder is highly heritable, making it much more frequent in some families (Kieseppa et al., 2004; NIMH, 2010b). The fact that bipolar disorder usually responds well to medication also suggests biological factors at work.

Oddly, the incidence of bipolar disorder has risen in recent years, particularly in children (Holden, 2008). This hints that the condition may have some environmental cause. Alternatively, some cases of bipolar disorder may have been overlooked in the past, or perhaps it is currently being overdiagnosed. Whatever is the truth of the matter, some sort of influence beyond genetics is at work.

Anxiety Disorders

Everyone has experienced anxiety in threatening or otherwise stressful situations. But would you pick up a snake? Or would you let a tarantula rest on your shoulder? For many people the mere thought of snakes or spiders is enough to send chills of fear down their spines.

Lots of people don't particularly like snakes or spiders, but that doesn't necessarily mean that they have an anxiety disorder. The pathological anxiety seen in the anxiety disorders is far more debilitating than the normal hesitancy associated with slithering, crawling things. Pathological anxiety is also relatively common—even more common than major depression (Barlow, 2000). One estimate says that over our lifetime, 30 percent of us—more women than men—will experience symptoms that are serious enough to qualify as one of the **anxiety disorders** recognized in the *DSM* (Hébert, 2006; Holden, 2005).

Here we will review four pathologies that have anxiety as their main feature: (1) *generalized anxiety disorder*, (2) *panic disorder*, (3) *phobic disorder*, and (4) *obsessive-compulsive disorder*. The major differences among them have to do with the target and the duration of anxiety: Does the anxiety seem to come from nowhere—unrelated to the individual's environment? Is it provoked by some object or situation, such as the sight of blood or a snake? Is the anxiety present most of the time or only occasionally?

Generalized Anxiety Disorder Some people spend months or years of their lives coping with anxiety. Charles, a heavy-equipment operator, says he has dizzy spells, headaches, cold sweats, and frequent feelings of "free-floating" anxiety. But he has no clue why he feels this way. A clinician would diagnose his condition as **generalized anxiety disorder.**

Charles and others with this problem are not worried or fearful about specific situations or objects, such as snakes or spiders. Rather, they have a pervasive and persistent sense of anxiety that seems to come from nowhere and lasts for long periods. They simply feel anxious much of the time, without knowing why.

How common is this condition? According to NIMH (2010b), about 6.8 million adult Americans have generalized anxiety disorder. As with depression, there is a gender difference, with generalized anxiety disorder affecting about twice as many women as men.

Panic Disorder While calmly eating lunch, an unexpected wave of panic sweeps over you, seemingly from nowhere. Your heart races, your body shakes, you feel dizzy, your hands become clammy and sweaty, you are afraid that you might be dying. You are having a *panic attack.*

The distinguishing feature of **panic disorder** is a recurring strong feeling of anxiety that occurs "out of the blue," with no connection to present events (Barlow, 2001). As in generalized anxiety disorder, the feeling is one of "free-floating anxiety." The difference is that the anxiety attacks in panic disorder usually last for only a few minutes and then subside (McNally, 1994).

Because of the unexpected nature of these "hit-and-run" attacks, *anticipatory anxiety* often develops as an added complication. The dread of the next attack and of being helpless and suddenly out of control can lead a person to avoid public places yet to fear being left alone. Cognitive–behavioral theorists view panic attacks as conditioned responses to physical sensations that may have initially been learned during a period of stress (Antony et al., 1992).

Biologically, we have strong evidence of genetic influences in panic disorder (Hettema et al., 2001). We also know that the brain pathways involved include the unconscious arousal pathway and, especially, the amygdala (Hébert, 2006; LeDoux, 1996; Mobbs et al., 2007). This "fear circuit" easily learns fear reactions but is reluctant to give them up—probably a good thing for our ancestors who had to avoid predators. It also appears that overstimulation of these emotion circuits can produce lasting physical changes that make the individual even more susceptible to future anxiety attacks (Rosen & Schulkin, 1998).

To complicate matters further, many people with panic disorder also have **agoraphobia,** a fearful reaction to crowded public places, open spaces, or other situations from which they fear that they cannot easily escape. The term *agoraphobia* literally translates from the ancient Greek as "fear of the marketplace." Victims of agoraphobia often fear that, if they have a panic attack in one of these locations, help might not be available or the situation will be embarrassing to them. These fears tend to grow and eventually deprive afflicted persons of their freedom, with some becoming essentially prisoners in their own homes, unable to hold a job or carry on normal daily activities.

It's entirely possible that you may know someone who has panic disorder or agoraphobia, because these disorders occur in nearly 4 percent of the population, again much more commonly in women than in men (Kessler et al., 2005). Fortunately, the

generalized anxiety disorder A psychological problem characterized by persistent and pervasive feelings of anxiety, without any external cause.

panic disorder A disturbance marked by panic attacks that have no obvious connection with events in the person's present experience. Unlike generalized anxiety disorder, the victim is usually free of anxiety between panic attacks.

CONNECTION CHAPTER 9

The brain has two main emotional pathways; one operates mainly at an unconscious level (p. 392).

agoraphobia A fear of public places and open spaces, commonly accompanying panic disorder.

treatment outlook is hopeful. Medical therapy involves antianxiety drugs to relieve the panic attacks. Psychological treatment is also effective: As we will see in the next chapter, cognitive–behavioral therapy may equal or outperform drug therapy in combating panic attacks.

Phobic Disorder In contrast with panic disorder and generalized anxiety disorder, **phobias** involve an irrational, debilitating fear of a specific object, activity, or situation—a response all out of proportion to the circumstances. (These are sometimes called *specific phobias,* as contrasted with the broader, nonspecific fears found in agoraphobia.) Phobias may center on spiders, snakes, thunder, lightning, germs, or any of dozens of objects or situations. 👁

By affecting more than 10 million Americans each year, phobias do cause substantial disruption to the lives of many people (Winerman, 2005b). Certain specific phobias are quite rare, e.g., fear of books, string, or even toads! Others, such as an extreme fear of closed spaces (claustrophobia), occur so commonly that they seem almost the norm. (Claustrophobia, for example, often prevents people from getting the needed MRI scans because of the confined space within the magnet.) Other common phobic disorders include *social phobias,* which are irrational fears of normal social situations, and fear of heights (acrophobia) and snakes (ophidiophobia). Still other phobias appear in Table 12.3.

What causes phobias? Long ago, John Watson and Rosalie Rayner demonstrated that fears can be learned. And we also have good evidence that fears and phobias can be *un*learned through cognitive–behavioral therapy based on conditioning

phobia One of a group of anxiety disorders involving a pathological fear of a specific object or situation.

👁 Watch the **Video** Phobias at **MyPsychLab**

CONNECTION CHAPTER 4

Watson and Rayner's infamous experiment with Little Albert showed that fears could be learned by classical conditioning (p. 139).

TABLE 12.3 Phobias

DSM-IV Category	Object/Situation	Incidence
Agoraphobia	Crowds, open spaces	Common (3.5–7% of adults)
Social Phobias	Fear of being observed or doing something humiliating	Common (11–15%)
Specific Phobias	Varies by category	(Up to 16% of adults have one or more specific phobias)
Animals	Cats (ailurophobia)	
	Dogs (cynophobia)	
	Insects (insectophobia)	
	Spiders (arachnophobia)	
	Birds (avisophobia)	
	Horses (equinophobia)	
	Snakes (ophidiophobia)	
	Rodents (rodentophobia)	
Inanimate objects or situations	Closed spaces (claustrophobia)	
	Dirt (mysophobia)	
	Thunder (brontophobia)	
	Lightning (astraphobia)	
	Heights (acrophobia)	
	Darkness (nyctophobia)	
	Fire (pyrophobia)	

(Continued)

TABLE 12.3 *(Continued)*

DSM-IV Category	Object/Situation	Incidence
Bodily conditions	Illness or injury (nosophobia)	(Up to 16% of adults have one or more specific phobias)
	Sight of blood (hematophobia)	
	Cancer (cancerophobia)	
	Venereal disease (venerophobia)	
	Death (thanatophobia)	
Other specific phobias	Numbers (numerophobia)	Rare
	The number 13 (triskaidekaphobia)	Rare
	Strangers, foreigners (xenophobia)	Rare
	String (linonophobia)	Rare
	Books (bibliophobia)	Rare
	Work (ergophobia)	Rare

Note: Hundreds of phobias have been described and given scientific names; this table provides only a sample. Some of the rare and strange-sounding phobias may have been observed in a single patient.

A common form of social phobia involves an extreme fear of public speaking.

(Mineka & Zinbarg, 2006). But learning may not tell the whole story, says Martin Seligman (1971), who has argued that humans are biologically predisposed to learn some kinds of fears more easily than others. This **preparedness hypothesis** suggests that we carry an innate biological tendency, acquired through natural selection, to respond quickly and automatically to stimuli that posed a survival threat to our ancestors (Öhman & Mineka, 2001). This explains why we develop phobias for snakes and lightning much more easily than we develop fears for automobiles and electrical outlets—objects that have posed a danger only in recent times. Again, the underlying brain mechanism includes the amygdala and the fast-and-unconscious emotion pathway mapped by Joseph LeDoux and his colleagues (Schafe et al., 2005; Wilensky et al., 2006).

preparedness hypothesis   The notion that we have an innate tendency, acquired through natural selection, to respond quickly and automatically to stimuli that posed a survival threat to our ancestors.

obsessive–compulsive disorder (OCD)   A condition characterized by patterns of persistent, unwanted thoughts and behaviors.

Obsessive–Compulsive Disorder In literature's most famous case of *obsessive compulsive disorder,* Lady Macbeth cries, "Out, damn'd spot! out, I say!" as she repeatedly washes her hands, trying to rid herself of guilt for the murder of King Duncan. Although people with **obsessive–compulsive disorder (OCD)** don't usually hallucinate about blood spots on their hands, Shakespeare got the rest spot-on. The main characteristics of OCD are persistent, unwelcome thoughts and ritual behaviors. Obsessive–compulsive disorder affects about 1 percent of us in any given year, regardless of culture (Steketee & Barlow, 2002).

The *obsession* component of OCD consists of thoughts, images, or impulses that recur or persist despite a person's efforts to suppress them. For example, a person with an obsessive fear of germs may avoid using bathrooms outside his or her home or refuse to shake hands with strangers. Others may obsess about keeping their houses clean and tidy or arranging shoes in their closets. And because people with OCD realize that their obsessive thoughts and compulsive rituals are senseless, they often go to great lengths to hide their compulsive behavior from other people. This, of course, places restrictions on their domestic, social, and work lives. Not surprisingly, people with OCD have extremely high divorce rates.

If you have ever been plagued by petty worries or persistent thoughts such as, "Did I remember to lock the door?" you have had a mild obsessional experience.

Obsessive–compulsive disorder makes people engage in senseless, ritualistic behaviors, such as repetitive hand washing.

A haunting phrase or melody that keeps running through your mind qualifies as a form of obsession too. Such thoughts are normal if they occur only occasionally and have not caused significant disruptions in your life. As we have noted in other disorders, it is a matter of degree.

Compulsions, the other half of obsessive–compulsive disorder, are repetitive, purposeful acts performed according to certain private "rules" in response to an obsession. People with OCD symptoms feel that their compulsive behavior will, somehow, reduce the tension associated with their obsessions. These urges may include an irresistible need to clean, to count objects or possessions, or to check and recheck "just to make sure" that lights or appliances have been turned off. When they are calm, individuals with OCD view these compulsions as senseless, but when their anxiety rises, they can't resist performing the compulsive behavior ritual to relieve tension. Part of the pain experienced by people with OCD comes from realizing the utter irrationality of their obsessions and their powerlessness to eliminate them. ◉

The tendency for OCD to run in families suggests a genetic link (Insel, 2010). Another hint comes from the finding that many people with OCD also display *tics,* unwanted involuntary movements, such as exaggerated eye blinks. In these patients, brain imaging often shows oddities in the deep motor control areas (Resnick, 1992). OCD expert Judith Rapoport tells us to think of compulsions as the brain's "fixed software packages," programmed for worry and repeated rituals. Once activated, she theorizes, the patient gets caught in a behavioral "loop" that cannot be switched off (Rapoport, 1989).

Again (at the risk of sounding obsessive!), we must note that biology cannot explain everything. Some people with OCD have clearly *learned* that their anxiety-provoking thoughts are connected to harmful consequences (Barlow, 2000). We can see further evidence that learning plays a role in behavioral therapy, which effectively reduces compulsive actions. A behavioral strategy for treating compulsive Lady Macbeth's ritual hand washing, for example, would call for a form of *extinction,* in which the therapist would prevent her from washing for progressively longer periods. Indeed, behavioral therapy can produce changes that show up in PET scans of OCD patients' brains (Schwartz et al., 1996). The general principle is this: When we change behavior, we inevitably change the brain, demonstrating once again that biology and behavior are inseparable.

Somatoform Disorders

"Soma" means *body.* Thus, the term **somatoform disorders** refers to psychological problems manifested in bodily symptoms, physical complaints, such as weakness, pain, or excessive worry about disease—as in the person who constantly frets about cancer. Not especially common, somatoform disorders occur in about 2 percent of the population. Still, they have captured the popular imagination under their more common names: "hysteria"[1] and "hypochondria" (Holmes, 2001).

The *DSM-IV* recognizes several types of somatoform disorders, but we will cover only two: *conversion disorder* and *hypochondriasis,* shown in the chart in the margin. And, while we're talking about somatoform disorders, please note their potential for confusion with *psychosomatic disorders,* in which mental conditions—especially stress—lead to actual physical disease. The *DSM-IV* places psychosomatic disorders under a separate heading, "Psychological Factors Affecting Medical Condition."

Conversion Disorder   Paralysis, weakness, or loss of sensation—with no discernible physical cause—distinguishes **conversion disorder** (formerly called "hysteria"). People with this diagnosis may, for example, be blind, deaf, unable to walk, or insensitive to

---

Watch the **Video** Margo: Obsessive-Compulsive Disorder at **MyPsychLab**

CONNECTION CHAPTER 4

In classical and operant conditioning, extinction involves the suppression of a response as the result of learning a competing response (p. 138).

---

somatoform disorders   Psychological problem appearing in the form of bodily symptoms or physical complaints, such as weakness or excessive worry about disease. The somatoform disorders include conversion disorder and hypochondriasis.

▶ **Somatoform Disorders:** Physical symptoms or overconcern with one's health

• Conversion disorder
• Hypochondriasis

---

conversion disorder   A type of somatoform disorder marked by paralysis, weakness, or loss of sensation but with no discernible physical cause.

---

[1]The original term *hysteria* had nothing to do with "going into hysterics." Rather, *hysteria* comes from the Greek word for "womb." At one time, physicians thought that only women could have hysteria, because they believed the physical symptoms to be caused by the womb migrating to the afflicted part of the body.

touch in part of their bodies. ("Glove anesthesia," shown in Figure 12.5, is a rare but classic form of sensory loss in conversion disorder.) Significantly, individuals with this condition have no organic disease that shows up on neurological examinations, laboratory tests, X-rays, or body scans. In conversion disorder, the problem really seems to be "all in the mind."

The term *conversion disorder* carries with it some baggage from the Freudian past. Originally, the term implied an unconscious displacement (or *conversion*) of anxiety into physical symptoms—although most clinicians no longer subscribe to that explanation. The diagnosis also has a reputation for being used as a "dumping ground" for those—especially females—who present physical symptoms but no obvious medical abnormality (Kinetz, 2006).

Some cases of conversion disorder are now thought to stem from physical stress responses. Another possibility, suggested by David Oakley (1999) of the University College in London, is that a common brain mechanism underlies conversion disorder and hypnosis. Accordingly, he suggests that conversion disorder and related mental problems be reclassified as *auto-suggestive disorders.*

Oddly, conversion disorder was much more common a century ago in Europe and the United States. More broadly, it has declined in industrialized countries, perhaps due to increased public understanding of physical and mental disorders (American Psychiatric Association, 1994; Nietzel et al., 1998). Meanwhile, conversion disorder is still relatively common in economically undeveloped regions, such as parts of China (Spitzer et al., 1989) and Africa (Binitie, 1975) and among poorly educated people in the United States (Barlow & Durand, 2005).

Hypochondriasis "Hypochondriacs" worry about getting sick. Every ache and pain signals a disease. Because of their exaggerated concern about illness, patients with **hypochondriasis** often bounce from physician to physician until they find one who will listen to their complaints and prescribe some sort of treatment—often minor tranquilizers or placebos. Naturally, these individuals represent easy marks for health fads and scams. They also find their way to the fringes of the medical community, where disreputable practitioners may encourage them to buy extensive and expensive treatments.

On the other side of the problem, we find the clinician who is too eager to conclude that the patient's concerns are imaginary—much as we found with conversion disorder. That is, some physicians seem to have a mental set to see hypochondria when they find no physical evidence of disease. This, of course, can have disastrous consequences, as when a mistaken impression of hypochondriasis blinds the physician to a very real and serious physical disease.

Dissociative Disorders

We may speak metaphorically of being "beside ourselves," but in the dissociative disorders, the feeling is no metaphor. The common denominator for all the **dissociative disorders** is "fragmentation" of the personality—a sense that some parts of the personality have become detached (dissociated) from one's sense of self. Among the dissociative disorders, we find some of the most fascinating forms of mental pathology, including *dissociative amnesia, dissociative fugue, depersonalization disorder,* and the controversial *dissociative identity disorder* (formerly called "multiple personality"), made famous by the fictional Dr. Jekyll and Mr. Hyde (see the chart in the margin). Unfortunately, the underlying causes of dissociative disorders remain unclear.

Dissociative Amnesia You may know an *amnesia* victim who has suffered a memory loss as the result of a severe blow to the head, perhaps in an auto accident. In many such cases, we find loss of recent memories, with well-established long-term memories preserved. But *dissociative amnesia* is different.

In **dissociative amnesia**, the memory loss typically is selective for specific personal events: for portions of episodic memory. The cause can be a stroke, alcoholic blackouts, head injuries, or a blood sugar crisis. But the origin is not always physical.

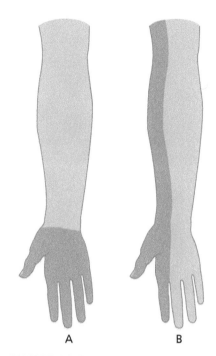

FIGURE 12.5
Glove Anesthesia

The form of conversion disorder known as "glove anesthesia" **(A)** involves a loss of sensation in the hand, as though the patient were wearing a thick glove. This cannot be a neurological disorder because the pattern of "anesthesia" does not correspond to the actual pattern of nerves in the hand, shown in **(B)**.

CONNECTION CHAPTER 6

A mental set is the tendency to respond to a new problem in the matter used for a previous problem (p. 225).

hypochondriasis A somatoform disorder involving excessive concern about health and disease; also called hypochondria.

dissociative disorders One of a group of pathologies involving "fragmentation" of the personality, in which some parts of the personality have become detached, or dissociated, from other parts.

dissociative amnesia A psychologically induced loss of memory of personal information, such as one's identity or residence.

▶ **Dissociative Disorders:** Nonpsychotic fragmentation of the personality

- Dissociative amnesia
- Dissociative fugue
- Depersonalization disorder
- Dissociative identity disorder

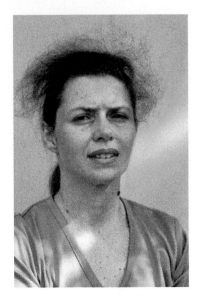

This is "Jane Doe," a victim of dissociative fugue who has never recovered the memory of her identity or her past.

dissociative fugue   Essentially the same as dissociative amnesia but with the addition of "flight" from one's home, family, and job. *Fugue* (pronounced *FEWG*) means "flight."

depersonalization disorder   An abnormality involving the sensation that mind and body have separated, as in an "out-of-body" experience.

dissociative identity disorder   A condition in which an individual displays multiple identities or personalities; formerly called "multiple personality disorder."

A purely psychological form of dissociative amnesia can result from a psychologically traumatic or a highly stressful experience.

As you might have guessed, dissociative amnesia has a close kinship with *posttraumatic stress disorder,* which we will discuss more extensively in Chapter 14. In both conditions, memory loss may relate to a particularly stressful incident or period in the person's life. We should note, however, that dissociative amnesia can be a controversial diagnosis when it is associated with recovered memories of childhood abuse, as we saw in the Memory chapter. As the *DSM-IV* states, dissociative amnesia may have "been overdiagnosed in individuals who are highly suggestible" (p. 479).

Dissociative Fugue   Now consider the real story of a woman with yet another dissociative disorder. "Jane Doe" was found near death in a Florida park, incoherent and suffering the effects of exposure. Unlike victims of dissociative amnesia, Jane Doe had a pervasive memory loss: no memory of her identity or any ability to read or write. Doctors diagnosed her with *dissociative fugue.* Therapy revealed only general information about the kind of past she must have had but no good clues as to her identity. After a nationwide television appeal, her doctors were flooded with calls. The most promising lead came from an Illinois couple, certain she was a daughter they had not heard from for more than 4 years. But despite their confidence that she was their daughter—even after meeting with her—Jane Doe was never able to remember her past (Carson et al., 2000).

Jane Doe's case was an extreme one: In most cases the fugue state lasts only hours or days, followed by complete and rapid recovery. Less often it may continue for months—or, as with Jane Doe, for years.

The diagnosis of **dissociative fugue** requires a combination of *amnesia* and *fugue* or "flight." In such persons, amnesia takes the form of a lost sense of identity, while the fugue component may cause them to flee their homes, families, and jobs. Some victims appear disoriented and perplexed. Others may travel to distant locations and take up new lives, appearing unconcerned about the unremembered past.

Heavy alcohol use may predispose a person to dissociative fugue. This suggests that the condition may involve some brain impairment—although no certain cause has been established. Like dissociative amnesia, fugue occurs more often in those under prolonged high stress, especially in times of war and other calamities. Some psychologists also suspect memory dissociation and repression accompany instances of sexual and physical childhood abuse (Spiegel & Cardeña, 1991). As with dissociative amnesia, this conjecture, however, is disputed.

Depersonalization Disorder   Yet another form of dissociation involves a sensation that mind and body have separated. People with **depersonalization disorder** commonly report "out-of-body experiences" or feelings of being external observers of their own bodies. Some feel as if they are in a dream. (Fleeting, mild forms of this are common, so there is no cause for alarm!) A study of 30 such cases found that obsessive–compulsive disorder and certain personality disorders often accompany this condition (Simeon et al., 1997). The causes are unknown.

People who have experienced severe physical trauma, such as a life-threatening injury in an auto accident, may also report symptoms of depersonalization. So do some individuals who have had near-death experiences. The effect is also common with those using recreational drugs. Usually the sensation passes rather quickly, although it can recur. In such individuals, investigators have attributed the disorder to hallucinations and to natural changes in the brain that occur during shock (Siegel, 1980), and one study has found people with depersonalization disorder to have abnormalities in the visual, auditory, and somatosensory cortex (Simeon et al., 2000).

Dissociative Identity Disorder   Robert Louis Stevenson's famous story of Dr. Jekyll and Mr. Hyde has become a misleading stereotype of **dissociative identity disorder.** In reality, most such cases occur in women, and most display more than two identities

(Ross et al., 1989). Unlike the homicidal Mr. Hyde in Stevenson's yarn, seldom do people with dissociative identity disorder pose a danger to others.

Although it was once thought to be rare, some specialists now believe that this controversial condition has always been common but hidden or misdiagnosed. Others believe that it is primarily the result of suggestion by the therapist—and not a real disorder at all (Piper & Mersky, 2004a,b). Proponents of the diagnosis say that dissociative identity disorder usually appears in childhood (Vincent & Pickering, 1988). Those with the disorder frequently report having been sexually abused (Putnam et al., 1986; Ross et al., 1990). If so, the formation of multiple identities or selves (sometimes referred to as *alters*) may be a defense by the dominant personality to protect itself from terrifying events or memories.

Dissociative identity disorder (DID) has now become a familiar diagnosis because of its portrayal in books such as *Sybil* (Schreiber, 1973) and *The Flock* (Casey & Wilson, 1991) and films such as the 1996 production *Primal Fear.* Each emerging personality contrasts in some significant way with the original self. For example, the new alter might be outgoing if the original personality is shy, tough if the original is weak, and sexually assertive if the other is fearful and sexually naive. These alternate identities, each apparently with its own consciousness, emerge suddenly—usually under stress.

What lies behind this mysterious disturbance? Psychodynamic theories explain it as a fracturing of the ego as a result of ego defense mechanisms that do not allow energy from conflicts and traumas to escape from the unconscious mind. Cognitive theories see it as a form of role playing or, perhaps, mood-state dependency, a form of memory bias in which events experienced in a given mood are more easily recalled when the individual is again in that mood state (Eich et al., 1997). Others suggest that at least some cases are frauds (as in the case of a student, charged with plagiarizing a term paper, who claimed that he had multiple personalities and that one of them copied the paper without the knowledge of his dominant personality).

To clear up a common point of confusion: In earlier editions of the *DSM,* dissociative identity disorder was called *multiple personality*—a term still heard occasionally. Adding to the confusion, DID is sometimes mistakenly called "split personality," an obsolete term for *schizophrenia*—which has *no* relationship to dissociative identity disorder at all. In schizophrenia (which literally means "split mind"), the "split" refers to a psychotic split from reality, not to a fracturing of one personality into many, which leads us to a discussion of schizophrenia . . . next.

Schizophrenia

Schizophrenia is the disorder that comes to mind when we hear the terms "madness," "psychosis," or "insanity." In psychological terms, **schizophrenia** encompasses several related forms of psychopathology in which personality seems to disintegrate, emotional life becomes disrupted, and cognitive processes grow distorted. (It was also the diagnosis given to all but one of Rosenhan's pseudopatients.)

The schizophrenic world may turn bleak and devoid of meaning, or it may become so filled with sensation that everything appears in a confusion of multiple realities layered with hallucinations and delusions. In schizophrenia, emotions often seem blunted, thoughts turn bizarre, language may take strange twists, and memory becomes fragmented (Danion et al., 1999). The disorder breaks the unity of the mind, often sending its victims on meaningless mental detours, sometimes spouting sequences of "clang" associations (associations involving similar-sounding words) and producing confused verbalizations that clinicians call "word salads." Here is an example of this type of speech:

> The lion will have to change from dogs into cats until I can meet my father and mother and we dispart some rats. I live on the front of Whitton's head. You have to work hard if you don't get into bed. . . . It's all over for a squab true tray and there ain't no squabs, there ain't no men, there ain't no music, there ain't no nothing besides my mother and my father who stand alone upon the Island of Capri where is no ice. Well it's my suitcase sir (Rogers, 1982).

schizophrenia (pronounced *skits-o-FRENNY-a*) A psychotic disorder involving distortions in thoughts, perceptions, and/or emotions.

▶ **Schizophrenia:** Psychotic deterioration of the personality, including disturbances in affect, thinking, and socialization

- Disorganized type
- Catatonic type
- Paranoid type
- Undifferentiated type
- Residual type

In a lifetime, more than one of every 100 Americans—more than 2 million over the age of 18—will become afflicted. Most will struggle with recurrent schizophrenic episodes all through their lives (Jobe & Harrow, 2010). For as yet unknown reasons, it happens to men more often, with the first appearance of schizophrenia typically occurring in men before they are 25 and in women between 25 and 45 years of age (Holden, 2005; NIMH, 2010b).

Major Types of Schizophrenia Many investigators consider schizophrenia a constellation of distinct disorders, with these five being the most common:

- **Disorganized type**—everyone's image of mental illness, featuring incoherent speech, hallucinations, delusions, and bizarre behavior. A person who talks to imaginary people most likely would receive this diagnosis.

- **Catatonic type**—appears in two forms: Persons with the more common *catatonic stupor* may remain motionless for hours—even days—sometimes holding rigid, statue-like postures. In the other form, called *catatonic excitement,* the patient becomes agitated and hyperactive.

- **Paranoid type**—features delusions and hallucinations but has no catatonic symptoms and little of the incoherence or confusion of disorganized schizophrenia. The paranoid delusions of persecution or of grandiosity (highly exaggerated self-importance) found in this type of schizophrenia are less well organized—more illogical—than those with a purely delusional disorder.

- **Undifferentiated type**—serves as a catchall category for schizophrenic symptoms that do not clearly meet the requirements for any of the other categories above.

- **Residual type**—the diagnosis for individuals who have had a schizophrenic episode in the past but currently have no major symptoms such as hallucinations or delusional thinking. Instead, their thinking is mildly disturbed, or their emotional lives are impoverished. The diagnosis of residual type may indicate that the disease is entering remission or becoming dormant. (This diagnosis was assumed in most of Rosenhan's pseudopatients, whom we met at the beginning of the chapter.)

In Table 12.4, you can see the criteria required for a diagnosis of schizophrenia according to criteria in the *DSM-IV.* Consider whether you think the symptoms presented by the Rosenhan's pseudopatients would warrant such a diagnosis under today's standards.

The fact that most such patients display a hodgepodge of symptoms places them into the "undifferentiated" category, further clouding our picture of the disorder.

TABLE 12.4 Criteria for a Diagnosis of Schizophrenia

A. *Characteristic symptoms:* Two (or more) of the following; each present for a significant portion of time during a 1-month period (or less if successfully treated):

1. delusions
2. hallucinations
3. disorganized speech (e.g., frequent derailment or incoherence)
4. grossly disorganized or catatonic behavior
5. negative symptoms, i.e., affective flattening, alogia, or avolition

. . . Only one Criterion A symptom is required if delusions are bizarre or hallucinations consist of a voice keeping up a running commentary on the person's behavior or thoughts, or two or more voices are conversing with each other.)

B. *Social/occupational dysfunction* . . . [Dysfunction in work, interpersonal relations, or self-care]

C. *Duration* . . . [Continuous signs of the disorder for at least six months]

Note: The *DSM-IV-TR* also qualifies the diagnosis of schizophrenia by excluding certain symptoms associated with medical conditions, drug abuse, and other mental disorders.

Source: American Psyciatric Association. (2000.) *Diagnostic and Statistical Manual of Mental Disorders* (4th ed., Text Revision, p. 312). Washington, DC: Author. 285–286.

Trying to make more sense of the problem, many investigators now merely divide the symptoms of schizophrenia into *positive* and *negative* categories (Javitt & Coyle, 2004; Sawa & Snyder, 2002). *Positive symptoms* refer to active processes, such as delusions and hallucinations, while *negative symptoms* refer to passive processes and deficiencies, such as social withdrawal, "flat" affect (lack of emotional expression), lack of pleasure in life, and poverty of thinking.

Patient responses to drug therapy support the positive–negative division: Those with positive symptoms usually respond to antipsychotic drugs, while those with negative symptoms do not (Andreasen et al., 1995; Heinrichs, 1993). But even this distinction has its problems because both positive and negative symptoms may occur in a single patient. Moreover, the negative form of schizophrenia often looks like major depression. All these difficulties have led some researchers to conclude that schizophrenia is probably a name covering a whole spectrum of disturbances.

Possible Causes of Schizophrenia No longer do most theorists look through the Freudian lens to see schizophrenia as the result of bad parenting or repressed childhood trauma (Walker & Tessner, 2008). Studies show that adopted children with no family history of the disorder run no increased risk of developing schizophrenia when placed in a home with a parent who has schizophrenia (Gottesman, 1991). Thus, an emerging consensus among psychiatrists and psychologists views schizophrenia as fundamentally a brain disorder—or a group of disorders (Grace, 2010; Karlsgodt et al., 2010; Walker et al., 2010).

Biological Factors in Schizophrenia Support for this brain-disorder view comes from many quarters. As we have noted, the antipsychotic drugs (sometimes called *major tranquilizers*)—which interfere with the brain's dopamine receptors—can suppress the positive symptoms of schizophrenia (Mueser & McGurk, 2004). On the other hand, drugs that stimulate dopamine production (e.g., the amphetamines) can actually produce schizophrenic reactions. Recently, attention has turned to deficiencies in the neurotransmitter glutamate (Berenson, 2008; Javitt & Coyle, 2004). Other evidence of a biological basis for schizophrenia comes in the form of abnormalities shown on brain scans, such as you see in Figure 12.6 (Conklin & Iacono, 2004; NIMH, 2005). In that vein, an especially provocative finding from MRI studies suggests that the schizophrenic brain fails to synchronize its neural firing across the cortex (Bower, 2005b; Symond et al., 2005).

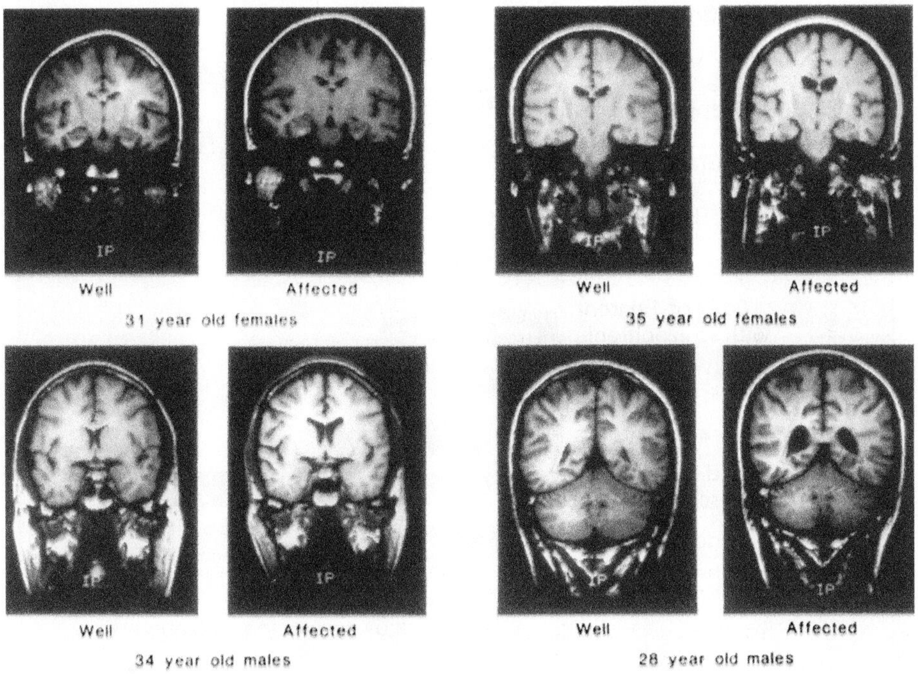

CONNECTION CHAPTER 13

Many antipsychotic drugs work by reducing the activity of the neurotransmitter dopamine in the brain (p. 578).

FIGURE 12.6

MRI Scans of a Twin with Schizophrenia and a Twin without Schizophrenia

The twin with schizophrenia is on the right. Note the enlarged ventricles (fluid-filled spaces) in the brain.

Yet another line of evidence for the biological basis of schizophrenia comes from family studies (Conklin & Iacono, 2004; Holden, 2003a). While no gene has been linked to schizophrenia with certainty, we do know that the closer one's relationship to a person with the disorder, the greater one's chances of developing it (Gottesman, 2001; Pogue-Gille & Yokley, 2010; Walker & Tessner, 2008).

Schizophrenia Is Not All Diathesis   Yet again, we sing the same refrain: Biology does not tell the whole story of schizophrenia. Ethnic background and geographic location also seem to be factors, although no clear cause-and-effect relationship has emerged (Minkel, 2009). We can see an environmental effect, too, in 90 percent of the relatives of people with schizophrenia, who do *not* develop the disorder (Barnes, 1987). Even in identical twins who share exactly the same genes, the *concordance rate* (the rate at which the disorder is shared by both) for schizophrenia is only about 50 percent. That is, in half the cases in which schizophrenia strikes identical twins, it leaves one twin untouched (see Figure 12.7).

So, can environment counterbalance heredity? Yes—to some extent—says a Finnish study. Being raised in a healthy family environment can actually *lower* the risk of schizophrenia in adopted children who have a genetic predisposition to the disease (Tienari et al., 1987). Apparently, schizophrenia requires a biological predisposition plus some unknown environmental agent to "turn on" the hereditary tendency (Cromwell, 1993; Iacono & Grove, 1993). This agent could be a chemical toxin, stress, or some factor we have not yet dreamed of. In view of all the evidence, we must remember that psychological disorder always requires an interaction of biological, cognitive, social-cultural, behavioral, and environmental factors, as our first Core Concept of the chapter suggested.

This broader perspective is often called the **diathesis–stress hypothesis.** In this view, biological factors put certain individuals at risk for mental disorder, but stressors in their lives transform the potential for psychopathology into an actual disorder

diathesis–stress hypothesis   In reference to schizophrenia, the proposal that genetic factors place the individual at risk while environmental stress factors transform this potential into an actual schizophrenic disorder.

FIGURE 12.7

Genetic Risk of Developing Schizophrenia

The graph shows average risks for developing schizophrenia in persons with a relative that has schizophrenia. Data were compiled from family and twin studies conducted in European populations between 1920 and 1987; the degree of risk correlates highly with the degree of genetic relatedness.

Source: Figure 10 from p. 96 of Gottesman, I. (1991). *Schizophrenia Genesis: The Origins of Madness.* New York, NY: W. H. Freeman/Times Books/Henry Holt & Co. Copyright © 1991. Reprinted by permission of W. H. Freeman and Company/Worth Publishers.

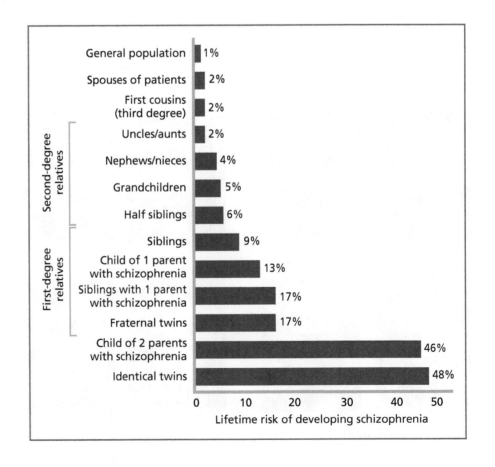

(Walker & Tessner, 2008). (The word *diathesis* refers to a predisposition or physical condition that makes one susceptible to disease, and *stress* can be caused by both psychological and biological stressors, including drugs and other chemicals.) Thus, we can see schizophrenia through this lens as a stress response in a person who is predisposed to the disorder. Conversely, susceptible individuals may never develop schizophrenia if they are spared certain damaging conditions or stressors that might push them "over the edge."

Developmental Disorders

Developmental problems can appear at any age, but several common ones first occur in childhood, including *autism, attention-deficit hyperactivity disorder (ADHD),* and *dyslexia*. All are specified on Axis II of the *DSM-IV*. Here, we will give only a brief description of these disorders, because you have already encountered them in earlier chapters.

Autism A complex and poorly understood disorder, **autism** involves an impoverished ability to "read" other people, use language, and interact socially. To illustrate, imagine the following situation: Sally and Shania are playing together, when Sally puts a piece of candy in a box and then leaves the room. While Sally is gone, Shania opens the box, removes the candy, and stashes it in her purse. When Sally comes back, where will she look for the candy?

Children without autism will say that Sally (who didn't see Shania switch the candy to her purse) will look in the box. That is, they realize that different people may hold different beliefs. But children with autism have a poorly developed *theory of mind* that, in normal children, helps them understand what others are thinking and feeling (Frith, 1993). Thus, children with autism are more likely to say (if they communicate at all) that Sally will look in the purse. They have difficulty imagining themselves in Sally's frame of mind, believing something they know is not the case. As a result of this deficit, they have difficulty in social relationships and are relegated to a world of social isolation.

Besides the theory-of-mind deficiencies and social isolation, most persons with autism also have language difficulties. In fact, many never achieve functional language at all. As a consequence of these multiple deficits, autism can easily be misclassified as mental retardation. (Most persons with mental retardation are *not* autistic.) In severe cases, autism may also involve destructive self-stimulation, such as head-banging. In addition, people with autism may display repetitive behavior, such as rocking, for extended periods. Typically, a physician or the parents first suspect the disorder at about 1½ to 2 years of age, when the child fails to develop language (Kabot et al., 2003).

Most experts believe that autism is fundamentally a brain disorder of undetermined cause. Some evidence suggests a link between autism and toxic materials in the environment (Neimark, 2007). Other studies suggest that children with autism have either fewer mirror neurons in their brains or else the mirror neurons they do have are defective (Miller, 2005; Ramachandran & Oberman, 2006). This finding has grabbed clinicians' interest because some of our mirror neurons purportedly do exactly what persons with autism cannot do: sense what other people's intentions are (Dobbs, 2006a; Rizzolatti et al., 2006). It remains to be seen whether these developments can be translated into effective therapies.

The National Institute of Health estimates that some form of the disorder occurs in about 1 in 500 children. Although you may have seen news reports of a rising incidence of autism in recent decades, experts attribute this primarily to an expanded definition of the disorder that came into wide use in the 1990s (Gernsbacher et al., 2005). There appears to be no "autism epidemic."

At present, the disorder has no cure. Behavioral treatment programs, involving both parents and the children with the disorder, can improve socialization and speech and diminish self-destructive behavior. Unfortunately, such programs are time consuming and relatively expensive.

autism A developmental disorder marked by disabilities in language, social interaction, and the ability to understand another person's state of mind.

▶ **Developmental Disorders:** Disorders usually first diagnosed in infancy, childhood, or adolescence

• Autism
• Dyslexia
• Attention-deficit hyperactivity disorder (ADHD)

CONNECTION CHAPTER 6

A *theory of mind* involves the understanding that others may have different beliefs, desires, and emotions that underlie their behavior (p. 247).

CONNECTION CHAPTER 2

Mirror neurons in the brain "reflect" other people's responses (p. 70).

dyslexia   A reading disability, thought by some experts to involve a brain disorder.

Dyslexia Reading is a key that opens many doors in a modern, information-driven society. But those doors can remain closed for people who have difficulty in reading—people with **dyslexia**. The disorder affects about one of five children to some degree, often leading to poor school performance. And because school is so important in our society, it often leads to diminished self-esteem and eventually to lost career opportunities (Shaywitz, 1996).

Contrary to popular presumption, dyslexia is not a visual disorder. It doesn't cause letters and words to "jump around" or reverse themselves. That is, dyslexia is *not* a problem of visual sensation or perception.

Instead, research over the past 15 years suggests that dyslexia involves abnormalities in the brain's language-processing circuits (Breier et al., 2003). Ironically, another "cause" may be language itself: Speakers of English—with its bizarre ways of spelling, including some 1,120 ways to spell only 40 different sounds—are much more likely to develop dyslexia than are Italian speakers, who must contend with only 33 combinations of letters for 25 sounds (Helmuth, 2001c; Paulesu et al., 2001).

According to some experts, we should not think of dyslexia as a distinct disorder at all. Researcher Sally Shaywitz and her colleagues (1990) have made a case that no diagnostic marker sets individuals with dyslexia clearly apart from others who are merely poor readers. She argues that dyslexia is simply the diagnosis we give to an arbitrarily defined group of people occupying the lower end of the reading-abilities spectrum.

Everyone does agree that dyslexia involves reading difficulties. Everyone also agrees that recent years have seen great strides made in understanding the neurological basis of the disorder, developing treatments, and debunking some of the myths surrounding dyslexia. (Smart people *can* have dyslexia: Einstein apparently did!) Currently, the most effective treatments include special reading programs that emphasize the matching of sounds to letter combinations.

CONNECTION CHAPTER 1

Hyperactivity is not caused by eating sugar (p. 9).

attention-deficit hyperactivity disorder (ADHD)   A developmental disability involving short attention span, distractibility, and extreme difficulty in remaining inactive for any period.

Attention-Deficit Hyperactivity Disorder (ADHD) Most children have trouble sitting still and focusing attention on a task, such as solving a math problem or listening to directions from the teacher—but some have more trouble than others. Many things can contribute to *attention deficit* and *hyperactivity*, including boring assignments, distracting problems at home, abuse from peers, or merely a cultural tradition that places low value on the tasks that demand quiet attention. Those distractions aside, some children apparently have a brain-based condition, known as **attention-deficit hyperactivity disorder (ADHD)**, that can interfere with even the best of intentions to focus attention and sit quietly (Barkley, 1998; Nigg, 2010). ADHD affects some 3 to 5 percent of school-age children (Brown, 2003b; NIMH, 2010b).

ADHD is a controversial diagnosis, and its treatment is even more controversial (Sax & Kautz, 2003). Critics claim that ADHD is overdiagnosed, often being used to describe normal rambunctiousness or to blame children for the mistakes made by unskilled parents and teachers. In addition, drug treatment consisting of stimulant drugs strikes many people as being wrongheaded. Yet many careful studies have demonstrated that properly administered drug therapy, along with behavioral therapy, an improve attention and diminish hyperactivity in a majority (about 70 percent) of individuals diagnosed with ADHD (Daley, 2004; MTA Cooperative Treatment Group, 2004). But do all hyperactive children need such treatment? It's an issue that can be resolved only by further research.

CONNECTION CHAPTER 10

Personality refers to the enduring set of characteristics and dispositions that provide a thread of consistency to an individual's attitudes and behaviors (p. 414).

personality disorder   Condition involving a chronic pervasive, inflexible, and maladaptive pattern of thinking, emotion, social relationships, or impulse control.

Personality Disorders

Disorders of personality account for the quirkiness of many historical and public figures, including the much-married King Henry VIII, numerous Hollywood bad boys and girls, and the fatal femme Lizzie Borden, who famously dispatched her parents with a hatchet. The **personality disorders** show themselves in chronic patterns of poor judgment, disordered thinking, emotional disturbances, disrupted social relationships, or lack of impulse control (Clark, 2009). The key element is a maladaptive personality pattern of long standing. And they, like the developmental disorders, are described on Axis II. Here we consider three of the better-known such conditions: *narcissistic personality disorder, antisocial personality disorder,* and *borderline personality disorder.*

Narcissistic Personality Disorder In Greek mythology, Narcissus was a man so enamored of his own good looks that, while admiring himself in a reflecting pool, he fell in and drowned. His sad legacy is the name for a disorder involving an exaggerated sense of self-importance, a need for constant attention or admiration, and often a preoccupation with fantasies of success or power. People with **narcissistic personality disorder** may respond inappropriately to criticism or minor defeat. They usually have problems in interpersonal relationships, feel entitled to favors without obligations, exploit others selfishly, and have difficulty understanding how others feel. Seldom do they want treatment. Judging from the (otherwise unreliable) entertainment tabloids, narcissistic personality disorder runs rampant in the film and recording industries.

Antisocial Personality Disorder Everyone from ruthless executives to con artists to serial killers is a candidate for this category, which afflicts some 1 percent of the adult population in the United States and some 70 to 80 percent of those in prison (Patrick, 2007). As we might guess from gender differences in criminality, men are four times more likely to be diagnosed with antisocial personality disorder than are women (Regier et al., 1988, 1993).

Persons with **antisocial personality disorder** seem to lack conscience or a sense of responsibility to others. Characteristically, their violations of social norms begin early in life: disrupting class, getting into fights, and running away from home. This pattern may progress to acts of cruelty and wanton disregard for others, such as vandalism, the abuse of animals, or setting fires. Other common signs of antisocial personality disorder include chronic lying and stealing.

Even though people with antisocial personalities may frequently find themselves in trouble, they may not feel anxiety, shame, or any other sort of intense emotion. Often, in fact, they can "keep cool" in situations that would arouse and upset normal people. Those who show a violent or criminal pattern of antisocial personality disorder, such as committing murders and other serious crimes, are popularly referred to as "psychopaths" or "sociopaths," although these labels are not recognized by the *DSM-IV* (Krueger & Markon, 2006; Miller, 2008).

While we commonly find antisocial personalities among convicted criminals, they are also well represented among successful politicians and businesspeople who put career, money, and power above everything and everyone (Babiak & Hare, 2006; Patrick, 2007). Some can be quite charming, having learned to use their charm to take advantage of people's tendency to be trusting. These same characteristics can also help them avoid getting caught for long periods of time—and when they do get caught, they are often able to manipulate their way out of trouble.

What causes antisocial personality disorder? Neuroimaging studies have recently suggested a malfunction in the amygdala and in a region of cortex just above the eyes (Kiehl & Buckholtz, 2010; Raine, 2008). We don't yet know, however, whether this is the cause or the effect of the disorder.

Borderline Personality Disorder A third form of personality disorder, **borderline personality disorder** manifests itself as instability, impulsivity, and chaotic relationships (Butcher et al, 2010; Selby & Joiner, 2009). People with this diagnosis have unpredictable moods and stormy interpersonal relationships, often becoming upset and abusive in response to perceived slights. They also have little tolerance for frustration. Their impulsivity may be seen in a tendency for substance abuse, gambling, sexual promiscuity, binge eating, reckless driving, self-mutilation, or suicide attempts. Imaging studies even show this volatility in the brain (Bower, 2009; Meyer-Lindenberg, 2008).

▶ **Personality Disorders:** Conditions involving a chronic and maladaptive pattern of thinking, emotion, social relationships, or impulse control

- Narcissistic personality disorder
- Antisocial personality disorder
- Borderline personality disorder

narcissistic personality disorder Condition involving an exaggerated sense of self-importance, a need for constant attention or admiration, and often a preoccupation with fantasies of success or power.

Narcissisism refers to the handsome Narcissus who, in Greek mythology, fell in love with his own reflection in a pool, as shown in this painting by Caravaggio.

antisocial personality disorder Condition involving a lack of conscience or a sense of responsibility to others.

borderline personality disorder Condition of instability and impulsivity; persons have unpredictable moods and stormy interpersonal relationships, with little tolerance for frustration.

One of these people probably lurks somewhere among your acquaintances. Indeed, borderline personality disorder accounts for about 2 percent of adults and between 10 and 20 percent of patients in clinical treatment (Meyer-Lindenberg, 2009, NIMH, 2010b). Unfortunately, as with the other personality disorders, the treatment outlook for borderline personality disorder is guarded.

Adjustment Disorders and Other Conditions: The Biggest Category of All

Although the majority of everyday psychological problems involve making choices and dealing with confusion, frustration, and loss, the *DSM-IV* gives these issues short shrift under *adjustment disorders* and under the awkwardly named category *other conditions that may be a focus of clinical attention*. Together, these categories represent a catch basin for relatively mild problems that do not fit well under other headings. They span a diverse range of conditions that include mild depression, physical complaints, marital problems, academic problems, job problems, parent–child problems, bereavement, and even *malingering* (faking an illness). Consequently, the largest group of people diagnosed with mental problems may fit these headings—even though the *DSM-IV* devotes disproportionately little space to them. Ironically, because these adjustment difficulties are so prevalent, those who turn to psychologists and psychiatrists account for a large proportion of the client load seen by professionals in private practice.

Gender Differences in Mental Disorders

No one knows exactly why, but the data show large gender differences in susceptibility to various mental disorders (Holden, 2005). We have seen, for example, that women more often are diagnosed with mood disorders, especially depression. Women also are diagnosed more often with anxiety disorders and eating disorders. In contrast, men are overwhelmingly more likely to have personality disorders that involve aggressive or control-related disorders, such as drug and alcohol abuse and violence. Thus men, far more often than women, are diagnosed as having antisocial personality disorder. As we have noted, one possibility is that social norms encourage more women than men to report feelings of depression. At the same time, social norms may encourage men to "act out" their feelings in a more physical manner.

Another possibility is that the differences originate in biology. For example, men's brains seem to be more strongly *lateralized* (that is, they tend to have specific cortical functions more localized on one side of the brain or the other). This may explain why men are less likely than women to recover language after a left-side stroke. Some neuroscientists also suspect that the "one-sidedness" of the male brain may contribute to the much higher incidence of schizophrenia and most developmental disorders, such as autism, dyslexia, and ADHD in males (Holden, 2005). Similarly, there may be some, as yet undiscovered, biological difference that underlies women's greater susceptibility to depression. Unfortunately, deciding between the social and biological explanations for gender differences in mental disorders awaits further research. Don't be surprised, however, if the final answer reflects the nature–nurture interaction: It probably involves both.

[PSYCHOLOGY MATTERS]

Shyness

Being shy is a common problem, but it is not a *DSM-IV* disorder in itself. Rather, **shyness** refers to a distressing pattern of avoiding or withdrawing from social contact. At the extreme, shy behavior can warrant a diagnosis of social phobia or an avoidant

shyness   A common temperamental condition but not a disorder recognized by the *DSM-IV.*

personality disorder, when afflicted individuals seek to isolate themselves from social interactions. As we have seen many times before, it is a matter of degree. For most shy people, however, the tragedy is that they suffer from loneliness and from lost opportunities to pursue interests and relationships.

What causes this often-painful problem? Shyness is one of three basic temperaments found in infants that, for many, will continue through life (Kagan et al., 1988, 1994). Kagan (2001) has proposed that this pattern may have its origin in biology—specifically in an overly excitable amygdala. But shyness and other forms of social anxiety can also be *learned* responses. Even those who are not "born shy" can acquire shy behavior patterns.

On a hopeful note, shyness does not have to be a permanent condition. Many people overcome it on their own. Organizations such as Toastmasters help people build verbal skills and confidence in social situations. Many others have found the help they need in cognitive–behavioral therapy groups. For more information, you may want to read *Shyness: What It Is, What to Do about It* by Philip Zimbardo (1990). Please forgive the shameless plug of a book by your senior author.

Shyness may be painful, but it is not a DSM-IV disorder.

Check Your Understanding

✓ Study and Review at MyPsychLab

1. **ANALYSIS:** What are the main differences between the medical model and the psychological model of mental disorder?

2. **RECALL:** Describe one kind of evidence suggesting that depression has a biological basis.

3. **APPLICATION:** According to the *preparedness hypothesis*, which one of the following phobias would you expect to be most common?

   a. fear of snakes (ophidiophobia)
   b. fear of books (bibliophobia)
   c. fear of horses (equinophobia)
   d. fear of the number 13 (triskaidekaphobia)

4. **RECALL:** Which of the following is most common: schizophrenia, depression, phobias, dissociative identity disorder?

5. **RECALL:** What mental processes may be disrupted by schizophrenia?

6. **RECALL:** In which type of anxiety disorder is the anxiety focused on a particular object or situation?

7. **UNDERSTANDING THE CORE CONCEPT:** The *DSM-IV* groups most mental disorders by their

   a. treatments.
   b. causes.
   c. symptoms.
   d. theoretical basis.

Answers 1. The medical model views mental disorders as diseases—as something wrong within the individual—while the psychological model encompasses biology, the environment, and mental processes. The medical model also tends to emphasize the patient receiving treatment, while the psychological model involves patients as partners in the treatment process. **2.** Depression runs in families and is more common in women than in men; the disorder often responds favorably to drugs; people with depression tend to have distinctive patterns on the EEG and on brain scans. **3. a.** All the others are relatively modern objects that have not existed long enough to be incorporated into our biological natures. **4.** Depression **5.** Schizophrenia may disrupt virtually all mental processes, including thinking, perception, motivation, and emotion. **6.** Phobias **7. c**

12.3 KEY QUESTION

What Are the Consequences of Labeling People?

"Mad." "Maniac." "Mentally ill." "Crazy." "Insane." "Disturbed." "Neurotic." These, along with all the official diagnostic terms that appear in the *DSM-IV*, represent labels used by the public, the courts, and mental health professionals to describe people who display mental disturbances. Ideally, of course, an accurate diagnostic label leads to good communication among mental health professionals and an effective treatment program for afflicted individuals. Sometimes, however, labels create confusion—or

labeling   Refers to the undesirable practice of attaching diagnoses of mental disorders to people and then using them as stereotypes—treating the afflicted individuals as if the labels explained their whole personalities. Psychiatric labels can also stigmatize people.

worse. **Labeling** can turn people into stereotypes, masking their personal characteristics and the unique circumstances that contribute to their disorders. And, if that were not enough, labels can provoke prejudices and social rejection.

In this section, we will begin with the problem of labeling as it affects the individual. Then we will pursue the issue of labeling in a larger context by asking: Does *psychological disorder* mean the same thing in all cultures? Finally, we will bring the topic home with a critical look at the dangers of applying diagnostic labels to your friends and family. The Core Concept that organizes all this states:

Core Concept 12.3

Ideally, accurate diagnoses lead to proper treatments, but diagnoses may also become labels that depersonalize individuals and ignore the social and cultural contexts in which their problems arise.

Diagnostic Labels, Labeling, and Depersonalization

Labeling a person as mentally disturbed can have both serious and long-lasting consequences aside from the mental disturbance itself. With most physical illnesses, a person may suffer a broken leg or an attack of appendicitis, but when the illness is over, the diagnosis moves into the past. Not so with mental disorders. A label of "depression" or "mania" or "schizophrenia" can be a stigma that follows a person forever (Farina et al., 1996; Wright et al., 2000). But what about a mistaken diagnosis? As Rosenhan pointed out, a mistaken diagnosis of cancer is cause for celebration, but almost never is a diagnosis of mental disorder retracted. As you will recall in the "pseudopatient" study, discussed at the beginning of the chapter, the glaring fact of normalcy never emerged—a situation that Rosenhan attributed to the label "schizophrenic."

A diagnostic label may also lead to a cycle of mistreatment and neglect caused by the second-class status accorded people with mental disorders. Sadly, in our society, to have severe mental problems is to be stigmatized and devalued. Even worse, mental hospital treatment can also involve **depersonalization**—as seen in the Rosenhan study. That is, treating people as a diagnostic category, such as "schizophrenic" or "bipolar," robs them of their individuality and identity by treating them as mere objects rather than as individuals. Depersonalization can easily result from labeling, but, as Rosenhan argued, it can also grow out of the impersonal environment of the mental hospital. All of this, of course, lowers self-esteem and reinforces disordered behavior. Thus, society extracts costly penalties from those who deviate from its norms—and in the process, it perpetuates the problem of mental disorder.

depersonalization   Depriving people of their identity and individuality by treating them as objects rather than as individuals. Depersonalization can be a result of labeling.

Perhaps the most extreme reaction against labeling has come from radical psychiatrist Thomas Szasz (1961, 1977), who claimed that mental illness is a "myth". Szasz argued that the symptoms used as evidence of mental illness are merely medical labels that give professionals an excuse to intervene in what is really the problem of people violating social norms. Once labeled, says Szasz, these people can be treated simply for their "problem of being different."

We must keep in mind, therefore, that the goal of diagnosis is not just to fit a person into a neat diagnostic box or to identify those who are "different." Instead, a diagnosis should initiate a process that leads to a greater understanding of a person and to the development of a plan to help. A diagnosis should be a beginning, not an end.

The Cultural Context of Psychological Disorder

ecological view   A perspective on mental disorder that emphasizes social and cultural context.

Few clinicians would go as far as Thomas Szasz, but many advocate an **ecological view** that takes the individual's external world into account (Levine & Perkins, 1987; Lilienfeld & Arkowitz, 2009). Unlike the medical model, this view sees abnormality as an interaction between individuals and their social and cultural context. Disorder results from a mismatch between a person's behavior and the needs of the situation. If you are a private investigator, for example, it might pay to have a slightly suspicious or paranoid complexion to your personality, but if you are a nurse or a teacher, this same characteristic might be called "deviant."

In support of this ecological view, studies show beyond doubt that culture influences both the prevalence of psychological disorders and the symptoms that disturbed people display (Jenkins & Barrett, 2004; Matsumoto, 1996). For example, work done by the World Health Organization (1973, 1979) in Colombia, Czechoslovakia, Denmark, India, Nigeria, Taiwan, Britain, the United States, and the former USSR has shown that the incidence of schizophrenia varies from culture to culture. More recent studies also support this conclusion (Jablensky, 2000).

Psychiatry, too, is beginning to note the effects of culture on psychopathology. The *DSM-IV,* in fact, has a section devoted to culture-specific disorders (although this section recognizes no disorders that are found specifically in the United States). According to psychiatrists Arthur Kleinman and Alex Cohen (1997), psychiatry has clung too long to three persistent myths:

1. The myth that mental disorders have a similar prevalence the world around.
2. The myth that biology creates mental disorder while culture merely shapes the way a person experiences it.
3. The myth that culture-specific disorders occur only in exotic places rather than at home.

But are cultural differences so great that a person who hallucinates might be labeled as having schizophrenia in our culture but a visionary or shaman (a healer or seer) in another? Jane Murphy (1976) set out to answer this question in a study of two non-Western groups, the Eskimos of northwest Alaska and the Yorubas of rural tropical Nigeria, societies selected because of their wide geographic separation and cultural dissimilarity. In both groups, she found separate terms and distinct social roles for the shaman and for the psychotic individual. Similar findings have since come from studies of cultures all over the world (Draguns, 1980). If mental illness is a socially defined myth, as Szasz asserts, it is a myth nurtured by cultures everywhere. 📖

Read about Personality and Mental Disorder in Africa at **MyPsychLab**

[PSYCHOLOGY MATTERS]

Using Psychology to Learn Psychology

Don't do it! Don't use your new knowledge of psychological disorders to diagnose your family and friends. Violating this caveat has caused grief for many an eager psychology student.

We realize how tempting it is to apply what you are learning to the people in your life. Some of the disorders that we have considered here are common. So, as you read through this chapter, you almost certainly have noticed signs of anxiety, paranoia, depression, mania, and various other impairments of perception, memory, or emotion that remind you of your friends and relatives. It is a variation on the tendency, discussed earlier, to see evidence of psychological disorder in oneself. You should recognize this as a sign that you are acquiring some new knowledge about psycholopathology. But we suggest that you keep these thoughts to yourself.

Remember that reading one chapter does not make you an expert on psychological disorders; so you should be cautious about making amateur diagnoses. What you especially should *not* do is to tell someone that you think he or she has schizophrenia, bipolar disorder, obsessive–compulsive disorder—or any other mental condition.

Having said that, we should also note that erring too far in the opposite direction by ignoring signs of pathology could also be hazardous. If someone you know is struggling with significant mental problems—and even if he or she asks for your opinion—you should refrain from putting a label on the problem. But you can—and should—encourage that person to see a competent professional for diagnosis and possible treatment.

We will discuss more about how such treatment is done—in the next chapter.

Check Your Understanding

✓●—Study and **Review** at **MyPsychLab**

1. **RECALL:** Which one of the following statements is true?

   a. Mental disorders have a similar prevalence in all cultures.

   b. In general, biology creates mental disorder, while culture merely shapes the way a person experiences it.

   c. Culture-specific stressors occur primarily in developing countries.

   d. Cultures around the world seem to distinguish between people with mental disorders and people who are visionaries or prophets.

2. **ANALYSIS:** Why did Rosenhan claim that mental patients are *depersonalized*?

3. **UNDERSTANDING THE CORE CONCEPT:** What are the positive and negative consequences of diagnostic labeling?

Answers 1. d **2.** Rosenhan found that the mental hospital staff rarely interacted with the patients; when they did, they treated the patients as objects or labels, not as persons. **3.** On the positive side, diagnostic labels help mental health professionals communicate about patients' symptoms and formulate a treatment plan. On the negative side, people who are labeled can be looked upon as a mere label ("a schizophrenic"). In addition, psychiatric labels carry a strong social stigma.

CRITICAL THINKING APPLIED

Insane Places Revisited—Another Look at the Rosenhan Study

Probably no other experiment in the history of psychology has caused such a furor as did Rosenhan's "pseudopatient" study. And no wonder: By raising questions about the reliability of psychiatric diagnosis, it threatened the very foundations of psychiatry and clinical psychology. Rosenhan summarized his study by saying, "It is clear that we cannot distinguish the sane from the insane in psychiatric hospitals." If Rosenhan was right, the whole mental health enterprise might be built on nothing but opinion. But was this the correct conclusion?

What Are the Critical Issues?

Our first task in evaluating Rosenhan is to identify the issues at the heart of the controversy. For Rosenhan, the issue was the reliability of psychiatric diagnosis and the question of whether mental disorder can be distinguished from normalcy. But his critics have claimed that his study was flawed. Let's examine their main arguments.

Insanity Is Not a Diagnosis   Robert Spitzer (1973), the leader of the charge against Rosenhan, pointed out that *sanity* and *insanity* are legal terms, as we have seen. Because these terms have no meaning in psychology or psychiatry, says Spitzer, Rosenhan's argument is essentially meaningless. While we can agree that Rosenhan was indeed sloppy with his terminology, your authors suggest that his conclusion has the effect of tossing the baby out with the bath water. In fact, Spitzer admits that Rosenhan apparently uses *insanity* to mean *psychosis*. Score one point for Rosenhan.

Unfair!   Rosenhan's critics also claimed that the study was unfair because people don't usually lie about their symptoms because they want to be admitted to mental hospitals. So we should not fault a psychiatrist for assuming that a person asking for help is sincere. Moreover, doctors and hospitals can be held liable if they don't admit people who might pose a danger to themselves or the community (Ostow, 1973). Rosenhan countered that, even if the doctors were erring on the side of caution, the fact that the patients were "sane" should have been detected, if not at admission, then at some time during their hospitalization. We score a tie on this one.

Not Enough Data

A third criticism targets the narrative approach Rosenhan used in his report of the pseudopatient study. The article tells a vivid story, but it is, in fact, sparse in data. Rosenhan's conclusions are mostly driven by his impressions rather than by facts—an irony, in view of his criticism of psychiatric diagnosis as contaminated by unreliable "impressions." We award this one to Rosenhan's critics.

Conclusions Applied to the Wrong Group

A fourth and most telling criticism accuses Rosenhan of making a rookie error. The failure of psychiatrists to detect "sanity" in the pseudopatients, said Spitzer (1973), tells us nothing about their ability to diagnose real patients—who aren't lying about their symptoms. True enough. But Rosenhan (1973b) replied that his study is only one small part of a vast literature attesting to the unreliability of psychiatric diagnosis: Different psychiatrists quite commonly give different diagnoses to the same patient. We give Rosenhan the edge on this point.

Bias

We can see the dispute as one between two camps that each perceived themselves under siege by the other. Psychiatrists thought the original study was a frontal assault on the integrity of their profession, so they responded in kind. The counterattack on Rosenhan impugned his integrity as a researcher. The relevant critical thinking question: Could each side's stance be contaminated by bias? The answer is a resounding Yes.

So, where does that leave us?

What Conclusions Can We Draw?

Without doubt, Rosenhan (1973a) is guilty of using the terms *sane* and *insane* inappropriately. He is also guilty of overstatement and sensationalism, as when he says:

> The facts of the matter are that we have known for a long time that [psychiatric] diagnoses are often not useful or reliable, but we have nevertheless continued to use them. We now know that we cannot distinguish insanity from sanity (p. 257).

Even so, the fact that not one of the pseudopatients was ever discovered to be mentally sound is a startling finding.

Power of the Situation in Mental Hospitals

More important, in our opinion, is a point to which the critics did not respond: Mental hospitals, said Rosenhan, are not primarily places of treatment. Rather, they are places in which patients are labeled, medicated, and ignored by the staff. Most of the time, Rosenhan found, ward attendants and nurses sequestered themselves in a small staff cubicle that patients called "the cage." Psychiatrists were even less available, making only rare appearances on the wards. When patients approached staff members with questions, they often received curt replies or were ignored.

Rosenhan was not the first person to decry mental hospitals as impersonal places, but he did offer reasons as to why this might be so. One rests on society's attitudes toward the mentally ill, attitudes that are colored by fear, distrust, and misunderstanding. These attitudes, said Rosenhan, have an effect on mental health workers.

A second factor involves *labeling:* the pernicious effect of a psychiatric diagnosis. Once they make a diagnosis, doctors are extremely reluctant to change their minds. Part of the reason has to do with pride, but an even bigger problem stems from the lack of contact the staff—and especially the doctors—have with patients. Therapy in mental hospitals, then, is largely a matter of medications.

As we noted at the beginning of the chapter, Rosenhan does not fault the doctors, nurses, ward attendants, or other staff members. He suggested that the problem lay in "the situation"—the whole hospital environment, which depersonalizes patients and discourages staff from interacting with patients. But that was 1973. What about now? Do these problems still plague mental hospitals?

A New Controversy Erupts

A brand new controversy erupted in 2005, with the publication of a book entitled *Opening Skinner's Box*. In it, author Lauren Slater describes her own reenactment of Rosenhan's classic experiment. In nine visits to different mental hospitals, Slater told doctors that she heard a voice saying, "Thud." Although she was never hospitalized, she claims that she was "prescribed a total of 25 antipsychotics and 60 antidepressants." In most cases, she was diagnosed as having "depression with psychotic features." Slater asserts that her experience supports Rosenhan.

Slater's assertion did not go unnoticed by Robert Spitzer, a critic who still sees the Rosenhan experiment as "an embarrassment" (Jaffe, 2006). Spitzer and two of his colleagues responded with a critique of Slater published in the *Journal of Nervous and Mental Disease* (2005). In that piece, they fired back a salvo consisting of their own study, in which they provided 74 psychiatrists with a written vignette based on Slater's "experiment." They claim that only three gave a diagnosis of psychotic depression. (We would note, however, that Slater's experiment has its own biases.)

The bottom line? Rosenhan put his finger on some important problems with mental hospitals and psychiatric diagnoses. But he did *not* prove that diagnoses of most mental patients are useless or completely unreliable. And, for our purposes, that conclusion makes the perfect transition to the next chapter, where we will study the treatment of mental disorders.

Do It Yourself! **RELATING DISORDERS TO THE PSYCHOLOGICAL PROCESSES THEY DISRUPT**

Every disorder involves a distortion or breakdown in one or more of the basic psychological functions, or processes, for which we have named chapters in this text. (You will remember that Wundt called them the "elements of conscious experience.") It will help you understand the disorders described in this chapter if, in the following table, you will write in the names of the disorders described in this chapter next to the process that is most disrupted by each. (You may place some disorders in more than one category and more than one disorder in each category.) We have written in a few to get you started.

Disrupted Processes	Psychological Disorders
Learning	phobia
Sensation and Perception	
Emotion	phobia
Personality and Self-concept	
Development	ADHD
Memory and Cognition	
Socialization	

CHAPTER SUMMARY

((•─[**Listen** to an audio file of your chapter at **MyPsychLab**

CHAPTER PROBLEM: Is it possible to distinguish mental disorder from merely unusual behavior? That is, are there specific signs that clearly indicate mental disorder?

- The line between mental disorder and merely unusual behavior is fuzzy. Everyone agrees that distress, maladaptiveness, irrationality, unpredictability, unconventionality, and undesirable behavior may be symptoms of mental disorder. There are no precise diagnostic tests for most mental disorders. Moreover, the causes of most mental disorders are either disputed or unknown.

- The "medical model," embodied in the *DSM-IV*, views mental disorders as specific diseases. The *DSM-IV* specifies mental and behavioral symptoms of over 300 mental disorders, classified on five axes. This classification system is widely used by the psychiatric community and other mental health professionals.

- The medical model is not universally accepted, however, especially by psychologists, who prefer to view mental disorder from a combination of biological, cognitive, social, behavioral, and developmental perspectives.

12.1 What Is Psychological Disorder?

[**Core Concept 12.1** The medical model views psychological disorders as "diseases," while the psychological view sees them as an interaction of biological, behavioral, cognitive, and social-cultural factors.]

Psychopathology is common in America. Three classic signs suggest severe psychological disorder: **hallucinations, delusions,** and extreme **affective disturbances.** But beyond these, the signs of disorder are more subtle, and a diagnosis depends heavily on clinical judgment.

Our modern conception of abnormality has evolved from attributing disorders to demon possession or imbalances of humors to the current **medical model,** which sees psychopathology as "illness" or "disease"—a perspective with which many psychologists disagree. An alternative psychological model includes social-cultural, cognitive, developmental, and behavioral factors as well as biological ones. Aside

from the three classic signs of disorder, psychopathology is usually judged by the degree to which a person exhibits distress, maladaptiveness, irrationality, unpredictability, and unconventionality.

It is normal to experience symptoms of psychological disorders on occasion, so psychology students are often unjustifiably concerned that they have a mental disorder. Frequent signs of abnormality, however, should prompt a consultation with a mental health professional.

The plea of **insanity** is often misunderstood by the public, because it is infrequently used and even more infrequently successful. The term *insanity* is a legal term, not a psychological or psychiatric diagnosis.

delusions (p. 517)
hallucinations (p. 517)
affective disturbances (p. 517)
insanity (p. 523)
medical model (p. 519)
psychopathology (p. 517)

12.2 How Are Psychological Disorders Classified in the *DSM-IV*?

[Core Concept 12.2 The *DSM-IV*, the most widely used system for classifying mental disorders, organizes them by their mental and behavioral symptoms.]

The **DSM-IV** derives from psychiatry and has a bias toward the medical model. The *DSM-IV* recognizes more than 300 specific disorders, categorized by symptoms rather than by cause. It has no category for "normal" functioning. Unlike its predecessor, it does not use the term neurosis; the term psychosis is restricted to a loss of contact with reality.

Among the *DSM-IV* categories are the **mood disorders** *(affective disorders),* which involve emotional disturbances. **Major depression** is the most common affective disorder, while **bipolar disorder** occurs less commonly. Strong gender differences have also been noted. All severe mental disorders are believed to have some biological basis.

The **anxiety disorders** include **generalized anxiety disorder, panic disorder, phobias,** and **obsessive–compulsive disorder.** Although they may have some basis in temperament, they are also affected by experience. The **somatoform disorders** involve the mind–body relationship in various ways. People with **conversion disorder** have physical symptoms but no organic disease, while those with **hypochondriasis** suffer from exaggerated concern about illness.

The controversial **dissociative disorders** include **dissociative amnesia, dissociative fugue, depersonalization disorder,** and **dissociative identity disorder.** All disrupt the integrated functioning of memory, consciousness, or personal identity. Among the *psychotic disorders,* **schizophrenia** is the most common. It is characterized by extreme distortions in perception, thinking, emotion, behavior, and language. It has five forms: *disorganized, catatonic, paranoid, undifferentiated,* and *residual types.* Evidence for the causes of schizophrenia has been found in a variety of factors including genetics, abnormal brain structure, and biochemistry.

The *DSM-IV* also lists a variety of *developmental disorders,* including **autism, dyslexia,** and **attention-deficit hyperactivity disorder,** which typically emerge as a distortion of the normal developmental processes, such as socialization, cognition, and attention. By contrast, the **personality disorders** involve distorted personality traits. Among the commonest are **narcissistic personality disorder, antisocial personality disorder,** and **borderline personality disorder.** There are significant gender differences across the spectrum of mental disorder, especially in depression and antisocial personality disorder.

The most common disorders of all are classified in the *DSM-IV* as the *adjustment disorders* and "other conditions that may be a focus of clinical attention." These include a wide range of problems in living. **Shyness** is a widespread problem—and a treatable one—but it is not officially a disorder unless it goes to the extreme of a *social phobia* or *avoidant personality disorder.*

agoraphobia (p. 531)
antisocial personality disorder (p. 543)
anxiety disorders (p. 530)
attention-deficit hyperactivity disorder (ADHD) (p. 542)
autism (p. 541)
bipolar disorder (p. 529)
borderline personality disorder (p. 543)
conversion disorder (p. 534)
depersonalization disorder (p. 536)
diathesis–stress hypothesis (p. 540)
dissociative amnesia (p. 535)
dissociative disorders (p. 535)
dissociative fugue (p. 536)
dissociative identity disorder (p. 536)
DSM-IV (p. 524)
dyslexia (p. 542)
generalized anxiety disorder (p. 531)
hypochondriasis (p. 535)
learned helplessness (p. 529)
major depression (p. 526)
mood disorders (p. 526)
narcissistic personality disorder (p. 543)
neurosis (p. 525)
obsessive–compulsive disorder (p. 533)
panic disorder (p. 531)
personality disorder (p. 542)
phobias (p. 532)
preparedness hypothesis (p. 533)
psychosis (p. 525)
schizophrenia (p. 537)
seasonal affective disorder (SAD) (p. 528)
rumination (p. 529)
shyness (p. 544)
somatoform disorders (p. 534)

12.3 What Are the Consequences of Labeling People?

[Core Concept 12.3 Ideally, accurate diagnoses lead to proper treatments, but diagnoses may also become labels that depersonalize individuals and ignore the social and cultural contexts in which their problems arise.]

Labeling someone as psychologically or mentally disordered is ultimately a matter of human judgment. Yet even professional judgments can be biased by prejudices. Those labeled with psychological disorders may suffer **depersonalization** in ways that most physically ill people do not.

Culture has an effect on whether a behavior is called normal, abnormal, or merely unusual, although cross-cultural research suggests that people everywhere distinguish between psychotic individuals and those whom they label shamans, prophets, or visionaries.

Ideally, accurate diagnoses lead to proper treatments, but diagnoses may also become labels that depersonalize individuals and ignore the social and cultural contexts in which their problems arise. Readers are cautioned not to apply diagnostic labels to people.

depersonalization (p. 546)
ecological view (p. 546)
labeling (p. 546)

CRITICAL THINKING APPLIED

Insane Places Revisited—Another Look at the Rosenhan Study

Rosenhan's "pseudopatient" study drew fire from many critics in the psychiatric community. Some objected that "insane" is not a diagnosis; some said it was unfair that the pseudopatients lied about psychotic symptoms; others noted that the study was sparse on data; and still others noted that the results didn't apply to patients with real mental disorders. Nevertheless, Rosenhan's study did point up the *power of the situation* and *labeling* to skew professional judgment in mental hospitals.

DISCOVERING PSYCHOLOGY **VIEWING GUIDE**

Watch the following video by logging into MyPsychLab (www.mypsychlab.com). After you have watched the videos, answer the questions that follow.

PROGRAM 21: **PSYCHOPATHOLOGY**

Program Review

1. Psychopathology is defined as the study of
   a. organic brain disease.
   b. perceptual and cognitive illusions.
   c. clinical measures of abnormal functioning.
   d. mental disorders.

2. What is the key criterion for identifying a person as having a mental disorder?
   a. The person has problems.
   b. The person's functioning is clearly abnormal.
   c. The person's ideas challenge the status quo.
   d. The person makes other people feel uncomfortable.

3. Which is true about mental disorders?
   a. They are extremely rare, with less than one-tenth of 1 percent of Americans suffering from any form of mental illness.
   b. They are not that uncommon, with about one-fifth of Americans suffering from some form of recently diagnosed mental disorder.

   c. The number of Americans with psychotic disorders fluctuates with the calendar, with more cases of psychosis during the weekends than during weekdays.
   d. The actions of people with mental disorders are unpredictable.

4. Fran is a mental health specialist who has a PhD in psychology. She would be classified as a
   a. psychiatrist.   **c.** social psychologist.
   b. clinical psychologist. **d.** psychoanalyst.

5. What happened after David Rosenhan and his colleagues were admitted to mental hospitals by pretending to have hallucinations and then behaved normally?
   a. Their sanity was quickly observed by the staff.
   b. It took several days for their deception to be realized.
   c. In most cases, the staff disagreed with each other about these "patients."
   d. Nobody ever detected their sanity.

6. Olivia is experiencing dizziness, muscle tightness, shaking, and tremors. She is feeling apprehensive. These symptoms most resemble those found in cases of
   a. anxiety disorders.
   c. psychoses.
   b. affective disorders.
   d. schizophrenia.

7. Prior to the 18th century, people with psychological problems were most likely to be
   a. placed in a mental hospital.
   b. tortured, trained, or displayed for public amusement.
   c. encouraged to pursue the arts.
   d. treated through psychotherapy only.

8. When Sigmund Freud studied patients with anxiety, he determined that their symptoms were caused by
   a. actual childhood abuse, both physical and sexual.
   b. imbalances in body chemistry.
   c. childhood conflicts that had been repressed.
   d. cognitive errors in the way patients viewed the world.

9. Which of the following statements about clinical depression is true?
   a. Most depressed people commit suicide.
   b. Depression is characterized by excessive elation of mood.
   c. Depression is often called the cancer of mental illness.
   d. In its milder forms, depression is experienced by almost everyone.

10. People lose touch with reality in cases of
    a. neurosis but not psychosis.
    b. psychosis but not neurosis.
    c. both psychosis and neurosis.
    d. all psychoses and some neuroses.

11. The term *neurosis* is no longer used by psychologists and psychiatrists as a diagnostic category because
    a. it has been replaced by the term *psychosis*.
    b. it is generally understood by everyone in our society.
    c. it does not include chronic anxiety.
    d. it is considered too general and imprecise.

12. Irving Gottesman and Fuller Torrey have been studying twins to learn more about schizophrenia. If the brain of a twin with schizophrenia is compared with the brain of a normal twin, the former has
    a. less cerebrospinal fluid.
    b. larger ventricles.
    c. a larger left hemisphere.
    d. exactly the same configuration as the latter.

13. For Teresa LaFromboise, the major issue influencing mental disorders among Native Americans is
    a. the prevalence of genetic disorders.
    b. alcohol's impact on family structure.
    c. the effect of imposing White American culture.
    d. isolation due to rural settings.

14. According to experts, what proportion of Americans suffer from some form of mental illness?
    a. about one-fifth
    b. less than one in 10,000
    c. about two-thirds
    d. about one in 1,000

15. Which of the following people would argue that psychopathology is a myth?
    a. Philippe Pinel
    b. Thomas Szasz
    c. Teresa LaFromboise
    d. Sigmund Freud

16. What might a severe viral infection do to a woman who has a genetic predisposition toward schizophrenia?
    a. make her schizophrenic
    b. destroy the genetic marker and make her mentally more stable
    c. redirect the predisposition toward a different class of mental illness
    d. kill her with greater likelihood than if she did not have a predisposition toward mental illness

17. Which of the following has been nicknamed "the common cold of psychopathology" because of its frequency?
    a. phobia
    b. personality disorder
    c. schizophrenia
    d. depression

18. All of the following are typically true about schizophrenia, *except* that
    a. less than one-third improve with treatment.
    b. the people who have it are aware that they are mentally ill.
    c. about 1 percent of the world's total population is schizophrenic.
    d. it is associated with impaired thinking, emotion, and perception.

19. Who is credited as being the first to introduce the idea that insane people are ill?
    a. Sigmund Freud
    b. Jean Charcot
    c. Emil Kraepelin
    d. Philippe Pinel

20. Which of the following is characterized by boundless energy, optimism, and risk-taking behavior?
    a. a manic episode
    b. paranoid schizophrenia
    c. anxiety disorders
    d. depression

13 Therapies for Psychological Disorders

CHAPTER PROBLEM What is the best treatment for Derek's depression: psychological therapy, drug therapy, or both? More broadly, the problem is this: How do we decide among the available therapies for any of the mental disorders?

CRITICAL THINKING APPLIED Evidence-Based Practice

OFF AND ON, DEREK HAD FELT TIRED AND UNHAPPY FOR MONTHS, AND he knew it was affecting not only his work but also the relationship with his partner. Michele, a coworker and friend, tactfully suggested he seek professional help, but Derek was unsure where to turn. As many people do, he asked for a recommendation from another friend, who he knew had sought therapy three years ago. And that is how he ended up, somewhat apprehensively, at Dr. Sturm's office.

She was easy to talk to, it turned out, and it didn't take long for both of them to agree that Derek was depressed. After some conversation about the nature of depression, Dr. Sturm said, "We have several treatment alternatives." She added, "The one in which I am trained is cognitive-behavioral therapy, which approaches depression as a learned problem to be treated by changing the way a person thinks about life events and interpersonal relationships. If we take that route, we will explore what is happening at work and at home that might trigger depressive episodes. I would also give you 'homework' every week—assignments designed to help you build on your strengths, rather than focusing on your weaknesses. Just like school," she added with a little laugh.

"As a second option," she said, "I could refer you to a colleague who does psychodynamic therapy. If you choose that approach, you and Dr. Ewing would explore your past, looking for events that may have pushed you down the path to the feelings you are experiencing now. Essentially, it would be a treatment aimed at bringing some unpleasant parts of your unconscious mind into the light of day."

"The other thing I could do is to arrange to get you some medication that has been proven effective in treating depression. It would probably be one of those antidepressants, like Prozac, that you have seen advertised in magazines and on TV. The problem there is that it takes several weeks for them to have an effect. And, besides, I'm not sure they really treat the problems that keep making you feel depressed."

"Oh, yes," she added, "There are some additional medical options, such as electroconvulsive therapy—people often call it 'shock treatment,' but I don't think it is needed in your case."

"Just hearing that makes me feel better," Derek sighed. "So, the choice is between drugs and psychological therapy?"

"Or perhaps a combination of the two," replied Dr. Sturm.

"How do I decide?" Derek asked.

PROBLEM: **What is the best treatment for Derek's depression: psychological therapy, drug therapy, or both? More broadly, the problem is this: How do we decide among the available therapies for any of the mental disorders?**

Despite the diversity of approaches that Dr. Sturm and her colleagues bring to their work, the overwhelming majority of people who enter **therapy** receive significant help. Not everyone becomes a success case, of course. Some people wait too long, until their problems become intractable. Some do not end up with the right sort of therapy for their problems. And, unfortunately, many people who could benefit from therapy do not get it because of the cost. Still, the development of a wide range of effective therapies is one of the success stories in modern psychology.

As you read through this chapter, we hope you will weigh the advantages and disadvantages of each therapy we discuss. Keep in mind, too, that you may sometime be asked by a friend or relative to use what you, like Derek, have learned here to recommend an appropriate therapy. It's even possible that you may sometime need to select a therapist for yourself.

> **therapy** A general term for any treatment process; in psychology and psychiatry, therapy refers to a variety of psychological and biomedical techniques aimed at dealing with mental disorders or coping with problems of living.

⌐13.1 KEY QUESTION
└──── What Is Therapy?

When you think of "therapy," chances are that a stereotype pops into mind, absorbed from countless cartoons and movies: a "neurotic" patient lying on a couch, with a bearded therapist sitting by the patient's head, scribbling notes and making interpretations. In fact, this is a scene from classic Freudian psychoanalysis, which is a rarity today, although it dominated the first half of the 20th century.

The reality of modern therapy differs from the old stereotype on several counts. First, most therapists don't have their patients (or *clients*) lie on a couch. Second, people now seek therapeutic help for a wide range of problems besides the serious *DSM-IV* disorders: Counselors or therapists also provide help in making difficult choices, dealing with academic problems, and coping with losses or unhappy relationships. And a third way in which the popular image of therapy is mistaken: Some forms of therapy now involve as much *action* as they do talk and interpretation—as you will see shortly.

At first, the therapeutic menu may appear to offer a bewildering list of choices. But you will see that one constant threads through them all—as our Core Concept suggests:

> **Core Concept 13.1**
>
> **Therapy for psychological disorders takes a variety of forms, but all involve a *therapeutic relationship* focused on improving a person's mental, behavioral, or social functioning.**

Let's set the stage for our exploration of these many therapies by looking at the variety of people who enter treatment and the problems they bring with them to the therapeutic relationship.

Entering Therapy

Why would you go into therapy? Why would anyone? Most often, people enter therapy when they have a problem that they are unable to resolve by themselves. They may seek therapy on their own initiative, or they may be advised to do so by family, friends, a physician, or a coworker.

Obviously, you don't have to be declared "crazy" to enter therapy. But you may be called either a "patient" or a "client." Practitioners who take a biological or medical model approach to treatment commonly use the term *patient,* while the term *client* is usually used by professionals who think of psychological disorders not as mental *illnesses* but as *problems in living* (Rogers, 1951; Szasz, 1961).

Access to therapy depends on several factors. People who have money or adequate health insurance can get therapy easily. For the poor, especially poor ethnic minorities, economic obstacles block the doorway to professional mental health care (Bower, 1998d; Nemecek, 1999). Another problem can be lack of qualified therapists. In many communities, it is still much easier to get help for physical health problems than for psychological problems. Even the nature of a person's psychological problems can interfere with getting help. An individual with agoraphobia, for example, finds it hard, even impossible, to leave home to seek therapy. Similarly, persons with paranoia may not seek help because they don't trust mental health professionals. Obviously, many difficulties stand in the way of getting therapy to all those who need it.

The Therapeutic Alliance and the Goals of Therapy

Sometimes, you simply need to talk out a problem with a sympathetic friend or family member, perhaps just to "hear yourself think." But friends and family not only lack the training to deal with difficult mental problems; they also have needs and agendas of their own that can interfere with helping you. In fact, they may sometimes be part of the problem. For many reasons, then, it may be appropriate to seek the help of a professionally trained therapist. You might also want professional help if you wish to keep your problems and concerns confidential. In all these ways, a professional relationship with a therapist differs from friendship or kinship.

What Are the Components of Therapy? In nearly all forms of therapy there is some sort of *relationship,* or **therapeutic alliance,** between the therapist and the client seeking assistance—as our Core Concept indicates. In fact, the quality of the therapeutic alliance is the biggest single factor in the effectiveness of therapy (Wampold & Brown, 2005). (We must admit, however, that there are experimental computer-therapy programs, where the idea of a "relationship" is stretching the point.)

What makes for a good therapeutic alliance? You and your therapist must be able to work together as allies, on the same side and toward the same goals, joining forces to cope with and solve the problems that have brought you to therapy (Horvath & Luborsky, 1993). Accordingly, trust and empathy are two of the essential ingredients. And, as clinicians have become more aware of gender and ethnic diversity among their clientele, research has shown that the most effective therapists are those who can connect with people in the context of their own culture, experience, and native language (Griner & Smith, 2006).

In addition to the relationship between therapist and client, the therapy process typically involves the following steps:

1. **Identifying the problem.** This may mean merely agreeing on a simple description of circumstances or feelings to be changed, or, in the case of a *DSM-IV* disorder, this step may lead to a formal diagnosis about what is wrong.

CONNECTION CHAPTER 12

The *medical model* assumes that mental disorders are similar to physical diseases (p. 519).

therapeutic alliance The relationship between the therapist and the client, with both parties working together to help the client deal with mental or behavioral issues.

2. **Identifying the cause of the problem or the conditions that maintain the problem.** In some forms of therapy, this involves searching the past, especially childhood, for the source of the patient's or client's discomfort. Alternatively, other forms of therapy emphasize the present causes—that is, the conditions that are keeping the problem alive.

3. **Deciding on and carrying out some form of treatment.** This step requires selecting a specific type of therapy designed to minimize or eliminate the troublesome symptoms. The exact treatment will depend on the nature of the problem and on the therapist's orientation and training.

Who Does Therapy? Although more people seek out therapy now than in the past, they usually turn to trained mental health professionals only when their psychological problems become severe or persist for extended periods. And when they do, they usually turn to one of seven main types of professional helpers: counseling psychologists, clinical psychologists, psychiatrists, psychoanalysts, psychiatric nurse practitioners, clinical (psychiatric) social workers, or pastoral counselors. The differences among these specialties are highlighted in Table 13.1. As you examine this table, note that each specialty has its own area of expertise. For example, in most states, the only therapists who are licensed to prescribe drugs are physicians (including psychiatrists) and psychiatric nurse practitioners.

TABLE 13.1 Types of Mental Health Care Professionals

Professional Title	Specialty and Common Work Settings	Credentials and Qualifications
Counseling psychologist	Provides help in dealing with the common problems of normal living, such as relationship problems, child rearing, occupational choice, and school problems. Typically counselors work in schools, clinics, or other institutions.	Depends on the state: typically at least a master's in counseling, but commonly private practice requires a PhD (Doctor of Philosophy), EdD (Doctor of Education), or PsyD (Doctor of Psychology).
Clinical psychologist	Trained primarily to work with those who have more severe disorders, but may also work with clients having less-severe problems; usually in private practice or employed by mental health agencies or by hospitals; not typically licensed to prescribe drugs.	Usually required to hold PhD or PsyD; often an internship and state certification are required.
Psychiatrist	A physician with a specialty in treating mental problems—most often by prescribing drugs; may be in private practice or employed by clinics or mental hospitals.	MD (Doctor of Medicine); may be required to be certified by medical specialty board.
Psychoanalyst	Practitioners of Freudian therapy; usually in private practice.	MD (some practitioners have doctorates in psychology, but most are psychiatrists who have taken additional training in psychoanalysis.)
Psychiatric nurse practitioner	A nursing specialty; licensed to prescribe drugs for mental disorders; may work in private practice or in clinics and hospitals.	Requires RN (Registered Nurse) credential, plus special training in treating mental disorders and prescribing drugs.
Clinical or psychiatric social worker	Social workers with a specialty in dealing with mental disorders, especially from the viewpoint of the social and environmental context of the problem.	MSW (Master of Social Work).
Pastoral counsellor	A member of a religious order or ministry who specializes in treatment of psychological disorders; combines spiritual guidance with practical counseling.	Varies.

Currently, through their professional organizations, clinical psychologists are seeking to obtain prescription privileges (Sternberg, 2003). In fact, New Mexico now grants prescription privileges to civilian psychologists who have completed a rigorous training program, including 850 hours of course work and a supervised internship (Dittmann, 2003). Similar legislation has been introduced in more than a dozen other states. Meanwhile, the U.S. military has embraced prescription privileges for psychologists (Dittmann, 2004). Nevertheless, the issue remains highly political, contested especially by the medical profession (Fox et al., 2009). Even some clinical psychologists oppose prescription privileges, fearing that psychology will "sell its soul" to serve a public that demands drug therapy. Said former APA President George Albee (2006):

> The current drive for people who are in practice to become drug prescribers is a matter of survival. Society has been sold the fallacy that mental/emotional disorders are all brain diseases that must be treated with drugs. The only way for psychology practitioners to survive is to embrace this invalid nonsense (p. 3).

Whether or not you agree with Albee, it appears that the era of prescription privileges for properly trained psychologists is coming. It remains to be seen how that will change the face of psychology.

Therapy in Historical and Cultural Context

How we treat mental disorder depends on how we *think* about mental disorder. If we believe, for example, that mental problems are *diseases,* we will treat them differently from those who believe that mental problems indicate a flaw in one's character or the influence of evil spirits. The way society has treated people with mental disorders has always depended on its prevailing beliefs.

History of Therapy

As we saw in the previous chapter, people in medieval Europe interpreted mental disorder as the work of devils and demons. In that context, then, the job of the "therapist" was to perform an exorcism or to "beat the devil" out of the person with the disorder—to make the body an inhospitable place for a spirit or demon. In more modern times, however, reformers have urged that people with mental illness be placed in institutions called asylums, where they could be shielded from the stresses of the world—and from the brutal "therapies" that had been common in a less-enlightened era. Unfortunately, the ideal of the "insane asylums" was not often realized.

One of the most infamous of the asylums was also one of the first: Bethlehem Hospital in London, where, for a few pence, weekend sightseers could observe the inmates, who often put on a wild and noisy "show" for the curious audience. As a result, "Bedlam," the shortened term Londoners used for "Bethlehem," became a word used to describe any noisy, chaotic place.

In most asylums, inmates received, at best, only custodial care. At worst, they were neglected or put in cruel restraints, such as cages and chains. Some even received beatings, cold showers, and other forms of abuse. It's not hard to guess that such treatment rarely produced improvement in people suffering from psychological disorders.

In this painting from the 1730s, we see the chaos of a cell in the London hospital, St. Mary of Bethlehem. Here, the upper classes have paid to see the horrors, the fiddler who entertains, and the mental patients chained, tortured, and dehumanized. The chaos of Bethlehem eventually became synonymous with the corruption of its name—Bedlam.

Modern Approaches to Therapy   Modern mental health professionals have abandoned the old demon model and frankly abusive treatments in favor of therapies based on psychological and biological theories of mind and behavior. Yet, as we will see, even modern professionals disagree on the exact causes and the most appropriate treatments—a state of the art that gives us a wide variety of therapies from which to choose. To help you get an overview of this cluttered therapeutic landscape, here is a preview of things to come.

The **psychological therapies** are often called simply *psychotherapy.*[1] They focus on changing disordered thoughts, feelings, and behavior using psychological techniques (rather than biomedical interventions). And they come in two main forms. One, called *insight therapy,* focuses on helping people understand their problems and change their thoughts, motives, or feelings. The other, known as *behavior therapy,* focuses primarily on behavior change. In fact, many psychotherapists use a combination of the two, known as *cognitive–behavioral therapy.*

In contrast, the **biomedical therapies** focus on treating mental problems by changing the underlying biology of the brain, using a variety of drugs, including antidepressants, tranquilizers, and stimulants. Occasionally the brain may be treated directly with electromagnetic stimulation or even surgery. Sometimes therapists use a combination approach involving both drugs and psychotherapy.

Disorder and Therapy in a Cultural Context   Ways of thinking about and treating mental disorder also vary widely across cultures (Matsumoto, 1996). People in individualistic Western cultures (that is, from Europe and North America) generally regard psychological disorders as the result of disease processes, abnormal genetics, distorted thinking, unhealthy environments, or stressors. But collectivist cultures often have quite different perspectives (Triandis, 1990; Zaman, 1992). Asian societies may regard mental disorder as a disconnect between the person and the group. Likewise, many Africans believe that mental disorder results when an individual becomes estranged from nature and from the community, including the community of ancestral spirits (Nobles, 1976; Sow, 1977).

In such cultures, treating mentally disturbed individuals by removing them from society is unthinkable. Instead, healing takes place in a social context, emphasizing a distressed person's beliefs, family, work, and life environment. An African use of group support in therapy has developed into a procedure called "network therapy," where a patient's entire network of relatives, coworkers, and friends becomes involved in the treatment (Lambo, 1978). Such treatments may also involve traditional shamans working alongside mental health professionals trained in modern psychology and psychiatry.

Had Derek been in such a culture, he would undoubtedly have received treatment from a sorcerer or *shaman* who was assumed to have special mystical powers. His therapy would have involved ceremonies and rituals that bring emotional intensity and meaning into the healing process. Combined with the use of symbols, these rituals connect the individual sufferer, the shaman, and the society to supernatural forces to be won over in the battle against madness (Devereux, 1981; Wallace, 1959).

[PSYCHOLOGY MATTERS]

Paraprofessionals Do Therapy, Too

Does the best therapy always require a highly trained (and expensive) professional? Or can **paraprofessionals**—persons who may have received on-the-job training in place of graduate training and certification—be effective therapists? If you are seeking

---

psychological therapy   Therapy based on psychological principles (rather than on the biomedical approach); often called "psychotherapy."

biomedical therapy   Treatment that focuses on altering the brain, especially with drugs, psychosurgery, or electroconvulsive therapy.

paraprofessional   Individual who has received on-the-job training (and, in some cases, undergraduate training) in mental health treatment in lieu of graduate education and full professional certification.

---

[1]No sharp distinction exists between counseling and psychotherapy, although in practice *counseling* usually refers to a shorter process, more likely to be focused on a specific problem, while *psychotherapy* generally involves a longer-term and wider-ranging exploration of issues.

treatment, these questions are important because hospitals, clinics, and agencies are increasingly turning to paraprofessionals as a cost-cutting measure: Those who lack full professional credentials can be hired at a fraction of the cost of those with professional degrees. They are often called "aides" or "counselors" (although many counselors do have professional credentials).

Surprisingly, a review of the literature has found no substantial differences in the effectiveness of the two groups across a wide spectrum of psychological problems (Christensen & Jacobson, 1994). This is good news in the sense that the need for mental health services is far greater than the number of professional therapists can possibly provide. And, because paraprofessional therapists can be effective, highly trained professionals may be freed for other roles, including prevention and community education programs, assessment of patients, training and supervision of paraprofessionals, and research. You should be cautioned about overinterpreting this finding, however. Professionals and paraprofessionals have been found to be equivalent only in the realm of the insight therapies, which we will discuss in a moment (Zilbergeld, 1986). Such differences have not yet been demonstrated in the areas of behavior therapies, which require extensive knowledge of operant and classical conditioning and of social learning theory.

Check Your Understanding

✓ Study and Review at MyPsychLab

1. **RECALL:** People in individualistic cultures often view mental disorder as a problem originating in a person's mind. In contrast, people in collectivist cultures are more likely to see mental disorder as a symptom of a disconnect between the person and _____.

2. **RECALL:** Identify three ways in which the relationship with a trained therapist would differ from that of a friendship.

3. **APPLICATION:** Which type of therapist would be most likely to treat depression by searching for the cause in the unconscious mind?

4. **UNDERSTANDING THE CORE CONCEPT:** In what respect are all therapies alike?
   a. All may be legally administered only by licensed, trained professionals.
   b. All make use of insight into a patient's problems.
   c. All involve the aim of altering the mind, behavior, or social relationships.
   d. All focus on discovering the underlying cause of the patient's problem, which is often hidden in the unconscious mind.

Answers 1. the family or community **2.** Unlike a friend, a therapist is a professional who (a) is trained in therapeutic techniques, (b) will not bring his or her own needs into the therapeutic relationship, and (c) will maintain confidentiality. **3.** A psychodynamic therapist **4.** c

13.2 KEY QUESTION
How Do Psychologists Treat Psychological Disorders?

In the United States and most other Western nations, the sort of therapy Derek receives would depend on whether he had gone to a medical or psychological therapist. By choosing a psychologist like Dr. Sturm, he would almost certainly receive one of the two types of therapy described by the Core Concept for this section of the chapter:

Core Concept 13.2

Psychologists employ two main forms of treatment, the insight therapies (focused on developing understanding of the problem) and the behavior therapies (focused on changing behavior through conditioning).

The *insight therapies,* we shall see, were the first truly psychological treatments developed, and for a long time, they were the only psychological therapies available.

insight therapy   Psychotherapy in which the therapist helps the patient/client understand (gain insight into) his or her problems.

> ▶ **Insight Therapies**
> • Freudian psychoanalysis
> • Neo-Freudian therapies
> • Humanistic therapies
> • Cognitive therapies
> • Group therapies

psychoanalysis   The form of psychodynamic therapy developed by Sigmund Freud. The goal of psychoanalysis is to release conflicts and memories from the unconscious.

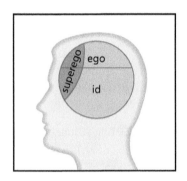

The psychodynamic therapies focus on the client's *motivation*—either conscious or unconscious.

◀ **CONNECTION CHAPTER 10**

The *ego defense mechanisms* include repression, regression, projection, denial, rationalization, reaction formation, displacement, and sublimation (p. 431).

Sigmund Freud's study, including the famous couch (right), is housed in London's Freud Museum. The 82-year-old Freud fled to London in 1938 upon the Nazi occupation of Austria and died there the following year.

In recent years, they have been joined by the *behavior therapies,* which are now among the most effective tools we have. But it is with the insight therapies that we begin.

Insight Therapies

The **insight therapies** attempt to change people on the *inside*—changing the way they think and feel. Sometimes called *talk therapies,* these methods share the assumption that distressed persons need to develop an understanding of the disordered thoughts, emotions, and motives that underlie their mental difficulties.

The insight therapies come in dozens of different "brands," but all aim at revealing and changing a patient's disturbed mental processes through discussion and interpretation. Some therapies, like Freudian *psychoanalysis,* assume that problems lie hidden deep in the unconscious, so they employ elaborate and time-consuming techniques to draw them out. Others, like Carl Rogers's *client-centered therapy,* minimize the importance of the unconscious and look for problems in the ways people consciously think and interact with each other. We have space here to sample only a few of the most influential ones, beginning with the legendary methods developed by Sigmund Freud himself.

Freudian Psychoanalysis   In the classic Freudian view, psychological problems arise from tension created in the unconscious mind by forbidden impulses and threatening memories. Therefore, Freudian therapy, known formally as **psychoanalysis,** probes the unconscious in an attempt to bring these issues into the "light of day"—that is, into consciousness, where they can be rendered harmless. The major goal of psychoanalysis, then, is to reveal and interpret the unconscious mind's contents.

To get at unconscious material, Freud sought ways to get around the defenses the ego has erected to protect itself. One ingenious method called for *free association,* by which the patient would relax and talk about whatever came to mind, while the therapist would listen, ever alert for veiled references to unconscious needs and conflicts. Another method involved *dream interpretation,* which you may recall from Chapter 8.

With these and other techniques, the psychoanalyst gradually develops a clinical picture of the problem and proceeds to help the patient understand the unconscious causes for symptoms. To give you the flavor of this process, we offer Freud's interpretation of a fascinating case involving a 19-year-old girl diagnosed with "obsessional neurosis" (now listed in the *DSM-IV* as *obsessive–compulsive disorder*). Please bear in mind that Freud's ideas no longer represent the mainstream of either psychology or psychiatry, but they remain important because many of his techniques have carried over into newer forms of therapy. Freud's ideas are also important because many of his concepts, such as *ego, repression, the unconscious, identification,* and *the Oedipus complex,* have become part of our everyday vocabulary. The following case, then—in which you may find Freud's interpretations shocking—will give you a sense of the way psychotherapy began about a century ago and is still practiced by a few orthodox psychoanalysts.

When Freud's patient entered treatment, she was causing her parents distress with a strange bedtime ritual that she performed each night. As part of this obsessional ritual, she first stopped the large clock in her room and removed other smaller clocks, including her wristwatch. Then, she placed all vases and flower pots together on her writing table, so—in her "neurotic" way of thinking—they could not fall and break during the night. Next, she assured that the door of her room would remain half open by placing various objects in the doorway. After these precautions, she turned her attention to the bed, where she was careful to assure that the bolster did not touch the headboard and a pillow must lie diagonally in the center of the bolster. Then, she shook the eiderdown in the quilt until all the feathers sank to the foot-end, after which she meticulously redistributed them evenly again. And, finally, she would crawl into bed and attempt to sleep with her head precisely in the center of the diagonal pillow.

To complicate matters, the girl was never sure that she had performed her ritual properly. She would do and then redo first one and then another aspect of the procedure—even though she acknowledged to Freud that all aspects of her nightly precautions were irrational. The result was that it took the girl about two hours to get ready for bed each night.

Before you read Freud's interpretation, you might think about how you would make sense of such strange behaviors. Now then, in Freud's (1957/1920) own words, here is the psychoanalytic interpretation of the case:

> The patient gradually learnt to understand that she banished clocks and watches from her room at night because they were symbols of the female genitals. Clocks, which we know may have other symbolic meanings besides this, acquire this significance of a genital organ by their relation to periodical processes and regular intervals. A woman may be heard to boast that menstruation occurs in her as regularly as clockwork. Now this patient's special fear was that the ticking of the clocks would disturb her during sleep. The ticking of a clock is comparable to the throbbing of the clitoris in sexual excitation. This sensation, which was distressing to her, had actually on several occasions wakened her from sleep; now her fear of an erection of the clitoris expressed itself by the imposition of a rule to remove all going clocks and watches far away from her during the night. Flower-pots and vases are, like all receptacles, also symbols of the female genitals. Precautions to prevent them from falling and breaking during the night are therefore not lacking in meaning. . . . Her precautions against the vases breaking signified a rejection of the whole complex concerned with virginity . . .
>
> One day she divined the central idea of her ritual when she suddenly understood her rule not to let the bolster touch the back of the bed. The bolster had always seemed a woman to her, she said, and the upright back of the bedstead a man. She wished therefore, by a magic ceremony, as it were, to keep man and woman apart; that is to say, to separate the parents and prevent intercourse from occurring . . .
>
> If the bolster was a woman, then the shaking of the eiderdown till all the feathers were at the bottom, making a protuberance there, also had a meaning. It meant impregnating a woman; she did not neglect, though to obliterate the pregnancy again, for she had for years been terrified that intercourse between her parents might result in another child and present her with a rival. On the other hand, if the large bolster meant the mother then the small pillow could only represent the daughter. . . . The part of the man (the father) she thus played herself and replaced the male organ by her own head.
>
> Horrible thoughts, you will say, to run in the mind of a virgin girl. I admit that; but do not forget that I have not invented these ideas, only exposed them . . . (pp. 277–279).

This case shows how Freud used the patient's symptoms as symbolic signposts pointing to underlying and unconscious conflicts, desires, and memories. In the course of treatment, then, he would help the patient understand how her ego defense mechanisms had morphed her unconscious problems into her obsessive rituals. Thus, by the ego defense mechanism of *displacement,* her fears about losing virginity became the ritual of protecting the vases in her bedroom. In this way, her ego was able to satisfy her unconscious needs. At the same time, it could keep the "real" problem blocked from consciousness by means of yet another defense mechanism called *repression.*

A psychoanalyst's main task, then, is to help a patient break through the barriers of repression and bring threatening thoughts to awareness. By doing so, the patient gains insight into the relationship between the current symptoms and the repressed conflicts. Freud argued that, when the patient comes to understand and accept these unconscious conflicts and desires, they will cease to cause trouble.

CONNECTION CHAPTER 10

Repression is the Freudian ego defense mechanism that causes forgetting by blocking off threatening memories in the unconscious (p. 431).

analysis of transference   The Freudian technique of analyzing and interpreting the patient's relationship with the therapist, based on the assumption that this relationship mirrors unresolved conflicts in the patient's past.

Ultimately, in the final stage of psychoanalysis, patients learn how the relationship they have established with the therapist reflects unresolved conflicts, especially problems they had with their parents. This projection of parental attributes onto the therapist is called *transference,* and so the final phase of therapy is known as the **analysis of transference.** According to psychoanalytic theory, this last step in recovery occurs when patients are finally released from the unconscious troubles established long ago in the relationship with their parents during early childhood (Munroe, 1955).

Neo-Freudian Psychodynamic Therapies Please pardon us for doing a bit of analysis on Freud: He obviously had a flair for the dramatic, and he also possessed a powerful, charismatic personality—or, as he himself might have said, a strong ego. Accordingly, Freud encouraged his disciples to debate the principles of psychoanalysis, but he would tolerate no fundamental changes in his doctrines. This inevitably led to conflicts with some of his equally strong-willed followers, such as Alfred Adler, Carl Jung, and Karen Horney, who eventually broke away from Freud to establish their own schools of therapy.

neo-Freudian psychodynamic therapy   Therapy for a mental disorder that was developed by psychodynamic theorists who embraced some of Freud's ideas but disagreed with others.

In general, the neo-Freudian renegades kept many of Freud's basic ideas and techniques while adding some and modifying others. In the true psychodynamic tradition, the **neo-Freudian psychodynamic therapies** have retained Freud's emphasis on motivation. Most now have abandoned the psychoanalyst's couch and treat patients face to face. Most also see patients once a week for a few months, rather than several times a week for several years, as in classical psychoanalysis.

So how do modern psychodynamic therapists get the job done in a shorter time? Most have shifted their emphasis to *conscious* motivation—so they don't spend so much time probing for hidden conflicts and repressed memories. Most have also made a break with Freud by emphasizing one or more of the following points:

- The significance of the self or *ego* (rather than the *id*)
- The influence of experiences occurring throughout life (as opposed to Freud's emphasis on early-childhood experience)
- The role of social needs and interpersonal relationships (rather than sexual and aggressive desires)

And, as we saw in Chapter 10, each of the neo-Freudians constructed a theory of disorder and therapy that had a different emphasis. We do not have space here to go into these approaches in greater detail, but let's briefly consider how a modern psychodynamic therapist might have approached the case of the obsessive girl that Freud described. Most likely, such a therapist would focus on the current relationship between the girl and her parents, perhaps on whether she has feelings of inadequacy for which she is compensating by becoming the center of her parents' attention for two hours each night. And, instead of working so intensively with the girl, the therapist might also work with the parents on changing the way they deal with the problem. And—to further illustrate the point—what about Derek, the depressed fellow whom we met at the beginning of the chapter? While an orthodox Freudian analyst would probe his early childhood memories for clues as to his depression, the modern psychodynamic therapist would be more likely to look for clues in his current relationships, assuming the cause to be social rather than sexual.

Humanistic Therapies In contrast with the psychodynamic emphasis on conflicting motives, the *humanistic* therapists believe that mental problems arise from low self-esteem, misguided goals, and unfulfilling relationships. Indeed, the primary symptoms for which college students seek therapy would include feelings of alienation, failure to achieve all they feel they should, difficult relationships, and general dissatisfaction with their lives. Therapists often refer to these problems in everyday existence as *existential crises,* a term emphasizing how many human problems deal with questions about the meaning and purpose of one's existence. The humanistic psychologists have developed therapies aimed specifically at such problems.

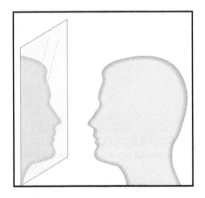

Humanistic therapists often help clients deal with low self-esteem, difficult relationships, and *existential crises.*

Again, in contrast with the psychodynamic view, humanistic therapists believe that people are generally motivated by *healthy* needs for growth and psychological well-being. They dispute Freud's assumption of a personality divided into conflicting parts, dominated by a selfish id, and driven by hedonistic instincts and repressed conflicts. Instead, the humanists emphasize the concept of a whole person engaged in a continual process of growth and change.

In the view of the humanistic psychologists, mental disorder occurs when conditions interfere with normal development and produce low self-esteem. **Humanistic therapies,** therefore, attempt to help clients confront their problems by recognizing their own freedom, enhancing their self-esteem, and realizing their fullest potential (Schneider & May, 1995). A humanistic therapist (if there had been one around a century ago) would probably have worked with Freud's patient to explore her self-concept and her feelings about her parents. As for Derek, a humanistic therapist might guess that his depression arose either from unsatisfying relationships or from a sense of personal inadequacy.

Client-centered therapy, perhaps the most widespread form of humanistic therapy, was developed by the legendary Carl Rogers (1951, 1977). His approach assumed that healthy development can be derailed by a conflict between one's desire for a positive self-image and criticism by self and others. This conflict creates anxiety and unhappiness. The task of Rogerian client-centered therapy, then, is to create a nurturing environment in which people can work through their concerns and finally achieve self-respect and self-actualization.

One of the main techniques used by Rogerian therapists involves **reflection of feeling** (also called *reflective listening*) to help clients understand their emotions. With this technique, therapists paraphrase their clients' words, acting as a sort of psychological "mirror" in which clients can see themselves. Notice how the therapist uses this technique to capture the emotional tone expressed by a young woman in the following excerpt from a therapy session (Rogers, 1951):

> CLIENT: It probably goes all the way back into my childhood. . . . My mother told me that I was the pet of my father. Although I never realized it—I mean, they never treated me as a pet at all. And other people always seemed to think I was sort of a privileged one in the family. . . . And as far as I can see looking back on it now, it's just that the family let the other kids get away with more than they usually did me. And it seems for some reason to have held me to a more rigid standard than they did the other children.
>
> THERAPIST: You're not so sure you were a pet in any sense, but more that the family situation seemed to hold you to pretty high standards.
>
> CLIENT: M-hm. That's just what has occurred to me; and that the other people could sorta make mistakes, or do things as children that were naughty . . . but Alice wasn't supposed to do those things.
>
> THERAPIST: M-hm. With somebody else it would be just—oh, be a little naughtiness; but as far as you were concerned, it shouldn't be done.
>
> CLIENT: That's really the idea I've had. I think the whole business of my standards . . . is one that I need to think about rather carefully, since I've been doubting for a long time whether I even have any sincere ones.
>
> THERAPIST: M-hm. Not sure whether you really have any deep values which you are sure of.
>
> CLIENT: M-hm. M-hm (p. 152).

Note how most of the therapist's statements in this example paraphrased, or "reflected," what the client has just said.

Is such an approach effective? In fact, client-centered therapy has abundant scientific support. An American Psychological Association task force, charged with finding science-based practices that contribute to the effectiveness of therapy, found that the common factor in therapies that work were precisely the Rogerian qualities of *empathy, positive regard, genuineness,* and *feedback* (Ackerman et al., 2001).

humanistic therapy   Treatment technique based on the assumption that people have a tendency for positive growth and self-actualization, which may be blocked by an unhealthy environment that can include negative self-evaluation and criticism from others.

client-centered therapy   A humanistic approach to treatment developed by Carl Rogers, emphasizing an individual's tendency for healthy psychological growth through self-actualization.

Humanistic therapist Carl Rogers (right center) facilitates a therapy group.

reflection of feeling   Carl Rogers's technique of paraphrasing the clients' words, attempting to capture the emotional tone expressed.

cognitive therapy Emphasizes rational thinking (as opposed to subjective emotion, motivation, or repressed conflicts) as the key to treating mental disorder.

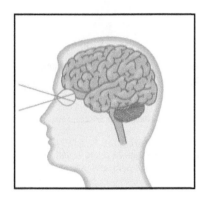

Cognitive therapies focus on changing the way clients *think* about themselves and their world.

Cognitive Therapies The insight therapies we have discussed so far focus primarily on people's emotions or motives (see Figure 13.1). **Cognitive therapy,** on the other hand, assumes that psychological problems arise from erroneous thinking and sees rational thinking as the key to positive therapeutic change (Butler et al., 2006). Cognitive therapy takes multiple forms, but we can give you some of its flavor with one example: Aaron Beck's cognitive therapy for depression.

Beck, who was originally trained in classical psychoanalysis, broke from the Freudian tradition when he began noticing that the dreams and free associations of his depressed patients were filled with negative thoughts (Beck, 1976; Bowles, 2004). Commonly they would make such self-deprecating statements as, "Nobody would like me if they really knew me" and "I'm not smart enough to make it in this competitive school." Gradually, Beck came to believe that depression occurs because of this negative self-talk. The therapist's job, then, is to help the client learn more positive ways of thinking.

Here's a sample of Beck's approach, taken from a therapy session with a college student of about Derek's age (Beck et al., 1979):

CLIENT: I get depressed when things go wrong. Like when I fail a test.

THERAPIST: How can failing a test make you depressed?

CLIENT: Well, if I fail, I'll never get into law school.

THERAPIST: Do you agree that the way you interpret the results of the test will affect you? You might feel depressed, you might have trouble sleeping, not feel like eating, and you might even wonder if you should drop out of the course.

CLIENT: I have been thinking that I wasn't going to make it. Yes, I agree.

THERAPIST: Now what did failing mean?

CLIENT: (tearful) That I couldn't get into law school.

THERAPIST: And what does that mean to you?

CLIENT: That I'm just not smart enough.

THERAPIST: Anything else?

CLIENT: That I can never be happy.

THERAPIST: And how do these thoughts make you feel?

CLIENT: Very unhappy.

THERAPIST: So it is the meaning of failing a test that makes you very unhappy. In fact, believing that you can never be happy is a powerful factor in producing unhappiness. So, you get yourself into a trap—by definition, failure to get into law school equals "I can never be happy" (pp. 145–146).

As you can see from this exchange, the cognitive therapist helps the individual confront the destructive thoughts that support depression. Studies have shown that Beck's

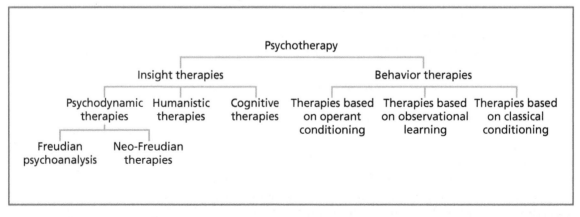

FIGURE 13.1

Types of Psychotherapy

Each of the two major branches of psychotherapy has many variations.

approach can be at least as effective in the treatment of depression as is medication (Antonuccio, 1995; Beck, 2005).

In Derek's case, a cognitive therapist would undoubtedly probe for negative self-talk that might be feeding his depression. And how might a cognitive therapist have approached Freud's 19-year-old obsessive patient? The focus would have been on irrational beliefs, such as the idea that flowerpots and vases could, by themselves, fall down in the night and break. A cognitive therapist would also challenge the assumption that something catastrophic might happen (such as not being able to sleep!) if she didn't perform her nightly ritual. In both cases, the assumption would be that the symptoms would disappear as positive thoughts replaced negative ones.

Group Therapies   The treatments we have discussed to this point usually involve one-to-one relationships between a patient or client and therapist. Most, however, can also be done with groups of two or more persons. Such **group therapy** offers real advantages over individual therapy, particularly in dealing with troubled interpersonal relationships. In fact, group therapy is often the preferred approach to therapy involving couples, families, or other groups of people who have similar problems, such as depression or drug addiction.

Therapy groups usually meet face to face once a week, although some groups are experimenting with sessions on the Internet (Davison et al., 2000). Most typically, the therapist employs a humanistic perspective, although psychodynamic and cognitive–behavioral groups are also common. Whatever the method, group therapy offers clients the opportunity to observe and imitate new social behaviors in a forgiving, supportive atmosphere. In the interest of brevity, we will touch on only two representative types of group therapy below: *self-help groups* and *marital and family therapy*.

Self-Help Support Groups   Perhaps the most noteworthy development in group therapy has been the surge of interest in **self-help support groups**. Thousands of such groups exist. Many are free, especially those that are not directed by a paid health care professional. Such groups give people a chance to meet under nonthreatening conditions to exchange ideas with others having similar problems and who are surviving and sometimes even thriving (Schiff & Bargal, 2000).

One of the oldest support groups, Alcoholics Anonymous (AA) pioneered the self-help concept, beginning in the mid-1930s. Central to the original AA process is the concept of "12 Steps" to recovery from alcohol addiction. It is noteworthy that the 12 Steps are based not on psychological theory but on the trial-and-error experience of early AA members.

In the 1960s, the feminist consciousness-raising movement brought the self-help concept to a wider audience. As a result, self-help support groups now exist for an enormous range of problems, including:

- Managing life transition or other crises, such as divorce or death of a child.
- Coping with physical and mental disorders, such as depression or heart attack.
- Dealing with addictions and other uncontrolled behaviors, such as alcoholism, gambling, overeating, sexual excess, and drug dependency.
- Handling the stress felt by relatives or friends of those who are dealing with addictions.

Group therapy also makes valuable contributions to the treatment of terminally ill patients. The goals of such therapy are to help patients and their families live their lives as fully as possible, to cope realistically with impending death, and to adjust to the terminal illness. One general focus of such support groups for the terminally ill is to help them learn "how to live fully until you say goodbye" (Nungesser, 1990).

Couples and Family Therapy   Perhaps the best setting in which to learn about relationships is in a group of people struggling with relationships. *Couples therapy* (or counseling), for example, may involve one or more couples who are learning to clarify their communication patterns and improve the quality of their interaction (Napier, 2000). By seeing couples together, a therapist can help the partners identify the verbal and nonverbal styles they use to dominate, control, or confuse each other (Gottman, 1994, 1999). The therapist then helps them to reinforce more desirable responses in the other

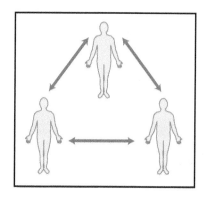

While practitioners from many perspectives use group therapy, they all capitalize on the social milieu of the group.

group therapy   Any form of psychotherapy done with more than one client/patient at a time. Group therapy is often done from a humanistic perspective.

self-help support groups   Groups, such as Alcoholics Anonymous, that provide social support and an opportunity for sharing ideas about dealing with common problems. Such groups are typically organized and run by laypersons, rather than professional therapists.

In couples therapy, the therapist can help people work together to improve the communication patterns that have developed in their relationship.

and withdraw from conflicts. Couples are also taught *nondirective* listening skills that help clarify and express feelings and ideas without being confrontational (Jacobson et al., 2000; Wheeler et al., 2001).

In *family therapy,* the "client" is an entire family group, with each family member being treated as part of a *system of relationships* (Fishman, 1993). A family therapist helps troubled family members perceive the issues or patterns that are creating problems for them. The goal is to alter the interpersonal dynamics (interactions) among the participants (Foley, 1979; Schwebel & Fine, 1994). Family therapy not only helps reduce tensions within a family, but it can also improve the functioning of individual members by helping them recognize their roles in the group. It is also proved to be effective in the treatment of anorexia nervosa, depression, and other mood disorders, and even as a boon to families struggling with schizophrenia (Miklowitz, 2007).

Behavior Therapies

> ▶ **Behavior Therapies**
>
> • Systematic desensitization
> • Aversion therapy
> • Contingency management
> • Token economies
> • Participant modeling

behavior modification   Another term for behavior therapy.

behavior therapy   Any form of psychotherapy based on the principles of behavioral learning, especially operant conditioning and classical conditioning.

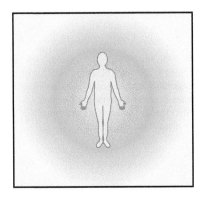

Behavior therapists focus on the person's environment and on problem *behaviors,* rather than on internal thoughts, motives, or feelings.

◀ **CONNECTION** CHAPTER 4

In *classical conditioning,* a CS comes to produce essentially the same response as the UCS (p. 137).

If the problem is overeating, bed wetting, shyness, antisocial behavior, or anything else that can be described in purely behavioral terms, the chances are good that it can be modified by one of the behavior therapies (also known as **behavior modification**). Based on the assumption that these undesirable behaviors have been learned and therefore can be *un*learned, **behavior therapy** relies on the principles of operant and classical conditioning. In addition to those difficulties listed above, behavior therapists report success in dealing with fears, compulsions, depression, addictions, aggression, and delinquent behaviors.

As the label suggests, behavior therapists focus on problem *behaviors* rather than inner thoughts, motives, or emotions. They seek to understand how unwanted behaviors might have been learned and, even more important, how they can be eliminated and replaced by more effective patterns. To see how this is done, we will look first at the behavior therapy techniques borrowed from *classical conditioning.*

Classical Conditioning Therapies   The first example of behavior therapy, reported by psychologist Mary Cover Jones (1924), treated a fearful little boy named Peter, who was afraid of furry objects. Jones was able to desensitize the boy's fear, over a period of weeks, by gradually bringing a rabbit closer and closer to the boy while he was eating. Eventually, Peter was able to allow the rabbit to sit on his lap while he petted it. (You may notice the similarity to John Watson's experiments on Little Albert. Indeed, Jones was an associate of Watson and knew of the Little Albert study. Unlike Albert, however, Peter came to treatment already possessing an intense fear of rabbits and other furry objects.)

Surprisingly, it was another 14 years before behavior therapy reappeared, this time as a treatment for bed wetting (Mowrer & Mowrer, 1938). The method involved a fluid-sensitive pad placed under the patient. When moisture set off an alarm, the patient would awaken. The treatment was effective in 75 percent of cases—an amazing success rate, in view of the dismal failure of psychodynamic therapy to prevent bed wetting by talking about the "meaning" of the symptom. And yet, it took yet another 20 years before behavior therapy entered the mainstream of psychological treatment.

Why the delay? The old Freudian idea—that every symptom has an underlying, unconscious cause that must be discovered and eradicated—was extremely well rooted in clinical lore. Therapists dared not attack symptoms (behaviors) directly for fear of *symptom substitution:* the idea that by eliminating one symptom, another, which could be much worse, could take its place. This concern was unfounded.

Systematic Desensitization   It took psychiatrist Joseph Wolpe to challenge the entrenched notion of symptom substitution. Wolpe reasoned that the development of irrational fear responses and other undesirable emotionally based behaviors might follow the classical conditioning model rather than the Freudian model. As you will recall, *classical conditioning* involves the association of a new stimulus with an unconditioned stimulus so that the person responds the same way to both. Thus, a fear

TABLE 13.2 A Sample Anxiety Hierarchy

The following is typical of anxiety hierarchies that a therapist and a patient might develop to desensitize a fear of public speaking. The therapist guides the deeply relaxed patient in imagining the following situations:

1. Seeing a picture or a video recording of another person giving a speech
2. Watching another person give a speech
3. Preparing a speech that I will give to a small group of friends
4. Having to introduce myself to a large group
5. Waiting to be called on to speak in a meeting or in a large class
6. Being introduced as a speaker to a group
7. Walking to the podium to make a speech
8. Making an important speech to a large group

response might be associated with, say, crowds or spiders or lightning. Wolpe also realized another simple truth: The nervous system cannot be relaxed and agitated at the same time because these two incompatible processes cannot be activated simultaneously. Putting these two ideas together formed the foundation for Wolpe's method, called **systematic desensitization** (Wolpe, 1958, 1973).

Systematic desensitization begins with a training program, teaching patients to relax their muscles and their minds (Rachman, 2000). With the patient in this deeply relaxed state, the therapist begins the process of *extinction* by having the patient imagine progressively more fearful situations. This is done in gradual steps, called an *anxiety hierarchy,* that move from remote associations to imagining an intensely feared situation.

To develop the anxiety hierarchy, the therapist and client first identify all the situations that provoke the patient's anxiety and then arrange them in levels, ranked from weakest to strongest (Shapiro, 1995). For example, a patient suffering from severe fear of public speaking constructed the hierarchy of unconditioned stimuli seen in Table 13.2.

Later, during desensitization, the relaxed client vividly imagines the weakest anxiety stimulus on the list. If it can be visualized without discomfort, the client goes on to the next stronger one. After a number of sessions, the client can imagine the most distressing situations on the list without anxiety (Lang & Lazovik, 1963)—hence the term *systematic* desensitization.

It turns out that Wolpe may have been too cautious about inducing anxiety in his clients. In a newer and more intense form of desensitization, known **exposure therapy,** the therapist may actually have the patient confront the feared object or situation, such as a spider or a snake, rather than just imagining it—and this seems to be even more effective than Wolpe's method (Barlow, 2010). You will recall that Sabra, whom you met at the beginning of Chapter 4, went through a form of exposure therapy to overcome her fear of flying. The technique has been used successfully with a multitude of patients with phobias and anxiety disorders, including many whose fears of blood, injections, and germs stand in the way of getting needed medical or dental treatment (Dittmann, 2005b).

In the past few years, some behavioral therapists have added a high-tech twist to exposure therapy. By using computer-generated images of fearful situations, their clients can explore and extinguish fears and anxieties in a virtual-reality environment that they know is safe. To enter the virtual-reality environment, patients don a helmet containing a video screen, on which are projected images to which they will be desensitized: spiders, snakes, high places, closed-in spaces—all the common phobia-producing objects or images (Winerman, 2005e).

Aversion Therapy So, desensitization and exposure therapy help clients deal with stimuli that they want to avoid. But what about the reverse? What can be done to help those who are attracted to stimuli that are harmful or illegal? Examples include drug addiction, certain sexual attractions, and tendencies to violence—all problems in

systematic desensitization   A behavioral therapy technique in which anxiety is extinguished by exposing the patient to an anxiety-provoking stimulus.

exposure therapy   A form of desensitization therapy in which the patient directly confronts the anxiety-provoking stimulus (as opposed to imagining the stimulus).

In "virtual reality," phobic patients can confront their fears safely and conveniently in the behavior therapist's office. On a screen inside the headset, the patient sees computer-generated images of feared situations, such as seeing a snake, flying in an airplane, or looking down from the top of a tall building.

aversion therapy As a classical conditioning procedure, aversive counterconditioning involves presenting the individual with an attractive stimulus paired with unpleasant (aversive) stimulation to condition a repulsive reaction.

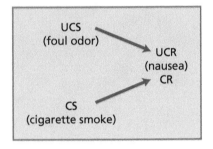

FIGURE 13.2

Conditioning an Aversion for Cigarette Smoke

Aversion therapy for smoking might simultaneously pair a foul odor with cigarette smoke blown in the smoker's face. The foul odor (such as rotten eggs) produces nausea. This response then becomes the conditioned response associated with cigarette smoke.

Source: Wolpe, J. (1991). *The practice of behavior therapy*, 4th ed. Boston, MA: Allyn & Bacon. Copyright © 1991 by Pearson Education. Reprinted by permission of the publisher.

▶ **CONNECTION** CHAPTER 4

In *operant conditioning*, behavior changes because of consequences, such as rewards and punishments (p. 143).

contingency management An operant conditioning approach to changing behavior by altering the consequences, especially rewards and punishments, of behavior.

which undesirable behavior is elicited by some specific stimulus. **Aversion therapy** tackles these problems with a conditioning procedure designed to make tempting stimuli repulsive by pairing them repeatedly with unpleasant (aversive) stimuli. For example, the therapist might use electric shocks or nausea-producing drugs, whose effects are highly unpleasant but not actually dangerous to the client. In time, the negative reactions (unconditioned responses) to the aversive stimuli come to be associated with the conditioned stimuli (such as an addictive drug), and so the client develops an aversion that replaces the desire.

To give another example, if you were to elect aversion therapy to help you quit smoking, you might be required to chain-smoke cigarettes while having a foul odor blown in your face—until you develop a strong association between smoking and nausea (see Figure 13.2). A similar conditioning effect occurs in alcoholics who drink while taking Antabuse, a drug often prescribed to encourage sobriety.

In some ways, aversion therapy resembles nothing so much as torture. So why would anyone submit voluntarily to it? Sometimes, the courts may assign a probationer to aversion therapy. Usually, however, people submit to this type of treatment because they have a troublesome addiction that has resisted other treatments.

Operant Conditioning Therapies Four-year-old Tyler has a screaming fit when he goes to the grocery store with his parents and they refuse to buy him candy. He acquired this annoying behavior through operant conditioning, by being rewarded when his parents have given in to his demands. In fact, most behavior problems found in both children and adults have been shaped by rewards and punishments. Consider, for example, the similarities between Tyler's case and the employee who chronically arrives late for work or the student who waits until the last minute to study for a test. Changing such behaviors requires operant conditioning techniques. Let's look at two therapeutic variations on this operant theme.

Contingency Management Tyler's parents may learn to extinguish his fits at the grocery store by simply withdrawing their attention—no easy task, by the way. In addition, the therapist may coach them to "catch Tyler being good" and give him all the attention he needs—but only for good behavior. Over time, the changing contingencies will work to extinguish the old, undesirable behaviors and help to keep the new ones in place. This approach is an example of **contingency management**: changing behavior by modifying its consequences. It has proved effective in treating behavior problems found in such diverse settings as families, schools, work, prisons, the military, and mental hospitals. The careful application of reward and punishment can also reduce the self-destructive behaviors in autistic children (Frith, 1997). And, if you would like to change some undesirable habit or acquire a new one, you can even apply contingency management techniques to yourself: See the accompanying box, *Do It Yourself! Behavior Self-Modification.*

Do It Yourself! BEHAVIOR SELF-MODIFICATION

Is there a behavioral habit that you would like to acquire—studying, initiating conversations with others, exercising to keep fit? Write this activity in behavioral terms on the lines below. (Don't use mentalistic words such as "feeling" or "wanting." Behaviorists require that you keep things objective by specifying only an observable behavior.)

The desired new behavior: _____

When or under what conditions would you like to engage in this new behavior? Below, write in the time or stimulus conditions

when you want to initiate the behavior (for example: in class, when relaxing with friends, or at a certain time every morning).

The time or conditions for the new behavior: _____

To increase your likelihood of producing the desired response, apply some positive reinforcement therapy to yourself. Choose an appropriate reward that you will give yourself when you have produced the desired behavior at the appropriate time. Write the reward that you will give yourself below.

Your reward: _____

Give yourself feedback on your progress by keeping a daily record of the occurrence of your new behavior. This could be done, for example, on a calendar or a graph. In time, you will discover that the desired behavior has increased in frequency. You will also find that your new habit carries its own rewards, such as better grades or more satisfying social interactions (Kazdin, 1994).

Token Economies   A special form of therapy called a **token economy** is commonly used in group settings such as classrooms and institutions. Think of it as the behavioral version of group therapy (Ayllon & Azrin, 1968; Martin & Pear, 1999). The method takes its name from the plastic tokens sometimes awarded by therapists or teachers as immediate reinforcers for desirable behaviors.

In a classroom application, for example, a student might earn a token for sitting quietly for several minutes, participating in a class discussion, or turning in an assignment. Later, recipients may redeem the tokens for food, merchandise, or privileges. Often, "points" or play money are used in place of tokens. The important thing is that the individual receives something as a reinforcer immediately after giving desired responses. With the appropriate modifications, the token economy also works well with children having developmental disabilities, with mental patients, and with correctional populations (Higgins et al., 2001).

Participant Modeling: An Observational-Learning Therapy

"Monkey see—monkey do," we say. And sure enough, monkeys learn fears by observation and imitation. One study showed that laboratory monkeys with no previous aversion to snakes could acquire a simian version of *ophidiophobia* by observing their parents reacting fearfully to real snakes and toy snakes. (You don't remember that phobia? Look back at Table 12.3 on pages 532–533.) The more disturbed the monkey parents were at the sight of the snakes, the greater the resulting fear in their offspring (Mineka et al., 1984). A follow-up study showed that such fears were not just a family matter. When other monkeys that had previously shown no fear of snakes were given the opportunity to observe unrelated adults responding to snakes fearfully, they quickly acquired the same response, as you can see in Figure 13.3 (Cook et al., 1985).

Like monkeys, people also learn fears by observing the behavior of others. But for therapeutic purposes, observational learning in the form of *participant modeling* can also encourage *healthy* behaviors. In **participant modeling**, then, the client, or *participant*, observes and imitates someone *modeling* desirable behaviors. Athletic coaches, of course, have used participant modeling for years. Similarly, a behavior therapist treating a snake phobia might model the desired behavior by first approaching a caged snake, then touching the snake, and so on. The client then imitates the modeled behavior—but at no time is forced to perform. If the therapist senses resistance, the client may return to a previously successful level. As you can see, the procedure is similar to systematic desensitization, with the important addition of observational learning. In fact, participant modeling draws on concepts from both operant and classical conditioning.

The power of participant modeling in eliminating snake phobias can be seen in a study that compared the participant modeling technique with several other approaches: (1) *symbolic modeling,* a technique in which subjects receive indirect exposure by watching a film or video in which models deal with a feared situation; (2) desensitization therapy, which, as you will remember, involves exposure to an imagined fearful stimulus; and (3) no therapeutic intervention (the control condition). As you can see in Figure 13.4, participant modeling was the most successful. The snake phobia was virtually eliminated in 11 of the 12 subjects in the participant modeling group (Bandura, 1970).

Cognitive–Behavioral Therapy: A Synthesis

Suppose you are having difficulty controlling feelings of jealousy every time the person you love is friendly with someone else. Chances are that the problem originates in your cognitions about yourself and the others involved ("Marty is stealing Terry away from me!") These thoughts may also affect your behavior, making you act in ways that could drive Terry away from you. A dose of therapy aimed at *both* your cognitions and your behaviors may be a better bet than either one alone.

In brief, **cognitive–behavioral therapy** (CBT) combines a cognitive emphasis on thoughts and attitudes with the behavioral strategies that we have just discussed. This dual approach assumes that an irrational self-statement often underlies maladaptive

token economy   An operant technique applied to groups, such as classrooms or mental hospital wards, involving the distribution of "tokens" or other indicators of reinforcement contingent on desired behaviors. The tokens can later be exchanged for privileges, food, or other reinforcers.

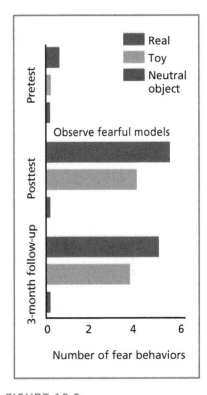

FIGURE 13.3

Fear Reactions in Monkeys

In a pretest, young monkeys raised in laboratories show little fear of snakes (top bars). But after observing other monkeys showing a strong fear of snakes, they are conditioned to fear both real snakes and toy snakes (middle bars). A follow-up test shows that the fear persists over a 3-month interval (bottom bars).

Source: Cook, M., Mineka, S., Wokenstein, B., & Laitsch, K. (1985). Observational conditioning of snake fear in unrelated rhesus monkeys. *Journal of Abnormal Psychology, 94,* pp. 591–610. Copyright © 1985 by American Psychological Association. Reprinted by permission of American Psychological Association.

participant modeling   A social learning technique in which a therapist demonstrates and encourages a client to imitate a desired behavior.

cognitive–behavioral therapy   A newer form of psychotherapy that combines the techniques of cognitive therapy with those of behavioral therapy.

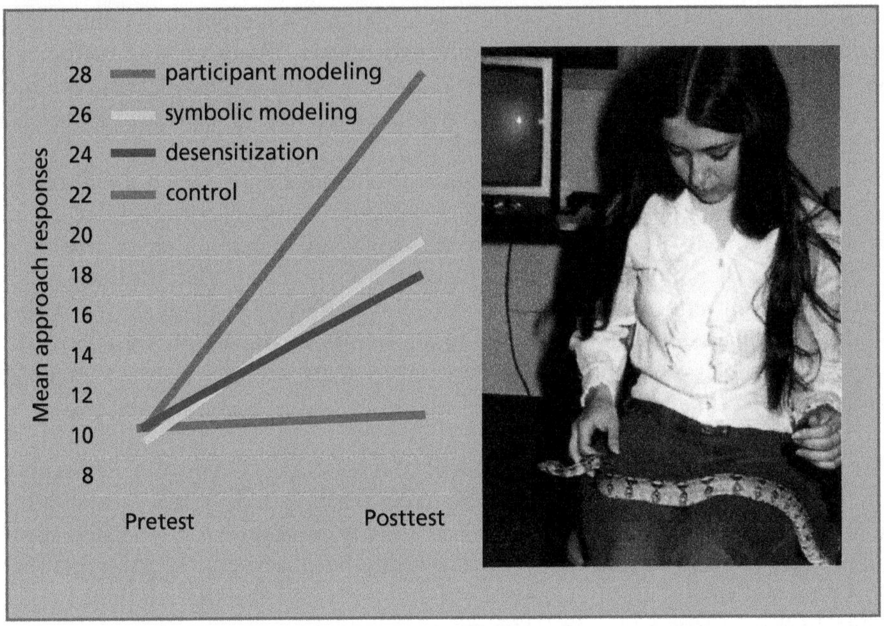

FIGURE 13.4
Participant Modeling Therapy

The client shown in the photo first watches a model make a graduated series of snake-approach responses and then repeats them herself. Eventually, she can pick up the snake and let it move about on her. The graph compares the number of approach responses clients made before and after receiving participant modeling therapy with the responses of those exposed to two other therapeutic techniques and a control group. The graph shows that participant modeling was far more effective in the posttest.

Source: Bandura, A. D. (1970). Modeling therapy. In W. S. Sahakian (Ed.), *Psychopathology today: Experimentation, theory, and research.* Itasca, IL: Peacock. Reprinted by permission of the author.

◉ Watch the **Video** Cognitive Behavioral Therapy at **MyPsychLab**

rational–emotive behavior therapy (REBT) Albert Ellis's brand of cognitive therapy, based on the idea that irrational thoughts and behaviors are the cause of mental disorders.

◀ **CONNECTION** CHAPTER 10

Compare Ellis's "neurotic" goals with Karen Horney's neurotic trends (p. 438).

behavior. Accordingly, the therapist and client work together to modify irrational self-talk, set attainable behavioral goals, develop realistic strategies for attaining them, and evaluate the results. In this way, people change the way they approach problems and gradually develop new skills and a sense of self-efficacy (Bandura, 1986, 1992; DeAngelis, 2008b; Schwarzer, 1992). **◉**

How well does cognitive–behavioral therapy work? Quite well, indeed, particularly for depression, anxiety disorders, alcoholism, bulimia nervosa, recurring nightmares, and posttraumatic stress disorder (Baker et al., 2008; Chamberlin, 2008). In fact, it is one of psychology's most prominent success stories. In all of these disorders, CBT can be at least as effective as medication—and sometimes *more* so. For certain other conditions, such as bipolar disorder and schizophrenia, a combination of CBT and medication is more effective than either one alone.

Rational–Emotive Behavior Therapy: Challenging the "Shoulds" and "Oughts" One of the most famous forms of cognitive–behavioral therapy was developed by the colorful and notorious Albert Ellis (1987, 1990, 1996) to help people eliminate self-defeating thought patterns. Ellis dubbed his treatment **rational–emotive behavior therapy (REBT)**, a name derived from its method of challenging certain "irrational" beliefs and behaviors.

What are the irrational beliefs challenged in REBT, and how do they lead to maladaptive feelings and actions? According to Ellis, maladjusted individuals base their lives on a set of unrealistic values and unachievable goals. These "neurotic" goals and values lead people to hold unrealistic expectations that they should *always* succeed, that they should *always* receive approval, that they should *always* be treated fairly, and that their experiences should *always* be pleasant. (You can see the most common irrational beliefs in the accompanying box, *Do It Yourself! Examining Your Own Beliefs.*) For example, in your own daily life, you may frequently tell yourself that you "should" get an A in math or that you "ought to" spend an hour exercising every day. Further, he says, if you are unable to meet your goals and seldom question this neurotic self-talk, it may come to control your actions or even prevent you from choosing the life you want. If you were to enter REBT, your therapist would teach you to recognize such assumptions, question how rational they are, and replace faulty ideas with more valid ones. Don't "should" on yourself, warned Ellis.

So, how might a cognitive–behavioral therapist have dealt with Freud's obsessive patient? First, taking a cognitive approach, the therapist would challenge the girl's irrational beliefs, as we suggested earlier. Then, switching to a behavioral mode, the

Do It Yourself! EXAMINING YOUR OWN BELIEFS

It may be obvious that the following are not healthy beliefs, but Albert Ellis found that many people hold them. Do you? Be honest: Put a check mark beside each of the following statements that accurately describes how you feel about yourself.

1. _____ I must be loved and approved by everyone.

2. _____ I must be thoroughly competent, adequate, and achieving.

3. _____ It is catastrophic when things do not go the way I want them to go.

4. _____ Unhappiness results from forces over which I have no control.

5. _____ People must always treat each other fairly and justly; those who don't are nasty and terrible people.

6. _____ I must constantly be on my guard against dangers and things that could go wrong.

7. _____ Life is full of problems, and I must always find quick solutions to them.

8. _____ It is easier to evade my problems and responsibilities than to face them.

9. _____ Unpleasant experiences in my past have had a profound influence on me. Therefore, they must continue to influence my current feelings and actions.

10. _____ I can achieve happiness by just enjoying myself each day. The future will take care of itself.

In Ellis's view, all these statements were irrational beliefs that can cause mental problems. The more items you have checked, the more "irrational" your beliefs. His cognitive approach to therapy, known as rational–emotive behavior therapy, concentrates on helping people see that they can "drive themselves crazy" with such irrational beliefs. For example, a student who parties rather than studying for a test holds belief #8. A person who is depressed about not landing a certain job holds irrational belief #3. You can obtain more information on Ellis's system from his books.

---

therapist might teach the girl relaxation techniques to use when she began to get ready for bed each evening. These techniques then would substitute for the obsessive ritual. It is also likely that the therapist would work with the parents, focusing on helping them learn not to reward the girl with attention for her ritual behavior.

Similarly, a cognitive–behavioral therapist would help depressed Derek by challenging the way he *thinks*—perhaps blaming himself less and focusing more on constructive plans for doing better—can ultimately change how he feels and how he acts. Indeed, Peter Lewinsohn and his colleagues have found that they can treat many cases of depression effectively with such cognitive–behavioral techniques (Lewinsohn et al., 1980, 1990; Lewinsohn & Gottlib, 1995). Their approach intervenes at several points in the cycle of depression to teach people how to change their helpless thinking, to cope adaptively with unpleasant situations, and to build more rewards into their lives.

Positive Psychotherapy (PPT) Derek might also be a good candidate for a newer form of cognitive–behavioral treatment called **positive psychotherapy (PPT)**, developed by Martin Seligman. Like the humanists, Seligman and his fellow *positive psychologists* see their mission as balancing psychology's negative emphasis on mental disorders with their own positive emphasis on growth, health, and happiness. So it was a "natural" for Seligman to tackle the problem of depression by accentuating the positive (Seligman et al., 2006). Unlike the humanists, however, the PPT approach is largely cognitive–behavioral, with an emphasis on research.

In both PPT and Lewinsohn's therapy sessions, Derek might find himself treated more like a student than a patient. For example, the therapist might give him a "homework" assignment, such as the "three good things" exercise: "Before you go to sleep, write down three things that went well today and why they went well." Derek would also learn to focus on positive emotions, respond constructively to others, and otherwise to seek more pleasure in his work and home life. How well does PPT work? Seligman and his group have applied PPT to dozens of clients and report preliminary results showing that it relieved depression far more effectively than did conventional therapy or antidepressant medication (Seligman et al., 2006).

Changing the Brain by Changing the Mind Brain scans now show that cognitive–behavioral therapy not only helps people change their minds, but it can also change the brain itself (Dobbs, 2006b). In one study, patients who experienced compulsive obsessions, such as worrying that they had not turned off their stoves or locked their

positive psychotherapy (PPT) A relatively new form of cognitive–behavioral treatment that seeks to emphasize growth, health, and happiness.

doors, were given cognitive behavior modification (Schwartz et al., 1996). When they felt an urge to run home and check on themselves, they were trained to relabel their experience as an obsession or compulsion—not a rational concern. They then focused on waiting out this "urge" rather than giving in to it, by distracting themselves with other activities for about 15 minutes. Positron emission tomography (PET) scans of the brains of subjects who were trained in this technique indicated that, over time, the part of the brain responsible for that nagging fear or urge gradually became less active.

As that study shows, psychology has come a long way since the days when we wondered whether thoughts and behavior were the product of nature *or* nurture. With cognitive–behavioral therapy, we now know that experience can change the biology behind behavior.

Evaluating the Psychological Therapies

Now that we have looked at a variety of psychological therapies (see Figure 13.5), let us step back and ask how effective therapy is. Think about it: How could you tell objectively whether therapy really works? The answer to this question hasn't always been clear (Kopta et al., 1999; Shadish et al., 2000).

Lots of evidence says that most people who have undergone therapy *like* it. This was shown, for example, by surveying thousands of subscribers to *Consumer Reports* (1995). Respondents indicated how much their treatment helped, how satisfied they

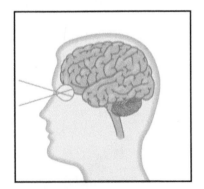

Behavior therapies
aim to change things *outside the individual*: rewards, punishments, and cues in the environment in order to change the person's external behaviors.

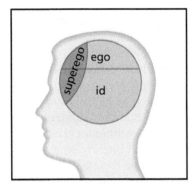

Psychodynamic therapies
aim to make changes *inside the person's mind*, especially the unconscious.

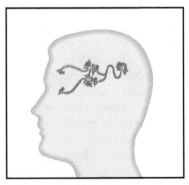

Humanistic therapies
aim to change the way people *see themselves and their relationships*.

Cognitive therapies
aim to change the way people *think and perceive*.

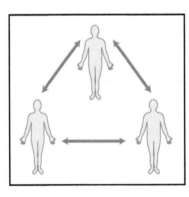

Group therapies
aim to change the way people *interact*.

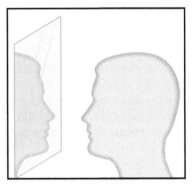

Biomedical therapies
aim to change the structure or function of the brain.

FIGURE 13.5

A Comparison of Different Types of Therapy

were with the therapist's treatment of their problems, how much their "overall emotional state" changed following therapy, as well as what kind of therapy they had undergone. Among the results: (a) Therapy works—that is, it was perceived to have helped clients diminish or eliminate their psychological problems; (b) long-term therapy is better than short-term therapy; and (c) all forms of therapy are about equally effective for improving clients' problems (see Jacobson & Christensen, 1996).

We can't give a thumbs-up to therapy, however, merely because people say they like it or that it helped them (Hollon, 1996). Testimonials don't make for good science—which is why psychologists now demand that therapy be judged by studies having a *comparison group* or *control group*. Let's turn, therefore, to the controlled studies of therapy's effectiveness, beginning with a report that nearly upset the therapeutic applecart.

Eysenck's Controversial Proclamation The issue of therapy's effectiveness came to a head in 1952, when British psychologist Hans Eysenck proclaimed that roughly two-thirds of all people who develop nonpsychotic mental disorders would recover within two years, *whether they get therapy or not*. Eysenck's evidence came from a review of several outcome studies of various kinds of insight therapy, all of which compared patients who received therapy to those who were on waiting lists, waiting their turn in treatment. What he noted was that just as many people on the waiting lists recovered as those in therapy. If taken at face value, this meant that psychotherapy was essentially worthless—no better than having no treatment at all! To say the least, this wasn't received happily by therapists. But Eysenck's challenge had an immensely productive result: It stimulated therapists to do a great deal of research on the effectiveness of their craft.

In Response to Eysenck Major reviews of the accumulating evidence on therapy began to be reported in 1970 (by Meltzoff & Kornreich), in 1975 (by Luborsky et al.), and in 1977 (by Smith and Glass). Overall, this literature—numbering some 375 studies—supported two major conclusions. First, therapy is, after all, more effective than no therapy—much to everyone's relief! And second, Eysenck had apparently overestimated the improvement rate in no-therapy control groups.

Gradually, then, a scientific consensus supporting the value of psychotherapy emerged (Meredith, 1986; VandenBos, 1986). In fact, for a broad range of disorders, psychotherapy has been demonstrated to have an effect comparable or superior to many established medical practices (Wampold, 2007). Moreover, research began to show that therapy was effective not only in Western industrialized countries (in the United States, Canada, and Europe) but also in a variety of cultural settings throughout the world (Beutler & Machado, 1992; Lipsey & Wilson, 1993).

New Questions But the new studies have raised new questions. Are some therapies better than others? Can we identify therapies that are best suited for treating specific disorders? The Smith and Glass (1977) survey hinted that the answers to those questions were "Yes" and "Yes." Smith and Glass found that the behavior therapies seemed to have an advantage over insight therapies for the treatment of many anxiety disorders. And as we noted earlier, the use of cognitive–behavioral therapies for treating depression, anxiety disorders, bulimia nervosa, and a few other disorders now has solid empirical support. In addition, recent evaluations have found that insight therapies can also be used effectively to treat problems such as marital discord, depression, and even the tough-to-treat personality disorders (Shedler, 2010). Indeed, there is now a clear trend toward matching specific therapies to specific conditions.

Finally, we should note that, in judging the effectiveness of various psychotherapies, it is important to realize that success does not necessarily mean a "cure." Sometimes just making an improvement is all the success we can expect. In the treatment of schizophrenia, mental retardation, or autism, for example, psychological therapies may be deemed effective when people with these afflictions learn more adaptive behaviors and report leading happier lives (Hogarty et al., 1997).

CONNECTION CHAPTER 1

A *control group* is treated exactly as the experimental group, except for the crucial independent variable (p. 27).

[PSYCHOLOGY MATTERS]

Where Do Most People Get Help?

The effectiveness of psychotherapy for a variety of problems seems to be established beyond doubt. Having said that, we should again acknowledge that *most people experiencing mental distress do not turn to professional therapists for help.* Rather, they turn to "just people" in the community (Wills & DePaulo, 1991). Those suffering from mental problems often look to friends, clergy, hairdressers, bartenders, and others with whom they have a trusting relationship. In fact, for some types of problems—perhaps the most common problems of everyday living—a sympathetic friend may be just as effective as a trained professional therapist (Berman & Norton, 1985; Christensen & Jacobson, 1994).

To put the matter in a different way: Most mental problems are not the crippling disorders that took center stage in the previous chapter. Rather, the psychological difficulties most of us face result from lost jobs, difficult marriages, misbehaving children, friendships gone sour, loved ones dying. . . . In brief, the most familiar problems involve chaos, confusion, choice, frustration, stress, and loss. People who find themselves in the throes of these adjustment difficulties may not need extensive psychotherapy, medication, or some other special treatment. They need someone to help them sort through the pieces of their problems. Usually, this means that they turn to someone like you.

So, what can you do when someone asks you for help? First, you should realize that some problems do indeed require immediate professional attention. These include a suicide threat or an indication of intent to harm others. You should not delay finding competent help for someone with such tendencies. Second, you should remember that most therapy methods require special training, especially those calling for cognitive–behavioral therapy techniques or psychodynamic interpretations. We urge you to learn as much as you can about these methods—but we strongly recommend that you leave them to the professionals. Some other techniques, however, are simply extensions of good human relationships, and they fall well within the layperson's abilities for mental "first aid." Briefly, we will consider three of these:

- **Listening.** You will rarely go wrong if you just listen. Sometimes listening is all the therapy a person in distress needs. It works by encouraging the speaker to organize a problem well enough to communicate it. Consequently, those who talk out their problems frequently arrive at their own solutions. As an **active listener,** you take the role a step farther by giving the speaker feedback: nodding, maintaining an expression that shows interest, paraphrasing, and asking for clarification when you don't understand. As we saw in the client-centered therapy excerpts on pages 565 and 566, active listening lets the speaker know that the listener is interested and *empathetic* (in tune with the other person's feelings). At the same time, you will do well to avoid the temptation of giving advice. Advice robs the recipient of the opportunity to work out his or her own solutions.

- **Acceptance.** Client-centered therapists call this a *nonjudgmental attitude.* It means accepting the person and the problem as they are. It also means suppressing shock, disgust, or condemnation that would create a hostile climate for problem solving.

- **Exploration of alternatives.** People under stress may see only one course of action, so you can help by identifying other potential choices and exploring the consequences of each. (You can point out that *doing nothing* is also a choice.) Remember that, in the end, the choice of action is not up to you but to the individual who owns the problem.

Beyond these basic helping techniques lies the territory of the trained therapist. Again, we strongly advise you against trying out the therapy techniques discussed in this chapter for any of the serious psychological disorders discussed in the previous chapter or listed in the *DSM-IV.*

active listener   A person who gives the speaker feedback in such forms as nodding, paraphrasing, maintaining an expression that shows interest, and asking questions for clarification.

Check Your Understanding

1. **RECALL:** On what form of behavioral learning is the behavioral technique of *counterconditioning* based?

2. **APPLICATION:** You could use *contingency management* to change the behavior of a child who comes home late for dinner by

   a. pairing food with punishment.
   b. having the child observe someone else coming home on time and being rewarded.
   c. refusing to let the child have dinner when he comes home late.
   d. having the child relax and imagine being home on time for dinner.

3. **RECALL:** What is the primary goal of psychoanalytic therapy? That is, what makes psychoanalytic therapy different from behavioral therapy or the cognitive therapies?

4. **RECALL:** Carl Rogers invented a technique to help people see their own thinking more clearly. Using this technique,

the therapist paraphrases the client's statements. Rogers called this _____.

5. **RECALL:** Which form of therapy directly confronts a client's self-defeating and irrational thought patterns?

6. **RECALL:** Eysenck caused a furor with his claim that people who receive psychotherapy _____.

7. **UNDERSTANDING THE CORE CONCEPT:** A phobia would be best treated by _____, while a problem of choosing a major would be better suited for _____.

   a. behavioral therapy/insight therapy
   b. cognitive therapy/psychoanalysis
   c. insight therapy/behavioral therapy
   d. humanistic therapy/behavioral therapy

Answers 1. Classical conditioning **2.** c **3.** Psychoanalysis seeks to reveal and resolve problems in the patient's unconscious, particularly repressed traumatic memories, unfulfilled desires, and unconscious conflicts. **4.** reflection of feeling **5.** Rational–emotive behavior therapy **6.** improve no more often than people who receive no therapy at all **7.** a

---

13.3 KEY QUESTION
How Is the Biomedical Approach Used to Treat Psychological Disorders?

The mind exists in a delicate biological balance. It can be upset by irregularities in our genes, hormones, enzymes, and metabolism, as well as by damage from accidents and disease. When something goes wrong with the brain, we can see the consequences in abnormal patterns of behavior or peculiar cognitive and emotional reactions. The biomedical therapies, therefore, attempt to treat these mental disorders by intervening directly in the brain. Our Core Concept specifies the targets of these therapies:

> ### Core Concept 13.3
> **Biomedical therapies seek to treat psychological disorders by changing the brain's chemistry with drugs, its circuitry with surgery, or its patterns of activity with pulses of electricity or powerful magnetic fields.**

Each of the biomedical therapies emerges from the medical model of abnormal mental functioning, which assumes an organic basis for mental illnesses and treats them as diseases—as we saw in Chapter 12. We begin our examination of these biomedical therapies with medicine's arsenal of prescription psychoactive drugs. ✳

✳● Explore the Concept Drugs Commonly Used to Treat Psychiatric Disorders at MyPsychLab

Drug Therapy

In the history of the treatment of mental disorder, nothing has ever rivaled the revolution created by the discovery of drugs that could calm anxious patients, elevate the mood of depressed patients, and suppress hallucinations in psychotic patients. This brave new therapeutic era began in 1953 with the introduction of the first antipsychotic drugs (often called "tranquilizers"). As these drugs found wide application, many unruly, assaultive patients almost miraculously became cooperative, calm, and sociable. In addition, many thought-disordered patients, who had previously been absorbed in their delusions and hallucinations, began to respond to the physical and social environment around them.

The effectiveness of drug therapy had a pronounced effect on the census of the nation's mental hospitals. In 1955, more than half a million Americans were living in mental institutions, each staying an average of several years. Then, with the introduction of tranquilizers, the numbers began a steady decline. In just over ten years, fewer than half that number actually resided in mental hospitals, and those who did were usually kept for only a few months.

Drug therapy has long since steamrolled out of the mental hospital and into our everyday lives. Currently, millions of people take drugs for anxiety, stress, depression, hyperactivity, insomnia, fears and phobias, obsessions and compulsions, addictions, and numerous other problems. Clearly, a drug-induced revolution has occurred. But what are these miraculous drugs?

You have probably heard of Prozac and Valium, but those are just two of scores of psychoactive drugs that can alter your mood, your perceptions, your desires, and perhaps your basic personality. Here, we will consider four major categories of drugs used today: *antipsychotics, antidepressants and mood stabilizers, antianxiety drugs,* and *stimulants.*

Antipsychotic Drugs   As their name says, the **antipsychotics** treat the symptoms of psychosis: delusions, hallucinations, social withdrawal, and agitation (Dawkins et al., 1999). Most work by reducing the activity of the neurotransmitter dopamine in the brain—although the precise reason why this has an antipsychotic effect is not known. For example, *chlorpromazine* (sold under the brand name Thorazine) and *haloperidol* (brand name: Haldol) are known to block dopamine receptors in the synapse between nerve cells. A newer antipsychotic drug, *clozapine* (Clozaril), both decreases dopamine activity and increases the activity of another neurotransmitter, serotonin, which also inhibits the dopamine system (Javitt & Coyle, 2004; Sawa & Snyder, 2002). While these drugs reduce overall brain activity, they do not merely "tranquilize" the patient. Rather, they reduce schizophrenia's "positive" symptoms (hallucinations, delusions, emotional disturbances, and agitated behavior), although they do little for the "negative" symptoms of social distance, jumbled thoughts, and poor attention spans seen in many patients (Wickelgren, 1998a). Newer drugs have come online in recent years, but a recent study suggests that, for reducing psychotic symptoms, these "second generation" antipsychotic drugs may be no more effective than the older ones (Lieberman et al., 2005; Rosenheck et al., 2006).

Unfortunately, long-term administration of any antipsychotic drug can have unwanted side effects. Physical changes in the brain have been noted (Gur & Maany, 1998). But most worrisome is **tardive dyskinesia**, which produces an incurable disturbance of motor control, especially of the facial muscles. Although some of the newer drugs, like clozapine, have reduced motor side effects because of their more selective dopamine blocking, they also can cause serious problems. Are antipsychotic drugs worth the risk? There is no easy answer. The risks must be weighed against the severity of the patient's current suffering.

Antidepressants and Mood Stabilizers   The drug therapy arsenal also includes several compounds that have revolutionized the treatment of depression and bipolar disorder. As with other psychoactive drugs, neither the *antidepressants* nor *mood stabilizers* can provide a "cure." Their use, however, has made a big difference in the lives of many people suffering from mood disorders.

Antidepressant Drugs   All three major classes of **antidepressants** work by "turning up the volume" on messages transmitted over certain brain pathways, especially those using norepinephrine and serotonin (Holmes, 2001). *Tricyclic* compounds such as Tofranil and Elavil reduce the neuron's reabsorption of neurotransmitters after they have been

---

Drug Therapies
- Antipsychotic drugs
- Antidepressants and mood stabilizers
- Antianxiety drugs
- Stimulants

---

antipsychotics   Medicines that diminish psychotic symptoms, usually by effects on the dopamine pathways in the brain.

CONNECTION CHAPTER 12

Positive symptoms of schizophrenia include active hallucinations, delusions, and extreme emotions; *negative symptoms* include withdrawal and "flat" emotions (p. 539).

tardive dyskinesia   An incurable disorder of motor control, especially involving muscles of the face and head, resulting from long-term use of antipsychotic drugs.

antidepressants   Medicines that treat depression, usually by their effects on the serotonin and/or norepinephrine pathways in the brain.

released in the synapse between brain cells—a process called *reuptake.* A second group includes the famous antidepressant Prozac (fluoxetine). These drugs, known as SSRIs (selective serotonin reuptake inhibitors), interfere with the reuptake of serotonin. As a result, the SSRIs keep serotonin available longer. For many people, this prolonged serotonin effect lifts depressed moods (Hirschfeld, 1999; Kramer, 1993). The third group of antidepressant drugs, the *monoamine oxidase (MAO) inhibitors,* limits the activity of the enzyme MAO, a chemical that breaks down norepinephrine in the synapse. When MAO is inhibited, more norepinephrine is available to carry neural messages across the synapse.

Strangely, most patients report that it takes at least a couple of weeks before antidepressants begin to lift the veil of depression. And recent research seems to suggest why. In animal studies, antidepressants stimulate the growth of neurons in the brain's hippocampus. No one is sure why the hippocampus seems to be involved in depression, but the animal studies offer another tantalizing clue: Stress slows the growth of new neurons in this part of the brain—and depression is believed to be a stress response (Santarelli et al., 2003).

The possibility of suicide poses a special concern in the treatment of depression. And now, it seems that the very drugs used for treating depression may provoke or amplify suicidal thoughts, particularly during the first few weeks of therapy and especially in children (Bower, 2004b). One study revived hopes by showing that the increased short-term risk is small—less than 1 percent (Bridge et al., 2007). And another study shows that patients taking antidepressants have a somewhat *lower* risk of suicide over the long haul (Bower, 2007). Obviously, the picture is confusing at the moment, and the Food and Drug Administration is advising prescribers to use caution (Bower, 2006b; Jick et al., 2004).

Controversy Over SSRIs   In his book, *Listening to Prozac,* psychiatrist and Prozac advocate Peter Kramer (1993) encourages the use of the drug to deal not only with depression but also with general feelings of social unease and fear of rejection. Such claims have brought heated replies from therapists who fear that drugs may merely mask the psychological problems that people need to face and resolve. Some worry that the wide use of antidepressants may produce changes in the personality structure of a huge segment of our population—changes that could bring unanticipated social consequences (Breggin & Breggin, 1994; Sleek, 1994). In fact, more prescriptions are being written for antidepressants than there are people who have been diagnosed with clinical depression (Coyne, 2001). The problem seems to be especially acute on college and university campuses, where increasing numbers of students are taking antidepressants (Young, 2003). At present, no one knows what the potential dangers might be of altering the brain chemistry of large numbers of people over long periods.

Just as worrisome for the medical model, another report suggests that antidepressants may owe nearly as much to their hype as to their effects on the brain. According to data mined from the Food and Drug Administration files, studies showing positive results find their way into print far more often than do studies showing no effects for these medicines. While these drugs do better overall than placebos, reports of their effects seem to be exaggerated by selective publication of positive results (Turner et al., 2008).

Mood Stabilizers   A simple chemical, *lithium* (in the form of *lithium carbonate*), has proved highly effective as a mood stabilizer in the treatment of bipolar disorder (Paulus, 2007; Schou, 1997). Not just an antidepressant, lithium affects both ends of the emotional spectrum, dampening swings of mood that would otherwise range from uncontrollable periods of hyperexcitement to the lethargy and despair of depression. Unfortunately, lithium also has a serious drawback: In high concentrations, it is toxic. Physicians have learned that safe therapy requires that small doses be given to build up therapeutic concentrations in the blood over a period of a week or two. Then, as a precaution, patients must have periodic blood analyses to ensure that lithium concentrations have not risen to dangerous levels. In a welcome development, scientists have

CONNECTION CHAPTER 2

Reuptake is a process by which neurotransmitters are taken intact from the synapse and cycled back into the terminal buttons of the axon. Reuptake, therefore, "tones down" the message being sent from one neuron to another (p. 53).

found a promising alternative to lithium for the treatment of bipolar disorder (Azar, 1994; Walden et al., 1998). *Divalproex sodium* (brand name: Depakote), originally developed to treat epilepsy, seems to be even more effective than lithium for most patients but with fewer dangerous side effects (Bowden et al., 2000).

Antianxiety Drugs   To reduce stress and suppress anxiety associated with everyday hassles, untold millions of Americans take **antianxiety drugs,** either *barbiturates* or *benzodiazepines.* Barbiturates act as central nervous system depressants, so they have a relaxing effect. But barbiturates can be dangerous if taken in excess or in combination with alcohol. By contrast, the benzodiazepines, such as Valium and Xanax, work by increasing the activity of the neurotransmitter GABA, thereby decreasing activity in brain regions more specifically involved in feelings of anxiety. The benzodiazepines are sometimes called "minor tranquilizers."

Many psychologists believe that these antianxiety drugs—like the antidepressants— are too often prescribed for problems that people should face rather than mask with chemicals. Nevertheless, antianxiety compounds can be useful in helping people deal with specific situations, such as anxiety prior to surgery. Here are some cautions to bear in mind about these compounds (Hecht, 1986):

- If used over long periods, barbiturates and benzodiazepines can be physically and psychologically addicting (Holmes, 2001; Schatzberg, 1991).
- Because of their powerful effects on the brain, these medicines should not be taken to relieve anxieties that are part of the ordinary stresses of everyday life.
- When used for extreme anxiety, antianxiety drugs should not normally be taken for more than a few days at a time. If used longer than this, their dosage should be gradually reduced by a physician. Abrupt cessation after prolonged use can lead to withdrawal symptoms, such as convulsions, tremors, and abdominal and muscle cramps.
- Because antianxiety drugs depress parts of the central nervous system, they can impair one's ability to drive, operate machinery, or perform other tasks that require alertness (such as studying or taking exams).
- In combination with alcohol (also a central nervous system depressant) or with sleeping pills, antianxiety drugs can lead to unconsciousness and even death.

Finally, we should mention that some antidepressant drugs have also been found useful for reducing the symptoms of certain anxiety disorders such as panic disorders, agoraphobia, and obsessive–compulsive disorder. (A modern psychiatrist might well have prescribed antidepressants for Freud's obsessive patient.) But because these problems may arise from low levels of serotonin, they may respond even better to drugs like Prozac that specifically affect serotonin function.

Stimulants   Ranging from caffeine to nicotine to amphetamines to cocaine, any drug that produces excitement or hyperactivity falls into the category of **stimulants.** We have seen that stimulants can be useful in the treatment of narcolepsy. They also have an accepted niche in treating *attention-deficit/hyperactivity disorder (ADHD).* While it may seem strange to prescribe stimulants (a common one is Ritalin) for hyperactive children, studies comparing stimulant therapy with behavior therapy and with placebos have shown a clear role for stimulants (American Academy of Pediatrics, 2001; Meyers, 2006). Although the exact mechanism is unknown, stimulants may work in hyperactive children by increasing the availability of dopamine, glutamate, and/or serotonin in their brains (Gainetdinov et al., 1999).

As you can imagine, the use of stimulants to treat ADHD has generated controversy (O'Connor, 2001). Some objections, of course, stem from ignorance of the well-established calming effect these drugs have in children with this condition. Other worries have more substance. For some patients, the drug will interfere with normal sleep patterns. Additionally, there is evidence that stimulant therapy can slow a child's growth (National Institute of Mental Health, 2004). Legitimate concerns also center on the potential for abuse

antianxiety drugs   A category of medicines that includes the barbiturates and benzodiazepines, drugs that diminish feelings of anxiety.

CONNECTION CHAPTER 2

GABA is the major inhibitory neurotransmitter in the brain (p. 54).

stimulants   Drugs that normally increase activity level by encouraging communication among neurons in the brain. Stimulants, however, have been found to suppress activity level in persons with attention-deficit/hyperactivity disorder.

that lurks in the temptation to see every child's behavior problem as a symptom of ADHD (Smith, 2002a). And finally, critics suggest that the prescription of stimulants to children might encourage later drug abuse (Daw, 2001). Happily, recent studies have found cognitive–behavioral therapy (CBT) to be comparable to stimulants as a treatment for ADHD (Sinha, 2005). Even better, say many experts, is a *combination therapy* regimen that employs both CBT and stimulants.

Evaluating the Drug Therapies The drug therapies have caused a revolution in the treatment of severe mental disorders, starting in the 1950s, when virtually the only treatments available were talk therapies, hospitalization, restraints, "shock treatment," and lobotomies. Of course, none of the drugs discovered so far can "cure" any mental disorder. Yet, in many cases, they can alter the brain's chemistry to suppress symptoms.

But is all the enthusiasm warranted? According to neuroscientist Elliot Valenstein (1998), a close look behind the scenes of drug therapy raises important questions (Rolnick, 1998). Valenstein believes that much of the faith in drug therapy for mental disorders rests on hype. He credits the wide acceptance of drug therapy to the huge investment drug companies have made in marketing their products. Particularly distressing are concerns raised about the willingness of physicians to prescribe drugs for children—even though the safety and effectiveness of many drugs has not been established in young people (K. Brown, 2003a).

Few question that drugs are the proper first line of treatment for certain conditions, such as bipolar disorder and schizophrenia. In many other cases, however, the apparent advantages of drug therapy are quick results and low cost. Yet some research raises doubts about simplistic time-and-money assumptions. Studies show, for example, that treating depression, anxiety disorders, and eating disorders with cognitive–behavioral therapy—alone or in combination with drugs—may be both more effective and more economical in the long run than reliance on drugs alone (Clay, 2000).

Other Medical Therapies for Psychological Disorders

Describing a modern-day counterpart to Phineas Gage, the headline in the *Los Angeles Times* read, ".22-Caliber Surgery Suicide Bid Cures Psychological Disorder" (February 23, 1988). The article revealed that a 19-year-old man suffering from severe obsessive–compulsive disorder had shot a 0.22 caliber bullet through the front of his brain in a suicide attempt. Remarkably, he survived, his pathological symptoms were gone, and his intellectual capacity was not affected.

We don't recommend this form of therapy, but the case does illustrate the potential effects of physical intervention in the brain. In this vein, we will look briefly at two medical alternatives to drug therapy that were conceived to alter the brain's structure and function, psychosurgery and direct stimulation of the brain.

Psychosurgery With scalpels in place of bullets, surgeons have long aspired to treat mental disorders by severing connections between parts of the brain or by removing small sections of brain. In modern times, **psychosurgery** is usually considered a method of last resort. Nevertheless, psychosurgery has a history dating back at least to medieval times, when surgeons might open the skull to remove "the stone of folly" from an unfortunate madman. (There is, of course, no such "stone"—and there was no anesthetic except alcohol for these procedures.)

In modern times, the best-known form of psychosurgery involved the now-discredited *prefrontal lobotomy*. This operation, developed by Portuguese psychiatrist Egas Moñiz,[2] severed certain nerve fibers connecting the frontal lobes with deep

Phineas Gage survived—with a changed personality—after a steel rod was blasted through his frontal lobe (p. 62).

psychosurgery The general term for surgical intervention in the brain to treat psychological disorders.

In medieval times, those suffering from madness might be treated by trephenation or making a hole in the skull. This painting portrays the operation as the removal of the "stone of folly."

[2]In an ironic footnote to the history of psychosurgery, Moñiz was shot by one of this disgruntled patients, who apparently had not become as pacified as Moniz had expected. This fact, however, did not prevent Moñiz from receiving the Nobel Prize for Medicine in 1949.

brain structures, especially those of the thalamus and hypothalamus—much as what happened accidentally to Phineas Gage. The original candidates for Moñiz's scalpel were agitated schizophrenic patients and patients who were compulsive and anxiety ridden. Surprisingly, this rather crude operation often produced a dramatic reduction in agitation and anxiety. On the down side, the operation permanently destroyed basic aspects of the patients' personalities. Frequently, they emerged from the procedure crippled by a loss of interest in their personal well-being and their surroundings. As experience with lobotomy accumulated, doctors saw that it destroyed patients' ability to plan ahead, made them indifferent to the opinions of others, rendered their behavior childlike, and gave them the intellectual and emotional flatness of a person without a coherent sense of self. Not surprisingly, when the antipsychotic drug therapies came on the scene in the 1950s, with a promise to control psychotic symptoms with no obvious risk of permanent brain damage, the era of lobotomy came to a close (Valenstein, 1980).

Psychosurgery is still occasionally done, but it is now much more limited to precise and proven procedures for very specific brain disorders. In the "split-brain" operation, for example, severing the fibers of the corpus callosum can reduce life-threatening seizures in certain cases of epilepsy, with relatively few side effects. Psychosurgery is also done on portions of the brain involved in pain perception in cases of otherwise intractable pain. Today, however, no *DSM-IV* diagnoses are routinely treated with psychosurgery.

Brain-Stimulation Therapies Electrical stimulation of the brain, also known as **electroconvulsive therapy (ECT),** is still widely used, especially in patients with severe depression who have not responded to drugs or psychotherapy for depression. (You will recall that the therapist said that Derek was not a good candidate for ECT.) The treatment induces a convulsion by applying an electric current (75 to 100 volts) to a patient's temples briefly—from one-tenth to a full second. The convulsion usually runs its course in less than a minute. Patients are prepared for this traumatic intervention by putting them to "sleep" with a short-acting barbiturate, plus a muscle relaxant. This not only renders them unconscious but minimizes any violent physical spasms during the seizure (Abrams, 1992; Malitz & Sackheim, 1984). Within half an hour, the patient awakens but has no memory of the seizure or of the events preparatory to treatment.

Does it work? Crude as it may seem to send an electric current through a person's skull and brain, studies have shown ECT to be a useful tool in treating depression, especially those in whom suicidal tendencies demand an intervention that works far more quickly than medication or psychotherapy (Shorter & Healy, 2007). Typically, the symptoms of depression often abate in a three- or four-day course of treatment, in contrast with the one- to two-week period required for drug therapy.

Although most clinicians regard ECT, properly done, as safe and effective, some critics fear that it also could be abused to silence dissent or punish patients who are uncooperative (Butcher et al., 2008; Holmes, 2001). Other worries about ECT stem from the fact that its effects are not well understood. To date, no definitive theory explains why inducing a mild convulsion should alleviate disordered symptoms, although there are some hints that it may stimulate neuron growth in parts of the brain, particularly the hippocampus.

Most worrisome, perhaps, are the memory deficits sometimes caused by electroconvulsive therapy (Breggin, 1979, 1991). Proponents claim, however, that patients generally recover full memory functions within months of the treatment (Calev et al., 1991). In the face of such concerns, the National Institute of Mental Health investigated the use of ECT and, in 1985, gave it a cautious endorsement for treating a narrow range of disorders, especially severe depression. Then, in 1990, the American Psychiatric Association also proclaimed ECT to be a valid treatment option. To minimize even short-term side effects, however, ECT is usually administered "unilaterally"—only to the right temple—to reduce the possibility of speech impairment.

Another promising new therapeutic tool for stimulating the brain with magnetic fields may offer all the benefits of ECT without the risk of memory loss. Still in the

electroconvulsive therapy (ECT)   A treatment used primarily for depression and involving the application of an electric current to the head, producing a generalized seizure; sometimes called "shock treatment."

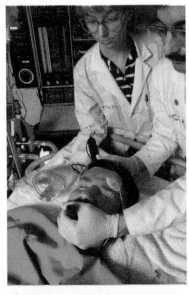

The sedated patient is about to receive electroconvulsive therapy. ECT involves a weak electrical current to a patient's temples, causing a convulsion. Some psychiatrists have found ECT successful in alleviating symptoms of severe depression, but it remains a treatment of last resort for most therapists.

CONNECTION CHAPTER 2

In most people, speech is controlled in the brain's left hemisphere (p. 74).

experimental stages, **transcranial magnetic stimulation (TMS)** involves directing high-powered magnetic stimulation to specific parts of the brain. Studies indicate that TMS may be useful for treating not only depression but also schizophrenia and bipolar disorder (George, 2003). Because TMS therapy does not require the induction of a seizure, researchers hope also that it offers a safer alternative to ECT.

Most recently, neurologist Helen Mayberg has reported using *deep brain stimulation,* which requires the surgical implantation of a microelectrode through a small hole in the skull and directly into the brain, where it delivers a continual trickle of electric current. Dr. Mayberg likens the treatment to a "pacemaker" for an area of cortex that seems to range out of control in depression (Gutman, 2006; Price, 2009). Although the treatment has been used on only a few patients, Mayberg reports highly encouraging outcomes (Mayberg et al., 2005). She views it not as an alternative to other therapies but as a promising last resort for severely depressed patients who have not responded to other approaches.

transcranial magnetic stimulation (TMS) A treatment that involves magnetic stimulation of specific regions of the brain. Unlike ECT, TMS does not produce a seizure.

Hospitalization and the Alternatives

We have seen that mental hospitals were originally conceived as places of refuge—"asylums"—where disturbed people could escape the pressures of normal living. In fact, they often worked very well (Maher & Maher, 1985). But by the 20th century, these hospitals had become overcrowded and, at best, little more than warehouses for the disturbed, with nowhere else to go. Rarely were people with money committed to these institutions; instead, they were given private care, including individual psychotherapy (Doyle, 2002a).

Read about The Therapeutic Community at **MyPsychLab**

The drugs that so profoundly altered treatment in mental hospitals did not appear until the 1950s, so prior to that time, institutionalized patients often found themselves controlled by straitjackets, locked rooms, and, sometimes, lobotomies. Meanwhile, in the large public mental hospitals, what passed for psychotherapy was a feeble form of "group therapy" performed on a whole ward—perhaps 50 patients—at a time. Too many patients, too few therapists, and too little time devoted to therapy meant that little, if any, real benefit accrued.

Deinstitutionalization and Community Mental Health The advent of antipsychotic drugs ushered in huge changes. Thousands of patients who responded to the new drugs were sent home for outpatient treatment. The goal of **deinstitutionalization** was to return as many patients as possible to their communities, where they would (it was hoped) thrive in a familiar and supportive environment. The concept also gained popularity with politicians, who saw large sums of money being poured into mental hospitals (filled, incidentally, with nonvoting patients). Thus, by the 1970s, a consensus formed among politicians and mental health professionals that the major locus of treatment should shift from mental hospitals back to the community. There, both psychological and drug therapies would be dispensed from walk-in clinics, and recovering patients could live with their families, in foster homes, or in group homes. This vision became known as the **community mental health movement.**

deinstitutionalization The policy of removing patients, whenever possible, from mental hospitals.

community mental health movement An effort to deinstitutionalize mental patients and to provide therapy from outpatient clinics. Proponents of community mental health envisioned that recovering patients could live with their families, in foster homes, or in group homes.

Unfortunately, the reality did not match the vision (Doyle, 2002a; Torrey, 1996, 1997). Community mental health clinics—the centerpieces of the community mental health movement—rarely received the full funding they needed. Chronic patients were released from mental hospitals, but they often returned to communities that could offer them few therapeutic resources and to families ill equipped to cope with them (Smith et al., 1993). Then, as patients returned to the community and needed care, they entered psychiatric wards at local general hospitals—rather than mental hospitals. As a result, hospital care has continued to consume a large share of mental health expenditures in the United States (Kiesler, 1993; U.S. Department of Health and Human Services, 2002).

Despite the dark picture we have painted, community treatment has had some successes. After a review of ten studies in which mental patients were randomly assigned to hospital treatment or to various community treatment programs, Kiesler (1982)

Deinstitutionalization put mental patients back in the community—but often without adequate resources for continued treatment.

The "telehealth" approach to therapy brings mental health services to clients in rural areas, where help might not otherwise be available.

reported that patients more often improved in the community-based programs. Further, those given community-based treatment were less likely to be hospitalized at a later date. When these programs have adequate resources, they can be highly effective (McGuire, 2000).

Unfortunately, some 60 million Americans in rural areas have no easy access to mental health services. But, thanks to the Internet and the telephone, some of them now can get help through remote "telehealth" sessions (Stambor, 2006; Winerman, 2006c). Using the telehealth approach, psychologists and other professionals can quickly establish a link with their rural clients to answer questions, make referrals, and even provide therapy.

[PSYCHOLOGY MATTERS]

What Sort of Therapy Would You Recommend?

Now that we have looked at both the psychological and biomedical therapies, consider the following situation. A friend tells you about some personal problems he or she is having and requests your help in finding a therapist. Because you are studying psychology, your friend reasons, you might know what kind of treatment would be best. How do you respond?

First, you can lend a friendly ear, using the techniques of active listening, acceptance, and exploration of alternatives, which we discussed earlier in the chapter. In fact, this may be all that your troubled friend needs. But if your friend wants to see a therapist or if the situation looks in any way like one that requires professional assistance, you can use your knowledge of mental disorders and therapies to help your friend decide what sort of therapist might be most appropriate. To take some of the burden from your shoulders, both of you should understand that any competent therapist will always refer the client elsewhere if the required therapy lies outside the therapist's specialty.

A Therapy Checklist

Here, then, are some questions you will want to consider before you recommend a particular type of therapist:

- **Is medical treatment needed?** While you should not try to make a diagnosis, you should encourage your friend to see a medical specialist, such as a psychiatrist or nurse practitioner, if you suspect that the problem involves a major mental disorder such as psychosis, mania, or bipolar disorder. Medical evaluation is also indicated if you suspect narcolepsy, sleep apnea, epilepsy, Alzheimer's disease, or other problems recognized to have a biological basis. If your suspicion is confirmed, the treatment may include a combination of drug therapy and psychotherapy.

- **Is there a specific behavior problem?** For example, does your friend want to eliminate a fear of spiders or a fear of flying? Is the problem a rebellious child? A sexual problem? Is she or he depressed—but not psychotic? If so, behavior therapy or cognitive–behavioral therapy with a counseling or clinical psychologist is probably the best bet. (Most psychiatrists and other medical practitioners are not usually trained in these procedures.) You can call a prospective therapist's office and ask for information on specific areas of training and specialization.

- **Would group therapy be helpful?** Many people find valuable help and support in a group setting, where they can learn not only from the therapist but also from other group members. Groups can be especially effective in dealing with shyness, lack of assertiveness, and addictions, and with complex problems of interpersonal relationships. (As a bonus, group therapy is often less expensive than individual therapy.) Professionals with training in several disciplines, including psychology, psychiatry, and social work, run therapy groups. Again, your best bet is a therapist who has had special training in this method and about whom you have heard good things from former clients.

- **Is the problem one of stress, confusion, or choice?** Most troubled people don't fall neatly into one of the categories that we have discussed in the previous points. More typically, they need help sorting through the chaos of their lives, finding a pattern, and developing a plan to cope. This is the territory of the insight therapies.

Some Cautions

We now know enough about human biology, behavior, and mental processes to avoid certain treatments. Here are some particularly important examples:

- **Drug therapies to avoid.** The minor tranquilizers (antianxiety drugs) are too frequently prescribed for patients leading chronically stressful lives. As we have said, because of their addicting and sedating effects, these drugs should only be taken for short periods—if at all. Similarly, some physicians ignore the dangers of sleep-inducing medications for their patients who suffer from insomnia. While these drugs have legitimate uses, many such prescriptions carry the possibility of drug dependence and of interfering with the person's ability to alter the conditions that may have caused the original problem.

- **Advice and interpretations to avoid.** Although psychodynamic therapy can be helpful, patients should also be cautioned that some such therapists may give ill-advised counsel in problems of anger management. Traditionally, Freudians have believed that individuals who are prone to angry or violent outbursts harbor deep-seated aggression that needs to be vented. But, as we have seen, research shows that trying to empty one's aggressions through aggressive behavior, such as shouting or punching a pillow, may actually increase the likelihood of later aggressive behavior.

With these cautions in mind, then, your friend can contact several therapists to see which has the combination of skills and manner that offer the best fit for her problem and her personality.

Check Your Understanding

✓—[Study and **Review** at **MyPsychLab**

1. **APPLICATION:** Imagine that you are a psychiatrist. Which type of drug would you prescribe for a patient diagnosed with attention-deficit/hyperactivity disorder (ADHD)?

2. **RECALL:** Which class of drugs blocks dopamine receptors in the brain? Which type magnifies the effects of serotonin?

3. **RECALL:** Name three types of medical therapies for mental disorder, including one that has now been largely abandoned as ineffective and dangerous.

4. **RECALL:** The community mental health movement followed a deliberate plan of _____ for mental patients.

5. **UNDERSTANDING THE CORE CONCEPT:** _____, _____, and _____ all are medical techniques for treating mental disorders by directly altering the function of the brain.

Answers 1. a stimulant **2.** Antipsychotic drugs block dopamine receptors in the brain. Antidepressants, particularly the selective serotonin reuptake inhibitors (SSRIs), amplify the effects of serotonin. **3.** Electroconvulsive therapy, drug therapy, and prefrontal lobotomy; the latter is no longer done as a treatment for mental disorders. **4.** deinstitutionalization **5.** Any three of the following would be correct: drug therapies, psychosurgery, ECT, and transcranial magnetic stimulation.

13.4 KEY QUESTION

How Do the Psychological Therapies and Biomedical Therapies Compare?

Now that we have looked at both the psychological and medical therapies, can we say which approach is best? In this section, we will see that the answer to that question depends on the disorder. But before we look at the treatment choices for several major conditions, we should acknowledge some other influences that cloud the issue of medical versus psychological treatments.

combination therapy   A therapeutic approach that involves both psychological and medical techniques—most often a drug therapy with a behavioral or cognitive–behavioral therapy.

We have seen that psychologists and psychiatrists have long been at odds over the best forms of treatment for mental disorders. In part, the dispute is over territory and money: Who gets to treat people with mental problems—and bill their insurance? The big pharmaceutical companies, with billions of dollars at stake, play a formidable role in this dispute, too. You can glimpse the sort of hardball game Big Pharma plays by noting the advertising for prescription drugs that is directed at the general public. Because of these conflicting interests and pressures, research on medical and psychological therapies has been done largely in parallel, with each side promoting its own approach and ignoring the other's. Unfortunately, this has meant that comparatively little research has focused on the effectiveness of **combination therapies**, involving both medication and psychotherapy used in concert.

That said, let's take a look at how we might weigh the options of medical and psychological treatment in some specific disorders with which you are now familiar. Here's the Core Concept:

> ### Core Concept 13.4
>
> **While a combination of psychological and medical therapies is often better than either one alone for treating mental disorders, most people who have unspecified "problems in living" are best served by psychological treatment alone.**

More specifically, what we will find is that a very large number of people with psychological problems do not have a *DSM-IV* disorder but need psychological counseling or therapy to help them work through difficult periods in their lives. On the other

Drug companies now do a hard sell on psychotropic drugs through advertisements like this one aimed at the general public. Here, the not-so-subtle message is that unhappy people can be treated with medication.

Kathy researched all the medications. She found out that ZOLOFT has helped millions with depression and anxiety. ZOLOFT is safe and effective. It has treated more people with more types of depression and anxiety than any brand of its kind. So she asked her doctor about ZOLOFT. ZOLOFT. #1 for millions of reasons.

hand, many of the well-known *DSM-IV* disorders, including the mood disorders and schizophrenia, are best treated by a combination of medical and psychological therapies. Let's begin with the latter.

Depression and Anxiety Disorders: Psychological versus Medical Treatment

Fluoxetine (Prozac) is the planet's most widely prescribed drug. Together with other SSRI medications, it represents a $10 billion, worldwide industry for the treatment of depression (Bower, 2006b). In addition, antidepressants are often used to treat panic disorder and other conditions marked by anxiety. These drugs may be worth every penny if they are effective in alleviating the suffering of these very common disorders. But just how effective are they? And how effective are they in comparison with psychological therapies?

CBT versus Drugs Studies show that antidepressant drugs and cognitive–behavioral therapy (CBT)—the psychological treatment for which we have the most evidence of efficacy—are equally effective ways of treating depression and panic disorder, at least in the short run. Significantly, however, CBT holds an edge over drug therapy in the long–term—particularly in depression, where the rate of patient relapse for CTB is about *half* that of antidepressant medications (Baker et al., 2009; DeRubeis et al., 2005; Hollon et al., 2002).

But what happens if depressed patients get antidepressants *and* CBT? The research shows that they may do even better than with either treatment alone (DeAngelis, 2008a; Keller et al., 2000; Thase et al., 1997). Oddly, combination therapy seems *not* to offer an advantage for those with anxiety disorders.

Advances in understanding the brain now suggest why such a combination therapy approach seems to be effective for depression. Neuroscientist Helen Mayberg has shown that CBT and the antidepressants work their wonders by affecting different parts of the brain. Antidepressants apparently target the limbic system—which contains the brain's main emotion pathways. In contrast, CBT affects a part the frontal cortex associated with reasoning. The common factor in both approaches is an "alarm switch" that gets turned off, either by the effect of drugs on the "fast" emotion pathway in the limbic system or by the effect of CBT on the brain's "slow" emotional circuitry in the cortex (Goldapple et al., 2004). Thus, as research from the clinic and the lab come together, many clinicians have come to favor a *combination therapy* approach for depression, using both drugs and CBT. In fact, a combined approach would be a reasonable option for Derek's depression (described at the beginning of the chapter). A recent study also supports a combined drug-and-medicine approach for bipolar patients (Miklowitz et al., 2007).

ECT And what about electroconvulsive therapy (ECT)? Although clinicians commonly assert that ECT is the most effective treatment for psychotic depression (Hollon et al., 2002), only one study, done in Sweden, has compared ECT head-to-head with antidepressants. The principal finding: Suicide attempts were less common among those patients receiving ECT than among those taking antidepressants (Brådvik & Berglund, 2006). As for transcranial magnetic stimulation, it is too early to tell. As of this writing, no studies have reported a one-on-one comparison of TMS with other therapies for depression.

Schizophrenia: Psychological versus Medical Treatment

Ever since the discovery of antipsychotics more than 50 years ago, these drugs have represented the front line of treatment for schizophrenia. Supplemental treatment, in the form of family therapy, social skills training (often in community residential treatment centers), and occupational therapy (through sheltered workshops, such as Goodwill Industries), has brought schizophrenic patients back into contact with their communities. But until recently, conventional psychological treatments were little used. In the past few years, however, advocates of cognitive–behavioral therapy have been trying their hands at treating schizophrenia, with encouraging results, even with patients who have not responded to medication (McGurk et al., 2007; Rector & Beck, 2001).

"The Worried Well" and Other Problems: Not Everyone Needs Drugs

While a combination of psychological therapy and drugs may be best for some disorders, we have seen that drugs are *not* useful for treating specific phobias. Likewise, medication has little value as a therapy for most learning disabilities, psychogenic sexual dysfunctions, most personality disorders, and most developmental disorders (with the exception of ADHD). In addition, we should remember that many people who have psychological problems do not have a diagnosed mental disorder, such as depression, a phobia, or schizophrenia. Rather, they may have financial difficulties, marital problems, stress on the job, out-of-control children—or perhaps they just experience loneliness and feelings of inadequacy: These are the people that clinicians sometimes call "the worried well."

That's not to say that those whose problems don't qualify as an "official" disorder are not suffering. They struggle with what we might term generic "problems in living." The difficulty is that people with such issues too often persuade a physician to prescribe antidepressants or antianxiety medications. What they really need is a referral to a mental health professional who could help them sort through their problems and choices.

Early Intervention and Prevention Programs: A Modest Proposal   A recent federal report suggests that the United States could save as much as $247 billion a year by instituting tried-and-true programs that would nip mental health problems of children and adolescents in the bud (BCYF, 2009; O'Connell et al., 2010). "The effects of prevention are now quite well documented," says Irwin Sandler, director of the Prevention Research Center at Arizona State University (Clay, 2009, p. 42).

The report recommends identifying young people who are at risk for emotional and behavior disorders and getting early help for them. Such preventive programs include stress management sessions for youth at risk for depression, cognitive–behavioral therapy for children exhibiting excessive anxiety, and parenting skills classes and counseling services for families dealing with adversities, such as divorce or poverty. At present, such programs exist on only a small scale. What we need now is research on moving such interventions from the lab into the field, notes Sandler.

But prevention is not just for kids. For adults, it may mean practicing the stress-reduction and wellness techniques that we will discuss in the next chapter. Here, we will take special note of the new research showing the value of exercise. Everyone knows, of course, that exercise is a powerful tool in conquering obesity. Yet, clearly, the connection between exercise and mental health hasn't registered in the public mind. Nor is it widely understood among mental health professionals. Still, for more than 20 years, evidence has been accumulating that regular exercise works just as well as medication in combating depression, anxiety, and many of the problems-in-living we discussed earlier (Blumenthal et al., 2007; Novotney, 2008; Ströhle, 2009). A few studies even suggest that exercise may help sharpen the mind and fend off dementia (Azar, 2010). Clinical training programs are just starting to take notice of this valuable old tool with a newly discovered use.

[PSYCHOLOGY MATTERS]

Using Psychology to Learn Psychology

Consider the ways in which psychotherapy is like your educational experiences in college:

- Most therapists, like most professors, are professionals with special training in what they do.
- Most clients are like students in that they are seeking professional help to change their lives in some way.
- Much of what happens in therapy and in the classroom involves learning: new ideas, new behaviors, new insights, and new connections.

Learning as Therapy

It may help you learn psychology (and other subjects as well) to think of your college education in therapeutic terms. As we have seen, therapy seems to work best when therapist and client have a good working relationship and when the client believes in the value of the experience—and the same is almost certainly true for the student–professor relationship. You can take the initiative in establishing a personal-but-professional relationship with your psychology professor by doing the following two things: (a) asking questions or otherwise participating in class (at appropriate times and without dominating, of course) and (b) seeking your instructor's help on points you don't understand or on course-related topics you would like to pursue in more detail (doing so during regular office hours). The result will be learning more about psychology because you will be taking a more active part in the learning process. Incidentally, an active approach to the course will also help you stand out from the crowd in the professor's mind, which could be helpful if you later need a faculty recommendation for a scholarship or admission to an advanced program.

Now consider a parallel between group therapy and education. In group therapy, patients learn from each other as well as from the therapist. Much the same can occur in your psychology course if you consider other students as learning resources. As we noted earlier in this book, the most successful students often spend part of their study time sharing information in groups.

Change Behavior, Not Just Thinking

One other tip for learning psychology we borrow from cognitive–behavioral therapy: the importance of changing behavior as well as thinking. It is easy to "intellectualize" a fact or an idea passively when you read about it or hear about it in class. But you are likely to find that the idea makes little impact on you ("I know I *read* about it, but I can't *remember* it!") if you don't use it. The remedy is to do something with your new knowledge: Tell someone about it, come up with illustrations from your own experience, or try acting in a different way. For example, after reading about active listening in this chapter, try it the next time you talk to a friend. Educators sometimes speak of this as "active learning."

And, we suggest, it's one of those psychological therapies that works best without drugs!

CRITICAL THINKING APPLIED

Evidence-Based Practice

The field of therapy for mental disorders is awash in controversy. Psychologists and psychiatrists dispute the value of drugs versus psychological therapies. Arguments rage over the advantages and disadvantages of electroconvulsive therapy for treating depression. And, as we saw in the previous chapter, debates still echo the issues Rosenhan raised more than three decades ago about the effectiveness of mental hospitals and the reliability of psychiatric diagnoses. But there is no dispute more acrimonious than the one over *evidence-based practice,* a dispute that is particularly bitter among clinical psychologists (Bower, 2005a).

What Is the Issue?

A decade ago, the American Psychological Association established a special task force charged with evaluating the effectiveness of various psychological therapies (Chambless et al., 1996). The thrust of their findings is that literally dozens of specific disorders can be treated successfully by therapies that have been validated in well-designed experiments (Barlow,

1996). Here are a few examples of therapies pronounced effective by the APA task force:

- Behavior therapy for specific phobias, enuresis (bed wetting), autism, and alcoholism
- Cognitive–behavioral therapy for chronic pain, anorexia, bulimia, agoraphobia, and depression
- Insight therapy for couples' relationship problems

More recently, a report by the Association for Psychological Science focused specifically on evidence-based treatments for depression (Hollon et al., 2002). That document asserts that several varieties of psychotherapy can be effective. These include cognitive–behavioral and family therapy. (The APS report also acknowledged that there is a legitimate role for both drug and electroconvulsive therapies in the treatment of depression.) As we have seen, some studies now suggest that, for depression, a combination of cognitive–behavioral therapy and drug therapy can have a greater effect than either treatment alone (Keller et al., 2000).

So, what's all the fuss about? At issue is whether counselors and therapists should be *limited* to the use of specific therapy methods known as **empirically supported treatments (EST)**, that is, to treatments that have been validated by research evidence showing that they actually work (Kazdin, 2008; Westen et al., 2005). So how could anyone possibly object to that, you might ask?

Surprisingly, psychologists line up on both sides of this issue (Johnson, 2006). Those in opposition say that the devil is in the details: They say that they are not antiscience, but they believe "empirically supported treatments" is a fuzzy concept (Westen & Bradley, 2005). They also worry about an overly strict interpretation that might inhibit a practitioner's freedom to meet the needs of an individual client. Let's take a critical look at these details.

What Critical Thinking Questions Should We Ask?

No one doubts that the people on both sides of the evidence-based practice issue are decent and honorable and that among them are genuine experts on therapy. So we won't question their credibility. But it might be a good idea to ask: What biases does each side have that might make them weigh the options differently?

The Evidence-Based Practice Movement   Those pushing the idea of evidence-based practice point to a long history of misguided and even harmful therapies—from beatings to lobotomies—to which people with mental problems have been subjected. Even in modern times, some practitioners continue to advocate techniques that can potentially harm their clients (Lilienfeld, 2007). These include "scared straight" interventions for juvenile offenders, facilitated communication for autism, recovered-memory therapies, induction of "alter" personalities in cases diagnosed as dissociative identity disorder, DARE (antidrug education) programs in the schools, boot-camp programs for conduct disorder in prisoner populations, sexual reorientation for homosexuality, and catharsis ("get-it-out-of-your-system") treatment for anger disorders. An even longer list (based on a survey of clinical psychologists), ranging from the merely ineffective to the crackpot, would include: angel therapy, past lives therapy, treatments for PTSD caused by alien abduction, aromatherapy, therapeutic touch, neuro-linguistic programming, primal scream therapy, and handwriting analysis (Norcross et al., 2006).

In 2009, the Association for Psychological science issued a major report on the current status of clinical psychology (Baker et al., 2009; West, 2009). In that report, the APS blasted clinicians for their failure to use treatments grounded in science, noting that an "alarming number" of clinicians are unaware of empirically validated treatments. The report states:

> Research has shown that numerous psychological interventions are efficacious, effective, and cost-effective. However, these interventions are used infrequently with patients who would benefit from them . . . (p. 67)

empirically supported treatment (EST)   Treatment regimen that has been demonstrated to be effective through research. Also called empirically supported therapies.

An independent report by clinical researchers R. Kathryn McHugh and David Barlow (2010) concurs, emphasizing the difficulty of moving new treatment methods out of the laboratory and into clinical practice.

Those Favoring Caution   While acknowledging that we have made great strides in developing highly effective treatments for a number of disorders, those urging caution point out that we are light-years from having the tools to treat all mental disorders—even with the use of drugs. Consequently, they fear that insurance companies and HMOs will be unwilling to pay for treatments not on the official list or for any deviations from "approved" treatments, no matter what the needs of the individual patient (Cynkar, 2007b). They also worry that the managed-care companies will force therapists into a one-size-fits-all approach that would ignore both the clinician's judgment and the client's complex needs (Shedler, 2006). Because therapy is such a time-consuming process, they also fear that nonmedical therapists will be squeezed out of the picture by drug prescribers who may take only a few minutes with each patient.

Those with reservations about evidence-based practice have several other, more subtle, concerns (Westen & Bradley, 2005). For example, they point out that therapy is much more than the application of specific *techniques:* Researchers find that a common element in successful therapy is a caring, hopeful relationship and a new way of looking at oneself and the world (Wampold et al., 2007). This conclusion has been supported by studies that find the effectiveness of therapy to depend less on the *type of therapy* used and more on the *quality of the relationship* (also called the *therapeutic alliance*) between the therapist and client (Wampold & Brown, 2005). Therapy also involves a host of *individual client factors,* such as motivation, intelligence, and the nature of the problem itself. We can represent these three aspects of therapy graphically, as in Figure 13.6. For some problems (such as a relationship issue or a vocational choice problem—the "problems in living" that we discussed earlier), no specific ESTs exist. Moreover, the specific type of therapy used in such cases may be less important than a supportive therapeutic relationship (DeAngelis, 2005; Martin et al., 2000).

Finally, the critics of evidence-based practice also point out that everyday clinical practice is usually messier than the controlled conditions of research on therapy. For one thing, most clinical patients/clients present themselves with multiple problems, such as an anxiety disorder *and* a personality disorder. Yet, most ESTs have been validated on "pure" samples of people having only one specific *DSM-IV* diagnosis (DeAngelis, 2010; Kazdin, 2008). Rarely do researchers target the largest population in most clinical practices: individuals with multiple "problems in living," such as marital difficulties *and* financial woes *and* child-rearing issues *and* low self-esteem. Moreover, most research aimed at validating therapeutic techniques is severely restricted to just

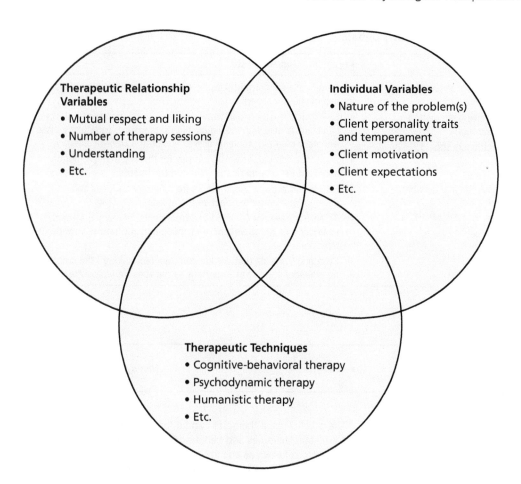

FIGURE 13.6
Three Aspects of Therapy

Therapy is more than a set of techniques. It also involves a number of individual variables (including the nature of the problem) and the relationship between the client and therapist—the *therapeutic alliance*. All must come together for therapy to be successful.

Therapeutic Relationship Variables
• Mutual respect and liking
• Number of therapy sessions
• Understanding
• Etc.

Individual Variables
• Nature of the problem(s)
• Client personality traits and temperament
• Client motivation
• Client expectations
• Etc.

Therapeutic Techniques
• Cognitive-behavioral therapy
• Psychodynamic therapy
• Humanistic therapy
• Etc.

a few sessions—usually no more than a dozen—after which most patients still have some residual problems.

To end this discussion on a more encouraging note: A recent study of 200 practitioners found that they all tended to modify their approach to treatment to fit the needs of their clients as the situation unfolds during counseling or psychotherapy (Holloway, 2003b). That is, despite our emphasis in this chapter on conflicting methods for the treatment of psychological disorders, most practitioners are quite willing to adapt their methods to the individual client rather than holding rigidly to a particular theoretical orientation. And that is good news, indeed, coming from a field that has traditionally had strongly divided allegiances. It appears that the emphasis on science-based practice is finally breaking down the old therapeutic boundaries.

What Conclusions Can We Draw?

Both sides make good points (see Table 13.3). On the one hand, practitioners should favor empirically validated treatments when they are clearly appropriate and effective. And they certainly should eschew treatments that are ineffective or harmful. But who is going to make that determination: the individual practitioners, the insurance companies, legislators, or professional organizations? Your authors think that the professional psychology associations, such as the APA, must

take stands against putting the therapist into a straitjacket by limiting him or her to a cast-in-stone list of treatments and disorders for which those treatments may be applied.

In fact, the American Psychological Association has a proposed policy under consideration (APA Presidential Task Force, 2006). The policy would define *evidence-based practice in psychology* as "the integration of the best available research with clinical expertise in the context of patient characteristics, culture, and preferences." Who wouldn't agree with that? Many people, it turns out. In particular, the evidence-based practice advocates are concerned that "clinical expertise" could trump "research," with the result that clinicians could ignore the science and do as they please (Stuart & Lilienfeld, 2007). It is a knotty issue that doesn't lend itself to easy answers.

Is there a solution in sight? A partial solution may lie in a proposal made by David Barlow (2004) who suggested that psychologists make a distinction between *psychological treatments* and what he calls "generic psychotherapy." The empirically validated therapies for specific disorders listed in the *DSM-IV* would fall under the heading of *psychological treatments,* while reserving the term *psychotherapy* for work with the nonspecific "problems-in-living" and the huge "Not Otherwise Specified" *DSM-IV* category that, together, make up a large proportion of the caseloads of many counselors and clinicians. Barlow's proposal would, at least, shrink the disputed territory.

TABLE 13.3 Summary of the Evidence-Based Practice (EBP) Debate

Arguments Favoring EBP	Arguments Opposing EBP
• Some treatments are clearly harmful, and practitioners should not be allowed to use them. • Specific empirically supported therapies (ESTs) have been demonstrated to be effective in dealing with certain disorders. • Psychology is a science, and psychological practitioners should follow what the research shows to be best. • Giving clinical judgment equal weight with science would lead to anarchy, in which clinicians could ignore the evidence and do what they please.	• Empirically supported therapies (ESTs) is a poorly defined, even meaningless, concept. • EBP is a "one-size-fits-all" approach that would limit the flexibility of clinicians to deal with individual clients' problems, particularly those who have multiple problems or who do not fit a *DSM-IV* category. • Insurance companies would not pay for therapy that was not on an approved list of empirically validated treatments. • EBP would prevent practitioners from trying new ideas and developing even more effective therapies. • Scientists have not yet validated treatments for many disorders, so under an EBP approach, many people might have to go without treatment. • Evidence suggests that certain common factors (e.g., the therapeutic alliance) are just as important as the specific type of treatment.

CHAPTER SUMMARY

((•—[Listen to an audio file of your chapter at **MyPsychLab**

PROBLEM: What is the best treatment for Derek's depression: psychological therapy, drug therapy, or both? More broadly, the problem is this: How do we decide among the available therapies for any of the mental disorders?

• The most basic choice is between one of the psychological therapies and a biological therapy—or a combination.

• Psychologists or other nonmedical practitioners opt for a psychological therapy when they believe the problem is learned or involves faulty cognitions, behaviors, or relationships.

• The psychological therapies can be further divided into the insight therapies and behavior therapies—or combined approaches known as cognitive-behavioral therapy and social learning. The specific therapy type depends primarily on the therapist's training and orientation.

• Biological therapies are delivered by psychiatrists and nurse practitioners when they believe the problem can best be treated by altering brain function through drugs or other biological interventions.

13.1 What Is Therapy?

> Core Concept 13.1 Therapy for psychological disorders takes a variety of forms, but all involve a *therapeutic relationship* focused on improving a person's mental, behavioral, or social functioning.

People seek **therapy** for a variety of problems, including *DSM-IV* disorders and problems of everyday living. Treatment comes in many forms, both psychological and biomedical, but most involve diagnosing the problem, finding the source of the problem, making a prognosis, and carrying out treatment. In earlier times, treatments for those with mental problems were usually harsh and dehumanizing, often based on the assumption of demonic possession. Only recently have people with emotional

problems been treated as individuals with "illnesses," which has led to more humane treatment.

Currently in the United States, there are two main approaches to therapy: the **psychological therapy** and the **biomedical therapy** approaches. Other cultures often have different ways of understanding and treating mental disorders, often making use of the family and community. In the United States, there is a trend toward increasing use of **paraprofessionals** as mental health care providers, and the literature generally supports their effectiveness.

biomedical therapy (p. 560)
paraprofessional (p. 560)
psychological therapy (p. 560)
therapeutic alliance (p. 557)
therapy (p. 556)

13.2 How Do Psychologists Treat Psychological Disorders?

> **Core Concept 13.2** Psychologists employ two main forms of treatment, the insight therapies (focused on developing an understanding of the problem) and the behavior therapies (focused on changing behavior through conditioning).

Psychoanalysis, the first of the *insight therapies,* grew out of Sigmund Freud's theory of personality. Using such techniques as *free association* and dream interpretation, its goal is to bring repressed material out of the unconscious into consciousness, where it can be interpreted and neutralized, particularly in the **analysis of transference**. Neo-Freudian psychodynamic therapies typically emphasize the patient's current social situation, interpersonal relationships, and self-concept.

Among other insight therapies, **humanistic therapy** focuses on individuals becoming more fully self-actualized. In one form, **client-centered therapy**, practitioners strive to be *nondirective* in helping their clients establish a positive self-image.

Another form of insight therapy, **cognitive therapy**, concentrates on changing negative or irrational thought patterns about oneself and one's social relationships. The client must learn more constructive thought patterns and learn to apply the new technique to other situations. This has been particularly effective for depression.

Group therapy can take many approaches. **Self-help support groups**, such as AA, serve millions, even though they are not usually run by professional therapists. *Family therapy* and *couples therapy* usually concentrate on situational difficulties and interpersonal dynamics as a total system in need of improvement rather than on internal motives.

The **behavior therapies** apply the principles of learning—especially operant and classical conditioning—to problem behaviors. Among the classical conditioning techniques, **systematic desensitization** and **exposure therapy** are commonly employed to treat fears. **Aversion therapy** may also be used for eliminating unwanted responses. Operant techniques include **contingency management**, which especially involves positive reinforcement

and extinction strategies. And, on a larger scale, behavior therapy may be used to treat or manage groups in the form of a **token economy**. **Participant modeling**, based on research in observational learning, may make use of both classical and operant principles, involving the use of models and social skills training to help individuals practice and gain confidence about their abilities.

In recent years, a synthesis of cognitive and behavioral therapies has emerged, combining the techniques of insight therapy with methods based on behavioral learning theory. **Rational–emotive behavior therapy** helps clients recognize that their irrational beliefs about themselves interfere with life and helps them learn how to change those thought patterns. **Positive psychotherapy (PPT)** is a similar approach coming out of the positive psychology movement. Brain scans suggest that **cognitive–behavioral therapy** produces physical changes in brain functioning.

The effectiveness of therapy was challenged in the 1950s by Eysenck. Since that time, however, research has shown that psychotherapy can be effective for a variety of psychological problems. Often, it is more effective than drug therapy. As the research on mental disorders becomes more refined, we are learning to match specific psychotherapies to specific disorders.

Most people do not get psychological help from professionals. Rather, they get help from teachers, friends, clergy, and others in their community who seem sympathetic. Friends can often help through **active listening**, acceptance, and exploration of alternatives, but serious problems require professional assistance.

active listener (p. 576)
analysis of transference (p. 564)
aversion therapy (p. 570)
behavior modification (p. 568)
behavior therapy (p. 568)
client-centered therapy (p. 565)
cognitive therapy (p. 566)
cognitive–behavioral therapy (p. 571)
contingency management (p. 570)
exposure therapy (p. 569)
group therapy (p. 567)
humanistic therapy (p. 565)

insight therapy (p. 562)
neo-Freudian psychodynamic therapy (p. 564)
participant modeling (p. 571)
positive psychotherapy (PPT) (p. 573)
psychoanalysis (p. 562)
rational–emotive behavior therapy (REBT) (p. 572)
reflection of feeling (p. 565)
self-help support groups (p. 567)
systematic desensitization (p. 569)
token economy (p. 571)

13.3 How Is the Biomedical Approach Used to Treat Psychological Disorders?

> **Core Concept 13.3** Biomedical therapies seek to treat psychological disorders by changing the brain's chemistry with drugs, its circuitry with surgery, or its patterns of activity with pulses of electricity or powerful magnetic fields.

Biomedical therapies concentrate on changing the physiological aspects of mental illness. Drug therapy includes **antipsychotic**, **antidepressant**, *mood stabilizing*, **antianxiety**, and **stimulant drugs**. Most affect the function of neurotransmitters. Such drugs have caused a revolution in the medical treatment of mental disorders such as schizophrenia, depression, bipolar

disorder, anxiety disorders, and ADHD. Critics, however, warn of their abuse, particularly in treating the ordinary stress of daily living.

Psychosurgery is rarely done anymore because of its radical, irreversible side effects. **Electroconvulsive therapy**, however, is still widely used—primarily with depressed patients—although it, too, remains controversial. A new and potentially less-harmful alternative involves **transcranial magnetic stimulation** of specific brain areas. Meanwhile, hospitalization has been a mainstay of medical treatment, although the trend is away from mental hospitals to community-based treatment. The policy of **deinstitutionalization** was based on the best intentions, but many mental patients have been turned back into their communities with few resources and little treatment. When the resources are available, however, community treatment is often successful.

If someone asks your advice on finding a therapist, you can refer him or her to any competent mental health professional. While you should avoid trying to make a diagnosis or attempting therapy for mental disorders, you may use your knowledge of psychology to steer the person toward a medical specialist, a behavior therapist, group therapy, or some other psychological treatment that you believe might be appropriate. There are, however, some specific therapies and therapeutic techniques to avoid.

antianxiety drugs (p. 580)
antidepressants (p. 578)
antipsychotics (p. 578)
community mental health movement (p. 583)
deinstitutionalization (p. 583)
electroconvulsive therapy (ECT) (p. 582)

psychosurgery (p. 581)
stimulants (p. 580)
tardive dyskinesia (p. 578)
transcranial magnetic stimulation (TMS) (p. 583)

13.4　How Do the Psychological Therapies and Biomedical Therapies Compare?

Core Concept 13.4　**While a combination of psychological and medical therapies is often better than either one alone for treating some (but not all) mental disorders, most people who have unspecified "problems in living" are best served by psychological treatment alone.**

Both medical and biological therapies can point to their successes, but until recently, few studies have compared medical and psychological therapies directly. New studies show that for depression, a **combination therapy**, consisting of CBT and medication, is often best. Comparative data for ECT and the new transcranial magnetic stimulation are sparse. As for the anxiety disorders, some studies have shown a combination of drugs and CBT to be effective. A clear exception involves the specific phobias, for which behavioral therapy is superior to drug therapy—which may actually aggravate the problem. For schizophrenia, medications are the front line of treatment, although they do not cure the disorder. Until recently, conventional psychotherapies were not often used with schizophrenia, but new research suggests that combination therapy may be effective.

Medication is not useful for treating many psychological problems, such as learning disabilities, many sexual dysfunctions, most personality disorders, and most developmental disorders. In addition, most people who have psychological problems do not have a *DSM-IV* disorder but rather suffer from "problems in living."

Education and psychotherapy have many points in common. In particular, both involve learning and the ultimate goal of changes in behavior. The authors suggest that both education and psychotherapy are more likely to be successful when the client takes an active role.

combination therapy (p. 586)
empirically supported treatment (EST) (p. 590)

CRITICAL THINKING APPLIED

Evidence-Based Practice

Psychological therapists are divided on the question of evidence based practice (EBP) and empirically supported treatments (ESTs). Opponents say that ESTs are not clearly defined, suppress innovative new treatments, offer no help in treating clients with multiple disorders, and deemphasize the importance of the therapeutic alliance. Proponents, however, counter that some treatments are clearly harmful and should be prohibited. They acknowledge that ESTs have not been found for all disorders. However, therapists as good scientists should be willing to practice those treatments for which science has found support.

DISCOVERING PSYCHOLOGY **VIEWING GUIDE**

Watch the following video by logging into MyPsychLab (www.mypsychlab.com). After you have watched the video, answer the questions that follow.

PROGRAM 22: **PSYCHOTHERAPY**

Program Review

1. What are the two main approaches to therapies for mental disorders?
   a. the Freudian and the behavioral
   b. the client-centered and the patient-centered
   c. the biomedical and the psychological
   d. the chemical and the psychosomatic

2. The prefrontal lobotomy is a form of psychosurgery. Although no longer widely used, it was at one time used in cases in which a patient

   a. was an agitated schizophrenic.

   b. had committed a violent crime.

   c. showed little emotional response.

   d. had a disease of the thalamus.

3. Leti had electroconvulsive shock therapy a number of years ago. She is now suffering a side effect of that therapy. What is she most likely to be suffering from?

   a. tardive dyskinesia

   b. the loss of her ability to plan ahead

   c. depression

   d. memory loss

4. Vinnie suffers from "manic-depressive" (bipolar) disorder, but his mood swings are kept under control because he takes the drug

   a. chlorpromazine.

   b. lithium.

   c. Valium.

   d. tetracycline.

5. The Silverman family is receiving genetic counseling because a particular kind of mental retardation runs in their family. What is the purpose of such counseling?

   a. to explain the probability of passing on defective genes

   b. to help eliminate the attitudes of biological biasing

   c. to repair specific chromosomes

   d. to prescribe drugs that will keep problems from developing

6. In psychodynamic theory, what is the source of mental disorders?

   a. biochemical imbalances in the brain

   b. unresolved conflicts in childhood experiences

   c. the learning and reinforcement of nonproductive behaviors

   d. unreasonable attitudes, false beliefs, and unrealistic expectations

7. Imagine you are observing a therapy session in which a patient is lying on a couch, talking. The therapist is listening and asking occasional questions. What is most likely to be the therapist's goal?

   a. to determine which drug the patient should be given

   b. to change the symptoms that cause distress

   c. to explain how to change false ideas

   d. to help the patient develop insight

8. Rinaldo is a patient in psychotherapy. The therapist asks him to free associate. What would Rinaldo do?

   a. describe a dream

   b. release his feelings

   c. talk about anything that comes to mind

   d. understand the origin of his present guilt feelings

9. According to Hans Strupp, in what major way have psychodynamic therapies changed?

   a. Less emphasis is now placed on the ego.

   b. Patients no longer need to develop a relationship with the therapist.

   c. Shorter courses of treatment can be used.

   d. The concept of aggression has become more important.

10. In the program, a therapist helped a girl learn to control her epileptic seizures. What use did the therapist make of the pen?

    a. to record data

    b. to signal the onset of an attack

    c. to reduce the girl's fear

    d. to reinforce the correct reaction

11. When Albert Ellis discusses with the young woman her fear of hurting others, what point is he making?

    a. It is the belief system that creates the "hurt."

    b. Every normal person strives to achieve fulfillment.

    c. Developing a fear-reduction strategy will reduce the problem.

    d. It is the use of self-fulfilling prophecies that cause others to be hurt.

12. What point does Enrico Jones make about investigating the effectiveness of different therapies in treating depression?

    a. All therapies are equally effective.

    b. It is impossible to assess how effective any one therapy is.

    c. The job is complicated by the different types of depression.

    d. The most important variable is individual versus group therapy.

13. What is the most powerful antidepressant available for patients who cannot tolerate drugs?

    a. genetic counseling

    b. electroconvulsive therapy

    c. psychoanalysis

    d. family therapy

14. All of the following appear to be true about the relation between depression and genetics, *except* that

    a. depression has been linked to a defect in chromosome #11.

    b. depression appears to cause genetic mutation.

    c. most people who show the genetic marker for depression do not exhibit depressive symptoms.

    d. genetic counseling allows families to plan and make choices based on their risk of mental illness.

15. For which class of mental illness would Chlorpromazine be prescribed?

    a. mood disorder

    b. psychosis

    c. personality disorder

    d. anxiety disorder

16. Which approach to psychotherapy emphasizes developing the ego?

    a. behavioral

    b. desensitization

    c. humanistic

    d. psychodynamic

17. In behavior modification therapies, the goal is to

    a. understand unconscious motivations.

    b. learn to love oneself unconditionally.

    c. change the symptoms of mental illness through reinforcement.

    d. modify the interpretations that one gives to life's events.

18. Which style of therapy has as its primary goal to make the client feel as fulfilled as possible?

    a. humanistic

    b. cognitive-behavioral

    c. Freudian

    d. social learning

19. Which psychologist introduced rational–emotive therapy?

    a. Carl Rogers

    b. Hans Strupp

    c. Albert Ellis

    d. Rollo May

20. Which type of client would be ideal for modern psychoanalytic therapy?

    a. someone who is smart, wealthy, and highly verbal

    b. someone who is reserved and violent

    c. someone who has a good sense of humor but takes herself seriously

    d. someone who grew up under stressful and economically deprived conditions

14 From Stress to Health and Well-Being

[Key Questions/ Chapter Outline]	[Core Concepts]	[Psychology Matters]
14.1 What Causes Distress? Traumatic Stressors Chronic Stressors	Traumatic events, chronic lifestyle conditions, major life changes, and even minor hassles can all cause a stress response.	**Student Stress** College students face some unique stressors in addition to typical developmental stressors.
14.2 How Does Stress Affect Us Physically? Physiological Responses to Stress Stress and the Immune System	The physical stress response begins with arousal, which stimulates a series of physiological responses that in the short term are adaptive but that can turn harmful if prolonged.	**Cognitive Appraisal of Ambiguous Threats** Threats to our well being are not always clear and obvious; thus how we identify and appraise them becomes vital for coping with them effectively.
14.3 Who Is Most Vulnerable to Stress? Type A Personality and Hostility Locus of Control Hardiness Optimism Resilience	Personality characteristics affect our individual responses to stressful situations and, consequently, the degree to which we are distressed when exposed to stressors.	**Using Psychology to Learn Psychology** Anyone—even people who don't think of themselves as "good writers"—can use writing as a valuable tool in the "coping strategies" toolbox.
14.4 How Can We Transform Negative Stress Into Positive Life Strategies? Psychological Coping Strategies Positive Lifestyle Choices: A "Two-for-One" Benefit to Your Health Putting It All Together: Developing Happiness and Subjective Well-Being	Effective coping strategies reduce the negative impact of stress on our health, while positive lifestyle choices can enhance our mental and physical health as well as our overall well-being.	**Behavioral Medicine and Health Psychology** These exciting new fields focus on how psychological and social factors influence health, and also on how these same factors can be applied to successful prevention of illness.

CHAPTER PROBLEM Were the reactions and experiences of the 9/11 firefighters and others at the World Trade Center attacks typical of people in other stressful situations? And what factors explain individual differences in our physical and psychological responses to stress?

CRITICAL THINKING APPLIED Is *Change* Really Hazardous to Your Health?

ON SEPTEMBER 11, 2001, AT 8:46 A.M., RETIRED FIREFIGHTER DENNIS Smith sat outside a New York clinic, waiting for his annual physical, when a nurse rushed in and announced that a plane had just crashed into the North tower of the World Trade Center in lower Manhattan (Smith, 2003b). The engine and ladder companies of New York's fire department (FDNY) were already responding to the alarms—trucks racing to the scene and firefighters running into the same buildings that hordes of people desperately sought to escape. Smith asked himself what conditions his coworkers were facing: the heat of the fire, the best access to the buildings, the stairwells' integrity. How many were already trapped inside and facing death?

One firefighter later described the chaos: "It looked like a movie scene, where the monster was coming . . . [W]e got showered with debris. . . . Things were hitting—bing, bang, boom—over your head" (Smith, 2003b, pp. 70–71). He had climbed high into the North Tower when the South Tower was hit, and "suddenly, there was this loud, loud noise overhead." He recalled huddling inside a stairwell, inventorying his resources: "I was thinking of my situation—what should I do, what can I do? What do I have that is positive? What tools do I have? . . . The main thing I had was my helmet. I remember thinking how important it was to have had that helmet" (p. 75).

But the critical need for the helmet was forgotten in one ironic moment by Smith's fellow firefighter, Father Mychael Judge. The FDNY chaplain was among the first to arrive and, after hearing that firefighters were trapped inside, rushed into the smoke. While performing last rites, he removed his helmet out of respectful habit—just as a shower of debris fell, killing him instantly (Downey, 2004).

In the weeks and months after the terrorist attacks, firefighters continued to search for bodies. They buried, memorialized, and mourned their brothers and sisters. Few of the 343 missing were ever recovered. Those who had made it—while others died just a few feet away—endured survivor's guilt, ambivalent and uncertain why they deserved to live, asking themselves, "Why me?" Some developed symptoms of posttraumatic stress disorder (PTSD), reliving the terrifying moments of the disaster again and again. And the aftereffects of that day weren't limited to those individuals personally involved: Millions of people around the world remained glued to their televisions for days, repeatedly watching the towers as they fell and hearing firsthand accounts from survivors.

The surviving firefighters continued to grieve. Many of them rejected false reverence or gloom in remembering their friends, preferring instead to laugh and joke about their fallen comrades' quirks and screw-ups. Manhattan's Engine 40/Ladder 35 lost 12 firefighters, more than any other firehouse and, like everyone else, wondered what really happened to the missing victims. Then, five months after 9/11, the members of 40/35 learned of a news tape that appeared to show their 12 lost partners entering the tower minutes before it collapsed on them. The video had been shot at a distance, but the moving figures gradually became recognizable. Staring intently at the screen, the surviving firefighters gazed once more on friends who had not returned. They played the video over and over again (Halberstam, 2002).

Firefighters are different from most other public servants because they spend much of their time in a shared communal house, their firehouse. Because fires and other emergencies are relatively rare, they spend lots of down time just hanging out with each other, playing cards and other games, as well as reading and watching TV. In most houses, a family sense evolves, with older guys becoming like dads and uncles or big brothers to the new guys. With this in mind, you can better appreciate the stressful impact on any of them from the sudden deaths of so many of their everyday families. In addition, each felt obligated to attend as many memorial services as possible, not only for their fallen house members but for all those they knew in recruit training or from other houses where they had served or had extended-family relatives working. For some, attending heart-wrenching church services was an enduring tribulation lasting more than a year—an unending source of secondary distress.

PROBLEM: **Were the reactions and experiences of the 9/11 firefighters and others at the World Trade Center attacks typical of people in other stressful situations? And what factors explain individual differences in our physical and psychological responses to stress?**

Of course, running into a falling building is not a typical human response; rather, it is a learned response of trained rescue workers. But what about the survivor's guilt and subsequent delayed stress reactions from repeated viewing of the disaster on websites and televisions around the world—are these "normal" stress responses? What connections can we make between these reactions and our own reactions to stress? In considering these questions, several related issues emerge:

- Stress isn't limited to major tragedies, traumas, and disasters. All of us encounter potentially stressful situations in our everyday lives—at our jobs, in our relationships, at school, in traffic, or as a result of illness. Have you ever noticed, though, that some people seem to get "stressed out" at even minor annoyances, while others appear calm, cool, and collected even in a crisis situation? In addition, some people bounce back quickly after major stress, while others have trouble regaining their equilibrium. How can we explain these individual differences in our reactions to stress?

- We must also consider how our stress responses have evolved over the years and millennia and how they functioned to aid our survival. Many cultures today live much faster-paced lives than those of previous generations. How are the stresses we face today different from those faced by our ancient ancestors? What impact might the differences in our environments have on the effectiveness of our stress response?

How do differences in our environments and cultures create stress and affect our responses to stress?

- Multiple perspectives are necessary to understand our human response to stress. What goes on in the body and the brain that influence our reactions to stress? And how are these physiological responses mediated by our thought processes, our prior learning, our personality, our stage in life, and our social context (see Figure 14.1)?

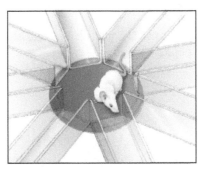

Behavioral Perspective:
Can certain stress responses — effective or ineffective — be learned?

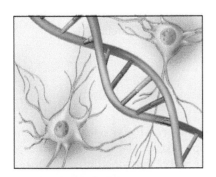

Biological Perspective:
Are some individuals just "hard-wired" in a way that makes them better able to cope with stress?

Developmental Perspective:
Do older people deal with stress more or less effectively than younger people?

STRESS

Cognitive Perspective:
Do some individuals perceive stress differently than others?

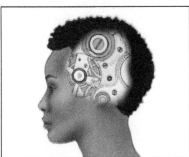

Whole-Person Perspective:
Do certain personality traits predict healthier coping?

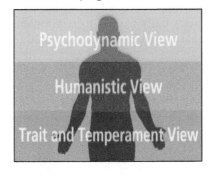

Psychodynamic View

Humanistic View

Trait and Temperament View

Sociocultural Perspective:
Are certain stress responses more prevalent in some cultures than in others?

FIGURE 14.1

The Multiple Perspectives Applied to Stress

This figure suggests just a few examples of the many ways that multiple perspectives are necessary to understand the complex nature of stress.

- Finally, to what extent do we have control over our own reactions to stress and to the potential toll stress is taking on our physical and mental health? The good news is that we are not "stuck" with our current stress level; there are specific changes we can make to help us meet the challenges of stress more effectively. Thus, we conclude this chapter on a more positive note by not only describing effective coping strategies but also introducing you to a new health psychology perspective promoting well-being, resilience, and happiness.

As we explore these questions, keep in mind the stresses you have faced and consider how this information can help you understand the sources of stress in your life—and improve the way you perceive and manage that stress. Although it would seem that college students' lives are less stressful than those of firefighters and other first responders, the recent increase in college students' visits to mental health facilities and higher rates of suicides forces us to examine, in a later section, where all this academic stress is coming from.

⌐14.1 KEY QUESTION
└──── What Causes Distress?

What images come to mind when you hear the word *stress?* Most people think of the pressures in their lives: difficult jobs, unhappy relationships, financial woes, health problems, and final exams. You may have some visceral associations with stress too: a churning stomach, perspiration, headache, or tension in your neck or upper back. We use the word *stress* loosely in everyday conversation, referring to a situation that confronts us (Lazarus et al., 1985). For example, if your employer or professor has been giving you a difficult time, you may say that you are "under stress," as though you were being squashed by a heavy object. You may also say you are "feeling stress" as a result. Thus, in everyday conversation, we use the word **stress** to refer both to an external threat and to our physical and mental response we feel when exposed to it.

Psychologists, however, make a distinction between the outer pressure or event that causes stress and its inner impact on us as individuals. **Stressors** are external events that cause internal stress responses, both psychological and emotional ones, termed **distress**, and biological and physiological reactions (Krantz et al., 1985). We will use the term *distress* to refer to our personal reactions, both physiological and psychological, to experienced stressors.

Thus, a stressor is the sight of a police officer climbing out of her car after you ran through a stop sign while texting. Your response to that sight of the cop about to ticket you—your racing heart, shaky hands, and sudden perspiration—are signs of the biological changes induced by this stressor. Your psychological stress, or distress, is the complex mix of shame, sense of stupidity, and worry about losing your license for this third moving violation if you cannot plead your way out of this unfortunate situation.

What are the common stressors faced by humans today? We begin this chapter with a review of stressors found to have the most impact on us. These include everything from petty daily hassles to relationship problems with family, friends, and romantic partners to terrorist attacks, as noted in our Core Concept for this section:

> ### Core Concept 14.1
> **Traumatic events, chronic lifestyle conditions, major life changes, and even minor hassles can all cause a stress response.**

Before embarking on our discussion of stressors and how we respond to them, we should first recall the concept of *cognitive interpretation* from our study of emotion in Chapter 9. There, we learned that a key component in our emotional response to a situation is the interpretation we make of that situation. Stress is a type of emotional response—consequently, interpretation or **cognitive appraisal** plays an important role in

---

stress   The physical and mental response to a stressor.

stressor   A stressful event or situation.

distress   The psychological reaction created by external stressors, which can be an emotional, cognitive, or behavioral response. It is part of the stress response that also includes biological and physiological reactions to stressors.

cognitive appraisal   Our interpretation of a stressor and our resources for dealing with it.

the degree of stress we feel when faced with a stressor. We will see later in this chapter that cognitive appraisal accounts for some individual differences in how people respond to stressors as well as in how effectively we succeed in dealing with them. In the previous paragraph, for example, a person who had never before received a ticket may interpret that situation as less stressful (and thus feel less distress) than one who had several recent tickets and was at risk for losing his driver's license or paying higher insurance rates.

Traumatic Stressors

Catastrophic events, such as natural disasters and terrorist attacks, qualify as **traumatic stressors**—situations that threaten your own or others' physical safety, arousing feelings of fear, horror, or helplessness. On a more personal level, a sudden major life change, such as the loss of a loved one, constitutes a trauma as well—despite the fact that death and separation are likely to affect everyone at some time. We will examine traumatic stress by first considering natural and human-made catastrophes, then personal loss, and finally posttraumatic stress.

Catastrophe In May 2008, shortly before the Olympics in Beijing, a massive earthquake in China killed more than 67,000 people. Subsequent quakes in Haiti and Chile also had devastating consequences on the population for many months after—as did the 2011 earthquake, tsunami, and resulting breach of nuclear reactors in Japan. Natural disasters such as these, as well as man-made tragedies like terrorist attacks and warfare, comprise the category of traumatic stressors known as **catastrophic events.** These sudden, violent calamities are inevitably accompanied by extreme stress and loss of loved ones or possessions. Moreover, the psychological and biological consequences can last far longer than the original event, as in the weeks after 9/11 when firefighters and emergency workers sometimes found themselves reliving the events in nightmares and in daytime flashbacks.

Studies of catastrophe survivors provide some insight into the ways individuals respond to these ordeals (Asarnow et al., 1999; Sprang, 1999). It's worth noting here that research of this type is difficult: Obviously, ethical considerations prevent psychologists from creating even minor traumatic events to study their effects on volunteer subjects. Instead, field researchers must wait for a catastrophe to occur and then get to the scene immediately to hear the story and observe survivors in the immediate aftermath.

A Natural Laboratory for Disaster One opportunity to understand disaster response presented itself in San Francisco in 1989, just as the baseball World Series was about to begin at Candlestick Park. Spectators were settling into their seats when the entire stadium began to shake violently. The lights went out, and the scoreboard turned black as a major earthquake struck. Elsewhere in the city, fires erupted, a bridge collapsed, highways were crushed—and people were dying.

One week after the quake, a team of research psychologists began a series of follow-up surveys with about 800 regional residents. Survey responses revealed a clear pattern: The lives of respondents who experienced the earthquake continued to revolve heavily around the disaster for about a month. After this period, they ceased obsessing, thinking, and talking about the quake, but simultaneously reported an increase in other stress-related symptoms including sleep disruption, relationship problems, and nightmares (Wood et al., 1992). Although most symptoms diminished gradually, one year later, as many as 20 percent of residents remained distressed (Pennebaker & Harber, 1991).

In contrast to natural disasters, human-made catastrophes such as crime and terrorism have an added dimension of threat because they are produced intentionally by other people. **Terrorism** has been defined as a type of disaster caused by "human malevolence" with the goal of disrupting society by creating fear and danger (Hall et al., 2002). Like survivors of natural disasters, terrorism survivors report elevated

CONNECTION CHAPTER 13

Cognitive appraisal is central to cognitive-behavioral therapy (p. 571).

traumatic stressor   A situation that threatens one's physical safety, arousing feelings of fear, horror, or helplessness.

catastrophic event   A sudden, violent calamity, either natural or manmade, that causes trauma.

The major recent earthquake in Japan, recorded as 9.0 on the Richter scale, triggered an enormous tsunami tidal wave of more than 33 feet that totally destroyed many towns in northern Japan, killing thousands of people. Consider the stresses it also created.

terrorism   A type of disaster caused by human malevolence with the goal of disrupting society by creating fear and danger.

symptoms of distress that substantially subside after several months (Galea et al., 2003). What appears to be different about surviving a terror attack, however, is the long-term change in perception of threat. Studies of individuals affected—both directly and indirectly—by the 9/11 attacks in America or by the 2005 bombings at the underground train station in London found that 50 to 75 percent of the public continued to worry about the safety of themselves and their families for a year or more following the attack (Rubin et al., 2005; Torabi & Seo, 2004; Weissman et al., 2005).

Psychological Response to Catastrophe   Psychological responses to natural and human-caused disasters have been theorized to occur in stages, as victims experience shock, feel intense emotion, and struggle to reorganize their lives (Beigel & Berren, 1985; Horowitz, 1997). Cohen and Ahearn (1980) identified five stages survivors typically pass through:

1. Immediately after the event, victims experience *psychic numbness,* including shock and confusion, and for moments to days cannot fully comprehend what has happened. Severe, sudden, and violent disasters violate our basic expectations about how the world is supposed to function. For some of us, the unimaginable becomes a stark reality.

2. During a phase of *automatic action,* victims have little awareness of their own experiences and later show poor recall for many details about what occurred.

3. In the *communal effort stage,* people pool resources and collaborate, proud of their accomplishments but also weary and aware they are using up precious energy reserves.

4. Next, survivors may experience a *letdown* as, depleted of energy, they comprehend and feel the tragedy's impact. Public interest and media attention fade, and survivors feel abandoned, although the state of emergency may continue.

5. An extended period of *recovery* follows as survivors adapt to changes created by the disaster. The fabric of the community changes as the natural and business environments are altered.

CONNECTION CHAPTER 7

Stage theories emphasize distinctive changes that occur as one develops or progresses through a life stage or event (p. 282).

narrative   A personal account of a stressful event that describes our interpretation of what happened and why.

Keep in mind, however, that *stage theories* don't necessarily apply to the entire population but attempt to summarize commonalities among a range of individual experiences. In this instance, stage theories of stress response are useful for organizing individual accounts into aggregate summaries and also because they help us anticipate what future survivors may go through and what kinds of assistance they may need.

Research also indicates the importance of stories or **narratives** in working through catastrophic experiences. To learn from and make sense of catastrophic loss, we formulate accounts that describe what happened and why. We are especially likely to develop narratives when an event is surprising or unpleasant (Holtzworth-Munroe & Jacobson, 1985) or violates our basic expectations (Zimbardo, 1999). And, as we'll see later in this chapter, narratives help us find meaning in loss, which in turn facilitates healing.

Catastrophic events merit extended news coverage, and in this Internet age, the sounds and images of others' pain are broadcast and viewed repeatedly. Viewers are not immune to such programs and may experience a sort of "secondhand" traumatization.

Trauma in the Media   Media news coverage expands the experience of catastrophe so all viewers can experience it. Students, like you, reported repeated viewing of the WTC towers collapsing on 9/11. Recall that, in our opening story, surviving members of the Manhattan firefighters' crew repeatedly viewed a videotape showing their now-dead comrades rushing into the World Trade Center just before the building collapsed. At last they knew for certain the fate of their friends. But was repeated viewing really therapeutic for them? Conventional wisdom suggests that identifying the figures on the tape as their friends might give them some closure, and their friends' heroism could help them find meaning in tragedy, but once that goal is achieved, how can repeated viewing be anything but stress enhancing?

Research clearly shows that revisiting and reliving catastrophe causes its own stress. **Vicarious traumatization** is severe stress caused when one is exposed to others' accounts of trauma and the observer becomes captivated by it (McCann & Pearlman, 1990). Whether it be plane crashes, riots in a far-off country, or natural disasters, what matters is the amount of exposure: Schuster and colleagues (2001) found that the more hours viewers spent watching television coverage of the 9/11 attacks, the more likely they were to report stress symptoms later. What's more, a whopping 90 percent of respondents all over the country—even those with no personal or job connection to New York—reported experiencing at least one symptom of stress in the aftermath of the attack. By reliving the disaster, heavy viewers of media coverage, including those who lived safely distant from the actual disaster site, nonetheless became engaged with the victims' suffering and experienced measurable stress as a result.

We will note later that one of the most widely mandated techniques for first responder stress reduction in police, fire, and military units is known as critical incident stress debriefing (CISD). Small groups of those affected by the disaster are essentially forced to share their horror stories, listening to others and telling their own tales of woe. Can you reflect on why such a process might backfire and *increase* rather than ameliorate distress? (Advance warning: It does not work, according to much solid research.)

Cultural Variations in Response to Catastrophes   The March 2011 disasters that befell Japan were the worst since its devastation in World War II from atomic bombing. It became a worst-case scenario of incredible proportions. Initially, the massive 9.0 earthquake that triggered a 33-foot tidal wave wiped out entire villages, killing thousands and leaving many homeless and without food in the winter cold. Then, radiation exposure from the meltdown of nuclear power plants posed long-term threats of widespread cancer among Japanese residents. Yet, despite these catastrophic experiences, the general response by most Japanese was a communal sense of calm, civility, and moral courage. Veteran reporters on the scene expressed amazement at the way in which Japanese people showed decorum and fought chaos with orderliness. There was no evidence of looting, and no increase in crime. Indeed, in 10-hour-long traffic jams caused by wrecked highways, not a single instance of honking was reported.

The collectivistic cultural focus on politeness, group consensus, and concern for others led to sharing, without complaint, of meager food supplies with strangers. Experts on Japanese culture trace such behaviors to the spiritual strength found in critical, comforting rituals of their religion. Most Japanese are Buddhists or follow ancient Shinto beliefs. Fundamental to these belief systems is alleviating mental and physical suffering through practicing compassion and acceptance of death as the end part of the life process. Buddhism as now practiced is less about spirits of the natural world and more about rituals of society, family, and state, according to scholar of Japanese religion Duncan Williams (Grossman, 2011).

Personal Loss   Like many other species, humans are social creatures: We depend on each other for survival. The loss of a loved one is very distressing, even if it is anticipated (such as after a long illness). A sudden, unexpected loss is traumatic: In a rated listing of life changes at the end of this section, you will see "death of spouse" is the most stressful of all life changes (Holmes & Rahe, 1967; Scully et al., 2000). **Grief** is the emotional response to interpersonal loss, a painful complex of feelings including sadness, anger, helplessness, guilt, and despair (Raphael, 1984). Whether grieving the death of a loved one, the breakup of a romantic relationship, or the betrayal of a trusted friend, you experience the jolt of separation and loneliness and have difficult questions to ponder. Some of our core assumptions about life may be challenged, and we may be forced to adapt to a different reality (Parkes, 2001). As a result, our identities and future plans may be permanently altered (Davis et al., 1998; Janoff-Bulman, 1992).

Psychologists view grieving as a normal, healthy process of adapting to a major life change, with no "right" method or "normal" time period (Gilbert, 1996; Neimeyer,

vicarious traumatization   Severe stress caused by exposure to traumatic images or stories that cause the observer to become engaged with the stressful material.

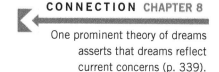

CONNECTION CHAPTER 8

One prominent theory of dreams asserts that dreams reflect current concerns (p. 339).

grief   The emotional response to loss, which includes sadness, anger, helplessness, guilt, and despair.

integration   A final phase of grieving, in which the
loss becomes incorporated into the self.

1995, 1999). Some experts recommend achieving closure, a Gestalt term for perceiving an incomplete stimulus as complete. But grief psychologists oppose the goal of closing off the pain and memories of loss and instead recommend **integration**. To understand this, think for a moment about someone you have lost: Perhaps you have "gotten over it" and don't think about it much any more—yet it is still there in your memory, with images, emotions, and thoughts still vivid and accessible and still part of who you are (Harvey, 1996; Harvey et al., 1990). Thus, the final phase of grieving is more accurately thought of as an ongoing process of integration in which each life loss becomes a part of the self-narrative and part of your memory storehouse of meaningful events, both negative and positive (Murray, 2002).

The mourning process also requires you to interact socially at a time when you feel especially vulnerable and socially withdrawn. Ironically, friends offering help or sympathy sometimes add to the stress. Hollander (2004) writes of losing first her husband and then, a few months later, her mother. "Am I all right? Everyone seems to be asking me that. . . .Often I find I don't know how to respond to the question" (pp. 201–202). Her friends feel uncomfortable when she weeps openly, and they encourage her to cheer up, to be herself again. Hollander concludes that her pain cannot and must not be rushed: "Closure is not my goal. . . . I am all right exactly because I weep" (p. 204).

Humiliation as Loss   Which would be more stressful: losing your romantic partner when he or she dies, or having that person leave you for another lover? Both tragedies involve losing your partner, but in addition, being rejected involves not only grief but also humiliation and abandonment. One study interviewed thousands of adults, categorizing their experiences of loss and other life-event stressors and diagnosing their symptoms of major depression and anxiety. Results indicated that rejected respondents were more likely to develop depression than those whose partners had died (Kendler et al., 2003). In discussing their findings, researchers observed that the death of one's partner is a "pure loss event," which does not represent a potential failure or deficiency on the part of the grieving person. In contrast, being left by your spouse or romantic partner "raises issues . . . [such] as humiliation, which is usually seen as the loss of status, the loss of a sense of self-esteem and the loss of a sense of your own worth" (National Public Radio, 2003a).

targeted rejection   The exclusive, active, and
intentional social rejection of an individual by others.

In a different, more recent study, researchers examined how quickly people became depressed following different types of stress. Life events were categorized by whether they involved **targeted rejection**, defined as the "exclusive, active, and intentional social rejection of an individual by others." Results revealed that people who experienced a recent targeted rejection event became depressed three times faster than those who experienced other types of stress (Slavich et al., 2009). Interestingly, these effects were similar regardless of whether the targeted rejection occurred at work (for example, the person was fired) or in the context of a personal relationship (such as a breakup). In sum, then, stressors that involve humiliation or social rejection are more likely to cause depression than are other stressors and also appear to bring about depression more quickly (Slavich et al., 2009, 2010a).

Why do we feel so bad about humiliation and rejection? Animal studies reveal that in primate colonies, such as free-roaming baboon groups, individuals who lose status withdraw, lose their appetite, become more submissive, and show immediate huge increases in measurable biological stress (Sapolsky, 1998). In evolutionary terms, loss of social status threatens survival and has serious consequences. By taking action to prevent such losses, humans and other primates increase their chances of survival. Thus, perhaps rejection makes us feel bad because we *need* to feel bad; in other words, perhaps the depression or loss of self-esteem that accompanies rejection keeps us from entering into unwise or insecure partnerships, thus protecting us from further rejection or humiliation.

Disenfranchised Grief   Grief is also especially stressful when others minimize your loss and fail to sympathize. Experiences such as death, divorce, and trauma are recognized with formal condolences, such as funerals, hospital visits, sentimental greeting cards, and professional attention from undertakers, attorneys, and physicians (Lensing, 2001). But other painful losses with no official "status" may be ignored or dismissed by the community. For example, adults who grieve after a miscarriage, young adults who have lost friends, and children saddened by the death of a favorite TV or movie star may find themselves alone in their sorrow, getting little sympathy or understanding from others. Their **disenfranchised grief,** the emotion surrounding a loss others do not understand, cannot be mourned through public rituals like memorials or funerals. Fearing others' negative reactions, even behind your back, disenfranchised grievers may try to hide their sorrow—but continue to suffer (Doka, 1989, 1995; Rickgarn, 1996).

disenfranchised grief The emotion surrounding a loss that others do not support, share, or understand.

Confiding in others can help people cope with loss and trauma (Harvey, 1996; Pennebaker, 1990). During these times, keep in mind the role of professional counselors or psychotherapists, who might be counted on to take your grief seriously. Also, it is therapeutically worthwhile to "confide" in other ways, such as by keeping a written private journal of your feelings and what triggers them over time (see the *Psychology Matters* section later in this chapter).

Posttraumatic Stress Individuals who have undergone severe ordeals—rape, combat, beatings, or torture, for example—may experience a belated pattern of stress symptoms that can appear months or even years after their trauma. Those delayed reactions, however, can last a lifetime. In **posttraumatic stress disorder (PTSD),** the individual re-experiences mental and physical responses that accompanied the trauma. Nearly one adult in 12 in the United States will experience PTSD at some time in his or her life, with symptoms lasting more than ten years in more than one-third of cases. Traumas described by PTSD victims most frequently include having witnessed another person being killed or badly injured, having lived through a natural disaster, and having survived a life-threatening accident. Men cite more experiences of physical attack, military combat, disaster or fire, or being held captive or hostage, whereas women cite more experiences of rape, sexual molestation, physical abuse, and neglect during childhood (Bower, 1995a). Women are more likely than men to develop symptoms of PTSD after experiencing a traumatic event (Tolin & Foa, 2006), and Hispanic Americans are more at risk than non-Hispanic Caucasian or Black Americans (Pole et al., 2005).

posttraumatic stress disorder (PTSD) A delayed stress reaction in which an individual involuntarily re-experiences emotional, cognitive, and behavioral aspects of past trauma.

What Are the Symptoms of PTSD? Victims of posttraumatic stress disorder typically become distracted and disorganized and experience memory difficulties (Arnsten, 1998). They may feel emotionally numb and alienated from others and experience less pleasure from positive events. Problems sleeping, guilt about surviving, and an exaggerated "startle response" (wide-eyed, gasping, surprised behavior upon perceiving a sudden threat) are common symptoms as well. Rape survivors, for example, may experience a barrage of psychological aftereffects, including feelings of betrayal by people close to them, anger about having been attacked, and fear of being alone (Baron & Straus, 1985; Cann et al., 1981). ◉

Posttraumatic stress disorder can also have lasting biological consequences (Crowell, 2002; Sapolsky, 1998). The brain undergoes physical changes when stress is extreme in intensity or duration. Specifically, the brain's hormone-regulating system may develop hair-trigger responsiveness, making the victim of posttraumatic stress overreact to mild stressors.

◉—**Watch** the **Video** 9/11 and PTSD at **MyPsychLab**

PTSD in Combat Personnel While the term *posttraumatic stress disorder* was coined fairly recently, historical accounts have noted similar symptoms, referred to as "combat fatigue," "shell-shock," or "soldier's heart," in soldiers for centuries. In the wake of the Vietnam War, where early estimates noted symptoms of PTSD in 30 percent of combat veterans, public attention on the disorder grew. Military psychologists now provide at least some minimal treatment for combat-related stress at deployment sites in Iraq, for instance, and a variety of educational programs aim to help soldiers and their families prepare more effectively for deployment and to cope better with the aftermath of war once the soldiers have returned home. And even though the military cultural norm has historically taught soldiers not to talk about combat experiences, which contributed to the stigma most veterans felt about asking for help with psychological symptoms, these new programs are helping participants slowly overcome that barrier to effective coping. A program entitled Battlemind, for example, was created to help soldiers develop realistic expectations of deployment prior to combat and also to help them readjust to life at home when they return from deployment. Initial research indicates that soldiers who participate in Battlemind report fewer symptoms of PTSD than their comrades who receive more traditional training (Munsey, 2007).

Increased scrutiny on PTSD in combat personnel has also unearthed a fascinating new finding about the brain's role in certain PTSD symptoms. Prompted by the groundbreaking research of neurologist Ibolja Cernak, U.S. military doctors now recognize that soldiers exposed to an explosion often develop cognitive symptoms such as memory loss, reduced ability to concentrate, slowed reaction time, and difficulty performing simple math tasks—even if the soldier wasn't hit by the blast. While researchers are still unsure exactly how the brain is affected by the blast, there is general agreement that the force of the explosion causes damage to brain functioning. Up to 20 percent of soldiers returning from Iraq and Afghanistan are estimated to experience some type of traumatic brain injury such as this, and researchers now think that neurological effects of blast exposure may account for the cognitive deficits seen in some veterans diagnosed with PTSD (Bhattacharjee, 2008).

Chronic Stressors

The stressors reviewed in the previous section—catastrophe, personal loss, and post-traumatic stress—involve events that, like the 9/11 attack, occur abruptly. In contrast, **chronic stressors** are relatively long lasting and may develop slowly over time. For example, they may involve ongoing financial problems, marital difficulties, or poor living conditions, such as one of the world's worse stress inducers—living in poverty. Here, we examine five different chronic stressors: societal stressors, burnout, compassion fatigue, major life changes, and daily hassles.

chronic stressor Long-lasting stressful condition.

societal stressor A chronic stressor resulting from pressure in one's social, cultural, or economic environment.

Societal Stressors
For most of us, stress comes not from sudden catastrophic events but from **societal stressors** or pressures in our social, cultural, and economic environment. These societal stressors often involve difficulties at home, work, or school that are chronic (recurring or continuing over time). Societal stressors also include unemployment, poverty, racism, and other conditions that handicap or oppress individuals because of their social group or status.

Societal stressors include unemployment, homelessness, and discrimination. Such conditions can exact a toll on both mental and physical health, especially among the poor and minorities.

For example, a study of work stress and health revealed that unemployed men experience more depression, anxiety, and worries about health than comparable men with jobs. Almost miraculously, these symptoms usually disappeared when the unemployed individuals found work (Liem & Rayman, 1982). The startling results of a recent survey powerfully illustrate the prevalence of stress related to money concerns: 83 percent of Americans aged 20 to 45 viewed their current financial situation as "very or somewhat stressful." Only 14 percent reported they were not at all stressed out by their financial situation (American Express ZYNC survey, reported in *USA Today*, March 15, 2011).

Prejudice and discrimination can also be significant sources of stress (Contrada et al., 2000). How? For one, high blood pressure among African Americans—long thought to be primarily genetic—is correlated with chronic stress caused by the daily negative impact of having menial jobs, limited education, and low socioeconomic status (Klag et al., 1991). Also, people living in poverty have less access to good health care and are more likely to live in areas containing greater health hazards such as environmental pollutants, lead in their house paint, greater noise, and drug-dealing gangs. Such situational factors affect cognitive development in children and create a variety of adverse physical and emotional factors in adults (Evans et al., 1998; Staples, 1996).

Burnout Having a job, however—even a high-paying one—does not inoculate one against stress. On the contrary, it can create stress of its own, both emotionally and physically. Continually stressful work can lead to **burnout**, a syndrome of overwhelming exhaustion, feelings of cynicism and detachment from the job, and a sense of ineffectiveness and lack of accomplishment (Maslach & Leiter, 1997). Christina Maslach (1998, 2003; Maslach et al., 2001), a leading researcher on this widespread problem, notes that burnout was first recognized in professions demanding high-intensity interpersonal contact, such as physicians with patients, teachers with students, and social workers with clients. We now know that burnout can occur anywhere—even among college students, stay-at-home parents, or volunteer workers. People experiencing burnout report feelings of detachment, failure, and cynicism about coworkers and clients. They seek escape and avoid their work, leading to decreased personal accomplishment. Burnout has been found to correlate with many negative consequences: absenteeism, job turnover, impaired performance, poor coworker relations, family problems, and decreased personal health (Maslach & Leiter, 1997; Schaufeli & Enzmann, 1998). In some nations where citizens get extended sick leave based on their level of stress-related burnout, the cost can run into hundreds of millions in required benefits.

burnout A syndrome of emotional exhaustion, physical fatigue, and cognitive weariness, often related to work.

More recently, research has focused on the positive alternative to burnout, labeled **job engagement** (Schaufeli & Bakker, 2004). The practical significance of this burnout–engagement continuum is that engagement represents a desired goal for burnout interventions. This new framework leads people to consider what factors in the workplace are likely to enhance employees' energy, vigor, and resilience; promote their involvement and absorption with work tasks; and ensure their dedication and sense of efficacy and success on the job.

job engagement An employee's sense of being part of a meaningful work setting where her or his contribution is valued and equitably rewarded (the opposite of job burnout).

Although there is some evidence for individual risk factors for burnout, there is far more evidence for the importance of situational variables. In other words, the workplace carries far more of the predictive weight for burnout than does personality. More than two decades of research on burnout across many occupations in various countries have identified a plethora of organizational risk factors (Maslach, et al., 2001; Schaufeli & Enzmann, 1998). However, rather than posing an "either/or" question ("is it the person *or* the job?")—it may well be that an "and" question is the better way to frame the issue. That is, there are both personal *and* situational variables that determine burnout, and the key issue is how best to conceptualize the combination or interaction of them.

Early models in the field of industrial-organizational psychology (French et al., 1974) theorized that a better fit between the employee and the workplace would predict better adjustment and less stress. Building on those models, Maslach and Leiter (1997) formulated a burnout model that measures the degree of match or mismatch between the individual and key aspects of his or her organizational environment. The greater the gap, or mismatch, the greater the likelihood of burnout; conversely, the greater the match (or fit), the greater the likelihood of job engagement.

> **CONNECTION** CHAPTER 1
>
> Industrial-organizational (I/O) psychologists focus on tailoring the work environment to maximize both productivity and morale (p. 5).

What are these key aspects of the organizational environment? Six major areas of work life have been found relevant to employee/workplace fit: workload, control, reward, community, fairness, and values (Maslach & Leiter, 2005). *Workload* and *control* refer to the amount of work and the degree of autonomy enjoyed by the worker. *Reward* refers to the relative match between the rewards offered by the job and those valued by the employee. The degree of social support and interpersonal conflict in the organization make up the fourth factor, which is *community*. *Fairness* is assessed by the match between the employee's sense of equity and social justice and that of the organization. The final factor, *values*, recognizes the cognitive and emotional power of job goals and expectations. Mismatches between the employee and the organization in these six key areas have been found to predict burnout, making researchers optimistic about the possibility of developing early-detection and intervention procedures to promote greater job engagement (Maslach & Leiter, 2008).

Thus, burnout is not a personal problem or a weakness in character, as was once thought. Effective burnout prevention requires both managers and workers to take responsibility for developing conditions that improve engagement with the job and

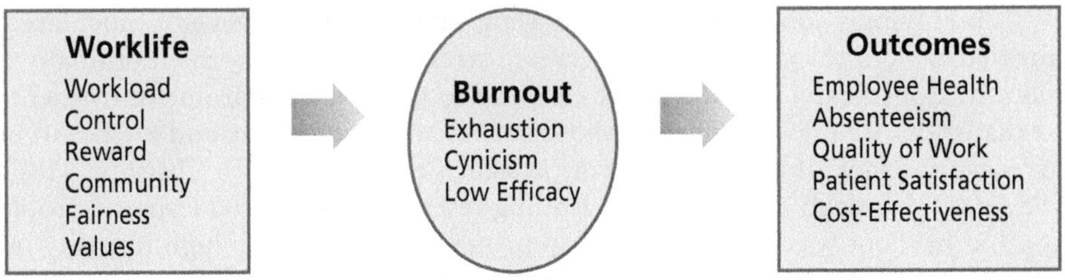

FIGURE 14.2

Worklife and Burnout

A schematic model of six input factors affecting burnout and four measurable outcomes.

Worklife
Workload
Control
Reward
Community
Fairness
Values

→

Burnout
Exhaustion
Cynicism
Low Efficacy

→

Outcomes
Employee Health
Absenteeism
Quality of Work
Patient Satisfaction
Cost-Effectiveness

create a better "fit" between employee and job and make decisions that focus on the long-term health of the employees and the organization (Berglas, 2001; Maslach & Goldberg, 1998).

Compassion Fatigue　After the 9/11 attacks, New York Ladder Company 5's Lieutenant O'Neill joined others in day after day of fruitless rescue searches. One day, instead of going home, O'Neill checked into a hospital and asked for help with stress-related symptoms he was experiencing. He met with a doctor to whom he poured out the story of the horrors he had seen. Contrary to O'Neill's assumption that, as a doctor, "He . . . could handle this," the doctor himself went to the hospital psychologist after treating O'Neill. "[H]e kind of lost it," O'Neill learned. "He had become freaked out from the story I told him, because he lost a friend from the tragedy. . . . He didn't show up for work for a couple of days" (Smith, 2003b, p. 259). Even medical professionals and therapists, though trained to be objective, are at risk for the stress of vicarious traumatization (Sabin-Farrell & Turpin, 2003).

When medical professionals, caregivers, and therapists are overexposed to trauma and its victims, they are at risk for **compassion fatigue,** a state of psychological exhaustion that leaves caregivers feeling stressed, numb, or indifferent to those in need after extended contact with sufferers (Figley, 2002). Compassion fatigue is also called *secondary traumatic stress* because it afflicts the helpers, who "catch" the stress suffered by the victims. Consequences are similar to burnout in that it leaves people unhappy with their work and resistant to contact with people they are supposed to help. Dreading further stories of trauma, fatigued helpers may emotionally withdraw from their clients and overuse the "silencing response," distracting, minimizing, or redirecting what their clients are saying to reduce their own discomfort and pain (Baranowsky, 2002). When therapists or religious counselors feel unable to listen to their clients or parishioners, they can no longer function as effective healers. Compassion fatigue and burnout harm not only the providers and receivers of care and attention but entire professions as well. Fortunately, healers can learn the warning signs in time to take action—and researchers can suggest what kinds of action to take:

compassion fatigue　A state of exhaustion experienced by medical and psychological professionals, as well as caregivers, which leaves the individual feeling stressed, numb, or indifferent.

compassion satisfaction　A sense of appreciation felt by a caregiver, medical or psychological professional, of the work he or she does.

- First, caregivers must focus on their sense of **compassion satisfaction,** an appreciation of the work they do that drew them to their professions in the first place. Compassion satisfaction can be increased by creating and maintaining a sense of team spirit with coworkers. Whenever possible, caregivers and rescue workers should be able to see clients recover so they realize their work is effective (Collins & Long, 2003).

- While it is important to care for those one is helping, helpers must avoid becoming overinvolved, or their lack of control over most of their clients' experiences can lead to a sense of defeat (Keidel, 2002).

- Novice trauma counselors may simply distance themselves from stressful exchanges; more experienced workers are better able to cope directly with their own stress (Pinto, 2003).

- Caregivers should resist overvolunteering. Volunteers who worked with more than one agency or effort after 9/11 were at greater risk for compassion fatigue than those who volunteered with only one organization, such as the American Red Cross (Roberts et al., 2003).

- Finally, professional helpers and emergency workers should use humor—but use it carefully! While tasteless jokes and dark humor with fellow workers can relieve anxiety and establish a sense of camaraderie among coworkers, workers must be cautious with these types of humor. Because it is not publicly acceptable to laugh in the face of tragedy, humor should be expressed selectively, with sensitivity to the environment, so as not to offend or further hurt those already suffering (Moran, 2002).

Major Life Events The beginning or end of a relationship is always a time of adjustment, accompanied by emotional ups and downs, tension, and turmoil. Earlier in this section, we discussed the effects of sudden interpersonal loss. Other changes can cause stress too: a new job, starting or finishing college, or—ironically—even taking a vacation! Even events we welcome, such as the birth of a child, often require major changes in our routines and adaptations to new demands and lifestyles. Especially when the events are considered positive events (such as an exciting new job or getting married), we may not recognize their potential impact on our stress level. In general, any change can generate distress; the bigger the change in our lives, the bigger the impact.

What if a simple questionnaire existed that would assess your current stress level? Several decades ago, psychologists Thomas Holmes and Richard Rahe (pronounced *RAY*) developed just such a tool. They first identified a variety of common stressful events and had a large number of respondents rate the events in terms of how stressful each one was in their own lives. After analyzing all the results, they created the **Social Readjustment Rating Scale (SRRS)**, which lists 43 life events—ranging from death of a spouse at the high end to pregnancy or a new job in the middle to getting a traffic ticket at the low end. Each life event is assigned a particular number of life-change units (LCUs), so anyone can calculate his or her current stress level by adding up the LCUs for each life change that was recently experienced.

Research has indeed found relationships between life changes and stress. The birth of a child, for example, is often associated with lower marital satisfaction (Cowan & Cowan, 1988). Since it was developed, the SRRS has been used in thousands of studies worldwide and has been found to apply cross-culturally. We must be cautious in interpreting our scores, though, in light of what we know about the role of cognitive appraisal in stress. We will examine the SRRS more closely at the end of this chapter. An undergraduate version of the scale, developed specifically to reflect student stress reactions, gives you the opportunity to assess your own stress level in the *Do It Yourself!* feature (Crandall, et al., 1992).

Social Readjustment Rating Scale (SRRS) Psychological rating scale designed to measure stress levels by attaching numerical values to common life changes.

Daily Hassles After a difficult workday, you get stuck in a traffic jam on your way to the grocery store. Finally arriving, you find they don't have the very item or brand you wanted. After selecting a substitute, you proceed to the checkout, only to be snapped at by an impatient clerk when you don't have exact change. Taken individually, such minor irritations and frustrations, known as **hassles**, don't seem like much in comparison to a natural disaster. But psychologists confirm that hassles can accumulate, especially when they are frequent and involve interpersonal conflicts (Bolger et al., 1989).

In our fast-moving, highly technological society, a major life hassle is "waiting." Waiting for anything, instead of having it instantly available, has become a modern stressor: waiting for public transportation, waiting for service in a store or restaurant, waiting in traffic, waiting for your computer to boot up or download files.

Any annoying incident can be a hassle, but some of the most common hassles involve frustrations—the blocking of some desired goal—at home, work, or school. In a diary study, a group of men and women kept track of their daily hassles over a one-year period, also recording major life changes and physical symptoms. A clear relationship emerged between hassles and health problems: The more frequent and intense the hassles people reported, the poorer their health, both physical and mental (Lazarus, 1981, 1984, 1999). The opposite was also true: As daily hassles diminish, people's sense of well-being increases (Chamberlain & Zika, 1990). Thus, a life filled with hassles can exact as great a price as that of a single, more intense stressor (Weinberger et al., 1987).

hassle Situation that causes minor irritation or frustration.

Traffic can be a hassle and consequently contribute to your stress—if you choose to interpret it that way.

Do It Yourself!   THE UNDERGRADUATE STRESS QUESTIONNAIRE: HOW STRESSED ARE YOU?

This scale, developed in 1992 specifically for undergraduates, initially contained an event about having problems with your typewriter—which we have removed for relevancy. For each of the following events, check off any item that describes a stressor that you have experienced in the past week. Tally up your check marks to compute your total (Crandell et al., 1992).

_____ Lack of money

_____ Someone broke a promise

_____ Death (family member or friend)

_____ Dealt with incompetence at the Registrar's office

_____ Can't concentrate

_____ Had a lot of tests

_____ Thought about unfinished work

_____ Someone did a "pet peeve" of yours

_____ It's finals week

_____ Living with boy-/girlfriend

_____ No sleep

_____ Applying to graduate school

_____ Felt need for transportation

_____ Sick, injury

_____ Bad haircut today

_____ Victim of a crime

_____ Had a class presentation

_____ Job requirements changed

_____ Applying for a job

_____ Assignments in all classes due the same day

_____ Fought with boy-/girlfriend

_____ No time to eat

_____ Have a hard upcoming week

_____ Felt some peer pressure

_____ Lots of deadlines to meet

_____ Went into test unprepared

_____ Working while in school

_____ Arguments, conflict of values with friends

_____ Have a hangover

_____ Problems with your computer

_____ Lost something (especially wallet)

_____ Death of a pet

_____ Bothered by having no social support of family

_____ Performed poorly at a task

_____ Did worse than expected on test

_____ Problem getting home from bar when drunk

_____ Used a fake ID

_____ Had an interview

_____ Had projects, research papers due

_____ Did badly on a test

_____ Can't finish everything you needed to do

_____ Heard bad news

_____ No sex for a while

_____ Someone cut ahead of you in line

_____ Had confrontation with an authority figure

_____ Maintaining a long-distance boy-/girlfriend

_____ Crammed for a test

_____ Parents getting divorce

_____ Dependent on other people

_____ Feel unorganized

_____ Breaking up with boy-/girlfriend

_____ Trying to decide on major

_____ Feel isolated

_____ Having roommate conflicts

_____ Checkbook didn't balance

_____ Visit from a relative and entertaining them

_____ Decision to have sex is on your mind

_____ Parents controlling with money

_____ Couldn't find a parking space

_____ Noise disturbed you while trying to study

_____ Someone borrowed something without permission

_____ Had to ask for money

_____ Got a traffic ticket

_____ Talked with a professor

_____ Change of environment (new doctor, dentist, etc.)

_____ Exposed to upsetting TV show, book, or movie

_____ Got to class late

_____ Erratic schedule

_____ Found out boy-/girlfriend cheated on you

_____ Can't understand your professor

_____ Trying to get into your major or college

_____ Missed your period and waiting

_____ Coping with addictions

_____ Registration for classes

_____ Stayed up late writing a paper

_____ Property stolen

_____ Someone you expected to call did not

_____ Holiday

_____ Sat through a boring class

_____ Favorite sporting team lost

_____ Thoughts about future

_____ TOTAL

How did you do? The following scale may be useful in providing you a general sense of how much stress you are experiencing as an undergraduate:

0–7: a very low level of stress
16–23: the amount of stress encountered by the average undergraduate
40+: a very high level of stress

You might want to compare your score at two different times, or with a friend.

Cognitive appraisal plays a role in the impact of hassles as well. If you interpret a frustrating situation as "too much" to deal with or as a major threat to well-being, it will affect you more than if you dismiss it as less important (Lazarus, 1984). Some people may be especially prone to see the world as hassle filled. One study showed that college students with a pessimistic outlook experienced both more hassles and poorer health (Dykema et al., 1995). This finding serves as a good reminder that correlation does not imply causation: In other words, we know a correlation exists between hassles and health but do not know what causes the link. On one hand, experiencing many hassles may have a negative impact on health—but on the other hand, having more health problems to begin with might increase a person's perception of minor annoyances as hassles. It is also possible that a third variable—something other than hassles or health—might be driving the correlation: For example, pessimists (as noted above) might be more likely to perceive minor annoyances as hassles and also more likely to have health problems.

One way to destress your life is to reconsider your own daily hassles. Look back on recent frustrations with a sense of humor, put problems in perspective, and consider just how unimportant such difficulties and delays really turned out to be. By reappraising everyday difficulties as minor, you enable yourself to remain good natured and productive and even to have a good laugh. Shake your head, put on the brakes, let the vending machine keep your dollar—and move along. Daily hassles are idiosyncratic: They are interpreted uniquely by each person experiencing them. What is a hassle or an annoyance to you may be unnoticed or even amusing to someone else. One person's agonizing traffic jam is another person's opportunity to listen to the radio, play a favorite CD, or engage in people watching. If your life seems hassle filled, some reappraisal of regularly irritating situations can save you psychological wear and tear. It almost always helps to connect with nature, take a walk in a park or on a beach, swim, hike, bike, even visit a local zoo. Later, we will see how cognitive reappraisal can play a central role in one's general strategies for coping with stress.

[PSYCHOLOGY MATTERS]

Student Stress

It's timely for you to be studying stress and well-being right now, because merely being a college student qualifies as a stressor. College freshmen in particular undergo major challenges in making the transition to college life. One study found that freshman stress unfolds in three phases. First, new students experience the shock and excitement of new roles, environments, and social relationships. Next comes a protracted period of disillusionment and struggle as students face both the serious work and mundane chores of academic life. Finally, as roles gel and mastery develops in at least some efforts, a sense of improved well-being and possibilities emerges (Rambo-Chroniak, 1999). But stress isn't limited to first-year students. All students experience a specific pattern of stress during the school year, with stress peaks at the beginning, middle, and end of each term (Bolger, 1997). Two points in time are particularly difficult, the "mid-winter crash" and the final exam period, when studying competes with regular sleep and healthy eating and when flu and cold viruses afflict those with low resistance.

Some causes of student stress are obvious, with academic pressure topping the list (Bolger, 1997). Also, new social interactions increase the possibility of problems in interpersonal relationships (Edwards et al., 2001). Romantic love, often a source of joy, can also be a source of stress and illness, especially among college women (Riessman et al., 1991). And when romance sours, breakup stress soars. An investigation of a large group of university students who had experienced a recent breakup of a romantic relationship was studied to determine its causes. Those who felt most distress from their breakup reported a *loss of intimacy* as the main cause for the breakup itself, leading to their failed romance; not as central were affiliation needs, sexuality, or autonomy reasons (Field et al., 2010).

Perhaps the essential source of stress for traditional-aged college students is freedom—specifically, the lack of structure in a college environment as contrasted with the structure of home and high school curriculum (*USA Today*, 1996). For students returning to college after years in the workforce or raising children, stress often involves the challenge of "retraining the brain" to process and retain massive amounts of new information—in quick time for exams.

And stress seems to be on the rise among college students. In a recent national survey, college freshmen and women reported record-low levels of emotional health: only 52 percent felt they had "good or above-average emotional health." This marks the lowest point since the survey first asked the question in 1985. The same survey also found that 76 percent rated their drive to achieve as "above average or in the highest 10 percent"—the highest point since 1985. More students than ever before admitted they frequently felt overwhelmed. Gender effects were also found: Only 46 percent of women reported their emotional health as "good" compared to a higher 59 percent of men. What do you think might account for this difference (Sieben, 2011)?

Solutions for student stress, fortunately, may be within arm's reach—the distance needed to reach for the phone and call a friend for support or the college health center, counseling office, or tutoring center for professional advice. Most students express a reluctance to seek help (Rambo-Chroniak, 1999); so simply overcoming this ambivalence—especially as an enlightened student of the many uses of psychology—can be a step toward feeling better. Young adults do better if they have positive attitudes about becoming independent individuals on a course of normal separation from their parents (Smith, 1995).

In terms of self-help, students report better results when taking specific action to resolve the problem rather than simply dwelling on their emotional response (Smith, 1995). Cultivating more hopeful attitudes and better self-esteem—for example, by setting and meeting realistic goals—also leads to lower stress and better adjustment. Students appear to be more adaptive if they report better social support and a greater sense of control in their lives (Rambo-Chroniak, 1999). Involvement in student organizations can offer both structure and social contact, but beware of the stress of excessive commitment (Bolger, 1997). Two qualities in particular characterize students who are most effective in preventing and coping with stress: *resilience*, based in part in self-acceptance, effective communication, and coping skills; and *cognitive hardiness*, an ability to interpret potential stressors as challenging rather than threatening (Nowack, 1983; Yeaman, 1995). We will examine these two characteristics in detail a little later in this chapter.

Check Your Understanding

✓● Study and Review at MyPsychLab

1. **RECALL:** External events or situations that cause stress are called _____, whereas the term _____ denotes the physical and mental changes that occur as a result.

2. **APPLICATION:** An example of a chronic societal stressor is _____.

   a. an earthquake
   b. vicarious trauma
   c. being stuck in traffic
   d. widespread unemployment

3. **ANALYSIS:** Which of the following statements about daily hassles is true?

   a. Some of the most common hassles involve threats to survival.
   b. As daily hassles diminish, people's sense of well-being increases.

   c. More frequent and intense hassles are associated with better health.
   d. The effects of hassles do not accumulate: Many hassles are no worse than a few.

4. **SYNTHESIS:** Your friend Rob recently lost his wife to cancer. Devon, another friend, recently found out his partner was cheating on him, and she left him for someone else. What difference would you predict between Rob and Devon in terms of the impact of these two different types of losses on their psychological well-being?

5. **UNDERSTANDING THE CORE CONCEPT:** Name four categories of common stressors, along with an example of each.

Answers 1. stressors; stress **2.** d **3.** b **4.** Both Rob and Devon have suffered a personal loss, which involves grief, stress, and mourning. Devon, however, is more at risk for depression due to the accompanying humiliation of being rejected, whereas Rob's loss is a "pure loss event." **5.** Traumatic events, such as catastrophe and personal loss; chronic stressors, such as societal stressors, burnout, and compassion fatigue; major life events, such as a new job or the birth of a child; and daily hassles, such as traffic jams or computer crashes.

14.2 KEY QUESTION
How Does Stress Affect Us Physically?

Since our earliest days on Earth, humans have survived by responding quickly and decisively to potentially lethal attacks by predators or hostile tribes. Our ancestors adapted to an enormous variety of environmental conditions worldwide, confronting climate extremes, scarce resources, and hostile neighbors. Faced with these challenges, quick action was necessary to obtain shelter and protection, to find food, and to defend themselves. The faster an individual was to feel fear or anger, appraise the situation accurately, and take appropriate action, the better his or her chances of success and survival. Those who responded most quickly and effectively to danger survived and passed those responsive genes to their offspring, whereas slower or less-clever individuals were less likely to survive and bear children in the course of human evolution.

Some of the serious stressors confronting our ancestors, such as catastrophe or combat, continue to face us today. Modern life, of course, adds some new dangers: demanding jobs, financial worries, and computer crashes. More often chronic in nature, these new threats aren't necessarily solved effectively with the same responses that suited our ancestors and their more immediate challenges. Yet, our stress response system remains the result of our ancestors' evolutionary legacy, because human physiology cannot evolve and change nearly as fast as our societies have. This ancient biological script is retained in our body's automatic responses to frightening or enraging conditions. If someone insults you, your face feels hot and your fists seem to clench by themselves, readying you for a physical contest. Or imagine a very different sort of "threat": Your instructor calls on you in a class discussion for which you are unprepared. Your heart races, your knees feel wobbly, and you feel the urge to run away.

These examples illustrate the two poles of the **fight-or-flight response**, a sequence of internal and behavioral processes triggered when a threat is perceived, preparing the organism for either struggle or escape. This response worked very well for our predecessors but doesn't always suit us as well today. After all, is running out of the classroom really an effective response to being called on in class? Our Core Concept summarizes this point:

fight-or-flight response   Sequence of internal responses preparing an organism for struggle or escape.

> ## Core Concept 14.2
> **The physical stress response begins with arousal, which stimulates a series of physiological responses that in the short term are adaptive but that can turn harmful if prolonged.**

Amazingly, we deal with stress effectively most of the time, managing to be not only healthy but even happy. But, as you will see in this section, there can be serious consequences when we don't deal effectively with stress—no matter what its source. On the positive side, we should emphasize that the emotional arousal we call stress usually works to our advantage. It brings threatening events into focus and readies us to respond. On the negative side, extreme or prolonged emotional arousal threatens our health. The results can include physical conditions such as heart disease, stroke, high blood pressure, and ulcers. Our mental health can also suffer.

Some of us are prone to "worrying ourselves sick" by anticipating what might go wrong, from minor irritants to major traumas (Sapolsky, 1994). Depression, as well as PTSD and other anxiety disorders, has direct linkages to stress. We see these consequences not only in emergency response workers and air traffic controllers but also in public- and private-sector employees at all status levels and in people of all ages and all walks of life. Let's take a closer look at the physiology of our stress response, which will lay the foundation for a clear understanding of exactly how this adaptive response triggers negative health consequences when chronic stress strains the limits of our resources.

In cases of acute stress, such as this woman faces as a forest fire nears her village in Portugal and threatens her home, the stressor arises suddenly, and the stress response begins with abrupt and intense physiological arousal.

CONNECTION CHAPTER 2

The autonomic nervous system (ANS) regulates our most basic vital functions (p. 57).

acute stress   A temporary state of arousal, caused by a stressor, with a distinct onset and limited duration.

Physiological Responses to Stress

Firefighters usually report that they love their work, and for some the job is a family tradition. But their camaraderie and commitment cannot lessen the threat, the risk of injury and death—the stress they experience—when they answer the alarm and race into harm's way. How does the body of an experienced firefighter respond to the perception of that stressor? And what about your own physical responses to stress?

The Fight-or-Flight Response   When a stressful situation begins suddenly—as when a professional firefighter first hears the alarm—the stress response begins with an abrupt and intense physiological arousal produced by the autonomic nervous system (ANS). Signs of this arousal include accelerated heart rate, quickened breathing, increased blood pressure, and profuse perspiration. This scenario illustrates a case of **acute stress**, a temporary pattern of stressor-activated arousal with a distinct onset and limited duration first described by physiologist Walter Cannon almost a century ago (Cannon, 1914).

Almost instantaneously, reactions in our nervous system, endocrine system, and muscles equip us to make an efficient and effective response—supplying, for example, extra strength if needed. Figure 14.3 provides a detailed illustration of the many ways the body prepares for an emergency response.

The fight-or-flight response can be a lifesaver when you need to escape from a fire, confront a hostile rival, or swerve to avoid an oncoming car. When faced with a chronic stressor, though, it has a cost: Staying physiologically "on guard" against a threat eventually wears down the body's natural defenses. In this way, facing frequent stress—or frequently interpreting experiences as stressful—can create a serious health risk: An essentially healthy stress response can become a health hazard. In the next section, we will explore exactly how and why this occurs.

FIGURE 14.3

Bodily Reactions to Stress

An amazing array of physiological reactions prepare us to fight or flee in acute stressful situations.

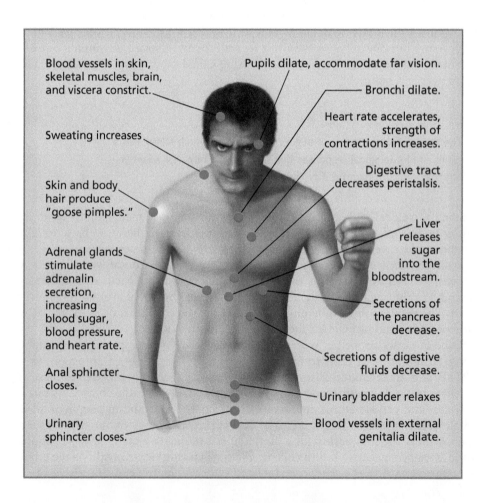

Blood vessels in skin, skeletal muscles, brain, and viscera constrict.

Pupils dilate, accommodate far vision.

Bronchi dilate.

Sweating increases

Heart rate accelerates, strength of contractions increases.

Skin and body hair produce "goose pimples."

Digestive tract decreases peristalsis.

Adrenal glands stimulate adrenalin secretion, increasing blood sugar, blood pressure, and heart rate.

Liver releases sugar into the bloodstream.

Secretions of the pancreas decrease.

Anal sphincter closes.

Secretions of digestive fluids decrease.

Urinary bladder relaxes

Urinary sphincter closes.

Blood vessels in external genitalia dilate.

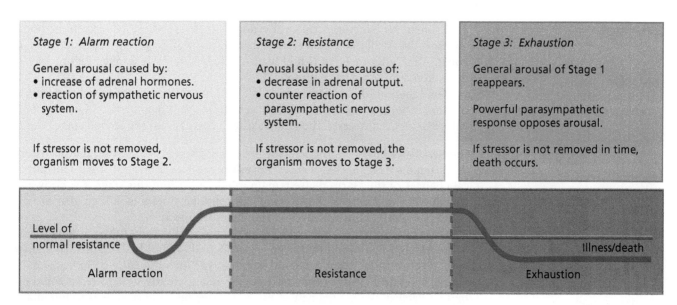

Stage 1: Alarm reaction	Stage 2: Resistance	Stage 3: Exhaustion
General arousal caused by: • increase of adrenal hormones. • reaction of sympathetic nervous system.	Arousal subsides because of: • decrease in adrenal output. • counter reaction of parasympathetic nervous system.	General arousal of Stage 1 reappears. Powerful parasympathetic response opposes arousal.
If stressor is not removed, organism moves to Stage 2.	If stressor is not removed, the organism moves to Stage 3.	If stressor is not removed in time, death occurs.

FIGURE 14.4

The General Adaptation Syndrome

In Stage 1, the body produces an emergency arousal response to a stressor. Then, in Stage 2, the body adapts to the continuous presence of the stressor. In Stage 3, if the stressor is not reduced, an arousal response begins again, although the body's defenses are depleted—with dangerous results.

The General Adaptation Syndrome Our understanding of how stress causes illness began in the mid-20th century with the work of Canadian endocrinologist Hans Selye (pronounced *SELL-yeh*). In brief, Selye discovered that different stressors trigger essentially the same systemic reaction, or general physical response, which mobilizes the body's resources to deal with the threat. Moreover, he found, all stressors provoke some attempt at adaptation or adjustment of the body to the stressor. Because the bodily response was a general rather than a specific adaptation effort, Selye dubbed it the **general adaptation syndrome (GAS)** (see Figure 14.4).

Normally, these responses are helpful, but under chronically stressful conditions, they can lead to heart disease, asthma, headache, gastric ulcers, arthritis, and a variety of other disorders (Carlson, 2007; Salovey et al., 2000). Selye's model of the GAS describes a three-phase response to any threat, consisting of an *alarm phase,* a *resistance phase,* and an *exhaustion phase* (Johnson, 1991; Selye, 1956, 1991).

The Alarm Phase In the first stage of stress, the body's warning system activates and begins to mobilize its resources against the stressor. Selye called this first stage the **alarm phase**—but it is similar to the pattern of reactions Cannon called the fight-or-flight response. The hypothalamus sets off two parallel emergency messages. One message signals the hormone system, especially the adrenal glands, through the pathway shown in Figure 14.5. The result is a flood of steroid hormones into the bloodstream—chemicals that support strength and endurance (the reason why some athletes might risk dangerous side effects by abusing steroids). Endorphins are also released, which reduce the body's awareness of pain signals. A concurrent message is relayed through the sympathetic division of the autonomic nervous system to internal organs and glands, arousing the body for action.

It's the cascade of messages through these two pathways—the sympathetic nervous system and the endocrine system—that readies us for action. Blood flow to the heart, brain, and muscles increases, enabling us to think and react better and faster. Blood flow to the digestive system, conversely, decreases—presumably so our bodies are not expending precious energy on nonessential functions during an emergency.

general adaptation syndrome (GAS) A three-phase pattern of physical responses to a chronic stressor.

alarm phase First phase of the GAS, during which body resources are mobilized to cope with the stressor.

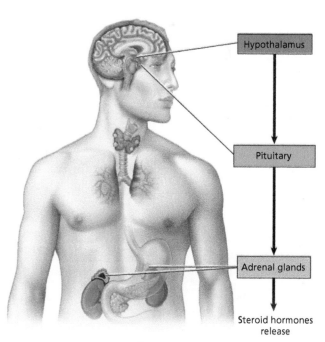

FIGURE 14.5

Hormonal Response in the Alarm Phase

In the alarm phase of the GAS, the hormone system response shown here is one of the two parallel response pathways set off by the hypothalamus.

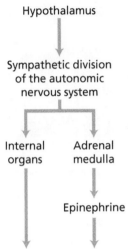

FIGURE 14.6

Sympathetic Nervous System Response in the Alarm Phase

This diagram shows the path of the sympathetic nervous system's response to acute stress, which occurs simultaneously with the parallel response of the hormone system.

resistance phase   Second phase of the GAS, during which the body adapts to and maintains resources to cope with the stressor.

exhaustion phase   Third phase of the GAS, during which the body's resources become depleted.

After responding to one stressor, such as finishing a difficult test, you may find your bodily resources somewhat depleted, leaving you less able to deal with another, unexpected stressor.

Pupils dilate, enhancing peripheral vision, and perspiration helps keep the body from overheating. Available blood sugar increases as well, to provide an additional energy boost. All in all, our body is highly attuned to immediate danger. Figure 14.6 details this autonomic series of responses.

The function of the alarm phase is to enable the organism to fight or to flee from the threat, which usually didn't last very long for our ancestors. Given the chronic nature of modern stresses, though, we often progress into the second stage—resistance.

The Resistance Phase   If the stressor persists—but is not so strong that it overwhelms us during the first stage—we enter the **resistance phase**, during which all the physiological changes of the alarm phase remain in effect. During this stage, the body attempts to fight off the effects of the stressor. The immune system is in high gear as well, and white blood cell count increases to help fight off infection.

Surprisingly, the resistance during this stage applies only to the original stressor. In his research, Selye found that if an experimental animal had adapted to one stressor (e.g., electric shock), but a second stressor was introduced (e.g., extreme cold), the animal soon died. The animal's resources were apparently so depleted it could not mobilize a defense against the new stressor. A tragic human example is found in a soldier who collapses and dies in response to the new stress of a prison camp after surviving months of stressful combat.

Thus, we see that our alarm and resistance defenses use physical energy. They reduce the resources available in case of additional stressors. Imagine this scenario, for example: You've just completed final exams; you've had minimal sleep, studying day and night, surviving on junk food and caffeine for a week. Now it's over. You can relax and rest at last. But the phone rings: It's the welcome voice of the love of your life, with an unwelcome note of some negative emotion. Before you can announce the good news that you survived your exams, the voice says, "I don't know how to say this, but—look, we have to talk . . ." This is probably not good news and may signal serious trouble, even a breakup—definitely a stressor. Already exhausted by the stresses of finals week, how will you handle this important conversation? You feel stricken, frightened, and even angry: Why this threat? Why now? Because your system is depleted, you may overreact and find yourself without the cognitive and emotional resources to handle the situation effectively.

The Exhaustion Phase   The resistance phase is the body's last-ditch effort to combat the stressor, and if the stressful situation is not ameliorated during that phase, the body can no longer keep up its intense physiological battle. In this third stage, the **exhaustion phase**, body functions drop back into normal range—and then fall below normal. At this point, the body requires rest and rejuvenation to bring our physiological functioning back up to acceptable levels. If it does not get that much-needed respite, as is often the case in today's world of chronic stressors, the very responses that were so adaptive in the first two phases put the body at risk for illness in the third phase.

Several processes may contribute to the physical and mental deterioration seen in the exhaustion phase. For example, increased blood pressure can cause headaches in the short term and, over an extended period of time, contribute to stroke and coronary heart disease (CHD)—two leading causes of death. Meanwhile, the compromised digestive system contributes to formation of certain types of ulcers and, over the long term, obesity. Chronic stress is also linked to increased fatty deposits in the bloodstream, which increases risk of stroke. Still other dangers lurk in the depleted immune system, making the stressed person a prime candidate for infections or other diseases. In addition, prolonged or repeated stress may produce long-term changes in the brain that provoke depression (Sapolsky, 1998; Schulkin, 1994). Stress hormones also act on the brain, interfering with its ability to regenerate neurons, especially in the hippocampus (Gould et al., 1998; Sapolsky, 1998). This helps explain why prolonged use of steroids—which are really stress hormones—is dangerous (except under certain medical conditions): Long-term steroid use effectively sends the body into the final stage of the GAS, the stage of exhaustion, producing perilous deterioration.

So we see that Selye's GAS model offers a useful explanation of how stress can lead not only to the initial fight-or-flight reaction but also to chronic and debilitating conditions. And while new research is beginning to reveal that not all stresses produce exactly the same response from the endocrine system (Kemeny, 2003), the model remains widely accepted as the key to understanding the link between stress and illness. Before we look more closely at the details of the chronic stress response, let's first consider an intriguing alternative to fight-or-flight: nurturance. ✳

✳—[Explore the Concept Selye's General Adaptation Syndrome at MyPsychLab

Tend and Befriend Psychologist Shelley Taylor noticed that the fight-or-flight model was developed by male theorists doing research with male subjects—male rats, mice, and humans. The fear and aggression so prominent in fight-or-flight may, noted Taylor, characterize the responses of males more than females (Taylor, 2003; Taylor et al., 2000b). A **tend-and-befriend** model may better explain the behavior of females in response to threats to themselves and their offspring. Taylor's theory argues that, because females are the primary caretakers of offspring, female biology assigns priority to protecting the survival of the young. From this perspective, fight-or-flight makes no sense. Aggression ("fight") can cause injury to oneself or one's children; escape ("flight") leaves children defenseless. Neither response promotes adaptation and survival from the female caretaker's point of view (Volpe, 2004).

tend-and-befriend   Stress response model proposing that females are biologically predisposed to respond to threat by nurturing and protecting offspring and seeking social support.

This tend-and-befriend model proposes that females are biologically predisposed—through brain and hormonal activity—to respond to threat by nurturing and protecting their offspring. Seeking social support creates networks that increase an individual's ability to protect and nurture (Eisler & Levine, 2002; Taylor et al., 2000b). One study in support of the tend-and-befriend model examined men's and women's hormonal changes and self-reports prior to an important examination. While reported anxiety levels did not differ, men had significantly higher levels of **cortisol** production—an important steroid in the fight-or-flight response—than did women (Ennis et al., 2001). Additional research reveals that **oxytocin**, another stress hormone released on exposure to a stressor, may combine with estrogen in females to prompt affiliation-seeking behavior (Taylor, 2006). Higher oxytocin levels are also associated with greater calmness and decreased anxiety, which are important components of effective nurturing.

cortisol   A steroid produced by the fight-or-flight response.

oxytocin   A hormone produced (by both women and men) in response to a stressor.

It might surprise you to know that both men and women seek social support as a stress response, although evidence at this point indicates women respond this way more frequently and consistently than men (Tamres et al., 2002). For women with early-stage breast cancer, for example, emotional support from their spouses buffered their daily stress (Gilmore et al., 2011). Importantly, however, the amount of support they needed from their spouses rose as their level of distress rose. Researchers urge spouses to understand the greater need and find ways to provide it rather than becoming disheartened and giving up. And doing so may benefit their own health; research indicates a lower mortality rate for older adults who give help and emotional support to friends, relatives, and neighbors (Brown et al., 2003).

The picture emerging from these complementary responses to stressful situations—fight-or-flight and tend-and-befriend—is of a more complex stress response than previously thought. We now see a response system that has evolved to enable both self-protection and reaching out to others in times of danger (Pitman, 2003). Tending and befriending powerfully complements the fight-or-flight pattern, together accounting for the survival not only of individuals but also of relationships and communities.

Stress and the Immune System

Earlier in this section, we noted that the immune system becomes compromised in the face of stress—specifically, when we enter the exhaustion phase of the GAS. Research has shown, for example, that individuals coping with the death of a spouse or the end of an important long-term relationship are frequently subject to both depression and **immunosuppression** (impairment in the function of the immune system), leaving them more vulnerable to disease (Cohen & Syme, 1985; Kiecolt-Glaser & Glaser, 1987, 2001).

immunosuppression   Impairment in the function of the immune system.

psycho-neuroimmunology   Multidisciplinary field that studies the influence of mental states on the immune system.

Psycho-Neuroimmunology   In recent years, advances in biotechnology have spurred the development of an exciting new field that seeks to understand how stress causes disease. **Psycho-neuroimmunology** pulls together psychologists with expertise in psychological factors of stress, such as cognition and emotion; neuroscientists, who study brain functioning; and immunologists, who have extensive knowledge of the immune system. While the field has an impressive multisyllabic title, interest in the mind–body connection is not new: In many ways, psycho-neuroimmunology is simply the rigorous study of questions pondered more than 2,000 years ago by ancient civilizations such as the Greeks and Chinese.

Bi-Directional Links between the Brain and Body   A primary goal of psycho-neuroimmunology is to examine how psychological and immunological processes influence each other and, in turn, how they are influenced by the external social world. Fundamental to this mission is the fact that the brain and periphery of the body communicate in a bidirectional fashion (Maier & Watkins, 1999). When a stressor is experienced, for example, the brain signals the adrenal glands to secrete cortisol, a major stress hormone. Cortisol then sends signals back to the brain to regulate its own production (Maier & Watkins, 2000). Psychological stress also activates the immune system. Among the chemical messengers shuttling between the brain and the immune system are proteins known as **cytokines.** One of the most interesting aspects of cytokines is that they signal the central nervous system to elicit behavioral changes that include fatigue, fever, and social-behavioral withdrawal. These changes are helpful because they help organisms recuperate and recover from illness or injury (DeAngelis, 2002a). If prolonged, however, these changes can increase risk for disorders, such as psychological depression. Again, we see the parallels with the functioning of the general adaptation syndrome, GAS.

cytokines   Hormone-like chemicals that fight infection and facilitate communication between the brain and immune system.

In one of the first studies to examine how the brain regulates cytokine responses to stress, psychologist George Slavich asked participants to give an impromptu speech in front of an imposing panel of raters wearing white lab coats. As expected, people's cytokine levels increased significantly during the impromptu speech (Slavich et al., 2010b). Next, he scanned participants' brains while they played a virtual ball-tossing game in which they were suddenly excluded by two other players. When Slavich examined the cytokine and brain data together, he noticed that people who had greater brain-activity responses to being rejected had also exhibited more cytokine activity during the speech. What conclusions can we draw from these results? You'll recall that in addition to acting as "chemical messengers," cytokines can promote specific behaviors such as social-behavioral withdrawal. Consequently, the Slavich study helps explain how social stressors outside the body are translated into biological changes that can increase some individuals' risk for disorders like depression.

Stress Ages Cells   Psychological stress can also affect physical health by accelerating the rate at which cells age. One way to assess a cell's age is to measure the length of its **telomeres.** Telomeres are DNA protein complexes that cap the ends of chromosomes and protect against damage to DNA. In humans, telomeres shorten across the lifespan. Importantly, however, their length is associated with a number of diseases, including cancer, cardiovascular disease, and several neurodegenerative diseases (Fitzpatrick et al., 2007). Shorter telomeres are even associated with early death (Cawthon et al., 2003).

telomeres   DNA protein complexes that cap the ends of chromosomes and protect against damage to DNA.

In a landmark study examining the effects of stress on telomere length, psychologist Elissa Epel found that women who cared for a child with a serious illness had an accelerated rate of immune cell telomere shortening (Epel et al., 2004). In fact, women reporting high levels of stress had telomeres that were nine to 17 years "older." Subsequent research demonstrated that this effect may be explained in part by people's level of pessimism or their tendency to expect negative outcomes in the future (O'Donovan et al., 2009). Thus, those women with high levels of pessimistic tendencies were more likely, when stressed, to have developed older telomeres than peers with more optimistic outlooks. This is an important point because it shows that cognitive appraisals play a critical role in the stress–illness relationship. What are other reasons for why some people get ill when faced with stress while others do not? We devote the second half of this chapter to answering that very question.

[PSYCHOLOGY MATTERS]

Cognitive Appraisal of Ambiguous Threats

In the aftermath of 9/11, many of the first responders continued to work on site at the WTC for months after the explosive destruction of the twin towers. When authorities from the Environmental Protection Agency (EPA) and the mayor of New York City announced that the air was safe to breathe, many workers took off their safety masks, which were hot and impaired visibility. But was that "all clear" announcement really accurate? Dust an inch thick covered window frames as far as a mile from the smoldering debris on the "pile" at the WTC. Think about what must have been the fall-out from two airliners crashing into and demolishing two 110-story office buildings. What would you expect to find upon close inspection of that site? And what do you imagine was the psychological reason for the upbeat, positive public announcement by the EPA when on the ground conditions were so unhealthy?

After the collapse of the twin towers on 9/11, many first responders continued to work on site for months without the protection of their safety masks.

Almost a decade later, the *New York Times* (2011) published this report on that "secondary tragedy"—the subsequent health damage to WTC first responders from having been encouraged by government officials that the air was safe to breathe when, in fact, it was lethal to do so.

> Scientists have called the dust, smoke and ash unleashed by the destruction of the World Trade Center on Sept. 11, 2001, the greatest acute environmental disaster in New York City history. Fires burning at 1,000 degrees created a toxic plume that clouded lower Manhattan and spread to adjoining areas. The collapsing towers pulverized cement and everything the buildings contained, including some asbestos, while the tremendous pressure of the collapsing floors fused materials together in potentially dangerous combinations that scientists had not seen before.
>
> Officials and medical experts estimate that in all, between 40,000 and 90,000 workers and volunteers spent time on the debris pile and may have been affected in some way by the dust. More than 9,000 workers at ground zero brought lawsuits against 90 government agencies and private companies related to illnesses and injuries they say stemmed from working at the site.

Were officials deliberately lying, then, when they made the announcement that the air was safe to breathe? Assuming they were fully cognizant of the dangers that were later discovered could be indicative of a judgment error known as the hindsight bias—similar to Monday-morning quarterbacks' analysis of what went wrong in the previous day's football game. While—with the benefit of hindsight—it may be easy to see the magnitude of the danger that workers faced, at the time, officials may have been overwhelmed by a variety of diverse predictions made in the face of a situation they had never before encountered. Similar processes may have been functioning in Japan's official optimistic announcements in the first few days following the 2011 quake, tsunami, and subsequent nuclear breach.

We must also acknowledge the power of cognitive appraisal. To make an effective cognitive appraisal of a situation, we must have a concrete understanding of the nature of the threat. For example, the victims of the 9/11 terrorist attacks indisputably experienced distress, recognizing the specific dangers in which they were immersed. But in the years following the attacks, airplane travelers also felt some distress when the government's color-coded warning system—created to assess terrorist threat level and keep the public informed—announced an increased terrorist threat level just before

CONNECTION CHAPTER 6

Hindsight bias is the tendency, after an event, to assume that signs were evident and that the event could have been predicted (p. 227).

flying. Curiously, the advisory system created enough public confusion and distress—as well as public distrust about possible political motives for alerts imposed just prior to national elections (Zimbardo, 2004a)—that the system was scrapped in 2011. Here's the point: Uncertainty can add to the perceived stress of a situation. Thus, interpretation, or *cognitive appraisal,* can make the accumulated distress from a series of vague threats evoke essentially the same stress response as a single major traumatic incident.

In light of what you learned in the previous section about the stress response and about stress and our immune system, if you were a government official, what decisions and announcements would you make to the public about potential threats if the nature of the true threat was not yet known?

Check Your Understanding

✓●─[Study and **Review** at **MyPsychLab**

1. **RECALL:** The first stage in Selye's GAS is.

   a. attention
   b. alertness
   c. alarm
   d. activity

2. **RECALL:** In George Slavich's research on social rejection as an external stressor that can lead to depression, what is the chemical messenger that mediates between the external event and the psychological state?

   a. cytokines
   b. telomeres
   c. oxytocin
   d. both a and b

3. **SYNTHESIS:** According to researcher Shelley Taylor, how might the responses of a man and a woman differ in the face of the same stressor?

4. **APPLICATION:** Which of the following stressors would be the most likely to cause the immune system to malfunction and even cause harm?

   a. accidentally slipping and falling on an icy surface
   b. caring for a dying family member for a prolonged period
   c. being rejected by someone you are romantically interested in
   d. receiving a bad grade on an important test

5. **UNDERSTANDING THE CORE CONCEPT:** Describe how our stress response system is well suited to acute stress but less effective in the face of chronic stress.

Answers 1. c **2.** a **3.** Taylor's tend-and-befriend model would predict that the woman would be more likely to seek social support, while the man would be more likely to respond with the aggression characteristic of the fight-or-flight response. **4.** b **5.** The short-lived alarm phase of the GAS sets off a host of physiological changes that help us combat stressors. We can maintain these high levels of "combat readiness" during the resistance phase, but if the stressor is chronic, the exhaustion phase kicks in, and our immune system suffers the effects of depleted resources.

14.3 KEY QUESTION
Who Is Most Vulnerable to Stress?

Why do some people bounce back after severely traumatic experiences such as 9/11 or the death of a loved one, while others are derailed by seemingly minor hassles? The stress we experience is determined not only by the quality and intensity of the stressful situation but also by how we interpret the stressor. In this section, we will focus our attention on the personality characteristics that influence our responses to stressors. A summary of what we will learn is captured in our Core Concept:

Core Concept 14.3

Personality characteristics affect our individual responses to stressful situations and, consequently, the degree to which we are distressed when exposed to potential stressors.

Before we delve into this fascinating field of study, we want to introduce to you a model of the stress–illness relationship that will serve as our guide for the remainder of this chapter.

Figure 14.7 gives you a visual picture of this model, showing how stressors can lead to stress, which in turn can cause physical and mental illness. Please take a close look at this figure before reading further. Note there are two opportunities for intervention: One lies between stressors and stress, and the other occurs between stress and illness. To put it another way, one set of factors can prevent stressors from causing us to feel stress; similarly, a second set of factors can prevent stress from escalating into physical or mental illness. The first set of factors—those that can intervene in the relationship between stressors and stress—we call **moderators** because they moderate or regulate the impact of stressors on our perceived level of stress. Most of them are variations on the concept of cognitive appraisal. In other words, these moderators influence the judgments and interpretations we make of the stressor. It is this set of possible interventions that we explore in this section, beginning with an example.

moderator Factor that helps prevent stressors from causing stress.

Consider this scenario: Demetria and Cory are newlyweds planning their life together. They want to buy a home as soon as possible and hope to start a family. They have recently begun to argue about these issues, however, as their outlooks toward their goals differ markedly. Demetria is optimistic they'll be able to afford the down payment on a home within a year and believes they can achieve this goal as long as they carefully manage their money. Cory is less positive. In his mind, it seems as though every time he gets close to reaching a goal, something gets in the way, and he's sure this will be no different. To him, "what's gonna happen will just happen," and he is afraid they risk disappointment if they get their hopes up about getting the house in a year.

Do you see yourself or someone you know in this example? If the different styles of approaching and perceiving events are long standing, consistent across situations, and similar to those of others, they could be called personality characteristics. Let's examine their impact on the stressor–stress relationship.

CONNECTION CHAPTER 10

Personality is the pattern of characteristics unique to an individual that persists over time and across situations (p. 414).

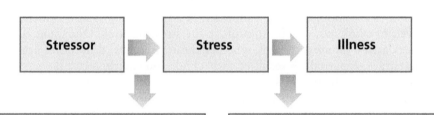

FIGURE 14.7

How Individual Factors Influence Our Stress Response

Oftentimes, stressors cause stress, which in turn can cause illness. However, three categories of psychological responses can intervene in the stress–illness relationship. *Moderators* can help keep stressors from causing stress, *coping strategies* can help prevent stress from leading to illness, and *positive lifestyle choices* can intervene in both places.

Stressor → **Stress** → **Illness**

Moderators
These personality characteristics reduce the impact of stressors on an individual's stress level:

1. Type A/B Personality
2. Locus of Control
3. Optimism
4. Hardiness
5. Resilience

Coping Strategies
These learned skills reduce the impact of perceived stress on physical and mental health:

1. Problem-Focused and Emotion-Focused Coping
2. Cognitive Restructuring
3. Social Comparisons
4. Positive Emotions
5. Finding Meaning

Positive Lifestyle Choices
These factors impact both sides of the equation, acting as moderators *and* as coping strategies:

1. Social Support
2. Exercise
3. Nutrition and Diet
4. Sleep and Meditation

Type A Personality and Hostility

When cardiologists Meyer Friedman and Ray Rosenman (1974) hired an upholsterer to repair furnishings in their waiting room, the upholsterer noticed something the doctors had not: Most of the chairs showed an unusually high degree of wear on the front edges of the seats. When they became aware of this, the doctors wondered whether their patients' heart problems might be related to a certain style of coping with stress—it was as if they were always "on the edge of their seats." The doctors began a series of studies to investigate their hypothesis, and interviews with patients revealed a striking pattern of common behaviors. Impatience, competitiveness, aggressiveness, and hostility—all stress-related responses—were noted again and again. Many also admitted they were notorious workaholics. Friedman and Rosenman ultimately found this collection of attitudes and behaviors not just correlated with heart disease but was actually predictive of it. They dubbed it the Type A pattern: Type A men and women were found to have twice as much risk of heart disease as the Type B individual, who takes a relaxed approach to life (Matthews, 1982).

Since the initial identification of the **Type A** personality, careful research has revealed that it is specifically the anger and hostility common in Type A people that increases risk of heart disease. Time urgency, perfectionism, and competitiveness, without the anger and hostility, are not risk factors. Hostile individuals are less trusting, quicker to anger, and more antagonistic than their nonhostile counterparts. If you're noticing a connection to cognitive appraisal, you are right: Hostile people would be more likely than most to perceive threat in a situation. This interpersonal style makes it more difficult to maintain relationships, which in turn reduces availability of social support. Hostility is also associated with a variety of risky health behaviors—such as smoking, drinking alcohol, and overeating—that themselves increase risk of heart disease (Taylor, 2006).

From a physiological perspective, those high in hostility become aroused more quickly in the face of a potential stressor, exhibit greater levels of arousal, and take more time for their arousal level to return to normal once the stressor has passed (Fredrickson et al., 2000; Guyll & Contrada, 1998). Hostility is also associated with higher levels of cytokines, which can prolong the stress response (Niaura et al., 2002). Researchers aren't yet sure, though, whether these biological differences are entirely genetic in nature or partially a result of early childhood environment: Boys who grow up in families rife with conflict and low in acceptance and support are at greater risk to develop hostility (Matthews et al., 1996). At this time, both nature and nurture are thought to play roles in development of hostility and later heart disease. Clearly, though, there are multiple channels through which hostility promotes heart disease.

Let us reassure you that, while many people may sometimes feel angry, there are important differences between normal anger and a truly hostile personality style. We all feel angry at times in response to a negative situation—in these instances, anger can be healthy and even adaptive: It signals us that something is wrong and provides the energy to take measures to correct the situation. That type of normal anger stands in marked contrast to the hostile personality style, which reflects a long-term pattern of hostile behavior that manifests frequently across a variety of situations. The level of arousal is a distinguishing factor as well: It is reasonable to feel irritated when a slow-moving vehicle blocks you in traffic, but feeling enraged is irrational and dangerous, especially if this becomes a common pattern in your life.

Besides cardiovascular diseases, other illnesses have been linked with Type A habits: allergies, head colds, headaches, stomach disorders, and mononucleosis (Suls & Marco, 1990; Suls & Sanders, 1988). Likewise, the perfectionism characteristic of Type A has been linked to anxiety (about reaching impossible goals) and to depression (from failing to reach them; Joiner & Schmidt, 1995).

Understanding the link between hostility and heart disease and between other Type A behaviors and their associated health risks can help in developing more effective disease prevention. Regular aerobic exercise, relaxation training, and even a program aimed at teaching hostile individuals to speak more slowly and quietly have proven effective at

Type A   Behavior pattern characterized by intense, angry, competitive, or hostile responses to challenging situations.

This basketball coach displays some Type A behaviors. What are they?

reducing risk of heart disease (Taylor, 2006). Comprehensive stress management training may offer some of the most promising benefits, however. One study in particular showed heart attack survivors given stress-management training had half as many heart attacks in the next three years as a control group who received no such training (Friedman & Ulmer, 1984). The researchers concluded: "No drug, food, or exercise program ever devised, not even a coronary bypass surgical program, could match the protection against recurrent heart attacks" afforded by learning to manage stress (p. 141). Thus, even though Type A behavior seems to show up early in life and persist into adulthood, well-designed interventions can be effective in helping Type As who are committed to change in their lifestyles.

Locus of Control

How confident are you that you can make your life turn out pretty much the way you want it to? In our example at the beginning of this section, newlyweds Cory and Demetria were struggling with their differences on this dimension of personality known as **locus of control** (from the Greek *loci,* meaning place). You probably remember our discussion of this concept in Chapter 9 on motivation and Chapter 10 on personality, so you already understand it is a relatively stable pattern of expectations about our ability to influence the outcomes in our life. **Internals** (those with an internal locus of control) generally believe that if they take certain action, they are likely to gain the outcome they desire—diligent studying, for example, will result in good grades. **Externals,** on the other hand, see an unpredictable relationship between their efforts and their outcomes. They are more likely to believe that factors outside their control, such as the fairness of the test or how much the professor likes them, will have a decisive effect on their grades—regardless of how much they study. In the face of a stressful event, internals are more likely to perceive the stressor as manageable than are externals, which leads to lower stress and, ultimately, to a variety of health benefits. And perception of control can, at least to some extent, be learned: Firefighters and other 9/11 personnel who were trained for such disasters experienced lower rates of PTSD in the years following the attacks (Perrin et al., 2007).

Locus of Control, Health, and Longevity A landmark study illuminating the importance of perceived control on health took place in a Connecticut nursing home 30 years ago. Elderly residents on one floor were offered a variety of choices about their daily lives. For example, they were allowed to choose whether and when to watch available movies, how they wanted the furniture and personal items in their rooms arranged, and whether or not to have a plant in their room—which they were responsible for watering. In communications with this group, nursing home staff emphasized the residents' personal responsibility for their own satisfaction; the nursing home staff was happy to help in any way (for example, moving the furniture) on request of a resident. Residents on a different floor, matched on important characteristics such as health and age, acted as the control group. Here the staff took full charge of the residents' care, watering all the plants, assigning movie times, and arranging furniture as per administrative decisions.

The results? After 18 months, the "more responsible" residents were more active, more alert, and happier than the control group. What's more—in an entirely unexpected outcome—locus of control actually affected the residents' life spans. By the end of the study, the mortality rate of the control group was 67 percent higher than that of the group with increased personal responsibility (Rodin, 1986).

Locus of control impacts a wide range of health-related outcomes. In addition to being more likely to wear seat belts, exercise regularly, and pay attention to their diets—all of which have obvious health benefits—internals have better immune systems than do externals (Chen et al., 2003). They get sick less often and recover more quickly from illnesses and surgeries alike (Skinner, 1996). What's more, a strong sense of internal control actually dissolves the well-documented relationship between social class and health: Low-income individuals who have an internal locus of control are just as healthy as those with higher incomes (Lachman & Weaver, 1998).

locus of control   A relatively stable pattern of behavior that characterizes individual expectations about the ability to influence the outcomes in life.

internals   People with an internal locus of control who believe they can do much to influence their life outcomes.

externals   People with an external locus of control who believe they can do little to influence their life outcomes.

CONNECTION CHAPTER 10

Longevity is highly related to the time perspective future orientation of those who are highly conscientious (p. 450).

primary control   Efforts aimed at controlling external events.

secondary control   Efforts aimed at controlling one's reactions to external events.

CONNECTION CHAPTER 10

Individualistic cultures value the individual over the group, whereas *collectivist cultures* prioritize group needs over individual needs (p. 418).

learned helplessness   Pattern of failure to respond to threatening stimuli after an organism experiences a series of ineffective responses.

In hospitals and nursing homes, patients may learn to feel helpless because they are not given opportunities to make decisions or exert control over their own lives.

hardiness   Attitude of resistance to stress, based on a sense of challenge (welcoming change), commitment (engagement), and control (maintaining an internal guide for action).

Culture Affects Locus of Control   Cultural studies have identified an interesting distinction between perceptions of control in Western and Eastern cultures. **Primary control**, prevalent in the West, is the type of control discussed previously: taking action aimed at controlling external events. Eastern cultures are more likely to engage in **secondary control**, which emphasizes controlling one's reactions to events (Rothbaum et al., 1982). A culture's general value system, such as the individualist and collectivist perspectives discussed in Chapter 10, influences the type of control most highly prized and promoted in that culture. In Japan, for example, traditionally a collectivist culture, child-rearing practices encourage development of secondary control. Children are taught to adjust their reactions to a situation to help maintain social harmony. This stands in direct contrast to the individualistic approach to child rearing, which fosters efforts to control the situation itself. Research indicates that both strategies work well in the context of their respective cultures (Weisz et al., 1984). Furthermore, when efforts at primary control fail or are not possible for an individual, engaging in secondary control improves health—a topic we will explore a little later in this chapter.

Is Locus of Control Innate or Learned?   While locus of control does tend to appear early and run in families—factors that often indicate a genetic component—our experiences also impact our expectations. Individuals who repeatedly experience failure when they attempt to escape threatening conditions may simply stop trying, a concept called **learned helplessness**. Evidence of learned helplessness originally came from animal studies performed by Martin Seligman and his colleagues. Dogs receiving inescapable electric shocks soon gave up their attempts to avoid the punishment and passively resigned themselves to their fate (Seligman, 1975, 1991; Seligman & Maier, 1967). Later, when given the opportunity to escape the shocks, the dogs typically did nothing but whimper and accept them. In contrast, a control group of dogs that had not been subjected to previous punishment was quick to escape. Seligman concluded that the experimental group of animals had already learned that nothing they did mattered or altered the consequences, so they passively accepted their fate (Seligman & Maier, 1967).

An experiment by Donald Hiroto (1974) employed human participants in a variation of Seligman's dog research. One at a time, students were placed in a very noisy room; some found a way to turn off the noise, but for others, the noise controls did not work. When the students were sent to a new room and exposed to a different irritating noise, those who had successfully turned off the noise in the previous room quickly found the simple solution in the second room. In contrast, those who had failed in their efforts to shut off the noise earlier just sat in the new room, making no effort to stop the latest stressor. They had already learned to be helpless. Seligman and other scholars see symptoms of the same learned helplessness syndrome in a variety of human populations, including abused and discouraged children, battered wives, and prisoners of war (Overmier, 2002; Yee et al., 2003). Conversely, workers at all skill levels in a variety of professions report greater well-being when given some measure of control over their environment and working conditions (Faulkner, 2001; Zarit & Pearlin, 2003).

Thus, although we may be born with an individual predisposition to an internal or external locus of control, our experiences play a role as well. Research with 9/11 rescue personnel and regarding learned helplessness are just two areas in which this important fact has been illustrated.

Hardiness

One of the most effective stress moderators is **hardiness**, an outlook based on distinctive attitudes toward stress and how to manage it. In contrast with risky Type A behavior, hardiness is a personality pattern that promotes healthy coping. Hardiness first emerged in a large-scale study of managers working for Illinois Bell Telephone (IBT) in the 1970s and 1980s. Salvatore Maddi and a team of researchers from the University of Chicago gathered extensive data from the managers over a period of years, during which federal deregulation of public utilities resulted in massive layoffs and downsizing of IBT. Working conditions, positions, and expectations changed frequently, creating a highly stressful work environment. Two-thirds of the managers experienced negative health consequences, including heart attacks, strokes, depression, and anxiety disorders. The other third—exposed to the same conditions—not only experienced no ill effects but actually appeared to thrive (Kobasa et al., 1979). The distinguishing factor, it turned out, came to be known as hardiness, a concept comprised of three specific characteristics:

- **Challenge.** Hardy people perceive change as a challenge to be overcome and an opportunity to learn and grow—rather than as a threat.
- **Commitment.** Hardy individuals become highly engaged in their lives, demonstrating a focused commitment to involvement in purposeful activity.
- **Control.** Hardy persons have an internal locus of control and are good at problem solving—that is, they have not become victims of learned helplessness.

Let's apply these three factors—known as "the three Cs" of hardiness—to the life of a college student. Suppose that on the day you must prepare for a major test, a friend confides in you about a terrible problem and begs for your help. These two stressors—an important test and a needy friend—could be overwhelming, especially if you are already stretching some of your resources to the limit. But a hardy individual would employ the "three Cs" to reduce the stress of the situation: commitment ("I'm committed to my friend and to preparing for this test; I'm not going to let either one down"); challenge ("Now I have two important things I need to do—what are my options for meeting both needs?"); and control ("I'll study all afternoon, talk to my friend over dinner—after all, I have to eat to keep my brain functioning—then review more before bed").

Hardiness has been shown to reduce the effects of stressful situations across a wide variety of populations: in businesspeople, children, couples, Olympic athletes, military, and law enforcement (Maddi, 2002). And—like locus of control—although some indications of a hardy personality show up early in life, hardiness can also be learned. Researchers have successfully developed hardiness training programs that help individuals learn more adaptive ways of reacting to stressors in their life (Beasley et al., 2003; Maddi, 1987).

Optimism

When you think about your future, do you generally expect good things to happen, or do you worry about all the things that could go wrong? Optimists see a future of bright possibilities; for them, "the glass is half full," whereas pessimists are far less positive, instead "seeing the glass as half-empty." And pessimism isn't simply a case of learned helplessness. "Life inflicts the same setbacks and tragedies on the optimist as on the pessimist," says psychologist Martin Seligman (1991), "but the optimist weathers them better." In general, optimistic people have fewer physical symptoms of illness, recover more quickly from certain disorders, are healthier, and live longer than pessimists do (Bennett & Elliott, 2002; Taylor et al., 2000a). What accounts for the differences? **Optimism** has a direct impact on health in that optimists feel more positive emotions, which in turn boosts their immune systems (Cohen et al., 2003). In addition, optimism aids in coping with stress via more active coping strategies, which we will discuss in the last section of this chapter.

A long-term research program by Seligman (2002) and associates indicates that an optimistic style of thinking makes three particular assumptions, or attributions, about negative events:

- They are the result of specific causes rather than global problems: *"I got a low grade on my last psychology test,"* instead of *"I'm doing badly in school."*
- They are situational rather than personal problems: *"It probably happened because I missed class the day before the exam when the professor gave a review session,"* rather than *"I'm not smart enough to do well."*

optimism An attitude that interprets stressors as external in origin, temporary, and specific in their effects.

• They are temporary, rather than permanent: *"If I'm careful not to miss class anymore, I'll do better on the next test,"* rather than *"I won't be able to recover from this low score."*

Seligman, one of the founders of the International Positive Psychology Association, believes that an optimistic thinking style can be learned. One way to do so, he advises, is by talking to yourself in a particular way when feeling depressed or helpless. Positive self-talk, says Seligman, should concentrate on the meaning and causes of personal setbacks. For example, if a person on a diet splurges on a piece of dessert, instead of thinking, *"Because I've ruined my whole diet, I might as well eat the whole cake!"* she or he should think, *"Well, I enjoyed that, but I know I'm strong enough to stick to this diet most of the time."* In essence, Seligman argues that optimism is learned by adopting a constructive style of thinking, self-assessment, and behavioral planning.

In considering this, you might be reminded of the importance of cognitive appraisal in our stress response and of our Problem for this chapter concerning individual variations in the stress response. Learning to think more optimistically, or to respond with greater hardiness, changes our interpretation of a potential stressor and, thus, lowers our perceived stress. ◉

Watch the **Video** Optimism and Resilience at **MyPsychLab**

Resilience

Actress Christina Applegate would seem to have a charmed life for her chosen profession. Born in Hollywood, California (1971), to an actress/singer mother and father who was a record producer, this beautiful, talented young woman went on to be the lead or supporting actress in dozens of films, television programs and Broadway stage shows. Winning numerous awards for her acting, with a popular fan base, she also hosted *Saturday Night Live* and was top of the list of the Most Beautiful People in 2009 of *People Magazine.*

Beneath that public surface is a life filled with many sources of extreme stress. Her parents divorced soon after her birth. She divorced her first husband a few years after their marriage. Her close friend and former boyfriend died of an apparent drug overdose. The next month, Applegate discovered she had breast cancer that was treated with a double mastectomy operation. Early detection saved her now cancer-free life. How did she deal with the knowledge that she, like her mother before her, had developed cancer? She is reported to have said after her initial diagnosis: "I was just shaking and—and then also immediately, I had to go into 'take-care-of-business-mode.'" In an interview with *USMagazine.com* (2010), Applegate also said she has turned her life around in response to that life-threatening disease. "Right away, you kind of go gung-ho—you don't let any stress in your life, you don't eat any crap (food), you do a total 180 from where you were. You look at life a little bit differently." She has now dedicated herself to raising money for cancer research and treatment through her charitable foundation Right Action for Women.

Like cyclist star Lance Armstrong, whom we met in Chapter 9 on emotion and motivation, Christina Applegate's life has been filled with successes and setbacks. Is luck at work here? Instead, psychologists recognize in the decisions, attitudes, and behavior of both of these celebrities something more precious to well being than either talent or genius: **resilience.**

Resilience is the capacity to adapt and achieve well-being in spite of serious threats to children's development (Masten, 2001). In fact, the word *resilience* comes from a Latin root meaning "buoyant"—literally bouncing amid waves. For more than two decades, most resilience research has focused on this quality in children and adolescents who have dealt with stressful life conditions, including parental neglect or abuse, parental mental illness, bereavement, and other serious risk factors. How could some at-risk children survive and even thrive when others became ill and failed *because* of the same types of risks?

Even at young ages, resilient children are distinguished by an assortment of qualities. They tend to have higher cognitive abilities, greater conscientiousness, better

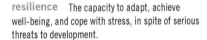

resilience The capacity to adapt, achieve well-being, and cope with stress, in spite of serious threats to development.

A cancer-free Christina Applegate arrives at the "Stand Up To Cancer" event in 2010.

social skills, greater competence, and access to better caretaking or parenting resources (Masten, 2001; Riolli, 2002). Identifying resilient qualities so early in life supports the inference that one is either born resilient or not—it is an innate human quality. More recently, however, attention has been focused on the quality of resilience among adult populations and also on whether resilience can be learned.

One study of resilience among adults examined survivors of the 1999 conflict in Kosovo in the former Yugoslavia. Resilience was related to a combination of personality traits, including extraversion, conscientiousness, and optimism (Riolli, 2002). Of these, optimism in particular holds promise for helping people to become more resilient and less vulnerable or brittle. Also, you may have noticed that resilience seems to overlap somewhat with hardiness, and indeed the two concepts are related. While hardiness is focused on three specific characteristics, though, resilience encompasses a broader range of qualities. And, because hardiness can be developed with the help of specific training programs, perhaps the future will bring similar findings to resilience.

Psychologist George Bonanno of Columbia University is a pioneering figure in the field of bereavement and trauma. His extensive longitudinal and interview research on survivors of all sorts of extremely stressful experiences—from children to adults, in personal loss and major catastrophes—leads to the conclusion that "The ability to rebound remains the norm throughout adult life" (Bonanno, 2009). Based on his research, Bonanno finds that resilience and recovery are far more common than chronic dysfunction or delayed trauma. More detail about Bonanno's findings can be found in Figure 14.8.

Bonanno also coined the term *coping ugly* to refer to a variety of coping strategies that are helpful in stressful situations but might be inappropriate in normal circumstances. Among them are: self-enhancement biases, ego boosting, laughing and smiling, thought suppression, beliefs in personal mastery to survive no matter what, and others. His main point is that most of us survive anything and everything surprising well, and we do so using a range of personally invented strategies. It is a testimony to our human adaptiveness under almost all challenges. (Bonanno & Mancini, 2008).

The adjustments to crises revealed in the stories of Christina Applegate and Lance Armstrong are rather extraordinary, but their resilience need not be rare. In fact, many everyday heroes and "unknown celebrities" overcome terrible difficulties without our awareness. Their ability to deal with pain and challenge is actually the result not of extraordinary forces but of *ordinary magic*. It is the term that resilience researcher Ann

Resilience: The ability of adults in otherwise normal circumstances who are exposed to an isolated and potentially highly disruptive event, such as the death of a close relative or a violent or life-threatening situation, to maintain relatively stable, healthy levels of psychological and physical functioning as well as the capacity for generative experiences and positive emotions.

Recovery: When normal functioning temporarily gives way to threshold or sub-threshold psychopathology (e.g., symptoms of depression or posttraumatic stress disorder [PTSD]), usually for a period of at least several months, and then gradually returns to pre-event levels.

Chronic Dysfunction: Prolonged suffering and inability to function, usually lasting several years or longer.

Delayed Grief or Trauma: When adjustment seems normal but then distress and symptoms increase months later. Researchers have not found evidence of delayed grief, but delayed trauma appears to be a genuine phenomenon.

FIGURE 14.8

Bonanno's Trajectories of Psychological Functioning

The first two trajectories, Resilience and Recovery, are common; the last two, Chronic Dysfunction and Delayed Grief or Trauma, are rare.

Source: Adapted from Bonanno, G. A. (2009). *The Other Side of Sadness: What the New Science of Bereavement Tells Us About Life After Loss.* New York: Basic Books; and Bonanno, G. A., & Mancini, A. D. (2008). The human capacity to thrive in the face of extreme adversity. *Pediatrics, 121,* 369–375.

Masten (2001) uses for normal adaptation processes, which, she argues, make people capable of greater outcomes than we might expect. By expecting more, perhaps we take a step toward greater optimism and resilience in our own lives.

[PSYCHOLOGY MATTERS]

Using Psychology to Learn Psychology

Imagine you have just suffered a loss: a friend picked a fight and insulted you, violating your sense of trust; the one you love doesn't return your feelings and has rejected you; or your family pet has died, leaving you grief stricken though friends insist you should "get over it." Whatever the stress, you aren't sure where to go or to whom you can talk—yet you feel a strong need to express your thoughts and feelings. What can you do? Here's a place to start: Write it out. In the process, you'll learn more about your own psychology.

Why write? Why not just rant and rave and get it out of your system? For one thing, aggressively venting emotions is not enough to relieve stress or support your health; on the contrary, it can even have aggravating or harmful effects (Gross & Psaki, 2004; Smythe, 1998). Conversely, writing about your fears and losses has therapeutic emotional effects (Pennebaker, 1990, 1997; Zimmerman, 2002), and writing about feelings and worries has been found to support the health of patients with immune disorders (Pennebaker, 1997). When you write out your thoughts and feelings, you talk only to and for yourself. With no audience to perform for and no patient listener to please, you can use frank language, tell all, and rest assured you don't have to explain anything. All you need is a place, a time, the materials you need, and commitment to maintain the habit. There are several ways to make the practice easier and more effective:

- Write in any medium that is efficient or comforting to you—it's OK to type at your keyboard, but you may not always have convenient access to your computer. Handwriting is more personally expressive, and you don't have to make it legible—it's for your eyes only. By using a pen and paper, you can not only write but draw or doodle, expressing yourself nonverbally. And a small notebook is inexpensive and easy to keep handy.

- Choose a topic or theme to get you started. If a loss or fear has prompted your writing exercise, start with that. If not, choose an "assignment" that prompts emotions and ideas about important challenges in your life. One professor asks students in a class on psychology of loss to develop a journal of loss, referring either to personal losses or to memorable events such as a terrorist attack or the death of a celebrity and what that has meant to the writer (Harvey & Hofmann, 2001).

- Write out your thoughts as well as your feelings. Focus on finding the meaning in difficult experiences. You may not know the answers (*"Why didn't our relationship last?"*), but you can reason and fantasize (*"Maybe this is a good time for me to be on my own anyway"*). An important purpose in therapeutic writing or talking is to achieve insight, growth, and change. It may also help to write out memories as if telling a story: with a beginning, middle, and end; descriptions of characters and events; and your own conclusions about the "moral of the story" and lessons you have learned (Harvey et al., 1990; Murray, 2002).

- Write in spare moments, setting a goal such as a few pages every week. Write as if you were a reporter, including whatever details seem important (DeSalvo, 2000). Experiment with various forms, such as writing love or hate letters. Identify blessings in disguise or categorize various things you do (e.g., things you do for others versus things you do for yourself; Zimmerman, 2002).

- Stick with it. Make writing a habit, not just a release for the bad times. One researcher found that writing only about trauma intensified the pain and left subjects less able to open up or work it through. So even at times when you don't "need" to write, write a few lines anyway—*because* you feel fine—so you can later remember that you have felt good and remind yourself how you got that way!

Your goal in writing is not to become a great writer (though it's possible!) but to work through your stress, learn about your responses and coping patterns, and heal. You set the goals, you make the rules. In doing so, you might consider how to incorporate some of what you have learned in this section about perceptions and hardiness. Perhaps, through writing, we can focus on improving our abilities to perceive stressors in an adaptive manner. In addition, remember our discussion in the first Core Concept of this chapter about the importance of narratives. But don't let it stress you out! Issue these writing "assignments" to yourself, so you can relax knowing there is no deadline pressure and no grade to worry about.

Check Your Understanding

✓●─ **Study** and **Review** at **MyPsychLab**

1. **RECALL:** In terms of health, the riskiest component of Type A behavior is _____.

   a. hostility   **c.** competitiveness

   b. perfectionism   **d.** time urgency

2. **ANALYSIS:** People who believe they can take action to affect their life outcomes have an _____ locus of control and are more likely to _____.

   a. internal; suffer more frequent frustrations

   b. external; suffer more frequent frustrations

   c. internal; live longer

   d. external; live longer

3. **APPLICATION:** Roz recently got a new assignment at work that she didn't really want. In responding to this change, she decided to see it as an opportunity for growth and to fully commit to doing whatever was necessary to do a good job with it. Which personality characteristic discussed in this section best describes Roz's response?

4. **APPLICATION:** Think of a recent negative event or situation in your own life. According to Martin Seligman, what three attributions should you make in perceiving the event/situation?

5. **UNDERSTANDING THE CORE CONCEPT:** Describe how personality characteristics fit into the stress–illness relationship.

Answers 1. a **2.** c **3.** Hardiness, as evidenced by Roz's high degree of commitment and challenge **4.** Specific (rather than global), situational (rather than personal), and temporary (rather than permanent) **5.** Personality characteristics moderate the relationship between stressors and stress by influencing the way we perceive and interpret stressors. People with more moderators feel less stressed when exposed to stressors and thus have greater resistance to stress.

14.4 KEY QUESTION
How Can We Transform Negative Stress Into Positive Life Strategies?

Is it possible to choose to live a long and healthy life? Or will your health be determined by factors out of your hands, such as your genetic background or your access to health care? After exposure to a traumatic stressor such as an earthquake or a chronic stressor such as the ones we have discussed in this chapter, is there something we can do to reduce its impact on our health?

By now, you've probably gathered that taking a hardy approach to these questions, with an internal locus of control and an optimistic attitude, will increase your odds of success! And there is more good news: Illness and mortality can also be affected by the coping strategies we employ and the lifestyle choices we make (Elliott & Eisdorfer, 1982; Taylor, 2006). As you can see by "reading between the lines" in Table 14.1, many early deaths result from behaviors over which we have control. Stress, of course, is part of the lifestyle equation too. In this section of the chapter, we will explore effective

TABLE 14.1 Number of Deaths for Twelve Leading Causes of Death

> 1. Heart disease: 616,067
> 2. Cancer: 562,875
> 3. Stroke (cerebrovascular diseases): 135,952
> 4. Chronic lower respiratory diseases: 127,924
> 5. Accidents (unintentional injuries): 123,706
> 6. Alzheimer's disease: 74,632
> 7. Diabetes: 71,382
> 8. Influenza and pneumonia: 52,717
> 9. Nephritis, nephrotic syndrome, and nephrosis (kidneys): 46,448
> 10. Septicemia: (bacterial infections): 34,828
> 11. Intentional self-harm (suicide): 34,598
> 12. Assault (homicide): 18,361

Note: In 2007, a total of 23,199 persons died of alcohol-induced causes in the United States. The age-adjusted death rate for alcohol-induced causes for males was 3.2 times the rate for females.

ways of coping with stress, as well as lifestyle choices that can help us ward off the devastating effects of stress through better health. As our Core Concept puts it:

> **Core Concept 14.4**
>
> **Effective coping strategies reduce the negative impact of stress on our health, while positive lifestyle choices can enhance our mental and physical health as well as our overall well-being.**

coping strategy   Action that reduces or eliminates the impact of stress.

Revisiting the model we introduced in the previous section (see Figure 14.7), **coping strategies** work by reducing the impact of stress—once we're feeling it—on our health. In other words, they decrease the effects of stress on our bodies. **Positive lifestyle choices** have the same power to help us cope effectively with stress and have an added benefit: They also act as stress moderators, diminishing the stress we perceive when exposed to stressors. That is, positive lifestyle choices increase our resistance to stress as well as our resistance to illness. We begin this section of the chapter by examining coping strategies that are most useful in combating stress. Then, we examine the lifestyle choices associated with stress reduction and disease prevention. Finally, we will look at the characteristics of people who say they have found happiness and a sense of well-being.

Psychological Coping Strategies

President Obama made a positive lifestyle choice in early 2010 when he was finally able to quit smoking cigarettes.

positive lifestyle choices   Deliberate decisions about long-term behavior patterns that increase resistance to both stress and illness.

defending   Efforts taken to reduce the symptoms of stress or one's awareness of them.

Earlier in the chapter, we saw how the Type A personality, pessimism, and learned helplessness can aggravate the stress response, just as hardiness, optimism, an internal locus of control, and resilience can moderate it. Certainly, we advise that for serious stressors and difficulties, you seek out professional advice and help. (If you don't know a psychotherapist or licensed counselor, ask a trusted instructor or health care provider for a referral.) What can you do on your own, however, to cope effectively with stress? And what exactly is meant by coping?

Defending versus Coping   There are two broad categories of stress management behaviors: defending and coping. **Defending** involves reducing the *symptoms* of stress or reducing one's awareness of them. For example, if you feel stress over an important psychology exam for which you feel unprepared, you might simply defend against that anxious feeling by distracting yourself with some activity that is fun—going to a party or visiting friends. Your defense won't make the problem go away—there will still be an exam, and now you'll be even less prepared for it! But for a brief period, you might feel less stress. Defending has the advantage of alleviating some symptoms like worry, discomfort, or pain; but it has the serious drawback of failing to deal with the stressor. Inevitably stress returns, only now it may be more difficult to alleviate.

In contrast with merely defending against stress, healthy **coping** involves taking action that reduces or eliminates the causes of stress, not merely its symptoms. To cope, you must confront the stress, identify the stressor, and develop a way of solving the problem or reducing the harm it causes you. This means not just feeling better but improving the entire stressful situation. To cope with stress over a looming psychology exam, you must (a) realize you feel unprepared for the exam, (b) identify effective strategies to study for the test, (c) implement the strategies in a timely manner, and (d) take the test. This way you will not only feel prepared, you will be prepared and feel less anxious. Of course, you may have to postpone having fun until after the exam, but you'll enjoy yourself more without the test anxiety. (Remember the Premack principle?)

coping Taking action that reduces or eliminates the causes of stress, not merely its symptoms.

Problem-Focused and Emotion-Focused Coping In general, there are two basic approaches to healthy coping: emotion-focused coping and problem-focused coping. **Problem-focused coping** involves clarifying the stressor and taking action to resolve it. This may involve some advance planning, such as when you are nervous about starting a new school. Problem-focused coping in that situation could involve a visit to the school to figure out where your classes are and to talk with an academic advisor to get some tips for success, thus reducing your anxiety about knowing your way around and about being able to do well. **Emotion-focused coping**, on the other hand, involves efforts to regulate your emotional response to the stressor by identifying your feelings, focusing on them, and working through them. Effective emotion-focused coping must be distinguished from **rumination**, which is dwelling on negative thoughts (rather than emotions); not surprisingly, rumination has been found to compromise our immune systems (Thomsen et al., 2004)—and it doesn't help us feel better either!

Both types of coping can be useful. In general, problem-focused coping is best when there is some concrete action that can be taken to reduce the stressor. In contrast, emotion-focused coping can help at times when you must simply accept a situation or when you need to work through your emotions before you can think clearly enough to act rationally (Folkman & Lazarus, 1980; Zakowski et al., 2001).

Sometimes, the two coping styles work best together. For example, if you get fired from your job, you might start looking for another job (problem-focused) but find you can't focus on the task because you are too angry and confused about being fired. In that type of situation, try some emotion-focused coping to help yourself calm down and think more clearly. You might go for a run or to the gym, talk to a trusted friend, write in your journal, or engage in some other task that helps you work through your feelings. Alternatively, you might take a hot bath, get some rest, or eat something nourishing. Such emotion-focused coping is not merely a defense (as in distracting yourself completely from the problem). Rather, it focuses on processing your emotional responses before they career out of control and become hazardous to your health. Then, when you feel calm and prepared, you can concentrate on what it takes to address the stressor and solve the problem.

> **CONNECTION CHAPTER 4**
>
> The *Premack principle* notes the strategy of using a preferred activity as a reward for completing a less-preferred activity (p. 148).

problem-focused coping Action taken to clarify and resolve a stressor.

emotion-focused coping Regulating one's emotional response to a stressor.

rumination Dwelling on negative thoughts in response to stress, a behavior that compromises the immune system.

Cognitive Restructuring Throughout this chapter, we have recognized the role of cognitive appraisal in the stress–illness relationship. And while the personality factors that make us less vulnerable to stress—such as hardiness and locus of control—are deeply ingrained in our general outlook, with a little conscious effort, we can apply their basic principles to our coping efforts (Kohn & Smith, 2003). **Cognitive restructuring** involves just that: cognitively reappraising stressors with the goal of seeing them from a less-stressful perspective (Meichenbaum & Cameron, 1974; Swets & Bjork, 1990). The approach involves recognizing the thoughts you have about the stressor that are causing anxiety, then challenging yourself to see the situation in a more balanced or realistic manner. Getting fired, for example, offers the opportunity to find a new job that is more enjoyable, offers better pay, or has more potential for advancement. Cognitive restructuring is especially suitable for people experiencing chronic stress. Indeed, it is one of the cornerstones of cognitive–behavioral therapy, which we discussed in the previous

cognitive restructuring Reappraising a stressor with the goal of seeing it from a more positive perspective.

social comparison A type of cognitive restructuring involving comparisons between oneself and others in similar situations.

downward social comparison Comparison between one's own stressful situation and others in a similar situation who are worse off, with the goal of gaining a more positive perspective on one's own situation.

upward social comparison Comparison between one's own stressful situation and others in a similar situation who are coping more effectively, with the goal of learning from others' examples.

Feeling and expressing positive emotions can lengthen your lifespan.

chapter. This approach is more than just putting on a happy face; it puts people into a constructive problem-solving mode that facilitates effective action strategies.

Making **social comparisons** is a type of cognitive restructuring that specifically compares your own situation to others in similar situations. Health psychologist Shelley Taylor (1983) first noted the use of social comparison in a study of breast cancer patients. Some of them engaged in **downward social comparison**, in which they compared their own situations to those of women worse off than they were, which in turn helped them see their illness in a more positive light. (Please note that, in making these downward comparisons, no one is taking pleasure in others' pain; the strategy is simply noticing and acknowledging the existence of grimmer possibilities.) Others engaged in **upward social comparison** and used breast cancer patients who were doing better than they were as models and inspiration for improvement. Corroborating research has demonstrated that both types are effective coping strategies. In a sense, downward social comparisons represent a type of emotion-focused coping—in that the comparison ultimately makes you feel less worried—whereas upward comparisons are a type of problem-focused coping because the models serve as a guide for specific action (Wills, 1991).

Positive Emotions If negative thinking and negative emotions such as hostility are stress inducing, then is the opposite true as well: Are positive emotions health inducing? Several areas of study indicate they may be.

One study investigated this question in a group of Catholic nuns who ranged in age from 75 to 95 years. Researchers gained access to autobiographies the nuns had written just prior to entering the convent (when most were in their early 20s) and measured the emotional content of the writings. Each one-page autobiography was rated for the number of positive, negative, and neutral emotional words used. Clear differences emerged: Nuns who used the most positive-emotion words lived an average of 9.4 years longer than those who expressed the fewest positive emotions! Moreover, expressing a wider variety of positive emotions in their autobiographies increased lifespan by an additional year (Danner et al., 2001).

Cultivating and expressing a sense of humor also buffers the effects of stress. The ability to find something to laugh about during exposure to a stressor not only improves mood but also decreases the physiological impact of the stressor (Dillard, 2007). Having a good sense of humor, as a personality characteristic, also appears to reduce an individual's cognitive appraisal of a stressor (Lefcourt, 2000; Kulper et al., 1993). These findings dovetail with work by Harvard psychologist George Vaillant, whose lifespan study of men noted joy in living as one of the key predictors of health and long life (Vaillant, 1990).

If you don't possess a naturally good sense of humor or don't characteristically experience a lot of positive emotions, you can still benefit from these tools in your coping efforts. Making a conscious effort to note positive moments in your life and to seek out situations in which you find humor and joy can and will improve your life, says positive psychology proponent Martin Seligman in his book *Authentic Happiness* (2002). A poignant expression of this was noted by an AIDS patient, who said this:

> Everyone dies sooner or later. I have been appreciating how beautiful the Earth is, flowers, and the things I like. I used to go around ignoring all those things. Now I stop to try and smell the roses more often, and just do pleasurable things (G. M. Reed, cited in Taylor, 1999).

Finding Meaning Viktor Frankl was a well-respected neurologist in Austria when Nazi forces deported him and his family to a concentration camp. They, along with thousands of other Jews, were subjected to various forms of deprivation, torture, and unspeakable atrocities, and many—including Frankl's wife and parents—died in the camps. Frankl, however, survived, and after the war ended, he made a significant contribution to the field of psychology with his work on the importance of finding meaning in seemingly inexplicable events such as what he had experienced in the camps.

In his seminal work, *Man's Search for Meaning* (Frankl, 1959), he says, "When we are no longer able to change a situation—just think of an incurable disease such as inoperable cancer—we are challenged to change ourselves."

Frankl's hypothesis spawned research investigating the benefit of finding meaning in loss, which has identified two specific types of meaning, **sense making** and **benefit finding.** Following a significant negative life event, people try to make sense of the event in some way so it fits our perception of the world as predictable, controllable, and nonrandom (Tait & Silver, 1989; Tedeschi & Calhoun, 1996). For example, a death might be explained as inevitable if the person had been battling a long illness or if he or she had a history of heavy smoking. In the wake of Hurricane Katrina, discussions of long-standing problems with New Orleans' levees reflected a similar attempt for sense making. Individuals with strong religious beliefs may make sense of loss by attributing it to God's will. A second path to finding meaning lies in recognizing some benefit that ultimately came from the loss, such as a renewed sense of appreciation for life or other loved ones, or discovery of a new path in life.

Successful coping appears to involve both sense making and benefit finding, although at different times. Sense making is the first task people struggle with, but ultimately working through the loss and regaining momentum in life seems to hinge on resolving this first question and moving on to the second (Janoff-Bulman & Frantz, 1997). This may explain why people who have lost a child, individuals coping with an accidental or violent death of a loved one, and others dealing with a loss that defies our perception of the natural order of life often have a harder time recovering from the loss (Davis et al., 1998).

Finding meaning in tragedy, then, is not an easy task. Is there anything that can help? Not surprisingly, perhaps, optimists have an easier time of it than do pessimists, especially with regard to benefit finding (Park et al., 1996). Strong religious beliefs appear to facilitate sense making, particularly with the loss of a child, as evidenced in a study of parents who had lost a child to sudden infant death syndrome (SIDS; McIntosh et al., 1993). And the benefits of social support—which we will explore shortly—are not limited to a particular personality type or to the religious but can play an important role in finding meaning of both types.

Psychological Debriefing: Help or Hindrance? On April 20, 1999, two heavily armed students at Columbine High School in Littleton, Colorado, carried out a planned massacre, fatally gunning down 12 students and a teacher before turning their guns on themselves. Those who survived needed help coping, but so did their horrified loved ones and the larger community. Although the vast majority of trauma survivors recover from early trauma without professional help, community leaders and mental health professionals may initiate counseling sessions—seeking out individuals or gathering groups in meeting spaces—in hopes of reducing posttraumatic stress. After the Columbine massacre, counselors visited all classes regardless of whether individual students had reported problems. Similarly, after the World Trade Center attacks, a program was funded to offer free counseling for New Yorkers—but only a fraction of the predicted number sought help, leaving $90 million in therapy funds unspent (Gittrich, 2003). Don't survivors want help—or isn't such help very effective?

This form of crisis intervention, called **psychological debriefing,** is a brief, immediate type of treatment focusing on venting emotions and discussing reactions to the trauma (McNally et al., 2003). This practice is based on the assumption that it is psychologically healthier to express negative feelings than to keep them inside. This belief, in turn, is based on the ancient concept of **catharsis,** which involves relieving emotional "pressure" by expressing feelings either directly (as by expressing them verbally or hitting a punching bag) or indirectly (as by watching a violent play or movie). Unfortunately, the theory of catharsis doesn't hold up to empirical scrutiny—rather than reducing arousal and feelings of distress, studies show it often prolongs them.

Critical Incident Stress Debriefing (CISD) Recently, a specific type of psychological debriefing known as **critical incident stress debriefing (CISD)** has emerged and taken

sense making One aspect of finding meaning in a stressful situation, which involves perceiving the stressor in a manner consistent with our expectations of the world as predictable, controllable, and nonrandom.

benefit finding The second phase of finding meaning in a stressful situation, which involves seeing some ultimate benefit from the stressor.

psychological debriefing Brief, immediate strategy focusing on venting emotions and discussing reactions to a trauma.

catharsis A theory suggesting that emotional pressure can be relieved by expressing feelings directly or indirectly.

critical incident stress debriefing (CISD) A specific type of psychological debriefing that follows a strict, step-by-step agenda.

center stage in the field of psychological debriefing. CISD programs typically offer group sessions to trauma survivors within 72 hours of the traumatic event; these sessions are two to three hours long and often mandated by organizations (such as by Columbine High School in the aftermath of the shooting and also in many police and fire departments). CISD programs follow a strict agenda that requires participants to first describe the facts of the traumatic event, then recount the immediate cognitive reactions they had to it, followed by their feelings and any symptoms of psychological distress they have begun to notice as a result. Next, program leaders offer information about frequently occurring symptoms and provide referrals for follow-up treatment. This is a commercial program that requires users to pay a fee to the CISD originators in order to employ these tactics.

Is CISD Effective?   Does it really work as advertised? As we have learned, extraordinary claims require extraordinary evidence. Also, remember that we are biased when it comes to emotionally charged topics—our strong desire to find a "cure" can interfere with our ability to think critically about the evidence. In cases like this, it is all too easy to jump on the bandwagon of an exciting new treatment before it has been soundly tested. And while proponents of CISD argue for its effectiveness, very few studies have followed sound methodological procedures to accurately measure the outcomes (Devilly et al., 2006). On the contrary, some trauma experts are cautioning that the procedures of CISD can actually strengthen the memory of a traumatic experience—the opposite of helpful intervention. Moreover, the procedures involved in CISD run contrary to some long-established findings regarding the ineffectiveness of catharsis, which casts further doubt on the true efficacy of the program. The initial skepticism of your authors about this technique has been justified by several systematic evaluations, which have concluded that there is no value of such debriefing after psychological trauma work in helping trauma survivors (Beverley, et al., 1995; McNally et al., 2003).

One comprehensive survey of the effects of such techniques on first responders to the World Trade Center terrorist disaster concludes:

> Psychological debriefing—the most widely used method—has undergone increasing empirical scrutiny, and the results have been disappointing. Although the majority of debriefed survivors describe the experience as helpful, there is no convincing evidence that debriefing reduces the incidence of PTSD, and some controlled studies suggest that it may impede natural recovery from trauma (McNally et al., 2003, p. 45).

CONNECTION CHAPTER 13

Cognitive–behavioral therapies treat maladaptive behavior by helping to change both unwanted cognitions and unwanted behaviors (p. 571).

Cognitive and behavioral therapies that focus on cognitive reappraisal and use well-established procedures to reduce emotional arousal associated with the event may be more effective than CISD, especially when therapy is delivered not immediately but many weeks after the traumatic event (McNally et al., 2003).

These, then, are the coping strategies found to be effective in keeping stress from taking a toll on our health—problem-focused and emotion-focused coping, cognitive restructuring, upward and downward social comparisons, positive emotions, and finding meaning. Each of these factors offers an additional clue to help us understand individual differences in how stress affects us. As you consider your own use of these tools, please remember two things. First, people facing chronic stressors often rely on a combination of strategies. Second, there are also a number of lifestyle choices we can add to our "coping strategies toolbox" and gain the added benefit of moderating stress as well. We turn our attention next to a review of those factors.

Positive Lifestyle Choices: A "Two-for-One" Benefit to Your Health

If you are like most people, you like a bargain! We want the most for our money, the most for our time, and the most for our efforts. The positive lifestyle choices we will discuss in this section are bargains for your health, in that each investment you make in this category gives you not one but two benefits: They act both as moderators and as coping strategies (see Figure 14.7). The more of these you integrate into your life, the better health you will enjoy. Let's start with a little help from our friends.

Social Support   One of the best antidotes for stress is **social support**: the psychological and physical resources others provide to help an individual cope with adversity. Research shows that people who encounter major life stresses, such as the loss of a spouse or job, experience fewer physical and psychological ailments if they have an effective network of friends or family for social support (Billings & Moos, 1985). They are less likely to contract colds and have less risk of depression or anxiety. Similarly, social support has demonstrable health benefits for those with physical disease (Davison et al., 2000; Kelley et al., 1997): Individuals diagnosed with conditions including heart disease, cancer, arthritis, and diabetes all recover more quickly with a good social support network (Taylor, 2006). By contrast, people with few close relationships die younger, on average, than people with good social support networks (Berkman & Syme, 1979; Pilisuk & Parks, 1986)—even when other factors known to affect lifespan, such as health and socioeconomic status, are controlled for. Remarkably, the lack of a reliable support network increases the risk of dying from disease, suicide, or accidents by about the same percentage as does smoking (House et al., 1988).

social support   Resources others provide to help an individual cope with stress.

These women are doing two things to improve their health: spending time with friends and laughing.

Benefits of Social Support   What is it about social support that gives it such power to enhance our health? Research has revealed three specific benefits. *Emotional support* may be what immediately comes to mind when you think of social support, and this indeed is one of its benefits. Having trusted friends and loved ones we can count on during difficult times lends immeasurable relief. *Tangible assistance* comes in the form of specific, task-oriented help, such as rides to the doctor's office or hospital, help with housecleaning, or cooking meals. Finally, *informational support* aims to help an individual better understand the nature of the stressor as well as available resources to cope with it. In the aftermath of a serious auto accident, for example, someone with spinal cord injuries might benefit from information regarding a typical timeline and strategies for recovery but not be mobile enough to get to a computer to research it. A friend can help. And even though social support networks often consist of family and close friends, support groups or other community resources can provide these benefits as well.

Physiologically, social support reduces the intensity and the duration of the arousal associated with the fight-or-flight response. This finding has emerged from experimental studies that first expose participants to a stressor, then measure such responses as their heart rate, blood pressure, and levels of stress hormones either in the presence of social support or alone (Christenfeld et al., 1997). Social support in the form of a friend or loved one provides optimal benefits, but arousal is also reduced when the support comes from a stranger, a video (Thorsteinsson et al., 1998), or even a pet—although dogs somewhat outperform cats in this regard (Allen et al., 2002). And when social support is not present, simply thinking about loved ones even provides some benefit (Broadwell & Light, 1999).

Physical affection, such as hugs, hand holding, and touch, helps combat stress as well. Several studies note lower arousal in women exposed to a stressor when their partners held their hand or gave them a hug—and, recently, this effect was found in men as well (Coan et al., 2006; Light et al., 2005). For both sexes, as in animals, physical contact with a trusted partner raises oxytocin levels, which decreases anxiety and stress. These findings fit nicely with the tend-and-befriend model we introduced earlier in this chapter.

Supporters Reap What They Sow   What impact does social support have on the supporter? People in need of social support sometimes worry they might raise their loved ones' stress levels by asking for help. And while this does sometimes occur—caregivers of Alzheimer's patients, for example, show greater risk of depression and disease—overall, support givers benefit from helping. In fact, one study of married couples measured amounts of support giving and receiving over a 5-year period and found that

Exercise is a good way to reduce stress and improve your general health.

📖⊙ Read about Transformative Exercise at **MyPsychLab**

those who provided more support lived longer (Brown et al., 2003). It is important to note, however, that supporters need support as well.

Exercise For better or worse, our bodies are still better adapted to the strenuous, Stone Age demands of hunting and gathering than to sedentary life in a digital, urban world. Spending our days in relative inactivity at a desk or computer terminal is not a formula for physical or mental health. Unfortunately, while many of us may know this, few are taking it seriously—two-thirds of Americans aren't getting enough exercise, according to the Center for the Advancement of Health (2004).

Just 30 minutes of aerobic exercise per day lowers risk of heart disease, stroke, and breast cancer, among others (Taylor, 2006). It can increase muscle tone and eliminate fat—changes that produce a variety of health benefits. Most importantly, perhaps, it can prolong your life. A long-term study of 17,000 middle-aged men showed that those who were on an exercise regimen (the equivalent of walking 5 hours a week) had mortality rates that were almost one-third lower than their couch-potato counterparts (Paffenbarger et al., 1986). Even smokers who exercised reduced their death rate by about 30 percent.

Regular exercise has not only physical but psychological benefits, including stress reduction (McDonald, 1998) and mental health. For example, a regular aerobic exercise program improved the emotional health of female college students who were mildly depressed (McCann & Holmes, 1984). Another study found that a 20-week physical fitness course could produce measurably lower levels of anxiety in sedentary women (Popejoy, 1967). Exercise programs have also been shown to have a positive effect on self-concept (Folkins & Sime, 1981). And a study of people with depression found that compared to a group receiving antidepressant medication, those assigned to an exercise-only regimen had a similar decline in symptoms. Even better, the exercisers maintained their improvement longer and were less likely to become diagnosed again with depression than were nonexercisers (Babyak et al., 2000). 📖

An exercise-for-health program has several big pluses. Exercise usually requires a change of environment, removing people from their daily hassles and other sources of stress. It also has a physical training effect by putting short-term physical stress on the body, which causes the body to rebound and become physically stronger. Third, when we exercise, we get a boost of endorphins and other pleasure chemicals such as serotonin, which improves our mood and makes us better able to respond effectively to potentially stressful situations. In this way, it moderates stress. The benefit of exercise as a coping strategy lies in its use as a healthy outlet for anger, as well as a facilitator of the cognitive functioning required for good problem solving. These benefits apply to all ages, from preschoolers to the elderly (Alpert et al., 1990).

Despite these advantages, most resolutions to increase exercise are short lived; people often find it difficult to maintain their motivation. Nevertheless, studies show that people can learn to make exercise a regular part of their lives (Myers & Roth, 1997). The keys are (a) finding an activity you like to do and (b) fitting exercise sessions into your schedule several times a week. Having an exercise partner often provides the extra social support people need to stick with their program.

Nutrition and Diet Good health and the ability to cope effectively with stress require a brain that has the nutrients it needs to function well. Fortunately, a balanced diet can provide all the nutrients necessary to accurately appraise potential stressors from a cognitive perspective. When we fuel ourselves with complex carbohydrates instead of simple sugars, for example, we metabolize the nutrients at a more stable pace, which may help keep us from overreacting. Many people, however, grab a fast-food meal or a candy bar instead of taking time for good nutrition. For example, a survey of students in 21 European countries revealed that only about half attempt to follow healthy eating practices. The same study found that women were more likely than men to be conscious of good nutrition (Wardle et al., 1997).

When chronic nutritional deficiencies occur in childhood—when the brain is growing fastest—development can be retarded (Stock & Smythe, 1963; Wurtman, 1982).

TABLE 14.2 Ten Steps to Personal Wellness

1. Exercise regularly.
2. Eat nutritious, balanced meals (high in vegetables, fruits, and grains, low in fat and cholesterol).
3. Maintain a sensible weight.
4. Sleep 7 to 8 hours nightly; rest/relax daily.
5. Wear seat belts and bike helmets.
6. Do not smoke or use drugs.
7. Use alcohol in moderation, if at all.
8. Engage only in protected, safe sex.
9. Get regular medical/dental check-ups; adhere to medical regimens.
10. Develop an optimistic perspective and supportive friendships.

Poor nutrition can have adverse affects on adults too. A diet high in saturated fat increases risk of heart disease and some types of cancer. Excessive salt intake increases risk of high blood pressure. Potassium deficiency can cause listlessness and exhaustion. One should be cautious, however, about going to the other extreme by ingesting large quantities of vitamins and minerals. Overdoses of certain vitamins (especially vitamin A) and minerals (such as iron) are easy to achieve and can cause problems that are even more severe than deficiencies.

What can you do to nurture your health through nutrition? The categories in Table 14.2 are good places to start. We suggest, also, you beware of nutritional fads, including dietary supplements that come with miraculous promises that seem almost too good to be true. Nutrition is a science in its infancy, and much remains to be discovered about its connections to physical and mental health.

Sleep and Meditation In Chapter 8, you learned about the benefits of good sleep. Sleep affects our health and stress in a variety of ways. First, given the link between REM sleep and cognitive functioning, we are reminded that to deal effectively with the cognitive demands of potential stressors, we must get enough sleep to enjoy the long REM periods that come only after about six hours of sleep. In addition to the increased risk of accidents we discussed in Chapter 8, chronic sleep deprivation has been linked to diabetes and heart disease, as well as decreased immune system functioning.

Meditation, which for many years was viewed with skepticism by Westerners, has earned increased consideration due to provocative new findings from a spate of studies. The ancient Buddhist practice of "mindful meditation" originated 2,500 years ago and, translated, means "to see with discernment" (Shapiro et al., 2005). Mindfulness-based stress reduction (MBSR), a modern variation on the Buddhist tradition, aims to increase awareness of one's reactions to stress, become at ease with them, and develop healthier responses. These goals are achieved in part through meditation that teaches the participant first to focus on body sensations and cognitions involved in stress reactions and then to let them go by fully accepting (rather than judging or resisting) them. Research on MBSR indicates that participation in an eight-week training program reduces stress; decreases risk of anxiety, depression, and burnout; and increases immune system functioning (Carlson et al., 2007; Shapiro et al., 2005). This fascinating work is just one example of how, in the 21st century, the pursuit of health is relying increasingly on East–West collaborations.

Putting It All Together: Developing Happiness and Subjective Well-Being

Making changes to live a healthier life can lead to a feeling-good state that researchers call **subjective well-being (SWB),** a psychologically more precise term for what you might call "happiness." Do you usually have that feeling?

subjective well-being (SWB)   An individual's evaluative response to life, commonly called happiness, which includes cognitive and emotional reactions.

| 20% | 46% | 27% | 4% | 2% | 1% | 0% |

FIGURE 14.9

The Faces Scale

"Which face comes closest to expressing how you feel about your life as a whole?" Researchers often use this simple scale to obtain people's ratings of their level of well-being. As the percentages indicate, most people select one of the happy faces.

Source: Andrews, F. M., & Withey, S. B. (1976). The faces scale. *Social indicators of well-being: Americans' perception of life quality* (pp. 207, 306). New York: Plenum Publishers. Copyright © 1976 by Plenum Publishers. Reprinted by permission of Springer Science and Business Media.

We cannot observe happiness directly. Instead, in SWB studies, researchers rely on respondents' own ratings of their experiences, answers to questions about what they find satisfying, and assessments of their well-being, mood, or success (Diener, 1984, 2000). To avoid confusion about what words like *well-being* mean, researchers also use nonverbal scales like the one in the smiley-faces in Figure 14.9 (Andrews & Withey, 1976).

Happiness, or SWB, is an increasingly popular subject of study with psychologists, evident in the emerging field of positive psychology. Accumulating research (Myers, 2000; Myers & Diener, 1995) shows that, despite many individual differences, SWB is defined by three central components:

1. **Satisfaction with present life.** People who are high in SWB like their work and are satisfied with their current personal relationships. They are sociable and outgoing, and they open up to others (Pavot et al., 1990). High-SWB people enjoy good health and high self-esteem (Baumeister et al., 2003; Janoff-Bulman, 1989, 1992).

2. **Relative presence of positive emotions.** High SWBs more frequently feel pleasant emotions, mainly because they evaluate the world around them in a generally positive way. They are typically optimistic and expect success (Seligman, 1991). They have an internal locus of control and are able to enjoy the "flow" of engaging work (Crohan et al., 1989; Csikszentmihalyi, 1990).

3. **Relative absence of negative emotions.** Individuals with a strong sense of subjective well-being experience fewer and less-severe episodes of negative emotions such as anxiety, depression, and anger. Very happy people are not emotionally extreme. They are positive (but not ecstatic) most of the time, and they do report occasional negative moods (Diener & Seligman, 2002).

What underlies a healthy response on these dimensions? Twin studies show that feelings of well-being are influenced by genetics (Lykken & Tellegen, 1996), but biology is not destiny: Environmental effects are revealed in studies showing that people feel unhappy if they lack social support, are pressured to pursue goals set by others, and infrequently receive positive feedback on their achievements. Accordingly, experts in this field suggest that feelings of well-being require the satisfaction of (a) a need to feel competent, (b) a need for social connection or relatedness, and (c) a need for autonomy or a sense of self-control (Baumeister et al., 2003; Ryan & Deci, 2000).

So who are the happy people? What characteristics and experiences are linked with feelings of subjective well-being and happiness? Before reading further, take a moment to consider whether you think some groups of people are happier than others. If so, which ones? A review of the SWB evidence by Myers and Diener (1995) shows that:

• **Younger (or older, or middle-aged) people are not happier than other age groups.** SWB cannot be predicted from someone's age. Although the causes of their happiness may change with age (Inglehart, 1990), an individual's SWB tends to remain relatively stable over a lifetime.

- **Happiness has no "gender gap."** While women are more likely than men to experience anxiety and depression, and men are more at risk for alcoholism and certain personality disorders, approximately equal numbers of men and women report being fairly satisfied with life (Fujita et al., 1991; Inglehart, 1990).

- **There are minimal racial differences in happiness.** African Americans and European Americans report nearly the same levels of happiness, with African Americans being slightly less vulnerable to depression (Diener et al., 1993). Despite racism and discrimination, members of disadvantaged minority groups generally seem to think optimistically—by making realistic self-comparisons and by attributing problems more to unfair circumstances than to themselves (Crocker & Major, 1989).

- **Money does not buy happiness.** It is true that people in wealthier societies report greater well-being. However, except for extremely poor nations like Bangladesh, once the necessities of food, shelter, and safety are provided, happiness is only weakly correlated with income. Poverty may be miserable, but wealth itself cannot guarantee happiness (Diener & Diener, 1996; Diener et al., 1993). The happiest people are not those who get what they want but rather those who want what they have (Myers & Diener, 1995).

- **Those who have a spiritual dimension in their lives most often report being happy (Myers & Diener, 1995).** This may result from many factors, including a healthier lifestyle, social support, and optimistic thinking. Whatever the reasons, spiritually involved people enjoy, on average, better mental and physical health (Seybold & Hill, 2001).

These findings tell us that life circumstances—one's age, sex, race, nationality, or income—do not predict happiness. The key factors in subjective well-being appear to be psychological traits and processes, many of which you have learned about in this chapter or elsewhere in this book. It is impressive to see how well people can adapt to major changes in their lives and still feel happy. For example, while the moods of victims of spinal cord injuries were extremely negative shortly after their accidents, several weeks later, they reported feeling even happier than they had been before sustaining their injuries (Silver, 1983).

It is possible to work at creating sustained happiness in your life, according to psychologist Sonja Lyubomirsky (2007), in the summary of her many years of scientific study of this elusive concept, *How of Happiness*. To do so involves a kind of social-emotional fitness training that encourages focusing on positive emotions, creating vibrant social support networks around yourself, goal setting, making and keeping commitments, working to stay healthy with an active life style, and being sociocentric, making others feel special. There is now a Happiness "app" you can buy for your mobile phone that gives daily exercises and activities that are fun and healthful.

Overall, studies of happiness and well-being show that people are exceedingly resilient. Those who undergo severe stress usually manage to adapt. Typically, they return to a mood and level of well-being similar to—or even better than—that prior to the traumatic event (Headey & Wearing, 1992). Using effective coping strategies and making smart lifestyle choices both increase the likelihood of positive outcomes. These, then, are the final components in our search to understand individual differences in the impact of stress on our health.

[PSYCHOLOGY MATTERS]

Behavioral Medicine and Health Psychology

Amazingly, 93 percent of patients don't follow the treatment plans prescribed by their doctors (Taylor, 1990). Obviously, this can have terrible consequences. Accordingly, the need to understand why people fail to take their medicine, get little exercise, eat too much fat, and cope poorly with stress has stimulated the development of two new fields: *behavioral*

behavioral medicine   Medical field specializing in the link between lifestyle and disease.

health psychology   Field of psychology that studies psychosocial factors that contribute to promoting health and well being, and also those that influence illness, with the goal of educating the public about developing healthier life styles.

medicine and *health psychology*. **Behavioral medicine** is the medical field that links lifestyle and disease. **Health psychology** is the comparable psychological specialty. Practitioners in both fields are devoted to understanding the psychosocial factors influencing health and illness (Taylor, 1990, 2006). Among their many concerns are health promotion and maintenance; prevention and treatment of illness; causes and correlates of health, illness, and dysfunction; and improvement of the health care system and health policy (Matarazzo, 1980).

Both behavioral medicine and health psychology are actively involved in the prevention and treatment of trauma and disease that result from stressful or dangerous environments and from poor choices with regard to nutrition, exercise, and drug use. Both are emerging disciplines in countries all over the world (Holtzman, 1992). The two fields overlap, and the differences between them are ones of emphasis. Psychologists have brought increased awareness of emotions and cognitive factors into behavioral medicine, making it an interdisciplinary field rather than an exclusively medical specialty (Miller, 1983; Rodin & Salovey, 1989). Both fields also recognize the interaction of mind and body and place emphasis on preventing illness as well as on changing unhealthy lifestyles after illness strikes (Taylor, 1990, 2006).

But—as the saying goes—old habits die hard. To help patients change long-held habits that are harmful to their health, social psychologists have identified the specific persuasive strategies that are most effective (Zimbardo & Leippe, 1991). For example, research shows that people are more likely to comply with requests when they feel they have freedom of choice. Therefore, instead of demanding that a patient strictly adhere to one course of treatment, a physician could offer the patient several options and ask him or her to choose one. Studies also suggest that patients are most likely to adhere to physicians' requests when they get active social support from friends and family (Gottlieb, 1987; Patterson, 1985). And one landmark study of heart disease prevention (see Figure 14.10) found that specific skills training, such as workshops designed to help participants implement positive changes to their health habits, was the key that resulted in greatest change (Maccoby et al., 1977).

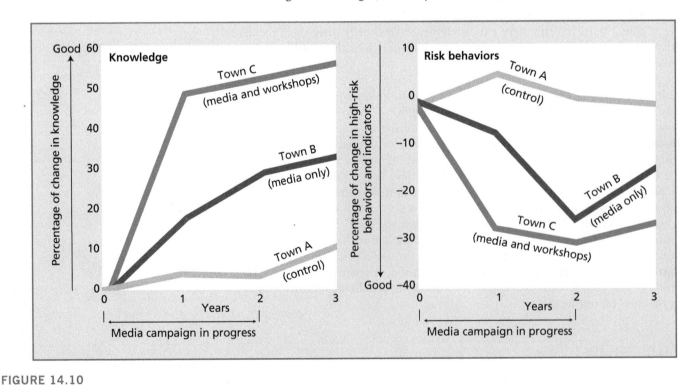

FIGURE 14.10

Response to Campaign for Healthy Change

Town A, whose residents received no mass media campaign for heart-healthy behavior, showed the least knowledge gain over two years. Town B residents, exposed to a media campaign, showed significant improvement. Knowledge gain was greatest for residents of Town C, whose residents participated in intense workshops and instruction sessions for several months prior to the media blitz. As knowledge increased, risk behaviors (bad health habits) and signs (indicators) decreased.

Overall, the field of psychology has contributed numerous findings and strategies—based on solid scientific evidence—that can be applied to our efforts to improve our health, both physically and mentally. For example, behavioral principles discussed in Chapter 4 can be combined with what we know about good thinking strategies (from Chapter 6) and, indeed, often are combined in cognitive–behavioral therapy. Principles of emotion and motivation—the topics of Chapter 9—provide additional insight into factors affecting our emotional health and the behaviors that support our basic needs for food, social support, and other basic needs. You can apply many of these same principles on your own as you work toward maximizing your health and wellness—and we wish you well on your journey!

Check Your Understanding

✓●─ **Study** and **Review** at **MyPsychLab**

1. **ANALYSIS:** Mai was recently in a car accident. In coping with the situation, she has focused on getting estimates for her car repair, seeking medical treatment, and working with her insurance agent to obtain compensation for the expenses of the car repair and her medical needs. What type of coping strategy is Mai employing?

2. **RECALL:** In coping with a loss, efforts to make sense of what happened or to find some ultimate benefit from the loss are examples of _____, which is an _____ coping strategy.

    a. finding meaning; effective
    b. finding meaning; ineffective
    c. emotion-focused coping; effective
    d. emotion-focused coping; ineffective

3. **APPLICATION:** Think of a recent stressor in your own life. Now identify at least two ways that you can use cognitive restructuring to reduce the impact of the stressor on your health.

4. **RECALL:** Name at least four lifestyle choices you can make that will reduce the impact of stress on your health.

5. **UNDERSTANDING THE CORE CONCEPT:** _____ reduce the effects of stress on our health, while _____ decrease our vulnerability to both stress and to stress-related illness.

    a. Stress moderators; coping strategies
    b. Positive lifestyle choices; stress moderators
    c. Positive lifestyle choices; coping strategies
    d. Coping strategies; positive lifestyle choices

Answers 1. Problem-focused coping **2.** a **3.** You can compare your situation to those who are worse off, which should make you see your situation in a different perspective. You can also observe people in similar situation who are coping better than you are and can learn from their examples. **4.** You can seek social support, exercise regularly, eat a healthy diet, get adequate sleep, and meditate. **5.** d

---

CRITICAL THINKING APPLIED

Is *Change* Really Hazardous to Your Health?

The more we hear about the links between stress and illness, the more we might wonder if our own stress levels put us at risk. In this chapter, we have discussed a variety of factors that impact the stress–illness relationship. At least one issue, however, remains in question: To what extent do major life changes impact our vulnerability to illness?

Recall the Social Readjustment Rating Scale (SRRS) introduced in the first section of this chapter. Like many students, you probably calculated your own score in the *Do It Yourself!* box on page 610. But how should you interpret your score? If you scored high, does that mean you are at greater risk for illness?

What Are the Critical Issues?

Recall, first, that the SRRS lists 43 life events that purport to be stressful. Given what we've learned about the importance of cognitive appraisal in determining how stressful a situation is to an individual, we should probably take a close look at the list of events to see if each one really would qualify as a stressor in our own lives.

Does the reasoning avoid common fallacies? The SRRS can allegedly predict your risk of illness based on the events of the past year of your life. In other words, it presents a cause–effect hypothesis that the number of LCUs you have experienced in the last year will cause a particular risk of illness. Are the research findings in support of the LCU–illness relationship really causal, or are they merely correlational?

Extraordinary Claims Require Extraordinary Evidence. Second, if the claim that a quick and simple self-administered test can determine your risk for illness strikes you as extraordinary, you might be right. As we have learned, answers to questions psychological are rarely simple—humans are complex, and so are the explanations for our thoughts, feelings, and behaviors. At the very least, we might wonder if the SRRS oversimplifies the relationship between life events and illness.

Does the Issue Require Multiple Perspectives?

Finally, we must acknowledge the many other factors involved in the link between stress and illness—such as those we have studied in this chapter—and ask what other perspectives might help explain the relationship between stress and illness.

What Conclusions Can We Draw?

In the first 15 years after it was published, the SRRS was used in more than 1,000 studies worldwide (Holmes, 1979), and research consistently found correlations between scores on the SRRS and both physical and behavioral symptoms. People with higher scores on the scale were more at risk for heart attacks, bone fractures, diabetes, multiple sclerosis, tuberculosis, complications of pregnancy and birth, decline in academic performance, employee absenteeism, and many other difficulties (Holmes & Masuda, 1974). High SRRS scores among federal prisoners were even associated with the length of their prison sentences. And the test was effective across cultural boundaries too: Both male and female respondents were found to rate events with similar scores (Holmes & Masuda, 1974), and ratings were also validated with Japanese, Latin American, European, and Malaysian samples.

However, the number of LCUs accumulated during the previous year is only a modest predictor of changes in a person's health (Johnson & Sarason, 1979; Rahe & Arthur, 1978). Many other factors—such as cognitive appraisal, stress moderators, and coping strategies—can intervene in the stress–illness relationship.

Moreover, the implication that stressful events cause illness is misleading (Dohrenwend & Shrout, 1985; Rabkin & Struening, 1976). The correlational data merely show a relationship between certain life changes and health; the research does not show that life changes are the cause of illness. The reverse could also be true: Illness can sometimes be the cause of life changes—someone who frequently gets colds or the flu is more likely to have problems at school, at work, and in relationships, for example. And remember the possibility of a third variable driving the relationship: Several other factors we've studied, such as economic status or Type-A hostility, could also be affecting both the frequency of life changes and the risk of illness.

The importance of multiple perspectives is critical to a thorough and accurate understanding of the stress–illness relationship. Let's review what we know about stress and health from the major perspectives we used to learn about psychology in this text:

- The *biological perspective* clearly plays a role in an individual's vulnerability to stress-related illness. We have seen that our hereditary makeup predisposes us to certain illnesses, such as heart disease, diabetes, obesity, and many forms of cancer. In addition, genetics probably gives some of us a better chance of being optimistic, hardy, or resilient—just as others of us are more at risk for hostility and other negative emotions.

- The *behavioral perspective* influences stress and illness in the health habits we learn as children growing up, in situations of learned helplessness, and in the coping strategies we see modeled by our parents and others in our immediate social environment. Likewise, the *sociocultural context*—the culture in which we live—creates social norms that influence these learned habits and strategies. Currently, for example, in Western culture, we receive mixed messages about health. On one hand, we hear a lot about the importance of a healthy diet and regular exercise. On the other hand, however, the fast-paced nature of our culture—combined with a barrage of ads for fast food—encourages us to grab a burger and fries, then sit on the couch and watch television instead of working out and preparing a healthy meal.

- The *cognitive perspective* helps us understand why, in a particular culture, individual health habits and perspectives vary. Someone with an internal locus of control, for example, would be more likely than an external to pay attention to diet and exercise in pursuit of a healthy life. Likewise, an optimistic thinker or someone high in hardiness would be more likely to perceive certain life events as possibilities than as threats. In general, people's chances of incurring an illness may be more related to their interpretations and responses to life changes than to the changes themselves (Lazarus et al., 1985).

- The *developmental perspective* illuminates certain aspects of stress and health as well. College students, for example—who are primarily in early adulthood—are at change points in their lives and tend to get high scores; it is not clear, however, if they are more at risk for illness. Youth may offer some protection. Similarly, as our bodies age and our cells become less effective at regeneration, we develop greater susceptibility to illness in late adulthood. It is possible, though, that older adults who have mastered the challenges of generativity and integrity may offset their physical vulnerability with a better system of stress moderators and coping strategies. Much research remains to be done at the intersection of developmental and health psychology.

- The *whole-person perspective* explains many of the personal qualities that have an impact on an individual's vulnerability to stress. Locus of control, optimism, hardiness, resilience, and Type A behavior all originated in the study of personality psychology, and we have seen how these factors moderate an individual's response to stressors. Likewise, traits such as openness to experience and conscientiousness probably affect the degree to which individuals are willing to try new coping strategies or lifestyle habits, as well as their likelihood of sticking to the changes once they've made them.

Clearly, then, there is much more to the relationship between stress and illness than the particular life events you experience. A high score does not mean that illness is certain, nor does a low score guarantee health. People differ in their abilities to deal with change because of genetic differences, general physical condition, personality and outlook, lifestyles, and coping skills. The SRRS takes none of these factors into account, but it remains the most widely used measure of stress-related risk for illness.

Should you, then, pay attention to your SRRS score? We offer it as one source of information about your own possible vulnerability—and we trust that you will interpret your score with caution. Overall, we hope you will keep in mind the many tools you have accumulated that, together, can help you respond more effectively to potential stressors—and ultimately live a longer and healthier life.

CHAPTER SUMMARY

((•—[**Listen** to an audio file of your chapter at **MyPsychLab**

PROBLEM: Were the reactions and experiences of the 9/11 firefighters and others at the World Trade Center attacks typical of people in other stressful situations? And what factors explain individual differences in our physical and psychological responses to stress?

- Surviving firefighters had a variety of responses to their involvement in the WTC disaster, including physical, behavioral, cognitive, and emotional stress responses. Aside from physical injuries and memories peculiar to this particular event, their responses were typical of others who have experienced stressful situations.

- Despite a cluster of similar symptoms that occur regardless of the stressor, research is revealing some response differences that depend on whether the stressor involves personal loss,

humiliation or rejection, experience of a catastrophe, and possibly other factors.

- Regardless of the cause, however, stress must be understood from multiple psychological perspectives, including the biological, behavioral, developmental, social-cultural, cognitive, and whole-person perspectives.

- There are also individual differences in our responses to stress. These depend on the intensity and duration of the stressor, culture background, coping strategies, social support, stress *moderators*, as well as other stressors present in our lives. Shelly Taylor has also suggested that women and men have different response styles in the face of stress.

14.1 What Causes Distress?

[Core Concept 14.1 **Traumatic events, chronic lifestyle conditions, major life changes, and even minor hassles can all cause a stress response.**]

Stressors are external events that cause internal stress responses, both psychological and emotional ones, termed **distress**, and biological and physiological reactions. And while **cognitive appraisal** influences our individual responses to stressors, there are several major categories of events that typically cause stress.

Traumatic stressors include natural disasters, acts of **terrorism**, or sudden personal loss such as the death of a loved one or an unforeseen breakup. All of these situations occur with little or no warning and almost always cause extreme stress in the immediate aftermath of the event. Research indicates that about 20 percent of survivors of natural disaster remain distressed after one year, while as many as 75 percent of those exposed to a terrorist attack report continued worry at the one-year mark. Repeated media coverage of the event often exacerbates and prolongs the effects and can also cause stress in people who were not directly exposed to the event in a phenomenon known as **vicarious traumatization. Grief** is a normal, healthy process in response to a personal loss, and the humiliation associated with rejection, such as that caused by **targeted rejection**, can put an individual at increased risk for depression.

Posttraumatic stress disorder (PTSD) can occur in individuals who have been exposed to severe circumstances such as

combat, rape, or other violent attack. Symptoms of PTSD can be cognitive, behavioral, and emotional, as evidenced (for example) by difficulty concentrating, an exaggerated "startle response," and survivor's guilt. About 8 percent of Americans will experience PTSD at some time in their lives, with symptoms lasting more than ten years in more than one-third of the cases. Combat personnel may be especially at risk for PTSD, and military psychologists are working increasingly to develop and provide more effective education and treatment for combat veterans and their families.

Chronic stressors have a more gradual onset and are longer lasting than traumatic events. **Societal stressors** such as poverty and unemployment, as well as difficulties at home, school, or work, are one type of chronic stressor. Another is **burnout**, which is a syndrome of emotional exhaustion, physical fatigue, and cognitive weariness that results from demanding and unceasing pressures at work, at home, or in relationships. **Compassion fatigue** is found in medical and psychological professionals as well as caregivers and other individuals who spend a great deal of time caring for others. Research in this area offers at least five steps caregivers and service providers can take to reduce their risk of compassion fatigue.

Major life changes—whether positive or negative—can be a source of stress as well, in that they involve changes in our daily routines and adaptation to new situations and environments. Finally, minor **hassles** such as computer crashes or an incessantly barking dog can accumulate and cause stress that adds up over time.

14.2   How Does Stress Affect Us Physically?

> **Core Concept 14.2** The physical stress response begins with arousal, which stimulates a series of physiological responses that in the short term are adaptive but that can turn harmful if prolonged.

When faced with **acute stressors**, our bodies are equipped with amazing abilities to meet the challenges effectively. The **fight-or-flight response** is produced by the autonomic nervous system and includes such immediate changes as accelerated heart rate, increased respiration and blood pressure, perspiration, and pupil dilation. A more comprehensive explanation of our response to stress is offered by Hans Selye's **GAS**. A three-phase system, the GAS begins with the **alarm phase**, then progresses into the **resistance phase** and finally the **exhaustion phase** if the stressor is chronic in nature. Under such circumstances, the resources that so effectively helped us combat an acute stressor become depleted, resulting in a host of physical and emotional symptoms. Consequently, we become more vulnerable to illness. While the fight-or-flight response has been well documented in both animals and humans, psychologist Shelley Taylor notes an alternative pattern of response to stress. Her **tend-and-befriend** theory suggests that social support seeking can be a more effective response to stress when protection or survival of offspring is involved. These models complement each other rather than competing with each other in helping us understand the complex human stress response.

The field of **psycho-neuroimmunology** tries to understand how stress causes illness by studying brain–body relationships. Research in this area has revealed that the central nervous system and the immune system remain in constant communication with each other in response to stress. **Cytokines** are proteins that fight infection but, under prolonged stress, produce feelings of listlessness and depression. One way in which stress affects physical health is by accelerating the rate at which cells age, which can be measured by examining the length of **telomeres**. Shorter telomeres are associated with several diseases as well as with early death. On the positive side, cognitive appraisals affect cell aging and thus play an important role in the stress–illness relationship.

14.3   Who Is Most Vulnerable to Stress?

> **Core Concept 14.3** Personality characteristics affect our individual responses to stressful situations and, consequently, the degree to which we are distressed when exposed to stressors.

Stress moderators reduce the impact of stressors on our perceived level of stress. Most of them function as variations of cognitive appraisal (although often on a nonconscious level). Hostile individuals are more likely to perceive stress in the face of a stressful situation and consequently have twice the risk of heart disease. Fortunately, stress-management programs have proven effective at reducing these individuals' response to stress and their resulting health vulnerability.

Locus of control is a second personality characteristic that has an impact on the stressor–stress relationship. People with an **internal** locus of control have greater resistance to stress than do **externals**, probably as a result of their perceived capability to take some action to ameliorate it. Locus of control has been found to affect not only stress but also health and longevity. While locus of control may have some genetic underpinnings, our experiences also influence it, as evidenced by research on **learned helplessness**. From a cultural perspective, **secondary control** involves controlling one's reactions to events rather than controlling the events themselves and is more prevalent in Eastern cultures. Research has found both types of control to be effective in the cultures in which they operate.

Hardiness is an outlook based on three Cs—a perception of internal control, of change as a challenge rather than a threat, and of commitment to life activities rather than alienation or withdrawal. Individuals with a hardy attitude exhibit greater resistance to stress. Similarly, optimistic people feel less stressed in the face of stressful situations, as they are more likely to focus on the positives rather than the negatives of the situation. **Optimism** is also characterized by specific, situational, and temporary attributions about negative situations. Both hardiness and optimism, like locus of control, appear to have some biological underpinnings but can be improved with well-designed training programs. **Resilience** is the ability to rebound and adapt to challenging circumstances and is related to optimism and hardiness, as well as social skills, cognitive abilities, and resources such as caring parents or support providers.

externals (p. 623)
hardiness (p. 624)

internals (p. 623)
learned helplessness (p. 624)
locus of control (p. 623)
moderator (p. 621)
optimism (p. 625)
primary control (p. 624)
resilience (p. 626)
secondary control (p. 624)
Type A (p. 622)

14.4 How Can We Transform Negative Stress Into Positive Life Strategies?

[Core Concept 14.4 **Effective coping strategies reduce the negative impact of stress on our health, while positive lifestyle choices can enhance our mental and physical health as well as our overall well-being.**]

Coping involves taking action that reduces or eliminates the causes of stress rather than just the symptoms of stress. **Problem-focused coping** is accomplished by specific actions aimed at resolving a problem or stressor, whereas **emotion-focused coping** relies on efforts to regulate our emotional response to stress. Both types of coping can be useful and sometimes best work together. **Cognitive restructuring** is another type of effective **coping strategy** and involves modifying our perceptions of the stressor or our reactions to it. Cognitive restructuring can include **upward** and **downward social comparisons**.

Cultivating positive emotions, including humor, also helps reduce the effects of stress on our health, as can efforts to find meaning in the stressful situation. In finding meaning, making sense of the event appears to be the first step, but those who ultimately succeed in finding meaning in tragedy must also identify some benefit of the event or situation. **Psychological debriefing**, which in some cases takes the form of **critical incident stress debriefing (CISD)**, has been found to be relatively ineffective in reducing the link between stress and illness.

A variety of **positive lifestyle choices** carry a two-for-one benefit to the stress–illness puzzle: They can increase our resistance to stress and also decrease our vulnerability to stress-related illness. **Social support** may be the most important of these lifestyle factors, as people with stronger social support live longer and healthier lives than those with little or no support. Social support is helpful in that it carries emotional, tangible, and informational benefits. Regular aerobic exercise has both physical and psychological benefits and has been found to reduce the impact of stress on our health. Similarly, a healthy diet, adequate sleep, and even meditation have been found to decrease our vulnerability to stress and illness.

Subjective well-being (SWB) includes satisfaction with life, prevalence of positive emotions, and absence of negative emotions. Like many of the concepts we have studied, an individual's SWB is influenced both by heredity and by environment. Neither age nor wealth predicts happiness—happy people can be found in the youngest and the oldest, the richest and the poorest, and even in victims of serious illness or life-changing injury.

behavioral medicine (p. 640)
benefit finding (p. 633)
catharsis (p. 633)
cognitive restructuring (p. 631)
coping (p. 631)
coping strategy (p. 630)
critical incident stress debriefing (CISD) (p. 633)
defending (p. 630)
downward social comparison (p. 632)
emotion-focused coping (p. 631)

health psychology (p. 640)
positive lifestyle choice (p. 630)
problem-focused coping (p. 631)
psychological debriefing (p. 633)
rumination (p. 631)
sense making (p. 633)
social comparison (p. 632)
social support (p. 635)
subjective well-being (SWB) (p. 637)
upward social comparison (p. 632)

CRITICAL THINKING APPLIED

Is *Change* Really Hazardous to Your Health?

The relationship between life change events and illness, as indexed by the SRRS, is much more complex than originally thought. While extreme high and low scores offer some useful predictions of probabilities of future stress-related effects, they do not include all the many other factors outlined in this chapter. Illness can be caused by prolonged exposure to situational stressors, but that link is moderated by a host of cognitive, affective, social and cultural factors. How we interpret the stressor, how we have learned to cope, the social support we can rely on, and other processes can alter that link of external stressor and personal health response.

DISCOVERING PSYCHOLOGY **VIEWING GUIDE**

Watch the following video by logging into MyPsychLab (www.mypsychlab.com).
After you have watched the video, answer the questions that follow.

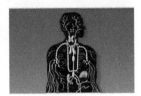

PROGRAM 23: **HEALTH, MIND, AND BEHAVIOR**

Program Review

1. How are the biopsychosocial model and the Navajo concept of *hozho* alike?
   a. Both are dualistic.
   b. Both assume individual responsibility for illness.
   c. Both represent holistic approaches to health.
   d. Both are several centuries old.

2. Dr. Wizanski told Thad that his illness was psychogenic. This means that
   a. Thad is not really sick.
   b. Thad's illness was caused by his psychological state.
   c. Thad has a psychological disorder, not a physical one.
   d. Thad's lifestyle puts him at risk.

3. Headaches, exhaustion, and weakness are
   a. not considered to be in the realm of health psychology.
   b. considered to be psychological factors that lead to unhealthful behaviors.
   c. usually unrelated to psychological factors.
   d. considered to be symptoms of underlying tension and personal problems.

4. When Judith Rodin talks about "wet" connections to the immune system, she is referring to connections with the
   a. individual nerve cells.
   b. endocrine system.
   c. sensory receptors.
   d. skin.

5. What mind–body question is Judith Rodin investigating in her work with infertile couples?
   a. How do psychological factors affect fertility?
   b. Can infertility be cured by psychological counseling?
   c. What effect does infertility have on marital relationships?
   d. Can stress cause rejection of *in vitro* fertilization?

6. When Professor Zimbardo lowers his heart rate, he is demonstrating the process of
   a. mental relaxation.
   b. stress reduction.
   c. biofeedback.
   d. the general adaptation syndrome.

7. Psychologist Neal Miller uses the example of the blindfolded basketball player to explain
   a. the need for information to improve performance.
   b. how chance variations lead to evolutionary advantage.
   c. the correlation between life-changing events and illness.
   d. how successive approximations can shape behavior.

8. In which area of health psychology has the most research been done?
   a. the definition of health
   b. stress
   c. biofeedback
   d. changes in lifestyle

9. Imagine a family is moving to a new and larger home in a safer neighborhood with better schools. Will this situation be a source of stress for the family?
   a. No, because the change is a positive one.
   b. No, because moving is not really stressful.
   c. Yes, because any change requires adjustment.
   d. Yes, because it provokes guilt that the family does not really deserve this good fortune.

10. Which response shows the stages of the general adaptation syndrome in the correct order?
    a. alarm reaction, exhaustion, resistance
    b. resistance, alarm reaction, exhaustion
    c. exhaustion, resistance, alarm reaction
    d. alarm reaction, resistance, exhaustion

11. What important factor in stress did Hans Selye *not* consider?
    a. the role of hormones in mobilizing the body's defenses
    b. the subjective interpretation of a stressor
    c. the length of exposure to a stressor
    d. the body's vulnerability to new stressors during the resistance stage

12. Today, the major causes of death in the United States are
    a. accidents.
    b. infectious diseases.
    c. sexually transmitted diseases.
    d. diseases related to lifestyle.

13. When Thomas Coates and his colleagues, in their study of AIDS, conduct interview studies, they want to gain information that will help them
    a. design interventions at a variety of levels.
    b. determine how effective mass media advertisements are.
    c. motivate AIDS victims to take good care of themselves.
    d. stop people from using intravenous drugs.

14. The body's best external defense against illness is the skin, whereas its best internal defense is
    a. the stomach.
    b. the heart.
    c. T-cells.
    d. the spinal cord.

15. In which stage of the general adaptation syndrome are the pituitary and adrenals stimulated?
    a. exhaustion
    b. alarm
    c. reaction
    d. resistance

16. Which stage of the general adaptation syndrome is associated with the outcome of disease?
    a. alarm
    b. reaction
    c. exhaustion
    d. resistance

17. What claim is Richard Lazarus most closely associated with?
    a. The individual's cognitive appraisal of a stressor is critical.
    b. The biopsychosocial model is an oversimplified view.
    c. Peptic ulcers can be healed through biofeedback.
    d. The general adaptation syndrome can account for 80% of heart attacks in middle-aged men.

18. Thomas Coates and Neal Miller are similar in their desire to
    a. eradicate AIDS.
    b. outlaw intravenous drug use.
    c. institute stress management courses as part of standard insurance coverage.
    d. teach basic skills for protecting one's health.

19. How should an advertising campaign ideally be designed in order to get people to use condoms and avoid high-risk sexual activities?
    a. It should be friendly, optimistic, and completely nonthreatening.
    b. It should have enough threat to arouse emotion but not so much that viewers will go into denial.
    c. It should contain a lot of humor.
    d. It should feature an older, white, male doctor and a lot of scientific terminology.

20. Neal Miller is to biofeedback as Judith Rodin is to
    a. analgesics.
    b. meditation.
    c. a sense of control.
    d. social support.

GLOSSARY

Absent-mindedness Forgetting caused by lapses in attention.

Absolute threshold The amount of stimulation necessary for a stimulus to be detected. In practice, this means that the presence or absence of a stimulus is detected correctly half the time over many trials.

Abu Ghraib Prison Prison in Iraq made famous by revelation of photos taken by Army Reserve MP guards in the acts of humiliating and torturing prisoners.

Accommodation A mental process that modifies schemas in order to include (or accommodate) new information.

Acoustic encoding The conversion of information, especially semantic information, to sound patterns in working memory.

Acquisition The initial learning stage in classical conditioning, during which the conditioned response comes to be elicited by the conditioned stimulus.

Action potential The nerve impulse caused by a change in the electrical charge across the cell membrane of the axon. When the neuron "fires," this charge travels down the axon and causes neurotransmitters to be released by the terminal buttons.

Activation-synthesis theory The theory that dreams begin (are activated) with random electrical activation coming from the brain stem. Dreams, then, are the brain's attempt to make sense of (to synthesize) this random activity.

Active listener A person who gives the speaker feedback in such forms as nodding, paraphrasing, maintaining an expression that shows interest, and asking questions for clarification.

Acute stress A temporary state of arousal, caused by a stressor, with a distinct onset and limited duration.

Addiction A condition in which a person continues to use a drug despite its adverse effects—often despite repeated attempts to discontinue using the drug. Addiction may be based on physical or psychological dependence.

Adolescence In industrial societies, a developmental period beginning at puberty and ending (less clearly) at adulthood.

Adoption study A method of separating the effect of nature and nurture by which investigators compare characteristics of adopted children with those of individuals in their biological and adoptive families.

Affective disturbances Disorders of emotion or mood.

Afterimages Sensations that linger after the stimulus is removed. Most visual afterimages are *negative afterimages,* which appear in reversed colors.

Agonists Drugs or other chemicals that enhance or mimic the effects of neurotransmitters.

Agoraphobia A fear of public places and open spaces, commonly accompanying panic disorder.

Alarm phase First phase of the GAS, during which body resources are mobilized to cope with the stressor.

Algorithms Problem-solving procedures or formulas that guarantee a correct outcome, if correctly applied.

All-or-none principle Refers to the fact that the action potential in the axon occurs either completely or not at all.

Alzheimer's disease A degenerative brain disease usually noticed first by its debilitating effects on memory.

Ambiguous figures Images that can be interpreted in more than one way. There is no "right" way to see an ambiguous figure.

Amplitude The physical strength of a wave. This is shown on graphs as the height of the wave.

Amygdala A limbic system structure involved in memory and emotion, particularly fear and aggression. Pronounced *a-MIG-da-la.*

Analysis of transference The Freudian technique of analyzing and interpreting the patient's relationship with the therapist, based on the assumption that this relationship mirrors unresolved conflicts in the patient's past.

Analytical intelligence According to Sternberg, the ability measured by most IQ tests; includes the ability to analyze problems and find correct answers.

Anchoring bias A faulty heuristic caused by basing (anchoring) an estimate on a completely irrelevant quantity.

Anecdotal evidence First-hand accounts that vividly describe the experiences of one or a few people, but may erroneously be assumed to be scientific evidence.

Animistic thinking A preoperational mode of thought in which inanimate objects are imagined to have life and mental processes.

Anorexia nervosa An eating disorder involving persistent loss of appetite that endangers an individual's health and stemming from emotional or psychological reasons rather than from organic causes.

Antagonists Drugs or other chemicals that inhibit the effects of neurotransmitters.

Anterograde amnesia The inability to form new memories (as opposed to retrograde amnesia, which involves the inability to remember information previously stored in memory).

Antianxiety drugs A category of medicines that includes the barbiturates and benzodiazepines, drugs that diminish feelings of anxiety.

Antidepressants Medicines that treat depression, usually by their effects on the serotonin and/or norepinephrine pathways in the brain.

Antipsychotics Medicines that diminish psychotic symptoms, usually by effects on the dopamine pathways in the brain.

Antisocial personality disorder Condition involving a lack of conscience or a sense of responsibility to others.

Anxiety disorder Mental problem characterized mainly by anxiety. Anxiety disorders include panic disorder, specific phobias, and obsessive–compulsive disorder.

Anxious-ambivalent attachment One of two primary response patterns seen in insecurely attached children in which a child wants contact with the caregiver, shows excessive distress when separated from the caregiver, and proves difficult to console even when reunited.

Applied psychologists Psychologists who use the knowledge developed by experimental psychologists to solve human problems.

Aptitudes Innate potentialities (as contrasted with abilities acquired by learning).

Archetype One of the ancient memory images in the collective unconscious. Archetypes appear and reappear in art, literature, and folktales around the world.

Artificial concepts Concepts defined by rules, such as word definitions and mathematical formulas.

Asch effect A form of conformity in which a group majority influences individual judgments of unambiguous stimuli, as with line judgments.

Assimilation A mental process that incorporates new information into existing schemas.

Association cortex Cortical regions throughout the brain that combine information from various other parts of the brain.

Attachment The enduring socio-emotional relationship between a child and a parent or other regular caregiver.

Attention A process by which consciousness focuses on a single item or "chunk" in working memory.

Attention-deficit hyperactivity disorder (ADHD) A developmental disorder involving short attention span, distractibility and difficulty concentrating, poor impulse control, and excessive activity.

Authoritarian parent One of the four parenting styles, characterized by demands for conformity and obedience, with little tolerance for discussion of rules, which the parent enforces with punishment or threats of punishment.

Authoritative parent One of the four parenting styles, characterized by high expectations of the children, which the parent enforces with consequences, rather than punitive actions. Authoritative parents combine high standards with warmth and respect for the child's views.

Autism A developmental disorder marked by disabilities in language, social interaction, and the ability to understand another person's state of mind.

Autokinetic effect The perceived motion of a stationary dot of light in a totally dark room; used by Muzafir Sherif to study the formation of group norms.

Autonomic nervous system The portion of the peripheral nervous system that sends communications between the central nervous system and the internal organs and glands.

Autonomy In Erikson's theory, autonomy is the major developmental task of the second stage in childhood. Achieving autonomy involves developing a sense of independence, as opposed to being plagued by *self-doubt*.

Availability bias A faulty heuristic strategy that estimates probabilities based on the availability of vivid mental images of the event.

Aversion therapy As a classical conditioning procedure, aversive counterconditioning involves presenting the individual with an attractive stimulus paired with unpleasant (aversive) stimulation to condition a repulsive reaction.

Avoidant attachment One of two primary response patterns seen in insecurely attached children, in which a child shows no interest in contact with the caregiver and displays neither distress when separated from the caregiver nor happiness when reunited.

Axon In a nerve cell, an extended fiber that conducts information from the soma to the terminal buttons. Information travels along the axon in the form of an electric charge called the *action potential*.

Babbling The production of repetitive syllables, characteristic of the early stages of language acquisition.

Base rate information The probability of a characteristic occurring in the general population period.

Basic anxiety An emotion, proposed by Karen Horney, that gives a sense of uncertainty and loneliness in a hostile world and can lead to maladjustment.

Basilar membrane A thin strip of tissue sensitive to vibrations in the cochlea. The basilar membrane contains hair cells connected to neurons. When a sound wave causes the hair cells to vibrate, the associated neurons become excited. As a result, the sound waves are converted (transduced) into nerve activity.

Behavior modification Another term for behavior therapy.

Behavior therapy Any form of psychotherapy based on the principles of behavioral learning, especially operant conditioning and classical conditioning.

Behavioral learning Forms of learning, such as classical conditioning and operant conditioning, that can be described in terms of stimuli and responses.

Behavioral medicine Medical field specializing in the link between lifestyle and disease.

Behavioral perspective A psychological viewpoint that finds the source of our actions in environmental stimuli rather than in inner mental processes.

Behaviorism A historical school (as well as a modern perspective) that has sought to make psychology an objective science focusing only on behavior—to the exclusion of mental processes.

Benefit finding The second phase of finding meaning in a stressful situation, which involves seeing some ultimate benefit from the stressor.

Binding problem Refers to the process used by the brain to combine (or "bind") the results of many sensory operations into a single percept. This occurs, for example, when sensations of color, shape, boundary, and texture are combined to produce the percept of a person's face. No one knows exactly how the brain does this. Thus, the binding problem is one of the major unsolved mysteries in psychology.

Binocular cues Information taken in by both eyes that aids in depth perception, including binocular convergence and retinal disparity.

Biological drive A motive, such as thirst, that is based primarily in biology. A *drive* is a state of tension that motivates an organism to satisfy a biological need.

Biological perspective The psychological perspective that searches for the causes of behavior in the functioning of genes, the brain and nervous system, and the endocrine (hormone) system.

Biomedical therapy Treatment that focuses on altering the brain, especially with drugs, psychosurgery, or electroconvulsive therapy.

Biopsychology The specialty in psychology that studies the interaction of biology, behavior, and mental processes.

Bipolar disorder A mental abnormality involving swings of mood from mania to depression.

Blind spot The point where the optic nerve exits the eye and where there are no photoreceptors. Any stimulus that falls on this area cannot be seen.

Blindsight The ability to locate objects despite damage to the visual system making it impossible for a person consciously to see and identify objects. Blindsight is thought to involve unconscious visual processing in the where pathway.

Blocking Forgetting that occurs when an item in memory cannot be accessed or retrieved. Blocking is caused by interference.

Body image An individual's perception of and feelings about their physical appearance.

Borderline personality disorder Condition of instability and impulsivity; persons have unpredictable moods and stormy interpersonal relationships, with little tolerance for frustration.

Bottom-up processing Perceptual analysis that emphasizes characteristics of the stimulus, rather than our concepts and expectations. "Bottom" refers to the stimulus, which occurs at step one of perceptual processing.

Brain stem The most primitive of the brain's three major layers. It includes the medulla, pons, and the reticular formation.

Brightness A psychological sensation caused by the intensity (amplitude) of light waves.

Bulimia nervosa An eating disorder characterized by eating binges followed by "purges," induced by vomiting or laxatives; typically initiated as a weight-control measure.

Bullying The act of tormenting others, in school classrooms or work settings, by one or more people, for personal, sadistic pleasure. It qualifies as a form of ordinary or everyday evil.

Burnout A syndrome of emotional exhaustion, physical fatigue, and cognitive weariness, often related to work.

Bystander intervention problem Laboratory and field study analogues of the difficulties faced by bystanders in real emergency situations.

Cannon–Bard theory The counterproposal that an emotional feeling and an internal physiological response occur at the same time: One is not the cause of the other. Both were believed to be the result of cognitive appraisal of the situation.

Case study Research involving a single individual (or, at most, a few individuals).

Catastrophic event A sudden, violent calamity, either natural or manmade, that causes trauma.

Catharsis A theory suggesting that emotional pressure can be relieved by expressing feelings directly or indirectly.

Central nervous system (CNS) The brain and the spinal cord.

Centration A preoperational thought pattern involving the inability to take into account more than one factor at a time.

Cerebellum The "little brain" attached to the brain stem. The cerebellum is responsible for coordinated movements.

Cerebral cortex The thin gray matter covering the cerebral hemispheres, consisting of a ¼-inch layer dense with cell bodies of neurons. The cerebral cortex carries on the major portion of our "higher" mental processing, including thinking and perceiving.

Cerebral dominance The tendency of each brain hemisphere to exert control over different functions, such as language or perception of spatial relationships.

Cerebral hemispheres The large symmetrical halves of the brain located atop the brain stem.

Chameleon effect The tendency to mimic other people, named after the animal that changes its skin color to fit into its varied environments.

Change blindness A perceptual failure to notice that a visual scene has changed from the way it had appeared previously. Unlike inattentional blindness, change blindness requires comparing a current scene to one from the past, stored in memory.

Childhood amnesia The inability to remember events during the first two or three years of life.

Chromosome Tightly coiled threadlike structure along which the genes are organized, like beads on a necklace. Chromosomes consist primarily of DNA.

Chronic stressor Long-lasting stressful condition.

Chronological age (CA) The number of years since the individual's birth.

Chunking Organizing pieces of information into a smaller number of meaningful units (or chunks)—a process that frees up space in working memory.

Circadian rhythm A physiological pattern that repeats approximately every 24 hours—such as the sleep–wakefulness cycle.

Classical conditioning A form of behavioral learning in which a previously neutral stimulus acquires the power to elicit the same innate reflex produced by another stimulus.

Client-centered therapy A humanistic approach to treatment developed by Carl Rogers, emphasizing an individual's tendency for healthy psychological growth through self-actualization.

Closure The Gestalt principle that identifies the tendency to fill in gaps in figures and to see incomplete figures as complete.

Cochlea The primary organ of hearing; a coiled tube in the inner ear, where sound waves are transduced into nerve messages.

Cognitive appraisal Our interpretation of a stressor and our resources for dealing with it.

Cognitive development The global term for the development of thought processes from childhood through adulthood.

Cognitive dissonance A highly motivating state in which people have conflicting cognitions, especially when their voluntary actions conflict with their attitudes or values. Leon Festinger was its originator.

Cognitive map In Tolman's work, a cognitive map was a mental representation of a maze or other physical space. Psychologists often used the term *cognitive map* more broadly to include an understanding of connections among concepts. Thus, a cognitive map can represent either a physical or a mental "space."

Cognitive neuroscience An interdisciplinary field involving cognitive psychology, neurology, biology, computer science, linguistics, and specialists from other fields who are interested in the connection between mental processes and the brain.

Cognitive perspective Another of the main psychological viewpoints distinguished by an emphasis on mental processes, such as learning, memory, perception, and thinking, as forms of information processing.

Cognitive restructuring Reappraising a stressor with the goal of seeing it from a more positive perspective.

Cognitive therapy Emphasizes rational thinking (as opposed to subjective emotion, motivation, or repressed conflicts) as the key to treating mental disorders.

Cognitive–behavioral therapy A newer form of psychotherapy that combines the techniques of cognitive therapy with those of behavioral therapy.

Cohesiveness Solidarity, loyalty, and a sense of group membership.

Collective unconscious Jung's addition to the unconscious, involving a reservoir for instinctive "memories," including the archetypes, which exist in all people.

Collectivism The view, common in Asia, Africa, Latin America, and the Middle East, that values group loyalty and pride over individual distinction.

Color Also called *hue*. Color is not a property of things in the external world. Rather, it is a *psychological sensation* created in the brain from information obtained by the eyes from the wavelengths of visible light.

Color blindness Typically a genetic disorder (although sometimes the result of trauma, as in the case of Jonathan) that prevents an individual from discriminating certain colors. The most common form is red–green color blindness.

Coma An unconscious state, during which a person lacks the normal cycles of sleep and wakefulness, that usually lasts only a few days. The comatose state differs from the *minimally conscious state* and the *persistent vegetative state*.

Combination therapy A therapeutic approach that involves both psychological and medical techniques—most often a drug therapy with a behavioral or cognitive–behavioral therapy.

Community mental health movement An effort to deinstitutionalize mental patients and to provide therapy from outpatient clinics. Proponents of community mental health envisioned that recovering patients could live with their families, in foster homes, or in group homes.

Compassion fatigue A state of exhaustion experienced by medical and psychological professionals, as well as caregivers, which leaves the individual feeling stressed, numb, or indifferent.

Compassion satisfaction A sense of appreciation felt by a caregiver, medical or psychological professional, of the work he or she does.

Computer metaphor The idea that the brain is an information-processing organ that operates, in some ways, like a computer.

Concept hierarchies Levels of concepts, from most general to most specific, in which a more general level includes more specific concepts—as the concept of "animal" includes "dog," "giraffe," and "butterfly."

Concepts Mental groupings of similar objects, ideas, or experiences.

Concrete operational stage The third of Piaget's stages, when a child understands conservation but still is incapable of abstract thought.

Conditioned reinforcer or **secondary reinforcer** A stimulus, such as money or tokens, that acquires its reinforcing power by a learned association with primary reinforcers.

Conditioned response (CR) In classical conditioning, a response elicited by a previously neutral stimulus that has become associated with the unconditioned stimulus.

Conditioned stimulus (CS) In classical conditioning, a previously neutral stimulus that comes to elicit the conditioned response. Customarily, in a conditioning experiment, the neutral stimulus is called a conditioned stimulus when it is first paired with an unconditioned stimulus (UCS).

Cones Photoreceptors in the retina that are especially sensitive to colors but not to dim light. You may have guessed that the cones are cone-shaped.

Confirmation bias The tendency to attend to evidence that complements and confirms our beliefs or expectations, while ignoring evidence that does not.

Conformity The tendency for people to adopt the behaviors, attitudes, and opinions of other members of a group.

Consciousness The process by which the brain creates a mental model of our experience. The most common, or ordinary, consciousness occurs during wakefulness, although there are can be altered states of consciousness.

Conservation The understanding that the physical properties of an object or substance do not change when appearances change but nothing is added or taken away.

Consolidation The process by which short-term memories become long-term memories over a period of time.

Contact comfort Stimulation and reassurance derived from the physical touch of a caregiver.

Contingency management An operant conditioning approach to changing behavior by altering the consequences, especially rewards and punishments, of behavior.

Continuous reinforcement A type of reinforcement schedule by which all correct responses are reinforced.

Contralateral pathways Sensory and motor pathways between the brain and the rest of the body cross over to the opposite side en route, so messages from the right side of the body are processed by the left side of the brain and vice versa.

Control group Participants who are used as a comparison for the experimental group. The control group is not given the special treatment of interest.

Conversion disorder A type of somatoform disorder marked by paralysis, weakness, or loss of sensation but with no discernible physical cause.

Coping Taking action that reduces or eliminates the causes of stress, not merely its symptoms.

Coping strategy An action that reduces or eliminates the impact of stress.

Corpus callosum The band of nerve cells connecting and enabling communication between the two cerebral hemispheres.

Correlational study A form of research in which the relationship between variables is studied, but without the experimental manipulation of an independent variable. Correlational studies cannot determine cause-and-effect relationships.

Cortisol A steroid produced by the fight-or-flight response.

Creative intelligence According to Sternberg, the form of intelligence that helps people see new relationships among concepts; involves insight and creativity.

Creativity A mental process that produces novel responses that contribute to the solutions of problems.

Critical incident stress debriefing (CISD) A specific type of psychological debriefing that follows a strict, step-by-step agenda.

Critical thinking skills This book emphasizes six critical thinking skills, based on the following questions: What is the source? Is the claim reasonable or extreme? What is the evidence? Could bias contaminate the conclusion? Does the reasoning avoid common fallacies? Does the issue require multiple perspectives?

Cross-cultural psychologists Those who work in this specialty are interested in how psychological processes may differ among people of different cultures.

Crystallized intelligence The knowledge a person has acquired plus the ability to access that knowledge.

CT scanning or **computerized tomography** A computerized imaging technique that uses X-rays passed through the brain at various angles and then combined into an image.

Culture A complex blend of language, beliefs, customs, values, and traditions developed by a group of people and shared with others in the same environment.

Cytokines Hormone-like chemicals that fight infection and facilitate communication between the brain and immune system.

Data Pieces of information, especially information gathered by a researcher to be used in testing a hypothesis. (Singular: datum.)

Daydreaming A common (and quite normal) variation of consciousness in which attention shifts to memories, expectations, desires, or fantasies and away from the immediate situation.

Declarative memory A division of LTM that stores explicit information; also known as *fact memory*. Declarative memory has two subdivisions, episodic memory and semantic memory.

Defending Efforts taken to reduce the symptoms of stress or one's awareness of them.

Dehumanization The psychological process of thinking about certain other people or groups as less than human, as like feared or hated animals. A basic process in much prejudice and mass violence.

Deinstitutionalization The policy of removing patients, whenever possible, from mental hospitals.

Delusion An extreme disorder of thinking, involving persistent false beliefs. Delusions are the hallmark of paranoid disorders.

Dendrite Branched fiber that extends outward from the cell body and carries information into the neuron.

Dependent variable The measured outcome of a study; the responses of the subjects in a study.

Depersonalization Depriving people of their identity and individuality by treating them as objects rather than as individuals. Depersonalization can be a result of labeling.

Depersonalization disorder An abnormality involving the sensation that mind and body have separated, as in an "out-of-body" experience.

Depressant Drug that slows down mental and physical activity by inhibiting transmission of nerve impulses in the central nervous system.

Developmental level of analysis Concerns changes in the organism's developmental progress that might change motivational priorities.

Developmental perspective One of the six main psychological viewpoints, distinguished by its emphasis on nature and nurture and on predictable changes that occur across the lifespan.

Developmental psychology The psychological specialty that studies how organisms grow and change over time as the result of biological and environmental influences.

Diathesis–stress hypothesis In reference to schizophrenia, the proposal that genetic factors place the individual at risk while environmental stress factors transform this potential into an actual schizophrenic disorder.

Difference threshold The smallest amount by which a stimulus can be changed and the difference be detected half the time.

Diffusion of responsibility Dilution or weakening of each group member's obligation to act when responsibility is perceived to be shared with all group members or accepted by the leader.

Discrimination A negative action taken against an individual as a result of his or her group or categorical membership. It is the behavior that prejudice generates.

Disenfranchised grief The emotion surrounding a loss that others do not support, share, or understand.

Display rules The permissible ways of displaying emotions in a particular society.

Disposition Relatively stable personality pattern, including temperaments, traits, and personality types.

Dispositional theory A general term that includes the temperament, trait, and type approaches to personality.

Dispositionism A psychological orientation that focuses primarily on the inner characteristics of individuals, such as personality dispositions, values, character, and

genetic makeup. Contrasted with situationism, the focus is on external causes of behavior.

Dissociative amnesia A psychologically induced loss of memory for personal information, such as one's identity or residence.

Dissociative disorders One of a group of pathologies involving "fragmentation" of the personality, in which some parts of the personality have become detached, or dissociated, from other parts.

Dissociative fugue Essentially the same as dissociative amnesia but with the addition of "flight" from one's home, family, and job. *Fugue* (pronounced *FEWG*) means "flight."

Dissociative identity disorder A condition in which an individual displays multiple identities or personalities; formerly called "multiple personality disorder."

Distress The psychological reaction created by external stressors, which can be an emotional, cognitive or behavioral response. It is part of the stress response that also includes biological and physiological reactions to stressors.

Distributed learning A technique whereby the learner spaces learning sessions over time rather than trying to learn the material all in one study period.

DNA (deoxyribonucleic acid) A long, complex molecule that encodes genetic characteristics.

Double-blind study An experimental procedure in which both researchers and participants are uninformed about the nature of the independent variable being administered.

Downward social comparison Comparison between one's own stressful situation and others in a similar situation who are worse off, with the goal of gaining a more positive perspective on one's own situation.

Drive Biologically instigated motivation.

Drive theory Developed as an alternative to instinct theory, drive theory explains motivation as a process in which a biological *need* produces a *drive* that moves an organism to meet the need. For most drives this process returns the organism to a balanced condition, known as *homeostasis.*

DSM-IV The fourth edition of the *Diagnostic and Statistical Manual of Mental Disorders,* published by the American Psychiatric Association; the most widely accepted psychiatric classification system in the United States.

Dyslexia A reading disability, thought by some experts to involve a brain disorder.

Eclectic Either switching theories to explain different situations or building one's own theory of personality from pieces borrowed from many perspectives.

Ecological view A perspective on mental disorder that emphasizes social and cultural context.

Ego defense mechanism A largely unconscious mental strategy employed to reduce the experience of conflict or anxiety.

Ego The conscious, rational part of the personality, charged with keeping peace between the superego and the id.

Egocentrism In Piaget's theory, the inability to realize that there are other viewpoints beside one's own.

Ego-integrity In Erikson's theory, the developmental task of late adulthood—involving the ability to look back on life without regrets and to enjoy a sense of wholeness.

Eidetic imagery An especially clear and persistent form of memory that is quite rare; sometimes known as "photographic memory."

Elaborative rehearsal A working-memory process in which information is actively reviewed and related to information already in LTM.

Electra complex Concept advanced by Carl Jung , highlighting a girl's psychosexual competition with mother for the father's love, which is resolved in psychoanalyitic theory when girl comes to identify with same sex adult. Equivalent to Oedipus Complex in males.

Electroconvulsive therapy (ECT) A treatment used primarily for depression and involving the application of an electric current to the head, producing a generalized seizure; sometimes called "shock treatment."

Electroencephalograph (EEG) A device for recording brain waves, typically by electrodes placed on the scalp. The record produced is known as an electroencephalogram (also called an EEG).

Electromagnetic spectrum The entire range of electromagnetic energy, including radio waves, X-rays, microwaves, and visible light.

Embryo In humans, the name for the developing organism during the first 8 weeks after conception.

Emerging adulthood A transition period between adolescence and adulthood.

Emotion A four-part process that involves physiological arousal, subjective feelings, cognitive interpretation, and behavioral expression. Emotions help organisms deal with important events.

Emotional bias   The tendency to make judgments based on attitudes and feelings, rather than on the basis of a rational analysis of the evidence.

Emotional intelligence   The ability to understand and control emotional responses.

Emotion-focused coping   Regulating one's emotional response to a stressor.

Empirical investigation   An approach to research that relies on sensory experience and observation as research data.

Empirically supported treatment (EST)   Treatment regimen that has been demonstrated to be effective through research.

Encoding specificity principle   The doctrine that memory is encoded and stored with specific cues related to the context in which it was formed. The more closely the retrieval cues match the form in which the information was encoded, the better it will be remembered.

Encoding   The first of the three basic tasks of memory, involving the modification of information to fit the preferred format for the memory system.

Endocrine system   The hormone system—the body's chemical messenger system, including the endocrine glands: pituitary, thyroid, parathyroid, adrenals, pancreas, ovaries, and testes.

Engram   The physical changes in the brain associated with a memory. It is also known as the *memory trace*.

Episodic memory   A subdivision of declarative memory that stores memory of personal events or "episodes."

Evolution   The gradual process of biological change that occurs in a species as it adapts to its environment.

Evolutionary psychology   A relatively new specialty in psychology that sees behavior and mental processes in terms of their genetic adaptations for survival and reproduction.

Executive function   Cognitive abilities in the frontal lobes necessary for complex thinking, planning, and goal-directed behavior.

Exhaustion phase   Third phase of the GAS, during which the body's resources become depleted.

Expectancy bias   The researcher allowing his or her expectations to affect the outcome of a study.

Expectancy-value theory   A social psychology theory that states how people decide

whether to pursue a relationship by weighing the potential value of the relationship against their expectation of success in establishing the relationship.

Experiment   A kind of research in which the researcher controls all the conditions and directly manipulates the conditions, including the independent variable.

Experimental group   Participants in an experiment who are exposed to the treatment of interest.

Experimental psychologists   Psychologists who do research on basic psychological processes—as contrasted with applied psychologists; experimental psychologists are also called research psychologists.

Experts   Individuals who possess well-organized funds of knowledge, including the effective problem-solving strategies, in a field.

Explicit memory   Memory that has been processed with attention and can be consciously recalled.

Exposure therapy   A form of desensitization therapy in which the patient directly confronts the anxiety-provoking stimulus (as opposed to imagining the stimulus).

Externals   People with an external locus of control who believe they can do little to influence their life outcomes.

Extinction (in classical conditioning)   The weakening of a conditioned response in the absence of an unconditioned stimulus.

Extinction (in operant conditioning)   A process by which a response that has been learned is weakened by the absence or removal of reinforcement. (Compare with *extinction in classical conditioning*.)

Extraversion   The Jungian personality dimension that involves turning one's attention outward, toward others.

Extrinsic motivation   The desire to engage in an activity to achieve an external consequence, such as a reward.

False positive   Mistaken identification of a person as having a particular characteristic. In polygraphy, a false positive is an erroneous identification of a truthful person as being a liar.

Family systems theory   A perspective on personality and treatment that emphasizes the family rather than the individual as the basic unit of analysis .

Feature detectors   Cells in the cortex that specialize in extracting certain features of a stimulus.

Fetal alcohol syndrome (FAS)   A set of physical and mental problems seen in children

whose mothers drink excessive amounts of alcohol during pregnancy.

Fetus   In humans, the term for the developing organism between the embryonic stage and birth.

Fight-or-flight response   Sequence of internal responses preparing an organism for struggle or escape.

Figure   The part of a pattern that commands attention. The figure stands out against the ground.

Five-factor theory   A trait perspective suggesting that personality is composed of five fundamental personality dimensions (also known as the Big Five): openness to experience, conscientiousness, extraversion, agreeableness, and neuroticism.

Fixation   Occurs when psychosexual development is arrested at an immature stage.

Fixed-action patterns   Genetically based behaviors, seen across a species, that can be set off by a specific stimulus. The concept of *fixed-action patterns* has replaced the older notion of instinct.

Fixed interval (FI) schedule   A program by which reinforcement is contingent upon a certain, fixed time period.

Fixed ratio (FR) schedule   A program by which reinforcement is contingent on a certain, unvarying number of responses.

Flashbulb memory   A clear and vivid long-term memory of an especially meaningful and emotional event.

Flow   In Csikszentmihalyi's theory, an intense focus on an activity accompanied by increased creativity and near-ecstatic feelings. Flow involves intrinsic motivation.

Fluid intelligence   The ability to see complex relationships and solve problems.

FMRI or functional magnetic resonance imaging   A newer form of magnetic resonance imaging that records both brain structure and brain activity.

Forgetting curve   A graph plotting the amount of retention and forgetting over time for a certain batch of material, such as a list of nonsense syllables. The typical forgetting curve is steep at first, becoming flatter as time goes on.

Formal operational stage   The last of Piaget's stages, during which abstract thought appears.

Fovea   The tiny area of sharpest vision in the retina.

Frequency   The number of cycles completed by a wave in a second.

Frontal lobes   Cortical regions at the front of the brain that are especially involved in movement and in thinking.

Fully functioning person   Carl Rogers's term for a healthy, self-actualizing individual who has a self-concept that is both positive and congruent with reality.

Functional fixedness   The inability to perceive a new use for an object associated with a different purpose; a form of mental set.

Functional level of analysis   Concerns the adaptive function of a motive in terms of the organism's survival and reproduction.

Functionalism   A historical school of psychology that believed mental processes could best be understood in terms of their adaptive purpose and function.

Fundamental attribution error (FAE)   The dual tendency to overemphasize internal, dispositional causes and minimize external, situational pressures. The FAE is more common in individualistic cultures than in collectivistic cultures.

G factor   A general ability, proposed by Spearman, as the main factor underlying all intelligent mental activity.

Gate-control theory   An explanation for pain control that proposes we have a neural "gate" that can, under some circumstances, block incoming pain signals.

Gene   Segment of a chromosome that encodes the directions for the inherited physical and mental characteristics of an organism. Genes are the functional units of a chromosome.

General Adaptation Syndrome (GAS)   A three-phase pattern of physical responses to a chronic stressor.

General anesthetic   Substance that suppresses consciousness and awareness of pain. Most anesthetics also produce sedation and immobility.

Generalized anxiety disorder   A psychological problem characterized by persistent and pervasive feelings of anxiety, without any external cause.

Generativity   The process of making a commitment beyond oneself to family, work, society, or future generations. In Erikson's theory, generativity is the developmental challenge of midlife.

Genetic leash   Edward Wilson's term for the constraints placed on development by heredity.

Genome   The complete set of genetic information contained with a cell.

Genotype   An organism's genetic makeup.

Gestalt psychology   From a German word (pronounced *gush-TAWLT*) that means "whole" or "form" or "configuration." (A Gestalt is also a *percept*.) The Gestalt psychologists believed that much of perception is shaped by innate factors built into the brain.

Giftedness   Often conceived as representing the upper 2 percent of the IQ range, commencing about 30 points above average (at about 130 IQ points).

Gist (pronounced *JIST*)   The sense or meaning, as contrasted with the exact details.

Glial cell   One of the cells that provide structural support for neurons. Glial cells also provide an insulating covering (the myelin sheath) of the axon for some neurons, which facilitates the electrical impulse.

Goal-directed behavior   An ability that emerges during the sensorimotor period by which infants develop the ability to keep a simple goal in mind as they pursue it.

Grammar   The rules of a language, specifying how to use the elements of language and word order to produce understandable sentences.

Grief   The emotional response to loss, which includes sadness, anger, helplessness, guilt, and despair.

Ground   The part of a pattern that does not command attention; the background.

Group therapy   Any form of psychotherapy done with more than one client/patient at a time. Group therapy is often done from a humanistic perspective.

Groupthink   The term for the poor judgments and bad decisions made by members of groups that are overly influenced by perceived group consensus or the leader's point of view.

Gustation   The sense of taste, from the same word root as "gusto;" also called the *gustatory sense*.

Habituation   Learning not to respond to the repeated presentation of a stimulus.

Hallucination   A false sensory experience that may suggest mental disorder. Hallucinations can have other causes, such as drugs or sensory isolation.

Hallucinogen   A drug that creates hallucinations or alters perceptions of the external environment and inner awareness.

Hardiness   Attitude of resistance to stress, based on a sense of challenge (welcoming change), commitment (engagement), and control (maintaining an internal guide for action).

Hassle   Situation that causes minor irritation or frustration.

Health psychology   Field of psychology that studies psychosocial factors that contribute to promoting health and well being, and also those that influence illness, with the goal of educating the public about developing healthier life styles.

Heritability   The amount of trait variation within a group raised under the same conditions, which can be attributed to genetic differences. Heritability tells us nothing about between-group differences.

Heroes   People whose actions help others in emergencies or challenge unjust or corrupt systems, doing so without concern for reward or likely negative consequences for them by acting in deviant ways.

Heuristics   Cognitive strategies or "rules of thumb" used as shortcuts to solve complex mental tasks. Unlike algorithms, heuristics do not guarantee a correct solution.

Hierarchy of needs   In Maslow's theory, the notion that needs occur in priority order, with the biological needs as the most basic.

Hindsight bias   The tendency, after learning about an event, to "second guess" or believe that one could have predicted the event in advance.

Hippocampus   A component of the limbic system, involved in establishing long-term memories.

Homeostasis   The body's tendency to maintain a biologically balanced condition, especially with regard to nutrients, water, and temperature.

Hormones   Chemical messengers used by the endocrine system. Many hormones also serve as neurotransmitters in the nervous system.

Humanistic psychology   A clinical approach emphasizing human ability, growth, potential, and free will.

Humanistic theories   A group of personality theories that focus on human growth and potential rather than on mental disorders. All emphasize the functioning of the individual in the present rather than on the influence of past events.

Humanistic therapy   Treatment technique based on the assumption that people have a tendency for positive growth and self-actualization, which may be blocked by an unhealthy environment that can include negative self-evaluation and criticism from others.

Humors   Four body fluids—blood, phlegm, black bile, and yellow bile—that, according to an ancient theory, control personality by their relative abundance.

Hypnosis   An induced state of awareness, usually characterized by heightened suggestibility, deep relaxation, and highly focused attention.

Hypochondriasis A somatoform disorder involving excessive concern about health and disease; also called hypochondria.

Hypothalamus A limbic structure that serves as the brain's blood-testing laboratory, constantly monitoring the blood to determine the condition of the body.

Hypothesis A statement predicting the outcome of a scientific study; a statement predicting the relationship among variables in a study.

Id The primitive, unconscious portion of the personality that houses the most basic drives and stores repressed memories.

Identification The mental process by which an individual tries to become like another person, especially the same-sex parent.

Identity In Erikson's theory, identity is a sense of who one is—a coherent self. Developing a sense of identity is the main goal of adolescence.

Illusion You have experienced an illusion when you have a demonstrably incorrect perception of a stimulus pattern, especially one that also fools others who are observing the same stimulus. (If no one else sees it the way you do, you could be having a *hallucination*.)

Immunosuppression Impairment in the function of the immune system.

Implicit memory A memory that was not deliberately learned or of which you have no conscious awareness.

Implicit personality theory A person's set of unquestioned assumptions about personality, used to simplify the task of understanding others.

Imprinting A primitive form of learning in which some young animals follow and form an attachment to the first moving object they see and hear.

Inattentional blindness A failure to notice changes occurring in one's visual field, apparently caused by narrowing the focus of one's attention.

Independent variable A stimulus condition so named because the experimenter changes it independently of all the other carefully controlled experimental conditions.

Individualism The view, common in the Euro-American world, that places a high value on individual achievement and distinction.

Industry Erikson's term for a sense of confidence that characterizes the main goal of the fourth developmental stage in childhood. Children who do not develop industry (confidence) will slip into a self-perception of *inferiority*.

Infancy In humans, infancy spans the time between the end of the neonatal period and the establishment of language—usually at about 18 months to 2 years.

Information-processing model A cognitive understanding of memory, emphasizing how information is changed when it is encoded, stored, and retrieved.

Informed consent Insures that research participants are informed of the procedures of the research, as well as any potential dangers involved, so they may opt out if desired.

In-group The group with which an individual identifies.

Initiative In Erikson's theory, initiative is the major developmental task in the third stage of childhood. Initiative is characterized by the ability to initiate activities oneself, rather than merely responding to others or feeling *guilt* at not measuring up to others' expectations.

Innate ability Capability of an infant that is inborn or biologically based.

Innate reflex Reflexive response present at birth.

Insanity A legal term, not a psychological or psychiatric one, referring to a person who is unable, because of a mental disorder or defect, to conform his or her behavior to the law.

Insight learning A form of cognitive learning, originally described by the Gestalt psychologists, in which problem solving occurs by means of a sudden reorganization of perceptions.

Insight therapy Psychotherapy in which the therapist helps the patient/client understand (gain insight into) his or her problems.

Insomnia The most common of sleep disorders—involving insufficient sleep, the inability to fall asleep quickly, frequent arousals, or early awakenings.

Instinct theory The now-outmoded view that certain behaviors are completely determined by innate factors. The instinct theory was flawed because it overlooked the effects of learning and because it employed instincts merely as labels rather than as explanations for behavior.

Instinctive drift The tendency of an organism's innate (instinctive) responses to interfere with learned behavior.

Integration A final phase of grieving, in which the loss becomes incorporated into the self.

Intelligence The mental capacity to acquire knowledge, reason, and solve problems effectively.

Intelligence quotient (IQ) A numerical score on an intelligence test, originally computed by dividing the person's mental age by chronological age and multiplying the result by 100.

Intermittent reinforcement A type of reinforcement schedule by which some, but not all, correct responses are reinforced; also called partial reinforcement.

Internals People with an internal locus of control who believe they can do much to influence their life outcomes.

Interneuron A nerve cell that relays messages between nerve cells, especially in the brain and spinal cord.

Interval schedule A program by which reinforcement depends on the time interval elapsed since the last reinforcement.

Intimacy In Erikson's theory, the main developmental task of early adulthood, involving the capacity to make a full commitment—sexual, emotional, and moral—to another person.

Intrinsic motivation The desire to engage in an activity for its own sake rather than for some external consequence, such as a reward.

Introspection The process of reporting on one's own conscious mental experiences.

Introversion The Jungian dimension that focuses on inner experience—one's own thoughts and feelings—making the introvert less outgoing and sociable than the extravert.

Intuition The ability to make judgments without consciously reasoning.

Inverted U function A term that describes the relationship between arousal and performance. Both low and high levels of arousal produce lower performance than does a moderate level of arousal.

Irreversibility The inability, in the preoperational child, to think through a series of events or mental operations and then mentally reverse the steps.

James–Lange theory The proposal that an emotion-provoking stimulus produces a physical response that, in turn, produces an emotion.

Job engagement An employee's sense of being part of a meaningful work setting where her or his contribution is valued and equitably rewarded (the opposite of job burnout).

Kinesthetic sense The sense of body position and movement of body parts relative to each other (also called *kinesthesis*).

Labeling Refers to the undesirable practice of attaching diagnoses of mental disorders to people and then using them as stereotypes—treating the afflicted individuals as if the labels explained their whole personalities. Psychiatric labels can also stigmatize people.

Language acquisition device (LAD) A biologically organized mental structure in the brain that facilitates the learning of language because (according to Chomsky) it is innately programmed with some of the fundamental rules of grammar.

Latent content The symbolic meaning of objects and events in a dream. Latent content is usually an interpretation based on Freud's psychoanalytic theory or one of its variants. For example, the latent content of a dream involving clocks might involve fear of the menstrual cycle and, hence, of one's sexuality.

Lateralization of emotion The two brain hemispheres process different emotions. The left hemisphere apparently focuses on positive emotions (for example, happiness), while the right hemisphere deals primarily with negative emotions (such as anger).

Law of common fate The Gestalt principle that we tend to group similar objects together that share a common motion or destination.

Law of continuity The Gestalt principle that we prefer perceptions of connected and continuous figures to disconnected and disjointed ones.

Law of effect The idea that responses that produced desirable results would be learned or "stamped" into the organism.

Law of Prägnanz The most general Gestalt principle, which states that the simplest organization, requiring the least cognitive effort, will emerge as the figure. *Prägnanz* shares a common root with *pregnant*, and so it carries the idea of a "fully developed figure." That is, our perceptual system prefers to see a fully developed Gestalt, such as a complete circle—as opposed to a broken circle.

Law of proximity The Gestalt principle that we tend to group objects together when they are near each other. *Proximity* means "nearness."

Law of similarity The Gestalt principle that we tend to group similar objects together in our perceptions.

Laws of perceptual grouping The Gestalt principles of similarity, proximity, continuity, and common fate. These "laws" suggest how our brains prefer to group stimulus elements together to form a percept (Gestalt).

Learned helplessness A condition in which depressed individuals learn to attribute negative events to their own personal flaws or external conditions that the person feels helpless to change. People with learned helplessness can be thought of as having an extreme form of *external locus of control*.

Learned helplessness Pattern of failure to respond to threatening stimuli after an organism experiences a series of ineffective responses.

Learning A lasting change in behavior or mental processes that results from experience.

Learning-based inference The view that perception is primarily shaped by learning (or experience), rather than by innate factors.

Levels-of-processing theory The explanation for the fact that information that is more thoroughly connected to meaningful items in long-term memory (more "deeply" processed) will be remembered better.

Libido The Freudian concept of psychic energy that drives individuals to experience sensual pleasure.

Limbic system The middle layer of the brain, involved in emotion and memory. The limbic system includes the hippocampus, amygdala, hypothalamus, and other structures.

Locus of control A relatively stable pattern of behavior that characterizes individual expectations about the ability to influence the outcomes in life; an individual's sense of whether control over his or her life is internal or external; An individual's sense of whether control over his or her life is internal or external.

Long-term memory (LTM) The third of three memory stages, with the largest capacity and longest duration; LTM stores material organized according to meaning.

Long-term potentiation A biological process involving physical changes that strengthen the synapses in groups of nerve cells that is believed to be the neural basis of learning.

Loudness A sensory characteristic of sound produced by the *amplitude* (intensity) of the sound wave.

Maintenance rehearsal A working-memory process in which information is merely repeated or reviewed to keep it from fading while in working memory.

Maintenance rehearsal involves no active elaboration.

Major depression A form of depression that does not alternate with mania.

Manifest content The story line of a dream, taken at face value without interpretation.

Matching hypothesis The prediction that most people will find friends and mates that are perceived to be of about their same level of attractiveness.

Maturation The process by which the genetic program manifests itself over time.

Medical model The view that mental disorders are diseases that, like ordinary physical diseases, have objective physical causes and require specific treatments.

Meditation A state of consciousness often induced by focusing on a repetitive behavior, assuming certain body positions, and minimizing external stimulation. Meditation may be intended to enhance self-knowledge, well-being, and spirituality.

Medulla A brain-stem structure that controls breathing and heart rate. The sensory and motor pathways connecting the brain to the body cross in the medulla.

Memory Any system—human, animal, or machine—that encodes, stores, and retrieves information.

Menarche The onset of menstruation.

Mental age (MA) The average age at which normal (average) individuals achieve a particular score.

Mental operation Solving a problem by manipulating images in one's mind.

Mental representation The ability to form internal images of objects and events.

Mental retardation Often conceived as representing the lower 2 percent of the IQ range, commencing about 30 points below average (below about 70 points). More sophisticated definitions also take into account an individual's level of social functioning and other abilities.

Mental set The tendency to respond to a new problem in the manner used for a previous problem.

Mere exposure effect A learned preference for stimuli to which we have been previously exposed.

Method of loci A mnemonic technique that involves associating items on a list with a sequence of familiar physical locations.

Mimicry The imitation of other people's behaviors.

Mindset The extent to which one believes abilities and talents are fixed by nature or can change and grow through practice, and that experience influences success that requires hard work and effort, and also one's reactions to failure.

Mirror neuron A recently discovered class of neuron that fires in response to ("mirroring") observation of another person's actions or emotions.

Misattribution A memory fault that occurs when memories are retrieved but are associated with the wrong time, place, or person.

Misinformation effect The distortion of memory by suggestion or misinformation.

MMPI-2 A widely used personality assessment instrument that gives scores on ten important clinical traits; also called the *Minnesota Multiphasic Personality Inventory*.

Mnemonic strategy Technique for improving memory, especially by making connections between new material and information already stored in long-term memory.

Moderator Factor that helps prevent stressors from causing stress.

Monocular cues Information about depth that relies on the input of just one eye—includes relative size, light and shadow, interposition, relative motion, and atmospheric perspective.

Mood-congruent memory A memory process that selectively retrieves memories that match (are congruent with) one's mood.

Mood disorder Abnormal disturbance in emotion or mood, including bipolar disorder and unipolar disorder. Mood disorders are also called affective disorders.

Morpheme A meaningful unit of language that makes up words. Some whole words are morphemes (example: *word*); other morphemes include grammatical components that alter a word's meaning (examples: *-ed*, *-ing*, and *un-*).

Motivation Refers to all the processes involved in initiating, directing, and maintaining physical and psychological activities.

Motive An internal mechanism that arouses the organism and then selects and directs behavior. The term *motive* is often used in the narrower sense of a motivational process that is learned, rather than biologically based (as are drives).

Motor cortex A narrow vertical strip of cortex in the frontal lobes lying just in front of the central fissure; controls voluntary movement.

Motor neuron A nerve cell that carries messages *away* from the central nervous system toward the muscles and glands; also called *efferent neurons*.

MRI or **magnetic resonance imaging** An imaging technique that relies on cells' responses in a high-intensity magnetic field.

Multiple intelligences A term used to refer to Gardner's theory, which proposes that there are seven (or more) forms of intelligence.

Myers–Briggs Type Indicator (MBTI) A widely used personality test based on Jungian types.

Narcissistic personality disorder Condition involving an exaggerated sense of self-importance, a need for constant attention or admiration, and often a preoccupation with fantasies of success or power.

Narcolepsy A disorder of REM sleep, involving sleep-onset REM periods and sudden daytime REM-sleep attacks, usually accompanied by cataplexy.

narrative A personal account of a stressful event that describes our interpretation of what happened and why.

Natural concepts Mental representations of objects and events drawn from our direct experience.

Natural language mediator Word associated with new information to be remembered.

Natural selection The driving force behind evolution by which the environment "selects" the fittest organisms.

Naturalistic observation A form of descriptive research involving behavioral assessment of people or animals in their natural surroundings.

Nature–nurture issue The long-standing discussion over the relative importance of nature (heredity) and nurture (environment) in their influence on behavior and mental processes.

Necker cube An ambiguous two-dimensional figure of a cube that can be seen from different perspectives: The Necker cube is used here to illustrate the notion that there is no single "right way" to view psychological processes.

Need In drive theory, a need is a biological imbalance (such as dehydration) that threatens survival if the need is left unmet. Biological needs are believed to produce drives.

Need for achievement (*n Ach*) In McClelland's theory, a mental state that produces a psychological motive to excel or to reach some goal.

Negative correlation A correlation coefficient indicating that the variables change simultaneously in opposite directions: As one becomes larger, the other gets smaller.

Negative punishment The removal of an attractive stimulus after a response.

Negative reinforcement The removal of an unpleasant or aversive stimulus, contingent on a particular behavior. Contrast with *punishment*.

Neo-Freudian Literally "new Freudian" refers to theorists who broke with Freud but whose theories retain a psychodynamic aspect, especially a focus on motivation as the source of energy for the personality.

Neo-Freudian psychodynamic therapy Therapy for a mental disorder that was developed by psychodynamic theorists who embraced some of Freud's ideas but disagreed with others.

Neonatal period In humans, the neonatal (newborn) period extends through the first month after birth.

Nervous system The entire network of neurons in the body, including the central nervous system, the peripheral nervous system, and their subdivisions.

Neural pathways Bundles of nerve cells that follow generally the same route and employ the same neurotransmitter.

Neuron Cell specialized to receive and transmit information to other cells in the body—also called a *nerve cell*. Bundles of many neurons are called *nerves*.

Neuroscience The field devoted to understanding how the brain creates thoughts, feelings, motives, consciousness, memories, and other mental processes.

Neurosis Before the *DSM-IV*, this term was used as a label for subjective distress or self-defeating behavior that did not show signs of brain abnormalities or grossly irrational thinking.

Neurotic needs Signs of neurosis in Horney's theory, the ten needs are normal desires carried to a neurotic extreme.

Neurotransmitter Chemical messenger that relays neural messages across the synapse. Many neurotransmitters are also hormones.

Neutral stimulus Any stimulus that produces no conditioned response prior to learning. When it is brought into a conditioning experiment, the researcher will call it a conditioned stimulus (CS). The assumption is that some conditioning occurs after even one pairing of the CS and UCS.

Night terrors Deep sleep episodes that seem to produce terror, although any terrifying mental experience (such as a dream) is usually forgotten on awakening. Night terrors occur mainly in children.

Nonconscious process Any brain process that does not involve conscious processing, including both preconscious memories and unconscious processes.

Non-REM (NREM) sleep The recurring periods, mainly associated with the deeper stages of sleep, when a sleeper is not showing rapid eye movements.

Normal distribution (or normal curve) A bell-shaped curve describing the spread of a characteristic throughout a population.

Normal range Scores falling near the middle of a normal distribution.

Object permanence The knowledge that objects exist independently of one's own actions or awareness.

Observational learning A form of cognitive learning in which new responses are acquired after watching others' behavior and the consequences of their behavior.

Obsessive–compulsive disorder (OCD) A condition characterized by patterns of persistent, unwanted thoughts and behaviors.

Occipital lobes The cortical regions at the back of the brain that house the visual cortex.

Oedipus complex According to Freud, a largely unconscious process whereby boys displace an erotic attraction toward their mother to females of their own age and, at the same time, identify with their fathers.

Olfaction The sense of smell.

Operant chamber A boxlike apparatus that can be programmed to deliver reinforcers and punishers contingent on an animal's behavior. The operant chamber is often called a "Skinner box."

Operant conditioning A form of behavioral learning in which the probability of a response is changed by its consequences—that is, by the stimuli that follow the response.

Operational definitions Objective descriptions of concepts involved in a scientific study. Operational definitions may restate concepts to be studied in behavioral terms (e.g., fear may be operationally defined as moving away from a stimulus). Operational definitions also specify the procedures used to produce and measure important variables under investigation (e.g., "attraction" may be measured by the amount of time one person spends looking at another).

Opiate Highly addictive drug, derived from opium, that can produce a profound sense of well-being and have strong pain-relieving properties.

Opponent-process theory The idea that cells in the visual system process colors in complementary pairs, such as red or green or as yellow or blue. The opponent-process theory explains color sensation from the bipolar cells onward in the visual system.

Optic nerve The bundle of neurons that carries visual information from the retina to the brain.

Optimism An attitude that interprets stressors as external in origin, temporary, and specific in their effects.

Out-group Those outside the group with which an individual identifies.

Overjustification The process by which extrinsic (external) rewards can sometimes displace internal motivation, as when a child receives money for playing video games.

Oxytocin A hormone produced (by both women and men) in response to a stressor.

Panic disorder A disturbance marked by panic attacks that have no obvious connection with events in the person's present experience. Unlike generalized anxiety disorder, the victim is usually free of anxiety between panic attacks.

Paraprofessional Individual who has received on-the-job training (and, in some cases, undergraduate training) in mental health treatment in lieu of graduate education and full professional certification.

Parasympathetic division The part of the autonomic nervous system that monitors the routine operations of the internal organs and returns the body to calmer functioning after arousal by the sympathetic division.

Parietal lobes Cortical areas lying toward the back and top of the brain; involved in touch sensation and in perceiving spatial relationships (the relationships of objects in space).

Participant modeling A social learning technique in which a therapist demonstrates and encourages a client to imitate a desired behavior.

Peer marriage Marriage in which the couple see each other as partners and friends, as contrasted with the older stereotypic roles of "husband" and "wife."

Percept The meaningful product of perception—often an image that has been associated with concepts, memories of events, emotions, and motives.

Perception A process that makes sensory patterns meaningful. It is perception that makes these words meaningful, rather than just a string of visual patterns. To make this happen, perception draws heavily on memory, motivation, emotion, and other psychological processes.

Perceptual constancy The ability to recognize the same object as remaining "constant" under different conditions, such as changes in illumination, distance, or location.

Perceptual set Readiness to detect a particular stimulus in a given context—as when a person who is afraid interprets an unfamiliar sound as a threat.

Peripheral nervous system (PNS) All parts of the nervous system lying outside the central nervous system. The peripheral nervous system includes the autonomic and somatic nervous systems.

Permissive parent One of the four parenting styles, characterized by setting few rules and allowing children to make their own decisions. While they may be caring and communicative, permissive parents give most decision-making responsibilities to their children.

Persistence A memory problem in which unwanted memories cannot be put out of mind.

Personal unconscious Jung's term for that portion of the unconscious corresponding roughly to the Freudian id.

Personality The psychological qualities that bring continuity to an individual's behavior in different situations and at different times.

Personality disorder Condition involving a chronic pervasive, inflexible, and maladaptive pattern of thinking, emotion, social relationships, or impulse control.

Personality process The internal working of the personality, involving motivation, emotion, perception, and learning, as well as unconscious processes.

Personality type Similar to a trait, but instead of being a *dimension*, a type is a *category* that is believed to represent a common cluster of personality characteristics.

Person–situation controversy Debate over the relative contributions to understanding human behavior from personality processes, like traits, versus social psychological processes, like the power of situational variables.

PET scanning or **positron emission tomography** An imaging technique that relies on the detection of radioactive sugar consumed by active brain cells.

Phenomenal field One's psychological reality, composed of one's perceptions and feelings.

Phenotype An organism's observable physical and behavioral characteristics.

Pheromones Chemical signals released by organisms to communicate with other members of their species. Pheromones are often used by animals as sexual attractants. It is unclear whether or not humans employ pheromones.

Phobia One of a group of anxiety disorders involving a pathological fear of a specific object or situation.

Photoreceptors Light-sensitive cells (neurons) in the retina that convert light energy to neural impulses. The photoreceptors are as far as light gets into the visual system.

Physical dependence A process by which the body adjusts to, and comes to need, a drug for its everyday functioning.

Pitch A sensory characteristic of sound produced by the *frequency* of the sound wave.

Pituitary gland The "master gland" that produces hormones influencing the secretions of all other endocrine glands, as well as a hormone that influences growth. The pituitary is attached to the brain's hypothalamus, from which it takes its orders.

Placebo *(pla-SEE-bo)* Substance that appears to be a drug but is not. Placebos are often referred to as "sugar pills" because they might contain only sugar, rather than a real drug.

Placebo effect A response to a placebo (a fake drug) caused by the belief that it is a real drug.

Placenta The organ interface between the embryo or fetus and the mother. The placenta separates the bloodstreams, but it allows the exchange of nutrients and waste products.

Plasticity The nervous system's ability to adapt or change as a result of experience. Plasticity may also help the nervous system adapt to physical damage.

Polygraph A device that records or graphs many ("poly") measures of physical arousal, such as heart rate, breathing, perspiration, and blood pressure. A polygraph is often called a "lie detector," even though it is really an arousal detector.

Pons A brain-stem structure that regulates brain activity during sleep and dreaming. The name *pons* derives from the Latin word for "bridge."

Positive correlation A correlation coefficient indicating that the variables change simultaneously in the same direction: As one grows larger or smaller, the other grows or shrinks in a parallel way.

Positive lifestyle choices Deliberate decisions about long-term behavior patterns that increase resistance to both stress and illness.

Positive psychology A recent movement within psychology, focusing on desirable aspects of human functioning, as opposed to an emphasis on psychopathology.

Positive psychotherapy (PPT) A relatively new form of cognitive–behavioral treatment that seeks to emphasize growth, health, and happiness.

Positive punishment The application of an aversive stimulus after a response.

Positive reinforcement A stimulus presented after a response and increasing the probability of that response happening again.

Posttraumatic stress disorder (PTSD) A delayed stress reaction in which an individual involuntarily re-experiences emotional, cognitive, and behavioral aspects of past trauma.

Practical intelligence According to Sternberg, the ability to cope with the environment; sometimes called "street smarts."

Preconscious Freud's notion that the mind has a special unconscious storehouse for information not currently in consciousness but readily available to consciousness. Example: your telephone number is stored in the preconscious.

Prejudice A negative attitude toward an individual based solely on his or her membership in a particular group or category, often without any direct evidence.

Premack principle The concept, developed by David Premack, that a more-preferred activity can be used to reinforce a less-preferred activity.

Prenatal period The developmental period before birth.

Preoperational stage The second stage in Piaget's theory, marked by well-developed mental representation and the use of language.

Preparedness hypothesis The notion that we have an innate tendency, acquired through natural selection, to respond quickly and automatically to stimuli that posed a survival threat to our ancestors.

Primary control Efforts aimed at controlling external events.

Primary reinforcer A reinforcer, such as food or sex, that has an innate basis because of its biological value to an organism.

Priming A technique for cuing implicit memories by providing cues that stimulate a memory without awareness of the connection between the cue and the retrieved memory.

Principle of proximity The notion that people at work will make more friends among those who are nearby—with whom they have the most contact. *Proximity* means "nearness."

Proactive interference A cause of forgetting by which previously stored information prevents learning and remembering new information.

Problem-focused coping Action taken to clarify and resolve a stressor.

Procedural memory A division of LTM that stores memories for how things are done.

Projective test Personality assessment instrument, such as the Rorschach and TAT, which is based on Freud's ego defense mechanism of projection.

Prospective memory The aspect of memory that enables one to remember to take some action in the future—as remembering a doctor's appointment.

Prototype An ideal or most representative example of a conceptual category.

Proximal level of analysis Concerns stimuli in the organism's immediate environment that can change motivational priorities. (In humans, *proximal* could also refer to things that the individual is thinking about.)

Pseudo-psychology Erroneous assertions or practices set forth as being scientific psychology.

Psychiatry A medical specialty dealing with the diagnosis and treatment of mental disorders.

Psychic determinism Freud's assumption that all our mental and behavioral responses are caused by unconscious traumas, desires, or conflicts.

Psychoactive drug Chemical that affects mental processes and behavior by its effect on the brain.

Psychoanalysis A method of treating mental disorders that is based on Sigmund Freud's psychoanalytic theory. The goal of psychoanalysis is to release unacknowledged conflicts, urges, and memories from the unconscious. (In common usage, the term often refers broadly both to Freud's psychoanalytic theory and to his psychoanalytic treatment method.)

Psychoanalytic theory Freud's theory of personality and mental disorder.

Psychodynamic psychology A clinical approach emphasizing the understanding of mental disorders in terms of unconscious needs, desires, memories, and conflicts.

Psychodynamic theory A group of theories that originated with Freud. All emphasize motivation—often unconscious motivation—and the influence of the past on the development of mental disorders.

Psychological debriefing Brief, immediate strategy focusing on venting emotions and discussing reactions to a trauma.

Psychological dependence A desire to obtain or use a drug, even though there is no physical dependence.

Psychological therapy Therapy based on psychological principles (rather than on the biomedical approach); often called "psychotherapy."

Psychology The science of behavior and mental processes.

Psycho-neuroimmunology Multidisciplinary field that studies the influence of mental states on the immune system.

Psychopathology Any pattern of emotions, behaviors, or thoughts inappropriate to the situation and leading to personal distress or the inability to achieve important goals. Other terms having essentially the same meaning include *mental illness, mental disorder,* and *psychological disorder.*

Psychosexual stages Successive, instinctive developmental phases in which pleasure is associated with stimulation of different bodily areas at different times of life.

Psychosis A disorder involving profound disturbances in perception, rational thinking, or affect.

Psychosocial stage In Erikson's theory, the developmental stages refer to eight major challenges that appear successively across the lifespan, which require an individual to rethink his or her goals, as well as relationships with others.

Psychosurgery The general term for surgical intervention in the brain to treat psychological disorders.

Puberty The onset of sexual maturity.

Punishment An aversive consequence which, occurring after a response, diminishes the strength of that response. (Contrast with *negative reinforcement.*)

Random assignment A process used to assign individuals to various experimental conditions by chance alone.

Ratio schedule A program by which reinforcement depends on the number of correct responses.

Rational–emotive behavior therapy (REBT) Albert Ellis's brand of cognitive therapy, based on the idea that irrational thoughts and behaviors are the cause of mental disorders.

Recall A retrieval method in which one must reproduce previously presented information.

Reciprocal determinism The process in which cognitions, behavior, and the environment mutually influence each other.

Recognition A retrieval method in which one must identify present stimuli as having been previously presented.

Redemptive self A common self-narrative identified by McAdams in generative Americans. The redemptive self involves a sense of being called to overcome obstacles in an effort to help others.

Reflection of feeling Carl Rogers's technique of paraphrasing the clients' words, attempting to capture the emotional tone expressed.

Reflex Simple unlearned response triggered by stimuli—such as the knee-jerk reflex set off by tapping the tendon just below your kneecap.

Reinforcement contingencies Relationships between a response and the changes in stimulation that follow the response.

Reinforcer A condition (involving either the presentation or removal of a stimulus) that occurs after a response and strengthens that response.

Reliability An attribute of a psychological test that gives consistent results.

REM rebound A condition of increased REM sleep caused by REM-sleep deprivation.

REM sleep A stage of sleep that occurs approximately every 90 minutes, marked by bursts of rapid eye movements occurring under closed eyelids. REM sleep periods are associated with dreaming.

Replicate In research, this refers to doing a study over to see whether the same results are obtained. As a control for bias, replication is often done by someone other than the researcher who performed the original study.

Representativeness bias A faulty heuristic strategy based on the presumption that, once people or events are categorized, they share all the features of other members in that category.

Repression An unconscious process that excludes unacceptable thoughts and feelings from awareness and memory.

Resilience The capacity to adapt, achieve well-being, and cope with stress, in spite of serious threats to development.

Resistance phase Second phase of the GAS, during which the body adapts to and maintains resources to cope with the stressor.

Resting potential The electrical charge of the axon in its inactive state, when the neuron is ready to "fire."

Reticular formation A pencil-shaped structure forming the core of the brain stem. The reticular formation arouses the cortex to keep the brain alert and attentive to new stimulation.

Retina The thin light-sensitive layer at the back of the eyeball. The retina contains millions of photoreceptors and other nerve cells.

Retrieval The third basic task of memory, involving the location and recovery of information from memory.

Retrieval cue Stimulus used to bring a memory to consciousness or to cue a behavior.

Retroactive interference A cause of forgetting by which newly learned information prevents retrieval of previously stored material.

Retrograde amnesia The inability to remember information previously stored in memory. (Contrast with anterograde amnesia.)

Reuptake The process by which unused neurotransmitters are drawn back into the vesicles of their originating neuron.

Revolution in aging A change in the way people think about aging in modern industrialized nations. This new perspective grows out of increased longevity, better health care, and more lifestyle choices available to older adults. It has also stimulated the psychological study of adult development.

Reward theory of attraction A social learning view that predicts we like best those who give us maximum rewards at minimum cost.

Rite of passage Social ritual that marks the transition between developmental stages, especially between childhood and adulthood.

Rods Photoreceptors in the retina that are especially sensitive to dim light but not to colors. Strange as it may seem, they are rod-shaped.

Romantic love A temporary and highly emotional condition based on infatuation and sexual desire.

Rorschach Inkblot Technique A projective test requiring subjects to describe what they see in a series of ten inkblots.

Rumination A pernicious form of negative self-reflection in which a person dwells on depressive thoughts and feelings in response to stress; can compromise the immune system.

Savant syndrome Found in individuals having a remarkable talent (such as the ability to determine the day of the week for any given date) even though they are mentally slow in other domains.

Scaffolding A teaching strategy that emphasizes the role of help from others in providing support for a person's learning.

Scapegoating Blaming an innocent person or a group for one's own troubles and then discriminating against or abusing them.

Schedule of reinforcement A program specifying the frequency and timing of reinforcements.

Schema Cluster of related information that represents ideas or concepts in semantic memory. Schemas provide a context for understanding objects and events; in Piaget's theory, a mental structure or program that guides a developing child's thought.

Schizophrenia (pronounced *skits-o-FRENNY-a*) A psychotic disorder involving distortions in thoughts, perceptions, and/or emotions.

Schlesinger Report Report issued by one of the official investigations of the Abu Ghraib Prison abuses, headed by James Schlesinger, former Secretary of Defense. It highlighted the social psychological factors that contributed to creating an abusive environment.

Scientific method A four-step process for empirical investigation of a hypothesis under conditions designed to control biases and subjective judgments.

Script Knowledge about the events, objects, and actions expected in a particular situation.

Seasonal affective disorder (SAD) A form of depression believed to be caused by deprivation of sunlight.

Secondary control Efforts aimed at controlling one's reactions to external events.

Secure attachment The attachment style of children who are relaxed and comfortable with their caregivers and tolerant of strangers and new experiences—as contrasted with children who are *insecurely attached*.

Selective social interaction Choosing to restrict the number of one's social contacts to those who are the most gratifying.

Self-actualizing personality A healthy individual who has met his or her basic needs and is free to be creative and fulfil his or her potentialities.

Self-consistency bias The commonly held idea that we are more consistent in our attitudes, opinions, and beliefs than we actually are.

Self-control The ability to delay instant gratification in pursuit of long-range positive outcomes.

Self-disclosure The sharing of personal information and feelings with another person as part of the process of developing trust.

Self-fulfilling prophecy Observations or behaviors that result primarily from expectations.

Self-help support groups Groups, such as Alcoholics Anonymous, that provide social support and an opportunity for sharing ideas about dealing with common problems. Such groups are typically organized and run by laypersons, rather than by professional therapists.

Self-narrative The "stories" one tells about oneself. Self-narratives help people sense a thread of consistency through their personalities over time.

Self-serving bias An attributional pattern in which one takes credit for success but denies responsibility for failure. (Compare with *fundamental attribution error.*)

Semantic memory A subdivision of declarative memory that stores general knowledge, including the meanings of words and concepts.

Sensation The process by which stimulation of a sensory receptor produces neural impulses that the brain interprets as a sound, a visual image, an odor, a taste, a pain, or other sensory image. Sensation represents the first series of steps in processing of incoming information.

Sensation seekers In Zuckerman's theory, individuals who have a biological need for higher levels of stimulation than do most other people.

Sense making One aspect of finding meaning in a stressful situation, which involves perceiving the stressor in a manner consistent with our expectations of the world as predictable, controllable, and nonrandom.

Sensitive period A span of time during which the organism is especially responsive to stimuli of a particular sort. Organisms may have sensitive periods for exposure to certain hormones or chemicals; similarly, they may have sensitive periods for learning language or receiving the visual stimulation necessary for normal development of vision.

Sensorimotor intelligence Piaget's term for the infant's approach to the world, relying on relatively simple physical (motor) responses to sensory experience.

Sensorimotor stage The first stage in Piaget's theory, during which the child relies heavily on innate motor responses to stimuli.

Sensory adaptation Loss of responsiveness in receptor cells after stimulation has remained unchanged for a while, as when a swimmer becomes adapted to the temperature of the water.

Sensory memory The first of three memory stages, preserving brief sensory impressions of stimuli.

Sensory neuron A nerve cell that carries messages *toward* the central nervous system from sense receptors; also called *afferent neurons*.

Separation anxiety A common pattern of distress seen in young children when separated from their caregivers.

Serial position effect A form of interference related to the sequence in which information is presented. Generally, items in the middle of the sequence are less well remembered than items presented first or last.

Set point Refers to the tendency of the body to maintain a certain level of body fat and body weight.

Sex chromosomes The X and Y chromosomes that determine our physical sex characteristics.

Sexual orientation The direction of one's sexual interests (usually for individuals of the same sex, the opposite sex, or both sexes).

Sexual response cycle The four-stage sequence of arousal, plateau, orgasm, and resolution, occurring in both men and women.

Shaping An operant learning technique in which a new behavior is produced by reinforcing responses that are similar to the desired response.

Shyness A common temperamental condition, but not a disorder, recognized by the *DSM-IV*.

Signal detection theory Explains how we detect "signals," consisting of stimulation affecting our eyes, ears, nose, skin, and other sense organs. Signal detection theory says that sensation is a judgment the sensory system makes about incoming stimulation. Often, it occurs outside of consciousness. In contrast to older theories from psychophysics, signal detection theory takes observer characteristics into account.

Similarity principle The notion that people are attracted to those who are most similar to themselves on significant dimensions.

Situationism The view that environmental conditions may influence people's behavior as much as or more than their personal dispositions do under some circumstances.

Skin senses   Sensory systems for processing touch, warmth, cold, texture, and pain.

Sleep apnea   A respiratory disorder in which the person intermittently stops breathing many times while asleep.

Sleep debt   A sleep deficiency caused by not getting the amount of sleep required for optimal functioning.

Sleep paralysis   A condition in which a sleeper is unable to move any of the voluntary muscles except those controlling the eyes. Sleep paralysis normally occurs during REM sleep.

Social comparison   A type of cognitive restructuring involving comparisons between oneself and others in similar situations.

Social context   The combination of (a) people, (b) the activities and interactions among people, (c) the setting in which behavior occurs, and (d) the expectations and social norms governing behavior in that setting.

Social distance   The perceived difference or similarity between oneself and another person.

Social neuroscience   An area of research that uses methodologies from brain sciences to investigate various types of social behavior, such as stereotyping in prejudice, attitudes, self-control, and emotional regulation.

Social norms   A group's expectations regarding what is appropriate and acceptable for its members' attitudes and behaviors.

Social psychology   The branch of psychology that studies the effects of social variables and cognitions on individual behavior and social interactions.

Social Readjustment Rating Scale (SRRS)   Psychological rating scale designed to measure stress levels by attaching numerical values to common life changes.

Social reality   An individual's subjective interpretation of other people and of one's relationships with them.

Social role   A socially defined pattern of behavior that is expected of persons in a given setting or group.

Social support   Resources others provide to help an individual cope with stress.

Social-cognitive theories   A group of theories that involve explanations of limited but important aspects of personality (e.g., locus of control). All grew out of experimental psychology.

Socialization   The lifelong process of shaping an individual's behavior patterns, values, standards, skills, attitudes, and motives to conform to those regarded as desirable in a particular society.

Societal stressor   A chronic stressor resulting from pressure in one's social, cultural, or economic environment.

Sociocultural perspective   A main psychological viewpoint emphasizing the importance of social interaction, social learning, and a culture in explaining behavior.

Soma   The part of a cell (such as a neuron) containing the nucleus, which includes the chromosomes; also called the *cell body*.

Somatic nervous system   A division of the peripheral nervous system that carries sensory information to the central nervous system and also sends voluntary messages to the body's skeletal muscles.

Somatoform disorders   Psychological problem appearing in the form of bodily symptoms or physical complaints, such as weakness or excessive worry about disease. The somatoform disorders include conversion disorder and hypochondriasis.

Somatosensory cortex   A strip of the parietal lobe lying just behind the central fissure. The somatosensory cortex is involved with sensations of touch.

Spontaneous recovery   The reappearance of an extinguished conditioned response after a time delay.

Stage of moral reasoning   Distinctive way of thinking about ethical and moral problems. According to Kohlberg, moral reasoning progresses through a series of developmental stages that are similar to Piaget's stages of cognitive development.

Stage theory   An explanation of development that emphasizes distinctive or rather abrupt changes. A stage theory of cognitive development, then, emphasizes revolutionary changes in thought processes.

Stanford Prison Experiment   Classic study of institutional power in directing normal, healthy college student volunteers playing randomly assigned roles of prisoners and guards to behave contrary to their dispositional tendencies, as cruel guards or pathological prisoners.

Stereotype threat   An expectation of being judged by the standard of a negative stereotype. Such expectations can adversely affect performance. Also the negative effect on performance that arises when an individual becomes aware that members of his or her group are expected to perform poorly in that domain.

Stimulant   A drug that arouses the central nervous system, speeding up mental and physical responses. Stimulants normally increase activity level by encouraging communication among neurons in the brain. Stimulants, however, have been found to suppress activity level in persons with attention-deficit/hyperactivity disorder.

Stimulus discrimination   Learning to respond to a particular stimulus but not to stimuli that are similar.

Stimulus generalization   The extension of a learned response to stimuli that are similar to the conditioned stimulus.

Storage   The second of the three basic tasks of memory, involving the retention of encoded material over time.

Stress   The physical and mental response to a stressor.

Stressor   A stressful event or situation.

Structuralism   A historical school of psychology devoted to uncovering the basic structures that make up mind and thought. Structuralists sought the "elements" of conscious experience.

Subjective well-being (SWB)   An individual's evaluative response to life, commonly called happiness, which includes cognitive and emotional reactions.

Subliminal perception   The process by which a stimulus that is below the awareness threshold can be sensed and interpreted outside of consciousness.

Suggestibility   The process of memory distortion as a result of deliberate or inadvertent suggestion.

Superego   The mind's storehouse of values, including moral attitudes learned from parents and from society; roughly the same as the common notion of the conscience.

Survey   A technique used in descriptive research, typically involving seeking people's responses to a prepared set of verbal or written items.

Sympathetic division   The part of the autonomic nervous system that sends messages to internal organs and glands that help us respond to stressful and emergency situations.

Synapse   The microscopic gap that serves as a communications link between neurons. Synapses also occur between neurons and the muscles or glands they serve.

Synaptic pruning   The process of trimming unused brain connections, making neurons available for future development.

Synaptic transmission   The relaying of information across the synapse by means of chemical neurotransmitters.

Synchronicity The close coordination between the gazing, vocalizing, touching, and smiling of infants and caregivers.

Synesthesia The mixing of sensations across sensory modalities, as in tasting shapes or seeing colors associated with numbers.

System power Influences on behavior that come from top-down sources in the form of creating and maintaining various situations that in turn have an impact on actions of individuals in those behavioral contexts.

Systematic desensitization A behavioral therapy technique in which anxiety is extinguished by exposing the patient to an anxiety-provoking stimulus.

Tardive dyskinesia An incurable disorder of motor control, especially involving muscles of the face and head, resulting from long-term use of antipsychotic drugs.

Targeted rejection The exclusive, active, and intentional social rejection of an individual by others.

Teachers of psychology Psychologists whose primary job is teaching, typically in high schools, colleges, and universities.

Telegraphic speech Short, simple sequences of nouns and verbs without plurals, tenses, or function words like *the* and *of*—somewhat like the language once used in telegrams.

Telomeres DNA protein complexes that cap the ends of chromosomes and protect against damage to DNA.

Temperament An individual's characteristic manner of behavior or reaction—assumed to have a strong genetic basis.

Temporal lobes Cortical lobes that process sounds, including speech. The temporal lobes are probably involved in storing long-term memories.

Tend-and-befriend Stress response model proposing that females are biologically predisposed to respond to threat by nurturing and protecting offspring and seeking social support.

Teratogen Substances from the environment, including viruses, drugs, and other chemicals, that can damage the developing organism during the prenatal period.

Terminal buttons Tiny bulblike structures at the end of the axon that contain neurotransmitters that carry the neuron's message into the synapse.

Terrorism A type of disaster caused by human malevolence with the goal of disrupting society by creating fear and danger.

Thalamus The brain's central "relay station," situated just atop the brain stem. Nearly all the messages going into or out of the brain go through the thalamus.

Thematic Apperception Test (TAT) A projective test requiring subjects to make up stories that explain ambiguous pictures.

Theory A testable explanation for a set of facts or observations. In science, a theory is not just speculation or a guess.

Theory of mind An awareness that other people's behavior may be influenced by beliefs, desires, and emotions that differ from one's own.

Therapeutic alliance The relationship between the therapist and the client, with both parties working together to help the client deal with mental or behavioral issues.

Therapy A general term for any treatment process; in psychology and psychiatry, therapy refers to a variety of psychological and biomedical techniques aimed at dealing with mental disorders or coping with problems of living.

Timbre The quality of a sound wave that derives from the wave's complexity (combination of pure tones). *Timbre* comes from the Greek word for "drum" as does the term *tympanic membrane* or eardrum.

Token economy An operant technique applied to groups, such as classrooms or mental hospital wards, involving the distribution of "tokens" or other indicators of reinforcement contingent on desired behaviors. The tokens can later be exchanged for privileges, food, or other reinforcers.

Tolerance The reduced effectiveness a drug has after repeated use.

Top-down processing Perceptual analysis that emphasizes the perceiver's expectations, concept memories, and other cognitive factors, rather than being driven by the characteristics of the stimulus. "Top" refers to a mental set in the brain—which stands at the "top" of the perceptual processing system.

TOT phenomenon The inability to recall a word, while knowing that it is in memory. People often describe this frustrating experience as having the word "on the tip of the tongue."

Trait and temperament psychology A psychological perspective that views behavior and personality as the products of enduring psychological characteristics.

Traits Multiple stable personality characteristics that are presumed to exist within the individual and that guide his or her thoughts and actions under various conditions.

Transcranial magnetic stimulation (TMS) A treatment that involves magnetic stimulation of specific regions of the brain. Unlike ECT, TMS does not produce a seizure.

Transduction Transformation of one form of information into another—especially the transformation of stimulus information into nerve signals by the sense organs. As a result of transduction, the brain interprets the incoming light waves from a ripe tomato as red.

Transience The impermanence of a long-term memory. Transience is based on the idea that long-term memories gradually fade in strength over time.

Transition An individual's redefinition or transformation of a life role.

Traumatic stressor A situation that threatens one's physical safety, arousing feelings of fear, horror, or helplessness.

Triangular theory of love Developed by Robert Sternberg, a theory that describes various kinds of love in terms of three components: passion (erotic attraction), intimacy (sharing feelings and confidences), and commitment (dedication to putting this relationship first in one's life).

Triarchic theory The term for Sternberg's theory of intelligence; so called because it combines three ("tri-") main forms of intelligence.

Trichromatic theory The idea that colors are sensed by three different types of cones sensitive to light in the red, blue, and green wavelengths. The trichromatic (three-color) theory explains the earliest stage of color sensation. In honor of its originators, this is sometimes called the Young-Helmholtz theory.

Trust The major developmental goal during the first 18 months of life. According to Erikson's theory, the child must choose between trusting or not trusting others.

Twin study A means of separating the effects of nature and nurture by which investigators may compare identical twins to fraternal twins or compare twins separated early in life and raised in different environments.

Two-factor theory The idea that emotion results from the cognitive appraisal of both physical arousal (Factor #1) and an emotion-provoking stimulus (Factor #2).

Tympanic membrane   The eardrum.

Type A   Behavior pattern characterized by intense, angry, competitive, or hostile responses to challenging situations.

Tyranny of choice   The impairment of effective decision making when confronted with an overwhelming number of choices.

Unconditioned response (UCR)   In classical conditioning, the response elicited by an unconditioned stimulus without prior learning.

Unconditioned stimulus (UCS)   In classical conditioning, UCS is the stimulus that elicits an unconditioned response.

Unconscious   In classic Freudian theory, a part of the mind that houses emotional memories, desires, and feelings that would be threatening if brought to consciousness. Many modern cognitive psychologists, however, view the unconscious in less sinister terms, as including all nonconscious mental processes.

Uninvolved parent   One of the four parenting styles, characterized by indifference or rejection, sometimes to the point of neglect or abuse.

Upward social comparison   Comparison between one's own stressful situation and others in a similar situation who are coping more effectively, with the goal of learning from others' examples.

Validity   An attribute of a psychological test that actually measures what it is being used to measure.

Variable interval (VI) schedule   A program by which the time period between reinforcements varies from trial to trial.

Variable ratio (VR) schedule   A reinforcement program by which the number of responses required for a reinforcement varies from trial to trial.

Vestibular sense   The sense of body orientation with respect to gravity. The vestibular sense is closely associated with the inner ear and, in fact, is carried to the brain on a branch of the auditory nerve.

Vicarious traumatization   Severe stress caused by exposure to traumatic images or stories that cause the observer to become engaged with the stressful material.

Visible spectrum   The tiny part of the electromagnetic spectrum to which our eyes are sensitive. The visible spectrum of other creatures may be slightly different from our own.

Visual cortex   The visual processing areas of cortex in the occipital and temporal lobes.

Wave metaphor   A way of conceptualizing cognitive development, as occurring more gradually—in "waves"—rather than abruptly, as the stage theory suggests.

Weber's law   The concept that the size of a JND is proportional to the intensity of the stimulus; the JND is large when the stimulus intensity is high and small when the stimulus intensity is low.

What pathway   A neural pathway, projecting from the primary visual cortex to the temporal lobe, that involves identifying objects.

Where pathway   A neural pathway that projects visu tion to the parietal lobe; responsible for locating objects in space.

Whole method   The mnemonic strategy of first approaching the material to be learned "as a whole," forming an impression of the overall meaning of the material. The details are later associated with this overall impression.

Whole-person perspectives   A group of psychological perspectives that take a global view of the person: Included are *psychodynamic psychology, humanistic psychology,* and *trait and temperament psychology.*

Wisdom   According to Sternberg, using one's intelligence toward a common good rather than a selfish pursuit.

Withdrawal   A pattern of uncomfortable or painful physical symptoms and cravings experienced by the user when the level of drug is decreased or when the drug is eliminated.

Working memory   The second of three memory stages and the one most limited in capacity. It preserves recently perceived events or experiences for less than a minute without rehearsal.

Zero correlation   When two variables have no relationship to each other.

Zygote   A fertilized egg.

REFERENCES

(2010). Lance Armstrong. *Encyclopedia of World Biography*. Retrieved from www.notablebiographies .com/news/A-Ca/Armstrong-Lance.html.

(2010). Lance's bio. Retrieved from http:// lancearmstrong.com/.

ABC News. (1995, June 30). My family, forgive me. *20/20*, Transcript #1526, pp. 6–10. New York: American Broadcasting Companies, Inc.

Abelson, R. P. (1981). Psychological status of the script concept. *American Psychologist, 36*, 715–729.

Abrams, A. R. (1992). *Electroconvulsive therapy.* New York: Oxford University Press.

Abrams, M. (2007, June). Born gay? *Discover, 28*(6), 58–83.

Acevedo, R. P., Aron, A., Fisher, H. E., & Brown, L. L. (2011, January 5). Neural correlates of long-term intense romantic love. *Social Cognitive and Affective Neuroscience Advance Access*, 1–15.

Ackerman, J. M., & Bargh, J. A. (2010). The purpose-driven life: Commentary on Kenrick et al. (2010). *Perspectives on Psychological Science, 5*, 323–326.

Ackerman, P. L. (2007). New developments in understanding skilled performance. *Current Directions in Psychological Science, 16*, 235–239.

Ackerman, S. J., Benjamin, L. S., Beutler, L. E., Gelso, C. J., Goldfried, M. R., Hill, C., Lambert, M. J., Norcross, J. C., Orlinsky, D. E., & Rainer, J. (2001). Empirically supported therapy relationships: Conclusions and recommendations of the Division 29 Task Force. *Psychotherapy, 38*, 495–497.

Adams, L. (2010, July 29). Top IVF doctor defends offering help for parents to pick babies' sex. *Daily Record*. Retrieved November 20, 2010, from Center for Genetics and Society www.geneticsandsociety .org/article.php?id=5316.

Adelson, R. (2004, July/August). Detecting deception. *Monitor on Psychology, 35*(7), 70–71.

Adelson, R. (2005, July/August). The power of potent steroids. *Monitor on Psychology, 36*(7), 20–22.

Adelson, R. (2006, January). Nationwide survey spotlights U.S. alcohol abuse. *Monitor on Psychology, 37*(1), 30–32.

Adler, J. (2006, March 27). Freud in our midst. *Newsweek, 157*(13), 43–49.

Adorno, T. W., Frenkel-Brunswick, E., Levinson, D. J., & Sanford, R. N. (1950). *The authoritarian personality.* New York: Harper.

Afftergood, S. (2000, November 3). Polygraph testing and the DOE National Laboratories. *Science, 290*, 939–940. [See also: Holden, 2001b; Saxe, 1991, 1994]

Agras, W. S., Brandt, H. A., Bulik, C. M., Dolan-Sewell, R., Fairburn, C. G., Halmi, K. A., Herzog, D. B., Jimerson, D. C., Kaplan, A. S., Kaye, W. H., le Grange, D., Lock, J., Mitchell, J., Rudorfer, M. V., Street, L. L., Striegel-Moore, R., Vitousek, K. M., Walsh, B. T., & Wilfley, D. E. (2004). Report of the National Institutes of Health workshop on overcoming barriers to treatment research in anorexia nervosa. *International Journal of Eating Disorders, 35*, 509–521.

Ahrons, C. R. (1994). *The good divorce: Keeping your family together when your marriage comes apart.* New York: HarperCollins.

Aiken, L. R. (1987). *Assessment of intellectual functioning.* Boston, MA: Allyn & Bacon.

Ainsworth, M. D. S. (1989). Attachments beyond infancy. *American Psychologist, 44*, 709–716.

Alanko, K., Santtila, P., Harlaar, N., Witting, K., Varjonen, M., Jern, P., Johansson, A., von der Pahlen, B., and Sandnabba, N. K. (2010). Common genetic effects of gender atypical behavior in childhood and sexual orientation in adulthood: A study of Finnish twins. *Archives of Sexual Behavior, 39*, 81–92.

Albee, G. W. (2006, Fall) Is it time for the Third Force in American psychology? *The General Psychologist, 41*(2), 1–3. Retrieved February 16, 2008, from www.apa.org/divisions/div1/archive.html.

Alferink, L. (2005, Spring). Behaviorism died today, again! *The General Psychologist, 40*(1), 7–8. [Electronic version available at www.apa.org/ divisions/div1/newspub.html]

Alison, S. T., & Goethals, G. R., Jr. (2011). *Heroes: Who they are and why we need them.* New York: Oxford University Press.

Allen, K., Blascovich, J., & Mendes, W. B. (2002). Cardiovascular reactivity and the presence of pets, friends, and spouses: The truth about cats and dogs. *Psychosomatic Medicine, 64*, 727–739.

Allen, M. J. (1995). *Introduction to psychological research.* Itasca, IL: Peacock.

Allen, V. S., & Levine, J. M. (1969). Consensus and conformity. *Journal of Experimental Social Psychology, 5*, 389–399.

Allport, G. W. (1954). *The nature of prejudice.* Cambridge, MA: Addison-Wesley.

Allport, G. W., & Odbert, H. S. (1936). Trait-names, a psycho-lexical study. *Psychological Monographs, 47*(1, Whole No. 211).

Alper, J. (1985, March). The roots of morality. *Science, 85*, 70–76.

Alper, J. (1993). Echo-planar MRI: Learning to read minds. *Science, 261*, 556.

Alpert, B., Field, T., Goldstein, S., & Perry, S. (1990). Aerobics enhances cardiovascular fitness and agility in preschoolers. *Health Psychology, 9*, 48–56.

Amabile, T. M. (1983). *The social psychology of creativity.* New York: Springer-Verlag.

Amabile, T. M. (1987). The motivation to be creative. In S. Isaksen (Ed.), *Frontiers in creativity: Beyond the basics.* Buffalo, NY: Bearly Limited.

Amabile, T. M. (2001). Beyond talent: John Irving and the passionate craft of creativity. *American Psychologist, 56*, 333–336.

Amabile, T. M., Hadley, C. N., & Kramer, S. J. (2002, August). Creativity under the gun. *Harvard Business Review, 80*(8), 52–60.

Ambady, N., & Rosenthal, R. (1993). Half a minute: Predicting teacher evaluations from thin slices of nonverbal behavior and physical attractiveness. *Journal of Personality and Social Psychology, 64*, 431–441.

Amedi, A., Merabet, L. B., Bermpohl, F., & Pascual-Leone, A. (2005, December). The occipital cortex in the blind. *Current Directions in Psychological Science, 14*, 306–311.

American Academy of Pediatrics, Subcommittee on Attention Deficit Hyperactivity Disorder, Committee on Quality Improvement. (2001). Clinical practice guideline: Treatment of the school-aged child with attention-deficit/hyperactivity disorder. *Pediatrics, 108*, 1033–1044. [See also: Henker & Whalen, 1989; Poling et al., 1991; Welsh et al., 1993.]

American Medical Association. (2010). Stem cell research: Human cloning. Retrieved November 19, 2010, from www.ama-assn.org/ama/pub/physician-resources/medical-science/genetics-molecular-medicine/related-policy-topics/stem-cell-research/ human-cloning.shtml.

American Psychiatric Association. (1994). *Diagnostic and statistical manual of mental disorders* (4th ed.). Washington, DC: Author.

American Psychological Association. (2002, June 26). *Is corporal punishment an effective means of discipline?* Retrieved July 2, 2007, from www.apa .org/releases/spanking.html.

American Psychological Association. (2003a). *Careers in psychology for the twenty-first century.* Retrieved October 14, 2004, from www.apa.org/students/ brochure/brochurenew.pdf.

American Psychological Association. (2003b). *Council policy manual.* Retrieved October 14, 2004, from www.apa.org/about/division/cpmscientific.html.

American Psychological Association. (2007). Frequently asked questions about teaching high school psychology. Retrieved April 17, 2007, from www.apa.org/ed/topss/topss_faqs.html.

American Psychiatric Association. (2010a). *DSM revision activities.* Retrieved from www.psych .org/MainMenu/Research/DSMIV/DSMV/ DSMRevisionActivities.aspx.

American Psychological Association (APA). (2010b). *Lesbian & gay parenting: APA amicus briefs.* Retrieved from www.apa.org/pi/lgbt/resources/ parenting.aspx.

Anand, K. J. S., & Hickey, P. R. (1987). Pain and its effects in the human neonate and fetus. *The New England Journal of Medicine, 317*, 1321–1329.

Anand, K. J. S., & Scalzo, F. M. (2000). Can adverse neonatal experiences alter brain development and subsequent behavior? *Biology of the Neonate, 77*, 69–82.

Anderson, C. A., & Bushman, B. J. (2001). Effects of violent video games on aggressive behavior, aggressive cognition, aggressive affect, physiological arousal, and prosocial behavior: A meta-analytic review of the scientific literature. *Psychological Science, 12*, 353–359.

Anderson, C., Gentile, D., & Buckley, K. (2007). *Violent video game effects on children and adolescents.* London: Oxford University Press.

Andreasen, N. C., Arndt, S., Alliger, R., Miller, D., & Flaum, M. (1995). Symptoms of schizophrenia: Methods, meanings, and mechanisms. *Archives of General Psychiatry, 52*, 341–351.

Andrews, F. M., & Withey, S. B. (1976). *Social indicators of well-being: Americans' perceptions of life quality.* New York: Plenum.

Andrews, J. D. W. (1967). The achievement motive and advancement in two types of organization. *Journal of Personality and Social Psychology, 6*, 163–168.

Andrews, P. W., & Thompson, J. A. (2009). The bright side of being blue: Depression as an adaptation for analyzing complex problems. *Psychological Review, 118*, 620–654.

Andrews, P. W., & Thompson, J. A. (2010, January/ February). Depression's evolutionary roots. *Scientific American Mind, 20*(7), 57–61.

Angell, M. (1985). Disease as a reflection of the psyche. *The New England Journal of Medicine, 312*, 1570–1572.

Anglin, J. M. (1993). Vocabulary development: A morphological analysis. *Monographs of the Society for Research in Child Development, 58*(Serial No. 238).

Anglin, J. M. (1995, March). Word learning and the growth of potentially knowable vocabulary. Paper presented at the biennial meetings of the Society for Research in Child Development, Indianapolis, IN.

Ansbacher, H. L., & Ansbacher, R. R., Eds. (1956). *The individual psychology of Alfred Adler: A systematic presentation in selections from his writings.* New York: Basic Books.

Antonova, I., Arancio, O., Trillat, A-C., Hong-Gang W., Zablow, L., Udo, H., Kandel, E. R., & Hawkins, R. D. (2001, November 16). Rapid increase in clusters of presynaptic proteins at onset of long-lasting potentiation. *Science, 294,* 1547–1550.

Antonuccio, D. (1995). Psychotherapy for depression: No stronger medicine. *American Psychologist, 50,* 450–452.

Antony, M. M., Brown, T. A., & Barlow, D. H. (1992). Current perspectives on panic and panic disorder. *Current Directions in Psychological Science, 1,* 79–82.

APA Presidential Task Force on Evidence-Based Practice. (2006). Evidence-based practice in psychology. *American Psychologist, 61,* 271–285.

Arnett, J. J. (1992). Reckless behavior in adolescence: A developmental perspective. *Developmental Review, 12,* 339–373.

Arnett, J. J. (1997). Young people's conceptions of the transition to adulthood. *Youth & Society, 29,* 1–23.

Arnett, J. J. (1999). Adolescent storm and stress, reconsidered. *American Psychologist, 54,* 317–326.

Arnett, J. J. (2000a). Emerging adulthood: A theory of development from the late teens through the twenties. *American Psychologist, 55*(5), 469–480.

Arnett, J. J. (2000b). High hopes in a grim world: Emerging adults' view of their futures and "Generation X." *Youth & Society, 31,* 267–286.

Arnett, J. J. (2001). Conceptions of the transition to adulthood: Perspectives from adolescence through midlife. *Journal of Adult Development, 8,* 133–144.

Arnsten, A. F. T. (1998, June 12). The biology of being frazzled. *Science, 280,* 1711–1712. [See also Caldwell, 1995; Mukerjee, 1995; Sapolsky, 1990]

Aronson, E. (1978). *The jigsaw classroom.* Beverly Hills, CA: Sage. Retrieved from www.jigsaw.org/history.htm.

Aronson, E. (1997). *Cooperation in the classroom: The jigsaw method* (with Shelley Patnoe). New York: Longman.

Aronson, E. (2000). *Nobody left to hate: Teaching compassion after Columbine.* New York: W. H. Freeman & Company.

Aronson, E. (2004). *The social animal* (9th ed.). New York: Worth. [See also: Feingold, 1990; Langlois et al., 1998; Tesser & Brodie, 1971]

Aronson, E., Helmreich, R., & LeFan, J. (1970). To err is humanizing—sometimes: Effects of self-esteem, competence, and a pratfall on interpersonal attraction. *Journal of Personality and Social Psychology, 16,* 259–264.

Aronson, E., & Patnoe, S. (1997). *Cooperation in the classroom: The jigsaw method.* New York, NY: Longman.

Aronson, E., Willerman, B., & Floyd, J. (1966). The effect of a pratfall on increasing interpersonal attractiveness. *Psychonomic Science, 4,* 227–228.

Aronson, J., Fried, C. B., & Good, C. (2001). Re ducing the effects of stereotype threat on African American college students by shaping theories of intelligence. *Journal of Experimental Social Psychology, 38,* 1–13.

Asarnow, J., Glynn, S., Pynoos, R. S., Nahum, J., Guthrie, D., Cantwell, D. P., & Franklin, B. (1999). When the earth stops shaking: Earthquake sequelae among children diagnosed for pre-earthquake psychopathology. *Journal of the American Academy of Child and Adolescent Psychiatry, 38,* 1016–1025.

Asch, S. E. (1940). Studies in the principles of judgments and attitudes: 11. Determination of judgments by group and by ego standards. *Journal of Social Psychology, 12,* 433–465.

Asch, S. E. (1955). Opinions and social pressure. *Scientific American, 193*(5), 31–35.

Asch, S. E. (1956). Studies of independence and conformity: A minority of one against a unanimous majority. *Psychological Monographs, 70*(9, Whole No. 416).

Aserinsky, E., & Kleitman, N. (1953). Regularly occurring periods of eye mobility and concomitant phenomena during sleep. *Science, 118,* 273–274.

Ashby, F., Isen, A., & Turken, A. (1999). A neuropsychological theory of positive affect and its influence on cognition. *Psychological Review, 106,* 529–550.

Ashby, F. G., & Waldron, E. M. (2000). The neuropsychological bases of category learning. *Current Directions in Psychological Science, 9,* 10–14. [See also: Beardsley, 1997a; Behrmann, 2000; Freedman et al., 2001; Thorpe & Fabre-Thorpe, 2001]

Athradhy, A. (2010, September 8). Pilot was asleep before crash: Black box. *Deccan Herald News Service.* Retrieved from www.deccanherald.com/content/95131/pilot-error-led-air-india.html.

Atkinson, R. C., & Schiffrin, R. M. (1968). Human memory: A control system and its control processes. In K. Spence (Ed.), *The psychology of learning and motivation* (Vol. 2). New York: Academic Press.

Austin, J. H. (1998). *Zen and the brain: Toward an understanding of meditation and consciousness.* Cambridge, MA: MIT Press.

Averill, J. A. (1980). A constructivist view of emotion. In R. Plutchik & H. Kellerman (Eds.), *Emotion: Theory, research, and experience: Vol. 1. Theories of emotion.* New York: Academic Press.

Axel, R. (1995, October). The molecular logic of smell. *Scientific American, 273,* 154–159.

Ayan, S. (2009, April/May). Laughing matters: Seeing the bright side of life may strengthen the psyche, ease pain and tighten social bonds. *Scientific American, 20*(2), 24–31.

Ayllon, T., & Azrin, N. H. (1965). The measurement and reinforcement of behavior of psychotics. *Journal of Experimental Analysis of Behavior, 8,* 357–383.

Ayllon, T., & Azrin, N. H. (1968). *The token economy: A motivational system for therapy and rehabilitation.* New York: Appleton-Century-Crofts.

Azar, B. (1994, October). Seligman recommends a depression "vaccine." *APA Monitor, 4.* [See also: Robins, 1988; Seligman, 1991; Seligman et al., 1979.]

Azar, B. (1995, June). New cognitive research makes waves. *APA Monitor, 16.*

Azar, B. (1996, November). Some forms of memory improve as people age. *APA Monitor, 27.*

Azar, B. (1997, October). Was Freud right? Maybe, maybe not. *American Psychological Association Monitor, 28,* 30.

Azar, B. (2002a, January). At the frontier of science. *Monitor on Psychology,* 40–43.

Azar, B. (2002b, September). Searching for genes that explain our personalities. *Monitor on Psychology, 33*(8), 44–45.

Azar, B. (2006, March). The faces of pride. *Monitor on Psychology, 37*(3). Retrieved March 30, 2008, from www.apa.org/monitor/mar06/pride.html.

Azar, B. (2007, April). A case for angry men and happy women. *Monitor on Psychology, 38*(4), 18–19.

Azar, B. (2010, June). Another reason to break a sweat. *Monitor on Psychology, 41*(6), 36–38.

Babiak, P., & Hare, R. D. (2006). *Snakes in suits: When psychopaths go to work.* New York: Harper Collins.

Babyak, M., Blumenthall, J. A., Herman, S., Khatri, P., Doraiswamy, M., Moore, K., Craighead, W. E., Baldewicz, T. T., & Krishnan, K. R. (2000). Exercise treatment for major depression: Maintenance of therapeutic benefit at 10 months. *Psychosomatic Medicine, 62,* 633–638.

Baddeley, A. (1998). *Human memory: Theory and practice.* Boston: Allyn & Bacon.

Baddeley, A. (2003). Working memory and language: An overview. *Journal of Communication Disorders, 36,* 189–208.

Baddeley, A. D. (2000). The episodic buffer: A new component of working memory? *Trends in Cognitive Sciences, 4,* 417–423.

Baddeley, A. D. (2001). Is working memory still working? *American Psychologist, 56,* 851–864.

Baddeley, A. D., & Hitch, G. (1974). Working memory. In G. A. Bower (Ed.), *Recent advances in learning and motivation* (Vol. 8). New York: Academic Press.

Bahrick, H. D. (1984). Fifty years of language attrition: Implications for programmatic research. *Modern language journal, 68,* 105–118.

Bahrick, H. P., Bahrick, L. E., Bahrick, A. S., & Bahrick, P. E. (1993). Maintenance of foreign language vocabulary and the spacing effect. *Psychology Science, 4,* 316–321.

Bahrick, H. P., Bahrick, P. O., & Wittlinger, R. P. (1975). Fifty years of memory for names and faces: A cross-sectional approach. *Journal of Experimental Psychology: General, 104,* 54–75.

Bailey, R. (2006, August 11). Don't be terrorized. *Reason Magazine.* Retrieved from http://reason.com/archives/2006/08/11/dont-be-terrorized.

Baillargeon, R., & DeVos, J. (1991). Object permanence in young infants: Further evidence. *Child Development, 62,* 1227–1246.

Baker, T. B., McFall, R. M., & Shoham, V. (2008). Current status and future prospects of clinical psychology: Toward a scientifically principled approach to mental and behavioral health care. *Psychological Science in the Public Interest, 9*(2).

Balch, P., & Ross, A. W. (1975). Predicting success in weight reduction as a function of locus of control: A uni-dimensional and multi-dimensional approach. *Journal of Consulting and Clinical Psychology, 43,* 119.

Baldwin, M. W. (1992). Relational schemas and the processing of social information. *Psychological Bulletin, 112,* 461–484.

Baltes, P. B. (1987). Theoretical propositions on life-span developmental psychology: On the dynamics between growth and decline. *Developmental Psychology, 23,* 611–626.

Baltes, P. B. (1990, November). Toward a psychology of wisdom. Invited address presented at the annual convention of the Gerontological Society of America, Boston, MA.

Baltes, P. B. (1993). The aging mind: Potential and limits. *The Gerontologist, 33,* 580–594.

Baltes, P. B., & Kliegl, R. (1992). Further testing of limits of cognitive plasticity: Negative age differences in a mnemonic skill are robust. *Developmental Psychology, 28,* 121–125.

Baltes, P. B., & Staudinger, U. M. (1993). The search for a psychology of wisdom. *Current Directions in Psychological Science, 2,* 75–80.

Bamshad, M. J., & Olson, S. E. (2003, December). Does race exist? *Scientific American, 289*(6), 78–85. [See also: Gould, 1996; Zuckerman, 1990]

Bandura, A. (1970). Modeling therapy. In W. S. Sahakian (Ed.), *Psychopathology today: Experimentation, theory and research.* Itasca, IL: Peacock.

Bandura, A. (1981). In search of pure unidirectional determinants. *Behavior Therapy, 12,* 30–40.

Bandura, A. (1986). *Social foundations of thought and action: A social cognitive theory.* Englewood Cliffs, NJ: Prentice Hall.

Bandura, A. (1992). Exercise of personal agency through the self-efficacy mechanism. In R. Schwarzer (Ed.), *Self-efficacy: Thought control of action* (pp. 3–38). Washington, DC: Hemisphere.

Bandura, A. (1999). Social cognitive theory of personality. In L. A. Pervin & O. P. John (Eds.), *Handbook of personality: Theory and research* (2nd ed., pp. 154–196). New York: Guilford Press.

Bandura, A., Ross, D., & Ross, S. A. (1963). Imitation of film-mediated aggressive models. *Journal of Abnormal and Social Psychology, 66,* 3–11.

Bandura, A., Underwood, B., & Fromson, M. E. (1975). Disinhibition of aggression through diffusion of responsibility and dehumanization of victims. *Journal of Personality and Social Psychology, 9,* 253–269.

Banich, M. T. (1998). Integration of information between the cerebral hemispheres. *Current Directions in Psychological Science, 7,* 32–37.

Banks, M. S., & Bennet, P. J. (1988). Optical and photoreceptor immaturities limit the spatial and chromatic vision of human neonates. *Journal of the Optical Society of America, 5,* 2059–2079.

Barab, S. A., & Plucker, J. A. (2002). Smart people or smart contexts? Cognition, ability, and talent development in an age of situated approaches to knowing and learning. *Educational Psychologist, 37,* 165–182.

Barach, J. (2003). Reorganization of the brain may provide blind with superior verbal memory. Retrieved May 16, 2007, from www.bioisrael.com/upload/research/blind_research.doc

Baranowsky, A. B. (2002). The silencing response in clinical practice: On the road to dialogue. In C. R. Figley (Ed.), *Treating compassion fatigue* (pp. 155–170). New York: Brunner-Routledge.

Barash, D. P. (2007, October 5). The targets of aggression. *The Chronicle of Higher Education,* B6–B9.

Barber, T. X. (1976). *Hypnosis: A scientific approach.* New York: Psychological Dimensions.

Barber, T. X. (1979). Suggested ("hypnotic") behavior: The trance paradigm versus an alternative paradigm. In E. Fromm & R. E. Shor (Eds.), *Hypnosis: Developments in research and new perspectives.* New York: Aldine.

Barber, T. X. (1986). Realities of stage hypnosis. In B. Zilbergeld, M. G. Edelstein, & D. L. Araoz (Eds.), *Hypnosis: Questions and answers.* New York: Norton.

Barinaga, M. (1997, June 27). New imaging methods provide a better view into the brain. *Science, 276,* 1974–1976.

Barinaga, M. (1998, April 17). Listening in on the brain. *Science, 280,* 376–377.

Barinaga, M. (2002, February 8). How the brain's clock gets daily enlightenment. *Science, 295,* 955–957.

Barinaga, M. (2003, October 3). Studying the well-trained mind. *Science, 302,* 44–46.

Barker, L. M., Best, M. R., & Domjan, M. (Eds.). (1978). *Learning mechanisms in food selection.* Houston: Baylor University Press.

Barkley, R. A. (1998, September). Attention-deficit hyperactivity disorder. *Scientific American, 279*(9), 66–71.

Barlow, D. H. (1996). Health care policy, psychotherapy research, and the future of psychotherapy. *American Psychologist, 51,* 1050–1058.

Barlow, D. H. (2000). Unraveling the mysteries of anxiety and its disorders from the perspective of emotion theory. *American Psychologist, 55,* 1247–1263.

Barlow, D. H. (2001). A modern learning theory perspective on the etiology of panic disorder. *Psychological Review, 108,* 4–32.

Barlow, D. H. (2004). Psychological treatments. *American Psychologist, 59,* 869–878.

Barlow, D. H. (2010). Negative effects from psychological treatments: A perspective. *American Psychologist, 65,* 13–20.

Barlow, D. H., & Durand, V. M. (2005). *Abnormal psychology: An integrative approach.* Belmont, CA: Wadsworth.

Barlow, J. (2008, February 15). *Parental intervention boosts education of kids at high risk of failure.* Retrieved March 16, 2008, from http://pmr.uoregon.edu/science-and-innovation/uo-research-news/research-news-2008/february-2008/parental-intervention-boosts-education-of-kids-at-high-risk-of-failure.

Barnes, D. M. (1987). Biological issues in schizophrenia. *Science, 235,* 430–433.

Barnett, R. C., & Hyde, J. S. (2001). Women, men, work, and family: An expansionist theory. *American Psychologist, 56,* 781–796.

Barnier, A. J., & McConkey, K. M. (1998). Posthypnotic responding away from the hypnotic setting. *Psychological Science, 9,* 256–262.

Barnouw, V. (1963). *Culture and personality.* Homewood, IL: Dorsey Press.

Baron, L., & Straus, M. A. (1985). *Four theories of rape in American society: A state-level analysis.* New Haven, CT: Yale University Press.

Barron, F., & Harrington, D. M. (1981). Creativity, intelligence and personality. *Annual Review of Psychology, 32,* 439–476.

Bartels, A., & Zeki, S. (2004). The neural correlates of maternal and romantic love. *NeuroImage, 22,* 419–433.

Bartlett, T. (2011). The case for play. *Chronicle of Higher Education.* Retrieved from http://chronicle.com/article/The-Case-for-Play/126382/.

Bartoshuk, L. (2000). Comparing sensory experiences across individuals: Recent psychophysical advances illuminate genetic variation in taste perception. *Chemical Senses, 25,* 447–460. doi: 10.1093/chemse/25.4.447.

Bartoshuk, L. (2009). *Do you taste what I taste? Some lessons about measurement that impact health.* Presentation given at the American Psychological Association annual convention in Toronto, August, 2009.

Bartoshuk, L. M. (1990, August–September). Psychophysiological insights on taste. *Science Agenda,* 12–13.

Bartoshuk, L. M. (1993). The biological basis of food perception and acceptance. *Food Quality and Preference, 4,* 21–32.

Bartoshuk, L. M., Duffy, V. B., & Miller, I. J. (1994). PCT/PROP tasting: Anatomy, psychophysics and sex effects. *Physiology and Behavior, 56,* 1165–1171.

Basbaum, A. I., & Julius, D. (2006, June). Toward better pain control. *Scientific American, 294*(6), 60–67.

Basic Behavioral Science Task Force of the National Advisory Mental Health Council. (1996). Basic behavioral science research for mental health: Family processes and social networks. *American Psychologist, 51,* 622–630.

Bass, E., & Davis, L. (1988). *The courage to heal.* New York: HarperCollins.

Batson, C. D. (1987). Prosocial motivation: Is it ever truly altruistic? In L. Berkowitz (Ed.), *Advances in experimental social psychology* (Vol. 20). Orlando, FL: Academic Press.

Bauer, P. J., Wiebe, S. A., Carver, L. J., Waters, J. M., & Nelson, C. A. (2003). Developments in long-term explicit memory late in the first year of life: Behavioral and electrophysiological indices. *Psychological Science, 14,* 629–635.

Baum, W. M. (1994). *Understanding behaviorism: Science, behavior, and culture.* New York: HarperCollins.

Baumeister, R. F. (Ed.). (1993). *Self-esteem: The puzzle of low self-regard.* New York: Plenum.

Baumeister, R. F. (2005). The unconscious is alive and well, and friendly too. *Journal of Social & Clinical Psychology, 24,* 293–295.

Baumeister, R. F. (2007, August). *Is there anything good about men?* Invited address given at the 2007 APA convention in San Francisco, CA. Retrieved November 16, 2007, from www.psy.fsu.edu/~baumeistertice/goodaboutmen.htm.

Baumeister, R. F., Bratslavsky, E., Muraven, M., & Tice, D. M. (1998). Ego depletion: Is the active self a limited resource? *Journal of Personality and Social Psychology, 74,* 1252–1265.

Baumeister, R. F., Campbell, J. D., Krueger, J. I., & Vohs, K. D. (2003). Does high self-esteem cause better performance, interpersonal success, happiness, or healthier lifestyles? *Psychological Science in the Public Interest, 4,* 1–44.

Baumeister, R. F., Smart, L., & Boden, J. M. (1996). Relation of threatened egotism to violence and aggression: The dark side of high self-esteem. *Psychological Review, 103,* 5–33.

Baumeister, R. F., Vohs, K. D., & Tice, D. M. (2007). The strength model of self-control. *Current Directions in Psychological Science, 16,* 351–355.

Baumrind, D. (1967). Child care practices anteceding three patterns of preschool behavior. *Genetic Psychology Monographs, 75,* 43–88.

Baumrind, D. (1971). Current patterns of parental authority. *Developmental Psychology Monograph, 4*(1, Part 2).

Baumrind, D. (1985). Research using intentional deception: Ethical issues revisited. *American Psychologist, 40,* 165–174.

Baynes, K., Eliassen, J. C., Lutsep, H. L., & Gazzaniga, M. S. (1998). Modular organization of cognitive systems masked by interhemispheric integration. *Science, 280,* 902–905.

Beaman, A. L., Barnes, P. J., Klentz, B., & McQuirk, B. (1978). Increasing helping rates through information dissemination: Teaching pays. *Personality and Social Psychology Bulletin, 4,* 406–411.

Beardsley, E. (2010, March 18). *Fake TV game show 'tortures' man, shocks France.* Retrieved from www.npr.org/templates/story/story.php?storyId=124838091.

Beardsley, T. (1996, July). Waking up. *Scientific American, 14,* 18.

Beardsley, T. (1997, March). Memories are made of … *Scientific American,* 32–33.

Beasley, M., Thompson, T., & Davidson, J. (2003). Resilience in response to life stress: The effects of coping style and cognitive hardiness. *Personality and Individual Differences, 34,* 77–95.

Bechara, A., Tranel, D., Damasio, H., Adolphs, R., Rockland, C., & Damasio, A. R. (1995, August 25). Double dissociation of conditioning and declarative knowledge relative to the amygdala and hippocampus in humans. *Science, 269,* 1115–1118.

Beck, A. T. (1976). *Cognitive therapy and emotional disorders.* New York: International Universities Press.

Beck, A. T. (2005). The current state of cognitive therapy: A 40-year retrospective. *Archives of General Psychiatry, 62,* 953–959.

Beck, A. T., Rush, A. J., Shaw, B. F., & Emery, G. (1979). *Cognitive therapy of depression.* New York: Guilford Press.

Beck, H. P., Levinson, S., & Irons, G. (2009). Finding little Albert: A journey to John B. Watson's infant laboratory. *American Psychologist, 64*(7), 605–614.

Beck, M. R., Angelone, B. L., & Levin, D. T. (2004). Knowledge about the probability of change affects change detection performance. *Journal of Experimental Psychology: Human Perception and Performance, 30,* 778–791.

Becker, D. V., Kenrick, D. T., Neuberg, S. L., Blackwell, K. C., & Smith, D. M. (2007). The confounded nature of angry men and happy women. *Journal of Personality and Social Psychology, 92,* 179–190.

Bédard, J., & Chi, M. T. H. (1992). Expertise. *Current Directions in Psychological Science, 1,* 135–139.

Bee, H. (1994). *Lifespan development.* New York: HarperCollins.

Behrmann, M. (2000). The mind's eye mapped onto the brain's matter. *Current Directions in Psychological Science, 9,* 50–54.

Beigel, A., & Berren, M. R. (1985). Human-induced disasters. *Psychiatric Annals, 15,* 143–150.

Beilin, H. (1992). Piaget's enduring contribution to developmental psychology. *Developmental Psychology, 28,* 191–204.

Bell, L. (2010, July 3). Fat chance: Scientists are working out ways to rev up the body's gut-busting machinery. *Science News, 178*(1), 18–21. doi: 10.1002/scin.5591780122.

Bem, D. J., & Allen, A. (1974). On predicting some of the people some of the time: The search for cross-situational consistencies in behavior. *Psychological Review, 81*(6), 506–520.

Benassi, V. A., Sweeney, P. D., & Dufour, C. L. (1988). Is there a relation between locus of control orientation and depression? *Journal of Abnormal Psychology, 97,* 357–367.

Benedetti, F., Mayberg, H. S., Wager, T. D., Stohler, C. S., & Zubieta, J. (2005, November 9). Neuro biological mechanisms of the placebo effect. *The Journal of Neuroscience, 25,* 10390–10402.

Benjamin, L. T., Jr., & Nielsen-Gammon, E. (1999). B. F. Skinner and psychotechnology: The case of the heir conditioner. *Review of General Psychology, 3,* 155–167.

Bennett, K. K., & Elliott, M. (2002). Explanatory style and health: Mechanisms linking pessimism to illness. *Journal of Applied Social Psychology, 32,* 1508–1526.

Benson, E. (2002, October). Pheromones, in context. *Monitor on Psychology, 33*(9), 46–49. [See also: Azar, 1998b; Holden, 1996b]

Benson, E. (2003, February) Intelligent intelligence testing. *Monitor on Psychology, 34*(2), 48–51.

Benson, H. (1975). *The relaxation response.* New York: Morrow.

Berenson, A. (2008, February 24). Daring to think differently about schizophrenia. *New York Times.* Retrieved from www.nytimes.com/2008/02/24/business/24drug.html.

Berglas, S. (2001). *Reclaiming the fire: How successful people overcome burnout.* New York: Random House.

Berk, L. (2002). *Infants, children, and adolescents* (4th ed.). Boston: Allyn & Bacon.

Berk, L. E. (2004). *Development through the lifespan* (4th ed.). Boston: Allyn & Bacon.

Berk, L. E. (2007). *Development through the lifespan,* (4th ed.) Boston: Allyn & Bacon.

Berkman, L. F., & Syme, S. L. (1979). Social networks, host resistance, and mortality: A nine-year follow-up study of Alameda County residents. *American Journal of Epidemiology, 109,* 186–204.

Berman, J. S., & Norton, N. C. (1985). Does professional training make a therapist more effective? *Psychological Bulletin, 98,* 401–407.

Berns, G. S. Chappelow, J., Zink, C. F., Pagnoni, G., Martin-Skurski, E. M., & Richards, J. (2005). Neurobiological correlates of social conformity and independence during mental rotation. *Biological Psychiatry, 58,* 245–253. [See also: www.nytimes.com/2005/06/28/science/28brai.html.]

Bernstein, I. L. (1988). What does learning have to do with weight loss and cancer? *Proceedings of the Science and Public Policy Seminar of the Federation of Behavioral, Psychological and Cognitive Sciences.* Washington, DC.

Bernstein, I. L. (1990). Salt preference and development. *Developmental Psychology, 26,* 552– 554.

Bernstein, I. L. (1991). Aversion conditioning in response to cancer and cancer treatment. *Clinical Psychology Review, 11,* 185–191.

Berry, J. (1992). Cree conceptions of cognitive competence. *International Journal of Psychology, 27,* 73–88.

Berry, J. W., Poortinga, Y. H., Segall, M. H., & Dasen, P. R. (1992). *Cross-cultural psychology: Research and applications.* New York: Cambridge University Press.

Berscheid, E. (1999). The greening of relationship science. *American Psychologist, 54,* 260–266.

Beutler, L. E., & Machado, P. P. (1992). Research on psychotherapy. In M. R. Rosenzweig (Ed.), *Inter national psychological science: Progress, problems, and prospects* (pp. 227–252). Washington, DC: American Psychological Association.

Beverley, R., Meldrum, L., & McFarlane, A. C. (1995). Does debriefing after psychological trauma work? *British Medical Journal, 310,* 1479–1480.

Bevins, R. A. (2001). Novelty seeking and reward: Implications for the study of high-risk behaviors. *Current Directions in Psychological Science, 10,* 189–193.

Bhattacharjee, Y. (2008, January 25). Shell shock revisited: Solving the puzzle of blast trauma. *Science, 319,* 406–408.

Biais, B., & Weber, M. (2009). Hindsight bias, risk perception, and investment performance. *Management Science, 55,* 1018–1029.

Bianchi, E. (1994). *Elder wisdom: Crafting your elderhood.* New York: Crossroad.

Bianchi, S. M., & Spain, D. (1996). Women, work, and family in America. *Population Bulletin, 51,* 1–48.

Bicklen, D. (1990). Communication unbound: Autism and praxis. *Harvard Educational Review, 60*(3), 291–314.

Biederman, I. (1989). Higher-level vision. In D. N. Osherson, H. Sasnik, S. Kosslyn, K. Hollerbach, E. Smith, & N. Block (Eds.), *An invitation to cognitive science.* Cambridge, MA: MIT Press.

Biehl, M., Matsumoto, D., Ekman, P., Hearn, V., Heider, K., Kudoh, T., & Ton, V. (1997). Matsumoto and Ekman's Japanese and Caucasian facial expressions of emotion (JACFEE): Reliability data and cross-national differences. *Journal of Nonverbal Behavior, 21,* 3–21. [See also: Ekman et al., 1987; Izard, 1994]

Billings, A. G., & Moos, R. H. (1985). Life stressors and social resources affect posttreatment outcomes among depressed patients. *Journal of Abnormal Psychology, 94,* 140–153.

Binet, A. (1911). *Les idées modernes sur les enfants.* Paris: Flammarion.

Binitie, A. (1975). A factor-analytical study of depression across cultures (African and European). *British Journal of Psychiatry, 127,* 559–563.

Bink, M. L., & Marsh, R. L. (2000). Cognitive regularities in creative activity. *Review of General Psychology, 4,* 59–78.

Bird, S. J. (2005). *The ethics of using animals in research.* Case Western Reserve University. Retrieved April 14, 2007, from http://onlineethics.org/reseth/mod/animalres.html.

Bjork, R. A. (2000). *Creating desirable difficulties for the learner. Implications for theory and practice.* Address given at the American Psychological Society's annual convention, Miami Beach, FL.

Bjorklund, D. F., & Shackelford, T. K. (1999). Differences in parental investment contribute to important differences between men and women. *Current Directions in Psychological Science, 8,* 86–89.

Blakeslee, S. (2005, November 22). This is your brain under hypnosis. *New York Times.* Retrieved December 4, 2007, from www.nytimes.com/2005/11/22/science/22hypno.html [See also: Kirsch & Lynn, 1995; Woody & Sadler, 1998]

Blanchard, R. (2008). Review and theory of handedness, birth order, and homosexuality in men. *Laterality: Asymmetries of Body, Brain and Cognition, 13,* 51–70. [See also: Blanchard & Bogaert, 1996.]

Blass, T. (1996). Experimental invention and controversy: The life and work of Stanley Milgram. *The General Psychologist, 32,* 47–55.

Blass, T. (2004). *The man who shocked the world: The life and legacy of Stanley Milgram.* New York: Basic Books.

Blum, D. (2002). *Love at Goon Park: Harry Harlow and the science of affection.* New York: Perseus Publishing.

Blumenthal, J. A., Babyak, M. A., Doraiswamy, P. M., Watkins, L., Hoffman, B. M., Barbour, K. A., Herman, S., Craighead, W. E., Brosse, A. L., Waugh, R., Hinderliter, A., Sherwood, A. (2007). Exercise and pharmacotherapy in the treatment of major depressive disorder. *Psychosomatic Medicine, 69*(7), 587–596.

Boahen, K. (2005, May). Neuromorphic microchips. *Scientific American, 292*(5), 56–63.

Board on Children, Youth, and Families (BCYF). (2009). Report brief for researchers: Preventing mental, emotional, and behavioral disorders among young people: Progress and possibilities. Retrieved from www.bocyf.org/prevention_researchers_brief.pdf.

Bocchiaro, P., & Zimbardo, P. G. (2008). Deciding to resist unjust authority. [Submitted for publication]

Bogaert, A. F. (2005). Sibling sex ratio and sexual orientation in men and women: New tests in two national probability samples. *Archives of Sexual Behavior, 34,* 111–116. doi: 10.1007/s10508-005-1005-9.

Bogaert, A. F. (2006, July 11). Biological versus non-biological older brothers and men's sexual orien tation. *Proceedings of the National Academy of Sciences, 103,* 10771–10774.

Bolger, M. A. (1997). An exploration of college student stress. *Dissertation Abstracts International, 58,* 5-A, 1597.

Bolger, N., DeLongis, A., Kessler, R. C., & Schilling, E. A. (1989). Effects of daily stress on negative mood. *Journal of Personality and Social Psychology, 57,* 808–818.

Bonanno, G. A. (2009). *The other side of sadness: What the new science of bereavement tells us about life after loss.* New York: Basic Books.

Bonanno, G. A., & Mancini, A. D. (2008). The human capacity to thrive in the face of extreme adversity. *Pediatrics, 121,* 369–375.

Bonanno, G. A., Papa, A., Lalande, K., Westphal, M., & Coifman, K. (2004). The importance of being flexible: The ability to both enhance and suppress emotional expression predicts long-term adjustment. *Psychological Science, 15,* 482–487.

Bond, C. F., Jr., & Atoum, A. O. (2000). International deception. *Personality and Social Psychology Bulletin, 26,* 385–395.

Bornstein, R. F. (1989). Exposure and affect: Overview and meta-analysis of research, 1968–1987. *Psy chological Bulletin, 106,* 265–289.

Bornstein, R. F. (2001). The impending death of psychoanalysis. *Psychoanalytic Psychology, 18,* 3–20. [See also: Bruner, 1992; Erdelyi, 1992;

Greenwald, 1992; Jacoby et al., 1992; Kihlstrom et al., 1992; Loftus & Klinger, 1992.]

Bostwick, J. M., & Pankratz, V. S. (2000). Affective disorders and suicide risk: A reexamination. *American Journal of Psychiatry, 157,* 1925–1932.

Bosveld, J. (2007, December). Sleeping like a hunter-gatherer. *Discover, 28*(12), 66–67.

Botvinick, M. (2004, August 6). Probing the neural basis of body ownership. *Science, 305,* 782–783.

Bouchard, T. J., Jr. (1994, June 17). Genes, environment, and personality. *Science, 264,* 1700–1701.

Bouchard, T. J., & McGue, M. (2003). Genetic and environmental influences on human psychological differences. *Journal of Neurobiology, 54,* 4–45.

Bouchard, T. J., Lykken, D. T., McGue, M., Segal, N. L., & Tellegen, A. (1990). Sources of human psychological differences: The Minnesota study of twins reared apart. *Science, 250,* 223–228.

Bowden, C. L., Calabrese, J. R., McElroy, S. L., Gyulai, L., Wassef, A., Petty, F., Pope, H. G., Jr., Chou, J. C., Keck, P. E. Jr., Rhodes, L. J., Swann, A. C., Hirschfeld, R. M., & Wozniak, P. J. (2000). A randomized, placebo-controlled 12-month trial of divalproex and lithium in treatment of outpatients with bipolar I disorder. Divalproex Maintenance Study Group. *Archives of General Psychiatry, 57,* 481–489.

Bower, B. (1992, August 22). Genetic clues to female homosexuality. *Science News, 142,* 117.

Bower, B. (1995a, December 23 & 30). Trauma disorder high, new survey finds. *Science News, 148,* 422.

Bower, B. (1995b, March 4). Virus may trigger some mood disorders. *Science News, 147,* 132.

Bower, B. (1996, April 27). Mom–child relations withstand day care. *Science News, 149,* 261.

Bower, B. (1997a, October 18). My culture, my self: Western notions of the mind may not translate to other cultures. *Science News, 152,* 248–249.

Bower, B. (1998b, November 28). Dr. Freud goes to Washington. *Science News, 154,* 347–349.

Bower, B. (1998d, June 20). Psychology's tangled web. *Science News, 153,* 394–395.

Bower, B. (2000a, January 22). Cultures of reason: Thinking styles may take Eastern and Western routes. *Science News, 157,* 56–58.

Bower, B. (2000b, September, 30). Memory echoes in brain's sensory terrain. *Science News, 158,* 213.

Bower, B. (2003, April 19). Words get in the way: Talk is cheap, but it can tax your memory. *Science News, 163,* 250–251. [See also Dodson et al., 1997]

Bower, B. (2004, July 24). Suicide watch: Antidepressants get large-scale inspection. *Science News, 166,* 51.

Bower, B. (2005a, November 5). Questions on the couch: Researchers spar over how best to evaluate psychotherapy. *Science News, 168,* 299–301.

Bower, B. (2005b, March 19). Schizophrenia syncs fast: Disconnected brain may lie at heart of disorder. *Science News, 167,* 180.

Bower, B. (2006a, July 1). Gay males' sibling link: Men's homosexuality tied to having older brothers. *Science News, 170*(1), 3.

Bower, B. (2006b, March 18). Prescription for controversy: Medications for depressed kids spark scientific dispute. *Science News, 169,* 168–172.

Bower, B. (2006c, February 11). Self-serve brains: Personal identity veers to the right hemisphere. *Science News, 169,* 90–92. [See also: Botvinick, 2004; Zimmer, 2005.]

Bower, B. (2007, July 28). Antidepressants trim suicide tries. *Science News, 172,* 61. [See also: Gibbons et al., 2007; Simon & Savarino, 2007]

Bower, B. (2009, February 14). Neural circuits foster oversensitivity: Borderline personality patients activate brain in specific ways. *Science News, 175*(4), 13.

Bower, B. (2010, May 22). Dream a little dream of recall. *Science News, 177*(11), 12–13.

Bower, B. (2010, June 19). Young kids can't face up to disgust. *Science News, 177*(13), 10.

Bower, G. H. (1972). A selective review of organizational factors in memory. In E. Tulving & W. Donaldson (Eds.), *Organization of memory.* New York: Academic Press.

Bower, J. M., & Parsons, L. M. (2003, August). Rethinking the "lesser brain." *Scientific American,* 50–57.

Bower, T. G. R. (1971, October). The object in the world of the infant. *Scientific American, 225*(4), 30–39.

Bowlby, J. (1969). *Attachment and loss: Vol. 1. Attachment.* New York: Basic Books.

Bowlby, J. (1973). *Attachment and loss: Vol. 2. Separation, anxiety and anger.* London: Hogarth.

Bowles, A. (2004). Beck in action: Grawemeyer-winning psychiatrist influential in psychology. *APS Observer, 17*(3), 7–8.

Boyatzis, C., Matillo, G., & Nesbitt, K. (1995). Effects of *The Mighty Morphin' Power Rangers* on children's aggression with peers. *Child Study Journal, 25,* 45–55.

Boyd, J., & Zimbardo, P. (2008). *The time paradox.* New York: Simon & Schuster.

Bradbury, J. (2001, May 19). Teasing out the genetics of bipolar disorder. *Lancet, 357,* 1596.

Bradley, G. W. (1978). Self-serving biases in the attribution process: A re-examination of the fact or fiction question. *Journal of Personality and Social Psychology, 35,* 56–71.

Bradshaw, G. (1992). The airplane and the logic of invention. In R. N. Giere (Ed.), *Minnesota studies in the philosophy of science* (pp. 2239–2250). Minneapolis: University of Minnesota Press.

Brådvik, L., & Berglund, M. (2006). Long-term treatment and suicidal behavior in severe depression: ECT and antidepressant pharmacotherapy may have different effects on the occurrence and seriousness of suicide attempts. *Depression and Anxiety, 23,* 34–41.

Brannon, L. (2008). *Gender: Psychological perspectives* (5th ed.). Boston: Allyn & Bacon.

Breckenridge, J. N., & Zimbardo, P. G. (2006). The strategy of terrorism and the psychology of mass-mediated fear. In B. Bongar, L. M. Brown, L. Beutler, J. N. Breckenridge, & P. G. Zimbardo (Eds.), *Psychology and terrorism* (pp. 116–133). New York: Oxford University Press.

Breggin, P. R. (1979). *Electroshock: Its brain-disabling effects.* New York: Springer.

Breggin, P. R. (1991). *Toxic psychiatry.* New York: St. Martin's Press.

Breggin, P. R., & Breggin, G. R. (1994). *Talking back to Prozac.* New York: St. Martin's Press.

Brehm, S. S. (1992). *Intimate relationships* (2nd ed.). Boston: McGraw-Hill.

Brehm, S. S., Miller, R., Perlman, D., & Campbell, S. M. (2002). *Intimate relationships* (3rd ed.). New York: McGraw-Hill.

Breier, J. I., Simos, P. G., Fletcher, J. M., Castillo, E. M., Zhang, W., & Papanicolaou, A. C. (2003). Abnormal activation of temporoparietal language areas during phonetic analysis in children with dyslexia. *Neuropsychology, 17,* 610–621.

Breland, K., & Breland, M. (1961). The misbehavior of organisms. *American Psychologist, 16,* 681–684.

Brett, A. S., Phillips, M., & Beary, J. F., III. (1986, March 8). Predictive power of the polygraph: Can the "lie detector" really detect liars? *Lancet, 1*(8480), 544–547.

Brewer, C. L. (1991). Perspectives on John B. Watson. In G. A. Kimble, M. Wertheimer, & C. L. White (Eds.), *Portraits of pioneers in psychology* (pp. 170–186). Washington, DC: American Psychological Association.

Brewer, M. B., Dull, V., & Lui, L. (1981). Perceptions of the elderly: Stereotypes and prototypes. *Journal of Personality and Social Psychology, 41,* 656–670.

Bridge, J. A., Satish, I., Salary, C. B., Barbe, R. P., Birmaher, B., Pincus, H. A., Ren, L., & Brent, D. A. (2007, April 18). Clinical response and risk for reported suicidal ideation and suicide attempts in pediatric antidepressant treatment: A meta-analysis of randomized controlled trials. *JAMA: Journal of the American Medical Association, 297,* 1683–1696.

Brislin, R. (1974). The Ponzo illusion: Additional cues, age, orientation, and culture. *Journal of Cross-Cultural Psychology, 5,* 139–161.

Brislin, R. (1993). *Understanding culture's influence on behavior.* Fort Worth, TX: Harcourt Brace Jovanovich.

Broadwell, S. D., & Light, K. C. (1999). Family support and cardiovascular responses in married couples during conflict and other interactions. *International Journal of Behavioral Medicine, 6,* 40–63.

Bronfenbrenner, U., & Ceci, S. J. (1994). Nature–nurture reconceptualized in developmental perspective: A bioecological model. *Psychological Review, 101,* 568–586.

Bronheim, S. (2000, January/February). The impact of the Human Genome Project on the science and practice of psychology. *Psychological Science Agenda, 13*(1), 12.

Brookhart, S. (2001). Persuasion and the "poison parasite." *APS Observer, 14*(8), 7.

Brown, A. M. (1990). *Human universals.* Unpublished manuscript, University of California, Santa Barbara.

Brown, C. (2003, October). The stubborn scientist who unraveled a mystery of the night. *Smithsonian,* 92–99.

Brown, J. D. (1991). Accuracy and bias in self-knowledge. In C. R. Snyder & D. F. Forsyth (Eds.), *Handbook of social and clinical psychology: The health perspective.* New York: Pergamon.

Brown, J. L., & Pollitt, E. (1996, February). Malnutrition, poverty and intellectual development. *Scientific American, 274*(2), 38–43.

Brown, K. (2003a, March 14). The medication merry-go-round. *Science, 299,* 1646–1649.

Brown, K. (2003b, July 11). New attention to ADHD genes. *Science, 301,* 160–161.

Brown, R., & Kulik, J. (1977). Flashbulb memories. *Cognition, 5,* 73–99.

Brown, R., & McNeill, D. (1966). The "tip of the tongue" phenomenon. *Journal of Verbal Learning and Verbal Behavior, 5,* 325–337.

Brown, S. L., Nesse, R. M., Vinokur, A. D., & Smith, D. M. (2003). Providing social support may be more beneficial than receiving it: Results from a prospective study of mortality. *Psychological Science, 14,* 320–327.

Brown, W. A. (1998, January). The placebo effect. *Scientific American, 278*(1), 90–95.

Bruck, M., & Ceci, S. (2004). Forensic developmental psychology: Unveiling four common misconceptions. *Current Directions in Psychological Science, 13,* 229–232. [See also: Loftus, 2004; Neimark, 2004.]

Bruin, J. E., Kellenberger, L. D., Gerstein, H. C., Morrison, K. M., & Holloway, A C. (2007). Fetal and neonatal nicotine exposure and postnatal glucose homeostasis: Identifying critical windows of exposure. *Journal of Endocrinology, 194,* 171–178.

Bruner, J. S., Olver, R. R., & Greenfield, P. M. (1966). *Studies in cognitive growth.* New York: Wiley.

Brunet, A., Orr, S. P., Tremblay, J., Robertson, K., Nader, K., & Pitman, R. K. (2007). Effect of post-retrieval propranolol on psychophysiologic responding during subsequent script-driven traumatic imagery in post-traumatic stress disorder. *Journal of Psychiatric Research, 42,* 503–506.

Brunner, H. G., Nelen, M., Breakefield, X. O., Ropers, H. H., & van Oost, B. A. (1993). Abnormal behavior associated with a point mutation in the structural gene for monoamine oxidase A. *Science, 262,* 578.

Büchel, C., Coull, J. T., & Friston, K. J. (1999). The predictive value of changes in effective connectivity for human learning. *Science, 283,* 1538–1541. [See also: Bower, 1999.]

Buckner, R., Andrews-Hanna, J., & Schacter, D. (2008). The brain's default network: Anatomy, function and relevance to disease. *Annals of the New York Academy of Sciences, 1124,* 1–38.

Buhrmester, D. (1996). Need fulfillment, interpersonal competence, and the developmental contexts of early adolescent friendship. In W. M. Bukowski, A. F. Newcomb, & W. W. Hartup (Eds.), *The company they keep: Friend In C. Murchison (Ed ship during childhood and adolescence* (pp. 158–185). New York: Cambridge University Press.

Bullock, T. H., Bennett, M. V. L., Johnston, D., Josephson, R., Marder, E., & Fields, R. D. (2005, November 4). The neuron doctrine, redux. *Science, 310,* 791–793.

Bureau of Justice Statistics, (2009). *Corrections statistics.* Retrieved January 13, 2011, from www.ojp .usdoj.gov/bjs/correct.htm.

Burger, J. M. (2009, January). Replication Milgram: Would people still obey today? *American Psychologist, 64,* 1–10.

Bushman, B. J., & Anderson, C. A. (2001). Media violence and the American public: Scientific facts versus media misinformation. *American Psychologist, 56,* 477–489.

Buss, D. M. (1999). *Evolutionary psychology: The new science of the mind.* Boston: Allyn & Bacon.

Buss, D. M. (2008). *Evolutionary psychology: The new science of the mind* (3rd ed.). Boston: Allyn & Bacon. [See also: Archer, 1996; Buss & Schmitt, 1993.]

Buss, D. M., Haselton, M. G., Shackelford, T. K., Bleske, A. L., & Wakefield, J. C. (1998). Adaptations, exaptations, and spandrels. *American Psychologist, 53,* 533–548.

Buss, D. M., & Schmitt, D. P. (1993). Sexual strategies theory: An evolutionary perspective on human mating. *Psychological Review, 100,* 204–232.

Butcher, J. N., Mineka, S., & Hooley, J. M. (2008). *Abnormal psychology: Core concepts.* Boston, MA: Allyn & Bacon.

Butcher, J. N., & Williams, C. L. (1992). *Essentials of MMPI-2 and MMPI-A interpretation.* Minneapolis: University of Minnesota Press.

Butcher, J. N., Mineka, S., & Hooley, J. M. (2010). *Abnormal Psychology* (14th ed.). Boston: Pearson.

Butler, A. C., Chapman, J. E., Forman, E. M. & Beck, A. T. (2006). The empirical status of cognitive-behavioral therapy: A review of meta-analyses. *Clinical Psychology Review, 26,* 17–31.

Button, T. M. M., Thapar, A., & McGuffin, P. (2005). Relationship between antisocial behavior, attention-deficit hyperactivity disorder, and maternal prenatal smoking. *British Journal of Psychiatry, 187,* 155–160.

Buzsáki, G. (2006). *Rhythms of the brain.* Oxford, UK: Oxford University Press.

Byne, W. (1995). The biological evidence challenged. *Scientific American, 270*(5), 50–55.

Byrne, D. (1969). Attitudes and attraction. In L. Berkowitz (Ed.), *Advances in experimental social psychology* (Vol. 4). New York: Academic Press.

Cabeza, R. (2002). Hemispheric asymmetry reduction in older adults: The HAROLD model. *Psychology & Aging, 17*(1), 85–100.

Cacioppo, J. T., & Brentson, G. G. (2005). *Essays in neuroscience.* Cambridge, MA: MIT Press.

Caldwell, M. (1995, June). Kernel of fear. *Discover, 16,* 96–102.

Caldwell, M. R., McCormick, D. J., Umstead, D., & VanRybroek, G. J. (2007). Evidence of treatment progress and therapeutic outcomes among adolescents with psychopathic features. *Criminal Justice and Behavior, 34,* 573–587.

Calev, A., Nigal, D., Shapira, B., Tubi, N., Chazan, S., Ben-Yehuda, Y., Kugelmass, S., & Lerer, B. (1991). Early and long-term effects of electroconvulsive therapy and depression on memory and other cognitive functions. *Journal of Nervous and Mental Disorders, 179,* 526–533.

Calkins, M. W. (1906). A reconciliation between structural and functional psychology. *Psychological Review, 13,* 61–81. Archived at the Classics in the History of Psychology site: http://psychclassics .yorku.ca/Calkins/reconciliation.htm.

Calkins, M. W. (1930). Autobiography of Mary Whiton Calkins. In C. Murchison (Ed.), *History of psychology in autobiography* (Vol. 1, pp. 31–61). Archived at the Classics in the History of Psychology site: http://psychclassics.yorku.ca/Calkins/ murchison.htm

Callaghan, E., Rochat, P., Lillard, A., Clau, M. L., Odden, H., Itakura, S., Tapanya, S., & Singh, S. (2005). Synchrony in the onset of mental-state reasoning: Evidence from five futures. *Psychological Science, 16,* 378–384.

Callahan, J. (1997, May/June). Hypnosis: Trick or treatment? *Health, 11*(1), 52–55. [See also: Miller & Bowers, 1993; Orne, 1980]

Calvert, J. D. (1988). Physical attractiveness: A review and reevaluation of its role in social skill research. *Behavioral Assessment, 10,* 29–42.

Cann, A., Calhoun, L. G., Selby, J. W., & Kin, H. E. (Eds.). (1981). Rape. *Journal of Social Issues, 37* (Whole No. 4).

Cannon, W. B. (1914). The interrelations of emotions as suggested by recent physiological researchers. *American Journal of Psychology, 25,* 256.

Caplow, T. (1982). *Middletown families: Fifty years of change and continuity.* Minneapolis: University of Minnesota Press.

Caporeal, L. R. (1976). Ergotism: The Satan loosed in Salem? *Science, 192,* 21–26.

Capps, J. G., & Ryan, R. (2005). It's not just polygraph anymore. *APA Online: Psychological Science Agenda.* Retrieved December 21, 2007, from www .apa.org/science/psa/polygraph_prnt.html.

Caprara, G. V., & Cervone, D. (2000). *Personality: Determinants, dynamics, and potentials.* New York: Cambridge University Press.

Carducci, B. J., & Zimbardo, P. G. (1995). Are you shy? *Psychology Today, 28,* 34 ff.

Carlat, D. (2010, March 30). Psychologists and prescription privileges: A conversation (part one). *The New Psychiatry.* Retrieved from www .psychologytoday.com/blog/the-new-psychiatry/ 201003/psychologists-and-prescription-privileges-conversation-part-one.

Carlsmith, K. M. (2006). The roles of retribution and utility in determining punishment. *Journal of Experimental Social Psychology, 42,* 437–451.

Carlson, L. E., Speca, M., Faris, P., & Patel, K. D. (2007). One year pre-post intervention follow-up of psychological, immune, endocrine and blood pressure outcomes of mindfulness-based stress reduction (MBSR) in breast and prostate cancer outpatients. *Brain, Behavior, and Immunity, 21,* 1038–1049.

Carlson, N. R. (2007). *Physiology of behavior* (9th ed.). Boston: Allyn & Bacon.

Carnagey, N. L., Anderson, C. A., & Bushman, B. J. (2007). The effect of video game violence on physiological desensitization to real-life violence. *Journal of Experimental Social Psychology, 43,* 489–496.

Carpenter, G. C. (1973). Differential response to mother and stranger within the first month of life. *Bulletin of the British Psychological Society, 16,* 138.

Carpenter, S. (1999, August 14). A new look at recognizing what people see. *Science News, 156,* 102.

Carpenter, S. (2000, September). Stoicism reconsidered. *Monitor on Psychology, 31*(8), 58–61.

Carskadon, M. A. (Ed.). (2002). *Adolescent sleep patterns: Biological, social, and psychological influences.* Cambridge, MA: Cambridge University Press.

Carson, R. C., Butcher, J. N., & Mineka, S. (2000). *Abnormal psychology and modern life* (11th ed.). Boston: Allyn & Bacon.

Carstensen, L. L. (1987). Age-related changes in social activity. In L. L. Carstensen & B. A. Edelstein (Eds.), *Handbook of clinical gerontology* (pp. 222–237). New York: Pergamon Press.

Carstensen, L. L. (1991). Selectivity theory: Social activity in life-span context. In K. W. Schaie (Ed.), *Annual review of geriatrics and gerontology* (Vol. 11). New York: Springer.

Carstensen, L. L., & Freund, A. M. (1994). Commentary: The resilience of the aging self. *Developmental Review, 14,* 81–92.

Cartwright, R. D. (1977). *Night life: Explorations in dreaming.* Englewood Cliffs, NJ: Prentice Hall.

Cartwright, R. D. (1984). Broken dreams: A study of the effects of divorce and depression on dream content. *Psychiatry, 47,* 251–259.

Carver, C. S., & Scheier, M. F. (2008). *Perspectives on personality* (6th ed.). Boston: Allyn & Bacon. [See also: Digman, 1990; Goldberg, 1981, 1993.]

Carver, P., Egan, S., & Perry, D. (2004). Children who question their heterosexuality. *Developmental Psychology, 40,* 43–53.

Casey, B. J., Jones, R. M., & Hare, T. A. (2008). The adolescent brain. *Annals of the New York Academy of Science, 1124,* 111–126.

Casey, J. F., & Wilson, L. (1991). *The flock.* New York: Fawcett Columbine.

Cash, T. F., & Janda, L. H. (1984, December). The eye of the beholder. *Psychology Today, 18,* 46–52.

Cassidy, J., & Shaver, P. R. (Eds.). (2008). *Handbook of attachment: Theory, research, and clinical applications* (2nd ed.). New York: Guilford Press.

Cassileth, B. R., Lusk, E. J., Strouse, T. B., Miller, D. S., Brown, L. L. and Cross, P. A. (1985), A psychological analysis of cancer patients and their next-of-kin. *Cancer, 55:* 72–76.

Cattell, R. B. (1963). Theory of fluid and crystallized intelligence: A critical experiment. *Journal of Educational Psychology, 54,* 1–22.

Cawthon, R. M., Smith, K. R., O'Brien, E., Sivatchenko, A., Kerber, R. A. (2003). Association between telomere length in blood and mortality in people aged 60 years or older. *Lancet, 361,* 393–395.

Ceci, S. J., & Williams, W. M. (1997). Schooling, intelligence, and income. *American Psychologist, 52,* 1051–1058.

Centers for Disease Control and Prevention. (2007). *Smoking and tobacco use.* Retrieved March 28, 2008, from www.cdc.gov/tobacco/data_statistics/ Factsheets/adult_cig_smoking.htm.

Cervone, D. (2004). The architecture of personality. *Psychological Review, 111,* 183–204.

Cervone, D., & Shoda, Y. (1999). Beyond traits in the study of personality coherence. *Current Directions in Psychological Science, 8,* 27–32.

Chalmers, D. J. (1995, December). The puzzle of conscious experience. *Scientific American, 273*(6), 80–86. [See also: Churchland, 1995; Crick, 1994]

Chamberlain, K., & Zika, S. (1990). The minor events approach to stress: Support for the use of daily hassles. *British Journal of Psychology, 81,* 469–481.

Chamberlin, J. (2004, July/August). Survey says: More Americans are seeking mental health treatment. *Monitor on Psychology, 35*(7), 17.

Chamberlin, J. (2008, December). The sleep aide: Jack Edinger helps patients remove the barriers to a good night's sleep. *Monitor on Psychology, 39*(11), 40–43.

Chambless, D. L., Sanderson, W. C., Shoham, V., Johnson, S. B., Pope, K. S., Crits-Christoph, P., Baker, M., Johnson, B., Woody, S. R., Sue, S., Beutler, L., Williams, D. A., & McCurry, S. (1996). An update on empirically validated therapies. *The Clinical Psychologist, 49*, 5–18.

Chan, L., Chiu, P. Y., & Lau, T. K. (2003). An in-vitro study of ginsenoside Rb1–induced teratogenicity using a whole rat embryo culture model. *Human Reproduction, 18*, 2166–2168.

Chapman, P. D. (1988). *Schools as sorters: Lewis M. Terman, applied psychology, and the intelligence testing movement, 1890–1930.* New York: New York University Press.

Charles, S. T., & Carstensen, L. L. (2010). Social and emotional aging. *Annual Review of Psychology, 61,* 383–409.

Chartrand, T. L., & Bargh, J. A. (1999). The chameleon effect: The perception–behavior link and social interaction. *Journal of Personality & Social Psychology, 76*, 893–910.

Chaudhari, N., Landin, A. M., & Roper, S. D. (2000). A metabotropic glutamate receptor variant functions as a taste receptor. *Nature Neuroscience, 3,* 113–119.

Chen, E., Fisher, E. B., Bacharier, L. B., & Strunk, R. C. (2003). Socioeconomic status, stress, and immune markers in adolescents with asthma. *Psychosomatic Medicine, 65*, 984–992.

Cherney, E. D., & London, K. (2006). Gender-linked differences in the toys, television shows, computer games, and outdoor activities of 5- to 13-year-old children. *Sex Roles, 54*, 717–726.

Chiaccia, K. B. (2007). Insanity defense. *Encyclopedia of Psychology.* Retrieved February 9, 2008, from http://findarticles.com/p/articles/mi_g2699/is_0005/ai_2699000509. [See also: Consensus Project (n. d.)]

Chisuwa, N., & O'Day, J. A. (2010). Body image and eating disorders amongst Japanese adolescents: A review of the literature. *Appetite, 54*(1), 5–15.

Chivers, M., Seto, M. C., & Blanchard, R. (2007). Gender and sexual orientation differences in sexual response to sexual activities versus gender of actors in sexual films. *Journal of Personality and Social Psychology, 93*, 1108–1121.

Chklovskii, D. B., Mel, B. W., & Svoboda, K. (2004, October 14). Cortical re-wiring and information storage. *Nature 431*, 782–788.

Chodzko-Zajko, W., Kramer, A. F., & Poon, L. W. (2009). *Enhancing cognitive functioning and brain plasticity.* Champaign, IL: Human Kinetics.

Chomsky, N. (1965). *Aspects of a theory of syntax.* Cambridge, MA: MIT Press.

Chomsky, N. A. (1977). On Wh-movement. In P. W. Culicover, T. Wasw, & A. Akmajian (Eds.), *Formal syntax.* San Francisco, London: Academic Press.

Chorney, M. J., Chorney, N. S., Owen, M. J., Daniels, J., McGuffin, P., Thompson, L. A., Detterman, D. K., Benbow, C., Lubinski, D., Eley, T., & Plomin, R. (1998). A quantitative trait locus associated with cognitive ability in children. *Psychological Science, 9*, 159–166.

Christenfeld, N., Gerin, W., Linden, W., Sanders, M., Mathus, J., & Deich, J. D., et al. (1997). Social support effects on cardiovascular reactivity: Is a stranger as effective as a friend? *Psychosomatic Medicine, 59*, 388–398.

Christensen, A., & Jacobson, N. S. (1994). Who (or what) can do psychotherapy: The status and challenge of nonprofessional therapies. *Psychological Science, 5*, 8–14.

Chua, H. F., Boland, J. E., & Nisbett, R. E. (2005, August 30). Cultural variation in eye movements during scene perception. *Proceedings of the National Academy of Sciences, 102*, 12629–12633.

Church, A. T., Katigbak, M. S., Del Prado, A. M., Ortiz, F. A., Mastor, K. A., Harumi, Y., Tanaka-Matsumi, J., De Jesús Vargas-Flores, J., Ibáñez-reyes, J., White, F. A., Miramontes, L. G., Reyes, J. A. S., & Cabrera, H. F. (2006). Implicit theories and self-perceptions of traitedness across cultures: Toward integration of cultural and trait psychology perspectives. *Journal of Cross-Cultural Psychology, 37*, 694–716.

Church, A. T., Katigbak, M. S., Ortiz, F. A., Del Prado, A. M., De Jesús Vargas-Flores, J., Ibáñez-Reyes, J., Pe-Pua, R., & Cabrera, H. F. (2005). Investigating implicit trait theories across cultures. *Journal of Cross-Cultural Psychology, 36*, 476–496.

Cialdini, R. B. (2001). *Influence: Science and practice* (4th ed.). Boston: Allyn & Bacon.

Cialdini, R. B. (2007). *Influence: The psychology of persuasion.* New York: HarperCollins.

Clark, L. A. (2009). Stability and change in personality disorder. *Current Directions in Psychological Science, 18*, 27–31.

Clark, M. S., Mills, J. R., & Corcoran, D. M. (1989). Keeping track of needs and inputs of friends and strangers. *Personality and Social Psychology Bulletin, 15*, 533–542.

Clark, R. E., & Squire, L. R. (1998, April 3). Classical conditioning and brain systems: The role of awareness. *Science, 280*, 77–81.

Clay, R. A. (2000, January). Psychotherapy is cost-effective. *Monitor on Psychology, 31*(1), 40–41.

Clay, R. A. (2003a, April). An empty nest can promote freedom, improved relationships. *Monitor on Psychology, 33*, 40–41.

Clay, R. A. (2003b, April). Researchers replace midlife myths with facts. *Monitor on Psychology, 34*, 38–39.

Clay, R. A. (2009a, September). Prevention works. *Monitor on Psychology, 40*(8), 42–44.

Clay, R. A. (2009b). Postgrad growth area: Forensic psychology. *GradPsych*, (7). Retrieved from www.apa.org/gradpsych/2009/11/postgrad.aspx.

Cleek, M. B., & Pearson, T. A. (1985). Perceived causes of divorce: An analysis of interrelationships. *Journal of Marriage and the Family, 47*, 179–191.

Clifton, S., & Myers, K. K. (2005). The socialization of emotion: Learning emotion management at the fire station. *Journal of Applied Communication Research, 33*, 67–92.

Coan, J. A., Schaefer, H., & Davidson, R. J. (2006). Lending a hand: Social regulation of the neural responses to threat. *Psychological Science, 17*, 1032–1039.

Coghill, R. C., McHaffie, J. G., & Yen, Y. (2003, July 8). Neural correlates of interindividual differences in the subjective experience of pain. *Proceedings of the National Academy of Sciences, 14*, 8538–8542.

Cohen, D., & Gunz, A. (2002). As seen by the other . . . : Perspectives on the self in the memories and emotional perceptions of Easterners and Westerners. *Psychological Science, 55–59.* [See also: Gardiner et al., 1998; Markus & Kitayama, 1994.]

Cohen, G. L., Garcia, J., Apfel, N., & Master, A. (2006). Reducing the racial achievement gap: A social-psychological intervention. *Science, 313,* 1307–1310.

Cohen, G. L., Garcia, J., Purdie-Vaughns, V., Apfel, N., & Brzustoski, P. (2009). Recursive processes in self-affirmation: Intervening to close the minority achievement gap. *Science, 324,* 400–403.

Cohen, J. (2002, February 8). The confusing mix of hype and hope. *Science, 295*, 1026.

Cohen, J. D., & Tong, F. (2001, 28 September). The face of controversy. *Science, 293*, 2405–2407.

Cohen, M. N. (1998). *Culture of intolerance: Chauvinism, class, and racism in the United States.* New Haven, CT: Yale University Press.

Cohen, R. E., & Ahearn, F. L., Jr. (1980). *Handbook for mental health care of disaster victims.* Baltimore: Johns Hopkins University Press.

Cohen, S., Doyle, W. J., Turner, R. B., Alper, C. M., & Skoner, D. P. (2003). Emotional style and susceptibility to the common cold. *Psychosomatic Medicine, 63*, 652–657.

Cohen, S., & Girgus, J. S. (1973). Visual spatial illusions: Many explanations. *Science, 179*, 503–504.

Cohen, S., & Syme, S. L. (Eds.). (1985). *Social support and health.* Orlando, FL: Academic Press.

Colby, A., Kohlberg, L., Gibbs, J., & Lieberman, M. (1983). A longitudinal study of moral judgment. *Monographs of the Society for Research in Child Development, 481*(1–2, Serial No. 200).

Colcombe, S. J., Kramer, A. F., Erickson, K. I., Scalf, P., McAuley, E., Cohen, N. J., Webb, A., Jerome, G. J., Marquez, D. X., & Elavsky, S. (2004). Cardiovascular fitness, cortical plasticity, and aging. *Proceedings of the National Academy of Sciences, 101,* 3316–3321.

Cole, M. (2006). Internationalism in psychology: We need it now more than ever. *American Psychologist, 61*, 904–917. [See also Fowers & Richardson, 1996; Gergen et al., 1996; Segall et al., 1998; Triandis, 1994, 1995]

Collins, A. W., Maccoby, E. E., Steinberg, L., Hetherington, E. M., & Bornstein, M. H. (2000). Contemporary research on parenting: The case for nature and nurture. *American Psychologist, 55*, 218–232.

Collins, G. P. (2001, October). Magnetic revelations: Functional MRI highlights neurons receiving signals. *Scientific American, 285*(4), 21.

Collins, N. L., & Read, S. J. (1990). Adult attachment, working models, and relationship quality in dating couples. *Journal of Personality and Social Psychology, 58*, 644–663.

Collins, S., & Long, A. (2003). Too tired to care? The psychological effects of working with trauma. *Journal of Psychiatric and Mental Health Nursing, 10*, 17–27.

Colom, R., Flores-Mendoza, C. E., & Abad, F. J. (2007). Generational changes on the draw-a-man test: A comparison of Brazilian urban and rural children tested in 1930, 2002 and 2004. *Journal of Biosocial Science, 39*, 79–89.

Coloroso, B. (2008). *The Bully, the bullied, and the bystander: From preschool to high school: How parents and teachers can break the cycle of violence.* New York: HarperCollins.

Committee on Substance Abuse and Committee on Children with Disabilities. (2000). Fetal alcohol syndrome and alcohol-related neurodevelopmental disorders. *Pediatrics, 106*, 358–361.

Conklin, H. M., & Iacono, W. G. (2004). Schizophrenia: A neurodevelopmental perspective. In T. F. Oltmans & R. E. Emery (Eds.), *Current Directions in Abnormal Psychology* (pp. 122–129). Upper Saddle River, NJ: Prentice Hall.

Conley, C. (2007). *Peak: How great companies get their Mojo from Maslow.* San Francisco: Jossey-Bass.

Conner, D. B., & Cross, D. R. (2003). Longitudinal analysis of the presence, efficacy, and stability of maternal scaffolding during informal problem-solving interactions. *British Journal of Developmental Psychology, 21*, 315–334.

Conrad, R. (1964). Acoustic confusions in immediate memory. *British Journal of Psychology, 55,* 75–84.

Consumer Reports. (1995, November). Mental health: Does therapy help? 734–739.

Contrada, R. J., Ashmore, R. D., Gary, M. L., Coups, E., Egeth, J. D., Sewell, A., Ewell, K., Goyal, T. M., & Chasse, V. (2000). Ethnicity-related sources of stress and their effects on well-being. *Current Directions in Psychological Science, 9,* 136–139.

Cook, M., Mineka, S., Wolkenstein, B., & Laitsch, K. (1985). Observational conditioning of snake fear in unrelated rhesus monkeys. *Journal of Abnormal Psychology, 94,* 591–610.

Cooper, R. S. (2005). Race and IQ: Molecular genetics as deus ex machina. *American Psychologist, 60,* 71–76.

Corkin, S. (2002). What's new with the amnesic patient H. M.? *Nature Reviews Neuroscience, 3,* 153–160. Retrieved March 10, 2008, from http://homepage.mac.com/sanagnos/corkin2002.pdf.

Costa, P. T., Jr., & McCrae, R. R. (1992a). Four ways five factors are basic. *Personality and Individual Differences, 13,* 653–665.

Costa, P. T., Jr., & McCrae, R. R. (1992b). *Revised NEO Personality Inventory (NEO-PI-R) and NEO Five-Factor Inventory (NEO-FFI) professional manual.* Odessa, FL: Psychological Assessment Resources.

Coughlin, E. K. (1994, October 26). Class, IQ, and heredity. *The Chronicle of Higher Education,* A12, A20.

Courchesne, E., Chisum, H., & Townsend, J. (1994). Neural activity-dependent brain cells in development: Implications for psychopathology. *Development and Psychopathology, 6,* 697–722.

Couzin, J. (2005, May 6). A heavyweight battle over CDC's obesity forecasts. *Science, 308,* 770–771.

Couzin, J. (2006, October 27). Unraveling pain's DNA. *Science, 314,* 585–586.

Covington, M. V. (2000). Intrinsic versus extrinsic motivation in schools: A reconciliation. *Current Direction in Psychology Science, 9,* 22–25.

Cowan, P., & Cowan, P. A. (1988). Changes in marriage during the transition to parenthood. In G. Y. Michaels & W. A. Goldberg (Eds.), *The transition to parenthood: Current theory and research.* Cambridge, UK: Cambridge University Press.

Coyne, J. C., Burchill, S. A. L., & Stiles, W. B. (1991). An interactional perspective on depression. In C. R. Snyder & D. O. Forsyth (Eds.), *Handbook of social and clinical psychology: The health perspective* (pp. 327–349). New York: Pergamon Press.

Coyne, J. C., Pajak,. T. F., Harris, J., Konski, A., Moysas, B., Ang, K., Bruner, D. W. and Radiation Therapy Oncology Group (2007). Emotional well-being does not predict survival in head and neck cancer patients: A Radiation Therapy Oncology Group study. *Cancer, 110*(11), 2568–2575.

Coyne, K. J. C. (2001, February). Depression in primary care: Depressing news, exciting research opportunities. *APS Observer, 14*(2), 1, 18.

Craik, F. I. M., & Lockhart, R. S. (1972). Levels of processing: A framework for memory research. *Journal of Verbal Learning and Verbal Behavior, 11,* 671–684.

Craik, F. I. M., & Tulving, E. (1975). Depth of processing and the retention of words in episodic memory. *Journal of Experimental Psychology: General, 104,* 268–294.

Cramer, P. (2000). Defense mechanisms in psychology today. *American Psychologist, 55,* 637–646.

Crandall, C. S., Preisler, J. J., & Aussprung, J. (1992). Measuring life event stress in the lives of college students: The Undergraduate Stress Questionnaire (USQ). *Journal of Behavioral Medicine, 15*(6), 627–662.

Cree, G. S., & McRae, K. (2003). Analyzing the factors underlying the structure and computation of the meaning of chipmunk, cherry, cheese, and cello (and many other such concrete nouns). *Journal of Experimental Psychology: General, 132,* 163–201. [See also: Posner & McCandliss, 1993; Raichle, 1994; Solso, 2001.]

Crick, F., & Mitchison, G. (1983). The function of dream sleep. *Nature, 304,* 111–114.

Crocker, J., & Major, B. (1989). Social stigma and self-esteem: The self-protective properties of stigma. *Psychological Review, 96,* 608–630.

Crohan, S. E., Antonucci, T. C., Adelmann, P. K., & Coleman, L. M. (1989). Job characteristics and well-being at mid-life. *Psychology of Women Quarterly, 13,* 223–235.

Cromwell, R. L. (1993). Searching for the origins of schizophrenia. *Psychological Science, 4,* 276–279.

Crowder, R. G. (1992). Eidetic images. In L. R. Squire (Ed.), *The encyclopedia of learning and memory* (pp. 154–156). New York: Macmillan.

Crowell, T. A. (2002). Neuropsychological findings in combat-related posttraumatic stress disorder. *Clinical Neuropsychologist, 16,* 310–321.

Csikszentmihalyi, M. (1990). *Flow: The psychology of optimal experience.* New York: Harper & Row.

Csikszentmihalyi, M. (1996, July/August). The creative personality. *Psychology Today, 29*(4), 34–40.

Csikszentmihalyi, M. (1998). *Finding flow.* New York: Basic Books.

Csikszentmihalyi, M., Larson, R., & Prescott, S. (1977). The ecology of adolescent activity and experience. *Journal of Youth and Adolescence, 6,* 281–294.

Csikszentmihalyi, M., Rathunde, K. R., Whalen, S., & Wong, M. (1993). *Talented teenagers: The roots of success and failure.* New York: Cambridge University Press.

Cynkar, A. (2007a, April). Low glucose levels compromise self-control. *Monitor on Psychology, 38*(4), 13.

Cynkar, A. (2007b, May). Demand a seat: Speak up about evidence-based practice to ensure public access to quality mental health care, SLC panelists advised. *Monitor on Psychology, 38*(5), 38–39.

Cytowic, R. E. (1993). *The man who tasted shapes.* Cambridge, MA: MIT Press.

Dabbs, J. M. (2000). *Heroes, rogues, and lovers: Testosterone and behavior.* New York: McGraw-Hill.

Dackman, L. (1986). Everyday illusions. *Exploratorium Quarterly, 10,* 5–7.

Dadds, M. R., & Fraser, J. A. (2006). Fire interest, fire setting and psychopathology in Australian children: A normative study. *Australian and New Zealand Journal of Psychiatry, 40,* 581–586.

Daily, D. K., Ardinger, H. H., & Holmes, G. E. (2000). Identification and evaluation of mental retardation. *American Family Physician, 61,* 1059–1067.

Daley, K. C. (2004). Update on attention-deficit/hyperactivity disorder. *Current Opinion in Pediatrics, 16,* 217–226.

Daley, T. C., Whaley, S. E., Sigman, M. D., Espinosa, M. P., & Neumann, C. (2003). IQ on the rise: The Flynn effect in rural Kenyan children. *Psychological Science, 14,* 215–219.

Dally, J. M., Emery, N. J., & Clayton, N. S. (2005). Cache protection strategies by western scrub-jays (*Aphelocoma californica*): Implications for social cognition. *Animal Behaviour, 70,* 1251–1263.

Dalton, A. (2010, October 26). Study: Half of teens admit bullying in last year. *Associated Press.*

Daly, R. C., Su, T.-P., Schmidt, P. J., Pagliaro, M., Pickar, D., & Rubinow, D. R. (2003). Neuroendocrine and behavioral effects of high-dose anabolic steroid administration in male normal volunteers. *Psychoneuroendocrinology, 28,* 317–331.

Damasio, A. R. (1994). *Descartes' error: Emotion, reason, and the human brain.* New York: Avon Books.

Damasio, A. R. (1999, December). How the brain creates the mind. *Scientific American, 281*(6), 112–117.

Damasio, A. R. (2000). *The feeling of what happens: Body and emotion in the making of consciousness.* New York: Harcourt Brace.

Damasio, A. R. (2003). *Looking for Spinoza: Joy, sorrow, and the feeling brain.* Orlando, FL: Harcourt. [See also LeDoux, 1996; Whalen, 1998]

Dana, R. H. (1993). *Multicultural assessment perspectives for professional psychology.* Boston: Allyn & Bacon.

Danion, J., Rizzo, L., & Bruant, A. (1999). Functional mechanisms underlying im paired recognition memory and conscious awareness in patients with schizophrenia. *Archives of General Psychiatry, 56,* 639–644.

Dannefer, D., & Perlmutter, M. (1990). Developmental as a multidimensional process: Individual and social constit uents. *Human Development, 33,* 108–137.

Danner, D. D., Snowdon, D. A., & Friesen, W. V. (2001). Positive emotions in early life and longevity: Findings from the nun study. *Journal of Personality and Social Psychology, 80,* 804–813.

Darwin, C. (1862/1998). *The expression of the emotions in man and animals* (3rd ed., with Introduction, Afterword, and Commentaries by P. Ekman). New York: Oxford University Press. (Original work published 1862.)

Darwin, C. (1963). *On the origin of species.* London: Oxford University Press. (Original work published 1859.)

Davidson, P. S. R., Cook, S. P., Clisky, E. L., Verfaellie, M., & Rapcsak, S. Z. (2005). Source memory in the real world: A neuropsychological study of flashbulb memory. *Journal of Clinical and Experimental Neuropsychology, 27,* 915–929.

Davidson, R. J. (1992a). Anterior cerebral asymmetry and the nature of emotion. *Brain and Cognition, 20,* 125–151.

Davidson, R. J. (1992b). Emotion and affective style: Hemispheric substrates. *Psychological Science, 3,* 39–43.

Davidson, R. J. (2000a). Affective neuroscience. Address given at the American Psychological Association's annual convention, Washington, DC.

Davidson, R. J. (2000b). Affective style, psychopathology, and resilience: Brain mechanisms and plasticity. *American Psychologist, 55,* 1196–1214.

Davidson, R. J., Jackson, D. C., & Kalin, N. H. (2000). Emotion, plasticity, context, and regulation: Perspectives from affective neuroscience. *Psychological Bulletin, 126,* 890–909. [See also: Adolphs et al., 2001; Ahern & Schwartz, 1985; Borod et al., 1988.]

Davidson, R. J., Kabat-Zinn, J., Schumacher, J., Rosenkranz, M., Muller, D., Santorelli, S. F., Urbanowski, F., Harrington, A., Bonus, K., & Sheridan, J. F. (2003). Alternations in brain and immune function produced by mindfulness meditation. *Psychosomatic Medicine, 65,* 564–570.

Davis, C. G., Nolen-Hoeksema, S., & Larson, J. (1998). Making sense of loss and benefiting from the experience: Two construals of meaning. *Journal of Personality and Social Psychology, 75,* 561–574.

Davis, J. L., & Rusbult, C. E. (2001). Attitude alignment in close relationships. *Journal of Personality & Social Psychology, 81,* 65–84.

Davison, K. P., Pennebaker, J. W., & Dickerson, S. S. (2000). Who talks? The social psychology of illness support groups. *American Psychologist, 55,* 205–217.

Daw, J. (2001, June). The Ritalin debate. *Monitor on Psychology, 32*(6), 64–65.

Dawes, R. M. (2001). *Everyday irrationality: How pseudoscientists, lunatics, and the rest of us fail to think rationally.* Boulder, CO: Westview Press.

Dawkins, K., Lieberman, J. A., Lebowitz, B. D., & Hsiao, J. K. (1999). Antipsychotics: Past and future. *Schizophrenia Bulletin, 25*, 395–405. [See also: Gitlin, 1990; Holmes, 2001; Kane & Marder, 1993.]

Day, N. L. (2002). Prenatal alcohol exposure predicts continued deficits in offspring size at 14 years of age. *Alcoholism: Clinical and Experimental Research, 26*, 1584–1591.

DeAngelis, T. (2002a, June). A bright future for PNI. *Monitor on Psychology*, 46–50.

DeAngelis, T. (2002b, February). New data on lesbian, gay, and bisexual mental health. *Monitor on Psychology, 33*(2), 46–47.

DeAngelis, T. (2004a, January). Family-size portions for one. *Monitor on Psychology, 35*(1), 50–51.

DeAngelis, T. (2004b, January). What's to blame for the surge in super-size Americans? *Monitor on Psychology, 35*(1), 46–49. [See also: Abelson & Kennedy, 2004; Marx, 2003; Newman, 2004; Taubes, 1998; Wickelgren, 1998c.]

DeAngelis, T. (2005, November). Where psychotherapy meets neuroscience. *Monitor on Psychology, 36*(11), 72–73.

DeAngelis, T. (2006, February). Promising new treatments for SAD. *Monitor on Psychology, 37*(2), 18–20.

DeAngelis, T. (2008a, February). When do meds make the difference? *Monitor on Psychology, 39*(2), 48–53.

DeAngelis, T. (2008b, October). One treatment for emotional disorders? Research suggests that a single protocol can successfully treat all anxiety and mood disorders. *Monitor on Psychology, 39*(9), 26–27.

DeAngelis, T. (2009, November 1). Understanding terrorism. *Monitor on Psychology, 40*, 60ff.

DeAngelis, T. (2010, June). Closing the gap between practice and research: Two efforts are addressing the reasons practitioners may not always use research findings. *Monitor on Psychology, 41*, 42–45.

DeCasper, A. J., & Spence, M. J. (1986). Prenatal maternal speech influences newborns' perception of speech sounds. *Infant Behavior and Development, 9*, 133–150.

Deckers, L. (2001). *Motivation: Biological, psychological, and environmental*. Boston: Allyn & Bacon.

de Gelder, B. (2000, August 18). More to seeing than meets the eye. *Science, 289*, 1148–1149. [See also: Barinaga, 1999; Batista et al., 1999; Maunsell, 1995.]

de Groot, A. D. (1965). *Thought and choice in chess*. The Hague: Mouton.

Delaney, P. F., Sahakyan, L., Kelley, C. M., & Zimmerman, C. A. (2010). Remembering to forget: The amnesic effect of daydreaming. *Psychological Science, 21*(7), 1036–1042.

Delgado, J. M. R. (1969). *Physical control of the mind: Toward a psychocivilized society*. New York: Harper & Row.

De Martino, B., Kumaran, D., Seymour, B., & Dolan, R. J. (2006, August 4). Frames, biases, and rational decision-making in the human brain. *Science, 313*, 684–687.

Dement, W. C. (1980). *Some watch while some must sleep*. San Francisco: San Francisco Book Company.

Dement, W. C. (2000, September 25). Sleep debt. Retrieved March 9, 2004, from SleepQuest website: www.sleepquest.com/d_column_archive6.html

Dement, W. C., & Kleitman, N. (1957). Cyclic variations in EEG during sleep and their relations to eye movement, body mobility and dreaming. *Electroencephalography and Clinical Neurophysiology, 9*, 673–690.

Dement, W. C., & Vaughan, C. (1999). *The promise of sleep*. New York: Delacorte Press.

DeMeyer, G., Shapiro, F., Vanderstichele, H., Vanmechelen, E., Engelborghs, S., DeDeyn, P. P., Coart, E., Hansson, O., Minthon, L., Zetterberg, H., Blennow, K., Shaw, L., Trojanowski, J. Q. (2010). Diagnosis-independent Alzheimer disease biomarker signature in cognitively normal elderly people. *Archives of Neurology, 67*, 949–956.

Dennis, W. (1960). Causes of retardation among institutionalized children: Iran. *Journal of Genetic Psychology, 96*, 47–59.

Dennis, W., & Dennis, M. G. (1940). The effect of cradling practices upon the onset of walking in Hopi children. *Journal of Genetic Psychology, 56*, 77–86.

DePaulo, B. M., Lindsay, J. J., Malone, B. E., Muhlenbruck, L., Charlton, K., & Cooper, H. (2003). Cues to deception. *Psychological Bulletin, 129*, 74–118.

Derbyshire, S. W. G., Whalley, M. G., Stenger, V. A., & Oakley, D. A. (2004). Cerebral activation during hypnotically induced and imagined pain. *Neuro image, 23*, 392–401.

Dermietzel, R. (2006, October/November). The electrical brain. *Scientific American Mind, 17*(5), 56–61.

DeRubeis, R. J., Hollon, S. D., Amsterdam, J. D., Shelton, R. C., Young, P. R., Salomon, R. M., O'Reardon, J. P., Lovett, M. L., Gladis, M. M., Brown, L. L., & Gallop, R. (2005). Cognitive therapy vs. medications in the treatment of moderate to severe depression. *Archives of General Psychiatry, 62*, 409–416.

DeSalvo, L. (2000). *Writing as a way of healing: How telling our stories transforms our lives*. Boston: Beacon Press.

Deutsch, M., & Collins, M. E. (1951). *Interracial housing: A psychological evaluation of a social experiment*. Minneapolis: University of Minnesota Press.

Deutsch, M., & Gerard, H. B. (1955). A study of normative and informational social influence upon individual judgment. *Journal of Abnormal and Social Psychology, 51*, 629–636.

Devereux, G. (1981). *Mohave ethnopsychiatry and suicide: The psychiatric knowledge and psychic disturbances of an Indian tribe*. Bureau of American Ethology Bulletin 175. Washington, DC: Smithsonian Institution.

Devilly, G. J., Gist, R., & Cotton, P. (2006). Ready! Fire! Aim! The status of psychological debriefing and therapeutic interventions: In the work place and after disasters. *Review of General Psychology, 10*, 318–345.

Devine, P. G., & Zuwerink, J. R. (1994). Prejudice and guilt: The internal struggle to overcome prejudice. In W. J. Lonner & R. Malpass (Eds.), *Psychology and culture* (pp. 203–207). Boston: Allyn & Bacon.

Devor, H. (1993). Sexual orientation identities, attractions, and practices of female-to-male transsexuals. *Journal of Sex Research, 30*, 303–315.

de Waal, F. B. M. (1999, December). The end of nature versus nurture. *Scientific American, 281*(6), 94–99.

DeWall, C. N., Macdonald, G., Webster, G. D., Masten, C. L., Baumeister, R. F., Powell, C., Combs, D., Schurtz, D. R., Stillman, T. F., Tice, D. M., & Eisenberger, N. I. (2010). Tylenol reduces social pain: Behavioral and neural evidence. *Psychological Science, 21*, 931–937.

Dewsbury, D. A. (1990). Early interactions between animal psychologists and animal activists and the founding of the APA Committee on Precautions in Animal Experimentation. *American Psychologist, 45*, 315–327.

Dewsbury, D. A. (1996) Beatrix Tugendhat Gardner (1933–1995): Obituary. *American Psychologist, 51*(12), 1332.

Dewsbury, D. A. (1997). In celebration of the centennial of Ivan P. Pavlov's (1897/1902) *The work of the digestive glands*. *American Psychologist, 52*, 933–935.

Diamond, L. (2008). Female bisexuality from adolescence to adulthood: Results from a 10-year longitudinal study. *Developmental Psychology, 44*, 5–14.

Diamond, M. (2007). *Psychosexual development— male or female?* Address given at the 2007 convention of the American Psychological Association in San Francisco.

Dickens, W. T., & Flynn, J. R. (2001). Heritability estimates versus large environmental effects: The IQ paradox resolved. *Psychological Review, 108*, 346–369.

Dickens, W. T., & Flynn, J. R. (2006). Black Americans reduce the racial IQ gap: Evidence from standardization samples. *Psychological Science, 17*, 913–920.

Dickinson, A. (2001). Causal learning: Association versus computation. *Current Directions in Psychological Science, 10*, 127–132.

Diehl, M., Coyle, N., & Labouvie-Vief, G. (1996). Age and sex differences in strategies of coping and defense across the life span. *Psychology and Aging, 11*, 127–139.

Diener, E. (1984). Subjective well-being. *Psychological Bulletin, 95*, 542–575.

Diener, E. (2000). Subjective well-being: The science of happiness and a proposal for a national index. *American Psychologist, 55*, 34–43.

Diener, E., & Diener, C. (1996). Most people are happy. *Psychological Science, 7*, 181–189.

Diener, E., Sandvik, E., Seidlitz, L., & Diener, M. (1993). The relationship between income and subjective well-being: Relative or absolute? *Social Indicators Research, 28*, 195–223.

Diener, E., & Seligman, M. E. P. (2002). Very happy people. *Psychological Science, 13*, 81–84.

DiFebo, H. (2002). *Psyography: Mary Whiton Calkins*. Retrieved January 11, 2008, from http://faculty.frostburg.edu/mbradley/psyography/marywhitoncalkins.html.

Dijksterhuis, A. (2004). Think different: The merits of unconscious thought in preference development and decision making. *Journal of Personality and Social Psychology, 87*, 586–598.

Dillard, A. J. (2007). Humor, laughter, and recovery from stressful experiences. *Dissertation Abstracts International: Section B: The Sciences and Engineering, 68*(5-B), 3432.

Dingfelder, S. F. (2004a, July/August). Gateways to memory. *Monitor on Psychology, 35*(7), 22–23. [See also: Azar, 1998a; Holloway, 1999.]

Dingfelder, S. F. (2004b, March). Pavlovian psychopharmacology. *Monitor on Psychology, 35*(3), 18–19.

Dingfelder, S. F. (2004c, March). To tell the truth. *Monitor on Psychology, 35*(3), 22–23. [See also: Aftergood, 2000; Holden, 2001b; Saxe, 1991, 1994.]

Dingfelder, S. F. (2005, September). Feelings' sway over memory. *Monitor on Psychology, 36*(8), 54–55.

Dingfelder, S. F. (2006, June). The formula for funny. *Monitor on Psychology, 37*(6), 54–56.

Dingfelder, S. F. (2007, January). Phantom pain and the brain. *Monitor on Psychology, 38*(1), 22–23.

Dingfelder, S. F. (2010). The scientist at the easel. *Monitor on Psychology, 41*(2), 34–38. Retrieved from www.apa.org/monitor/2010/02/painters.aspx.

Dittmann, M. (2003). Psychology's first prescribers. *Monitor on Psychology, 34*(2), 36.

Dittmann, M. (2004). Prescriptive authority. *Monitor on Psychology, 35*(5), 34–35.

Dittmann, M. (2005, July/August). When health fears hurt health. *Monitor on Psychology, 36*(7), 100–103.

Dixon, R. A., Kramer, D. A., & Baltes, P. B. (1985). Intelligence: A life-span developmental perspective. In B. B. Wolman (Ed.), *Handbook of intelligence* (pp. 301–352). New York: Wiley.

Dobbins, A. C., Jeo, R. M., Fiser, J., & Allman, J. M. (1998, July 24). Distance modulation of neural activity in the visual cortex. *Science, 281*, 552–555.

Dobbs, D. (2006a). A revealing reflection. *Scientific American Mind, 17*(2), 22–27.

Dobbs, D. (2006b, August/September). Turning off depression. *Scientific American, 17*(4), 26–31.

Dodson, C. S., Johnson, M. K., & Schooler, J. W. (1997). The verbal overshadowing effect: Why descriptions impair face recognition. *Memory & Cognition, 25*, 129–139.

Dohrenwend, B. P., & Shrout, P. E. (1985). "Hassles" in the conceptualization and measurement of life stress variables. *American Psychologist, 40*, 780–785.

Doka, K. J. (1989). *Disenfranchised grief: Recognizing hidden sorrows.* Lexington, MA: Lexington Books.

Doka, K. J. (1995). Friends, teachers, movie stars: The disenfranchised grief of children: Friends, teachers, movie stars. In E. A. Grollman (Ed.), *Bereaved children and teens: A support guide for parents and professionals* (pp. 37–45). Boston: Beacon Press.

Dolan, R. J. (2002). Emotion, cognition, and behavior. *Science, 298*, 1191–1194.

Domhoff, G. W. (1996). *Finding meaning in dreams: A quantitative approach.* New York: Plenum Press.

Doob, L. W. (1964). Eidetic images among the Ibo. *Ethnology, 3*, 357–363.

Dowling, J. E. (1992). *Neurons and networks: An introduction to neuroscience.* Cambridge, MA: Harvard University Press.

Downey, T. (2004). *The last men out: Life on the edge at Rescue 2 Firehouse.* New York: Henry Holt and Co.

Downing, J., & Bellis, M. A. (2009). Early pubertal onset and its relationship with sexual risk taking, substance use and anti-social behaviour: A preliminary cross-sectional study. *BMC Public Health, 9*, 446.

Doyère, V., Débiec, J., Monfils, M.-H., Schafe, G. E., & LeDoux, J. E. (2007, November 1). Synapse-specific reconsolidation of distinct fear memories in the lateral amygdala. *Nature Neuroscience, 10*, 414–416. [See also: Riccio et al., 2003; Wixted, 2005.]

Doyle, R. (2001, June). The American terrorist. *Scientific American, 285*(6), 28.

Doyle, R. (2002a). Deinstitutionalization: Why a much maligned program still has life. *Scientific American, 287*, 38.

Doyle, R. (2002b, January). Going solo: Unwed motherhood in industrial nations rises. *Scientific American, 286*(1), 24.

Doyle, R. (2006, February). Sizing up: Roots of obesity epidemic lie in the mid-20th century. *Scientific American, 294*(2), 32.

Doyle, R. (2007, January). Teen sex in America: Virginity into the third millennium takes an uptick. *Scientific American, 296*(1), 30.

Draguns, J. (1980). Psychological disorders of clinical severity. In H. Triandis & J. Draguns (Eds.), *Handbook of cross-cultural psychology, Vol. 6: Psychopathology* (pp. 99–174). Boston: Allyn & Bacon.

Draguns, J. G. (1979). Culture and personality. In A. J. Marsella, R. G. Tharp, & T. J. Ciborowski (Eds.), *Perspectives on cross-cultural psychology* (pp. 179–207). New York: Academic Press.

Driscoll, E. V. (2008, June/July). Bisexual species. *Scientific American Mind, 19*(3), 68–73.

Druckman, D., & Bjork, R. A. (1991). *In the mind's eye: Enhancing human performance.* Washington, DC: National Academy Press.

Duenwald, M. (2005, March). Building a better grapefruit. *Discover, 26*(3), 26–27.

Dugoua, J., Mills, E., Perri, D., & Koren, G. (2006). Safety and efficacy of ginkgo (Ginkgo biloba) during pregnancy and lactation. *Canadian Journal of Clinical Pharmacology, 13*, e277–e284.

Duncan, J., Seitz, R. J., Kolodny, J., Bor, D., Herzog, H., Ahmed, A., Newell, F. N., & Emslie, H. (2000, July 21). A neural basis for general intelligence. *Science, 289*, 457–460.

Dunn, K. (2006, December). Runners-up: John Donoghue, neuroscientist at Brown University. *Discover, 27*(2), 39.

Dutton, D. G., & Aron, A. P. (1974). Some evidence for heightened sexual attraction under conditions of high anxiety. *Journal of Personality and Social Psychology, 30*, 510–517.

Dweck, C. (2006). *Mindset: The new psychology of success.* New York: Random House.

Dweck, C. S. (December 2007/January 2008). The secret to raising smart kids. *Scientific American Mind, 18*(6), 37–43.

Dykema, J., Bergbower, K., & Peterson, C. (1995). Pessimistic explanatory style, stress, and illness. *Journal of Social and Clinical Psychology, 14*, 357–371.

Eagly, A. H. (1987). *Sex differences in social behavior: A social-role interpretation.* Hillsdale, NJ: Erlbaum.

Eagly, A. H., Ashmore, R. D., Makhijani, M. G., & Kennedy, L. C. (1991). What is beautiful is good, but ... : A meta-analytic review of the social psychological literature. *Psychological Bulletin, 100*, 283–308. [See also: Dion, 1986; Hatfield & Sprecher, 1986.]

Eagly, A. H., & Carli, L. L. (1981). Sex of researchers and sex-typed communications as determinants of sex differences in influenceability: A meta-analysis of social influence studies. *Psychological Bulletin, 90*, 1–20.

Eagly, A. H., & Wood, W. (1999). The origins of sex differences in human behavior: Evolved dispositions versus social roles. *American Psychologist, 54*, 408–423.

Ebbinghaus, H. (1908/1973). *Psychology: An elementary textbook.* New York: Arno Press. (Original work published 1908.)

Eberhardt, J. L., & Randall, J. L. (1997). The essential notion of race. *Psychological Science, 8*, 198–203.

Eckensberger, L. H. (1994). Moral development and its measurement across cultures. In W. J. Lonner & R. Malpass (Eds.), *Psychology and culture* (pp. 71–78). Boston, MA: Allyn & Bacon.

Edwards, A. E., & Acker, L. E. (1962). A demonstration of the long-term retention of a conditioned galvanic skin response. *Psychosomatic Medicine, 24*, 459–463.

Edwards, K. J., Hershberger, P. J., Russell, R. K., & Markert, R. J. (2001). Stress, negative social exchange, and health symptoms in university students. *Journal of American College Health, 50*, 75–86.

Ehrlich, P. R. (2000a). *Genes, cultures and the human prospect.* Washington, DC: Island Press.

Ehrlich, P. R. (2000b, September 22). The tangled skeins of nature and nurture in human evolution. *The Chronicle of Higher Education*, B7–B11.

Eich, E., Macaulay, D., Loewenstein, R. J., & Dihle, P. H. (1997). Memory, amnesia, and dissociative identity disorder. *Psychological Science, 8*, 417–422.

Einstein, G. O., & McDaniel, M. A. (2005). Prospective memory: Multiple retrieval processes. *Current Directions in Psychological Science 14*, 286–290.

Eisenberger, R., & Cameron, J. (1996). Detrimental effects of reward: Reality or myth? *American Psychologist, 51*, 1153–1166.

Eisler, R., & Levine, D. S. (2002). Nurture, nature, and caring: We are not prisoners of our genes. *Brain and Mind, 3*, 9–52.

Ekman, P. (1984). Expression and the nature of emotion. In K. R. Scherer & P. Ekman (Eds.), *Approaches to emotion.* Hillsdale, NJ: Erlbaum.

Ekman, P. (1992). Facial expressions of emotion: New findings, new questions. *Psychological Science, 3*, 34–38.

Ekman, P. (1994). Strong evidence for universals in facial expressions: A reply to Russell's mistaken critique. *Psychological Bulletin, 115*, 268–287.

Ekman, P. (2003). *Emotions revealed: Recognizing faces and feelings to improve communication and emotional life.* New York: Times Books, Henry Holt and Company. [See also: Ekman, 1984, 1992, 1993; Ekman & Friesen, 1971, 1986; Ekman & Rosenberg, 1997; Ekman et al., 1969, 1987; Keating, 1994.]

Elbert, T., Pantev, C., Wienbruch, C., Rockstroh, B., & Taub, E. (1995, October 13). Increased cortical representation of the fingers of the left hand in string players. *Science, 270*, 305–307.

Elfenbein, H. A., & Ambady, N. (2003). Universals and cultural differences in recognizing emotions. *Current Directions in Psychological Science, 12*, 159–164.

Elias, C. L., & Berk, L. E. (2002). Self-regulation in children: Is there a role for sociodramatic play? *Early Childhood Research Quarterly, 17*(2), 216–238.

Elliott, G. R., & Eisdorfer, C. (Eds.). (1982). *Stress and human health: Analysis and implications of research (A study by the Institute of Medicine/National Academy of Sciences).* New York: Springer.

Ellis, A. (1987). *The practice of rational emotive therapy (RET).* New York: Springer.

Ellis A. (1990). *The essential Albert Ellis: Seminal writings on psychotherapy.* New York: Springer.

Ellis, A. (1996). *Better, deeper, and more enduring brief therapy: The rational emotive behavior therapy approach.* New York: Brunner/Mazel.

Ellison, J. (1984, June). The seven frames of mind. *Psychology Today, 18*, 21–24, 26.

Ellsworth, P. C. (1994). William James and emotion: Is a century of fame worth a century of misunderstanding? *Psychological Review, 101*, 222–229.

Engle, R. W. (2002). Working memory capacity as executive attention. *Current Directions in Psychological Science, 11*, 19–23.

Ennemoser, M., & Schneider, W. (2007). Relations of television viewing and reading: Findings from a 4-Year longitudinal study. *Journal of Educational Psychology, 99*, 349–368.

Ennis, M., Kelly, K. S., & Lambert, P. L. (2001). Sex differences in cortisol excretion during anticipation of a psychological stressor: Possible support for the tend-and-befriend hypothesis. *Stress and Health, 17*, 253–261.

Epel, E. S., Blackburn, E. H., Lin, J., Dhabhar, F. S., Adler, N. E., Morrow, J. D., & Cawthon, R. M. (2004, December 7). Accerated telomere shortening in response to life stress. *Proceedings of the National Academy of Science, 101, 17*, 312–17, 315.

Epel, E. S., Blackburn, E. H., Lin, J., Dhabhar, F. S., Adler, N. E., Morrow, J. D., et al. (2004, December 7). Accelerated telomere shortening in response to life stress. *Proceedings of the National Academy of Sciences of the United States of America, 101*, 17312–17315.

Epstein, S. (1980). The stability of confusion: A reply to Mischel and Peake. *Psychological Review, 90*, 179–184.

Erdberg, P. (1990). Rorschach assessment. In G. Goldstein & M. Hersen (Eds.), *Psychological assessment* (2nd ed.). New York: Pergamon.

Ericsson, K. A., & Charness, N. (1994). Expert performance: Its structure and acquisition. *American Psychologist, 49*, 725–747.

Ericsson, K. A., Charness, N., Feltovich, P. J., & Hoffman, R. R. (Eds.). (2006). *The Cambridge handbook of expertise and expert performance.* New York: Cambridge University Press. [See also: Bransford et al., 1986; Gardner, 1993; Glaser, 1984; Greeno, 1989; Klahr & Simon, 2001; Mayer, 1983; Who Wants to Be a Genius?, 2001.]

Ericsson, K. A., Krampe, R. T., & Tesch-Römer, C. (1993). The role of deliberate practice in the acquisition of expert performance. *Psychological Review, 100,* 363–406.

Erikson, E. H. (1963). *Childhood and society* (2nd ed.). New York: Norton.

Evans, G. W., Bullinger, M., & Hygge, S. (1998). Chronic noise exposure and physiological response: A prospective study of children living under environmental stress. *Psychological Science, 9,* 75–77.

Everitt, B. J., & Robbins, T. W. (2005). Neural systems of reinforcement for drug addiction: From actions to habits to compulsion. *Nat Neurosci, 8*(11), 1481–1489.

Ezzell, C. (2003, February). Why??? The neuroscience of suicide. *Scientific American, 288,* 45–51. [See also: Hirschfeld & Goodwin, 1988; Nemeroff, 1998.]

Fadiman, J., & Frager, R. (2001). *Personality and personal growth.* Upper Saddle River, NJ: Prentice Hall.

Fallon, A., & Rozin, P. (1985). Sex differences in perceptions of desirable body states. *Journal of Abnormal Psychology, 94,* 102–105.

Fancher, R. E. (1979). *Pioneers of psychology.* New York: W. W. Norton.

Fantz, R. L. (1963). Pattern vision in newborn infants. *Science, 140,* 296–297.

Farah, M. J., Betancourt, L., Shera, D. M., Savage, J. H., Giannetta, J. M., Brodsky, N. L., Malmud, E. K., & Hurt, H. (2008). Environmental stimulation, parental nurturance and cognitive development in humans. *Developmental Science, 11*(5), 793–801.

Faraone, S. V., Sergeant, J., Gillberg, C., & Biederman, J. (2003). The worldwide prevalence of ADHD: Is it an American condition? *World Psychiatry, 2,* 104–113.

Farina, A., Fischer, E. H., Boudreau, L. A., & Belt, W. E. (1996). Mode of target presentation in measuring the stigma of mental disorder. *Journal of Applied Social Psychology, 26,* 2147–2156.

Faris, R., & Felmlee, D. (2011). Status struggles: Network centrality and gender segregation in same and cross-gender aggression. *American Sociological Review, 76,* 48–73.

Fariva, R. (2009). Dorsal–ventral integration in object recognition. *Brain Research Reviews, 61,* 144–153.

Faulkner, A. H., & Cranston, K. (1998). Correlates of same-sex sexual behavior in a random sample of Massachusetts high school students. *American Journal of Public Health, 88*(2), 262–266.

Faulkner, M. (2001). The onset and alleviation of learned helplessness in older hospitalized people. *Aging and Mental Health, 5,* 379–386.

Feingold, A. (1988). Matching for attractiveness in romantic partners and same-sex friends: A meta-analysis and theoretical critique. *Psychological Bulletin, 104,* 226–235. [See also: Cash & Killcullen, 1985; Folkes, 1982; Hatfield & Sprecher, 1986.]

Feingold, A. (1990). Gender differences in effects of physical attractiveness on romantic attraction: A comparison across five research paradigms. *Journal of Personality and Social Psychology, 59,* 981–993.

Festinger, L. (1957). *A theory of cognitive dissonance.* Stanford, CA: Stanford University Press.

Festinger, L., Schachter, S., & Back, K. (1950). *Social pressures in informal groups: A study of a housing community.* New York: Harper & Row.

Field, E. (2007). *Bully blocking: Six secrets to help children deal with teasing and bullying.* Warriewood, Australia: Finch Publisher.

Field, T., Diego, M., Pelaez, M., Deeds, O., & Delgado, J. (2010). Breakup distress and loss of intimacy in university students. *Psychology, 1,* 173–177.

Fields, H. (2010, May 17). Golden years truly are golden. *Science Now.* Retrieved from http://news.sciencemag.org/sciencenow/2010/05/golden-years-truly-are-golden.html.

Fields, H. L. (1978, November). Secrets of the placebo. *Psychology Today,* 172.

Fields, H. L. (2009, September/October). The psychology of pain. *Scientific American Mind, 21*(5), 43–49.

Fields, H. L., & Levine, J. D. (1984). Placebo analgesia: A role for endorphins. *Trends in Neuroscience, 7,* 271–273.

Fields, R. D. (2004, April). The other half of the brain. *Scientific American, 290*(4), 54–61.

Figley, C. R. (2002). *Treating compassion fatigue.* New York: Brunner-Routledge.

Finckenauer, J. O., Gavin, P. W., Hovland, A., & Storvoll, E. (1999). *Scared straight: The panacea phenomenon revisited.* Prospect Heights, IL: Waveland Press.

Findley, M. J., & Cooper, H. M. (1983). Locus of control and academic achievement: A literature review. *Journal of Personality and Social Psychology, 44,* 419–427.

Finer, B. (1980). Hypnosis and anaesthesia. In G. D. Burrows & L. Donnerstein (Eds.), *Handbook of hypnosis and psychosomatic medicine.* Amsterdam: Elsevier/North Holland Biomedical Press.

Fiorillo, C. D., Tobler, P. N., & Schultz, W. (2003, March 21). Discrete coding of reward probability and uncertainty by dopamine neurons. *Science, 299,* 1898–1902.

Fiorito, G., & Scotto, P. (1992). Observational learning in Octopus vulgaris. *Science, 256,* 545–547.

Fischer, A. H. (1993). Sex differences in emotionality: Fact or stereotype? *Feminism & Psychology, 3,* 303–318.

Fischer, A. H., Rodriguez Mosquera, P. M., van Vianen, A. E. M., & Manstead, A. S. R. (2004). Gender and culture differences in emotion. *Emotion, 4,* 87–94. [See also: Baumeister et al., 1990; Fischer et al., 1993; Gottman, 1994; Gottman & Krokoff, 1989; Gottman & Levenson, 1986; Oatley & Duncan, 1994; Polefrone & Manuck, 1987; Rusting & Nolen-Hoeksema, 1998; Shaver & Hazan, 1987; Shields, 1991.]

Fischhoff, B. (1975). Hindsight AD foresight: The effect of outcome knowledge on judgment under uncertainty. *Journal of Experimental Psychology: Human Perception and Performance, 1,* 288–299.

Fisher, H. E. (1992). *Anatomy of love: The natural history of monogamy, adultery, and divorce.* New York: W. W. Norton and Company.

Fishman, H. C. (1993). *Intensive structural therapy: Treating families in their social context.* New York: Basic Books.

Fiske, S. T., Cuddy, A. J. C., & Glick, P. (2007). Universal dimensions of social cognition: Warmth and competence. *Trends in Cognitive Science, 11,* 77–83.

Fiske, S. T., & Neuberg, S. L. (1990). A continuum of impression formation, from category-based to individuating processes: Influences of information and motivation on attention and interpretation. In M. P. Zanna (Ed.), *Advances in experimental social psychology* (Vol. 23). San Diego, CA: Academic Press.

Fitzpatrick, A. L., Kronmal, R. A., Gardner, J. P., Psaty, B. M., Jenny, N. S., Tracy R. P., et al. (2007). Leukocyte telomere length and cardiovascular disease in the Cardiovascular Health Study. *American Journal of Epidemiology, 165,* 14–21.

Fleeson, W. (2004). Moving personality beyond the person-situation debate: The challenge and the opportunity of within-person variability. *Current Directions in Psychological Science, 13,* 83–87.

Fleischman, J. (2002). *Phineas Gage: A gruesome but true story about brain science.* Boston: Houghton Mifflin.

Fletcher, A., Lamond, N., van den Heuvel, C. J., & Dawson, D. (2003). Prediction of performance during sleep deprivation and alcohol intoxication using a quantitative model of work-related fatigue. *SleepResearch Online, 5,* 67–75. Retrieved November 6, 2004, from www.sro.org/2003/Fletcher/67/.

Fletcher, G. J. O., & Ward, C. (1988). Attribution theory and processes: A cross-cultural perspective. In M. H. Bond (Ed.), *The cross-cultural challenge to social psychology* (pp. 230–244). Newbury Park, CA: Sage.

Flier, J. S. (2006, May 12). Regulating energy balance: The substrate strikes back. *Science, 312,* 861–864.

Flier, J. S., & Maratos-Flier, E. (2007, September). What fuels fat. *Scientific American, 297*(3), 72–81. [See also: Campfield et al., 1998; Comuzzie & Allison, 1998; Gura, 1998, 2003; Hill & Peters, 1998; Levine et al., 1999; Ravussin & Danforth, 1999.]

Flynn, J. R. (1987). Massive IQ gains in 14 nations: What IQ tests really measure. *Psychological Bulletin, 101,* 171–191.

Flynn, J. R. (2003, June). Movies about intelligence: The limitations of g. *Current Directions in Psychological Science, 12,* 95–99.

Flynn, J. R. (2007, October/November). Solving the IQ puzzle. *Scientific American Mind, 18*(5), 25–31.

Fogel, A. (1991). Movement and communication in human infancy: The social dynamics of development. *Human Movement Science, 11,* 387–423.

Foley, H. J., & Matlin, M. W. (2010). *Sensation and perception* (5th ed.). Boston: Allyn & Bacon.

Foley, V. D. (1979). Family therapy. In R. J. Corsini (Ed.), *Current psychotherapies* (2nd ed., pp. 460–469). Itasca, IL: Peacock.

Folkins, C. H., & Sime, W. (1981). Physical fitness training and mental health. *American Psychologist, 36,* 373–389.

Folkman, S., & Lazarus, R. S. (1980). An analysis of coping in a middle-aged community sample. *Journal of Health and Social Behavior, 21,* 219–239.

Forgas, J. P. (2008). Affect and cognition. *Perspectives on Psychological Science, 3,* 94–101.

Foster, J. B. (2006, November 1). Racial, ethnic variables shape the experience of chronic pain. *Applied Neurology.* Retrieved November 26, 2007, from http://appneurology.com/showArticle.jhtml?articleId=196604178.

Fouts, R. (1997). *Next of kin: What chimpanzees have taught me about who we are.* New York: William Morrow.

Fox, R. E., DeLeon, P. H., Newman, R., Sammons, M. T., Dunivin, D. L., & Baker, D. C. (2009). Prescriptive authority and psychology: A status report. *American Psychologist, 64,* 257–268.

Frankl, V. (2006/1964). *Man's Search for Meaning.* Boston, MA: Beacon Press.

Franklin, M. S., & Zyphur, M. J. (2005). The role of dreams in the evolution of the human mind. *Evolutionary Psychology, 3,* 59–78.

Fraser, S. (Ed.). (1995). *The bell curve wars: Race, intelligence, and the future of America.* New York: Basic Books.

Fredrickson, B. L., Maynard, K. E., Helms, M. J., Haney, T. L., Siegler, I. C., & Barefoot, J. C. (2000). Hostility predicts magnitude and duration of blood pressure response to anger. *Journal of Behavioral Medicine, 23,* 229–243.

French, J. R. P., Jr., Rodgers, W., & Cobb, S. (1974). Adjustment as person-environment fit. In G. V. Coelho, D. A. Hamburg, & J. E. Adams (Eds.), *Coping and adjustment* (pp. 316–333). New York, NY: Basic Books.

Freud, S. (1925). The unconscious. In S. Freud (Ed.), *The collected papers* (Vol. 4). London: Hogarth.

Freud, S. (1953). *The interpretation of dreams.* New York: Basic Books. (Original work published 1900.)

Freud, S. (1957). *A general introduction to psychoanalysis.* New York: Permabooks. (J. Riviere, Trans. Original work published 1920 by Horace Liveright.)

Friedman, J. M. (2003, February 7). A war on obesity, not the obese. *Science, 299,* 856–858.

Friedman, M., & Rosenman, R. F. (1974). *Type A behavior and your heart.* New York: Knopf.

Friedman, M., & Ulmer, D. (1984). *Treating Type A behavior—and your heart.* New York: Knopf.

Friend, R., Rafferty, Y., & Bramel, D. (1990). A puzzling misinterpretation of the Asch "conformity" study. *European Journal of Social Psychology, 20,* 29–44.

Frincke, J. L., & Pate, W. E., II. (2004). *Yesterday, today, and tomorrow careers in psychology, 2004: What students need to know.* Retrieved October 14, 2004, from http://research.apa.org.

Frith, C. D., & Frith, U. (1999, November 26). Interacting minds—A biological basis. *Science, 286,* 1692–1695.

Frith, U. (1993, June). Autism. *Scientific American, 268,* 108–114.

Frith, U. (1997). Autism. *Scientific American* [Special Issue: *The Mind*], 7(1), 92–98.

Fromm, E., & Shor, R. E. (Eds.). (1979). *Hypnosis: Developments in research and new perspectives* (2nd ed.). Hawthorne, NY: Aldine.

Fujita, F., Diener, E., & Sandvik, E. (1991). Gender differences in dysphoria and well-being: The case for emotional intensity. *Journal of Personality and Social Psychology, 61,* 427–434.

Funder, D. C. (1983a). The "consistency" controversy and the accuracy of personality judgments. *Journal of Personality, 51,* 346–359.

Funder, D. C. (1983b). Three issues in predicting more of the people: A reply to Mischel & Peake. *Psychological Review, 90,* 283–289.

Funder, D. C., & Ozer, D. J. (1983). Behavior as a function of the situation. *Journal of Personality and Social Psychology, 44,* 107–112.

Furnham, A., Moutafi, J., & Crump, J. (2003). The relationship between the revised NEO-Personality Inventory and the Myers-Briggs Type Indicator. *Social Behavior and Personality, 31,* 577–584. [See also: McCrae & Costa, 1989; Pittenger, 1993]

Furumoto, L. (1979). Mary Whiton Calkins (1863–1930), fourteenth president of the American Psychological Association. *Journal of the History of the Behavioral Sciences, 15,* 346–356. [Cited in Milar, K. S. (n.d.). An historical view of some early women psychologists and the psychology of women. Archived at the Classics in the History of Psychology site: http://psychclassics.yorku.ca/Special/Women/variability.htm.]

Furumoto, L., & Scarborough, E. (1986). Placing women in the history of psychology: The first American women psychologists. *American Psychologist, 41,* 35–42.

Gadsby, P. (2000, July). Tourist in a taste lab. *Discover, 21,* 70–75.

Gage, F. H. (2003, September). Brain, repair yourself. *Scientific American, 289*(3), 46–53. [See also Barinaga, 2003a; Kempermann & Gage, 1999.]

Gahlinger, P. M. (2004). Club drugs: MDMA, gamma-hydroxybutyrate (GHB), rohypnol, and ketamine. *American Family Physician, 69,* 2619–2626.

Gailliot, M. T., Baumeister, R. F., DeWall, C. N., Maner, J. K., Plant, E. A., Tice, D. M., Brewer, L. E., & Schmeichel, B. J. (2007). Self-control relies on glucose as a limited energy source: Willpower is more than a metaphor. *Journal of Personality and Social Psychology, 92,* 325–336.

Gainetdinov, R. R., Wetsel, W. C., Jones, S. R., Levin, E. D., Jaber, M., & Caron, M. G. (1999). Role of serotonin in the paradoxical calming effect of psychostimulants on hyperactivity. *Science, 283,* 397–401. [See also: Barkley, 1998; Wu, 1998]

Galambos, N. L. (1992). Parent–adolescent relations. *Current Directions in Psychological Science, 1,* 146–149.

Galea, S., Vlahov, D., Resnick, H., Ahern, J., Susser, E., Gold, J., Bucuvalas, M., & Kilpatrick, D. (2003). Trends of probable post-traumatic stress disorder in New York City after the September 11th terrorist attacks. *American Journal of Epidemiology, 158,* 514–524.

Gallagher, W. (1994, September). How we become what we are. *The Atlantic Monthly,* 39–55.

Gallo, P. S., & McClintock, C. G. (1965). Cooperative and competitive behavior in mixed-motive games. *Journal of Conflict Resolution, 9,* 68–78.

Gallo, V., & Chittajallu, R. (2001, May 4). Unwrapping glial cells from the synapse: What lies inside? *Science, 292,* 872–873.

Gallup, Inc. (2010). *In U.S., 62% exceed ideal weight, 19% at their goal.* Retrieved from www.gallup.com/poll/144941/exceed-ideal-weight-goal.aspx.

Gambrel, P. A., & Cianci, R. (2003). Maslow's hierarch of needs: Does it apply in a collectivist culture? *Journal of Applied Management and Entrepreneurship, 8,* 143–161. Retrieved April 4, 2008, from www3.tjcu.edu.cn/wangshangketang/lyxgl/yuedu/21.pdf.

Gamer, M. (2009, February/March). Portrait of a lie. *Scientific American Mind, 26*(1), 50–55.

Gami, A. S., Howard, D. E., Olson, E. J., & Somers, V. K. (2005, March 24). Day-night pattern of sudden death in obstructive sleep apnea. *New England Journal of Medicine, 352,* 1206–1214. [See also Dement, 1999; Benson, 2003c.]

Ganchrow, J. R., Steiner, J. E., & Daher, M. (1983). Neonatal facial expressions in response to different qualities and intensities of gustatory stimuli. *Infant Behavior and Development, 6,* 189–200.

Garces, E., Thomas, D., & Currie, J. (2002, September). Longer-term effects of head start. *American Economic Review, 92*(4), 999–1012.

Garcia, J. (1990). Learning without memory. *Journal of Cognitive Neuroscience, 2,* 287–305.

Garcia, J. (1993). Misrepresentations of my criticisms of Skinner. *American Psychologist, 48,* 1158.

Garcia, J., & Koelling, R. A. (1966). The relation of cue to consequence in avoidance learning. *Psychonomic Science, 4,* 123–124.

Gardiner, H. W., Mutter, J. D., & Kosmitzki, C. (1998). *Lives across cultures: Cross-cultural human development.* Boston: Allyn & Bacon.

Gardner, H. (1983). *Frames of mind.* New York: Basic Books.

Gardner, H. (1985). *The mind's new science: A history of the cognitive revolution.* New York: Basic Books.

Gardner, H. (1993). *Creating minds: An anatomy of creativity seen through the lives of Freud, Einstein, Picasso, Stravinsky, Eliot, Graham, and Gandhi.* New York: Basic Books.

Gardner, H. (1999a). *Intelligence reframed.* New York: Basic Books.

Gardner, H. (1999b, February). Who owns intelligence? *The Atlantic Monthly, 283,* 67–76.

Gardner, R. A., & Gardner, B. T. (1969). Teaching language to a chimpanzee. *Science, 165,* 664–672.

Garland, A., & Zigler, E. (1993). Adolescent suicide prevention: Current research and social policy implications. *American Psychologist, 48,* 169–182.

Garnsey, S. M. (1993). Event-related brain potentials in the study of language: An introduction. *Language and Cognitive Processes, 8,* 337–356.

Garry, M., & Gerrie, M. P. (2005). When photographs create false memories. *Current Directions in Psychological Science, 14,* 321–325.

Gazzaniga, M. S. (1970). *The bisected brain.* New York: Appleton-Century-Crofts.

Gazzaniga, M. S. (1998a). *The mind's past.* Berkeley: University of California Press.

Gazzaniga, M. S. (1998b, July). The split brain revisited. *Scientific American, 279,* 50–55.

Gazzaniga, M. S. (2005). Forty-five years of split-brain research and still going strong. *Nature Reviews Neuroscience, 6,* 653–659.

Gelman, R., & Shatz, M. (1978). Appropriate speech adjustments: The operation of conversational constraints on talk to two-year-olds. In M. Lewis & L. A. Rosenblum (Eds.), *Interaction, conversation, and the development of language* (pp. 27–61). New York: Wiley.

Gelman, S. A., & Wellman, H. M. (1991). Insides and essences: Early understandings of the non-obvious. *Cognition, 38,* 213–244.

Gentner, D., & Stevens, A. L. (1983). *Mental models.* Hillsdale, NJ: Erlbaum.

George, M. S. (2003, September). Stimulating the brain. *Scientific American, 289*(3), 67–73. [See also: George et al., 1999; Helmuth, 2001b; Travis, 2000b; Wassermann & Lisanby, 2001.]

Gernsbacher, M. A., Dawson, M., & Goldsmith, H. H. (2005). Three reasons not to believe in an autism epidemic. *Current Directions in Psychological Science, 14,* 55–58.

Getzels, J. W., & Csikszentmihalyi, M. (1976). *The creative vision.* New York: Wiley.

Giambra, L. M. (2000). Daydreaming characteristics across the life-span: Age differences and seven- to twenty-year longitudinal changes. In R. G. Kunzendorf & B. Wallace (Eds.), *Individual differences in conscious experience* (pp. 147–206). Amsterdam, Netherlands: John Benjamins Publishing Company.

Gibbs, W. W. (2001). Side splitting. *Scientific American, 284,* 24–25.

Gibbs, W. W. (2003, December). The unseen genome: Beyond DNA. *Scientific American, 289*(6), 106–113.

Gibbs, W. W. (2005, June). Obesity: An overblown epidemic. *Scientific American, 292*(6), 70–77.

Gibney, A. (Director). (2006). *The Human Behavior Experiments* [Documentary]. USA: Fearful Symmetry.

Gibson, E. J., & Walk, R. D. (1960, April). The "visual cliff." *Scientific American, 202,* 64–71.

Gieler, U., & Walter, B. (2008, June/July). Scratch this! *Scientific American Mind, 19*(3), 52–59.

Gilbert, K. R. (1996). "We've had the same loss, why don't we have the same grief?" Loss and differential grief in families. *Death Studies, 20,* 269–283.

Gilbert, R. M. (1992). *Extraordinary relationships: A new way of thinking about human interactions.* New York: Wiley.

Gilbertson, J., Dindia, K., & Allen, M. (1998). Relational continuity, constructional units, and the maintenance of relationships. *Journal of Social and Personal Relationships, 15,* 774–790.

Gilchrist, A. (2006, June/July). Seeing in black & white. *Scientific American Mind, 17*(3), 42–49.

Gilligan, C. (1982). *In a different voice: Psychological theory and women's development.* Cambridge, MA: Harvard University Press.

Gilmore, T. M., Baucom, D. H., Kirby, J. S., Porter, L. S., Atkins, D. C., & Keefe, F. J. (2011). Stress buffering effects of daily spousal support on women's daily emotional and physical experiences in the context of breast cancer concerns. *Health Psychology, 30,* 20–30.

Gist, R. & Devilly, G. J. (2002, September 7). Post-trauma debriefing: the road too frequently travelled. *The Lancet, 360,* 741. Retrieved from www.pitt.edu/~kconover/ftp/Lancet-CISM.pdf.

Gittrich, G. (2003, May 27). Trauma aid in limbo: Millions unspent as relative few seek counseling. *New York Daily News,* 8.

Gladwell, M. (2005). *Blink.* New York: Little Brown and Company. [See also: Bechara et al., 1997; Gehring & Willoughby, 2002; Vogel, 1997a.]

Gladwell, M. (2008). *Outliers: The story of success.* New York: Little Brown.

Glanz, J. (1998, April 3). Magnetic brain imaging traces a stairway to memory. *Science, 280,* 37.

Glaser, D. (2003). Child abuse and neglect and the brain: A review. *Journal of Child Psychology and Psychiatry, 41,* 97–116.

Glaser, R. (1990). The reemergence of learning theory within instructional research. *American Psychologist, 45,* 29–39.

Gleitman, H. (1991). Edward Chace Tolman: A life of scientific and social purpose. In G. A. Kimble, M. Wertheimer, & C. L. White (Eds.), *Portraits of pioneers in psychology* (pp. 226–241). Washington, DC: American Psychological Association. [See also: Kesner & Olton, 1990; Olton, 1992; Tolman, 1932.]

Goel, V., & Dolan, R. J. (2001). The functional anatomy of humor: Segregating cognitive and affective components. *Nature Neuroscience, 4,* 237–238. [See also: Winerman, 2006]

Gold, D. R., Rogacz, S., Bock, N., Tosteson, T. D., Baum, T. M., Speizer, F. E., & Czeisler, C. A. (1992). Rotating shift work, sleep, and accidents related to sleepiness in hospital nurses. *American Journal of Public Health, 82*(7), 1011–1014.

Goldapple, K., Segal, Z., Garson, C., Lau, M., Bieling, P., Kennedy, S., & Mayberg, H. (2004). Modulation of cortical-limbic pathways in major depression: Treatment-specific effects of cognitive behavior therapy. *Archives of General Psychiatry, 61,* 34–41.

Goldberg, C. (2008, March 3). Brain scans support surprising differences in perception between Westerners and Asians. *The Boston Globe,* p. C1.

Golden, C., & Figueroa, M. (2007). Facing cultural challenges in personality testing: A review of *Assessing hispanic clients using the MMPI-2 and MMPI-A.* Retrieved April 16, 2008, from Psyc-Critiques at http://content.apa.org/critiques/52/41/1.html?sid=7903CA01-0711-4940-886C-9E3D3DB7D4AA.

Golden, O. (2000). The federal response to child abuse and neglect. *American Psychologist, 55,* 1050–1053.

Goldin-Meadow, S., & Mylander, C. (1990). Beyond the input given: The child's role in the acquisition of language. *Language, 66,* 323–355.

Goldman-Rakic, P. S. (1992, September). Working memory and the mind. *Scientific American, 267,* 110–117.

Goleman, D. (1980, February). 1528 little geniuses and how they grew. *Psychology Today, 14,* 28–53.

Golombok, S., & Tasker, F. (1996). Do parents influence the sexual orientation of their children? Findings from a longitudinal study of lesbian families. *Developmental Psychology, 32,* 3–11. [See also: Bailey et al., 1995; Bell et al., 1981; Isay, 1990]

Gomez, R., & McLaren, S. (2007). The inter-relations of mother and father attachment, self-esteem and aggression during late adolescence. *Aggressive Behavior, 33,* 160–169.

Gonzalvo, P., Cañas, J. J., & Bajo, M. (1994). Structural representations in knowledge acquisition. *Journal of Educational Psychology, 86,* 601–616.

Goodale, M. A., & Milner, A. D. (1992). Separate visual pathways for perception and action. *Trends in Neuroscience, 15,* 20–25.

Goodall, J. (1986). *The chimpanzees of Gombe: Patterns of behavior.* Cambridge, MA: Harvard University Press.

Goodman, G. S., Quas, J. A., & Ogle, C. M. (2010). Child maltreatment and memory. *Annual Review of Psychology, 61,* 325–351.

Goodwyn, S. W., & Acredolo, L. P. (2000). *Baby minds.* New York: Bantum Books.

Gottesman, I. I. (1991). *Schizophrenia genesis: The origins of madness.* New York: Freeman.

Gottesman, I. I. (2001). Psychopathology through a life span–genetic prism. *American Psychologist, 56,* 867–878.

Gottlieb, B. H. (1987). Marshalling social support for medical patients and their families. *Canadian Psychology, 28,* 201–217.

Gottman, J. M. (1994). *What predicts divorce?: The relationship between marital processes and marital outcomes.* Hillsdale, NJ: Lawrence Erlbaum.

Gottman, J. M. (1995). *Why marriages succeed or fail.* New York: Fireside.

Gottman, J. M. (1999). *Seven principles for making marriages work.* New York: Crown.

Gould, E., Tanapat, P., McEwen, B. S., Flüge, G., & Fuchs, E. (1998). Proliferation of granule cell precursors in the dentate gyrus of adult monkeys is diminished by stress. *Proceedings of the National Academy of Science, 99,* 3168–3171.

Grace, A. A. (2010). Ventral hippocampus, interneurons, and schizophrenia: A new understanding of the pathophysiology of schizophrenia and its implications for treatment and prevention. *Current Directions in Psychological Science, 19,* 232–237.

Graham, J. R. (1990). *MMPI-2: Assessing personality and psychopathology.* New York: Oxford University Press.

Grant, B. F., & Dawson, D. A. (2006). Introduction to the national epidemiologic survey on alcohol and related conditions. *National Epidemiologic Survey on Alcohol and Related Conditions: Selected Findings.* [Special issue: *Alcohol Research & Health*], 29, 74–78.

Gray, C. R., & Gummerman, K. (1975). The enigmatic eidetic image: A critical examination of methods, data, and theories. *Psychological Bulletin, 82,* 383–407.

Gray, J. R. (2004). Integration of emotion and cognitive control. *Current Directions in Psychological Science, 13,* 46–48.

Graziano, M. S. A., Cooke, D. F., & Taylor, C. S. R. (2000, December 1). Coding the location of the arm by sight. *Science, 290,* 1782–1786.

Greeley, A., & Sheatsley, P. (1971). The acceptance of desegregation continues to advance. *Scientific American, 225*(6), 13–19.

Green, C. S., & Bavelier, D. (2007). Action-video-game experience alters the spatial resolution of vision. *Psychological Science, 18,* 88–94.

Green, D. M., & Swets, J. A. (1966). *Signal detection theory and psychophysics.* New York: Wiley.

Greenberg, B. S. (1986). Minorities and the mass media. In J. Bryant & D. Zillman (Eds.), *Perspectives in media effects* (pp. 17–40). Hillsdale, NJ: Erlbaum.

Greenberg, G. (1997). Right answers, wrong reasons: Revisiting the deletion of homosexuality from the *DSM. Review of General Psychology, 1,* 256–270.

Greene, R. L. (1991). *The MMPI-2/MMPI: An interpretive manual.* Boston: Allyn & Bacon.

Greenhoot, A. F., Bunnell, S. L., Curtis, J. S., & Beyer, A. M. (2008). Trauma and autobiographical memory function: Findings from a longitudinal study of family violence. In M. L. Howe, G. S. Goodman, & D. Cichetti (Eds.), *Stress, trauma, and children's memory development.* New York: Oxford University Press.

Greenwald, A. G. (1992). New look 3: Unconscious cognition reclaimed. *American Psychologist, 47*(6), 766–779.

Greenwald, A. G., Draine, S. C., & Abrams, R. L. (1996, September 20). Three cognitive markers of unconscious semantic activation. *Science, 273,* 1699–1702.

Greer, M. (2004a, September). People don't notice unexpected visual changes—though they predict they will. *Monitor on Psychology, 35*(8), 10.

Greer, M. (2004b, July/August). Strengthen your brain by resting it. *Monitor on Psychology, 35*(7), 60–62. [See also: Maquet, 2001; Siegel, 2001; Stickgold et al., 2001.]

Greer, M. (2005, March). When intuition misfires. *Monitor on Psychology, 36*(3), 58–60.

Gregory, R. (1997). *Mirrors in mind.* New York: W. H. Freeman.

Gregory, R. L. (1977). *Eye and brain: The psychology of seeing* (3rd ed.). New York: World University Library.

Grevert, P., & Goldstein, A. (1985). Placebo analgesia, naloxone, and the role of en dogenous opioids. In L. White, B. Turks, & G. E. Schwartz (Eds.), *Placebo* (pp. 332– 351). New York: Guilford. [See also: Mayer, 1979; Watkins & Mayer, 1982.]

Grimm, O. (2007, April/May). Addicted to food? *Scientific American Mind, 18*(2), 36–39. [See also: Gura, 2000; Woods et al., 1998.]

Griner, D., & Smith, T. B. (2006). Culturally adapted mental health intervention: A meta-analytic review. *Psychotherapy: Theory, Research, Practice, Training, 43,* 531–548.

Grinspoon, L., Bakalar, J. B., Zimmer, L., & Morgan, J. P. (1997, August 8). Marijuana addiction. *Science, 752,* 748.

Gross, A. E., & Psaki, J. (2004, June 25). *Venting: Its role in mediation.* Annual Conference, Association for Conflict Resolution of Greater New York, Columbia Law School.

Gross, J. J. (1998). The emerging field of emotion regulation: An integrative review. *Review of General Psychology, 2,* 271–299.

Grossman, C. L. (2011, March 15). Japanese look to ancient traditions for strength. *USA Today.*

Grossmann, K., Grossmann, K. E., Spangler, S., Suess, G., & Unzner, L. (1985). Maternal sensitivity and newborn attachment orientation responses as related to quality of attachment in northern Germany. In I. Bretherton & E. Waters (Eds.), *Growing points of attachment theory: Monographs of the society of research in child development, 50* (1–2, Serial No. 209).

Gruben, D., & Madsen, L. (2005, June). Lie detection and the polygraph: A historical review. *The Journal of Forensic Psychiatry & Psychology, 16,* 357–369.

Guisinger, S. (2003). Adapted to flee famine: Adding an evolutionary perspective on anorexia nervosa. *Psychological Review, 110,* 745–761.

Guisinger, S., & Blatt, S. J. (1994). Individuality and relatedness: Evolution of a fundamental dialectic. *American Psychologist, 49,* 104–111.

Gur, R. E., & Maany, V. (1998). Subcortical MRI volumes in neuroleptic-naive and treated patients with schizophrenia. *American Journal of Psychiatry, 155,* 1711–1718.

Guterman, L. (2005, December 2). Duping the brain into healing the body. *The Chronicle of Higher Education,* A12–A14.

Guthrie, R. V. (1998). *Even the rat was white*. Boston: Allyn & Bacon.

Gutman, A. R. (2006, January 5). Deep brain stimulation for treatment-resistant depression: An expert interview with Helen S. Mayberg, MD. Retrieved February 16, 2008, from www.Medscape.com/viewarticle/520659.

Guyll, M., & Contrada, R. J. (1998). Trait hostility and ambulatory cardiovascular activity: Responses to social interaction. *Health Psychology, 17*, 30–39.

Haber, R. N. (1969, April). Eidetic images. *Scientific American, 220*, 36–44.

Haber, R. N. (1970, May). How we remember what we see. *Scientific American, 222*, 104–112.

Haber, R. N. (1980, November). Eidetic images are not just imaginary. *Psychology Today, 14*, 72–82.

Haberlandt, K. (1999). *Human memory: Exploration and application*. Boston: Allyn & Bacon.

Hagen, E. (2004). The evolutionary psychology FAQ. On *Buss Lab: Evolutionary psychology at the University of Texas*. Retrieved November 19, 2010, from www.anth.ucsb.edu/projects/human/evpsychfaq.html.

Haidt, J. (2001). The emotional dog and its rational tail: A social intuitionist approach to moral judgment. *Psychological Review, 108*, 814–834.

Haier, R. J., Jung, R. E., Yeo, R. A., Head, K., & Alkire, M. T. (2004). Structural brain variation and general intelligence. *Neuroimage, 23*, 425–433.

Haimov, I., & Lavie, P. (1996). Melatonin—A soporific hormone. *Current Directions in Psychological Science, 5*, 106–111.

Halberstam, D. (2002). *Firehouse*. New York: Hyperion.

Hall, C. (1951). What people dream about. *Scientific American, 184*, 60–63.

Hall, C. (1953/1966). *The meaning of dreams*. New York: Harper & Row/McGraw-Hill.

Hall, C. S. (1984). "A ubiquitous sex difference in dreams" revisited. *Journal of Personality and Social Psychology, 46*, 1109–1117.

Hall, M. J., Norwood, A. E., Ursano, R. J., Fullerton, C. S., & Levinson, C. J. (2002). Psychological and behavioral impacts of bioterrorism. *PTSD Research Quarterly, 13*, 1–2.

Halpern, D. F. (2002). *Thought & knowledge: An introduction to critical thinking*. Mahwah, NJ: Erlbaum.

Hamann, S. (2005). Sex differences in the responses of the human amygdale. *Neuroscientist, 11*, 288–293.

Hamann, S. B., Ely, T. D., Hoffman, J. M., & Clinton, D. K. (2002). Ecstasy and agony: Activation of the human amygdala in positive and negative emotion. *Psychological Science, 13*, 135–141.

Hamlin, K., Wynn, K., & Bloom, P. (2007). Social evaluation by preverbal infants. *Nature, 450*, 557–559.

Harder, B. (2004, June 19). Narcolepsy science reawakens. *Science News, 165*, 394–396.

Harder, B. (2005, November 26). Staring into the dark: Research investigates insomnia drugs. *Science News, 168*, 344–345.

Harder, B. (2006, April 1). XXL from too few Zs? *Science News, 169*, 195–196.

Hariri, A. R., Mattay, V. S., Tessitore, A., Kolachana, B., Fera, F., Goldman, D., Egan, M. F., & Weinberger, D. R. (2002, July 19). Serotonin transporter genetic variation and the response of the human amygdala. *Science, 297*, 400–403.

Harlow, H. F. (1965). Sexual behavior in the rhesus monkey. In F. Beach (Ed.), *Sex and behavior*. New York: Wiley.

Harlow, H. F., & Harlow, M. K. (1966). Learning to love. *American Scientist, 54*, 244–272.

Harris, B. (1979). Whatever happened to Little Albert? *American Psychologist, 34*, 151–160.

Harris, G., Thomas, A., & Booth, D. A. (1990). Development of salt taste in infancy. *Developmental Psychology, 26*, 534–538.

Harris, J. A. (2004). Measured intelligence, achievement, openness to experience, and creativity. *Personality & Individual Differences, 36*, 913–929.

Harris, J. R. (1995). Where is the child's environment? A group socialization theory of development. *Psychological Review, 102*, 458–489.

Harris, M. J., & Rosenthal, R. (1986). Four factors in the mediation of teacher expectancy effects. In R. S. Feldman (ed.), *The social psychology of education: Current research and theory*. New York: Cambridge University Press.

Hartman, P. S. (2000). *Women developing wisdom: Antecedents and correlates in a longitudinal sample*. Unpublished doctoral dissertation, University of Michigan, Ann Arbor.

Hartmann, E. L. (1973). *The functions of sleep*. New Haven, CT: Yale University Press.

Harvey, A. G. (2008). Insomnia, psychiatric disorders, and the transdiagnostic perspective. *Current Directions in Psychological Science, 17*, 299–303.

Harvey, J. H. (1996). *Embracing their memory: Loss and the social psychology of storytelling*. Boston: Allyn & Bacon.

Harvey, J. H., & Hofmann, W. J. (2001). Teaching about loss. *Journal of Loss and Trauma, 6*, 263–268.

Harvey, J. H., & Pauwels, B. G. (1999). Recent developments in close-relationships theory. *Current Directions in Psychological Science, 8*, 93–95.

Harvey, J. H., Weber, A. L., & Orbuch, T. L. (1990). *Interpersonal accounts: A social psychological perspective*. Cambridge, MA: Basil Blackwell.

Harvey, S. M., & Spigner, C. (1995). Factors associated with sexual behavior among adolescents: A multivariate analysis. *Adolescence, 30*, 253–264.

Hasin, D. S., Goodwin, R. D., Stinson, F. S., & Grant, B. F. (2005, October). Epidemiology of major depressive disorder: Results from the National Epidemiologic Survey on Alcoholism and Related Conditions. *Archives of General Psychiatry, 62*, 1097–1106. Retrieved from http://archpsyc.ama-assn.org/cgi/reprint/62/10/1097.

Haslam, S. A. (2007, April/May). I think, therefore I err? *Scientific American Mind, 18*(2), 16–17.

Haslam, S. A., Salvatore, J., Kessler, T., & Reicher, S. D. (2008, April/May). The social psychology of success. *Scientific American Mind, 19*, 24–31.

Hasler, G., Buysse D. J., Klaghofer R., Gamma, A., Ajdacic, V., Eich D., Rössler W., & Angst J. (2004). The association between short sleep duration and obesity in young adults: A 13-year prospective study. *Sleep, 27*, 661–666.

Hassebrauck, M. (1988). Beauty is more than "name" deep: The effect of women's first names on ratings of physical attractiveness and personality attributes. *Journal of Applied Social Psychology, 18*, 721–726. [See also: Brigham, 1980; Cash & Duncan, 1984; Moore et al., 1987.]

Hatfield, E., & Rapson, R. (1993). *Love, sex, and intimacy: Their psychology, biology, and history*. New York: HarperCollins.

Hatfield, E., & Rapson, R. (1998). On love and sex in the 21st century. *The General Psychologist, 33*(2), 45–54.

Hatfield, E., Rapson, R. L., & Rapson, R. (1995). *Love and sex: Cross-cultural perspectives*. Boston: Allyn & Bacon.

Hatzfeld, J. (2005). *Machete season: The killers in Rwanda speak*. New York: Farrar, Strauss, and Giroux.

Hauser, M. D., Chomsky, N., & Fitch, W. T. (2002, November 22). The faculty of language: What is it, who has it, and how did it evolve? *Science, 298*, 1569–1579.

Hawkins, S. A., & Hastie, R. (1990). Hindsight: Biased judgments of past events after the outcomes are known. *Psychological Bulletin, 108*, 311–327.

Haworth, C. M., Wright, M. J., Luciano, M., Martin, N. G., de Geus, E. J., van Beijsterveldt, C. E., Bartels, M., Posthuma, D., Boomsma, D., Davis, O. S., Kovas, Y., Corley, R .P., DeFries, J. C., Hewitt, J. K., Olson, R. K., Rhea, S. A., Wadsworth, S. J., Iacono, W. G., McGue, M., Thompson, L. A., Hart, S. A., Petrill, S., Lubinski, D., & Plomin, R. (2010). The heritability of general cognitive ability increases linearly from childhood to young adulthood. *Molecular Psychiatry, 15*, 1112–1120.

Hazan, C., & Diamond, L. M. (2000). The place of attachment in human mating. *Review of General Psychology, 4*, 186–204.

Hazan, C., & Shaver, P. R. (1990). Love and work: An attachment-theoretical perspective. *Journal of Personality and Social Psychology, 59*, 270–280.

Hazeltine, E., & Ivry, R. B. (2002, June 14). Can we teach the cerebellum new tricks? *Science, 296*, 1979–1980. [See also Raymond, Lisberger, & Mauk, 1996; Seidler et al., 2002.]

Headey, B., & Wearing, A. (1992). *Understanding happiness: A theory of well-being*. Melbourne, Australia: Longman Cheshire.

Heatherton, T. F., Macrae, C. N., & Kelley, W. M. (2004). What the social brain sciences can tell us about the self. *Current Directions in Psychological Science, 13*, 190–193.

Hébert, R. (2005, January). The weight is over. *APS Observer, 18*(1), 20–24.

Hébert, R. (2006, October). We love to be scared on Halloween but fears and phobias are no laughing matter. *APS Observer, 19*(10), 14–19.

Hecht, A. (1986, April). A guide to the proper use of tranquilizers. *Healthline Newsletter, 5–6*.

Heckler, S. (1994). Facilitated communication: A response by child protection. *Child Abuse and Neglect: The International Journal, 18*(6), 495–503.

Hedden, T., Ketay, S., Aron, A., Markus, H. R., & Gabrieli, J. D. E. (2008.) Cultural influences on neural substrates of attentional control. *Psychological Science, 19*, 12–17. doi: 10.1111/j.1467-9280 .2008.02038.x.

Heine, S. J., Lehman, D. R., Markus, H. R., & Kitayama, S. (1999). Is there a universal need for positive self-regard? *Psychological Review, 106*, 766–794.

Heinrichs, R. W. (1993). Schizophrenia and the brain: Conditions for a neuropsychology of madness. *American Psychologist, 48*, 221–233.

Helmes, E., & Reddon, J. R. (1993). A perspective on developments in assessing psychopathology: A critical review of the MMPI and MMPI-2. *Psychological Bulletin, 113*, 453–471. [See also: Butcher et al., 1989; Butcher & Williams, 1992; Greene, 1991.]

Helms, J. E. (1992). Why is there no study of cultural equivalence in standardized cognitive ability testing? *American Psychologist, 47*, 1083–1101. [See also: Garcia, 1981; Miller-Jones, 1989]

Helmuth, L. (2000, December 1). Where the brain monitors the body. *Science, 290*, 1668.

Helmuth, L. (2001a, November 2). Beyond the pleasure principle. *Science, 294*, 983–984.

Helmuth, L. (2001b, March 16). Dyslexia: Same brains, different languages. *Science, 291*, 2064–2065.

Helmuth, L. (2002, June 21). A generation gap in brain activity. *Science, 296*, 2131–2133.

Helmuth, L. (2003a, November 14). Brain model puts most sophisticated regions front and center. *Science, 302*, 1133.

Helmuth, L. (2003b, April 25). Fear and trembling in the amygdala. *Science, 300*, 568–569. [See also: Bechara et al., 1995; Johnson, 2003]

Helmuth, L. (2003c, February 28). The wisdom of the wizened. *Science, 299,* 1300–1302.

Hendrick, S. S., & Hendrick, C. (1992). *Liking, loving, and relating* (2nd ed.) Pacific Grove, CA: Brooks/Cole.

Herek, G. M. (2000). The psychology of sexual prejudice. *Current Directions in Psychological Science, 9,* 19–22.

Herek, G., Norton, A., Allen, T., & Sims, C. (2010). Demographic, psychological, and social characteristics of self-identified lesbian, gay, and bisexual adults in a U.S. probability sample. *Sexuality Research and Social Policy, 7,* 176–200.

Herrnstein, R. J., & Murray, C. (1994). *The bell curve.* New York: Free Press.

Hersen, M., & Thomas, J. C. (2005). *Comprehensive handbook of personality and psychopathology* (Vol. 2). Hoboken, NJ: Wiley and Sons.

Hersh, S. M. (2004a, May 5). American soldiers brutalize Iraqis: How far up does the responsibility go? Torture at Abu Ghraib. *The New Yorker.*

Hersh, S. M. (2004b). *Chain of command: The road from 9/11 to Abu Ghraib.* New York: HarperCollins.

Hetherington, E. M., & Parke, R. D. (1975). *Child psychology: A contemporary viewpoint.* New York: McGraw-Hill.

Hettema, J. M., Neale, M. C., & Kendler, K. S. (2001). A review and meta-analysis of the genetic epidemiology of anxiety disorders. *American Journal of Psychiatry, 158,* 1568–1578.

Heyman, K. (2006, May 5). The map in the brain: Grid cells may help us navigate. *Science, 312,* 680–681.

Hibbard, S. (2003). A critique of Lilienfeld et al.'s (2000) "The scientific status of projective techniques." *Journal of Personality Assessment, 80,* 260–271. [See also: Exner, 1974, 1978; Exner & Weiner, 1982]

Hickok, G. (2009). Eight problems for the mirror neuron theory of action understanding in monkeys and humans. *Journal of Cognitive Neuroscience, 21,* 1229–1243.

Hickok, G. (2010, March 26). *Self-destruction of mirror neurons. Talking brains blog.* Retrieved November 16, 2010, from www.talkingbrains.org/2010/03/self-destruction-of-mirror-neuron.html

Hicks, R. A. (1990). *The costs and benefits of normal insomnia.* Paper presented to the annual meeting of the Western Psychological Association, Los Angeles, CA.

Higgins, J. W., Williams, R. L., & McLaughlin, T. F. (2001). The effects of a token economy employing instructional consequences for a third-grade students with learning disabilities: A data-based case study. *Education and Treatment of Children, 24,* 99–106. [See also: Corrigan, 1995; Le Blanc et al., 2000; Morisse et al., 1996.]

Hilgard, E. R. (1992). Dissociation and theories of hypnosis. In E. Fromm & M. R. Nash (Eds.), *Contemporary hypnosis research.* New York: Guilford.

Hill, J. O., & Peters, J. C. (1998, May 29). Environmental contributions to the obesity epidemic. *Science, 280,* 1371–1374.

Hilts, P. J. (1995). *Memory's ghost: The strange tale of Mr. M. and the nature of memory.* New York: Simon & Schuster.

Hiroto, D. S. (1974). Locus of control and learned helplessness. *Journal of Experimental Psychology, 102,* 187–193.

Hirschfeld, L. A. (1996). *Race in the making: Cognition, culture, and the child's construction of human kinds.* Cambridge, MA: MIT Press.

Hobson, J. A. (1988). *The dreaming brain.* New York: Basic Books.

Hobson, J. A. (2002). *Dreaming: An introduction to the science of sleep.* New York: Oxford University Press.

Hobson, J. A., & McCarley, R. W. (1977). The brain as a dream state generator: An activation-synthesis hypothesis of the dream process. *American Journal of Psychiatry, 134,* 1335–1348.

Hochberg, L. R., Serruya, M. D., Friehs, G. M., Mukand, J. A., Saleh, M., & Caplan, A. H. (2006). Neuronal ensemble control of prosthetic devices by a human with tetraplegia. *Nature, 442,* 164–171. [See also Nicolelis & Chapin, 2002; Taylor, Helms Tillery, & Schwartz, 2002; Wickelgren, 2003.]

Hochwalder, J. (1995). On stability of the structure of implicit personality theory over situations. *Scandinavian Journal of Psychology, 36,* 386–398.

Hofling, C. K., Brotzman, E., Dalrymple, S., Graves, N., & Pierce, C. M. (1966). An experimental study in nurse-physician relationships. *Journal of Nervous and Mental Disease, 143,* 171–180.

Hogan, R., Hogan, J., & Roberts, B. W. (1996). Personality measurement and employment decisions: Questions and answers. *American Psychologist, 51,* 469–477.

Hogarty, G. E., Kornblith, S. J., Greenwald, D., DiBarry, A. L., Cooley, S., Ulrich, R. F., Carter, M., & Flesher, S. (1997). Three-year trials of personal therapy among schizophrenic patients living with or independent of family, I: Description of study and effects on relapse rates. *American Journal of Psychiatry, 154,* 1504–1513.

Holden, C. (1978). Patuxent: Controversial prison clings to belief in rehabilitation. *Science, 199,* 665–668.

Holden, C. (1980a). Identical twins reared apart. *Science, 207,* 1323–1325.

Holden, C. (1980b, November). Twins reunited. *Science, 80,* 55–59.

Holden, C. (2000, April 7). Global survey examines impact of depression. *Science, 288,* 39–40.

Holden, C. (2003, January 17). Deconstructing schizophrenia. *Science, 299,* 333–335. [See also: Lencer et al., 2000; Plomin et al., 1994]

Holden, C. (2004, October 29). Mystics and synesthesia. *Science, 306,* 808.

Holden, C. (2005, June 10). Sex and the suffering brain. *Science, 308,* 1574–1577. [See also: Leut-wyler, 1995; Strickland, 1992; Weissman et al., 1996.]

Holden, C. (2008, July 11). Poles apart. *Science, 321,* 193–195.

Hollander, E. M. (2004). Am I all right? *Journal of Loss and Trauma, 9,* 201–204.

Hollon, S. D. (1996). The efficacy and effectiveness of psychotherapy relative to medications. *American Psychologist, 51,* 1025–1030.

Hollon, S. D., Thase, M. E., & Markowitz, J. C. (2002, November). Treatment and prevention of depression. *Psychological Science in the Public Interest, 3,* 39–77.

Holloway, J. D. (2003, December). Snapshot from the therapy room. *Monitor on Psychology, 34*(11), 31.

Holloway, M. (2003, September). The mutable brain. *Scientific American, 289*(3), 78–85.

Holmes, D. S. (2001). *Abnormal psychology* (4th ed.). Boston: Allyn & Bacon. [See also: Linsheid et al., 1990; Lovaas, 1977; Lovaas et al., 1974.]

Holmes, T. H. (1979). Development and application of a quantitative measure of life change magnitude. In J. E. Barrett, R. M. Rose, & G. L. Klerman (Eds.), *Stress and mental disorder.* New York: Raven.

Holmes, T. H., & Masuda, M. (1974). Life change and stress susceptibility. In B. S. Dohrenwend & B. P. Dohrenwend (Eds.), *Stressful life events: Their nature and effects* (pp. 45–72). New York: Wiley.

Holmes, T. H., & Rahe, R. H. (1967). The social readjustment rating scale. *Journal of Psychosomatic Research, 11*(2), 213–218.

Holstege, G., Georgiandis, J. R., Paans, A. M. J., Meiners, L. C., van der Graff, F. H. C. E., & Reinders, A. A. T. S. (2003). Brain activation during human male ejaculation. *Journal of Neuroscience, 23,* 9185–9193.

Holtzman, W. H. (1992). Health psychology. In M. A. Rosenzweig (Ed.), *International psychological science* (pp. 199–226). Washington, DC: American Psychological Association.

Holtzworth-Munroe, A., & Jacobson, N. S. (1985). Causal attributions of marital couples: When do they search for causes? What do they conclude when they do? *Journal of Personality and Social Psychology, 48,* 1398–1412.

Hölzel, B. K., Carmody, J., Vangel, M., Congleton, C., Yerramsetti, S. M., Gard, T., & Lazar, S. W. (2011). Mindfulness practice leads to increases in regional brain gray matter density. *Psychiatry Research, 191*(1), 36–43.

Homme, L. E., de Baca, P. C., Devine, J. V., Steinhorst, R., & Rickert, E. J. (1963). Use of the Premack principle in controlling the behavior of nursery school children. *Journal of the Experimental Analysis of Behavior, 6,* 544.

Horgan, J. (1993, June). Eugenics revisited. *Scientific American, 268,* 122–131.

Horne, J. A. (1988). *Why we sleep: The functions of sleep in humans and other animals.* Oxford: Oxford University Press.

Horney, K. (1939). *New ways in psychoanalysis.* New York: Norton.

Horney, K. (1942). *Self-analysis.* New York: Norton.

Horney, K. (1967). *Feminine psychology.* New York: Norton.

Horowitz, M. J. (1997). *Stress response syndromes: PTSD, grief, and adjustment disorders* (3rd ed.). Northvale, NJ: Jason Aronson.

Horvath, A. O., & Luborsky, L. (1993). The role of the therapeutic alliance in psychotherapy. *Journal of Consulting and Clinical Psychology, 61,* 561–573.

House, J. S., Landis, K. R., & Umberson, D. (1988). Social relationships and health. *Science, 241,* 540–545.

Howes, C., Rodning, C., Galluzzo, D. C., & Myers, L. (1988). Attachment and child care: Relationships with mother and care-giver. *Early Childhood Research Quarterly, 3,* 403–416.

Hu, F. B., Li, T. Y., Colditz, G. A., Willett, W. C., & Manson, J. E. (2003, April 9). Television watching and other sedentary behaviors in relation to risk of obesity and Type 2 diabetes mellitus in women. *Journal of the American Medical Association, 289,* 1785–1791.

Huesmann, L. R., & Moise, J. (1996, June). Media violence: A demonstrated public health threat to children. *Harvard Mental Health Letter, 12*(12), 5–7.

Huesmann, L. R., Moise-Titus, J., Podolski, C-L., & Eron, L. D. (2003). Longitudinal relations between children's exposure to TV violence and their aggressive and violent behavior in young adulthood: 1977–1992. *Developmental Psychology, 39,* 201–221. [See also: Bushman & Anderson, 2001; Johnson et al., 2001.]

Hull, C. L. (1943). *Principles of behavior: An intro duction to behavior theory.* New York: Appleton-Century-Crofts.

Hull, C. L. (1952). *A behavior system: An introduction to behavior theory concerning the individual organism.* New Haven, CT: Yale University Press.

Humphreys, L. G. (1988). Trends in levels of academic achievement of blacks and other minorities. *Intelligence, 12,* 231–260.

Hunt, E. (1989). Cognitive science: Definition, status, and questions. *Annual Review of Psychology, 40,* 603–629. [See also: Medin, 1989; Mervis & Rosch, 1981; Rosch & Mervis, 1975.]

Hunter, I. (1964). *Memory.* Baltimore: Penguin.

Huss, M. T. (2001). Psychology and law, now and in the next century: The promise of an emerging area of psychology. In J. S. Halonen & S. F. Davis (Eds.), *The many faces of psychological research in the 21st century.* Retrieved from http://teachpsych.org/resources/e-books/faces/script/Ch11.htm.

Huston, T. L., Ruggiero, M., Conner, R., & Geis, G. (1981). Bystander intervention into crime: A Study based on naturally-occurring episodes. *Social Psychology Quarterly, 44,* 14–23.

Huttenlocher, J., Haight, W., Bryk, A., Seltzer, M., & Lyons, T. (1991). Early vocabulary growth: Relation to language input and gender. *Developmental Psychology, 27,* 236–248.

Hyde, J. S. (2007). New directions in the study of gender similarities and differences. *Current Directions in Psychological Science, 16,* 259–263.

Hyde, J. S., & Jaffe, S. (2000). Becoming a heterosexual adult: The experiences of young women. *Journal of Social Issues, 56,* 283–296.

Hyman, I. A. (1996). Using research to change public policy: Reflections on 20 years of effort to eliminate corporal punishment in schools. *Pediatrics, 98,* 818–821. [See also: Hyman et al., 1977.]

Hyman, R. (1989). The psychology of deception. *Annual Review of Psychology, 40,* 133–154.

Iacono, W. G., & Grove, W. M. (1993). Schizophrenia reviewed: Toward an integrative genetic model. *Science, 4,* 273–276.

Ineichen, B. (1979). The social geography of marriage. In M. Cook & G. Wilson (Eds.), *Love and attraction.* New York: Pergamon Press.

Inglehart, R. (1990). *Culture shift in advanced industrial society.* Princeton, NJ: Princeton University Press.

Insel, T. R. (2010, April). Faulty circuits. *Scientific American, 302*(4), 44–51.

Insko, C., Thibaut, J. W., Moehle, D., Wilson, M., & Diamond, W. D. (1980). Social evolution and the emergence of leadership. *Journal of Personality and Social Psychology, 39,* 441–448.

Institute of Medicine. (2002). *Dietary reference intakes for energy, carbohydrate, fiber, fat, fatty acids, cholesterol, protein, and amino acids.* Washington, DC: National Institutes of Health.

Ishai, A., & Sagi, D. (1995). Common mechanisms of visual imagery and perception. *Science, 268,* 1772–1774.

Iverson, P., Kuhl, P. K., Akahane-Yamada, R., Diesch, E., Tohkura, Y., Kettermann, A., & Siebert, C. (2003). A perceptual interference account of acquisition difficulties for non-native phonemes. *Cognition, 87,* B47–B57.

Izard, C. E. (2007). Basic emotions, natural kinds, emotion schemas, and a new paradigm. *Perspectives on Psycho logical Science, 2,* 260–280.

Jablensky, A. (2000). Epidemiology of schizophrenia: The global burden of disease and disability. *Euro pean Archives of Psychiatry & Clinical Neuroscience, 250,* 274–283.

Jacobs, B. L. (1987). How hallucinogenic drugs work. *American Scientist, 75,* 386–392.

Jacobs, B. L. (2004). Depression: The brain finally gets into the act. *Current Directions in Psychological Science, 13,* 103–106.

Jacobs, L. F., & Schenk, F. (2003). Unpacking the cognitive map: The parallel map theory of hippocampal function. *Psychological Review, 110,* 285–315.

Jacobs, R. C., & Campbell, D. T. (1961). The permanence of an arbitrary tradition through several generations of a laboratory microculture. *Journal of Abnormal and Social Psychology, 62,* 649–658.

Jacobson, N. S., & Christensen, A. (1996). Studying the effectiveness of psychotherapy: How well can clinical trials do the job? *American Psychologist, 51,* 1031–1039.

Jacobson, N. S., Christensen, A., Prince, S. E., Cordova, J., & Eldridge, K. (2000). Integrative behavioral couple therapy: An acceptance-based, promising new treatment for couple discord. *Journal of Consulting and Clinical Psychology, 68,* 351–355.

Jaffe, E. (2006, March). Opening Skinner's Box causes controversy. *APS Observer, 19*(3), 17–19.

Jaffe, E. (2007, May). Mirror neurons: How we reflect on behavior. *APS Observer, 20*(5), 20–25.

James, W. (1884). What is an emotion? *Mind 9,* 188–205.

James, W. (1890/1950). *The principles of psychology* (2 vols.). New York: Holt, Rinehart & Winston. (Original work published 1890.)

Janis, I. (1972). *Victims of groupthink: A psychological study of foreign-policy decisions and fiascoes.* Boston: Houghton Mifflin.

Janis, I., & Mann, L. (1977). *Decision making: A psychological analysis of conflict, choice and commitment.* New York: The Free Press.

Janoff-Bulman, R. (1989). The benefits of illusions, the threat of disillusionment, and the limitations of inaccuracy. *Journal of Social and Clinical Psychology, 8,* 158–175.

Janoff-Bulman, R. (1992). *Shattered assumptions: Towards a new psychology of trauma.* New York: The Free Press.

Janoff-Bulman, R., & Frantz, C. M. (1997). The impact of trauma on meaning: From meaningless world to meaningful life. In M. Power & C. R. Brewin (Eds.), *The transformation of meaning in psychological therapies* (pp. 91–106). New York: Wiley.

Janus, S. S., & Janus, C. L. (1993). *The Janus report on sexual behavior.* New York: Wiley.

Javitt, D. C., & Coyle, J. T. (2004). Decoding schizophrenia. *Scientific American, 290,* 48–55.

Jenkins, J. H., & Barrett, R. J., (Eds.). (2004). *Schizophrenia, culture, and subjectivity: The edge of experience.* Cambridge, UK: Cambridge University Press.

Jensen, A. R. (1969). How much can we boost IQ and scholastic achievement? *Harvard Educational Review, 39,* 1–123.

Jensen, A. R. (1998). The g factor and the de sign of education. In R. J. Sternberg & W. M. Williams (Eds.), *Intelligence, instruction, and assessment: Theory into practice.* Mahwah, NJ: Erlbaum.

Jensen, A. R. (2000). Testing: The dilemma of group differences. *Psychology, Public Policy, and Law, 6,* 121–127.

Jensen, A. R., & Figueroa, R. A. (1975). Forward and backward digit-span interaction with race and IQ: Predictions from Jensen's theory. *Journal of Educational Psychology, 67,* 882–893.

Jick, H., Kaye, J. A., & Jick, S. S. (2004, July 21). Antidepressants and the risk of suicidal behaviors. *JAMA: Journal of the American Medical Association, 292,* 338–343.

Jitendra, A. K., Griffin, C. C., Haria, P., Leh, J., Adams, A., & Kaduvettoor, A. (2007). A comparison of single and multiple strategy instruction on third-grade students' mathematical problem solving. *Journal of Educational Psychology, 99,* 115–127.

Jobe, T. H., & Harrow, M. (2010). Schizophrenia course, long-term outcome, recovery, and prognosis. *Current Directions in Psychological Science, 19,* 220– 225.

Jog, M. S., Kubota, Y., Connolly, C. I., Hillegaart, V., & Grabiel, A. M. (1999, November 26). Building neural representations of habits. *Science, 286,* 1745–1749.

John, O. P., & Srivastava, S. (1999). *The Big-Five trait taxonomy: History, measurement, and theoretical perspectives.* Retrieved January 24, 2008, from www.uoregon.edu/~sanjay/pubs/bigfive.pdf. [See also: Caprara et al., 1993; Costa & McCrae, 1992a, b]

Johnson, J. H., & Sarason, I. B. (1979). Recent developments in research on life stress. In V. Hamilton & D. M. Warburton (Eds.), *Human stress and cognition: An information processing approach* (pp. 205–233). Chichester, UK: Wiley.

Johnson, M. (1991). Selye's stress and the body in the mind. *Advances in Nursing Science, 7,* 38–44.

Johnson, M. H. (1998). The neural basis of cognitive development. In D. Kuhn & R. S. Siegler (Eds.), *Handbook of child psychology: Vol. 2. Cognition, perception, and language* (5th ed., pp. 1–49). New York: Wiley.

Johnson, P. M., & Kenny, P. J. (2010, March 28). Dopamine D2 receptors in addiction-like reward dysfunction and compulsive eating in obese rats. *Nature Neuroscience, 13,* 635–641. doi:10.1038/nn.2519.

Johnson, R. L. (2006, Fall). Editorial: The science-practice divide. *The General Psychologist, 41*(2), 4.

Johnson, R. L., & Rudmann, J. L. (2004). Psychology at community colleges: A survey. *Teaching of Psychology, 31,* 183–185.

Johnson, W., McGue, M., & Iacono, W. G. (2009). School performance and genetic and environmental variance in antisocial behavior at the transition from adolescence to adulthood. *Developmental Psychology, 45,* 973–987.

Johnson, W., teNijenhuis, J., & Bouchard, T. J. (2008). Still just 1 *g*: Consistent results from five test batteries. *Intelligence, 36,* 81–95.

Joiner, T. E., Jr., & Schmidt, N. B. (1995). Dimensions of perfectionism, life stress, and depressed and anxious symptoms: Prospective support for diathesis-stress but not specific vulnerability among male undergraduates. *Journal of Social and Clinical Psychology, 14,* 165–183.

Jones, M. C. (1924). A laboratory study of fear: The case of Peter. *Pedagogical Seminary, 31,* 308–315.

Jonides, J., Lacey, S. C., & Nee, D. E. (2005). Processes of working memory in mind and brain. *Current Directions in Psychological Science, 14,* 2–5.

Joseph, R. (1988). Dual mental functioning in a split-brain patient. *Journal of Clinical Psychology, 44,* 770–779.

Juliano, S. L. (1998, March 13). Mapping the sensory mosaic. *Science, 279,* 1653–1654.

Julien, R. M. (2007). *A primer of drug action* (11th ed.). New York: W. H. Freeman.

Jung, C. G. (1936/1959). The concept of the collective unconscious. In H. E. Read & M. Fordham (Eds.), *The archetypes and the collective unconscious, collected works* (Vol. 9, Part 1, pp. 54–77). Princeton, NJ: Princeton University Press. (Original work published 1936.)

Kabot, S., Masi, W., & Segal, M. (2003). Advances in the diagnosis and treatment of autism spectrum disorders. *Professional Psychology: Research and Practice, 34,* 26–33.

Kagan, J. (1996). Three pleasing ideas. *American Psychologist, 51,* 901–908.

Kagan, J. (1998). *Three seductive ideas.* Cambridge, MA: Harvard University Press.

Kagan, J. (2001). Temperamental contributions to affective and behavioral profiles in childhood. In S. G. Hofmann & P. M. DiBartolo (Eds.), *From social anxiety to social phobia: Multiple perspectives* (pp. 216–234). Boston: Allyn & Bacon.

Kagan, J., Herschkowitz, N., & Herschkowitz, E. (2005). *Young mind in a growing brain.* Mahwah, NJ: Erlbaum Associates.

Kagan, J., Reznick, J. S., & Snidman, N. (1988). Biological basis of childhood shyness. *Science, 20,* 167–171.

Kagan, J., & Snidman, N. (1998). Childhood derivatives of high and low reactivity in infancy. *Child Development, 69,* 1483–1493.

Kagan, J., Snidman, N., Arcus, D., & Reznick, J. S. (1994). *Galen's prophecy: Temperament in human nature.* New York: Basic Books.

Kahneman, D. (2003). A perspective on judgment and choice: Mapping bounded rationality. *American Psychologist, 58,* 697–720.

Kahneman, D., & Tversky, A. (2000). *Choice, values, and frames.* New York: Cambridge University Press. [See also: Jacowitz & Kahneman, 1995; Tversky & Kahneman, 2000.]

Kairys, A. (2010). *Time perspective: Its links to personality traits, age, and gender.* Dissertation summary, Vilnius University, Lithuania, Social Sciences, Psychology (06S).

Kaiser Family Foundation. (2005). Generation M: Media in the lives of 8–18-year-olds. Retrieved from www.kff.org/entmedia/7250.cfm.

Kalman, I. (2008). *Bullies 2 buddies: Victim proof your school.* New York: The Wisdom Press. Also see www.Bullies2Buddies.com

Kamil, A. C., Krebs, J., & Pulliam, H. R. (1987). *Foraging behavior.* New York: Plenum.

Kamin, L. (1994, November 23). Intelligence, IQ tests, and race. *Chronicle of Higher Education,* p. B5.

Kamin, L. J. (1995, February). Book review: Behind the curve. *Scientific American, 272,* 99–103.

Kandel, D. B. (1978). Similarity in real-life adolescent friendship pairs. *Journal of Personality and Social Psychology, 36,* 306–312.

Kandel, E. (2000, November 10). Neuroscience: Breaking down scientific barriers to the study of brain and mind. *Science, 290,* 1113–1120.

Kandel, E. R., & Hawkins, R. D. (1992, September). The biological basis of learning and individuality. *Scientific American, 267,* 79–86.

Kandel, E. R., & Squire, L. R. (2000, November 10). Neuroscience: Breaking down scientific barriers to the study of brain and mind. *Science, 290,* 1113–1120. [See also: Heeger, 1994; Hubel & Wiesel, 1979; Lettvin et al., 1959; Maunsell, 1995; Zeki, 1992]

Kantrowitz, B. (1992, January 27). A head start does not last. *Newsweek, 119,* pp. 44–45.

Kanwisher, N. (2006, February 3). What's in a face? *Science, 311,* 617–618. [See also Gross, 2005.]

Karlsen, C. F. (1998). *The devil in the shape of a woman: Witchcraft in colonial New England.* New York: W. W. Norton & Company.

Karlsgodt, K. H., Sun, D., & Cannon, T. D. (2010). Structural and functional brain abnormalities in schizophrenia. *Current Directions in Psychological Science, 19,* 226–231. [See also: Sawa & Snyder, 2002.]

Kasamatsu, A., & Hirai, T. (1966). An electroencephalographic study on the Zen meditation (Zazen). *Folia Psychiatrica et Neurological Japonica, 20,* 315–336.

Kassin, S. (2001). Confessions: Psychological and forensic aspects. In N. J. Smelser & P. B. Baltes (Eds.), *International encyclopedia of the social & behavioral sciences.* Amsterdam: Elsevier.

Kaufman, G., Raphael, L., & Espeland, P. (1999). *Stick up for yourself: Every kid's guide to personal power and positive self-esteem.* Minneapolis, MN: Free Spirit Publishing.

Kazdin, A. E. (1994). *Behavior modification in applied settings* (5th ed.). Pacific Grove, CA: Brooks/Cole.

Kazdin, A. E. (2008). Evidence-based treatment and practice: New opportunities to bridge clinical research and practice, enhance the knowledge base, and improve patient care. *American Psychologist, 63,* 146–159.

Keating, D. P. (2004). Cognitive and brain development. In R. M. Lerner & L. Steinberg (Eds.), *Handbook of adolescent psychology* (2nd ed., pp. 45–84). Hoboken, NJ: Wiley.

Keel, P. K., & Klump, K. L. (2003). Are eating disorders culture-bound syndromes? Implications for conceptualizing their etiology. *Psychological Bulletin, 129,* 747–769.

Keen, S. (1991). *Faces of the enemy: Reflections of the hostile imagination.* San Francisco: Harper.

Keidel, G. C. (2002). Burnout and depressioin among hospice caregivers. *American Journal of Hospice and Palliative Care, 19,* 200–205.

Keller, M. B., McCullough, J. P., Klein, D. N., Arnow, B., Dunner, D. L., Gelenberg, A. J., Markowitz, J. C., Nemeroff, C. B., Russell, J. M., Thase, M. E., Trivedi, M. H., & Zajecka, J. (2000, May 18). A comparison of nefazodone, the cognitive behavioral-analysis system of psychotherapy, and their combination for the treatment of chronic depression. *New England Journal of Medicine, 342,* 1462–1470.

Kelley, J. E., Lumley, M. A., & Leisen, J. C. C. (1997). Health effects of emotional disclosure in rheumatoid arthritis patients. *Health Psychology, 16,* 331–340.

Kemeny, M. E. (2003). The psychobiology of stress. *Current Directions, 12,* 124–129.

Kendler, H. H. (2005). Psychology and phenomenology: A clarification. *American Psychologist, 60,* 318–324.

Kendler, K. S., & Gardner, C. O., Jr. (1998). Boundaries of major depression: An evaluation of DSM-IV criteria. *American Journal of Psychiatry, 155,* 172–177.

Kendler, K. S., Hettema, J. M., Butera, F., Gardner, C. O., & Prescott, C. A. (2003). Life event dimensions of loss, humiliation, entrapment, and danger in the prediction of onsets of major depression and generalized anxiety. *Archives of General Psychiatry, 60,* 789–796.

Kenealy, P. (1997). Key components of the Mozart Effect. *Perceptual and Motor Skills, 86,* 835–841.

Kenrick, D. T., & Funder, D. C. (1988). Profiting from controversy: Lessons from the person–situation debate. *American Psychologist, 43,* 23–34.

Kenrick, D. T., Griskevicius, V., Neuberg, S. L., & Schaller, M. (2010). Renovating the pyramid of needs: Contemporary extensions built upon ancient foundations. *Perspectives on Psychological Science, 5,* 292–314.

Kenrick, D. T., & Stringfield, D. O. (1980). Personality traits and the eye of the beholder: Crossing some traditional philosophical boundaries in the search for consistency in all of the people. *Psychological Review, 87,* 88–104.

Kern, M. L., & Friedman, H. S. (2008). Do conscientious individuals live longer? A quantitative review. *Health Psychology, 27,* 505–512.

Kershaw, S. (2010, January 9). The terrorist mind: An Update. *New York Times.* Retrieved from www.nytimes.com/2010/01/10/weekinreview/10kershaw.html?emc=eta1&pagewanted=print.

Kesebir, S., Graham, J., & Oishi, S. (2010). A theory of human needs should be human-centered, not animal-centered: Commentary on Kenrick et al. (2010). *Perspectives on Psychological Science, 5,* 315–319.

Kessler, R. C., Berglund, P., Demler, O., Jin, R., Koretz, D., Merikangas, K. R., Rush, A. J., Walters, E. E., & Wang, P. S. (2003, June). The epidemiology of major depressive disorder: Results from the National Comorbidity Survey Replication (NCS-R). *Journal of the American Medical Association, 289,* 3095–3105.

Kessler, R. C., Chiu, W. T., Demler, O., & Walters, E. E. (2005). Prevalence, severity, and comorbidity of twelve-month *DSM-IV* disorders in the National Comorbidity Survey Replication (NCS-R). *Archives of General Psychiatry, 62,* 617–27.

Keynes, R. (2002). *Darwin, his daughter, and human evolution.* New York: Penguin Putnam.

Keysers, C. (2010). Mirror neurons. *Current Biology, 19,* 971–973.

Kiecolt-Glaser, J. K., & Glaser, R. (1987). Psychosocial moderators of immune function. *Annals of Behavioral Medicine, 9,* 16–20.

Kiecolt-Glaser, J. K., & Glaser, R. (2001). Stress and immunity: Age enhances the risks. *Current Directions in Psychological Science, 10,* 18–21.

Kiehl, K. A., & Buckholtz, J. W. (2010, September/October). Inside the mind of a psychopath. *Scientific American Mind, 21*(4), 22–29.

Kierein, N. M., & Gold, M. A. (2000). Pygmalion in work organizations: A meta-analysis. *Journal of Organizational Behavior, 21,* 913–928.

Kieseppa, T., Partonen, T., Haukka, J., Kaprio, J., & Lonnqvist, J. (2004). High concordance of bipolar I disorder in a nationwide sample of twins. Retrieved from http://ajp.psychiatryonline.org/cgi/reprint/161/10/1814.

Kiesler, C. A. (1982). Mental hospitals and alternative care: Noninstitutionalization as potential public policy for mental patients. *American Psychologist, 37,* 349–360.

Kiesler, C. A. (1993). Mental health policy and mental hospitalization. *Current Directions in Psychological Science, 2,* 93–95.

Kiester, E. (1980, May/June). Images of the night. *Science, 80,* 36–42.

Kihlstrom, J. F. (1985). Hypnosis. *Annual Review of Psychology, 36,* 385–418.

Kihlstrom, J. F. (1987). The cognitive unconscious. *Science, 237,* 1445–1452.

Kihlstrom, J. F. (1990). The psychological unconscious. In L. Pervin (Ed.), *Handbook of personality: Theory and research* (pp. 445–464). New York: Guilford Press.

Kihlstrom, J. F. (in press). The Person–situation interaction. In D. Carlston (Ed.), *Oxford handbook of social cognition.* New York: Oxford University Press.

Kihlstrom, J. F., Barnhardt, T. M., & Tataryn, D. J. (1992). The psychological unconscious: Found, lost, and regained. *American Psychologist, 47,* 788–791.

Killingsworth, M. A., & Gilbert, D. T. (2010). A wandering mind is an unhappy mind. *Science, 330,* 932.

Kim, H. S. (2002). We talk, therefore we think? A cultural analysis of the effects of talking on thinking. *Journal of Personality and Social Psychology, 83,* 828–842.

Kim, J., & Hatfield, E. (2004). Love types and subjective well-being. *Social Behavior and Personality: An International Journal, 32,* 173–182.

Kimble, G. A. (1991). The spirit of Ivan Petrovich Pavlov. In G. A. Kimble, M. Wertheimer, & C. L. White (Eds.), *Portraits of pioneers in psychology* (pp. 26–40). Washington, DC: American Psychological Association.

Kincade, K. (1973). *A Walden Two experiment: The first five years of Twin Oaks Community.* New York: Morrow.

Kindt, M., Soeter, M., & Vervliet, B. (2009). Beyond extinction: Erasing human fear responses and preventing the return of fear. *Nature Neuroscience, 12,* 256–258.

Kinetz, E. (2006, September 26). Is hysteria real? Brain images say yes. *New York Times.* Retrieved February 5, 2008, from www.nytimes.com/2006/09/26/science/26hysteria.html?pagewanted=1&sq=Is%20hysteria%20real?&st=nyt&scp=1.

King, P. M., & Kitchener, K. S. (1994). *Developing reflective judgment: Understanding and promoting intellectual growth and critical thinking in adolescents and adults.* San Francisco, CA: Jossey-Bass.

Kinsey, A. C., Pomeroy, W. B., & Martin, C. E. (1948). *Sexual behavior in the human male.* Philadelphia: Saunders.

Kinsey, A. C., Pomeroy, W. B., Martin, C. E., & Gebhard, P. H. (1953). *Sexual behavior in the human female.* Philadelphia: Saunders.

Kirkpatrick, L. A., & Shaver, P. R. (1992). An attachment-theoretical approach to romantic love and religious belief. *Personality and Social Psychology Bulletin, 18,* 266–275.

Kirsch, I., & Braffman, W. (2001). Imaginative suggestibility and hypnotizability. *Current Directions in Psychological Science, 10,* 57–61.

Kirsch, I., & Lynn, S. J. (1995). Altered state of hypnosis: Changes in the theoretical landscape. *American Psychologist, 50,* 846–858.

Kirsch, I., & Lynn, S. J. (1998). Dissociation theories of hypnosis. *Psychological Bulletin, 123,* 100–115. [See also: Kihlstrom, 1998; Woody & Sadler, 1998.]

Klag, M. J., Whelton, P. K., Grim, C. E., & Kuller, L. H. (1991). The association of skin color with blood pressure in U.S. blacks with low socioeconomic status. *Journal of the American Medical Association, 265,* 599–602.

Klagsbrun, F. (1985). *Married people: Staying together in the age of divorce.* New York: Bantam Books.

Klein, P. J., & Meltzoff, A. M. (1999). Long-term memory, forgetting, and deferred imitation in 12-month-old infants. *Developmental Science, 2,* 102–113.

Kleinman, A., & Cohen, A. (1997). Psychiatry's global challenge. *Scientific American, 276*(3), 86–89.

Kleinmuntz, B., & Szucko, J. J. (1984). Lie detection in ancient and modern times: A call for contemporary scientific study. *American Psychologist, 39,* 766–776.

Klinger, E. (1987, May). The power of daydreams. *Psychology Today,* 37–44.

Kluger, J. (2010, August 16). What animals think. *Time, 176*(7).

Klüver, H., & Bucy, P. C. (1939). Preliminary analysis of temporal lobes in monkeys. *Archives of Neurology and Psychiatry, 42,* 979–1000.

Knapp, S., & VandeCreek, L. (2003). An overview of the major changes in the 2002 APA Ethics Code. *American Psychologist, 34,* 301–308. [See also: Ilgen & Bell, 1991; Rosenthal, 1994a.]

Knecht, S., Flöel, A., Dräger, B., Breitenstein, C., Sommer, J., Henningsen, H., Ringelstein, E. B., & Pascual-Leone, A. (2002, July 1). Degree of language lateralization determines susceptibility to unilateral brain lesions. *Nature Neuroscience, 5,* 695–699.

Knox, D., & Schact, C. (2008). *Choices in relationships: An introduction to marriage and the family.* Belmont, CA: Thomson.

Kobasa, S. O., Hilker, R. R., & Maddi, S. R. (1979). Who stays healthy under stress? *Journal of Occupational Medicine, 21,* 595–598.

Kochanska, G., Barry, R. A., Jimenez, N. B., Hollatz, A. L., & Woodard, J. (2009). Guilt and effortful control: Two mechanisms that prevent disruptive developmental trajectories. *Journal of Personality and Social Psychology, 97,* 322–333.

Kochanska, G., Barry, R. A., Stellern, S. A., & O'Bleness, J. J. (2009). Early attachment organization moderates the parent–child mutually coercive pathway to children's antisocial conduct. *Child Development, 80,* 1288–1300.

Koechlin, E., Ody, C., & Kouneiher, F. (2003, November 14). The architecture of cognitive control in the human prefrontal cortex. *Science, 302,* 1181–1185.

Kohlberg, L. (1964). Development of moral character and moral ideology. In M. L. Hoffman & L. W. Hoffman (Eds.), *Review of child development research* (Vol. 1). New York: Russell Sage Foundation.

Kohlberg, L. (1968, April). The child as a moral philosopher. *Psychology Today, 2*(4), 25–30.

Kohlberg, L. (1981). *The philosophy of moral development.* New York: Harper & Row.

Köhler, W. (1925). *The mentality of apes.* New York: Harcourt Brace Jovanovich.

Köhler, W. (1947). *Gestalt psychology* (2nd ed.). New York: LiveRight.

Kohn, P. M., Barnes, G. E., & Hoffman, F. M. (1979). Drug-use history and experience seeking among adult male correctional inmates. *Journal of Consulting and Clinical Psychology, 47,* 708–715.

Kohn, S. J., & Smith, G. C. (2003). The impact of downward social comparison processes on depressive symptoms in older men and women. *Ageing International, 28,* 37–65.

Kohout, J. (2001, February). Facts and figures: Who's earning those psychology degrees? *Monitor on Psychology, 32*(2). Retrieved October 14, 2004, from www.apa.org/monitor/feb01/facts.html.

Kohout, J., & Wicherski, M. (2000, December). Where are the new psychologists working? *Monitor on Psychology,* 13.

Kolb, B. (1989). Development, plasticity, and behavior. *American Psychologist, 44,* 1203–1212.

Koltko-Rivera, M. E. (2006). Redisovering the later version of Maslow's hierarchy of needs: Self-transcendence and opportunities for theory, research, and unification. *Review of General Psychology, 10,* 302–317.

Kopta, S. M., Lueger, R. J., Saunders, S. M., & Howard, K. I. (1999). Individual psychotherapy outcome and process research: Challenges leading to greater turmoil or a positive transition? *Annual Review of Psychology, 30,* 441–469.

Kosko, B., & Isaka, S. (1993, July). Fuzzy logic. *Scientific American, 269,* 76–81.

Kosslyn, S. M. (1976). Can imagery be distinguished from other forms of internal representation? Evidence from studies of information retrieval times. *Memory and Cognition, 4,* 291–297.

Kosslyn, S. M., Cacioppo, J. T., Davidson, R. J., Hugdahl, K., Lovallo, W. R., Speigel, D., & Rose, R. (2002). Bridging psychology and biology: The analysis of individuals in groups. *American Psychologist, 57,* 341–351. [See also: Davidson, 1992a, b; 2000a, b; Heller et al., 1998.]

Kotchoubey, B. (2002). Do event-related brain potentials reflect mental (cognitive) operations? *Journal of Psychophysiology, 16,* 129–149.

Koyama, T., McHaffie, J. G., Laurienti, P. J., & Coghill, R. C. (2005, September 6). The subjective experience of pain: Where expectations become reality. *Proceedings of the National Academy of Sciences, 102,* 12950–12955.

Krackow, A., & Blass, T. (1995). When nurses obey or defy inappropriate physician orders: Attributional differences. *Journal of Social Behavior and Personality, 10,* 585–594.

Krakovsky, M. (2005, February 2). Dubious "Mozart effect" remains music to many Americans' ears. *Stanford Report.* Retrieved September 7, 2008, from http://news-service.stanford.edu/news/2005/february2/mozart-020205.html.

Krakovsky, M. (2007, February). Unsettled scores. *Scientific American, 296*(2), 13–14.

Kramer, P. D. (1993). *Listening to Prozac: A psychiatrist explores antidepressant drugs and the remaking of the self.* New York: Viking.

Krampe, R. T., & Ericsson, K. A. (1996). Maintaining excellence: Deliberate practice and elite performance in young and older pianists. *Journal of Experimental Psychology: General, 125,* 331–359.

Krantz, D. S., Grunberg, N. E., & Baum, A. (1985). Health psychology. *Annual Review of Psychology, 36,* 349–383.

Krätzig, G. P., & Arbuthnott, K. D. (2006). Perceptual learning style and learning proficiency: A Test of the Hypothesis. *Journal of Educational Psychology, 98,* 238–246.

Kringen, J. A. (2006, April 3). How we've improved intelligence: Minimizing the risk of "groupthink." Editorial. *Washington Post,* p. A19.

Krueger, R. F., & Markon, K. E. (2006). Understanding psychopathology: Melding behavior genetics, personality, and quantitative psychology to develop an empirically based mode. *Current Directions in Psychological Science, 15,* 113–117.

Kuiper, N. A., et. al. (1993). Coping humor, stress, and cognitive appraisals. *Canadian Journal of Behavioral Science, 25*(1), 81–96.

Kukla, A. (1989). Nonempirical issues in psychology. *American Psychologist, 44,* 785–794.

Kurdek, L. A. (2005). What do we know about gay and lesbian couples? *Current Directions in Psychological Science, 14,* 251–254.

Kurth, S., Ringluim M., Geiger, A., LeBourgeois, M., Jennie, O. G., & Huber, R. (2010). Mapping of cortical activity in the first two decades of life: A high-density sleep electroencephalogram study. *Journal of Neuroscience, 30*(40), 13211–13219.

Lacey, M., & Herszenhorn, D. M. (2011, January 8). In attack's wake, political repercussions. *New York Times.* Retrieved from www.nytimes.com/2011/01/09/us/politics/09giffords.html?_r=1.

Lachman, M. E., & Weaver, S. L. (1998). The sense of control as a moderator of social class differences in health and well-being. *Journal of Personality and Social Psychology, 74,* 763–773.

Lachman, R., Lachman, J. L., & Butterfield, E. C. (1979). *Cognitive psychology and information processing: An introduction.* Hillsdale, NJ: Erlbaum.

Lama, D. (His Holiness). (2007). *How to see yourself as you really are* (J. Hopkins, Trans.). New York: Simon & Schuster.

Lamb, M. E. (1999, May/June). Mary D. Salter Ainsworth, 1913–1999, attachment theorist. *APS Observer, 32,* 34–35.

Lambo, T. A. (1978). Psychotherapy in Africa. *Human Nature, 1*(3), 32–39.

Landesman, S., & Butterfield, E. C. (1987). Normalization and deinstitutionalization of mentally retarded individuals: Controversy and facts. *American Psychologist, 42,* 809–816.

Landry, D. W. (1997, February). Immunotherapy for cocaine addiction. *Scientific American, 276*(2), 42–45.

Lane, E. (2006, July 28). Neuroscience in the courts—A revolution in justice? *Science, 313,* 458.

Lang, F. R., & Carstensen, L. L. (1994). Close emotional relationships in late life: Further support for proactive aging in the social domain. *Psychology and Aging, 9,* 315–324.

Lang, P. J., & Lazovik, D. A. (1963). The experimental desensitization of a phobia. *Journal of Abnormal and Social Psychology, 66,* 519–525.

Langens, T. A. (2003). Daydreaming mediates between goal commitment and goal attainment in individuals high in achievement motivation. *Imagination, Cognition and Personality, 22*(2), 103–115.

Langleben, D. D., Schroeder, L., Maldjian, J. A., Gur, R. C., McDonald, S., Ragland, J. D., O'Brien, C. P., & Childress, A. R. (2002). Brain activity during imulated deception: An event-related functional magnetic resonance study. *NeuroImage, 15,* 727–732.

Langlois, J. H., Roggman, L. A., Casey, R. J., Ritter, J. M., Rieser-Danner, L. A., & Jenkins, V. Y. (1987). Infant preferences for attractive faces: Rudiments of a stereotype. *Developmental Psychology, 23,* 363–369.

Larson, R. W. (2001). How U.S. children and adolescents spend time: What it does (and doesn't) tell us about their development. *Current Directions in Psychological Science, 10,* 160–164.

Lash, J. (2001). Dealing with the tinder as well as the flint. *Science, 294,* 1789.

Latané, B., & Darley, J. M. (1968). Group inhibition of bystander intervention in emergencies. *Journal of Personality and Social Psychology, 10,* 215–221.

Laumann, E. O., Gagnon, J. H., Michael, R. T., & Michaels, S. (1994). *The social organization of sexuality: Sexual practices in the United States.* Chicago: University of Chicago Press.

Lazarus, R. S. (1981, July). Little hassles can be hazardous to your health. *Psychology Today,* 58–62.

Lazarus, R. S. (1984). On the primacy of cognition. *American Psychologist, 39,* 124–129.

Lazarus, R. S. (1999). *Stress and emotion: A new synthesis.* London, UK: Free Association Press.

Lazarus, R. S., DeLongis, A., Folkman, S., & Gruen, R. (1985). Stress and adaptational outcomes: The problem of confounded measures. *American Psychologist, 40,* 770–779.

Leach, A. (2010, November 16). *The problem with cyber-bullying is the bullying not the cyber bit, says social researcher Danah Boyd.* www.shinyshiny.tv/2010/11/social_researcher_cyber_bullying.html.

Leaper, C., Anderson, K. J., & Sanders, P. (1998). Moderators of gender effects on parents' talk to their children: A meta-analysis. *Developmental Psychologist, 34,* 3–27.

Learman, L. A., Avorn, J., Everitt, D. E., Rosenthal, R. (1990, July). Pygmalion in the nursing home. The effects of caregiver expectations on patient outcomes. *Journal of American Geriatrics Society, 38*(7), 797–803.

LeDoux, J. (2002). *Synaptic self: How our brains become who we are.* New York: Viking. [See also: Canli et al., 2002; Carpenter, 2001a; Craik et al., 1999; Davidson, 2002; Zuckerman, 1995]

LeDoux, J. E. (1994). Emotion, memory and the brain. *Scientific American, 270*(6), 50–57.

LeDoux, J. E. (1996). *The emotional brain: The mysterious underpinnings of emotional life.* New York: Simon & Schuster. [See also Barinaga, 1996; Singer, 1995.]

LeDoux, J. E. (2000). Emotion circuits in the brain. *Annual Review of Neuroscience, 23,* 155–184.

Lee, J. L. (2009, August 29). What do you see? *Science News, 176*(5), 22–25.

Lehrer, J. (2010, December, 11/12) Are heroes born, or can they be are made? *Wall Street Journal,* p. C12. Retrieved from http://online.wsj.com/article/SB10001424052748704156304576003963233286324.html.

Leichtman, M. D. (2006). Cultural and maturational influences on long-term event memory. In C. Tamis-LeMonda & L. Balter (Eds.), *Child psychology: A handbook of contemporary issues* (2nd ed.). Philadelphia, PA: Psychology Press.

Lefcourt, H. M. (2000). *Humor: The psychology of living buoyantly.* Kluwer.

Lensing, V. (2001). Grief support: The role of funeral service. *Journal of Loss and Trauma, 6,* 45–63.

Leonard, J. (1998, May–June). Dream-catchers: Understanding the biological basis of things that go bump in the night. *Harvard Magazine, 100,* 58–68.

Lepper, M. R., Greene, D., & Nisbett, R. E. (1973). Undermining children's intrinsic interest with extrinsic reward: A test of the over-justification hypothesis. *Journal of Personality and Social Psychology, 28*(1), 129–137.

Lerner, R. M., Orlos, J. R., & Knapp, J. (1976). Physical attractiveness, physical effectiveness and self-concept in adolescents. *Adolescence, 11,* 313–326.

Lesgold, A. (1988). Problem solving. In R. J. Sternberg & E. E. Smith (Eds.), *The psychology of human thought.* New York: Cambridge University Press.

Leshner, A. I. (1997, October 3). Addiction is a brain disease, and it matters. *Science, 278,* 45–47.

Leslie, M. (2000, July/August). The vexing legacy of Lewis Terman. *Stanford, 28*(4), 44–51.

Levenson, R. W. (1992). Autonomic nervous system differences among emotions. *Psychological Science, 3,* 23–27.

Leventhal, H., & Tomarken, A. J. (1986). Emotion: Today's problems. *Annual Review of Psychology, 37,* 565–610.

Levine, K., Shane, H. C., & Wharton, R. H. (1994). What if . . . : A plea to professionals to consider the risk–benefit ratio of facilitated communication. *Mental Retardation, 32*(4), 300–304.

Levine, L. J. (1997). Reconstructing memory for emotions. *Journal of Experimental Psychology: General, 126,* 165–177.

Levine, L. J., & Bluck, S. (2004). Painting with broad strokes: Happiness and the malleability of event memory. *Cognition & Emotion, 18,* 559–574.

Levine, L. J., & Safer, M. A. (2002). Sources of bias in memory for emotions. *Current Directions in Psychological Science, 11,* 169–173.

Levine, M., & Perkins, D. V. (1987). *Principles of community psychology: Perspectives and applications.* New York: Oxford University Press.

Levinson, D. J. (1978). *The seasons of a man's life.* New York: Knopf.

Levinson, D. J. (1986). A conception of adult development. *American Psychologist, 41*(1), 3–13.

Levinson, D. J. (1996). *The seasons of a woman's life.* New York: Knopf.

Levinthal, C. F. (2008). *Drugs, behavior, and modern society.* Boston: Pearson Education.

Levitt, S. D., & Dubner, S. J. (2005). *Freakonomics: A rogue economist explores the hidden side of everything.* New York: HarperCollins.

Levy, S. R., Stroessner, S. J., & Dweck, C. S. (1998). Stereotype formation and endorsement: The role of implicit theories. *Journal of Personality and Social Psychology, 74,* 1421–1436.

Lewinsohn, P. M., Clarke, G. N., Hops, H., & Andrews, J. A. (1990). Cognitive-behavioral treatment for depressed adolescents. *Behavior Therapy, 21,* 385–401.

Lewinsohn, P. M., & Gotlib, I. H. (1995). Behavioral theory and treatment of depression. In E. E. Beckham, & W. R. Leber (Eds.), *Handbook of depression* (2nd ed., pp. 352–375). New York: Guilford Press.

Lewinsohn, P. M., Sullivan, J. M., & Grosscup, S. J. (1980). Changing reinforcing events: An approach to the treatment of depression. *Psychotherapy: Theory, Research and Practice, 17,* 322–334.

Lewis, T. L., & Maurer, D. (2005). Multiple sensitive periods in human visual development: Evidence from visually deprived children. *Developmental Psychobiology, 46,* 163–183.

Lewy, A. J., Lefler, B. J., Emens, J. S., & Bauer, V. K. (2006). The circadian basis of winter depression. *PNAS Proceedings of the National Academy of Sciences of the United States of America, 103,* 7414–7419. [See also Wehr & Rosenthal, 1989]

Ley, R. (1990). *A whisper of espionage; Wolfgang Kohler and the apes of Tenerife.* Garden City Park, NY: Avery Publishing Group Inc.

Li, J. (2005). Mind or virtue: Western and Chinese beliefs about learning. *Current Directions in Psychological Science, 14,* 190–194.

Lieberman, J. A., Stroup, T. S., McEvoy, J. P., Schwartz, M. S., Rosenheck, R. A., Perkins, D. O., Keefe, R. S. E., Davis, S. M., Davis, C. E., Lebowitz, B. D., Severe, J., & Hsiao, J. K. (2005). Effectiveness of antipsychotic drugs in patients with chronic schizophrenia. *The New England Journal of Medicine, 353,* 1209–1223.

Lieberman, M. D., & Rosenthal, R. (2001). Why introverts can't always tell who likes them: Multitasking and nonverbal decoding. *Journal of Personality and Social Psychology, 80,* 294–310.

Liegeois, F., Baldeweg, T., Connelly, A., Gadian, D. G., Mishkin, M., & Vargha-Khadem, F. (2001). Language fMRI abnormalities associated with FOXP2 gene mutation. *Nature Neuroscience, 11,* 1230–1237.

Liem, R., & Rayman, P. (1982). Health and social costs of unemployment: Research and policy considerations. *American Psychologist, 37,* 1116–1123.

Light, K. C., Grewen, K. M., & Amico, J. A. (2005). More frequent partner hugs and higher oxytocin levels are linked to lower blood pressure and heart rate in premenopausal women. *Biological Psychology, 69,* 5–21.

Lilienfeld, S. O. (2007). Psychological treatments that cause harm. *Perspectives on Psychological Science, 2,* 53–70. doi: 10.1111/j.1745-6916.2007.00029.x.

Lilienfeld, S. O., & Arkowitz, H. (2009, November/December). Foreign afflictions: Do psychological disorders differ across cultures? *Scientific American Mind, 20*(6), 68–69.

Lilienfeld, S. O., Lynn, S. J., Ruscio, J., & Beyerstein, B. L. (2010). *50 great myths of popular psychology.* West Sussex, UK: Wiley-Blackwell.

Lillard, A. (1999). Developing a cultural theory of mind: The CIAO approach. *Current Directions in Psychological Science, 8,* 57–61.

Lillard, A. S. (1997). Other folks' theories of mind and behavior. *Psychological Science, 8,* 268–274. [See also: Miller, 1984; Morris & Peng, 1994]

Linebarger, D. L., Kosanic, A. Z., Greenwood, C. R., & Docku, N. S. (2004). Effects of viewing the television program "Between the Lions" on the emergent literacy skills of young children. *Journal of Educational Psychology, 96,* 297–308.

Lipsey, M. W., & Wilson, D. B. (1993). The efficacy of psychological, educational, and behavioral treatment: Confirmation from meta-analysis. *American Psychologist, 48,* 1181–1209.

Lipsitt, L. P., Reilly, B., Butcher, M. G., & Greenwood, M. M. (1976). The stability and interrelationships of newborn sucking and heart rate. *Developmental Psychobiology, 9,* 305–310.

Liu, W., Vichienchom, K., Clements, M., DeMarco, S. C., Hughes, C., McGucken, E., Humayun, M. S., De Juan, E., Weiland, J. D., & Greenberg, R. (2000, October). A neuro-stimulus chip with telemetry unit for retinal prosthetic device. *IEEE Journal of Solid-State Circuits, 35,* 1487–1497.

Liu, Z., Richmond, B. J., Murray, E. A., Saunders, R. C., Steenrod, S., & Stubblefield, B. K. (2004, August 9). DNA targeting of rhinal cortex D2 receptor protein reversible blocks learning of cues that predict reward. *PNAS Online, 101*(33). Retrieved from www.pnas.org/cgi/content/full/101/33/12336?hits=10&FIRSTINDEX=0&FULLTEXT=rhinal+cortex+D2+receptor&SEARCHID=1094432333655_2912&gca=pnas%3B101%2F33%2F12336&.

Loftus, E. F. (1979). *Eyewitness testimony.* Cambridge, MA: Harvard University Press.

Loftus, E. F. (1984). The eyewitness on trial. In B. D. Sales & A. Alwork (Eds.), *With liberty and justice for all.* Englewood Cliffs, NJ: Prentice Hall.

Loftus, E. F. (1997). Creating false memories. *Scientific American, 277,* 70–75. Retrieved from http://faculty.washington.edu/eloftus/Articles/sciam.htm.

Loftus, E. F. (2003a). Make-believe memories. *American Psychologist, 58,* 867–873. [See also: Hyman et al., 1995; Loftus, 1997a, 1997b; Loftus & Ketcham, 1994.]

Loftus, E. F. (2003b). Our changeable memories: Legal and practical implications. *Nature Reviews: Neuroscience, 4,* 231–234.

Loftus, E. F., & Ketcham, K. (1994). *The myth of repressed memory: False memories and allegations of sexual abuse.* New York: St. Martin's Griffin. [See also: Loftus, 1993; Ofshe & Watters, 1994]

Loftus, E. F., & Klinger, M. R. (1992). Is the unconscious smart or dumb? *American Psychologist, 47,* 761–765.

Loftus, E. F., & Palmer, J. C. (1973). Reconstruction of automobile destruction: An example of the interaction between language and memory. *Journal of Verbal Learning and Verbal Behavior, 13,* 585–589.

Lonner, W. J., & Malpass, R. (1994). *Psychology and culture.* Boston: Allyn & Bacon.

Lourenço, O., & Machado, A. (1996). In defense of Piaget's theory: A reply to 10 common criticisms. *Psychological Review, 103,* 143–164.

Lovibond, S. H., Adams, M., & Adams, W. G. (1979). The effects of three experimental prison environments on the behavior of nonconflict volunteer subjects. *Australian Psychologist, 14,* 273–285.

Luborsky, L., Singer, B., & Luborsky, L. (1975). Comparative studies of psycho therapies: Is it true that everyone has won and all must have prizes? *Archives of General Psychiatry, 32,* 995–1008.

Lykken, D., & Tellegen, A. (1996). Happiness is a stochastic phenomenon. *Psychological Science, 7,* 186–189.

Lykken, D. T., McGue, M., Tellegen, A., & Bouchard, T. J. (1992). Emergenesis: Genetic traits that may not run in families. *American Psychologist, 47,* 1565–1577.

Lytton, H., & Romney, D. M. (1991). Parents' differential socialization of boys and girls: A meta-analysis. *Psychological Bulletin, 109,* 267–296.

Lyubomirsky, S. (2007). *The how of happiness: A scientific approach to getting the life you want.* New York: Penguin Press.

Lyubomirsky, S., & Boehm, J. K. (2010). Human motives, happiness, and the puzzle of parenthood: Commentary on Kenrick et al. (2010). *Perspectives on Psychological Science, 5,* 327–334.

Maas, J. B. (1999). *Power sleep: The revolutionary program that prepares your mind for peak performance.* New York: HarperPerennial.

Maccoby, E. (1998). *The two sexes: Growing up apart, coming together.* Cambridge, MA: Belknap Press.

Maccoby, E. (2000). *Gender differentiation in childhood: Broad patterns and their implications.* Address given at the American Psychological Association annual convention, Washington, DC.

Maccoby, E. E., & Martin, J. A. (1983). Socialization in the context of the family: Parent–child interaction. In E. M. Hetherington (Ed.), *Handbook of child psychology: Vol. 4, Socialization, personality, and social development* (4th ed., pp. 1–101). New York: Wiley.

Maccoby, N., Farquhar, J. W., Wood, P. D., & Alexander, J. K. (1977). Reducing the risk of cardiovascular disease: Effects of a community-based campaign on knowledge and behavior. *Journal of Community Health, 3,* 100–114.

MacCoun, R. J. (1998). Toward a psychology of harm reduction. *American Psychologist, 53,* 1199–1208.

Macmillan, J. C. (2000). *An odd kind of fame: Stories of Phineas Gage.* Cambridge, MA: MIT Press.

Macrae, C. N., Milne, A. B., & Bodenhausen, G. V. (1994). Stereotypes as energy-saving devices: A peek inside the cognitive toolbox. *Journal of Personality and Social Psychology, 66,* 37–47.

Maddi, S. R. (1987). Hardiness training at Illinois Bell Telephone. In J. P. Opatz (Ed.), *Health promotion evaluation* (pp. 101–115). Stevens Point, WI: National Wellness Institute.

Maddi, S. R. (2002). The story of hardiness: Twenty years of theorizing, research and practice. *Consulting Psychology Journal, 54,* 173–185.

Maguire, E. A., Spiers, H. J., Good, C. D., Hartley, T., Frackowiak, R. S., & Burgess, N. (2003). Navigation expertise and the human hippocampus: A structural brain imaging analysis. *Hippocampus, 13,* 250–259.

Maher, B. A., & Maher, W. B. (1985). Psychopathology: II. From the eighteenth century to modern times. In G. A. Kimble & K. Schlesinger (Eds.), *Topics in the history of psychology* (Vol. 2, pp. 295–329). Hillsdale, NJ: Erlbaum.

Maier, S. F., & Watkins, L. R. (1999). Bidirectional communication between the brain and the immune system: Implications for behaviour. *Animal Behaviour, 57,* 741–751.

Maier, S. F., & Watkins, L. R. (2000). The immune system as a sensory system: Implications for psychology. *Current Directions in Psychological Science, 9,* 98–102.

Maisto, S. A., Galizio, M., & Connors, G. J. (1995). *Drug use and abuse* (2nd ed.). Fort Worth, TX: Harcourt Brace.

Malatesta, V. J., Sutker, P. B., & Treiber, F. A. (1981). Sensation seeking and chronic public drunkenness. *Journal of Consulting and Clinical Psychology, 49,* 282–294.

Malitz, S., & Sackheim, H. A. (1984). Low dosage ECT: Electrode placement and acute physiological and cognitive effects. *American Journal of Social Psychiatry, 4,* 47–53.

Manfredi, M., Bini, G., Cruccu, G., Accor nero, N., Beradelli, A., & Medolago, L. (1981). Congenital absence of pain. *Archives of Neurology, 38,* 507–511.

Mann, T., Tomiyama, A. J., Westling, E., Lew, A., Samuels, B., & Chatman, J. (2007). Medicare's search for effective obesity treatments: Diets are not the answer. *American Psychologist, 62,* 220–233.

Manning, R., Levine, M., & Collins, A. (2007). The Kitty Genovese murder and the social psychology of helping. *American Psychologist, 62,* 555–562.

Maquet, P. (2001, November 2). The role of sleep in learning and memory. *Science, 294,* 1048–1052.

Marcotty, J. (2010, September 22). "Savior sibling" raises a decade of life-and-death questions. *Star Tribune.* Retrieved November 20, 2010, from Center for Genetics and Society www.geneticsandsociety.org/article.php?id=5388

Marcus, G. B. (1986). Stability and change in political attitudes: Observe, recall, and "explain." *Political Behavior, 8,* 21–44.

Marcus, G. F. (1996). Why do children say "breaked"? *Current Directions in Psychological Science, 3,* 81–85.

Markman, H. J., & Notarius, C. I. (1993). *We can work it out.* Berkeley, CA: Berkeley Publishing Group.

Marks, J. (2004, June). Ask *Discover:* How closely related are people to each other? And how closely does our genome match up with those of other primates? *Discover, 25*(6), 17.

Markus, H. R., & Kitayama, S. (1994). The cultural construction of self and emotion: Implications for social behavior. In H. R. Markus & S. Kitayama (Eds.), *Emotion and culture: Empirical studies of mutual influence* (pp. 89–130). Washington, DC: American Psychological Association.

Markus, H. R., Uchida, Y., Omoregie, H., Townsend, S. S. M., & Kitayama, S. (2006). Going for the gold: Models of agency in Japanese and American contexts. *Psychological Science, 17,* 103–112.

Marschall, J. (2007, February/March). Seduced by sleep. *Scientific American Mind, 18*(1), 52–57.

Marsh, H. W., Hau, K. T., Sung, R. Y. T., & Yu, C. W. (2007). Childhood obesity, gender, actual–ideal body image discrepancies, and physical self-concept in Hong Kong children: Cultural differences in the value of moderation. *Developmental Psychology, 43,* 647–662.

Marsh, P. (1988). Detecting insincerity. In P. Marsh (Ed.), *Eye to eye: How people interact.* (Ch. 14, pp. 116–119). Oxford, UK: Oxford Andromeda.

Martin, D. J., Garske, J. P., & Davis, M. K. (2000). Relation of the therapeutic alliance with outcome and other variables: A meta-analytic review. *Journal of Consulting and Clinical Psychology, 68,* 438–450.

Martin, G., & Pear, J. (1999). *Behavior modification: What it is and how to do it* (6th ed.). Upper Saddle River, NJ: Prentice Hall.

Martin, J. A. (1981). A longitudinal study of the consequences of early mother–infant interaction: A microanalytic approach. *Monographs of the Society for Research in Child Development, 46* (203, Serial No. 190).

Martinez-Conde, S., & Macknik, S. L. (2008, December). Magic and the brain. *Scientific American, 299*(6), 72–79.

Martins, Y., Preti, G., Crabtree, C. R., Runyan, T., Vainius, A. A., & Wysocki, C. J. (2005). Preference for human body odors is influenced by gender and sexual orientation. *Psychological Science, 16,* 694–701.

Maruyama, G., & Miller, N. (1975). *Physical attractiveness and classroom acceptance (Research Report 75-2).* Los Angeles: University of Southern California, Social Science Research Institute.

Marx, J. (2004, July 16). Prolonging the agony. *Science, 305,* 326–329.

Marx, J. (2005). Preventing Alzheimer's: A lifelong commitment? *Science, 309,* 864–866.

Marx, J. (2006, January 20). Drugs inspired by a drug. *Science, 311,* 322–325.

Maslach, C. (1998, April). *The truth about burnout.* The G. Stanley Hall Lecture given at the Western Psychological Association convention in Albuquerque, NM.

Maslach, C. (2003). Job burnout: New directions in research and intervention. *Current Directions in Psychological Science, 12,* 189–192.

Maslach, C., & Goldberg, J. (1998). Prevention of burnout: New perspectives. *Applied and Preventive Psychology, 7,* 63–74.

Maslach, C., & Leiter, M. P. (1997). *The truth about burnout: How organizations cause personal stress and what to do about it.* San Francisco: Jossey-Bass Publishers.

Maslach, C., & Leiter, M. P. (2005). Stress and burnout: The critical research. In C. L. Cooper (Ed.), *Handbook of stress medicine and health* (2nd ed., pp. 153–170). Boca Raton, FL: CRC Press LLC.

Maslach, C., & Leiter, M. P. (2008). Early predictors of job burnout and engagement. *Journal of Applied Psychology, 93,* 498–512.

Maslach, C., Schaufeli, W. B., & Leiter, M. P. (2001). Job burnout. *Annual Review of Psychology, 52,* 397–422.

Maslow, A. (1943). A theory of human motivation. *Psychological Review, 50,* 370–396. Retrieved April 4, 2008, from http://psychclassics.yorku.ca/Maslow/motivation.htm.

Maslow, A. H. (1968). *Toward a psychology of being* (2nd ed.). New York: Van Nostrand.

Maslow, A. H. (1970). *Motivation and personality* (Rev. ed.). New York: Harper & Row.

Maslow, A. H. (1971). *Farther reaches of human nature.* New York: Viking Penguin.

Mason, M. F., Norton, M. I., Van Horn, J. D., Wegner, D. M., Grafton, S. T., & Macrae, C. N. (2007, January 19). Wandering minds: The default network and stimulus-independent thought. *Science, 315*, 393–395.

Massimini, M., Ferrarelli, F., Huber, R., Esser, S. K., Singh, H., & Tononi, G. (2005, September 30). Breakdown of cortical effective connectivity during sleep. *Science, 309*, 2228–2232. [See also: Miller, 2005; Roser & Gazzaniga, 2004.]

Masten, A. S. (2001). Ordinary magic: Resilience processes in development. *American Psychologist, 56*, 227–238.

Masters, W. H., & Johnson, V. E. (1966). *Human sexual response.* Boston: Little, Brown.

Masters, W. H., & Johnson, V. E. (1970). *Human sexual inadequacy.* Boston: Little, Brown.

Masters, W. H., & Johnson, V. E. (1979). *Homo sexuality in perspective.* Boston: Little, Brown.

Matarazzo, J. D. (1980). Behavioral health and behavioral medicine: Frontiers for a new health psychology. *American Psychologist, 35*, 807–817.

Mather, M. (2007). Emotional arousal and memory binding: An object-based framework. *Perspectives on Psychological Science, 2*, 33–52.

Matossian, M. K. (1982). Ergot and the Salem witch-craft affair. *American Scientist, 70*, 355–357.

Matossian, M. K. (1989). *Poisons of the past: Molds, epidemics, and history.* New Haven, CT: Yale University Press.

Matsumoto, D. (1996). *Culture and psychology.* Pacific Grove, CA: Brooks/Cole. [See also: Jenkins, 1994; Manson, 1994]

Matthews, K. A. (1982). Psychological perspectives on the Type-A behavior pattern. *Psychological Bulletin, 91*, 293–323.

Matthews, K. A., Woodall, K. L., Kenyon, K., & Jacob, T. (1996). Negative family environment as a predictor of boys' future status on measures of hostile attitudes, interview behavior, and anger expression. *Health Psychology, 15*, 30–37.

Mauron, A. (2001, February 2). Is the genome the sec-ular equivalent of the soul? *Science, 291*, 831–833.

May, R. (1996). *The meaning of anxiety.* New York: Norton.

Mayberg, H. S. (2006). Defining neurocircuits in depression. *Psychiatric Annals, 36*, 259–268.

Mayberg, H. S. (2009). Targeted electrode-based modulation of neural circuits for depression. *Journal of Clinical Investigation, 119*, 717–725. Retrieved July 4, 2011, from www.jci.org/articles/view/38454.

Mayberg, H. S., Lozano, A. M., Voon, V., McNeely, H. E., Seminowicz, D., Hamani, C., Schwalb, J. M., & Kennedy, S. H. (2005, March 3). Deep brain stimula-tion for treatment-resistant depression. *Neuron, 45*, 651–660.

Mayberry, R. I. (1991). The importance of childhood to language acquisition: Evidence from American Sign Language. In J. C. Goodman & H. C. Nusbaum (Eds.). *The development of speech perception: The transition from speech sounds to spoken words* (pp. 57–90) Cambridge, MA: MIT Press.

Mayr, E. (2000, July). Darwin's influence on modern thought. *Scientific American, 283*(1), 79–83.

McAdams, D. P. (1992). The five-factor model in per-sonality: A critical appraisal. *Journal of Personality, 60*, 239–361.

McAdams, D. P. (2006). *The redemptive self: Stories Americans live by.* New York: Oxford University Press.

McAdams, D. P., & Pals, J. L. (2006). A new Big Five: Fundamental principles for an integrative science of personality. *American Psychologist, 61*, 204–217.

McAdams, D. P., de St. Aubin, E., & Logan, R. L. (1993). Generativity among young, midlife, and older adults. *Psychology and Aging, 8*, 221–230.

McAnulty, R. D., & Burnette, M. M. (2004). *Exploring human sexuality: Making healthy decisions* (2nd ed.). Boston: Allyn & Bacon.

McArdle, J. J., Ferrer-Caja, E. Hamagami, F., & Woodcock, R. W. (2002). Comparative longitudinal structural analyses of the growth and decline of multiple intellectual abilities over the life span. *Develop mental Psychology, 38*, 115–142.

McCann, I. L., & Holmes, D. S. (1984). Influence of aerobic exercise on depression. *Journal of Personality and Social Psychology, 46*, 1142–1147.

McCann, I. L., & Pearlman, L. A. (1990). Vicarious traumatization: A framework for understanding the psychological effects of working with victims. *Journal of Traumatic Stress, 3*, 131–149.

McCarley, N., & Carskadon, T. G. (1983). Test–retest reliabilities of scales and subscales of the Myers–Briggs Type Indicator and of criteria for clinical interpretive hypotheses involving them. *Research in Psychological Type, 6*, 24–36.

McCarthy, K. (1991, August). Moods—good and bad—color all aspects of life. *APA Monitor, 13.*

McCartney, K., Harris, M. J., & Bernieri, F. (1990). Growing up and growing apart: A developmental meta-analysis of twin studies. *Psychological Bulletin, 107*, 226–237.

McClelland, D. C. (1958). Methods of measuring human motivation. In J. W. Atkinson (Ed.), *Motives in fantasy, action and society.* Princeton, NJ: D. Van Nostrand.

McClelland, D. C. (1965). Achievement and entrepreneurship: A longitudinal study. *Journal of Personality and Social Psychology, 1*, 389–392.

McClelland, D. C. (1975). *Power: The inner experi-ence.* New York: Irvington.

McClelland, D. C. (1985). *Human motivation.* New York: Scott Foresman.

McClelland, D. C. (1987a). Characteristics of success-ful entrepreneurs. *The Journal of Creative Behavior, 21*, 219–233.

McClelland, D. C. (1987b). *Human motivation.* New York: Cambridge University Press. [See also: Cooper, 1983; French & Thomas, 1958]

McClelland, D. C. (1993). Intelligence is not the best predictor of job performance. *Current Directions in Psychological Science, 2*, 5–6.

McClelland, D. C., & Boyatzis, R. E. (1982). Lead-ership motive pattern and long-term success in management. *Journal of Applied Psychology, 67*, 737–743.

McClure, S. M., Laibson, D. I., Loewenstein, G., & Cohen, J. D. (2004). Separate neural systems value immediate and delayed monetary rewards. *Science, 306*, 503–507.

McCook, A. (2006, July 24). Conflicts of interest at federal agencies. *TheScientist.com.* Retrieved October 18, 2007, from www.the-scientist.com/news/display/24056/.

McCrae, R. R., Terraciano, A., & 78 members of the Personality Profiles of Cultures Project. (2005). Universal features of personality traits from the observer's perspective: Data from 50 cultures. *Journal of Personality and Social Psychology, 88*, 547–561.

McCullough, M. L. (2001). Freud's seduction theory and its rehabilitation: A saga of one mistake after another. *Review of General Psychology, 5*, 3–22.

McDonald, K. A. (1998, August 14). Scientists consider new explanations for the impact of exercise on mood. *The Chronicle of Higher Education,* A15–A16.

McGaugh, J. L. (2000, January 14). Memory—A century of consolidation. *Science, 287*, 248–251.

McGlone, M. S., & Aronson, J. (2006). Stereotype threat, identity salience, and spatial reasoning. *Journal of Applied Developmental Psychology, 27*, 486–493.

McGuire, P. A. (2000, February). New hope for people with schizophrenia. *Monitor on Psychology, 31*(2), 24–28.

McGurk, S. R., Mueser, K. T., Feldman, K., Wolfe, R., & Pascaris, A. (2007). Cognitive training for supported employment: 2–3 year outcomes of a randomized controlled trial. *American Journal of Psychiatry, 164*, 437–441. [See also: Butcher et al., 2008]

McHugh, R. K. & Barlow, D. (2010). The dissemina-tion and implementation of evidence-based psychological treatments: A review of current efforts. *American Psychologist, 65*, 73–84.

McIntosh, D. N., Silver, R. C., Wortman, C. B. (1993). Religion's role in adjustment to a negative life event: Coping with the loss of a child. *Journal of Personality and Social Psychology, 65*, 812–821.

McKeachie, W. J. (1990). Research on college teaching: The historical background. *Journal of Educational Psychology, 82*, 189–200.

McKeachie, W. J. (1997). Good teaching makes a difference—and we know what it is. In R. B. Perry & J. C. Smart (Eds.), *Effective teaching in higher education: Research and practice* (pp. 396–408). New York: Agathon Press.

McKeachie, W. J. (1999). *McKeachie's teaching tips: Strategies, research, and theory for college and university teachers* (10th ed.). Boston: Houghton Mifflin.

McLeod, F. (2008, March 8). *Bullying affects girls far more than boys.* Retrieved on September 8, 2008, from http://news.scotsman.com/bullyingatschool/Bullying-affects-girls-far-more.3857607.jp.

McNally, R. J. (1994, August). Cognitive bias in panic disorder. *Current Directions in Psychological Science, 3*, 129–132.

McNally, R. J., Bryant, R. A., & Anke, E. (2003). Does early psychological intervention promote recovery from posttraumatic stress? *Psychological Science in the Public Interest, 4*(2), 45–79. doi: 10.1111/1529-1006.01421.

McNally, R. J., Bryant, R. A., & Ehlers, A. (2003). Does early psychological intervention promote recovery from posttraumatic stress? *Psychology Science in the Public Interest, 4*, 45–79.

McNamara, P., McLaren, D., Smith, D., Brown, A., & Stickgold, R. (2005). A "Jekyll and Hyde" within: Aggressive versus friendly interactions in REM and non-REM dreams. *Psychological Science, 16*, 130–136.

Medin, C., Lynch, J., & Solomon, H. (2000). Are there kinds of concepts? *Annual Review of Psychology, 52*, 121–147.

Medin, D. L., & Ross, B. H. (1992). *Cognitive psychology.* Fort Worth, TX: Harcourt Brace Jovanovich.

Meeus, W. H. J., & Raaijmakers, Q. A. W. (1986). Administrative obedience: Carrying out orders to use psychological-administrative violence. *European Journal of Social Psychology, 16*, 311–324.

Mehl, M. R., Gosling, S. D. & Pennebaker, J. W. (2006). Personality in its natural habitat: Manifes-tations and implicit folk theories of personality in daily life. *Journal of Personality and Social Psychology, 90*, 862–877.

Meichenbaum, D. H., & Cameron, R. (1974). The clinical potential and pitfalls of modifying what clients say to themselves. In M. J. Mahoney & C. E. Thoreson (Eds.), *Self-control: Power to the person* (pp. 263–290). Monterey, CA: Brooks-Cole.

Meier, R. P. (1991). Language acquisition by deaf children. *American Scientist, 79*, 60–70.

Meltzoff, J., & Kornreich, M. (1970). *Research in psychotherapy.* New York: Atherton.

Melzack, R. (1990, February). The tragedy of needless pain. *Scientific American, 262*, 27–33.

Melzack, R., & Wall, P. D. (1965). Pain mechanisms: A new theory. *Science, 150,* 971–979.

Melzack, R., & Wall, P. D. (1983). *The challenge of pain.* New York: Basic Books.

Merari, A. (2006). Psychological aspects of suicidal terrorism. In B. Bongar, L. M. Brown, L. Beutler, J. N. Breckenridge, & P. G. Zimbardo (Eds.), *Psychology and terrorism,* (pp. 101–115). New York: Oxford University Press.

Mercado, C. C. (2006, November). Expert testimony in insanity cases. *Monitor on Psychology, 37*(10), 58.

Meredith, N. (1986, June). Testing the talking cure. *Science 86, 7,* 30–37.

Merikle, P. M., & Reingold, E. M. (1990). Recognition and lexical decision without detection: Unconscious perception? *Journal of Experimental Psychology: Human Perception & Performance, 16,* 574–583.

Mervis, C. B., & Rosch, E. (1981). Categorization of natural objects. *Annual Review of Psychology, 32,* 89–115.

Meyer-Lindenberg, A. (2008, August 8). Trust me on this. *Science, 321,* 778–780.

Meyer-Lindenberg, A. (2009, April/May). Perturbed personalities. *Scientific American Mind, 20*(2), 41–43.

Meyer, S. (n.d.). The story behind *Twilight.* In *The official website of Stephanie Meyer.* Retrieved from www.stepheniemeyer.com/twilight.html.

Meyers, L. (2006, November). Medicate or not? An APA working group reports on use of medications when treating children. *Monitor on Psychology, 37*(10), 24–25.

Meyers, L. (2007, June). Of mind and matter: Understanding consciousness. *Monitor on Psychology, 38*(6), 32–35.

Michael, R. T., Gagnon, J. H., Laumann, E. O., & Kolata, G. (1994). *Sex in America: A definitive survey.* New York: Little, Brown.

Miklowitz, D. J. (2007) The role of the family in the course and treatment of bipolar disorder. *Current Directions in Psychological Science, 16,* 192–196.

Milgram, S. (1965). Some conditions of obedience and disobedience to authority. *Human Relations, 18,* 56–76.

Milgram, S. (1974). *Obedience to authority.* New York: Harper & Row.

Miller, G. (2004, April 2). Learning to forget. *Science, 304,* 34–36.

Miller, G. (2005, May 13). Reflecting on another's mind. *Science, 308,* 945–946.

Miller, G. (2006a, August 4). The emotional brain weighs its options. *Science, 313,* 600–601.

Miller, G. (2006b, May 12). Probing the social brain. *Science, 312,* 838–839.

Miller, G. (2006c, January 27). The unseen: Mental illness's global toll. *Science, 311,* 458–461.

Miller, G. (2007, March 9). Hunting for meaning after midnight. *Science, 315,* 1360–1363.

Miller, G. (2008, September 5). Investigating the psychopathic mind. *Science, 321,* 1284–1286.

Miller, G. A. (1956). The magic number seven plus or minus two: Some limits in our capacity for processing information. *Psychological Review, 63,* 81–97.

Miller, K. E., Barnes, G. M., Sabo, D. F., Melnick, M. J., & Farrell, M. P. (2002). Anabolic-androgenic steroid use and other adolescent problem behaviors: Rethinking the male athlete assumption. *Sociological Perspectives, 45,* 467–489.

Miller, M. W. (1993, December 2). Dark days: The staggering cost of depression. *The Wall Street Journal,* B1.

Miller, N. E. (1983). Behavioral medicine: Symbiosis between laboratory and clinic. *Annual Review of Psychology, 34,* 1–31.

Miller, P. Y., & Simon, W. (1980). The development of sexuality in adolescence. In J. Adelson (Ed.), *Handbook of adolescent psychology.* New York: Wiley.

Miller, S. L., & Maner, J. K. (2010). Scent of a woman: Men's testosterone responses to olfactory ovulation cues. *Psychological Science, 21,* 276–283. doi: 10.1177/0956797609357733.

Miller, W. R., & Brown, S. A. (1997). Why psychologists should treat alcohol and drug problems. *American Psychologist, 52,* 1269–1279.

Milner, B., Corkin, S., & Teuber, H. H. (1968). Further analysis of the hippocampal amnesic syndrome: 14-year follow-up study of H. M. *Neuropsychologia, 6,* 215–234.

Mineka, S., Davidson, M., Cook, M., & Keir, R. (1984). Observational conditioning of snake fear in rhesus monkeys. *Journal of Abnormal Psychology, 93,* 355–372.

Mineka, S., & Zinbarg, R. (2006). A contemporary learning theory perspective on the etiology of anxiety disorders: It's not what you thought it was. *American Psychologist, 61,* 10–26.

Minkel, J. R. (2009, November). Putting madness in its place. *Scientific American, 301*(5), 16, 19.

Mintz, L. B., & Betz, N. E. (1986). Sex differences in the nature, realism, and correlates of body image. *Sex Roles, 15,* 185–195.

Mischel, W. (1968). *Personality and assessment.* New York: Wiley.

Mischel, W. (1973). Toward a cognitive social learning conceptualization of personality. *Psychological Review, 80,* 252–283.

Mischel, W. (1990). Personality dispositions revisited and revised: A view after three decades. In L. A. Pervin (Ed.), *Handbook of personality: Theory and research.* New York: Guilford Press.

Mischel, W. (1993). *Introduction to personality* (5th ed.). Fort Worth, TX: Harcourt Brace Jovanovich College Publishers.

Mischel, W. (2003). Challenging the traditional personality psychology paradigm. In R. J. Sternberg, (Ed.), *Psychologists defying the crowd: Stories of those who battled the establishment and won* (pp. 139–156). Washington, DC: American Psychological Association.

Mischel, W., & Shoda, Y. (1995). A cognitive-affective system theory of personality: Reconceptualizing situations, dispositions, dynamics, and invariance in personality structure. *Psychological Review, 102,* 246–268.

Miyake, A., Kost-Smith, L. E., Finkelstein, N. D., Pollock, S. J., Cohen, G. L., & Ito, T. A. (2010). Reducing the gender achievement gap in college science: A classroom study of values affirmation. *Science, 330,* 1234–1237.

Miyake, K. (1993). Temperament, mother–infant interaction, and early emotional development. *Japanese Journal of Research on Emotions, 1,* 48–55.

Miyake, K., Cen, S., & Campos, J. J. (1985). Infant temperament, mother's mode of interaction, and attachment in Japan: An interim report. In J. Bretherton & E. Waters (Eds.), *Growing points of attachment theory: Monographs of the Society of Research in Child Development, 50* (1-2, Serial No. 209).

Miyashita, Y. (1995). How the brain creates imagery: Projection to primary visual cortex. *Science, 268,* 1719–1720.

Mizukami, K., Kobayashi, N., Ishii, T., & Iwata, H. (1990). First selective attachment begins in early infancy: A study using telethermography. *Infant Behavior and Development, 13,* 257–271.

Mobbs, D., Petrovic, P., Marchant, J. L., Hassabis, D., Weiskopf, N., Seymour, B., Dolan, R. J., & Frith, C. D. (2007, August 24). When fear is near: Threat imminence elicits prefrontal-periaqueductal gray shifts in humans. *Science, 317,* 1079–1083. [See also: Barlow, 2000, 2001; Maren, 2007.]

Moen, P., & Wethington, E. (1999). Midlife development in a life-course context. In S. L. Willis & J. D. Reid (Eds.), *Life in the middle: Psychological and social development in middle age* (pp. 3–25). San Diego, CA: Academic Press.

Moffitt, T. E., Arseneault, L., Belsky, D., Kickson, N., Hancox, R. J., Harrington, H., Houts, R., Poulton, R., Roberts, B., Ross, S., Sears, M. R., Thomson, W. M., & Caspi, A. (2011). A gradient of childhood self-control predicts health, wealth, and public safety. *Proceedings of the National Academy of Sciences, 108*(7), 2693–2698.

Mogelonsky, M. (1996). The rocky road to adulthood. *American Demographics, 18,* 26–36, 56.

Moghaddam, E. (2007). *Multiculturalism and intergroup relations: Psychological implications for democracy.* Washington, DC: APA Press.

Moghaddam, F. M., Taylor, D. M., & Wright, S. C. (1993). *Social psychology in cross-cultural perspective.* New York: W. H. Freeman.

Molden, D. C., & Dweck, C. S. (2006). Finding "meaning" in psychology: A lay theories approach to self-regulation, social perception, and social development. *American Psychologist, 61,* 192–203.

Monaghan, P. (1999, February 26). Lessons from the "marriage lab." *The Chronicle of Higher Education,* A9.

Mones, A. G., Schwartz, R. C. (2007). The functional hypothesis: A family systems contribution toward an understanding of the healing process of the common factors. *Journal of Psychotherapy Integration, 17,* 314–329.

Money, J. (1987). Sin, sickness, or status? Homosexual gender identity and psychoneuroendocrinology. *American Psychologist, 42,* 384–399.

Monroe, S. M., & Reid, M. W. (2009). Life stress and major depression. *Current Directions in Psychological Science, 18,* 68–72.

Monte, C. F. (1980). *Beneath the mask: An introduction to theories of personality* (2nd ed.). New York: Holt, Rinehart and Winston.

Moore, M. K., & Meltzoff, A. M. (2004). Object permanence after a 24-hour delay and leaving the locale of disappearance: The role of memory, space, and identity. *Developmental Psychology, 40,* 606–620.

Moore-Ede, M. (1993). *The twenty-four-hour society: Understanding human limits in a world that never stops.* Reading, MA: Addison-Wesley.

Moran, J. M., Wig, G. S., Adams, R. B., Jr., Janata, P., & Kelley, W. M. (2002). Neural correlates of humor detection and appreciation. *Neuroimage, 21,* 1055–1060.

Morgan, A. H., Hilgard, E. R., & Davert, E. C. (1970). The heritability of hypnotic susceptibility of twins: A preliminary report. *Behavior Genetics, 1,* 213–224.

Mori, K., & Arai, M. (2010, December). Out of the Asch study. *The Psychologist, 23,* 960.

Mori, K., Nagao, H., & Yoshihara, Y. (1999). The olfactory bulb: Coding and processing of odor molecule information. *Science, 286,* 711–715.

Moriarity, T. (1975). Crime, commitment and the responsive bystander: Two field experiments. *Journal of Personality and Social Psychology, 31,* 370–376.

Morrell, E. M. (1986). Meditation and somatic arousal. *American Psychologist, 41*(6), 712–713. [See also: Dillbeck & Orme-Johnson, 1987; Holmes, 1984]

Morris, W. N., & Miller, R. S. (1975). The effects of consensus-breaking and consensus-preempting partners on reduction of conformity. *Journal of Experimental Social Psychology, 11,* 215–223.

Moskowitz, C. (2009). Teen brains clear out childhood thoughts. *LiveScience*, March 23, 2009. Retrieved from www.livescience.com/3435-teen-brains-clear-childhood-thoughts.html.

Moss, R. (1996). *Conscious dreaming: A spiritual path to everyday life.* New York: Crown Publishing.

Mowrer, O. H., & Mowrer, W. M. (1938). Enuresis—a method for its study and treatment. *American Journal of Orthopsychiatry, 8,* 436–459.

Mroczek, D. K. (2001). Age and emotion in adulthood. *Current Directions in Psychological Science, 10,* 87–90.

MTA Cooperative Group. (1999). A fourteen-month randomized clinical trial of treatment strategies for attention-deficit/hyperactivity disorder. *Archives of General Psychiatry, 56,* 1073–1086.

MTA Cooperative Treatment Group. (2004). National Institute of Mental Health Multimodal Treatment Study of ADHD Follow-up: 24-Month Outcomes of Treatment Strategies for Attention-Deficit/Hyperactivity Disorder. *Pediatrics, 113,* 754–761.

Mueser, K. T., & McGurk, S. R. (2004, June 19). Schizophrenia. *The Lancet, 363,* 2063–2072. doi: 10.1016/S0140-6736(04)16458-1

Muhle R., Trentacoste S. V., & Rapin, I. (2004). The genetics of autism. *Pediatrics, 113*(5), 472–486.

Munakata, Y., McClelland, J. L., Johnson, M. H., & Siegler, R. S. (1997). Rethinking infant knowledge: Toward an adaptive process account of successes and failures in object permanence tasks. *Psychological Review, 104,* 686–713.

Munroe, R. L. (1955). *Schools of psychoanalytic thought.* New York: Dryden.

Munsey, C. (2006, July/August). Frisky, but more risky. *Monitor on Psychology, 37*(7), 40–42.

Munsey, C. (2007). Armor for the mind. *Monitor on Psychology, 38.*

Munsey, C. (2009, October). Insufficient evidence to support sexual orientation change efforts. *Monitor on Psychology, 40*(9), 29.

Murphy, G., & Murphy, L. B. (Eds.). (1968). *Asian psychology.* New York: Basic Books.

Murphy, J. M. (1976, March 12). Psychiatric labeling in cross-cultural perspective. *Science, 191,* 1019–1028.

Murray, B. (1995, October). Americans dream about food, Brazilians dream about sex. *APA Monitor,* 30.

Murray, B. (2002, June). Writing to heal. *APA Monitor,* 54–55.

Murray, H. A. (1938). *Explorations in personality.* New York, NY: Oxford University Press.

Murray, J. P., & Kippax, S. (1979). Children's social behavior in three towns with differing television experience. *Journal of Communication, 28,* 19–29.

Myers, D. G. (2000). The funds, friends, and faith of happy people. *American Psychologist, 55,* 56–67.

Myers, D. G. (2002). *Intuition: Its powers and perils.* New Haven, CT: Yale University Press.

Myers, D. G., & Diener, E. (1995). Who is happy? *Psychological Science, 6,* 10–19.

Myers, I. B., & Myers, P. B. (1995). *Gifts differing: Understanding personality type.* Palo Alto, CA: Consulting Psychologists Press. [See also: Myers, 1962, 1976, 1987.]

Myers, R. S., & Roth, D. L. (1997). Perceived benefits of and barriers to exercise and stage of exercise adoption in young adults. *Health Psychology, 16,* 277–283.

The mysteries of twins. (1998, January 11). *The Washington Post.* Retrieved November 8, 2004, from www.washingtonpost.com/wpsrv/national/longterm/twins/twins2.htm.

Nachson, I., & Zelig, A. (2003). Flashbulb and factual memories: The case of Rabin's assassination. *Applied Cognitive Psychology, 17,* 519–531.

Nahemow, L., & Lawton, M. P. (1975). Similarity and propinquity in friendship formation. *Journal of Personality and Social Psychology, 32,* 205–213.

Naigles, L. (1990). Children use syntax to learn verb meanings. *Child Language, 17,* 357–374.

Naigles, L. G., & Kako, E. T. (1993). First contact in verb acquisition: Defining a role for syntax. *Child Development, 64,* 1665–1687.

Naik, G. (2009, February 12). A baby, please. Blond, freckles—and hold the colic. *Wall Street Journal.* Retrieved November 20, 2010 from Center for Genetics and Society www.geneticsandsociety.org/article.php?id=4519.

Nairne, J. S. (2003). Sensory and working memory. In A. F. Healy and R. W. Proctor (eds.), *Handbook of Psychology, Volume 4: Experimental Psychology.* New York: Wiley.

Nairne, J. S. (2009). *Psychology* (5th ed.). Belmont, CA: Thomson.

Nantais, K. M., & Schellenberg, E. G. (1999). The Mozart effect: An artifact of preference. *Psychological Science, 10,* 370–373.

Napier, A. Y. (2000). Making a marriage. In W. C. Nichols, M. A. Pace-Nichols, D. S. Becvar, & A. Y. Napier (Eds.), *Handbook of family development and intervention* (pp. 145–170). New York: Wiley.

Nash, M. R. (2001, July). The truth and the hype of hypnosis. *Scientific American, 285,* 46–49, 52–55.

Nash, M. R., & Tasso, A. (2010). The effectiveness of hypnosis in reducing pain and suffering among women with metastatic breast cancer and among women with temporomandibular disorder. *International Journal of Clinical and Experimental Hypnosis, 58*(4), 497–504.

National Academies of Science. (2003). *The polygraph and lie detection.* Washington, DC: National Academies Press.

NICHD Early Child Care Research Network. (2000). The relation of child care to cognitive and language development. *Child Development, 71,* 960–980.

NICHD Early Child Care Research Network. (2003). Does quality of child care affect child outcomes at age 4 1/2? *Developmental Psychology, 39,* 451–469.

NICHD Early Child Care Research Network. (2007). Age of entry to kindergarten and children's academic and socioemotional development. *Early Education & Development, 18*(2), 337–368.

National Institute of Medicine. (2006). *Sleep disorders and sleep deprivation: an unmet public health problem.* Retrieved March 19, 2008, from www.iom.edu/CMS/3740/23160/33668.aspx

National Institute of Mental Health (NIMH). (2003, December 22). *Mental illness genetics among science's top "breakthroughs" for 2003.* Retrieved February 6, 2008, from www.nimh.nih.gov/science-news/2003/mental-illness-genetics-among-sciences-top-breakthroughs-for-2003.shtml [See also: Plomin, 2003.]

National Institute of Mental Health (NIMH). (2005, April 21). *Brain scans reveal how gene may boost schizophrenia risk.* Retrieved February 6, 2008, from www.nimh.nih.gov/science-news/2005/brain-scans-reveal-how-gene-may-boost-schizophrenia-risk.shtml

National Institute of Mental Health (NIMH). (2006, January). *Statistics. Questions and answers about the NIMH sequenced treatment alternatives to relieve depression (STAR*D) study—Background.* Retrieved February 5, 2008, from www.nimh.nih.gov/health/trials/practical/stard/questions-and-answers-about-the-nimh-sequenced-treatment-alternatives-to-relieve-depression-stard-study-background.shtml

National Institute of Mental Health (NIMH). (2008a, April 3). *Anxiety disorders.* Retrieved April 20, 2008, from http://nimh.nih.gov/health/publications/anxiety-disorders/complete-publication.shtml#pub7

National Institute of Mental Health (NIMH). (2008b, February). *Schizophrenia.* Retrieved February 6, 2008, from www.nimh.nih.gov/health/publications/schizophrenia/summary.shtml [See also: Javitt & Coyle, 2004; Sawa & Snyder, 2002.]

National Institute of Mental Health (NIMH). (2008c, February). *Statistics.* Retrieved February 5, 2008, from www.nimh.nih.gov/statistics/index.shtml.

National Institute of Mental Health (NIMH). (2010a). *Major depressive disorder among adults.* Retrieved July 4, 2011, from www.nimh.nih.gov/statistics/1MDD_ADULT.shtml.

National Institute of Mental Health (NIMH). (2010b). *Statistics.* Retrieved July 4, 2011, from www.nimh.nih.gov/statistics/index.shtml

National Institute of Mental Health, MTA Cooperative Group. (2004). National Institute of Mental Health multimodal treatment study of ADHD follow-up: Changes in effectiveness and growth after the end of treatment. *Pediatrics, 113,* 762–769.

National Institute of Neurological Disorders and Stroke (NINDS). (2007, February). *Coma and persistent vegetative state information page.* Retrieved December 4, 2007 from www.ninds.nih.gov/disorders/coma/coma.htm

National Institute on Aging. (2004). *Alzheimer's disease education & referral center.* Retrieved November 8, 2004, from www.alzheimers.org/generalinfo.htm

National Institute on Aging. (2010). *Alzheimer's disease medications fact sheet.* Retrieved November 15, 2010, from www.nia.nih.gov/Alzheimers/Publications/medicationsfs.htm

National Institutes of Health. (2011). *Multiple sclerosis: Hope through research.* Retrieved August 8, 2011, from www.ninds.nih.gov/disorders/multiple_sclerosis/detail_multiple_sclerosis.htm.

National Public Radio. (2003a, August 19). Interview: Kenneth Kendler on study about severity of depression depends on the cause. *Morning Edition.*

National Safety Council (2010). Understanding the distracted brain: Why driving while using hands-free cell phones is risky behavior. Retrieved from www.fnal.gov/pub/traffic_safety/files/NSC%20White%20Paper%20-%20Distracted%20Driving%203-10.pdf.

Neal, D. (Producer). (2000, September 20). [Television broadcast of Olympic Games]. New York: NBC. [As cited in Markus et al., 2006]

Needleman, H., Schell, A., Belinger, D., Leviton, A., & Allred, E. (1990). The long-term effects of exposure to low doses of lead in childhood: An 11-year follow-up report. *New England Journal of Medicine, 322,* 83–88.

Neimark, J. (2005, October). Can the flu bring on psychosis? *Discover, 26*(10), 70–71.

Neimark, J. (2007, April). Autism: It's not just in the head. *Discover, 28*(4), 33–36, 38, 75.

Neimeyer, R. A. (1995). An invitation to constructivist psychotherapies. In R. A. Neimeyer & M. J. Mahoney (Eds.), *Constructivism in psychotherapy.* Washington, DC: American Psychological Association.

Neimeyer, R. A. (1999). Narrative strategies in grief therapy. *Journal of Constructivist Psychology, 12,* 65–85.

Neisser, U. (1967). *Cognitive psychology.* New York: Appleton-Century-Crofts.

Neisser, U. (1997). Never a dull moment. *American Psychologist, 52,* 79–81.

Neisser, U., Boodoo, B., Bouchard, T. J. Jr., Boyukin, A. W., Brody, N., Ceci, S. J., Halpern, D. F., Loehlin, J. C., Perloff, R., Sternberg, R. J., & Urbina, S. (1996). Intelligence: Knowns and unknowns. *American Psychologist, 51,* 77–101.

Nelson, C. A. (1987). The recognition of facial expressions in the first two years of life: Mechanisms of development. *Child Development, 58,* 889–909.

Nelson, C. A., III, Zeanah, C. H., Fox, N. A., Marshall, P. J., Smyke, A. T., & Guthrie, D. (2007, December 21). Cognitive recovery in socially deprived young children: The Bucharest early intervention project. *Science, 318,* 1937–1940. [See also: Millum & Emanuel, 2007.]

Nelson, T. D. (1993). The hierarchical organization of behavior: A useful feedback model of self-regulation. *Current Directions in Psychological Science, 2,* 121–126.

Nemecek, S. (1999, January). Unequal health. *Scientific American, 280*(1), 40–41.

Nesse, R. M., & Berridge, K. C. (1997, October 3). Psychoactive drug use in evolutionary perspective. *Science, 278,* 63–66.

Nestler, E. J., & Malenka, R. C. (2004, March). The addicted brain. *Scientific American, 290,* 78–85. [See also: Koob & Le Moal, 1997; Nestler, 2001]

Neuman, S. B. (2003). From rhetoric to reality: The case for high quality compensatory prekindergarten programs. *Phi Delta Kappan, 85,* 286–291.

Neville, H. J., Bavelier, D., Corina, D., Rauschecker, J., Karni, A., Lalwani, A., Braun, A., Clark, V., Jezzard, P., & Turner, R. (1998, February 3). Cerebral organization for language in deaf and hearing subjects: Biological constraints and effects of experience. *Proceedings of the National Academy of Sciences, 95,* 922–929.

Newberg, A. B., Alavi, A., Baime, M., Pourdehnad, M., Santanna, J., & d'Aquili, E. G. (2001a). The measurement of regional cerebral blood flow during the complex cognitive task of meditation: A preliminary SPECT study. *Psychiatry Research: Neuroimaging, 106,* 113–122.

Newberg, A., D'Aquili, E., & Rouse, V. (2001b). *Why God won't go away: Brain science and the biology of belief.* New York: Ballantine Books.

Newcomb, T. M. (1943). *Personality and social change.* New York: Holt.

Newcomb, T. M., Koenig, D. E., Flacks, R., & Warwick, D. P. (1967). *Persistence and change: Bennington College and its students after twenty-five years.* New York: Wiley.

Newman, B. S., & Muzzonigro, P. G. (1993). The effects of traditional family values on the coming out process of gay male adolescents. *Adolescence, 28,* 213–226.

Newman, C. (2004, August). Why are we so fat? *National Geographic, 206,* 46–61.

New York Times. (2011, Feb. 8). "9/11 Health and Environmental Issues." (*Times Topics*).

Niaura, R., Todaro, J. F., Stroud, L., Spiro, A., 3rd, Ward, K. D., & Weiss, S. (2002). Hostility, the metabolic syndrome, and incident coronary heart disease. *Health Psychology, 21*(6), 588–593.

Nicholson, I. (2007, Fall). Maslow: Toward a psychology of being. *The General Psychologist, 42*(2), 25–26. [See also: Baumeister & Leary, 1995; Brehm, 1992; Hatfield & Rapson, 1993; Kelley et al., 1983; Weber & Harvey, 1994a,b.]

Nickerson, R. S. (1998). Confirmation bias: A ubiquitous phenomenon in many guises. *Review of General Psychology, 2,* 175–220.

Nickerson, R. S., & Adams, M. J. (1979). Long-term memory for a common object. *Cognitive Psychology, 11,* 287–307.

Nicoll, R. A., & Alger, B. E. (2004, December). The brain's own marijuana. *Scientific American, 291*(6), 68–71.

Niedenthal, P. M. (2007, May 18). Embodying emotion. *Science, 316,* 1002–1005.

Niemi, M. (2009, February/March). Cure in the mind. *Scientific American Mind, 20*(1), 42–49.

Nietzel, M. T., Speltz, M. L., McCauley, E. A., & Bernstein, D. A. (1998). *Abnormal psychology.* Boston, MA: Allyn & Bacon.

Nigg, J. T. (2010). Attention-deficit/hyperactivity disorder: Endophenotypes, structure, and etiological pathways. *Current Directions in Psychological Science, 19,* 24–29.

Nippold, M. A., Duthie, J. K., & Larsen, J. (2005). Literacy as a leisure activity: Free time preferences of older children and young adolescents. *Language, Speech, and Hearing Services in Schools, 36,* 93–102.

Nisbett, R. E. (2000). *Culture and systems of thought: Holistic versus analytic cognition in East and West.* Master Lecture presented at the annual convention of the American Psychological Association, Washington, DC.

Nisbett, R. E. (2003). *The geography of thought: How Asians and Westerners think differently . . . and why.* New York: Free Press. [See also: Chua et al., 2005; Nisbett & Norenzayan, 2002; Winerman, 2006.]

Nisbett, R. E. (2005). Heredity, environment, and race differences in IQ: A commentary on Rushton and Jensen. *Psychology, Public Policy, and Law, 11,* 302–310.

Nisbett, R. E., & Norenzayan, A. (2002). Culture and cognition. In D. L. Medin (Ed.), *Stevens' Handbook of Experimental Psychology* (3rd ed.). New York: John Wiley & Sons.

Nisbett, R. E., Peng, K., Choi, I., & Norenzayan, A. (2001). Culture and systems of thought: Holistic versus analytic cognition. *Psychological Review, 108,* 291–310.

Nobles, W. W. (1976). Black people in white insanity: An issue for black community mental health. *Journal of Afro-American Issues, 4,* 21–27.

Nolen-Hoeksema, S. (2001). Gender differences in depression. *Current Directions in Psychological Science, 10,* 173–176.

Nolen-Hoeksema, S., & Davis, C. G. (1999). "Thanks for sharing that": Ruminators and their social support networks. *Journal of Personality and Social Psychology, 77,* 801–814.

Nolen-Hoeksema, S., Wisco, B. E., & Lyubomirsky, S. (2008). Rethinking rumination. *Perspectives on Psychological Science, 3,* 400–424. [See also Law, 2005; Nolen-Hoeksema & Davis, 1999]

Norcross, J. C., Koocher, G. P., & Garofalo, A. (2006). Discredited psychological treatments and tests: A Delphi poll. *Professional Psychology: Research and Practice, 37,* 515–522.

Norenzayan, A., & Nisbett, R. E. (2000). Culture and causal cognition. *Current Directions in Psychological Science, 9,* 132–135. [See also: Fletcher & Ward, 1988; Miller, 1984; Triandis, 1996]

Notarius, C. I. (1996). Marriage: Will I be happy or sad? In N. Vanzetti & S. Duck (Eds.), *A lifetime of relationships.* Pacific Grove, CA: Brooks/Cole.

Nova Online. (1996). *Kidnapped by UFOs?* Retrieved August 2, 2007, from www.pbs.org/wgbh/nova/aliens/carlsagan.html.

Novak, M. A., & Suomi, S. J. (1988). Psychological well-being of primates in captivity. *American Psychologist, 43,* 765–773.

Novotney, A. (2008, July–August). Get your clients moving: Ten tips to incorporate exercise into your treatment arsenal. *Monitor on Psychology, 39*(7), 68–69.

Novotney, A. (2008, March). Preventing harassment at schools. *Monitor on Psychology,* 18–20.

Novotney, A. (2009, April). New solutions. *Monitor on Psychology, 40*(4), 47–51.

Novotney, A. (2009). Postgrad growth area: Environmental psychology. *GradPsych* (7). Retrieved from www.apa.org/gradpsych/2009/09/postgrad.aspx.

Nowack, K. M. (1983). The relationship between stress, job performance, and burnout in college resident assistants. *Journal of College Student Personnel, 24,* 545–550.

Nungesser, L. G. (1990). *Axioms for survivors: How to live until you say goodbye.* Santa Monica, CA: IBS Press.

Nurnberger, J. I. Jr., & Bierut, L. J. (2007, April). Seeking the connections: Alcoholism and our genes. *Scientific American, 296*(4), 46–53.

Oakland, T., & Glutting, J. J. (1990). Examiner observations of children's WISC-R test-related behaviors: Possible socioeconomic status, race, and gender effects. *Psychological Assessment, 2,* 86–90.

Oakley, D. A. (1999). Hypnosis and conversion hysteria: A unifying model. *Cognitive Neuropsychiatry, 4,* 243–265.

Oakley, D. A. (2006). Hypnosis as a tool in research: Experimental psychopathology. *Contemporary Hypnosis 23,* 3–14. [See also: Bowers, 1983; Hilgard, 1968, 1973; Miller & Bowers, 1993; Nash, 2001.]

O'Connell, M. E., Boat. T., & Warner, K. E. (Eds.). (2010). *Preventing mental, emotional, and behavioral disorders among young people: Progress and possibilities.* Washington, DC: National Academies Press. Retrieved July 5, 2011, from www.nap.edu/openbook.php?record_id=12480&page=R1#.

O'Connor, E. M. (2001, December). Medicating ADHD: Too much? Too soon? *Monitor on Psychology, 32*(11), 50–51.

Oden, G. C. (1968). The fulfillment of promise: 40-year follow-up of the Terman gifted group. *Genetic Psychology Monographs, 77,* 3–93.

Oden, G. C. (1987). Concept, knowledge, and thought. *Annual Review of Psychology, 38,* 203–227.

O'Doherty, J., Dayan, P., Schultz, J., Deichmann, R., Friston, K., & Dolan, R. J. (2004, April 16). Dissociable roles of ventral and dorsal striatum in instrumental conditioning. *Science, 304,* 452–454.

O'Donovan, A., Lin, J., Dhabhar, F. S., Wolkowitz, O., Tillie, J. M., Blackburn, E., & Epel, E. (2009). Pessimism correlates with leukocyte telomere shortness and elevated interleukin-6 in postmenopausal women. *Brain, Behavior, & Immunity, 23,* 446–449.

Offer, D., Ostrov, E., & Howard, K. I. (1981). *The adolescent: A psychological self-portrait.* New York: Basic Books.

Offer, D., Ostrov, E., Howard, K. I., & Atkinson, R. (1988). *The teenage world: Adolescents' self-image in ten countries.* New York: Plenum Medical.

Office of the Surgeon General, U.S. Department of Health and Human Services. (2005). Advisory on alcohol use in pregnancy. Retrieved from www.surgeongeneral.gov/pressreleases/sg02222005.html.

Ofshe, R., & Watters, E. (1994). *Making monsters: False memories, psychotherapy, and sexual hysteria.* New York: Charles Scribner's Sons.

Öhman, A., & Mineka, S. (2001). Fears, phobias, and preparedness: Toward an evolved module of fear and fear learning. *Psychological Review, 108,* 483–522.

Olds, M. E., & Fobes, J. L. (1981). The central basis of motivation: Intracranial self-stimulation studies. *Annual Review of Psychology, 32,* 523–574.

Oliner, S. P. (2001). Heroic Altruism: Heroic and Moral Behavior in a Variety of Settings. In *Remembering for the Future 2000: Papers and Proceedings.* London: Palgrave.

Olton, D. S. (1992). Tolman's cognitive analyses: Predecessors of current approaches in psychology. *Journal of Experimental Psychology: General, 121,*

427–428. [See also: Menzel, 1978; Moar, 1980; Olton, 1979]

Olweus. D. (1993). *Bullying at school: What we know and what we can do.* Oxford, UK: Blackwell.

Oren, D. A., & Terman, M. (1998, January 16). Tweaking the human circadian clock with light. *Science, 279,* 333–334.

Orne, M. T. (1980). Hypnotic control of pain: Toward a clarification of the different psychological processes involved. In J. J. Bonica (Ed.), *Pain* (pp. 155–172). New York: Raven Press.

Ornstein, R., & Sobel, D. (1989). *Healthy pleasures.* Reading, MA: Addison-Wesley.

Orser, B. A. (2007, June). Lifting the fog around anesthesia. *Scientific American, 296*(6), 54–61.

Ortmann, A., & Hertwig, R. (1997). Is deception acceptable? *American Psychologist, 52,* 746–747. [See also: Bower, 1998d]

Osterhout, L., & Holcomb, P. J. (1992). Event-related brain potentials elicited by syntactic anomaly. *Journal of Memory and Language, 31,* 785–806.

Ostow, M. (1973, April 27). (Untitled letter to the editor). *Science, 180,* 360–361. [See also other critiques of the Rosenhan study among other letters in the same issue.]

Ouattara, K., Lemasson, A., & Zuberbuhler, K. (2009). Campbell's monkeys concatenate vocalizations into context-specific call sequences. *Proceedings of the National Academy of Sciences, USA,* December 9, 2009. Retrieved from www.pnas.org/content/early/2009/12/08/0908118106.short.

Overmier, J. B. (2002). On learned helplessness. *Integrative Behavioral and Physiological Science, 37,* 4–8.

Overmier, J., & Seligman, M. (1967). Effects of inescapable shock on subsequent escape and avoidance learning. *Journal of Comparative and Physiological Psychology, 63,* 23–33.

Owen, A. M., Schiff, N. D., & Laureys, S. (2009). A new era of coma and consciousness science. In S. Laureys et al. (eds.), *Progress in brain research* (Vol. 177, pp. 399–411). Elsevier: Amsterdam, The Netherlands.

Paffenbarger, R. S., Hyde, R. T., Wing, A. L., & Hsieh, C. C. (1986, March). Physical activity, all-cause mortality, and longevity of college alumni. *New England Journal of Medicine, 314,* 605–613.

Paikoff, R. L., & Brooks-Gunn, J. (1991). Do parent-child relationships change during puberty? *Psychological Bulletin, 110,* 47–66.

Palmer, S. E. (2002). Perceptual grouping: It's later than you think. *Current Directions in Psychological Science, 11,* 101–106.

Park, C. L., Cohen, L. H., & Murch, R. L. (1996). Assessment and prediction of stress-related growth. *Journal of Personality, 64,* 71–105.

Park, D. C. (2007). Eating disorders: A call to arms. *American Psychologist, 62,* 158.

Parker-Pope, T. (2009, June 23). How the food makers captured our brains. *New York Times.* Retrieved from www.nytimes.com/2009/06/23/health/23well.html.

Parkes, C. M. (2001). *Bereavement: Studies of grief in adult life.* New York: Routledge.

Parr, W. V., and Siegert, R. (1993). Adults' conceptions of everyday memory failures in others: Factors that mediate the effects of target age. *Psychology and Aging, 8,* 599–605.

Patenaude, A. F., Guttmacher, A. E., & Collins, F. S. (2002). Genetic testing and psychology: New roles, new responsibilities. *American Psychologist, 57,* 271–282. [See also Fackelmann, 1998.]

Patrick, C. J. (2007). Getting to the heart of psychopathy. In H. Hervé & J. C. Yuille (Eds.), *Psychopathy: Theory, research, and social implications,* pp. 207–252. Hillsdale, NJ: Erlbaum.

Patterson, C. J. (2006). Children of lesbian and gay parents. *Current Directions in Psychological Science, 15,* 241–244.

Patterson, D. R. (2004, December). Treating pain with hypnosis. *Current Directions in Psychological Science, 13,* 252–255.

Patterson, D. R. (2010). *Clinical hypnosis for pain control.* Washington, DC: American Psychological Association.

Patterson, D. R., Jensen, M. P., Wiechman, S. A., & Sharar, S. R. (2010). Virtual reality hypnosis for pain associated with recovery from physical trauma. *International Journal of Clinical and Experimental Hypnosis, 58*(3), 288–300.

Patterson, F., & Linden, E. (1981). *The education of Koko.* New York: Holt, Rinehart and Winston.

Patterson, J. M. (1985). Critical factors affecting family compliance with home treatment for children with cystic fibrosis. *Family Relations, 34,* 74–89.

Patton, G. C., Carlin, J. B., Shao, Q., Hibbert, M. E., Rosier, M., Selzer, R., et al. (1997). Adolescent dieting: Healthy weight control or borderline eating disorder? *Journal of Child Psychology and Psychiatry and Allied Disciplines, 38*(3), 299–306.

Patzer, G. L. (1985). *The physical attractiveness phenomena.* New York: Plenum Press.

Paulesu, E. D., Démonet, J.-F., Fazio, F., McCrory, E., Chanoine, V., Brunswick, N., Cappa, S. F., Cossu, G., Habib, M., Frith, C. D., & Frith, U. (2001, March 16). Dyslexia: Cultural diversity and biological utility. *Science, 291,* 2165–2167.

Paulus, J. (2007, April/May). Lithium's healing power. *Scientific American Mind, 18*(2), 70–75.

Pavlov, I. P. (1928). *Lectures on conditioned reflexes: Twenty-five years of objective study of higher nervous activity (behavior of animals)* (Vol. 1, W. H. Gantt, Trans.). New York: International Publishers.

Pavot, W., Diener, E., & Fujita, F. (1990). Extraversion and happiness. *Personality and Individual Differences, 1,* 1299–1306.

Pawlik, K., & d'Ydewalle, G. (1996). Psychology and the global commons: Perspectives of international psychology. *American Psychologist, 51,* 488–495.

Pearman, R. R. (1991, November 13). Disputing a report on "Myers–Briggs" test. *Chronicle of Higher Education,* B7.

Pearson, H. (2006, June 22). Lure of lie detectors spooks ethicists. *Nature, 441,* 918–919. [See also: McKhann, 2006; Neuroethics Needed, 2006]

Pedersen, P. (1979). Non-Western psychology: The search for alternatives. In A. J. Marsella, R. G. Tharp, & T. J. Ciborowski (Eds.), *Perspectives on cross-cultural psychology* (pp. 77–98). New York: Academic Press.

Penfield, W. (1959). The interpretive cortex. *Science, 129,* 1719–1725.

Penfield, W., & Baldwin, M. (1952). Temporal lobe seizures and the technique of subtotal lobectomy. *Annals of Surgery, 136,* 625–634.

Peng, K., & Nisbett, R. E. (1999). Culture, dialectics, and reasoning about contradiction. *American Psychologist, 54,* 741–754.

Pennebaker, J. W. (1990). *Opening up: The healing power of confiding in others.* New York: William Morrow.

Pennebaker, J. W. (1997). Writing about emotional experiences as a therapeutic process. *Psychological Science, 8,* 162–166.

Pennebaker, J. W., & Harber, K. D. (1991, April). Coping after the Loma Prieta earthquake: A preliminary report. Paper presented at the Western Psychological Association Convention, San Francisco, CA.

Pennisi, E. (2001, February 16). The human genome. *Science, 291,* 1177–1180.

Pennisi, E. (2006, September 29). Mining the molecules that made our mind. *Science, 313,* 1908–1913.

Pennisi, E. (2007, April 3). Genomicists tackle the primate tree. *Science, 316,* 218–221.

Peplau, L. A. (2003). Human sexuality: How do men and women differ? *Current Directions in Psychological Science, 12,* 37–40.

Perkins, D. F., & Lerner, R. M. (1995). Single and multiple indicators of physical attractiveness and psychosocial behaviors among young adolescents. *Journal of Early Adolescence, 15,* 268–297.

Perrin, M. A., DiGrande, L., Wheeler, K., Thorpe, L., Farfel, M., & Brackbill, R. (2007). Differences in PTSD prevalence and associated risk factors among World Trade Center disaster rescue and recovery workers. *American Journal of Psychiatry, 164,* 1385–1394.

Perry, W. G. Jr. (1970). *Forms of intellectual and ethical development in the college years: A scheme.* New York: Holt, Rinehart and Winston.

Perry, W. G. Jr. (1994). Forms of intellectual and ethical development in the college years: A scheme. In B. Puka (Ed.), *Defining perspectives in moral development: Vol. 1. Moral development: A compendium* (pp. 231–248). New York: Garland Publishing.

Pervin, L. A. (1985). Personality: Current controversies, issues, and directions. *Annual Review of Psychology, 36,* 83–114.

Peterson, C., & Park, N. (2010). What happened to self-actualization? Commentary on Kenrick et al. (2010). *Perspectives on Psychological Science, 5,* 320–322.

Peterson, C., & Seligman, M. E. P. (2004). *Character strengths and virtues.* Washington, DC: American Psychological Association & Oxford University Press.

Petitto, L. A., & Marentette, P. (1991). Babbling in the manual mode: Evidence for the ontogeny of language. *Science, 251,* 1483–1496.

Petrosino A., Turpin-Petrosino, C., & Buehler, J. (2003, November). "Scared Straight" and other juvenile awareness programs for preventing juvenile delinquency. (Updated C2 Review). *The Campbell Collaboration Reviews of Intervention and Policy Evaluations (C2-RIPE).* Philadelphia: Campbell Collaboration. Retrieved August 2, 2007, from www.campbellcollaboration.org/doc-pdf/ssrupdt.pdf.

Petrovic, P., Kalso, E., Petersson, K. M., & Ingvan, M. (2002, March 1). Placebo and opioid analgesia—Imaging a shared neuronal network. *Science, 295,* 1737–1740.

Pettigrew, T. F. (1998). Intergroup contact theory. *Annual Review of Psychology, 49,* 65–85.

Pham, M. T. (2007). Emotion and rationality: A critical review and interpretation of empirical evidence. *Review of General Psychology, 11,* 155–178.

Phelan, J. (2009). *What is life? A guide to biology.* New York: W. H. Freeman.

Phelps, J. A., Davis, J. O., & Schartz, K. M. (1997). Nature, nurture, and twin research strategies. *Current Directions in Psychological Science, 6,* 117–121.

Pifer, A., & Bronte L. (Eds.). (1986). *Our aging society: Paradox and promise.* New York: Norton.

Pilcher, J. J., & Walters, A. S. (1997). How sleep deprivation affects psychological variables related to college students' cognitive performance. *Journal of American College Health, 46,* 121–126.

Pilisuk, M., & Parks, S. H. (1986). *The healing web: Social networks and human survival.* Hanover, NH: University Press of New England.

Pillard, R., & Bailey, M. (1991). A genetic study of male sexual orientation. *Archives of General Psychiatry, 48,* 1089–1096.

Pillemer, D. B. (1984). Flashbulb memories of the assassination attempt on President Reagan. *Cognition, 16*, 63–80.

Pinel, J. P. J. (2005). *Biopsychology* (6th ed.). Boston: Allyn & Bacon.

Pinel, J. P. J., Assanand, S., & Lehman, D. R. (2000). Hunger, eating, and ill health. *American Psychologist, 55*, 1105–1116.

Pines, A., & Zimbardo, P. G. (1978). The personal and cultural dynamics of shyness: A comparison between Israelis, American Jews and Americans. *Journal of Psychology and Judaism, 3*, 81–101.

Pinker, S. (1994). *The language instinct: How the mind creates language.* New York: Morrow.

Pinker, S. (2002). *The blank slate: The modern denial of human nature.* New York: Viking.

Pinker, S. (2006, Spring). The blank slate. *The General Psychologist, 41*(1), 1–8. Retrieved July 5, 2011, from www.apa.org/divisions/div1/news/Spring2006/GenPsychSpring06.pdf.

Pinto, R. M. (2003). The impact of secondary traumatic stress on novice and expert counselors with and without a history of trauma. *Dissertation Abstracts International, Section A: Humanities and Social Sciences, 63*, 3117.

Piper, A., & Merskey, H. (2004a). The persistence of folly: A critical examination of dissociative identity disorder. Part I. The excesses of an improbable concept. *Canadian Journal of Psychiatry, 49*, 592–600.

Piper, A., & Merskey, H. (2004b). The persistence of folly: A critical examination of dissociative identity disorder. Part II. The defence and decline of multiple personality or dissociative identity disorder. *Canadian Journal of Psychiatry, 49*, 678–683.

Pitman, G. E. (2003). Evolution, but no revolution: The "tend-and-befriend" theory of stress and coping. *Psychology of Women Quarterly, 27*, 194–195.

Plomin, R. (2000, September). Psychology in a postgenomics world: It will be more important than ever. *American Psychological Society Observer, 3*, 27. [See also Boomsma, Anokhin, & de Geus, 1997.]

Plomin, R., & DeFries, J. C. (1998). The genetics of cognitive abilities and disabilities. *Scientific American, 278*(5), 62–69.

Plomin, R., Owen, M. J., & McGuffin, P. (1994). The genetic basis of complex human behaviors. *Science, 264*, 1733–1739.

Plous, S. (1996). Attitudes toward the use of animals in psychological research and education: Results from a national survey of psychologists. *American Psychologist, 51*, 1167–1180. [See also: Blum, 1994]

Plutchik, R. (1980). *Emotion: A psychoevolutionary synthesis.* New York: Harper & Row.

Plutchik, R. (1984). Emotions: A general psychoevolutionary theory. In K. Scherer & P. Ekman (Eds.), *Approaches to emotion.* Hillsdale, NJ: Erlbaum.

Pogue-Geile, M. F., & Yokley, J. L. (2010). Current research on the genetic contributors to schizophrenia. *Current Directions in Psychological Science, 19*, 214–219.

Poldrack, R. A., Wagner, A. D., Phelps, E. A., & Sharot, T. (2008). How (and why) emotion enhances the subjective sense of recollection. *Current Directions in Psychological Science, 17*, 147–152.

Pole, N., Best, S. R., Metzler, T., & Marmar, C. R. (2005). Why are Hispanics at greater risk for PTSD? *Cultural Diversity and Ethnic Minority Psychology, 11*, 144–161.

Pollak, S. D. (2008). Mechanisms linking early experience and the emergence of emotions: Illustrations from the study of maltreated children. *Current Directions in Psychological Science, 17*, 370–375.

Poole, D. A., Lindsay, D. S., Memon, A., & Bull, R. (1995). Psychotherapy and the recovery of memories of childhood sexual abuse: U.S. and British practitioners' opinions, practices, and experiences. *Journal of Consulting and Clinical Psychology, 63*, 426–437.

Poon, L. W. (1985). Differences in human memory with aging: Nature, causes, and clinical implications. In J. E. Birren & W. K. Schaie (Eds.), *Handbook of the psychology of aging* (pp. 427–462). New York: Van Nostrand Reinhold.

Popejoy, D. I. (1967). *The effects of a physical fitness program on selected psychological and physiological measures of anxiety.* Unpublished doctoral dissertation. University of Illinois.

Popkin, B. M. (2007, September). The world is fat. *Scientific American, 297*(3), 88–95.

Porreca, F., & Price, T. (2009, September/October). When pain lingers. *Scientific American Mind, 21*(5), 34–41. [See also: Craig & Reiman, 1996; Vogel, 1996]

Portner, M. (2008). The orgasmic mind. *Scientific American Mind, 19*(2), 67–71.

Practice Directorate Staff. (2005, February). Prescription for success. *Monitor on Psychology, 36*(2), 25–29.

Premack, D. (1965). Reinforcement theory. In D. Levine (Ed.), *Nebraska Symposium on Motivation* (pp. 128–180). Lincoln: University of Nebraska Press.

Prentice, D. A., & Miller, D. T. (1993). Pluralistic ignorance and alcohol use on campus: Some consequences on misperceiving the social norm. *Journal of Personality and Social Psychology, 64*, 243–256.

Pretz, J. (2008). Intuition versus analysis: Strategy and experience in complex everyday problem solving. *Memory and Cognition, 36*, 554–566.

Price, M. (2009, March). A pacemaker for your brain? *Monitor on Psychology, 40*(3), 36–39.

Priest, R. F., & Sawyer, J. (1967). Proximity and peership: Bases of balance in interpersonal attraction. *American Journal of Sociology, 72*, 633–649.

Primavera, L. H., & Herron, W. G. (1996). The effect of viewing television violence on aggression. *International Journal of Instructional Media, 23*, 91–104.

Prinzmetal, W. (1995). Visual feature integration in a world of objects. *Current Directions in Psychological Science, 5*, 90–94.

Provine, R. R. (2004). Laughing, tickling, and the evolution of speech and self. *Current Directions in Psychological Science, 13*, 215–218.

Putnam, F. W., Guroff, J. J., Silberman, E. K., Barban, L., & Post, R. M. (1986). The clinical phenomenology of multiple personality disorder: Review of 100 recent cases. *Journal of Clinical Psychiatry, 47*, 285–293.

Qualls, S. H., & Abeles, N. (2000). *Psychology and the aging revolution: How we adapt to longer life.* Washington, DC: American Psychological Association.

Quiñones-Vidal, E., Lõpez-García, J. J., Peñaranda-Ortega, M., & Tortosa-Gil, F. (2004). The nature of social and personality psychology as reflected in JPSP, 1965–2000. *Journal of Personality and Social Psychology, 86*, 435–452.

Rabkin, J. G., & Struening, E. L. (1976). Life events, stress, and illness. *Science, 194*, 1013–1020.

Rachman, S. (2000). Joseph Wolpe (1915–1997). *American Psychologist, 55*, 431–432.

Rahe, R. H., & Arthur, R. J. (1978, March). Life change and illness studies: Past history and future directions. *Journal of Human Stress*, 3–15.

Raichle, M. E. (1994). Visualizing the mind. *Scientific American, 270*(4), 58–64.

Raine, A. (2008). From genes to brain to antisocial behavior. *Current Directions in Psychological Science, 17*, 323–328.

Ramachandran, V. S., & Blakeslee, S. (1998). *Phantoms in the brain.* New York: William Morrow.

Ramachandran, V. S., & Hirstein, W. (1999). The science of art: A neurological theory of aesthetic experience. *Journal of Consciousness Studies, 6*(6–7), 15–51.

Ramachandran, V. S., & Hubbard, E. M. (2001). Synaesthesia—A window into perception, thought and language. *Journal of Consciousness Studies, 8*, 3–34.

Ramachandran, V. S., & Hubbard, E. M. (2003, May). Hearing colors, tasting shapes. *Scientific American (Special Edition), 16*(3), 76–83. [See also Ramachandran & Hubbard, 2001.]

Ramachandran, V. S., & Oberman, L. M. (2006, November). Broken mirrors. *Scientific American, 295*(5), 62–69.

Ramachandran, V. S., & Rogers-Ramachandran, D. (2008, December/2009, January). I see, but I don't know. *Scientific American Mind, 19*(6), 20–22.

Ramachandran, V. S., & Rogers-Ramachandran, D. (2010, September/October). Reading between the lines. *Scientific American Mind, 21*(5), 18–20.

Rambo-Chroniak, K. M. (1999). Coping and adjustment in the freshman year transition. Unpublished dissertation, Northwestern University, Chicago, IL. (*Dissertation Abstracts International, 59* [June], 12-A, 4378.)

Ramey, C. T., & Ramey, S. L. (1998a). Early intervention and early experience. *American Psychologist, 53*, 109–120.

Ramey, C. T,. & Ramey, S. L. (1998b). In defense of special education. *American Psychologist, 53*, 1159–1160.

Randerson, J. (2002, January 26). Sleep scientists discount sheep. *New Scientist*, Issue #2327. Retrieved December 8, 2007, from www.newscientist.com/article/dn1831-sleep-scientists-discount-sheep.html

Raphael, B. (1984). *The anatomy of bereavement: A handbook for the caring professions.* London, UK: Hutchinson.

Rapoport, J. L. (1989, March). The biology of obsessions and compulsions. *Scientific American, 263*, 83–89.

Rauschecker, J. P., & Tian, B. (2000). Mechanisms and streams for processing of "what" and "where" in auditory cortex. *Proceedings of the National Academy of Sciences, 97*, 11800–11806.

Rauscher, F. H., Shaw, G. L., & Ky, K. N. (1993, October 14). Music and spatial task performance. *Nature, 365*, 611.

Rawlins, W. K. (1992). *Friendship matters: Communication, dialectics, and the life course.* New York: DeGruyter.

Raymond, C. (1989, September 20). Scientists examining behavior of a man who lost his memory gain new insights into the workings of the human mind. *The Chronicle of Higher Education*, A4, A6.

Raynor, J. O. (1970). Relationships between achievement-related motives, future orientation, and academic performance. *Journal of Personality and Social Psychology, 15*, 28–33.

Raz, A., Shapiro, T., Fan, J., & Posner, M. I. (2002). Hypnotic suggestion and the modulation of Stroop interference. *Archives of General Psychiatry, 59*, 1151–1161.

Ready, D. D., LoGerfo, L. F., Burkan, D. T., & Lee, V. E. (2005). Explaining girls' advantage in kindergarten literacy learning: Do classroom behaviors make a difference? *The Elementary School Journal, 106*, 21–38.

Reber, A. S. (1993). *Implicit learning and tacit knowledge: An essay on the cognitive unconscious. (Oxford Psychology Series No. 19).* Oxford, UK: Oxford University Press.

Rechtschaffen, A. (1998). Current perspectives on the function of sleep. *Perspectives in Biology and Medicine, 41*, 359–390. [See also: Pinel, 2005.]

Rector, N. A., & Beck, A. T. (2001). Cognitive behavioral therapy for schizophrenia: An empirical review. *Journal of Nervous & Mental Disease, 189,* 278–287.

Regier, D. A., Boyd, J. H, Burke, J. D., Rae, D. S., Myers, J. K., Kramer, M., Robins, L. N., George, L. K., Karno, M., & Locke, B. Z. (1988). One-month prevalence of mental disorders in the United States. *Archives of General Psychiatry, 45,* 977–986.

Regier, D. A., Narrow, W. E., Rae, D. S., Manderscheid, R. W., Locke, B. Z., & Goodwin, F. K. (1993). The de facto U.S. mental and addictive disorders service system: Epidemiologic Catchment Area prospective 1-year-prevalence rates of disorders and services. *Archives of General Psychiatry, 50,* 85–94.

Rescorla, R. A., & Wagner, A. R. (1972). A theory of Pavlovian conditioning: Variations in the effectiveness of reinforcement and nonreinforcement. In A. H. Black & W. F. Prokasy (Eds.), *Classical conditioning, II: Current research and theory* (pp. 64–94). New York: Appleton-Century-Crofts.

Resnick, S. M. (1992). Positron emission tomography in psychiatric illness. *Current Directions in Psychological Science, 1,* 92–98.

Rest, J. R., & Thoma, S. J. (1976). Relation of moral judgment development to formal education. *Developmental Psychology, 21,* 709–714.

Reuter-Lorenz, P. A., & Miller, A. C. (1998). The cognitive neuroscience of human laterality: Lessons from the bisected brain. *Current Directions in Psychological Science, 7,* 15–20.

Reynolds, C. R. (2000). Why is psychometric research on bias in mental testing so often ignored? *Psychology, Public Policy, and Law, 6,* 144–150.

Rhodes, G., Sumich, A., & Byatt, G. (1999). Are average facial configurations attractive only because of their symmetry? *Psychological Science, 10,* 52–58. [See also: Langlois & Roggman, 1990; Langlois et al., 1994.]

Rich, L. E. (2004, January). Bringing more effective tools to the weight-loss table. *Monitor on Psychology, 35*(1), 52–55.

Rickgarn, R. L. V. (1996). The need for postvention on college campuses: A rationale and case study findings. In C. A. Corr & D. E. Balk (Eds.), *Handbook of adolescent death and bereavement* (pp. 273–292). New York: Springer Publishing.

Richards, J. M., & Gross, J. J. (2000). Emotion regulation and memory: The cognitive costs of keeping one's cool. *Journal of Personality & Social Psychology, 79,* 410–424.

Riessman, C. K., Whalen, M. H., Frost, R. O., & Morgenthau, J. E. (1991). Romance and help-seeking among women: "It hurts so much to care." *Women and Health, 17,* 21–47.

Riolli, L. (2002). Resilience in the face of catastrophe: Optimism, personality and coping in the Kosovo crisis. *Journal of Applied Social Psychology, 32,* 1604–1627.

Ripple, C. H., Gilliam, W. S., Chanana, N., & Zigler, E. (1999). Will fifty cooks spoil the broth? The debate over entrusting Head Start to the states. *American Psychologist, 54,* 327–343.

Ripple, C. H., & Zigler, E. (2003). Research, policy, and the Federal role in prevention initiatives for children. *American Psychologist, 58,* 482–490. [See also: Ripple et al., 1999; Schweinhart & Weikart, 1986; Smith, 1991.]

Rips, L. J. (1997). Goals for a theory of deduction: Reply to Johnson-Laird. *Minds and Machines, 7,* 409–424.

Rizzolatti, G., Fogassi, L., & Gallese, V. (2006, November). Mirrors in the mind. *Scientific American, 295*(5), 54–61.

Robbins, D. (1971). Partial reinforcement: A selective review of the alleyway literature since 1960. *Psychological Bulletin, 76,* 415–431.

Robbins, J. (2000, April). Wired for sadness. *Discover, 21*(4), 77–81.

Roberts, S. B., Flannelly, K. J., Weaver, A. J., & Rigley, C. R. (2003). Compassion fatigue among chaplains, clergy, and other respondents after September 11th. *Journal of Nervous and Mental Disease, 191,* 756–758.

Robins, L. N., Locke, B. Z., & Regier, D. A. (1991). An overview of psychiatric disorders in America. In L. N. Robins & D. A. Regier (Eds.), *Psychiatric disorders in America: The epidemiologic catchment area study.* New York: Free Press.

Robins, R. W. (2005, October 7). The nature of personality: Genes, culture, and national character. *Science, 310,* 62–63.

Robinson, N. M., Zigler, E., & Gallagher, J. J. (2000). Two tails of the normal curve: Similarities and differences in the study of mental retardation and giftedness. *American Psychologist, 55,* 1413–1424. [See also Baumeister, 1987; Detterman, 1999; Greenspan, 1999.]

Roche, S. M., & McConkey, K. M. (1990) Absorption: Nature, assessment, and correlates. *Journal of Personality & Social Psychology, 59,* 91–101.

Rock, I., & Palmer, S. (1990, December). The legacy of Gestalt psychology. *Scientific American, 263,* 84–90.

Rodin, J. (1986). Aging and health: Effects of the sense of control. *Science, 233,* 1271–1276.

Rodin, J., & Salovey, P. (1989). Health psychology. *Annual Review of Psychology, 40,* 533–579.

Roediger, H. L., III, & McDermott, K. B. (1995). Creating false memories: Remembering words not presented in lists. *Journal of Experimental Psychology: Learning, Memory, and Cognition, 21,* 803–814.

Roediger, H. L., III, & McDermott, K. B. (2000, January/February). *Psychological Science Agenda,* 8–9.

Roediger, R. (2004, March). What happened to behaviorism? *APS Observer, 17*(3), 5, 40–42.

Roesch, M. R., & Olson, C. R. (2004, April 9). Neuronal activity related to reward value and motivation in primate frontal cortex. *Science, 304,* 307–310.

Rogers, C. R. (1951). *Client-centered therapy: Its current practice, implications and theory.* Boston: Houghton Mifflin.

Rogers, C. R. (1961). *On becoming a person: A therapist's view of psychotherapy.* Boston: Houghton Mifflin. [See also: Rogers, 1951, 1980.]

Rogers, C. R. (1977). *On personal power: Inner strength and its revolutionary impact.* New York: Delacorte.

Rogers, C. R. (1982, July/August) Roots of madness. In T. H. Carr & H. E. Fitzgerald (Eds.), *Psychology 83/84* (pp. 263–267). Guilford, CT: Dushkin. (Originally published in *Science 82,* July/August, 1982).

Rogoff, B. (2003). *The cultural nature of human development.* New York: Oxford University Press.

Rohrer, M., et al. (1954). The stability of autokinetic judgment. *Journal of Abnormal and Social Psychology, 49,* 595–597.

Roll, S., Hinton, R., & Glazer, M. (1974). Dreams and death: Mexican Americans vs. Anglo-American. *Interamerican Journal of Psychology, 8,* 111–115.

Rollman, G. B., & Harris, G. (1987). The detectability, discriminability, and perceived magnitude of painful electrical shock. *Perception & Psychophysics, 42,* 257–268.

Rolls, B. J., Federoff, I. C., & Guthrie, J. F. (1991). Gender differences in eating be havior and body weight regulation. *Health Psychology, 10,* 133–142.

Rolnick, J. (1998, December 4). Treating mental disorders: A neuroscientist says no to drugs. *The Chronicle of Higher Education,* A10.

Roozendaal, B., McEwen, B. S., & Chattarji, S. (2009, June). Stress, memory, and the amygdale. *Nature reviews neuroscience, 10,* 423–433.

Rosch, E. (1999). Is wisdom in the brain? *Psychological Science, 10,* 222–224.

Rosen, J. B., & Schulkin, J. (1998). From normal fear to pathological anxiety. *Psychological Review, 105,* 325–350.

Rosenhan, D. L. (1969). Some origins of concern for others. In P. Mussen, J. Langer, & M. Covington (Eds.), *Trends and issues in developmental psychology.* New York: Holt, Rinehart & Winston.

Rosenhan, D. L. (1973a). On being sane in insane places. *Science, 179,* 250–258.

Rosenhan, D. L. (1973b, April 27). (Untitled letter to the editor). *Science, 180,* 360–361. [See also the critiques of Rosenhan's study among other letters in the same issue.]

Rosenhan, D. L., & Seligman, M. E. P. (1995). *Abnormal psychology* (3rd ed.). New York: Norton.

Rosenheck, R. A., Leslie, D., L., Sindelar, J., Miller, E. A., Lin, H., Stroup, T. S., McEvoy, J., Davis, S. M., Keefe, R. S. E., Swartz, M., Perkins, D. O., Hsiao, J. K., & Lieberman, J. (2006). Cost-effectiveness of second-generation antipsychotics and perphenazine in a randomized trial of treatment for chronic schizophrenia. *American Journal of Psychiatry, 163,* 2080–2089.

Rosenthal, R. (2002). Covert communication in classrooms, clinics, courtrooms, and cubicles. *American Psychologist, 57,* 839–849.

Rosenthal, R., & Lawson, R. (1964). A longitudinal study of the effects of experimenter bias on the operant learning of laboratory rats. *Journal of Psychiatric Research, 2,* 61–72.

Rosenzweig, M. R. (1992). Psychological science around the world. *American Psychologist, 47,* 718–722.

Rosenzweig, M. R. (1999). Continuity and change in the development of psychology around the world. *American Psychologist, 54,* 252–259.

Ross, C. A., Miller, S. D., Reagor, P., Bjornson, L., Fraser, G. A., & Anderson, G. (1990). Structured interview data on 102 cases of multiple personality disorder from four centers. *American Journal of Psychiatry, 147,* 596–601.

Ross, C. A., Norton, G. R., & Wozney, K. (1989). Multiple personality disorder: An analysis of 236 cases. *Canadian Journal of Psychiatry, 34,* 413–418.

Ross, P. (2003, September). Mind readers. *Scientific American, 289,* 74–77.

Ross, P. E. (2006, August). The expert mind. *Scientific American, 295*(8), 64–71. [See also: Bédard & Chi, 1992; Bransford et al., 1986; Chi et al., 1982; Glaser, 1990; Greeno, 1989; Klahr & Simon, 2001.]

Rothbaum, F. M., Weisz, J. R., & Snyder, S. S. (1982). Changing the world and changing the self: A two-process model of perceived control. *Journal of Personality and Social Psychology, 42,* 5–37.

Rothenberger, A., & Banaschewski, T. (2007). Informing the ADHD debate. *Scientific American Reports, 17,* 36–41.

Rotter, J. B. (1966). Generalized expectancies for internal versus external control of reinforcement. *Psychological Monographs, 80* (Whole no. 609).

Rotter, J. B. (1971, June). External control and internal control. *Psychology Today, 4,* 37–42, 58–59.

Rotter, J. B. (1990). Internal versus external control of reinforcement: A case history of a variable. *American Psychologist, 45,* 489–493.

Roush, W. (1996, July 5). Live long and prosper? *Science, 273,* 42–46.

Rozin, P. (1996). Towards a psychology of food and eating: From motivation to module to model to marker, morality, meaning, and metaphor. *Current Directions in Psychological Science, 5,* 18–24.

Rubenstein, J., Meyer, D., & Evans, J. (2001). Executive control of cognitive processes in task switching. *Journal of Experimental Psychology: Human Perception and Performance, 27*(4), 763–797.

Rubin, G. J., Brewin, C. R., Greenberg, N., Simpson, J., & Wessely, S. (2005). Psychological and behavioural reactions to the bombings in London on 7 July 2005: Cross sectional survey of a representative sample of Londoners. *British Medical Journal, 331,* 606.

Rumbaugh, D. M., & Savage-Rumbaugh, E. S. (1994). Language and apes. *The Psychology Teacher Network, 4,* 2–5.

Rushton, J. P., & Jensen, A. R. (2005). Thirty years of research on race differences in cognitive ability. *Psychology, Public Policy, and Law, 11,* 235–294. [See also Nisbett, 2005; Shiraev & Levy, 2007]

Russell, A., Mize, J., & Bissaker, K. (2002). Parent-child relationships. In P. K. Smith & C. H. Hart (Eds.), *Handbook of childhood social development.* Oxford, UK: Blackwell.

Russell, J. A., & Widen, S. C. (2002). Words versus faces in evoking preschool children's knowledge of the causes of emotions. *International Journal of Behavioral Developement, 28,* 97–103. doi: 10.1080/0165025004000582.

Rutter, M. (2006). *Genes and behavior: Nature–nurture interplay explained.* Malden, MA: Blackwell Publishing. [See also Bouchard, 1994; Caspi et al., 2002; DeAngelis, 1997; Gelernter, 1994; Hamer, 1997; Hamer, 2002; Lai et al., 2001; Plomin, 2003; Plomin, Owen, & McGuffin, 1994; Plomin & Rende, 1991; Saudino, 1997.]

Ryan, R. M., & Deci, E. L. (2000). Self-determination theory and the facilitation of intrinsic motivation, social development, and well-being. *American Psychologist, 55,* 68–78.

Ryff, C. D. (1989). In the eye of the beholder: Views of psychological well-being among middle-aged and older adults. *Psychology and Aging, 4,* 195–210.

Ryff, C. D., & Heidrich, S. M. (1997). Experience and well-being: Explorations on domains of life and how they matter. *International Journal of Behavioral Development, 20,* 193–206.

Ryff, C. D., & Heincke, S. G. (1983). The subjective organization of personality in adulthood and aging. *Journal of Personaltiy and Social Psychology, 44,* 807–816.

Saarinen, T. F. (1987). *Centering of mental maps of the world: Discussion paper.* Tucson: University of Arizona, Department of Geography and Regional Development.

Sabin-Farrell, R., & Turpin, G. (2003). Vicarious traumatization: Implications for the mental health of health workers? *Clinical Psychology Review, 23,* 449–480.

Sakaki, M. (2007). Mood and recall of autobiographical memory: The effect of focus of self-knowledge. *Journal of Personality, 75,* 421–450. [See also: Blaney, 1986; Bower, 1981; Eich et al., 1997; Gilligan & Bower, 1984; Goodwin & Sher, 1993; Lewinsohn & Rosenbaum, 1987; MacLeod & Campbell, 1992; Matt et al., 1992; Ruiz-Caballero & Bermúdez, 1995.]

Salovey, P., & Grewal, D. (2005). The science of emotional intelligence. *Current Directions in Psychological Science, 14,* 281–285.

Salovey, P., & Mayer, J. D. (1990). Emotional intelligence. *Imagination, Cognition, and Personality, 9,* 185–211. [See also Mayer & Salovey, 1997, 1995.]

Salovey, P., Rothman, A. J., Detweiler, J. B., & Steward, W. T. (2000). Emotional states and physical health. *American Psychologist, 55,* 110–121.

Saltzstein, H. D., & Sandberg, L. (1979). Indirect social influence: Change in judgmental processor anticipatory conformity. *Journal of Experimental Social Psychology, 15,* 209–216. [See also: Deutsch & Gerard, 1955; Lott & Lott, 1961.]

Sanders, L. (2009, April 25). Specialis revelio! It's not magic, it's neuroscience. *Science News, 175*(9), 22–25.

Sanders, L. (2010, July 29). Sadness response strengthens with age. *Science News.* Retrieved from www.sciencenews.org/view/generic/id/61613.

Santarelli, L., Saxe, M., Gross, C., Surget, A., Battaglia, F., Dulawa, S., Weisstaub, N., Lee, J., Duman, R., Arancio, O., Belzung, C., & Hen, R. (2003, August 8). Requirement of hippocampal neurogenesis for the behavioral effects of antidepressants. *Science, 301,* 805–809. [See also: Dubuc, 2002; Vogel, 2003]

Sapolsky, R. (2002, November). The loveless man . . . who invented the science of love. *Scientific American, 287*(5), 95–96.

Sapolsky, R. M. (1992). *Stress: The aging brain and the mechanisms of neuron death.* Cambridge, MA: MIT Press.

Sapolsky, R. M. (1994). *Why zebras don't get ulcers: An updated guide to stress, stress-related disease, and coping.* New York: Freeman.

Sarbin, T. R., & Coe, W. C. (1972). *Hypnosis: A social psychological analysis of influence communication.* New York: Holt, Rinehart & Winston.

Savage-Rumbaugh, E. S. (1990). Language acquisition in a non-human species: Implications for the innateness debate. *Developmental Psychobiology, 23,* 559–620. [See also: Patterson, 1978; Premack, 1971, 1976; Rumbaugh, 1977.]

Savin-Williams, R. C. (2006). Who's gay? Does it matter? *Current Directions in Psychological Science, 15,* 40–44.

Savitsky, J. C., & Lindblom, W. D. (1986). The impact of the guilty but mentally ill verdict on juror decisions: An empirical analysis. *Journal of Applied Social Psychology, 16,* 686–701.

Sawa, A., & Snyder, S. H. (2002, April 26). Schizophrenia: Diverse approaches to a complex disease. *Science, 296,* 692–695.

Sax, B. (2002). *Animals in the Third Reich: Pets, scapegoats, and the Holocaust.* London: Continuum International Publishers.

Sax, L., & Kautz, K. J. (2003). Who first suggests the diagnosis of attention-deficit/hyperactivity disorder? *Annals of Family Medicine, 1,* 171–174.

Saxe, L., Dougherty, D., & Cross, T. (1985). The validity of polygraph testing: Scientific analysis and public controversy. *American Psychologist, 40,* 355–366.

Scarr, S. (1998). American child care today. *American Psychologist, 53,* 95–108.

Scarr, S., & Weinberg, R. (1976). IQ test performance of black children adopted by white families. *American Psychologist, 31,* 726–739.

Scarr, S., & Weinberg, R. A. (1978, April). Attitudes, interests, and IQ. *Human Nature, 1,* 29–36.

Schachter, S., & Singer, J. E. (1962). Cognitive, social, and physiological determinants of emotional state. *Psychological Review, 69*(5), 379–399.

Schacter, D. L. (1992). Understanding implicit memory: cognitive neuroscience approach. *American Psychologist, 47,* 559–569.

Schacter, D. L. (1996). *Searching for memory: The brain, the mind, and the past.* New York: Basic Books. [See also: Anderson, 1982; Tulving, 1983]

Schacter, D. L. (1999). The seven sins of memory: Insights from psychology and cognitive neuroscience. *American Psychologist, 54,* 182–203.

Schacter, D. L. (2001). *The Seven Sins of Memory: How the Mind Forgets and Remembers.* Boston: Houghton Mifflin.

Schafe, G. E., Doyère, V., & LeDoux, J. E. (2005). Tracking the fear engram: The lateral amygdala is an essential locus of fear memory storage. *Journal of Neuroscience, 25,* 10,010–10,015.

Schaller, M., Neuberg, S. L., Griskevicius, V., & Kenrick, D. T. (2010). Pyramid power: Response to commentaries. *Perspectives on Psychological Science, 5,* 335–337.

Schank, R. C., & Abelson, R. (1977). *Scripts, plans, goals and understanding: An inquiry into human knowledge and structures.* Hillsdale, NJ: Erlbaum.

Scharfe, E., & Bartholomew, K. (1998). Do you remember? Recollections of adult attachment patterns. *Personal Relationships, 5,* 219–234.

Schatzberg, A. F. (1991). Overview of anxiety disorders: Prevalence, biology, course, and treatment. *Journal of Clinical Psychiatry, 42,* 5–9.

Schaufeli, W. B., & Bakker, A. B. (2004). Job demands, job resources, and their relationship with burnout and engagement: A multi-sample study. *Journal of Organizational Behavior, 25,* 293–315.

Schaufeli, W. B., & Enzmann, D. (1998). *The burnout companion to study and practice: A critical analysis.* London: Taylor & Francis.

Schick, T., Jr., & Vaughn, L. (2001). *How to think about weird things: Critical thinking for a new age* (3rd ed.). New York: McGraw-Hill.

Schiff, M., & Bargal, D. (2000). Helping characteristics of self-help and support groups: Their contribution to participants' subjective well-being. *Small Group Research, 31,* 275–304.

Schlenker, B. R., Weingold, M. F., Hallam, J. R. (1990). Self-serving attributions in social context: Effects of self-esteem and social pressure. *Journal of Personality and Social Psychology, 58,* 855–863. [See also: Epstein & Feist, 1988; Ickes & Layden, 1978.]

Schmidt, R. A., & Bjork, R. A. (1992). New conceptualizations of practice: Common principles in three paradigms suggest new concepts for training. *Psychological Science, 3,* 207–217.

Schmitt, D. P., Allik, J., McCrae, R. R., & Benet-Martínez, V. (2007). The geographic distribution of Big Five personality traits: Patterns and profiles of human self-description across 56 nations. *Journal of Cross-Cultural Psychology, 38,* 173–212. [See also: Birenbaum & Montag, 1986; Guthrie & Bennet, 1970; McCrae & Costa, 1997; Paunonen et al., 1992.]

Schmolck, H., Buffalo, E. A., & Squire, L. R. (2000). Memory distortions develop over time: Recollections of the O. J. Simpson trial verdict after 15 and 32 months. *Psychological Science, 11,* 39–45.

Schneider, K., & May, R. (1995). *The psychology of existence: An integrative, clinical perspective.* New York: McGraw-Hill.

Schooler, J. W., Falshore, M., & Fiore, S. M. (1995). Putting insight into perspective. In R. J. Sternberg & J. E. Davidson (eds.), *The nature of insight* (pp. 589–597). Cambridge: Massachusetts Institute of Technology Press.

Schou, M. (1997). Forty years of lithium treatment. *Archives of General Psychiatry, 54,* 9–13.

Schreiber, F. R. (1973). *Sybil.* New York: Warner Books.

Schroeder, D. A., Penner, L. A., Dovidio, J. F., & Piliavin, J. A. (1995). *The psychology of helping and altruism.* New York: McGraw-Hill.

Schroeder, D. A., & Prentice, D. A. (1995). *Pluralistic ignorance and alcohol use on campus II: Correcting misperceptions of the social norm.* Unpublished manuscript, Princeton University.

Schroeder, S. R., Schroeder, C. S., & Landesman, S. (1987). Psychological services in educational settings to persons with mental retardation. *American Psychologist, 42,* 805–808.

Schulkin, J. (1994). Melancholic depression and the hormones of adversity: A role for the amygdala.

Current Directions in Psychological Science, 3, 41–44.

Schultz, D. P., & Schultz, S. E. (2006). *Psychology and work today: An introduction to industrial and organizational psychology* (9th ed.). Upper Saddle River, NJ: Prentice Hall.

Schulz, R., & Heckhausen, J. (1996). A life span model of successful aging. *American Psychologist, 51,* 702–714.

Schuster, M. A., Stein, B. D., Jaycox, L. H., Collins, R. L., Marshall, G. N., Elliott, M. N., Zhou, A. J., Kanouse, D. E., Morrison, J. L., & Berry, S. H. (2001). A national survey of stress reactions after the September 11th, 2001, terrorist attacks. *New England Journal of Medicine, 345,* 1507–1512.

Schwartz, B. (1997). Psychology, idea technology, and ideology. *Psychological Science, 8,* 21–27.

Schwartz, C. E., Wright, C. I., Shin, L. M., Kagan, J., & Rauch, S. L. (2003, June 20). Inhibited and uninhibited infants "grown up": Adult amygdalar response to novelty. *Science, 300,* 1952–1953.

Schwartz, J., & Wald, M. L. (2003, March 9). Smart people working collectively can be dumber than the sum of their brains: "Groupthink" is 30 years old, and still going strong. *New York Times.* Retrieved December 15, 2004, from www.mindfully.org/Reform/2003/Smart-People-Dumber9mar03.htm.

Schwartz, J. M., Stoessel, P. W., Baxter, L. R., Martin, K. M., & Phelps, M. E. (1996). Systematic changes in cerebral glucose metabolic rate after successful behavior modification treatment of obsessive–compulsive disorder. *Archives of General Psychiatry, 53,* 109–116.

Schwartz, P. (1994). *Peer marriage: How love between equals really works.* New York: The Free Press.

Schwarz, N. (1999). Self-reports: How the questions shape the answers. *American Psychologist, 54,* 93–105.

Schwarzer, R. (Ed.). (1992). *Self-efficacy: Thought control of action.* Washington, DC: Hemisphere.

Schwebel, A. I., & Fine, M. A. (1994). *Understanding and helping families: A cognitive behavioral approach.* Hillsdale, NJ: Erlbaum.

Scott, K. G., & Carran, D. T. (1987). The epidemiology and prevention of mental retardation. *American Psychologist, 42,* 801–804.

Scoville, W. B., & Milner, B. (1957). Loss of recent memory after bilateral hippocampal lesions. *Journal of Neurology, Neurosurgery, & Psychiatry, 20,* 11–21. Retrieved March 10, 2008, from http://homepage.mac.com/sanagnos/scovillemilner1957.pdf

Scully, J. A., Tosi, H., & Banning, K. (2000). Life events checklist: Revisiting the Social Readjustment Rating Scale after 30 years. *Educational and Psychological Measurement, 60,* 864–876.

Searleman, A. (2007, March 12). Is there such a thing as a photographic memory? And if so, can it be learned? *Scientific American.* Retrieved January 13, 2011, from www.scientificamerican.com/article.cfm?id=is-there-such-a-thing-as.

Seeman, T. E., Dubin, L. F., & Seeman, M. (2003). Religiosity/spirituality and health: A critical review of the evidence for biological pathways. *American Psychologist, 58,* 53–63.

Segal, M. W. (1974). Alphabet and attraction: An unobtrusive measure of the effect of propinquity in a field setting. *Journal of Personality and Social Psychology, 30,* 654–657.

Segall, M. H., Dasen, P. R., Berry, J. W., & Poortinga, Y. H. (1990). *Human behavior in global perspective: An introduction to cross-cultural psychology.* Boston: Allyn & Bacon. [See also: Deregowski, 1980; Kitayama et al., 2003; Segall, 1994; Segall et al., 1966; Stewart, 1973.]

Segall, M. H., Dasen, P. R., Berry, J. W., & Poortinga, Y. H. (1999). *Human behavior in global perspective: An introduction to cross-cultural psychology* (2nd ed.). Boston: Allyn & Bacon.

Segall, M. H., Lonner, W. J., & Berry, J. W. (1998). Cross-cultural psychology as a scholarly discipline: On the flowering of culture in behavioral research. *American Psychologist, 53,* 1101–1110.

Seider, B. H., Shiota, M. N., Whalen, P., & Levenson, R. W. (2010). Greater sadness reactivity in late life. *Social Cognitive and Affective Neuroscience.* Retrieved from http://scan.oxfordjournals.org/content/early/2010/07/22/scan.nsq069.full.pdf+html.

Selby, E. A., & Joiner, T. E., Jr. (2009). Cascades of emotion: The emergence of borderline personality disorder from emotional and behavioral dysregulation. *Review of General Psychology, 13,* 219–229.

Selfridge, O. G. (1955). Pattern recognition and modern computers. In *Proceedings of the Western Joint Computer Conference.* New York: Institute of Electrical and Electronics Engineers.

Seligman, M. E. P. (1971). Preparedness and phobias. *Behavior Therapy, 2,* 307–320.

Seligman, M. E. P. (1973, June). Fall into helplessness. *Psychology Today, 7,* 43–48.

Seligman, M. E. P. (1975). *Helplessness: On depression, development and death.* San Francisco: Freeman.

Seligman, M. E. P. (1991). *Learned optimism.* New York: Knopf.

Seligman, M. E. P. (2002). *Authentic happiness: Using the new positive psychology to realize your potential for lasting fulfillment.* New York: Free Press.

Seligman, M. E. P., & Maier, S. F. (1967). Failure to escape traumatic shock. *Journal of Experimental Psychology, 74,* 1–9.

Seligman, M. E. P., Rashid, T., & Parks, A. (2006). Positive psychotherapy. *American Psychologist, 61,* 774–788.

Seligson, S. V. (1994, November/December). Say good night to snoring. *Health, 8*(7), 89–93.

Selye, H. (1956). *The stress of life.* New York: McGraw-Hill.

Selye, H. (1991). *Stress without distress.* New York: Signet Books.

Sethi-Iyengar, S., Huberman, G., & Jiang, W. (2004). How much choice is too much? Contributions to 401(k) retirement plans. In Mitchell, O. S. & Utkus, S. (Eds.), *pension design and structure: new lessons from behavioral finance* (pp. 83–95). Oxford: Oxford University Press.

Seybold, K. S., & Hill, P. C. (2001). The role of religion and spirituality in mental and physical health. *Current Directions in Psychological Science, 10,* 21–24.

Shadish, W. R., Matt, G. E., Navarro, A. M., & Phillips, G. (2000). The effects of psychological therapies under clinically representative conditions: A meta-analysis. *Psychological Bulletin, 126,* 512–529.

Shapiro, F. (1995). *Desensitization and reprocessing: Basic principles, protocols, and procedures.* New York: Guilford.

Shapiro, S. L., Astin, J. A., Bishop, S. R., & Cordova, M. (2005). Mindfulness-based stress reduction for health care professionals: Results from a randomized trial. *International Journal of Stress Management, 12,* 64–176.

Sharps, M. J., & Wertheimer, M. (2000). Gestalt perspectives on cognitive science and on experimental psychology. *Review of General Psychology, 4,* 315–336.

Shatz, M., Wellman, H. M., & Silber, S. (1983). The acquisition of mental verbs: A systematic investigation of the first reference to mental state. *Cognition, 14,* 301–321.

Shaver, P. R., & Hazan, C. (1993). Adult attachment: Theory and research. In W. Jones & D. Perlman (Eds.), *Advances in personal relationships (Vol. 4),* pp. 29–70. London, UK: Jessica Kingsley.

Shaver, P. R., & Hazan, C. (1994). Attachment. In A. L. Weber & J. H. Harvey (Eds.), *Perspectives on close relationships* (Chapter 6, pp. 110–130). Boston: Allyn & Bacon.

Shaw, P., Eckstrand, K., Sharp, W., Blumenthal, J., Lerch, J. P., Greenstein, D., Clasen, L., Evans, A., Giedd, J., & Rapoport, J. L. (2007). Attention-deficit/hyperactivity disorder is characterized by a delay in cortical maturation. *Proceedings of the National Academy of Sciences, 104,* 19,649–19,654.

Shaywitz, S. E. (1996, November). Dyslexia. *Scientific American,* 98–104.

Shaywitz, S. E., Shaywitz, B. A., Fletcher, J. M., & Escobar, M. D. (1990). Prevalence of reading disability in boys and girls: Results of the Connecticut Longitudinal Study. *Journal of the American Medical Association, 264,* 998–1002.

Shea, C. (1998, January 30). Why depression strikes more women than men: "Ruminative coping" may provide answers. *The Chronicle of Higher Education,* 14.

Shedler, J. (2006, Fall). Why the scientist-practitioner split won't go away. *The General Psychologist, 41*(2), 9–10.

Shedler, J. (2010). The efficacy of psychodynamic psychotherapy. *American Psychologist, 65,* 98–109.

Shepard, R. N., & Metzler, J. (1971). Mental rotation of three-dimensional objects. *Science, 171,* 701–703.

Sherif, C. W. (1981, August). *Social and psychological bases of social psychology.* The G. Stanley Hall Lecture on social psychology, presented at the annual convention of the American Psychological Association, Los Angeles, CA.

Sherif, M. (1935). A study of some social factors in perception. *Archives of Psychology, 27,* 187.

Shermer, M. (2006, July). The political brain. *Scientific American, 295*(1), 36.

Sherrer, H. (2008). *Dehumanization is not an option: An inquiry into the exercise of authority against perceived wrongdoers.* Seattle, WA: Justice Institute.

Sherrill, R., Jr. (1991). Natural wholes: Wolfgang Köhler and Gestalt theory. In G. A. Kimble, M. Wertheimer, & C. L. White (Eds.), *Portraits of pioneers in psychology* (pp. 256–273). Washington, DC: American Psychological Association.

Shih, M., Pittinsky, T., & Ambady, N. (1999). Stereotype susceptibility: Identity salience and shifts in quantitative performance. *Psychological Science, 10,* 80–83.

Shiffrin, R. M. (1993). Short-term memory: A brief commentary. *Memory and Cognition, 21*(2), 193–197.

Shiraev, E., & Levy, D. (2001). *Coss-cultural psychology: Critical thinking and contemporary applications.* Boston: Allyn & Bacon.

Shiraev, E., & Levy, D. (2006). *Cross-cultural psychology: Critical thinking and contemporary applications* (3rd ed.). Boston: Allyn & Bacon.

Shizgal, P., & Arvanitogiannis, A. (2003, March 21). Gambling on dopamine. *Science, 299,* 1856–1858.

Shorter, E., & Healy, D. (2007). *Shock therapy: A history of electroconvulsive treatment in mental illness.* New Brunswick, NJ: Rutgers University Press. [See also: Glass, 2001; Holden, 2003; Hollon et al., 2002; Sackheim et al., 2000; Scovern & Kilmann, 1980]

Shrader, B. (2001). Industrial/organizational psychology 2010: A research odyssey. In J. S. Halonen & S. F. Davis (Eds.), *The many faces of psychological research in the 21st century.* Retrieved July 6, 2011, from http://teachpsych.org/resources/e-books/faces/script/Ch03.htm.

Shweder, R. A. (1991). *Thinking through cultures.* Cambridge, MA: Harvard University Press.

Sieben, L. (2011, January 27). College freshmen report record-low levels of emotional health. *Chronicle of Higher Education.* Retrieved from http://topics.nytimes.com/top/reference/timestopics/subjects/s/sept_11_2001/health_and_environmental_issues/index.html?scp=11&sq=sieben%209/11&st=cse.

Siegel, J. M. (1990). Stressful life events and use of physician services among the elderly: The moderating role of pet ownership. *Journal of Personality and Social Psychology, 58,* 1081–1086.

Siegel, J. M. (2003, November). Why we sleep. *Scientific American, 289,* 92–97.

Siegel, R. K. (1980). The psychology of life after death. *American Psychologist, 35,* 911–931.

Siegler, R. S. (1994). Cognitive variability: A key to understanding cognitive development. *Current Directions in Psychological Science, 3,* 1–5.

Sigelman, C. K., Thomas, D. B., Sigelman, L., & Robich, F. D. (1986). Gender, physical attractiveness, and electability: An experimental investigation of voter biases. *Journal of Applied Social Psychology, 16,* 229–248.

Silver, R. L. (1983). Coping with an undesirable life event: A study of early reactions to physical disability. *Dissertation Abstracts International, 43,* 3415.

Simeon, D., Gross, S., Guralnik, O., Stein, D. J., Schmeidler, J., & Hollander, E. (1997). Feeling unreal: 30 cases of *DSM-III-R* depersonalization disorder. *American Journal of Psychiatry, 154,* 1107–1113.

Simeon, D., Guralnik, O., Hazlett. E. A., Spiegel-Cohen, J., Hollander E., & Buchsbaum, M. S. (2000). Feeling unreal: A PET study of depersonalization disorder. *American Journal of Psychiatry, 157,* 1782–1788.

Simon, H. A. (1992). What is an "explanation" of behavior? *Psychological Science, 3,* 150–161.

Simons, D. J., & Levin, D. T. (1998). Failure to detect changes to people during a real-world interaction. *Psychonomic Bulletin & Review, 4,* 644–649.

Simonton, D. K. (2001). Talent development as a multidimensional, multiplicative, and dynamic process. *Current Directions in Psychological Science, 10,* 39–43.

Simpson, J. A. (1990). The influence of attachment styles on romantic relationships. *Journal of Personality and Social Psychology, 59,* 971–980.

Simpson, J. A., & Harris, B. A. (1994). Interpersonal attraction. In A. L. Weber & J. H. Harvey (Eds.), *Perspectives on close relationships* (pp. 45–66). Boston: Allyn & Bacon.

Sinclair, R. C., Hoffman, C., Mark, M. M., Martin L. L., & Pickering, T. L. (1994). Construct accessibility and the misattribution of arousal: Schacter and Singer revisited. *Psychological Sciences, 5,* 15–18.

Singer, J. L. (1966). *Daydreaming: An introduction to the experimental study of inner experience.* New York: Random House.

Singer, J. L. (1975). Navigating the stream of consciousness: Research in daydreaming and related inner experience. *American Psychologist, 30,* 727–739.

Singer, J. L., Singer, D. G., & Rapaczynski, W. S. (1984). Family patterns and television viewing as predictors of children's beliefs and aggression. *Journal of Communication, 34,* 73–89.

Singer, J. L., & McCraven, V. J. (1961). Some characteristics of adult daydreaming. *Journal of Psychology, 51,* 151–164.

Singer, T., Seymour, B., O'Doherty, J., Kaube, H., Dolan, R. J., & Frith, C. D. (2004, February 20). Empathy for pain involves the affective but not sensory components of pain. *Science, 303,* 1157–1162.

Singhal, A., & Rogers, E. M. (2002). A theoretical agenda for entertainment—Education. *Communication Theory, 12*(2), 117–135.

Singleton, J. L., & Newport, E. L. (2004). When learners surpass their models: The acquisition of American Sign Language from inconsistent input. *Cognitve Psychology, 49,* 370–407.

Sinha, G. (2005, July). Training the brain. *Scientific American, 293*(1), 22–23.

Skinner, B. F. (1948). *Walden Two.* Indianapolis, IN: Hackett Publishing Company.

Skinner, B. F. (1953). Some contributions of an experimental analysis of behavior to psychology as a whole. *American Psychologist, 8,* 69–78.

Skinner, B. F. (1956). A case history in scientific method. *American Psychologist, 11,* 221–233. (Reprinted in S. Koch [Ed.], *Psychology: A study of a science* [Vol. 2, pp. 359–379]. New York: McGraw-Hill.)

Skinner, B. F. (1989). The origins of cognitive thought. *American Psychologist, 44,* 13–18.

Skinner, B. F. (1990). Can psychology be a science of mind? *American Psychologist, 45,* 1206–1210. [See also: Skinner, 1987.]

Skinner, E. A. (1996). A guide to constructs of control. *Journal of Personality and Social Psychology, 71,* 549–570.

Skotko, B. G., Kensinger, E. A., Locascio, J. J., Einstein, G., Rubin, D. C., Tupler, L. A., Krendl, A., Corkin, S. (2004). Puzzling thoughts for H. M.: Can new semantic information be anchored to old semantic memories? *Neuropsychology, 18,* 756–769.

Slater, L. (2005). *Opening Skinner's box: Great psychological experiments of the twentieth century.* New York: W. W. Norton.

Slavich, G. M., O'Donovan, A., Epel, E. S., & Kemeny, M. E. (2010a). Black sheep get the blues: A psychobiological model of social rejection and depression. *Neuroscience and Biobehavioral Reviews, 35,* 39–45.

Slavich, G. M., Thornton, T., Torres, L. D., Monroe, S. M., & Gotlib, I. H. (2009). Targeted rejection predicts hastened onset of major depression. *Journal of Social and Clinical Psychology, 28,* 223–243.

Slavich, G. M., Way, B. M., Eisenberger, N. I., & Taylor, S. E. (2010b). Neural sensitivity to social rejection is associated with inflammatory responses to social stress. *Proceedings of the National Academy of Sciences of the United States of America, 107,* 14817–14822.

Sleek, S. (1994, April). Could Prozac replace demand for therapy? *APA Monitor, 28.*

Slobin, D. I. (1985a). Introduction: Why study acquisition crosslinguistically? In D. I. Slobin (Ed.), *The crosslinguistic study of language acquisition. Vol. 1: The data* (pp. 3–24). Hillsdale, NJ: Erlbaum.

Slobin, D. I. (1985b). Cross-linguistic evidence of the language making capacity. In D. I. Slobin (Ed.), *The crosslinguistic study of language acquisition. Vol. 2: Theoretical issues* (pp. 1157–1256). Hillsdale, NJ: Erlbaum.

Slyper, A. H. (2006). The pubertal timing controversy in the USA, and a review of the possible causative factors for the advance in timing of onset of puberty. *Clinical Endocrinology, 65,* 1–8.

Smith, A. W. (1995). Separation-individuation and coping: Contributions to freshman college adjustment. Unpublished doctoral dissertation, University of North Carolina at Greensboro. *Dissertation Abstracts International, 56,* 3-A, 0831.

Smith, C. (2004). Consolidation enhancement: Which stages for which tasks? *Behavior and Brain Sciences, 28,* 83–84.

Smith, C. A., & Ellsworth, P. C. (1987). Patterns of appraisal and emotion related to taking an exam. *Journal of Personality and Social Psychology, 52,* 475–488.

Smith, D. (2001, October). Sleep psychologists in demand. *Monitor on Psychology, 36*–39.

Smith, D. (2002a, January). Guidance in treating ADHD. *Monitor on Psychology, 33*(1), 34–35. [See also: Angold et al., 2000; Marshall, 2000.]

Smith, D. (2002b). The theory heard "round the world." *Monitor on Psychology, 33*(9), 30–32.

Smith, D. (2003a, January). Five principles for research ethics. *Monitor on Psychology, 34*(1), 56–60.

Smith, D. (2003b). *Report from Ground Zero.* New York: Penguin.

Smith, E. E. (2000). Neural bases of human working memory. *Current Directions in Psychological Science, 9,* 45–49.

Smith, E. E., & Jonides, J. (1999, March 12). Storage and executive processes in the frontal lobes. *Science, 283,* 1657–1661.

Smith, E. E., & Medin, D. L. (1981). *Cognitive Science Series: 4. Categories and concepts.* Cambridge, MA: Harvard University Press.

Smith, G. B., Schwebel, A. I., Dunn, R. L., & McIver, S. D. (1993). The role of psychologists in the treatment, management, and prevention of chronic mental illness. *American Psychologist, 48,* 966–971.

Smith, G. T., Spillane, N. S., & Annus, A. M. (2006). Implications of an emerging integration of universal and culturally specific psychologies. *Perspectives on Psychological Science, 1,* 211–233. [See also: Matsumoto, 1994, 1996]

Smith, M. L., & Glass, G. V. (1977). Meta-analysis of psychotherapy outcome studies. *American Psychologist, 32,* 752–760.

Smythe, J. (1998). Written emotional expression: Effect sizes, outcome types, and moderator variables. *Journal of Consulting and Clinical Psychology, 66,* 174–184.

Snow, C. P. (1998). *The Two Cultures.* Cambridge, UK: Cambridge University Press.

Solms, M. (2004, May). Freud returns. *Scientific American, 17*(2), 28–35.

Solso, R. L. (2001). *Cognitive psychology* (6th ed.). Boston: Allyn & Bacon.

Sommer, I. E. C., Aleman, A., Bouma, A., & Kahn, R. S. (2004). Do women really have more bilateral language representation than men? A meta-analysis of functional imaging studies. *Brain: A Journal of Neurology, 127,* 1845–1852.

Sow, I. (1977). *Psychiatrie dynamique africaine.* Paris, France: Payot.

Sparling, J. W., Van Tol, J., & Chescheir, N. C. (1999). Fetal and neonatal hand movement. *Physical Therapy, 79,* 24–39.

Spear, L. P. (2000). Neurobehavioral changes in adolescence. *Current Directions in Psychological Science, 9,* 111–114.

Spearman, C. (1927). *The abilities of man.* New York: Macmillan.

Spelke, E. S. (2000). Core knowledge. *American Psychologist, 55,* 1233–1243.

Spencer, R. M. C., Zelaznik, H. N., Diedrichsen, J., & Ivry, R. B. (2003, May 30). Disrupted timing of discontinuous but not continuous movements by cerebellar lesions. *Science, 300,* 1437–1439.

Sperling, G. (1960). The information available in brief visual presentations. *Psychological Monographs, 74,* 1–29.

Sperling, G. (1963). A model for visual memory tasks. *Human Factors, 5,* 19–31.

Sperry, R. W. (1964). The great cerebral commissure. *Scientific American, 210,* 42–52.

Sperry, R. W. (1968). Mental unity following surgical disconnection of the cerebral hemispheres. *The Harvey Lectures, Series 62.* New York: Academic Press.

Sperry, R. W. (1982). Some effects of disconnecting the cerebral hemispheres. *Science, 217,* 1223–1226.

Spiegel, A. (2008). Old-fashioned play builds serious skills. NPR, February 21, 2008. Retrieved February 25, 2011, from www.npr.org/templates/story/story.php?storyId=19212514&ps=rs.

Spiegel, D., & Cardeña, E. (1991). Disintegrated experience: The dissociate disorders revisited. *Psychological Bulletin, 100,* 366–378.

Spinweber, C. (1990). *Insomnias and parasomnias in young adults*. Paper presented to the annual meeting of the Western Psychological Association, Los Angeles, CA.

Spiro, R. J. (1980). Accomodative reconstruction in prose recall. *Journal of Verbal Learning and Verbal Behavior, 19*, 84–95.

Spitz, R. A. (1946). Hospitalism: A follow-up report on investigation described in Volume I, 1945. *The Psychoanalytic Study of the Child, 2*, 113–117.

Spitzer, R. L. (1973). On pseudoscience in science, logic in remission, and psychiatric diagnosis: A critique of Rosenhan's "On being sane in insane places." *Journal of Abnormal Psychology, 84*, 442–452.

Spitzer, R. L., Gibbon, M., Skodol, A. E., Williams, J. B. W., & First, M. B. (1989). *DSM-III-R casebook*. Washington, DC: American Psychiatric Press.

Spitzer, R. L., Lilienfeld, S. O., & Miller, M. B. (2005). Rosenhan revisited: The scientific credibility of Lauren Slater's pseudopatient diagnosis study. *Journal of Nervous and Mental Disease, 193*, 734–739.

Sprang, G. (1999). Post-disaster stress following the Oklahoma City bombing: An examination of three community groups. *Journal of Interpersonal Violence, 14*, 169.

Sprecher, S., Barbee, A., & Schwartz, P. (1995). "Was it good for you, too?": Gender differences in first sexual intercourse experiences. *Journal of Sex Research, 32*, 3–15.

Springen, K. (2010, January/February). Daring to die. *Scientific American Mind, 20*(7), 40–47.

Sprock, J., & Blashfield, R. K. (1991). Classification and nosology. In M. Hersen, A. E. Kazdin, & A. S. Bellack (Eds.), *The clinical psychology handbook* (2nd ed., pp. 329–344). New York: Pergamon Press.

Squier, L. H., & Domhoff, G. W. (1998). The presentation of dreaming and dreams in introductory psychology textbooks: A critical examination with suggestions for textbook authors and course instructors. *Dreaming: Journal of the Association for the Study of Dreams, 8*, 149–168.

Squire, L. R. (2007, April 6). Rapid consolidation. *Science, 316*, 57–58. [See also: Balter, 2000; Beardsley, 1997; Bilkey, 2004; Fyhn et al., 2004; Haberlandt, 1999; Heyman, 2006; Kandel, 2001; Leutgeb et al., 2004; McGaugh, 2000; Travis, 2000a.]

Srivastava, S., John, O. P., Gosling, S. D., Potter, J. (2003). Development of personality in early and middle adulthood: Set like plaster or persistent change? *Journal of Personality and Social Psychology, 84*, 1041–1053.

St. George-Hyslop, P. H. (2000). Piecing together Alzheimer's. *Scientific American, 283*(6), 76–83. [See also: Morrison-Bogorad & Phelps, 1997; Plomin, Owen, & McGuffin, 1994; Skoog et al., 1993.]

Stahl, S. A. (1999, Fall). Different strokes for different folks? A critique of learning styles. *American Educator, 23*(3), 27–31.

Stambor, Z. (2006, November). The forgotten population: Psychologists are testing telehealth and home-based health-care interventions to turn around a mental health crisis among elderly Americans in rural areas. *Monitor on Psychology, 37*(10), 52–53.

Staples, S. L. (1996). Human response to environmental noise: Psychological research and public policy. *American Psychologist, 51*, 143–150.

Stavish, S. (1994, Fall). Breathing room. *Stanford Medicine, 12*(1), 18–23.

Steele, C. M. (1997). A threat in the air: How stereotypes shape intellectual identity and performance. *American Psychologist, 52*, 613–629.

Steele, C. M., Spencer, S. J., & Aronson, J. (2002). Contending with group image: The psychology of stereotype and social identity threat. In M. P. Zanna (Ed.), *Advances in experimental social psychology, Vol. 34* (pp. 379–440). San Diego, CA: Academic Press.

Steele, K. M., Bass, K. E., & Crook, M. D. (1999). The mystery of the Mozart effect: failure to replicate. *Psychological Science, 10*, 366–369.

Steele, K., & Johnson, C. (2009, April/May). Ask the brains. *Scientific American Mind, 20*(2), 70. [See also Campbell & Murphy, 1998; Oren & Terman, 1998.]

Steinberg, L. D., & Silk, J. S. (2002). Parenting adolescents. In M. H. Bornstein (Ed.) *Handbook of parenting* (Vol. 1, pp. 103–134). Mahwah, NJ: Erlbaum.

Steketee, G., & Barlow, D. H. (2002). Obsessive compulsive disorder. In D. H. Barlow (Ed.), *Anxiety and its disorders* (2nd ed., pp. 516–550). New York: Guilford.

Stern, J. A., Brown, M., Ulett, G. A., & Sletten, I. (1977). A comparison of hypnosis, acupuncture, morphine, valium, aspirin, and placebo in the management of experimentally induced pain. *Annals of the New York Academy of Sciences, 296*, 175–193.

Sternberg, R. J. (1994). A triarchic model for teaching and assessing students in general psychology. *The General Psychologist, 30*, 42–48.

Sternberg, R. J. (1998). *Cupid's arrow: The course of love through time*. New York: Cambridge University Press.

Sternberg, R. J. (1999). The theory of successful intelligence. *Review of General Psychology, 3*, 292–316.

Sternberg, R. J. (2000). Implicit theories of intelligence as exemplar stories of success: Why intelligence test validity is in the eye of the beholder. *Psychology, Public Policy, and Law, 6*, 159–167.

Sternberg, R. J. (2001). What is the common thread of creativity? Its dialectical relation to intelligence and wisdom. *American Psychologist, 56*, 360–362.

Sternberg, R. J. (2003). *Wisdom, intelligence, and creativity synthesized*. New York: Cambridge University Press.

Sternberg, R. J. (2003). It's time for prescription privileges. *Monitor on Psychology, 34*(6), 5.

Sternberg, R. J. (2004). Culture and intelligence. *American Psychologist, 59*, 325–338. [See also: Kleinfeld, 1994; Neisser et al., 1996; Rogoff, 1990; Segall et al., 1999; Serpell, 1994]

Sternberg, R. J. (2007). Assessing what matters. *Informative Assessment, 65*(4), 20–26.

Sternberg, R. J., & Grigorenko, E. L. (1997). Are cognitive styles still in style? *American Psychologist, 52*, 700–712.

Sternberg, R. J., Grigorenko, E. L., & Kidd, K. K. (2005). Intelligence, race, and genetics. *American Psychologist, 60*, 46–59. [See also: Chorney et al., 1998; McClearn et al., 1997; Neisser et al., 1996; Petrill et al., 1998; Plomin, 1989; Scarr, 1998.]

Sternberg, R. J., & the Rainbow Project Collaborators. (2006). The Rainbow Project: Enhancing the SAT through assessments of analytical, practical, and creative skills. *Intelligence, 34*(4), 321–350.

Sternberg, R. J., & Lubart, T. I. (1991). An investment theory of creativity and its development. *Human Development, 34*, 1–31.

Sternberg, R. J., Wagner, R. K., Williams, W. M., & Horvath, J. A. (1995). Testing common sense. *American Psychologist, 50*, 912–927.

Stevenson, H. W., Chen, C., & Lee, S. Y. (1993). Mathematics achievement of Chinese, Japanese, and American children: Ten years later. *Science, 259*, 53–58.

Stickgold, R. (2011). Memory in sleep and dreams: The construction of meaning. In S. Nalbantian, P. M. Matthews, & J. L. McClelland (Eds.), *The memory process: Neuroscientific and humanistic perspectives*.

Stickgold, R., & Walker, M. (2004). To sleep, perchance to gain creative insight? *Trends in Cognitive Sciences, 85*(5), 191–192.

Stix, G. (2008, August). Lighting up the lies. *Scientific American, 229*, 18, 20.

Stock, M. B., & Smythe, P. M. (1963). Does undernutrition during infancy inhibit brain growth and subsequent intellectual development? *Archives of Disorders in Childhood, 38*, 546–552.

Stone, A. A., Schwartz, J. E., Broderick, J. E., & Deaton, A. (2010). A snapshot of the age distribution of psychological well-being in the United States. *Proceedings of the National Academy of Sciences, USA*, published online May 17, 2010. Retrieved from www.pnas.org/content/early/2010/05/04/1003744107.full.pdf+html.

Stone, J., Lynch, C. I., Sjomeling, M., & Darley, J. M. (1999). Stereotype threat effects on Black and White athletic performance. *Journal of Personality and Social Psychology, 77*, 1213–1227.

Ströhle, A. (2009). Physical activity, exercise, depression and anxiety disorders. *Journal of Neural Transmission, 116*, 777–784. doi: 10.1007/s00702-008-0092-x.

Strasburger, V. C. (1995). *Adolescents and the media*. Thousand Oaks, CA: Sage.

Strauss, E. (1998). Writing, speech separated in split brain. *Science, 280*, 827.

Strayer, D. L., Drews, F. A., & Johnston, W. A. (2003). Cell phone-induced failures of visual attention during simulated driving. *Journal of Experimental Psychology: Applied, 9*, 23–32.

Strickland, B. R. (2000). Misassumptions, misadventures, and the misuse of psychology. *American Psychologist, 55*, 331–338.

Striegel-Moore, R. H., & Bulik, C. M. (2007). Risk factors for eating disorders. *American Psychologist, 62*, 181–198.

Striegel-Moore, R. H., Silberstein, L. R., & Rodin, J. (1993). The social self in bulimia nervosa: Public self-consciousness, social anxiety, and perceived fraudulence. *Journal of Abnormal Psychology, 102*, 297–303.

Stromeyer, C. F., & Psotka, J. (1970). The detailed texture of eidetic images. *Nature, 225*, 346–349.

Stuart, R. B., & Lilienfeld, S. O. (2007). The evidence missing from evidence-based practice. *American Psychologist, 62*, 615–616.

Styron, W. (1990). *Darkness visible: A memoir of madness*. New York: Random House.

Substance Abuse and Mental Health Services Administration. (2009). *Many baby boomers are continuing illicit drug use into their later years according to new analytic publication*. Office of Applied Studies, August 19, 2009. Retrieved from www.samhsa.gov/newsroom/advisories/0908182855.aspx.

Substance Abuse and Mental Health Services Administration. (2010). *Results from the 2009 National Survey on Drug Use and Health: Volume I. Summary of National Findings* (Office of Applied Studies, NSDUH Series H-38A, HHS Publication No. SMA 10-4586 Findings). Rockville, MD.

Sue, S. (1983). *The mental health of Asian Americans*. San Francisco: Jossey-Bass.

Sue, S. (1991). Ethnicity and culture in psychological research and practice. In J. D. Goodchilds (Ed.), *Psychological perspectives on human diversity in America* (pp. 47–86). Washington, DC: American Psychological Association.

Sue, S., & Okazaki, S. (1990). Asian-American educational achievements: A phenomenon in search of an explanation. *American Psychologist, 45*, 913–920.

Sugarman, L. (2001). *Life-span development. Frameworks, accounts, and strategies* (2nd ed.). East Sussex, UK: Psychology Press.

Sulloway, F. J. (1992). *Freud, biologist of the mind: Beyond the psychoanalytic legend.* Cambridge, MA: Harvard University Press.

Sulloway, F. J. (1996). *Born to rebel: Birth order, family dynamics and creative lives.* New York: Pantheon Books.

Sulloway, F. J., & Zweigenhaft, R. (2010). Birth order and risk taking in athletics: A meta-analysis and study of major league baseball. *Personality and Social Psychology Review, 14,* 402–416.

Suls, J., & Marco, C. A. (1990). Relationship between JAS- and FTAS-Type A behavior and non-CHD illness: A prospective study controlling for negative affectivity. *Health Psychology, 9,* 479–492.

Suls, J., & Sanders, G. S. (1988). Type A behavior as a general risk factor for physical disorder. *Journal of Behavioral Medicine, 11,* 201–226.

Swann, W. B., Jr., Hixon, J. G., & De La Ronde, C. (1992). Embracing the bitter "truth": Negative self-concepts and marital commitment. *Psychological Science, 3,* 118–121.

Swanson, J. M., Elliott, G. R., Greenhill, L. L., Wigal, T., Arnold, L. E., Vitiello, B., et al. (2007a). Effects of stimulant medication on growth rates across 3 years in the MTA follow-up. *Journal of the American Academy of Child and Adolescent Psychiatry, 46,* 1015–1927.

Swanson, J. M., Hinshaw, S. P., Arnold, L. E., Gibbons, R. D., Marcus, S., HUR, K., et al. (2007b). Secondary evaluations of MTA 36-month outcomes: Propensity score and growth mixture model analyses. *Journal of the American Academy of Child and Adolescent Psychiatry, 46,* 979–988.

Swets, J. A., & Bjork, R. A. (1990). Enhancing human performance: An evaluation of "new age" techniques considered by the U.S. Army. *Psychological Science, 1,* 85–96.

Symond, M. B., Harris, A. W. F., Gordon, E., & Williams, L. M. (2005), "Gamma synchrony" in first-episode schizophrenia: A disorder of temporal connectivity? *American Journal of Psychiatry, 162,* 459–465.

Szasz, T. S. (1961). *The myth of mental illness.* New York: Harper & Row.

Szasz, T. S. (1977). *The manufacture of models.* New York: Dell.

Tait, R., & Silver, R. C. (1989). Coming to terms with major negative life events. In J. S. Uleman & J. A. Bargh (Eds.), *Unintended thought* (pp. 357–381). New York: Guilford Press.

Talarico, J. M., and Rubin, D. C. (2003). Confidence, not consistency, characterizes flashbulb memories. *Psychological Science, 14,* 465–461.

Tamres, L., Janicke, D., & Helgeson, V. S. (2002). Sex diffferences in coping behavior: A meta-analytic review. *Personality and Social Psychology Review, 6,* 2–30.

Tangney, J. P., Baumeister, R. F., & Boone, A. L. (2004). High self-control predicts good adjustment, less pathology, better grades, and interpersonal success. *Journal of Personality, 72,* 271–324.

Tavris, C. (1989). *Anger: The misunderstood emotion.* New York: Touchstone.

Tavris, C. (1991). The mismeasure of woman: Paradoxes and perspectives in the study of gender. In J. D. Goodchilds (Ed.), *Psyc hological perspectives on human diversity in America* (pp. 87–136). Washington, DC: American Psychological Association.

Tavris, C. (1995). From excessive rage to useful anger. *Contemporary Psychology, 40*(11), 1101–1102.

Tavris, C., & Aronson, E. (2007). *Mistakes were made, but not by me.* Orlando, FL: Harcourt.

Taylor, J. B. (2009). *My stroke of insight.* New York: Penguin Books.

Taylor, L. C., Hinton, I. D., & Wilson, M. M. (1995). Parental influences of academic performance in African-American Students. *Journal of Child and Family Studies, 4,* 293–302.

Taylor, L. S., Fiore, A. T., Mendelshon, G. A., & Chesire, C. (2011, In Press). "Out of my league:" A real-world test of the matching hypothesis. *Personality and Social Psychology Bulletin, 39,* 456–467.

Taylor, S. E. (1983). Adjusting to threatening events: A theory of cognitive adaptation. *American Psychologist, 38,* 1161–1173.

Taylor, S. E. (1990). Health psychology: The science and the field. *American Psychologist, 45,* 40–50.

Taylor, S. E. (2003). *The tending instinct: Women, men, and the biology of relationships.* New York: Owl Books/Henry Holt.

Taylor, S. E. (1999). *Health psychology.* 4th ed. New York: McGraw-Hill.

Taylor, S. E., Kemeny, M. E., Reed, G. M., Bower, J. E., & Gruenewald, T. L. (2000a). Psychological resources, positive illusions, and health. *American Psychologist, 55,* 99–109.

Taylor, S. E., Klein, L., Lewis, B. P., Gruenewald, T. L., Gurung, R. A. R., & Updegraff, J. A. (2000b). Biobehavioral responses to stress in females: Tend-and-befriend, not fight-or-flight. *Psychological Review, 107,* 411–429.

Teasdale, T. W., & Owen, D. R. (1987). National secular trends in intelligence and education: A twenty-year cross-sectional study. *Nature, 325,* 119–21.

Teasdale, T. W., & Owen, D. R. (2008). Secular declines in cognitive test scores: A reversal of the Flynn effect. *Intelligence, 36,* 121–126.

Tedeschi, R. G., & Calhoun, L. G. (1996). The Post-traumatic Growth Inventory: Measuring the positive legacy of trauma. *Journal of Traumatic Stress, 9,* 455–471.

Tellegen, A., Lykken, D. T., Bouchard, T. J., Wilcox, K. J., Segal, N. L., & Rich, S. (1988). Personality similarity in twins reared apart and together. *Journal of Personality and Social Psychology, 54,* 1031–1039.

Teller, D. Y. (1998). Spatial and temporal aspects of infant color vision. *Vision Research, 38,* 3275–3282.

Terman, L. M. (1916). *The measurement of intelligence.* Boston: Houghton Mifflin.

Terman, L., & Oden, M. H. (1959). *Genetic studies of genius: Vol. 4. The gifted group at midlife.* Stanford, CA: Stanford University Press.

Terry, K. J., & Tallon, J. (2004). Child Sexual Abuse: A Review of the Literature. Retrieved from www.usccb.org/nrb/johnjaystudy/litreview.pdf.

Terry, W. S. (2000). *Learning and memory: Basic principles, processes, and procedures.* Boston: Allyn & Bacon.

Thabet, A. A. M., Abed, Y., & Vostanis, P. (2004). Comorbidity of PTSD and depression among refugee children during war conflict. *Journal of Child Psychology and Psychiatry, 45,* 533–542. [See also: Horgan, 1996; Weissman et al., 1996]

Thase, M. E., Greenhouse, J. B., Reynolds F. E., III, Pilkonis, P. A., Hurley, K., et al. (1997). Treat ment of major depression with psychotherapy or psychotherapy-pharmacotherapy combinations. *Archives of General Psychiatry, 54,* 1009–1015.

The man with two brains. (1997, January 22). *Scientific American Frontiers: Pieces of Mind.* Retrieved November 26, 2010, from www.pbs.org/saf/transcripts/transcript703.htm.

Thio, A. (1995). *Deviant behavior.* New York: HarperCollins.

Thomas, F. F. (1991). *Impact on teaching: Research with culturally diverse populations.* Symposium conducted at the Western Psychological Association Convention, San Francisco.

Thomas, J., Khan, S., & Abdulrahman, A. A, (2010). Eating attitudes and body image concerns among female university students in the United Arab Emirates. *Appetite, 54*(3), 595–598.

Thompson, D. M. (1988). Context and false recognition. In G. M. Davies & D. M. Thompson (Eds.), *Memory in context: Context in memory* (pp. 285–304). New York: Wiley.

Thompson, J. K. (1986, April). Larger than life. *Psychology Today,* 38–44.

Thompson, M. R., Callaghan, P. D., Hunt, G. E., Cornish, J. L., & McGregor, I. S. (2007). A role for oxytocin and 5-HT(1A) receptors in the prosocial effects of 3,4 methylenedioxymethamphetamine ('ecstasy'). *Neuroscience, 146*(2), 509–514.

Thompson, R., Emmorey, K., & Gollan, T. H. (2005). "Tip of the fingers" experiences by deaf signers: Insights into the organization of a sign-based lexicon. *Psychological Science, 16,* 856–860.

Thompson, W. R., Schellenberg, E. G., & Husain, G. (2001). Arousal, mood, and the Mozart effect. *Psychological Science, 12,* 248–251.

Thomsen, D. K., Mehlsen, M. Y., Hokland, M., Viidik, A., Olesen, F., Avlund, K., Munk, K., & Zachariae, R. (2004). Negative thoughts and health: Associations among rumination, immunity, and health care utilization in a young and elderly sample. *Psychosomatic Medicine, 66,* 363–371

Thorsteinsson, E. B., James, J. E., & Gregg, M. E. (1998). Effects of video-relayed social support on hemodynamic reactivity and salivary cortisol during laboratory-based behavioral challenge. *Health Psychology, 17,* 436–444.

Tienari, P., Sorri, A., Lahti, I., Naarala, M., Wahlberg, K.-E., Moring, J., Pohjola, J., & Wynne, L. C. (1987). Genetic and psychosocial factors in schizophrenia: The Finnish adoptive family study. *Schizophrenia Bulletin, 13,* 476–483.

Tirozzi, G. N., & Uro, G. (1997). Education reform in the United States: National policy in support of local efforts for school improvement. *American Psychologist, 52,* 241–249. [See also: Zigler & Muenchow, 1992; Zigler & Styfco, 1994.]

Todes, D. P. (1997). From the machine to the ghost within: Pavlov's transition from digestive physiology to conditional reflexes. *American Psychologist, 52,* 947–955.

Tolin, D. F., & Foa, E. B. (2006). Sex Differences in Trauma and Post-Traumatic Stress Disorder: A quantitative review of 25 years of research. *Psychological Bulletin, 132,* 959–992.

Tolman, E. C. (1948). Cognitive maps in rats and men. *Psychological Review, 55,* 189–208.

Tolman, E. C., & Honzik, C. H. (1930). "Insight" in rats. *University of California Publications in Psychology, 4,* 215–232.

Tolman, E. C., Ritchie, B. G., & Kalish, D. (1946). Studies in spatial learning: I. Orientation and the short-cut. *Journal of Experimental Psychology, 36,* 13–24.

Toneatto, T., & Nguyen, L. (2007). Does mindfulness meditation improve anxiety and mood symptoms? A review of the controlled research. *The Canadian Journal of Psychiatry, 52,* 260–266.

Tononi, G., & Edelman, G. M. (1998, December 4). Consciousness and complexity. *Science, 282,* 1846–1850.

Torabi, M. R., & Seo, D. C. (2004). National study of behavioral and life changes since September 11. *Health Education Behavior, 31,* 179–192.

Torrey, E. F. (1996). *Out of the shadows: Confronting America's mental illness crisis.* New York: Wiley.

Torrey, E. F. (1997). The release of the mentally ill from institutions: A well-intentioned disaster. *The Chronicle of Higher Education,* B4–B5.

Totterdell, P. (2000). Catching moods and hitting runs: Mood linkage and subjective performance in professional sport. *Journal of Applied Psychology, 85,* 848–859.

Totterdell, P., Kellett, S., Briner, R. B., & Teuchmann, K. (1998). Evidence of mood linkage in work groups. *Journal of Personality and Social Psychology, 74,* 1504–1515.

Tracy, J. L., & Robins, R. W. (2004). Show your pride: Evidence for a discrete emotion expression. *Psychological Science, 15,* 194–197.

Trainor, L. J. (2005). Are there critical periods for musical development? *Developmental Psychobiology, 46,* 262–278.

Travis, J. (2004, January 17). Fear not. *Science News, 165,* 42–44.

Treffert, D. A., & Wallace, G. L. (2002, June). Islands of genius. *Scientific American, 286,* 76–85.

Triandis, H. (1990). Cross-cultural studies of individualism and collectivism. In J. Berman (Ed.), *Nebraska Symposium on Motivation, 1989* (pp. 42–133). Lincoln: University of Nebraska Press.

Triandis, H. C. (1995). *Individualism & collectivism.* Boulder, CO: Westview Press. [See also: Triandis, 1989, 1990, 1994; Triandis & Gelfand, 1998]

Tronick, E., Als, H., & Brazelton, T. B. (1980). Moradic phases: A structural description analysis of infant-mother face to face interaction. *Merrill-Palmer Quarterly, 26,* 3–24.

Trope, I., Rozin, P., Nelson, D. K., & Gur, R. C. (1992). Information processing in separated hemispheres of the callosotomy patients: Does the analytic–holistic dichotomy hold? *Brain and Cognition, 19,* 123–147.

Tse, D., Langston, R. F., Kakeyama, M., Bethus, I., Spooner, P. A., Wood, E. R., Witter, M. P., & Morris, R. G. M. (2007, April 6). Schemas and memory consolidation. *Science, 316,* 76–82.

Tsao, D. (2006, October 6). A dedicated system for processing faces. *Science, 314,* 72–73. [See also: Downing et al., 2001; Holden, 1997; Tsao et al., 2006; Turk et al., 2002)

Turin, L. (2006). *The secret of scent: Adventures in perfume and the science of smell.* New York: Ecco. [See also: Mombaerts, 1999.]

Turk, D. C. (1994). Perspectives on chronic pain: The role of psychological factors. *Current Directions in Psychological Science, 3,* 45–48.

Turkheimer, E., Haley, A., Waldron, M., D'Onofrio, B., & Gottesman, I. I. (2003). Socioeconomic status modifies heritability of IQ in young children. *Psychological Science, 14,* 623–628.

Turkington, C. (1993, January). New definition of retardation includes the need for support. *APA Monitor,* 26–27.

Turner, E. H., Matthews, A. M., Linardatos, E., Tell, R. A., & Rosenthal, R. (2008, January 17). Selective publication of antidepressant trials and its influence on apparent efficacy. *New England Journal of Medicine, 358,* 252–260.

Turner, J. C., & Oakes, P. J. (1989). Self-categorization theory and social influence. In P. B. Paulus (Ed.), *Psychology of group influence* (2nd ed.). Hillsdale, NJ: Erlbaum.

Turvey, M. T. (1996). Dynamic touch. *American Psychologist, 51,* 1134–1152.

Twin Oaks Intentional Community Homepage. (2007). Retrieved June 19, 2007, from www.twinoaks.org/index.html.

Tyler, L. (1988). Mental testing. In E. R. Hilgard (Ed.), *Fifty years of psychology* (pp. 127–138). Glenview, IL: Scott, Foresman.

Ulrich, R. E., & Azrin, N. H. (1962). Reflexive fighting in response to aversive stimulation. *Journal of the Experimental Analysis of Behavior, 5,* 511–520.

U.S. Bureau of the Census. (2002). *Statistical abstract of the United States* (122nd ed.). Washington, DC: U.S. Government Printing Office.

U.S. Bureau of the Census. (2011). *Statistical abstracts of the United States. Table 227.* Washington, DC: U.S. Government Printing Office.

U.S. Department of Health and Human Services, Health Resources and Services Administration, Maternal and Child Health Bureau. (2009). *Child health USA 2008–2009.* Rockville, MD: U.S. Department of Health and Human Services.

U.S. Department of Health and Human Services. (2002). *Hospitalization in the United States, 2002.* Retrieved February 20, 2008, from http://ahrq.gov/data/hcup/factbk6/factbk6b.htm#common.

U.S. Department of Health and Human Services. (2011). Head Start Program Information Report for the 2009–2010 Program Year, National Level Survey Summary Report.

U.S. Department of Justice. (1999). *Eyewitness Evidence: A Guide for Law Enforcement.* Retrieved July 14, 2007, from www.ncjrs.gov/pdffiles1/nij/178240.pdf.

U.S. Senate Select Committee on Intelligence. (2004). *Report on the U.S. Intelligence Community's Prewar Intelligence Assessments on Iraq: Conclusions.* Retrieved on November 23, 2004, from http://intelligence.senate.gov/conclusions.pdf.

USA Today. (1996, December). College freedom can trigger illness. *125*(1), 7.

USMagazine.com. (2010, January 29). Christina Applegate "Did a 180" after beating Cancer. Retrieved from www.usmagazine.com/healthylifestyle/news/christina-applegate-did-a-180-after-cancer-2010291.

Vaillant, G. E. (1990). Avoiding negative life outcomes: Evidence from a forty-five year study. In P. B. Baltes & M. M. Baltes (Eds.), *Successful aging: Perspectives from the behavioral sciences.* Cambridge, MA: Cambridge University Press.

Valenstein, E. S. (Ed.). (1980). *The psychosurgery debate.* New York: Freeman.

Valenstein, E. S. (1998). *Blaming the brain: The truth about drugs and mental health.* New York: The Free Press.

Vallee, B. L. (1998, June). Alcohol in the Western world. *Scientific American, 278*(6), 80–85.

van Dam, L. (1996, October 1). Mindful healing: An interview with Herbert Benson. *Technology Review, 99*(7), 31–38. [See also: Bjork, 1991; Shapiro, 1985]

Van de Castle, R. L. (1983). Animal figures in fantasy and dreams. In A. Katcher & A. Beck (Eds.), *New perspectives on our lives with companion animals.* Philadelphia: University of Pennsylvania Press.

Van de Castle, R. L. (1994). *Our dreaming mind.* New York: Ballantine Books.

VandenBos, G. R. (1986). Psychotherapy research: A special issue. *American Psychologist, 41,* 111–112.

van den Hurk, P. A. M, Giommi, F., Gielen, S. C., Speckens, A. E. M., & Barendregt, H. P. (2010). Greater efficiency in attentional processing related to mindfulness meditation. *Quarterly Journal of Experimental Psychology, 63*(6), 1168–1180.

Van Dongen, H. P. A., Maislin, G., Mullington, J. M., & Dinges, D. F. (2003). The cumulative cost of additional wakefulness: Dose-response effects on neurobehavioral functions and sleep physiology from chronic sleep restriction and total sleep deprivation. *Journal Sleep, 26,* 117–126.

van Praag, H. (2009). Exercise and the brain: Something to chew on. *Trends in Neurosciences, 32*(5), 283–290.

Verbaten, M. N. (2003). Specific memory deficits in ecstasy users? The results of a meta-analysis. *Human Psychopharmacology: Clinical and Experimental, 18,* 281–290.

Vernon, P. A., Petrides, K. V., Bratko, D., & Schermer, J. A. (2008). A behavioral genetic study of trait emotional intelligence. *Emotion 8*(5), 635–64.

Viegas, J. (2011, January 4). Border collie breaks vocabulary record. *Discovery News.* Retrieved from http://news.discovery.com/animals/border-collie-breaks-vocabulary-record.html#mkcpgn=rssnws1.

Vincent, M., & Pickering, M. R. (1988). Multiple personality disorder in childhood. *Canadian Journal of Psychiatry, 33,* 524–529.

Vingerhoets, G., Berckmoes, C., & Stroobant, N. (2003). Cerebral hemodynamics during discrimination of prosodic and semantic emotion in speech studied by transcranial doppler ultrasonography. *Neuropsychology, 17,* 93–99.

Vogel, G. (1997, February 28). Scientists probe feelings behind decision-making. *Science, 275,* 1269.

Vogel, G. (2003, August 8). Depression drugs' powers may rest on new neurons. *Science, 301,* 757.

Vokey, J. R. (2002). Subliminal messages. In John R. Vokey and Scott W. Allen (Eds.), *Psychological Sketches* (6th ed., pp. 223–246). Lethbridge, Alberta: Psyence Ink. Retrieved November 27, 2007, from http://people.uleth.ca/~vokey/pdf/Submess.pdf.

Volpe, K. (2004). Taylor takes on "fight-or-flight." *Psychological Science, 17,* 391.

Von Fritsch, K. (1974). Decoding the language of the bee. *Science, 185,* 663–668.

Vuilleumier, P., & Huang, Y. (2009). Emotional attention: Uncovering the mechanisms of affective biases in perception. *Current Directions in Psychological Science, 18,* 148–152.

Vygotsky, L. S. (1934, 1987). Thinking and speech. In R. W. Rieber & A. S. Carton (Eds.) and N. Minick (Trans.), *The collected works of L. S. Vygotsky: Vol. 1. Problems of general psychology* (pp. 37–285). New York: Plenum.

Wade, K. A., Garry, M., Read, J. D., & Lindsay, D. S. (2002). A picture is worth a thousand lies: Using false photographs to create false childhood memories. *Psychonomic Bulletin & Review, 9,* 597–603.

Wade, T. J. (1991). Race and sex differences in adolescent self-perceptions of physical attractiveness and level of self-esteem during early and late adolescence. *Journal of Personality and Individual Differences, 12,* 1319–1324.

Wagar, B. M., & Thagard, P. (2006). Spiking Phineas Gage: A neurocomputational theory of cognitive-affective integration in decision making. *Psychological Review, 111,* 67–79.

Wager, T. D. (2005). The neural bases of placebo effects in pain. *Current Directions in Psychological Science, 14,* 175–179.

Wager, T. D., Rilling, J. K., Smith, E. E., Sokolik, A., Casey, K. L., Davidson, R. J., Kosslyn, S. M., Rose, R. M., & Cohen, J. D. (2004, February 20). Placebo-induced changes in fMRI in the anticipation and experience of pain. *Science, 303,* 1162–1167.

Wagner, U., Gais, S., Haider, H., Verleger, R., & Born, J. (2004, January 22). Sleep in spires insight. *Nature, 427,* 352–355.

Walden, J., Normann, C., Langosch, J., Berger, M., & Grunze, H. (1998). Differential treatment of bipolar disorder with old and new antiepileptic drugs. *Neuropsychobiology, 38,* 181–184.

Walker, E., Shapiro, D., Esterberg, M., & Trotman, H. (2010). Neurodevelopment and schizophrenia: Broadening the perspective, *Current Directions in Psychological Science, 19,* 204–208.

Walker, E., & Tessner, K. (2008). Schizophrenia. *Perspectives on Psychological Science, 3,* 30–37.

Walker, L. J. (1989). A longitudinal study of moral reasoning. *Child Development, 60,* 157–166.

Walker, L. J. (1991). Sex differences in moral reasoning. In W. M. Kurtines & J. L. Gewirtz (Eds.), *Handbook of moral behavior and development: Research* (Vol. 2, pp. 333–364). Hillsdale, NJ: Erlbaum.

Walker, L. J., & de Vries, B. (1985). *Moral stages/ moral orientations: Do the sexes really differ?* Paper presented at the annual meeting of the American Psychological Association, Los Angeles.

Wallace, A. F. C. (1959). Cultural determinants of response to hallucinatory experience. *Archives of General Psychiatry, 1,* 58–69.

Wallace, B., & Fisher, L. E. (1999). *Consciousness and behavior.* Boston: Allyn & Bacon.

Wallbott, H. G., Ricci-Bitti, P., & Banniger-Huber, E. (1986). Non-verbal reactions to emotional experiences. In K. R. Scherer, H. G. Wallbott, & A. B. Summerfield (Eds.), *Experiencing emotion: A cross-cultural study* (pp. 98–116). *European monographs in social psychology.* New York: Cambridge University Press.

Walsh, R. (1984). Asian psychologies. In R. Corsini (Ed.), *Encyclopedia of Psychology,* (pp. 90–94). New York: Wiley.

Walton, G. M., & Cohen, G. L. (2003). Stereotype lift. *Journal of Experimental Social Psychology, 39,* 456–467.

Wampold, B. E. (2007). The humanistic (and effective) treatment. *American Psychologist, 62,* 857–873. [See also: Barker et al., 1988; Jones et al., 1988.]

Wampold, B. E., & Brown, G. S. (2005). Estimating variability in outcomes attributable to therapists: A naturalistic study of outcomes in managed care. *Journal of Consulting and Clinical Psychology, 73,* 914–923. [See also: Blatt et al., 1996; Krupnick et al., 1996.]

Wampold, B. E., Goodheart, C. D., & Levant, R. F. (2007). Clarification and elaboration on evidence-based practice in psychology. *American Psychologist, 62,* 616–618.

Wardle, J., Steptoe, A., Bellisle, F., Davou, B., Reschke, K., & Lappalainen, M. (1997). Healthy dietary practices among European students. *Health Psychology, 16,* 443–450.

Wargo, E. (2009). Resisting temptation: Psychological research brings new strength to understanding willpower. *Observer, 22*(1), 10–17.

Warren, J. (2007). *The head trip.* New York: Random House.

Watkins, L. R., & Maier, S. F. (2003). When good pain turns bad. *Current Directions in Psychological Science, 12,* 232–236.

Watson, J. B., & Rayner, R. (2000). Conditioned emotional reactions. *American Psychologist, 55,* 313–317. (Original work published by J. B. Watson and R. Rayner, 1920, *Journal of Experimental Psychology, 3,* 1–14.)

Watson, J. D. (1968). *The double helix.* New York: The New American Library (Signet).

Watson, K. K., Matthews, B. J., & Allman, J. M. (2007, February). Brain activation during sight gags and language-dependent humor. *Cerebral Cortex, 17,* 314–324. [See also: Johnson, 2002; Mobbs et al., 2006; Moran et al., 2004.]

Watters, E. (2010, January 8). The Americanization of mental illness. *The New York Times.* Retrieved from www.nytimes.com/2010/01/10/magazine/10psyche-t.html.

Wegner, D. M., Wenzlaff, R. M., & Kozak, M. (2004). Dream rebound: The return of suppressed thoughts in dreams. *Psychological Science, 15,* 232–236.

Weil, A. T. (1977). The marriage of the sun and the moon. In N. E. Zinberg (Ed.), *Alternate states of consciousness* (pp. 37–52). New York: Free Press.

Weinberger, M., Hiner, S. L, & Tierney, W. M. (1987). In support of hassles as a measure of stress in predicting health outcomes. *Journal of Behavioral Medicine, 10,* 19–31.

Weiner, I. B., Freedheim, D. K., & Goldstein, A. M. (2003). *Handbook of psychology: Forensic psychology.* Hoboken, NJ: Wiley and Sons.

Weiner, J. (1994). *The beak of the finch.* New York: Vintage Books.

Weiss, R. (2007, November 11). Study debunks theory on teen sex, delinquency. *Washington Post.* Retrieved December 15, 2007, from www .washingtonpost.com/wp-dyn/content/article/2007/11/10/AR2007111001271_pf.html.

Weissman, M. M., Neria, Y., Das, A., Feder, A., Blanco, C., Lantigua, R., et al. (2005). Gender differences in posttraumatic stress disorder among primary care patients after the World Trade Center attack of September 11, 2001. *Gender Medicine, 2,* 76–87.

Weisz, J, R., Rothbaum, F. M., & Blackburn, T. C. (1984). Standing out and standing in: The psychology of control in America and Japan. *American Psychologist, 39,* 955–969.

Wellman, H. M., & Estes, D. (1986). Early understanding of mental entities: A reexamination of childhood realism. *Child Development, 57,* 910–923.

Wells, B. E., & Twenge, J. M. (2005). Changes in young people's sexual behavior and attitudes, 1943–1999: A cross-temporal meta-analysis. *Review of General Psychology, 9,* 249–261.

Werblin, F., & Roska, B. (2007, April). Movies in our eyes. *Scientific American, 296*(4), 73–79.

Wertheimer, M. (1923). *Untersuchungen zur Lehre von der Gestalt, II. Psychologische Forschung, 4,* 301–350.

Wesson, D. R., Smith, D. E., & Seymour, R. B. (1992). Sedative-hypnotics and tricyclics. In J. H. Lowinson, P. Ruiz, R. B. Millman, & J. G. Langrod (Eds.), *Substance abuse: A comprehensive textbook* (2nd ed., pp. 271–279). Baltimore: Williams & Wilkins.

West, C. (2009, October). 'An unconscionable embarrassment.' *Observer, 22*(8), 9, 11.

Westen, D. (1998). The scientific legacy of Sigmund Freud: Toward a psychodynamically informed psychological science. *Psychological Bulletin, 124,* 333–371.

Westen, D., Blagov, P. S., Harenski, K. Kilts, C., & Hamann, S. (2006). Neural bases of motivated reasoning: An fMRI study of emotional constraints on partisan political judgment in the 2004 U.S. presidential election. *Journal of Cognitive Neuroscience, 18,* 1947–1958.

Westen, D., & Bradley, R. (2005). Empirically supported complexity: Rethinking evidence-based practice in psychotherapy. *Current Directions in Psychological Science, 14,* 266–271.

Westen, D., Novotny, C. M., & Thompson-Brenner, H. (2005). EBP ≠ EST: Reply to Crits-Christoph et al. (2005) and Weisz et al. (2005). *Psychological Bulletin, 131,* 427–433.

Whalen, P. J. (1998) Fear, vigilance, and ambiguity: Initial neuroimaging studies of the human amygdala. *Current Directions in Psychological Science, 7,* 177–188.

Wheeler, J. G., Christensen, A., & Jacobson, N. S. (2001). Couple distress. In Barlow, D. H. (Ed.) *Clinical handbook of psychological disorders: A step-by-step treatment manual* (3rd ed., pp. 609–630). New York: Guilford.

Whitley, B. E., Jr. (1999). Right-wing authoritarianism, social dominance orientation, and prejudice. *Journal of Personality and Social Psychology, 7,* 126–134.

Whyte, W. F. (1972, April). Skinnerian theory in organizations. *Psychology Today,* 67–68, 96, 98, 100.

Wicherski, M., Michalski, D., & Kohout, J. (2009). *2007 Doctorate employment survey.* APA Center for Workforce Studies. Retrieved from www.apa.org/workforce/publications/07-doc-empl/index.aspx.

Wickelgren, I. (1997, June 27). Marijuana: Harder than thought? *Science, 276,* 1967–1968.

Wickelgren, I. (1998a, August 28). A new route to treating schizophrenia? *Science, 281,* 1264–1265.

Wickelgren, I. (1998b, May 29). Obesity: How big a problem? *Science, 280,* 1364–1367.

Wickelgren, I. (1998c, June 26). Teaching the brain to take drugs. *Science, 280,* 2045–2047.

Wickelgren, I. (1999, March 19). Nurture helps mold able minds. *Science, 283,* 1832–1834.

Wickelgren, I. (2001, March 2). Working memory helps the mind focus. *Science, 291,* 1684–1685.

Wickelgren, I. (2006, May 26). A vision for the blind. *Science, 312,* 1124–1126. [See also Leutwyler, 1994; Service, 1999]

Wickelgren, W. (1974). *How to solve problems: Elements of a theory of problems and problem solving.* San Francisco: W. H. Freeman.

Wiggins, J. S. (1973). *Personality and prediction: Principles of personality assessment.* Reading, MA: Addison-Wesley.

Willford, J. A. (2006). Moderate prenatal alcohol exposure and cognitive status of children at Age 10. *Alcoholism: Clinical and Experimental Research 30,* 1051–1059.

Wills, T. A. (1991). Similarity and self-esteem in downward comparisons. In J. Suls & T. A. Wills (Eds.), *Social Comparison: Contemporary Theory and Research* (pp. 51–78). Hillsdale, NJ: Erlbaum.

Wills, T. A., & DePaulo, B. M. (1991). Interpersonal analysis of the help-seeking process. In C. R. Snyder & D. R. Forsyth (Eds.), *Handbook of social and clinical psychology: The health perspective* (pp. 350–375). New York: Pergamon Press.

Wilner, D., Walkley, R., & Cook, S. (1955). *Human relations in interracial housing.* Minneapolis: University of Minnesota Press.

Wilson, D. A., & Stevenson, R. J. (2006). *Learning to smell: Olfactory perception from neurobiology to behavior.* Baltimore: Johns Hopkins.

Wilson, E. O. (1998). *Consilience: The Unity of Knowledge.* New York: Alfred A. Knopf.

Wilson, E. O. (2004). *On Human Nature (25th Anniversary Edition).* Cambridge, MA: Harvard University Press.

Wilson, R. I., & Nicoll, R. A. (2002, April 26). Endocannabinoid signaling in the brain. *Science, 296,* 678–682.

Wilson, S. M., & Medora, N. P. (1990). Gender comparisons of college students' attitudes toward sexual behavior. *Adolescence, 25,* 615–627.

Wilson, T. D. (2002). *Strangers to ourselves: Discovering the adaptive unconscious.* Cambridge, MA: Belknap Press/Harvard University Press.

Windholz, G. (1997). Ivan P. Pavlov: An overview of his life and psychological work. *American Psychologist, 52,* 941–946.

Winerman, L. (2005a, September). The culture of memory. *Monitor on Psychology, 36*(8), 56–57.

Winerman, L. (2005b, July/August). Fighting phobias: Figuring out phobia. *Monitor on Psychology; 36*(7), 96–98.

Winerman, L. (2005c, June). Intelligence, sugar and the car-lot hustle headline WPA meeting. *Monitor on Psychology, 36*(3), 38–39.

Winerman, L. (2005d, July/August). A virtual cure. *Monitor on Psychology, 36*(7), 87–89. [See also: Hoffman, 2004; Rothbaum & Hodges, 1999; Rothbaum et al., 2000]

Winerman, L. (2006a, January). Brain, heal thyself. *Monitor on Psychology, 37*(1), 56–57.

Winerman, L. (2006b, April). Bringing recovery home: Telehealth initiatives offer support and rehabilitation services in remote locations. *Monitor on Psychology, 37*(4), 32–34.

Winerman, L. (2006d, February). The culture-cognition connection. *Monitor on Psychology, 37*(2), 64–65.

Winkielman, P., Knutson, B., Paulus, M., & Trujillo, J. L. (2007). Affective influence on judgments and decisions: Moving toward core mechanisms. *Review of General Psychology, 11*, 179–192.

Winn, P. (ed.). (2001). *Dictionary of biological psychology.* New York: Routledge.

Winner, E. (2000). The origins and ends of giftedness. *American Psychologist, 55*, 159–169.

Winter, D. G., John, O. P., Stewart, A. J., & Klohnen, E. C. (1998). Traits and motives: Toward an integration of two traditions in personality research. *Psychological Review, 105*, 230–250.

Winters, J. (2002, January). Hey birder, this phone's for you. *Discover, 75.*

Wirth, S., Yanike, M., Frank, L. M., Smith, A. C., Brown, E. N., & Suzuki, W. A. (2003, June 6). Single neurons in the monkey hippocampus and learning of new associations. *Science, 300,* 1578–1581.

Wolfson, A. (2005, October 19). A hoax most cruel. *The Courier-Journal* (Louisville, Kentucky).

Wolpe, J. (1958). *Psychotherapy by reciprocal inhibition.* Stanford, CA: Stanford University Press.

Wolpe, J. (1973). *The practice of behavior therapy* (2nd ed.). New York: Pergamon.

Wolpe, J., & Plaud, J. J. (1997). Pavlov's contributions to behavior therapy: The obvious and the not so obvious. *American Psychologist, 52,* 966–972.

Wong, M. M., & Csikszentmihalyi, M. (1991). Motivation and academic achievement: The effects of personality traits and the quality of experience. *Journal of Personality, 59*, 539–574.

Wood, J. M., Bootzin, R. R., Rosenhan, D., & Nolen-Hoeksema, S. (1992). Effects of the 1989 San Francisco earthquake on frequency and content of nightmares. *Journal of Abnormal Psychology, 101,* 219–224.

Woodworth, R. S. (1918). *Dynamic psychology.* New York: Columbia University Press.

World Health Organization. (1973). *Report of the International Pilot Study of Schizophrenia (Vol. 1).* Geneva, Switzerland: Author.

World Health Organization. (1979). *Schizophrenia: An international follow-up study.* New York: Wiley.

Wright, E. R., Gronfein, W. P., & Owens, T. J. (2000). Deinstitutionalization, social rejection, and self-esteem of former mental patients. *Journal of Health and Social Behavior, 41*, 68–90.

Wurtman, R. J. (1982, April). Nutrients that modify brain functions. *Scientific American, 242,* 50–59.

Wynn, K. (1992). Addition and subtraction by human infants. *Nature, 358,* 749–759.

Wynn, K. (1995). Infants possess a system of numerical knowledge. *Current Directions in Psychological Science, 4,* 172–177.

Yacoubian, G. S. Jr., Deutsch, J. K., & Schumacher, E. J. (2004). Estimating the prevalence of ecstasy use among club rave attendees. *Contemporary Drug Problems, 31,* 163–177.

Yalom, I. D., & Greaves, C. (1977). Group therapy with the terminally ill. *American Journal of Psychiatry, 134,* 396–400.

Yamamoto, A. (Producer). (2000, October 8). *NHK Special* [Television broadcast of Olympic Games]. Tokyo: NHK. [As cited in Markus et al., 2006.]

Yeaman, J. (1995). Who is resilient? Who is vulnerable? *Dissertation Abstracts International, Section A: Humanities and Social Sciences, 55,* 3110.

Yee, A. H. (1995). Evolution of the nature–nurture controversy: Response to J. Philippe Rushton. *Educational Psychology Review, 7,* 381–390.

Yee, P. L., Pierce, G. R., Ptacek, J. R., & Modzelesky, K. L. (2003). Learned helplessness, attributional style, and examination performance: Enhancement effects are not necessarily moderated by prior failure. *Anxiety, Stress & Coping, 16,* 359–373.

Yerkes, R. M. (1921). Psychological examining in the United States Army. In R. M. Yerkes (Ed.), *Memoirs of the National Academy of Sciences: Vol. 15.* Washington, DC: U.S. Government Printing Office.

Young, J. R. (2003, February 14). Prozac campus. *The Chronicle of Higher Education,* A-37–A-38.

Zajonc, R. B. (1968). Attitudinal effects of mere exposure. *Journal of Personality and Social Psychology. Monograph Supplement, 9*(2, Part 2), 1–27.

Zajonc, R. B. (2001). Mere exposure effects explained … finally! Address given at the Western Psychological Association annual convention in Lahaina (Maui), Hawaii.

Zakowski, S. G., Hall, M. H., Klein, L. C., & Baum, A. (2001). Appraised control, coping, and stress in a community sample: A test of the goodness-of-fit hypothesis. *Annals of Behavioral Medicine, 23,* 158–165.

Zaman, R. M. (1992). Psychotherapy in the third world: Some impressions from Pakistan. In U. P. Gielen, L. L. Adler, & N. A. Milgram (Eds.), *Psychology in international perspective* (pp. 314–321). Amsterdam: Swets & Zeitlinger.

Zaragoza, M. S., Mitchell, K. J., Payment, K., & Drivdahl, S. (2011). False memories for suggestions: The impact of conceptual elaboration. *Journal of Memory and Language, 64,* 18–31.

Zarit, S. H., & Pearlin, L. I. (Eds.). (2003). *Personal control in social and life course contexts: Societal impact on aging* (pp. 127–164). New York: Springer Publishing.

Zigler, E., & Styfco, S. J. (1994). Head Start: Criticisms in a constructive context. *American Psychologist, 49,* 127–132.

Zilbergeld, B. (1986, June). Psychabuse. *Science, 86,* 7, 48.

Zimbardo, P. G. (1953). The dynamics of prejudice and assimilation among two underprivileged minority groups in New York City. *Alpha Kappa Delta, XXIV (1),* 16–22.

Zimbardo, P. G. (1977). *Shyness: What it is, what to do about it.* Reading, MA: Addison Wesley. (Reprinted in 1991.)

Zimbardo, P. G. (1990). *Shyness: What it is, what to do about it* (Rev. ed.). Reading, MA: Perseus Books. (Original work published 1977.)

Zimbardo, P. G. (1999). Discontinuity theory: Cognitive and social searches for rationality and normality—may lead to madness. In M. P. Zanna (Ed.), *Advances in experimental social psychology* (Vol. 31, pp. 345–486). San Diego, CA: Academic Press.

Zimbardo, P. G. (2004a, July). *The politics of fear.* Address given at the annual convention of the American Psychological Association, Honolulu, HI.

Zimbardo, P. G. (2004b, May 9). Power turns good soldiers into "bad apples." *Boston Globe,* D11.

Zimbardo, P. G. (2007). *The Lucifer effect: Understanding how good people turn evil.* New York: Random House. [See also: Haney et al., 1973; Haney & Zimbardo, 1998; Zimbardo, 1973, 1975; Zimbardo et al., 1999; replicated in Australia by Lovibond et al., 1979]

Zimbardo, P. G. (2008). On being "Shoe" at Yale: A study in institutional conformity. In preparation. Stanford University.

Zimbardo, P. G., Andersen, S. M., & Kabat, L. (1981). Induced hearing deficit generates experimental paranoia. *Science, 212,* 1529–1531.

Zimbardo, P. G., & Boyd, J. N. (1999). Putting time in perspective: A valid, reliable individual-differences metric. *Journal of Personality and Social Psychology, 77,* 1271–1288.

Zimbardo, P. G., & Leippe, M. (1991). *The psychology of attitude change and social influence.* New York: McGraw-Hill.

Zimbardo, P. G., & Montgomery, K. D. (1957). The relative strengths of consummatory responses in hunger, thirst, and exploratory drive. *Journal of Comparative and Physiological Psychology, 50,* 504–508.

Zimmer, C. (2010, May). The brain: The first yardstick for measuring smells. *Discover, 31*(4), 28–29.

Zimmerman, F. J., & Christakis, D. A. (2007). Associations between content types of early media exposure and subsequent attentional problems. *Pediatrics, 120,* 986–992.

Zimmerman, F. J., Christakis, D. A., & Meltzoff, A. N. (2007). Television and DVD/video viewing in children younger than 2 years. *Archives of Pediatrics and Adolescent Medicine, 16,* 473–479.

Zimmerman, S. (2002). *Writing to heal the soul: Transforming grief and loss through writing.* New York: Three Rivers Press/Crown Publishing.

Zucker, G. S., & Weiner, B. (1993). Conservatism and perceptions of poverty: An attributional analysis. *Journal of Applied Social Psychology, 23,* 925–943.

Zuckerman, M. (1974). The sensation-seeking motive. In B. Maher (Ed.), *Progress in experimental personality research* (Vol. 7). New York: Academic Press.

Zuckerman, M. (2004). The shaping of personality: Genes, environments, and chance encounters. *Journal of Personality Assessment, 82,* 11–22. [See also: Zuckerman, 1995; Zuckerman et al., 1978, 1980, 1993.]

ANSWERS TO DISCOVERING PSYCHOLOGY

Program Review Questions

CHAPTER 1

1. c, 2. c, 3. c, 4. c, 5. b, 6. b, 7. d, 8. c, 9. c, 10. b, 11. d, 12. b

CHAPTER 2

1. d, 2. a, 3. b, 4. c, 5. c, 6. a, 7. a, 8. d, 9. b, 10. a, 11. a, 12. b, 13. d, 14. a, 15. b, 16. b, 17. c, 18. a, 19. c, 20. c

CHAPTER 3

1. d, 2. c, 3. c, 4. a, 5. d, 6. a, 7. a, 8. a, 9. c, 10. c, 11. b, 12. b, 13. c, 14. b, 15. a, 16. d, 17. c, 18. a, 19. d, 20. a

CHAPTER 4

1. b, 2. d, 3. d, 4. a, 5. b, 6. c, 7. c, 8. a, 9. d, 10. c, 11. b, 12. d, 13. c, 14. a, 15. b, 16. d, 17. a, 18. c, 19. b, 20. d

CHAPTER 5

1. d, 2. c, 3. b, 4. b, 5. d, 6. a, 7. b, 8. a, 9. b, 10. b, 11. c, 12. c, 13. d, 14. a, 15. b, 16. d, 17. a, 18. a, 19. b, 20. d

CHAPTER 6

1. d, 2. a, 3. a, 4. c, 5. c, 6. b, 7. a, 8. d, 9. b, 10. a, 11. c, 12. a, 13. b, 14. b, 15. a, 16. d, 17. c, 18. a, 19. a, 20. c

CHAPTER 7

1. d, 2. b, 3. c, 4. d, 5. d, 6. b, 7. b, 8. a, 9. d, 10. d, 11. c, 12. c, 13. a, 14. a, 15. c

CHAPTER 8

1. c, 2. c, 3. b, 4. c, 5. d, 6. b, 7. c, 8. a, 9. d, 10. d, 11. b, 12. d, 13. b, 14. a, 15. d, 16. c, 17. b, 18. a, 19. c, 20. d

CHAPTER 9

1. d, 2. b, 3. b, 4. c, 5. a, 6. c, 7. c, 8. a, 9. d, 10. b, 11. a, 12. b, 13. c, 14. a, 15. d, 16. c, 17. d, 18. b, 19. a, 20. c

CHAPTER 10

1. c, 2. b, 3. a, 4. b, 5. a, 6. d, 7. d, 8. b, 9. c, 10. b, 11. a, 12. c, 13. d, 14. a, 15. b, 16. b, 17. a, 18. a, 19. c, 20. d

CHAPTER 11

1. a, 2. c, 3. d, 4. a, 5. b, 6. a, 7. c, 8. d, 9. a, 10. b, 11. b, 12. c, 13. d, 14. a, 15. a, 16. c, 17. b, 18. c, 19. a, 20. d

CHAPTER 12

1. d, 2. b, 3. b, 4. b, 5. d, 6. a, 7. b, 8. c, 9. d, 10. b, 11. d, 12. b, 13. c, 14. a, 15. b, 16. a, 17. d, 18. b, 19. d, 20. a

CHAPTER 13

1. c, 2. a, 3. d, 4. b, 5. a, 6. b, 7. d, 8. c, 9. c, 10. d, 11. a, 12. c, 13. b, 14. b, 15. b, 16. d, 17. c, 18. a, 19. c, 20. a

CHAPTER 14

1. c, 2. b, 3. d, 4. b, 5. d, 6. c, 7. a, 8. b, 9. c, 10. d, 11. b, 12. d, 13. a, 14. c, 15. b, 16. c, 17. a, 18. d, 19. b, 20. c

PHOTO CREDITS

NAME INDEX

SUBJECT INDEX

Note: Page numbers followed by f or t refer to figures or tables.